THE ESCOFFIER COOK BOOK

The

ESCOFFIER

C·O·O·K·B·O·O·K

*A Guide to the Fine Art
of French Cuisine*

*The Classic Work
by the Master Chef*

Auguste Escoffier

CROWN PUBLISHERS, INC.

NEW YORK

Copyright © 1969, 1989 by Crown Publishers, Inc.

Published by Crown Publishers, Inc.,
201 East 50th Street, New York, New York 10022.
Member of the Crown Publishing Group.

Random House, Inc. New York, Toronto,
London, Sydney, Auckland
www.randomhouse.com

CROWN and colophon are trademarks of
Crown Publishers, Inc.

Printed in the United States of America

Library of Congress Cataloging-in-Publication Data
Escoffier, Auguste, 1846–1935.
  The escoffier cookbook / by Auguste Escoffier.
  Translation of Le guide culinaire.
  Includes index.
  1. Cookery, French. I. Title.
TX719.E832   1975   641.5'944   75-1321

ISBN 0-517-50662-9

80 79 78 77 76

PUBLISHERS' NOTE

THE ESCOFFIER COOK BOOK is the American edition of the great French Master Chef's world famous *Guide Culinaire*. It is more than a direct translation, however, for everything is stated in American terms and according to American usage.

Nevertheless the publishers have been careful to retain the precise sense of Escoffier's writing. Therefore, Escoffier's recipes for certain foreign foods that are not usually obtainable in the U. S. have been retained for the benefit of those who may desire them. In such cases the American equivalents of the foreign foods are stated.

Likewise certain French cooking terms have been used throughout the book because they do not bear exact translation (for example, *poëling* which means roasting with butter). They are fully explained, however, both in the recipes where they appear and in the Glossary.

THE ESCOFFIER COOK BOOK is arranged in two major sections: I. The Fundamental Elements of Cooking and II. The Recipes. The Table of Contents will indicate the pages covering any class of foods—Soups, Meats, Poultry, etc. The Index will indicate the page number and recipe number of any specific dish. Titles are in both French and English and are indexed in both languages.

Terms that are defined in the Glossary are printed in italics. When, in one recipe, M. Escoffier refers to another recipe, the number of that recipe is given in parentheses.

The discussions preceding each type of food are eminently interesting and informing and the publishers suggest that readers consult these discussions before proceeding to prepare any of the excellent dishes described.

WEIGHTS AND MEASUREMENTS

1 quart	=	4 cups	=	64 tbsp.
1 pint	=	2 cups	=	32 tbsp.
$\frac{1}{2}$ pint	=	1 cup	=	16 tbsp.
$\frac{1}{3}$ pint	=	$\frac{2}{3}$ cup	=	$10\frac{2}{3}$ tbsp.
$\frac{1}{4}$ pint	=	$\frac{1}{2}$ cup	=	8 tbsp.
$\frac{1}{5}$ pint	=	$\frac{2}{5}$ cup	= app.	$6\frac{1}{2}$ tbsp.
1 tbsp.	=			3 tsp.

BUTTER, One pound	=	2 cups
FLOUR, One pound	=	4 cups
SUGAR, One pound	=	$2\frac{1}{4}$ cups
1 tbsp. CORNSTARCH	=	$\frac{1}{2}$ ounce
1 tbsp. FLOUR	=	$\frac{1}{4}$ ounce

CONTENTS

PART I

The Fundamental Elements of Cooking

PART II

Recipes and Methods of Procedure

GLOSSARY

(GLOSSARY OF TERMS PRINTED IN ITALICS)

Abats, refers to such butcher's specialties as heads, hearts, liver, kidneys, giblets, etc.

Aiguilettes, these are simply the breasts of the fowl cut into very thin slices.

Ailerons (wings), see No. 1583.

Amourettes, see No. 1288. This is the spinal marrow of the calf.

Anglaise, to treat à la Anglaise, see No. 174. Or to cook à la Anglaise, means to cook plainly in water. Also a preparation of beaten eggs and seasoning and oil.

Aromatics, No. 174a, this term mainly pertains to seasonings and herbs, but in many cases the author has used it to indicate a vegetable garnish, such as carrots, onions, etc., as in the preparation of a *Poëlé,* see No. 250.

Attereaux, see No. 1219. Bits of meat cooked on small skewers.

Baba mould, see Drawing.

Bain-marie, a hot water bath used for cooking or for keeping warm various preparations. At times an ordinary double-boiler will serve the same purpose, if the recipe indicates small quantities.

Barquettes, see No. 314, these are simply boat-shaped pastry shells used for garnishing.

Bavarois, this is the Bavarian Cream.

Biscottes, these are a light kind of dry rusk.

Bisque, see No. 241.

Blanched, see No. 273.

Blanquette, see Nos. 1273–4–5.

Bombe mould, see Drawing.

Border mould, see Drawing.

Braising, see Nos. 247 and 248. The traditional French method of braising is apt to be confusing so it is best to consult the chapters on this subject, which explain in detail. For other types of braisings consult the index.

Brandade, see No. 127, a mixture of a sauce and shredded fish, usually salt cod.

Brioche mould, see Drawing.

Brochettes, means to stick small pieces of meat on a skewer and cook in this manner.

Brunoise fashion, to cut food into small dice.

Canapés, see No. 316.

Caramel Sugar or Stage, see No. 2344.

Casserole (En), see No. 250.

Cassolet Mould, see Drawing.

Cèpes, see Nos. 2068–71. A kind of mushroom.

Charlotte Mould, see Drawing.

Chartreuse, see No. 1220.

Chiffonade, see No. 215.

Choux, a kind of cake made from pâte a Choux. (Cream Puff Paste).

Civet, this is jugged hare.

ix

Cocotte Mould, see Drawing.

Court-Boullion, see page 64.

Crepinettes, see No. 1410.

Crimp, see No. 783.

Croustade, see No. 2393.

Croustade Mould, see Drawing.

Croutons, pieces of bread in various shapes and sizes, fried in butter. Aspic jelly croutons are used to garnish cold dishes or salads.

Cullis, see No. 240.

Cutlet Mould, see Drawing.

Dariole Mould, see Drawing.

Darne, see No. 270, this is simply a large slice or cut, usually of salmon or other large fish.

Dome Mould, see Drawing.

Duxelles, see page 94.

Egg Mould, see Drawing.

Émincé, this simply means that the food is cut into a fine mince.

Essence, see Nos. 13 and 2354. The word essence when applied to meats, vegetables, etc., means a concentrate of that particular product, but when indicated in a pastry or dessert recipe it means flavoring or extract.

Fecula, this is pure starch and is principally used for thickening. Cornstarch, flour, etc., may be used.

Feuilletés, these are little pastries made of puff pastry in oval, round, or other shapes, used for appetizers, soups, etc.

Fines Herbes, see No. 174a. Minced fine dry herbs. But if the recipe calls for a herb sauce, see No. 132.

Flawn-ring (Spring-form), see Drawing.

Flute, a long crisp French dinner roll used in soups.

Foie-Gras, see No. 1726. Fat goose liver which is sometimes used uncooked or cooked in the recipes. At other times it is the prepared pâté type which is called for.

Fondue, it is either a cheese preparation or a pulpy state to which vegetables like tomatoes, sorrel, etc., are reduced by cooking.

Forcemeat, see page 78 under stuffings and forcemeat.

Frangipan Cream, see No. 2399.

Fricandeau, see No. 1206. This is a large larded slice of veal from off the rump similar to the Wiener Schnitzel.

Fumet, see No. 11. This is a kind of concentrated essence extracted from fish, game, by slow cooking.

Galatines, see No. 1708.

Galette, any food formed into the shape of a small cake or patty.

Garbures, this is nothing more than a thick vegetable soup or hodge-podge.

Gaufrette, a thin wafer used in dessert preparations and for garnishes.

Genoise, see No. 2376.

Glaze, the author has used this term to indicate a method of procedure in the use of concentrated essence which gives a glossy covering, and it may differ according to the recipe in which it is used. Therefore it is important that the reader refer to the index, according to whether the recipe calls for meat, game, fish, etc.

Godiveau, see No. 198

Granité, see No. 2930. It is very much like a sherbet.

Gratin or Gratined, see Nos. 268 to 272 inclusive.

Gratin Dish or Mould, see Drawing.

Grenadin, see No. 1216. They are small slices of veal on the order of very small veal cutlets, prepared according to the given recipe.

GLOSSARY

Ice Cream Mould, see Drawing.

Jardinières, this is a vegetable soup or sauce, or a mode of garnishing with garden vegetables.

Julienne, means to cut a product into long matched-shaped sticks.

Lard, See Stud (Glossary).

Larding Needle, see Drawing.

Lenten, simply means cooking without meat.

Macédoine, this is a mixture of early season vegetables and/or fruit.

Madeleine Mould, see Drawing.

Maigre (lean), refers to any dish prepared in the Lenten style, meaning without meat.

Maintenon, see No. 226.

Manié (butter and flour), see No. 151.

Manque Mould, a fancy mould.

Marinade or Marinate, see pages 64 to 69, inclusive. Means the liquid and to soak or steep the product in a prepared sauce or liquid prior to cooking it.

Matelotes, see Nos. 1037–38.

Matignon, see No. 227.

Meringue, see No. 2382 (ordinary) and No. 2383 (Italian).

Mignonette, this is a peeled finest quality peppercorn.

Milt, this is another name for fish roe.

Minion Fillets, when used in a recipe for poultry or fowl of any kind, game birds, etc., it pertains to that part of the breast meat that lies right next to the *Suprême,* the largest muscles in the poultry breast. In the four footed animals it is the tenderloin.

Mirepoix, see No. 228.

Mise-en-Place, a general name given to those elementary preparations which are constantly resorted to during the various stages of most culinary operations.

Mollet Eggs, see page 167.

Mousses, a class of light, hot or cold preparations of fish, meat, poultry, etc., and sweets, formed in large moulds large enough to serve a number of persons.

Mousselines, this is the same preparation as the *Mousse,* except that it is made in individual moulds.

Noisettes, these are small kernels of meat like the center part of a rib chop. It is really a part of the tenderloin like the tournedos of beef.

Oxalis Roots, this is a Mexican vegetable with a leaf similar to sorrel. It is a tuberous plant and the roots are very much like the ordinary potato and the latter or the Jerusalem artichoke may be used to replace it.

Orgeat, this is a preparation from orange-flower water, sugar and almonds, made into a thick syrup.

Ornamented Border Mould, see Drawing.

Paillettes au Parmesan, see No. 2322.

Palmettes, palm-shaped pieces of puff paste used in decorating.

Panada, see No. 189 under stuffings and forcemeat.

Panés à la Anglaise, see No. 174. Means covered with bread-crumbs.

Pannequets, see No. 2403. Similar to pancakes.

Papillote, see No. 1259. Means wrapping the preparation in vegetable parchment and cooking it that way in the oven.

Parfait, see No. 2918.

Parfait Mould, see Drawing.

Pâte a Choux, see No. 2373. This is the kind of paste used for ordinary cream puff shells.

Pauppiette, any preparation rolled into a roulade or scroll and cooked in a like manner.

Paysanne, to cut the food or product into triangles.

Petit Four Mould, see Drawing.

Pig's Caul, this is the investing membrane, with fatty veins, which covers the intestinal organs of the pig. It is used by butchers in the preparation of certain cuts of meat for cooking and is therefore difficult to procure except at slaughter houses.

Pluches, principally applied to Chervil, but they may be the serrated portions of any leaves, such as tarragon, mint, etc.

Poach, see No. 249. This term means cooking very slowly in small amounts of water at the lowest temperature. It is best to refer to the description when in doubt about the method used.

Poëlé, see No. 250. A method of cooking used in France which should be called simply "butter roasting." It applies not only to meats, but to eggs, etc., see No. 395.

Porcelain Cases, see Drawing.

Pound Cake Mould, see Drawing.

Pralin, see No. 2352.

Printanier, this usually means a garnish or filling of early spring vegetables cut into various shapes. It may also apply to preparations comprising the same.

Profiterolles, see No. 218.

Provençale, see No. 235. This is a special blend of Bechamel, with eggs and seasoning, used for stuffing foods, particularly cutlets a la Provençale.

Purée, a purée is any food that is strained through a sieve, so that it forms a complete mass. The consistency of the product referred to in the recipe and its use governs this. Purée not only applies to soups or sauces, etc., but to fruits, vegetables, meats, etc. In other words, any food.

Pyramid Mould, see Drawing.

Quenelle, see No. 205. These are forcemeat balls used for garnishing soup, etc.

Râble, the back or saddle of a hare.

Raspings, see No. 178. Simply the grated crusts of bread, etc., used for gratins, a l'Anglaise, etc.

Ravioli, see No. 2376. An Italian form of filled paste, which is boiled and covered with a sauce.

Relevé, see page 359. The term Relevé is noncommittal. The author explains in the chapter referred to that it is merely a "relief." It is better to read the text.

Richelieu Mould, a deep fluted mould.

Risotta or Rizotto, see No. 2258. This is an Italian national dish. Rice, cooked with saffron and olive oil.

Rissole, this term when pertaining to meats means to sear or brown with a protective crust. In regard to cakes, fritters, etc., it means to coat them with a golden brown crust.

Roulade, this is the more general name for *Pauppiette.*

Royales, see No. 213.

Salamander, this is a large sheet of iron on which are heaped red hot coals, so that if one holds this against a dish it browns or glazes it, almost at once. A clean coal shovel may be used for the same purpose. See Drawing.

Salpicon, a compound of various products, cut into dice and generally combined with a sauce or a forcemeat.

Sauté, see No. 251.

Savarin Mould, see Drawing.

Soufflé, a name given to a class of light, hot or cold preparations of fish, meat, poultry, etc. Also to sweets to which the whites of eggs are added if the preparation is served hot, and to which whipped cream is added if it is served cold.

Spring-Form, see Drawing.

Star Mould, see Drawing.

Swashing or Swirling, when referred to, it actually means scraping from the utensil used the adhered particles and diluting it with the wine or liquid indicated in the recipe.

Stud or Lard, studding is done by injecting protruding pieces of fat into the incisions made in the meat with a sharp knife. Larding uses the same strip of fat or bacon, which are inserted into a larding needle. With this, one pinches the meat at regular intervals allowing the larding fat to show at the point of its entry. See Drawing.

Subrics, see No. 2137. The recipe referred to gives the preparation of Subrics, which are really spinach puffs.

Supreme, this is the name given to the fillet or the breast of fowl. The term has been extended to include the best parts of meat, fish, etc.

Tart Mould, see Drawing.

Tartlets, see No. 387.

Tartlet Mould, see Drawing.

Tazza Mould, Fancy cup mould.

Terrine, this is a patty and its container. But a terrine à pâté is an earthenware dish in which a patty or food is cooked. See Drawing.

Timbale, may mean a *Timbale* Mould and it may mean a food cooked in the Mould or crust, and formed in such a manner. See Drawing.

Verjuice, this is the juice of unripe fruit, such as grapes, etc. Sometimes used as a substitute for vinegar in acidulating water.

Vesiga, this is the dried spine-marrow of the sturgeon and very difficult to procure.

Zest, the outermost, colored glossy film of the rind of an orange or lemon.

MOULDS

Easter Egg   Gratin   Pound Cake

Ice Cream   Bombe   Dome

Terrine à pâté

Ornamental Border   Star

Charlotte   Parfait   Spring-form-flawn-ring

MOULDS

Petit-fours

Tart

Madeleine

Brioche

Savarin-
Ring ~ Border

Tartlett~
croustade

Cutlet

Dariole ~ Baba
Timbale

Porcelain Cases

Cocotte

Conical~
pyramid

Cassolet

Salamander

Larding needle

THE ESCOFFIER COOK BOOK

PART I

FUNDAMENTAL ELEMENTS OF COOKING

CHAPTER I

BASIC PRINCIPLES OF COOKERY

BEFORE undertaking the description of the different kinds of dishes whose recipes I intend giving in this work, it will be necessary to reveal the groundwork whereon these recipes are built. And, although this has already been done again and again, and is wearisome in the extreme, a text-book on cooking that did not include it would be not only incomplete, but in many cases incomprehensible.

Notwithstanding the fact that it is the usual procedure, in culinary matters, to insist upon the importance of the part played by stock, I feel compelled to refer to it at the outset of this work, and to lay even further stress upon what has already been written on the subject.

Indeed, stock is everything in cooking, at least in French cooking. Without it, nothing can be done. If one's stock is good, what remains of the work is easy; if, on the other hand, it is bad or merely mediocre, it is quite hopeless to expect anything approaching a satisfactory result.

The cook mindful of success, therefore, will naturally direct his attention to the faultless preparation of his stock, and, in order to achieve this result, he will find it necessary not merely to make use of the freshest and finest products, but also to exercise the most scrupulous care in their preparation, for, in cooking, care is half the battle. Unfortunately, no theories, no formulæ, and no recipes, however well written, can take the place of practical experience in the acquisition of a full knowledge concerning this part of the work—the most important, the most essential, and certainly the most difficult part.

1

In the matter of stock it is, above all, necessary to have a sufficient quantity of the finest materials at one's disposal. Every cook knows this, and any master or mistress of a house who stints in this respect forfeits the right to make any remark whatsoever to the *chef* concerning his work, for, let the talent or merits of the latter be what they may, they are crippled by insufficient or inferior material. It is just as absurd to exact excellent cooking from a *chef* whom one provides with defective or scanty goods, as to hope to obtain wine from a bottled decoction of logwood.

The Principal Kinds of Fonds de Cuisine (Foundation Sauces and Stocks)

The principal kinds of fonds de cuisine are:—

1. Ordinary and clarified consommés.
2. The brown stock or *"estouffade,"* game stocks, the bases of thickened gravies and of brown sauces.
3. White stock, basis of white sauces.
4. Fish stock.
5. The various essences of poultry, game, fish, &c., the complements of small sauces.
6. The various *glazes:* meat, game and poultry.
7. The basic sauces: Espagnole, Velouté, Béchamel, Tomato, and Hollandaise.
8. The savory jellies or aspics of old-fashioned cooking.

To these kinds of stock, which, in short, represent the buttresses of the culinary edifice, must now be added the following preparations, which are, in a measure, the auxiliaries of the above:—

1. The *roux,* the thickening element in sauces.
2. The *"Mirepoix"* and *"Matignon"* aromatic and flavoring elements.
3. The *"Court-Bouillon"* and the *"Blancs."*
4. The various stuffings.
5. The *marinades.*
6. The various garnishes for soups, for *relevés,* for entrées, &c. ("Duxelle," "Duchesse," "Dauphine," *Pâte à choux,* frying batters, various *Salpicons, Profiteroles, Royales,* Œufs filés, *Diablotins,* Pastes, Dough or Batters, etc.).

1—ORDINARY OR WHITE CONSOMME *Fonds Blancs Ordinaires*

Quantities for making Four Quarts

3 lbs. of shin of beef.	¾ lb. of leeks and 1 stalk of celery.
3 lbs. of lean beef.	
1½ lbs. of fowls' skeletons.	¼ lb. of parsnips.
1 lb. of carrots.	1 medium-sized onion with a clove stuck in it.
½ lb. of turnips.	

Preparation.—Put the meat into a stock-pot of suitable dimensions, after having previously tied it together; add the fowl skeletons, five quarts of water, and one-half oz. of table salt. Place the stock-pot on a moderate fire in such a manner that it may not boil too quickly, and remember to stir the meat from time to time. Under the influence of the heat, the water gradually reaches the interior of the meat, where, after having dissolved the liquid portions, it eventually combines with them. These liquid portions contain a large proportion of albumen, and as the temperature of the water rises this substance has a tendency to coagulate. It also increases in volume, and, by virtue of its lightness, escapes from the water and accumulates on the surface in the form of scum. Carefully remove this scum as it forms, and occasionally add a little cold water before the boil is reached in order that, the latter being retarded, a complete expulsion of the scum may be effected. The clearness of the consommé largely depends upon the manner in which this skimming has been carried out. Then the vegetable garnishing is added. The scum from this is removed as in the previous case, and the edge of the stock-pot should be carefully wiped to the level of the fluid, so as to free it from the deposit which has formed there. The stock-pot is then moved to a corner of the fire where it may continue cooking slowly for four or five hours. At the end of this time it should be taken immediately from the fire, and, after half a pint of cold water has been added to its contents, it should be left to rest a few minutes to permit the grease to accumulate on the surface of the liquid, whence it must be carefully removed before the consommé is strained. This last operation is effected by means of a very fine strainer, placed on the top of a white tureen (clean and wide), which should be chilled to hasten the cooling of the consommé. The tureen should not on any account be covered, and this more particularly in summer, when rapid cooling is a precautionary measure against fermentation.

Remarks upon the Different Causes which Combine to Influence the Quality of a Consommé

It will be seen that I have not made any mention in the above recipe of the meat and the vegetables which have helped to make the consommé, my reason being that it is preferable to remove them from the stock-pot only after the broth has been strained, so as not to run the risk of disturbing the latter.

The quality of the meat goes a long way towards establishing the quality of the consommé. In order that the latter be perfect, it is essential that the meat used should be that of comparatively old animals whose flesh is well set and rich in flavor.

Now to extract that gelatinous element from bone which produces the mellowness characteristic of all good consommés, it is necessary that the gelatigenous bodies should be cooked for twelve hours at least, and even after that time has elapsed they are still not entirely spent.

I therefore believe that, in the case of either consommé or stock, the recipe of which I shall give later, it would be advisable for the bones to stew at least twelve hours, and this only after they have been well broken up, while the quantity of water used should be sufficient to allow exactly for the immersion of the meat that must follow. The contents of this first stock-pot should include half of the vegetables mentioned, and the consommé thus obtained, after having been strained and cooled, will take the place of the water in the recipe, in accordance with the directions I have given above.

The Uses of White Consommé

White consommé is used in the preparation of clarified consommés, in which case it undergoes a process of clearing, the directions for which will be given later. It also serves as the liquor for thick soups, poached fowls, etc. It must be transparent, as colorless as possible, and very slightly salted, for, whatever the use may be for which it is intended, it has to undergo a process of concentration.

2—THE PREPARATION OF CLARIFIED CONSOMME FOR CLEAR SOUPS   *La Préparation des Fonds Clarifiés*

Quantities for making four quarts.—Five quarts of ordinary consommé, one and one-half lbs. of very lean beef, the white of an egg, one fowl's skeleton (roasted if possible). First, mince the beef and put through a grinder with the fowl's skeleton and the white of egg, adding a little cold white consommé. Put the whole into a tall, narrow, and thick-bottomed saucepan or pot; then gradually add the cold, white broth, from which all grease has been removed, that the whole may be well mixed. Then the pot may be put on the fire, and its contents thoroughly stirred, to prevent their burning at the bottom. When boiling-point almost is reached, move the saucepan to a corner of the fire, so that the soup may only simmer, for anything approaching the boil would disturb the contents. A good hour should be enough to complete the consommé, and any longer time on the fire would be rather injurious than helpful, as it would probably impair the flavor of the preparation. Now carefully remove what little grease may have collected on the surface of the consommé, and strain the latter through muslin into another clean saucepan. It is now ready for the addition of the garnishes that are to form part of it, which I shall enumerate in due course.

REMARKS UPON CLARIFICATIONS

For clarified consommés, even more than for the ordinary kind, it is eminently advisable that the meat should be that of old animals. Indeed, it is safe to say that one lb. of meat coming from an animal of eight years will yield much better consommé than two lbs. would, coming from a fattened animal of about three or four years. The consommé will be stronger, mellower, and certainly more tasty, as the flesh of young animals has absolutely no richness of flavor.

It will be seen that I do not refer to any vegetable for the clarification. If the white consommé has been well carried out, it should be able to dispense with all supplementary flavoring, and, the customary error of cooks being rather to overdo the quantity of vegetables—even to the extent of disguising the natural aroma of the consommé—I preferred to entirely abandon the idea of vegetable garnishes in clarifications, and thus avoid a common stumbling-block.

3—CHICKEN CONSOMME   *Fonds de Volaille*

White chicken consommé is prepared in exactly the same way as ordinary white consommé. There need only be added to the meat, the quantity of which may be lessened, an old hen or a cock, slightly browned on the spit or in the oven.

For the clarification, the quantity of roast fowl skeletons used may be increased, provided the latter be not too fat. The process, however, is the same as in the clarification of ordinary consommés.

The color of chicken consommé should be lighter than that of the ordinary kind—namely, a light, amber yellow, transparent and warm.

4—FISH CONSOMME *Fonds de Poisson*

These consommés are rarely used, for *Lenten* soups with a fish basis are generally thick soups, for the preparation of which the fish *fumet* (Recipe 11) should avail. Whenever there is no definite reason for the use of an absolutely *Lenten* consommé, it would be advisable to resort to one of the ordinary kind, and to finish off the same by means of a good fish essence extracted from the bones of a sole of whiting. An excellent consommé is thus obtained, more palatable and less flat than the plain fish consommé.

If, however, one were obliged to make a plain fish consommé, the following procedure should be adopted:—

CLARIFICATION OF FISH CONSOMMÉ

Quantities for making Four Quarts.—Four and one-half quarts of ordinary fish *fumet* having a decided taste; one-half lb. of good caviar, or pressed caviar.

Mode of Procedure.—Pound the caviar and mix the pulp with the cold fish *fumet.* Put the whole into a saucepan, place it on the fire, and stir with a spatula until the contents reach the boil. Then move the saucepan to a corner of the fire. and let the consommé simmer gently for twenty minutes, after which strain it through muslin with great caution, and keep it well covered and in the warmth, to prevent the formation of a gelatinous film on the surface.

Fish consommés are greatly improved by the addition of such aromatics as saffron or curry, both of which considerably add to their quality.

5—GAME CONSOMME *Fonds de Gibier*

The necks, breasts, and shoulders of venison and of hare, old wild rabbits, old pheasants, and old partridges may be used in the production of game consommés. An ordinary consommé may likewise be made, in which half the beef can be replaced by veal, and to which may be added, while clarifying, a succulent game *essence.* This last method is even preferable when dealing with game birds, but in either case it is essential that the meat used should be half-roasted beforehand, in order to strengthen the *fumet*.

The recipe that I give below must therefore only be looked upon as a model, necessarily alterable according to the resources at one's disposal, the circumstances, and the end in view.

Quantities for making Four Quarts of Plain Game Consommé.

3 lbs. of neck, shoulder, or breast of venison.

1½ lbs. of hare-trimmings.

1 old pheasant or 2 partridges.

4 oz. of sliced carrots, browned in butter.

½ lb. of mushrooms browned in butter.

1 medium-sized leek and 2 stalks of celery.

1 herb bunch with extra thyme and bay leaves.

1 onion, oven-browned, with 2 cloves stuck into it.

Liquor.—Five and one-half quarts of water.

Seasoning.—One oz. of salt and a few peppercorns, these to be added ten minutes previous to straining the consommé.

Time allowed for cooking.—Three hours.

Mode of Procedure.—Proceed in exactly the same way as for ordinary consommés (1), taking care only to half-roast the meat, as I pointed out above, before putting it in the saucepan.

THE CLARIFICATION OF GAME CONSOMMÉS

The ingredients of the clarification of game consommés vary according to the kind desired. If it is to have a partridge flavor, one partridge should be allowed for each quart of the consommé, whereas if its flavor is to be that of the pheasant, half an old pheasant will be required per each quart of the liquid. Last, in the case of plain game consommés, one lb. of lean venison, hare, or wild rabbit should be allowed for each quart required.

Mode of Procedure.—Whatever be the kind of game used, the latter must be thoroughly boned and the meat well ground, together with the white of an egg per four quarts of consommé. About two oz. per quart of dried mushrooms should now be added if they can be procured, while the bones and the meat of the game should be browned in the oven and completely drained of all grease. The whole can now be mixed with the cold game consommé (5). The clarification is then put over a fire (stirring constantly), and as soon as the boil is reached the saucepan must be moved to a corner of the fire, where its contents may gently boil for three-quarters of an hour longer. The fat should then be removed, and the consommé strained through muslin, after which cover until wanted.

6—SPECIAL CONSOMME FOR SUPPERS　　*Potages pour les Soupers*

The consommés whose recipes I have just given are intended more particularly for dinners. They are always finished off by some kind of garnish, which, besides lending them an additional touch of flavor, gives them their special and definite character when they are served.

But the case is otherwise with the consommés served for suppers. These, being only served in cups, either hot or cold, do not allow for any garnishing, since they are to be drunk at table. They must therefore be perfect in themselves, delicate, and quite clear.

These special consommés are made in a similar manner to the others, though it is needful to slightly increase the quantity of meat used for the clarification, and to add to that clarification the particular flavor mentioned on the menu—to wit, a few stalks of celery, if the consommé is that type; a small quantity of curry, if the consommé is made "à l'Indienne"; or a few old roast partridges if it is to be termed "Consommé au *fumet* de perdreau"; and so on.

The means by which one may vary the aroma of consommés are legion, but it is highly important, whatever aroma used, that it be not too pronounced. It should only lend a distinctive and, at the same time, subtle finish to the consommé, which, besides sharpening the latter, should increase its succulence.

When the consommé is served cold it ought to have the qualities of an extremely light and easily-melting jelly, barely firm; but when it is too liquid, it rarely gives that sensation of perfection and succulence to the palate of the consumer which the latter expects. When too firm and too gelatinous it is positively disagreeable; therefore, if it is to be relished, it should be of just the right consistency.

7—BROWN STOCK OR ESTOUFFADE   *Fonds Brun ou Estouffade*

Quantities for making Four Quarts

4 lbs. of shin of beef (flesh and bone).

4 lbs. of shin of veal (flesh and bone).

½ lb. of lean, raw ham.

½ lb. of fresh pork rind, *blanched*.

¾ lb. of minced carrots, browned in butter.

¾ lb. of minced onions, browned in butter.

1 herb bunch, containing a little parsley, a stalk of celery, a small sprig of thyme, and a bay leaf.

Preparation.—Bone and tie the meat, and keep it handy. Break the bones as finely as possible, and, after having sprinkled them with a little stock-fat, brown them in an oven; also stir them repeatedly. When they are slightly browned, put them in a conveniently large saucepan with the carrots, the onions, and the herb bunch. Add five quarts of cold water, and put the saucepan on to boil. As soon as the boil is reached skim carefully; wipe the edge of the saucepan; put the lid half on, and allow the stock to cook gently for twelve hours; then roughly remove the fat; strain the liquid through a sieve, and let it cool.

This being done, put the meat in a saucepan just large enough to hold it. Brown it a little in some stock-fat and drain off fat entirely. Add half a pint of the prepared stock, cover the saucepan, and let the meat simmer on the side of the fire until the stock is almost entirely reduced. Meanwhile the meat should have been repeatedly turned, that it may be equally affected throughout. Now pour the remainder of the stock, prepared from bones, into the saucepan, bring the whole to a boil, and continue very slowly and regularly with the lid off. As soon as the meat is well cooked the fat should be removed from the stock, and it should be strained or rubbed through a sieve, after which it should be put aside to be used when required.

Remarks Relative to the Making of Brown Stock.—Instead of tying the meat after having boned it, if time presses, it may be cut into large cubes before browning. In this case one hour and a half would suffice to cook it and to extract all its juice.

Whether brown or white, stock should never be salted, because it is never served in its original state. It is either reduced in order to make *glazes* or sauces—in which case the concentration answers the purpose of seasoning—or else it is used to cook meat which must be salted before being cooked and which, therefore, imparts the necessary salt to its surrounding liquor.

Brown stock ought to be the color of fine burnt amber, and it must be transparent. It is used in making meat *glazes* (14) after reduction, also to moisten meat for *braising* and to prepare brown sauces.

8—BROWN GAME STOCK   *Fonds de Gibier Brun*

There is no difference between the game consommés and game stock, or, otherwise stated, ordinary game consommé and brown game stock are one and the same thing. The distinction lies in the ultimate use of this preparation; it is clarified, as we have shown (5), if it be intended for a clear soup, and it is used in its original state if it is to be used for a thick game soup, for a sauce, or for reducing.

9—BROWN VEAL STOCK   *Fonds de Veau Brun*

Brown veal stock requires the same quantities of shin and trimmings of veal as white veal stock (10). The time allowed for cooking is, however, a little shorter, and this operation may be completed within eight hours. This stock is mostly used as the liquor for poultry and *poëled* game, while it may also serve in the preparation of thickened veal stock. Being quite neutral in taste, it lends itself to all purposes, and readily takes up the aroma of the meat with which it may happen to be combined. It is admirably suited to the *poaching* of quails, and nothing can supplant it in this particular.

10—WHITE VEAL STOCK AND POULTRY STOCK
Fonds de Veau Blanc et de Volaille

Quantities for making Four Quarts

8 lbs. of shin of veal, or lean and fresh veal trimmings.
1 or 2 fowls' skeletons, uncooked if they are handy.
12 oz. of carrots.
6 oz. of onions stuck with a clove.

5½ quarts of cold water.
4 oz. of leeks tied with a stalk of celery.
1 herb bunch, including 1 oz. of parsley, 1 bay leaf, and a small sprig of thyme.

Preparation.—Bone the shins, string the meat, break up the bones as small as possible, and put them in a saucepan with the water. Place on an open fire, allow to boil, skim carefully, and then move to a side of the fire to cook very gently for five hours. At the end of this time put the stock into another saucepan, add the meat and the vegetables, add water, if necessary, to keep the quantity of liquid at five quarts, let it boil, and allow it to cook slowly for another three hours, after which remove all grease from the stock, pass it through a fine strainer or a colander, and put it aside until wanted.

Remarks upon White Stock.—One should contrive to make this stock as gelatinous as possible. It is therefore an indispensable measure that the bones be well broken up and cooked for at least eight hours. Veal never yields such clear stock as beef; nevertheless, the consommé obtained from veal should not be cloudy. It must, on the contrary, be kept as clear and as white as possible.

Poultry Stock is made by adding two old fowls to the above veal stock, and these should be put into the liquor with the meat.

Fish Stock

11—WHITE FISH STOCK   *Fumet Blanc de Poisson*

Quantities for making Four Quarts

4 lbs. of trimmings and bones of sole or whiting.	2 oz. of parsley root or stalks.
½ lb. of sliced *blanched* onions.	½ bottle of white wine.

Preparation.—Butter the bottom of a thick, deep saucepan, put in the *blanched* onions and the parsley-stalks, and upon these lay the fish remains. Add the juice of a lemon, cover the saucepan, put it on the fire, and allow the fish to exude its essence, shaking the pan at intervals. Moisten, in the first place, with the white wine; then, with the lid off, reduce the liquid to about half. Now add four quarts of cold water, bring to a boil, skim, and then leave to cook for twenty minutes, only, on a moderate fire. The time allowed is ample for the purpose of extracting the aromatic and gelatinous properties contained in the bones, and a lengthened stewing would only impair the savor of the stock.

Remarks upon White Fish Stock.—The recipe which I give above diverges considerably from that commonly used, for, as a rule, fish stock is diluted far too much, and is cooked for much too long a time. I have observed that fish stock may be greatly improved by rapid cooking, and it was this consideration that led me to dilute it scantily, so as to avoid prolonged reduction.

It is likewise necessary to remember that in order to make perfect fish stock, only the sole or whiting should be used. In a case of emergency, however, if the supply of the latter were to run short, a quarter of their weight of turbot bones might be added to them. But all other kinds of fish should be avoided in the preparation.

12—FISH STOCK WITH RED WINE *Fumet de Poisson au Vin Rouge*

This stock is comparatively rarely used, because, in practice, it is naturally obtained in the cooking of the fish itself, as, for instance, in the case of the *"Matelotes"* (1037). Be this as it may, with the recent invasion of a custom which seems to demand, ever more and more, the serving of fish without bones, the following recipe will be worthy of interest, as it is likely that its need will henceforth be felt with increasing urgency.

Fish *fumet* with red wine may be prepared from all fresh-water fish, as well as from the remains of sole, whiting, chicken-turbot, and turbot. It is generally better, however, to have recourse to the bones and remains of that fish which happens to be constituting the dish —that is to say, the bones and trimmings of sole in a stock for fillet of sole, the bones and trimmings of a chicken-turbot in a *fumet* for a chicken-turbot, and so on. The preparatory recipe remains the same, whatever kind of fish used may be.

Quantities for making Four Quarts of Fumet with Red Wine.— Four lbs. of bones, heads, and trimmings of the fish to be served; three-quarters lb. of minced white onions; three oz. of parsley stalks, two bay leaves, four small sprigs of thyme, and four cloves of garlic; two bottles of red wine and four pints of water.

Mode of Procedure.—Put all the above-mentioned ingredients in a heavy and deep saucepan, boil, skim carefully, and allow to cook twenty to thirty minutes on a moderate fire; then strain the stock through a colander into a tureen, to be used when required.

Remarks upon Fish Stock with Red Wine.—This stock stands reduction far better than white fish stock. Nevertheless, I urge the advisability of trying to obtain the required quantity without too much cooking. In its preparation, one may use some mushroom peelings, as in the case of white stock, if these are handy, and they will be found to lend an agreeable flavor to the fish *fumet*.

13—VARIOUS ESSENCES   *Essences Diverses*

As their name implies, *essences* are stock which hold a large proportion of a substance's aroma in a concentrated form. They are, in fact, ordinary stock, only less diluted, with the idea of intensifying the flavor of the treated ingredients; hence their utility is *nil* if the stock which they are intended to complete has been properly treated. It is infinitely simpler to make savory and succulent stock in the first place than to produce a mediocre stock, and finally complete it by a specially prepared *essence*. The result in the first instance is better, and there is economy of time and material.

The most one can do is to recommend, in certain circumstances, the use of essences extracted from particularly well-flavored products, as, for instance, mushrooms, truffles, morels, and celery. But it would be well to remember that, nine times out of ten, it is preferable to add the product itself to the stock during the preparation of the same rather than to prepare *essences*.

For this reason I do not think it necessary to enlarge upon the subject of *essences,* the need of which should not be felt in good cooking.

14—VARIOUS GLAZES

The various *glazes* of meat, fowl, game, and fish are merely stock reduced to the point of glutinous consistency. Their uses are legion. Occasionally they serve in decorating dishes with a brilliant and smooth coating which makes them appetizing; at other times they may help to strengthen the consistency of a sauce or other culinary preparation, while again they may be used as sauces proper after they have been correctly creamed or buttered.

Glazes are distinguished from *essences* by the fact that the latter are only prepared with the object of extracting all the flavor of the product under treatment, whereas the former are, on the contrary, constituted by the whole base of the substance itself. They therefore have not only its savor, but also its succulence and mellowness, whereby they are superior to the *essences*, and cooking can but be improved by substituting them for the latter. Nevertheless, many *chefs* of the old school do not permit the use of *glazes* in culinary preparations, or, rather, they are of opinion that each cooking operation should produce them on its own account, and thus be sufficient unto itself. Certainly, the theory is correct when neither time nor cost is limited. But nowadays the establishments are scarce where these theories may be applied, and, indeed, if one does not make an abuse of *glazes,* and if they be prepared with care, their use gives excellent results, while they lend themselves admirably to the very complex demands of modern customs.

15—MEAT GLAZE   *Glace de Viande*

Meat *glaze* is made by reducing brown stock (7) in a large saucepan upon an open fire. As often as the stock is appreciably reduced, during boiling, it may be transferred to smaller pots, taking care to strain it through muslin at each change. The *glaze* may be considered sufficiently reduced when it evenly coats a withdrawn spoon. The fire used for reducing should gradually diminish as the concentration progresses, and the last phase must be done slowly and on a moderate fire.

When it is necessary to obtain a lighter and clearer *glaze,* the brown veal stock (9) should be reduced instead of the *"Estouffade."*

16—POULTRY GLAZE   *Glace de Volaille*

Reduce the poultry base indicated in (10), and proceed in exactly the same way as for meat *glaze* (15).

17—GAME GLAZE   *Glace de Gibier*

Use the game base (8), and proceed as for meat *glaze* (15).

18—FISH GLAZE   *Glace de Poisson*

This *glaze* is used less often than the preceding ones. As it is only used to intensify the savor of sauces, it is sufficient for this purpose to prepare a white fish stock (11), which may be diluted with the stock already prepared, and which may be reduced according to the requirements. The name of fish *fumet* or fish *essence* is given to this preparation; its flavor is more delicate than that of fish *glaze,* which it replaces with advantage.

CHAPTER II

THE LEADING WARM SAUCES

WARM sauces are of two kinds: the leading sauces, also called "mother sauces," and the small sauces, which are usually derived from the first-named, and are generally only modified forms. Cooking stock only includes the leading sauces, but I shall refer to the small hot sauces and the cold sauces at the end of the auxiliary stock.

Experience, which plays such an important part in culinary work, is nowhere so necessary as in the preparation of sauces, for not only must the latter flatter the palate, but they must also vary in savor, consistency and viscosity, in accordance with the dishes they accompany. By this means, in a well-ordered dinner, each dish differs from the preceding ones and from those that follow.

Furthermore, sauces must, through the perfection of their preparation, obey the general laws of a rational hygiene, wherefore they should be served and combined in such a way as to allow for easy digestion by the frequently disordered stomachs of their consumers.

Carême was quite justified in priding himself upon the fact that during his stay at the English Court his master—the Prince Regent —had assured him that he (Carême) was the only one among those who had served his Highness whose cooking had been at all easy to digest. Carême had grasped the essential truth that the richer the cooking is, the more speedily do the stomach and palate tire of it. And, indeed, it is a great mistake to suppose that, in order to do good cooking, it is necessary to be extravagant in one's use of all things. In reality, practice dictates fixed and regular quantities, and from these one cannot diverge without upsetting the hygienic and taste balance on which the value of a sauce depends. The requisite quantities of each ingredient must, of course, be used, but neither more nor less, as there are objections to either extreme.

Any sauce whatsoever should be smooth, light (without being liquid), glossy to the eye, and decided in taste. When these condi-

15

tions are fulfilled it is always easy to digest even for tired stomachs.

An essential point in the making of sauces is the seasoning, and it would be impossible for me to lay sufficient stress on the importance of not indulging in any excess in this respect. It too often happens that the insipidness of a badly-made sauce is corrected by excessive seasoning; this is an absolutely deplorable practice.

Seasoning should be so calculated as to be merely a complementary factor, which, though it must throw the savor of dishes into relief, may not form a recognizable part of them. If it be excessive, it modifies and even destroys the taste peculiar to every dish—to the great detriment of the latter and of the consumer's health.

It is therefore desirable that each sauce should possess its own special flavor, well defined, the result of the combined flavors of all its ingredients.

THE ROUX

The *roux* being the thickening element of leading sauces, it is necessary to reveal its preparation and ingredients before giving one's attention to the latter.

Three kinds of *roux* are used—namely, brown *roux*, for brown sauces; pale *roux*, for veloutés, or cream sauces; and white *roux*, for white sauces and Béchamel.

19—BROWN ROUX   *Roux Brun*

Quantities for making about One lb.—Eight oz. of clarified butter (175), nine oz. of best-quality flour.

Preparation.—Mix the flour and butter in a very thick saucepan, and put it on the side of the fire or in a moderate oven. Stir the mixture repeatedly so that the heat may be evenly distributed throughout.

The time allowed for the cooking of brown *roux* cannot be precisely determined, as it depends upon the degree of heat employed. The more intense the latter, the more speedy will be the cooking, while the stirring will of necessity be more rapid. Brown *roux* is known to be cooked when it has acquired a fine, light brown color and when it exudes an odor resembling that of the hazel-nut, characteristic of baked flour.

It is very important that brown *roux* should not be cooked too rapidly. As a matter of fact, among the various constituent elements of flour, the starch alone acts as the binding principle. This starch is contained in little cells, which tightly constrain it, but which are sufficiently porous to permit the percolation of liquid and fatty substances. Under the influence of moderate heat and the infiltered butter, the cells burst through the swelling of the starch, and the latter thereupon completely combines with the butter to form a mass capable of absorbing six times its own weight of liquid when cooked.

When the cooking takes place with a very high heat in the beginning the starch gets burned within its shrivelled cells, and swelling is then possible only in those parts which have been least burned.

The binding principle is thus destroyed, and double or treble the quantity of *roux* becomes necessary in order to obtain the required consistency. But this excess of *roux* in the sauce chokes it up without binding it, and prevents it from clearing. At the same time, the cellulose and the burnt starch lend a bitterness to the sauce of which no subsequent treatment can rid it.

From the above it follows that, starch being the only one from among the different constituents of flour which really affects the thickening of sauces, there would be considerable advantage in preparing *roux* either from a pure form of it, or from substances with kindred properties, such as *fecula*, arrowroot, cornstarch, etc. It is only habit that causes flour to be still used as the binding element of *roux*, and, indeed, the hour is not so far distant when the advantages of the changes I propose will be better understood—changes which have been already recommended by Favre in his dictionary.

With a *roux* well made from the purest starch—in which case the volume of starch and butter would equal about half that of the flour and butter of the old method—and with strong and succulent brown stock, a Spanish sauce or Espagnole may be made in one hour. And this sauce will be clearer, more brilliant, and better than that of the old processes, which needed three days at least to throw off the scum.

20—PALE ROUX   *Roux Blond*

The quantities are the same as for brown *roux*, but cooking must cease as soon as the color of the *roux* begins to change, and before the appearance of any coloring whatsoever.

The observations I made relative to brown *roux*, concerning the thickening element, apply also to pale *roux*.

21—WHITE ROUX   *Roux Blanc*

Same quantities as for brown (19) and pale *roux* (20), but the time of cooking is limited to a few minutes, as it is only needful, in this case, to do away with the disagreeable taste of flour which is typical of those sauces whose *roux* has not been sufficiently cooked.

22—BROWN SAUCE OR ESPAGNOLE SAUCE

Sauce Brun ou Sauce Espagnole

Quantities Required for Four Quarts.—One lb. of brown (19) *roux* dissolved in a deep, thick saucepan with six quarts of brown stock (7) or estouffade. Put the saucepan on an open fire, and stir the sauce with a spatula or a whisk, and do not stop until it begins to boil. Then remove the whisk, and put the saucepan on a corner of the fire, letting it lean slightly to one side with the help of a wedge, so that boiling may only take place at one point, and that the scum thrown out by the sauce may accumulate high up in the saucepan, whence they can be easily removed as they collect.

It is advisable during the skimming to change saucepans twice or even three times, straining every time, and adding a quart of brown stock (7) to replace what has evaporated. At length, when the sauce begins to get lighter, and about two hours before finally straining it, two lbs. of fresh tomatoes, roughly cut up, should be added, or an equivalent quantity of tomato purée, and about one lb. of *Mirepoix* (228). The sauce is then reduced so as to measure four quarts when strained, after which it is poured into a wide tureen, and must be kept in motion until quite cool lest a skin should form on its surface.

The time required for the skimming of an Espagnole varies according to the quality of the stock and *roux*. We saw above that one hour sufficed for a concentrated stock and starch *roux*, in which case the *Mirepoix* and the tomato are added from the first. But much more time is required if one is dealing with a *roux* whose base is flour. In the latter case six hours should be allowed, provided one have excellent stock and well-made *roux*. More often than not this work is done in two stages, thus: after having skimmed the Espagnole for six or eight hours the first day, it is put on the fire the next day with half its volume of stock, and it is left to settle a few hours more before it is finally strained.

Summing up my opinion on this subject, I can only give cooks the following advice, based upon long experience:—

1. Only use strong, clear stock with a decided taste.

2. Be scrupulously careful of the *roux*, however it may be made. By following these two rules, a clear, brilliant, and consistent Espagnole will always be obtained in a fairly short time.

23—HALF GLAZE   *Demi-Glace*

This is the Espagnole sauce, having reached the limit of perfection by final skimming. It is obtained by reducing one quart of Espagnole and one quart of first-class brown stock (7) until its volume is reduced to nine-tenths of a quart. It is then strained into a double-boiler of convenient dimensions, and it is finished, away from the fire, with one-tenth of a quart of excellent sherry. Cover the double-boiler, or slightly butter the top to avoid the formation of a skin. This sauce is the base of all the smaller brown sauces.

24—LENTEN ESPAGNOLE   *Espagnole Maigre*

Practical men are not agreed as to the need of *Lenten* Espagnole. The ordinary Espagnole being really a neutral sauce in flavor, it is quite simple to give it the necessary flavor by the addition of the required quantity of fish *fumet*. It is only, therefore, when one wishes to conform with the demands of a genuine Lent sauce that a fish Espagnole is needed. And, certainly in this case, nothing can take its place.

The preparation of this Espagnole does not differ from that of the ordinary kind, except that the bacon is replaced by mushroom peelings in the *Mirepoix,* and that the sauce must be skimmed for only one hour.

This sauce takes the place of the ordinary Espagnole, for *Lenten* preparations, in every case where the latter is generally used, in *Gratins,* in the Genevoise sauce, etc.

25—ORDINARY VELOUTE SAUCE   *Velouté (Sauce Blanche)*

Quantities Required for Four Quarts.—One lb. of pale *roux* (20), five quarts of white veal stock (10).

Dissolve the *roux* in the cold white veal stock and put the saucepan containing this mixture on an open fire, stirring the sauce with a spatula or whisk, so as to avoid its burning at the bottom. Add one oz. of table-salt, a pinch of nutmeg and white powdered pepper, together with one-quarter lb. of nice white mushroom peelings, if these are handy. Now boil and move to a corner of the fire to scum slowly for one and a half hours, at the same time observing the precautions advised for ordinary Espagnole (22). Strain through muslin into a smaller saucepan, add one pint of white stock, and allow to settle for another half hour. Strain it again through a fine sieve into a wide tureen, and keep stirring it with a spatula until it is quite cold.

I am not partial to garnishing Velouté Sauce with carrots, an onion with a clove stuck into it, and an herb bunch, as many do. The stock should be sufficiently fragrant itself, without requiring the addition of anything beyond the usual condiments. The only exception I should make would be for mushroom peelings, even though it is preferable, when possible, to replace these by mushroom liquor. But this is always scarce in kitchens where it is used for other purposes; wherefore it is often imperative to have recourse to mushrooms instead. The latter may not, however, be added to the stock itself, as they would blacken it; hence I advise their addition to the Velouté during its preparation.

26—CHICKEN VELOUTE   *Velouté de Volaille*

This is identical with ordinary Velouté, except that instead of having white veal stock (10) for its liquor, it is diluted with white poultry stock (10). The mode of procedure and the time allowed for cooking are the same.

26a—FISH VELOUTE   *Velouté de Poisson*

Velouté is the base of various fish sauces whose recipes will be given in Part II.

Prepare it in precisely the same way as poultry velouté, but instead of using poultry stock, use very clear fish *fumet,* and let it scum for twenty minutes only. (See fish *fumet* No. 11.)

27—THICKENED VELOUTE   *Sauce Allemande*

Allemande Sauce or thickened Velouté is not, strictly speaking, a basic sauce. However, it is so often resorted to in the preparation of other sauces that I think it necessary to give it after the Veloutés, from which it is derived.

Quantities Required for One Quart

The yolks of 5 eggs.
1 pint of cold white stock (1).
1 quart of Velouté (25), well cleared.

½ the juice of a lemon.
¼ pint of mushroom liquor.

Mode of Procedure.—Put the various ingredients in a thick-bottomed saucepan and mix them carefully. Then put the pan on an open fire, and stir the sauce with a metal spatula, lest it burn at the bottom. When the sauce has been reduced to about one quart, add one-third pint of fresh cream to it, and reduce further for a few minutes. It should then be passed through a fine strainer into a tureen and kept agitated until quite cold.

Prepared thus, the Allemande Sauce is ready for the preparation of the smaller sauces. Butter must only be added at the very last moment, for if it were buttered any earlier it would most surely separate. The same holds true with this sauce when it is to be served in its original state; it should then receive a small addition of cream, and be buttered so that it may attain its required delicacy; but this addition of butter and cream ought only to be made at the last moment, and away from the fire. When a sauce thickened with egg yolks has any fat substance added to it, it cannot be exposed to a higher temperature than 140 degrees Fahrenheit without risking curdling.

28—BECHAMEL SAUCE   *Sauce Béchamel*

Quantities Required for Four Quarts

1 lb. of white *roux* (21).
4½ quarts of boiling milk.
½ lb. of lean veal.

⅔ oz. of salt, 1 pinch of *mignonette* pepper, and grated nutmeg, and 1 small sprig of thyme.
1 minced onion.

Preparation.—Pour the boiling milk on the *roux,* which should be almost cold, and whisk it well to avoid lumping. Let it boil, then cook on the side of the fire. Meanwhile the lean veal should have been cut into small cubes, and fried with butter in a saucepan, together with the minced onion. When the veal has cooked without becoming browned, it is added to the Béchamel, together with salt and the other seasonings. Let the sauce boil slowly for about one hour in all, and then strain it through a fine sieve into a tureen; butter the top, lest a crust should form.

When Béchamel is intended for *Lenten* preparations, the veal must be omitted.

There is another way of making the sauce. After having boiled the milk, the seasoning and herbs should be added; the saucepan is then covered and placed on a corner of the stove, so as to ensure a thorough infusion. The boiling milk must now be poured on to the *roux* which has been separately prepared, and the sauce should then cook for one quarter of an hour only.

29—TOMATO SAUCE   *Sauce Tomatée*

Quantities Required for Four Quarts

5 oz. of salt pork, rather fat.
6 oz. of carrots cut into cubes.
6 oz. of onions cut into cubes.
1 bay leaf and 1 small sprig of thyme.
5 oz. of flour.

2 oz. of butter, ½ oz. of salt, 1 oz. of sugar, a pinch of pepper.
10 lbs. of raw tomatoes or 4 quarts canned.
2 quarts of white stock (10).

Preparation.—Fry the pork with the butter in a deep, thick-bottomed saucepan. When the pork is nearly melted, add the carrots, onions, and seasonings. Cook and stir the vegetables, then add the flour, which should be allowed to cook until it begins to brown. Now put in the tomatoes and white stock, mix the whole well, and set to boil on an open fire. At this point add the seasoning and a crushed clove of garlic, cover the saucepan, and place in a moderate oven, where it may cook for one and one-half hours. At the end of this time the sauce should be passed through a sieve, and it should boil while being stirred. Finally, pour it into a tureen, and butter its surface to avoid the formation of a skin.

Remarks.—A *purée* of tomatoes is also used in cookery; it is prepared in precisely the same fashion, except that the flour is omitted and only one pint of white stock is added.

30—HOLLANDAISE SAUCE   *Sauce Hollandaise*

Quantities Required for One Quart.—One and one-half lbs. of butter, the yolks of six eggs, one pinch of *mignonette* pepper and one-quarter oz. of salt, three tablespoons of good vinegar.

Preparation.—Put the salt, the *mignonette* pepper, the vinegar, and equal amount of water in a small saucepan, and reduce by three-quarters on the fire. Move the saucepan to a corner of the fire or into a double-boiler, and add a spoonful of cold water and the yolks. Beat with a whisk until the yolks thicken and have the consistency of cream. Then remove the pot to a tepid place and gradually pour the butter on the yolks while briskly stirring the sauce.

When the butter is absorbed, the sauce ought to be thick and firm. It is brought to the correct consistency with a little water, which also lightens it slightly, but the addition of water is optional. The sauce is completed by a drop of lemon juice, and it is rubbed through a fine sieve.

Remarks.—The consistency of sauces whose processes are identical with those of the Hollandaise may be varied at will; for instance, the number of yolks may be increased if a very thick sauce is desired, and it may be lessened in the reverse case. Also similar results may be obtained by cooking the eggs either more or less. As a rule, if a thick sauce be required, the yolks ought to be well cooked and the sauce kept almost cold in the making. Experience alone—the fruit of long practice—can teach the various devices which enable the skilled chef to obtain different results from the same kind and quality of material.

CHAPTER III

THE SMALL COMPOUND SAUCES

Remarks.—In order that the classification of the small sauces should be clear and methodical, I divide them into three parts.

The first part includes the small brown sauces; the second deals with the small white sauces and those suited to this part of the classification; while the third is concerned with the English sauces.

THE SMALL BROWN SAUCES

31—BIGARRADE SAUCE *Sauce Bigarrade*

This sauce is principally used to accompany *braised* and *poëled* ducklings. In the first case, the duckling's *braising* stock, being thickened, constitutes a sauce. In the second case, the stock is clear, and the procedure in both cases is as follows:—

1. After having strained the *braising* sauce, completely remove its grease, and reduce it until it is very thick. Strain it once more through muslin, twisting it; then, in order to bring the sauce to its normal consistency, add the juice of six oranges and one lemon per quart of sauce. Finish with a small piece of lemon and orange rind cut regularly and finely, *Julienne*-fashion, and scalded for five minutes.

2. Strain the poëled stock, for ducklings or wild ducks, through linen; entirely remove the grease, and add four teaspoons of caramelized sugar (2344) dissolved in one tablespoon of vinegar per one-half point of stock, the juice of the oranges and the lemon and the *Julienne* of rinds, as for the braised-ducklings sauce indicated above.

32—BORDELAISE SAUCE *Sauce Bordelaise*

Put into a saucepan two oz. of very finely minced shallots, one-half pint of good red wine, a pinch of *mignonette* pepper, and bits of thyme and bay leaf. Reduce the wine by three-quarters, and add one-half pint of half-*glaze* (23). Keep the sauce simmering for half an hour; skin it from time to time, and strain it through linen or a sieve. When ready to serve, finish it with two tablespoons of dissolved meat glaze (15), a few drops of lemon-juice, and four oz. of beef-marrow, cut into slices or cubes and *poached* in slightly salted boiling water. This sauce may be buttered to the extent of about three oz. per pint, which makes it smoother, but less clear. It is especially suitable for grilled meat.

33—CHASSEUR SAUCE   *Sauce Chasseur*

Peel and mince six medium-sized mushrooms. Heat one-half oz. of butter and as much olive oil in a saucepan; put in the mushrooms, and fry the latter quickly until they are slightly browned. Now add a teaspoonful of minced shallots, and immediately remove half the butter; pour one-half pint of white wine and one glass of liqueur brandy into the saucepan; reduce this liquid to half, and finish the sauce with: one-half pint of half-glaze (23), one-quarter pint of tomato sauce (29), and one tablespoon of meat-glaze (15). Set to boil for five minutes more, and complete with a teaspoon of chopped parsley.

34—BROWN CHAUD-FROID SAUCE   *Sauce Chaud-Froid Brune*

Put one quart of half-glaze (23) into a saucepan with one-fifth pint of truffle *essence*. Put the pan on an open fire, and reduce its contents; while making same add to the sauce, in small quantities at a time, one and one-half pints of aspic.

The degree of reduction in this sauce is a good third, but, to be quite certain, a test of its consistency may be made by allowing it to cool a little. After the reduction, carefully taste, and rectify the seasoning if necessary; mix a little Madeira or Port with the sauce, away from the fire, and strain through muslin or, preferably, through the finest possible sieve. Stir the sauce now and then while it cools, until it is sufficiently liquid, and at the same time consistent enough, to coat a spoon evenly with a film. Its use will be explained among the recipes of the different kinds of Chaud-froids.

35—VARIETIES OF THE CHAUD-FROID SAUCE
Diverses Sauces Chaud-Froid

For Ducks.—Prepare the sauce as for (34), adding to it (for the prescribed quantity) one-half pint of duck *fumet* obtained from the skeletons and remains of roast duckling, and finish it, away from the fire, with the juice of four oranges and a heaped tablespoon of orange rind, cut finely, *Julienne*-fashion, and scalded for five minutes.

For Game Birds.—Treat the Chaud-Froid sauce as indicated in 34, adding one-half pint of the *fumet* of the game constituting the dish in order to lend it that game's characteristic taste. Observe the same precaution for the cooling.

For Fish.—Proceed as in (34), but substitute the Espagnole of fish (22) for the half glaze; intensify the first Espagnole with one-half pint of very clear fish *essence;* use *Lenten* jelly instead of meat jelly.

Remarks upon the Use of Chaud-Froid Sauces.—The chaud-froid sauce may be prepared beforehand, and when it is wanted it need only be gently melted without heating it too much. It ought simply to be made sufficiently liquid to give a good coating to substances immersed in it.

36—DEVILLED SAUCE   *Sauce Diable*

Put in a saucepan two oz. of sliced shallots and one-third pint of white wine. Reduce the latter to two-thirds, add one-half pint of half-glaze (23), reduce to two-thirds again, season strongly with cayenne pepper, and strain through muslin. This sauce may be served with grilled fowls or pigeons. It also forms an excellent accompaniment to left-over meat which needs a spicy sauce.

37—ESCOFFIER DEVILLED SAUCE   *Sauce Diable Escoffier*

This sauce, which may be bought ready-made, is admirably fitted to accompany grilled fish and grills in general. In order to make it ready, all that is needed is to add an equal amount of fresh butter to it, the latter being previously well softened so as to ensure its perfect mixture with the sauce.

38—GENEVOISE SAUCE   *Sauce Genevoise*

Heat two oz. of butter in a saucepan; add one lb. of *Mirepoix* (228) without bacon. Slightly brown, add two lbs. of head of salmon and trimmings or bones of fish, and cook with lid on for twenty minutes. Let the saucepan lean slightly to one side, so that the butter may be drained; moisten with one bottle of excellent red wine; reduce the latter by half; add one pint of *Lenten* Espagnole (24), and allow to cook gently for half an hour.

Rub the sauce through a sieve, pressing it so as to extract all the *essence.* Let it rest awhile; carefully remove the fat which has risen to the surface, and add one liqueur-glass of burnt brandy, one-half pint of red wine, and as much fish *fumet*. Boil again, then move saucepan to the side of fire and skim for one and one-half hours. Frequently remove what the boiling causes to rise to the surface, this second period of cooking being only to ensure the purification of the sauce. If the boiling has been properly handled, the sauce should reach the proper degree of reduction and can be skimmed at the same time. It is then strained through muslin or a fine sieve, and it is finished at the last minute with a few drops of anchovy *essence* and four oz. of butter per quart of sauce.

N.B.—The Genevoise Sauce, like all red-wine sauces, may be served without being buttered. It is thus clearer and more pleasing in color, but the addition of butter in small quantities makes it mellower and more palatable.

38a—REMARKS ON RED WINE SAUCES
Reflexions sur des Sauces au Vin Rouge

In the general repertory of cooking we also have, in the way of red-wine sauces, the "Bourguignonne," "Matelote," and "Red-Wine" sauces, which are closely allied to the "Genevoise," and only differ from it in details of procedure.

The "Bourguignonne" Sauce is composed of red-wine accompanied by seasonings, and reduced by half. In accordance with ordinary principles, it is thickened by means of three oz. of *manié* butter per quart of reduced wine. This sauce is buttered with four oz. of butter per quart, and is especially regarded as a domestic preparation for *poached,* moulded, and hard-boiled eggs.

"Matelote" Sauce is made from Court-bouillon (166) with red wine which has been used for cooking fish. This Court-bouillon, with the mushroom peelings added, is reduced by two-thirds, and is thickened with one pint of *Lenten* Espagnole (24) per pint of the reduced Court-bouillon.

This sauce should be reduced by a third, strained through a fine sieve, and finished by means of two oz. of butter and a little cayenne per pint of sauce.

The Red-Wine Sauce resembles the two preceding ones in so far as it contains *Mirepoix* browned in butter and diluted with red wine. The wine is reduced by half, thickened by a pint of *Lenten* Espagnole per pint of the reduction, and the sauce is skimmed for about twenty minutes. It is strained through a fine sieve, and finished, when ready, by a few drops of anchovy *essence,* a little cayenne, and two oz. of butter per pint of sauce.

39—GRAND-VENEUR SAUCE   *Sauce Grand-Veneur*

Take one pint of Poivrade Sauce (49) and boil it, adding one pint of game stock (5) to keep it light; reduce the sauce by a good third; remove it from the fire, and add four tablespoons of redcurrant jelly. When the latter is well dissolved, complete the sauce by adding one-quarter pint of cream per pint of sauce.

This sauce is the proper accompaniment for joints of venison.

40—ITALIAN SAUCE   *Sauce Italienne*

Ordinary Italian Sauce.—Put into a saucepan six tablespoons of Duxelles (223), two oz. of very lean, cooked ham, cut very finely, *brunoise*-fashion, and one pint of half-glaze (23) tomato. Boil for ten minutes, and complete, at the moment of serving, with one teaspoon of parsley, chervil, and tarragon, minced and mixed.

Lenten Italian Sauce.—Same preparation, only omit the ham, and substitute *Lent* Espagnole (24) (combined with fish *fumet* made from the fish for which the sauce is intended) for half-glaze (23) with tomatoes.

41—THICKENED GRAVY   *Jus Lié*

Boil one pint of poultry or veal stock (10) (according to the nature of the dish the gravy is intended for). Thicken this sauce by means of three-quarters oz. of *fecula* (cornstarch, etc.), diluted with a little cold water or gravy, and pour this binding into the boiling gravy, being careful to stir briskly.

The thickened gravy with the veal-stock (10) base is used for choicest cuts of butcher's meat; the same gravy with a poultry-stock base is for breasts of poultry.

42—TOMATOED VEAL GRAVY   *Jus Lié Tomaté*

Add to one pint of veal stock (10) two oz. of *purée* and one-quarter pint of tomato juice, and reduce by a fifth. Strain the gravy through linen. This gravy is used for various meat.

43—LYONNAISE SAUCE   *Sauce Lyonnaise*

Finely mince two oz. of onions and brown them slightly in two oz. of butter. Moisten with one-quarter pint of white wine and as much vinegar; reduce the liquid; add one and one-half pints of clear half-glaze (23), and set to cook slowly for half an hour. Rub the sauce through a fine sieve.

N.B.—The onion may be left in the sauce or not, according to the preparation for which it is intended and to suit the taste.

44—MADEIRA SAUCE *Sauce Madère*

Put one and one-half pints of half-glaze (23) into a saucepan, and reduce it on a brisk fire to a stiff consistency. When it reaches this point, take it off the fire and add one-fifth pint of Madeira to it, which brings it back to its normal consistency. Strain through a fine sieve, and keep it warm without allowing it to boil.

45—MARROW SAUCE *Sauce Moelle*

Follow the proportions as indicated under "Sauce Bordelaise" (32) for the necessary quantity of this sauce, the Marrow Sauce being only a variety of the Bordelaise. Finish it with six oz. per quart of beef marrow, cut into cubes, *poached* and well drained, and one teaspoon of chopped parsley, scalded for a second. If the sauce is to accompany vegetables, finish it, away from the fire, with three oz. of butter, and then add the cubes of marrow and the parsley.

46—PINE-NUT SAUCE *Sauce Pignons*

Take the necessary amount of Poivrade Sauce (49), and let it boil. Now, for one pint of sauce, prepare an infusion of juniper berries, with one-quarter pint of water and two oz. of coarsely chopped berries; one oz. of toasted pine-nuts, and one oz. of raisins, seeded and washed, and left to soak in tepid water for about an hour. Finish the sauce, when serving, by adding the infusion of juniper berries strained through linen, the toasted pine-nuts, the soaked raisins, and one-eighth pint of Madeira wine.

This sauce is specially suited to joints of venison.

47—PERIGUEUX SAUCE *Sauce Perigueux*

Prepare a "Sauce Madère" (44), and add to the half-glaze (23), to be reduced, half its volume of very strong veal stock (10), and keep it a little thicker than usual. Finish this sauce by adding one-sixth pint of truffle *essence* and three oz. of chopped truffles per quart of Madeira Sauce (44). It is used for numerous small entrées, timbales, hot pâtés, etc.

48—PIQUANTE SAUCE *Sauce Piquante*

Put into a saucepan two oz. of minced shallots, one-quarter pint of vinegar, and as much white wine. Reduce the liquid by a good half, and add one pint of half-glaze (23); set the sauce to boil, and skim it for half an hour. At the last moment finish it, away from the fire, with two oz. of gherkins, one oz. of capers, and a teaspoon of chervil, parsley, and tarragon, mixed; all the ingredients to be finely chopped. This sauce generally accompanies grilled or boiled pork, and cold left-over meat minced, which needs spicy flavoring.

49—ORDINARY POIVRADE SAUCE   *Sauce Poivrade Ordinaire*

1. Heat two oz. of butter in a saucepan, and add one lb. of raw *Mirepoix* (228). Fry the vegetables until they are well browned; moisten with one-quarter pint of vinegar and one-half pint of *Marinade* (169); reduce to two-thirds; add one pint of Espagnole Sauce (22), and cook for three-quarters of an hour. Ten minutes before straining the sauce, put in a few crushed peppercorns. If the pepper were put in the sauce earlier, it might make it bitter.

2. Strain the sauce through a sieve, pressing the seasonings; add a further one-half pint of *Marinade,* and skim for one-quarter of an hour, keeping it simmering the while. Strain again through a fine sieve, and finish the sauce, when ready for serving, with two oz. of butter.

This sauce is suitable for joints marinated or not.

50—POIVRADE SAUCE FOR VENISON   *Sauce Poivrade pour Gibier*

Fry, with two oz. of butter and two oz. of oil, one lb. of raw *Mirepoix* (228) to which are added four lbs. of well-broken bones and ground-game trimmings. When the whole is well browned, drain off the grease, and dilute with one pint of vinegar and one pint of white wine. Reduce this liquid by three-quarters, then add three quarts of game stock and a quart of Espagnole Sauce (22). Boil, cover the saucepan, and put into a moderate oven, where it should stay for at least three hours. At the end of this time take out the saucepan and pour its contents through a fine sieve placed over a tureen; press the remains so as to expel all the sauce they hold, and pour the sauce into a tall, thick saucepan. Add enough game stock (8) and *Marinade,* mixed in equal parts, to produce three quarts in all of sauce, and gently reduce the latter while skimming it. As it diminishes in volume, it should be passed through muslin into smaller saucepans, and the reduction should be stopped when only a quart of sauce remains.

N.B.—This sauce, like red-wine sauces, may be served as it stands. It is brilliant, clear, and perhaps more pleasing, but the addition of a certain quantity of butter (four oz. per quart) makes it perfectly mellow, and admirably completes its fragrance.

51—PROVENCALE SAUCE   *Sauce Provençale*

Peel, remove the seeds, press and coarsely chop twelve medium tomatoes. Heat in a saucepan one-fifth pint of oil, until it begins to smoke a little; add the tomatoes seasoned with pepper and salt; add a crushed garlic clove, a pinch of powdered sugar, one teaspoon of chopped parsley, and allow to cook gently for half an hour. In reality, true Provençale is nothing but a fine *fondue* of tomatoes with garlic.

52—ROBERT SAUCE   *Sauce Robert*

Finely mince a large onion and put it into a saucepan with butter. Fry the onion gently and without letting it brown. Dilute with one-third pint of white wine, reduce the latter by one-third, add one pint of half-glaze (23), and leave to simmer for twenty minutes. When serving, finish the sauce with one tablespoon of meat glaze (15), one teaspoon of dry mustard, and one pinch of powdered sugar. If, when finished, the sauce has to wait, it should be kept warm in a double-boiler, as it must not boil again. This sauce—of a spicy flavor—is best suited to grilled and boiled pork. It may also be used for a mince of the same meat.

53—ROBERT SAUCE ESCOFFIER   *Sauce Robert Escoffier*

This sauce may be bought ready-made. It is used either hot or cold. It is especially suitable for pork, veal, poultry, and even fish, and is generally used hot with grills after the equal quantity of excellent brown stock (7) has been added to it. It may also be served cold to accompany cold meat.

54—ROUENNAISE SAUCE   *Sauce Rouennaise*

Prepare a "Bordelaise" sauce (32). The diluting liquid of this sauce must be an excellent red wine. For one pint of sauce, pass four raw ducks' livers through a sieve; add the resulting *purée* to the Bordelaise, and heat the latter for a few minutes in order to *poach* the liver. Be careful, however, not to heat the sauce too much nor too long, lest the liver be cooked. Serve this sauce with duckling à la Rouennaise (1754).

55—SALMIS SAUCE   *Sauce Salmis*

The base of this sauce, which rather resembles the *cullis,* is unchangeable. Its diluting liquid only changes according to the kind of birds or game to be treated, and whether this game is to be considered ordinary or *Lenten.*

Cut and gently brown in butter five oz. of *Mirepoix* (228). Add the skin detached from the limbs and the chopped skeleton of the bird being used, and moisten with one pint of white wine. Reduce the latter to two-thirds, add one-half pint of half-glaze (23), and boil gently for three-quarters of an hour. Pass through a strainer, while pressing down the bird and the seasonings, with the view of extracting their *essence,* and thin the *cullis* thus obtained by means of one-half pint of game stock (5) or mushroom liquor, if the game be *Lenten.* Now skim for about one hour, finally reduce the sauce, bring it to its proper consistency with a little mushroom liquor and truffle *essence,* rub it through a fine sieve, and butter it slightly at the last moment.

56—TURTLE SAUCE   *Sauce Tortue*

Boil one-half pint of veal stock (9), adding a small sprig of sage, sweet marjoram, rosemary, basil, thyme, and as much bay leaf, two oz. of mushroom peelings, and one oz. of parsley. Cover and allow to steep for half an hour. Two minutes before straining the infusion, add four coarsely chopped peppercorns.

After straining through fine linen, add one-half pint of half-glaze (23) and as much tomato sauce (29) (away from the fire) with four tablespoons of sherry, a little truffle (29) *essence,* and a good pinch of cayenne.

N.B.—As this sauce must be spicy, the use of cayenne suggests itself, but great caution should be observed, as there must be no excess of this condiment.

57—VENISON SAUCE   *Sauce Venaison*

Prepare a Poivrade sauce (50) for game. Finish this sauce with two tablespoons of red-currant jelly, previously dissolved, and mixed with five tablespoons of fresh cream per pint of sauce. This addition of cream and red-currants must be made away from the fire.

Serve this sauce with large-game.

SMALL WHITE AND COMPOUND SAUCES

58—AMERICAN SAUCE   *Sauce Americaine*

This sauce is that of lobster prepared "à l'Américaine" (939). As it generally accompanies a fish, the meat of the lobster or lobsters which have served in its preparation is sliced and used as the garnish of the fish.

59—ANCHOVY SAUCE *Sauce Anchois*

Put into a small saucepan one pint of unbuttered "Normande Sauce" (99), and finish it, away from the fire, with three oz. of anchovy butter (281), and one oz. of anchovy fillets, washed, dried, and cut into small pieces.

60—AURORE SAUCE *Sauce Aurore*

Into one-half pint of boiling velouté (25) put the same quantity of very red tomato *purée* (29), and mix the two. Let the sauce boil a little, pass it through a fine sieve, and finish, away from the fire, with three oz. of butter.

61—LENTEN AURORE SAUCE *Sauce Aurore Maigre*

This sauce is made like the preceding one, with the same quantities of velouté and tomato *purée,* replacing ordinary velouté by fish velouté (26a).

62—BEARNAISE SAUCE *Sauce Béarnaise*

Put into a small saucepan one teaspoon of chopped shallots, two oz. of chopped tarragon stalks, three oz. of chervil, some *mignonette* pepper, a pinch of salt, and four tablespoons of vinegar. Reduce the vinegar by two-thirds, take off the fire, let the pan cool a little, and add to this reduction the yolks of five eggs. Now put the saucepan on a low fire and gradually combine with the yolks six oz. of melted butter. Whisk the sauce briskly, to ensure the cooking of the yolks, which alone, by gradual cooking, effect the thickening of the sauce.

When the butter is combined with the sauce, rub it through a fine sieve, and finish it with a teaspoon of chervil and chopped tarragon leaves. Complete the seasoning with a pinch of cayenne. This sauce should not be served very hot, as it is really a mayonnaise with butter. It need only be tepid, for it would probably curdle if it were over-heated. Serve it with grilled meat or poultry.

63—BEARNAISE SAUCE WITH MEAT GLAZE, CALLED VALOIS SAUCE OR FOYOT SAUCE
Sauce Béarnaise à la Glace de Viande, dite Valois ou Foyot

Prepare a Béarnaise sauce as explained in (62). Complete it with three tablespoons of dissolved pale meat glaze (15), which may be added in small quantities at a time. Serve it with various meats.

64—TOMATOED BEARNAISE SAUCE OR CHORON SAUCE

Sauce Béarnaise Tomatée ou Sauce Choron

Proceed in exactly the same way as for Béarnaise (62). When the sauce is made and rubbed through a fine sieve, finish it with one-third pint of very red tomato *purée*. In this case the final addition of chervil and tarragon should not be made.

This is proper to "Tournedos Choron," but it may accompany grilled poultry and veal or pork.

65—BERCY SAUCE　　　　　　　　*Sauce Bercy*

Heat two oz. of chopped shallots. Moisten with one-half pint of white wine and as much fish *fumet,* or, when possible, the same quantity of fish liquor, the latter being, of course, that of a fish similar to the one the sauce is to accompany. Reduce to a good third, add one-third pint of velouté (25), let the sauce boil some time, and finish it, away from the fire, with four oz. of butter (added by degrees), a few drops of fish *glaze,* half the juice of a lemon, and one oz. of chopped parsley.

Serve with medium-sized *poached* fish.

66—BUTTER SAUCE　　　　　　　　*Sauce au Beurre*

Mix two oz. of sifted flour with two oz. of melted butter. Dilute with one quart of boiling water, salted to the extent of one-quarter oz. per quart. Stir briskly to ensure a perfect blending, and do not allow to boil. Add immediately the yolks of six eggs mixed with one-quarter pint of cream and the juice of half a lemon. Rub through a fine sieve, and finish the sauce with five oz. of best fresh butter.

Be careful that the sauce does not boil after it has been thickened.

67—BONNEFOY SAUCE, OR WHITE BORDELAISE SAUCE

Sauce Bonnefoy, ou Sauce Bordelaise Blanche

Put in a saucepan two oz. of minced shallots and one-half pint of Graves, Sauterne, or any other excellent white Bordeaux. Reduce the wine almost entirely, add one-quarter pint of velouté (25), let it simmer twenty minutes, and rub it through a fine sieve. Finish it, away from the fire, with six oz. of butter and a little chopped tarragon.

Serve it with grilled fish or grilled white meat.

68—CAPER SAUCE
Sauce aux Capres

This is a derivative of the Butter Sauce (66), and there need only be added two tablespoons of capers per pint of sauce. It frequently accompanies boiled fish of all kinds.

69—CARDINAL SAUCE
Sauce Cardinal

Boil one pint of Béchamel (28), to which add one-half pint of fish *fumet* and a little truffle *essence,* and reduce by a quarter. Finish the sauce, when serving, with three tablespoons of cream and three oz. of very red lobster butter (149).

70—MUSHROOM SAUCE
Sauce aux Champignons

If this be intended for poultry, add one-fifth pint of mushroom liquor and eight oz. of button-mushroom caps turned or grooved and cooked, to one pint of very stiff Allemande Sauce (27).

If it be intended for fish, take one pint of fish velouté (26a) thickened with the yolks of four eggs, and finish it with mushroom liquor, as above.

The sauce that I suggest for poultry may also be used for fish, after adding the necessary quantity of fish *fumet.*

71—CHÂTEAUBRIAND SAUCE
Sauce Châteaubriand

Put one oz. of chopped shallots, a sprig of thyme and a bit of bay leaf, one oz. of mushroom peelings, and one-quarter pint of white wine into a saucepan. Reduce the wine almost entirely, add one-half pint of veal gravy, and reduce again until the liquid only measures one-quarter pint. Strain through muslin, and finish the sauce away from the fire with four oz. of butter "Maître d'Hotel" (150), to which may be added a little chopped tarragon. Serve with grilled fillet of beef, otherwise "Châteaubriand."

72—WHITE CHAUD-FROID SAUCE
Sauce Chaud-Froid Blanche

Boil one pint of velouté (25) in a saucepan, and add three-quarters pint of melted white poultry aspic (159). Put the saucepan on an open fire, reduce the sauce by a third, stirring constantly, and gradually add one-half pint of very fresh cream. When the sauce has reached the desired degree of consistency rub it through a fine sieve, and stir it frequently while it cools, for fear of a skin forming on its surface, for if this happened it would have to be strained again. When serving, this sauce should be cold, so that it may properly coat a spoon and yet be liquid enough to permit the latter being easily dipped into it.

73—ORDINARY CHAUD-FROID SAUCE   *Sauce Chaud-Froid Ordinaire*

Proceed exactly as above, substituting Allemande Sauce (27) for the velouté, and reducing the quantity of cream to one-quarter pint. Observe the same precautions while cooling.

74—CHAUD-FROID SAUCE, A L'AURORE

Sauce Chaud-Froid à l'Aurore

Prepare a white Chaud-Froid (72). The same may be colored by the addition of fine red tomato *purée* (29)—more or less to match the desired shade—or by an infusion of paprika, according to the use for which it is intended. This last product is preferable when not too deep a shade is required.

75—CHAUD-FROID SAUCE VERT-PRE

Sauce Chaud-Froid, au Vert-Pré

Add to the velouté (25) of the white Chaud-Froid (72) sauce, at the same time as the jelly aspic, an infusion prepared thus:—Boil one-quarter pint of white wine, and add to it one pinch of chervil stalks, a similar quantity of tarragon leaves, chives, and parsley leaves. Cover, allow infusion to proceed away from the fire for ten minutes, and strain through linen.

Treat the sauce as explained, and finish with spinach-green (143). The shade of the sauce must not be too pronounced, but must remain a pale green. The coloring principle must therefore be added with caution and in small quantities, until the correct shade is obtained. Use this sauce for Chaud-Froids of fowl, particularly that kind distinguished as *"Printanier."*

76—LENT CHAUD-FROID SAUCE   *Sauce Chaud-Froid Maigre*

Proceed as for white Chaud-Froid (22), using the same quantities, and taking note of the following modifications:—

1. Substitute fish velouté (26a) for ordinary velouté.

2. Substitute white fish jelly for poultry aspic.

Remarks.—I have adopted the use of this ordinary Chaud-Froid sauce for the glazing of fillets and scallops of fish and shell-fish, instead of cleared Mayonnaise, formerly used, which had certain inconveniences—not the least being the oozing out of the oil under the shrinkage of the gelatine. This difficulty does not obtain in the ordinary Chaud-Froid, the definite and pronounced flavor of which is better than that of the cleared Mayonnaise.

77—CHERRY SAUCE ESCOFFIER   *Sauce aux Cerises Escoffier*

This sauce may be bought ready-made. Like the Robert Sauce, it can be served hot or cold. It is an excellent addition to venison, and even to small ground-game. Saddle of venison with this sauce constitutes one of the greatest delicacies that an epicure could desire.

78—CHIVRY SAUCE   *Sauce Chivry*

In one-half pint of boiling poultry stock (10) put a large pinch of chervil *pluches,* tarragon and parsley leaves, a head of young pimpernel (the qualification here is very important, for this aromatic plant grows bitter as it matures), and a good pinch of chives. Cover, and let infusion proceed for ten to twelve minutes; then add the liquid (strained through linen) to one pint of velouté (25). Boil, reduce by a quarter, and complete it with two oz. of Green Butter (143). Chivry Sauce is admirably suited to boiled or *poached* poultry.

79—CREAM SAUCE   *Sauce à la Crème*

Boil one pint of Béchamel Sauce (28), and add one-quarter pint of cream to it. Reduce on an open fire until the sauce has become very thick; then strain through a fine sieve. Bring to its normal degree of consistency by gradually adding, away from the fire, one-quarter pint of very fresh cream and a few drops of lemon-juice. Serve this sauce with boiled fish, poultry, eggs, and various vegetables.

80—SHRIMP SAUCE   *Sauce aux Crevettes*

Boil one pint of fish velouté (26a) or, failing this, Béchamel sauce (28), and add to it one-quarter pint of cream and one-quarter pint of very clear fish *fumet.* Reduce to one pint, and finish the sauce, away from the fire, with two oz. of Shrimp Butter (145) and two oz. of shelled shrimps' tails.

81—CURRY SAUCE   *Sauce Currie*

Slightly brown the following vegetables in butter:—Twelve oz. of minced onions, one oz. of parsley roots, four oz. of minced celery, a small sprig of thyme, a bit of bay leaf, and a little mace. Sprinkle with two oz. of flour and a teaspoon of curry powder. Cook the flour for some minutes without letting it brown, and dilute with one and one-half pints of white stock (10). Boil, cook gently for three-quarters of an hour, and rub through a fine sieve. Now heat the sauce, remove its grease, and keep it in a double-boiler. Serve this sauce with fish, shell-fish, poultry, and various egg-preparations.

N.B.—This sauce is sometimes flavored with cocoa-nut water or milk in the proportion of one-quarter of the liquid.

82—DIPLOMATE SAUCE   *Sauce Diplomate*

Take one pint of Normande Sauce (99), and finish it with two oz. of lobster butter (149) and three tablespoons of lobster meat, and truffles cut into small, regular cubes.

83—HERB SAUCE   *Sauce aux Fines Herbes*

Prepare one pint of white-wine sauce (111). Finish it away from the fire with three oz. of shallot butter (146), a tablespoon of parsley, chervil, tarragon, and chives, chopped and mixed. Serve this sauce with boiled or *poached* fish.

84—GOOSEBERRY SAUCE   *Sauce aux Groseilles*

Prepare one pint of butter sauce (66). Meanwhile put one lb. of green gooseberries into a small copper saucepan containing boiling water. Boil for five minutes, then drain the gooseberries, and put them in a little saucepan with one-half pint of white wine and three oz. of powdered sugar. Gently cook the gooseberries, rub them through a fine sieve, and add the pulp to the butter sauce. This sauce is excellent with grilled mackerel and the *poached* fillets of that fish.

85—HUNGARIAN SAUCE   *Sauce Hongroise*

Gently fry in butter, without browning, two tablespoons of chopped onions seasoned with table-salt and half a teaspoon of paprika. Moisten with one-quarter pint of white wine, add a small herb bunch, reduce the wine by two-thirds, and remove the herbs.

Finish with one pint of ordinary or *Lenten* Velouté (26a), according to the use for which the sauce is intended, and boil moderately for five minutes. Then rub the sauce through a fine sieve, and complete it with two oz. of butter. Remember this sauce should be of a tender, pink shade, which it must owe to the paprika alone.

It forms an ideal accompaniment to choice morsels of lamb and veal, eggs, poultry, and fish.

86—OYSTER SAUCE   *Sauce aux Huîtres*

Take one pint of Normande Sauce (99), finish it as directed in that recipe, and complete it with one-quarter pint of reduced oyster liquor, strained through linen, and twelve *poached* and trimmed oysters.

87—IVORY SAUCE, OR ALBUFERA SAUCE   *Sauce Albufera*

Take the necessary quantity of Suprême Sauce (106a). Add to this four tablespoons of dissolved, pale, meat glaze (15) per quart of sauce, in order to lend the latter that ivory-white tint which characterizes it. Serve this sauce chiefly with poultry and *poached* sweetbread.

88—JOINVILLE SAUCE   *Sauce Joinville*

Prepare one pint of Normande Sauce (99), as given in the first part of the recipe, and complete it with two oz. of shrimp butter (45) and two oz. of crayfish butter (147). If this sauce is to accompany a fish à la Joinville, which includes a special garnish, it is served as it stands. If it is served with a large, boiled, ungarnished fish, one oz. of very black truffles cut *Julienne*-fashion should be added. As may be seen, Joinville Sauce differs from similar preparations in the final operation where crayfish and shrimp butter are combined.

89—MALTESE SAUCE   *Sauce Maltaise*

To the Hollandaise Sauce (30), add, when serving up, the juice of two blood oranges (these late-season oranges being especially suitable for this sauce) and half a teaspoonful of grated orange-rind.

Maltese Sauce is the finest for asparagus.

90—MARINIERE SAUCE   *Sauce Marinière*

Take the necessary quantity of Bercy Sauce (65), and add, per pint of sauce, one-quarter pint of mussel liquor and a binding composed of the yolks of three eggs.

Serve this with small *poached* fish and more particularly with mussels.

91—MORNAY SAUCE   *Sauce Mornay*

Boil one pint of Béchamel Sauce (28) with one-quarter pint of the *fumet* of the fish, poultry, or vegetable, which is to constitute the dish. Reduce by a good quarter, and add two oz. of Gruyère and two oz. of grated Parmesan.

Put the sauce on the fire again for a few minutes, and ensure the melting of the cheese by stirring with a small whisk. Finish the sauce away from the fire with two oz. of butter added by degrees.

92—MOUSSELINE SAUCE   *Sauce Mousseline*

To a Hollandaise Sauce (30), add, just before serving up, one-half pint of stiffly-whipped cream per pint of sauce.

93—MOUSSEUSE SAUCE   *Sauce Mousseuse*

Scald and wipe a small pan, and put into it one-half lb. of stiff *manié* butter, properly softened. Season this butter with table-salt and a few drops of lemon-juice, and whisk it while gradually adding one-third pint of cold water. Finish with two tablespoons of very firm, whipped cream. This preparation, though classified as a sauce, is really a compound butter, which is served with boiled fish. The heat of the fish is sufficient to melt it, and its appearance is infinitely more agreeable than that of plain, melted butter.

94—MUSTARD SAUCE   *Sauce Moutarde*

Take the necessary quantity of butter sauce and complete it, away from the fire, with one tablespoon of mustard per pint of sauce.

N.B.—If the sauce has to wait, it must be kept in a double-boiler, for it should not on any account boil. It is served with certain small grilled fish, especially fresh herrings.

95—NANTUA SAUCE   *Sauce Nantua*

Boil one pint of Béchamel Sauce (28), add one-half pint of cream, and reduce by a third. Rub it through a fine sieve, and finish it with a further addition of two tablespoons of cream, three oz. of very fine crayfish butter (147), and one tablespoon of small, shelled crayfishes' tails.

96—NEWBURG SAUCE   *Sauce Newburg*

First Method (with Raw Lobsters).—Divide a two lb. lobster into four parts. Remove its creamy parts, chop them finely with two oz. of butter, and put them aside.

Heat in a saucepan one and one-half oz. of butter and as much oil, and add the pieces of lobster, well seasoned with salt and cayenne. Fry until the pieces assume a fine, red color; entirely drain away the butter, and add two tablespoons of burnt brandy and one-third pint of Marsala or old Sherry.

Reduce the wine by two-thirds, and douse the lobster with one-third pint of cream and one-half pint of fish *fumet*. Now add a herb bunch, cover the saucepan, and gently cook for twenty-five minutes. Then drain the lobster in a sieve, remove the meat and cut it into cubes, and finish the sauce by adding the creamy portions put aside from the first. Boil so as to ensure the cooking of these latter portions; add the meat, cut into cubes, and test for the seasoning.

N.B.—The addition of the meat to the sauce is optional; instead of cutting it into cubes it may be cooked and arranged on the fish constituting the dish.

97—NEWBURG SAUCE WITH COOKED LOBSTER
Sauce Newburg avec Homard Cuit

The lobster having been cooked in a *Court-bouillon* (166), shell the tail and slice it up. Arrange these slices in a saucepan liberally buttered; season them strongly with salt and cayenne, and heat them on both sides so as to effect the reddening of the skin. Immerse, to cover, in a good Sherry, and almost entirely reduce same.

When serving, pour on the slices a binding mixture composed of one-third pint of fresh cream and the yolks of two eggs. Gently stir, away from the fire, and roll the saucepan about until the blending is completed.

Originally, these two sauces, like the American, were exclusively composed of, and served with, lobster. They were one with the two very excellent preparations of lobster which bear their name. In its two forms lobster may only be served at lunch, many people with delicate stomachs being unable to digest it at night. To obviate this serious difficulty, I have made it a practice to serve lobster sauce with fillets or Mousselines of sole, adding the lobster as a garnish only. And this innovation proved most welcome to the public.

By using such condiments as curry and paprika, excellent varieties of this sauce may be obtained, which are particularly suited to sole and other white *Lenten* fish. In either of these cases it is well to add a little rice "à l'Indienne" (2254) to the fish.

98—NOISETTE SAUCE   *Sauce Noisette*

Prepare a Hollandaise Sauce (30). Add two oz. of hazel-nut butter (155) at the last moment.

Serve this with salmon, trout, and all boiled fish in general.

99—NORMANDY SAUCE   *Sauce Normandie*

Put in a saucepan one pint of fish velouté (26a), three tablespoons of mushroom liquor, as much oyster liquor, and twice as much sole *fumet* (11), the yolks of three eggs, a few drops of lemon-juice, and one-quarter pint of cream. Reduce by a good third over an open fire, season with a little cayenne, rub through a fine sieve, and finish with two oz. of butter and four tablespoons of good cream.

This sauce is proper to fillet of sole "à la Normande" (856), but it is also frequently used as the base of other small sauces.

100—ORIENTAL SAUCE   *Sauce Orientale*

Take one pint of American sauce (58), season with curry, and reduce to a third. Then add, away from the fire, one-quarter pint of cream per pint of sauce.

Serve this sauce in the same way as American Sauce.

101—POULETTE SAUCE   *Sauce Poulette*

Boil for a few minutes one pint of Sauce Allemande (27), and add six tablespoons of mushroom liquor. Finish, away from the fire, with two oz. of butter, a few drops of lemon-juice, and one teaspoonful of chopped parsley. Use this sauce with certain vegetables, but more generally with sheep's shanks.

102—RAVIGOTE SAUCE   *Sauce Ravigote*

Reduce by half, one-quarter pint of white wine with half as much vinegar. Add one pint of ordinary velouté (25), boil gently for a few minutes, and finish with one and one-half oz. of shallot butter (146) and one teaspoon of chervil, tarragon, and chopped chives. This sauce accompanies boiled poultry (1444) and certain white "*abats*" (lights of veal, pork, and lamb).

103—REGENCY SAUCE   *Sauce Régence*

If this sauce is to garnish poultry, boil one pint of Allemande Sauce (27) with six tablespoons of mushroom *essence* and two tablespoons of truffle *essence*. Finish with four tablespoons of poultry *glaze* (16).

If it is to garnish fish, substitute for the Allemande Sauce (27) some fish velouté (26a) thickened with egg-yolks and the *essences* of mushroom and truffle. Complete with some fish *essence*.

104—SOUBISE SAUCE   *Sauce Soubise*

Cook in butter two lbs. of finely-minced onions, scalded for three minutes and well dried. This cooking of the onions in butter increases their flavor. Now add one-half pint of thickened Béchamel (28); season with salt and a teaspoon of powdered sugar. Cook gently for half an hour, rub through a fine sieve, and complete the sauce with some tablespoons of cream and two oz. of butter.

105—SOUBISE SAUCE WITH RICE   *Sauce Soubise au Riz*

The same quantity as above of minced onions, scalded and well drained. Garnish the bottom and the sides of a tall, medium saucepan with some thin slices of fat bacon. Add the onions, together with one-quarter lb. of Carolina or Southern rice, one pint of white consommé, a large pinch of powdered sugar, and the necessary salt. Cook gently in the front of the oven for three-quarters of an hour. Then put the onions and rice through a grinder, rub the resulting *purée* through a fine sieve, and finish with cream and butter as in the preceding case.

N.B.—This sauce, being more consistent than the former, is used as a garnish just as often as a sauce.

106—TOMATOED SOUBISE SAUCE   *Sauce Soubise Tomatée*

Prepare a Soubise in accordance with the first of the two above recipes, and add to it one-third of its volume of very red tomato *purée* (29).

REMARKS

1. The Soubise is rather a *cullis* than a sauce, and its consistency must be greater than that of a sauce.
2. The addition of Béchamel (28) in Soubise is preferable to that of rice, since it makes it smoother. If, in certain cases, rice is used as a binding element, it is to give the Soubise more consistency.
3. In accordance with the uses to which it may be put, the Tomato Soubise may be finally seasoned either with curry or paprika.

106a—SUPREME SAUCE   *Sauce Suprême*

The salient characteristics of Suprême Sauce are its perfect whiteness and delicacy. It is generally prepared in small quantities only.

Preparation.—Put one and one-half pints of very clear poultry stock (10) and one-quarter pint of mushroom cooking liquor into a saucepan. Reduce to two-thirds; add one pint of "poultry velouté" (26); reduce on an open fire, stirring with the spatula, and combine one-half pint of excellent cream with the sauce, this last ingredient being added little by little.

When the sauce has reached the desired consistency, strain it through a sieve, and add another one-quarter pint of cream and two oz. of best butter. Stir with a spoon, from time to time, or keep the pan well covered.

107—VENETIAN SAUCE *Sauce Venitienne*

Put into a saucepan one tablespoon of chopped shallots, one tablespoon of chervil, and one-quarter pint of white wine and tarragon vinegar, mixed in equal quantities. Reduce the vinegar by two-thirds; add one pint of white wine sauce (111); boil for a few minutes; rub through a fine sieve, and finish the sauce with a sufficient quantity of herb juice (183) and one teaspoon of chopped chervil and tarragon. This sauce accompanies various fish.

108—VILLEROY SAUCE *Sauce Villeroy*

Put into a saucepan one pint of Allemande Sauce (27) to which have been added two tablespoons of truffle *essence* and as much ham *essence*.

Reduce on an open fire and constantly stir until the sauce is sufficiently thick to coat immersed solids thickly.

109—VILLEROY SOUBISE SAUCE *Sauce Villeroy Soubisée*

Put into a saucepan two-thirds pint of Allemande Sauce (27) and one-third pint of Soubise *purée* (105). Reduce as in the preceding case, as the uses to which this is put are the same. Now, according to the circumstances and the nature of the dish it is intended for, a few teaspoons of very black, chopped truffles may be added to this sauce.

110—VILLEROY TOMATOED SAUCE *Sauce Villeroy Tomatée*

Prepare the sauce as explained under (108) and add to it the third of its volume of very fine tomato *purée* (29). Reduce in the same way.

Remarks.—Villeroy sauce, of any kind, is solely used for the coating of preparations said to be "à la Villeroy."

The Villeroy Tomato may be finally seasoned with curry or paprika, according to the preparation for which it is intended.

111—WHITE WINE SAUCE *Sauce au Vin Blanc*

The three following methods are employed in making it:—

1. Add one-quarter pint of fish *fumet* to one pint of thickened

Velouté (27), and reduce by half. Finish the sauce, away from the fire, with four oz. of butter. Thus prepared, this white wine sauce is suitable for *glazed* fish.

2. Almost entirely reduce one-quarter pint of fish *fumet*. To this reduction add the yolks of four eggs, mixing them well, and follow with one lb. of butter, added by degrees, paying heed to the precautions indicated under sauce Hollandaise (30).

3. Put the yolks of five eggs into a small saucepan and mix them with one tablespoon of cold fish-stock. Put the pan in a water-bath and finish the sauce with one lb. of butter, meanwhile adding from time to time, and in small quantities, six tablespoons of excellent fish *fumet*. The procedure in this sauce is, in short, exactly that of the Hollandaise, with this distinction, that here fish *fumet* takes the place of the water.

HOT ENGLISH AND AMERICAN SAUCES

112—APPLE SAUCE   *Sauce aux Pommes*

Quarter, peel, core, and chop two lbs. of medium-sized apples; place these in a saucepan with one tablespoon of powdered sugar, a bit of cinnamon, and a few tablespoons of water. Cook the whole gently with lid on, and smooth the *purée* with a whisk before serving.

Serve this sauce lukewarm with duck, goose, roast hare, etc.

113—BREAD SAUCE   *Sauce de Pain*

Boil one pint of milk, and add three oz. of fresh, white breadcrumbs, a little salt, a small onion with a clove stuck in it, and one oz. of butter. Cook gently for about a quarter of an hour, remove the onion, smooth the sauce by beating, and finish it with a few tablespoons of cream.

This sauce is served with roast fowl and roast feathered game.

114—CELERY SAUCE   *Sauce Céleri*

Clean six stalks of celery (only use the hearts), put them in a saucepan, immerse in consommé, add a herb bunch and one onion with a clove stuck in it, and cook gently. Drain the celery, put it through a grinder, then rub it through a fine sieve and put the *purée* in a saucepan. Now thin the *purée* with an equal quantity of cream sauce and a little reduced celery liquor. Heat it moderately, and, if it has to wait, put it in a double-boiler.

This sauce is suited to boiled or *braised* poultry. It is excellent, and has been adopted in French cookery.

115—CRANBERRY SAUCE   *Sauce aux Airelles*

Cook one pint of cranberries with one quart of water in a saucepan, and cover. When the berries are cooked mash them through a fine sieve. To the *purée* add the necessary quantity of their cooking liquor, so as to make a somewhat thick sauce. Sugar should be added according to taste.

This sauce is mostly served with roast turkey. It can be bought ready-made, and, if this kind be used, it need only be heated with a little water.

116—FENNEL SAUCE   *Sauce Fenouil*

Take one pint of butter sauce (66) and finish it with two table-spoons of chopped fennel, scalded for a few seconds.

This is principally used with mackerel.

117—EGG SAUCE WITH MELTED BUTTER
Sauce aux Oeufs au Beurre Fondu

Dissolve one-quarter pound of butter, and add to it the necessary salt, a little pepper, half the juice of a lemon, and three hard-boiled eggs (hot and cut into large cubes); also a teaspoon of chopped and scalded parsley.

118—SCOTCH EGG SAUCE   *Sauce Ecossaise*

Make a white *roux* (21) with one and one-half oz. of butter and one oz. of flour. Mix in one pint of boiling milk, season with salt, white pepper, and nutmeg, and boil gently for ten minutes. Then add three hot hard-boiled eggs, cut into cubes (the whites and the yolks).

This sauce usually accompanies boiled fish, especially fresh haddocks and fresh and salted cod.

119—HORSE-RADISH OR ALBERT SAUCE
Sauce Raifort ou Albert

Grate five oz. of horse-radish and place in a saucepan with one-quarter pint of white consommé (1). Boil gently for twenty minutes and add a good one-half pint of butter sauce (66), as much cream, and one-half oz. of bread-crumbs; thicken by reducing on a brisk fire and rub through a fine sieve. Then thicken with the yolks of two eggs, and complete the seasoning with a pinch of salt and pepper, and a teaspoon of dry mustard dissolved in a tablespoon of vinegar.

Serve this sauce with *braised* or roast beef—especially fillets.

119a—PARSLEY SAUCE *Sauce Persil*

This is the Butter Sauce (66), to which is added, per pint, a heaped tablespoon of freshly-chopped parsley.

120—REFORM SAUCE *Sauce Réforme*

Put into a small saucepan and boil one pint of half-glaze sauce (23) and one-half pint of ordinary Poivrade sauce (19). Complete with a garnish composed of one-half oz. of gherkins, one-half oz. of the hard-boiled white of an egg, one oz. of smoked tongue, one oz. of truffles, and one oz. of mushrooms. All these to be cut *julienne*-fashion and short.

This sauce is for mutton cutlets when these are "à la Reforme" (1316a).

CHAPTER IV

COLD SAUCES AND COMPOUND BUTTERS

121—AIOLI SAUCE OR PROVENCE BUTTER

Sauce Aioli ou Beurre Provençale

Chop one oz. of garlic cloves as finely as possible, and add the yolk of one raw egg, a pinch of salt, and one-half pint of oil, letting it trickle in a thread and stirring meanwhile, so as to effect a complete cohesion of the mixture. Add a few drops of lemon juice and cold water to the sauce as it thickens, this being done to avoid its turning.

Should it separate in the process of making or when made, the only thing to be done is to begin again with another egg yolk.

122—ANDALOUSE SAUCE   *Sauce Andalouse*

Take the required quantity of Mayonnaise sauce (126) and add to it the quarter of its volume of very red and concentrated tomato *purée* (29), and finally add two oz. of pimento cut finely, *Julienne*-fashion, per pint of sauce.

123—BOHEMIAN SAUCE   *Sauce Bohémienne*

Put in a bowl one-quarter pint of cold Béchamel (28), the yolks of four eggs, a little table salt and white pepper. Add a quart of oil and three tablespoons of tarragon vinegar, proceeding as for the Mayonnaise (126).

Finish the sauce with a tablespoon of dry mustard.

124—GENOA SAUCE   *Sauce Génoise*

Pound in a mortar, and make into a smooth, fine paste, one oz. of pistachios and one oz. of pine-nuts, or, if these are not available, one oz. of sweet almonds; add one-half tablespoon of cold Béchamel (28). Put this paste into a bowl, add the yolks of six eggs, a little salt and pepper, and finish the sauce with one quart of oil, the juice of two lemons, and proceed as for the Mayonnaise (126).

Complete with three tablespoons of *purée* of herbs (132), prepared with equal quantities of chervil, parsley, tarragon, and fresh pimpernel, scalded for one minute. Cool quickly, press so as to expel the water, and pass through a fine sieve.

Serve this sauce with cold fish.

125—GRIBICHE SAUCE   *Sauce Gribiche*

Crush in a bowl the yolks of six hard-boiled eggs, and work them into a smooth paste, together with a large tablespoon of French mustard, the necessary salt, a little pepper, and make up the sauce with one pint of oil. Complete with two teaspoons of parsley, chervil, and tarragon (chopped and mixed), as many capers and gherkins, evenly mixed, and the hard-boiled whites of three eggs, cut in short, *Julienne* strips.

This sauce is chiefly used with cold fish.

126—MAYONNAISE SAUCE   *Sauce Mayonnaise*

Put in a bowl the yolks of six raw eggs, after having removed the cores. Season them with one-half oz. of table-salt and a little cayenne pepper. Gradually pour one-fifth pint of vinegar on the yolks while beating them briskly. When the vinegar is absorbed add one quart of oil, letting the latter trickle down in a thread, constantly stirring the sauce meanwhile. The sauce is finished by the addition of the juice of a lemon and three tablespoons of boiling water—the purpose of the latter being to ensure the cohesion of the sauce and to prevent it separating.

Mayonnaise prepared in this way is rather liquid, but it need only be left to rest a few hours in order to thicken considerably. Unless it be exposed to too low a temperature, the Mayonnaise, prepared as above, never separates, and may be kept for several days without the fear of anything happening to it. Merely cover it and put away.

Remarks.—In the matter of that sauce there exist endless prejudices, which I must attempt to refute:—

1. If the sauce mixes badly, or not at all, the reason is that the oil has been added too rapidly at first, before the addition of the vinegar, and that its assimilation by the yolks has not functioned normally.

2. It is quite an error to suppose that it is necessary to work over ice or in a cold room. Cold is rather injurious to Mayonnaise, and is invariably the cause of this sauce separating in winter. In the cold season the oil should be slightly warmed, or, at least, kept at the

temperature of the kitchen, though it is best to make it in a moderately warm place.

3. It is a further error to suppose that the seasoning interferes with the making of the sauce, for salt, in solution, rather aids the cohering force of the yolks.

Causes of the Separation of the Mayonnaise:—

1. The too rapid addition of the oil at the start.

2. The use of congealed, or too cold, an oil.

3. Excess of oil in proportion to the number of yolks, the assimilating power of an egg being limited to two and one-half oz. of oil (if the sauce be made some time in advance), and three oz. if it is to be used immediately.

Means of Bringing Separated Mayonnaise Back to its Normal State.—Put the yolks of an egg into a bowl with a few drops of vinegar, and mix the separated Mayonnaise in it, little by little. If it be a matter of only a small quantity of Mayonnaise, one-half a teaspoon of prepared mustard can take the place of the egg-yolk. Finally, with regard to acid seasoning, a whiter sauce is obtained by the use of lemon juice instead of vinegar.

127—CLEARED MAYONNAISE SAUCE   *Sauce Mayonnaise Collée*

Take the necessary quantity of Mayonnaise (126) and gradually add to it, per one and one-half pints of the sauce, one-half pint of cold and rather firm melting aspic jelly—*Lenten* or ordinary, according to the nature of the products for which the sauce is intended.

Remarks.—It is this very Mayonnaise, formerly used almost exclusively for coating entrées and cold *relevées* of fish, filleted fish, scallops of common and spiny-lobster, etc., which I have replaced with the *Lenten* Chaud-Froid (76).

128—WHISKED MAYONNAISE   *Sauce Mayonnaise Broyée*

Put into a copper basin or other bowl three-quarters pint of melted jelly aspic, two-thirds pint of Mayonnaise (126), one tablespoon of tarragon vinegar, and as much grated or finely-chopped horse-radish. Mix up the whole and place the utensil on ice, and beat gently until the contents become very frothy. Stop beating as soon as the sauce begins to solidify, for it must remain almost liquid to enable it to mix with the foods for which it is intended.

This sauce is used principally for vegetable salads.

129—RAVIGOTE SAUCE, OR VINAIGRETTE

Sauce Ravigote, ou Vinaigrette

Put into a bowl one pint of oil, one-third pint of vinegar, a little salt and pepper, two oz. of small capers, three tablespoons of fine herbs, comprising some very finely chopped onion, as much parsley, and half as much chervil, tarragon, and chives. Mix thoroughly. The Ravigote accompanies calf's head or feet, sheep's shanks, etc.

Two or three tablespoons of the liquor or stock with which the accompanying foods have been cooked, are often added to this sauce when serving.

130—REMOULADE SAUCE

Sauce Remoulade

To one pint of Mayonnaise (126) add one large tablespoon of prepared mustard, another of gherkins, and yet another of chopped and pressed out capers, one tablespoon of fine herbs, parsley, chervil, and tarragon, all chopped and mixed, and a teaspoon of anchovy *essence* or a bit of anchovy paste.

This sauce accompanies cold meat and poultry, and more particularly, common and spiny lobster.

131—GREEN SAUCE

Sauce Verte

Take the necessary quantity of thick Mayonnaise (126) and spicy seasoning, and add to these, per pint of sauce, one-third pint of herb juice (132).

This is suitable for cold fish and shell fish.

132—VINCENT SAUCE

Sauce Vincent

Prepare and carefully wash the following herbs:—One oz. each of parsley, chervil, tarragon, chives, sorrel-leaves, and fresh pimpernel, two oz. of water-cress and two oz. of spinach. Put all these herbs into a copper bowl containing salted, boiling water. Boil for two minutes only; then drain the herbs through a sieve and cover them with fresh water. When they are cold they are once more drained until quite dry; then they must be finally chopped with the yolks of eight hard-boiled eggs. Rub this *purée* through a strainer first, then through a fine sieve, add one pint of very stiff Mayonnaise (126) to it and finish the sauce with two teaspoons of Worcestershire sauce.

COLD ENGLISH AND AMERICAN SAUCES

133—CAMBRIDGE SAUCE   *Sauce Cambridge*

Pound together the yolks of six hard-boiled eggs, the washed and dried fillets of four anchovies, a teaspoon of capers, two teaspoons of chervil, tarragon, and chives, mixed. When the whole forms a fine paste, add one tablespoon of mustard, one-fifth pint of oil, one tablespoon of vinegar, and proceed as for a Mayonnaise (126). Season with a little cayenne; rub through a fine sieve, applying pressure with a spoon, and put the sauce in a bowl. Stir it awhile with a whisk to smooth it, and finish with one teaspoon of chopped parsley.

It is suited to cold meats in general; in fact, it is an Anglicized version of Vincent Sauce (132).

134—CUMBERLAND SAUCE   *Sauce Cumberland*

Dissolve four tablespoons of red-currant jelly, to which are added one-fifth pint of port wine, one teaspoon of finely-chopped shallots, scalded for a few seconds and pressed, one teaspoon of small pieces of orange rind and as much lemon rind (cut finely, *Julienne*-fashion, scalded for two minutes, well-drained, and cooled), the juice of an orange and that of half a lemon, one teaspoon of dry mustard, a little cayenne pepper, and as much powdered ginger. Mix the whole well.

Serve this sauce with cold venison.

135—GLOUCESTER SAUCE   *Sauce Gloucester*

Take one pint of very thick Mayonnaise (126) and complete it with one-fifth pint of sour cream with the juice of a lemon added, and combine with the Mayonnaise by degrees; one teaspoon of chopped fennel leaves and as much Worcestershire sauce.

Serve this with all cold meats.

136—MINT SAUCE   *Sauce de Menthe*

Cut finely, *Julienne*-fashion, or chop, two oz. of mint leaves. Put these in a bowl with a little less than one oz. of white granulated or powdered sugar, one-quarter pint of fresh vinegar, and four tablespoons of water.

Special sauce for hot or cold lamb.

137—OXFORD SAUCE   *Sauce Oxford*

Make a Cumberland (134) with this difference: that the *Julienne* of orange and lemon rinds should be replaced by grated or finely-chopped rinds, and that the quantities of same should be less, *i.e.*, two-thirds of a teaspoonful of each.

138—HORSE-RADISH SAUCE   *Sauce au Raifort*

Dilute one tablespoon of mustard with two tablespoons of vinegar in a basin, and add one lb. of finely grated horse-radish, two oz. of powdered sugar, a little salt, one pint of cream, and one lb. of bread-crumbs steeped in milk and pressed out. Stir this together vigorously. Serve this sauce very cold.

It accompanies boiled and roast joints of beef.

COMPOUND BUTTER FOR GRILLS AND FOR THE COMPLETION OF SAUCES

With the exception of those of the shell-fish order, the butters, whose recipes I am about to give, are not greatly used in kitchens. Nevertheless, in some cases, as, for instance, in accentuating the savor of sauces, they answer a real and useful purpose, and I therefore recommend them, since they enable one to give a flavor to the derivatives of the Velouté (25) and Béchamel (28) sauces which these could not acquire by any other means.

With regard to shell-fish butters, and particularly those of the common and spiny lobster (Rock lobsters) and the crayfish, experience has shown that when they are prepared with heat (that is to say, by melting in a double-boiler a quantity of butter which has been previously pounded with shell-fish remains and afterwards strained through muslin into a basin of ice water where it has solidified) they are of a finer color than the other kind and quite free from shell particles. But the heat, besides dissipating a large proportion of their delicacy, involves considerable risk, for the slightest neglect gives the above preparation quite a disagreeable taste. To obviate these difficulties I have adopted a system of two distinct butters, one which is colorful and prepared with heat, and the other which is prepared with all the creamy parts, the trimmings and the remains of common and spiny lobsters (Rock lobsters) without the shells, pounded with the required quantity of fresh butter and passed through a sieve. The latter is used to complete sauces, particularly those with a Béchamel base to which it lends a perfect savor.

I follow the same procedure with shrimp and crayfish butters, sometimes substituting for the butter good cream, which, I find, absorbs the aromatic principles perhaps better than the former.

With the above method it is advisable to pass the butter or the cream through a very fine strainer first and afterwards through a very fine sieve, so as to avoid small particles of the pounded shell being present in the sauce.

139—BERCY BUTTER   *Beurre Bercy*

Put into a small saucepan one-quarter pint of white wine and one oz. of finely-chopped shallots, scalded a moment. Reduce the wine by one-half, and add one-half lb. of butter softened into a cream; one teaspoon of chopped parsley, two oz. of beef marrow cut into cubes, *poached* in slightly salted water and well drained, the necessary table-salt, and, when serving, add a little ground pepper and a few drops of lemon-juice.

This butter must not be completely melted, and it is principally served with grilled beef.

140—CHIVRY OR RAVIGOTE BUTTER   *Beurre Chivry ou Ravigote*

Put into a small saucepan of salted, boiling water six oz. of chervil, parsley, tarragon, fresh pimpernel, and chives, in equal quantities, and two oz. of chopped shallots. Boil quickly for two minutes, drain, cool in cold water, press in a towel to completely remove the water, and pound in a mortar. Now add one-half lb. of half-melted butter, mix well with the *purée* of herbs (132), and strain through a fine sieve.

This butter is used to complete Chivry sauce and other sauces that contain herb juices, such as the Venetian, etc.

140a—CHÂTEAUBRIAND BUTTER   *Beurre Châteaubriand*

Reduce by two-thirds four-fifths pint of white wine containing four chopped shallots, fragments of thyme and bay leaf, and four oz. of mushroom peelings. Add four-fifths pint of veal gravy, reduce the whole to half, rub it through a fine sieve, and finish it away from the fire with eight oz. of Maître d'Hôtel butter (150) and half a tablespoon of chopped tarragon.

141—COLBERT BUTTER   *Beurre Colbert*

Take one lb. of Maître d'Hôtel butter (150) and add six tablespoons of dissolved, pale meat *glaze* (15) and one teaspoon of chopped tarragon.

Serve this sauce with fish prepared à la Colbert.

142—RED COLORING BUTTER   *Beurre Rouge*

Put on to a dish any available left over shells of shell-fish after having thoroughly cleaned them of meat and dried them in the oven. Pound them until they form a very fine powder, and add their weight of butter.

Put the whole into a double-boiler and melt, stirring frequently. When the butter is quite clear strain it through muslin, twisting the latter over a tureen of ice water in which the strained butter solidifies. Put the congealed butter in a towel, press it heavily so as to expel the water, and keep cool in a small bowl.

Remarks.—A very fine and decided red color is obtained by using paprika as a condiment for sauces intended for poultry and certain meats, in accordance with the procedure I recommend for Hungarian paprika. But only the very best quality of paprika should be used—that which is mild and at the same time produces a nice pink color without entailing any excess of the condiment.

143—GREEN COLORING BUTTER   *Beurre Vert*

Peel, wash, and thoroughly shake (so as to get rid of every drop of water) two lbs. of spinach. Pound it raw and then press it in a strong towel, twisting the latter so as to extract all the vegetable juice. Pour this juice into a double-boiler and let it coagulate, and then pour it on to a napkin stretched over a bowl in order to drain away the water. Collect the remains of the coloring substance on the napkin, using a spatula for the purpose, and put these into a mortar; mix with half the weight of butter, strain through a fine sieve, and put aside to cool. This green butter should in all cases take the place of the liquid green found on the market.

144—VARIOUS CULLISES   *Coulis Divers*

Finely pound shrimp and crayfish shells, and combine with these the available creamy parts and spawn of the common and spiny or Rock lobsters; add one-quarter pint of rich cream per lb. of the above remains, and strain, first through a fine sieve and then through a fine hair sieve. This *cullis* is prepared just in time for serving, and is used as a refining element in certain fish sauces.

145—SHRIMP BUTTER   *Beurre de Crevette*

Finely pound any available shrimp remains, add to these their weight of butter, and strain through a fine sieve. Place in a bowl and put aside to chill.

146—SHALLOT BUTTER
Beurre d'Echalote

Put eight oz. of roughly minced shallots in the corner of a clean towel, and wash them quickly in boiling water. Cool, and press them heavily. Then pound them finely with their own weight of fresh butter and strain through a very fine sieve.

This butter accentuates the savor of certain sauces, such as Bercy, Ravigote, etc.

147—CRAYFISH BUTTER
Beurre d'Ecrevisse

Pound, very finely, the remains and shells of crayfish cooked in *Mirepoix*. Add their weight of butter, and strain through a fine sieve, and again through a fine hair sieve, so as to avoid the presence of any shell particles. This latter precaution applies to all shell-fish butters.

148—TARRAGON BUTTER
Beurre d'Estragon

Quickly scald and cool eight oz. of fresh tarragon, drain, press in a towel, pound in a mortar, and add to them one lb. of butter. Strain through a very fine sieve, and put aside to chill if it is not to be used immediately.

149—LOBSTER BUTTER
Beurre de Homard

Reduce to a paste in the mortar the spawn, shell, and creamy parts of lobster. Add their equal in weight of butter and strain through a very fine sieve.

150—BUTTER A LA MAITRE D'HOTEL
Beurre à la Maitre d'Hotel

First *manie* and then soften into a cream one-half lb. of butter. Add a tablespoon of chopped parsley, a little salt and pepper, and a few drops of lemon-juice.

Serve this with grills in general.

151—MANIE BUTTER
Beurre Manié

Knead, until perfectly combined, four oz. of butter and three oz. of sifted flour. This butter is used for quick bindings like in the *Matelotes,* etc.

The sauce to which *manie* butter has been added should not boil too long if this can possibly be avoided, but long enough to cook the flour otherwise it would have a very disagreeable taste of uncooked flour.

151a—MELTED BUTTER   *Beurre Fondu*

This preparation, which is used principally as a fish sauce, should consist of butter, just melted, and combined with a little table-salt and a few drops of lemon-juice. It should therefore be prepared only at the last minute; for, should it wait and be allowed to clarify, besides losing its flavor it will be found to disagree with certain people.

152—BUTTER A LA MEUNIERE   *Beurre à la Meunière*

Put into a saucepan the necessary quantity of butter, and cook it gently until it has acquired a golden tint and exudes a slightly nutty odor. Add a few drops of lemon-juice, and pour on the fish being prepared, which should have been previously sprinkled with chopped parsley.

This butter is proper to fish "à la Meunière" and is always served on the fish.

153—MONTPELIER BUTTER   *Beurre Montpelier*

Put into a saucepan containing boiling water equal quantities of watercress leaves, parsley, chervil, chives, and tarragon (six oz. in all), one and one-half oz. of chopped shallots, and one-half oz. of fresh spinach leaves. Boil for two minutes, then drain, cool, press in a towel to expel water, and pound in a mortar with one tablespoon of pressed capers, four oz. of gherkins, a garlic clove, and the fillets of four anchovies well washed.

Mix this paste with one and one-half lbs. of butter; then add the yolks of three boiled eggs and two raw eggs, and finally pour in, by degrees, two-fifths pint of oil. Strain through a very fine sieve, put the butter into a bowl, and stir it well with a wooden spoon to make it smooth. Season with table-salt and a little cayenne.

Use this butter to decorate large fish, such as salmon and trout; but it is also used for smaller pieces and slices of fish.

Remarks.—When this butter is specially prepared to form a coating on fish, the oil and the egg yolks are omitted and only butter is used.

154—BLACK BUTTER   *Beurre Noir*

Put into a saucepan the necessary amount of butter, and cook it until it has assumed a brown color and begins to smoke. At this moment add a large pinch of chopped parsley leaves and spread it immediately over the object to be treated.

155—HAZEL-NUT BUTTER   *Beurre de Noisette*

Put eight oz. of shelled hazel-nuts, in the front of the oven, in order to slightly grill their skins and make them easily removable. Now crush the nuts in a mortar until they form a paste, and add a few drops of cold water with a view to preventing their producing any oil. Add an equal weight of butter and rub through a fine sieve.

156—PISTACHIO BUTTER   *Beurre de Pistache*

Put into boiling water eight oz. of pistachio nuts, and heat them over the fire until the peel may be easily removed. Drain, cool in cold water, clean the pistachios, and finely pound while moistening them with a few drops of water.

Add two oz. of butter and pass through a fine sieve.

157—PRINTANIER BUTTER   *Beurre Printanier*

These butters are made from all early-season vegetables, such as carrots, string beans, peas, and asparagus tips.

When dealing with green vegetables cook quickly in boiling, salted water, drain, dry, pound with their weight of butter, and rub through a fine sieve.

With carrots: Mince and cook with consommé, a little sugar, and butter until the liquid is quite reduced. After cooling they are pounded with their own weight of butter and rubbed through a fine sieve.

CHAPTER V

ASPIC JELLIES

Aspic jellies are to cold cookery what consommés and stock are to hot. If anything, the former are perhaps more important, for a cold entrée—however perfect it may be in itself—is nothing without its accompanying jelly or aspic.

In the recipes which I give hereafter I have made a point of showing how melting jellies may be obtained, that is, served in a sauce-boat simultaneously with the cold food, or actually poured over it when the latter rests in a deep dish—a common custom nowadays.

This method of serving cold entrées, which I inaugurated at the Savoy Hotel in London with the "Suprême de Volaille Jeannette," is the only one which permits serving an aspic jelly in a state of absolute perfection.

Nevertheless, if a more solid jelly were required, either for the decorating of cold dishes or for a moulded entrée, there need only be added to the following recipes a few tablespoons of granulated gelatine—more or less—according to the required firmness of the aspic.

But it should not be forgotten that the greater the glutinous consistency of the jelly the less value will the same possess.

The various uses of aspics are dealt with in Part II. of this work, where the recipes of their various accompanying dishes will also appear.

158—ORDINARY ASPICS *Gelées Ordinaires*

Stock for Ordinary Aspic—Quantities for Making Four Quarts

4 lbs. of tied knuckle of veal.
3 lbs. of tied knuckle of beef.
3 lbs. of veal bones, well broken up.

3 calf's feet, boned and blanched.
½ lb. of fresh pork rind, well blanched and with fat removed.

Mode of Procedure.—Put the meat in a very clean stockpot or saucepan. Add eight quarts of cold water, boil, and skim after the manner indicated under (1). Having well skimmed the stock add one oz. of salt, put it on a low fire, and let it boil gently for four hours. Then remove the meat, taking care not to disturb the stock. Carefully remove the fat, and garnish with one-half lb. of carrots, six oz. of onions, two oz. of leeks, a stalk of celery, and a large herb bunch. Put the whole back on to the fire and cook gently for a further two hours. Strain through a sieve into a very clean bowl and leave it to cool.

Clarification of Aspic.—When the stock, prepared according to the above directions, has cooled, the grease that has formed on its surface should be removed. Then pour off gently into a saucepan of convenient size in such a way as to prevent the deposit at the bottom from mixing with the clear liquor. Test the consistency of the aspic, when it should be found that the quantities given above have proved sufficient to form a fairly firm jelly. If, however, this be not the case, a few ounces of granulated gelatine steeped in cold water should be added, being careful not to overdo the quantity. Now add to the stock two lbs. of lean beef (first minced and then ground together with the white of an egg), a little chervil and tarragon, and a few drops of lemon-juice. Place the saucepan on a fire, stir its contents with a spatula until the liquid begins to boil, remove it from the fire, and place it on a low flame, where it may boil gently for half an hour longer.

At the end of this time take the saucepan off the fire and remove what little grease has formed on the aspic while cooking. Strain through a napkin stretched across a frame and let the aspic fall into a bowl placed beneath it. Make certain whether the liquid is quite clear, and if, as frequently happens, this be not the case, what has already been strained should once more be passed through the napkin, repeating the operation until the aspic becomes quite transparent.

Flavoring the Aspic.—The aspic obtained as above is transparent, has an agreeable savor, and is the color of fine amber. It now only requires flavoring according to the tastes of the consumer and the purpose for which it is intended. For this operation it should be allowed to become quite tepid, and the following quantities of choice wine are added to it, viz.:—

If the wine is of a liqueur kind, such as Sherry, Marsala, Madeira, etc., one-fifth pint per quart.

If it is another kind of wine, for example, champagne, hock, etc., one-fourth pint per quart.

The wine used should be very clear, free from any deposit and as perfect as possible in taste.

159—CHICKEN ASPIC *Gelée de Volaille*

The quantities of meat are the same as for ordinary aspic; there need only be added to it either two oven-browned hens, or their equivalent in weight of roasted fowl skeletons, and poultry giblets if these are handy. It is always better, however, to prepare the stock with the hens and giblets and to keep the skeletons for the clarification. This clarification follows the same rules as that of the ordinary aspic, except that a few roasted-fowl skeletons, previously well freed from fat, are added to it.

In the case of this particularly delicate aspic, it is more than ever necessary not to overdo the amount of gelatine. It should be easily soluble to the palate in order to be perfect.

160—GAME ASPIC *Gelée de Gibier*

Prepare this aspic stock in exactly the same way as that of ordinary aspic, only substitute game, such as deer, roebuck, doe, or hare, or wild rabbit (previously browned in the oven), for the beef. When possible also add to this stock a few old game birds, such as partridges or pheasants that are too tough for other purposes and which suit admirably here.

The clarification changes according to the different flavors which are to be given to the aspic. If it is not necessary to give it a special characteristic, it should be prepared with the meat of the game which happens to be most available at the time, adding to the quantity used roast bones and pickings of game birds, the respective amounts of both ingredients being the same as for ordinary aspic. If, on the other hand, the aspic is to have a well-defined flavor, the meat used for the clarification should naturally be that producing the flavor in question, either partridge or pheasant, or grouse, etc.

Some aspics are greatly improved by being flavored with a small quantity of old brandy. Rather than use an inferior kind of this ingredient, however, I should advise its total omission from the aspic.

Without flavoring the aspic, though imperfect, is passable; but flavored with bad brandy it is invariably spoilt.

LENTEN ASPICS

161—FISH ASPIC WITH WHITE WINE *Gelée de Poisson au Vin Blanc*

The stock for this aspic is prepared in precisely the same manner as fish stock (4). The saucepan need not, however, be buttered previous to the adding of the onions, parsley-stalks, and fish-bones. If the aspic is not required to be quite white, a little saffron may be added to it, as the flavor of this condiment blends so perfectly with that of fish.

When the stock is prepared its consistency should be tested, and rectified, if necessary, by means of gelatine. The quantity of this substance should on no account exceed three and three-quarters ounces per quart of aspic, and, at the risk of repeating myself, I remind the reader that the less gelatine is used the better the aspic will be.

The clarification should be made with fresh caviar if possible, but pressed caviar is also admirably suited to this purpose. The quantities are the same as for the clarification of fish consommé (4).

In flavoring white fish aspics either dry champagne or a good Bordeaux or Burgundy may be used. Take care, however—

1. That the wine used be of an unquestionably good quality.

2. That it be only added to the aspic when the latter is already cold and on the point of coagulating, as this is the only means of preserving all the aroma of the wine.

Finally, in certain cases, a special flavor may be obtained by the use of crayfish, which are cooked, as for *bisque,* then pounded, and added to the fish stock (11) ten minutes before straining it. A proportion of four little crayfish *à bisque* per quart of aspic is sufficient to secure an excellent flavor.

162—FISH ASPIC WITH RED WINE *Gelée de Poisson au Vin Rouge*

This aspic stock is the *Court-bouillon* with red wine (165), which has served in cooking the fish for which the aspic is intended; this fish is generally either trout or salmon; sometimes also, but less commonly, a carp or a pike.

This stock must first of all have its grease thoroughly removed; it should then be carefully poured off, reduced if necessary, and the required quantity of gelatine added. This cannot be easily determined, as all gelatines are not alike, and the stock may have contracted a certain consistency from its contact with the fish. One can, therefore, only be guided by testing small quantities cooled in ice, but care should be taken that the aspic be not too firm.

The clarification of this aspic is generally made with white of egg in the proportion of one white per quart. The white, slightly beaten, is added to the cold stock, and the latter is put over a fire and stirred with a spatula. As soon as it boils, the aspic is poured through a napkin on a frame. The first drippings of the fluid aspic are put back through the napkin if they do not seem clear, and this operation is repeated until the required clarity is reached.

It almost invariably happens that, either during the cooking of the fish or during the clarification, the wine loses its color through the precipitation of the coloring elements derived from the tannin.

The only way of overcoming this difficulty is to add a few drops of liquid carmine or red vegetable coloring; but, in any case, it is well to remember that the color of red-wine aspic must never be deeper than a dark pink.

CHAPTER VI

THE COURT-BOUILLONS OR SHORT BROTHS AND THE MARINADES

163—COURT-BOUILLON WITH VINEGAR   *Court-Bouillon au Vinaigre*

Court-Bouillon au Vin Blanc

Quantities Required for Five Quarts

5 quarts of water.	¾ lb. of carrots.
½ pint of vinegar.	1 lb. of onions.
2 oz. of salt.	A little thyme and bay leaf.
½ oz. of peppercorns.	2 oz. of parsley stalks.

Preparation.—Put into a saucepan the water, salt, and vinegar, the minced carrots and onions, and the parsley, thyme, and bay leaf, in a bunch. Bring to a boil, allow to simmer for one hour, rub through a fine sieve, and put aside until wanted.

Remarks.—Put the peppercorns into the court-bouillon only twelve minutes before straining the latter. If the pepper were in for too long a time it would give a bitterness to the preparation. This rule also applies to the recipes that follow, in which the use of pepper-corns is also required.

This court-bouillon is principally used for cooking trout and salmon, as well as for various shell-fish.

164—COURT-BOUILLON WITH WHITE WINE
Court-Bouillon au Vin Blanc

Quantities Required for Two Quarts

1 quart of white wine.	1 large herb bunch.
1 quart of water.	½ oz. of salt.
3 oz. of minced onions.	A few peppercorns.

64

Preparation.—This is the same as for the court-bouillon with vinegar, except that it is boiled for half an hour and is strained through a fine sieve.

Remarks.—If the court-bouillon has to be reduced the quantity of salt should be proportionately less. This preparation is principally used for *poaching* fresh-water fish.

165—COURT-BOUILLON WITH RED WINE

Court-Bouillon au Vin Rouge

Use the same quantities as for court-bouillon with white wine, taking care—

1. To replace white wine by excellent red wine.
2. To add four oz. of minced carrots.
3. To apportion the wine and water in the ratio of two-thirds to one-third.

Preparation.—The same as that of the former, with the same time for boiling.

Remarks.—If the court-bouillon is to be reduced, the salt should be less accordingly. When the court-bouillon with red wine is to constitute an aspic stock, fish *fumet* with enough gelatine takes the place of the water.

The uses of court-bouillon with red wine are similar to those of the white-wine kind.

166—PLAIN COURT-BOUILLON   *Court-Bouillon Ordinaire*

The quantity of court-bouillon is determined by the size of the food which it is to cover. It is composed of cold, salt water (the salt amounting to a little less than one-half oz. per quart of water), one-quarter pint of milk per quart of water, and one thin slice of peeled lemon in the same proportion. The fish is immersed while the liquor is cold; the latter is very slowly brought to the boil, and as soon as this is reached, the pot is moved to the slowest fire, where the cooking of the fish is completed.

This court-bouillon, which is used with large pieces of turbot, is never prepared beforehand.

167—SPECIAL OR WHITE COURT-BOUILLON

Court-Bouillon Special, ou Blanc

This preparation is a genuine court-bouillon, though it is not used in cooking fish.

The Quantities Required for Five Quarts of this
Court-bouillon are:—

A little less than 2 oz. of flour.   The juice of 3 lemons or ⅛ pint
1½ oz. of salt.   of good vinegar.
                                        5 quarts of cold water.

Gradually mix the flour and the water; add the salt and the lemon juice, and pass through a strainer. Set to boil, and stir the mixture, in order to prevent the flour from lumping; as soon as the boil is reached, immerse the objects to be treated. These are usually calf's head or feet, previously *blanched*; sheep's shanks, cock's kidneys or combs, or such vegetables as salsify, oyster plant, cardoon, etc.

REMARKS UPON THE USE OF COURT-BOUILLON

1. Court-bouillon must always be prepared in advance for all fish, as the time for *poaching* is less than half an hour, except turbots.

2. When a fish is of such a size as to need more than half an hour's *poaching*, proceed as follows:—Place under the trivet or drainer of the fish-kettle the minced carrots and onions and the herb bunch; put the fish on the trivet, and cover it with water and vinegar, or white wine, in accordance with the kind of court-bouillon wanted and the quantity required. Add the salt, boil, and keep the court-bouillon gently simmering for a period of time according to the size of the fish. The time allowed for *poaching* will be given in the respective recipes.

3. Fish, when whole, should be immersed in cold court-bouillon; when sliced, in the same liquor that is boiling. The exceptions to this rule are small trout *"au bleu"* and shell-fish.

4. If fish be cooked in a small amount of liquor the carrots, onions, etc. are put under the drainer and the liquid elements of the selected court-bouillon (as, for example, that with red or white wine) are so calculated as to cover only one-third of the solid body. Fish cooked in this way should be frequently basted.

5. Court-bouillon for ordinary and spiny (Rock) lobsters should always be at full boiling pitch when these are immersed. The case is the same for small or medium fish *"au bleu."*

6. Fish which is to be served cold, also shell-fish (crustaceans), should cool in the court-bouillon itself; the cooking period is conse·quently curtailed.

MARINADES AND BRINES

Marinades play but a small part in English and American cookery, venison or other game being generally preferred fresh. However, in the event of its being necessary to resort to these methods of preparation, I shall give two recipes for venison and two for mutton.

The use of the *marinade* for venison is very much debated. Certainly it is often desirable that the fibre of those meats that come from old specimens of the deer be softened, but there is no doubt that what the meat gains in tenderness it loses in flavor. On the whole, therefore, it would be best to use only those joints which come from young beasts.

In the case of the latter, the *marinade* may well be dispensed with. It would add nothing to the savor of a haunch of venison, while it would be equally ineffectual in the case of the roebuck or hare. A summary treatment of these two, with raw *marinade*, may well be adopted, as also for deer.

As for cooked *marinade*, its real and only use lies in the fact that during summer weather it enables one to preserve meat which would otherwise spoil. It may, moreover, be used for *braised* venison, but this treatment of game is very uncommon nowadays.

168—COOKED MARINADE FOR VENISON

Marinade Cuite pour Venaison

Quantities Required for Five Quarts

¼ lb. of minced carrots.
½ lb. of minced onions.
2 oz. of minced shallots.
1 crushed garlic clove.

1 herb bunch, including 1 oz. of parsley stalks, 2 sprigs of rosemary, as much thyme, and 2 bay leaves.

Preparation.—Heat one-half pint of oil in a saucepan, add the carrots and onions, and fry them while stirring frequently. When they begin to brown add the shallots, the garlic, and the herb bunch, then one pint of vinegar, two bottles of white wine, and three quarts of water. Cook this *marinade* for twenty minutes, and add a further two oz. of salt, one-half oz. of peppercorns, and four oz. of brown sugar. Ten minutes afterwards pass it through a strainer and let it cool before laying in the meats.

N.B.—In summer the *marinade* very often decomposes, because of the blood contained by the meat under treatment in it. The only means of averting this is to boil the *marinade* every two or three days at least and keeping it well chilled.

169—RAW MARINADE FOR MEAT OR VENISON

Marinade Crue pour Viandes ou Venaison

This *marinade* is prepared immediately before using. The meat
to be treated is first salted and peppered on all sides, then it is put
in a receptacle just large enough to hold it, and laid on a bed of
aromatics, including minced carrots and onions, a few chopped
shallots, parsley stalks, thyme, and bay leaf in proportion to the rest.
Now sprinkle the meat copiously with oil and half as much vinegar;
cover the dish with oiled paper, and put it somewhere to keep cool.
Turn the meat over three or four times a day, covering it each time
with a layer of vegetables.

This *marinade* is very active, and is admirably suited to all meat
and venison, provided they are not allowed to remain in it for too
long a time. It is very difficult to say how long the meat must stay in
these *marinades;* the time varies according to the size and quality of
the joints, and the taste of the consumer. All that can be said is that
three hours should be sufficient to *marinate* a cutlet or pieces of
roebuck, and that for big joints such as saddle or leg the time should
not exceed four days.

170—MARINADE FOR MUTTON, ROEBUCK-STYLE

Marinade pour le Mouton, en Chevreuil

This is exactly the same as cooked *marinade* (168). There need
only be added one oz. of juniper berries, a few sprigs of rosemary,
wild thyme, and basil, two more garlic cloves, and one quart less
of water.

171—MARINADE WITH RED WINE FOR MUTTON

Marinade pour le Mouton au Vin Rouge

By substituting red wine for white in the preceding recipe—the
quantity of the liquid equalling that of the water—and by slightly
increasing the quantity of *aromatics,* etc. an excellent *marinade* for
mutton is obtained, which in summer enables one to preserve meat,
otherwise perishable, for some days.

172—BRINE   *Grande Saumure*

Quantities Required for Fifty Quarts

56 lbs. of kitchen or rock salt.	6 lbs. of saltpeter.
50 quarts of water.	$3\frac{1}{2}$ lbs. of brown sugar.

Mode of Procedure.—Put the salt and the water in a lined copper pan, and put it over an open fire. When the water boils, throw in a peeled potato, and, if it floats, add water until it begins to sink. If, on the contrary, the potato should sink immediately, reduce the liquid until it is able to buoy the potato up. At this stage the sugar and saltpeter are added; let them dissolve, and the brine is then removed from the fire and is allowed to cool. It is then poured into the receptacle intended for it, which must be either of earthenware, stone, or cement. It is well to place in the bottom of this reservoir a wooden lattice, where the meats to be salted may be laid, for, were the immersed objects to lie directly on the bottom of the receptacle, the under parts would be entirely shielded from the brine.

If the meats to be salted are of an appreciable size, they should be inoculated with brine by means of a special syringe. Without this measure it would be impossible to salt evenly, as the sides would already be over-saturated before the center had even been properly reached.

Eight days should be allowed for salting a piece of beef of any size, above eight or ten lbs., since the process of inoculation equalizes the salting.

Ox-tongue intended for salting, besides having to be as fresh as possible, must be trimmed of almost all the cartilage of the throat, and carefully pounded either with a wooden mallet or rolling pin. Then it must be pricked on all sides with a heavy needle, and immersed in the liquid, where it should be slightly weighted by some means or other in order to prevent its rising to the surface. A medium-sized tongue would need about seven days' immersion in the brine.

Though brine does not turn as easily as the cooked *marinades*, it would be well, especially in warm weather, to watch it and occasionally to boil it. But, as the process of boiling invariably concentrates the brine, a little water should be added to it every time it is so treated, and the test of the potato, described above, should always be resorted to. (Of course there is no reason to have spoilage today because of modern refrigeration.—Ed.)

CHAPTER VII

1. ELEMENTARY PREPARATIONS

BEFORE broaching the question of the numerous preparations which constitute the various soup, *relevés*, and entrée garnishes, it will be necessary to give the recipes of the elementary preparations, or what are technically called the *mise en place*. If the various operations which go to make the *mise en place* were not, at least summarily, discussed here, I should be compelled to repeat them in each formula for which they are required—that is to say, in almost every recipe. I should thus resemble those bad cooks who, having neglected their *mise en place*, are obliged to make it in the course of other work, and thereby not only run the risk of making it badly, but also of losing valuable time which might be used to better advantage.

Elementary preparations consist of those things of which one is constantly in need, which may be prepared in advance, and which are kept available for use at a moment's notice.

173—FILLETS OF ANCHOVIES
Filets d'Anchois

Whether they be for hors d'œuvres or for culinary use, it is always best to have these handy.

After having washed and well wiped them, in order to remove the white powder resulting from the little scales with which they are covered, they should be neatly trimmed to the shape of extended oblongs. Then detach the fillets from the bones by gentle pulling, divide each fillet lengthwise into three or four smaller fillets, put the latter into a small narrow dish or a little bowl, and cover them with oil. The fillets may also be kept whole with a view to rolling them into rings.

174—ANGLAISE (FOR EGG-AND-BREAD-CRUMBLING)
Panés à l'Anglaise

It is well to have this always ready for those dishes which are to be *panés à l'anglaise* (breaded), or as many of the recipes direct: *treated à l'anglaise*.

70

It is made of well-beaten eggs, salt, pepper and one teaspoon of oil per egg.

Its Uses.—The solids to be *panés à l'anglaise* (breaded) are dipped into the preparation described above taking care that the latter coats them thoroughly; whereupon, according to the requirements, they are rolled either in bread-crumbs or in fine *raspings*. From this combination of egg with bread-crumbs or *raspings* there results a kind of coat which, at the moment of contact with the hot fat, is immediately converted into a resisting crust. In croquettes this crust checks the escape, into the fat, of the substances it encloses, and this is more especially the case when the croquettes contain some reduced sauce, or are composed of uncooked meats or fish whose juices are thereby entirely retained. A solid food prepared *à l'anglaise* and cooked in fat should always be put into the fat when this is very hot, so as to ensure the instantaneous solidification of the egg and bread-crumbs.

N.B.—Foods to be treated *à l'anglaise* are generally rolled in flour before being immersed in the *anglaise,* for the flour helps the bread-crumbs and egg to adhere to the food.

The crust formed over the food thus acquires a density which is indispensable.

174a—AROMATICS   *Aromatiques*

Aromatics play a very prominent part in cookery, and their combination with the condiments constitutes, as Grinod de la Reynière said, "the hidden soul of cooking." Their real object, in fact, is to throw the savor of dishes into relief, to intensify that savor, and to give each culinary preparation its particular stamp.

They are all derived from the vegetable kingdom; but, while some are used dry, others are used fresh.

The first-named should belong to the permanent kitchen stock; they are: *sage, basil, rosemary, sweet marjoram, thyme,* and *bay leaf.*

Also to be included in the permanent stock are: *cinnamon, ginger, juniper-berries, nutmeg, cloves, mace* and *vanilla bean.*

The last-named comprise those *aromatic* herbs used fresh, such as: *parsley, chervil, tarragon, pimpernel,* and *common savory;* while, under this head, there may also be included: bits of orange and lemon rind and *zests* of lemon.

174b—SEASONING AND CONDIMENTS   *Assaisonnement*

Seasonings are divided into several classes, which comprise:—

1. *Saline seasonings.*—Salt, spiced salt, saltpeter.

2. *Acid seasonings.*—Plain vinegar, or the same aromatized with tarragon; *verjuice,* lemon and orange juices.

3. *Hot seasonings.*—Peppercorns, ground or coarsely chopped pepper, or *mignonette* pepper; paprika, curry, cayenne, and mixed pepper spices.

4. *Saccharine seasonings.*—Sugar and honey.

Condiments are likewise subdivided, the three classes being:—

1. *The pungents.*—Onions, shallots, garlic, chives, and horse-radish.

2. *Hot condiments.*—Mustard, gherkins, capers, English sauces, such as Worcestershire, Harvey, Ketchup, Escoffier's sauces, etc. and American sauces such as Chili, Tabasco, A-One, Beefsteak, etc.; the wines used in reductions and *braisings;* the finishing elements of sauces and soups.

3. *Fatty substances.*—Most animal fats, butter, vegetable greases (edible oils and margarine).

Remarks.—In cookery it should be borne in mind that both excellence and edibility depend entirely upon a judicious use and a rational blending of the *aromatics,* seasonings, and condiments. And, according as the latter have been used and apportioned, their action will be either beneficial or injurious to the health of the consumer.

In the matter of seasoning there can be no question of approximation or half measures; the quantities must be exact, allowing only of slight elasticity in respect of the various tastes to be satisfied.

175—CLARIFIED BUTTER *Beurre Clarifié*

A certain quantity of clarified butter should always be kept ready and handy.

To prepare this butter, put one lb. to melt in a saucepan large enough to hold twice that amount. Place the saucepan on the fire, over moderate heat; remove all the scum which rises to the surface, and, when the butter looks quite clear and all foreign substances have dropped to the bottom, strain it through muslin and put the liquid carefully away.

176—HERB BUNCHES *Bouquets Garnis*

These little bunches of *aromatics* which, when the contrary is not stated, are generally composed (in order to weigh one ounce) of eight-tenths oz. of parsley sprigs and roots, one-tenth oz. of bay leaves, and one-tenth oz. of thyme. These various *aromatics* are tied neatly together so that no sprig of the one sticks out beyond the others.

177—CHERVIL *Cerfeuil*

Chopped Chervil.—Clean the chervil and remove the stalks; wash, dry it well while tossing it, then chop it finely and put it aside on a plate in a cool place, if it is not for immediate use.

Concassed Chervil.—Proceed as above, except that, instead of chopping it, compress it between the fingers and slice it with a shredding knife. *Concassed* and chopped chervil are, if possible, only prepared at the last moment.

Chervil Pluches.—The pluches are greatly used in the finishing off of soups. They are, practically, the serrated portions only of the leaves, which are torn away in such a manner as to show no trace of the veinings. They are immersed in water, and at the last moment withdrawn, so as to be added, raw, to either soups or boiling consommés.

178—RASPINGS *Chapelure*

Golden raspings are obtained by pounding and passing through a fine sieve bread-crusts which have been previously well dried in the oven.

White raspings are similarly prepared, except that very dry, white crumb is used.

179—PEELED, CHANNELLED, AND ZESTED LEMONS

Citrons, écorcés, creusés et zestés

Lemons are greatly used in cookery, as a decorative and edible garnish. When a whole lemon is used for marinades of fish, for the *"blancs,"* etc., it is well to remove the peel and the whole of the underlying white. The lemon is then cut into more or less large slices, according to the use for which it is intended.

The rind of a lemon thus peeled may be cut into bits and used in this form as the necessity arises. When cutting it up, flatten the rind inside uppermost on the table, and, with a very sharp and flexible knife, scrape off all the white; then slice the remaining peel (which constitutes what is called *zest*) into strips about one inch wide, and cut these across *julienne*-fashion.

Scald the bits of lemon for five minutes, cool them, drain them carefully, and put them aside until wanted. Sometimes, instead of cutting *julienne*-fashion, the *zest* may be finely chopped, but the rest of the process remains the same.

Lemons are grooved by means of a little knife, or a special instrument for the purpose, which cuts out parallel ribbons from the surface of the rind and lays the white bare. A lemon grooved in this way is cut in two, lengthwise with the core; its two ends are removed, and the two halves are cut across into thin, regular slices to look like serrated half-discs.

Fried fish, oysters, and certain game are generally garnished with lemon slices fashioned according to the taste of the cook; but the simplest, and perhaps the best, way is to cut the lemon through the center, after having trimmed the two ends quite straight, and then to remove the rind roughly from the edge.

For whatever purpose the lemon be intended, it should be, as far as possible, only prepared at the last moment. If it must be prepared beforehand, it would be well to keep it in a bowl of fresh water or covered in the refrigerator.

180—SHALLOTS   *Echalotes*

Chopped Shallots.—Peel the shallots, and, by means of a very sharp knife, cut them lengthwise into thin slices; let these cling together by not allowing the knife to cut quite through them, and, this done, turn them half round and proceed in the same way at right angles to the other cuts.

Finally, cut them across, and this will be found to produce very fine and regular, small cubes.

Sliced Shallots.—These are merely sliced across, the result of which operation is a series of thin, regular slices. Chopped shallots should, when possible, only be prepared when required; if, however, they must be treated in advance, they should be kept somewhere in a cool place until wanted.

181—SPICES   *Epices*

Strictly speaking, spices include cinnamon, nutmeg, ginger, mace; and the many varieties of peppers and pimentos, cayenne, paprika, etc.

These various condiments are found ready-made on the market, and they need only be kept dry in air-tight boxes in order to prevent the escape of their aroma.

But there is another kind of preparation, in cookery, to which the name of spice or all-spice is more especially given. Nowadays several market varieties of this preparation exist, and vie with each other for custom, though in most cases they deserve it equally well.

Formerly this was not so, and every chef had his own formula.

The following is a recipe for the spice in question, which would be found useful if it had to be prepared at a moment's notice:—

Obtain the following, very dry

5 oz. of bay leaves.	4 oz. of cloves.
3 oz. of thyme (half of it wild, if possible).	3 oz. of ginger-root.
3 oz. of coriander.	3 oz. of mace.
4 oz. of cinnamon.	10 oz. of mixed pepper (half black and half white).
6 oz. of nutmeg.	1 oz. of cayenne.

Put all these ingredients into a mortar and pound them until they are all able to pass through a very fine sieve. Put the resulting powder into an air-tight box, which must be kept dry.

Before being used, this spice is generally mixed with salt (188).

182—FLOUR   *Farine*

For whatever use the flour is intended, it is always best to sift it. This is more particularly necessary in the case of flour used for coating objects to be fried; for the latter, being first dipped into milk, must of necessity let a few drops of the milk fall into the flour they are rolled in. Lumps would therefore form, which might adhere to the objects to be fried if the flour were not sifted.

183—HERB JUICE   *Jus d'Herbes*

This is to finish or intensify certain preparations.

To prepare it, throw into a small saucepan of boiling water some parsley, chervil, and tarragon and chive leaves, in equal quantities, according to the amount of juice required.

Set to boil for two minutes, drain, cool, press the herbs in a towel, twisting it; pound very finely, and extract the juice from the resulting paste by twisting it in a strong towel.

Keep this juice in a cool place.

(In the United States the use of a juicer simplifies the method of obtaining herb juice.—Ed.)

184—BREAD-CRUMBS   *Mie de Pain*

Thoroughly rub, in a folded towel, some stale bread-crumbs well broken up. Pass them through a fine sieve or colander, according to whether they are required very fine or not, and put them aside in a convenient container.

185—CHOPPED ONION   *Oignon Haché*

Cut the onion finely, like the shallots, but if it is to be minced to make it even finer, it should be freed of its pungent juice, which would cause it to blacken with exposure to the air.

To accomplish this, put the onion in the corner of a towel, pour plenty of cold water over it, and twist the towel in order to press out the water. By this means the onion remains quite white.

186—TURNED OR PITTED OLIVES   *Olives Tournées en Spirale*

There are special instruments for pitting olives, but, lacking these, cut the fruit spirally from the pit with the point of a small knife.

Keep the olives in slightly salted water.

187—PARSLEY   *Persil*

Chopped Parsley.—If parsley be properly chopped, no juice should be produced. If, on the contrary, this is badly done, and amounts to a process of pounding which would press out the juice.

In the latter case the particles stick together, and they are sprinkled with difficulty over an object. To remedy this shortcoming, wash the choppings in fresh water, as in the case of the onion, pressing in a similar manner so as to expel the water.

Concassed Parsley is that kind which is roughly chopped. When a culinary preparation is dressed with *concassed* parsley, the latter should be added to it a few moments before serving, in order to undergo a slight cooking process; whereas chopped parsley may be strewn over a dish at the last moment.

It should be remembered that parsley, when quite fresh and used in moderation, is an excellent thing; but, should it have remained too long in the heat, it becomes quite insufferable.

I cannot, therefore, too strongly urge the advisability of using it in the freshest possible state, and it would even be wiser to discard it entirely than to be forced to ignore this condition. (Modern refrigeration keeps it from wilting.)

Parsley Sprigs.—These are chiefly used in garnishing dishes, and it is well for the purpose to make as much use as possible of the curl-leaf kind, after having removed the long stalks. Keep the sprigs in fresh water until required.

Fried Parsley.—This consists of the sprigs, well drained of water after washing, and immersed for an instant in very hot fat. The moment it is fried drain it carefully, salt it, and place it in a clean towel, where it may get rid of any superfluous fat. It is used to dress fried meats.

188—SALT *Sel*

Two kinds of salt are used in cooking, grey, or sea-salt, and rock-salt. Grey-salt is used more especially for Brines and in the preparation of ices, as its grey color does not allow of its being used indiscriminately.

Be this as it may, many prefer it to rock-salt (coarse white culinary salt) for the salting of stock-pots, roasts, and grills. For the last two purposes it is crushed with a rolling pin, without being pounded, and the result should be such that every grain is distinctly perceptible to the touch. This makes it a coarse salt.

This salt, in melting over a roast or a grill, certainly imparts a supplementary flavor to the latter which could not be had with the use of rock-salt. (The white culinary salt.)

Rock-salt.—This is found on the market in the forms of cooking and table-salt. If the kitchen is only supplied with cooking salt, the quantity required for several days should be dried, pounded in the mortar, and passed through a fine sieve; and then put aside in a dry place for use when wanted. Even table-salt, as it reaches one from the grocer, sometimes needs drying and passing through a sieve before being used.

Spiced Salt.—This condiment, which serves an important purpose in the preparation of meat pies and galantines, is obtained from a mixture of one lb. of table salt with three and one-half oz. of spices (181).

This kind of salt should be carefully kept in a very dry place.

(In the United States we have salt which is already prepared and dried finely ground and packed in containers.—Ed.)

189—VARIOUS PANADAS FOR STUFFINGS

Les Panades Diverses pour Farces

Panadas are those preparations which bind the *forcemeats* and which ensure their proper consistency when they are cooked. They are not necessary to every *forcemeat;* for the *mousseline* kind, which are the finest and lightest, do not require them. Nevertheless, they are useful for varying the taste and the uses of *forcemeats,* and I thought it advisable to introduce them here. The reader will thus be able to use either *forcemeats* with a *panada* base or *mousseline* forcemeats; in accordance with the requirements and his resources.

190—BREAD PANADA　　　　　*Panade au Pain*

Put one-half lb. of the soft crumb of bread and one-half oz. of salt into one-half pint of boiling milk. When the crumb has absorbed all the milk, place the saucepan over a brisk fire and stir with a spatula until the paste has become so thick it does not cling any longer to the end of the spatula. Turn the contents of the saucepan into a buttered platter, and lightly butter the surface of the *panada* in order to avoid its drying out while it cools.

191—FLOUR PANADA　　　　　*Panade à la Farine*

Put into a small saucepan one-half pint of water, a little salt, and two oz. of butter. When the liquid boils add five oz. of sifted flour, stirring over a brisk fire until it reaches the consistency described in the case of bread *panada*. Use the same precautions with regard to cooling.

192—FRANGIPAN PANADA　　　　　*Panade à la Frangipan*

Put into a saucepan four oz. of sifted flour, the yolks of four eggs, a little salt, pepper, and nutmeg. Now add by degrees three oz. of melted butter and dilute with one-half pint of boiled milk. Pass through a strainer, stir over the fire until the boil is reached; set to cook for five minutes while gently whisking, and cool as in the preceding cases.

This is a special *forcemeat* for fowl or fish.

193—CHICKEN FORCEMEAT WITH PANADA AND BUTTER

Farce de Volaille à la Panade et au Beurre

Remove the sinews and cut into cubes, one lb. of chicken-meat. Pound or grind finely and add one-third oz. of salt, a little pepper and nutmeg. When the meat is well pounded remove it from the mortar, and place in its stead one-half lb. of very cold *panada* (190). Finely pound this *panada,* and then add one-half lb. of butter, taking care that the two ingredients mix thoroughly. Now put in the chicken-meat, and wield the pestle or spoon vigorously until the whole mass is completely mixed. Finally, add consecutively two whole eggs and the yolks of four, stirring constantly and seeing that each egg is only added when the one preceding it has become perfectly incorporated with the mass. Rub through a sieve, put the *forcemeat* into a bowl, and smooth it with a wooden spoon and chill.

Test the *forcemeat* by *poaching* a small portion of it in salted, boiling water. This test, which is indispensable, permits rectifying the seasoning and the consistency if necessary. If it be found that the *forcemeat* is too light, a little white of egg could be mixed with it; if, on the other hand, it should be too stiff add a little softened butter.

N.B.—By substituting for chicken veal, game, or fish, etc., any kind of forcemeat may be made; for the quantities of the other ingredients remain the same whatever the basic meat may be.

194—CHICKEN FORCEMEAT WITH PANADA AND CREAM

Farce de Volaille à la panade et a la creme

(For Fine Quenelles.)

Finely pound in a mortar or grind fine one lb. of chicken-meat after having removed the sinews, and seasoned with one-quarter oz. of salt, a little pepper and nutmeg.

When the meat has been reduced to a fine paste, add, very gradually, two oz. of white of egg. Finish with seven oz. of Frangipan *panada* (192), and work vigorously with the pestle or spoon until the whole is blended. Strain through a fine sieve, put the *forcemeat* into a pan sufficiently large to permit working it with ease, and place it on ice for a good hour.

This done, stir the *forcemeat* (still on the ice) for a few seconds with a wooden spoon, then add, in small quantities at a time, one pint of cream. At this stage complete the mixture by adding one-half pint of whipped cream. It should then be found to be very white, smooth, and mellow. Test as directed in the preceding recipe, and add a little white of egg if it is too light, and a little cream if it is too stiff.

N.B.—This *forcemeat* may be prepared from all meats, game, or fish.

195—FINE CHICKEN FORCEMEAT, OR "MOUSSELINE"
Farce Fine de Volaille, ou Mousseline

Remove the sinews, trim, and cut into cubes, one lb. of chicken-meat. Season with one oz. of salt, a little pepper and nutmeg.

Finely pound, in mortar or grind and, when it is reduced to a paste, gradually add the whites of two eggs, vigorously working with the pestle or wooden spoon.

Strain through a fine sieve, put the *forcemeat* into a dish, stir it once more with the wooden spoon for a moment or two, and combine with it, gradually, one pint of thick, fresh cream, working with great caution and keeping the receptacle on ice.

Remarks Relative to Mousseline Forcemeat.—This, like the preceding forcemeats, may be prepared from any kind of meat. The addition of the white of egg is not essential if the meats used already possess a certain quantity of albumen; but without the white of egg the *forcemeat* absorbs much less cream.

This *forcemeat* is particularly suited to preparations with a shell-fish base. Incomparable delicate results are obtained by the process, while it also furnishes ideal *quenelles* for the purpose of garnishing soup. In a word, it may be said of *mousseline forcemeat* that, where it can replace all other kinds, none of these can replace it.

N.B.—*Mousseline forcemeats* of all kinds, with meat, poultry, game, fish, or shell-fish, may be made according to the principles and quantities given above.

196—PORK FORCEMEAT FOR VARIOUS USES
Farce de Porc pour Pièces Diverses

Remove the sinews, and cut into large cubes, two lbs. of tenderloin of pork, and the same weight of fresh, fat bacon. Season with one and three-quarter oz. of spiced salt (188), chop the tenderloin and bacon up, together or separately, pound them finely in the mortar or grind, and finish with two eggs and two tablespoons of brandy.

This *forcemeat* is used for ordinary meat pies and *terrines*. Strictly speaking, it is "sausage-meat." The inclusion of eggs in this *force-*

meat really only obtains when it is used to stuff joints that are to be *braised,* such as stuffed breast of veal; or in the case of meat pies and *terrines.* The addition of the egg in these cases prevents the fat from melting too quickly, and thus averts the drying out of the *forcemeat.*

197—FORCEMEAT FOR GALANTINES, PIES, AND TERRINES
Farces pour Galantines, Pâtés, et Terrines

Remove the sinews, and cut into cubes, one lb. of fillet of veal and as much tenderloin of pork; add to these two lbs. of fresh, fat bacon, also cut into cubes. Season with three oz. of spiced salt, chop the three ingredients together or apart, and then finely pound or grind them. Finish with three eggs and three tablespoons of burnt brandy, strain through a sieve, and place in a bowl.

When about to serve this stuffing, add to it a little *fumet* corresponding with the meat that is to constitute the dish. For *terrines,* meat pies, and *galantines* of game, one-quarter or one-fifth of the *forcemeat's* weight of *gratin* stuffing (proper to the game in preparation) is added.

198—VEAL FORCEMEAT WITH FAT, OR GODIVEAU
Farce de Veau à la Graisse, ou Godiveau

Remove the tendons and cut into cubes, one lb. of fillet of veal; also detach the skin and filaments from two lbs. of the very dry fat of beef kidneys. First, chop these up separately, then combine and pound them in the mortar or grind. Season with one-half oz. of salt, a little pepper, some nutmeg, and pound again until the veal and fat become completely mixed. Now add four eggs, consecutively, and at intervals of a few minutes, without ceasing to pound, and taking care to add each egg after the preceding one has been properly mixed with the mass. Spread the *forcemeat* thus prepared on a dish, and put it covered on ice until the next day.

The next day pound once more, and add little by little fourteen oz. of very clean ice (in small pieces); or, instead, an equal weight of iced water, adding this also very gradually.

When the *godiveau* is properly moistened, *poach* a small portion of it in boiling water in order to test its consistency. If it is too firm, add more ice to it; if, on the other hand, it seem too flimsy, add a little of the white of an egg. For the uses of *godiveau* and *quenelles* see No. 205.

199—VEAL FORCEMEAT WITH FAT AND CREAM
Farce de Veau à la Graisse et à la Crême

Chop finely and separately one lb. of very white fillet of veal, with sinews removed, cut into cubes, and one lb. of the fat pared from a beef kidney.

Combine the veal and the fat in the mortar, and pound or grind through chopper until the two ingredients form a fine and even paste. Season with one-half oz. of salt, a little pepper, and some nutmeg, and add consecutively two eggs and two yolks, after the manner of the preceding recipe and without ceasing to pound. Strain through a sieve, spread the forcemeat on a dish, and keep it on ice until the next day.

Next day pound the forcemeat again for a few minutes, and add to it, little by little, one and one-half pints of cream.

Test as before, and rectify if necessary, either by adding cream or by thickening with the white of an egg.

200—CHICKEN FORCEMEAT FOR GALANTINES, PIES, and TERRINES
Farce de Volaille pour Galatines, Pâtés, et Terrines

The exact weight of chicken-meat used as the base of this *forcemeat* determines the quantities of its other ingredients. Thus the weight of meat afforded by a fowl weighing four lbs. is estimated at twenty oz. after deducting the breasts which are always reserved. Hence the quantities for the *forcemeat* are regulated thus:—

Chicken-meat, twenty oz.; lean pork, eight oz.; tenderloin of veal, eight oz.; fresh, fat bacon, thirty oz.; five whole eggs, spiced salt, two oz.; brandy, one-fifth pint.

Chop up, either together or separately, the chicken-meat, the veal, the pork, and the bacon. Put all these into the mortar, pound them very finely with the seasoning, or grind through chopper, add the eggs consecutively, and, last of all, pour in the brandy.

REMARKS

1. The quantity of spiced salt varies, a few grains either way, according as to whether the atmosphere be dry or damp.

2. According to the purpose of the *forcemeat*, and with a view to giving it a finer flavor, one may, subject to the resources at one's disposal, add a little raw trimmings of *foie gras* to it; but the latter must not, in any case, exceed one-fifth of the *forcemeat* in weight.

3. As a rule, *forcemeat* should always be rubbed through a sieve so as to ensure its being fine and even.

4. Whether the *foie gras* is added or not, chicken *forcemeat* may always be completed with two or three oz. of chopped truffles per lb. of its volume, if desired and available.

201—GAME FORCEMEAT FOR PIES AND TERRINES
Farce de Gibier pour Pâtés et Terrines

This follows the same principles as the chicken *forcemeat,* as, the weight of the game-meat determines the quantities of the other ingredients. The proportions are precisely the same amount of veal, pork, bacon, and the seasoning. The procedure is also the same, while the appended remarks likewise apply.

202—GRATIN FORCEMEAT FOR ORDINARY HOT, RAISED PIES
Farce Gratin pour Pâtés Chauds

Put into a saucepan containing one oz. of very hot butter, one-half lb. of fresh, fat bacon, cut into large cubes, brown quickly, and drain.

Quickly brown in the same butter one-half lb. of fillet of veal cut like the bacon and drain in the same way.

Now rapidly brown one-half lb. of pale calf's liver, also cut into large cubes. Put the veal and the bacon back into the saucepan with the liver, add the necessary quantity of salt and pepper, two oz. of mushroom peels, one oz. of truffle peels (raw if possible), chopped shallots, a sprig of thyme, and a small piece of bay leaf. Put the whole on the fire for two minutes, drain the bacon, the veal, and the liver, and put the gravy aside. Stir into and swash the saucepan with one-quarter pint of Madeira.

Pound or grind the bacon, veal, and liver quickly and finely, while adding consecutively six oz. of butter, the yolks of six eggs, the gravy that has been put aside, one-third pint of cold, reduced Espagnole (22), and the Madeira from the pan.

Strain through a sieve, place in a tureen, and smooth with the wooden spoon.

N.B.—To make a *gratin forcemeat* with game, substitute for the veal that game-meat which may happen to be required.

203—PIKE FORCEMEAT FOR QUENELLES LYONNAISE
Farce de Brochet pour Quenelles Lyonnaise

Forcemeats prepared with the flesh of the pike are extremely delicate. Subject to circumstances, they may be prepared according to any one of the three recipes (193, 194, 195). There is another excel.

lent method of preparing this *forcemeat* which I shall submit here, as it is specially used for the preparation of pike *forcemeat* à la Lyonnaise.

Pound in a mortar one lb. of the meat of a pike, without the skin or bones; combine with this one-half lb. of stiff frangipan (192), season with salt and nutmeg, pass through a sieve, and put back into the mortar.

Vigorously work the *forcemeat* in order to make it combine, and gradually add to it one-half lb. melted beef-suet. The whole half-pound, however, need not necessarily be beef-suet; beef-marrow or butter may form part of it in the proportion of half the weight of the beef-suet.

When the *forcemeat* is very fine and smooth, remove it from the mortar and place it in a bowl surrounded with ice until wanted, or keep it in the refrigerator.

204—SPECIAL STUFFINGS FOR FISH   *Farces Spéciales pour Poisson*

These preparations diverge slightly from the *forcemeats* given above, and they are of two kinds. They are used to stuff such fish as mackerel, herring, shad, etc., to which they lend a condimentary touch that makes these fish more agreeable to the taste, and certainly more digestible.

First Method.—Put into a bowl four oz. of raw, chopped *milt*, two oz. of bread-crumbs, steeped in milk and well pressed out, and one and one-half oz. of the following fine herbs, mixed in equal quantities and finely chopped:—Chives, parsley, chervil, shallots, sweet basil, half a garlic clove (crushed), then two whole eggs, salt, pepper, and nutmeg.

Chop up all these ingredients together so as to mix them thoroughly.

Second Method.—Put into a bowl four oz. of bread-crumbs soaked in milk and well pressed out; one-half oz. of onion and one-half oz. of chopped shallots, slightly cooked in butter, and cold; one oz. of fresh mushrooms, chopped and well pressed in a towel; a tablespoon of chopped parsley; a clove of garlic the size of a pea, crushed; salt, pepper, and nutmeg, and two eggs.

Mix it as above.

205—FORCEMEAT BALLS OR QUENELLES   *Quenelles*

Various Ways of Moulding and Poaching.—Whatever be the required size or shape of *quenelles* there are four ways of making them:—(1) By rolling them; (2) by moulding them with a spoon; (3) by forming them with a pastry-bag; (4) by moulding them by hand into the shape of a kidney.

1. *To roll quenelles* it is necessary to keep the *forcemeat* somewhat stiff, and therefore this process could not well apply to the *mousseline* forcemeats. Place one-quarter lb. of *forcemeat,* when ready, on a floured board, and, hands covered with flour, roll the preparation until it has lengthened itself into the form of a sausage, the thickness of which depends upon the required size of the intended *quenelles.*

Cut the sausage of *forcemeat* in slices with a floured knife, and roll each section with the finger-tips until the length it assumes is three times that of its diameter. The balls should be put aside on a floured tray as soon as they are made.

The Poaching of Rolled Quenelles.—When all the *forcemeat* has been used up, the balls are gently tilted into a saucepan containing boiling, salted water, so calculated in quantity to not be too tightly squeezed. The saucepan is covered and kept on the side of the fire until all the balls have risen to the surface and are almost out of the water. They are then lifted out with a skimmer and placed in a bowl of cold water.

At last, when they have properly cooled, they are carefully drained on a cloth and put aside on a dish until required.

When the *quenelles* are needed for immediate use it would be better not to cool them.

2. *To Mould Quenelles with a Spoon.*—This method may be applied to all *forcemeats,* and makes the balls much softer, as the *forcemeat* need not be so stiff. First, butter the saucepan or the tray, on which the balls are to be laid, by means of a brush, and let the butter cool.

Put the saucepan on the table in front of you and a little to the right; on the left, place the saucepan or bowl containing the *forcemeat,* and on the further side of the buttered saucepan there should be a receptacle containing hot water, into which the spoon used for moulding is placed. For ordinary *quenelles* two large teaspoons are used, one of which is kept in the hot water as stated above. Now, with the other held in the left hand, take up a little of the *forcemeat* just enough to fill the spoon); withdraw the second spoon from the hot water and place it, upside down, on the other spoon.

This smooths the top of the *forcemeat.* Now, with the help of the second spoon, remove the whole of the contents of the first spoon, and overturn the second spoon on the spot in the tray or saucepan which the ball is supposed to occupy. The second spoon, being at once moist and hot, allows the *forcemeat* to leave it quite easily in the shape of a large olive. Renew this operation until the whole of the forcemeat has been used up.

The Poaching of Spoon-moulded Quenelles.—When all the balls have been moulded, place the tray on the side of the stove and pour enough boiling, salted water over them to moisten them abundantly. Leave them to *poach,* and from time to time move and shake the tray or pan; then, when they have swollen sufficiently and seem soft and firm to the touch, drain them. If they are to be used at once they should be placed directly in the sauce. If they have been prepared in advance, it would be well to cool them as directed under rolled *quenelles.*

3. *To Form Quenelles with a Pastry-bag.*—This process is especially recommended for small, fine, and light *forcemeat* balls intended for soup garnish. For, besides being extremely quick, it permits making them in any desirable size or shape.

Butter a tray or a pan, and leave to cool. Put the *forcemeat* into a bag fitted with a tube at its narrowest end. The tube may be grooved or smooth, and its size must be in accordance with that intended for the proposed balls. Now squeeze out the latter, proceeding in the usual way and laying them very closely.

The Poaching of Quenelles made by the above Process, with ordinary or Mousseline Forcemeat.—These *quenelles* are *poached* in exactly the same way as the spoon-moulded ones.

The Poaching of Godiveau Quenelles made with a Pastry-bag.—These quenelles or balls are laid on a piece of fine, buttered paper, which is placed upon a buttered tray. The *godiveau* must not be too stiff, and the balls are laid by means of the pastry-bag side by side and slightly touching one another. When the tray is covered place it in a very moderate oven for a few minutes. The balls are *poached* when a thin condensation of grease may be seen to glisten on their surfaces. On the appearance of this greasy film remove them from the oven and overturn the tray, carefully, upon a marble slab, taking care that the tray does not press at all upon the balls, lest it crush them. When the latter are nearly cold the paper which covers them is taken off with caution, and all that remains to be done is to put them carefully away on a dish until they are wanted.

4. *To Mould Forcemeat with the Fingers.*—This excellent process is as expedient as that of the pastry bag. and it produces beautifully

shaped balls. Place on the edge of a table, in front of you, a saucepan three-quarters full of boiling, salted water, the handle being turned to the opposite side of you. Now take a piece of string one yard in length, double it over, and tie the free ends to a weight of two lbs., letting the two strands twist round each other and hang down.

This done, there should be a loop at the top of the string. Put this loop over the handle of the saucepan, and draw the string diametrically across to you, letting the weight pull the string tightly down on the side opposite to the handle. When this has been done, with the left hand, take some of the *forcemeat*, smoothing it with a spoon, and, placing the spoon near the string with the right, first finger, then take a portion of the preparation about equal to the intended size of the balls. This portion of the *forcemeat* remaining suspended on your first finger, now scrape it across the string, and the ball falls beneath into the saucepan containing the water. When all the stuffing has been moulded in this way the saucepan is placed on the fire to complete the *poaching* of the balls, and the precautions indicated in the preceding processes are observed.

CHAPTER VIII

The Various Garnishes for Soups

ROYALES

206—ORDINARY ROYALE   *Royale Ordinaire*

Put one oz. of chervil into one pint of boiling consommé, cover the saucepan, and let infusion proceed away from the fire for twenty minutes. Now pour this infusion over two eggs and six yolks, beaten briskly in a bowl, and mix with the beater. Strain through muslin, and carefully remove the froth that has formed. Pour into buttered moulds; *poach* in a *bain-marie* (water-bath), as in the case of cream, and take great care that the water in the *bain-marie* does not boil.

According to the way in which the *royale* is to be divided, it may be *poached* either in large or small "Charlotte" (custard) moulds; but the latter, large and small alike, must be well buttered.

If the preparation be put into large moulds, thirty-five or forty minutes should be allowed for *poaching;* if, on the other hand, the moulds are small, about fifteen minutes would suffice.

Always let the *royale* cool in the moulds.

207—DESLIGNAC OR CREAM ROYALE *Deslignac or Royale à la Crème*

Bring to a boil one pint of thin cream, and pour it, little by little, over one egg and six yolks, well beaten in a bowl. Season with a little salt and nutmeg, strain through muslin, and, for the *poaching,* follow the directions given above.

208—CHICKEN ROYALE   *Royale de Volaille*

Finely pound three oz. of cooked white chicken-meat, and add three tablespoons of cold Béchamel (28). Put this paste in a bowl, season with a little salt and a dash of nutmeg, dilute with one-fifth pint of cream, and strain through a fine sieve.

Thicken this preparation with one egg and the yolks of three,

88

and *poach* in small or large moulds, in accordance with the procedure already described.

209—GAME ROYALE   *Royale de Gibier*

Finely pound or grind three oz. of the cooked meat of game which gives its name to the preparation, and add three tablespoons of cold Espagnole Sauce (22) and one-fifth pint of rich cream, in small quantities at a time. Warm the seasoning with a very little cayenne, strain through a fine sieve, thicken with one egg and three yolks, and *poach* as before.

210—FISH ROYALE   *Royale de Poisson*

Stew in butter four oz. of fillet of sole cut into cubes, or the same quantity of any other fish suited to the nature of the intended soup. Cool, pound finely, and add, little by little, two tablespoons of cold Béchamel (28) and one-quarter pint of cream. Season with salt and a pinch of nutmeg, and strain through a fine sieve. Thicken with the yolks of five eggs, and *poach* in large or small moulds.

211—CARROT OR CRECY ROYALE   *Royale de Carotte ou Crécy*

Stew gently in butter five oz. of the outside part of carrots. Cool, crush in a mortar or grind and gradually add two tablespoons of Béchamel (28) and one-fifth pint of rich cream. Season with table-salt and a pinch of sugar, and deepen the tint of the *royale* with a few drops of vegetable red coloring. Strain through a fine sieve, thicken with one egg and four yolks, put into moulds, and *poach*.

212—FRESH PEAS OR ST. GERMAIN ROYALE
Royale Saint-Germain de Purée de Pois Frais

Cook one-half lb. of fresh, small peas in boiling water with a bunch of chervil and a few leaves of fresh mint. Pass through a sieve, and dilute the *purée* (in a saucepan) with two-fifths of its volume of the liquor it has been cooked in and one-fifth of cream. Add a little sugar, the necessary salt, one egg, and two yolks. Pass through a fine strainer, and *poach* in well-buttered moulds.

213—VARIOUS ROYALES   *Royales Diverses*

Royales may also be made with leeks, celery, etc., the procedure being as follows:—

Finely mince or grind six or seven oz. of the chosen vegetables; stew the same gently and thoroughly in butter, and press through a fine sieve. Add to the resulting *purée* three tablespoons of Béchamel (28), one-fifth pint of cream, two eggs, and four yolks. Put into large or small moulds, and *poach*.

Remarks.—In order that these *royales* may have the required delicacy, I should urge the reader not to exceed the prescribed quantities of eggs and yolks, these being so calculated as to exactly produce the consistency required.

214—THE DIVIDING UP OF ROYALES   *La Division des Royales*

When the *poaching* is done take the mould or moulds out of water, and leave the *royale* to cool in them. Do not turn out the moulds while the preparation is hot, as it would surely separate. It only assumes the necessary solidity for being cut up by means of the cohesion and condensation of its various ingredients during the cooling process.

If the royale has been poached in small moulds, slightly trim the cylinders of *royale,* cut them across into slices, and stamp them uniformly with a plain or fancy cutter.

If the royale has been poached in large moulds, remove it from these, and place it on a napkin; trim the tops, cut into half-inch slices, and stamp with small, fancy cutters of different shapes. These little portions of *royale* must always be stamped very neatly and quite regularly.

215—CHIFFONADE   *Chiffonade*

The name *"Chiffonade"* is given to a mince of sorrel or lettuce, intended as a complement for such soups as "Potage de santé," "le Germiny," etc., or various clear consommés like *"Julienne."*

To prepare *Chiffonade,* first carefully shred the sorrel or lettuce, and remove all the leaf-ribs. Carefully wash the leaves, and squeeze them tightly between the fingers of the left hand and the table top. Now cut them into fine strips with a sharp knife.

If the *Chiffonade* is intended for a consommé, add it to the latter half an hour before serving; it is thus actually cooked in the soup itself. If, as is most often the case, it is intended for a thick soup, it is better to let it melt well in butter, to moisten it with a little consommé, and to let it boil for ten minutes before adding it to the soup.

Whatever the purpose is for which it is made, *chiffonade* should always be prepared with very tender sorrel or lettuce.

216—DIRECTIONS FOR SOUPS WITH PASTES

Potages avec des Croutes

Vermicelli and the various Italian pastes should be used in the proportion of about three oz. per quart of consommé. They should first be thrown into boiling, salted water, where they are left to *poach* for three minutes, then they are drained, cooled, and their cooking is completed in the consommé.

The parboiling of these pastes is necessary in order to get rid of the little flecks of flour which adhere to them, and which would otherwise make the consommé cloudy.

Tapioca, sago, salep (edible orchid root) etc., should also be apportioned at about three oz. per quart. But this is only an average, for the quality of this kind of products varies greatly, and it is best to choose the products of an excellent maker, and, in order to avoid surprises, to abide by that choice.

These products need no parboiling; they are merely sprinkled into the boiling consommé while stirring it, and they are left to cook until the soup is quite clear. The boiling should be gentle, and the scum should be removed as often as it forms.

The time allowed for cooking naturally varies in accordance with the quality of the products, but the absolute transparency of the consommé is an infallible sign of its having been completed.

Brazilian or Japanese pearls are similar to large sago and could be used in the same quantities, but they should *poach* for thirty minutes if required to be very transparent.

217—THREADED EGGS   *Oeufs Filés*

Beat up three eggs in a bowl, season with salt and pepper, and strain through a sieve. Now pour the eggs through a fine strainer, hold same over a saucepan containing some boiling consommé, and shift it about in such a way as to let the egg fall in threads into the boiling liquid beneath, and thus immediately coagulate. Drain the egg-threads very carefully lest they break and use to garnish clear soups.

218—PROFITEROLLES FOR SOUPS   *Profiterolles pour Potages*

These consist of little *choux* (puff shells) about the size of a large hazel-nut, stuffed with some kinds of *purée,* such as that of *foie gras* with cream, or of chicken, or of vegetables, etc. Four *profiterolles* should be allowed for each person.

To make *profiterolles,* put a few tablespoons of *"pâte à choux"* (cream puff paste) without sugar (2374) into a pastry-bag fitted with a smooth tube, whose opening should be about one-quarter inch in diameter. Squeeze out portions of the preparation on to a baking sheet, so as to form balls about the size of a small hazel-nut; brush with beaten egg and bake in a moderate oven until a light golden brown.

Do not take the *profiterolles* from the oven until they are quite dry.

CHAPTER IX

GARNISHING PREPARATIONS FOR RELEVÉS AND ENTRÉES

219—POTATO CROQUETTES   *Croquettes à Pommes*

Cook quickly in salted water two lb. of peeled and quartered potatoes. As soon as they seem soft to the finger, drain them, place them in the front of the oven for a few minutes in order to dry, and then turn them into a sieve lying on a cloth, and press them through without rubbing.

Place the *purée* in a saucepan; season with salt, pepper, and nutmeg; add one oz. of butter, and dry; stirring over a brisk fire until the *purée* becomes a well blended paste.

Take off the fire, complete with the yolks of three eggs, well mixed with the rest, and turn the paste out on to a buttered dish, taking care to spread it in a rather thin layer, so as to hasten its cooling. Butter the surface to prevent drying out.

To make croquettes, equal parts of this paste, portions weighing about one and one-half oz. are rolled on a flour-dusted board into the shape of a cork, a ball, or a patty. These are now dipped into an *Anglaise* (174) and rolled in bread-crumbs or raspings, the latter being well patted on to the surface of the croquettes, lest they should fall into the frying fat. Let the patting also help to finish off the selected shape of the objects. These are then plunged into hot fat, where they should remain until they have acquired a fine, golden color.

220—DAUPHINE POTATOES   *Pommes Dauphine*

Prepare as above the required quantity of paste, and add per lb. six oz. of *pâte à choux*, without sugar (2374).

Mix the two pastes thoroughly.

Dauphine potatoes are moulded in the shape of small cylinders, and they are treated *à l'Anglaise*, like the croquettes.

221—DUCHESS POTATOES   *Pommes Duchesse*

These are the same as the croquettes, though they are differently treated. They are made on a floured board in the shape of diminu-

93

tive cottage-loaves, little shuttle-shaped loaves, small patties, and diamonds or rectangles. They are brushed with beaten egg, and when their shape is that of patties, rectangles, or diamonds, they are decorated by means of a small knife.

After this operation, which is to prevent the brushed egg from blistering, they are baked in the oven for a few minutes previous to being used in garnishing the dishes they accompany.

222—MARQUIS POTATOES   *Pommes Marquise*

Take one lb. of croquette paste (219) and add six oz. of very red, thick tomato-*purée* (29). Pour this mixture into a pastry bag fitted with a large, grooved tube, and squeeze it out upon a baking-tray in shapes resembling large meringue shells.

Slightly brush their surfaces with beaten egg and put them into the oven for a few minutes before using them to decorate the dish.

223—ORDINARY OR DRY DUXELLE   *Duxelle Sèche*

The uses of *Duxelle* are legion, and it is prepared thus:—Slightly fry one teaspoon of onions in one tablespoon of butter and oil mixed. Add to this four tablespoons of mushroom stalks and peels, chopped and well pressed in a towel to expel their moisture. Stir over a brisk fire until the latter has completely evaporated; season with salt, pepper, and nutmeg, and one teaspoon of well-chopped parsley, mixing the whole thoroughly.

Transfer to a bowl, cover with a piece of white, buttered paper, and put aside until wanted.

224—DUXELLE FOR STUFFED VEGETABLES
Duxelle pour Légumes Farcis

Put six tablespoons of dry *duxelle* into a small saucepan, and add three tablespoons of half-glaze sauce (23) containing plenty of tomato, crushed garlic the size of a pea, and two tablespoons of white wine. Set to simmer until the required degree of consistency is reached.

N.B.—A tablespoon of fine, fresh bread-crumbs may be added to the *duxelle* in order to thicken it.

225—DUXELLE FOR GARNISHING SMALL PIES, ETC.
Duxelle pour Garnitures Diverses

To four tablespoons of dry *duxelle* add four tablespoons of ordinary pork *forcemeat* (196).

226—MAINTENON PREPARATION USED IN STUFFING
Préparation à la Maintenon

Put one pint of Béchamel (28) into a saucepan with one-half pint of Soubise (104), and reduce to half while stirring over a brisk fire. Thicken, away from the fire, by means of the yolks of five eggs, and add four tablespoons of minced mushrooms, either cooked in the ordinary way or stewed in butter.

227—MATIGNON
Matignon

This preparation serves chiefly for covering certain large joints of meat, or fowl, to which it imparts an appropriate flavor. It is made as follows:—Finely mince two medium carrots (the outside part only), two onions, and two stalks of celery taken from the heart. Add one tablespoon of raw lean ham, cut *paysanne*-fashion, a sprig of thyme, and half a bay leaf, crushed.

Stew in butter, and finally stir into the saucepan two tablespoons of Madeira and swash and scrape the pan.

228—MIREPOIX
Mirepoix

The purpose of *Mirepoix* in culinary preparations is the same as that of *Matignon,* but its mode of use is different.

Its ingredients are the same as those of the *Matignon,* but instead of being minced they are cut up into more or less fine dice, in accordance with the use for which the preparation is intended.

Instead of the ham, fresh and slightly-salted pork or fresh bacon may be used, while both the ham and the bacon may be excluded under certain circumstances.

229—FINE OR BORDELAISE MIREPOIX *Mirepoix Bordelaise Fine*

Coarse *Mirepoix,* which are added to certain preparations in order to lend these the proper flavor, are generally made immediately before being used, but this is not so in the case of the finer *Mirepoix,* which chiefly serves as an accompaniment to crayfish and lobsters. This is made in advance, and as follows:—

Cut into dice four oz. of the outside part only of carrots, the same quantity of onion, and one oz. of parsley. In order that the *Mirepoix* may be still finer, these ingredients may now be chopped, but in this case it is advisable to thoroughly press them in a corner of a towel, so as to squeeze out their juice, the mere process of stewing not being sufficient for this purpose.

Should this juice be allowed to remain in the *Mirepoix,* more particularly if it must be kept some time, it would probably give rise to mustiness or fermentation.

Put the ingredients into a small stewpan with one and one-half oz. of butter and a little powdered thyme and bay leaf, and stew until all is well cooked. This done, turn the preparation out into a small bowl, heap it together with the back of a fork, cover it with a piece of wax paper, and put aside until wanted.

230—VARIOUS SALPICONS   *Salpicons Divers*

Salpicon is a term applied to a number of diced preparations which may be either simple or compound.

Salpicons are simple or compound. Simple if they only contain one product, such as the meat of a fowl, or of game, of beef, *foie gras,* various fish, ham or tongue, mushrooms, truffles, etc. Compound if they consist of two or more of the above-mentioned ingredients which may happen to combine suitably.

The preparatory method consists in cutting the various ingredients into dice.

The series of preparations arises from the many possible combinations of the products, each particular combination bearing its own name.

Thus *Salpicons* may be Royal, Financier, Chasseur, Parisien, Montglas, etc.; of whichever kind, however, *Salpicons* are always mixed with a blending sauce which is in accordance with their purpose and ingredients.

231—BATTER FOR VARIOUS FRITTERS
Pâté à Frire pour Beignets Divers

Put into a bowl one lb. of sifted flour, one-quarter oz. of salt, one tablespoon of oil or melted butter, and the necessary quantity of barely lukewarm water. If the batter is to be used at once mix the ingredients by turning them over and over without stirring with a spoon, for stirring would give the batter an elasticity which would prevent its adhering to immersed solids. Should the batter be prepared beforehand, however, it may be stirred, since it loses its elasticity when left to stand any length of time.

Before using it add the whites of two eggs whisked to a froth.

232—BATTER FOR VEGETABLES *Pâté à Frire pour Légumes*

Put one lb. of sifted flour into a bowl with one-quarter oz. of salt and two tablespoons of oil or melted butter. Dilute with one egg and the necessary quantity of cold water. Keep this batter somewhat thin, do not stir it, and let it rest for a few hours before using.

233—BATTER FOR FRUIT AND FLOWER FRITTERS

Pâté à Frire pour Beignets de Fruits et de Fleurs

Put one lb. of flour into a bowl with one-quarter oz. of salt and two tablespoons of oil or melted butter. Dilute gradually with one-quarter pint of beer and a little tepid water.

When about to use the batter mix in the whites of two eggs whisked to a froth.

N.B.—Keep this batter thin, if anything, and above all do not stir too much.

234—BATTER FOR OVEN-GLAZED FRUIT FRITTERS

Pâté à Frire pour Beignets Glacés au Four

Mix one lb. of flour with two tablespoons of oil, a few grains of salt, two eggs (added one after the other), the necessary quantity of water, and one oz. of sugar. Keep this preparation in a lukewarm place to let it ferment, and stir it with a wooden spoon before using it to cover the food.

Remarks.—Batter for fruit fritters may contain a few tablespoons of brandy, in which case an equal quantity of the water must be eliminated.

235—PREPARATION FOR STUFFING CUTLETS A LA PROVENCALE

Préparations pour Farce Provençale

Put one pint of Béchamel (28) into a saucepan and reduce it until it has become quite thick. Add the yolks of four eggs, and finish it away from the fire with a crushed piece of garlic as large as a pea, and one-quarter lb. of grated cheese.

CHAPTER X

LEADING CULINARY OPERATIONS

236—THE PREPARATION OF SOUPS   *Préparation des Potages*

The nutritious liquids known under the name of Soups are of comparatively recent origin. Indeed, as they are now served, they do not date any further back than the early years of the nineteenth century.

The soups of old cookery were, really, complete dishes, wherein the meats and vegetables used in their preparation were assembled. They, moreover, suffered from the effects of the general confusion which reigned in the menus of those days. These menus seem to have depended in no wise, for their items, upon the progressive satisfaction of the diner's appetites, and a long procession of dishes was far more characteristic of the meal than their judicious order and diversity.

In this respect, as in so many others, Carême was the reformer, and, if he were not, strictly speaking, the actual initiator of the changes which ushered in our present methods, he certainly had a large share in the establishment of the new theories.

Nevertheless, it took his followers almost a century to bring soups to the perfection of to-day, for modern cookery has replaced those stodgy dishes of yore by comparatively simple and savory preparations which are veritable wonders of delicacy and taste. Now, my attention has been called to the desirability of drawing up some sort of classification of soups, if only with the view of obviating the absurdity of placing such preparations as are indiscriminately called *Bisque, Purée, Cullis,* or Cream under the same head. Logically, each preparation should have its own special formula, and it is impossible to admit that one and the same can apply to all.

It is generally admitted that the terms *Veloutés* and *Creams,* whose introduction into the vocabulary of cookery is comparatively recent, are peculiarly well suited to supplant those of *Bisque* and *Cullis,* which are steadily becoming obsolete, as well as that too

98

vulgar term *Purée*. Considerations of this kind naturally led me to a new classification of soups, and this I shall disclose later.

I shall not make any lengthy attempt here to refute the arguments of certain autocrats of the dinner-table who, not so many years ago, urged the total abolition of soups. I shall only submit to their notice the following quotation from Grimod de la Reynière, one of our most illustrious gastronomists: "Soup is to a dinner what the porch or gateway is to a building," that is to say, it must not only form the first portion thereof, but it must be so devised as to convey some idea of the whole to which it belongs; or, after the manner of an overture in a light opera, it should divulge what is to be the dominant phrase of the melody throughout.

I am at one with Grimod in this, and believe that soups have come to stay. Of all the items on a menu, soup is that which exacts the most delicate perfection and the strictest attention, for upon the first impression it gives to the diner the success of the latter part of the meal largely depends.

Soups should be served as hot as possible in very warm plates or cups, especially in the case of consommés when these have been preceded by cold hors-d'œuvres.

Hors-d'œuvres are pointless in a dinner, and even when oysters stand as such they should only be allowed at meals which include no soup.

Those hors-d'œuvres which consist of various fish, smoked or in oil, and strongly seasoned salads, leave a disagreeable taste on the diner's palate and make the soup which follows seem flat and insipid if the latter be not served boiling hot.

CLASSIFICATION OF SOUPS

This includes (1) clear soups, (2) thick soups, (3) special soups of various kinds, (4) classical vegetable soups, including some local preparations.

237—CLEAR SOUPS   *Les Potages Clairs*

Clear soups, of whatever nature the base may be, whether meat, poultry, game, fish, shell-fish, or turtle, etc., are made according to one method only. They are always clear consommés to which has been added a slight garnish in keeping with the nature of the consommé.

238—THICK SOUPS   *Les Potages Liés*

These are divided into three leading classes as follows:—(1) The *Purées, Cullises,* or *Bisques.* (2) Various *Veloutés.* (3) Various Creams.

Remarks.—Though the three preparations of the first class are practically the same, and, generally speaking, the *Cullises* and the *Bisques* may be considered as *purées* of fowl, game, or shell-fish, it is advisable to distinguish one from another by giving each a special name of its own.

Thus the word *purée* is most suitably applied to any preparation with a vegetable base. The term *Cullis* or *Coulis* is best fitted to preparations having either poultry, game, or fish for base, while *bisque,* in spite of the fact that in former days it was applied indiscriminately to *purées* of shell-fish, poultry, pigeons, etc., distinctly denotes a *purée* of shell-fish (either lobster, crayfish, or shrimp, etc.).

In short, it is imperative to avoid all confusion and to give everything its proper name, or, at least, that name which identifies it most correctly.

239—PUREES   *Les Purées*

Starchy vegetables, such as dried beans and lentils, and the mealy ones, such as the potato, need no additional thickening ingredient, since the flour or *fecula* which they contain amply suffices for the binding of their *purées.*

On the other hand, succulent vegetables like carrots, pumpkins, turnips, celery, etc., and herbs cannot dispense with a thickening ingredient, as their *purées* of themselves do not hold together and bind.

Binding or Thickening Elements; Quantities.—In order to effect the binding of vegetable *purées,* either rice, potato, or soft crumb of bread cut into dice and fried in butter may be used.

The proportion of these per pound of vegetables should be respectively three oz., ten oz., and ten oz. Soft bread dice, prepared as described above, were greatly used in old cookery, and they lend a mellowness to a *purée* which is quite peculiar to them.

The Dilution of Purées.—Generally this is done by means of ordinary white consommé, though in certain cases, as, for instance, if the soup is a *Lenten* one, milk is used.

The Finishing.—When the *purées* have been strained and brought to the required consistency they should be boiled and stirred. Then they are placed on the side of the fire to simmer for twenty-five or thirty minutes. It is at this stage that they are purified by means of the careful removal of all the scum that forms on their surface.

When ready to serve complete them, away from the fire, with three oz. of butter per quart of soup, and pass them once more through a strainer.

Purée Garnishes.—These are usually either small fried crusts, small dice of potato fried in butter, a *chiffonade,* some kind of little *brunoise,* or, more generally, chervil *pluches.*

240—CULLISES *Les Coulis*

Cullises have for their base either poultry, game, or fish.

The thickening ingredients used are:—

For fowl, two or three oz. of rice, or three-quarters pint of poultry *velouté* (26) per lb. of fowl.

For game, three or four oz. of lentils, or three-quarters pint of game Espagnole (22) per lb. of game.

For fish, a clear *panada* made of French bread soaked in boiling salted milk. Use five oz. of bread and one good pint of milk per lb. of fish. Having strained and made up the *Cullises,* boil them while stirring (except in the case of fish *cullises,* which must not boil, and must be served as soon as they are made), then place them in a *bain-marie* (water-bath) and butter their surfaces lest a skin should form.

At the last moment complete them with two or three oz. of butter per quart.

The garnish of poultry or game *cullises* consists of either small dice of game or fowl breasts, which should be kept aside for the purpose; a fine *julienne* of these uncooked breasts, or small *quenelles* made from them.

The garnish of fish *cullis* is generally fish-fillets *poached* in butter and cut up into small dice or in *julienne-*fashion.

241—BISQUES *Les Bisques*

The invariable base of *Bisques* is shell-fish cooked in *mirepoix.*

Their thickening ingredients may be rice, fish *velouté,* or crusts of bread fried in butter, the proportion being three oz. of rice, ten oz. of bread-crusts, or three-quarters pint of fish *velouté* (26a) per lb. of shell-fish cooked in *mirepoix* (228).

When the soup is strained, treat it in precisely the same way as the *cullises.*

The garnish consists of small dice of the meat from the shell-fish used. These pieces should be put aside from the first.

242—THE VELOUTES *Les Veloutés*

These differ from the *purées, cullises,* and *bisques* in that their invariable thickening element is a *velouté* whose preparation is in harmony with the nature of the ingredients of the soup, these being either vegetables, poultry, game, fish, or shell-fish.

The Preparation of the Velouté.—Allow three and one-half oz. of white *roux* per quart of the diluting liquid. This liquid should be ordinary consommé for a *velouté* of vegetables or herbs, chicken consommé for a poultry *velouté,* or very clear fish fumet for a fish or shell-fish *velouté.* The procedure is exactly the same as that described under (25) of the leading sauces.

The Apportionment of the Ingredients.—In general, the quantities of each ingredient are in the following proportion:—*Velouté,* one-half; the *purée* of the substance which characterizes the soup, one-quarter; the consommé used to bring the soup to its proper consistency, one-quarter. In respect of finishing ingredients, use, for thickening, the yolks of three eggs and one-fifth pint of cream per quart of soup.

Thus for four quarts of poultry *velouté* we arrive at the following quantities:—

Poultry *velouté,* three pints; *purée* of fowl obtained from a cleaned and drawn hen weighing about three lbs., one quart; consommé for regulating consistency, one quart; binding, twelve egg yolks and four-fifths pint of cream.

Rules Relative to the Preparation.—If the *velouté* is to be of lettuce, chicory, celery, or mixed herbs, these ingredients are scalded for five minutes, drained, gently stewed in butter, and added to the prepared *velouté* in which their cooking is completed.

If carrots, turnips, onions, etc., are to be treated, finely mince them, stew them in butter without allowing them to acquire any color, and add them to the *velouté.*

If fowl be the base, cook it in the *velouté.* This done, withdraw it, remove the meat, finely pound or grind, and add it to the *velouté,* which is then rubbed through a fine sieve.

In the case of fish the procedure is the same as for fowl. For game, roast or *sauté* the selected piece, bone it, finely pound or grind the meat, and combine the latter with the *velouté,* which should then be rubbed through a fine sieve.

For shell-fish, cook these in a *mirepoix,* finely pound them together with the latter, add to the *velouté,* and pass the whole through a fine sieve.

The Completing of Velouté.—Having passed the soup through a fine sieve, bring it to its proper degree of consistency with the necessary quantity of consommé, boil while stirring, and place in a *bain-marie* or water-bath.

At the last moment finish the soup with the binding and two oz. of butter per quart of liquid.

Garnish for Velouté.—In the case of vegetables: *Chiffonade,* fine *printaniers,* or *brunoise.*

For fowl and game: The breasts of one or the other, *poached* and cut into small dice or in *julienne*-fashion; little *quenelles* made with the raw breasts, or either fowl or game royales (208).

For fish: Small dice or fine *julienne* of fish fillets *poached* in butter.

For shell-fish: Small dice of cooked shell-fish meat put aside for the purpose.

Remarks.—In certain cases these garnishes are increased by means of three tablespoons of *poached* rice per quart of the soup.

243—THE CREAMS   *Les Crèmes*

Practically speaking, the preparation of the creams is the same as that of the *veloutés,* but for the following exceptions:—

1. In all cases, whatever be the nature of the soup, *velouté* is substituted for clear Béchamel.

2. The correct consistency of the soup is made by means of milk instead of consommé.

3. Creams do not require egg-yolk bindings.

4. They are not buttered, but they are finished with one-fifth or two-fifths pint of fresh cream per quart.

Creams permit the same garnishes as the *veloutés.*

244—SPECIAL SOUPS AND THICKENED CONSOMMES
Les Potages Spéciaux et les Consommés Liés

These are of different kinds, though their preparation remains the same, and they do not lend themselves to the requirements of *veloutés* or creams. I should quote as types of this class the Ambassador, à l'Américaine, Darblay, Faubonne, etc.

The same holds good with thickened consommés, such as "Germiny," "Coquelin," etc.

245—VEGETABLE SOUPS   *Les Potages à Légumes*

These soups, of which the *"Paysanne"* (peasant type) is the radical type, do not demand very great precision in the apportionment of the vegetables of which they are composed; but they need great care and attention, notwithstanding.

The vegetables, in the majority of cases, must undergo a long stewing in butter, an operation the object of which is to expel their vegetable juice and to saturate them with butter.

In respect of others which have a local character, the vegetables should be cooked with the liquid, without a preparatory stewing.

246—FOREIGN SOUPS   *Potages Etrangères*

In the course of Part II of this book I shall refer to certain soups which have a foreign origin, and whose use, although it may not be general, is yet sufficiently common. If only for the sake of novelty or variety, it is occasionally permissible to poach upon the preserves of foreign nations; but apart from this there exist among the recipes of foreigners many which can but enrich their adopter, besides being generally appreciated.

Braising, Poaching, Sautés, and Poëles

Except for the roasts, grills, and fryings, which will be discussed later, all culinary operations dealing with meat are related to one of the four following methods: *Braising, poëles, poaching,* and *sautés.*

These four methods of cooking belong, however to the sauces, and this explains how it is that the latter hold such a pre-eminent position in French cookery.

Before devoting any attention to particular recipes, which will be given in the second part of this work, it seemed desirable to me to recapitulate in a general way the theory of each of these cooking methods. These theories are of paramount importance, since it is only with a complete knowledge of them that good results may be obtained by the chef or cook.

247—ORDINARY BRAISINGS   *Les Braises Ordinaires*

Of all the various culinary operations, *braisings* are the most expensive and the most difficult. Long and assiduous practice alone can teach the many difficulties that this mode of procedure entails, for it is one which demands extraordinary care and the most constant attention. Over and above the question of care and that of the quality of meat used, which latter consideration is neither more nor less important here than in any other cooking operation, there are also these conditions to be fulfilled in order that a good *braising* may be obtained, namely, that excellent stock should be used in moistening, and that the *braising* base be well prepared.

Meats that are Braised.—Mutton and beef are *braised* in the ordinary way, but veal, lamb, and poultry are *braised* in a manner which I shall treat of later.

Meat intended for *braising* need not, as in the case of roasts, be that of young beasts. The best for the purpose is that derived from an animal of three to six years of age in the case of beef, and one to two years in the case of mutton. Good meat is rarely procured from animals more advanced than these in years, and, even so, should it be used, it would not only be necessary to lengthen the time of cooking a great deal, but the resulting food would probably be fibrous and dry.

Properly speaking, meat derived from old or ill-nourished beasts only answers two purposes in cookery, the preparation of consommés and that of various kinds of stock.

The Larding of Meats for Braising.—When the meat to be *braised* is ribs or fillet of beef, it is always *interlarded,* and consequently never dry if of good quality. But this is not the case with the meat of the rumps, or with leg of mutton. These meats are not sufficiently fat of themselves to allow for prolonged cooking without becoming dry. For this reason they are *larded* with square strips of bacon fat, which should be the length of the meat under treatment, and about half an inch thick. These strips of fat are first seasoned with pepper, nutmeg, and spices, sprinkled with chopped parsley, and then *marinated* for two hours in a little brandy. They should be inserted into the meat at equal distances apart by means of special larding needles. The proportion of fat to the meat should be about three oz. per lb.

To Marinate Braisings.—Larded or not, the meats intended for *braising* gain considerably from being *marinated* for a few hours in the wines which are to supply their moistening and the *aromatics* (herbs and vegetables) constituting the base of their liquor. Before doing this season them with salt, pepper, and spices, rolling them over and over in these in order that they may absorb the seasoning thoroughly. Then place them in a receptacle just large enough to contain them, between two beds of prepared vegetables and herbs, which will be detailed hereafter; cover them with the wine which forms part of their *braising*-liquor, and which is generally a white or red "vin ordinaire," in the proportion of one-quarter pint per lb.

of meat, and leave them to *marinate* for about six hours, taking care to turn them over three or four times during that period.

The Aromatics or Base of the Braising.—These are thickly sliced and fried carrots and onions, in the proportion of one oz. per lb. of meat, one herb bunch (176), including one garlic clove and one and one-half oz. of fresh, *blanched* bacon-rind.

To Fry, Prepare, and Cook Braised Meat.—Having sufficiently *marinated* the meat, drain it on a sieve for half an hour, and wipe it dry with a clean piece of linen. Heat some clarified fat skimmed from white consommé (2) in a thick saucepan of convenient size, or a braising-pan, and when it is sufficiently hot put the meat in the saucepan and let it brown on all sides. The object of this operation is to cause a contraction of the pores of the meat, thereby surrounding the meat with a kind of crust, which prevents the inner juices from escaping too soon and converting the braising into a boiling process. The frying should, therefore, be a short or lengthy process according to whether the amount of meat to be braised be small or large.

Having properly fried the meat, remove it from the braising-pan, cover it with slices of larding-bacon if it be lean, and tie it. In the case of fillets and ribs of beef, this treatment may be dispensed with, as they are sufficiently well supplied with their own fat.

Now pour the *marinade* prepared for the meat into the braising-pan, and place the meat on a bed composed of the vegetables the *marinade* contained. Cover the pan and rapidly reduce the wine. When this has assumed the consistency of syrup add sufficient brown stock (7) to cover the meat (it being understood that the meat only just conveniently fills the pan), cover the braising pan, set to boil, and then put it in a moderate oven. Let the meat cook until it may be deeply pricked with a testing needle without any blood being drawn. At this stage the first phase of *braising*, of which the theory shall be given after, comes to an end, and the meat is transferred to another clean utensil just large enough to hold it.

With respect to the cooking liquor, either of the two following modes of procedure may now be adopted:—

1. If the liquor is required to be clear it need only be strained, over the meat, through muslin, while the braising-pan should be placed in the oven, where the cooking may go on until completed, interrupting it only from time to time in order to baste the meat. This done, thicken the liquor with arrowroot or flour, after the manner of an ordinary thickened gravy (41).

2. If, on the contrary, a sauce be required, the liquor should be reduced to half before being put back on the meat, and it is restored to its former volume by means of two-thirds of its quantity of Espagnole sauce (7) and one-third of tomato *purée*, or an equivalent quantity of fresh tomatoes.

The cooking of the meat is completed in this sauce, and the basting should be carried on as before. When it is cooked—that is to say, when the point of a knife may easily be thrust into it without meeting with any resistance whatsoever—it should be carefully withdrawn from the sauce; the latter should be again strained through muslin and then left to rest, with a view to letting the grease settle on the surface.

Carefully remove this grease, and rectify the sauce with a little excellent stock if it is too thick, or by reduction if it is too thin.

The Glazing of Braised Meat.—*Braised* meat is *glazed* in order to make it more appetizing, but this operation is by no means essential, and it is quite useless when the meat is cut up previous to being served.

To *glaze* meat place it as soon as cooked in the front of the oven, sprinkle it slightly with its cooking liquor (gravy or sauce), and put it into the oven so that this liquor may dry. Being very gelatinous, the latter adheres to the meat, while its superfluous water evaporates, and thus coats the solid with a thin film of meat-*glaze*. This operation is renewed eight or ten times, whereupon the meat is taken from the oven, placed on a dish, and covered until it is served.

Various Remarks relative to Braising.—When a braised meat is to be accompanied by vegetables, as in the case of beef à la mode, these vegetables may either be cooked with the meat during the second *braising* phase, after they have been duly browned in butter with a little salt and sugar, or they may be cooked separately with a portion of the *braising*-liquor. The first procedure is the better, but it lends itself less to a correct final dressing. It is, therefore, the cook's business to decide according to circumstances which is the more suitable of the two.

I pointed out above that the cooking of *braised* meat consists of two phases, and I shall now proceed to discuss each of these, so that the reader may thoroughly understand their processes.

It has been seen that meat, to be *braised*, must in the first place be browned all over, and this more particularly when it is very thick. The object of this operation is to hold in the meat's juices, which would otherwise escape from the cut surfaces. Now, this searing produces a kind of protective coating around the flesh, which gradually thickens during the cooking process until it reaches the center. Under the influence of the heat of the surrounding liquor the meat fibres contract, and steadily drive the contained juices towards the center. Soon the heat reaches the center, where, after having effected a change in the juices therein collected, the latter release the superfluous water they contain. This water quickly vaporizes, and by so doing distends and separates the tissues surrounding it. Thus, during this first phase, a concentration of juices takes place in the center of the meat. It will now be seen that they undergo an absolutely different process in the second.

As shown, the disintegration of the muscular tissue begins in the center of the meat as soon as the temperature which reaches there is sufficiently intense to vaporize the collected juices. The tension of the vapor given off by the latter increases by less resistance; it therefore exerts considerable pressure upon the tissues, though now its direction is the reverse of what it was in the first place, from the center to the outside surface.

Gradually the tissues relax under the pressure and the effects of cooking, and, the work of disintegration having gradually reached the browned surface, the latter also relaxes in its turn and allows the constrained juices to escape and to mix with the sauce. At the same time, however, the latter begins to filter through the meat, and this it does in accordance with a well-known physical law, namely, capillarity. This stage of the *braising* demands the most attentive care. The *braising*-liquor is found to be considerably reduced and no longer covers the meat, for the operation is nearing its end. The bared meat would, therefore, dry very quickly, if care were not taken to baste it constantly and to turn it over and over, so that the whole of the muscular tissue is moistened and thoroughly saturated with the sauce. By this means the meat acquires that mellowness which is typical of *braisings* and distinguishes them from other preparations.

I should be loath to dismiss this subject before pointing out two practices in the cooking of braisings which are as common as they are absolutely wrong. The first of these is the *"pinçage"* of the braising base. Instead of laying the fried meat on a bed of *aromatics* (vegetables and herbs), likewise fried beforehand, many cooks place the meat, which they often fail to brown, on raw *aromatics* at the bottom of the braising-pan. The whole is sprinkled with a little melted fat, and the *aromatics* are left to fry, on one side only, until they begin to burn on the bottom of the receptacle.

If this operation were properly conducted it might be tolerated, even though *aromatics* which are only fried on one side cannot exude the same savor as those which are fried all over. But nine times out of ten the frying is too lengthy a process; from neglect or absent-mindedness the *aromatics* are left to burn on the bottom of the pan, and there results a bitterness which pervades and spoils the whole sauce.

As a matter of fact, this process of *"pinçage"* is an absurd caricature of a method of preparing *braisings* which was very common in old cookery, the custom of which was not to prepare the *braising*-liquor in advance, but to cook it and its ingredients simultaneously with the meat to be *braised*. This method, though excellent, was very expensive, the meats forming the base of the *braising*-liquor consisting of thick slices of raw ham or veal. The observance of economy, therefore, long ago compelled cooks to abandon this procedure. But routine has perpetuated the form of the latter without insisting upon the use of its ingredients, which were undoubtedly its essential part. Routine has even, in certain cases, aggravated the first error by instituting a habit consisting of substituting bones for the meats formerly employed—an obviously ridiculous practice.

In the production of ordinary consommé (1) we saw that bones, even when taken from veal, as is customary in the case of *braising*-liquor, require, at the very least, ten to twelve hours of cooking before they can yield all their soluble properties. As a proof of this it is interesting to note that, if bones undergo only five or six hours of cooking, and are moistened again and cooked for a further six hours, the liquor of the second cooking yields more meat-*glaze* than that of the first; though it must be admitted that, while the latter is more gelatinous, it has less savor. But this gelatinous property of bones is no less useful to *braisings* than is their savor, since it is the former that supplies the mellowness, which nothing can replace and without which the sauce can have no quality.

Since, therefore, the longest time that a *braising* can cook is from four to five hours, it follows that, if bones be added, their properties will scarcely have begun disintegrating when the meat is cooked. They will, in fact, have yielded but an infinitesimal portion of these properties; wherefore their addition to the *braising* is, to say the least, quite useless.

It now remains to be proved that the above method is bad from another point of view.

I suppose I need not fear contradiction when I assert that, in order that a *braising* may be good, its sauce should be short and cor-respondingly substantial; also that the sauce obtained from a piece of meat moistened with a quart of liquid cannot be so good as that resulting from the moistening of a pint only.

It is more particularly on this account that I advise a braising utensil which can only just hold the meat, for since, in the first stage, the meat is only moistened with the *braising*-liquor, the smaller the receptacle may be the less liquor will it require, and the latter will in consequence be the tastier. Hence, if bones be added to the *braising*, the utensils must necessarily be larger, and a greater quantity of *braising*-liquor must be used. But this liquor will not be nearly so savory as that obtained from the process I recommend; in fact, it will be but a rather strong broth, quite unfit for the im-pregnation of the meat, and the final result will be a tasteless lump of fibre instead of a succulent *braising*.

I must apologize to the reader for my insistence with regard to these questions, but their importance is such that success is beyond reach in the matter of brown sauces and *braisings* unless the above details have been thoroughly grasped. Moreover, the explanations given will afford considerable help in the understanding of opera-tions which I shall give later; therefore it is to be hoped that the examination of the theories involved, however long this has been, will prove of use and assistance.

248—BRAISING OF WHITE MEATS   *Les Braises de Viandes Blanches*

The braising of white meats as it is now effected in modern cookery is, strictly speaking, not *braising* at all, inasmuch as the cooking is stopped at the close of the first of the two phases which I mentioned when discussing brown *braisings*. True, old cookery did not understand *braising* in the way that the modern school does, and under the ancient régime large pieces, especially of veal, were frequently cooked until they could almost be scooped out with a spoon. This practice has been generally, though mistakenly, shunned, but its name survives.

White *braisings* are made with the neck, the saddle, the loin, the fillets, the *fricandeaus*, and the sweet-bread of veal, young turkeys and fat pullets, and sometimes, though less frequently, *relevés* of lamb, hindquarters or saddle. The procedure is the same for all these meats; the time of cooking alone varies in accordance with their size. The *aromatics* are the same as those of the brown *brais-ings*, but the frying of them is optional.

The moistening liquor is brown veal stock (9).

Mode of Procedure.—Except for the veal sweet-breads, which are always *blanched* before being *braised,* the meats or poultry to be treated may always be slightly cooked and browned in butter, on all sides. This is not essential in all cases, but I think that when they do undergo something of the kind they dry less quickly. Now place them in a utensil just large enough to hold them and deep enough to keep the lid from touching them. Place the *aromatics* under them and moisten with a little veal stock (9); set to boil on a moderate fire, and reduce the veal stock with the lid on. When this stock has assumed the consistence of a *glaze,* add a further similar quantity of fresh stock, and reduce as before. The third time moisten the veal until it is half covered, and put the pan into a moderate oven.

The meat needs constant basting while it cooks, in order to avoid its drying; and, as the stock is very gelatinous, it forms a coating on the surface which resists the evaporation of the contained juices; for these, being insufficiently constrained by the slight browning the meat has undergone, tend to vaporize under the influence of the heat.

It is for this reason that the stock must be reduced to a *glaze* before finally moistening. If the moistening were all done at once, the liquor would not be sufficiently dense to form the coating mentioned, and the meat would consequently dry on being set to cook.

Braised white meat is known to be cooked when, after having deeply pricked it with a testing needle, it exudes an absolutely colorless liquid. This liquid denotes that the meat is cooked to the center, and as a result the blood has decomposed.

There lies the great difference between brown *braisings* and white-meat *braisings.* The latter are practically roasts, and they should not be made with any but young poultry or meats, very fat and tender, for they cannot go beyond their correct time of cooking, which equals that of roasts, without immediately losing all their quality. A quarter of an hour too much in the cooking of a roast of veal weighing about six lbs. is enough to make the meat dry and unpalatable, and to thoroughly spoil it, whereas a brown *braising* cannot be over-cooked, provided it does not burn.

White *braised* meats are generally *glazed,* and this process is especially recommended for larded pieces, which, though less common nowadays than formerly, can still claim many advantages.

249—POACHINGS *Les Pochés*

However nonsensical it may sound, the best possible definition of a *poaching* is a boiling that does not boil. The term *poach* is extended to all slow processes of cooking which involve the use of a liquor, however small. Thus the term *poach* applies to the cooking in *court-bouillon* of large pieces of turbot and salmon, as well as to fillets of sole cooked with a little fish *fumet,* to hot *mousselines* and *mousses,* cooked in moulds, to *quenelles* which are cooked in salted water, to eggs announced as *"poached,"* to creams, various *royales,* etc. It will readily be seen that among so many different products, the time allowed for the cooking in each case must differ sometimes widely from the rest. The treatment of them all, however, is subject to this unalterable principle, namely, that the *poaching* liquor must not boil, though it should reach a degree of heat as approximate as possible to the boiling-point. Another principle is that large pieces of fish or poultry be set to boil in cold liquor, after which the latter is brought to the required temperature as rapidly as possible. The case may be the same with fillets of sole, or poultry, which are *poached* almost dry; but all other preparations whose mode of cooking is *poaching* gain by being immersed in liquor which has reached the required temperature beforehand.

Having regard to the many forms and kinds of products that are *poached,* it would be somewhat difficult to state here the details and peculiarities proper to each in the matter of *poaching;* I think, therefore, I should do better to leave these details to the respective recipes of each product, though it will now be necessary to disclose the way of *poaching* poultry, if only with a view to thoroughly acquainting the reader with the theory propounded above.

Properly prepare the piece of poultry to be *poached,* and truss it with its legs folded back alongside of the breast.

If it is to be stuffed, this should be done before trussing.

If it is to be *larded* or *studded,* either with truffles, ham, or tongue, rub it when trussed on the breasts and legs with half a lemon, and dip the same portions of its body (namely, those to be *larded* or *studded*) for a few moments in boiling white stock (10). The object of this operation is to slightly stiffen the skin, thus facilitating the *larding* or *studding.*

The Cooking of the Piece of Poultry.—Having stuffed, *larded,* or *studded* it, if necessary, and having, in any case, trussed it, place it in a receptacle just large enough to hold it, and moisten with some excellent white stock previously prepared.

Set to boil, skim, put the lid on, and continue the cooking at a low simmer. It is useless to work too quickly, as the cooking would not be shortened a second by so doing. The only results would be:—

1. Too violent evaporation, which would reduce the liquor and disturb its transparency.

2. The running of a considerable risk of bursting the piece of poultry, especially when the latter is stuffed.

The fowl, or whatever it may be, is known to be cooked when, after pricking the thick of the leg close to the "drumstick," the oozing liquid is white.

Remarks.—(*a*) The need of *poaching* poultry in a receptacle just large enough to hold the bird is accounted for as follows: (1) The piece must be wholly immersed in the stock during the cooking process. (2) As the liquor used is afterwards served as an accompanying sauce to the dish, the less there is of it the more saturated does it become with the juices of the meat, and, consequently, the better it is.

(*b*) (1) The white stock used in *poaching* should be prepared beforehand, and be very clear.

(2) If the poultry were set to cook with the products constituting the stock, even if these were more than liberally apportioned, the result would be bad, for inasmuch as a fowl, for example, can only take one and one-half hours, at the most, to cook, and the time required for extracting the nutritious and flavoring principles from the ingredients of the stock would be at least six hours, it follows that the fowl would be cooking in little more than hot water, and the resulting sauce would be quite devoid of savor.

250—POELES   *Les Poêlés*

Poêlés are, practically speaking, roasts, for the cooking periods of each are the same, except that the former are cooked entirely or almost entirely with butter. They represent a simplified process of old cookery, which consisted in enveloping the object to be treated, after frying it, in a thick coating of *Matignon*. It was then wrapped with thin slices of pork fat, covered with buttered paper, placed in the oven or on a spit, and basted with melted butter while it cooked. This done, its grease was drained away, and the vegetables of the *Matignon* were put in the braising-pan wherein the piece had cooked, or in a saucepan, and were moistened with excellent Madeira or highly seasoned stock. Then, when the liquor had thoroughly absorbed the aroma of the vegetables, it was strained, and its grease was removed just before serving. This excellent method is worthy of continued use in the case of large pieces of poultry.

Preparation of Poëléd Meats.—Place in the bottom of a deep and thick receptacle, just large enough to hold the piece to be poëléd, a layer of raw *Matignon* (227). The meat or poultry is placed on the vegetables after it has been well seasoned, and is copiously sprinkled with melted butter; cover the pan, and put it into an oven whose heat is not too hot. Set it to cook gently in this way, after the manner of a stew, and frequently sprinkle with melted butter.

When the meats or the pieces of poultry are cooked, the pan is uncovered so that the former may brown; then they are transferred to a dish which should be kept covered until taken to the table. Now add to the vegetables (which must not be burned) a sufficient quantity of brown veal stock (9), transparent and highly seasoned; set the whole to boil gently for ten minutes, strain through a napkin, carefully remove all grease from the *poëléd* stock and send it to the table in a sauceboat at the same time as the meat or poultry, which, by the way, is generally garnished.

Remarks on Poëlés.—It is of paramount importance that these be not moistened during the process of cooking, for in that case their savor would be the same as that of *braised* white meats.

Nevertheless, an exception may be made in the case of such game birds as pheasants, partridges, and quails, to which is added, when nearly cooked, a small quantity of burnt brandy.

It is also very important that the vegetables should not have their grease removed before their moistening stock is added to them. The butter used in the cooking absorbs a large proportion of the savor of both the vegetables and the meat which is being cooked, and, to make good this loss, it is essential that the moistening stock remain at least ten minutes in contact with the butter. At the end of this time it may be removed without in the least impairing the aroma of the stock.

Special Poëlés known as "En Casserole," or "En Cocotte."—The preparations of meats, of poultry, or game, known as *"en casserole"* or *"en cocotte,"* are actual poëlés cooked in special earthenware utensils and served in the same. Generally, preparations known as *"en casserole"* are simply cooked in butter, without the addition of vegetables.

When the cooking is done, the piece being prepared is removed for a moment, and some excellent brown veal stock (9) is poured into the pan. This is left to simmer for a few minutes; the super-fluous butter is then removed; the piece is returned to the earthen-ware utensil, and it is kept hot, without being allowed to boil, until it is served.

For preparations termed *"en cocotte,"* the procedure is the same, except that the piece is garnished with such vegetables as mush-rooms, the hearts of artichokes, small onions, carrots, turnips, etc., which are either cut out or pared, and half cooked in butter before being used.

One should endeavor to use only fresh vegetables, and these should be added to the meat constituting the dish in such a way as to complete their cooking with it.

The earthenware utensils used for this purpose improve with use, provided they be cleaned with clean, fresh water, without any soda or soap. If new utensils have to be used, these should be filled with water, which is set to boil, and they should then undergo at least twelve hours' soaking. For the prescribed time this water should be kept gently boiling, and then the utensil should be well wiped and soaked again, in fresh water, before being used.

251—THE SAUTES   *Les Sautés*

What characterizes the process we call *"sauté"* is that the object treated is cooked dry—that is to say, solely by means of a fatty substance such as butter, oil, or grease.

Sautés are made with cut-up fowl or game, or with meat suitably divided up for the purpose.

All products treated in this way must be frizzled—that is to say, they must be put into the fat when it is very hot in order that a hardened coating may form on their surfaces which will keep their juices in. This is more particularly desirable for red meats such as beef and mutton.

The cooking of fowl *sautés* must, after the meats have been seared, be completed on the stove or, with lid off, in the oven, where they should be basted with butter after the manner of a roast.

The pieces are withdrawn from the cooking utensil with a view to swashing and scraping it, after which, if they be put back into the sauce or accompanying garnish, they should only remain therein a few moments or just sufficiently long to become properly warm.

The procedure is the same for game *sautés*.

Sautés of red meats, such as tournedos, kernels, cutlets, fillets, and noisettes, are always made on the stove; the meats are quickly browned and cooked with a small quantity of clarified butter.

The thinner and smaller they are, the more rapidly should the searing process be done.

When blood appears on the surface of their uncooked side, they should be turned over; when drops of blood begin to gather on their other side, they are known to be cooked.

The swashing or swirling of the pan happens in all *sautés*. After having removed the treated product from the saucepan, remove the grease and pour the flavoring liquid (a wine), that forms part of the accompanying sauce, into the saucepan.

Set to boil and scrape the pan, so that the solidified gravy lying on the bottom may dissolve, and add the sauce; or simply add the flavoring liquid to the prepared sauce or accompanying garnish of the *sauté*. The utensil used must always be just large enough to hold the objects to be cooked. If it be too large, the parts left uncovered by the cooked meats burn, and swashing is then impossible, whence there results a loss of the solidified gravy which is an important ingredient in the sauce.

Sautés of white meats, such as veal and lamb, must also be quickly browned in hot fat, but their cooking must be completed gently on the side of the fire, and in many cases with the lid on.

Preparations of a mixed nature, which partly resemble *sautés* and partly *braisings*, are also called *sautés*. Stews, however, is their most suitable name.

These dishes are made from beef, veal, lamb, game, etc., and they are to be found in Part II under the headings Estouffade; Goulash; Sautés: Chasseur, Marengo, Bourgeoise; Navarin; Civet; etc.

In the first stage of their preparation, the meats are cut up small and fried like those of the *sautés;* in the second, slow cooking with sauce or garnish makes them similar to *braised* meats.

ROASTS, GRILLS, FRYINGS

Roasts

OF the two usual methods of roasting, the spit will always be used in preference to the oven, if only on account of the conditions under which the cooking is done, and whatever be the kind of fuel used—wood, coal, gas or electricity.

The reason of this preference is clear if it be remembered that, in spite of every possible precaution during the progress of an oven roast, it is impossible to avoid an accumulation of vapor around the cooking object in a closed oven. And this steam is more particularly objectionable inasmuch as it is excessive in the case of delicately flavored meats, which are almost if not entirely impaired thereby.

The spitted roast, on the contrary, cooks in the open in a dry atmosphere, and by this means retains its own peculiar flavor. Hence the unquestionable superiority of spitted roasts over the oven kind, especially in respect of small game birds.

In certain circumstances and places there is no choice of methods, and, like it or not, the oven has to be used; but, in this case at least, all possible precautions should be observed in order to counteract the effects of the steam above mentioned.

252—LARDING BACON FOR ROASTS *Lardons pour Larder les Viandes*

Poultry and game to be roasted ought generally to be partly covered with a large thin slice of larding bacon, except those pieces of game which in special cases are *larded*.

The object and use of these slices is not only to shield the breasts of fowl and game from the severe heat of the fire, but also to prevent these from drying, while the legs, which the heat takes much longer to penetrate than the other parts, are cooking. The slices of bacon should therefore completely cover the breasts of fowl and game, and they should be tied on to the latter by means of string.

In some cases roasts of meat are covered with layers of veal- or beef-fat, the object of which is similar to that of the bacon mentioned above.

253—SPITTED ROASTS *Les Rôtis en Broche*

The whole theory of roasts on the spit might be condensed as follows:—

In the case of meat, calculate the intensity of the heat used according to the cut to be roasted, the latter's size and quality, and the time it has hung. Experience, however, is the best guide, for any theory, whatever be its exactness, can only give the leading principles and general rules, and cannot pretend to supply the place of the practised eye and the accuracy which are the result of experience alone.

Nevertheless, I do not say with Brillat Savarin that a good roaster is born and not made; I merely state that one may become a good roaster with application, observation, care, and a little aptitude.

The three following rules will be found to cover all the necessary directions for spitted roasts:—

1. All red meats containing a large quantity of juice should be properly set or browned, and then, according to their size, made to undergo the action of a fire capable of radiating a very penetrating heat with little or no flame.

2. In the case of white meats, whose cooking should be thorough, the fire ought to be so regulated as to allow the roast to cook and brown simultaneously.

3. With small game the fuel should be wood, but whatever fuel be used the fire ought to be burning in such a way as to produce more flame than glowing embers.

254—OVEN ROASTS   *Les Rôtis au Four*

The degree of heat used for each roast must be regulated according to the nature and size of the latter after the manner of spitted roasts.

An oven roast, in the first place, should always be placed on a meat rack or trivet, and this should be of such a height that at no given moment during the cooking process the meat may come in contact with the juices and fat which have drained from it into the utensil beneath. Lacking proper equipment, a spit resting upon the edges of the pan may be used.

No liquid of any kind, gravy or water, need be put in the pan. The addition of any liquid is rather detrimental, since by producing vapor which hangs over the roast it transforms the latter into a stew.

Remarks.—Whether spitted or in the oven, a roast must always be frequently basted with a fatty substance, but never with any other liquid.

255—THE GRAVY OF ROASTS   *Le Fonds de Braise*

The real and most natural gravy for roasts is made from the swashing and scraping (Fr. *deglaçage*) of the baking or dripping-pan, even if water is used as the liquid, since the contents of these utensils represent a portion of the essential principles of the roast fallen from it in the process of cooking. But to obtain this result neither the utensils nor the gravy ought to have burned; the latter should merely have solidified, and for this reason a roast cooked in a very hot oven ought to be laid in a pan only just large enough to hold it, so that the fat may not burn.

The swashing and scraping can in any case only produce a very small quantity of gravy, consequently, when it happens that a greater quantity is required, the need is met beforehand by preparing a stock made from bones and trimmings of a similar nature to the roast for which the gravy is required. The procedure for this is as follows:—

Place the bones and trimmings in a pan with a little fat and literally roast them. Then transfer them to a saucepan, moisten so as to cover with tepid, slightly-salted water, and add the residue of the pan where they were roasted. Boil, skim, and set to cook gently for three or four hours, according to the nature of the products used. This done, almost entirely remove the grease, strain through muslin, and put aside for the purpose of swashing the dripping or baking-pan of the roast.

Swashing and Scraping.—Having removed the roast from the spit or oven, take off a portion of the grease from the baking or dripping-pan, scrape the sides and bottom, and pour into it the required quantity of prepared gravy. Reduce the whole by half, strain through muslin, and almost entirely remove grease.

It is a mistake to remove all the grease from, and to clarify, the gravy of roasts. Treated thus they are certainly clearer and more sightly, but a large proportion of their savor is lost, and it should be borne in mind that the gravy of a roast is not a consommé.

In the matter of roast game birds, the accompanying gravy is supplied by the swashing of the utensil, either with water or a small quantity of brandy. This is a certain means of obtaining a gravy whose savor is precisely that of the game; but occasionally veal gravy is used, as its flavor is neutral, and it therefore cannot impair the particular flavor of the reduced game gravy lying on the bottom of the utensil. The use of stock prepared from the bones and trimmings of game similar to that constituting the dish is also common.

256—THE DRESSING AND ACCOMPANIMENTS OF ROASTS
Le Dressage et les Garnitures des Rôtis

As a rule, a roast ought not to wait. It ought only to leave the spit or oven in order to be served. All roasts should be placed on very hot dishes, slightly sprinkled with fresh butter, and surrounded by bunches of watercress (this is optional). The gravy is invariably served separately.

Roasts of meat and poultry are served as simply as possible.

Small roasted game may be set on fried slices of bread covered with *gratin* stuffing (202).

When lemons accompany a roast, they should be served separately. Pieces of lemon that have once served to garnish a dish must not be used again, for they have mostly been tainted by grease.

The mediæval custom of serving game with the plumage has been abandoned.

Roast game birds *à l'anglaise* are served with or without potato chips, and the three accompaniments are gravy, bread-crumbs, and bread-sauce, particularly in England.

In northern countries game roasts are always accompanied either by slightly sugared stewed apples, or by cherry or apricot jam or currant jelly.

257—GRILLS *Les Grillades*

Those culinary preparations effected by means of grilling belong to the order called cooking by concentration. And, indeed, in almost all cases, the great object of these operations, I might even say the greatest object, is the concentration, in the center, of the juices and *essences* which represent, most essentially, the nutritive principles of the products cooked.

A grill, which is, in short, but a roast on an open fire, stands, in my opinion, as the remote starting-point, the very genesis of our art.

It was the primæval notion of our forefathers' infantile brains; it was progress born of an instinctive desire to eat with greater pleasure; and it was the first culinary method ever employed.

A little later, and following naturally, as it were, upon this first attempt, the spit was born of the grill; gradually, intelligence supplanted rude instinct; reason began to deduce effects from supposed causes; and thus cooking was launched forth upon that highroad along which it has not yet ceased steadily to advance.

Fuel for Grills.—That mostly used, and certainly the best for the purpose, is live coal or small pieces of charcoal. Whatever fuel be used, however, it is essential that it produce no smoke, even though the grill fire be ventilated by powerful blowers which draw the smoke off. More especially is this necessary, though I admit the contingency is rare, when artificial ventilation has to be effected owing to the fire's burning in the open without the usual help of systematic draughts; for if smoke occasioned by foreign substances or by the falling of the fat itself on to the glowing embers were not immediately carried away, either artificially or by a convenient draught, the grills would most surely acquire a very disagreeable taste.

The Bed of Charcoal.—The arrangement of the bed of charcoal under the grill is of some importance, and it must not only be regulated according to the size and kind of the products to be grilled, but also in such a way as to allow for the production of more or less heat under given circumstances.

The bed should therefore be set in equal layers in the center, but varying in thickness according to whether the fire has to be more or less high and fierce; it should also be slightly raised on those sides which are in contact with the air, in order that the whole burning surface may radiate equal degrees of heat.

The grill must always be placed over the glowing fuel in advance, and it should be very hot when the objects to be grilled are placed upon it, otherwise they would stick to the bars, and would probably be spoiled when turned.

(In the United States the finest grilling equipment is sold for gas, electricity and charcoal which makes the method much easier.—Ed.)

GRILLS CLASSIFIED

Grills may be divided into four classes, of which each demands particular care. They are: (1) Red-meat grills (beef and mutton); (2) White-meat grills (veal, lamb, poultry); (3) Fish; (4) Grills coated with butter and bread-crumbs.

258—RED MEAT GRILLS *Grillades de Viandes Noires*

I submit as a principle that the golden rule in grills is to strictly observe the correct degree of heat which is proper to each treated food, never forgetting that the larger and richer in nutrition the piece of meat, the quicker and more thorough must be its initial setting.

I have already explained, under *braisings,* the part played by, and the use of, *rissoling* or searing; but it is necessary to revert to this question and its bearing upon grills.

If large pieces of meat (beef or mutton) are in question, the better their quality and the richer they are in juices, the more resisting must be the *rissoled* coating they receive. The pressure of the contained juices upon the *rissoled* coating of this meat will be proportionately great or small according to whether the latter be rich or poor, and this pressure will gradually increase with the rising heat.

If the grill fire be so regulated as to ensure the progressive penetration of heat into the cooking object, this is what happens:—

The heat, striking that surface of the meat which is in direct
contact with the fire, penetrates the tissues, and spreads through the
layers of meat, driving the latter's juices in front of it. When these
reach the opposite, *rissoled,* or seared side of the meat, they are
checked, and thereupon, absorbing the incoming heat, effect the
cooking of the inner parts.

Of course, if the piece of meat being cooked is very thick, the heat
of the fire should be proportionately lessened the moment the
initial process of *rissoling* or searing of the meat's surface has been
done, the object being to allow the heat to penetrate the cooking
body more regularly. If the high temperature of the fire were maintained, the *rissoled* coating on the meat would probably char, and
the resulting thickness of carbon would so successfully resist the
passage of any heat into the interior that, in the end, while the
meat would probably be found to be completely burnt on the outside, the inside would be quite raw.

If somewhat thinner pieces are in question, a quick *rissoling* of
their surfaces over a hot fire, and a few minutes of subsequent cooking, will be all they need. No alteration in the intensity of the fire
need be sought in this case.

Examples.—A rumpsteak or Châteaubriand (1076), in order to
be properly cooked, should first have its outside surface *rissoled* on
a very hot fire with a view to preserving its juices, after which cooking may proceed over a moderate fire so as to allow the gradual
penetration of the heat into the center of the steak.

Small pieces such as tournedos, small fillets, noisettes, chops, may,
after the preliminary process of *rissoling,* or searing, be cooked over
the same degree of heat as cooked the outside, because the thickness
of meat to be penetrated is less.

The Care of Grills while Cooking.—Before placing the meats on
the grill, baste them slightly with clarified butter (175), and repeat
this operation frequently during the cooking process, so as to avoid
the possible drying of the *rissoled* surfaces.

Grilled red meat should always be turned by means of special
tongs, and great care should be observed that its surface is not torn
or pierced, lest the object of the preliminary precautions be defeated,
and the contained juices escape.

Time of Cooking.—This, in the case of red meats, is arrived at
by the following test: if, on touching the meat with one's finger,

it resists any pressure, it is sufficiently cooked: if it gives, it is clear that in the center, at least, it is still rare. The most certain sign, however, that cooking has been completed is the appearance of little beads of blood upon the *rissoled* surface of the meat.

259—WHITE MEAT GRILLS   *Grillades de Viandes Blanches*

That superficial *rissoling* or searing which is so necessary in the case of red meats is not at all so in the case of white, for in the latter there can be no question of the concentration of juices, since these are only present in the form of albumen—that is to say, in the form of juices "in the making," so to speak, which is peculiar to veal and lamb.

For this kind of grills keep a moderate fire, so that the cooking and browning of the meat may take place simultaneously.

White meat grills should be fairly often basted by means of a brush, with clarified butter (175), while cooking, lest their outside dries.

They are known to be cooked when the juice issuing from them is quite white.

260—FISH GRILLS   *Poissons Grillés*

Use a moderate fire with these, and only grill after having copiously sprinkled them with clarified butter (175) or oil. Sprinkle them again while cooking.

A grilled fish is cooked when the bones are easily separated from the meat. Except for the fatty kind, such as mackerel, gray mullet, or herrings, always roll fish to be grilled in flour before sprinkling them with melted butter. The object of so doing is to give them a golden crust, which, besides making them more pleasing, keeps them from drying.

261—THE GRILLING OF PRODUCTS COATED WITH BUTTER AND BREAD CRUMBS   *Grillades d'Eléments Panés*

These grills generally consist of only small objects; they must be cooked on a very moderate fire, with the view of enabling them to cook and acquire brown simultaneously. They should also be frequently sprinkled with clarified butter (175), and turned with care, so as not to break their coating, the object of which is to withhold their contained juices.

262—FRYINGS   *Les Fritures*

Frying is one of the principal cooking processes, for the number of preparations that are accomplished by this means is very considerable. Its procedure is governed by stringent laws and rules which it is best not to break, lest the double danger of failure and impairment of material be the result.

The former is easily averted if one is familiar with the process, and pays proper attention to it, while the latter is obviated by precautions which have every *raison d'être,* and the neglect of which only leads to trouble.

The question of the kind of utensil to employ is not so immaterial as some would think, for very often accidents result from the mere disregard of the importance of this matter.

Very often imprudence and excitement on the part of the cook may be the cause of imperfections, the greatest care being needed in the handling of utensils containing overheated fat.

Utensils used in frying should be made of copper, or other resisting metal; they should be in one piece, oval or round in shape, and sufficiently large and deep to allow, while only half-filled with fat, the food being properly cooked by it. The necessity of this condition is obvious, seeing that if the utensil contain too much fat the slightest jerking of it on the stove would spill some of the liquid, and the cook would probably be badly burnt.

Finally, utensils with vertical sides are preferable to those of the slanting kind; more especially is this so in large kitchens where, the work involving much frying, enormous receptacles are required.

(In the United States the finest utensils for frying have been created of stainless metal and the most heat retaining alloys. Both for ordinary and deep fat frying the chef and the household cook alike find utensils to suit their needs and the danger of spilling fat, etc., is eliminated to the greatest degree.—Ed.)

263—FRYING FAT—ITS PREPARATION *La Graisse pour Fritures*

Any animal or vegetable fat is suitable for frying, provided it be quite pure and possesses a resisting force allowing it to reach a very high temperature without burning. But for frying on a large scale, the use of drippings and clarified fats, such as the fat skimmed from the *"pot-au-feu"* and roasts, should be avoided.

A frying medium is only perfect when it is able to meet the demands of an extended operation, and consists of fresh or raw fats, chosen with care and thoroughly purified by cooking.

Under no circumstances may butter be used for frying on a large scale; even when thoroughly purified, it can only reach a comparatively low degree of heat. It may be used only for small, occasional fryings.

The fat of beef kidney generally forms the base of the grease intended for frying on a large scale. It is preferable to all others on account of its cheapness and the great length of time it can be used, provided it receives the proper care.

Veal-fat yields a finer frying medium, but its resistance is small, and it must, moreover, always be mixed with the beef-fat.

Mutton-fat should be deliberately discarded, for, if it happen to be that of an old animal, it smells of tallow, and, if it is that of a young one, it causes the hot grease to foam and to overflow down the sides of the utensil, this leading to serious accidents.

Pork-fat (lard) is also used for frying, either alone, or combined with some other kind.

In brief, the fat of beef kidney is that which is best suited to frying on a large scale. Ordinary household frying, which does not demand a very resisting grease, may well be effected by means of the above, combined with an equal quantity of veal-fat, or a mixture composed of the fat of beef kidney, veal, and pork in the proportions of one-half, one-quarter, and one-quarter respectively.

The grease used for frying ought not only to be melted down, but also thoroughly cooked, so that it may be quite pure. If insufficiently cooked, it foams on first being used, and so demands all kinds of extra precautions, which only cease to be necessary when constant heating at last rectifies it. Moreover, if it is not quite pure, it easily penetrates immersed solids and makes them indigestible.

All fat used in frying should first be cut into pieces and then put into the saucepan with one pint of water per every ten lbs.

The object of the water is to assist in the melting, and this it does by filtering into the fat, vaporizing, and thereby causing the latter to swell. So long as the water has not completely evaporated, the grease only undergoes the action of liquefaction, the dissolution of its molecules; but its thorough cooking process, ending with its purification, only begins when all the water is gone.

The grease is cooked when the membranes which enveloped it alone remain intact and are converted into cracklings; it gives off smoke which has a distinct smell.

At this stage it has reached such a high temperature that it is best to remove it from the fire for about ten minutes, so that it may cool; then it must be strained through a sieve, or a coarse towel, which must be tightly twisted.

264—THE VARIOUS DEGREES OF HEAT REACHED BY THE FRYING MEDIUM, AND THEIR APPLICATION

Degrés de la Friture et leur Application

The temperature reached by a frying medium depends upon the fat's components and its purity. The various degrees may be classified as moderately hot, hot, very hot.

The expression "boiling hot" is unsuitable, seeing that fat never boils. Butter (an occasional frying medium) cannot go over 248° F. without burning, whereas if it be thoroughly purified it can attain from 269° to 275° F.—a temperature which is clearly below what would be needed for work on a large scale.

Animal fats used in ordinary frying reach from 275° to 284° F. when moderately hot, 320° F. when hot, and 356° F. when very hot; in the last case they smoke slightly.

Pork-fat (lard), when used alone, reaches 392° F. without burn-ing. Very pure goose dripping withstands 428° F.; and, finally, vegetable fats may reach, without burning, 482° F. in the case of cocoa-nut butter, 518° F. with ordinary oils, and 554° in the case of olive oil.

The temperature of ordinary frying fat may be tested thus: it is moderately hot when, after throwing a sprig of parsley or a crust of bread into it, it begins to bubble immediately; it is hot if it crackles when a slightly moist object is dropped into it; it is very hot when it gives off a thin white smoke perceptible to the smell.

The first temperature, "moderately hot," is used for all products containing vegetable water the complete evaporation of which is necessary; for fish whose volume exacts a cooking process by means of penetration, previous to that with concentration.

In the first degree of heat with which it is used the frying fat therefore only effects a kind of preparatory operation.

The second temperature, "hot," is used for all products which have previously undergone an initial cooking process in the first temperature, either for evaporation or penetration, and its object is either to finish them or to cover them with a crisp coating.

It is also applicable to those products upon which the frying fat must act immediately by concentration—that is to say, by forming a set coating around them which prevents the escape of the con-tained substances.

Objects treated with this temperature are: all those *panés à l'an-glaise* or covered with batter, such as various croquettes, *cromesquis,* cutlets, and collops à la Villeroy, fritters of all kinds, fried creams, etc.

In this case the frying medium acts by setting, which in certain cases is exceedingly necessary.

1. If the objects in question are *panés à l'anglaise* (dipped in beaten eggs and rolled in bread-crumbs), the sudden contact of the hot grease converts this coating of egg and bread-crumbs into a resisting crust, which prevents the escape of the substances and the liquefied sauce contained within.

If these objects were plunged in a fat that was not sufficiently hot, the coating of egg and bread-crumbs would not only absorb the frying medium, but it would run the risk of breaking, thereby allowing the escape of the very substances it was intended to with-hold.

2. The same holds with objects treated with batter. Hence the absolute necessity of ensuring that setting which means that the covering of batter solidifies immediately. As the substances consti-tuting these various dishes are cooked in advance, it follows that their second heating and the browning of the coating (egg and bread-crumbs or batter) take place at the same time and in a few minutes.

The third temperature, "very hot," is used for all objects that need a quick and firm setting; for all small objects the setting of which is of supreme importance, and whose cooking is affected in a few minutes, as in the case of whitebait.

265—FRYING MEDIUM FOR FISH   *Fritures pour Poisson*

Every frying medium, used for work on a large scale, which has acquired a too decided coloring through repeated use, may serve in the preparation of fish even until its whole strength is exhausted.

Oil is best suited to the frying of fish, especially the very small kind, owing to the tremendous heat it can withstand without burn-ing, for this heat guarantees that setting which is so indispensable.

Except in this case, however, the temperature of the frying medium should be regulated strictly in accordance with the size of the fish to be fried, in order that its cooking and browning may be done simultaneously.

Except whitebait, which is simply rolled in flour, fish to be fried are previously soaked in slightly salted milk and then rolled in flour. From this combination of milk and flour there results a crisp coating which holds those particular principles that the fish exude while cooking.

When finished, fried fish are drained, dried, slightly salted, and served on a napkin or on paper, with a garnish of fried parsley-sprigs and sections of grooved lemon.

266—THE QUANTITY OF THE FRYING MEDIUM
La Quantité de Friture à Employer

This should always be in proportion to the quantity or size of the foods to be fried, bearing in mind that these must always be entirely submerged.

Without necessarily exaggerating, the quantity should invariably be rather in excess of the requirements, and for this reason, the greater the amount of fat, the higher will be the temperature reached, and the less need one fear a sudden cooling of the fat when the objects to be treated are immersed. This sudden cooling is often the cause of great trouble, unless one be working over a fire of such intensity that the fat can return in a few seconds to the temperature it was at before the food were immersed.

267—THE CARE OF THE FRYING MEDIUM
Soins à Donner aux Fritures

Every time the frying fat is used it should, after having been melted, be strained through a towel, for the majority of foods which it has served to cook must have left some particles behind them which might prove injurious to the foods that are to follow.

Objects that are breaded always leave a residue, for instance, which in time assume the form of black powder, while those that have been treated with flour likewise drop some of their coating, which, in accumulating, produces a muddy deposit on the bottom of the utensil.

Not only do these foreign substances disturb the clearness of the fat and render it liable to burn, but they are exceedingly detrimental to the objects that are fried in it later.

Therefore, always strain the fat whenever it is used—in the first place because the proper treatment of the foods demands it, and, secondly, because its very existence as a serviceable medium depends upon this measure.

268—GRATINS *Les Gratins*

This culinary operation plays a sufficiently important part in the work to warrant my detailing at least its leading points.

The various kinds of the order "Gratins" are (1) the Complete *Gratin;* (2) the Rapid *Gratin;* (3) the Light *Gratin;* (4) *Glazing,* which is a form of Rapid *Gratin.*

269—COMPLETE GRATIN *Le Gratin Complet*

This is the first example of the series; it is that whose preparation is longest and most tiresome; for its principal ingredient, whatever this is, must be completely cooked. Its cooking must moreover be coincident with the reduction of the sauce, which is the base of the *gratin,* and with the formation of the *gratin* proper, the crisp crust which forms on the surface and is the result of the combination of the sauce with the raspings (crumbs) and the butter, under the direct influence of the heat.

In the preparation of complete *gratin,* two things must be taken into account:—The nature and size of the food to be treated, and the degree of heat which must be used in order that the cooking of the food, the reduction of the sauce, and the formation of the *gratin* may be done simultaneously.

The base of complete *gratin* is almost invariably ordinary or *Lenten duxelle* sauce (223), in accordance with the requirements.

The object to be treated with the *gratin* is laid on a buttered dish, surrounded with slices of fresh mushrooms and chopped shallots, and covered with *duxelle* sauce (223). The surface is then sprinkled with raspings (178), and copiously moistened with melted butter. Should the piece be large, the amount of sauce used will be proportionately greater, and the reverse, of course, applies to medium or smaller sizes.

Take note of the following remarks in the making of complete *gratins:*—

1. If too much sauce were used in proportion to the size of the food, the latter would cook and the *gratin* form before the sauce could reach the correct degree of consistency by means of reduction. Hence it would be necessary to reduce the sauce still further on the stove, and thereby give rise to steam which would soften the coating of the *gratin.*

2. If the sauce used were insufficient, it would be reduced before the cooking of the object had been effected, and, more sauce having to be added, the resulting *gratin* would be uneven.

3. The larger the piece, and consequently the longer it takes to cook, the more moderate should be the heat used. Respectively, the smaller it is, the hotter should the fire be.

When taking the *gratin* from the oven squeeze a few drops of lemon-juice over it, and sprinkle it with chopped parsley.

270—RAPID GRATIN　　　　　　*Le Gratin Rapide*

Proceed as above, with *duxelle* sauce (223), but the foods treated with it, meats, fish, or vegetables, are always cooked and warmed in advance. All that is required, therefore, is to effect the formation of the *gratin* as quickly as possible.

To do this, cover the food under treatment with the necessary quantity of salt, sprinkle with raspings (crumbs) and butter, and set the *gratin* to form in a very hot oven.

271—LIGHT GRATIN　　　　　　*Le Gratin Léger*

This is proper to use for starchy products, such as macaroni, lazagnes, noodles, gnocchi (dumplings), and consists of a combination of grated cheese, bread-crumbs, and butter. In this case, again, the only end in view is the formation of the *gratin* coating, which must be evenly browned, and is the result of the cheese melting. A moderate heat is all that is wanted for this kind of *gratin*.

Also considered as light *gratins* are those which serve as the complement of stuffed vegetables such as tomatoes, mushrooms, egg-plant, and cucumber, etc. With these the *gratin* is composed of bread-crumbs sprinkled with butter or oil, and it is placed in a more or less intense heat according to whether the vegetables have already been cooked or partially cooked, or are quite raw.

272—GLAZINGS　　　　　　*Les Glaçages*

These are of two kinds—they either consist of a heavily buttered sauce, or they form from a sprinkling of cheese upon the sauce with which the food to be glazed is covered.

In the first case, after having poured sauce over the food to be treated, place the dish on another dish containing a little water. This is to prevent the sauce separating and boiling. The greater the quantity of butter used, the more intense will be the heat required, in order that a slight golden film may form almost instantaneously.

In the second case, the sauce used is always a Mornay (91). Cover the food in preparation with the sauce, sprinkle with grated cheese and melted butter, and place in fairly intense heat, so that a slight golden crust may form almost immediately, this crust being the result of the combined cheese and butter.

273—BLANCHINGS   *Blanchissages*

The essentially unsuitable term *blanchings* is applied in the culinary technology of France to three classes of operations which entirely differ one from the other in the end they have in view.

1. The *blanching* of meats.

2. The *blanching*, or, better, the parboiling of certain v getables.

3. The *blanching* of certain other vegetables, which in reality amounts to a process of cooking.

The blanching of meats obtains mostly in the case of calf's head and feet and the sweet-breads of veal, sheeps' and lambs' shanks, and lamb's sweet-bread. These meats are first set to soak in cold, running water until they have got rid of the blood with which they are naturally saturated. They are then placed on the fire in a saucepan containing enough cold water to abundantly cover them, and the water is gradually brought to the boil.

For calf's head or feet, boiling may last for fifteen or twenty minutes; veal sweet-breads must not boil for more than ten or twelve minutes; while lamb sweet-breads are withdrawn the moment the boil is reached.

As soon as *blanched,* the meats are cooled in plenty of fresh water before undergoing their final treatment.

The blanching of cocks' combs is exceptional in this, namely, that after the combs have been cleansed of blood—that is to say, soaked in cold water, they are placed on the fire in cold water, the temperature of which must be carefully kept below 113° F. When this degree is approached, take the saucepan off the fire and rub each comb with a cloth, dusted with table-salt, in order to remove the skins; then cool the combs with fresh water before cooking them.

Many people use the *blanching* process with meats intended for "blanquette" or "fricassée." I regard this procedure as quite erroneous, as also the preliminary soaking in cold water.

If the meats or pieces of poultry intended for the above-mentioned preparations be of a good quality (and no others should be used), they need only be set to cook in cold water, or cold stock, and gradually brought to the boil, being stirred repeatedly. The scum formed should be carefully removed, and, in this way, perfectly white meats and stock, with all their savor, are obtained.

As to meats or pieces of poultry of an inferior quality, no soaking and no *blanching* can make good their defects. Whichever way they are treated they remain dry, gray, and savorless. It is therefore simpler and better to use only the finest quality products.

An excellent proof of the futility of soaking and *blanching* meats intended for "fricassées" and "blanquettes" lies in the fact that these very meats, if of good quality, are always perfectly white when they are *braised, poëléd,* or roasted, notwithstanding the fact that these three operations are less calculated to preserve their whiteness than the kind of treatment they are subjected to in the case of "blanquettes" and "fricassées."

Mere routine alone can account for this practice of soaking and *blanching* meats—a practice that is absolutely condemned by common sense.

The term *blanching* is wrongly applied to the cooking of green vegetables, such as string beans, green peas, Brussels sprouts, spinach, etc. The cooking of these, which is effected by means of boiling salted water, ought really to be termed *à l'anglaise.* All the details of the procedure, however, will be given when I deal with the vegetables to which the latter apply.

Lastly, under the name of *blanching,* there exists another operation which consists in partly cooking certain vegetables in plenty of water, in order to rid them of any bitter or pungent flavor they may possess. The time allowed for this *blanching* varies according to the age of the vegetables, but when the latter are young and in season, it amounts to little more than a mere scalding.

Blanching is chiefly resorted to for lettuce, chicory, endives, celery, artichokes, cabbages, and the green vegetables; carrots, turnips, and small onions when they are out of season. In respect of squash, cucumbers, and chayotes, *blanching* is often left to the definite cooking process, which should then come under the head of the *à l'anglaise* cooking.

After the process of *blanching,* the vegetables I have just enumerated are always cooled—that is to say, steeped in cold water until they are barely lukewarm. They are then left to drain through a sieve, previous to undergoing the final cooking process to which they are best suited, this generally being *braising.*

VEGETABLES AND GARNISHES

Various Preparations

274—THE TREATMENT OF DRY VEGETABLES

Préparation des Légumes Secs

It is wrong to soak dried vegetables. If they are of good quality, and the produce of the year, they need only be put into a saucepan with enough cold water to completely cover them, and with one oz. of salt per five quarts of water.

Set to boil gently, skim, add the seasoning, quartered carrots, onions, with or without garlic cloves, and an herb bunch, and set to cook gently with lid on.

Remarks.—If the vegetables used are old or inferior in quality, they might be put to soak in bicarbonated water; but this only long enough to swell them slightly, about one and one-half hours.

A prolonged soaking of dried vegetables may give rise to incipient germination, and this, by impairing the principles of the vegetables, depreciates the value of the food, and may even cause some harm to the diner.

275—BRAISED VEGETABLES

Légumes Braisés

Vegetables to be *braised* must be first *blanched,* cooled, pared, and tied.

Garnish the bottom of a saucepan with *blanched* pork-rind, sliced carrots and onions, and an herb bunch, and cover the sides of the utensil with thin slices of bacon. Lay the vegetables upon the prepared bed, and leave them to sweat in the oven for about ten minutes with lid on. The object of this oven-sweating is to expel the water. Now moisten enough to cover with white stock (10), and set to cook gently.

This done, drain, remove string, and cut to the shape required. Lay them in a saucepan, and, if they are to be served soon, cover them with their reduced stock from which the grease has been removed.

If they are prepared in advance, simply put them aside in suitable bowls, cover them with their cooking-liquor, which should be strained over them, boiling, and without its grease removed, and cover with waxed paper.

AUXILIARY HELPS TO BRAISED VEGETABLES

According to the case, the auxiliary is either the *braising*-liquor, reduced and with all grease removed, or the same completed by means of an addition of meat-*glaze* (15).

Occasionally, it may be the *braising*-liquor slightly thickened with half-*glaze* (23) and finished with butter and the juice of a lemon.

276—BINDING OF GREEN VEGETABLES WITH BUTTER
Liaison des Légumes Verts au Beurre

First thoroughly drain the cooked vegetables and toss them over the fire for a few minutes, in order to completely rid them of their moisture. Season according to the kind of vegetable; add the butter away from the fire, and toss lightly, rolling the saucepan meanwhile on the stove with the view of effecting the blending by means of the mixing of the butter with the treated vegetables.

277—BINDING OF VEGETABLES WITH CREAM
Liaison des Légumes à la Crème

Vegetables to be treated in this way must be kept somewhat firm in cooking. After having thoroughly drained them, put them into a saucepan with enough boiling fresh cream to well moisten without covering them.

Finish their cooking process in the cream, stirring occasionally.

When the cream is almost entirely reduced, finish, away from the fire, with a little butter.

The binding may be slightly stiffened, if necessary, by means of a few tablespoons of cream sauce (79).

278—VEGETABLE CREAMS AND PUREES
Crèmes de Légumes et Purées

Purées of dry and starchy vegetables may be obtained by rubbing the latter through a sieve.

Put the *purée* into a saucepan, and dry it over a brisk fire, adding one and one-half oz. of butter per pint of *purée;* then add milk or cream in small quantities at a time, until the *purée* has reached the required degree of consistency.

For *purées* of succulent vegetables, such as string beans, cauliflowers, celery, etc., a quarter of their volume of mashed potatoes should be added to them in order to effect the binding.

In the case of vegetable creams, substitute for the thickening of mashed potatoes an equivalent quantity of succulent and stiff Béchamel sauce (28).

279—GARNISHES   *Garnitures*

In cookery, although garnishes only play a minor part, they are, nevertheless, very important, for, besides being the principal accompaniments to dishes, they are very often the adornment, while it frequently happens that their harmonious arrangement considerably helps to throw the beauty of a fine joint or bird into relief.

A garnish may consist of one or more products. Be this as it may, its name, as a rule, distinctly denotes, in a word, what it is and how it is made.

In any case, it should always bear some relation to the piece it accompanies, either in the ingredients of its preparation or with regard to the size of the piece constituting the dish.

I merely add that, since the ingredients of garnishes are strictly denoted by the name the latter bear, any addition of products foreign to their nature would be a grave mistake. Likewise, the omission of any parts is to be avoided, as the garnish would thereby be out of keeping with its specified character.

Only in very exceptional circumstances should any change of this kind be allowed to take place.

The ingredients of garnishes are supplied by vegetables, starchy products, *quenelles* of all kinds, cocks' combs and kidneys, truffles and mushrooms, plain or stuffed olives, molluscs (mussels or oysters), shell-fish (crayfish, shrimps, lobster, etc.), butcher's supplies, such as lamb's sweet-bread, calf's brains, and calf's spinal-marrow.

As a rule, garnishes are independent of the dish itself—that is to say, they are prepared entirely apart. At other times they are mixed with it, playing the double part of garnish and condimentary principle, as in the case of *Matelotes, Compotes,* Civets, etc.

Vegetables for garnishing are fashioned and treated in accordance with the use and shape implied by the name of the dish, which should always be the cook's guide in this respect.

The starchy ones, the molluscs and shell-fish, undergo the customary preparation.

I have already described (189 et seq.) the preparation of *quenelles* and *forcemeats* for *garnishing*. Other recipes which have the same purpose will be treated in their respective order.

PART II

RECIPES AND METHODS OF PROCEDURE

In Part I of this work I treated the general principles on which the science of cookery is founded, and the leading operations constituting the basis of the work.

In Part II I shall proceed from the general to the particular—in other words, I shall set forth the recipes of every dish I touch upon, its method of preparation, and its composing parts.

With the view of making reference as easy as possible, without departing from a certain logical order, I have adopted the method of classifying these recipes in accordance with the position the dishes they represent hold in the ordinary menu, and thus, starting with the hors-d'œuvres, I go straight on to the dessert. I was compelled, however, to alter my plan in the case of eggs, which never appear on the menu of a dinner except in *Lent*.

These I have therefore placed immediately after the hors-d'œuvres, which, like eggs, should only be served at luncheons, for reasons I shall explain later.

It will be seen that I have placed the Savories before the Sweets, instead of after the Ices (as is customary in England). My reason for this apparent anomaly is that I consider it a positive gastronomical heresy to eat fish, meats, fowl-remains, etc., after delicate Sweets and Ices, the subtle flavor of the latter, which form such an agreeable item in a dinner, being quite destroyed by the high seasoning of the Savories.

Moreover, the very pretext brought forward in support of this practice, so erroneous from the gastronomical standpoint, namely, "that after a good dinner it is necessary to serve something strange and highly seasoned, in order to whet the diner's thirst," is its own condemnation.

For. if appetite is satiated and thirst is quenched, it follows that the diner has taken all that is necessary. Therefore, anything more that he may be stimulated to take will only amount to excess, and excess in gastronomy, as in everything else, is a fault that can find no excuse.

At all events, I could agree to no more than the placing of the Savories before mild Sweets, and, even so, the former would have to consist of light, dry preparations, very moderately seasoned, such as *Paillettes* with Parmesan, various kinds of dry biscuits, crackers and small tartlets garnished with cheese *soufflé*.

In short, if I expressed my plain opinion on the matter, I should advise the total omission of Savories in a dinner.

(This explanation having been written especially for England it does not apply to the United States as we are not in the habit of serving Savories after the desserts, if at all.—Ed.)

CHAPTER XI

GENERAL REMARKS

THE preparations described hereafter all belong to the order of cold hors-d'œuvres or appetizers. I did not think it necessary to touch upon the hot kind, for they are mostly to be found either among the hot Entrées or the Savories proper.

Generally speaking, hors-d'œuvres should only form part of a meal that does not comprise soup, while the rule of serving them at luncheons only, ought to be looked upon as absolute.

It is true that restaurants à la carte deliberately deviate from this rule, but it should be remembered, in their case, that, in addition to the fact that "hors-d'œuvres de luxe," such as caviar, oysters, plovers' eggs, etc., are mostly in question, they also find the use of hors-d'œuvres expedient if only as a means of whiling away the guests' time during the preparation of the various dishes that may have been ordered.

Moreover, the hors-d'œuvres enumerated are not subject to the same objection as those composed of fish, salads, and *marinated* vegetables. The use of cold hors-d'œuvres in these special cases is thus, to a certain extent, justified, but it is nevertheless to be regretted that an exception of this kind should degenerate into a habit, and that it should be made to prevail under circumstances which, in themselves, are insufficient warrant for the abuse.

In Russia it is customary to have a sideboard in a room adjoining the dining-room, decorated with all kinds of special pastries, smoked fish, and other products, and these the diners partake of, standing, together with strong liqueurs, before taking their seats at the table. The general name given to the items on the sideboard is "Zakouski." Caterers and hotel-keepers in different parts of the world, more zealous than judicious, introduced the custom of the Zakouski without allowing for the differences of race, which are due, to some extent, to the influence of climate; and at first, probably owing to everybody's enthusiasm for things Russian, the innovation enjoyed a certain vogue, in spite of the fact that, in many cases, the dishes served resembled the Zakouski in name alone, and consisted of cold and very ordinary hors-d'œuvres, served at the dining-table itself.

At length the absurdity of investing such common things as hors-d'œuvres with an exotic title began to be perceived, and nowadays the occasions are rare when the Russian term is to be found on a menu; nevertheless, the custom unfortunately survives.

(In the United States the same custom is being carried out with the introduction of the Swedish smörgasbord.—Ed.)

For my own part, I regard cold hors-d'œuvres as quite unnecessary in a dinner; I even consider them counter to the dictates of common sense, and they are certainly injurious to the flavor of the soup that follows.

At the most, caviar might be tolerated, the nutty taste of which, when it is quite fresh, can but favorably impress the diner's palate, as also certain fine oysters, provided they are served with very dry Rhine wine or white Bordeaux. But I repeat that hors-d'œuvres consisting of any kind of fish, salad, *marinated* vegetables, etc., should be eliminated from the items of a dinner.

The custom of serving cold hors-d'œuvres at lunch is, on the contrary, not only traditional, but indispensable, and their varied combinations, thrown into relief by tasteful and proper arrange ment, besides lending a cheerful aspect to the table, beguile the diner's attention and fancy from the very moment of his entering the dining-room. It has been said, with reason, that soups should foretell the dominant note of the whole dinner, and cold hors-d'œuvres should in the same way reveal that of a luncheon.

Possibly it was with a sense of the importance of hors-d'œuvres, from this standpoint, that their preparation was transferred from the *office* (the exclusive concern of which used, formerly, to be the hors-d'œuvres) to the kitchen.

The results of this change manifested themselves immediately in prodigious variations and transformations of the hors-d'œuvres, both in respect of their preparation and serving, so much so, indeed, that perhaps in no other department of culinary art has there been such progress of recent years.

Their variety is infinite, and it would be impossible to compute, even approximately, the number of combinations an ingenious cook could effect in their preparation, seeing that the latter embraces almost every possible use of every conceivable edible and appetizing product.

Well may it be said that a good hors-d'œuvres artist is a man to be prized in any kitchen, for, although his duties do not by any means rank first in importance, they nevertheless demand of the chef the possession of such qualities as are rarely found united in one person, reliable and experienced taste, originality, keen artistic sense, and professional knowledge.

The hors-d'œuvre should be able to produce something appetizing and good out of very little, and the beauty and attractiveness of a hors-d'œuvre should depend to a much greater degree upon his work and the judicious treatment of his material than upon the nature of the latter.

Preparations for Appetizers or Hors-d'œuvres

(All of the following preparations must be well chilled before serving.—Ed.)

280—BUTTERS AND CREAMS   *Beurres et Crèmes*
The seasoning of butters for hors-d'œuvres is done just before serving. When prepared in advance, they ought to be placed in a bowl and put aside somewhere in a cool spot and covered with a piece of wax paper.

281—ANCHOVY BUTTER   *Beurre d'Anchois*
Wash twelve or fifteen anchovies in cold water, and dry them thoroughly. Remove the fillets from the bones, pound them smoothly with four oz. of butter, rub through a fine sieve, smooth it with a spoon, and put aside.

282—CAVIAR BUTTER   *Beurre de Caviare*
Pound three oz. of pressed caviar with four oz. of butter, and rub through a fine sieve.

283—SHRIMP BUTTER   *Beurre de Crevettes*
Pound four oz. of shrimps with four oz. of butter; rub through a fine sieve first, then through muslin, after having softened the preparation.

This may also be made from the shelled tails of crayfish, which process, though it is easier, does not yield a butter of such delicate taste as the former.

284—CURRY BUTTER *Beurre au Currie*

Soften four oz. of butter in a bowl, and add sufficient curry-powder to ensure a decided taste. The exact quantity of curry cannot be prescribed, since the quality of the latter entirely governs the proportion.

285—CRAYFISH BUTTER *Beurre d'Ecrevisses*

Cook the crayfish with *mirepoix,* as for *Bisque.* Finely pound the shells after having removed the tails, and add four oz. of butter per two oz.; rub through a fine sieve first, then through muslin.

N.B.—The whole crayfish may be pounded, but the tails are usually laid aside with a view to supplying the garnish of the toasts for which the butter is intended.

286—RED-HERRING BUTTER · *Beurre de Hareng*

Take the fillets of three red Matjes herrings; remove the skins, and pound finely with three oz. of butter. Rub through a fine sieve.

287—LOBSTER BUTTER *Beurre de Homard*

Pound four oz. of lobster trimmings and spawn, and a little of the coral with four oz. of butter. Rub through a fine sieve.

288—MILT BUTTER *Beurre de Laitance*

Poach four oz. of *milt* in a covered and buttered saucepan, with the juice of half a lemon; pound in the mortar, and add to the preparation its weight of butter and a teaspoon of dry mustard. Rub through a fine sieve.

289—MONTPELIER BUTTER (GREEN BUTTER)

Beurre Montpelier (Beurre Vert)

See Compound Butter for Sauces (153).

290—HORSE-RADISH BUTTER *Beurre de Raifort*

Grate two oz. of horse-radish and pound with four oz. of butter. Rub through a fine sieve.

291—SMOKED SALMON BUTTER *Beurre de Saumon Fume*

Finely pound four oz. of smoked salmon with as much butter, and rub through a fine sieve.

292—PAPRIKA BUTTER *Beurre Paprika*

Soften four oz. of butter in a bowl, and mix with a small teaspoon of paprika infused in a few drops of white wine or consommé, with a view to strengthening the color of the paprika.

293—PIMENTO BUTTER *Beurre Piment*

Pound four oz. of canned or freshly-cooked red peppers; add as much butter, and rub through a fine sieve.

294—CAVIAR CREAM *Crème de Caviare*

Pound four oz. of preserved caviar and add, little by little, two tablespoons of fresh cream and two oz. of softened butter. Rub through a fine sieve, and finish the preparation by an addition of three tablespoons of whipped cream.

N.B.—This cream and those that follow often take the place of the butters in the preparation of hors-d'œuvres. The addition of previously well-softened butter to these creams is necessary in order to make them sufficiently consistent when they cool.

295—LOBSTER CREAM *Crème de Homard*

Pound four oz. of lobster trimmings, spawn, and coral, and add three tablespoons of fresh cream and two oz. of softened butter.

Rub through a sieve, and complete the preparation with whipped cream, as above.

296—GAME CREAM *Crème de Gibier*

Pound four oz. of cold, cooked game-meat with three tablespoons of fresh cream and two oz. of softened butter. Rub through a sieve, and finish the preparation with three tablespoons of whipped cream.

297—SMOKED SALMON CREAM *Crème de Saumon Fumé*

Finely pound four oz. of smoked salmon, and add, little by little, three tablespoons of fresh cream and two oz. of softened butter. Rub through a sieve, and finish with an addition of three tablespoons of whipped cream.

298—TUNA CREAM *Crème de Thon*

Finely pound four oz. of tuna fish in oil, and finish the cream similarly to that of the Smoked Salmon.

299—CHICKEN CREAM *Crème de Volaille*

Finely pound four oz. of cold fowl (white part only) and add two tablespoons of fresh cream and two oz. of softened butter. Rub through a sieve, and finish with three tablespoons of whipped cream.

N.B.—This cream ought to be made and seasoned with salt immediately before being served.

299a—MUSTARD SAUCE WITH CREAM *Sauce Moutarde à la Crème*

Put three tablespoons of prepared mustard in a bowl with a little salt, pepper, and a few drops of lemon-juice. Mix and add, little by little, the necessary quantity of very fresh cream.

APPETIZERS OR HORS-D'ŒUVRES

300—ANCHOVY STICKS *Allumettes d'Anchois*

Roll some puff-paste trimmings (2366) into rectangular strips two and one-half inches wide and one-eighth inch thick. Spread on them a thin coating of fish stuffing, finished with anchovy butter (281); lay the anchovy fillets, prepared beforehand, lengthwise on this stuffing, and cut into pieces about one inch wide. Place the pieces on a baking-sheet, and set to bake in the oven for twelve minutes.

301—ANCHOVY FILLETS *Filets d'Anchois*

Cut each halved anchovy, which should have been previously *marinated* in oil, into two or three little fillets. Place them across each other in a hors-d'œuvre dish, after the manner of a lattice; garnish with chopped parsley and the chopped white and yolk of a hard-boiled egg, alternating the colors. Put a few capers on the fillets, and sprinkle moderately with oil. Anchovy fillets may also be served on a salad of shredded lettuce, for the sake of variety.

302—FRESH MARINATED ANCHOVIES *Anchois Frais Marines*

Take live anchovies, cleanse them, and put them in salt for two hours. This done, plunge them in hot smoking oil, where they may remain only just long enough to stiffen. Drain, place them in a moderately acid *marinade,* and serve on a hors-d'œuvre dish with a little *marinade.*

303—ROLLED ANCHOVIES *Anchois Roulés*

Pit some fine olives and stuff them with anchovy butter (281)· when quite cold, encircle them with a ring of anchovy fillet, kept whole.

304—ANCHOVY MEDALLIONS *Medaillons d'Anchois*

Cut into slices, about the size of half-a-dollar, potatoes boiled in water or baked beets. Cover their edges with fine anchovy fillets *marinated* in oil, and garnish their centers either with caviar, chopped hard-boiled egg, or *milt purée,* etc.

305—ANCHOVY ROULADES *Paupiettes d'Anchois*

Prepare some thick slices of *blanched* and *marinated* cucumber, about the size of half-dollars, and hollow their center slightly. Place rings composed of the fillets of anchovies in oil upon these slices, and fill their centers with tuna fish cream (298) or the cream of any fish or shell-fish.

306—ANCHOVY WITH PIMENTOS *Anchois au Pimento*

Prepare some anchovy fillets in oil, and place them across each other in a lattice, using strips of pimento alternately with those of the anchovies. Garnish in the same way as for anchovy fillets, with the chopped white and yolk of a hard-boiled egg, and chopped parsley.

307—NORWEGIAN ANCHOVIES, CALLED KILKIS

Anchois Norvegiens, dit Kilkis

These are found ready-prepared on the market. Place them on a hors-d'œuvre dish with some of their liquor, and without any garnish.

308—SMOKED EEL *Anguille Fumée*

Serve it plain, cut into fillets.

309—EEL WITH WHITE WINE AND PAPRIKA

Anguille au Vin Blanc et Paprika

Divide the eel into lengths of three and one-half inches; poach these in exactly the same way as for *matelote,* but with white wine and paprika seasoning. Let them cool in their cooking-liquor; cut the pieces lengthwise into large fillets, and cover them with the liquor after all grease has been removed and it has been clarified and cleared.

310—GREEN EEL *Anguille au Vert*

Stew in butter two oz. of sorrel, one-quarter oz. of parsley, as much chervil, a few tarragon leaves, a little fresh pimpernel, two oz. of tender nettle (a pot herb), one-quarter oz. of savory, a sprig of green thyme, and a few sage-leaves, all of which must be coarsely chopped. Remove the skins from two lbs. of small eels, cut off the heads, and cut into pieces two inches long. Put these pieces with the herbs, cook, and add one pint of white wine and a little salt and pepper. Set to cook for ten minutes longer, thicken with the yolks of four eggs and a few drops of lemon-juice, and leave to cool in a bowl. This preparation of eel is served very cold.

311—GREEN EEL A LA FLAMANDE   *Anguille au Vert à la Flamande*

Remove the skin from, and cut into small pieces, two lbs. of small eels. Lightly brown the pieces in butter, moisten with one pint of beer, season, and set to cook for ten minutes. Add the herbs enumerated in (310), raw and roughly chopped. Once more set to cook for seven or eight minutes, thicken with flour or cornstarch if the sauce is too thin, and transfer the whole to a bowl to cool. Serve very cold.

312—ARTICHOKES A LA GRECQUE   *Artichauts à la Grecque*

Take some very small and tender artichokes. Pare them, cut the leaves short, and plunge them into a large saucepan of water, adding a little lemon or vinegar. Parboil for eight or ten minutes, drain, cool in fresh water, and drain once more in a sieve.

For twenty artichokes prepare the following liquor:—one pint of water, one-quarter pint of oil, a little salt, the juice of three lemons, a few fennel and coriander seeds, some peppercorns, a sprig of thyme, and a bay leaf. Set to boil, add the parboiled artichokes, and leave to cook for twenty minutes. Transfer to a bowl.

Serve these artichokes very cold upon an hors-d'œuvre dish, accompanied by a few tablespoons of their cooking-liquor.

313—SMALL ARTICHOKE BOTTOMS   *Petits Fonds d'Artichauts*

Remove the leaves and the hearts of some little artichokes; trim their remaining bases, and plunge each as soon as trimmed into water to which lemon juice has been added lest they blacken. Cook them *"au blanc"* (167), and leave them to cool in their liquor.

Drain them well, dry them, place them in a pan, and *marinate* them for twenty minutes in oil and lemon-juice. This done, garnish them either with a *salpicon* thickened with mayonnaise, a *milt* or other *purée*, a small *macédoine*, or a vegetable salad, etc. Place on a hors-d'œuvre dish with a garnish of parsley sprigs.

314—BARQUETTES   *Barquettes*

These are a kind of small Croustades with scalloped edges, made in very small, boat-shaped moulds, and they may be garnished in any conceivable way.

As their preparation is the same as that of Tartlets, see the latter (387); also refer to "Frivolities" (350).

315—SMOKED BEEF   *Boeuf Fumé*

Cut it into very thin slices; divide these up into triangles, and roll the latter into the shape of cones. The slices of chipped beef may also be served flat.

Prepare up at the last moment, and serve very cold.

316—CANAPES AND TOAST   *Canapés et Toast*

In the matter of hors-d'œuvres, the two above names have the same meaning. The preparation consists of small slices of bread, about one-quarter inch thick, slightly toasted and with a garnish on one side. The garnish is subject to taste and the resources at the disposal of the cook, or the latter's fancy, which may here be fully indulged.

But the garnish, par excellence, for Canapés or Toast, is fresh butter combined with a fine mince of white roast chicken-meat, the meat of shell-fish or fish, or cheese, etc., as I pointed out under the butters for hors-d'œuvres.

Whatever be the garnish of Canapés or Toast, and even when it would be unreasonable to let butter form a part of it, as, for example, in the case of *marinated* fish, anchovies, herring fillets, etc., it is always best to put plenty of butter on the pieces of toast while they are still hot, with the view of keeping them soft.

When the garnish consists of a *purée,* or a compound butter, I should advise the use of a pastry-bag fitted with a decorating tube, for piping the preparation upon the toast. This method is both clean and expeditious, and lends itself to any fanciful arrangement which the varying shape of the toast may suggest.

The principal shapes given to the toast are as follows: round, square, rectangular, oval, triangular, crescent or star-shaped, etc.

They should never exceed one and one-half inches in diameter, and a corresponding size in the other shapes.

I shall only indicate here a few kinds of specially garnished toast, and leave the thousand and one other kinds for the chef himself to discover.

317—ANCHOVY TOAST   *Canapé d'Anchois*

Make the pieces of toast oval. Cover with anchovy butter (281), and place, lattice like, some fillets of anchovy cut to the length of the toast. Garnish the pieces of toast all round with the separately chopped whites and yolks of hard-boiled eggs, alternating the colors.

318—CAVIAR TOAST   *Canapés de Caviare*

Make the pieces of toast round; cover with caviar butter (282); garnish the edges with a band of softened butter, piped on by means of a pastry-bag fitted with a decorating tube. Put fresh caviar in the center.

319—SHRIMP TOAST   *Canapés de Crevettes*

Make the pieces of toast round; cover with shrimp butter (283), and garnish by means of a border composed of shelled shrimps' tails with a caper in the center.

320—CITY TOAST   *Canapés City*

Make the pieces of toast round, and cover with a thick coating of the following preparation:—Four oz. of fresh butter, softened; two oz. of fresh Gruyère and two oz. of Parmesan, both grated; two spoons of cream, and a little salt and cayenne. Cover this preparation with two half-rounds cut respectively from a Lyons sausage and a Gruyère cheese; both should be thin, and equal in thickness and just cover the toast.

321—DANISH TOAST   *Canapés à la Danoise*

Prepare some slices of dark or whole rye bread, equal in thickness to toast; but only heat, do not grill them. Spread some horse-radish butter (290) over them, and cover with alternate strips of smoked salmon, caviar, and herring fillets *marinated* in white wine. Now stamp the garnished slices with a sharp fancy-cutter, the shape of which is optional.

322—CRAYFISH TOAST   *Canapés d'Ecrevisses*

Make the pieces crescent-shaped; cover with crayfish butter (285), decorate the edges with a ribbon of softened butter, and garnish with a crayfish tail, cut into two lengthwise. The two halves of the tail should be placed in the middle of each crescent, close together and with their thickest side innermost.

323—TONGUE TOAST   *Canapés de Langue*

Prepare some slices of bread, equal in thickness, and toast them.
Now garnish with a coating, half as thick as the slices themselves, of
mustard butter. Cover the butter with thin slices of very red, cured
and smoked tongue, and let the butter harden.

Stamp out the pieces of toast with a star-shaped fancy-cutter.
Finally, make a rosette of mustard butter in the middle of each piece
of toast.

324—LUCILE TOAST   *Canapés Lucile*

Make the pieces of toast oval, cover with mustard butter, and
border their edges with a line of finely chopped and very red tongue.
Garnish the middle of each with chopped white chicken-meat, and
in the center drop a pinch of chopped truffle.

325—VARIOUS CAROLINES   *Carolines Diverses*

These are very small éclairs of *pâte à choux* (cream puff paste)
without sugar (2373). When quite cold, fill them with a *purée*, either
of tongue, fowl, game, or *foie gras,* etc., then coat them thinly with
a chaud-froid sauce (35) in keeping with the *purée* forming the
inside filling.

When the sauce has cooled, *glaze* it, with a brush, with a little cold
melted jelly, with a view to making it glossy.

N.B.—Carolines are also used as a garnish for certain cold dishes,
aspics, etc.

326—CAVIAR AND BLINIS   *Caviar et Blinis*

Caviar is undoubtedly the richest and most delicate of hors-
d'œuvres, granted, of course, that it be of good quality and consist
of large, light-colored, and transparent sturgeon roe. Its price is
always high, owing to the difficulty connected with its importation.
It is served very simply, either in a silver dish or in its original
receptacle, surrounded with ice, and accompanied by a dish of
Blinis, which the preparation of is as follows:—

Make a thin paste with one oz. (two cakes) of compressed yeast
and one lb. of sifted flour diluted with one pint of lukewarm milk.
Leave this paste to raise for two hours in a lukewarm atmosphere,
and then add one-half lb. of flour, the yolks of four eggs, a pinch of
salt, one-half pint of tepid milk; mix the whole without letting it
thicken, and finally add the whites of four eggs, beaten. Let the
mixture raise for half an hour, and, when about to serve, cook the
Blinis quickly, after the manner of pancakes, in special little pans

or on a griddle. Serve them very hot on a napkin. (These are often eaten with just melted butter, Matjes herring and sour cream.—Ed.)

Failing fresh caviar, the pressed and salted kind may also be used for hors-d'œuvres. Some cooks serve finely-chopped onions with fresh caviar, but a worse practice could not be imagined. Fresh caviar, the flavor of which is perfect, does not need any supplementary condiment.

327—CELERY "A LA BONNE FEMME"   *Céleri à la Bonne Femme*

Take equal quantities of very tender celery stalks and peeled and cored quartered russet apples. Mince the celery and apples finely, season with a mustard-and-cream sauce (299a), and place on a hors-d'œuvre dish.

328—CELERY A LA GRECQUE   *Céleri à la Grecque*

Select a few hearts of celery, in size equal; trim, wash, and parboil them in water in which lemon juice or vinegar has been added, as directed under "artichokes à la Grecque" (312). Prepare the cooking-liquor from the same ingredients, using the same quantities, and cook similarly.

Serve very cold on a crystal hors-d'œuvre dish with a portion of the cooking-liquor.

329—CELERY KNOBS OR CELERIAC   *Céleri—Rave*

Quarter, peel, and cut the knobs in *julienne*-fashion. Prepare the seasoning with dry mustard, salt, pepper, and vinegar; add the *julienne* of the celeriac and mix thoroughly. When the roots are quite soft, a seasoning consisting of mustard-and-cream sauce (299a) is preferable.

329a—MARINATED CEPES   *Cèpes Marinés*

Select some very small and fresh *cèpes*. Parboil them for eight minutes, drain and cool them, put them into a bowl, and cover them with the boiling *marinade* after having passed the latter through a strainer.

Marinade for Two lbs. of Cèpes.—Put into a saucepan one pint of vinegar, one-third pint of oil, a crushed clove of garlic, a piece of bay leaf, and a little thyme, six peppercorns, a pinch of coriander, a few fennel leaves, and a small parsley root. Set to boil for five minutes. Leave the mushrooms to *marinate* for five or six hours before using them.

329b—CHERRIES IN VINEGAR
Cerises a l'Allemande

Take five lbs. of not quite ripe Morella cherries, which are dark red and sour, and put them into a bottle, as in the case of cherry brandy, and add three cloves, a small stick of cinnamon, some grated nutmeg, and a sprig of tarragon. Pour over the cherries two quarts of vinegar, boiled with one-half lb. of brown sugar and properly cooled. Cork the bottle, and leave the fruit to steep for a fortnight.

329c—BRAINS A LA ROBERT
Cervelle Robert

Soak in lemon water, then cook the well-cleaned sheep's or lamb's brains in *court-bouillon* (166), and cool. Divide them up into thin and regular slices, and place them on an hors-d'œuvre dish. Rub the brain trimmings through a fine sieve, combine the resulting *purée* with a mustard-and-cream sauce (299a), and add thereto a fine *julienne* of the white part only of celery stalks.

Cover the slices of brain with the sauce.

329d—CUCUMBER A LA DANOISE
Concombres à la Danoise

Cut the cucumber in the shape of small cups or boats, *blanch* and *marinate* them.

Garnish with a preparation composed of a *purée* of smoked salmon mixed with herring fillets and chopped, hard-boiled eggs in equal quantities.

Sprinkle a little grated horse-radish over the garnish.

330—STUFFED CUCUMBERS
Concombres Farcis

Prepare them as above, in the shape of small boats or cups. Cook them, at the same time keeping them firm. When they are quite cold *marinate* them for twenty minutes in oil and vinegar, and garnish them, by means of a pastry-bag, either with a thick *purée,* of some minced-meat thickened with mayonnaise, or a small vegetable *macédoine,* etc.

331—CUCUMBER SALAD
Concombres en Salade

Carefully peel the cucumbers, cut them into two lengthwise, remove their seeds, and mince them finely. Place them in a bowl, sprinkle with table-salt, and leave them to exude their moisture for twenty-five minutes. This done, drain them, press them in a towel, season with pepper, oil, and vinegar, and add some chopped chervil.

332—CUCUMBER AND PIMENTO SALAD

Concombres et Pimentos en Salade

Select some very fresh, medium-sized cucumbers, peel them, and cut them into slices two inches in length. Cut these pieces spirally, beginning at their outer edges and working towards their centers; then cut them across, so as to produce curved strips of the cucumber. Add an equal quantity of pimentos cut into strips, and season as in the case of cucumber salad.

333—YORK CONES

Cornets d'York

Cut slices from a fine baked smoked ham as thinly as possible, and trim off the fat and cut them to the shape of triangles. Roll the triangles into cones, and garnish the insides (by means of a pastry-bag fitted with a decorating tube) with any butter or cream (280 to 299).

334—TONGUE CONES

Cornets de Langue

Proceed as for Ham Cones.

335—MOULDED CREAMS

Les Crèmes Moulées

Prepare a hors-d'œuvre cream in accordance with any one of the recipes (294 to 299). Put this cream into very small, slightly-oiled, and ornamented moulds, and leave it to set in the cool or on ice. Empty the moulds, at the moment of serving, either directly upon a dish, on *tartlets* garnished with a *purée* in keeping with the cream, or on toast. With these moulded creams, endless varieties of delicate and recommendable little hors-d'œuvres may be prepared, while in their preparation the moulds used in pastry for *"petits fours"* may serve a useful purpose.

336—SHRIMPS AND PRAWNS

Crevettes et Ecrevisses

Have these cooked very fresh and serve them in their shells on boat-shaped hors-d'œuvre dishes, arranging them so that they over-lap one another. Either garnish the middle of the dishes with curled-leaf parsley, or lay the crustacean directly upon parsley.

337—DUCHESSES

Duchesses

This hors-d'œuvre is almost equivalent to the Carolines (325), except that the shape of the Duchesses is that of little *choux*, about the size of a pigeon's egg, and that, as a rule, they are merely *glazed* with some melted jelly aspic, and not covered with a chaud-froid sauce. Sprinkle them with chopped pistachios, and serve them very cold on ornamented doilies.

338—NANTUA DUCHESSES   *Duchesses Nantua*

Stuff the little *choux,* referred to above, with crayfish *purée,* and sprinkle them, again and again, with cold, melted jelly aspic, in order to cover them with a transparent film.

339—DUCHESSES A LA REINE   *Duchesses à la Reine*

Stuff the little *choux* with a *purée* of fowl with cream. *Glaze* with jelly aspic, and sprinkle some very black, finely-chopped truffles over the jelly.

340—DUCHESSES A LA SULTANE   *Duchesses à la Sultane*

Stuff the little *choux* with a *purée* of fowl, completed with pistachio butter. *Glaze* with aspic-jelly, and sprinkle a little chopped pistachio upon each.

341—CAVIAR DUCHESSES   *Duchesses Caviare*

Stuff with fresh caviar or caviar cream (294). *Glaze* with aspic-jelly and serve iced.

342—SMOKED SALMON DUCHESSES   *Duchesses Saumon Fumé*

Stuff the little *choux* with a *purée* of smoked salmon and butter, and *glaze* them with a lean, degreased aspic-jelly.

343—NORWEGIAN DUCHESSES   *Duchesses Norvegiennes*

Stuff the *choux* with a *purée* of Kilkis (307) and butter, and *glaze* with jelly.

344—KAROLY ECLAIRS   *Eclairs Karoly*

These are little éclairs stuffed with a *purée* made from the entrails of woodcock with champagne. The *purée* is buttered and slightly seasoned. Cover the éclairs with a brown chaud-froid sauce (34), mask them with game aspic (160), and serve them, iced, on ornamented doilies.

345—CRAYFISH EN BUISSON   *Ecrevisses en Buisson*

Prepare them in accordance with the recipes "à la nage" (968) or "à la marinière" (967), and serve them very cold.

346—MARINATED SMELTS　　　　　　　　　*Eperlans Marinés*

Fry some well-dried and floured smelts in oil; as soon as this is done, put them in a deep dish or a bowl. Add to the oil, per pint (which quantity should be allowed for every two lbs. of the fish), eight unpeeled garlic-cloves, an onion, and a carrot cut into thin, round slices, all of which vegetables should be slightly fried. Drain off the oil, moisten with one-quarter pint of vinegar and as much water, and season with a little salt, two small red peppers, a small bay leaf, a sprig of thyme, and a few parsley stalks. Dip the smelts for twelve minutes in this *marinade,* and transfer them to the dish, where they may be left to *marinate* for twenty-four hours.

Serve very cold with a portion of the *marinade.*

347—FENNEL A LA GRECQUE　　　　　*Fenouil à la Grecque*

Same process as for artichokes and celery à la Grecque (312).

348—FRESH FIGS　　　　　　　　　　　*Figues Fraîches*

Place them on a layer of very green leaves, and surround them with cracked ice.

349—FOIE GRAS　　　　　　　　　　　　*Foie Gras*

If in the form of a sausage, cut it into thin slices. If potted, shape it into little balls, after the manner in which butter is sometimes served, only a little smaller. In all cases serve it iced, and as soon as it is ready.

350—FRIVOLITIES　　　　　　　　　　　*Frivolités*

I adopted the above term for those small, light, and elegant little preparations, the radical types of which are *barquettes* (boats) (314) and *tartlets* (387), which often take the place of hors-d'œuvres on a menu. The term seems plain, clear, and explicit, and no other could denote more happily this series of trifles which constitute mere gewgaws of the dining-table.

351—FROGS OR NYMPHS A L'AURORE　　*Nymphes à l'Aurore*

For various reasons, I thought it best, in the past, to substitute the mythological name "Nymphs" for the more vulgar term "Frogs" on menus, and the former has been universally adopted, more particularly in reference to the following "Chaud-froid à l'Aurore" (74):—

Poach the frogs' legs in an excellent white-wine *court-bouillon* (164). When cooled, trim them properly, dry them thoroughly in a piece of fine linen, and steep them, one after the other, in a chaud-froid sauce of fish with paprika, the tint of which should be golden. This done, arrange the treated legs on a layer of champagne aspic-jelly, which should have set beforehand on the bottom of a square, silver dish or crystal bowl. Now lay some chervil *pluches* and tarragon leaves between the legs in imitation of water-grasses, and cover the whole with champagne aspic-jelly to imitate water.

Send the dish to the table, set in a block of ice, fashioned as fancy may suggest.

352—SALAD OF FILLETED SALTED HERRINGS

Harengs Salés en Salade

Remove the fillets whole; skin them; soak and then trim them. For serving cover them with the following sauce:—Add the *purée* of eight soft roes or *milts*, moistened with two tablespoons of vinegar, to four tablespoons of mayonnaise. Season with onion, parsley, chervil, chives, and tarragon, all finely minced; flavor moderately with cayenne.

353—FRESH HERRINGS MARINATED IN WHITE WINE

Hareng Frais Marinés au Vin Blanc

For twelve herrings, put one pint of white wine into a saucepan, with one-quarter pint of vinegar, an onion cut into thin slices, half a carrot cut into grooved rounds, an herb bunch, the necessary salt, and a few peppercorns. Set to boil gently for twenty minutes.

Place the cleaned herrings in a saucepan, pour the boiling *marinade* over them, and let them *poach* for fifteen minutes.

Serve them very cold with the *marinade,* the rounds of carrot, and thin strips of onion.

354—LUCAS HERRINGS
Harengs Lucas

Detach the fillets from fine salted herrings, soak them first in cold water, and then in milk for an hour.

Prepare a sauce as follows:—Beat up the yolks of two eggs in a bowl with salt and pepper and one tablespoon of mustard; add five tablespoons of oil and two of vinegar, proceeding as in the case of mayonnaise (126), and complete with shallots and two teaspoons of chopped chervil and gherkins. Season with cayenne, immerse the drained and dried fillets of herrings in this sauce, and send them to the table on an hors-d'œuvre dish.

355—HERRINGS A LA LIVONIENNE   *Harengs à la Livonienne*

Take some fine salted herring fillets, clean them, and cut them into dice. Place these in a bowl, and add, in equal quantities, some cold, boiled potatoes and russet or tart apples cut into dice, parsley, chervil, and chopped fennel and tarragon. Season with oil and vinegar, salt and pepper; form the mixture into shapes resembling herrings, and place the heads and tails, which should have been put aside for the purpose, at each extremity of every supposed herring.

356—HERRINGS A LA RUSSE   *Harengs à la Russe*

Cut some fine, cleaned fillets of salted herrings into thin slices. Put in a dish, and alternate the rows of sliced fillets with rows of sliced, cold, boiled potatoes. Season with oil and vinegar, and finish up with chopped chervil, fennel, tarragon, and shallots.

357—HERRINGS WITH FRENCH BEANS   *Harengs aux Haricots Verts*

This appetizer can only be served at their best in the months of September and October, when the first runs of herrings (Dutch) begin to appear. Dutch fishermen know of a means of salting and *marinating* this virgin fish, which greatly increases its value, and it is not unusual to pay as much as twenty-five cents for one in the early part of the season. They form an excellent dish, and their flavor is rich and exquisite. Before serving them, it is only necessary to skin them, whereupon they may be served with a little chopped parsley. Send a bowl of string beans to the table with them, the vegetables having been freshly cooked, kept somewhat firm, buttered, and not cooled. Some cooks serve the beans cold, in the form of a salad, but as a rule they are preferred hot with butter, while the herrings should be very cold.

358—OYSTERS   *Huîtres*

Oysters are the dish par excellence; their delicacy satisfies the most fastidious of epicures, and they are so easily digested that the most delicate invalid can partake of them freely. With the exception of caviar, they are the only hors-d'œuvres which should ever appear on the menu of a well-ordered dinner.

Oysters ought to be served very cold; hence the prevailing custom of serving them on ice. In England they are served plain on the flat half of the shell, whereas in France and in the United States they are left in the hollow half, which is better calculated to retain the natural liquor of the oyster, held in high esteem by many. Send some slices of dark or whole rye bread and butter to the table with the oysters.

The various methods of treating oysters will be given hereafter in the chapter dealing with fish. I have given them merely because consumers and caterers alike may wish to have them; but the real and best way of serving oysters is to send them to the table raw.

(These are often served in the United States with lemon, grated and prepared horse-radish, as well as with cock-tail sauce and chili sauce, and oyster crackers are then served with the raw oysters.—Ed.)

359—ARDENNES HAM   *Jambon d'Ardennes*

This is served like smoked breast of goose, cut, raw, into thin and even slices.

360—CANTALOUP MELON   *Le Melon Canteloup*

A cantaloup makes an excellent hors-d'œuvre for summer luncheons. It should be just ripe, and have a nice fragrance. Serve it as fresh and cold as possible.

361—ENGLISH MELONS   *Melons Anglais*

Their shape is round, their peel is greenish yellow, thin, and smooth, and their flesh, which is light green and sweet and delicate, more nearly resembles the transparency of the water-melon flesh than that of the cantaloup in flavor.

362—MELON WITH PORT, MARSALA, OR SHERRY

Melon au Porto, Marsala, ou Sherry

Select a cantaloup or other melon and let it be just ripe. Make a round incision about the stem end, three inches in diameter; withdraw the plug cut, and through the hole remove all the pips with a silver spoon.

Now pour one-half pint of best Port, Marsala, or Sherry into the melon, replace the plug, and keep the melon iced for two or three hours. Do not cut the melon into slices when serving it. It should be taken to the table, whole, and then the plug is withdrawn and the fruit is cut into shell-like slices with a silver spoon, and served with a little of the accompanying wine upon iced plates.

363—VARIOUS MELONS   *Melons Divers*

France produces a large variety of melons, of which the principal kinds are the Sucrins of Tours, the St. Laud melon, the black melons of the Carmes, etc. They are all excellent, and are served like the Cantaloups, Honey Dews, Water-melon, etc.

364—OYSTERS WITH CAVIAR   *Huîtres au Caviare*

This is a typically luxurious hors-d'œuvre. Make some little *tartlet crusts* for hors-d'œuvre (387). When about to serve, garnish these with a tablespoon of fine, fresh caviar; make a hollow in the center and place a Bluepoint oyster, bearded, seasoned with a little pepper and a drop of lemon-juice.

365—SMOKED BREAST OF GOOSE   *Poitrine d'Oie Fumée*

Cut it into the thinnest possible slices, and garnish with very green parsley.

366—PLAIN OLIVES   *Olives Ordinaires*

Olives of all kinds are suitable for hors-d'œuvres, and they are served plain. Three are known, green, ripe and green-ripe, all of which are excellent, provided they be fleshy, firm, very green, and moderately salted.

367—STUFFED OLIVES   *Olives Farcis*

For this purpose, select large Spanish olives and pit them, either by cutting them spirally, or by means of a special machine. In the place of the pit, put one of the butters or creams for hors-d'œuvres (280 to 299). Before serving these olives, it is well to let them rest awhile in a moderately warm atmosphere. For, since stuffed olives are generally kept cool, immersed in oil with which they become thoroughly saturated, it follows that the moment they are put into contact with a slightly higher temperature they will exude that oil. Wherefore, if the above precaution were not observed, by the time the olives reached the table they would, more often than not, be swimming in oil, when they would be neither nice nor appetizing.

368—PLAIN PLOVERS' EGGS   *Oeufs de Pluvier*

Though the plover and the lapwing are different in respect of their plumage, they are, nevertheless, birds of similar habits and haunts, and their eggs are remarkably alike. The former, which are a little larger than pigeons' eggs, have a light-green shell covered with black spots.

When cooked, the albuminous portions acquire a milky color, and never assume the solidity of the whites of other eggs.

When served as an hors-d'œuvre, these eggs are always boiled hard.

Put them in a saucepan of cold water, and leave them to cook for eight minutes after the boil is reached. Cool them, shell their pointed ends, and serve them in a nest composed of watercress or curled-leaf parsley.

N.B.—Test the freshness of the eggs before boiling them by plunging them in a bowl of cold water. If they float, their freshness is doubtful, and they should be discarded.

(Lapwing eggs cannot be purchased in the United States, whereas Plovers' eggs are imported for use.—Ed.)

369—PLOVERS' EGGS IN ASPIC   *Oeufs de Pluviers en Gelée*

Decorate a border-mould according to taste, and let a thin coating of very clear aspic jelly set on the bottom of the utensil. Sprinkle the articles used in decorating with a few drops of melted jelly, in order to keep them from shifting; then cover them with a few tablespoons of aspic jelly, and let it set. On this coating arrange the shelled, hard-boiled plovers' eggs with their points downwards, so that they may appear upright when the aspic is unmoulded. Fill up the mould by means of successive layers of melted aspic-jelly.

When about to serve, dip the mould into hot water; quickly dry it, and then turn the aspic out on to a folded napkin on a dish.

370—PLOVERS' EGGS A LA MODERNE   *Oeufs de Pluviers à la Moderne*

Boil the eggs soft; mould them in *dariole-moulds,* coated with aspic-jelly, and garnished in *Chartreuse* fashion. Heap a vegetable-salad, thickened with mayonnaise, in the middle of the dish, and place the eggs unmoulded all round.

371—PLOVERS' EGGS A LA CHRISTIANA

Oeufs de Pluviers à la Christiana

Cook the eggs hard; shell them; slice a piece off their blunt ends to make them stand, and arrange them on a dish, placing them upon little *tartlet-crusts* (387), garnished with a *foie-gras purée.*

For twelve eggs put two tablespoons of *foie-gras purée* in a small saucepan; add one tablespoon of chopped truffles and as much melted jelly, the latter with a view to making the preparation more liquid. Take some of this preparation in a tablespoon and pour it over the eggs, taking care that each of these is well covered. Let the coating set in the refrigerator, and serve the *tartlets* on a napkin, arranging them in the form of a circle with curled parsley as a center-garnish.

372—PLOVERS' EGGS A LA MUSCOVITE

Oeufs de Pluviers à la Muscovite

Boil the eggs hard; cool and shell them. Prepare as many *tartlet-crusts* as there are eggs. When serving, garnish the *tartlets* with a teaspoon of caviar, and place one egg in the middle of each.

373—VARIOUS HARD-BOILED EGGS   *Les Oeufs Durs Divers*

With hard-boiled eggs for base, a large number of hors-d'œuvres may be made. I shall limit myself to a few only, which, by means of a small change in their form, garnish, or decoration, may be varied at will:—

Egg Discs.—Cut the eggs across into slices one-third inch thick, and discard the two end-pieces of each egg, in order that the shapes may be almost uniform, and that the yolks may appear about the same size throughout. In the center of each slice make a little rosette of butter, by means of a pastry-bag with a small, fancy tube. Different butters, such as the Shrimp, Montpellier, Caviar, and other kinds, may be used with the view of varying the colors.

Halved, Stuffed Eggs.—Take some very small, hard-boiled eggs; cut them into two, lengthwise; remove the yolks, and trim the oval hollow of each of the remaining whites to the shape of an oblong, the edges of which may then be scalloped.

Garnish, either with a *purée* of tuna, salmon, *milt,* etc., or a hash or *salpicon* of lobster, shrimp, etc., thickened with mayonnaise with jelly, or a fine *macédoine* of vegetables with mayonnaise, or a *purée* composed of the removed yolks combined with a little butter, some cold Béchamel sauce (28), and herbs.

Quartered, Stuffed Eggs.—The simplest way of doing this is to proceed as above, to stuff the halved white with a buttered *purée,* or a *purée* mixed with aspic-jelly, to leave the stuffing to set and chill, and then to cut the halves in two.

Salad of Eggs.—With alternate rows of sliced eggs and either tomatoes, potatoes, cucumbers, or beets, and a salad-seasoning composed of oil and vinegar or cream, a dozen different salads may be prepared, each of which constitutes an excellent hors-d'œuvre.

374—LARK PATE   *Pâté d'Alouettes*

For this hors-d'œuvre use the ready-made pâté, which is obtained either in earthenware pots or in crusts. Thoroughly congeal it by means of ice; turn it out of its receptacle, cut it into very small and thin slices, and arrange them on an hors-d'œuvre dish with a little chopped aspic-jelly in the middle.

375—SWEET GRILLED PEPPERS   *Pimentos Douces Grillées*

Grill the peppers over a moderate fire until the skins are so scorched as to be easily removed. Remove the seed also.

Now cut them *julienne*-fashion, and season with oil and vinegar.

376—RADISHES   *Radis*

In the preparation of hors-d'œuvres by the kitchen, radishes are used chiefly as a garnish. When they constitute a hors-d'œuvre of themselves, their preparation is relegated to the pantry.

They are cut in imitation of roses; sometimes they are sliced and placed on cut cucumber to form a dish-border; but their uses in garnishing are as numerous as they are various.

377—AMERICAN RELISHES   *Relishes Americains*

These consist of various kinds of fruit and of small onions and gherkins, prepared with vinegar, seasoned with sugar and cinnamon, and flavored with cayenne.

They resemble what the Italians call "Aceto-dolce" (sweet and sour). This hors-d'œuvre is accompanied by special cinnamon buns, and remains on the table throughout the meal.

378—RILLETTES   *Rillettes de Tours*

This is finely chopped pork-meat and fat paté which is made up by the pork butcher and may be found in the markets of France.

The *rillettes* are served in their pots, and are always sent to the table very cold.

379—RED MULLET A L'ORIENTALE   *Rougets au Safran à l'Orientale*

Select small ones, as far as possible. Place them in an oiled pan, and add peeled and chopped tomatoes, parsley-root, fennel, thyme, bay leaf, a little garlic, peppercorns, coriander, and saffron, the latter being the dominating ingredient.

Cover the whole with white wine; salt moderately, set to boil, and then leave to *poach* on the side of the fire for twelve or eighteen minutes, in accordance with the size of the mullet.

Leave the fish to cool in their cooking-liquor, and serve them with a little of the liquor and a few slices of peeled lemon.

(Only grey mullet can be purchased in the United States.—Ed.)

380—SARDINES　　　　　*Sardines*

The various kinds of sardines for hors-d'œuvres may be found on the market.

381—SALADS　　　　　*Salades*

Salads for hors-d'œuvres may consist of an endless variety of foods, and their preparation varies so that it would be impossible to prescribe fixed rules for them. I shall therefore restrict myself to saying merely that they should be made as light and as appetizing as possible, in order that they may be in keeping with the general idea and purpose of hors-d'œuvre.

382—SALAMIS　　　　　*Les Salamis*

Cut these into very thin slices, and place them, one on top of the other, on an hors-d'œuvre dish, in the form of a crown, with a sprig of curly parsley in the middle. They may also be laid flat upon a bed of parsley.

383—VARIOUS BOLOGNAS AND SAUSAGES　　　*Saucissons Divers*

Cut these up and arrange them like the Salami.

384—FOIE-GRAS SAUSAGES　　　　*Saucissons Foie-Gras*

Cut into thin slices and serve with chopped aspic jelly as a center-garnish.

385—SMOKED SALMON　　　　*Saumon Fumé*

Cut into triangular, thin slices; roll these into cones, and arrange in the form of a crown with curly parsley in the middle.

386—SPRATS　　　　　*Royans*

These are smoked sardines (not in oil). Select the very fleshy ones, for there are many kinds, a few of which are dry and quite flavorless.

In order to prepare them, take off the heads and remove or leave on the skins, in accordance with the diner's taste. Put them on a dish with some finely-chopped shallots, chopped parsley, and oil and vinegar, using a very little of each ingredient. Leave them to *marinate* for five or six hours, taking care to turn them over from time to time so as to thoroughly saturate them with the *marinade*.

(You can use smoked herring fillets instead.—Ed.)

387—TARTLETS AND BARQUETTES   *Tartelettes et Barquettes*

These articles play an important part in the service of hors-d'œuvres, and represent the class I designated under the name of *Frivolities*.

The garnishes suitable for *tartlets* are likewise used with *barquettes* (boat type crusts), the latter only differing from the former in their shape. The directions which follow, and which should be carefully noted, apply equally to both.

Special Paste for Tartlets and Barquettes.—Sift one lb. of flour on to a mixing-board; make a hole in the center, into which put one-eighth oz. of salt, one-half lb. of cold, melted butter, one egg, the yolks of two, and a few drops of water. Mix the whole into a paste, handling it as little as possible; roll it into a ball, and put it aside to chill for two hours.

The Preparation of Tartlet- and Barquette-crusts.—Roll out the paste to the thickness of one-eighth inch, and stamp it with a scalloped fancy-cutter into pieces of the same size as the *tartlet-moulds* to be used, which in this case are the same as for *"petits fours,"* and, therefore, very small.

The fancy-cutter should be round for *tartlets,* and oval for *barquettes.* Lay the paste in the moulds, prick the bottoms, lest they should blister, lay out the inside with pieces of kitchen-paper to protect the paste, and fill them with rice or flour. Bake in a moderate oven; remove the rice or flour, the sole object of which was to preserve the shape of the *tartlets* or *barquettes;* turn the latter out of their moulds, and set them to cool.

The Garnishes of Tartlets and Barquettes.—These may be divided into two classes, viz., those with a compound butter for base, those with an aspic jelly base.

The first class comprises all the garnishes I gave for *Canapés* (316) and Toast, as also all those which the cook's fancy, taste, and inventiveness may devise.

The second class generally consists of a layer, on the bottom, of some kind of *mousse,* upon which a whole piece of a different color from the *mousse* is placed, and which is then coated with a very clear aspic jelly.

Example.—Garnish the bottom of a *tartlet* or *barquette* with a coating of pink, shrimp, crayfish or lobster *mousse.* Upon this lay a very white *poached* oyster, or a slice of hard-boiled egg, cut out with a scalloped fancy-cutter. In the center of the yolk put a little lobster coral, and coat the whole with jelly to the level of the *tartlet* edges.

The explanations given above warrant my refraining from a more detailed discussion of these delicate preparations. Sufficient has been said to allow of any cook, with a little taste and inventiveness, easily making an endless variety of combinations.

388—TUNA IN OIL   *Thon à l'Huile*

This is found on the market, and it may be served as it stands. It is very greatly used as a garnish for hors-d'œuvres.

389—TUNA WITH TOMATOES   *Thon aux Tomates*

Lay alternate slices of tuna and tomato upon an hors-d'œuvres dish, and between each slice lay a thin slice of onion. Garnish the edge of the dish with a border composed of sliced cold potato, and sprinkle the whole with an ordinary salad dressing.

390—TOMATOES   *Tomates au Naturel*

Select some about the size of a walnut, and peel them carefully. Press them in a piece of linen, and set them to *marinate* for half an hour in oil and vinegar. Then stick a small piece of parsley stalk into each tomato, in imitation of the stem, and surround it with little leaves made from green butter (153) by means of a small pastry bag.

391—TOMATOES A L'AMERICAINE   *Tomates à l'Americaine*

Select some firm, medium-sized tomatoes, and cut them into thin slices. Put them into a dish with salt, pepper, oil, and a few drops of vinegar, and leave them to *marinate* for twenty minutes. Then arrange them on a hors-d'œuvre dish, garnishing the border with fine rings of onion.

392—TOMATOES A LA MONEGASQUE   *Tomates à la Monégasque*

Select some small tomatoes about the size of walnuts, and cut a slice from each in the region of the stalk. Squeeze out all their liquid and seeds, and *marinate* them, inside, for twenty minutes. Prepare a mince of tuna with oil, and add to it, per two oz. of the fish, half a tablespoon of finely-chopped onion, a tablespoon of chopped parsley, chervil, and tarragon, and a small, hard-boiled egg, also chopped.

Thicken the whole with a tablespoon of thick mayonnaise; put it into a pastry bag fitted with a smooth, medium-sized tube, and garnish the tomatoes with the mixture, using enough of it to form a kind of dome upon each tomato.

393—QUARTERED TOMATOES   *Tomates en Quartiers*

Use medium-sized tomatoes, somewhat firm and with very smooth skins. Peel them and remove the pulp and seeds, and then fill them, either with a fish *purée* cleared with aspic jelly (158), or with a *macédoine* of vegetables thickened by means of a mayonnaise with jelly. Place on ice for half an hour, and cut the tomatoes into regular quarters. The tomatoes may also be cut into four, previous to stuffing them, whereupon they may, with the help of a pastry bag fitted with a fancy tube, be filled with one of the compound butters.

394—MARINATED TROUT   *Truites Marinées*

Select some very small trout, clean and dress them, and *poach* them in a white-wine *court-bouillon* (164) to which vinegar has been added in the proportion of one-third of its volume.

Leave the fish to cool in the liquor, and serve it with a few tablespoons of the liquid, placing some thin, grooved slices of lemon upon the fish.

CHAPTER XII

EGGS

Of all the products put to use by the art of cookery, not one is so fruitful of variety, so universally liked, and so complete in itself as the egg. There are very few culinary recipes that do not include eggs, either as a principal constituent or as an ingredient.

The many and various egg-preparations constitute chiefly breakfast or luncheon dishes; nevertheless, at a *Lenten* dinner they may be served as entrées with advantage, for, at a time when fish, shellfish and game fish are the only resources in this respect, eggs form a pleasant and welcome change.

395—EGGS ON THE DISH *Oeufs sur-le-Plat*

Eggs cooked in this way, on a earthenware dish, derive all their quality from the way in which the cooking process is conducted. They must be evenly cooked, on top and underneath, and should remain soft. An important condition of the process is that the eggs should be fresh. After having heated sufficient butter in the dish to cover the whole bottom, break two eggs into it, baste the yolks with a little very hot butter, salt them slightly, and put them into the oven. As soon as the white of the eggs assumes a milky-white color, they are cooked and should be withdrawn from the oven to be served immediately.

Great attention should be given to the cooking process, a few seconds more or less than the required time is sufficient to spoil the eggs. Special care ought to be taken that they do not cook either too much or too quickly, for it should be remembered that, even were the cooking checked before the proper time, the heat of the dish does, to a certain extent, make up for it.

Eggs *à la poêle*, which are called "fried eggs," are a variety of eggs served on a dish, very often served on toast, or accompanied by sausages or fried bacon. They are cooked in an open pan, trimmed neatly with a fancy-cutter, and placed, by means of a spatula, upon the prepared toast.

166

About one-half oz. of butter should be allowed for every two eggs, which number constitutes the working-base of the following recipes.

396—BERCY EGGS   *Oeufs Bercy*

Put half of the butter to be used in a dish; melt it, drop in the eggs, taking care not to break the yolks; baste the latter with the rest of the butter, and season. Cook as directed—or, until the whites are quite done and the yolks are glossy. Garnish with a small, grilled sausage, placed between the yolks, and surround with a ribbon of tomato sauce (29).

397—EGGS WITH BROWN BUTTER   *Oeufs au Beurre Noir*

There are two methods: Cook the eggs in a dish as usual, and then cover them with one-quarter oz. of brown butter (154) and a few drops of vinegar, which should be added after the butter.

2. Put one-half oz. of butter into a small open pan, and cook it until it is almost black. Break the eggs into it, season, cook, tilt them gently on to a dish, and sprinkle with a few drops of vinegar, which has been stirred in the pan.

398—EGGS HUNTERS' STYLE   *Oeufs Chasseur*

Cook the eggs as (395). This done, garnish on either side with a tablespoon of sliced chicken's liver, rapidly *sautéd* and mixed with a little Chasseur sauce (33).

399—DEVILLED EGGS   *Oeufs à la Diable*

Cook the eggs in the open pan; turn them, after the manner of pancakes on both sides, taking care lest they break. Slide them gently into a dish, and sprinkle them with brown butter (154) and a few drops of vinegar which has been stirred into the pan.

400—FLORENTINE EGGS   *Oeufs à la Florentine*

Garnish the bottom of a dish with spinach-leaves cooked in butter; sprinkle over it two pinches of grated cheese; break the eggs on this garnish, and cover them with two tablespoons of Mornay sauce (91). Place in a hot oven, so that the cooking and *glazing* of the eggs may be effected simultaneously.

401—EGGS AU GRATIN   *Oeufs au Gratin*

Put a tablespoon of very hot Mornay sauce (91) into a dish. Break the eggs into it, cover them with Mornay sauce, sprinkle with grated cheese mixed with fine bread crumbs, and cook in a hot oven, in order that the eggs and the *gratin* may be done at the same time.

402—ISOLINE EGGS   *Oeufs Isoline*

Cook the eggs according to 395. Place between them, and all around the dish, some small, halved tomatoes à la *Provençale* (2268). Put in the center of each halved tomato a fine chicken's liver *sautéd* with Madeira.

403—JOCKEY CLUB EGGS   *Oeufs Jockey Club*

Cook the eggs in an open pan; tilt them gently on to a dish, and trim them with a round fancy-cutter. Place each egg upon a round, thin piece of toast, and then cover them with *foie-gras purée*. Arrange them in the form of a crown, on a dish, and pour into the middle a garnish of veal kidneys cut into dice and *sautéd,* and truffles similarly cut, the latter being put on the garnish by means of some dense half-*glaze* (23).

404—LULLY EGGS   *Oeufs Lully*

Cook the eggs in an open pan, and cut them with a round fancy-cutter. Place each egg on a slice of uncooked ham, cut to the same shape as the egg, and fried in butter. Then place the egg and ham on toast of the same shape and size. Arrange the eggs in a circle round the dish, and garnish the middle of it with macaroni combined with chopped tomatoes stewed in butter.

405—MEYERBEER EGGS   *Oeufs Meyerbeer*

Cook the eggs as in (395). Place a small, grilled sheep's or lamb's kidney between each yolk, and surround with a ribbon of Périgueux sauce (47).

406—MIRABEAU EGGS   *Oeufs Mirabeau*

Substitute for ordinary butter, anchovy butter (281). Break the eggs and cook them. Surround each yolk with anchovy fillets, and garnish each of these with a spray of parboiled tarragon leaves. Place a large olive stuffed with tarragon butter (148) on either side of the yolks.

407—OMAR-PACHA EGGS   *Oeufs Omar-Pacha*

Garnish a dish with a large tablespoon of minced onions cooked in butter but not browned. Break the eggs over the garnish, sprinkle them with a small tablespoon of dry, grated Parmesan cheese, and cook in a fairly hot oven for a slight *gratin* to form as soon as the eggs are done.

408—PARMENTIER EGGS   *Oeufs Parmentier*

Bake some fine Irish potatoes in the oven. Cut them open at the top, with an oval fancy-cutter; remove the pulp from the inside, rub it through a sieve, and make a smooth *purée* of it. Half-fill the potato-shells with this *purée,* break an egg into each, sprinkle with cream, and cook in the oven. Replace the oval top part of the baked shell, and serve on a napkin.

409—PORTUGUESE EGGS   *Oeufs à la Portuguise*

Put a tablespoon of tomato *fondue* into a dish. Break the eggs upon this, season, and cook. Between the eggs and at each end of the dish put a little tomato *fondue,* and on each of the mounds drop a pinch of chopped parsley.

410—EGGS A LA REINE   *Oeufs à la Reine*

Cook the eggs in an open pan, and trim them with a round fancy-cutter. Put each egg upon a small round thin cake of Duchesse potatoes (221), the same size as the egg, previously browned in the oven. Arrange the eggs in a circle round the dish; in the middle put some minced chicken, and surround with a border of Suprème sauce (106a).

POACHED AND MOLLET EGGS

All the recipes given hereafter apply equally to poached and *mollet* eggs, wherefore I shall only mention *"poached"* in the titles, leaving *mollet* to be understood.

411—PROCEDURE FOR POACHED EGGS   *Pour Faire les Oeufs Pochés*

The one and only essential condition in this case is the use of absolutely fresh eggs, for it is quite impossible to expect an even *poaching* if this condition is not fulfilled.

Have ready a saucepan containing boiling salted water (one-third oz. of salt per quart of water), with vinegar added. Break the eggs into that part of the water which is actually boiling.

In order that the eggs may *poach* freely, do not put more than eight or ten at a time into the same large saucepan; better even *poach* them six at a time, for then the *poaching* will be effected more equally.

As soon as the eggs are in the water, let the water simmer only. The egg is *poached* when the white has enveloped the yolk, reassuming, as it were, the form of a raw egg, and when it may be touched without breaking. The usual time allowed for *poaching* is three minutes.

Remove the eggs by means of a skimmer; dip them into cold water, and put them back into moderately warm water slightly salted until ready to serve.

412—THE COOKING OF MOLLET EGGS   *La Cuisson des Oeufs Mollets*

These must be strictly fresh. The *mollet* eggs are used in the same way as *poached* eggs, and their quality and consistency are nearly alike. While the *poached* egg is prepared quicker without its shell, the *mollet* egg is barely hardened enough to handle, but is cooked in its shell, and must be peeled at once after running cold water over the cooked egg. While the egg white is congealed enough to make the handling possible, the yolk is so soft as to make the task difficult. To make the cooking even use a colander perforated with large holes, whereby they may be plunged into and withdrawn from the water together. Keep the water boiling; plunge the eggs into the water as directed; leave them to simmer from four to six minutes from the time the water has regained the boiling-point; drain, run cold water over them, and shell the eggs carefully. Keep them in moderately-salted hot water until ready to serve.

413—THE DISHING OF POACHED MOLLET EGGS
Le Service des Oeufs Pochés et Mollets

There are many ways of doing this, viz.:—

On thick croutons of toast, slightly hollowed in the center, and fried in clarified butter (175). Their shape is oval for *poached* eggs, and round for *mollet* eggs, the latter being generally served standing on end.

On little *feuilletés* for *poached* eggs, on *feuilletés* in the shape of indented crowns, or in small patties for *mollet* eggs.

In borders of *forcemeat* or other preparations, the kind of which is indicated by the name of the particular egg-preparation. These borders are laid on the dish by means of a pastry-bag or by hand; they are either oval or round, plain or scalloped, poached or oven-browned, according to the nature of the preparation used.

On *tartlet-crusts* which are garnished so as to be in keeping with the method of dressing the eggs.

Remarks.—Poached or *mollet* eggs, when served on fried croutons, *feuilletés,* or *tartlets,* should, before being placed on these, be covered with sauce. Also before being treated with sauce they should be well drained.

Having given the general outlines of the procedure, I shall now pass on to the particular recipes, stating them briefly, and reminding the reader that all of them apply equally to *poached* and *mollet* eggs. Thus "Poached Eggs Mireille" stands for *"Poached* or *Mollet* Eggs Mireille."

414—ARGENTEUIL POACHED EGGS   *Oeufs Pochés Argenteuil*
Garnish the bottom of some *tartlet-crusts* with asparagus cut into pieces and cooked, and six green asparagus-tips, about one and one-half inches in length, arranged like a star. Place an egg, coated with cream sauce (79) mixed with half its volume of asparagus *purée,* upon each *tartlet.*

415—POACHED EGGS A L'AURORE   *Oeufs Pochés à l'Aurore*
Coat the eggs with Aurora sauce (60), and dish them on oval *feuilletés* if *poached,* or upright on *feuilletés* in the shape of rings if *mollet* eggs.

416—POACHED EGGS IN THE CRADLE   *Oeufs Pochés en Berceau*
Bake some fine large Irish potatoes in the oven. Cut each potato in half, lengthwise, with the point of a small knife, and remove the pulp. Emptied, the halved potatoes resemble little cradles. Coat the interior of each with a fine minced chicken mixed with cream, and place an egg coated with Aurora sauce (60) in each.

417—BOHEMIAN POACHED EGGS   *Oeufs Pochés à la Bohemienne*
Garnish the bottom of some *tartlet-crusts* with a *salpicon* of *foie-gras* and truffles mixed with a few tablespoons of the following sauce:—For six eggs, dissolve one teaspoon of white-meat *glaze* (15); add half a teaspoon of truffle *essence,* and finish with a lump of butter about the size of a pigeon's egg. Take enough of this sauce to hold together the *salpicon;* coat the eggs with Hungarian sauce (85), and place one upon each garnished *tartlet.*

418—BOILDIEU POACHED EGGS   *Oeufs Pochés Boildieu*
Garnish the *tartlets* with a white-chicken-meat, *foie-gras,* and truffle *salpicon* held together with poultry velouté (26). Coat the eggs with a reduced and thickened poultry gravy.

419—BRUSSELS POACHED EGGS   *Oeufs Pochés à la Bruxelloise*
Garnish some *tartlet-crusts* with *braised,* minced endives thickened with cream. Place an egg, coated with cream sauce (79), upon

each; sprinkle moderately with rusk *raspings*, and set to *glaze* quickly in a hot oven.

420—CLAMART POACHED EGGS   *Oeufs Pochés à la Clamart*

Garnish some *tartlet-crusts* with small, green peas, cooked à la française (2193), and mixed with finely shredded lettuce with the peas. Place an egg, coated with cream sauce (79) which has been finished with fresh-pea butter (348), upon each.

421—COLBERT POACHED EGGS   *Oeufs Pochés Colbert*

Garnish some *tartlet-crusts* with a *macédoine* mixed with Béchamel (28). Place a plain poached egg upon each, and serve Colbert butter (141), separately, with the tartlets.

422—COUNTESS POACHED EGGS   *Oeufs Pochés à la Comtesse*

Garnish some *tartlet-crusts* with white asparagus *purée*. Place an egg coated with Allemande sauce (27) upon each, and sprinkle with very black chopped truffles.

423—GRAND DUKE POACHED EGGS   *Oeufs Pochés Grand Duc*

There are two methods of procedure:—(*a*) Place the eggs on large fried croutons, with a nice slice of truffle on each; arrange them in a circle round the dish, coat with Mornay sauce (91), and set to *glaze* in a hot oven. On removing the dish from the oven, put in the center a garnish composed of asparagus tips and a small bunch of the latter, very green and cooked. (*b*) Prepare a *croustade* crust in a spring-form pan, the size of which must be in proportion to the number of eggs to be served. Arrange the eggs in a circle in the *croustade*, coat them with Mornay sauce (91), and set to *glaze* in a hot oven. On withdrawing the *croustade* from the oven, garnish its center with asparagus tips and a small bunch of asparagus.

424—MAINTENON POACHED EGGS   *Oeufs Pochés Maintenon*

Garnish some *tartlet-crusts* with a Soubise à la Béchamel (104), slightly thickened by reduction. Coat the eggs with Mornay sauce (91), sprinkle with grated cheese, and place them in the crusts by means of a spatula.

Set to *glaze* in a hot oven, and, on withdrawing the dish from the oven, surround the crusts with a ribbon of melted meat-*glaze* (15).

425—MASSENA POACHED EGGS   *Oeufs Pochés Masséna*

Heat some medium-sized artichoke-bottoms in butter. Slightly hollow them, if necessary, and garnish each with a tablespoon of Béarnaise sauce (62). Place an egg, coated with tomato sauce (29), upon each artichoke-bottom; then place a slice of *poached* marrow upon each egg, and a little chopped parsley upon each slice.

426—MIREILLE POACHED EGGS   *Oeufs Pochés Mireille*

Slightly press some saffroned pilaff rice (2255) in buttered *tartlet* moulds.

Prepare as many pieces of toast of the same size as the *tartlets,* and fry them in oil. Place an egg, coated with cream sauce (79), finished with saffron, upon each. Turn the rice-*tartlets* out of the moulds, and arrange them in a circle on a dish, alternating them with the eggs on toast; put a teaspoon of chopped tomatoes, stewed in butter and kept rather thick, upon each rice-*tartlet.*

427—MORNAY POACHED EGGS   *Oeufs Pochés Mornay*

Coat the eggs with Mornay sauce (91), and sprinkle with grated Gruyère and Parmesan cheese mixed with fine bread crumbs. Carefully transfer the eggs to pieces of toast fried in oil. Arrange them in a circle on a dish, sprinkle each egg with a few drops of melted butter, and set to *glaze* quickly in a hot oven.

428—POACHED EGGS D'ORSAY   *Oeufs Pochés D'Orsay*

Place the eggs upon toast fried in butter. Arrange them in a circle on a dish, and coat them with Châteaubriand sauce (71).

429—ROSSINI POACHED EGGS   *Oeufs Pochés Rossini*

Garnish some *tartlet-crusts,* each with a slice of *foie gras* (raw if possible) seasoned, dredged with flour, and fried in butter. Place an egg, coated with thickened veal gravy (41) with Madeira, on each *tartlet,* and complete by means of a large slice of very black truffle on each egg.

430—SEVIGNE POACHED EGGS   *Oeufs Pochés Sévigné*

Prepare some thin large bread *croutons;* fry them in clarified butter (175), and stuff them with minced *braised* lettuce. Place an egg on each stuffed *crouton;* coat with *velouté* (26) mixed with poultry *essence;* arrange in a circle on a dish, and complete with a ring of very black truffle on each egg.

431—VICTORIA POACHED EGGS   *Oeufs Pochés Victoria*

Garnish some *tartlet-crusts* with a *salpicon* made from three oz. of spiny or Rock lobster meat and one-half oz. of truffles, mixed with three tablespoons of Diplomate sauce (82). Place an egg, coated with the Diplomate sauce, on each *tartlet*. Arrange, and set to *glaze* in a hot oven.

432—POACHED EGGS WITH RED WINE *Oeufs Pochés au Vin Rouge*

These eggs may either be *poached* in red wine, or in the ordinary way.

In the first case, the wine used for *poaching* may serve to prepare the red wine or Bordelaise sauce (32). In either case, the eggs are served on oval thick *croutons*, slightly hollowed and fried in butter; they are coated with the sauce, after having been prepared, and they are quickly *glazed.*

433—HARD-BOILED EGGS *Oeufs Durs*

Boiling eggs hard may seem an insignificant matter, but, like the other methods of procedure, it is, in reality, of some importance, and should be effected in a given period of time. If, for a special purpose, they have to be just done, it is pointless and even harmful to cook them beyond a certain time-limit, seeing that any excess in the cooking only makes them tough, and the whites particularly so, owing to their albuminous nature. In order to boil many eggs uniformly, they should be put into a colander with large holes, whereby they may be plunged at the same moment of time into the boiling water. From the time the water begins to boil, eight minutes should be allowed in the case of medium-sized eggs, and ten minutes in the case of larger ones; but these times should never be exceeded. As soon as they are done drain the eggs and dip them in cold water, and then shell them carefully.

434—CAREME HARD-BOILED EGGS *Oeufs Durs Carème.*

Have ready beforehand a *timbale* crust (2394), somewhat shallow.

For six hard-boiled eggs, slice four artichoke-bottoms of medium size, and cook them in butter; cut some truffles into slices, allowing four slices to each egg, and cut up the eggs into slices about one-half inch thick. Prepare also in advance one-half pint of Nantua sauce (95).

Garnish the crust with alternate layers of sliced artichoke-bottoms, egg-slices, and sliced truffles. Finish with a coating of sauce and a ring of sliced truffles.

Serve the crust on a napkin.

435—CHIMAY HARD-BOILED EGGS   *Oeufs Durs Chimay*

Cut the eggs, lengthwise, in two. Remove the yolks, pound them into a paste, and add an equal quantity of dry *Duxelle* (223). Fill the empty whites with the preparation; place them on a buttered *gratin-dish;* cover them with Mornay sauce (91); sprinkle with grated cheese; pour a few drops of melted butter on the sauce, and set to *glaze* in a hot oven.

436—HARD-BOILED EGGS IN CROQUETTES

Oeufs Durs en Croquettes

Cut the eggs into small dice (white and yolks). For six eggs add five oz. of cooked mushrooms and one oz. of truffles, cut in dice.

Thicken the whole with one-quarter pint of reduced Béchamel (28), and spread on a plate to cool.

When cold, divide the preparation into portions weighing about two oz.; roll these portions into balls on a floured bread board, and then shape them like eggs. Dip them into an *anglaise* (174), taking care to cover them well with it, and then roll them in fine and fresh bread-crumbs, letting this operation permit the perfecting of the shape. Put them into hot fat seven or eight minutes before serving; drain, salt moderately, place on a napkin, with a center garnish of very green, fried parsley, and send a cream sauce (79) to the table with them.

437—HARD-BOILED EGGS IN RISSOLES   *Oeufs Durs en Rissoles*

Make a preparation of eggs, as for the croquettes, using a little more sauce. Roll some puff-paste trimmings (2366) to a thickness of one-quarter inch, and stamp it with a round scalloped cutter two and one-half inches in diameter.

Place a small tablespoon of the preparation in the middle of each piece of paste; moisten slightly all round, and make the *rissoles* by folding the outside edges of the paste over one another to look like a closed purse, taking care to press them well together, completely enclosing the preparation. Treat them *à l'anglaise;* put them into hot fat eight minutes before serving, and place on a napkin, with a center garnish of parsley.

438—EGGS WITH TRIPE   *Oeufs à la Tripe*

For six eggs, finely mince two onions, and stew them in butter, without letting them brown. Add one-half pint of Béchamel sauce

(28), and set to cook gently for ten minutes. A few minutes before serving add the eggs, cut into large slices, to the sauce.

Serve in a *timbale*.

439—EGGS WITH TRIPE, BOURGEOISE   *Oeufs à la Tripe, Bourgeoise*

For six eggs chop up two large onions and stew them in butter without browning. Sprinkle them with one-half oz. of flour, moisten with one pint of boiling milk, and season with salt, pepper, and nutmeg.

Set to cook, gently, for twenty minutes; rub through a fine sieve or hair sieve, and transfer the mixture to a saucepan, and heat it well. Serve the eggs, which should be quartered, in a *timbale*, and cover them with the mixture of onions, very hot.

440—EGGS IN COCOTTE   *Oeufs en Cocotte*

The *poaching* of eggs *en cocotte* is done in the *bain-marie* (water-bath).

Cocottes for eggs, which may be replaced by little china cases or ramekins, are a kind of small saucepan in earthenware, in porcelain, or in silver, provided with a little handle. The time generally allowed for the cooking or *poaching* of eggs in this way is ten minutes, but this time is subject to variations either way. In order to hasten the process I should advise the warming of the *cocottes* before putting in the eggs.

Method of Procedure.—Having garnished the *cocottes* and broken the eggs into them, as directed in the recipes given hereafter, set them in a saucepan and pour in enough boiling water to reach within one-half inch of the brims of the *cocottes*. Place in the oven and cover, just leaving sufficient opening for the steam to escape.

The eggs are done when the whites are almost set and the yolks are glossy. After having properly wiped the *cocottes*, serve them on a napkin or on a fancy dish-paper.

441—EGGS IN COCOTTE WITH CHAMBERTIN
Oeufs en Cocotte au Chambertin

Prepare a red-wine sauce with Chambertin. Fill the *cocottes*, one-third full, with this sauce. Set to boil on a corner of the stove; break the eggs into the boiling sauce, season with a few grains of salt, and put the *cocottes*, one by one, into a saucepan containing the necessary amount of boiling water.

Poach as directed, and set to *glaze* quickly at the last moment.

442—EGGS IN COCOTTE WITH CREAM *Oeufs en Cocotte à la Crème*

This preparation constitutes the radical type of this series of eggs, and, for a long time, was the only one in use. Heat the *cocottes* beforehand; pour a tablespoon of boiling cream into each, followed by an egg, broken; season, and add two little lumps of butter, the size of peas. Place the *cocottes* in a pan with water, and *poach* as before.

443—EGGS IN COCOTTE JEANNETTE *Oeufs en Cocotte à la Jeannette*

Garnish the bottom and the sides of the *cocottes* with a thickness of one-third inch of chicken-*forcemeat* (194) with cream, mixed with a fifth of its volume of *foie gras*. Break the egg over the center, season, and *poach* in the usual way. When about to serve, surround the eggs with a ribbon of poultry *velouté* (26).

444—EGGS IN COCOTTE WITH GRAVY *Oeufs en Cocotte au Jus*

Break the eggs into buttered *cocottes*. Season, *poach,* and, when about to serve, surround the yolks with a ribbon of reduced veal gravy (42).

445—EGGS IN COCOTTE LORRAINE *Oeufs en Cocotte à la Lorraine*

Put a teaspoon of bacon, cut into dice and fried, into each *cocotte,* also three thin slices of Gruyère cheese and one tablespoon of boiling cream. Break the eggs, season, and *poach* in the usual way.

446—EGGS IN COCOTTE MARAICHERE

Oeufs en Cocotte à la Maraichère

Garnish the bottom and sides of the *cocottes* with cooked spinach, chopped and pressed, and sorrel and lettuce leaves, both of which should be stewed in butter. Break the eggs, season, *poach* in the usual way, and, when about to send the eggs to the table, drop a fine chervil *pluche* on each yolk.

447—EGGS IN COCOTTE WITH MORELS *Oeufs en Cocotte aux Morilles*

Garnish the bottom and sides of the *cocottes* with minced morels (French mushrooms) fried in butter and thickened with a little reduced half-*glaze* (23). Break the eggs, season, *poach,* and surround the yolks with a ribbon of half-*glaze* when serving.

448—EGGS IN COCOTTE SOUBISE *Oeufs en Cocotte à la Soubise*

Garnish the bottom and sides of the *cocottes* with a coating of thick (104) Soubise *purée*. Break the eggs, season, and *poach*. When serving, surround the yolks with a ribbon of melted meat-*glaze*.

449—MOULDED EGGS   *Oeufs Moulés*

These form a very decorative dish, but the time required to prepare them being comparatively long, *poached, mollet,* and other
kinds of eggs are generally preferred instead. They are made in variously shaped moulds, decorated according to the nature of the
preparation, and the eggs are broken into them direct, or they may
be added in the form of scrambled eggs, together with raw eggs
poached in a *bain-marie* (water-bath).

Whatever be the method of preparation, the moulds should always be liberally buttered. The usual time allowed for the *poaching*
of the eggs in moulds is from ten to twelve minutes, but when withdrawn from the *bain-marie* it is well to let the moulds stand awhile
permitting them to congeal and facilitate the turning out of the
moulded eggs.

Turn out the moulds on small pieces of toast or *tartlets,* and
arrange these in a circle round the dish.

450—MOULDED EGGS CARIGNAN   *Oeufs Moulés à la Carignan*

Butter some *Madeleine-moulds,* shaped like elongated shells, and
garnish them with a thin coating of chicken-stuffing (189) or crayfish
butter (147). Break the eggs in the center of the *forcemeat;* season,
place carefully in a *bain-marie* (water-bath), and *poach,* with cover
on, in the oven, leaving a small opening for the escape of the steam.
Turn out the moulds on toast cut to the same shape and fried in
butter; arrange them on the dish, and coat with a Châteaubriand
sauce (71).

451—MOULDED EGGS DUCHESSE   *Oeufs Moulés à la Duchesse*

Butter some *baba-moulds;* garnish the bottom of each with a large
slice of truffle; break an egg into each, and *poach* in the *bain-marie.*
Turn out the moulds on to little fluted patty cakes made from
Duchesse potatoes (221) and browned in the oven after having been
brushed with egg.

Arrange up in the form of a crown, and coat with a thickened
veal gravy (41).

452—MOULDED EGGS GALLI-MARIE   *Oeufs Moulés Galli-Marié*

For four people: Prepare five scrambled eggs, keeping them very
soft; add three raw, beaten eggs and one teaspoon of pimento, cut
into dice. Mould this preparation in four little shallow *cassolettes,*
well buttered, and *poach* in the *bain-marie* (water-bath).

Have ready and hot as many cooked artichoke-bottoms as there are *cassolettes;* the former should have had their edges fluted. Have also ready a "Rice à la Grecque" (2253).

Garnish the artichoke-bottoms with the rice; turn out the *casso-lettes* upon the latter; arrange on a dish, and cover with highly-seasoned and buttered Béchamel sauce (28). Put the dish in a hot oven, so as to *glaze* quickly, and serve immediately.

453—MOULDED EGGS MORTEMART   *Oeufs Moulés à la Mortemart*

Scramble five eggs, keeping them soft, and add three raw, beaten eggs. Butter some shallow, *timbale* moulds; garnish their bottoms with a fine slice of truffle, and fill them with the preparation of eggs. *Poach* in a *bain-marie* (water-bath).

Turn out each mould on a *tartlet*-crust, garnished with mushroom *purée* à la crème (2079), and arrange in a circle on a round dish. Send a sauceboat containing some melted and buttered meat-*glaze* (15) to the table with the eggs.

454—NEAPOLITAN MOULDED EGGS   *Oeufs Moulés à la Napolitain*

Make a preparation consisting of scrambled eggs and Parmesan cheese, keeping it very soft; add, per five scrambled eggs, two raw eggs. Fill some little, well-buttered *brioche-moulds* with this preparation, and *poach* in the *bain-marie*. As soon as their contents are properly set, turn out the moulds on to a buttered *gratin* dish. sprinkle with grated Parmesan cheese, and coat the eggs with reduced and buttered half-*glaze* (23), well saturated with tomato.

455—MOULDED EGGS PALERMITAINE   *Oeufs Moulés Palermitaine*

Butter some *baba-moulds;* garnish the bottoms with a slice of truffle, and sprinkle the sides with very red, chopped cured tongue. Put the moulds on ice for a while, in order that the tongue may set in the butter. Break an egg into each mould, season, and *poach* in the *bain-marie* (water-bath). Turn out the moulds on *tartlet*-crusts garnished with macaroni with cream.

456—MOULDED EGGS POLIGNAC   *Oeufs Moulés Polignac*

Butter some *baba-moulds,* and garnish the bottoms with a slice of truffle. Break an egg into each; season, and *poach* in a *bain-marie.*

Turn out the moulds upon little round pieces of toast; arrange them in a circle on a dish, and coat the eggs with Maître-d'Hôtel butter (150), the latter being dissolved and mixed with three table-spoons of melted meat-*glaze* (15) per every one-quarter lb. of its weight.

457—MOULDED EGGS PRINCESS   *Oeufs Moulés Princesse*

Butter some narrow and deep *dariole-moulds;* garnish their bottoms with a slice of very black truffle, and their sides with a very thin coating of chicken *forcemeat* (195).

Make a preparation of scrambled eggs, asparagus-tips, and truffles cut into dice, keeping them very soft, and add to raw, beaten eggs in the proportion of one raw egg to every four scrambled.

Fill the moulds, two-thirds full, with this preparation; cover the eggs with a coating of *forcemeat,* and *poach* in a *bain-marie* (water-bath) for twelve minutes.

Turn out the moulds upon little, round pieces of toast; set these in a circle on a dish, and surround them with a ribbon of clear poultry *velouté* (26). Or the *velouté* may be sent to the table separately, in a sauceboat.

458—MOULDED EGGS PRINTANIER   *Oeufs Moulés Printanier*

Butter some *hexagonal* moulds, and garnish them, *Chartreuse*-fashion, with cut-up, cooked vegetables, varying the colors. Break an egg into each mould; season, and *poach* in a *bain-marie*. Turn out the moulds upon little, round pieces of toast; arrange these in a circle on a dish, and pour in their midst a cream sauce finished by means of a *Printanier* butter (157) with herbs, in the proportion of one oz. of butter to one-quarter pint of sauce.

459—SCRAMBLED EGGS   *Oeufs Brouillés*

This dish is undoubtedly the finest of all egg-preparations, provided the eggs are not over-cooked, and they be kept soft and creamy.

Scrambled eggs are mostly served in silver *timbales,* but, in certain cases, they may also be served in special little *croustades,* in little receptacles made from hollowed *brioches,* or in *tartlet*-crusts. Formerly, it was customary to garnish scrambled eggs served in a silver *timbale* with small, variously-shaped pieces of toast, or with small scraps of puff-paste, cooked without browning, and shaped like crescents, diamonds, rings, *palmettes,* etc. This method has something to recommend it, and may always be adopted. In old cookery, scrambled eggs were sanctioned only when cooked in a *bain-marie* (water-bath). This measure certainly ensured their being properly cooked, but it lengthened the procedure. The latter may therefore be shortened by cooking the eggs the usual way, in a pan in direct contact with the fire; but in this case the heat must be moderate, in order that, the process of cooking being progressive and gradual, perfect incorporation of the eggs (effecting the smoothness of the preparation) may result.

460—METHOD OF SCRAMBLING EGGS

Préparation des Oeufs Brouillès

For six eggs, slightly heat one oz. of butter in a thick-bottomed saucepan. Add the six eggs, beaten moderately, together with a large pinch of salt and a little pepper, place the pan on a moderate fire, and stir constantly with a wooden spoon, taking care to avoid cooking too quickly, which, by instantaneously solidifying the egg-molecules, would cause lumps to form in the mass—a thing which, above all, should be guarded against.

When the eggs have acquired the proper consistency, and are still smooth and creamy, take the saucepan off the fire, and finish the preparation by means of one and one-half oz. of butter (divided into small quantities) and three tablespoons of cream. Only whisk the eggs to be scrambied when absolutely necessary.

N.B.—Having given the method of procedure, which is unalterable for scrambled eggs, I shall now pass on to the various garnishes suited to this kind of dish. The quantities I give are those required for six scrambled eggs.

461—SCRAMBLED EGGS A LA BOHEMIENNE

Oeufs Brouillés à la Bohémienne

Take one large brioche for every two eggs. Remove the tops of the brioches, and the inside crumb from the remaining portions, so as to form cases. Add one-half oz. of *foie gras* to the scrambled eggs, and half as much truffles, cut into dice, for every two eggs. Fill the emptied brioche cases with this preparation, and place a slice of truffle coated with meat-*glaze* (15) on each.

462—SCRAMBLED EGGS WITH MUSHROOMS

Oeufs Brouillés aux Champignons

Add to the scrambled eggs one oz. of cooked mushrooms cut into dice, or raw mushrooms, minced and *sautéd* in butter, for every two eggs.

Serve in a *timbale;* put a fine, cooked, and grooved mushroom in the middle, and surround with a crown of sliced mushrooms, also cooked.

463—SCRAMBLED EGGS HUNTERS' STYLE

Oeufs Brouillés Chasseur.

Dress the scrambled eggs in a *timbale*. Make a well in the middle, and place in it a garnish of one fine chicken liver, *sautéd,* per every two eggs. Sprinkle a pinch of chervil and tarragon on the garnish, and surround with a ribbon of chasseur sauce (33).

464—SCRAMBLED EGGS CHATILLON   *Oeufs Brouillés Chatillon*

Place the eggs in a *timbale,* and place a garnish of mushrooms in the center. The mushrooms should first be minced raw, and then *sautéd* in butter. Sprinkle a pinch of chopped parsley on the garnish, and surround with a ribbon of melted meat-*glaze* (15). Border the whole, close to the sides of the *timbale,* with small crescents of puff-paste (2360), baked lightly.

465—SCRAMBLED EGGS WITH SHRIMPS

Oeufs Brouillés aux Crevettes

Serve the scrambled eggs in a silver *timbale*. Place a little mound of shrimp tails bound with a few tablespoons of shrimp sauce (80) in the middle, and surround with a ribbon of the same.

466—SCRAMBLED EGGS WITH HERBS

Oeufs Brouillés aux Fines Herbes

Add to the scrambled eggs a tablespoon of parsley, chervil *pluches,* chives, and tarragon leaves in equal quantities and chopped.

467—SCRAMBLED EGGS WITH CHEESE   *Oeufs Brouillés au Fromage*

Break the eggs, beat them, season, and add, for every two eggs, one-half oz. of fresh grated Gruyère cheese, and as much grated Parmesan. Cook the eggs in the usual way or a very moderate fire, in order to keep them creamy.

468—SCRAMBLED EGGS GRAND-MERE   *Oeufs Brouillés Grand-Mère*

Add to the scrambled eggs a tablespoon of little bread crusts, cut into dice, fried in clarified butter (175), and prepared in time to be added to the eggs very hot. Put in a *timbale* with a pinch of chopped parsley in the middle.

469—SCRAMBLED EGGS GEORGETTE   *Oeufs Brouillés Georgette*

Bake three large Irish potatoes, or six smaller ones, in the oven. Open them by means of an incision on their tops, take out the pulp with the handle of a spoon, and keep the remaining shells hot. Prepare the scrambled eggs in the usual way, and finish them away from the fire with one and one-half oz. of crayfish butter (147), and eight or ten shelled crayfish tails. Garnish the potato shells with this preparation, and serve on a napkin.

470—SCRAMBLED EGGS FOR HOT LUNCHEON HORS-D'ŒUVRE

Oeufs Brouillés pour Hors-d'œuvre du Lunch Chaud

I only give one recipe of this kind, but the series may be extended at will without involving much deep research, since all that is needed for the purpose of variety is the modification of the garnish and a change in the *soufflé* preparation. The method of procedure remains the same. Prepare the scrambled eggs, and garnish them as fancy may suggest. Also make a "Soufflé with Parmesan Cheese" (2295a).

Put the scrambled eggs into a large *tartlet-crust,* bake without browning, and fill them only two-thirds full. Cover with the *soufflé* preparation, taking care to make it peak in a mound above the *tartlets;* place these on a tray, *poach* quickly in a hot oven, and *glaze* at the same time.

471—SCRAMBLED EGGS WITH MORELS

Oeufs Brouillés aux Morilles

Add to the scrambled eggs some minced morels (type of mushroom), *sautéd* in butter and seasoned. Serve in *timbales,* and place a fine, cooked morel in the center of each.

472—SCRAMBLED EGGS WITH SMALL MUSHROOMS

Oeufs Brouillés aux Mousserons

Proceed as for (471).

473—SCRAMBLED EGGS ORLOFF   *Oeufs Brouillés Orloff*

Break the eggs, beat them, and add a little fresh, thick cream. Cook them in the usual way, and add three crayfishes tails per every two eggs. Serve in little ramekins and place a fine slice of truffle in each, and arrange these upon a napkin on a dish.

474—SCRAMBLED EGGS PIEDMONT *Oeufs Brouillés à la Piemontise*

Add to the scrambled eggs, for every two eggs, one-half oz. of grated Parmesan cheese and a teaspoon of raw, grated, Piedmont truffles. Serve in a *timbale,* and garnish with a fine crown of sliced truffles of the same kind as the above.

475—SCRAMBLED EGGS PORTUGUESE

Oeufs Brouillés à la Portugaise

Serve the eggs in a *timbale,* and place, in the middle, some fine, chopped tomatoes, seasoned and *sautéed* in butter. Sprinkle a pinch of chopped parsley on the tomatoes, and surround with a ribbon of meat-*glaze* (15).

476—SCRAMBLED EGGS PRINCESS MARY

Oeufs Brouillés Princess Mary

Prepare some small *timbales* in *dariole-moulds* from puff-paste scraps (2366), and bake them without browning; also some little covers of puff-paste, stamped out with a scalloped fancy-cutter, two inches in diameter. Set the covers on a tray, brush them with egg slightly, place on each a cover of scalloped paste, and leave this uncolored. Bake the *timbales* and the covers in a moderate oven.

Make a preparation of scrambled eggs and Parmesan cheese; add to this, away from the fire, two tablespoons of reduced *velouté* (242) with truffle *essence* and truffles cut into dice.

Garnish the *timbales,* put a cover on each, and serve on a napkin.

477—SCRAMBLED EGGS RACHEL   *Oeufs Brouillés Rachel*

Add some *truffles,* cut into dice, and some asparagus-tips to the scrambled eggs. Place on a *timbale;* put a fine little bunch of asparagus-tips in the middle, and surround with a crown of sliced truffles.

478—SCRAMBLED EGGS REINE MARGOT

Oeufs Brouillés Reine Margot

Prepare the scrambled eggs in the usual way, and finish them with the necessary quantity of almond butter. Place this preparation in small *tartlet-crusts,* baked without browning, and surround the *tartlets* with a ribbon of Béchamel sauce (28), finished with pistachio butter (156), the ribbon of sauce being close up to the edge of the *tartlets.*

480—SCRAMBLED EGGS ROTHSCHILD   *Oeufs Brouillés Rothschild*

Finely pound the remains of six crayfish (cooked in *Mirepoix*) the tails of which have been put aside, and add, little by little, two tablespoons of thick cream. Rub through a very fine sieve.

Add this crayfish cream to the six beaten eggs; season, and cook on a moderate fire with the object of obtaining a smooth, soft, and creamy preparation. Serve in a *timbale* and garnish, first with a small bunch of asparagus-tips placed in the center of the eggs, second with crayfish tails arranged in a circle round the asparagus, and third with large slices of very black truffles arranged in a crown around the crayfish tails.

481—SCRAMBLED EGGS WITH TRUFFLES
Oeufs Brouillés aux Truffles

Add one tablespoonful of truffles, cooked in Madeira and cut into dice, to the scrambled eggs. Place these in a *timbale,* and garnish with a crown of sliced truffles.

Or place the preparation in *tartlet-crusts,* made from trimmings of puff-paste (2366) and bake without browning, with a large slice of truffle on the eggs, in each *tartlet.*

482—FRIED EGGS
Oeufs Frits

In the long series of egg-preparations, fried eggs are those which hold the least important place, for the fried eggs which are so commonly served at breakfast in England and America are really eggs *à la poêle.* The real fried egg is almost unknown in England and America. As a rule, the garnish given to this kind of eggs is served separately, while the latter are served, either on a napkin or on pieces of toast, with a little fried parsley laid in the middle of the dish.

483—THE PREPARATION OF FRIED EGGS
La Préparation des Oeufs Frits

Any fat, provided it be well purified, may be used for these eggs, but oil is the more customary frying medium. To cook these eggs properly, only one at a time should be dealt with.

Heat some oil in an open pan until it begins to smoke slightly; break the egg on a plate; season it, and let it slide into the pan. Then, with a wooden spoon, quickly cover up the yolk with the white, in order to keep the former soft.

Drain the egg on a piece of stretched linen, and proceed in the same way with the other eggs until the required quantity has been treated.

484—FRIED EGGS BORDELAISE
Oeufs Frits à la Bordelaise

Prepare as many halved tomatoes *à la Provençale* (2268) as there are eggs, adding a pinch of chopped shallots to each halved tomato. When cooked, garnish them with *cèpes,* finely minced and *sautéd* à la Bordelaise (2068); place a fried egg on each garnished half-tomato, and arrange them in a circle on a dish, with fried parsley in the middle.

485—HARVESTERS FRIED EGGS   *Oeufs Frits Moissoneur*

Fry as many *blanched* slices of bacon as there are eggs. Arrange in a circle on a dish, alternating the bacon with the eggs. Garnish the center with large peas, cooked with shredded lettuce and finely-sliced potatoes.

486—FRIED POACHED EGGS   *Oeufs Pochés Frits*

This kind is recommended, because it may be served with various garnishes—either vegetables of the same nature, a *macédoine,* vegetable *purées,* or various *cullises,* sauces in keeping with the eggs, artichoke-bottoms, mushrooms, morels, etc. (sliced and *sautéd* in butter), or tomato-*fondue,* etc.

After having properly drained and dried the *poached* eggs, which should have been prepared beforehand, dip them carefully in a Villeroy sauce (108), and arrange them, one by one, on a dish. When the sauce has set, pass the point of a small knife round the eggs to remove any excess of sauce; take them from the dish to dip them in an *anglaise* (174), and then roll them in very fine, fresh bread-crumbs.

Plunge them into very hot fat three or four minutes before serving; drain them on a piece of paper; salt slightly, arrange in a circle on a dish, and set the selected garnish in the center.

487—FRIED EGGS PORTUGUESE   *Oeufs Frits à la Portugaise*

Place each of the fried eggs upon a half-tomato *à la Portugaise* (2267), stuffed with rice after having been previously half-baked in the oven. Arrange in a circle on a dish, and garnish the center with chopped tomatoes *sautéd* in butter.

488—FRIED EGGS PROVENCALE   *Oeufs Frits à la Provençale*

Put each fried egg on a half-tomato on a large, thick slice of egg-plant, seasoned, rolled in flour, and fried in oil.

Set in a circle on a dish, with fried parsley in the center.

489—FRIED EGGS ROMAINE   *Oeufs Frits à la Romaine*

Place the eggs, fried in oil, on little, oval *subrics* (puffs) of spinach (2137). The preparation of spinach should have anchovy fillets, cut into dice, added to it.

490—FRIED EGGS VERDI *Oeufs Frits à la Verdi*

Cut six hard-boiled eggs lengthwise. Remove the yolks, pound them with two oz. of butter, and add two tablespoons of thick, cold Béchamel (28), two tablespoons of cooked herbs, and one table-spoonful of lean smoked ham, cooked and chopped. Garnish each half-white of egg with a good tablespoon of this preparation, and smooth it with the blade of a small knife, mounding it in such a way as to represent the other half of the egg. Dip each whole egg, thus formed, into an *anglaise,* and roll in fine, fresh bread-crumbs. Plunge in hot fat six minutes before serving, and place on a napkin, with fried parsley in the center. Send, separately, to the table a garnish composed of asparagus tips.

491—FRIED POACHED EGGS VILLEROY

Oeufs Pochés Frits à la Villeroy

Prepare the eggs, *poached* beforehand, as explained under (486). Fry them, and serve them on a napkin, with a garnish of fried parsley in the center.

Omelets

The procedure for omelets is at once very simple and very difficult, for tastes differ considerably in respect to their preparation. Some like them well done, others insist upon their being just done enough, while there are yet others who only enjoy them when they are almost liquid.

Nevertheless, the following conditions apply to all—namely, that there should be complete incorporation of the egg-molecules; that the whole mass should be smooth and soft; and that it should be borne in mind that an omelet is really scrambled eggs enclosed in a coating of coagulated egg.

I take as my standard an omelet consisting of three eggs, the seasoning of which comprises a small pinch of table-salt and a little pepper, and which requires one-half oz. of butter for its preparation. The quantities of garnishing ingredients given are based upon this standard.

492—THE PREPARATION OF OMELETS

La Préparation des Omelettes

Heat the butter in the omelet-pan, until it gives off the characteristic nutty smell. This will not only lend an exquisite taste to the omelet, but the degree of heat reached in order to produce the aroma will be found to ensure the perfect setting of the eggs.

Pour in the beaten and seasoned eggs, and stir briskly with a fork, in order to heat the whole mass evenly. If the omelet is to be filled inside, this ought to be done now, and then the omelet should be speedily rolled up and transferred to a dish, to be finished in accordance with the taste of the diner.

When the omelet is on the dish, a piece of butter may be quickly drawn across its surface, to make it glossy.

493—AGNES SOREL OMELET   *Omelette Agnes Sorel*

Fill the omelet with one tablespoon of mushrooms, minced and *sautéd* in butter. Roll it up, and transfer it to a dish.

Then lay eight small slices of very red smoked tongue upon it, letting their edges overlap; surround with a ribbon of veal gravy (42).

494—OMELET BRUXELLOISE   *Omelette à la Bruxelloise*

Fill the omelet with two tablespoons of braised endives, shredded and thickened with cream. Surround with a band of cream sauce (79).

495—OMELET WITH CEPES   *Omelette aux Cèpes*

Finely mince two oz. of *cèpes;* toss them in butter in an omelet-pan until they have acquired a brown color; add a pinch of chopped shallots, and toss them again for a moment.

Pour the eggs into the omelet-pan; make the omelet; put on a dish, and surround with a ribbon of half-*glaze* (23).

496—OMELET WITH MUSHROOMS   *Omelette aux Champignons*

Mince two oz. of raw mushrooms; toss them in butter in an omelet-pan; add the eggs, and make the omelet. Transfer it to a dish, lay three little cooked and grooved mushrooms upon it, and surround with a band of half-*glaze* (23).

497—OMELET CHOISY   *Omelette à la Choisy*

Fill the omelet with two tablespoons of *braised* lettuce; the latter should have been shredded and bound by means of cream sauce.

Roll and dish the omelet, and surround it with a thread of cream sauce (79).

498—OMELET CLAMART *Omelette à la Clamart*

Fill the omelet with two tablespoons of fresh peas, bound by means of butter and combined with a portion of the lettuce used in cooking them, finely shredded. Roll the omelet, make an opening lengthwise in the center, and fill the space with a tablespoon of fresh peas.

499—OMELET WITH CRUSTS *Omelette aux Croûtes*

Combine with the beaten and seasoned eggs two tablespoons of small crusts of bread, cut into dice, fried in clarified butter (175), and very hot.

Make the omelet very quickly.

500—OMELET WITH SPINACH *Omelette aux Epinards*

Fill the omelet with two tablespoons of spinach with cream, and surround with a band of cream sauce (79).

501.—OMELET FERMIERE *Omelette à la Fermière*

Add to the beaten and seasoned eggs one tablespoon of very lean, cooked ham cut into dice. Pour the eggs into the omelet-pan, and cook them quickly, taking care to keep them very soft. Let the outside harden slightly; tilt into the dish after the manner of a pancake, and sprinkle the surface with a pinch of chopped parsley.

502—OMELET WITH HERBS *Omelette aux Fines Herbes*

Add to the eggs one tablespoon of parsley, chervil, chive, and tarragon leaves, all to be finely chopped and almost equally apportioned.

Make the omelet in the usual way.

503—OMELET WITH SQUASH BLOSSOMS

Omelette aux Fleurs de Courge

Add to the eggs one and one-half oz. of the blossoms of freshly-plucked and young squash or pumpkin plants; shred and cook them, and add a pinch of chopped parsley. Surround the omelet with a ribbon of tomato sauce (29).

N.B.—This omelet may be cooked with oil, as well as with butter.

504—OMELET WITH CHICKEN LIVERS

Omelette aux Foies de Volaille

Fill the omelet with two tablespoons of chicken's liver, which should be cut into dice or finely sliced, seasoned, quickly *sautéd* in butter, and bound with half-*glaze* (23). Put the omelet on a dish, make an opening lengthwise in the center, and place one tablespoon of chicken's liver, prepared as above, in the opening. Sprinkle with chopped parsley, and surround the omelet with a band of half-*glaze* (23).

505—OMELET WITH ARTICHOKE-BOTTOMS
Omelette aux Fonds d'Artichauts

Finely mince two small artichoke-bottoms (raw if possible), season them, and slightly brown them in butter. Add the beaten and seasoned eggs, and make the omelet in the usual way.

506—OMELET WITH YOUNG SHOOTS OF HOPS
Omelette aux Jets de Houblons

Fill the omelet with two tablespoons of young shoots of hops, mixed with cream, and finish it in the usual way. Open it slightly along the top, and garnish with a few young shoots of hops put aside for the purpose.

The omelet may be surrounded with a ribbon of cream sauce (79), but this is optional.

507—OMELET LYONNAISE *Omelette à la Lyonnaise*

Finely mince half an onion, and cook it with butter in an omelet-pan, letting it brown slightly. Add the eggs, with which a large pinch of chopped parsley has been mixed, and make the omelet in the usual way.

508—OMELET MAXIM *Omelette Maxim*

Make the omelet in the usual way. Lay upon it alternate rows of crayfish tails and slices of truffle. Surround the omelet with a fine border of frogs' legs "*sautéd* à la Meunière," seasoned raw, rolled in flour, and *sautéd* in butter until quite cooked and a golden brown.

509—OMELET WITH MORELS *Omelette aux Morilles*

Mince and toss in butter two oz. of very firm morels (French mushrooms). Two should be put aside, which, after having been cut in two, lengthwise, and *sautéd* with the others, should be placed on a dish when the omelet is about to be made. Having placed it on a dish, put the four *sautéd* and reserved pieces of morels upon it, and surround it with a band of half-*glaze* (23).

510—OMELET MOUSSELINE *Omelette Mousseline*

Beat the yolks of three eggs in a bowl with a small pinch of salt and a tablespoon of very thick cream. Add the three whites, beaten to a stiff froth, and pour this into a wide omelet-pan containing one' oz. of very hot butter. *Sauté* the omelet, tossing it very quickly, and taking care to turn the outside edges of the preparation constantly towards the center; when the whole mass seems uniformly set, roll the omelet up quickly. This omelet should be served immediately.

510a—OMELET WITH SMALL MUSHROOMS

Omelette aux Mousserons

Mince two oz. of very fresh *mousserons* (a kind of mushroom); toss them in butter in the omelet-pan; add the eggs mixed with a pinch of chopped parsley; make the omelet, put it on a dish, and surround it with a ribbon of half-*glaze* (23).

511—OMELET NANTUA *Omelette à la Nantua*

Add to the omelet six little crayfishes' tails or shrimps, each of which must be cut into three, and the whole mixed with a little Nantua sauce (95). Put two fine crayfishes' or shrimps' tails on the omelet, making them touch at their thicker ends, and surround with a ribbon of Nantua sauce (95).

512—OMELET PARMENTIER *Omelette Parmentier*

Add a pinch of chopped parsley to the eggs, and, when about to pour the latter into the omelet-pan, add two tablespoons of potato cut into dice, seasoned, *sautéd* in butter, and very hot. Make the omelet in the usual way.

513—OMELET PAYSANNE *Omelette à la Paysanne*

Frizzle with butter, in the omelet-pan, two oz. of bacon cut into dice. Add to the eggs one tablespoon of finely-sliced potatoes *sautéd* in butter, one-half tablespoon of shredded sorrel stewed in butter, and a pinch of chopped chervil.

Pour the whole over the bacon-dice; cook the eggs quickly, keeping them soft; turn the omelet after the manner of a pancake, and tilt it immediately on to a round dish.

514—OMELET WITH ASPARAGUS TIPS

Omelette aux Pointes d'Asperges

Add one and one-half tablespoons of *blanched* asparagus-tips, stewed in butter, to the omelet. Having placed the omelet on a dish, open it along the middle, and lay a nice little bundle of asparagus-tips in the opening.

515—OMELET PROVENCALE   *Omelette à la Provençale*

Rub the bottom of the omelet-pan lightly with a clove of garlic; put two tablespoons of oil in the pan, and heat it until it smokes.

Throw into the oil a fine, peeled, pressed, and seeded tomato, cut into dice and sprinkled with a pinch of chopped parsley. Cook it quickly, tossing it the while, and add it to the beaten and seasoned eggs. Make the omelet in the usual way.

N.B.—The nature of this preparation demands the use of oil in treating the tomato, but, lacking oil, clarified butter (175) may be used.

516—OMELET WITH KIDNEYS   *Omelette aux Rognons*

Add to the omelet a tablespoon of calf's or sheep's kidney, cut into dice, seasoned with salt and pepper, *sautéd* quickly in butter, and bound by means of half-*glaze* (23). Having dished the omelet, divide it down the middle, lay some reserved kidney-dice in between, and surround with a ribbon of half-*glaze*.

517—OMELET ROSSINI   *Omelette à la Rossini*

Add to the beaten and seasoned eggs two teaspoons of cooked *foie gras* and as much truffle, cut into small dice. Having placed the omelet on a dish, place in the middle a small rectangular piece of heated *foie gras,* and two slices of truffle on either side of it. Surround it with a ribbon of half-*glaze* (23) flavored with truffle *essence.*

518—OMELET WITH TRUFFLES   *Omelette aux Truffles*

Add to the omelet one tablespoon of truffles, cut into dice. Make the omelet, and lay a row of fine slices of truffles upon it. Surround it with a ribbon of melted meat-*glaze* (15).

519—HOT PLOVERS' EGGS   *Oeufs de Pluviers Chauds*

Note.—In the chapter on hors-d'œuvres (368), where recipes were given which deal with lapwings' eggs, I made a few remarks relative to their freshness, and indicated the procedure for boiling them soft and hard.

520—SCRAMBLED PLOVERS' EGGS   *Oeufs de Pluviers Brouillés*

Proceed as for ordinary scrambled eggs, all the recipes given (460) for the latter being perfectly applicable to plovers' eggs. They require, however, very great care in their preparation, and it should be borne in mind that one ordinary hen's egg is equal to about three plovers' eggs.

521—PLOVERS' EGGS DANISH   *Oeufs de Pluvier à la Danoise*

Poach (411) the eggs as directed in the recipe dealing with the process, and place them in *tartlet-crusts* garnished with a *purée* of smoked salmon.

522—OMELET OF PLOVERS' EGGS   *Omelette d'Oeufs de Pluvier*

Proceed as for other omelets, but one ordinary hen's egg is generally added to every six plovers' eggs in order to give more body to the preparation. All the omelet recipes already given may be applied to plovers' eggs.

523—PLOVERS' EGGS ROYALE   *Oeufs de Pluvier à la Royale*

Garnish as many small *tartlet moulds* as there are eggs with chicken-*forcemeat* (195). *Poach,* turn out the moulds, and hollow out the centers of the *tartlets* in such a way as to be able to set an egg upright in each.

Place a soft or hard-boiled egg on each *forcemeat tartlet,* coat the eggs with a light *purée* of mushrooms, sprinkle with chopped truffles, and arrange in a circle on a dish.

524—PLOVERS' EGGS AU TROUBADOUR
Oeufs de Pluvier au Troubadour

Select as many large morels (French mushrooms) as there are eggs. Remove the stalks, and widen the openings of the morels; season them, and stew them in butter. Boil the plovers' eggs soft.

Garnish each stewed morel with an egg; set them on little *tartlet-crusts* garnished with a light, *foie-gras purée,* and arrange them in a circle on a dish.

COLD EGGS

The preparation of cold eggs is not limited by rigid rules; it rests with the skill and artistic imagination of the cook, and, since fancifulness and originality are always closely allied to artistic imagination, it follows that the varieties evolved may be infinite.

Indeed, so various and numerous are the recipes dealing with this kind of egg-preparations that I must limit myself to a selection only of the more customary ones, culled as far as possible from my own repertory.

525—COLD EGGS ALEXANDRA
Oeufs Froids Alexandra

Take some cold, well-trimmed, *poached* eggs; dry them and cover them with a white chaud-froid sauce (72). Place a fine scalloped slice of truffle in the center of each, and sprinkle with a cold, white, melted aspic jelly until they are thinly coated. Slip the point of a small knife round each egg and transfer them to oval *tartlet-crusts* made from puff-paste trimmings (2366), baked without browning.

Lay a border of caviar round the eggs; serve them in the form of a crown, and put some chopped jelly in the center.

526—COLD EGGS ANDALUSIAN
Oeufs Froids à l'Andalouse

Cover some cold, well-dried, *poached* eggs with a tomato *purée* (29) combined with a full third of its volume of Soubise *purée* (104) and one-half pint of melted aspic jelly per pint of sauce. Cut some pimentos, *marinated* in oil, into very thin strips, and lay these, after the manner of a lattice, upon each egg.

Now garnish as many oiled, oval *tartlet-moulds* as there are eggs with tomato *purée*, thickened with jelly, and let the garnish set on ice. Turn out the moulds, and put an egg upon each of the tomato *tartlets*; arrange the latter in a circle on a dish surrounded with a chain composed of linked rings of onion, and garnish the center with chopped, white aspic jelly.

527—COLD EGGS ARGENTEUIL
Oeufs Froids Argenteuil

Coat some well-dried, *mollet* eggs, slightly cut at their base to make them stand, with a white chaud-froid sauce (72) combined with a good third of its volume of asparagus-tips *purée*. Sprinkle repeatedly with cold, melted, white aspic jelly, until a glossy coating is obtained.

Garnish the center of a dish with a salad of asparagus tips; surround this with fine slices of cold potato, cooked in water and cut with an even fancy-cutter, one inch in diameter, and arrange the eggs all round.

528—COLD EGGS CAPUCINE
Oeufs Froids Capucine

Carefully dry some cold, *poached* eggs, and half-coat them lengthwise with a white chaud-froid sauce (72); complete the coating on the other side with a smooth *purée* of truffles, thickened with aspic-jelly. Leave these two coats to set, placing the eggs in a cool place or on the ice for that purpose.

Garnish the center of a round dish with a small pyramid of cold, truffled Brandade of codfish (1027), and set the eggs round the latter.

529—COLD EGGS CAREME   *Oeufs Froids Carème*

Cook the eggs on the dish, leave them to cool, and trim them with an even fancy-cutter, oval in shape. Place each egg on an oval *tartlet crust,* garnished with dice of cooked salmon, mixed with mayonnaise.

Surround with a ribbon of caviar, and lay a thin slice of very black truffle on each egg.

530—COLD EGGS COLBERT   *Oeufs Froids Colbert*

Garnish some small, oval moulds in *Chartreuse fashion,* like a checker-board. Put a small, cold, *poached* egg into each mould, fill up with melted, white aspic-jelly, and leave to set. Garnish the center of a dish with a heaped vegetable salad; arrange the eggs taken from their moulds around this, and surround with a little chopped aspic.

531—COLD EGGS COLINETTE   *Oeufs Froids Colinette*

Let a thin coat of white jelly set upon the bottom and sides of some small, oval moulds. Garnish the latter with some small dice, consisting of white of egg and truffles, placing them so as to simulate a checker-board; now insert a very small, cold, *poached* egg into each mould, and fill up with a melted aspic-jelly.

Garnish the center of a dish with a "Rachel" salad (2019), encircled by a ring of sliced, cold potatoes, cooked in water, and place the eggs, removed from their moulds, all round. Border the dish with scalloped crescents of white aspic-jelly.

532—COLD EGGS TARRAGON   *Oeufs Froids à l'Estragon*

Mould these in *baba-moulds,* or in porcelain *cocottes;* sometimes they may simply be served in small *tartlet-crusts.*

The preparation consists of *poached* or *mollet* eggs, garnished with *blanched* tarragon leaves, or coated or moulded with a very fine tarragon aspic-jelly.

533—COLD EGGS FROU-FROU   *Oeufs Froids Frou-Frou*

Select some very small *poached* eggs of equal size, cover them with a white chaud-froid sauce (72) combined with about a third of its volume of a *purée* of hard-boiled egg-yolks.

Garnish the top of each egg with a scalloped ring of very black truffle, and surround the base of the eggs with a narrow ribbon composed of chopped truffles. *Glaze* with aspic-jelly, and leave to set on ice.

Prepare a salad of green vegetables (peas, string beans cut into dice or diamonds, asparagus-tips); thicken it with a very little mayonnaise mixed with melted jelly. Pour this preparation into an oiled mould, and leave it to set. For serving, turn out the salad in the middle of a dish; surround the base with a line of chopped jelly; encircle the whole with the eggs, letting them rest on the jelly, and garnish the dish with a border of dice cut in very clear, white aspic jelly.

534—COLD EGGS MUSCOVITE   *Oeufs Froids Muscovite*

Slightly level both ends of some shelled, hard-boiled eggs. Surround the tops and the bases with three little anchovy fillets, and place a bit of truffle just half-way along each egg. Eggs prepared in this way resemble little barrels, the anchovy fillets imitate the iron hoops, and the bits of truffle the bungs. With a small corer empty the eggs with care; garnish them with caviar, and shape to a point, on the ends of the egg.

Lay each egg in an artichoke-bottom, cooked white, and garnished with finely-chopped jelly, and arrange them in a circle on a dish with chopped jelly in the center.

535—COLD EGGS NANTUA   *Oeufs Froids à la Nantua*

Prepare some hard-boiled eggs to resemble little barrels, after the manner described above. For every six eggs keep ready and cold eighteen crayfish or giant shrimp cooked *à la Bordelaise* (32). Shell the tails, put two aside for each egg, and cut the remainder into dice; finely pound the bodies and remains, add three tablespoons of thick cream, and rub through a fine sieve. Add to this *cullis* one tablespoon of thick mayonnaise.

Bind the crayfish tails, cut into dice, with a few tablespoons of this sauce, and garnish the eggs, emptied by the method indicated in (534), with the preparation of dice, making it stand out of the eggs in the shape of a small dome. Garnish each dome with a rosette composed of four halved crayfish tails or shrimp and four truffle slices.

Glaze well with aspic jelly; set the eggs upon artichoke-bottoms garnished with a mayonnaise with crayfish *cullis,* and arrange in a circle on a dish.

536—COLD EGGS POLIGNAC   *Oeufs Froids Polignac*

Prepare some eggs *à la Polignac* (456), as explained under "Moulded Eggs," and leave them to cool. Select some moulds a little larger than those used in the cooking of the eggs; pour into each half a tablespoon of melted, white aspic jelly, and leave to set. Then put an egg into each mould, and fill up the space around the eggs with melted, white jelly.

Leave to set, unmould, arrange on a dish, and surround them with dice of faintly colored aspic-jelly.

537—COLD EGGS A LA REINE *Oeufs Froids à la Reine*

Prepare some *mollet* eggs, and leave them to cool. Take as many large *brioches* as there are eggs; trim them to the level of the fluting, and remove the inside, so as to form little *croustades* of them. Garnish the bottom and the sides of these *croustades* with a fine mince of white chicken-meat, thickened with mayonnaise, and season moderately with cayenne. Place a shelled, *mollet* egg in each *croustade;* coat thinly with mayonnaise slightly thickened by means of an aspic-jelly; lay a fine piece of truffle on each egg, and, when the sauce has set, *glaze* with jelly, using a fine brush for the purpose.

Serve on a napkin.

538—COLD EGGS RUBENS *Oeufs Froids Rubens*

Season some cooked young shoots of hops with salt and freshly-ground pepper; add some chopped parsley and chervil, and a *purée* of plainly-cooked tomatoes combined with just enough aspic-jelly to ensure the binding of the hops. Mould in oiled *tartlet-moulds*.

Coat some well-dried, cold, *poached* eggs with white chaud-froid sauce (72); garnish with pieces of tarragon leaves, and *glaze* with aspic-jelly.

Turn out the *tartlet-moulds*; set an egg on each one, and arrange them in a circle on a dish, placing between each egg a piece of very clear jelly, cut to the shape of a cock's comb.

Garnish the center of the dish with chopped aspic-jelly.

CHAPTER XIII

Soups are divided into two leading classes:—

1. Clear soups, which include plain and garnished consommés.
2. Thick soups, which comprise the *Purées,* Veloutés, and Creams.

A third class, which is independent of either of the above, inasmuch as it forms part of plain, household cookery, embraces vegetable soups and *Garbures* or *gratined* soups. But in important dinners—by this I mean rich dinners—only the first two classes are recognized.

When a menu contains two soups, one must be clear and the other thick. If only one is to be served, it may be either clear or thick, in which case the two kinds are represented alternately at different meals.

In Part I of this work I indicated the general mode of procedure for consommés and thick soups; I explained how the latter might be converted from plain *purées* into veloutés or creams, or from veloutés into creams; and all that now remains is to reveal the recipes proper to each of those soups.

Remarks.—In the course of the recipes for consommés, given hereafter, the use of *Royales* (206 to 213) and of *Quenelles,* variously prepared (193 to 195 and 205), will often be used. For the preparation of these garnishes the reader will have to refer to the numbers indicated.

The quantities for the clear soups that follow are all calculated to be sufficient for six people, and the quantity of *Royales* is always given in so many *dariole-moulds,* which contain about one-eighth pint, or *baba-moulds,* which hold about one-fifth pint.

Of course, it will be understood that the *poaching* need not necessarily have been effected in these moulds, for very small *"Charlotte"* moulds would do quite as well. But I had reference to the particular utensils mentioned above, in order that there might be no sort of doubt as to the exact quantity of *royale* it would be necessary to prepare for any one of the soups.

198

CLEAR SOUPS AND GARNISHED CONSOMMÉS

539—ALEXANDRA CONSOMME *Consommé Alexandra*

Have a quart of excellent chicken consommé (3) ready; add, in order to thicken it slightly, three tablespoons of *poached* tapioca, strained through muslin, and very clear.

Put the following garnish into the soup-tureen: One tablespoon of white chicken-meat cut in fine *julienne*-fashion, one tablespoon of small chicken *quenelles,* grooved and long in shape, and one tablespoon of lettuce *chiffonade.*

Pour the boiling consommé upon this garnish, and send to the table immediately.

540—AMBASSADRESS CONSOMME *Consommé Ambassadrice*

Have one quart of chicken consommé (3) ready; also there should have been prepared beforehand, with the view of using them quite cold, three different kinds of *royales,* consisting respectively of truffle *purée,* tomato *purée,* and *purée* of peas, each of which should have been *poached* in a *dariole-mould.*

Cut these *royales* up into regular dice, and put them in the soup-tureen with one tablespoon of chicken breast and an equal quantity of small, freshly-cooked mushrooms, finely minced. Pour the boiling consommé over these garnishes, and serve at once.

541—ANDALUSIAN CONSOMME *Consommé Andalouse*

Prepare a *baba-mould* of *royale* made from tomato *purée.* When quite cold, cut it into dice, and put these in the soup-tureen with one small tablespoon of cooked ham cut *julienne*-fashion, one tablespoon of boiled rice, with every grain distinct and separate, and two tablespoons of threaded eggs (217).

When about to serve, pour one quart of very clear chicken consommé (3) over the garnish.

542—ARENBERG CONSOMME *Consommé d'Arenberg*

With a small ball-cutter, cut out a spoonful of small carrot balls and the same quantity of turnip balls. Cook these vegetables by boiling them in consommé, taking care that the latter be reduced to a *glaze* when the vegetables are cooked. With the same cutter shape the same quantity of very black truffle; also prepare a *dariole-mould* of *royale* made from asparagus tips, and a dozen small chicken-*forcemeat quenelles* (194), which should be moulded to the shape of large balls.

Poach the *quenelles,* cut the *royales* into slices, which must be stamped with a fluted fancy-cutter, and put the whole into the soup-tureen with the carrots, turnips, and truffle balls, and one tablespoon of very green peas.

Pour a quart of chicken consommé (3) over the garnish, and send to the table at once.

543—BOHEMIAN CONSOMME　　*Consommé à la Bohémienne*

Prepare three *dariole-moulds* of *foie-gras royale,* and twelve *profiterolles* (218) of the size of hazel-nuts, the latter being made very crisp.

When the *royale* is cold, cut it into little, regular squares, and put these into the soup-tureen.

When about to serve, pour over this garnish a quart of chicken consommé (3), thickened by means of three tablespoons of tapioca, *poached* and strained through a cloth or fine sieve.

Send the *profiterolles* to the table separately, and very hot.

544—BOILDIEU CONSOMME　　*Consommé Boildieu*

Prepare eighteen chicken-*forcemeat quenelles,* moulded with a small teaspoon; some should be stuffed with *foie-gras purée,* moistened with a little velouté (25); others with chicken *purée;* and yet others with truffle *purée*—in short, six of each kind.

Place these, one by one, in a buttered saucepan; *poach* them, drain, then put them in the soup-tureen with a tablespoon of white chicken-meat, cut into dice.

When about to serve, pour one quart of chicken consommé (3) thickened with tapioca, over the garnish.

545—BOUQUETIERE CONSOMME　　*Consommé Bouquetière*

Prepare a garnish of carrots and turnips, cut with a spoon; string beans cut, asparagus-tips, and green peas, all of which vegetables should be fresh and young. Cook each vegetable according to its nature, and put the whole into the soup-tureen.

When about to serve, pour over the garnish one quart of chicken consommé (3) thickened with two tablespoons of tapioca, *poached* and strained through fine cloth.

546—BOURDALOUE CONSOMME   *Consommé Bourdaloue*

Prepare a *dariole-mould* of each of the four following *royales*:—

1. Of a *purée* of dried-beans with a slight addition of tomato.

2. Of a chicken *purée* moistened with velouté (25).

3. Of a *purée* of asparagus-tips combined with a few cooked spinach leaves, to deepen the color.

4. Of a carrot *purée (Purée Crécy* (630).

Having *poached* and cooled the *royales,* cut them as follows:—

(1) Into dice, (2) into diamonds, (3) into little leaves, and (4) into stars.

Place them all in the soup-tureen, and, when about to serve, pour one quart of boiling and very clear chicken consommé (3) over them.

547—BORSCHT SOUP   *Potage Bortsch*

Cut in *julienne*-fashion the heads of two leeks, one carrot, half of an onion, four oz. of the white of cabbage leaves, half a root of parsley, the white part of a stalk of celery, and four oz. of beets; set the whole to stew gently in butter.

Moisten with one quart of white consommé (2) and two or three tablespoons of the juice of grated beets; add a small bunch of fennel and sweet marjoram, two lbs. of moderately fat brisket of beef, and the half of a partly roasted duck; set to cook gently for four hours.

When about to serve, cut the beef into large dice, and cut the duck into small slices; finish the soup with one-quarter pint of beet juice, extracted from grated beets pressed through linen, and a little *blanched* and chopped fennel and parsley. Put the beef dice and sliced duck into the soup, with twelve grilled *chipolatas* (Italian or Polish sausages).

Serve, separately, a sauceboat of sour cream.

N.B.—The *chipolatas* may be replaced by very small patties with duck *forcemeat,* which should be served separately.

548—BRUNOISE CONSOMME   *Consommé Brunoise*

Cut into small dice the outside part only of two small carrots, one small turnip, the heads of two leeks, a small stalk of celery, and the third of an onion of medium size.

Season the vegetables moderately with salt and a pinch of sugar, and stew them in butter. Moisten with one-half pint of consommé, and complete the cooking of the Brunoise gently. Five minutes before serving, finish with one quart of boiling, ordinary consommé

(2), a scant tablespoon of peas, and the same quantity of string beans, cut into dice and kept very green.

Pour into the soup-tureen, and add a pinch of fine chervil *pluches*.

549—CARMEN CONSOMME *Consommé Carmen*

Prepare one quart of consommé (2), to which add, while clarifying, one-quarter pint of raw tomato *purée*, in order to give it a faint, pink tinge.

Also peel and press a small and rather firm tomato; cut into dice, and *poach* the latter in some of the consommé; put them in the soup-tureen with a small tablespoon of mild sweet pepper, cut in fine *julienne* strips, and one tablespoon of plain-boiled rice.

When about to serve, pour the boiling consommé over the garnish, and add a small pinch of chervil *pluches*.

550—CASTILIAN CONSOMME *Consommé Castellane*

Prepare one quart of game consommé (5), flavored with a *fumet* of woodcock; two *baba-moulds* of *royale*, two-thirds of which consists of a *purée* of woodcock and one-third of lentils, with half the yolk of a hard-boiled egg, chopped and thickened with the usual thickening.

Cut this *royale* into slices, about the size of a half-dollar, one-half inch thick. Put these into the soup-tureen, together with one tablespoon of a *julienne* of roast woodcock breasts, and pour on the boiling game consommé.

551—CELESTINE CONSOMME *Consommé Célestine*

Prepare one quart of chicken consommé (3), and add three small tablespoons of *poached* tapioca, strained through fine linen.

For the garnish make three *pannequets* (2403 and 2476) without sugar, and spread over each a thin coating of chicken *forcemeat* with cream. Place one on top of the other, sprinkle the layer of *forcemeat* on the uppermost one with finely-chopped, very black truffles, and place in the front of the oven for a few minutes, in order to *poach* the *forcemeat*.

Stamp the *pannequets* out with a plain rimmed cutter about one inch in diameter. Put the pieces into a soup-tureen, and, when about to serve, pour in the boiling consommé.

552—CHARTREUSE CONSOMME *Consommé Chartreuse*

Prepare eighteen small *raviolis* (2296)—six from spinach *purée*, six from *foie-gras purée*, and the remaining six from chopped mushrooms; two small tablespoons of tomatoes diced. Ten minutes before serving, *poach* the *raviolis* in boiling, salted water, and the tomato dice in some of the consommé.

Put the *raviolis* and the tomato (well drained) into the soup-tureen, and pour over them one quart of consommé with a moderate addition of tapioca. Add a pinch of chervil *pluches*.

553—ANGELS' HAIR CONSOMME   *Consommé auc Cheveux d'Ange*

About two minutes before serving, plunge three oz. of the very finest vermicelli into one quart of excellent, boiling consommé (2).

An instant only is needed to *poach* the vermicelli, and the latter does not require to be *blanched*.

This soup, like those containing pastes, should be accompanied by freshly-grated Parmesan cheese.

554—COLBERT CONSOMME   *Consommé Colbert*

Have ready one quart of excellent *Printanier* chicken consommé (601). Also *poach* six small eggs in slightly salted and vinegared water. The eggs should be as small and as fresh as possible, both of which conditions are absolutely necessary for a proper *poaching* (see poached eggs, 411). Set these eggs in a small dish with a little consommé, and send them to the table with the *Printanier* consommé. Having poured it into the plates, put one of the eggs into each.

555—COLUMBINE CONSOMME   *Consommé Columbine*

Prepare a full tablespoon of carrot balls, and as many turnip balls, keeping the latter very white. Cook them in the customary way, and put them in the soup-tureen with one tablespoon of very green peas, one tablespoon of a *julienne* of roast-pigeon breasts, and six *poached* pigeons' eggs, which should be sent to the table in a dish at the same time as the consommé.

Pour over the other garnish one quart of very clear, boiling, chicken consommé (3), and serve immediately.

This soup can only appear on summer and spring menus, when the pigeons' eggs are in season.

556—CROUTE-AU-POT   *Croûte-au-Pot*

Prepare a freshly-cooked vegetable garnish for a stock-pot:—Carrots and turnips cut *julienne* and trimmed; a few heads of leeks, and cabbage, parboiled, minced, and cooked in very fat consommé (2).

Put these vegetables in a somewhat greasy broth for ten minutes.

Also prepare seven or eight crusts of French soup rolls *"flutes"*; sprinkle them with the fat from the stock, and dry them in the oven. Put the vegetable garnish into the soup-tureen; pour on one quart of consommé of the Petite Marmite (598), and add the dried French roll crusts.

557—CYRANO CONSOMME
Consommé Cyrano

Prepare one quart of consommé with a *fumet* of duck; twelve small *quenelles* of duck *forcemeat,* which should be made flat and oval. Having *poached* the *quenelles,* drain them, and set them in a small, shallow earthen pan or *timbale;* sprinkle with a little grated Parmesan cheese and a few drops of chicken *glaze* (16), and set to *glaze* in the oven.

The *quenelles* are served separately in the pan in which they have been *glazed,* and the consommé is sent to the table in a soup-tureen.

558—DEMIDOFF CONSOMME
Consommé Demidoff

With the small ball-cutter, cut out a good tablespoon of carrot, and the same quantity of turnip. Cook these vegetables in the customary way, and put them in the soup-tureen with one tablespoon of truffle, the same quantity of peas, and small, *poached,* chicken-*forcemeat quenelles* with herbs. Pour one quart of boiling chicken consommé (3) over this garnish, and add a pinch of chervil *pluches.*

559—DESLIGNAC CONSOMME
Consommé Deslignac

Prepare two small, stuffed lettuces, rolled into sausage form and *poached;* two *baba-moulds* of *royale* with cream. Cut the *royale* into small, regular dice; trim the lettuce, and cut it into slices; put this garnish into the soup-tureen, and pour on one quart of boiling chicken consommé (3), thickened with three tablespoons of *poached* tapioca, strained through linen. Add a pinch of chervil *pluches.*

560—CONSOMME WITH DIABLOTINS
Consommé aux Diablotins

Cut a French roll for soup *"flute"* into twelve slices one-quarter inch thick. Reduce about one-quarter pint of Béchamel (28) to a thick consistency; add, away from the fire, two heaped tablespoons of grated Gruyère cheese, and season with a little cayenne.

Garnish the slices of soup French rolls *"flute"* with this preparation, arranged in the form of a dome, upon a tray, and set to *glaze* a few minutes before serving.

Pour one quart of chicken consommé (3) into the soup-tureen, and add the *croutons*.

561—DIPLOMAT CONSOMME   *Consommé Diplomate*

Roll into small sausage-form three oz. of chicken *forcemeat*, finished with crayfish butter (147). *Poach* the sausages, cut them into thin slices, and put them into the soup-tureen with two teaspoons of very black truffle, cut *julienne*-fashion.

Pour over this garnish one quart of boiling chicken consommé (3), thickened with two tablespoons of *poached* tapioca, strained through linen.

562—DIVETTE CONSOMME   *Consommé Divette*

Prepare two *baba-moulds* of *royale* made from crayfish velouté, eighteen small *quenelles* of smelt *forcemeat*, moulded in the shape of balls, and one tablespoon of small balls of very black truffle.

Cut the *royale* into oval slices, and put these into the soup with the *poached quenelles* and the truffle balls.

Pour one quart of very clear, boiling consommé (2) over the garnish.

563—DORIA CONSOMME   *Consommé Doria*

Prepare the following garnish:—Thirty small balls of cucumber; eighteen small *quenelles* of chicken *forcemeat*, long in shape and grooved; six little balls, about the size of a large pea, of *pâte à choux*, combined with grated cheese, rolled by hand; and one and one-half tablespoons of sago or large tapioca, *poached* in some of the consommé.

Put the cucumber balls, cooked in consommé, into the soup-tureen; add the *poached quenelles* and the sago.

Four minutes before serving, plunge the balls of *pâte à choux* into hot fat, keeping them crisp.

When about to serve, pour over the garnish one quart of boiling chicken consommé; complete with a pinch of chervil *pluches*, and serve the little, fried puff balls separately.

564—DOUGLAS CONSOMME   *Consommé Douglas*

With a plain cutter, the size of a quarter, cut out some *braised* and cooled sweetbreads into twelve rounds one-third inch thick; with the same cutter cut out twelve more round slices from some cooked artichoke-bottoms, and put the whole into the soup-tureen with two tablespoons of very green asparagus tips.

When about to serve, pour one quart of boiling, highly sea-soned, ordinary consommé (2) upon the garnish.

565—SCOTCH BROTH   *Consommé à l'Ecossaise*

Prepare a special mutton broth, like a good beef broth and, at the same time, cook a fine piece of breast of mutton for the garnish.

Per two quarts of broth, put into the soup-tureen four table-spoons of pearl-barley, cooked very gently beforehand; two table-spoons of string beans, cut in diamonds, and the breast of mutton cut in dice of one-half inch, in the proportion of one tablespoon for each person.

Pour the boiling mutton broth over this garnish, after having removed all the grease and strained it through linen.

566—FAVORITE CONSOMME   *Consommé Favori*

With a ball-cutter, cut from out some new kidney potatoes eighteen balls the size of small hazel-nuts, and cook them in salted water in good time for them to be ready for the serving up of the soup. Put them in the soup-tureen with two tablespoons of a *julienne* of artichoke-bottoms and the same quantity of cooked mushrooms, also cut in *julienne*-fashion.

Pour over the garnish one quart of chicken consommé (3), thickened with three tablespoons of *poached* tapioca strained through linen. Add a pinch of chervil *pluches*.

566a—CONSOMME FERMIERE   *Consommé à la Fermière*

Mince, somewhat finely, one small carrot, one small turnip, the heads of two leeks, and the half of an onion. Slightly stew these vegetables in one and one-half oz. of butter; moisten with one and one-half pints of white consommé (2); add two oz. of parboiled cabbage, cut roughly into *julienne*, and complete the cooking gently, taking care to remove all grease, to obtain a very clear consommé.

Pour into the soup-tureen, and add a few thin slices of French bread, soup *"flute,"* slightly dried.

567—FLORENTINE CONSOMME   *Consommé Florentine*

With fine chicken *forcemeat* make twenty-four small *quenelles* on a buttered tray, their shape being that of small loaves. To the *forcemeat* of six of these *quenelles* add some very finely chopped tongue; add white chicken-meat to that of another six; and to that of the remaining twelve add some very reduced spinach *purée*. The *quenelles* with spinach should number twice those with the other two ingredients, in order that the preparation may be in keeping with its name "à la Florentine."

Poach the *quenelles;* put them in the soup-tureen with two tablespoons of very green, cooked peas.

When about to serve, pour one quart of very clear, boiling chicken consommé (2) over this garnish, and add a pinch of chervil *pluches.*

568—GALLIC CONSOMME   *Consommé Gauloise*

Prepare two *dariole-moulds* of ham *royale,* and *poach* the latter in a small, well-buttered *Charlotte mould.* When quite cold, cut it into large diamonds, and put these into the soup-tureen with six small cocks' combs and six small cocks' kidneys (these latter as small as possible).

When about to serve, pour over this garnish one quart ot chicken consommé, (3) thickened slightly with two tablespoons of *poached* tapioca, strained through linen.

569—GEORGE SAND CONSOMME   *Consommé George Sand*

Have ready one quart of consommé (2) flavored with very clear fish *fumet.* Also prepare twelve small *quenelles* of whiting *force-meat,* finished with crayfish butter (147); stew twelve morels (French mushrooms), which should be left whole if very small, and cut into two if they are of medium size; twelve small slices of *poached* carps' *milt,* and twelve little rounds of French rolls for soup.

Put the *poached quenelles* and the stewed morels into the soup-tureen; pour on the boiling fish consommé, and send the slices of carps' *milt* set on the rounds of French rolls for soup *"flute"* separately to the table.

570—GERMAINE CONSOMME   *Consommé Germaine*

Prepare two *dariole-moulds* of *royale* made from a *purée* of very green peas, combined with a tablespoon of *Mirepoix* stewed in butter, and a strong pinch of small, chervil *pluches;* eighteen small *quenelles* of chicken *forcemeat* with cream, moulded to the form of *pastils.*

When the *royale* is cold, cut it into regular slices, and put these into the soup-tureen with the *poached quenelles.*

When about to serve, pour one quart of boiling chicken consommé (3) over the garnish.

571—GIRONDINE CONSOMME   *Consommé Girondine*

Prepare one quart of highly-seasoned beef consommé (1); two *baba-moulds* of ordinary *royale* made with whole eggs and combined with two tablespoons of cooked and finely-chopped lean ham; three tablespoons of a *julienne* of carrots stewed in butter, the cooking of which should be completed in the consommé.

Put the *royale*, cut into large, regular diamond shapes, and the *julienne* of carrots into the soup-tureen, and pour in the boiling beef consommé.

572—GRIMALDI CONSOMME *Consommé Grimaldi*

Have ready one quart of excellent ordinary consommé (2) to which have been added, while clarifying, four tablespoons of raw tomato *purée*, strained through fine linen.

Also prepare two *dariole-moulds* of ordinary *royale*, and three tablespoons of a fine *julienne* of the white parts of celery, stewed in butter, finally cooked in the consommé, and with all grease removed.

Put the *royale*, cut into large dice, and the *julienne* of celery into the soup-tureen, and pour on the boiling consommé with tomatoes.

573—IMPERIAL CONSOMME *Consommé Imperiale*

Prepare three *dariole-moulds* of *mousseline forcemeat* of fowl (195), and put it to *poach* in a small *Charlotte* mould.

When quite cold, cut it into rounds the size of a quarter, and put these in the soup-tureen with six small *blanched* cocks' combs and three sliced cocks' kidneys, and two tablespoons of very green peas.

Pour over this garnish one quart of chicken consommé (3), thickened with three tablespoons of *poached* tapioca strained through linen.

574—INDIAN CONSOMME *Consommé à l'Indienne*

Have ready one quart of ordinary consommé (2) seasoned with curry. Also prepare three *baba-moulds* of *royale* made from cocoanut water or milk, and, when quite cold, cut into small dice.

Put this *royale* into the soup-tureen; pour on it the boiling consommé with curry, and send to the table, separately, four tablespoons of Rice à l'Indienne (2254).

575—INFANTA CONSOMME *Consommé à l'Infante*

With some *pâte à choux* (2374) prepare eighteen *profiterolles* of the size of hazel-nuts. Cook them, taking care to keep them very crisp, and stuff them when cold with *purée de foie gras* moistened with velouté (25).

Put two tablespoons of a fine *julienne* of sweet pepper into the soup-tureen, and pour on one quart of boiling chicken consommé (3), moderately thickened with *poached* tapioca strained through linen.

Serve the *profiterolles* of *foie gras* separately, after having heated them in the front of the oven.

N.B.—The garnish of Consommé à l'Infante may consist only of the *profiterolles*, and the *julienne* of pepper may be omitted; this is a matter of taste.

576—JACQUELINE CONSOMME   *Consommé Jacqueline*

With a small spoon, cut out from some carrots twenty-four little balls, which should be cooked in the consommé. Prepare two *baba-moulds* of *royale* with cream.

Put into the soup-tureen the carrot balls and the *royale* cut to the shape of *pastils,* one tablespoon of peas, the same quantity of very green asparagus tips, and one tablespoon of rice.

When about to serve, pour one quart of boiling chicken consommé (3) over this garnish.

576a—JULIENNE CONSOMME   *Consommé Julienne*

Cut into strips, two inches in length, two medium-sized carrots, one medium-sized turnip, one leek, half a stalk of celery, some cabbage leaves, and half an onion. Season these vegetables with a pinch of salt and as much sugar; stew them in one oz. of butter; moisten with one and one-half pints of white consommé (2), and then add two oz. of small parboiled cabbages, cut after the manner of the other vegetables.

Finish the cooking gently, removing the grease the while, and complete with one small tablespoon of very green, cooked peas, one tablespoon of sorrel and lettuce *chiffonade,* and one pinch of chervil *pluches.*

577—LORETTE CONSOMME   *Consommé Lorette*

Have ready one quart of chicken consommé (3). Also prepare two tablespoons of a fine *julienne* of celery stewed in butter and cooked in the consommé; twelve small "potatoes à la lorette" (2226), the size of hazel-nuts, and shaped like small crescents. These potatoes should be fried in hot fat four minutes before serving.

Put into the soup-tureen the *julienne* of celery, twelve small, freshly-*poached* cocks' kidneys, and one tablespoon of a *julienne* of pimentos: pour the boiling consommé over this garnish; add a

pinch of chervil *pluches,* and send the potatoes to the table separately.

578—MACDONALD CONSOMME   *Consommé MacDonald*

Prepare one quart of highly seasoned beef consommé (1), two
dariole-moulds of calf's brain-*purée royale;* two tablespoons of
cucumbers cut in small dice and cooked in consommé until the
latter is reduced to a *glaze;* five little *raviolis* garnished with chicken
forcemeat combined with a third of its volume of spinach. Put
these *raviolis* to *poach* in salted boiling water twelve minutes before
serving.

Put into the soup-tureen the *royale* of brains cut into slices
one-third inch thick, the cucumber dice, and the *raviolis poached*
and well drained.

Pour the boiling beef consommé over this garnish just before
serving.

579—MARGUERITE CONSOMME   *Consommé Marguerite*

Take two tablespoons of chicken *forcemeat* with cream, and
roll it into sausage-form on the floured mixing-board. Put the
sausage to *poach.* Rub the yolk of a hard cooked egg through a
fine sieve, and mix it with half a teaspoon of raw *forcemeat.*

Having *poached* and cooled the chicken sausage, cut it into thin
round slices, and stamp each slice with a fancy-cutter in the shape
of a daisy. Arrange the daisies on a dish, and lay in the middle of
each a bit of the egg and *forcemeat* mixture, in imitation of the
flower-center.

Put these marguerites (daisies) into the soup-tureen with one
tablespoon of small, green asparagus cut into lengths of one inch.
When about to serve, pour one quart of very clear, boiling chicken
consommé (3) over this garnish.

580—MARQUISE CONSOMME   *Consommé Marquise*

Prepare one quart of good, ordinary consommé (2), to which
three stalks of celery have been added, while clarifying, in order
that the taste of the celery may be very decided.

Make thirty small *quenelles* of chicken *forcemeat* combined with
finely-chopped filberts, giving them the shape of *pastils.*

Poach these *quenelles* ten minutes before serving. Also *poach* in
court-bouillon two calf's spine marrows, and cut them into thin
slices.

Put the poached *quenelles* and the slices of calf's marrow into the soup-tureen, and pour on the boiling consommé.

581—MERCEDES CONSOMME *Consommé Mercédes*

Prepare one quart of chicken consommé (3) with pimentos, combined, at the last minute, away from the fire, with one-half pint of sherry.

Put into the soup-tureen two tablespoons of green pepper, cut in fine *julienne*-fashion and short, and some small, freshly-cooked cocks' combs.

When about to serve, pour the consommé over this garnish.

582—MESSALINE CONSOMME *Consommé Messaline*

Prepare one quart of chicken consommé (3), and add, while clarifying, one-quarter pint of tomato *essence,* obtained by reducing tomato juice to a syrup.

Put into the soup-tureen twelve small, freshly-*poached* cocks' combs, two tablespoons of Spanish peppers cut into a *julienne* and *poached* in the consommé if fresh (this should have been previously grilled to remove the skin), and two tablespoons of *poached* rice, every grain of which should be separate.

Pour the boiling consommé over this garnish.

583—METTERNICH CONSOMME *Consommé Metternich*

Prepare one quart of game consommé (5) with pheasant *fumet*. Also *poach* two *dariole-moulds* of *royale*, made from a *purée* of artichokes combined with some tablespoons of the reduced game Espagnole (22). Cut this *royale* into dice; put these into a soup-tureen with one tablespoon of a *julienne* of pheasant breasts, and pour on the boiling consommé.

584—MILANESE CONSOMME *Consommé à la Milanaise*

Cook in slightly salted boiling water two oz. of moderately thick macaroni. As soon as it is cooked, drain it, lay it on a piece of linen, and cut it into small rings. Also prepare one-quarter pint of Béchamel (28), thickened with the yolk of one egg combined with one oz. of grated cheese, and keep it very thick.

Mix the rings of macaroni with this sauce; spread the whole on a dish, and leave to cool. Now divide up the preparation into portions the size of walnuts; roll these into balls, and then flatten them out to form little cakes about the size of a half-dollar. Treat these cakes with an *anglaise,* and very fine bread-crumbs, and plunge into hot fat four minutes before serving. Drain them when they have acquired a fine golden brown.

Pour one quart of boiling chicken consommé (3) into the soup-tureen, and send to the table, separately, the fried macaroni cakes and one and one-half oz. of Gruyère and Parmesan cheese, in equal quantities, grated and mixed.

585—MIREILLE CONSOMME   *Consommé Mireille*

Add one tablespoon of very concentrated tomato *purée* to three oz. of chicken *forcemeat;* roll this preparation into the form of a somewhat large sausage, and *poach* it. When cold, cut it into slices, one-quarter inch thick, and stamp each slice with an oval fancy-cutter in the shape of a half-dollar. Put these slices in the soup-tureen with two tablespoons of saffroned pilaff rice (2255), and, when about to serve, pour on one quart of very clear, boiling chicken consommé (3).

586—MIRETTE CONSOMME   *Consommé Mirette*

Make eighteen *quenelles* of chicken *forcemeat* in the shape of large balls, and *poach* them. Prepare two tablespoons of lettuce *chiffonade* (the heart of one lettuce cut *julienne*-fashion and stewed in butter); make eighteen *paillettes* with Parmesan (2322), and put them in a very hot oven eight or ten minutes before serving.

Put the poached *quenelles* and the lettuce *chiffonade* into the soup-tureen; pour on one quart of boiling consommé of the Petite Marmite (598), and one pinch of chervil *pluches*.

Send the *paillettes* au Parmesan to the table separately, and have them very hot.

587—MONTE CARLO CONSOMME   *Consommé Monte Carlo*

Make and *poach* thirty small *quenelles* of chicken *forcemeat;* shred and stew in butter the heart of one lettuce; prepare twelve little *profiterolles* of *pâte à choux,* the size of hazel-nuts, and cook them, taking care to keep them crisp.

Put the *quenelles* and the lettuce *chiffonade* into the soup-tureen; pour on one quart of very clear, boiling, chicken consommé (3), and add a pinch of chervil *pluches*.

Serve the *profiterolles* separately and very hot.

588—MONTMORENCY CONSOMME   *Consommé Montmorency*

Have ready one quart of chicken *consommé* (3) thickened with three tablespoons of *poached* tapioca, strained through linen.

Prepare eighteen small grooved *quenelles* of chicken *forcemeat.*
Poach, drain, and put them into the soup-tureen with two tablespoons of very green asparagus tips and two tablespoons of *poached*
rice, every grain of which should be distinct and separate.

589—MUSCOVITE CONSOMME   *Consommé à la Moscovite*
Prepare one quart of sturgeon consommé, as other fish consommé
and add some cucumber *essence,* obtained by pounding a cored
and peeled cucumber, and straining the resulting *purée* through
linen.

Put into the soup-tureen two tablespoons of a *julienne* of salted
mushrooms, one oz. of soaked *vesiga* (sturgeon marrow) cut into
dice and cooked in broth, and pour on the boiling consommé.

N.B.—*Vesiga* or the spine-marrow of the sturgeon ought to be
soaked in cold water for a few hours in order to soften and swell
it, after which it should be cut into dice and cooked in broth. For
every four tablespoons of cooked *vesiga,* one oz. of dry *vesiga* should
be allowed.

590—NESSELRODE CONSOMME   *Consommé Nesselrode*
Have ready one quart of game consommé (5), prepared with
hazel-hen *fumet. Poach* two *baba-moulds* of *royale* made from
chestnut *purée* with two small tablespoons of game salmis sauce (55)
added; cut it into round slices half-inch thick, and trim these with
a grooved fancy-cutter.

Put them into the soup-tureen with two tablespoons of a *julienne*
of hazel-hen breasts, the same quantity of a *julienne* of mushrooms,
and pour on the boiling game consommé.

591—ENGLISH BIRDS' NESTS SOUP
Consommé aux Nids d'Hirondelles
The nests used for this soup are those of the tropical swallow,
and their shape somewhat resembles that of the rind of a quartered,
dry orange.

In the first place, prepare a chicken consommé (3) containing a
large proportion of nutritious ingredients. Set three nests to soak
in cold water for twenty-four hours, the object being to swell the
glutinous elements of which they are composed and to make them
transparent.

When they have soaked sufficiently remove any pieces of feather
which may have remained in them, using for this purpose the
point of a needle, and, when the nests are quite clean, drain them

and put them into the consomme. At this stage set the consommé
to boil, gently, for thirty or thirty-five minutes without interruption.
During this time the gummy portions of the nests will melt into
the consommé, giving the latter its characteristic sticky consistency,
and there will only remain visible those portions which, in the
natural state, constitute the framework of the nests; little threads
not unlike superfine transparent vermicelli.

592—CONSOMME WITH WARBLERS' EGGS
Consommé aux Oeufs de Fauvette

I introduced this consommé in honor of the illustrious singer,
Adelina Patti.

It consists of a chicken consommé (3), which should be made as
perfect as possible, and a garnish composed of the *poached* eggs
of small birds, pigeons, or other tiny birds.

593—OLGA CONSOMME
Consommé Olga

Prepare one quart of excellent ordinary consommé (2), and add
when about to serve and away from the fire, one-quarter pint of
port wine.

Also cut into a fine *julienne* the quarter of a small knob of celery,
the white of a leek, and the outside only of a small carrot. Stew
this *julienne* in butter and complete its cooking in consommé,
reducing the latter to a *glaze*.

When about to serve put this *julienne* in a soup-tureen, add a
few tablespoons of a *julienne* of salted gherkins, and pour on the
consommé with port.

594—ORLEANS CONSOMME
Consommé d'Orléans

Lay on a buttered tray ten small *quenelles* of ordinary chicken
forcemeat, ten others of chicken *forcemeat* combined with a very
red tomato *purée*, and ten more of the same *forcemeat*, combined
with a *purée* of spinach, all the *quenelles* being grooved.

Ten minutes before serving *poach* these *quenelles*, drain them,
put them in the soup-tureen, and pour in one quart of chicken
consommé (3) thickened with three tablespoons of *poached* tapioca
strained through linen. Add a pinch of chervil *pluches*.

595—CONSOMME D'ORSAY
Consommé d'Orsay

Prepare one quart of very clear chicken consommé (3), also make
fifteen small *quenelles* of pigeon *forcemeat* moulded to the shape

ot eggs by means of a very small spoon, and *poach* the yolks of ten eggs, taking care to keep them very soft.

Put the *quenelles* and the *poached* yolks into the soup-tureen with a *julienne* of three breasts of pigeon and a tablespoon of asparagus tips, and pour on the boiling consommé. Serve at once.

596—OX-TAIL SOUP   *Potage Queue de Boeuf*

For Ten People.—Garnish the bottom of a small stock-pot or saucepan with one small carrot and two medium-sized onions cut into slices and browned in butter, and one herb bunch. Add two small ox-tails, or one of medium size weighing about four lbs. (The tails should be cut into sections, each of which should contain one of the tail bones, and they should then be browned in the oven.) Also add two lbs. of gelatinous bones, broken very small and likewise browned in the oven.

Now proceed exactly as for brown veal stock (9), taking note that the whole moistening must consist of no more than two and one-half quarts of ordinary broth and one quart of water.

Set to boil very gently for four and one-half or five hours. This done, strain the broth, which should be reduced to two and one-half quarts, and completely remove its grease. Transfer the largest sections of the tails, by means of a fork, one by one to another saucepan. Cover them with broth, and keep them warm for the garnish.

Finely chop one lb. of very lean beef; put this mince into a saucepan with the white of a leek cut into dice and half the white of an egg, and mix thoroughly. Add the broth, the grease of which has been removed, set to boil, stirring constantly the while, and then leave to simmer for one hour, which is the time required for the beef to exude all its juices and for the clarification of the broth.

While the clarification is in progress cut a small carrot in dice. Cook this garnish in a little water with butter, salt, and sugar.

A few minutes before serving strain the ox-tail broth through a napkin, put the sections of ox-tail and the carrot into the soup-tureen, and pour on the prepared broth. This soup may be flavored with port or sherry, but this is optional.

N.B.—If a thickened ox-tail soup be required add to the broth per every quart of it one-third of an oz. of arrowroot or other starch diluted with a little of the broth or some cold water.

597—PARISIAN CONSOMME　　　*Consommé Parisienne*

Have one quart of chicken consommé (3) ready.

For the garnish prepare two *dariole-moulds* of *royale* made from a *purée* of ordinary *julienne* of vegetables and a small *macédoine* of vegetables, comprising one heaped tablespoon each of carrots and turnips cut up by means of a small grooved knife and cooked in the usual way, one tablespoon of small peas, the same quantity of fine string beans cut into short bits, and one tablespoon of asparagus tips.

Cut the *royale* into regular round slices; put these in the soup-tureen with the *macédoine* of vegetables, and, when about to serve, pour on the boiling chicken consommé. Add a pinch of fine chervil *pluches*.

598—THE PETITE MARMITE　　　*La Petite Marmite*

For Ten People.—Prepare a consommé in a special earthen-ware stock-pot in accordance with the procedure indicated in recipe (1), but with the following quantities, two lbs. of lean beef and as much breast of beef, one marrow-bone tied in a muslin-bag, and the necks, the wings, and the gizzards of six large fowls, these giblets being put in the earthenware stock-pot one hour before serving up.

Moisten with three and one-half quarts of water and add three-quarters of an oz. of salt. Set to boil, skim as indicated, and cook gently to obtain a very clear broth. One hour before serving add six oz. of carrots and the same quantity of turnips, both cut to the shape of large olives, five oz. of the white of leeks, and a heart of celery.

Cook a quarter of a very white, properly *blanched* cabbage, separately, in a saucepan with a little consommé and some fat from stock.

When about to serve test the seasoning of the consommé, which should be very clear; thoroughly clean the stock-pot, which may even be covered with a clean napkin; lift out the marrow-bone; take it out of its muslin-bag, and send it and the cabbage to the table separately, accompanied by a plate of small pieces of hot toast for the marrow.

599—THE POT-AU-FEU　　　*Pot-au-Feu*

Prepare this exactly like the Petite Marmite.

600—POULE AU POT   *Poule au Pot, ou Pot Henri IV*

This is a variation of the Petite Marmite, in which a tender and very fleshy hen is substituted for the giblets of fowl.

Strictly observe the rule of never using a new earthenware stock-pot before having boiled water in it for at least twelve hours. Also bear in mind that earthenware stock-pots should be washed in hot water only, without any soda or soap.

601—PRINTANIER CONSOMME   *Consommé Printanier*

Have ready one quart of chicken consommé (3), also cut one carrot and one turnip into round slices one-half inch thick. Cut these round slices into little sticks, making a sufficient number to fill one tablespoon with each vegetable. Cook these little sticks in consommé, and reduce the latter to a *glaze*.

Put the carrot and turnip sticks into the soup-tureen with one tablespoon of small peas, the same quantity of small string beans and asparagus tips, ten sorrel leaves, and as many of lettuce leaves, the latter being *poached* in some consommé. When about to serve pour the boiling consommé over these garnishes and add a large pinch of small chervil *pluches*.

602—SPRING CONSOMME WITH DUMPLINGS
Consommé Printanier aux Quenelles

Prepare the vegetable garnish exactly as directed above, but slightly lessen the quantities.

Make eighteen small *quenelles* of chicken *forcemeat* in the shape of little grooved meringue shells, and *poach* them ten minutes before serving.

Drain them, put them into the soup-tureen with the other garnishes, pour on the boiling consommé.

603—CONSOMME WITH PROFITEROLLES
Consommé aux Profiterolles

Prepare forty very dry *profiterolles* (218), and add an excellent chicken consommé (3) to them at the last moment.

The *profiterolles* may also be made to the size of walnuts, in which case they may be stuffed with a *purée* of chicken, *foie gras,* etc.

604—RACHEL CONSOMME   *Consommé Rachel*

Prepare one quart of chicken consommé (3) and thicken it with three tablespoons of *poached* tapioca strained through linen. With a cutter stamp out twelve round slices of bread the size of a half dollar and one-half inch thick. *Poach* in consommé as many slices of very fresh beef-marrow as there are slices of bread.

Six minutes before serving fry the slices of bread in clarified butter (175), hollow out their centers, and place on each a slice of *poached* beef-marrow trimmed evenly.

Put three tablespoons of a *julienne* of cooked artichokes into the soup-tureen, pour on the thickened consommé, and add the slices of bread garnished with the marrow.

605—REJANE CONSOMME   *Consommé Réjane*

Prepare one quart of excellent white consommé (2), set it to boil, and add a *julienne* of the white meat of half a fowl and the heads of two leeks cut likewise. Set to cook gently for ten minutes, disturbing the consommé as little as possible, add three oz. of potatoes cut into a *julienne,* complete the cooking, and serve immediately.

606—RENAISSANCE CONSOMME   *Consommé Renaissance*

Prepare one quart of clear chicken consommé (3).

For the garnish make two *dariole-moulds* of *royale* with a *purée* of early-season herbs (vegetables) thickened with velouté (25) and whole eggs; with a small sharp spoon cut out one tablespoon of balls from a turnip and the outside part of a carrot. Cook these vegetables in the usual way. Cut the *royale* with a fancy-cutter into pieces of the shape of small leaves. Put the leaves of *royale* into the soup-tureen with the carrot and turnip balls, one tablespoon of very green peas, the same quantity of string beans cut, one tablespoon of asparagus tips, and twelve very small particles of very white cauliflower. Pour the boiling consommé over these garnishes, and add a pinch of chervil *pluches.*

607—RICHELIEU CONSOMME   *Consommé Richelieu*

Have ready one quart of highly-seasoned beef consommé (2). Also prepare twelve *quenelles* of chicken *forcemeat* moulded by means of a small teaspoon, proceeding as follows:—Line the spoon with a thin coating of the forcemeat, and in the middle lay some chopped, reduced, cold chicken aspic. Cover the jelly with a layer of *forcemeat,* shaping it like a dome; insert another spoon (first dipped in hot water) under the *quenelle,* and place the latter upon a buttered saucepan. Repeat the operation until the required number of *quenelles* have been moulded. Treated in this way, the *quenelles,* when *poached,* contain, so to speak, a liquid core. Five minutes before serving, *poach* the *quenelles.*

Cut six rectangles from lettuce leaves; spread a thin layer of *forcemeat* over each; roll into *paupiettes* (roulades), and *poach* in some of the consommé.

Prepare two tablespoons of a coarse *julienne* of carrots and turnips, stew them in butter, and complete their cooking in the consommé, which should be thoroughly cleared of grease.

Put the *julienne,* the *paupiettes,* and the stuffed *quenelles* into the soup-tureen; pour in the boiling beef consommé, and add a pinch of chervil *pluches.*

608—ROSSINI CONSOMME   *Consommé Rossini*

Prepare one quart of chicken consommé (3), slightly thickened with two tablespoons of *poached* tapioca strained through linen.

Make eighteen *profiterolles,* from *pâte à choux* without sugar (2374), to the size of hazel-nuts. Bake them in a moderate oven, keeping them very crisp, and stuff them, inside, with a *foie-gras* and truffle *purée.*

When about to serve, pour the consommé into the soup-tureen, and serve the *profiterolles* separately, after having placed them in the oven, so that they may reach the table very hot.

609—ROTHSCHILD CONSOMME   *Consommé Rothschild*

Have ready one quart of game consommé (5), prepared with pheasant *fumet.* Add, when about to serve, one-quarter pint of reduced Sauterne. Make two *dariole-moulds* of *royale* from a preparation consisting of one-third of the whole of *purée* of pheasant, one-third of chestnut *purée,* and one-third of pheasant salmis sauce (55). *Poach* the *royale;* cut it into grooved slices, and place these in the soup-tureen with one tablespoon of a *julienne* of breasts of pheasant.

When about to serve, pour the boiling consommé over the garnish.

610—ST. HUBERT CONSOMME   *Consommé Saint-Hubert*

Take one quart of game consommé (5), prepared with venison *fumet.* Finish the consommé, at the time of serving, with one-quarter pint of Marsala.

Make three *dariole-moulds* of *royale* from a preparation consisting of one-third of the whole of venison *purée,* one-third of lentil *purée,* and one-third of reduced game Espagnole (22). *Poach* the *royale* in a small *Charlotte* mould, and, when it has cooled, cut it up with a fancy-cutter in the shape of a cross. Put the crosses of *royale* into the soup-tureen with two tablespoons of a *julienne* consisting of fillets of hare, and pour on the boiling consommé.

611—SARAH BERNHARDT SOUP   *Potage Sarah Bernhardt*

Sprinkle three tablespoons of tapioca into one quart of boiling chicken consommé (3) and leave to poach gently for fifteen or eighteen minutes.

Make twenty small *quenelles* from chicken *forcemeat*, finished by means of crayfish butter (147), and mould them into the shape of small, grooved mounds. *Poach* these *quenelles*. Cut twelve slices, the size of a half-dollar, from a piece of beef-marrow, and *poach* them in the consommé.

Put the drained *quenelles* and the *poached* slices of marrow into the soup-tureen; add one tablespoon of a *julienne* of very black truffles, and the same quantity of asparagus tips. Pour the boiling consommé, with tapioca, over this garnish.

612—SEVIGNE CONSOMME   *Consommé Sévigné*

Keep one quart of very clear chicken consommé (3) very warm.

Prepare ten *quenelles* of chicken *forcemeat*, moulded by means of a small teaspoon, and *poach* them; also have ready four *braised* small heads of lettuces.

Put the *quenelles*, the lettuce cut into small sections and properly trimmed, and one tablespoon of peas into the soup-tureen; pour in the boiling consommé and a pinch of chervil *pluches*.

613—SOVEREIGN CONSOMME   *Consommé Souveraine*

Have ready one quart of chicken consommé (3).

Make ten large *quenelles* from chicken *forcemeat*, and stuff them with very fine diced vegetables, proceeding as follows:—Line a tablespoon with a thin coat of *forcemeat*, and garnish the center with the *brunoise*, previously cooked in consommé, and cold. Cover the *brunoise* with a layer of *forcemeat*, shaping it like a dome; insert another tablespoon dipped into hot water under the *quenelle*, and transfer the latter to a buttered saucepan. Repeat the operation until the required number of *quenelles* have been moulded.

Allow eight minutes for the *poaching* of these *quenelles;* put them into the soup-tureen with two tablespoons of peas; pour on the boiling consommé, and add a pinch of chervil *pluches*.

614—TURTLE SOUP   *Consommé de Tortue*

Turtle soup is very rarely prepared in the kitchens of catering establishments. It is more generally obtained ready-made, either fresh or preserved, and as a rule of exceptional quality, from firms whose specialty it is to make it, and who usually deliver it in excellent condition.

From among the New York firms who have deservedly earned a reputation for this soup, Moore and Co., 137 Beekman St., New York may be quoted as one whose produce is quite irreproachable.

When a comparatively small quantity of this soup is required, it is best to buy it ready-made; in the event of its being desirable to prepare it oneself, the following recipe will be found the simplest and most practical for the purpose.

PARTICULARS OF THE OPERATION

The Slaughtering of the Turtle.—For soup, take a turtle weigh ing from 120 to 180 lbs., and let it be very fleshy and full of life.

To slaughter it, lay it on its back on a table, with its head hanging over the side. By means of a double butcher's hook, one spike of which is thrust into the turtle's lower jaw, while the other suspends an adequately heavy weight, make the animal hold its head back; then, quickly as possible, sever the head from the body.

Now immediately hang the body over a receptacle, that the blood may be collected, and leave it thus for one and one-half or two hours.

Then follows the dismemberment:—To begin with, thrust a strong knife between the carapace or upper shell and the plastron or lower shell, exactly where the two meet, and separate the one from the other. The turtle being on its back, cut all the adhering flesh from the plastron, and put the latter aside. Now cut off the flippers; remove the intestines, throw them away, and carefully collect all the green fat. Whereupon cut away the flesh adhering to the carapace; once more remove all fat, and keep both in reserve.

The Treatment of the Carapace, the Plastron, and the Flippers. —The carapace and plastron, which are the outside bony framework of the turtle, constitute the only portions wherefrom the gelatinous flesh, used as the garnish of the soup, are obtained.

Saw the carapace into six or eight pieces, and the plastron into four.

Put these pieces with the flippers into boiling water or into steam, to *blanch*. Withdraw the flippers as soon as they are sufficiently stiff for their skin to be removed, and lease the pieces of carapace and plastron to *blanch* for five minutes, in order that they may admit of being scraped. Now cool the pieces of carapace and plastron and the flippers, and put them into a pot containing enough water to abundantly cover them. Set to boil; garnish with vegetables, as in the case of an ordinary broth, and add a small quantity of *turtle herbs*.

Five or six hours should be allowed for the cooking of the carapace and the plastron, but the flippers, which are put to further uses in other culinary preparations, should be withdrawn at the end of five hours.

When the pieces are taken from the cooking-liquor, remove all the flesh from the bones, and cool the former; then trim it carefully, and cut it into little squares of one and one-half inches. It is these squares together with the green fat (*poached* in salted water and sliced) which constitute the garnish of the soup.

The Preparation of Turtle Soup.—There are two modes of procedure, though their respective results are almost identical.

1. Make a broth of the flesh of turtle alone, and then add a very gelatinous beef consommé (1) to it, conforming to the method employed when the turtle soup is bought ready-made.

This procedure is practically the best, more particularly if the soup has to be kept some time.

2. Make an ordinary broth of shin of beef, using the same quantity of the latter as of turtle. Also include half a calf's foot and one-half lb. of calf's shin per 3 lbs. of the beef. Add the flesh of the turtle, or, in the event of its being thought necessary to clarify, which operation I do not in the least advise, reserve it for that purpose.

The condiments and *aromatics* being the same for both methods, I shall now describe the procedure for method No. 1.

The Ingredients of the Soup.—Put into a stewpan of convenient size the flesh of the turtle and its head and bones. Moisten partly with the cooking-liquor of the carapace, and complete the moistening, in the case of a turtle weighing 120 lbs., with enough water to bring the whole to 50 quarts. By this means a soup of about thirty to thirty-five quarts will be obtained at the end of the operation. Add salt in the proportion of one oz. per every five quarts; set to boil; skim, and garnish with twelve carrots, a bunch of leeks (about \en bound with a bunch of celery), one lb. of parsley stalks, eight onions with ten cloves stuck into them, two lbs. of shallots, and one head of garlic. Set to boil gently for eight hours. An hour before straining the soup, add to the garnish four strips of lemon-peel, a bunch of herbs, comprising sweet basil, sweet marjoram, sage, rosemary, savory, and thyme, and a bag containing four oz. of coriander and two oz. of pepper-corns.

Finally, strain the soup through a napkin; add the pieces of meat from the carapace and plastron which were put aside for the garnish, and keep it until wanted in specially-made stone crocks.

The Serving of the Soup.—When about to serve this soup, heat it; test and rectify its seasoning, and finish it off by means of a port wine glass of very old Madeira to every quart.

Very often a milk punch is served with turtle soup, the recipe being:—

Milk Punch.—Prepare a syrup from one-half pint of water and three oz. of sugar; allow to come to a boil (17° Baumé's Hydrometer). Set to infuse in this syrup two orange and two lemon *zests*. Strain at the end of ten minutes, and add one-half pint of rum, one-fifth pint of kirsch, two-thirds pint of milk, and the juice of three oranges and three lemons. Mix thoroughly. Let it stand for three hours; filter, and serve cold.

615—TOSCA CONSOMME   *Consommé Tosca*

Have ready one quart of chicken consommé (3) thickened with three tablespoons of *poached* tapioca strained through linen.

Also prepare two tablespoons of a *julienne* of carrots stewed in butter, the cooking of which is completed in the consommé; ten small *quenelles* of chicken *forcemeat,* combined, in the proportion of one-third, with *foie gras* and chopped truffles; ten small, very crisp *profiterolles,* stuffed with a *purée* of chicken with pistachio kernels.

Put the *quenelles* and the *julienne* into the soup-tureen, pour in the boiling consommé, and send the *profiterolles* to the table separately, and very hot.

616—CONSOMME VERT-PRE   *Consommé Vert-Pré*

Sprinkle two tablespoons of tapioca into one quart of boiling consommé (2), and set to cook gently for a quarter of an hour.

Put into the soup-tureen one tablespoon of asparagus tips, the same quantity of peas and of string beans cut into bits, a few pieces of sorrel leaves, and as many *poached* lettuce leaves.

Pour the boiling consommé, with tapioca, over this garnish, and add a large pinch of chervil *pluches*.

617—VILLENEUVE CONSOMME *Consommé Villeneuve*

Have ready one quart of chicken consommé (3).

Prepare the following garnish:—Two small heads of *blanched* lettuces, stuffed with chicken *forcemeat* combined with *braised* and chopped smoked tongue; two *dariole-moulds* of ordinary *royale*, and two pancakes coated with a layer of chicken *forcemeat*, which should be placed in the front of the oven for a few moments with the view of *poaching* the *forcemeat*.

Put the cut-up lettuce, the pancakes cut into small, narrow squares, and the *royale* cut into *pastils*, into the soup-tureen; and, when about to serve, pour the boiling consommé over the whole.

SPECIAL COLD CONSOMMÉ FOR SUPPERS

Remarks Relative to the Consommés.—I gave the recipes of these consommés in Part I of this work (6), and shall now, therefore, limit myself to the following remarks, which are of paramount importance:—

1. These consommés must be perfect in transparency and quality.

2. The flavor which typifies them should be very decided and yet not too pronounced.

3. When the flavor is imparted by a wine, the latter should be of the best possible quality. Rather than make use of inferior wines, the presence of which in the soup would tend to depreciate its quality, completely discard wine flavorings.

4. Supper consommés never contain any garnish.

618—ESSENCE OF QUAIL CONSOMME
Consommé à l'Essence de Cailles

Use roast quails in the proportion of two for each pint of consommé; the breasts may be reserved for a cold entrée.

619—ESSENCE OF CELERY CONSOMME
Consommé à l'Essence of Céleri

It is impossible to state exactly how much celery should be used, the quantity being entirely subject to the more or less decided flavor of the vegetables at one's disposal.

Experience alone can guide the cook in this matter.

620—ESSENCE OF MORELS CONSOMME
Consommé à l'Essence de Morilles

Allow five oz. of small fresh morels (French mushroom), or three oz. of dry ones per quart of the consommé. Pound them and mix them with the consommé before clarification.

621—ESSENCE OF TRUFFLES CONSOMME
Consommé à l'essence de Truffles

Use fresh truffles only in this case. Allow two oz. of peelings and trimmings per quart of the consommé; pound them and mix them in before the clarification.

622—ESSENCE OF PARTRIDGE CONSOMME
Consommé au Fumet de Perdreau

Proceed as in (618); allow one partridge for each quart of the consommé.

623—GOLD LEAF CONSOMME   *Consommé aux Paillettes d'Or*
Take a very superior chicken consommé (3); add, per quart, a glass of excellent liqueur brandy, and, in the same proportion, one small sheet of real gold-leaf cut into small spangles.

624—SWEET RED PEPPER CONSOMME *Consommé aux Piments Doux*
Add one-half oz. of fresh or canned pimentos to every quart of the consommé. The product should be pounded and mixed in before the clarification.

625—MADRID CONSOMME   *Consommé à la Madrilène*
Add four oz. of raw tomato and one oz. of pimentos to the consommé per every quart of the latter. Mix these ingredients with the clarification, and serve as cold as possible.

626—PORTUGUESE CONSOMME   *Consommé à la Portugaise*
Add to the consommé for every quart one-third pint of raw tomato *purée* and one-sixth pint of tomato juice. Cook with lid on for twenty minutes, taking care not to let it reach the boil; strain through muslin, pressing lightly the while, and season moderately with cayenne. Set to cool, and serve very cold.

627—CONSOMME WITH WINE   *Consommé aux vins*
By adding a port wine glass full of the chosen wine to one pint of excellent cold chicken consommé, the following series of consommés may be made:—

Consommé au vin de Chypre.
Consommé au vin de Madère.
Consommé au vin de Malvoisie.
Consommé au vin de Marsala.
Consommé au vin de Porto doré.
Consommé au vin de Porto rose.
Consommé au vin de Samos.
Consommé au vin de Zucco.

628—JELLIED TOMATO SOUP *Gelée aux Pommes d'Amour*

Proceed as for the "Consommé Portugaise" (626), and use that variety of small tomatoes which are called "Pommes d'amour" (plum tomatoes).

629—NEAPOLITAN JELLIED CHICKEN CONSOMME
Gelée de Volaille à la Napolitaine

Proceed as for the "Consommé Portugaise" (626), but finish it with one port wine-glass of port or old Marsala per quart.

THICK SOUPS

In Part I, Chapter I, of this work I pointed out what thick soups consist of. I likewise touched upon the general rules which should be observed in the preparation of each class of these soups, and showed how most of them could, if necessary, be converted into and served as *cullises, purées, bisques,* veloutés, or creams. The principles governing these alterations are very simple, and after a moment's reflection the cook will thoroughly grasp their import. Be this as it may, the reader will find the necessary directions at the end of each recipe that permits various methods of preparation.

With regard to those recipes which are not followed by any directions of the sort referred to, and which I simply class under the name of Potages, these are unalterable preparations which may only be served in accordance with the directions given. This being clear, the reader will understand that I have refrained from repeating the quantities of butter, cream, thickening ingredients, etc., in each recipe. These particulars having been given in Part I, it will be necessary to refer to that part of the book for them.

630—PUREE OF CARROTS, CALLED CRECY
Purée de Carottes, dite Crécy

Cut one lb. of the outer part only of carrots into fine slices: chop

one onion, and put the whole into a saucepan with a sprig of
thyme and two oz. of butter. Stew gently for twenty minutes, and
season with a pinch of salt and sugar. Add for the thickening
ingredient, either two oz. of rice or five and one-half oz. of bread
dice fried in butter; also add one and one-half pints of white consommé (2), and set to cook very gently.

Rub through a fine sieve, test the consistency, skim, and add
butter when serving.

Ordinary garnish: small *croutons* fried in butter.

Occasional garnish: *poached* large sago in the proportion of two
tablespoons per quart of the soup.

This soup may also be prepared as a cream or a velouté à la
Nivernaise (674).

631—PUREE OF CARROTS WITH TAPIOCA, CALLED VELOURS
Purée de Carottes au tapioca, dite Velours

Make one pint of carrot *purée* as (630), and *poach* two tablespoons
of tapioca in a pint of white consommé (2).

When about to serve, and after having buttered the *purée* of
carrots, mix with the prepared tapioca.

632—PUREE OF CELERY ROOT   *Purée de Céleri-Rave*

Finely mince one lb. of celery root; *blanch* it; thoroughly drain it,
and stew it gently in one oz. of butter. Moisten with one quart of
white consommé (2); add two medium-sized potatoes, minced, and
set to cook gently. Rub through a fine sieve; skim the *purée* gently
for half an hour, and add butter when serving.

Garnish: small bread dice fried in butter.

633—PUREE OF BRUSSELS SPROUTS, CALLED FLAMANDE
Purée de choux de Bruxelles, dite Flamande

Parboil and drain one lb. of very fresh Brussels sprouts. Set them
to stew gently in three oz. of butter; moisten with one pint of white
consommé (2); for the thickening add two medium-sized quartered
potatoes, and complete the cooking.

Rub through a fine sieve, finish the *purée* with milk, skim it in the
usual way, and add butter when serving. Garnish with small
croutons fried in butter.

634—PUREE OF CAULIFLOWER, CALLED DU BARRY
Purée de choux-fleurs, dite Du Barry

Parboil one lb. head of cauliflower divided into flowerets.

Drain them and put them in a saucepan with one pint of boiled

milk and two medium-sized minced potatoes for the thickening. Set
to cook gently, rub through a fine sieve, finish with boiled milk,
skim, and add butter.

Garnish with small *croutons* fried in butter.

This soup may also be prepared as a velouté or a cream with small
pieces of cauliflower as garnish.

635—PUREE OF JAPANESE ARTICHOKES OR STACHYS, CALLED
JAPANESE   *Purée de crosnes ou stachys, dite Japonaise*

Parboil and drain one lb. of well-cleaned Japanese artichokes.
Stew them in one oz. of butter; moisten with one pint of boiled milk
or white consommé (2), according to whether the *purée* is to be a
Lenten one or not; add two medium-sized minced potatoes, and
complete the cooking gently.

Rub through a fine sieve, test the consistency, and add, if necessary, either a little boiled milk or some consommé; skim, and add
butter.

Garnish with two tablespoons of large sago *poached* in consommé
or milk.

This soup may also be prepared as a velouté or a cream.

636—PUREE OF YOUNG KIDNEY BEANS, CALLED MUSARD
Purée de flageolets, dite Musard

Cook together with the ordinary *aromatic* garnish three-quarters
pint of dry kidney beans, or, if they are in season, use twice that
quantity of fresh ones (wax beans).

Drain, pound, and moisten the *purée* with a little of the cooking-
liquor of the beans, rub through a fine sieve, and rectify the consistency with some white consommé (2) and the necessary quantity
of boiled milk. Skim, and butter it when about to serve.

Garnish with two tablespoons of small *croutons* fried in butter.

This soup may also be prepared as a velouté or a cream, but for
either of the latter it is preferable to use fresh wax beans, the garnish
for both consisting of very small kidney beans and chervil *pluches*.

637—PUREE OF WHITE BEANS, CALLED SOISSONNAISE
Purée de haricots blancs, dite Soissonnaise

Cook in the usual way, that is to say, with carrots, an herb bunch,
and one onion stuck with a clove, a good half-pint of dry white
beans.

Crush all these, moisten with a few tablespoons of their cooking-
liquor, and rub through a fine sieve.

Rectify the consistency of the *purée* with the necessary quantity of white consommé (2) and milk, skim, add butter when about to serve, and garnish with small *croutons*.

This soup may also be prepared as a velouté or a cream.

638—PUREE OF STRING BEANS, CALLED CORMEILLES
Purée de haricots verts, dite Cormeilles

Parboil one and one-half lbs. of string beans and keep them very green. After having well drained them, stew them for ten or twelve minutes in one oz. of butter, moisten with one pint of white consommé (2), and add two medium-sized minced potatoes for the thickening.

Set to cook gently, rub through a fine sieve, rectify the consistency of the *purée* with a little boiled milk, skim, and add butter when serving.

Garnish with two tablespoons of cooked string beans cut into narrow lengths.

This soup may also be prepared as a velouté or a cream.

639—PUREE OF RED KIDNEY BEANS, CALLED CONDE
Purée de haricots rouges, dite Conde

Put a heaped pint of red kidney beans into cold water, set to boil slowly, skim, add three oz. of carrots, one small herb bunch, one onion stuck with a clove, and a quart of boiling red wine. Set to cook gently.

Drain the beans and mash them. Moisten the *purée* with a few tablespoons of the cooking-liquor from the beans, rub through a sieve. Dilute the consistency of the *purée* with some white consommé (2), follow the procedure of all *purées*, and add butter when about to serve.

Garnish with *croutons* fried in butter.

640—PUREE OF LENTILS, CALLED CONTI
Purée de lentilles, dite Conti

Soak three-quarters of a pint of lentils in lukewarm water for two hours. Put them in a pot with two oz. of very lean bacon, *blanched,* cooled, and cut into dice, and one quart of white consommé (2). Set to boil, skim, add three oz. of carrots, one onion, and one herb bunch, and cook very gently.

Drain the lentils, pound them together with the bacon, moisten the *purée* with a few tablespoons of cooking-liquor, and rub through a sieve. Dilute the consistency with some reserved cooking-liquor, then treat the *purée* in the usual way and add butter when about to serve.

Garnish with two tablespoons of *croutons* fried in butter and a pinch of chervil *pluches*.

N.B.—It should be borne in mind that the *aromatic* garnish used in cooking dry vegetables of any kind should be taken out before the *purée* is rubbed through a sieve.

641—PUREE OF WHITE TURNIPS, CALLED FRENEUSE
Purée de navets, dite Freneuse

Finely mince one lb. of very firm white turnips, parboil, drain, and stew them in one and one-half oz. of butter, the necessary salt, and one-half oz. of sugar, until they are almost completely cooked. Moisten with one-half pint of white consommé (2), and complete the cooking. Meantime, cook two medium-sized, peeled and quartered potatoes in some consommé.

Now put the turnips and the potato into the same saucepan; crush them, and rub them through a sieve. Bring the *purée* to the proper consistency by means of boiled milk, and finish it in the usual way.

Garnish with some small *croutons* fried in butter.

This soup may also be prepared as a velouté or a cream.

642—PUREE OF SORREL AND VERMICELLI WITH CREAM
Purée d'Oseille et de Vermicelle à la Crème

Sprinkle three oz. of well-separated vermicelli into one pint of boiling milk or white consommé (2) (according to whether the preparation be a *Lenten* one or not). Let the vermicelli *poach* gently for twenty-five minutes, and then add four tablespoons of sorrel cooked in butter.

Rub the whole through a sieve; finish the *purée* with sufficient milk or thin cream; heat until the boil is reached, and, when about to serve, complete by means of a thickening composed of the yolks of two eggs and one-quarter pint of very fresh cream.

For the garnish, refer to the remarks under (646).

643—PUREE OF SORREL AND SAGO WITH CREAM
Purée d'Oseille et de Sagou à la Crème

Proceed exactly as directed in the preceding recipe; but instead of vermicelli use three oz. of sago. Allow the usual time for cooking, and add the same quantity of sorrel cooked in butter.

Use the same quantities of milk or consommé in order to bring the *purée* to the proper consistency, and make use of a similar thickening.

644—PUREE OF SORREL AND SEMOLINA (FARINA) WITH CREAM
Purée d'Oseille et de Semoule à la Crème

The same as the above, but use three oz. of semolina or heavy farina. All other ingredients remain the same.

645—PUREE OF SORREL AND TAPIOCA WITH CREAM
Purée d'Oseille et de Tapioca à la Crème

Procedure like (642), using instead of the vermicelli three oz. of tapioca.

646—REMARKS RELATIVE TO THE POSSIBLE VARIATIONS OF THE FOUR PRECEDING RECIPES
Variations des quatre recettes précédentes

A large variety of this kind of soups may be prepared by using the quantity prescribed of buckwheat, oatmeal, barley-meal, etc.

These soups derive a particular and agreeable flavor from their diluting element.

The chief point to be remembered in their preparation is their consistency, which should be that of a thin cream.

When too thick, these soups are pasty and disagreeable; when too thin, they are insipid; hence the desirability of aiming at a happy medium.

Their garnish is exceedingly variable, the more preferable forms being small bread dice *croutons* fried in clarified butter (175), pressed; peeled tomatoes cut into dice and tossed in butter; small *printaniers, brunoises, juliennes, paysannes,* or well-*poached* rice.

Thus, from a typical recipe of these soups, a whole series may be prepared, which need not be gone into separately here.

647—PUREE OF PEAS WITH CROUTONS   *Purée de Pois aux Croûtons*

Wash three-quarters of a pint of split peas, green or yellow, in cold water and put them into a saucepan with one quart of cold water, a little salt, and one-half lb. of ham. Set to boil, skim, and add two oz. of *mirepoix,* the minced green leaves of three leeks, a fragment of thyme and bay leaf, salt, and one-half oz. of sugar. Set to cook very gently.

Rub through a fine sieve, bring the *purée* to the proper consistency by means of white consommé (2), skim it, and add butter to it when serving.

Garnish with two tablespoons of small *croutons* fried in butter.

648—PUREE OF FRESH PEAS CALLED ST. GERMAIN
Purée de Pois Frais, dite Saint-Germain

The two following methods may be employed:—

Cook quickly one and one-quarter pints of fresh peas, just shelled, in boiling, salted water. Drain them, mash them, moisten the *purée* with one pint of white consommé (2), and rub it through a fine sieve. Bring it to the proper degree of heat, and add butter when about to serve. Prepared in this way, the *purée* should be of a perfect shade of green.

Or stew one and one-quarter pints of fresh peas in one and one-half oz. of butter, a little lettuce *chiffonade,* one and one-half oz. of the green part of leeks, a pinch of chervil, a little salt and sugar, and one-seventh pint of water.

Mash the peas as soon as they are cooked, moisten the *purée* with one pint of white consommé, and rub through a fine sieve. Bring the preparation to the proper degree of heat and add butter at the last moment.

Treated thus, the *purée* will be of a fainter shade than the preceding one, but its flavor will be more delicate.

Garnish, in both cases, with one and one-half tablespoons of very green, small peas, and some chervil *pluches.* This soup may also be prepared as a velouté or a cream.

649—PUREE OF FRESH PEAS WITH MINT
Purée de pois frais à la menthe

Make the *purée* according to one of the mentioned methods, and add to the peas, while cooking, a bunch of three little sprigs of fresh mint. Finish with consommé (2), and add butter in the usual way.

Garnish with small peas, as above, and some very tender mint leaves, chopped, instead of the chervil *pluches.*

Remarks Relative to those Soups which have a Purée of Peas for Base.—A large number of soups may be made from *purées* of fresh peas; among others I may mention the following, with brief directions as to their ingredients and garnish.

650—AMBASSADORS' SOUP   *Potage Ambassadeurs*

Purée of fresh peas, ready for soup; finish with a small tablespoon of sorrel and lettuce *chiffonade,* and two tablespoons of *poached* rice per quart of *purée.*

651—CAMELIA SOUP   *Potage Camelia*

Prepare this after the recipe of potage Lamballe (653); finish with one tablespoon of a *julienne* of the white of a leek and one tablespoon of white chicken meat, cut *julienne*-fashion, per quart of the soup.

652—FONTANGES SOUP   *Potage Fontanges*

Purée of fresh peas ready for soup; add two tablespoons of a *chiffonade* of sorrel and a pinch of chervil *pluches* per quart of the *purée,* and two tablespoons of *poached* rice.

653—LAMBALLE SOUP   *Potage Lamballe*

Half of this consists of a finished *purée* of peas, and the other half of tapioca *poached* in consommé as for the ordinary "potage au tapioca" (660).

654—LONGCHAMPS SOUP   *Potage Longchamps*

This is the "potage Fontange," kept somewhat clear, and with a garnish composed of one and one-half oz. of vermicelli, *poached* in consommé (2), and a pinch of chervil *pluches* per quart of the soup.

655—MARIGNY SOUP   *Potage Marigny*

Proceed as for "potage Fontange" (652), and add a garnish of one tablespoon of peas and one tablespoon of string beans cut into small pieces.

656—MARCILLY SOUP   *Potage Marcilly*

Half of this consists of a *purée* of peas and the other half of a *purée* of chicken. Prepare these *purées* in the usual way and mix them together when about to serve.

Garnish with two tablespoons of large sago *poached* in consommé (2) and twelve small *quenelles* of chicken *forcemeat,* in the shape of small balls, per quart of the soup.

657—SAINT-MARCEAU SOUP   *Potage Saint-Marceau*

This is an ordinary *purée* of peas with butter, combined with two tablespoons of a *julienne* consisting of the white part of a leek and some chervil *pluches* per quart of the *purée*. This list could be considerably lengthened, but what there is of it amply suffices to show the great number of soups that may be obtained from the combination of other suitable products with the *purée* of peas and the modification of the garnish in each case.

658—PUREE OF POTATOES, CALLED PARMENTIER
Purée de pommes de terre, dite Parmentier

Finely mince the white of two medium-sized leeks, and fry them without browning in one oz of butter. Add three medium-sized peeled and quartered potatoes, one pint of white consommé (2), and cook quickly. The moment the potatoes seem soft to the touch crush them and rub them through a sieve.

Finish the *purée* with some boiled milk or thin cream, heat until the boil is reached, and add butter when serving.

Garnish with two tablespoons of small *croutons* fried in butter and some chervil *pluches*.

This soup may also be prepared as a velouté or a cream.

659—PUREE OF TOMATOES, CALLED PORTUGUESE
Purée de Tomates, dite Portugaise

Fry in one oz. of butter a somewhat finely-cut *mirepoix* consisting of one oz. of bacon cut into dice, one-third of a carrot, half an onion, a fragment of thyme and bay leaf. Add to this fried *mirepoix* eight medium-sized tomatoes, pressed and cut into pieces, a pinch of sugar, two and one-half oz. of rice, and one pint of white consommé (2). Set to cook gently, rub through a sieve, and finish with the necessary quantity of consommé.

When about to serve complete the *purée* by adding, away from the fire, two oz. of butter.

Garnish with two tablespoons of *poached* rice, each grain being separate, and the same quantity of peeled tomatoes cut into dice and briskly tossed in butter.

This soup may also be prepared as a velouté or a cream.

660—PUREE OF TOMATOES WITH TAPIOCA, CALLED WALDEZE
Purée de tomates au tapioca, dite Waldèze

Prepare one and one-half pints of tapioca in white consommé (2), and keep it a little lighter than ordinary tapioca. Also press, peel, and cut into dice the pulp of three medium-sized, very red tomatoes; *poach* these in some consommé and mix them with the tapioca.

Or, lacking fresh tomatoes, add to the tapioca two tablespoons of concentrated tomato *purée* diluted in a bowl with some white consommé.

Send two oz. of grated cheese to the table separately.

661—PUREE OF JERUSALEM ARTICHOKES, CALLED PALESTINE
Purée de topinambours, dite Palestine

Finely mince two lbs. of Jerusalem artichokes and stew them in one oz. of butter. Add five roasted and crushed filberts, moistened with one pint of white consommé (2), and set to cook gently. Rub through a sieve; finish the *purée* with one-quarter pint of milk, in which one tablespoon of *fecula* or other starch has been diluted, with cold water. Set to boil and add butter when serving.

Garnish with small bread dice fried in butter.

This soup may also be prepared as a velouté or a cream.

662—BISQUE OF CRAYFISH OR ROCK LOBSTER
Bisque d'Ecrevisses

Cut into very small dice one oz. of carrot, one oz. of onion, and two parsley stalks. Add a fragment of thyme and bay leaf; brown this *mirepoix* with butter, in a saucepan; throw in fifteen crayfish for *"Bisque"* (their average weight being about one and one-third oz.), and toss them in the *mirepoix* until they acquire a very red color. Sprinkle with two tablespoons of burnt brandy and one-quarter pint of white wine, season with a large pinch of salt and a pinch of ground pepper, and set to reduce.

This done, moisten with one-quarter pint of white consommé (2) and leave to cook for ten minutes.

Also cook three oz. of rice in one and one-half pints of white consommé.

Shell the crayfishes' tails and put them aside; also reserve eight crayfish shells. Drain the crayfish of all their cooking-liquor; finely pound them and their remains and the *mirepoix*. Add the rice, properly cooked, and the cooking-liquor of the crayfish, and rub through a strainer, first, and then through a very fine sieve.

Add to the resulting *purée* one-half pint of white consommé, set to boil, stirring with a whisk the while, pass through a strainer, and then keep the preparation in a *bain-marie* (double-boiler), taking care to place a few lumps of butter on its surface lest a skin should form while the *bisque* is waiting to be served.

Finish the preparation when serving with two and one-half oz.

of butter, three tablespoons of excellent thick cream, and a very little cayenne.

Garnish with the crayfish tails cut into dice, and the eight shells stuffed with a fish *forcemeat* with cream and *poached* seven or eight minutes previously.

This soup may also be prepared as a velouté or a cream.

663—LOBSTER BISQUE　　　　　　　　　*Bisque de Homard*

After substituting for the crayfish an uncooked lobster weighing three lbs., cut into small sections, the procedure is the same as that of (662). It is only necessary, therefore, to refer to that recipe for all particulars relating to preparation and quantities.

Garnish with the meat taken from the tail; this should have been kept aside and cut into small dice.

This soup may also be prepared as a velouté or a cream.

664—SHRIMP BISQUE　　　　　　　　　*Bisque de Crevettes*

The mode of procedure for this *bisque*, the *mirepoix*, the thickening ingredients, the moistening, and the finishing of the soup are identical with those of (662).

All that is needed, therefore, is to substitute for the crayfish two lbs. of shrimps.

Instead of using ordinary butter in finishing this *bisque*, use three oz. of shrimp butter (145). Garnish with twenty-five shrimp tails, shelled and trimmed.

This soup may also be prepared as a velouté or a cream.

665—CULLIS OF GAME, HUNTERS' STYLE
Coulis de Gibier, dit au Chasseur

Prepare six oz. of the meat of a wild rabbit, six oz. of that of a partridge, and six oz. of that of a pheasant. These meats should be roasted and the roasting pans swashed and scraped with a liqueur-glass of burnt brandy. The resulting gravy should be added to the soup.

Now finely grind these meats together with one-half pint of cooked and drained lentils. When the whole has become a smooth *purée* add the cooking-liquor of the lentils and the pan gravy referred to and rub through a fine sieve.

Finish the *cullis* with the necessary quantity of consommé (2), heat it, and pass it through a strainer. Add butter at the last moment and season moderately.

Garnish with three tablespoons of small, very fresh mushrooms; these to be finely minced and tossed in butter.

666—CULLIS OF CRACKLINGS WITH BLACK BREAD, CALLED

A L'ARDENNAISE *Coulis de Grives au Pain Noir, dit à l'Ardennaise*

Fry four fine thrushes in butter and complete their cooking in one pint of game bird consommé (5) containing five oz. of rye-bread dice fried in butter. These dice constitute in this case the thickening element of the soup. Remove and put aside the thrushes' breasts, finely grind the rest together with two juniper-berries, add the thickening of bread dice, and rub through a sieve.

Add to the resulting *purée* one-quarter pint of game bird consommé, set to boil, and pass through a strainer. Finish the *cullis* with two and one-half oz. of butter and four tablespoons of cream.

Garnish with the reserved breasts cut into thin slices or into a *julienne*.

667—CULLIS OF GROUSE OLD STYLE

Coulis de Gelinotte à l'Ancienne

Proceed as in (666) in so far as the preparatory details and the quantities are concerned, but take note of the following changes in other directions:—

Substitute for the thrushes, two grouse or two hazel-hens, taking care to discard the legs and the skeletons.

Use ordinary bread dice instead of those of rye-bread.

668—CULLIS OF RABBIT WITH CURRY *Coulis de Lapereau au Currie*

Cut the legs of a young wild rabbit into small pieces, brown in butter, and put them into the saucepan with a few slices of carrot and onion, one small bunch of parsley and celery, and one quart of white consommé (2). Set to cook gently.

Also lightly brown in butter two tablespoons of chopped onion, sprinkle with one-half tablespoon of *fecula* or other starch, etc., and a sufficient quantity of curry, moisten with the strained cooking-liquor of the rabbit, bring to the boil, and set to simmer for seven or eight minutes. Rub through a sieve and then skim for twenty minutes, adding from time to time one or two tablespoons of consommé to clarify the *cullis*. When about to serve finish with three or four tablespoons of cream.

Garnish with eighteen very small slices of rabbit meat and two oz. of rice à l'Indienne (2254), serving the latter separately.

669—CULLIS OF PARTRIDGE WITH CHESTNUT PUREE, CALLED A LA MANCELLE

Coulis de Perdreau à la Purée de Marrons, dit à la Mancelle

Split the shells of fifteen fine chestnuts, put them in a saucepan with water, boil them for five minutes, and shell and peel them quickly while they are still very hot. Then cook them gently in one-half pints of boiling water, add an herb bunch, a pinch of salt, a celery, minced, and one teaspoon of sugar.

Poêle a partridge, remove the breasts for the purpose of garnish, bone the rest, and grind it together with the skeleton and the *poêle* liquor. Add the chestnuts, pound the whole, and add some consommé to the *purée,* rubbing it through a fine sieve. This done, add to the preparation about one-quarter pint of very clear game stock (8), bring the whole to the boil, pass it through a strainer, and finish the *cullis,* when serving, with a very little cayenne and one and one-half oz. of butter.

Garnish with the breasts of partridge cut into a small *julienne.*

670—CULLIS OF CHICKEN CALLED A LA REINE

Coulis de Volaille, dit à la Reine

Poach in one quart of white consommé (2) a cleaned fowl weighing about three lbs. and two oz. of rice previously *blanched.* Having cooked the fowl, withdraw it, take off its breasts, and put them aside. Bone the remainder and finely grind the meat. When it is a smooth paste mix with the rice, which should be very well cooked, add the necessary amount of white consommé to the *purée,* and rub through a fin. sieve. Bring the *cullis* to the boil and pass it through a fine strainer.

Finish the preparation, when serving, with a binding composed of the yolks of three eggs, one-sixth pint of cream, and three oz. of butter.

Garnish with the reserved breasts cut into small, regular dice.

This soup may also be prepared as a velouté or a cream.

671—AGNES SOREL VELOUTE
Velouté Agnes Sorel

Prepare one and one-half pints of poultry velouté (56), keeping it somewhat thin.

Clean, wash, peel, and mince eight oz. of very fresh mushrooms, newly gathered if possible.

Rub through a fine sieve, and add the resulting *purée* of raw mushrooms to the velouté. Bring the whole to the boil once or twice, and this done rub through a fine sieve immediately. Finish with the thickening and add butter when serving.

Garnish with one tablespoon of a *julienne* of raw mushrooms tossed in butter, one tablespoon of breast of chicken, and as much smoked tongue, both of which should be cut in *julienne*-fashion.

N.B.—With regard to veloutés I remind the reader that the velouté of ordinary consistency represents one-half of the soup, the *purée* typifying the latter represents one-quarter, while the consommé required to bring the soup to the correct degree of consistency should be in the proportion of the remaining quarter.

The thickening, per quart of the soup, should consist of the yolks of three eggs and one-sixth pint of cream, while the average quantity of butter should measure about two and one-half oz. (see 242).

This soup may also be prepared as a cream.

672—VELOUTE OF WHITEBAIT WITH CURRY
Velouté de Blanchaille au Currie

Bear in mind that this soup ought to be made and served within the space of twenty minutes, for if it be left to stand for however short a time, it will most probably curdle, in spite of every possible precaution.

Cook three oz. of finely chopped onion in butter without browning, sprinkle with one-half teaspoon of curry, moisten with one and one-half pints of boiling water, add an herb bunch, a pinch of salt, a few sprigs of saffron (or a little of it powdered), and two oz. of Vienna bread.

Set to boil for ten minutes; this done add three-quarters lb. of very fresh Blanchailles (small white bait), and cook over a brisk fire.

Rub through a hair-sieve, finish by means of a thickening consist of the yolks of three eggs and one-fifth pint of cream, and pour the whole into the soup-tureen over some dried slices of bread (buttered), over rice, or over some previously *poached* vermicelli. Serve at once.

673—CARMELITE VELOUTE   *Velouté Carmelite*

Prepare one and one-half pints of fish velouté (26a), cook four oz. of fillets of sole and the same quantity of fillets of whiting in one and one-half oz. of butter and lemon juice. Pound the fish, add it to the velouté, and rub through a fine sieve.

Add the necessary quantity of consommé, heat the velouté, and finish it, when about to serve, with a thickening and butter.

Garnish with one tablespoon of a *julienne* of *poached* fillets of sole and twelve small *quenelles* of smelt *forcemeat*.

This soup may also be prepared as a cream.

674—CARROT VELOUTE, CALLED NIVERNAISE
Velouté aux Carottes, dit Nivernaise

Cut into thin slices one lb. of the outer part only of carrots, season with a pinch of table-salt and twice that amount of powdered sugar, and cook in one oz. of butter.

Add one pint of ordinary thin velouté (25) and let the cooking of the carrots be completed therein. Rub through a fine sieve, finish with one-half pint of white consommé (2), set to boil, and complete the preparation, when serving, with the thickening and butter.

Garnish with one and one-half tablespoons of a fine *brunoise* of carrots.

This soup may also be prepared as a cream.

675—COUNTESS VELOUTE
Velouté Comtesse

Prepare one pint of ordinary velouté (25), parboil one and one-half lbs. of white asparagus, and put them into the velouté. Complete the cooking gently. Rub through a fine sieve, add one-half pint of white consommé (2), heat, and finish the preparation, when serving, with the thickening and butter.

Garnish with one tablespoon of a lettuce *chiffonade* and twelve small white asparagus tips.

This soup may also be prepared as a cream.

676—CUCUMBER VELOUTE, CALLED DANOISE
Velouté au Conconbres, dit Danoise

Peel, remove the seeds from, mince, and stew in butter one lb. of parboiled cucumbers. Add this to one pint of ordinary velouté (25), which should have been prepared at the same time, and complete the cooking quickly. Rub through a sieve, add the necessary quantity of white consommé (2), heat, and finish the preparation, when serving, with a thickening and butter in the usual quantities.

Garnish with small *croutons* fried in butter.

This soup may also be prepared as a cream.

677—WATERCRESS VELOUTE
Velouté Cressonière

After having slightly parboiled it, stew one lb. of very fresh watercress in one and one-half oz. of butter, add them to one pint of ordinary velouté (25). Set to simmer for seven or eight minutes, rub through a sieve, add one and one-half pints of ordinary white consommé (2), heat, and finish the preparation, when serving, with a thickening and butter.

Garnish with one oz. of watercress leaves parboiled for three minutes.

This soup may also be prepared as a cream.

678—WHITE LADY VELOUTE   *Velouté Dame-Blanche*

Prepare one and one-half pints of clear poultry velouté (26). Also finely pound ten or twelve well-washed sweet almonds, moisten them, little by little, with one-sixth pint of fresh water, and rub through a strong towel, twisting it to assist the process. This also can be done with a grinder or sieve.

Add this almond milk to the velouté, and finish it, when serving, with the thickening and butter.

Garnish with one tablespoon of the white meat of chicken cut into small dice, and twelve small *quenelles* of chicken *forcemeat* (in the shape of balls) *poached* just before serving.

679—ARTOIS VELOUTE   *Velouté d'Artois*

Prepare one pint of ordinary velouté (25), and mix with one-half pint of a *purée* of white beans. Rub through a sieve; add one-half pint of white consommé (2); heat, and finish, when serving, with the thickening and butter.

Garnish with two tablespoons of an ordinary *julienne* and a pinch of chervil *pluches.*

This soup may also be prepared as a cream.

680—VELOUTE OF SMELTS   *Velouté d'Eperlans*

Prepare a thin *panada* (189) with one pint of boiled milk and two and one-half oz. of crumbled bread. Season with a pinch of salt and a very small quantity of *mignonette* pepper. Also cook gently, in one oz. of butter, two tablespoons of chopped onion, two and one-half oz. of fillets of smelt, one-half lb. of fillets of sole, or the meat of a wall-eyed pike, and the juice of the quarter of a lemon.

Add the fish, stewed in butter and pounded, to the *panada,* together with one-half pint of ordinary thin velouté (25).

Rub through a fine sieve; heat; season with a very little cayenne, and finish, when serving, with an ordinary thickening and one and one-half oz. of butter.

N.B.—In view of the decided flavor of the smelt, and the really disagreeable taste it imparts to a preparation which contains too much of it, never permit it to exceed the proportion of one-third of the required quantity of fish. The remaining two-thirds should be supplied by a fish of neutral flavor, such as the sole or wall-eyed pike, both of which are admirably suited to this purpose.

The *velouté d'éperlans* should, like almost all fish veloutés, be prepared as quickly as possible, and at the last moment. The process should not last longer than thirty minutes, for, if there be any delay, the preparation will curdle and lose its flavor.

For this soup I elected to use a *panada* as the thickening element, instead of a fish velouté, the reason being that, were the latter used, the taste of fish would be too pronounced.

681—JOINVILLE VELOUTE OF SMELTS   *Velouté d'Eperlans Joinville*

Proceed in the matter of the base of the soup as in (680).

Finish the velouté with an ordinary thickening and one and one-half oz. of shrimp butter (145).

Garnish with six crayfish tails or giant shrimp cut into four pieces, and one tablespoon of a short *julienne* of truffles and mushrooms.

682—PRINCESS VELOUTE OF SMELTS   *Velouté d'Eperlans Princesse*

Prepare same as above, with twelve small *quenelles* of smelt *forcemeat* with crayfish butter (147), and one tablespoon of very green asparagus tips per quart of velouté.

683—FROG VELOUTE, CALLED SICILIAN

Velouté aux Grenouilles, dit Sicilienne

Prepare one and one-half pints of delicate and rather thin fish velouté (26a).

Trim fifteen or twenty frogs' legs; toss them in butter without letting them brown, and set them to *poach* for ten minutes in two tablespoons of white wine and the juice of a lemon. Pound them in a mortar or put through a grinder; add the resulting *purée* to the velouté; set to simmer for seven or eight minutes, and rub through a fine sieve.

Heat the velouté, and finish it, when serving, with the ordinary thickening and three and one-half oz. of best butter.

Do not garnish this velouté.

This soup may also be prepared as a cream.

684—LOBSTER VELOUTE, CALLED CARDINAL
Velouté d'Homard, dit Cardinal

Prepare one and three-quarter pints of *bisque* de homard (lobster) (663), but substitute velouté (25) for the thickening with rice. Rub through a fine sieve; heat, and complete, when serving, with two and one-half oz. of lobster butter (149) and three-quarters oz. of red butter (142).

Garnish with two *baba-moulds* of a *royale* of lobster, cut with a fancy-cutter in the shape of a cross.

Shell-fish veloutés do not permit an egg-yolk thickening.

685—LOBSTER VELOUTE A LA CLEVELAND
Velouté de Homard à la Cleveland

Break up two small live lobsters or one medium-sized one, and prepare it à l'Américaine (see "Lobster à l'Américaine" (939)). Reserve a few slices of the meat for garnishing purposes. Finely pound the rest with the shell; combine the *purée* with one quart of ordinary velouté (25) prepared beforehand, and add the lobster sauce. Rub through a strainer, first, then through a fine sieve; heat without allowing to boil; add the required quantity of consommé, and once more pass all through a strainer.

Complete, when serving, with three oz. of best butter.

Garnish with one-half tablespoon of peeled tomato pulp, cut into dice and half-melted in butter, and the reserved slices of lobster cut into dice.

686—LOBSTER VELOUTE INDIAN   *Velouté de Homard à l'Indienne*

Prepare the lobster à l'Américaine (939), and flavor it with curry. Preserve a sufficient quantity of meat from the tail to allow for an abundant garnish.

For the rest of the process proceed exactly as the preceding recipe directs.

Garnish with the reserved meat cut into dice, and four tablespoons of rice à l'Indienne (2254); send it to the table separately.

687—LOBSTER VELOUTE ORIENTAL   *Velouté de Homard à l'Orientale*

Prepare a medium-sized lobster after the manner directed in "Homard à la Newburg with raw lobster" (948), and season with curry.

Reserve a few slices of the meat of the tail for the garnish; finely pound the remaining portions and the shell; add the lobster sauce,

and combine with one quart of ordinary velouté (25), kept somewhat light.

Rub through a strainer, first, then through a fine sieve; heat the
velouté without letting it boil; add the necessary quantity of consommé (4), and finish the preparation, when about to serve, with
three oz. of butter.

Garnish with the reserved lobster cut into dice, and two tablespoons of rice à l'Indienne (2254), each grain of which should be
kept distinct and separate.

688—LOBSTER VELOUTE WITH PAPRIKA

Velouté de Homard au Paprika

Prepare a medium-sized lobster àl'Américaine (939), and, in addition to the usual ingredients of the preparation, include two
chopped tomatoes and two roughly chopped onions. Season with
paprika.

For the rest of the operation, proceed exactly as directed under
"Velouté à la Cleveland" (685).

Garnish with lobster meat cut into dice, two tablespoons of rice,
and one tablespoon of pimentos cut into dice.

689—LOBSTER VELOUTE PERSIAN　*Velouté de Homard à la Persane*

Proceed exactly as for "Velouté de Homard à l'Orientale" (687).

Garnish with lobster meat in dice, one tablespoon of pimentos in
dice, and two tablespoons of pilaff rice (2255), to which add a very
little saffron.

Remarks Relating to the Variation of these Veloutés.—By merely
substituting an equivalent quantity of crayfish, shrimps, or crabs,
for the lobster, the recipes dealing with veloutés of lobster, given
above, may be applied to *Veloutés of Crayfish, Shrimps,* or *Crabs.*

It would therefore be pointless to repeat them, since all that is
needed is to read crayfish, shrimps, or crabs wherever the word
lobster appears.

Thus I shall only point out that the number of these veloutés may
be increased at will, the only requisites being the change of the basic
ingredient and the modification of the garnish.

690—OYSTER VELOUTE　　　　　*Velouté aux Huîtres*

Prepare one quart of very delicate fish velouté (26a), and bear in
mind that the preparation must be made as speedily as possible.
(See the remarks dealing with this question which follow upon the
model recipe of the *velouté d'éperlans* (680).)

Add to the velouté the carefully collected liquor of the twenty-four oysters constituting the garnish, and complete, when about to serve, with a thickening and butter.

Garnish with four poached oysters, bearded, for each person.

691—ISOLINE VELOUTE   *Velouté Isoline*

Prepare one quart of poultry velouté (26). Complete it, when serving, with an ordinary thickening and three oz. of crayfish butter (147).

Garnish with three tablespoons of large sago *poached* in white consommé (2).

692—MARIE LOUISE VELOUTE   *Velouté Marie Louise*

Prepare one pint of poultry velouté (26); mix with one-half pint of barley cream (712), and rub through a sieve. Add one-half pint of white consommé (2), and heat the velouté without letting it boil.

Finish it, when about to serve, with a thickening and butter. Garnish with one and one-half tablespoons of best macaroni, *poached* and cut.

This soup may also be prepared as a cream.

693—MARY STUART VELOUTE   *Velouté Marie Stuart*

Prepare a poultry velouté (26) with barley cream (712). Finish it, when about to serve, with a thickening and butter.

Garnish with two tablespoons of a *brunoise,* and the same quantity of fine pearl barley cooked in white consommé (2).

This soup may also be prepared as a cream.

694—VELOUTE AU POURPIER   *Velouté au Pourpier*

Proceed exactly as directed under "Velouté Cressonière" (677), but substitute *purslane* for the watercress.

695—SULTAN VELOUTE   *Velouté à la Sultane*

Prepare one quart of poultry velouté (26). Finish it, when serving, with a binding composed of the yolks of three eggs diluted with one-fifth pint of sweet-almond milk (made by pounding eighteen sweet almonds, mixed with one-fifth pint of water, and straining through a twisted towel), and three oz. of pistachio butter (156). The velouté should be of a pale green shade.

Garnish with small crescents of chicken *forcemeat* prepared with crayfish butter (147), kept a pink shade. These crescents should be piped, by means of a pastry-bag, upon thin round slices of truffle, and *poached* in consommé (2).

This soup may also be prepared as a cream.

695a—COLD CHICKEN VELOUTE FOR SUPPERS
Velouté de Volaille Froid pour Soupers

The preparation of these veloutés requires the utmost care, but, as a rule, they are very much liked.

Prepare a white *roux* from one oz. of butter and one and one-sixth oz. of flour per quart of the liquid. Dilute with some very strong clear consommé (2), thoroughly cleared of grease; boil, and skim during one and one-half hours of cooking, adding meanwhile half as much consommé as served in the diluting of the velouté.

When the velouté is thoroughly cleared and entirely free of grease, strain it through a silk sieve, and add, per quart, one-quarter pint of very fresh thin cream. Cool, stirring incessantly; once more strain the velouté through the sieve when it is cold, and, if necessary, add some of the consommé already used, in order to give the velouté the consistency of a thickened consommé. Serve it in cups, and see that it be sufficiently thin so as not to be pasty to the taste.

This velouté is usually served as it stands, but it allows for various condimentary additions. Such are:—Tomato and red or green pepper *essences;* crayfish, shrimp, or game creams. These creams or *essences* should be of consummate delicacy, and ought to lend only a very delicate flavor to the velouté.

696—CREAM OF ARTICHOKES WITH HAZEL-NUT BUTTER
Crème d'Artichauts au Beurre de Noisette

Have ready one and one-half pints of Béchamel (28). Parboil, finely mince, and stew in butter four large artichoke-bottoms. Pound these; put them in the Béchamel, and rub through a fine sieve.

Add the necessary quantity of white consommé (2) or milk, and set to heat without allowing to boil. Finish the preparation, when serving, with one-quarter pint of cream and one oz. of hazel-nut butter (155).

Remarks Relative to Creams.—I remind the reader here that the thickening element of creams is a Béchamel prepared in the usual way (28); in the preparation of a cream, of any kind, the Béchamel should constitute half of the whole quantity, the basic ingredient a quarter, and the white consommé or milk the remaining quarter.

As a rule, they contain no butter, but are finished by means of one-third pint of very fresh cream per quart. Be this as it may, if it be desirable to butter them, one may do so, but in very small quantities, and taking care to use the very best butter.

This class of soups is more particularly suited to *Lenten* menus.

697—CREAM OF ASPARAGUS, CALLED ARGENTEUIL

Crème d'Asperges, dit Argenteuil

Parboil for five or six minutes one and one-half lbs. of white asparagus, the tough parts removed. Drain them, and set them to complete their cooking gently in one and one-quarter pints of previously prepared Béchamel (28).

Rub through a fine sieve; add the necessary quantity of white consommé (2), and heat without allowing to boil.

Finish with cream when serving.

Garnish with two tablespoons of white asparagus tips and a pinch of chervil *pluches.*

698—CREAM OF GREEN ASPARAGUS   *Crème d'Asperges Vertes*

Proceed exactly as for "Crème Argenteuil" (697), but substitute green asparagus for white asparagus.

699—CREAM OF GREEN WHEAT, CALLED CERES

Crème au Blé Vert, dit Cerès

Put one lb. of dehydrated, green wheat to soak in cold water for four hours. Then cook it slowly in one-half pint of water and as much white consommé (2). Mix with one and one-quarter pints of Béchamel (28) and rub through a fine sieve.

Add the necessary amount of white consommé to the *purée;* heat the whole without boiling, and finish it with cream when dishing up.

Garnish with a pinch of chervil *pluches.*

This soup may also be prepared as a *purée* or a velouté.

700—CREAM OF CELERY   *Crème de Céleri*

Mince one lb. white celery stalks; parboil for seven or eight minutes; drain, and stew in one oz. of butter. Mix one and one-quarter pints of Béchamel (28) with it; complete the cooking slowly, and rub through a fine sieve.

Add one-half pint of white consommé (2); heat without allowing to boil, and finish the preparation with cream when about to serve.

Garnish with two tablespoons of a chopped and cooked celery. This soup may also be prepared as a *purée* or a velouté.

701—CREAM OF CHERVIL, CALLED CHEVREUSE
Crème de Cerfeuil Bulbeux, dit Chevreuse

Mince and stew in butter one lb. of bulbous chervil roots, and mix with one and one-quarter pints of Béchamel (28). Complete the cooking slowly; rub through a fine sieve; add sufficient white consommé (2); heat, and finish with cream when serving. Garnish with one tablespoon of a fine *julienne* of breast of chicken and the same quantity of a *julienne* of truffles.

This soup may also be prepared as a velouté.

702—CREAM OF BELGIAN ENDIVE, CALLED BRUXELLOISE
Crème de Chicorée de Bruxelles, dit Bruxelloise

Take one lb. of very fresh chicory (Belgian endive), and stew it for a good half-hour in one and one-half oz. of butter and the juice of one lemon.

Now mix one and one-quarter pints of Béchamel (28) with it, and finish the cooking very slowly. Rub through a sieve; add the necessary quantity of white consommé (2); heat, and complete with cream when serving.

Garnish with a *julienne* of Belgian chicory (endive), stewed and well drained.

703—CREAM OF SPINACH, CALLED FLORENTINE
Crème d'Epinards, dit Florentine

Quickly parboil one lb. of shredded and well-washed spinach to which a little sorrel may be added; drain, press, and add one and one-half pints of somewhat thin Béchamel (28). Complete the cooking; rub the whole through a sieve, and finish it with the necessary amount of fresh cream.

Garnish with a *julienne* of spinach, quickly parboiled and stewed in butter.

704—CREAM OF NEW SHELLED BEANS   *Crème de Fèves Nouvelles*

Shell two-thirds lb. of new broad beans, freshly picked, if possible. Cook them for ten minutes in boiling salted water containing a sprig of savory, and then add one and one-quarter pints of Béchamel (28). Complete the cooking of the broad beans in the Béchamel; rub through sieve; add one-half pint of white consommé or milk; heat without allowing to boil, and finish the preparation with cream when dishing up.

Garnish with very small shelled broad beans, split in two and parboiled with a sprig of savory.

This soup may also be prepared as a velouté.

705—CREAM OF YAMS, CALLED BRESILIENNE

Crème d'Ignames, dit Brésilienne

Bake the yams in the oven in their skins. As soon as this is done, cut them in two, remove their pulp, and quickly rub it through a sieve while it is still hot. Dilute the *purée* with one pint boiling milk or one-half pint thin Béchamel (28) per lb. of the yam *purée*. (This Béchamel should be made from one and one-half oz. of butter and one oz. of flour per quart of milk.)

Rub the whole through a fine sieve, and finish the preparation in the usual way. Garnish with two tablespoons of large sago, *poached* in consommé.

This soup may also be prepared as a velouté.

706—CREAM OF LETTUCE, CALLED JUDIC

Crème de Laitues, dit Judic

Parboil and stew in butter two medium-sized heads of shredded lettuce, the greenest leaves of which should have been discarded. Add these to one and one-half pints of Béchamel (28).

Rub through a fine sieve; add one pint of white consommé (2); heat, and finish as usual with cream.

Garnish with lettuce leaves, lightly coated with chicken *forcemeat,* a bit of truffle laid in their center, and the whole *poached* at the last minute.

This soup may also be prepared as a velouté.

707—CREAM OF CORN, CALLED WASHINGTON

Crème de Maïs, dit Washington

Cook some fresh corn in salted water (or use the canned kind if the fresh is out of season), and combine with an equal quantity of thin Béchamel (28). Rub through a fine sieve; heat, and finish with cream when serving.

Garnish with kernels of corn cooked in salted water.

This soup may also be prepared as a velouté by substituting for the Béchamel an excellent poultry velouté (26).

708—CREAM OF SORREL WITH OATMEAL

Crème d'Oseille a l'Avoine

Pour one-quarter lb. of oatmeal diluted with one-half pint of cold milk into one quart of slightly salted boiling milk. Stir over the fire until the boil is reached; move the saucepan to the side of the fire, and simmer for two hours.

This done, add six tablespoons of a *fondue* of sorrel and butter; set to simmer again for one-quarter hour, and rub the whole through a fine sieve.

Complete the operation after the manner common to all creams.

709—CREAM OF SORREL WITH BARLEY   *Crème d'Oseille a l'Orge*

Proceed exactly as for (708), using the same quantities, but substituting barley-meal for oatmeal.

Remarks upon the Two above Creams.—They may also be prepared as veloutés. Their garnish may be greatly varied, and may consist of *chiffonade* of lettuce and sorrel; pressed peeled tomatoes, cut into dice and cooked in butter; *poached* rice or pastes (vermicelli, etc.); fine well-cooked pearl barley; *brunoise;* small *printaniers* of spring vegetables.

They belong, in fact, to the same order of soups as the *purées* of sorrel with pastes, the recipes of which were given earlier in the chapter.

710—CREAM OF OXALIS   *Crème d'Oxalis*

Peel and slice the *oxalis* roots (similar to potatoes), and half-cook them in salted water. Drain, add it to one and one-half pints of Béchamel (28), and complete its cooking gently in the sauce.

Rub through a fine sieve; add one-half pint of white consommé (2), and finish after the manner of other creams. Garnish with chervil *pluches*.

This soup may also be prepared as a *purée* or a velouté.

711—CREAM OF RICE   *Crème de Riz*

Wash one-half lb. of rice in cold water; *blanch* it; cool it, and cook it very gently in one quart of white consommé (2). Mash and rub through a fine sieve, and dilute the rice *purée* with one pint of white consommé. Heat and finish the preparation, when serving, with the necessary quantity of cream.

Or pour four tablespoons of rice cream soup, diluted with one-half pint of cold milk, into three pints of boiling milk; set to boil.

stirring the while, and leave to cook very gently for twenty-five minutes. Rub through a fine sieve, and finish the preparation, when serving, with the required quantity of cream.

This soup may also be prepared as a velouté.

712—CREAM OF BARLEY   *Crème d'Orge*

Wash three-quarters lb. of coarse pearl barley in lukewarm water, and cook it gently for about two and one-half hours in one pint of white consommé (2) containing one stalk of white celery.

Mash and rub through a sieve; dilute the *purée* of barley with one pint of white consommé (2); heat, and finish the preparation, when serving, with the necessary quantity of cream.

This soup may also be prepared with barley-meal, the procedure in that case being the same as that of the "Crème de Riz" (711).

Garnish with very fine, well-cooked pearl barley.

This soup may also be prepared as a velouté.

713—PRINCESS CREAM OF CHICKEN   *Crème de Volaille Princesse*

Mix one and one-half pints of thin Béchamel (28) with one-half pint of chicken *purée*. Rub through a fine sieve; add one-half pint of white consommé (2), or the same quantity of boiled milk; heat without allowing to boil, and finish with cream when serving.

Garnish with twenty very small slices of chicken breasts, white asparagus tips, and chervil *pluches*.

This soup may also be prepared as a velouté.

714—REINE MARGOT CREAM   *Crème Reine Margot*

Mix one-half pint of chicken *purée* with one pint of thin Béchamel (28). Rub through a fine sieve; add one and one-half pints of white consommé (2) and one-quarter pint of almond milk (678). Heat without allowing to boil, and finish with cream.

Garnish with very small grooved *quenelles* of chicken *forcemeat* combined with one oz. of pistachio *purée* per three oz. of *forcemeat*.

This soup may also be prepared as a velouté.

715—AURORA SOUP   *Potage à l'Aurore*

Wash one-quarter lb. of fine pearl barley in plenty of water. Put it into a saucepan with one quart of consommé, as much water, an herb bunch comprising parsley, celery, and chervil, and set to cook very gently for five hours. While the cooking progresses, take care to remove all the scum which forms on the surface, in order that the cooking-liquor may remain very clear.

When the barley is well cooked, transfer it to another saucepan, and add to it four tablespoons of a thick and very red tomato *purée*, strained through muslin, and two tablespoons of celery, minced in *paysanne*-fashion, stewed in butter, and finally cooked in con‐ sommé (2).

This excellent soup should not be made too thick.

716—BAGRATION RICH VEAL SOUP   *Potage Bagration Gras*

Cut two-thirds lb. of very white tenderloin of veal into large dice, and cook in butter without letting them brown. Add one and one-quarter pints of thin velouté (25) with a veal base, and set to cook very gently.

Finely grind the veal; dilute the *purée* with velouté, and rub through a fine sieve. Add one pint of white consommé (2); heat without boiling, and complete the preparation, when serving, with a binding of the yolks of three eggs diluted with four tablespoons of cream and two oz. of butter.

Garnish with thin macaroni cut into short lengths, and send some grated cheese to the table separately.

717—BAGRATION LENTEN SOUP   *Potage Bagration Maigre*

Prepare one and one-half pints of fresh velouté (25), and mix with one-quarter pint of mushroom velouté. (For making this, see "Velouté Agnès Sorrel," 671.)

Heat without boiling; pass through a strainer, and finish, when about to serve, with the same thickening as for ordinary velouté, and two and one-half oz. of butter. Garnish with one fillet of sole, *poached* very white, and cut into a *julienne;* twelve small *quenelles* of sole or whiting *forcemeat* finished with crayfish butter (147), and six crayfishes' tails and shrimps cut into small pieces.

718—CHOISEUL SOUP   *Potage Choiseul*

Prepare a *"purée* Conti" (640) with an excellent *fumet* of game.

Garnish with two tablespoons of sorrel, chopped and cooked in butter, and two tablespoons of *poached* rice.

719—COMPIEGNE SOUP   *Potage Compiègne*

Prepare a light *"Purée* Soissonaise" (637); butter it well, and add as a garnish three tablespoons of chopped sorrel cooked in butter, and chervil *pluches*.

720—DERBY SOUP   *Potage Derby*

Add one-half pint of Soubise *purée* (104) to one pint of "Crème de Riz" (711) flavored with a very little curry. Rub the whole through a fine sieve.

Add one-half pint of white consommé (2), and heat without boiling. Complete, when about to serve, with an ordinary thickening and three oz. of butter.

Garnish with twelve small *quenelles* of chicken *forcemeat* combined with one-third of its volume of *foie-gras purée,* one tablespoon of little truffle balls, and an equal quantity of *poached* rice, each grain of which must be kept distinct and separate.

721—DIANA SOUP   *Potage à la Diane*

Cook one-half lb. of lentils in the usual method. Roast two medium-sized partridges, keeping them slightly underdone, and remove their breasts. Complete the cooking of the partridges with the lentils, drained of their cooking-liquor, in one pint of game consommé (5).

Prepare a *royale* (209) with the reserved breasts.

When the birds are cooked, bone them; grind the meat, and add the lentils and the cooking-liquor; rub through a fine sieve.

Finish the *purée* with one and one-half pints of excellent thin game stock (8), and complete the soup, when serving, with two oz. of butter and two tablespoons of reduced Madeira.

Garnish with the *royale,* cut into small regular crescents, and twelve small crescents of very black truffle.

722—ELISA SOUP   *Potage Elisa*

Prepare one and one-half pints of poultry velouté (26), and rub it through a fine sieve. Complete with one-half pint of white consommé (2); heat without boiling, and finish, when serving, with an ordinary thickening, two and one-half oz. of butter, and two tablespoons of a *fondue* of sorrel.

723—FAVORITE SOUP   *Potage Favori*

Prepare one pint of a velouté of green asparagus; one-half pint of a velouté of lettuce, and one-half pint of poultry velouté (26). Put all three into a saucepan; add the necessary quantity of white consommé (2) to bring the soup to the correct degree of consistency; heat without boiling, and pass through a strainer.

Finsh the soup, when serving, with an ordinary thickening and two oz. of butter. Garnish with one tablespoon of a *chiffonade* of sorrel, and one tablespoon of green asparagus tips.

724—GERMINY SOUP   *Potage Germiny*

Cook in butter three oz. of shredded sorrel, and add one and one-half pints of white consommé (2). A few minutes before serving, pour into the consommé a thickening composed of the yolks of six eggs diluted with one-quarter pint of cream; set on the fire and stir, until the preparation begins to show signs of boiling.

Finish, away from the fire, with two and one-half oz. of butter, and add a pinch of chervil *pluches.*

Remarks concerning the Possible Variation of this Soup.—The mode of procedure adopted in the case of the "Potage Germiny" could, if necessary, be applied to all thick soups, and it would then constitute a class to which the term "Cream" would be better suited than it is at present to the soups so called.

Instead of the ordinary white consommé, which is used in its preparation, a consommé may be used in which such vegetables as carrots, turnips, peas, etc., are cooked, the vegetable being reserved for the garnish, while the cooking-liquor is thickened with egg-yolks and cream in accordance with the quantities and directions given in the above recipe.

A carrot cream, a cream of fresh peas, or of asparagus tips, prepared in this way, would be much more delicate than those prepared from the ordinary recipes.

The essential point in this series of soups is the thickening; this should consist of enough egg-yolks to make the soups sufficiently thick and creamy.

725—HERB SOUP   *Potage aux Herbes*

Cut two oz. of sorrel leaves into a *julienne,* and stew them in butter with one oz. of watercress leaves, one oz. of chervil *pluches,* and young pimpernel. Add one and one-half pints of water, the necessary salt, three medium-sized, peeled, and quartered potatoes, and cook gently.

Drain and reserve the cooking-liquor; mash the potatoes; dilute the *purée* with the cooking-liquor, and rub through a fine sieve. Set to boil, and finish, when serving, with three oz. of *printanier* (157) butter with herbs, combined with a few leaves of sweet basil.

Add a pinch of chervil *pluches.*

726—JUBILEE SOUP, CALLED BALVET   *Potage Jubilee, dit Balvet*

Prepare, according to the directions given (648), one and one-half pints of a *purée* of fresh peas, and add one-half pint of consommé of "La Petite Marmite" (598). Set to boil, and finish with two oz. of butter.

Garnish with the vegetables from the Marmite, prepared as for Croûte au Pot (556).

727—LONGCHAMPS SOUP   *Potage Longchamps*

Refer to the derivative soups of the "Purée of Peas" (654).

728—LAVALLIERE SOUP   *Potage Lavallière*

Prepare one and one-half pints of "Crème de Volaille" (713), finished with a thickening of egg-yolks and cream; also two-thirds pint of "Crème de Céleri" (750), similarly finished, and combine the two creams.

Garnish with twelve small *profiterolles,* stuffed with chicken *forcemeat,* and a *royale* of celery in dice.

729—MADELEINE SOUP   *Potage Madeleine*

Prepare and combine the following *purées*:—One-third pint of artichoke *purée,* one-fifth pint of dried bean *purée,* one-seventh pint of Soubise (104) *purée.* Add one pint of white consommé (2); set to boil; pass through a strainer, and finish, when serving, with two oz. of butter.

Garnish with two tablespoons of sago *poached* in one-half pint of white consommé.

730—MISS BETSY SOUP   *Potage Miss Betsy*

Proceed exactly as for "Potage à l'Aurore" (715), but flavor "potage Miss Betsy" with curry; substitute for the celery, peeled, cored apples cut into dice and cooked in butter.

N.B.—Both these soups ("Aurore" and "Miss Betsy") are subject to much variation. All that is needed is to alter the flavoring element and the garnish. Thus the quantity of tomato may be reduced by half, and combined with one-quarter lb. of peas and their cooking-liquor (the peas in this case being cooked in one pint of water with a little salt and sugar); or with the same quantity of string beans, asparagus tips, or sorrel cooked in butter, etc.

731—MONTESPAN SOUP *Potage Montespan*

Add one-half pint of somewhat thick tapioca to one and one-half pints of "Crème d'Asperges" (697), prepared as directed. Garnish with very fine cooked peas.

732—NELUSKO SOUP *Potage Nelusko*

Mix one and one-half pints of rather liquid poultry velouté (26) with one-half pint of chicken *purée*. When serving, add an ordinary thickening, and finish with two and one-half oz. of hazel-nut butter (155).

Garnish with very small *quenelles* of chicken *forcemeat* combined with one tablespoon of finely ground hazel-nut per three oz. of the *forcemeat*.

733—LITTLE DUKE SOUP *Potage Petit Duc*

Take a fine woodcock; lift and reserve one of its breasts, and roast it, taking care to keep it very underdone. Then remove the other breast and with it prepare two *dariole-moulds* of *royale* (209). Finely grind what remains of the woodcock, and combine with the resulting *purée* one and one-half pints of game velouté (242) prepared with *essence* of woodcock. Cover the saucepan and place it in the water-bath for thirty-five minutes. Now rub the whole through a fine sieve; heat without boiling, and finish, when serving, with one and one-half oz. of butter, one and one-half oz. of cooked *foie-gras purée,* diluted with a few tablespoons of the soup, one and cne-half tablespoons of cream, and one and one-half tablespoons of burnt liqueur brandy.

Garnish with the *royale* cut into dice, and the reserved breast of woodcock, slightly cooked in butter at the last moment, and cut into thin slices.

734—REGENCY SOUP *Potage Régence*

Prepare one quart of barley cream (712). Finish it, when serving, with an ordinary thickening and one and one-half oz. of crayfish butter.

Garnish with twelve small, grooved *quenelles* of chicken *forcemeat* finished with crayfish butter (147); one tablespoon of small pearl barley, well cooked; and six small cocks' combs, freshly *poached* and very white.

735—RUSSIAN ROSSOLNIK *Potage Rossolnik*

Prepare one quart of light, poultry velouté (26) combined with the juice of a cucumber; ten pieces of parsley root and the same quantity of celery root, cut to the shape of small, new carrots, and split crosswise at their base; twenty small slices of salted cucumber.

Parboil the celery and parsley roots and the cucumber slices for fifteen minutes, and add them to the velouté when about to cook it. Cook the whole gently for forty minutes, skimming the velouté the while. Finish with one and one-half tablespoons of cucumber juice, and an ordinary thickening.

Garnish with small chicken-*forcemeat quenelles*.

736—HEALTH SOUP   *Potage de Santé*

Cook quickly, in salted water, three medium-sized, peeled, and quartered potatoes. When they seem soft to the touch, drain them; rub them through a fine sieve, and dilute the resulting *purée* with one and one-half pints of white consommé (2). Add two tablespoons of sorrel cooked in butter, and finish the preparation with an ordinary thickening and one oz. of butter.

Garnish with very thin round slices of French dinner rolls and chervil *pluches*.

737—SIGURD SOUP   *Potage Sigurd*

Prepare one pint of "Velouté Parmentier" and one pint of tomato velouté (242). Combine the two; heat, and finish, when serving, with two and one-half oz. of butter.

Garnish with twenty small *quenelles* of chicken *forcemeat,* combined with one teaspoonful of chopped green pepper, or peppers cut in dice, per three oz. of the *forcemeat.*

738—SOLFERINO SOUP   *Potage Solferino*

Mince the white part of two leeks, the third of a medium-sized carrot, and half an onion, and stew the whole in one and one-half oz. of butter. Add one-half lb. of pressed tomatoes cut into pieces, two medium-sized, peeled potatoes, minced; moisten with two-thirds pint of white consommé (2), and cook gently. Crush the vegetables; rub them through a fine sieve; complete the *purée* with the necessary quantity of white consommé; set to boil, and finish, when serving, with two and one-half oz. of butter.

Garnish with twelve little balls of potato, cut with a ball-cutter, and cooked in salted water; two tablespoons of string beans cut into small pieces; and some chervil *pluches*.

739—VIVIANE SOUP　　　　　　　　　　*Potage Viviane*

Prepare one quart of "Crème de Volaille" (713), and finish it with the usual thickening. Garnish with one tablespoon of artichoke-bottoms, cut into dice, the same quantity of carrot dice, both gently cooked in butter, and one tablespoon of truffle dice.

740—WINDSOR SOUP　　　　　　　　　　*Potage Windsor*

Blanch and cool one small, boned calf's foot, and cook it gently in a good white-wine *mirepoix*. Prepare one and one-half pints of "Crème de Riz" (711), and add the cooking-liquor of the calf's foot, strained through muslin.

Finish this cream, when about to serve, with an ordinary thickening, one and one-half tablespoons of a slight infusion of *turtle-soup herbs,* and one and one-half oz. of butter.

Garnish with a *julienne* of half of the calf's foot and twenty small *quenelles* consisting of a *purée* of hard-boiled egg-yolks and chicken *forcemeat,* these two preparations being in the proportion of two-thirds and one-third respectively.

741—ENGLISH GIBLET SOUP

Soupe aux Abatis de Volaille à l'Anglaise

Cut the chicken necks into three, the gizzards into four, and the wings into two. Brown one-half lb. of these giblets in a thick-bottomed saucepan with one oz. of butter. Sprinkle with one tablespoon of flour; slightly brown it, and dilute with one quart of white consommé (2) and one pint of water. Add an herb bunch containing also one stalk of celery, and set to cook gently for three hours.

When the giblets are cooked, drain them, trim them, and put them into a pot with two teaspoons of parboiled rice and a heaped tablespoon of celery-heart, minced and fried in butter. Strain the cooking-liquor of the giblets, through a strainer, over the garnishes, set to cook gently for another quarter of an hour; season strongly with pepper, and serve.

742—CHERRY SOUP　　　　　　　　　　*Soupe aux Cerises*

Pit two-thirds lb. of small, fleshy cherries and save the pits, and put twenty cherries aside for garnishing purposes. Put the others into a heavy pot with two-thirds pint of hot water, a small strip of lemon rind, and a small piece of cinnamon, and set to boil quickly for eight minutes.

Also boil in another heavy pot one-half pint of Port or Bordeaux wine. Crush half of the cherry-stones in the mortar; put them into the boiled wine, and let them infuse, away from the fire.

Rub the cooked cherries through a fine sieve; dilute the *purée* with the juice thickened by means of one tablespoon of *fecula* or cornstarch moistened with cold water; add the cherries put aside for the garnish, and one-half tablespoonful of powdered sugar, and again set to boil for four minutes.

Complete the preparation with the infusion strained through muslin; pour it into the soup-tureen, and add a few *biscottes*.

For the sake of variety, lady's-fingers may be substituted for *biscottes*.

743—COCKIE-LEEKIE SOUP   *Potage Cocki-Lecki*

Set half a stewing fowl to cook very gently in one and one-half pints of light and clear veal stock (10) with a few *aromatics*.

Also prepare a *julienne* of the white part of three leeks; stew this in butter without browning, and complete the cooking in the cooking-liquor of the fowl, strained and poured carefully away.

Pour the soup into the soup-tureen, and add the meat of the fowl, cut into a *julienne*.

Serve some stewed prunes separately, but this is optional.

744—CHICKEN LIVER SOUP   *Soupe aux Foies de Volaille*

Make a *roux* from one and one-half oz. of butter and as much flour. When it has acquired a nice, light-brown color, moisten it with one quart of white consommé (2) or brown stock (7), and set to boil, stirring the while.

Add one-half lb. of raw chicken livers rubbed through a sieve, and set to cook for fifteen minutes. Rub the whole through a fine sieve; season strongly with pepper; heat, and complete the preparation, at the last moment, with one-quarter lb. of sliced chickens' livers, tossed in butter, and one wineglass of good Madeira.

745—JULIENNE DARBLAY SOUP   *Soupe Julienne Darblay*

Cook quickly in salted water two small, peeled, and quartered potatoes. Drain them, rub them through a fine sieve, and dilute the *purée* with one and one-half pints of white consommé (2). Add three tablespoons of a *julienne* made in accordance with the above recipe; heat, and finish the preparation with an ordinary thickening and one and one-half oz. of butter.

746—MINESTRONE   *Minestrone*

Brown the minced white parts of two small leeks and one-third of an onion, also minced, in one oz. of chopped, fresh lean bacon, and one-half oz. of grated, fat bacon. Moisten with one and one-half pints of white consommé (2), and add one-third of a carrot, one-third of a turnip, half a stalk of celery, two oz. of small cabbage, and one small potato, or one-half of a medium-sized one, all of which must be finely minced.

About twenty-five minutes after the soup has started cooking, complete it with two tablespoons of peas, a few string beans cut into one-half inch pieces, and one and one-half oz. of rice, or the same quantity of very thin macaroni broken into very small pieces.

This done, set to cook again for thirty minutes. A few minutes before serving, add to the soup one small, crushed clove of garlic, three leaves of sweet basil, and a small pinch of chopped chervil *pluches;* mix the whole with one-half tablespoon of grated bacon.

Send to the table, separately, at the same time as the soup some freshly grated Gruyère.

747—MILLE-FANTI   *Mille-Fanti*

First make the following preparation:—Beat two small eggs until thick, and mix with one and one-half oz. of fresh crumbs of white bread, one oz. of grated Parmesan, and a little nutmeg. Boil one and two-thirds pints of white consommé (2), and pour the above preparation in, little by little, stirring briskly the while with the whisk. Then move the pot to the side of the fire, put the lid on, and set to cook gently for seven or eight minutes.

When about to serve, stir the soup with a whisk again, and pour it into the soup-tureen.

748—MULLIGATAWNY SOUP   *Soupe Mulligatawny*

Cut a small fowl, or half a medium-sized one, into little pieces, and put these in a pot with a few round slices of carrot and onion, a small bunch of parsley and celery, one-half oz. of mushroom peelings and one quart of white consommé (2). Set to boil, and then let cook gently.

Also lightly brown in butter half a medium-sized onion, chopped; sprinkle it with two teaspoons of *fecula,* flour, etc., and one teaspoon of curry; moisten with the cooking-liquor of the fowl, strained through a sieve; boil, and set to cook gently for seven or eight minutes. Now rub the whole through a fine sieve, and skim for twenty minutes, adding one tablespoon of consommé, from time to time, to clarify the soup.

When about to serve, finish the preparation with three or four tablespoons of cream. Pour the whole into the soup-tureen; add a portion of the meat of the fowl, cut into thin slices, and serve separately two oz. of rice à l'Indienne (2254).

749—GUMBO OR OKRA SOUP   *Soupe aux Gombos ou Okra*

This soup is held in high esteem by Americans. It is served either with garnish, as I direct below, or as a consommé, hot or cold, or in cups, after it has been strained.

Fry one medium-sized chopped onion in two oz. of butter, without letting it brown. Add one-quarter lb. of fresh lean bacon, or ham cut into medium-sized dice; fry for a few minutes, and add about one lb. of boned chicken-meat cut into large dice (the white parts of the chicken are used in preference); let these ingredients brown well; take care to stir fairly often, and moisten with two quarts of white chicken consommé (3). Boil, and set to cook gently for twenty or twenty-five minutes with lid on.

Now add about one-half lb. of peeled okras, cut in coarse *paysanne*-fashion, and three or four medium-sized tomatoes, peeled, seeded and coarsely chopped.

When the okras are well cooked, carefully remove all grease from the preparation; test the seasoning, and, if necessary, add a few drops of Worcestershire sauce.

Garnish the soup with two or three tablespoons of plainly-cooked rice.

N.B.—This soup is excellent if it is finished with one-quarter pint of cream per quart. A cream of gumbo may also be prepared, which may be garnished with diced chicken meat. In the latter case, the garnish of rice is optional.

750—PAYSANNE SOUP   *Soupe à la Paysanne*

Finely mince one small carrot, one small turnip, one leek, one-third of a stalk of celery, one-third of an onion, and some cabbage leaves. Stew the vegetables in one oz. of butter; moisten with one and one-half pints of white consommé (2), and set to boil. After a few minutes, add two small potatoes minced like the other vegetables, and complete the cooking gently. Send separately some slices of French rolls.

751—LEEK AND POTATO SOUP, CALLED A LA BONNE FEMME OR VICHYSOISSE OR CREME GAULOISE

Soupe aux Poireaux et Pommes de Terre, dit à la Bonne Femme

Finely mince the white part of four medium-sized leeks. Put this into a pot with one oz. of butter, and stew gently for a quarter of an hour. Then add three medium-sized quartered potatoes, cut into slices the thickness of a quarter. Moisten with one pint of white consommé (2); add the necessary quantity of salt, and set to cook gently. When about to serve, finish the soup with one pint of boiled milk and one and one-half oz. of butter; pour it into the soup-tureen, and add twelve slices of French dinner rolls, cut as thinly as possible.

Vichysoisse, now called Crème Gauloise, is made by adding cream and chilling.

752—KIDNEY SOUP   *Soupe aux Rognons*

Proceed exactly as for "Soupe aux Foies de Volaille" (744), but substitute for the garnish of sliced livers one of calf's or sheep's kidney cut into large dice, or sliced, and briskly tossed in butter just before serving.

Finish the soup similarly to the preceding one, with Madeira.

CHAPTER XIV

FISH AND SEAFOOD

IN matters culinary, fish comprise not only the vertebrates of the sea and river, but also the edible crustaceans, mollusks, and terrapins and turtles, and frogs. Of course, the animals representing these various classes differ enormously in respect of their importance as articles of diet. Regarding fish, although certain species, such as salmon, trout, sole and the turbot, are in great demand, many other and excellent ones which are looked upon as inferior are seldom put into use by first-class cookery. Thus, chicken-turbot, Grey Mullet, and Bass are not nearly so popular as they deserve to be, and never appear on a menu of any importance. No doubt, Fashion—ever illogical and wayward—exercises her tyrannical sway here, as in other matters of opinion; for it will be found, even when the distinctions among fish are once established, that there exist a host of incongruities in the unwritten law. Fresh cod is a case in point; should this fish appear on the menu of a grand dinner given by Royalty, the guests would not think it at all out of place; but if the chef of a large modern hotel ventured to include it among the items of a plain table-d'hôte dinner he would most probably incur the scorn and indignation of his clientele.

This example, than which none could be better suited to our case, successfully shows that the culinary value of the fish has far less to do with the vogue the latter enjoys than the very often freakish whims of the public.

One can but deplore the arbitrary proscription which so materially reduces the resources at the disposal of a cook, more particularly at a time when the universally imperious cry is for novelty and variety in dishes and menus respectively; and one can only hope that reason and good sense may, at no remote period, intervene to check the purposeless demands of both entertainers and their guests in this respect.

Having regard to these considerations, I have omitted from this

263

work, which is really a thesaurus of selected recipes and not a complete formulary, all those fish enumerated below, which are very rarely eaten in France, and the recipes for which could therefore serve no purpose:—

753—SHAD *Alose*
Chiefly served grilled, baked, planked.

754—FRESH ANCHOVIES *Anchois Frais*
Extremely rare, and may be grilled or fried.

755—EELS *Anguilles*
Considered as common, and principally used in the preparation of a pie and in aspics. (Small eels are also pickled, smoked and fried.)

756—PIKE *Brochet*
Plentiful and of excellent quality; only used in the preparation of *forcemeat* and *quenelles;* the directions for the latter will be given later. They are sometimes served *crimped,* gashed or cooked whole in a *court-bouillon au bleu,* accompanied by parsley or caper sauce, etc. Small pike are generally prepared "à la Meunière" (778), or fried.

757—CARP *Carpe*
In still less demand than the pike, and only prized for its *milt*. It must, however, be admitted this fish is too often spoilt by the taint of mud.

758—DORADO (BREAM) *Dorade*
Served boiled with any of the fish sauces; but, in my opinion, it is best grilled.

759—STURGEON *Esturgeon*
Very rare; it is *braised,* like veal.

760—FERA *Féra*
Very scarce on the market; comes from the Swiss or Savoy lakes, and is only served à la Meunière (778).

761—SMELTS *Eperlans*
Very abundant.

762—FROGS *Grenouilles*

Not generally accepted as an article of first-class food by non-French people; nevertheless "Nymphes à l'Aurore" (351), the recipe of which I gave among the hors-d'œuvres, are generally appreciated.

763—FRESH HERRINGS *Harengs Frais*

Abundant and of excellent quality; seldom used in first-class cookery, except, perhaps, for their *milt*. Bloaters and kippered herrings are, with reason, preferred; of these I shall speak later.

764—LAMPREYS (EELS) *Lamproie*

Chiefly used in preparing pies similar to those referred to in 755.

765—FRESH WATER HERRINGS *Hareng d'eau douce*

Like the Féra, come from Switzerland or Savoy, and are very scarce on the market. Prepared especially *à la Meunière*

766—LOTE OR BURBOT *Lotte*

Very scarce on the market; only prized for its liver.

767—MOSTELE *Mostele*

Only caught in the region of Monaco; cannot bear transport; especially served *à la Meunière* or *à l'Anglaise.*

768—MUSSELS *Moules*

Chiefly used as garnish. See 2979–81.

769—NONAT *Nonnat*

Replaced by whitebait, which it greatly resembles.

770—PERCH *Perche*

Very moderately appreciated; chiefly served fried, when small, and boiled with some fish sauce when large.

771—SKATE *Raie*

Generally served boiled, with caper sauce; occasionally with brown butter. The smaller specimens are better fried.

772—SARDINES *Sardines*

Generally of inferior quality; used in the preparation of sprats.

773—STERLET *Sterlet*

Almost unknown in the United States.

774—TURTLE   *Tortue*

With the exception of those firms which make this their specialty, is almost exclusively used in preparing Turtle Soup. The flippers are sometimes served braised au Madère.

I do not think it at all necessary to lay any further stress upon the series of preparations bearing the names of *Croquettes, Cromesquis, Cotelettes* (cotelettes here only mean those prepared from cooked fish, and which are really but a form of croquettes), *Coquilles, Bouchées, Palets,* etc., which may be made from any kind of cooked fish.

775—VARIOUS WAYS OF COOKING FISH
Les Différents Modes de Cuisson des Poissons

The various ways of cooking fish are all derived from one or another of the following methods:—

(1) Boiling in salted water, which may be applied equally well to large pieces and slices of fish.

(2) Frying, particularly suited to small specimens and thin slices of larger ones.

(3) Cooking in butter, otherwise *"à la Meunière,"* best suited to the same pieces as No. 2.

(4) *Poaching,* with a little moistening, especially suited to fillets or small specimens.

(5) *Braising,* used particularly for large pieces.

(6) Grilling, for small specimens and slices.

(7) Cooking *au Gratin,* same as grilling.

776—THE BOILING OF FISH IN SALTED WATER
Cuisson des Poissons à l'Eau salée

The procedure changes according to whether the fish is to be cooked whole or in slices. If whole, after having been properly cleaned, washed, and trimmed, lay it on the drainer or trivet of the utensil best suited to its shape; like a fish-kettle. Cover it with water, salt it in the proportion of one-quarter oz. of salt per quart of water, cover the utensil, and bring the liquid to the boil. As soon as this is done skim and move the kettle to the side of the fire, where the cooking of the fish may be completed without boiling.

If the fish is cut into slices, which should never be cut too thin, plunge these into boiling salted water, and lower the flame; complete their cooking slowly without allowing the water to just simmer.

The object of this process is to concentrate, inside the fish, all the juices contained in it, whereas a large portion escapes when the cut fish is plunged in cold water gradually brought to the boil. If this method is not applied to large fish, cooked whole, the reason is that the sudden immersion of these in boiling water would cause such a shrinking of their flesh that they would burst and thereby be spoiled.

In the case of certain kinds of fish, such as Turbot, milk is added to the water in the proportion of one eighth of the latter, the object being to increase the whiteness of the fish.

For the various kinds of Salmon and Trout, the *court-bouillon* (163) is used in the place of salted water, but the general working process remains the same.

The boiled fish is served on a napkin and platter; it is garnished with fresh parsley; and the sauce, together with some plain-boiled and mealy potatoes, are sent to the table separately.

777—THE FRYING OF FISH *Friture des Poissons*

In Part I of this work I explained the general theory of frying (Chapter X, No. 262); I shall now, therefore, only concern myself with the details of the operation in its relation to fish.

As a rule, frying should never be resorted to for very large fish or very thick slices of the latter, for, owing to the very high temperature that the operation demands, the outside of the fish would be dried up before the inside had even become affected.

If the fish to be fried is somewhat thick, it is best to cut several gashes in it, lengthwise and across, these being deeper and closer together, according to the thickness of the fish. The object of this measure is to facilitate the cooking, but the process itself is quite unnecessary when dealing with small fish. In the case of flat-fish, partly detach the two underlying fillets on either side of the back-bone instead of gashing them.

All fish intended for frying (except Whitebait) should first be steeped in salted milk, then rolled in flour before being plunged into the hot fat. If they are *"panés à l'anglaise,"* the milk may be dispensed with, in which case, after they have been lightly coated with flour, they are completely dipped in egg mixture and afterwards rolled in white bread-crumbs. They should then be patted with the blade of a knife so as to ensure the adhesion of the coating, and, finally, the latter should be criss-crossed with the back of a knife with the view of improving the appearance when fried.

Fried fish are served either on a napkin, on a drainer, or on special doilies. They are garnished with fried parsley and properly trimmed half-lemons.

778—THE COOKING OF FISH A LA MEUNIERE
Cuisson des Poissons à la Meunière

This excellent mode of procedure is only suited to small fish or the slices of larger ones. Nevertheless, it may be resorted to for chicken-turbots, provided their weight does not exceed four lbs.

The operation consists in cooking the fish (or slices or fillets of fish) in the frying-pan with very hot butter, after having seasoned them and sprinkled them with flour. If the fish are very small, ordinary butter is used; if, on the other hand, they are large, the procedure demands clarified butter (175). When the fish is sufficiently browned on one side, it is turned over for the completion of the browning. This done, it is transferred, by means of a spatula, to a hot dish, when, after having been salted, it is sent to the table.

It may be served as it is with a garnish of trimmed half-lemons.

Fish prepared in this way are termed "Soles Golden Brown," "Turbotins Golden Brown," etc., in order to distinguish them from those prepared *à la Meunière.*

If the fish is announced *"à la Meunière,"* a few drops of lemon should be sprinkled upon it; it should be seasoned with salt and pepper, and garnished with chopped, scalded parsley. At the last moment a piece of butter, in proportion to the size of the fish, is put in the frying-pan, and is heated until it begins to brown slightly. This is poured over the fish immediately, and it is sent to the table at once while still covered by the froth resulting from the contact of the butter with the parsley.

779—THE POACHING OF FISH
Le Poché des Poissons

This method is best suited to sole, chicken-turbots, as well as to the fillets of various fish.

Having laid the fish to be *poached* in a baking-tray or a roasting-pan, which should have been previously buttered, season it moderately with salt and moisten with a little very white fish or mushroom *fumet;* very often the two are mixed. Cover the pan, put it into a moderate oven, and baste from time to time, especially when a large fish is cooking. When the fish is done, drain it carefully, place it on a dish, and, as a rule, reduce the *poaching*-liquor and add it to the sauce. *Poached* fish are always served sauced; covered with the sauce which properly forms their accompaniment. More often than not they are garnished after the manner which will be described later.

I most emphatically urge the use of very little fish *fumet* for the *poaching,* but this *fumet* should be perfect and should, above all, not be cooked for longer than the required time; and that the fish should be covered with vegetable parchment paper.

The use of this paper not only applies to fish, but to all those foods with which paper is used at some stage in their cooking process.

780—THE BRAISING OF FISH   *Le Braisage des Poissons*

This method is generally applied to whole or sliced salmon, trout, and chicken-turbot. Sometimes the fish treated in this way is *larded* on one side with strips of bacon-fat, truffles, gherkins, or carrots. The mode of procedure is exactly the same as that described under the "Braising of White Meats" (248). Moisten these *braisings* in the proportion of one-half with white wine or red wine (according as to how the fish is to be served), and for the other half use a light fish *fumet.* Place the fish on the drainer or trivet in a fish-kettle just large enough to hold it, and moisten in such a way that the cooking-liquor at the beginning of the operation does not cover more than three-quarters of the depth of the fish. Unless it be for a *Lenten* dish, the fish may be covered with slices of bacon while cooking. In any case, baste it often. Take care not to close the lid down too tightly, in order that the liquor may be reduced simultaneously with the cooking of the fish.

When the operation is almost completed, take the lid off the fish-kettle with the view of *glazing* the fish; then take the kettle from the fire. Now remove the trivet with the fish upon it, and lay it across the top of the fish-kettle, and let it drain; tilt the fish on to a dish, and cover it until it is sent to the table. Strain the stock remaining in the fish-kettle through a strainer; let it stand for ten minutes, remove all the grease that has formed on its surface, and use it to complete the sauce as I directed above.

Braised fish are generally accompanied by a garnish, the ingredients of which I shall give in the particular recipes relating to *braising.*

781—THE GRILLING OF FISH   *Le Grillage des Poissons*

This method is best suited to small fish, to medium-sized chicken-turbots, halibut and to large-sectioned fish.

Unless they are very small, it is best to gash both sides of fish intended for grilling; the reasons given above for this measure like-wise apply here.

All white and naturally dry fish should be rolled in flour and sprinkled with butter or very good oil before being placed on the grill to be exposed to the heat. The flour forms a crust around the fish, which keeps it from drying and gives it that golden brown quite peculiar to food thus prepared.

Salmon, trout, grey mullet, mackerel, and herrings, the flesh which is fatty, need not be floured, but only sprinkled with melted butter.

Owing to the somewhat fragile texture of most fish, a special double gridiron is used, by means of which they may be turned without fear of damage. This gridiron is placed upon the ordinary grill. I have already given in Part I. of this work the radical princi-ples of grilling (257 and 260); to this, therefore, the reader is asked to refer.

Grilled fish are served on a very hot dish, without paper or a napkin; they are garnished with fresh parsley and grooved slices of lemon.

Butter à la Maître d'Hôtel, anchovy butter, devilled sauce, Roberts' sauce Escoffier, and butter à la Ravigote constitute the best accompaniments to grilled fish.

782—THE COOKING OF FISH AU GRATIN
Cuisson des Poissons au Gratin

I described all the details of this method under Complete *Gratin* (269), to which I must ask the reader to refer. This process is best suited to small fish, such as sole, whiting, grey mullet, chicken-turbot, etc.

783—THE CRIMPING OF FISH *Cuisson des Poissons "Crimped"*

Crimped fish is quite an English specialty. This method of prep-aration is applied more particularly to salmon, fresh cod, haddock, and skate. The first three of these fish may be prepared whole or in slices, while skate is always cut into more or less large pieces after it has been skinned on both sides.

In order to *crimp* a whole fish, it should be taken as it leaves the water. Lay it on something flat, and make deep gashes across it on both its sides from head to tail. Allow a space of about one and one-half inches to two inches between each gash. This done, put the fish to soak in very cold water for an hour or so. When the fish is to be cooked sliced, divide it up as soon as it is caught, and put the slices to soak in very cold water, as in the case of the whole fish.

But does this barbarous method, which stiffens and contacts the flesh of the fish, affect its quality so materially as connoisseurs would have us believe?

It is very difficult to say, and opinions on the matter are divided. This, however, is certain, that fish prepared in the way described is greatly relished by many.

Whether whole or sliced, *crimped* fish is always boiled in salted water. Its cooking presents a real difficulty, in that it must be stopped at the precise moment when it is completed and any delay would impair the quality of the dish.

Crimped fish is served like the boiled kind, and all the sauces suit both kinds. Besides the selected sauce, send a sauceboat to the table containing some of the cooking-liquor of the fish.

SALMON (SAUMON)

Salmon is served as plainly as possible, either boiled, cold or hot, grilled, or à la Meunière (778); but whatever be the method of preparation, it is always accompanied by cucumber salad.

784—BOILED SALMON   *Saumon Bouilli*

Boiled salmon, whether whole or sliced, should be cooked in *court-bouillon* (163) in accordance with directions given at the beginning of the chapter (776). All fish sauces are suited to it, but more especially the following, viz.:—Hollandaise sauce, Mousseline sauce, Melted butter, Shrimp sauce, Nantua sauce, Cardinal sauce, etc.

Crimped salmon requires the same sauces.

785—BROILED SALMON   *Saumon Grillé*

Cut the salmon to be grilled in slices from one inch to one and one-half inches thick. Season with table-salt, sprinkle with melted butter or oil, and grill it for the first part on a rather brisk fire, taking care to moderate heat towards the close of the operation. Allow about twenty-five minutes for the grilling of a salmon steak one and one-half inches thick. Butter à la Maître d'Hôtel (150), anchovy butter (281), and devilled sauce (37) Escoffier are the most usual additions to grilled salmon.

786—SALMON A LA MEUNIERE *Saumon à la Meunière*

Having cut the salmon into moderately thick slices, season these, dredge them slightly, and cook them in the frying-pan with very hot clarified butter (175).

It is important that the salmon brown quickly and that the cooking be rapid.

Serve it in either of the two ways indicated above (778).

Various Ways of Preparing Salmon

In addition to the three methods of serving salmon described above, and those cold preparations with which I shall deal later, the fish in question lends itself to a whole host of preparations which are of the greatest value in the varying of menus. The principles of these preparations I shall now give.

787—SALMON KEDGEREE *Cadgerée de Saumon*

Prepare one lb. of cooked salmon, cleared of bones and skin, and cut into small pieces; four hard-boiled eggs cut into dice; one lb. of well-cooked pilaff rice (2255); and three-quarters pint of Béchamel (28) flavored with curry.

Serve in a hot *timbale,* alternating the various foods, and finish with a coating of sauce.

788—SALMON STEAKS *Côtelettes de Saumon*

Prepare some *mousseline forcemeat* for salmon, the quantity in accordance with the number of cutlets to be made, and rub it through a coarse sieve. Line the bottom and sides of some buttered tin moulds, shaped like cutlets, with a coating one-half inch thick of the prepared *forcemeat.*

Fill the moulds to within one-third inch of their brims with a cold *salpicon* of mushrooms and truffles, thickened by means of reduced Allemande sauce (27), and cover this with the *forcemeat.*

Set the cutlets to *poach,* turn out the moulds; treat the cutlets *à l'anglaise,* and cook them with clarified butter (175).

Arrange in a circle round a dish, put a frill on a piece of fried bread imitating the bone of each cutlet, garnish with fried parsley, and send to the table, separately, a "Dieppoise" sauce, Shrimp sauce, or a *purée* of fresh vegetables, such as peas, carrots, etc. In the latter case, serve at the same time a sauce in keeping with the garnish.

789—SALMON LOAF IN BRIOCHE PASTE (RUSSIAN)

Coulibiac de Saumon

Preparation.—Have ready two lbs. of ordinary *brioche* paste without sugar (2368). Brown in butter one and one-half lbs. of small salmon pieces, and prepare one-sixth lb. of mushrooms and one chopped onion (both of which should be fried in butter), one-half lb. of semolina kasha (2292) or the same weight of rice cooked in consommé; two hard-boiled eggs, chopped; and one lb. of *vesiga,* coarsely chopped and cooked in consommé.

For this weight of cooked *vesiga* about two and one-half oz. of dried *vesiga* will be needed, which should be soaked for at least four hours in cold water, and then cooked for three and one-half hours in white consommé (2). It may also be cooked in water.

Roll the brioche paste into rectangles twelve inches long by eight inches wide, and spread with successive layers the kasha or the rice, the pieces of salmon, the chopped *vesiga,* the eggs, the mushrooms, and the onion, and finish with a layer of kasha or rice. Moisten the edges of the paste and draw the longest ends of it towards each other over the layers of filling, and join them so as to properly enclose the latter.

Now fold the two remaining ends over to the center in the same way. Place the pastry loaf thus formed on a baking-sheet, and take care to turn it over in order that the joining parts of the paste lie underneath.

Set the paste to rise for twenty-five minutes, sprinkle some melted butter over the loaf, sprinkle with some very fine *raspings,* make a slit in the top for the escape of steam, and bake in a moderate oven for forty-five or fifty minutes. Fill the salmon pastry loaf with freshly-melted butter when taking it from the oven.

790—CHAMBORD SALMON CUT   *Darne de Saumon Chambord*

The term *"darne"* stands for a piece of salmon cut from the middle of that fish, and the size of a *darne* slice, or steak, is in proportion to the number of people it is intended for.

Proceed after the manner directed under *Braising* of Fish (780); moisten in the proportion of two-thirds with excellent red wine and one-third with fish stock, calculating the quantity in such wise that it may cover no more than two-thirds of the depth of the cut. Bring to a boil, then set to *braise* gently, and *glaze* the cut at the last moment.

Garnish and Sauce.—Garnish with *quenelles* of truffled *mous-*

seline forcemeat for fish, moulded by means of a spoon; two large ornamented *quenelles;* truffles fashioned like olives; pieces of *milt* dipped in Villeroy sauce (174), treated *à l'anglaise* and fried when about ready to serve; small smelts treated similarly to the *milt,* and trussed crayfish cooked in *court-bouillon* (163).

The sauce is a Genevoise (38), made from the reduced cooking-liquor of the salmon.

Serving.—Surround the salmon cut with the garnishes enumerated, arranging them tastefully, and pierce it with two decorative skewers, each garnished with a small truffle, an ornamented *quenelle,* and a crayfish.

Send the sauce to the table separately.

791—DAUMONT SALMON CUT   *Darne de Saumon Daumont*

Poach the cut of salmon in a *court-bouillon* (163) prepared beforehand.

Serving and Garnish.—Surround the fish by medium-sized mushrooms stewed in butter and garnished with small crayfish tails or large shrimp mixed with a few tablespoons of Nantua sauce (95); small round *quenelles* of *mousseline forcemeat* for fish, decorated with truffles, and some slices of *milt* treated *à l'anglaise,* and fried when about to serve.

Serve the Nantua sauce separately.

792—LUCULLUS SALMON CUT   *Darne de Saumon Lucullus*

Skin one side of the salmon cut, *lard* it with truffles, and *braise* it in champagne.

The Garnish.—Very small patties of crayfish tails or giant shrimp; small *cassolettes* of *milt;* small *mousselines* of oysters, *poached* in *dariole-moulds.*

Sauce.—The *braising*-liquor of the salmon finished by means of ordinary and crayfish butter (147) in equal quantities. Send it to the table separately.

793—NESSELRODE SALMON CUT   *Darne de Saumon Nesselrode*

Remove the back-bone and all other smaller bones. Stuff the salmon with raw lobster *mousse* stiffened by means of a little pike *forcemeat.*

Line a well-buttered, round and even deep-dish pie mould with a thin layer of hot-water, raised-pie paste (this is made from one lb. of flour, four oz. of lard, one egg, and a little lukewarm water), which should be prepared in advance and made somewhat stiff.

Now garnish the inside of the pie with thin slices of bacon and place the salmon upright in it. (To simplify the operation the fish may be stuffed at this stage.) Cover the pie with a layer of the same paste, pinch its edges, make a slit in the top for the steam to escape, and cook in a good oven.

When the pie is almost baked, prick it repeatedly with a testing needle; when it is withdrawn clean the pie should be taken from the oven. This done, turn it upside down in order to drain away the bacon fat and other liquids inside it, but do not let it drop from the mould. Then tilt it on to a dish and take off the mould. Do not break the crust except at the dining-table.

Sauce.—Serve an American sauce (58) with the pie, the former being prepared from the remains of the lobsters used in making the *mousse,* finished with cream, and garnished with very fine bearded oysters, *poached* when about ready to serve.

794—REGENCE SALMON CUT   *Darne de Saumon Régence*

Braise the salmon cut in white wine in accordance with the directions given in (780).

Garnish.—Surround the cut by spoon-moulded *quenelles* of whiting *forcemeat* prepared with crayfish butter (147), oysters bearded and *poached,* small, very white mushrooms, and *poached* slices oi *milt.*

Normande sauce (42) finished with truffle *essence.*

795—ROYAL SALMON CUT   *Darne de Saumon Royale*

Braise the salmon in Sauterne wine.

Garnish.—Bunches of crayfishes' tails or shrimp, small *quenelles* of *mousseline forcemeat* for fish, small mushrooms, slices of truffle, and little balls of potato cut with a spoon, and cooked *à l'anglaise.*

Send a Normande sauce (42) separately.

796—VALOIS SALMON CUT   *Darne de Saumon Valois*

Poach the salmon in a white wine *court-bouillon.*

Garnish.—Potato balls cut with a spoon or turned to the shape of olives, and cooked in salted water, *poached* slices of *milt,* and trussed crayfish cooked in *court bouillon.*

Serve a Valois sauce (63) separately.

797—SALMON MOUSSELINE   *Mousseline de Saumon*

In Part I I dealt with the preparation of *mousseline forcemeat* (195), and also the method of *poaching* spoon-moulded *quenelles*

(205). Now *mousselines* are only large *quenelles* which derive their name from the very light *forcemeat* of which they are composed. These *mousseline quenelles* are always moulded with the ordinary tablespoon, they are garnished on top with a fine, raw slice of the fish being used, and *poached* after the manner already described.

798—SALMON MOUSSELINE ALEXANDRA

Mousseline de Saumon Alexandra

Having made the salmon *mousseline forcemeat,* mould the *quenelles* and place them, one by one, in a buttered saucepan. Place a small, round and very thin slice of salmon on each, and *poach* them in a very moderate oven with lid on the utensil containing them.

Drain on a piece of linen, arrange them in a circle on a dish, place a slice of truffle upon each slice of salmon, coat with Mornay sauce (191), and *glaze.*

Garnish the center of the dish with very small peas or asparagus tips mixed with butter just before serving.

799—SALMON MOUSSELINE A LA TOSCA

Mousseline de Saumon à la Tosca

Combine one and one-half oz. of crayfish cream-*cullis* with each pound of the salmon *mousseline forcemeat.* Mould and *poach* as above, drain, and arrange in a circle on a dish.

Garnish each *mousseline* with a thin slice of *milt* cooked in lightly-browned butter, four crayfish tails or shrimp cut lengthwise into two, and a slice of truffle at each end. Coat with a light Mornay sauce (91), finished with crayfish butter (147), and *glaze* quickly.

N.B.—In addition to these two recipes, all the garnishes suitable for fillets of sole may be applied to *mousselines.* Garnishes of early-season vegetable *purées* also suit them admirably, and therein lies an almost inexhaustible source of variety.

800—COLD SALMON   *Saumon Froid*

When salmon is to be served cold it should, as far as possible, be cooked, either whole or in large pieces, in the *court-bouillon* given under (163) and cooled in the latter. Pieces cooked separately may seem better or may be more easily made to look appetizing, but their meat is more dry than that of the salmon cooked whole. And what is lost in appearance with the very large pieces is more than compensated for by their extra quality.

In serving cold salmon the skin may be removed and the fillets bared, so that the fish may be more easily decorated, but the real gourmet will always prefer the salmon served in its natural silver vestment.

In decorating cold salmon use pieces of cucumber, anchovy fillets, capers, slices of tomato, curly parsley, etc.

I am not partial to the decorating of salmon with softened butter, colored or not, laid on by means of the pastry-bag. Apart from the fact that this method of decoration is rarely artistic, the butter used combines badly with the cold sauces and the meat of the salmon on the diner's plate. Very green tarragon leaves, chervil, lobster coral, etc., afford a more natural and more delicate means of decoration. The only butter fit to be served with cold salmon is Montpellier butter (153), though this, ir fact, is but a cold sauce often resorted to for the coating of the cold fish in question.

Among the garnishes which suit cold salmon, I might mention small peeled, and seeded tomatoes garnished with some kind of salad; hard-boiled eggs, either wholly stuffed, or stuffed in halves or in quarters, *barquettes, tartlets* and *cassolettes* made from cucumber or beets, parboiled until almost completely cooked and garnished with a *purée* of tuna, of sardines, of anchovies, etc.; small aspics of shrimps or of crayfishes' tails; small slices of lobster, etc.

Almost all the cold sauces may accompany cold salmon.

801—COLD SALMON OR CUT OF COLD SALMON A LA ROYALE
Saumon Froid où Darne de Saumon à la Royale

Having drained and dried the salmon, remove the skin from one of its sides, and coat the bared fillets with a layer of a preparation of *mousse de saumon* (797), putting it more thickly over the middle than the sides. Coat the layer of *mousse* with mayonnaise sauce thickened by means of fish aspic-jelly, and leave to set.

Now let some clear fish jelly set on the bottom of the dish to be sent to the table; place the salmon on this jelly, and surround the piece with a border consisting of Montpellier butter (153), using for the purpose a pastry-bag fitted with a fancy tube.

Decorate the center of the piece by means of a fine fleur-de-lis made from truffles, and encircle it with two *royale* crowns made from anchovy fillets.

802—PARISIAN COLD SALMON OR CUT OF SALMON

Saumon Froid où Darne de Saumon à la Parisienne

Remove the skin in a way as to leave the bared portion in the shape of a rectangle, equally between the tail and the head; or, in the case of a cut, only two-thirds of its surface.

Cover the bared meat with mayonnaise sauce thickened with fish aspic-jelly and leave it to set.

Now set the fish on a small bed of rice or semolina, shaping it like the piece itself; trim the sauced rectangle with a border of Montpellier butter (153), laid on by means of a pastry-bag fitted with a small grooved tube. Garnish the center with pieces of lobster coral, the chopped, hard-boiled white and yolk of an egg, chervil leaves, etc.

Encircle the piece with a border of small artichoke-bottoms, garnished, in the form of a dome, with a small *macédoine* of vegetables mixed with cleared mayonnaise.

Send a mayonnaise sauce to the table separately.

803—COLD SALMON OR CUT OF COLD SALMON A LA RIGA

Saumon Froid où Darne de Saumon Froid à la Riga

Prepare a whole salmon or a cut as in the preceding recipe, and put it on a layer of rice or semolina.

Surround it with grooved sections of cucumber hollowed to represent small *timbales,* well parboiled, *marinated* with a few drops of oil and lemon-juice and filled with a vegetable salad thickened with mayonnaise; scooped out, halved eggs filled with caviar; and *tartlets* of vegetable salad mixed with mayonnaise, and garnished, each with a crayfish-shell stuffed with crayfish *mousse* (976); alternate these various garnishes, and encircle with a border of chopped aspic.

804—COLD SALMON OR CUT OF COLD SALMON EN BELLE-VUE

Saumon Froid où Darne de Saumon Froid en Belle-Vue

Skin the salmon and set upright on the belly side, and decorate the fillets with pieces of truffles, *poached* white of egg, chervil leaves, and tarragon, etc.

Coat the garnish with a little melted fish aspic so as to fix it.

This done, sprinkle the fish, again and again, with the same melted aspic jelly in order to cover it with a transparent coating.

Place the piece thus prepared in a crystal platter shaped like the fish, and fill it to the brim with very clear, melted jelly.

When serving, incrust the receptable containing the fish in a block of clean ice which, in turn, is laid on another dish to be sent to the table. Another way is to place the crystal platter directly upon the dish and to surround the former with cracked ice.

805—COLD SALMON OR CUT OF COLD SALMON IN CHAMBERTIN
Saumon Froid où Darne de Saumon Froid au Chambertin

Poach the salmon in a *court-bouillon* consisting of very clear fish *fumet* and Chambertin wine, in equal quantities, and leave to cool. Prepare an aspic jelly from the *court-bouillon.*

Skin and decorate the salmon and *glaze* it with white aspic jelly, exactly as directed above, in the case of the Belle-vue (804).

Serve in the same way, in a crystal receptacle, and fill it with the prepared aspic jelly. Serve on a block of ice, or with cracked ice around the utensil.

806—NORWEGIAN COLD SALMON OR CUT OF COLD SALMON
Saumon Froid ou Darne de Saumon Froid à la Norvégienne

Skin and decorate the salmon, and *glaze* it with white aspic jelly as in (804).

Let a coating of very clear jelly set on the bottom of the dish to be sent to the table. Upon this aspic jelly lay a bed the same shape as the fish, of semolina, or of cooked rice.

Set the piece of salmon, decorated and *glazed,* upon this bed, and lay on a row of fine prawns or large shrimps, cleared of their shells.

Surround with a garnish of small cucumber *timbales,* well parboiled, *marinated,* and garnished dome-fashion, with a *purée* of smoked salmon; halved, hard-boiled eggs, *glazed* with aspic; very small tomatoes, or halved medium-sized ones, peeled, pressed in a towel to their original shape, stuck with a bit of parsley, and decorated with leaves of green butter (289) moulded by means of the pastry-bag; and small *barquettes* of cooked and *marinated* beets, garnished with shrimps' tails attached with mayonnaise.

Send a Russe sauce separately.

807—COLD SALMON STEAKS OR CUTLETS
Côtelettes Froides de Saumon

Liberally butter some tin cutlet-shaped *moulds.* Line their bottoms and sides with a very red slice of salmon, as thin as a piece of cardboard. This slice should be long enough to project outside the brim of the mould to the extent of one-half inch.

Garnish the insides of the moulds with well-seasoned salmon

meat, and draw the projecting lengths of salmon across this meat so as to enclose it and finish off the cutlets.

Arrange the moulds on a baking-tray; *poach* the cutlets, dry, in a moderate oven; turn them out of their moulds on to another tray as soon as they are *poached,* and let them cool. Then coat them with a half-melted aspic, and decorate them according to fancy, either with very green peas or a leaf of chervil with a bit of lobster coral in its center.

These cutlets, which are generally served at ball-suppers, may be served on a long shallow plate, on a bed of rice, semolina, corn-meal, and laid almost vertically against a pyramid of vegetable salad formed by means of mayonnaise with aspic. In this case the dish is finished off with an ornamental skewer stuck into the middle of the pyramid.

The cutlets may also be arranged in a circle on a flat, shallow, silver or crystal dish, and covered with a delicate cold melted jelly.

Whatever be the selected method of serving, always send to the table with the cutlet a sauceboat of cold sauce.

808—SALMON MEDALLION CUTLETS *Médaillons de Saumon*

These médaillons have the same purpose as the cutlets already described, and are prepared thus:—

Cut some small slices, one-third inch thick, from a fillet of salmon.

Arrange them on a buttered pan; *poach* them, dry, in a moderate oven, and cool them and press.

Now trim them neatly, with an even cutter, oval or round, in accordance with the shape they are intended to have.

Coat them, according to their purpose, either with mayonnaise sauce or one of its derivatives, thickened with aspic, or a white, pink, or green chaud-froid sauce (73). Decorate it in any way that may be fancied, and *glaze* them with cold melted aspic jelly.

Serve after the manner described under *"Côtelettes"* (807).

809—SALMON MAYONNAISE *Mayonnaise de Saumon*

Garnish the bottom of a salad-bowl with moderately seasoned, shredded lettuce. Cover with cold, cooked and flaked salmon, cleaned of all skin and bones.

Coat with mayonnaise sauce, and decorate with anchovy fillets, capers, olives, small slices or quartered of hard-boiled eggs, small hearts of lettuce, a border of little slices of radish, etc.

810—SALMON SALAD   *Salade de Saumon*

This preparation comprises the same ingredients as the above, with the exception of the mayonnaise sauce. The decorating garnish is placed directly upon the salmon, and the whole is seasoned in the same way as an ordinary salad.

TROUT

From the culinary standpoint, trout are divided into two distinct classes, large trout, of which the typical specimen is Salmon-trout, and small or fresh-water trout.

811—SALMON TROUT   *Truite Saumonée*

In its many preparations, salmon-trout may be replaced by salmon, and all the recipes relating to the former may be adapted to the latter.

In any case, however, as its size is less than that of salmon, it is very rarely cut into slices, being more generally served whole.

The few recipes that follow are proper to salmon-trout.

812—TROUT CAMBACERES   *Truite a la Cambacerès*

Select a male trout in preference; clean it, and remove its gills without opening it in the region of the belly.

Skin it on one side, starting at a distance of one inch from the head and finishing within two and one-half inches of the tail.

Lard the bared portions with truffles and the outside part only of carrots cut into rods.

This done, spread out a napkin, lay the trout on, belly down, and with a sharp knife, separate the two fillets from the bones, beginning in the region of the head and proceeding straight down to where the body converges towards the tail.

The spine being thus liberated, sever it at both ends; from the tail and the head, and withdraw it, together with all the rib bones. The intestines are then removed, the inside of the fish is well cleaned, the fillets are seasoned on their insides, and the trout is stuffed with a *mousseline forcemeat* of raw crayfish. The two fillets are drawn together, and the trout, thus reconstructed, is covered with thin slices of bacon and laid on the drainer or trivet of the fish-kettle and *braised* in Sauterne wine.

When the fish is done, remove the slices of bacon, *glaze* it, and put it on dish. Surround it with alternate heaps of morels (French mushrooms) tossed in butter and *milt* à la Meunière (778).

Send to the table, separately, a fine Béchamel sauce (28), combined with the *braising*-liquor of the trout, strained and reduced,
and finished with crayfish butter (147).

813—COLD SALMON TROUT *Truites Saumonées Froides*

We are now concerned with a whole series of unpublished
"Trout" preparations, which are of superfine delicacy, and which
permit of clean and easy serving.

Cook a trout weighing from two to three lbs. in *court-bouillon,*
and let it cool in the latter. Then drain it; sever the head and tail
from the body, and put them aside. Completely skin the whole fish,
and carefully separate the two fillets from the bones.

Garnish each fillet with tarragon and chervil leaves, lobster coral,
hard-boiled white of eggs, etc., and set them, back to back, upon a
mousse of tomatoes spread in a special, long white or colored
porcelain platter about one and one-half to two inches deep.

Replace the head and tail, and cover the whole with a coating
of half-melted, succulent fish aspic, somewhat clear. Let the aspic
set, and incrust the dish containing the trout in a block of ice, or
surround it with chopped ice.

814—PREPARATION OF THE TOMATO MOUSSE

Préparation de la Mousse de Tomates

This *mousse,* like those which I shall give later, is really a *bavarois*
without sugar. Its recipe is exactly the same as that of the *"bavarois*
of fruit"* (2615), except with regard to the question of sugar.

Cook one-half lb. of tomato pulp (cleared of skin and seeds, and
roughly chopped) in one oz. of butter. When the pulp has thoroughly mixed with the butter, add two tablespoons of velouté (25)
thickened with about three and three-quarter ounces of gelatine per
quart of the sauce.

Rub through tammy, and add to the preparation, when almost
cold, half of its volume of barely-whipped cream. Taste the *mousse;*
season with a few drops of lemon juice, and if it still seems flat, add
the necessary salt and a very little cayenne.

N.B.—It will be seen that I prescribe cream only half-whipped.
This precaution, however, does not apply to "Mousse de Tomates"
alone, but to all *mousses.* Well-whipped cream imparts a dry and
woolly taste to them, whereas, when it is only half-whipped, it gives
them a bland taste, fresh to the palate.

From the point of view of delicacy, the respective results of the
two methods do not bear comparison.

815—OTHER PREPARATIONS OF TROUT AFTER THE SAME RECIPE
Autres Préparations de Truites

By proceeding exactly as directed in the foregoing recipe, and by substituting one of the following *mousses* for the "Mousse de Tomates," it will be found that considerable variety may be introduced into menus:—

1. Crayfish Mousse with fillets of trout, garnished with crayfish tails and tarragon leaves.

2. Lobster Mousse with fillets of trout, garnished with slices of lobster, coral, and chervil.

3. Shrimp Mousse with fillets of trout, garnished with crayfish tails and capers.

4. Red Pepper Mousse with fillets of trout, garnished with strips of grilled red peppers.

5. Physalia Mousse (made with strawberry tomatoes) with fillets of trout, garnished with chervil, tarragon, and bunches of physalia around the fillets.

6. Green pimentos Mousse with fillets of trout, garnished with strips of green pimentos.

7. Early-season Vegetable Mousse with fillets of trout, garnished with chopped, hard-boiled eggs, and chopped parsley.

8. Volnay Mousse with fillets of trout, garnished with anchovy fillets, capers, and olives.

9. Chambertin Mousse with fillets of trout garnished like (8).

N.B.—In the making of "Mousse au Volnay" and "au Chambertin" the base of the preparations is supplied by cleared velouté (25), to which is added the reduced cooking-liquor of the trout.

All these recipes are equally suitable for sole or chicken-turbot.

815a—ONDINES OF PINK SHRIMPS   *Ondines aux Crevettes Roses*

Prepare a very delicate trout *mousse*, mould it in egg-*moulds*, and garnish the center with trimmed prawns' tails or shrimp. Let the *mousse* set; then speedily turn the *mermaids* out of their moulds, and lay them in a deep entrée-dish. Between each of them lay a few prawns or shrimp, the tails of which should be shelled. Cover the whole, little by little, with some excellent, half-melted aspic-jelly; here and there add a few sprigs of chervil, and then fill the dish with jelly, so as to completely cover the *mousse*.

816—FRESH WATER TROUT   *Truite d'Eau Douse*

The best are those procured in mountainous districts, where the clear water they inhabit is constantly refreshed by strong currents.

The two leading methods of preparing them are called, respectively, "Au bleu" and "à la Meunière." Having already described the latter, I shall now give my attention to "Truite au bleu."

817—TROUT BLUE   *Truites au Bleu*

The essential condition for this dish consists in having live trout. Prepare a *court-bouillon* with plenty of vinegar (163), and keep it boiling in a rather shallow pan.

About ten minutes before serving them, take the trout out of water; stun them by a blow on the head; clean them very quickly, and plunge them into the boiling liquid, where they will immediately shrivel, and their skins will break in all directions.

A few minutes will suffice to cook trout the average weight of which is one-third lb.

Drain them and place them immediately upon a napkin, with parsley. Serve them with a Hollandaise sauce (30) or melted butter.

N.B.—Fresh-water trout may also be served fried or grilled, but neither of these methods of preparation suits them so well as "à la Meunière" or "au bleu," which I have given.

SOLES

Sole may be served whole or filleted, and a large number of the recipes given for the whole fish may be adapted to its fillets.

As a rule, the fillets are used on the menu of a dinner owing to the fact that they can be served more elegantly and are more easily handled than the whole fish, the latter being generally served at luncheons.

Nevertheless, in cases where great ceremony is not observed at a dinner, soles may well be served whole, as no hard-and-fast rule is observed in this matter.

(The real Dover sole (Limande) is rare here and a fine fillet of flounder might do to replace it although of course it can never replace the fine quality and firmness of the real sole.—Ed.)

818—SOLE ALICE   *Sole Alice*

This sole is prepared, or rather its preparation is completed, at the table.

Have an excellent fish *fumet* (11), short and very white. Trim the sole; put it into a special, deep earthenware dish, the bottom of which should be buttered; pour the *fumet* over it and *poach* gently.

Now send it to the table with a plate containing separate heaps of one finely-chopped onion, a little powdered thyme, and three finely-crushed *biscottes*.

In the dining-room the waiter places the dish on a chafing dish, and, taking off the sole, he takes out the fillets, and places them between two hot plates. He then adds to the cooking-liquor of the sole the chopped onion, which he leaves to cook for a few moments, the powdered thyme and a sufficient quantity of the *biscotte raspings* to allow of thickening the whole.

At the last minute he adds six raw oysters and one oz. of butter divided into small pieces.

As soon as the oysters are cooked, he returns the fillets of sole to the dish, sprinkles them copiously with the sauce, and then serves them very hot.

N.B.—In order to promote the *poaching* of the soles, more particularly when they are large, the fillets on the upper side of the fish should be slightly separated from the bones. By this means the heat is able to reach the inside of the fish very quickly, and the operation is hastened.

The sole is always laid on the dish on its back.

819—SOLE MORNAY *Sole Mornay*

Lay the sole on a buttered dish; sprinkle a little fish *fumet* over it, and add one-half oz. of butter divided into small pieces. *Poach* gently.

Coat the bottom of the dish on which the sole is to be served with Mornay sauce (91); drain the fish, lay it on the prepared dish; cover it with the same sauce; sprinkle with grated Gruyère and Parmesan cheese, and *glaze* at a Salamander.

820—SOLE MORNAY DES PROVENCAUX

Sole Mornay des Provençaux

This sole, which used to be served at the famous restaurant of the "Frères Provençaux," was prepared, and always may be prepared, as follows:—

Poach the sole in fish *fumet* and butter, as directed in the preceding recipe; drain it, and place it on a dish; cover it with white-wine sauce (111); sprinkle liberally with grated cheese, and *glaze* quickly.

821—SOLE IN CHAMPAGNE   *Sole au Champagne*

Poach the sole in a buttered dish with one-half pint of champagne. Reduce its cooking-liquor to half; add one-sixth pint of velouté (25), and complete with one and one-half oz. of best butter.

Cover the sole with this sauce; *glaze,* and garnish each side of the dish with a little heap of a *julienne* of filleted sole, seasoned, dredged, and tossed in clarified butter (175) at the last moment in order to have it very crisp.

N.B.—By substituting a good white wine for the champagne, a variety of dishes may be made, among which may be mentioned: Soles au Chablis, Soles au Sauterne, Sole au Samos, Sole au Chateau Yquem, etc.

822—COLBERT SOLE   *Sole Colbert*

On the upper side of the fish separate the fillets from the back-bone, and break the latter in several places. Dip the sole in milk; roll it in flour; treat it *à l'anglaise,* and roll the separated fillets back a little, so that they may be quite free from the bones.

Fry; drain on a piece of linen; remove the bones, and fill the resulting space with butter à la Maitre d'Hôtel (150).

Serve the sole on a very hot dish.

823—SOLE A LA DAUMONT   *Sole à la Daumont*

Bone the sole; severing the back-bone near the tail and the head; remove it, and leave those portions of the fillets which lie on the remaining parts of it intact. Garnish the inside with whiting *forcemeat* finished with crayfish butter (147), and rearrange the fillets in such a way as to give a natural and untouched appearance to the fish. *Poach* it on a buttered dish with one-sixth pint of white wine, the same quantity of the cooking-liquor of mushrooms, and one oz. of butter cut into small lumps.

Drain and cover it with Nantua sauce (95). Place around it four mushrooms stewed in butter and garnished with crayfish tails in Nantua sauce; four small, round *quenelles* of whiting *forcemeat* with cream, garnished with truffles; and four slices of *milt* treated *à l'anglaise* and fried at the last moment.

824—SOLE DOREE   *Sole Dorée*

As I explained under "Fish à la Meunière" (778), "Sole Dorée" is a sole fried in clarified butter (175), served dry, and garnished with slices of carefully peeled lemon.

825—SOLE DUGLERE *Sole Duglére*

All fish treated according to this recipe, with the exception of soles, should be cut up.

Put the sole in a buttered dish with one and one-half oz. of chopped onion, one-half lb. of peeled and coarsely chopped tomatoes, a little chopped parsley, a pinch of table salt, a very little pepper, and one-eighth pint of white wine. Set to *poach* gently, and then place on a dish.

Reduce the cooking-liquor; thicken it with two tablespoons of fish velouté (26a); complete with one oz. of butter and a few drops of lemon juice, and cover the fish with this sauce.

826—GRILLED SOLE *Sole Grillée*

Season the sole; sprinkle with oil, and grill the fish very gently. Serve, garnished with slices of lemon, on a very hot dish.

827—GRILLED SOLE WITH OYSTERS AMERICAN STYLE

Sole Grillée aux Huîtres à l'Americaine

This sole may be either grilled or *poached,* almost dry, in butter and lemon juice. With the procedure remaining the same, it may also be prepared in fillets. Whatever be the mode of procedure, serve it on a very hot dish, and surround it at the last moment with six oysters *poached* in a little boiling Worcestershire sauce and oyster liquor.

Cover the sole immediately with very hot fried bread-crumbs, and add to these a pinch of chopped parsley.

828—SOLE A LA FERMIERE *Sole à la Fermière*

Put the sole, seasoned, on a buttered dish with a few *aromatics.* Add one-third pint of excellent red wine, and *poach* gently with lid on.

Put on a dish; strain the cooking-liquor, and reduce it to half; thicken it with a lump of *manié* butter the size of a hazel-nut, and finish the sauce with one oz. of butter.

Encircle the sole with a border of mushrooms sliced raw and tossed in butter. Pour the prepared sauce over the sole, and set to *glaze* quickly.

829—HOLLANDAISE SOLE *Sole à la Hollandaise*

Break the back-bone of the sole by folding it over in several places. Put the fish in a deep dish; cover it with slightly salted water; set to boil, and then *poach* gently for ten minutes with lid on.

Drain and place on a napkin with very green parsley all round. Serve at the same time some plainly boiled potatoes, freshly done, and two oz. of melted butter.

830—ST. GERMAIN SOLE *Sole Saint-Germain*

Season the sole; dip it in melted butter, and cover it with fresh bread-crumbs, taking care to pat them in with the flat of a knife, in order that they may combine with the butter to form a crust. Sprinkle with some more melted butter, and grill the fish gently so that its coating of bread-crumbs may acquire a nice golden brown. Surround it with potatoes cut in the shape of olives, and cooked in butter.

Send a Béarnaise sauce (62) to the table separately.

831—FLORENTINE SOLE *Sole Florentine*

Poach the sole in a fish *fumet* and butter. Spread a layer of shredded spinach, stewed in butter, on the bottom of a dish; place the sole on it; cover it with Mornay sauce (91); sprinkle with a little grated cheese, and set to *glaze* quickly in the oven or at a *salamander*.

832—MONTREUIL SOLE *Sole Montreuil*

Poach the sole in one-sixth pint of fish *fumet,* one-sixth pint of white wine, and one-half oz. of butter.

Drain as soon as *poached,* and surround with potato-balls the size of walnuts, cooked in salted water, and kept whole. Cover the sole with white-wine sauce (111), and lay a ribbon of shrimp sauce (80) over the garnish.

833—SOLE AU GRATIN *Sole au Gratin*

Partly separate the fillets from the bones on the upper side of the fish, and slip a lump of butter, the size of a walnut, under each.

This done, place the sole on a well-buttered *gratin* dish, on the bottom of which a pinch of chopped shallots and parsley has been sprinkled, together with one or two tablespoons of *Gratin* sauce (269).

Lay four cooked mushrooms along the sole, and surround it with one oz. of raw mushrooms, cut into rather thin slices.

Add two tablespoons of white wine; cover the sole with *Gratin* sauce; sprinkle with fine *raspings* followed by melted butter, and set the *gratin* to form in accordance with the directions given under complete *Gratin* (269).

When taking the sole from the oven, sprinkle a few drops of lemon juice and a pinch of chopped parsley on it, and serve at once.

834—SOLE IN CHAMBERTIN *Sole au Chambertin*

Season the sole and *poach* it on a buttered dish with one-third pint of Chambertin wine.

As soon as it is *poached,* drain it, put it on a dish, and keep it hot. Reduce the cooking-liquor to half, add a little freshly-ground pepper and two or three drops of lemon-juice, thicken with a lump of *manié* butter the size of a walnut, and finish the sauce with one and one-half oz of butter.

Cover the sole with the sauce, set to *glaze* quickly, and garnish both sides of the dish with a little heap of *julienne* of filleted sole, seasoned, dredged, and tossed in clarified butter (175) at the last moment so that it may be very crisp.

835—REMARKS CONCERNING SOLE WITH FINE WINES
Soles aux Grands Vins

Taking recipe (834) as a model, and putting into use all the good wines of Burgundy and Bordeaux, the following varieties are obtained, viz.:—Soles au Volnay, au Pommard, au Romanée, au Clos-Vougeot, or soles au Saint-Estèphe, au Château-Larose, au Saint-Émilion, etc.

836—SOLE MONTGOLFIER *Sole Montgolfier*

Poach the sole in one-sixth pint of white wine and as much of the cooking-liquor of mushrooms. Drain, and cover it with a white wine sauce (111) combined with the reduced cooking-liquor of the sole and one tablespoon of a fine *julienne* of spiny (Rock) lobster's tail, mushrooms, and very black truffles. Surround the sole with a border of little *palmettes* made from puff-paste and baked without browning.

837—SOLE ON THE DISH *Sole-sur-le-Plat*

Partly separate the fillets from the bones on the upper side of the fish, and slip a piece of butter the size of a walnut under each.

Lay the sole on a liberally buttered dish, moisten with one-fifth pint of the cooking-liquor of fish, and add a few drops of lemon-juice.

Cook in the oven, basting often, until the cooking-liquor has by reduction acquired the consistency of a syrup and covers the sole with a translucent and glossy coat.

N.B.—By substituting for the mushroom cooking-liquor a good white or red wine, to which a little melted pale meat-*glaze* (15) has been added, the following series of dishes may be prepared, viz.:— Sole sur le plat au Chambertin. Sole sur le plat au vin rouge, Sole sur le plat au Champagne, Sole sur le plat au Chablis, etc.

838—REGENCY SOLE   *Sole Régence*

Poach the sole in a little white wine and two-thirds oz. of butter cut into small pieces.

Drain the sole, put it on a dish, and surround it with six *quenelles* of whiting *forcemeat* finished with crayfish butter (147), moulded with a small spoon; four *poached* oysters, bearded; four small cooked and very white mushrooms; four small truffles, cut into the shape of olives; and four small *poached* slices of *milt*. Cover the sole and the garnish with a Normande sauce (99) finished with a little truffle *essence*.

839—PORTUGUESE SOLE   *Sole Portugaise*

Poach the sole in white wine (111) and the cooking-liquor of fish. Drain, dish, and surround with a garnish consisting of two medium-sized tomatoes, peeled, pressed, minced, cooked in butter, and combined with minced and cooked mushrooms, and a large pinch of chopped chives.

Coat the sole with the white wine sauce, plentifully buttered, and take care that none of the sauce touches the garnish.

Set to *glaze* quickly, sprinkle the garnish with a pinch of chopped parsley when taking the sole from the oven, and serve immediately.

840—SOLE CUBAT   *Sole Cubat*

Poach the sole in one-fifth pint of the cooking-liquor of mushrooms and one-half oz. of butter cut into small pieces.

Coat the bottom of the dish intended for the sole with a *purée* of mushrooms, place the drained sole on this *purée*, lay six fine slices of truffle along the fish, coat with Mornay sauce (91), sprinkle with cheese, and *glaze* quickly.

841—SOLE WITH OYSTERS   *Sole aux Huîtres*

Shuck and *poach* six oysters. *Poach* the sole in the liquor of the oysters, drain it, place on a dish, and surround it with the oysters bearded.

Coat with a white wine sauce (111) combined with the reduced cooking-liquor of the sole, and *glaze* quickly.

842—MEUNIERE SOLE *Sole à la Meunière*

Proceed for this dish as directed under "Fish à la Meunière" (778).

843—MEUNIERE SOLE WITH CUCUMBERS, CALLED DORIA

Sole Meunière aux Conconbres, dit Doria

Prepare a sole à la Meunière. Garnish it at both ends with little heaps of cucumber, cut in pieces and cooked in butter with a little salt and a pinch of sugar.

844—MEUNIERE SOLE WITH EGGPLANT

Sole Meunière aux Aubergines

Prepare a sole à la Meunière in the usual way. Surround it with a fine border of eggplant slices one-third inch thick, seasoned, dredged, and fried in clarified butter (175), just in time to be arranged round the sole when it is ready. The question of time is important, for if the fried eggplant be allowed to wait at all they very quickly lose their crispness.

845—MEUNIERE SOLE WITH CEPES MUSHROOMS

Sole Meunière aux Cèpes

Prepare the sole à la Meunière in the usual way and surround it with a border of sliced *cèpes* frizzled in butter just before serving.

846—MEUNIERE SOLE WITH MORELS *Sole Meunière aux Morilles*

Surround the sole with very fresh morels (French mushrooms) cooked in salted water and then tossed in butter just before serving. Sprinkle a pinch of chopped parsley over the morels.

847—SOLE MEUNIERE WITH GRAPES *Sole Meunière aux Raisins*

The sole being ready, circle it with fresh skinned Muscatel grapes prepared in advance.

848—MEUNIERE SOLE WITH ORANGE *Sole Meunière à l'Orange*

When the sole is cooked and ready, lay on a row of orange slices, peeled to the pulp and thoroughly seeded, or some sections of oranges, likewise peeled to the pulp and carefully seeded. This done, cover the sole and the garnish with lightly-browned butter and serve instantly.

849—LUTECE SOLE *Sole Lutèce*

Line the bottom of the dish intended for the sole with a coating of shredded spinach tossed in lightly-browned butter. Place the sole, prepared *à la Meunière,* upon the spinach; lay a few onion rings and slices of artichoke-bottoms tossed in butter upon the fish; and on either side of the sole lay a border of potato-slices, freshly cooked in salted water and fried brown in butter.

At the last moment cover the whole with lightly-browned butter.

850—MURAT SOLE   *Sole Murat*

Sauté in butter, separately, one medium-sized potato cut into dice; two small raw artichoke-bottoms, likewise cut into dice. Prepare the sole *à la Meunière,* and surround it with the potato and artichoke-bottom, mixed when cooked. Lay on the sole five slices of tomato, one-half inch thick, seasoned, dredged, and sautéd in very hot oil; sprinkle a few drops of pale melted meat-*glaze,* a little lemon-juice, and a pinch of chopped parsley over the sole, and cover the whole with slightly-browned butter. Serve instantly.

851—PROVENCALE SOLE   *Sole Provençale*

Poach the sole in one-sixth pint of fish *fumet,* two tablespoons of oil and a piece of garlic, well crushed. Drain and put on a dish. Coat it with Provençale sauce (51) combined with the reduced cooking-liquor, and sprinkle a little chopped parsley over it.

Surround the sole with four little tomatoes and four medium-sized mushrooms stuffed with *duxelles* flavored with a bit of garlic; these should be put in the oven just in time for them to be ready for the serving of the fish.

852—ARLESIAN SOLE   *Sole Arlésienne*

Poach the sole in a little fish *fumet.* Put it on a dish, reduce the *fumet,* and add the following garnish:—Cook a little chopped onion in butter, add two medium-sized, peeled, seeded and chopped tomatoes, a bit of garlic, and some chopped parsley. Cook with lid on, add the reduced *fumet* and twelve pieces of vegetable-marrow (squash), cut in the shape of olives and cooked in butter.

Cover the sole with this garnish and place a little heap of fried onion at each end of the dish.

853—ROYAL SOLE   *Sole à la Royale*

Poach the sole in a few tablespoons of fish *fumet* and two-thirds oz. of butter cut into small lumps. Put on a dish and set on it four small cooked mushrooms, four small *quenelles* of fish *forcemeat,* four crayfish tails, shrimps, and four slices of truffle.

Surround the sole with potato-balls, cooked *à l'anglaise,* and coat the sole and garnish with Normande sauce (99).

854—RUSSIAN SOLE *Sole à la Russe*

Prepare twelve grooved and very thin round slices of carrots, and cut a small onion into fine slices. Put these vegetables into one-seventh pint of white wine, and one-third pint of fish *fumet.* Cook and, in the process, reduce the moistening by half, and pour this preparation into a deep dish.

Partly separate the fillets from the bones on the upper side of the sole, slip a piece of butter, the size of a walnut, under each fillet, and put the fish into a deep dish containing the preparation. *Poach* and baste frequently.

As soon as it is *poached,* put it on a dish, also the vegetables used in cooking, and keep the whole hot.

Reduce the cooking-liquor to one-eighth pint, add a few drops of lemon juice, and finish it away from the fire with one and one-half oz. of butter. Coat the sole and the garnish with this sauce.

855—RICHELIEU SOLE *Sole Richelieu*

Prepare the sole exactly as directed under "Sole à la Colbert" (822). When it is fried, remove the bones and put it on a dish. Garnish the inside with butter à la maître-d'hôtel (150), and lay on a row of sliced truffles.

856—NORMAN SOLE *Sole Normande*

Poach the sole on a buttered dish with one-sixth pint of fish *fumet,* and the same quantity of the cooking-liquor of mushrooms. Drain, and surround it with mussels, *poached* oysters bearded, shrimps' tails, and small cooked mushrooms. Put the sole in the oven for a few minutes, tilt the dish in order to pour off all liquid, and coat the sole and the garnish with Normande sauce (99). Make a little garland of pale meat-*glaze* (15) on the sauce, and finish the garnish with the following:—Six fine slices of truffle set in a row upon the sole; six small bread crusts in the shape of diamonds, fried in clarified butter (175) and arranged round the truffles; four smelts treated *à l'anglaise* and fried at the last moment; and four medium-sized trussed crayfish cooked in *court-bouillon.*

Set the smelts and the crayfish round the dish.

857—MARGUERY SOLE   *Sole Marguéry*

Poach the sole in white wine and fish *fumet* in the proportions already given.

Drain and put on a dish, and surround it with a border of mussels and shrimp tails. Coat the sole and the garnish with white wine sauce (111), well finished with butter, and set to *glaze* quickly.

858—MARINIERE SOLE   *Sole Marinière*

Liberally butter a dish, sprinkle a teaspoon of chopped shallots on the bottom, lay the sole on, and *poach* the latter with one-sixth pint of white wine and the same quantity of the very clear cooking-liquor of mussels. Drain the sole, surround it with mussels bearded, and keep it hot.

Reduce the cooking-liquor to half; thicken with a tablespoon of velouté (25), and the yolks of two eggs, and finish it, away from the fire, with two and one-half oz. of butter and a pinch of chopped parsley.

Tilt the dish, pour off the liquid accumulated on the bottom, coat the sole and the garnish with the prepared sauce, and *glaze* quickly.

859—SOLE IN WHITE WINE   *Sole au Vin Blanc*

Partly separate the fillets from the bones on the upper side of the sole, and slip a piece of butter, as large as a walnut, under each fillet. Lay the sole in a dish, the bottom of which should be buttered and garnished with a small onion, chopped. Moisten with one-quarter pint of ordinary white wine, as much fish *fumet,* and a few tablespoons of the cooking-liquor of mushrooms. *Poach* gently with lid on.

Drain and coat the sole with a white wine sauce, prepared in accordance with one of the methods given in the chapter on Sauces (111). *Glaze* quickly, or serve without glazing.

N.B.—"Sole au Vin Blanc" may be prepared according to the above recipe, but ordinary white wine may be replaced by one of the Rhine wines or Moselle, by some Johannisberg, or by a good white Burgundy or Bordeaux wine, such as Chablis, Savigny, Montrachet, Barsac, Sauternes, and even Château-Yquem or Château-Latour.

In any of these cases the name of the wine may be mentioned, and on the menu may be written Sole au Barsac, Sole au Château-Yquem, etc.

860—DIEPPE SOLE   *Sole Dieppoise*

Poach the sole with one-sixth pint of fish *fumet* and a few table-spoons of the cooking-liquor of mussels.

Drain and surround the sole with *poached* mussels (bearded and shelled), and shrimp tails, and coat the fish and the garnish with a white wine sauce (111) combined with the reduced cooking-liquor.

861—DIPLOMAT SOLE   *Sole Diplomate*

Poach the sole in very clear fish *fumet*.

Drain it, and put it on a dish, coat with Diplomate sauce (82).

Set upon it a row of six fine slices of black truffle; these should have been previously *glazed* with pale meat-*glaze* (15).

862—SOLE BONNE FEMME   *Sole Bonne Femme*

Butter the bottom of the dish intended for the sole, and sprinkle it with two chopped shallots, one pinch of parsley, and one and one-half oz. of raw minced mushrooms. Lay the sole upon this garnish, Moisten with one-quarter pint of white wine and as much fish *fumet,* and *poach* gently, taking care to baste from time to time.

When the sole is *poached,* drain off the cooking-liquor into a pan, and reduce it quickly to half; thicken with two tablespoons of fish velouté (26a), and finish the sauce with two oz. of butter. Coat the sole with this sauce and set it to *glaze* in a hot oven or at a *salamander.*

863—PARISIAN SOLE   *Sole Parisienne*

Poach the sole in white wine, the cooking-liquor of mushrooms, and some butter. Drain it thoroughly, put it on a dish, and coat it with white wine sauce (111) combined with the reduced cooking-liquor of the sole. Garnish with a row of six slices of truffle and six fine round slices of cooked mushrooms kept very white, and finish with four medium-sized crayfish or giant shrimp.

864—NANTUA SOLE   *Sole Nantua*

Poach the sole in one-sixth pint of fish *fumet* and a few table-spoons of the cooking-liquor of mushrooms.

Drain the sole, surround it with twelve shelled crayfish tails or giant shrimp, and coat it with Nantua sauce (95).

Lay a row of very black truffle slices along the middle of the fish.

FILLETS OF SOLE

Subject to the kind of dish required, fillets of sole are either kept in their natural state, they are stuffed and folded over, or they are simply folded over without being stuffed, each of which methods of preparation will be specially referred to in the recipes.

Whatever the method adopted, always skin the fillets thoroughly, removing the thin membrane which lies beneath the skin, which has a tendency, during the cooking process, to shrink and disfigure the fillet.

This done, flatten out the fillets with the broad side of a wet knife, and trim them slightly if necessary. The *poaching* of fillets of sole must be done without allowing the cooking-liquor to boil, the object being to prevent the pieces losing their shape. Fillets should also be kept very white.

In cases where the exact amount of the *poaching*-liquor is not given, allow one-quarter pint to every four fillets.

865—AMERICAN FILLETS OF SOLE   *Filets de Soles Americaine*
Arrange the folded fillets in a deep, buttered dish, and *poach* them in fish *fumet*.

Drain, and arrange them in the form of an oval, letting them overlap one another with their tail-ends hidden. Garnish the center of the dish with slices of lobster prepared à l'Américaine (939), and coat the whole with the sauce.

866—ENGLISH FILLETS OF SOLE   *Filets de Soles Anglaise*
Treat the fillets à *l'anglaise* with fresh and fine bread-crumbs. Pat the bread-crumbs over the egg with the flat of a knife, that the two may be well combined; and, with the back of a knife, criss-cross the coating of the fillets.

Cook them gently in clarified butter. Serve on a hot dish, and sprinkle the fillets with half-melted butter à la maître-d'hôtel (150).

867—ANDALUSIAN FILLETS OF SOLE   *Filets de Soles Andalouse*
Coat the upper sides of the fillets with fish *forcemeat* combined, per pound, with three oz. of chopped green peppers. Roll them up, after the manner of a *roulade* (914), and smooth the *forcemeat* on the top. *Poach* the fillets in butter and fish *fumet*.

The following should have been prepared beforehand:—As many small half-tomatoes, stewed in butter and garnished by means of *rizotto* with peppers, as there are fillets of sole; the same number of slices of egg-plant, seasoned, dredged, and fried in oil.

When serving, arrange the egg-plant slices round the dish; place a stuffed tomato on each slice of egg-plant, and a *poached* fillet of sole upon each tomato. Sprinkle with lightly-browned butter, and serve at once.

868—CAPRICE FILLETS OF SOLE   *Filets de Soles Caprice*

Dip the fillets in melted, seasoned butter, and then roll them in fresh and fine bread-crumbs. Pat the bread-crumbs with the flat of the knife and criss-cross the surface of the fillets. Sprinkle with melted butter, and set to grill gently, taking care that the coating of bread-crumbs acquires a nice, light-brown color.

Lay on each grilled fillet the half of a peeled banana, cooked in butter, and send to the table, separately, a Roberts sauce Escoffier (53), finished with butter.

869—CATALAN FILLETS OF SOLE   *Filets de Soles Catalane*

Poach, in the oven, as many seeded and seasoned half-tomatoes as there are fillets of sole. Cook some very finely-minced onion in oil, without letting it brown, and allow one tablespoon of the onion to each half-tomato.

Fold the fillets of sole, and *poach* them in fish *fumet* just a few minutes before serving them. Garnish the half-tomatoes with onion; arrange them in a circle on a dish, and place a fillet of sole upon each. Quickly reduce the cooking-liquor of the fillets, and finish it with butter in the proportion of one oz. per one-eighth pint of reduced *fumet*.

Coat the fillets and set to *glaze* quickly.

870—CLARENCE FILLETS OF SOLE   *Filets de Soles Clarence*

Fold the fillets, and *poach* them in fish *fumet*.

They may be prepared after the two following methods:—

1. Put a preparation of Duchesse potatoes (221) in a pastry-bag fitted with a large, grooved tube, and squeeze on an ornamental design containing as many divisions as there are fillets of sole. Lightly brush with egg and brown in the oven. This design, consisting of scroll-work, should be prepared before *poaching* the fillets. Lay a fillet in each division of the design, and coat with American sauce (58), prepared with curry and combined with the small diced meat of the lobster which has served in the preparation of the sauce. Take

care that no sauce touches the scroll-work, which should remain in-tact.

2. Bake some large potatoes in the oven. Open them; remove their pulp, and put into each baked shell a tablespoon of American sauce with curry referred to above. Add a *poached* fillet of sole; coat with American sauce; arrange these garnished potatoes on a napkin, and serve very hot.

871—FILLETS OF SOLE WITH MUSHROOMS
Filets de Soles aux Champignons

Stew two oz. of small mushrooms in butter. Fold the fillets, and *poach* them in one-sixth pint of the cooking-liquor of mushrooms, and a piece of butter the size of a walnut. Arrange the fillets in an oval, and garnish the center of the dish with the stewed mushrooms.

Reduce the cooking-liquor of the fillets to one-third; add two tablespoons of velouté (25); finish the sauce with one oz. of butter, and coat the fillets and the garnish.

872—FILLETS OF SOLE WITH SHRIMPS *Filets de Soles aux Crevettes*

Fold the fillets, and *poach* them in fish *fumet*.

Arrange them in an oval; garnish the middle with one oz. of shelled shrimps' tails, kept very hot, and coat the fillets and the garnish with shrimp sauce (80).

873—CHAUCHAT FILLETS OF SOLE *Filets de Soles Chauchat*

Poach the fillets of sole, folded, in butter and lemon juice.

Coat the bottom of a dish with Mornay sauce (91), and set the fillets of sole on in the form of an oval. Surround the fish with cooked potatoes cut in the shape of corks or cylinders.

Cover the fillets and the garnish with Mornay sauce, and *glaze* quickly in a hot oven or at the *salamander*.

874—BERCY FILLETS OF SOLE *Filets de Soles Bercy*

Butter the bottom of the dish intended for the soles, and sprinkle it with two finely-chopped shallots. Lay the fillets lengthwise upon the dish, side by side; moisten with three tablespoons of white wine and as much fish *fumet*, and add one-half oz. of butter cut into small pieces.

Cook in the oven, basting frequently, and *glaze* at the last minute. Sprinkle with a few drops of lemon juice, and when about to serve drop a pinch of chopped parsley upon each fillet.

Or, *poach* the fillets with chopped shallots, and increase the moistening. As soon as the fillets are ready, drain off their cooking-liquor into a pan; reduce it speedily to one-third, and add a few drops of meat-*glaze* (15), a little lemon juice, one-half oz. of butter, and one pinch of chopped parsley.

Coat the fillets, and set to *glaze* quickly.

N.B.—Sole à la Bercy may be prepared after either of the two methods.

875—DEJAZET FILLETS OF SOLE   *Filets de Soles Dejazet*

Treat the fillets of sole *à l'anglaise* and grill them as explained under (830).

Put them on a dish, cover them thinly with half-melted tarragon butter (148), and decorate each fillet with five or six parboiled, tarragon leaves.

876—GRAND DUKE FILLETS OF SOLE   *Filets de Soles Grand Duc*

Fold the fillets of sole over, and *poach* them in fish *fumet* and the cooking-liquor of mushrooms. Arrange them in an oval on a dish, with their tails pointing inwards; place a fine slice of truffle in the middle of each fillet, and between each of the latter three shelled crayfish tails or shrimp.

Coat with Mornay sauce (91), and set to *glaze* quickly.

When taking the dish from the oven, set in its center a fine heap of very green asparagus tips, mixed with butter at the moment of serving.

877—JOINVILLE FILLETS OF SOLE   *Filets de Soles Joinville*

Select some fine fillets of sole; fold them, and *poach* them in the cooking-liquor of mushrooms, and butter, taking care to keep them very white. Arrange them in an oval, with their tails pointing upwards and the shell of a crayfish fixed on each fillet; and garnish the center of the dish with a *salpicon* or a short *julienne,* consisting of one and one-half oz. of cooked mushrooms, one-half oz. of truffle, and one and one-half oz. of shrimp tails mixed with a few tablespoons of Joinville sauce (88). Coat the fillets and the garnish with the same sauce, and decorate each fillet with a fine slice of truffle coated with meat-*glaze* (15).

They may also be served in the old-fashioned way, as follows:—

Set the garnish in the center of the dish, shaping it like a dome; coat it with Joinville sauce, and surround it with the fillets of sole, which should slightly overlap one another and have their tails uppermost. Fix a shell of crayfish on the tail of each fillet, and decorate each with a slice of very black truffle.

With this method of serving, the garnish alone is coated with sauce, the fillets thus forming a white, encircling border.

878—JUDIC FILLETS OF SOLE   *Filets de Soles Judic*

Fold, and *poach* the fillets in butter and lemon juice.

Arrange them in an oval round a dish, laying each upon a nice little *braised* and trimmed lettuce cut in half, and place upon each fillet a *quenelle* of sole *mousseline-forcemeat* in the shape of a flattened oval, *poached* at the time of serving.

Coat with Mornay sauce (91) and *glaze* quickly. When taking the dish out of the oven, encircle the fillets of sole with a ribbon of buttered meat-*glaze* (15).

879—HUNGARIAN FILLETS OF SOLE   *Filets de Soles Hongroise*

Fry in butter, without browning, one small tablespoon of chopped onion seasoned with a very little paprika; moisten with three tablespoons of white wine and one-sixth pint of fish *fumet;* add two small peeled, pressed, and roughly-chopped tomatoes, and set to cook for seven or eight minutes.

Fold the fillets of sole; lay them on a buttered dish; pour the above preparation on, and *poach* them. Arrange them in a circle on a dish; reduce their cooking-liquor to a thick consistency; add a few tablespoons of cream and a few drops of lemon juice, and coat the fillets with this sauce.

880—LADY EGMONT FILLETS OF SOLE   *Filets de Soles Lady Egmont*

Fold the fillets, and *poach* them in a few tablespoons of excellent fish *fumet.*

Also for every four fillets finely mince one oz. of well-cleaned mushrooms, and cook them quickly in butter, lemon juice, a little salt, and pepper. This done, add the cooking-liquor to the fish *fumet,* and keep the cooked minced mushrooms hot.

Reduce the combined cooking-liquor and fish *fumet* to half; add one oz. of butter and two tablespoons of cream; and to the resulting sauce add the reserved minced mushrooms and two tablespoons of freshly-cooked and well-drained asparagus tips.

Serve the fillets of sole on an earthenware dish, coat them with the above garnish, and set to *glaze* quickly in a hot oven or at the *salamander.*

881—MARINETTE FILLETS OF SOLE   *Filets de Soles Marinette*

Poach a sole in fish *fumet* and the cooking-liquor of mushrooms, and drain on a napkin. When it is still lukewarm, carefully lift out its fillets and trim them.

Break an egg into a bowl; beat it well, and add enough grated Gruyère and Parmesan cheese to it (mixed in equal quantities) to produce a thick paste. Mix two teaspoons of cold Béchamel sauce (28) with this paste; add salt and cayenne pepper; spread an even thickness of one inch over two of the fillets of sole; lay on the two remaining fillets, and put aside to cool.

When the egg and cheese paste is very stiff, dip the fillets in a Villeroy sauce (108), and leave the latter to cool. Then treat the stuffed and sauced fillets *à l'anglaise,* and fry them, just before serving, in very hot fat.

Arrange on a napkin with very green parsley all round.

882—MARY STUART FILLETS OF SOLE   *Filets de Soles Marie Stuart*

Fold the fillets, and *poach* them in fish *fumet.* Arrange them in an oval on a dish; coat them with the sauce given under "Filets de soles à la Newburg" (890), and place on each fillet a *quenelle* of fish *forcemeat* in the shape of a patty and decorated with a slice of truffle. These *quenelles* should, if possible, be *poached* just before serving, and well drained before being laid on the fillets of sole.

883—MIGNONETTE FILLETS OF SOLE   *Filets de Soles Mignonette*

Cook the fillets in butter, and set them in a hot *timbale.*

Surround them with potato-balls the size of peas, cut by means of a round, sharp spoon, and cooked beforehand in butter.

Lay upon the fillets eight or ten slices of fresh truffle heated in one-sixth pint of very light meat-*glaze* (15).

Finish the *glaze* in which the slices of truffle have been heated with two-thirds oz. of butter and a few drops of lemon juice, and pour it over the fillets and the garnish. Serve very hot.

884—MIMI FILLETS OF SOLE   *Filets de Soles Mimi*

Divide a live lobster into two, lengthwise, and prepare it à l'Américaine (939), taking care to keep the sauce thick.

When the lobster is cooked, take the meat from the tail; cut it into as many slices as there are fillets of sole, and keep them hot.

Remove all the meat from the claws, and that remaining in the lobster shell; pound or grind all of it smoothly, add two tablespoons

of cream, and rub through a fine sieve. Prepare a garnish of spaghetti with cream, and add the *purée* of lobster.

Fold the fillets of sole, and *poach* them in Chablis wine and
butter. This done, lay the two emptied shells of the lobster on a
napkin on a dish, setting them back to back. Fill these lobster shells
to the brim with the prepared filling of spaghetti. Upon this filling
lay the *poached* fillets of sole, sandwiching a slice of lobster between
every two; sprinkle the whole with a short and fine *julienne* of very
black truffle.

Send the lobster sauce, finished with a few tablespoons of cream,
to the table separately. Proceed as quickly as possible with the
serving, in order that the dish may reach the table very hot.

885—MEXICAN FILLETS OF SOLE　　　*Filets de Soles Mexicaine*

Coat the fillets with fish *forcemeat,* and roll them to resemble
roulades (914). *Poach* them in fish *fumet* as directed for the *paupiettes.* Lay each rolled fillet in a grilled mushroom garnished with
one-half tablespoon of peeled, pressed, and chopped tomato cooked
in butter, and arrange them in an oval on a dish.

Coat them with Béchamel sauce (28) combined with a *purée* of
tomatoes and red peppers cut into small dice, in the proportion of
two tablespoons of the *purée* and two-thirds oz. of the peppers per
pint of the sauce.

886—MIRABEAU FILLETS OF SOLE　　　*Filets de Soles Mirabeau*

Poach the fillets, left in their natural state, in fish *fumet.*

Arrange them and coat with white wine (111) and Genévoise
sauces (38), alternating the two, white and brown. Lay a thin strip
of anchovy fillet between each of the fillets of sole; decorate those
of the latter coated with white sauce with a slice of truffle, and
those coated with brown sauce with a star of *blanched* tarragon
leaves.

887—MIRAMAR FILLETS OF SOLE　　　*Filets de Soles Miramar*

Divide each of the fillets into slices; season them and cook them
in butter. Cut fifteen round slices (one-third inch thick) of egg-
plant; season, dredge, and fry them in butter, taking care to keep
them very crisp.

Take a *timbale* of suitable size, and line its sides with a layer
(three-quarters inch thick) of pilaff rice (2255).

Put the slices of egg-plant and the fillets of sole (mixed and sautéd
together for a moment) in the center of the dish.

Just before serving, sprinkle with one oz. of lightly-browned butter.

888—FILLETS OF SOLE WITH OYSTERS *Filets de Soles aux Huîtres*

Shuck and *poach* twelve oysters. *Poach* the fillets of sole, folded, in the oyster liquor strained through cheesecloth, and a piece of butter as large as a walnut.

Arrange in an oval on a dish; garnish the center with the *poached* oysters, bearded, and coat the fillets of sole and the oysters with Normande sauce (99) combined with the reduced cooking-liquor of the fillets.

889—NELSON FILLETS OF SOLE *Filets de Sole Nelson*

Fold the fillets, and *poach* them in fish *fumet*.

Arrange them in a circle on a dish; coat them with white-wine sauce (111), and *glaze* quickly.

Garnish the center of the dish with a pyramid of potato-balls cooked in butter and of a light-brown color. Surround the fillets with *poached milt*.

890—FILLETS OF SOLE NEWBURG *Filets de Soles Newburg*

Prepare a lobster à la Newburg, in accordance with one of the recipes given (948 and 949). Cut the tail into as many slices as there are fillets of sole, and keep them hot.

Cut the remainder of the lobster meat into dice, and add these to the sauce. Fold the fillets of sole, and *poach* them in fish *fumet*. Arrange them in an oval on a dish; lay a slice of lobster upon each fillet, and coat with the lobster-sauce combined with the dice, prepared as directed above.

391—ORIENTAL FILLETS OF SOLE *Filets de Soles Orientale*

Prepare the fillets exactly as those à la Newburg, but season the sauce with curry.

Having arranged and sauced the fillets, set a pyramid of rice à l'Indienne (2254) in the middle of the dish, or send the rice to the table separately, in a *timbale;* either way will be satisfactory.

892—PERSIAN FILLETS OF SOLE *Filets de Soles Persane*

Prepare the fillets as in the case of those à la Newburg, but season the sauce with paprika, and add one oz. of pimentoes cut into large dice. Send some pilaff rice (2255) with saffron to the table separately.

893—ORLY FILLETS OF SOLE   *Filets de Soles Orly*

Season the fillets; dip them into batter and, a few minutes before serving, put them into very hot fat. Drain them; place them on a napkin with fried parsley, and serve a tomato sauce (29) separately.

N.B.—There are several ways of preparing these fillets of sole. Thus they may be simply dipped in milk, dredged, and stuck on an ornamental skewer. They may also be *marinated,* treated *à l'anglaise,* and twisted into cork-screw shapes.

Always, however, serve them on a napkin with fried parsley and, in every case, send the tomato sauce to the table separately.

This last accompaniment is essential.

894—FILLETS OF SOLE OLGA, OR "OTERO"

Filets de Soles Olga, ou "Otero"

Bake beforehand, in the oven, as many fine, well-washed potatoes as there are fillets of sole. As soon as they are done, remove a piece of the baked shell, and withdraw the pulp in such a way as to leave nothing but the long, parched shells. Fold the fillets, and *poach* them with a little excellent fish *fumet.* Garnish the bottom of each prepared shell with a tablespoon of shelled shrimp tails, combined with a white-wine sauce (111).

Put a *poached* fillet of sole upon this garnish; cover with sufficient Mornay sauce (91) to completely fill the shell; sprinkle with grated cheese, and *glaze* quickly. Put on a napkin the moment the fillets have been taken from the oven, and serve immediately.

895—POLIGNAC FILLETS OF SOLE   *Filets de Soles Polignac*

Fold the fillets, and *poach* them in one-quarter pint of white wine, a few tablespoons of the cooking-liquor of mushrooms, and a piece of butter about the size of a walnut.

Arrange the fillets in an oval. Reduce the cooking-liquor to half; thicken it by means of two scant tablespoons of fish velouté (26a); finish the sauce with one oz. of butter, and add three small, cooked, finely-minced mushrooms, and one tablespoon of a *julienne* of truffles.

Coat the fillets with sauce, and set to *glaze.*

896—PAYSANNE FILLETS OF SOLE   *Filets de Soles Paysanne*

For the fillets of sole, cut two small carrots, two new onions, a stalk of celery, and the white of one leek in *paysanne* fashion. Season these vegetables with a very little table-salt and a pinch of sugar; stew them in butter; cover them with lukewarm water; and add a few flowerets of broccoli, a tablespoon of peas, and the same quantity of cut string beans.

Complete the cooking of the vegetables while reducing the cooking-liquor. Season the fillets of sole, and lay them on a buttered earthenware dish. Pour on the garnish of vegetables; put the cover on the dish, and gently *poach* the fillets.

When they are cooked, tilt the dish to pour all the liquor away into a vegetable-pan; this done, reduce the liquor to one-fifth pint, and add to it three oz. of butter.

Pour this sauce into the dish containing the fillets and the vege-table garnish, and serve immediately.

897—LEVANTINE FILLETS OF SOLE IN PILAFF
Filets de Soles en Pilaw à la Levantine

Cut the fillets into pieces, and sauté these in butter. Prepare some pilaff rice after the usual recipe (2255), and add one oz. of mild pepper cut into dice.

Also toss in butter one and one-half oz. of eggplant, cut into dice and seasoned, and put these in with the fillets of sole. Mould the rice into a border round the dish; put the fillets and the eggplant in the middle, and coat with curry sauce (81) without letting it touch the rice.

N.B.—In the case of pilaff rice with fillets of sole, the rice should border the dish, and the fillets of sole, sautéd in butter, should be laid in the middle and coated with brown butter (154).

898—POMPADOUR FILLETS OF SOLE   *Filets de Soles Pompadour*

Prepare the fillets with butter and bread-crumbs, and grill them. Garnish them all round with a ribbon of very firm Béarnaise tomatée (64), and surround them with a border of Château potatoes (2208).

Lay a fine slice of truffle, moistened with melted meat-*glaze* (15), on each fillet.

899—RACHEL FILLETS OF SOLE   *Filets de Soles Rachel*

Coat the fillets with some delicate fish *forcemeat*; put four slices of truffle on the *forcemeat* of each of the fillets; fold the latter, and *poach* them in one-sixth pint of the cooking-liquor of mushrooms, and a piece of butter the size of a walnut, cut into small pieces.

Arrange the fillets in an oval on a dish. and coat them with white-wine sauce (111) combined with one tablespoon of freshly-cooked asparagus tips, and one tablespoon of truffle in dice per every one-half pint of the sauce.

900—VENETIAN FILLETS OF SOLE   *Filets de Soles Vénitienne*

Fold the fillets, and *poach* them in fish *fumet*.

Arrange them in a circle on a dish, alternating them with thin crusts (croutons), in the shape of hearts, fried in butter. Coat with Venetian sauce (107) combined with the reduced cooking-liquor of the fillets.

901—VERDI FILLETS OF SOLE   *Filets de Soles Verdi*

Prepare a garnish of macaroni cut into dice; mix this with cream and grated Gruyère and Parmesan cheese, and add three oz. of lobster meat and one and one-half oz. of truffles in dice per every one-half lb. of the macaroni.

Poach the fillets of sole in fish *fumet*, keeping the fillets in their natural state. Lay the macaroni very evenly on the dish; set the *poached* fillets of sole upon it; coat with Mornay sauce (91), and set to *glaze* quickly.

902—VICTORIA FILLETS OF SOLE   *Filets de Soles Victoria*

Fold the fillets, and *poach* them in fish *fumet*.

Arrange them in an oval on a dish, and garnish the center with three oz. of the meat from the tail of the spiny or Rock lobster, and one oz. of truffle in dice per every four fillets.

Coat the fillets and the garnish with Victoria sauce, and set to *glaze* quickly.

903—VERONIQUE FILLETS OF SOLE   *Filets de Soles Véronique*

Lift out the fillets of a fine sole; beat them slightly; fold and season them, and put them in a special earthenware, buttered dish.

With the bones, some of the trimmings of the fish, a little minced onion, some parsley stalks, a few drops of lemon juice, and white wine and water, prepare two spoonfuls of *fumet*.

This done, strain it over the fillets, and *poach* them gently.

Drain them carefully; reduce the *fumet* to the consistency of syrup, and finish it with one and one-half oz. of butter. Arrange the fillets in an oval on the dish where they have been *poached;* cover them with the buttered *fumet,* and set to *glaze* quickly. When about to serve, set a pyramid of skinned and very cold Muscatel grapes in the middle of the dish.

Put a cover on the dish, and serve immediately.

904—WALEWSKA FILLETS OF SOLE   *Filets de Soles Walewska*

Poach the fillets in fish *fumet,* keeping them in their natural state.

Arrange on a dish, and surround them with three spiny or Rock lobster tails cut into two lengthwise, and stewed in butter (covered) with six fine slices of raw truffle.

Coat with a delicate Mornay sauce (91), and set to *glaze* quickly.

N.B.—The Mornay sauce may, according to circumstances, be combined with one and one-half oz. of lobster butter (149) per pint.

905—WILHELMINE FILLETS OF SOLE   *Filets de Soles Wilhelmine*

Prepare some potato shells, as directed under "Filets de soles Olga" (894). Garnish them with a tablespoon of cucumber with cream; put a fillet of sole into each garnished shell, a fine blue point oyster on each fillet. and cover with Mornay sauce (91).

Set to *glaze* quickly, and serve on a napkin.

VARIOUS PREPARATIONS OF SOLES AND FILLETS OF SOLE

906—MOUSSELINE OF SOLE   *Mousselines de Soles*

The directions given under *"Mousselines de Saumon"* (797) apply in all circumstances to *Mousselines of Sole*. I shall therefore refrain from repeating the recipe, since, the quantities remaining the same, all that is needed is the substitution of the meat of sole for that of salmon. Thus, I shall only state here, by way of reminding the reader, that these excellent preparations permit of all the fish sauces and garnishes, and that they also be accompanied by all *purées* of fresh vegetables.

907—TURBAN OF FILLETS OF SOLE VILLARET

Turban de Filets de Soles à la Villaret

Lift out the fillets of three soles; flatten them slightly with a moistened wooden potato masher, and trim them very straight on either side.

Liberally butter a medium-sized *savarin-mould.* Lay the fillets slantwise in this mould, with their tail-ends over its inner edge and their other ends projecting over its outer edge; slip a fine slice of truffle between each, and let them slightly overlap one another.

When the mould is completely lined with the fillets of sole, fill it with lobster *mousseline forcemeat.* Gently tap the mould on a folded napkin lying on the table, with the object of settling the *forcemeat,* and then draw the overhanging ends of the fillets across the latter.

Set to *poach* in a *bain-marie* (water-bath) in a moderate oven.

This done, take the mould out of the *bain-marie;* let it stand for a few minutes, and then turn it upside-down upon the dish. Leave it to drain; soak up the liquid that has leaked out on to the dish; take off the mould, and moisten the surface of the fillets by means of a small brush dipped in melted butter. The object of this last measure is to *glaze* the fish and to remove the froth resulting from its *poached* albumen.

Now garnish the center of the mould with shrimp tails, mushrooms, *poached milt,* and slices of truffle, the whole mixed with Béchamel sauce (28) finished with lobster butter (149).

Send a sauceboat of Béchamel sauce, finished with lobster butter, to the table at the same time as the fish.

908—TURBAN OF FILLETS OF SOLE AND SALMON VILLARET

Turban de Filets de Soles et Saumon Villaret

Proceed as in the preceding recipe, but alternate the fillets of sole with very red slices of salmon of the same size as the fillets.

The combination is excellent, and the varying strips of white and orange which constitute the body of the moulded crown make it attractive.

N.B.—The designation "à la Villaret," relating to the crown alone, in no way affects the ingredients of the garnish; these may either remain the same as those of the preceding recipe, or may be replaced by something similar. The sauce alone remains unalterable, and this should be a good Béchamel (28) finished with lobster butter (149).

909—TIMBALE OF FILLETS OF SOLE CARDINAL

Timbale de Filets de Soles Cardinal

For ten people, prepare a *timbale* crust (2394) the diameter of which should be greater than the height; line it with fine, short paste, and decorate it with noodle paste (2291).

Lift out the fillets of three medium-sized soles, flatten them slightly; coat them with whiting *forcemeat* prepared with crayfish butter (147), and roll them into *roulades.* Also prepare ten small slices of the meat of a medium-sized ordinary or spiny (Rock) lobster tail, ten small grooved and cooked mushrooms, fifteen slices of truffle, and three-quarters pint of Cardinal sauce (69) finished with a lobster butter (149).

When about to serve, lay the *poached,* rolled fillets of sole (well drained) in a circle round the bottom of the *timbale;* put the slices of lobster and the mushrooms in the center, and cover with the Cardinal sauce.

Set in the sauce, just over the center of the *timbale,* a large, grooved mushroom (cooked and kept very white), and encircle the latter with fifteen slices of truffle.

Place the *timbale,* thus garnished, on a folded napkin lying on a dish, and serve at once.

910—TIMBALE OF FILLETS OF SOLE CARMELITE
Timbale de Filets de Soles Carmelite

Prepare a *timbale* crust as above; a lobster à la Newburg made from raw lobster (948); twelve rolled fillets of sole stuffed with fish *forcemeat* finished with lobster butter (149); three oz. of sliced truffles.

Poach the rolled fillets in fish *fumet;* slice the meat of the lobster tail, and put the *poached* fillets, the slices of lobster and the slices of truffle into the lobster sauce. Heat the whole well, without boiling; pour the sauce and seafood into the *timbale* crust, and garnish the top with twelve fine slices of truffle.

Place the *timbale* on a folded napkin, and serve instantly.

911—TIMBALE OF FILLETS OF SOLE GRIMALDI
Timbale de Filets de Soles Grimaldi

Prepare a rather deep *timbale* crust, and decorate it with noodle paste. Cook, as for *bisque,* twenty-four small crayfish or spiny (Rock) lobster; take off their tails; cut them into two lengthwise, and keep them hot in butter. Finely pound the shells, and add one-third pint of fine Béchamel (28). Rub through a fine strainer first, and then through a fine sieve. Put the resulting *cullis* into a saucepan, and heat without boiling it; intensify the seasoning; add a few table-spoons of cream, little by little; put the prepared tails in the *cullis,* and keep it in the *bain-marie* (double-boiler). Cut four oz. of *blanched* and somewhat stiff macaroni into pieces, and add one-sixth pint of cream and three oz. of sliced truffle. Heat until the macaroni has completely absorbed the cream; thicken with one-sixth pint of Béchamel sauce (28) finished with fish *fumet;* add one and one-half oz. of butter cut into small lumps, and keep hot. Coat sixteen fillets of sole with truffled fish *forcemeat;* roll the fillets into *roulades,* and, at the last minute, *poach* them in fish *fumet.*

To garnish the *timbale,* spread a layer of macaroni on the bottom, lay half of the rolled fillets upon the macaroni, and cover these with half of the spiny (Rock) lobster tails in the *cullis*.

Repeat the procedure, in the same order, with what is left of the garnishes, and finish the *timbale* with a layer of the lobster tails.

Set the *timbale* on a folded napkin on a dish, and serve immediately.

912—TIMBALE OF FILLETS OF SOLE CAREME
Timbale de filets de soles Carème

Flatten the fillets of three medium-sized soles, and trim them neatly.

Liberally butter a pound-cake (round) mould, and line it with the fillets, placing them side by side with their tails lying round the center of the bottom of the mould, and their opposite ends projecting above the brim. Press them well into the shape of the mould.

Completely coat the fillets with a layer, one-half inch thick, of fish *forcemeat*.

Put the mould in the front of the oven for a few minutes in order to *poach* the *forcemeat*, which, in combining the fillets, gives the required firmness to the *timbale*.

When the *forcemeat* has been *poached* and is stiff, take out the *timbale* trom the oven, and cut off the pieces of fillet that project above the edges of the mould. Fill the *timbale* to within one-third inch of its brim with a garnish of shrimps and *poached* oysters and mussels, small button-mushrooms, and slices of truffle, all of which should be mixed with a thick and highly-seasoned Béchamel sauce (28). Cover this garnish with the projecting pieces of fillets, already cut off, and close the *timbale* by means of a thin layer of that *forcemeat* which served in coating the fillets. *Poach* for thirty minutes in a *bain-marie* (water-bath) and in a moderate oven. After taking the *timbale* out of the *bain-marie*, let it stand for a few minutes; overturn it on a round dish; take off the mould; garnish it on top with a garland consisting of six little *paupiettes* of salmon, each stuffed with a crayfish tail, and surrounded by an encrusted crayfish shell.

Serve a Nantua sauce (95).

913—TIMBALE OF FILLETS OF SOLE MARQUISE
Timbale de Filets de Soles Marquise

For a *timbale* large enough for ten people, prepare a plain or fluted *timbale* crust.

And a garnish consisting of twelve rolled or folded fillets of sole *poached* in fish *fumet,* twelve *poached* oysters bearded, twenty-four small *quenelles* of salmon, and twenty slices of truffle.

Heat this garnish after after having added a few drops of fish *fumet* to it, and then thicken it with one-half pint of white-wine sauce (111) prepared with paprika.

Put the above garnish into the *timbale,* which should be very hot; set it on a folded napkin, and serve at once.

914—THE PREPARATION OF ROULADES OF FILLETS OF SOLE, SALMON, ETC.

La Préparation des paupiettes de Filets de Soles, Saumon, etc.

The *paupiettes* or fillets rolled in a *roulade* are served either as entrées like fillets of sole or as a garnish. For the second purpose, not only should they be smaller than for the first, but very small fillets are generally selected for the preparation of the *paupiettes.*

In order to make *paupiettes,* first remove the nerve tissue from the outside surfaces of the fillets, and then slightly flatten the latter with the blade of a large knife; trim them on both sides, and coat them on their flattened side with a thin layer of fish *forcemeat,* truffled or not, in accordance with the requirements.

Now roll them up; smooth the *forcemeat* that projects from the top end, and the *paupiettes* are ready to cook.

Stand them upright in a buttered saucepan to *poach,* and take care to place them snugly together lest they lose their shape while the operation is in progress. Moisten them with sufficient fish *fumet* (11) to cover them; *poach* them in a moderate oven, and remember, as in the case of fillets of sole, not to let the *poaching*-liquor boil.

All the garnishes and sauces suited to fillets of sole likewise pertain to *paupiettes,* provided the difference in their shape be taken into account when serving.

For salmon *paupiettes,* cut slices two-thirds inch wide, one-half inch thick, and the length of a fillet of sole, from a skinned fillet of salmon. In view of the unusual fragility of salmon's flesh, the slices of fillets should be carefully flattened in order to give them the width and thickness of a fillet of sole. This done, spread *forcemeat* on them, and roll them as explained above.

SOLES AND FILLETS OF SOLE (COLD)

915—ASPIC OF FILLETS OF SOLE   *Aspic de Filets de Soles*

An essential point in the making of an aspic is the clearness of the fish jelly. For a sole aspic, take some white fish aspic (158), which is at once succulent, transparent, and just sufficiently glutinous to permit of it being turned out of a mould without breaking.

For the purpose under consideration, moulds with plain or decorated borders are generally used, and there are two methods of procedure:—

For a mould capable of holding one quart, fold twelve small fillets of sole and *poach* them in butter and lemon juice, taking care to keep them very white. This done, set them to cool and press lightly.

Pour a few tablespoons of melted fish aspic-jelly into the mould, which should be standing in cracked ice. As soon as the jelly begins to set, decorate it tastefully with crescents, diamonds, etc., of very black truffle and the *poached* white of an egg. Capers, tarragon leaves, thin slices of small radishes, etc., may also be used for the purpose of decoration.

When this part of the procedure has been satisfactorily effected, sprinkle a few drops of the same jelly over the decorating particles, in order to fix them and prevent their shifting during the subsequent stages of the process. Now add enough melted aspic-jelly to cover the bottom of the mould with a layer one inch thick, and leave this to set.

On this set jelly, arrange the six fillets of sole; let their tail-ends overlap, and cover them with jelly. Continue adding coat upon coat of jelly until the thickness covering the fillets measures about one-half inch.

Now arrange the remaining fillets in the reverse order, and fill up the mould with cold, melted jelly. Leave to cool for one hour.

When about to serve, quickly dip the mould in a saucepan of hot water; wipe it, and turn out the aspic upon a folded napkin lying on a dish.

916—ANOTHER METHOD OF PREPARING ASPICS OF FILLETS OF SOLE

Deuxième Methode de Préparation des Aspics de Filets de Sole

Coat ten fine fillets of sole with a thin layer of truffled fish *force-meat* finished with crayfish butter (147), and roll them round a little rod of truffle, twice as thick as an ordinary penholder. Tie these *paupiettes*, once or twice round, with cotton string; *poach* them very gently in fish *fumet* and cool them on ice. Take a *border-mould*, even if possible; pour in a few tablespoons of melted fish jelly, and then rock it about in cracked ice, with the object of evenly coating it with a thin layer of the aspic-jelly.

This operation is technically called "coating the mould."

Decorate the bottom of the mould as explained above; fix the decorating garnishes, and cover them with a layer one-half inch thick of fish jelly.

After having properly trimmed the ends of the *paupiettes,* cut them into round slices one-half inch thick; set these upright against the sides of the mould, keeping them close together; add a few drops of melted jelly to fix the slices, and as soon as this has set, add more slices, sufficient to completely cover them.

As soon as this jelly sets, repeat the operation with the *paupiette* slices and the jelly, and do it again and again until the mould is filled. For turning out the aspic, proceed as directed in (915).

917—BORDER OF FILLETS OF SOLE ITALIAN
Bordure de Filets de Soles à l'Italienne

Line a *border-mould* with jelly and coat the bottom and sides with a thin layer of fish jelly, rocking it in cracked ice as already explained.

Now fill it, two-thirds full, with a garnish consisting of a *julienne* of cold, *poached* fillets of sole, a *julienne* of truffles (two oz. per two filleted soles), and a *julienne* of mild peppers (one and one-half oz. per two filleted soles). Fill up the mould with melted fish jelly, and leave it to set.

When about to serve, turn out the mould upon a little, low bed of rice, lying on a dish, and set an Italian salad in the center.

Serve a Mayonnaise sauce (126) with this dish.

918—CALYPSO FILLETS OF SOLE   *Filets de Soles Calypso*

Flatten the fillets, and roll them into *paupiettes* around little rods of wood two-thirds inch thick. Lay the *paupiettes* in a buttered saucepan, with their joined sides down, and *poach* them in very clear fish *fumet* and lemon juice, taking care to keep them very white.

Let them cool, and remove the pieces of wood, and they will have the appearance of rings.

Take as many small tomatoes as there are *paupiettes;* cut them in two at a point two-thirds of their height below their stem-end; seed, and peel them. Set a *paupiette,* upright, in each tomato; fill the center with crayfish *mousse* combined with crayfish tails in dice; lay a round piece of *milt* (stamped out with a cutter, *poached*, and cold) on each, and, finally, the shelled tail of a crayfish on each slice of *milt*.

Arrange the tomatoes in a circle round a dish; surround them with little triangles of white fish aspic-jelly, and garnish the center of the dish with the same fish jelly, chopped.

919—CHARLOTTE FILLETS OF SOLE   *Filets de Soles Charlotte*

Fold the fillets; *poach* them in fish *fumet,* and let them cool.

Trim them; coat them with pink chaud-froid sauce (35); decorate each fillet by means of a rosette of chervil leaves, in the center of which rests a bit of lobster coral, and *glaze* them with fish jelly.

Set them, tail end up, against a *mousse* of *milt* with horse-radish, moulded in a narrow dome-mould, which should have been coated with fish jelly and sprinkled with chopped lobster coral.

Surround with a border of regularly-cut jelly dice.

920—MUSCOVITE FILLETS OF SOLE   *Filets de Soles à la Moscovite*

Prepare some *paupiettes* of filleted sole, in rings, as explained under "Filets de Soles à la Calypso" (918); and as many round, fluted cases made from hollowed cucumber as there are *paupiettes.* The cucumber cases should be well *blanched* and *marinated* inside. Set each *paupiette* in a cucumber case; garnish their center with caviar, and arrange them in a circle on a dish.

Send a sauce Russe to the table, separately, at the same time as the dish.

921—DOMINOES OF FILLETS OF SOLE   *Dominos de Filets de Soles*

Select some fine, fleshy fillets; slightly flatten them; *poach* them in a little of the cooking-liquor of mushrooms, some lemon juice and butter, and set them to cool under a light weight. When the fillets are cold, trim them and cut them into regular rectangles the size of dominoes.

Coat these with a *maigre,* white, chaud-froid sauce (72); decorate them in imitation of dominoes, with little spots of truffle; *glaze* them with cold, melted fish jelly, and put them aside.

Pound the trimmings of the fish together with their weight of caviar, and rub the whole through a fine sieve. Add to this preparation half its weight of highly-colored aspic, and leave it to set in a somewhat deep and moderately-oiled tray, the thickness of the preparation on the tray being not greater than that of a fillet of sole.

When the jelly is set, cut it into rectangles exactly the same size as the prepared dominoes, and then, by means of a little melted, cold jelly, fix the dominoes of sole to the rectangles just prepared.

Put some chopped jelly in the center of the dish, and on this heap the dominoes.

922—COLD FILLETS OF SOLE GARNISHED IN MOUSSES
Filets de Soles Froids Dressés sur Mousses

What I pointed out above, I repeat here for the reader's guidance —namely, that fillets of sole may be prepared after all the recipes given for trout (813).

As the fillets of sole in this dish remain very conspicuous, it is advisable to keep them very white in the *poaching*. Set them to cool under a light weight, and decorate them in a way that will be in keeping with the *mousse* on which they are served. This *mousse* is set on a special dish, as already explained, and the decorated fillets are laid upon it and covered with melted jelly.

For the variation of *mousses,* see the table given under (814).

923—TURBOT   *Turbot*

Turbot is generally served boiled, accompanied by freshly cooked, mealy potatoes, and the cases are exceptional when, cooked in this way, it is served with any other garnish.

All fish sauces may be served with turbot. When, for the sake of variety, turbot has to be *braised* or garnished, it is best to select a medium-sized fish, one weighing from eight to twelve lbs. thick, very fleshy, and white.

Unless expressly ordered, it is best to avoid surrounding the piece with its garnish. Preferably, send it to the table in a separate dish, as also the sauce. By this means the service is hastened, and, more important still, the fish is quite hot when it reaches the table. It is granted that the sight of a dish containing a fine, richly garnished and tastefully arranged piece is flattering to the host, but it would be a pity that the quality of the fish should suffer, more particularly as the gourmet is not satisfied with the appearance alone.

I explained at the beginning of this chapter, under "Boiled Fish" (776 and 779), the details relating to this method of cooking, especially with regard to its application to turbot. For the *braising* and garnishing of turbot, the reader is asked to refer to the recipes concerned with chicken-turbot (925–38). These recipes may be applied to turbot, provided the difference in the size of the fish be taken into account in reference to the time allowed for *braising* and the quantities of the garnishing ingredients.

924—COLD TURBOT   *Turbot Froid*

Whether whole or sliced, cold turbot makes an excellent dish, if the fish have not been cooked too long beforehand. It will be found that turbot, especially when sliced, tends to harden, crumple, and lose its flavor while cooling. It is therefore of the greatest importance that the fish should have just cooled after cooking, and that the cooking-liquor should have barely time to set; otherwise the evil effects of cooling, mentioned above, will surely ensue. When served, just cooled, with one of the cold sauces suited to fish, turbot can vie in delicacy even with such fish as salmon or trout, which are usually served cold.

925—CHICKEN TURBOT   *Turbotin*

Chicken turbots may rank among the most delicate and nicest of fish. Their varying sizes allow for their being served either for three, four, or ten, or twelve people; they are, moreover, tender and white, and they lend themselves to quite a vast number of culinary preparations.

They may be served boiled, like the turbot; grilled; à la Meunière; fried; *au gratin,* like the soles; or *braised,* like the salmon and the trout. They are most often served whole, garnished with sauce; but, in order to simplify the process, they may be filleted, the fillets being *poached* and served with a garnish and the selected sauce.

(Chicken-halibut may be used to replace chicken turbot if the latter is not available.—Ed.)

Whatever be the method of preparing the chicken turbot or chicken-halibut, whether it be boiled, *poached,* or *braised,* the backbone should always be cut in one or two places. The gash should be just in the middle of the back where the flesh is thickest, and the fillets on either side of the gash should be partly separated from the bone. The object of this measure is to prevent deformation during the cooking process and, also, to hasten the cooking.

926—ADMIRAL CHICKEN TURBOT   *Turbotin à l'Amiral*

Gash the back of the fish, and partly separate the under fillets from the bones. Lay it on a grill, and moisten, sufficiently to cover it, with previously-cooked *court-bouillon* with Sauterne wine. As soon as the *court-bouillon* boils, allow the fish to cook ten or twelve minutes for every two lbs. of its weight.

This done, drain it, and coat it twice with melted, red butter (142).

Now surround it with the following garnish, which should be in proportion to the size of the fish, little heaps of large mussels and oysters, prepared à la Villeroy (108), and fried at the time of serving; small patties of crayfish tails; large mushroom-heads grooved and cooked, and slices of truffle.

Serve, separately, a *timbale* of potatoes à *l'Anglaise;* Normande sauce (99), combined with one-sixth pint of reduced *court-bouillon* per quart of sauce, finished with crayfish butter (147) and seasoned with cayenne.

927—ANDALUSIAN CHICKEN TURBOT   *Turbotin à l'Andalouse*

Cut it in the region of the back; season it, and lay it in a deep earthenware dish of convenient size, liberally buttered. In the case of a chicken turbot weighing two and one-half lbs., moisten with one-third pint of white wine and one-quarter pint of fish *fumet.*

Finely mince two medium-sized onions, and sauté them in butter until they have acquired a yellow color.

Peel, press and mince three tomatoes, and add three large, raw, sliced mushrooms. Cut two mild peppers into strips.

Spread the onion on the chicken-turbot; put the tomatoes and the sliced mushrooms on top, and upon these arrange the grilled strips of mild pepper. Sprinkle moderately with *raspings;* lay one oz. of butter, cut into small pieces, on the top, and set to cook gently in the oven.

Allow thirty minutes for the cooking. By reducing the moistening-liquor, which has absorbed some of the gelatinous properties of the fish, and it thickens itself.

928—BONNE FEMME CHICKEN TURBOT   *Turbotin Bonne Femme*

For a chicken turbot weighing from two to two and one-half lbs. sprinkle on the bottom of a buttered tray two teaspoons of chopped shallots, one pinch of chopped parsley, and three oz. of minced mushrooms.

Cut the chicken turbot in the back, and partly separate the fillets from the bone; lay it on the tray, and moisten with one-third pint of white wine and one-third pint of fish *fumet.* Cook gently in the oven, and baste frequently.

When the chicken turbot is cooked, put it on a dish and keep it hot. Pour the cooking-liquor into a saucepan; reduce it to half, and add three tablespoons of fish velouté (26a) and three oz. of butter.

Cover the fish with this sauce and the garnish, and *glaze* quickly.

929—COMMODORE CHICKEN TURBOT   *Turbotin Commodore*

Poach the chicken turbot in salted water.

Prepare the following garnish per one person:—Three potato balls cut to the size of hazel-nuts and cooked *à l'anglaise;* one medium-sized, trussed crayfish; one *quenelle* of fish; one small lobster *croquette;* and one oyster prepared à la Villeroy (108).

All these products should be treated according to their nature, and just in time to be ready for the serving. A few moments before, drain the turbot; put it on a dish, and surround it with the garnish detailed above, arranged in alternate heaps.

Serve a Normande sauce (99), finished with anchovy butter (281), separately.

930—DAUMONT CHICKEN TURBOT   *Turbotin Daumont*

Proceed exactly as directed under "Sole Daumont" (823), taking into account the size of the fish, and increasing the sauce and the garnishing ingredients accordingly.

931—CHICKEN TURBOT FERMIERE   *Turbotin Fermière*

Sprinkle on the bottom of a buttered pan two minced shallots, a few slices of carrot and onion, some parsley stalks, thyme, and bay leaf.

Lay the chicken-turbot on these *aromatics,* and season moderately. For a fish weighing two lbs. moisten with two-thirds pint of excellent red wine; add one-half oz. of butter, cut into small pieces, and *poach* gently, taking care to baste frequently.

Meantime sauté three oz. of minced mushrooms in three oz. of butter. When the turbot is ready, drain it; put it on a dish; surround it with the mushrooms, and keep it hot.

Strain the cooking-liquor into a pan, and reduce it to half. Thicken it with a piece of *manié* butter the size of a walnut; add three oz. of butter; pour this sauce over the chicken-turbot and its garnish, and set to *glaze* quickly.

932—HOLLAND STYLE CHICKEN TURBOT
Turbotin à la Mode Hollande

Poach the chicken turbot in salted water. Drain it, put it on a dish, and upon it lay a lobster cooked in *court-bouillon.* The shell of the lobster should have been opened along the top of the tail, and the meat of the tail should have been quickly sliced and returned to its place.

Send to the table at the same time a *timbale* of mealy potatoes, freshly cooked *à l'anglaise;* a sauceboat containing egg sauce with melted butter (117).

933—MIRABEAU CHICKEN TURBOT *Turbotin Mirabeau*

Poach the fish in *court-bouillon* with Sauterne wine, as directed under "Turbotin à l'Amiral" (926).

Drain it; put it on a dish, and coat it in alternate bands with white wine (111) and Genèvoise sauces (38). Along the lines formed by the meeting of the sauces lay thin strips of anchovy fillets placed end to end. Decorate the bands of white sauce with slices of truffle, and the bands of brown sauce with blanched tarragon leaves.

934—PARISIAN CHICKEN TURBOT *Turbotin Parisienne*

Poach the fish in *court-bouillon* with Sauterne wine. Drain it, put it on a dish, and round it arrange a border composed of alternate slices of truffles and mushrooms. Coat the fish with white-wine sauce (111), and surround it with trussed crayfish cooked in *court-bouillon.*

N. B.—For fish *à la Parisienne,* the garnish of sliced truffles and mushrooms may be set on the dish, either conspicuously or the reverse. It may be laid round the fish and covered by the sauce, or arranged in the form of an oval on the fish after it has been sauced. In either case the slices of truffles and mushrooms should be laid alternately.

935—REGENCY CHICKEN TURBOT *Turbotin Régence*

Poach the chicken turbot in a sufficient quantity of previously-prepared *court-bouillon* with Chablis wine.

For a fish weighing three lbs. (enough for ten people), prepare the following garnish:—Twenty small spoon-moulded *quenelles* of whiting *forcemeat* with crayfish butter (147); ten *poached* oysters, bearded; ten small mushroom-heads (very white); ten truffles in the shape of olives, and ten *poached* slices of *milt.*

Drain the chicken turbot just before serving, and slip it on to a dish. Surround it with the garnish detailed above, arranged in alternate heaps, and serve a Normande sauce (99), finished with two tablespoons of truffle *essence* per pint, separately.

936—CHICKEN TURBOT SOUFFLE REYNIERE

Turbot soufflé à la Reynière

Lay the chicken turbot on its belly, and make two gashes in its back, on either side of the back-bone, from the head to the tail. Completely separate the fillets from the bones; cut the back-bone at both ends; carefully lift it from the underlying, ventral fillets, and entirely remove it.

Season the inside of the fish, and garnish it with enough fish *mousseline forcemeat* to give it a rounded appearance. Close in the *forcemeat* by drawing the two separated fillets over it; turn the fish over, and lay it on a well-buttered, deep, oval dish, the size of which should be in proportion to that of the chicken-turbot.

Poach it gently, almost dry, with lid on, in fish *fumet* and the cooking-liquor of mushrooms mixed, with two-thirds pint of the one and one-third pint of the other. This done, put it on a dish carefully, and lay a row of grooved and white mushroom-heads down the center of it. On either side put some very white, *poached milt,* alternating the latter with whole anchovy fillets, in such a way as to form an oval framing the row of mushrooms.

Send to the table, separately, a sauce composed of Soubise *cullis* (104) and white-wine sauce (111), in the proportion of one-third and two-thirds respectively, combined with the reduced cooking-liquor of the chicken-turbot.

937—CHICKEN TURBOT FEUILLANTINE

Turbotin à la Feuillantine

Stuff the chicken turbot after the method described in the preceding recipe, but substitute lobster *mousseline forcemeat* for that mentioned above.

Poach as directed above, and arrange on a dish.

Coat the fish with lobster butter (149), made as red as possible, from the shell of the lobster whose meat has been used for the *forcemeat.*

From head to tail and down the center of the fish lay a row of fine slices of truffle, letting them overlap each other slightly. Frame the row of truffle with two lines of very white, *poached* oysters, so placed as to form a regular oval.

Send to the table, separately, a fine Béchamel sauce (28) seasoned with cayenne.

938—COLD CHICKEN TURBOT *Turbotin Froid*

May remarks relative to cold turbot apply here with even greater force, for chicken turbots are particularly well suited to cold dishes.

The chicken turbots to be served cold should not be too small; the best for the purpose would be those weighing four lbs. or more.

In dismissing the subject I can but recommend cold chicken turbot as a dish permitting the most tasteful arrangement and decoration.

Lobster (Homard)

Whereas the ordinary lobster is a very favorite dish with gourmets, the spiny kind has scarcely any vogue. This is no doubt accounted for by the fact that the former is not only very plentiful, but also of excellent quality, while the latter is comparatively scarce.

939—LOBSTER AMERICAN STYLE *Homard à l'Américaine*

The first essential condition is that the lobster should be alive. Sever and slightly crush the claws, with the view of withdrawing their meat after cooking; cut the tail into sections; split the shell in two lengthwise, and remove the queen (a little bag near the head containing some gravel). Put aside, on a plate, the intestines and the coral, which will be used in the finishing of the sauce, and season the pieces of lobster with salt and pepper.

Put these pieces into a saucepan containing one-sixth pint of oil and one oz. of butter, both very hot. Fry them over an open fire until the meat has cooked well and the shell is of a fine red color.

Then remove all fat by tilting the saucepan on its side with its lid on; sprinkle the pieces of lobster with two chopped shallots and one crushed clove of garlic; add one-third pint of white wine, one-quarter pint of fish *fumet,* a small glassful of burnt brandy, one tablespoon of melted meat-*glaze* (15), three small, fresh pressed, and chopped tomatoes (or, failing fresh tomatoes, two tablespoons of tomato *purée*), a pinch of chopped parsley, and a very little cayenne. Cover the saucepan, and set to cook in the oven for eighteen or twenty minutes.

This done, transfer the pieces of lobster to a dish; take out the meat from the section of the tail and the claws, and put them in a *timbale;* set upright the two halves of the shell, and let them lie against each other. Keep the whole hot.

Now reduce the cooking-sauce of the lobster to one-third pint;

add the intestines and the chopped coral, together with a piece of butter the size of a walnut; set to cook for a moment, and pass through a strainer.

Put this *cullis* into a pot; heat it without letting it boil, and add, away from the fire, three oz. of butter cut into small pieces.

Pour this sauce over the pieces of lobster which have been kept hot, and sprinkle with a pinch of chopped and scalded parsley.

940—LOBSTER BORDELAISE   *Homard à la Bordelaise*

Section the live lobster as directed above.

Cook the meat and color the shell in a saucepan with two oz. of clarified butter (175). When the meat is quite done and the shell is red, pour away two-thirds of the butter. Then add two tablespoons of chopped shallots, a crushed piece of garlic the size of a pea, one-sixth pint of white wine, three tablespoons of burnt brandy, and reduce the whole to half. Complete with one-half pint of fish *fumet,* one-third pint of *maigre* Espagnole (22), one-quarter pint of tomato sauce (29), one small herb bunch, one pinch of salt, and a very little cayenne.

Put the lid on, and set to cook for one-quarter hour more.

Take the meat from the sections of the tail and the claws, as in the case of the preparation à l'Américaine (939); put these into a small saucepan, and keep them hot. Add the intestines and the chopped coral, reduce the sauce to one-third pint; pass it through a strainer, and pour it over the pieces of lobster.

Heat without boiling; add a few drops of lemon juice, two and one-half oz. of butter cut into small pieces, and one-half tablespoon of chopped chervil and tarragon, and stir over the fire, thoroughly mixing it.

Serve as directed in the preceding recipe.

941—BOILED LOBSTER HOLLANDAISE   *Homard à la Hollandaise*

Cook the lobster in a *court-bouillon* (163), allowing twenty minutes for a lobster weighing two lbs.

As soon as the lobster is cooked, drain it; split it in two lengthwise without completely severing the two halves; lay it on a platter covered with a napkin, and surround it with very green, curly parsley.

Serve with it, at the same time, a *timbale* of mealy potatoes freshly cooked à *l'anglaise,* and a sauceboat of melted butter.

942—LOBSTER ON THE SPIT — *Homard à la Broche*

Select a lobster that seems full of life, and, after killing it, fix it on a spit. Put into the dripping-pan six oz. of butter, one-half bottle of champagne, salt, and peppercorns. In order to cook it to perfection, frequently baste it with this mixture, and allow one hour before a red fire for a specimen weighing three lbs. It may be served with two accompaniments:—

A hot ravigote sauce (102) combined with the gravy of the lobster, from which all grease has been removed.

Or strain the contents of the dripping-pan (cleared of all grease) through a fine sieve; reduce it by a quarter over a brisk fire; add three tablespoons of meat-*glaze* (15), two tablespoons of Worcestershire sauce, and a little chopped parsley, and finish this sauce with three oz. of butter and a few drops of lemon juice.

943—CARDINAL LOBSTER — *Homard Cardinal*

Plunge the live lobster into boiling *court-bouillon,* and cook it after the manner directed under "Homard à la Hollandaise" (941).

The moment it is cooked, cut it in two lengthwise; take out the meat from the tail, slice it, and keep it hot in a little Cardinal sauce (69). Disconnect the claws; open them sideways, and take out all their meat without breaking them. Cut the meat into dice, as also the creamy parts from the shell, and add their weight of cooked mushrooms and half that quantity of truffles—both of which products should also be in dice. Thicken this *salpicon* with a few tablespoons of lobster sauce, and spread it in even layers on the bottom of each half-shell.

Reserve, however, two tablespoons of it for garnishing the emptied claws.

Upon the *salpicon* lay the slices of lobster, kept hot, alternating these with fine slices of truffles. Set the two half-shells, thus garnished, on a dish, and wedge them upright by means of the two claws.

Coat the slices and the claws with the Cardinal sauce; sprinkle with grated cheese and melted butter; set to *glaze* quickly in a hot oven or at the *salamander,* and serve instantly.

944—CLARENCE LOBSTER — *Homard Clarence*

Cook the lobster in *court-bouillon,* and drain it as soon as it is done.

When it is lukewarm, split it open lengthwise; take the meat from the tail; slice it, and keep it hot in a pot with a few drops of fish *fumet* or the cooking-liquor of mushrooms.

Remove the remains of meat and the creamy parts from the shell; pound the two together with two tablespoons of cream; strain through a fine sieve, and add to the resulting *cullis* one-half pint of Béchamel sauce with curry (28).

Garnish the two half-shells, two-thirds full, with rice à l'Indienne (2254); set the slices of lobster on this rice, inserting them with slices of truffle; coat thinly with the prepared Béchamel sauce, and set the two garnished and sauced half-shells on a long, hot dish.

Send to the table, at the same time, a sauceboat containing Béchamel with curry.

945—CREAMED LOBSTER   Homard à la Crème

Proceed as for "Homard à la Newburg à cru" (948), but swash the pan with brandy only, and add, immediately, four oz. of fresh, peeled truffles cut into slices.

Moisten, almost to cover, with very fresh, thin cream; season with salt and cayenne, and cook the lobster. Then take the meat from the shells, and put it into a *timbaie,* reduce the cream to one-third pint, and mix with three tablespoons of melted, white meat-*glaze* (15) and a few drops of lemon juice.

Strain this sauce through muslin, and pour it over the pieces of lobster.

946—BROILED LOBSTER   Homard Grillé

For this purpose, the lobster may be taken raw, but it is better, first, to have it three-quarters cooked in *court-bouillon*.

Now split it into two lengthwise; sprinkle it with melted butter, and set it on the grill for its cooking to be completed.

Treated thus, the meat of the lobster does not harden as when it is grilled raw. Serve the grilled lobster on a napkin or on a drainer, after having broken the shell of the claws in order to facilitate the withdrawal of the meat, and surround with curly parsley.

Serve a "Devilled sauce Escoffier" (37), or any other sauce suited to grilled fish, with the lobster, but remember that the first-named sauce is the best that could be found for this particular dish.

947—MORNAY LOBSTER, CALLED AU GRATIN
Homard à la Mornay, dit au Gratin

Proceed in all points as directed under "Homard Cardinal" (943), but substitute Mornay sauce (91) for Cardinal.

HOMARD À LA NEWBURG

This dish may be prepared in two ways—with raw lobster or with the lobster cooked some time beforehand. The second way is more correct, but the first, which is less troublesome to prepare, is more suited to the work of large establishments.

948—LOBSTER NEWBURG WITH FRESH LOBSTER
Homard à la Newburg with Fresh Lobster

Cut up the live lobster, and fry it in oil and butter as explained under "Homard à l'Américaine" (939). When the pieces of lobster are cooked and colored, clear them of all grease; swash the saucepan with one tablespoon of burnt brandy and one-half pint of Marsala.

Reduce by a third; season, and add two-thirds pint of cream and one-sixth pint of fish *fumet*. Cover and set to cook for fifteen minutes.

Take out the pieces of lobster; withdraw the meat, and keep it hot in a covered *timbale*. Thicken the sauce with the reserved intestines and coral of the lobster, which should be chopped in combination with one oz. of butter.

Set to boil a second time; rub the sauce through a fine sieve, and pour it over the pieces of lobster.

949—LOBSTER NEWBURG WITH BOILED LOBSTER
Homard à la Newburg with Boiled Lobster

Cook the lobster in *court-bouillon*. Remove the shell from the tail; take out the meat, and cut it into regular slices. Lay these slices in a liberally-buttered saucepan, season highly, and heat the slices on both sides until the outside membrane acquires a fine red color.

Moisten with enough Madeira to almost cover the slices, and reduce the liquid almost entirely. When serving, pour a thickening, composed of one and one-quarter pints of cream and two egg-yolks, over the slices. Stir gently on the side of the fire until it is thickened, and serve in a lukewarm *timbale*.

950—PALESTINE LOBSTER
Homard à la Palestine

Cut up the live lobster and toss it in butter with a *mirepoix* prepared in advance, as for crayfish intended for potage *bisque* (662).

Moisten with two-thirds pint of white wine, one pint of fish *fumet,* and three tablespoons of burnt brandy. Cover and cook for fifteen minutes.

Now detach the sections of the tail and the claws; take out the meat from them, and keep them hot in a small covered saucepan with a little butter. Pound the shell and remains of the lobster in a mortar; fry them in four tablespoons of very hot oil, and add an ordinary *mirepoix,* cut very fine. Moisten with the cooking-liquor of the lobster, and set to cook for one-quarter hour. Strain through muslin; leave to stand for five minutes, that the oil may rise to the surface, and then completely remove it. Reduce this liquid to one-quarter pint; thicken it with the reserved creamy parts of the lobster, rubbed through a fine sieve, and two tablespoons of fish velouté (26a), and finish this sauce with two and one-half oz. of curry butter (284).

Arrange a border of pilaff rice (2255) on the dish intended for the lobster; set the pieces of lobster, kept hot, in the center, and coat these with a few tablespoons of curry sauce (81).

Serve the remainder of the sauce separately.

951—MOUSSELINES OF LOBSTER   *Mousselines de Homard*

In the matter of crustaceans, the term *mousse* stands, as a rule, for a cold preparation, whereas the term *mousseline* is only applied to warm dishes. The special *mousselines* or *quenelles* of lobster are made with a *mousseline forcemeat,* the recipe for which I gave under (195). This *forcemeat* is prepared with the raw meat of the lobster.

As with the other crustaceans, their meat produces *forcemeat* which is somewhat too flimsy to be spoon-moulded, and it is preferable to *poach* it in special well-buttered *quenelle* or *dariole-moulds.*

Mousselines are *poached* under cover in a moderate oven.

All the garnishes and sauces given in respect of salmon *mousselines* may be applied here. The reader will therefore refer to:

Mousselines de Saumon Alexandra (798).

Mousselines de Saumon à la Tosca (799).

952—SOUFFLES OF LOBSTER   *Soufflés de Homard*

For lobster *soufflés* the same *forcemeat* is used as for the *mousselines;* but, unlike the latter, it is poached in the half-shells of the lobster, the meat of which has served in its preparation. The procedure is as follows:—First cook the two half-shells carefully, that they may not lose their shape in the process.

After having drained and dried them, fill them with *mousseline forcemeat* and surround them with strong, buttered vegetable parchment, which should be tied on with string, and should extend over the edges of the shells by one inch.

The object of this measure is to prevent the *forcemeat* from spilling out during the *poaching*.

Lay the two filled shells in a pan containing just enough boiling water to moisten its whole surface. Put the pan in a moderate oven or in a steamer, and allow from fifteen to twenty minutes for the *soufflé* to *poach*.

This done, carefully drain the two shells; remove the paper holding in the *forcemeat;* place them on a napkin, and surround them with bunches of very green, curly parsley. Serve separately a sauce in keeping with the preparation, a Normande (99), a white-wine (111), a Diplomate (82), or a Béchamel (28) finished with lobster butter (149), etc.

N.B.—The above constitutes the model-recipe of lobster *soufflé,* and I need scarcely point out that the latter may be varied almost indefinitely in accordance with the fancy of the cook and the taste of the diner.

Thus the *forcemeat* may be garnished with truffles in dice, slices of lobster, *milt,* or *poached* oysters, etc., which garnishes may also be laid on the *soufflé* when it is finished. I therefore leave to the cook, who should now see his way quite clearly, the task of imagining the various possible combinations.

953—COLD LOBSTER WITH VARIOUS SAUCES

Homard Froid aux Sauces Diverses

Cook the lobster in *court-bouillon,* and let it cool in the latter. Drain it, sever the claws, and break them open in order to take out the meat. Split the lobster into two lengthwise, remove the intestines and the queen, and arrange it on a napkin. Lay the claws on either side of it, and surround it either with curly parsley or with a few hearts of lettuce.

Send to the table separately one of the derivative sauces of the Mayonnaise (122 to 132).

954—ASPIC OF LOBSTER

Aspic de Homard

Under "Aspic de filets de soles" (915), I pointed out the preparatory principles of an aspic; in this case, therefore. I shall only refer to the various details very cursorily.

Let a thin coating of white fish aspic jelly set on the bottom of an aspic-mould incrusted in ice. The reader is reminded of the great care that must be observed in the preparation of an aspic jelly, that the latter be transparent, succulent, and just sufficiently firm not to break when taken from the mould. Decorate the bottom of the mould with bits of truffle, *poached* white of egg, lobster coral, capers, and tarragon leaves.

The decorative design cannot be described; it must be left to the taste and fancy of the chef; all I can urge is that it be as regular and symmetrical as possible.

Fix the decoration by means of a few drops of jelly; then cover the whole with a thickness of one inch of the same jelly, and leave the latter to set. Upon this layer of jelly arrange rows of thin slices of lobster meat and slices of truffles placed alternately and slightly overlapping. Now add enough jelly to cover these slices, and continue filling up the mould with varying layers consisting respectively of jelly (one inch thick) and the slices of lobster.

When about to serve, dip the mould in hot water; dry it, and turn out the aspic upon a dish covered with a napkin.

955—ARCHANGEL (RUSSIAN) LOBSTER CUTLETS
Côtelettes de Homard Arkhangel

Prepare a *salpicon* of lobster meat in dice combined with its weight of caviar, the whole quantity being in proportion to the number of *côtelettes* required.

Thicken the *salpicon* with an equal quantity of lobster *mousse* (956), and at once garnish some moderately oiled *cutlet-moulds* with the preparation. As soon as the latter has set, turn out the cutlets; coat them with a fish chaud-froid (35) sauce, finished with lobster butter (149); and deck each with a fine, grooved slice of truffle. *Glaze* them with cold melted jelly, and keep them in a cool place until required to be served.

Arrange them in a circle on a round dish; garnish the center with chopped white jelly, and serve a Russian salad separately (2021).

956—LOBSTER MOUSSE
Mousse de Homard

Cook the lobster in a few tablespoons of previously-prepared fine *mirepoix,* one half-bottle of white wine, and a small glass of burnt brandy. Leave to cool in the cooking-liquor. Now split the lobster in two, take out the meat. Finely pound the latter while adding, little by little, one-third pint of cold fish velouté (26a) per lb. of meat. Rub through a sieve; put the resulting *purée* in a pan lying on ice, and stir for a few minutes. This done, add a little good fish jelly, melted and cold, and one-third pint of barely-whipped cream. Taste; rectify the seasoning, and add a dash of cayenne.

957—MOULDED LOBSTER MOUSSE   *Mousse de Homard Moulée*

When the *mousse* is intended for moulding, it is well to decorate and coat the mould with fish jelly some time in advance. I have already explained that to coat a mould with jelly, all that is needed is to pour in a few tablespoons of melted jelly, and then to rock the mould standing on ice. By this means a thin even coating sets on the bottom and sides of the mould, which, when the mould is turned out, swathes the latter in a transparent film.

This coating of jelly may be made more or less thick, according to the requirements, by simply using more or less of it, and by proportionately lengthening or shortening the time.

When the mould is coated, decorate the sides with large slices of very black truffle dipped in melted jelly, that they may stick.

This done, fill the receptacle with the prepared *mousse* (see the preceding recipe), and leave to set in a cold place.

For the turning out of the mould and the serving of the dish, proceed as for the aspic.

958—INDIVIDUAL LOBSTER MOUSSES   *Petites Mousses de Homard*

For these small *mousses,* use little *cassolettes* or silver *timbales.* First let a thin layer of jelly (one or two tablespoons, according to their size) set on the bottom of each, and then surround the latter with bands of white paper, the ends of which should be stuck together, and should reach one inch above the brims of the *cassolettes.* The preparation of *mousse* may now be placed in the *cassolettes* in a sufficient quantity to rise above the brims, so that, when the paper is removed, their appearance is that of small *soufflés.*

When the *cassolettes* have been filled, put them aside on ice or in a refrigerator until they are served.

959—GRAMMONT LOBSTER   *Homard à la Grammont*

Split the lobster open lengthwise down the middle. Take out the meat from the tail; trim it, and cut it into regular pieces. Coat them again and again with aspic jelly, that they may be well covered with it; decorate each with a slice of truffle, and *glaze* it with the same aspic.

Also coat with jelly as many very white *poached* and dried oysters as there are slices.

Now take the creamy parts and the meat of the claws, and pound them finely with one tablespoon of cold Béchamel sauce (28); rub through a sieve, and, with the resulting *purée* combined with melted fish jelly and cream (see lobster mousse 956), prepare a *mousse* "au paprika" of a decided pink color.

Fill the two half-shells to their edges with this *mousse*, and leave it to set on ice.

When about to serve, lay the pieces, *glazed* with jelly, upon this *mousse*, and place an oyster between each pair. Serve the two filled half-shells, back to back, upon a napkin, and put the heart of a lettuce in the middle, and a bunch of curly parsley at either end.

Serve a mayonnaise or other cold sauce separately.

960—PARISIAN LOBSTER   *Homard à la Parisienne*

Tie a lobster to a little board; stretch out its tail to the fullest extent; cook it in *court-bouillon,* and leave it to cool in the latter.

When it is quite cold, carefully cut a strip of the shell from the back of the head to the tail. The aperture left by the removed strip of shell ought to be sufficiently wide to allow the meat of the tail to be removed without breaking it. Having emptied the tail, refill it with lettuce leaves, and return the strip of shell (upside down) to its place. Cut the meat of the tail into even slices, and lay on each a slice of truffle stamped out with the fancy-cutter, and dipped in half-melted jelly. Then coat these slices, again and again, with cold melted jelly until they are well covered with it.

Now break the claws and remove their meat, and that remaining in the shell, and cut the meat into dice. Take the creamy parts, and rub them through a sieve.

Prepare a small vegetable salad; add the meat dice, and mix the two with a mayonnaise sauce combined with melted jelly and the creamy parts rubbed through a sieve. When the salad begins to set, garnish twelve small artichoke-bottoms with it, arranging the salad in a pyramid. Set a bit of truffle on each pyramid, and sprinkle the salad with melted fish jelly to make it glossy.

Serving.—Place the lobster on a bed of buttered bread on which a *julienne* of lettuce has been placed, or on one of moulded rice. The bed should have the shape of a wedge, in order that the lobster may lie at an angle of about 45°, with its head raised, when laid upon it. Arrange the slices (slightly overlapping one another) along the back of the lobster, beginning at its head with the smallest, and progressing down towards the tail, gradually increasing their size.

Surround the lobster alternately with artichoke-bottoms garnished with salad, and quartered hard-boiled eggs, or halved hard-boiled eggs (set upright with their yolks facing outwards).

Border the dish with very clear aspic-jelly in large cubes or triangles, etc.

961—RUSSIAN LOBSTER _Homard à la Russe_

Proceed exactly as above with regard to the cooking of the lobster, the extraction of the meat, and the cutting of it into slices. Coat the slices with mayonnaise sauce combined with melted jelly; or, better still, with a white fish chaud-froid sauce (76) combined with the lobster's creamy parts rubbed through a sieve.

Decorate each slice with a bit of coral and two little chervil leaves; coat them again and again with cold melted aspic, and put them aside to cool. Coat ten _dariole-moulds,_ and decorate the bottom of each with a slice of truffle. Also prepare ten hard-boiled eggs.

Prepare a Salade Russe (without meat) (2021); add to this the remains of the lobster meat cut into dice, and thicken with mayonnaise and melted aspic, mixed. With this thickened salad fill the _dariole-moulds,_ and leave to set in a cool place.

Serving.—Set the lobster on a bed, after the manner of the preceding recipe. Trim the slices, and lay them, as before, on the lobster's back, taking care to graduate their sizes. Surround the lobster with the small moulded salads, and alternate these with the hard-boiled eggs. The latter should be cut in two at a point one-third of their height above their base; their yolks should be removed, the space filled with caviar moulded to the form of a pyramid, and, this done, the eggs should be set upright.

Border the dish with slices of very clear fish jelly, stamped out by a fancy-cutter, and lay a bit of truffle upon each.

N.B.—The moulds of salad must, of course, be dipped in hot water before being turned out.

The lobster may also be served "à la Néva," "à la Moscovite," "à la Sibérienne," etc., but these preparations are only minor forms of "Homard à la Russe" under different names.

Changes may be made in the preparation by altering the ingredients of the salad and its serving. It may, for instance, be made in small cucumber or beets _barquettes,_ while the caviar, instead of being laid in hard-boiled eggs, may be served in little fluted paper cases.

As these preparations, however, are based neither on fixed principles nor on rigid rules, I shall refrain from giving them.

962—MAYONNAISE OF LOBSTER   *Mayonnaise de Homard*

Proceed as for Mayonnaise de Saumon (809)—that is to say, garnish the bottom of a salad-bowl with shredded lettuce leaves, and season them moderately.

Upon this salad lay the remains of the lobster, and upon the latter place the thin slices of the tail. Cover with mayonnaise sauce, and decorate with strips of anchovy fillets, capers, olives, hard-boiled eggs, slices of pink radishes, the hearts of lettuce, etc.

N.B.—I have already pointed out the futility of describing a decorative design. As a rule, the matter is so intimately connected with the taste and fancy of the individual, and the products used for the purpose lend themselves to such infinite variations, that I prefer merely to enumerate these garnishes, and to leave their arrangement to the artistic ingenuity of the cook.

963—LOBSTER SALAD   *Salade de Homard*

See "Salade de Saumon" (810). As the preparation and seasoning of the latter are identical with those of the dish under consideration, all that is needed is to replace the salmon of the recipe by the pieces of lobster.

SPINY LOBSTERS OR ROCK LOBSTERS (LANGOUSTE)

All culinary preparations dealing with lobsters may be adapted to spiny lobsters. There is, therefore, no need to repeat them here. Of the cold recipes, two are much better suited to the spiny than to the ordinary kind, though, as they are used for both specimens, I gave them earlier in the book. The two recipes referred to are:—

964—PARISIAN ROCK LOBSTER   *Langouste à la Parisienne*

See LOBSTER, recipe 960.

965—RUSSIAN ROCK LOBSTER   *Langouste à la Russe*

See LOBSTER, recipe 961.

CRAYFISH (ÉCREVISSES)

Crayfish, prepared whole, are rather popular on the European continent. But crayfish dishes are not much known in the United States. This is doubtless accounted for by the fact that they only exist in a few places as in the states of Louisiana and Wisconsin.

They are therefore only served in the form of an aspic, a *mousse, mousselines, timbales,* etc., or as the garnish of some other fish; for in all these cases they are shelled.

I give below the various recipes relating to them, and from among these it ought to be possible to choose one which will meet the requirements of any particular menu.

966—BORDELAISE CRAYFISH OR ROCK LOBSTERS
Ecrevisses à la Bordelaise

N.B.—Whatever be their mode of preparation, crayfish should always be thoroughly cleansed and cleared of their intestines, the extreme end of which is to be found under the middle of the tail. In order to remove the intestines, take the tail-segment between the point of a small knife and the thumb, and pull gently. If this were not done, the intestines, especially in the breeding season, might make the crayfish disagreeably bitter.

As soon as their intestines have been removed, the crayfish should be set to cook, otherwise if they be left to wait, their juices escape through the tail wound, and they empty.

For twelve crayfish, after having cleaned and drawn them, put them into a pot with one tablespoon of very fine *mirepoix,* completely cooked beforehand, and two-thirds oz. of butter. Toss them over an open fire until the shells have acquired a fine, red color. Moisten with three tablespoons of burnt brandy and one-quarter pint of white wine; reduce by a third, and complete with one tablespoon of Espagnole (22), two tablespoons of fish *fumet,* the same quantity of tomato *purée,* and one spoonful of special *mirepoix* (229).

Put the lid on, and set to cook for ten minutes.

Serve the crayfish in a *timbale;* reduce the sauce by a quarter, and finish it with a few drops of meat *glaze* (15), one oz. of butter, a very little cayenne, chopped chervil, and tarragon. Pour this over the crayfish, and serve instantly.

967—CRAYFISH OR ROCK LOBSTER MARINIERE

Ecrevisses à la Marinière

In the case of twelve crayfish, *sauté* them in two-thirds oz. of butter over an open fire, until the shells are of a fine red. Season with salt and pepper; add two finely chopped shallots, a bit of thyme and a bit of bay leaf; moisten with one-third pint of white wine; cover; cook for ten minutes, and serve in a *timbale*.

Reduce the cooking-liquor to half; thicken with two tablespoons of fish velouté (26a); finish the sauce with one oz. of butter, and pour it over the crayfish.

Sprinkle with a pinch of chopped parsley, and serve at once.

968—"SWIMMING" CRAYFISH   *Ecrevisses à la Nage*

For twelve crayfish, ten minutes beforehand prepare a *court-bouillon* of one-half pint of white wine, one-quarter pint of fish *fumet*, a few slices of carrot and onion, one sprig of parsley cut into dice, a small pinch of powdered thyme and bay leaf, and a very little salt and cayenne pepper.

Put the crayfish into the boiling *court-bouillon;* cover, and leave to cook for ten minutes, taking care to toss the crayfish from time to time.

When about to serve, pour the crayfish with the *court-bouillon* and the *aromatics* into a *timbale*.

969—CRAYFISH OR ROCK LOBSTER LIEGEOISE

Ecrevisses à la Liègoise

Cook the crayfish in *court-bouillon* as explained in the preceding recipe. Place them in a *timbale,* and keep them hot. Strain the *court-bouillon;* reduce it by a quarter; add one oz. of butter, and pour it over the crayfish.

Sprinkle with a pinch of chopped parsley.

970—MOUSSELINE OF CRAYFISH OR ROCK LOBSTER

Mousselines d'Ecrevisses

What I said with reference to "Mousseline de Homard" (951) applies perfectly here, and my remarks relative to the variation of the garnishing ingredients, which are the same as those in (951), also hold good.

971—TIMBALE OF CRAYFISH TAILS NANTUA

Timbale de Queues d'Ecrevisses à la Nantua

For ten people prepare a shallow *timbale crust,* and a cover decorated with a design of leaves or some other ornamental treatment; toss sixty crayfish in butter with two tablespoons of very fine *mirepoix* cooked in butter beforehand. When the crayfish are of a distinct red, moisten with one glass of white wine and three table-spoons of burned brandy; season with salt and cayenne pepper; cover them, and keep them on a low flame for ten minutes, taking care to toss them again from time to time; shell the tails and put them into a small saucepan with twenty small *quenelles* of whiting *forcemeat,* finished with crayfish butter (147); fifteen small, grooved mushrooms, cooked and very white, and three oz. of truffles in slices. Add a few drops of the mushroom cooking-liquor to this garnish, and keep it hot; pound the remains and shells of the crayfish very finely; add two-thirds pint of cream sauce (79) to the resulting *purée;* rub it through a fine sieve, and add it to the garnish; when about to serve, pour this garnish into the *timbale crust,* which should be very hot, and decorate the top with a crown of fine slices of very black truffle. Close the *timbale* with its cover, and serve it on a napkin.

972—CRAYFISH SOUFFLE FLORENTINE
Soufflé d'Ecrevisses à la Florentine

Make a preparation of Soufflé au Parmesan (2295a) combined with two tablespoons of crayfish cream per pint. The cream is pre-pared after the manner of lobster cream (295).

Put this preparation in a buttered *timbale* in alternate layers separated by layers of sliced truffle and crayfish tails. Cook the *soufflé* after the manner of an ordinary one.

973—CRAYFISH SOUFFLE LEOPOLD DE ROTHSCHILD
Soufflé d'Ecrevisses Leopold de Rothschild

Prepare a *soufflé* as above, and add a scant tablespoon of freshly-cooked asparagus and slices of truffle, and crayfish tails placed be-tween the layers of the *soufflé* preparation. Cook as above.

974—CRAYFISH SOUFFLE PIEDMONT
Soufflé d'Ecrevisses à la Piémontaise

This is identical with (972), except that the ordinary truffles are replaced by peelings of Piedmont truffles.

975—ASPIC OF CRAYFISH TAILS MODERN
Aspic de Queues d'Ecrevisses à la Moderne

Cook twelve fine crayfish in accordance with the directions under (966), but substitute champagne for the white wine.

Shell the tails; trim them evenly; cut them in two lengthwise, and keep them in a cool place until they are wanted. Remove the creamy parts from the shells of the crayfish; add the trimmings of the tails, the meat from the claws, and the *mirepoix* in which the crayfish have cooked.

Pound the whole very finely in a mortar, and rub it through a sieve. Put the resulting *purée* in a receptacle; add one-quarter pint of very cold, melted aspic, and three tablespoons of lightly beaten cream. Leave this preparation to set.

Trim the crayfish shells; fill them with a little prepared *mousse,* and decorate each shell with a small roundel of truffle.

Put the remainder of the *mousse* in the middle of a little crystal bowl, and mould it to the shape of a cone, narrow towards the base, and as high as possible.

Arrange the garnished crayfish shells on their backs in the bowl around the cone of *mousse,* and set some crayfish tails in rings encircling the cone. The crayfish tails should be dipped in half-melted aspic-jelly, that they may stick fast to the cone. Lay a small, very round truffle on the top of the cone to complete the decoration. This done, coat the whole again and again by means of a spoon with half-melted, succulent, clear fish jelly (161), and incrust the *timbale* in a block of ice, or set it in cracked ice.

976—MOUSSE OF CRAYFISH   *Mousse d'Ecrevisses*

For ten people cook thirty crayfish as for potage *Bisque.* This done, remove the tails, and reserve a dozen fine shells. Finely pound the remainder, together with the *mirepoix* in which the crayfish have cooked, and add one-half oz. of butter, one oz. of red butter (142), one-quarter pint of cold fish velouté (26a), and six tablespoons of melted fish jelly (161). Rub through a fine sieve, and put the resulting *purée* in a saucepan; stir it over ice for two or three minutes; add three-quarters pint of lightly-beaten cream, and the crayfish tails cut into dice or finely sliced.

Before beginning to prepare the *mousse,* line the bottom and side of a *Charlotte-mould* with paper, that the *mousse* may be moulded as soon as ready.

Pour the preparation into the mould, taking care to reserve enough for the twelve shells already put aside, and put the *mousse* on ice or in a refrigerator until needed. Fill the twelve trimmed shells with the reserved *mousse,* and decorate each with a round slice of truffle. When about to serve, turn out the *mousse* on a small, round bed of semolina or rice, one-half inch thick, on a dish. Remove all the paper, and decorate the top of the *mousse* with a crown of the fine slices of truffle dipped in melted jelly, that they may be glossy.

Surround the semolina or rice bed with a border of chopped aspic-jelly, and arrange the garnished shells upon this jelly, setting them almost upright.

N.B.—Instead of being served on a bed, the crayfish *mousse* may be sent to the table in a deep silver dish with a border of chopped aspic-jelly, and surrounded by the garnished shells. The utensil is then laid on a flat dish in a bed of cracked ice, or it is incrusted direct in a block of carved ice.

For the moulding of crayfish *mousse,* the mould may be coated with fish jelly (161) and decorated with slices of truffle, as directed under "Mousse de Homard moulée" (957).

A *mousse* prepared in this way may be either served on a semolina or rice bed, or in a deep silver entrée dish, as described above.

976a—SUPREME OF CRAYFISH WITH CHAMPAGNE
Suprêmes d'Ecrevisses au Champagne

Select forty medium-sized crayfish that seem full of life; cook them quickly in a highly-seasoned *mirepoix,* moistened with one half-bottle of dry champagne. This done, shell them; trim their tails, and keep them cool in a small bowl. Pound their shells as finely as possible with one-quarter lb. of fresh butter, and put the resulting *purée* in a saucepan, together with one-half pint of boiling velouté (25) containing about two and one-half ounces of gelatine, and the cooking-liquor of the crayfish passed through a fine strainer

Set to boil for a few minutes, that the remains may bring out all their flavor; rub through a fine sieve over a bowl set in cracked ice, and whisk the preparation in order to hasten its cooling. As soon as it begins to thicken, add one pint of half-whipped cream to it. Then pour the whole into a silver or porcelain *timbale,* taking care that the utensil be not more than three-quarters full.

When the *mousse* has set, decorate the surface with the reserved crayfish tails, to which are added, as a finish, bits of truffle and chervil leaves. Cover the decoration with a thin coating of easily-melting (soft) and amber-colored fish jelly (161), and put the *timbale* on ice. When about to serve, incrust it in a block of carved ice, or place it on a silver dish with cracked ice all round.

977—CRAYFISH MOUSSE CARDINAL   *Mousse d'Ecrevisses Cardinal*

For ten people cook the crayfish as explained in (976), but take forty instead of thirty. Shell the tails; trim them and cut them into dice. Prepare the *mousse* in the same way, but use twice as much red butter (142). Garnish twelve shells after the same manner, and decorate each with a slice of truffle.

Coat a dome or *Charlotte-mould* somewhat thickly with aspic; garnish its bottom and sides with crayfish tails, previously dipped in half-melted jelly, and lined in rows; and place the crayfish so that the tails of the first row lie to the left, those of the second row to the right, and so on. As often as possible, do this work before preparing the *mousse,* in order that the latter may be put into the mould as soon as ready.

When about to fill the mould, add twenty fine slices of truffle to the *mousse.* Serve after one of the two methods directed in the appended note to (970), and take care to dip the mould quickly into hot water before attempting to turn out its contents.

978—COLD INDIVIDUAL SOUFFLES OF CRAYFISH

Petits soufflés froids d'Ecrevisses

Prepare the crayfish *mousse* as directed under (976) and replace the fish velouté by cold Béchamel (28). The addition of sauce is unnecessary in this case, and the preparation may be all the more delicate for consisting only of the crayfish *cullis* and two tablespoons of fish jelly (161).

For the moulding of these small *soufflés* I can only repeat what I said under "Petites Mousses de Homard" (958). Let a thin coating of jelly set on the bottom of the small *cassolettes* or *timbales* used; garnish their insides with a band of white paper, reaching one inch above their brims; stick the end of this band with a little batter.

Now garnish the *timbales* with *mousse,* letting it project above their edges to the extent of two-thirds of an inch, and leave it to set in a cool place. When about to serve, remove the band of paper, holding in the projecting *mousse,* and the appearance of the garnished *timbales* is exactly that of small, hot *soufflés.* Allow one *soufflé* for each person.

979—SHRIMPS AND PRAWNS   *Crevettes Grises et Crevettes Roses*

Prawns are chiefly used for hors-d'œuvres, but they may, nevertheless, be prepared in Aspics; *Mousses;* small cold *Soufflés,* etc.

As regards shrimps, their use in Europe is generally limited to garnishes, hors-d'œuvres, and to the preparation of soups, shrimp butters, and creams.

OYSTERS (HUITRES)

Though oysters are best raw, there are so many culinary preparations of which they form the leading ingredient, and such a number of garnishing uses to which they may be put, that I feel compelled to mention some of these.

980—OYSTERS FAVORITE   *Huîtres à la Favorite*

Poach the oysters bearded in their own liquor, which should have been carefully collected when opening them. Clean their hollow shells, and place them on a tray covered with a layer of rock salt one-half inch thick. Garnish them with Béchamel (28); upon the latter, in each shell, lay an oyster decorated with a slice of truffle; cover with the same sauce; sprinkle with grated Parmesan cheese and melted butter, and set to *glaze* quickly. Serve immediately.

981—OYSTERS AU GRATIN   *Huîtres au Gratin*

Open the oysters; cut them free, and lay them in the hollow halves of their shells, which should be incrusted in a layer of rock salt covering the tray. On each oyster put a drop of lemon juice, a pinch of fried bread-crumbs, a little melted butter, and a piece of fresh butter the size of a pea.

Set the *gratin* to form in a hot oven or at the *salamander,* and serve immediately.

982—OYSTERS MORNAY   *Huîtres à la Mornay*

Poach the oysters, and allow two per shell.

Set the hollow shells, thoroughly cleansed, on a tray covered with rock salt. Cover the bottom of the shells with Mornay sauce (91); put two *poached* oysters into each; cover with the same sauce; sprinkle with grated cheese and melted butter, and set to *glaze* quickly. Serve instantly.

983—OYSTER SOUFFLE   *Huîtres soufflées*

Make a preparation of *Soufflé au Parmesan* (2295a). Slightly *poach* the oysters, clean their hollow shells, and set these on a tray covered with rock salt. Spread a layer of the preparation on each shell; put on an oyster, and cover the latter with the *soufflé au Parmesan.*

Heat the base of the tray on the stove, and, when the *soufflé* be-gins to rise, put the tray in the oven, that the *soufflé* may cook and color at the same time. Serve at once.

984—OYSTERS FLORENTINE   *Huîtres à la Florentine*

Poach the oysters. Set their hollow shells on a tray as above; garnish the bottom of each of these with shredded spinach stewed in butter; lay an oyster on the spinach in each shell; cover with Mornay sauce (91), and set to *glaze* quickly. Serve immediately.

985—BROILED OYSTERS   *Huîtres Grillées*

Open the oysters, and leave them in their hollow shells; lay them (very straight) on a tray covered with rock salt, incrusting them in the latter; sprinkle with a drop of lemon juice and a little *mignon-ette* pepper and put them in a hot oven, that their top surfaces may be speedily *poached.*

Serve them on a napkin; pour a teaspoon of "Sauce Diable Escof-fier" (37) over each, and serve directly.

986—QUENELLES OF OYSTERS REINE   *Quenelles d'Huîtres à la Reine*

With four oz. of breast of chicken and six raw oysters, prepare a *mousseline forcemeat* in accordance with the directions given under (195). Mould this *forcemeat,* by means of a tablespoon, into large *quenelles,* in the center of which lay two cold *poached* oysters.

Poach these *quenelles* after the manner of ordinary *mousselines.* This done, drain them; arrange them in a circle on a round dish, and cover them with highly-seasoned Suprême sauce (106a). Decorate each *quenelle* with a fine slice of truffle, and garnish the center of the dish with some asparagus tips, mixed with butter.

987—BASS   *Bar*

The large specimens are served, boiled, with the same kind of sauce as for turbot. The smaller ones are chiefly served à la Meunière (778) or fried.

988—BRILL   *Barbue*

Served whole, brill may be looked upon as the understudy, as it were, of the chicken-turbot, and all the preparations given for the latter may be adapted to the former.

If it be preferred filleted, it may be treated after the recipes given for fillets of sole. Hence for brill cooked whole refer to chicken-turbot and the recipes (925 to 938), and for filleted brill see recipes (865 to 922).

(Brill is not procurable in the United States.—Ed.)

989—BLOATERS
Harengs Fumés

Bloaters, or herrings partially dried in smoke, form one of the finest breakfast dishes. As a rule, they are simply grilled over a moderate fire. It should be borne in mind that, as these fish are only partially salted and smoked, they will not keep very long.

COD (CABILLAUD)

If cod were less common, it would be held in as high esteem as salmon; for, when it is really fresh and of good quality, the delicacy and delicious flavor of its flesh ranks it among the finest of fish.

990—BOILED COD
Cabillaud Bouilli

Fresh cod is mostly served boiled, either whole, in sections, or in steaks, and the directions given under "The Boiling of Fish" (776) apply particularly to this fish.

Boiled fresh cod is always accompanied by its liver, *poached* in salted water, and very mealy potatoes, boiled at the last minute, must always be sent to the table with it.

Served thus with an oyster sauce (86), a Hollandaise sauce (30), or melted butter, fresh cod constitutes a *Relevé* which would satisfy the most exacting of gourmets.

991—GRILLED COD
Cabillaud Grillé

Cut the fish into slices one inch or two inches thick. Season these slices; dredge them; sprinkle them copiously with melted butter, and set them to grill, remembering to baste them frequently with melted butter.

Serve them on a hot dish; garnish them with slices of lemon, and surround with bunches of parsley.

Send a Maître-d'Hôtel (991) or Anchovy Butter (281), or a grilled-fish sauce to the table with the dish.

992—FRIED COD
Cabillaud Frit

Cut some slices of fresh cod, from one inch to one and one-half inches thick. Season them, treat them *à l'anglaise,* and fry them sufficiently to allow their being well cooked all through. Serve them on a napkin with fried parsley and lemon, and send a butter sauce

(66), a tartar sauce, or a tomato sauce (29) to the table at the same time as the fish.

993—CREAMED COD AU GRATIN   *Cabillaud Crème Gratin*

For ten people take two lbs. of boiled fresh cod divided into small pieces; clean of all bones and skin, and keep them hot in a little of their cooking-liquor.

Now, with the necessary quantity of Duchesse potatoes (221), and by means of a pastry-bag fitted with a fancy tube, lay a border, one and one-half inches high, round a dish, shaping it in such a way that it is thickest at its base. The dish may be either round or oval. Carefully brush this border with egg-yolks.

This done, pour a few tablespoons of Mornay sauce (91) on the dish; lay on the drained pieces of cod, and cover with enough Mornay sauce to reach within one-third of an inch of the brim of the border. If more sauce were used, it would flow over the border during the process of *glazing*.

Sprinkle with grated Parmesan cheese and melted butter; set to *glaze*, and see that the border gets evenly browned.

Serve the moment the dish is taken from the oven.

N.B.—This mode of preparation is not restricted to fresh cod. It may be applied to all other boiled fish—turbot, chicken-turbot, brill, bass, salmon, etc.

994—COD FLEMISH STYLE   *Cabillaud à la Flamande*

Cut the fresh cod into slices one inch thick; season them with salt, pepper, and nutmeg, and put them in a saucepan or a deep, liberally-buttered tray. Moisten with white wine to the height of the slices; add chopped shallots and *"fines herbes,"* and garnish the fish with slices of seeded lemon, peeled to the pulp.

Set to boil, and then *poach* in the oven for twelve minutes. Place the slices on a dish; thicken their cooking-liquor with crushed *biscotte;* cook it for five minutes; pour it over the slices, and serve.

995—PORTUGUESE COD   *Cabillaud à la Portugaise*

For ten people, cut five slices of fresh cod, each weighing one-half lb., and season them with salt and pepper. Put these slices into a saucepan containing the following garnish, into which they should be pressed:—Three oz. of butter and one-sixth pint of oil; one large onion, chopped and lightly browned in butter; a bit of crushed garlic the size of a pea; one herb bunch; two pinches of chopped parsley; eight medium-sized, peeled, pressed, and minced tomatoes, and one-third pint of white wine.

Cover the saucepan, and set to boil on an open fire for five minutes.

Now take the lid off the saucepan, and leave it to cook for twelve minutes on the side of the fire, in order that the liquid may be reduced and the fish cooked at the same moment of time.

Set the slices on a long dish; take out the herb bunch, and pour the garnish and the cooking-liquor over the fish.

996—CARP MILT   *Laitances de Carpe*

The *milt* of a carp makes a very delicate dish. It is served either as a second fish at a dinner; as a garnish to large fish *Relevés*, after having been *poached* in salted water; or cut raw into slices which are generally treated *à la Meunière* (778).

997—FISH MILT MEUNIERE   *Laitances à la Meunière*

Prepare them whole or in slices, in pursuance of the directions given under "The Cooking of Fish à la Meunière" (778).

998—FISH MILT IN BARQUETTES FLORENTINE
Barquettes de Laitances à la Florentine

Poach the *milts* in salted water; cut them into small, long slices, and set them in *barquette* crusts prepared in advance.

Cover the sliced *milts* with a *soufflé au Parmesan* (2295a), and shape the latter slightly after the manner of a dome.

Arrange the *barquettes* on a dish, and put them in a moderate oven, that they may cook and the *soufflé* be *glazed* at the same time. When taking them out of the oven, place them on a napkin and serve immediately.

999—RAMEKINS OF MILT A LA NANTUA
Caisses de Laitances à la Nantua

Poach the *milts* in salted water. Drain them, and cut them into small slices thicker than their length.

Place these slices in small ramekins with two crayfish tails in each. Fill up the ramekins with Nantua sauce (95), and lay a fine slice of truffle over the center of each ramekin.

1000—JOHN DORY (WALL-EYED PIKE)   *Dorée St. Pierre*

This fish, which is in the highest degree unsightly, has flesh whose firmness, whiteness, and delicacy are of the rarest excellence; and, when quite fresh, its fillets are certainly equal in quality to those of the chicken-turbot and the sole.

Although the dory (wall-eyed pike) is not as popular as it deserves to be, this is owing either to its unsightliness, which may prejudice the opinion of gourmets against it, or to people's indifference to it, or to a mere trick of fashion.

While I admit its unpopularity, however, I should strongly recommend all lovers of fish to give it a trial. Let them prepare the fillets after the recipes given under Fillets of Sole (992) and Chicken-turbot (925), and, provided the directions be properly carried out, I venture to say that the prevailing aversion to it will very soon be found to have no reason.

1001—FRESH HADDOCK *Frais Eglefin*

When it is fresh, it may be prepared after the recipes given for cod, to which it is quite equal in the matter of delicacy.

1002—SMELTS *Eperlans*

Owing to their small size, smelts only lend themselves to a very limited number of preparations. They are usually served either on little skewers or placed in a heap on a napkin, with fried parsley and grooved half-lemons; those on skewers are served flat with the same garnish.

Large smelts may be treated after the recipes immediately following.

1003—SMELTS ENGLISH STYLE *Eperlans à l'Anglaise*

Open the smelts down the back and carefully bone, without marring them. Treat them *à l'anglaise* with fine bread-crumbs, and pat them lightly with the flat of a knife, that the bread-crumbs may hold well.

Cook them in clarified butter (175); set them on a long hot dish, and sprinkle them with half-melted butter à la Maître-d'Hôtel (150).

1004—SMELTS AU GRATIN *Eperlans au Gratin*

Proceed as for Merlans au Gratin (1018), but allowing for the difference between the sizes of the two fish, put the smelts in a hotter oven than the whiting, in order that they may be cooked simultaneously with the formation of the *gratin*.

1005—GRILLED SMELTS *Eperlans Grillés*

Open them down the back, and remove the bulk of their backbone, leaving a small piece only in the region of the tail. and another small piece at the head. Season, dredge, and sprinkle them with melted butter, and grill them quickly.

Set them on a long, hot platter; surround them with slices of lemon and bunches of fried parsley, and serve separately either some half-melted butter à la Maître-d'Hôtel (150), or a sauce suited to grilled fish.

1006—MOUSSELINES OF SMELTS *Mousselines d'Eperlans*

Proceed exactly as for Mousselines de Saumon (797). To prepare the *forcemeat,* follow the directions under (195); but note the following changes:—Of the whole quantity of the meat of fish, that of the smelt should only measure one-third; the other two-thirds should be supplied by the sole, wall-eyed pike, or whiting.

The reason for this proportion has already been explained under "Velouté d'Éperlans" (680). The flesh of the smelt is of a much too decided flavor to be used alone, and when this flavor predominates, it becomes positively disagreeable; hence the need of a fish whose flesh is almost neutral in so far as taste is concerned. But this addition of a fish foreign to the base of the preparation fulfils a double purpose; for, while it effectually weakens the pungency of the smelt's flesh, it also enables the whole preparation to absorb a much larger quantity of cream, and this allows the *mousselines* to be lighter and mellower.

1007—HOT MOUSSE OF SMELTS A LA ROYAL
Mousse Chaude d'Eperlans à la Royale

Take a *Charlotte-mould,* of a size in proportion to the number of people to be served, and butter its bottom and sides. Cover the bottom of the mould with a round piece of buttered kitchen paper, and do the same with the sides.

Prepare the required quantity of smelts' fillets; slightly flatten them in order to break the fibres, and trim them all to the same length and width.

Then garnish the bottom of the mould with the fillets of smelt, placing them so that their skin-sides are down. Between each of the fillets set a small strip of truffle, one quarter of the width of the former.

Garnish the sides in the same way, putting a strip of truffle between each; but take care to place the fillets slantwise instead of upright. Having lined the mould with fillets of smelt and truffle, cover with a layer of *mousseline forcemeat,* one-half inch thick.

Now fill the mould in the following way:—On the layer of *force-meat* covering the fillets at the bottom of the mould set as many slices of truffle as will cover it; spread another layer of *forcemeat* on the truffle, and over that lay, alternately, a sufficient quantity of fillets of smelt and anchovy. Follow with a fresh layer of *forcemeat,* slices of truffle, etc., until the mould is full, and finish with a layer of *forcemeat.*

Poach the *mousse* (covered) in a moderate oven, and allow fifty minutes for one prepared in a quart-mould. It is very easy, however, to tell when the *mousse* is done, simply by thrusting a small knife into it; if the blade of the knife withdraws quite clean, the *mousse* is cooked.

As soon as it is ready, turn the mould upside-down on a dish, and raise it a little in order to allow the liquid, which always accumulates in more or less large quantities, to drain away. Soak up this liquid; gently draw off the mould; take off the paper, and remove the froth which may have formed on the fillets by means of a wet brush.

Lay a fine, grooved mushroom on the top of the *mousse;* surround it with *mousseline* sauce (92), finished with crayfish butter (147), and send a sauceboat of the same *mousseline* sauce to the table with the dish.

N.B.—This *mousse* may also be prepared with fillets of sole, of salmon, or of trout, etc.

1008—HADDOCK   *Eglefin*

Sometimes this fish is grilled, but, after having boned it and removed its fins and the greater part of its belly, it is more often cooked in water or milk, either of which liquid is usually scant.

It is plunged in slightly salted boiling water, and then it is moved to the side of the fire to *poach*, with lid on. Allow about fifteen minutes for a fish weighing one and one-half lbs.

Serve it with a few tablespoons of its cooking-liquor, and, subject to the diner's taste, serve some fresh or melted butter separately.

When haddock is served at lunch, send to the table with it an egg-sauce and a *timbale* of potatoes, freshly cooked *à l'anglaise*.

MACKEREL (MAQUEREAU)

1009—BOILED MACKEREL WITH GOOSEBERRY SAUCE

Maquereau Bouilli, Sauce aux Groseilles

Cut the mackerels into three, crosswise, and *poach* them in *court-bouillon* with vinegar (163), seasoned with a pinch of fennel per pint. Drain them on a napkin; skin them, and serve them with curly leaf parsley all round.

With the mackerels serve a gooseberry sauce prepared as follows:—

Green Gooseberry Sauce for Mackerel.—Cook one lb. of green gooseberries in a copper preserving kettle with three oz. of sugar and enough water to cover them, and then rub them through a fine sieve.

1010—GRILLED MACKEREL   *Maquereau Grillé*

Cut off the extremity of the mackerels' mouths; open them down the back, without dividing them into two.

Season them; sprinkle them with melted butter, and grill them gently, taking care to baste them by means of a brush with melted butter while they are cooking.

Set them on a round, hot dish, and sprinkle them with half-melted butter à la Maître-d'Hôtel (150), after having drawn their halves together, that they may seem natural and untouched.

Or surround them with grooved slices of lemon, and send a "Sauce Diable Escoffier" (37) to the table separately. This sauce constitutes an excellent accompaniment to grilled mackerel.

1011—FILLETS OF MACKEREL WITH HERBS
Filets de Maquereau aux fines herbes

Lift out some mackerels' fillets in such wise as to leave the bones quite clean. Arrange the fillets on a buttered dish, and *poach* them in white wine and the cooking-liquor of mushrooms in equal quantities. Take care to cover them while they are being *poached.*

This done, drain them; skin them; lay them on a long platter, and cover them with an herb sauce (83), combined with their cooking-liquor strained through linen and reduced.

1012—FILLETS OF MACKEREL WITH PARSLEY
Filets de Maquereau au persil

Lift out the fillets as before, and *poach* them in a white-wine *court-bouillon* (164) with one-half oz. of parsley leaves per pint. Drain them; skin them; set them on a long platter, and cover them with a parsley sauce. This is a butter sauce (66) to which some freshly-chopped parsley is added at the last moment.

1013—FILLETS OF MACKEREL VENETIAN STYLE

Filets de Maquereau à la Vénitienne

Poach the fillets in a *court-bouillon* with white wine. Drain them; skin them; set them on a long platter, and cover them with a Venetian sauce (107).

Whiting (Merlan)

1014—WHITING ENGLISH STYLE *Merlan à l'anglaise*

Open the whitings down the back; loosen the backbone, and competely remove it. Season them inside, and treat them *à l'anglaise* with very fresh and fine bread-crumbs.

Cook the whitings very quickly in clarified butter (175); lay them on a long platter, and sprinkle them with half-melted butter à la Maître-d'Hôtel (150).

N.B.—Whitings *à l'anglaise* may also be grilled, but it is preferable to cook them in clarified butter.

1015—WHITING A LA BERCY *Merlan à la Bercy*

Make a short slit down the backs of the whitings with the view of aiding their cooking process. Lay them on a buttered dish sprinkled with finely-chopped shallots, and moisten them with white wine and fish *fumet*. Add one-half oz. of butter per whiting, and cook in the oven, basting often. The moment when the whitings are quite done should be coincident with the almost complete reduction of their cooking-liquor.

Set to *glaze* at the last moment.

When taking the whitings out of the oven, sprinkle them with a few drops of lemon juice and a little chopped parsley.

1016—WHITING A LA COLBERT *Merlan à la Colbert*

Make a short slit down the backs of the whitings and bone them. Season and dip them in milk; roll them in flour; and treat them *à l'anglaise*. Fry them; drain them; set them on a long platter; garnish the openings in their backs with butter à la Maître-d'Hôtel (150) and border the dish with grooved slices of lemon.

1017—MOUSSELINES OF WHITING *Mousselines de Merlan*

For the preparation of the *mousseline forcemeat*, refer to (195). The moulding and *poaching* of these *mousselines* are the same as for salmon *mousselines*, and the preparations suited to the latter may likewise be applied to *mousselines* de merlans. (See Mousselines de Saumon, 797 to 799.)

1018—FILLETS OF WHITING AU GRATIN   *Filets de Merlan au Gratin*

Lift out the fillets from some whitings, and leave the bones quite clean. Lay the fillets on a buttered dish sprinkled with chopped shallots, the bottom of which should have been covered with a few tablespoons of *gratin* sauce. Surround the fillets with slices of raw mushrooms, set two small, cooked mushrooms upon each fillet; pour a few tablespoons of white wine into the dish, and cover with *gratin* sauce.

Sprinkle with fine *raspings* and melted butter, and put the dish in a hot enough oven to reduce the sauce; allow the *gratin* to form; and cook the fillets at the same time. In respect of this operation, refer to Complete *Gratin* (269).

When taking the dish from the oven, sprinkle a little chopped parsley and a few drops of lemon juice over it.

N.B.—If the whiting be treated whole, the procedure remains the same.

1019—ROULADES OF WHITING AU GRATIN
Paupiettes de Merlan au Gratin

Lift out some fillets of whiting; coat them with a fish *forcemeat* combined with fine herbs, and roll them into *roulades*. Set these rolled fillets on a round, buttered *gratin* dish sprinkled with chopped shallots, the bottom of which should have been covered with *gratin* sauce (269).

Surround them with a border of sliced, raw mushrooms; place a small, cooked mushroom on each fillet, and proceed for the rest of the operation exactly as explained under "Filets de Merlan au Gratin" (1018).

1020—WHITING EN LORGNETTE AU GRATIN
Merlan en Lorgnette au Gratin

Separate the fillets from the bones, proceeding from the tail to the head, and completely remove the spine near the head. Cover the fillets with fish *forcemeat* "*aux fines herbes*," and roll them into *roulades* with their tail-ends inside.

Set them on a round dish sprinkled with chopped shallots and covered with *gratin* sauce, placing them side by side, all round the dish, with the whitings' heads in the center; and proceed for the rest of the operation as explained under (1018).

N.B.—Whitings prepared in this way may be treated with white wine, Dieppoise, Bercy, fried, etc.

1021—ORLY FILLETS OF WHITING   *Filets de Merlan Orly*
Lift out the fillets and proceed as for "Filets de Soles Orly" (893).

1022—WHITING ON THE DISH   *Merlan sur le Plat*
Proceed as for "Sole sur le Plat" (837).

1023—RICHELIEU WHITING   *Merlan à la Richelieu*
Prepare six "Merlans à l'anglaise" (1014). Lay on a few slices of truffle. Or serve them simply on their sides; garnish their top surfaces with the butter prescribed above, and put a row of truffle slices on the butter.

1024—SALT COD   *Morue*
Salt cod bought in the United States has generally been caught somewhere along the New England coast, and is, as a rule, of recent salting. It has not the peculiar flavor and grain of the Newfoundland specimens, and it does not always lend itself to such a large variety of preparations as the latter.

At the end of each of the following recipes, I shall indicate the kind of cod which is preferable but not necessarily so.

Salt cod, especially the Newfoundland kind, must be set to soak at least twelve hours before being used, and the water during that time should be frequently changed, unless otherwise directed.

When about to cook it, remove its fins, and cut it up in a way suiting the selected mode of preparation.

Allow four oz. gross of the fish for each person.

1024a—SALT COD ENGLISH STYLE   *Morue à l'Anglaise*
Put the fish into cold water; set to boil, and as soon as this point is reached, leave the fish to *poach* on the side of the fire for fifteen minutes.

Drain, skin, place on a napkin, and serve, separately, a *timbale* of parsnips and an egg-sauce à l'Écossaise (118).

Both kinds of cod may be used for this dish.

1025—SALT COD BENEDICTINE   *Morue à la Benedictine*
Poach one and one-half lbs. of salt cod as above; drain it and cut into small pieces, cleared of all skin and bone. Pound it quickly while it is still hot, and add to it half its weight of potatoes cooked

as for a *purée,* drained, and dried in the oven for a few minutes. When the whole has been reduced to a fine paste, add one-sixth pint of oil, and one-quarter pint of boiled milk. The oil and the milk should be added little by little, and the paste should be more mellow than stiff.

Serve in a buttered *gratin* dish; arrange the preparation in the form of a dome; sprinkle with melted butter, and set to brown in the oven.

Preferably Newfoundland salt cod.

1026—SALT COD IN BLACK BUTTER OR NUT BUTTER
Morue au Beurre Noir ou Beurre Noisette

Cut the salt cod into squares or rectangles; roll these into *paupiettes* or *roulades,* and bind these with a piece of string. *Poach* them in the usual way; drain them; scrape off their skins, and put on a dish. Sprinkle with chopped parsley; add lemon juice, and cover with brown or lightly-browned butter. Either kind of cod may be used.

1027—ENGLISH BRANDADE OF SALT COD   *Brandade de Morue*

Cut one lb. of salt cod into pieces, and *poach* these for eight minutes. The eight minutes should be counted from the time the water begins to boil.

Drain on a sieve, and clear the pieces of all skin and bones. Heat in a saucepan one-sixth pint of oil until it smokes; throw the cleaned pieces of salt cod into the oil; add a piece of crushed garlic the size of a navy bean, and stir over a brisk fire with a wooden spoon until the salt cod is reduced to shreds and becomes a thick paste.

Then take the saucepan off the fire, and, without ceasing to stir the paste, add, little by little, as for a mayonnaise, about one-half pint of oil. When the paste begins to stiffen through the addition of the oil, now and again add a tablespoon of milk. For the amount of salt cod used, one-quarter pint of boiling milk should thus be added by degrees.

When the *Brandade* is finished, it should have the consistency of an ordinary potato *purée.* When about to serve, taste the preparation, and rectify its seasoning.

Serve the *Brandade* in a hot *timbale,* building it up in the shape of a pyramid, and set on a crown of bread-crumb triangles fried in butter just before serving.

N.B.—The triangles of fried bread may, with advantage, be replaced by diamond shapes made from puff-paste (2366), which are baked without browning. For the *Brandade* use only well soaked, best quality Boston or Newfoundland salt cod.

1028—BRANDADE OF SALT COD WITH CREAM
Brandade de Morue à la Crème

Follow the directions given above, but instead of oil and milk, use two-thirds pint of cream, which should be added to the salt cod paste by spoonfuls.

1029—SALT COD CREOLE STYLE *Morue à la Creole*

Finely mince an onion, and cook it gently in butter until it is of a nice golden brown. Spread it on the bottom of a little oval earthenware dish, and set three tomatoes prepared à la Provençale (2268) upon it.

Poach one lb. of salt cod; drain it as soon as ready, and flake it while clearing it of all skin and bones. Lay this flaked cod on the slices of tomato; cover it with three mild peppers, split and broiled; sprinkle the whole with a few drops of lemon juice and one oz. of lightly-browned butter, and put the dish in the oven for a few minutes. Serve very hot.

Preferably Newfoundland salt cod may be used.

1030—SALT COD HOLLAND STYLE *Morue à la Hollandaise*

Proceed exactly as for "Sole à la Hollandaise" (829). Both kinds of salt cod suit this preparation.

1031—SALT COD INDIAN STYLE *Morue à l'Indienne*

Poach one lb. of salt cod, and flake it while clearing it of all skin and bones. Mix this flaked fish with two-thirds pint of Indienne sauce (81), and serve it in a hot *timbale*.

Serve some rice à l'Indienne (2254) separately.

Both kinds of salt cod fish are suited to this dish.

1032—SALT COD LYONNAISE *Morue à la Lyonnaise*

Poach one lb. of salt cod, and flake it as explained above. Finely mince a medium-sized onion, and toss it in butter. Also toss three medium-sized potatoes cut into slices. Heat one oz. of butter and two tablespoons of oil in a frying-pan; put in the flaked cod and the potatoes, and toss the whole over a brisk fire for a few minutes.

When about to serve, add a few drops of vinegar.

Put in a hot *timbale,* and sprinkle the cod with a pinch of chopped parsley. Use either the Boston or the Newfoundland salt cod for this preparation.

1033—SALT CODFISH SOUFFLE *Soufflé de Morue*

Finely pound one-quarter lb. of freshly *poached* and flaked salt cod, and add, little by little, two tablespoons of hot and very thick Béchamel sauce (28). When the paste is very smooth, season it; put into a saucepan, heat it, and add the yolks of three eggs, and four whites beaten to a stiff froth.

Put the whole into a buttered casserole, and cook after the manner of an ordinary *soufflé*. Take either Boston or Newfoundland salt cod for this dish.

1034—CHAR *Ombre Chevalier*

The char is a fish of the salmon trout family, which is treated in exactly the same way as the trout. When it is large, the recipes given for salmon trout may be adapted to it, but it is mostly used small— that is to say, from five inches to ten inches long. Char is found chiefly in mountain lakes in Scotland and Switzerland, and it is only in season during two months of the year. Moreover, as this fish loses much of its quality in transit, its scarcity on all markets will be easily understood. The lake of Zug, in Switzerland, supplies the most famous specimens, which are called Röthel by the people of the locality. The delicacy of the fish is remarkable, and in this it vies with the best river or brook trout. A typical English recipe follows.

1035—POTTED CHAR *Potted Char*

Cook the chars in a fine *mirepoix* with white wine, exactly after the manner of trout. When the fish are cooked, leave them to cool completely in their cooking-liquor. Drain them; skin them; separate their fillets, and thoroughly bone them. Set the fillets in a special earthenware pot; entirely cover them with clarified butter (175), and put them in a moderate oven for one quarter of an hour.

Leave them to cool until the next day, and add sufficient clarified butter to cover them with a layer one-third inch thick.

If Potted Char be kept in a cool place, it will keep for considerable time.

RED MULLETS (ROUGETS)

Red mullet, especially the Mediterranean rock kind, is one of the greatest fish delicacies known; and the surname "Sea Woodcock," which gourmets sometimes give it, is quite justified, not only by its quality, but by the fact that, except for its gills, it is generally left whole, and not even cleaned.

It is best grilled.

1035a—GRILLED RED MULLET   *Rouget Grillé*

Carefully wipe the mullet; gash it on either side to a depth in proportion to the thickness of its flesh and at closer intervals the thicker it is, in order to facilitate the cooking; season it with salt and pepper; sprinkle it with a little oil and a few drops of lemon-juice; spread a few slices of lemon and a few parsley sprigs upon and underneath it; and let it *marinate* for an hour or two, turning it over frequently.

Twenty minutes before serving, set the red mullet on a double fish grill, and cook it over a rather hot fire, sprinkling it often the while with its *marinade*. Put on a dish and serve it as soon as it is ready, and serve a little half-melted *maître-d'hôtel* butter (150) separately.

1035b—MULLET A LA BORDELAISE   *Rouget à la Bordelaise*

Grill or *sauté* the red mullet. At the same time serve a sauce Bordelaise Bonnefoy (67).

1035c—MULLET WITH FENNEL   *Rouget au Fenouil*

Gash and *marinate* the red mullet as directed under (1035a), and add a certain quantity of chopped fennel to the seasonings. Twenty minutes before serving, add two oz. of roughly-chopped raw pork fat and a little parsley to the *marinade;* wrap the red mullets in strong, oiled paper, together with its *marinade,* grill it gently, and serve it as it stands.

1035d—MULLET OF NICOISE   *Rouget à la Niçoise*

Grill it as directed above, and serve it with the garnish given under "Sole à la Niçoise."

1035e—MULLET IN PAPER   *Rouget en Papillote*

Grill and wrap it in strong, oiled paper bag made from vegetable parchment between two layers of somewhat thick Duxelle sauce (225). When about to serve, put the *papillote* for five minutes in the oven, that it may be *souffléd.*

1036—WHITEBAIT *Nonats et Blanchailles*

Whitebait, which has many points in common with the Thames whitebait and "Nonat" of the Mediterranean, is one of the riddles of ichthyology; for, while it is generally admitted that it is the fry of one of the many species of fish, its real parentage is quite unknown.

At dinners in Europe it usually stands as a second fish-course, and, fried after the customary manner, it constitutes a dish the delicacy of which is incomparable. Whitebait, like the nonat, are extremely fragile, and ought to be cooked as soon as they are caught. They are always served fried, and the frying fat used in their preparation should be fresh, abundant, and just smoking when the fish are plunged into it. Previous to this operation, however, the whitebait ought to be thoroughly dredged with flour and placed in a special sieve frying basket, which should be well shaken, in order to rid the fish of any superfluous flour.

They are then plunged into the smoking frying fat, in small quantities at a time, and one minute's stay suffices to make them sufficiently crisp.

Draining is the next operation, done upon a piece of absorbent paper, that the fish may be easily seasoned with table-salt and cayenne, mixed. This done, the whitebait are placed upon a napkin and sent to the table with very green, fried parsley.

Various Preparations of Fish

1037—MATELOTE WITH RED WINE *Matelote au Vin Rouge*

The fish used for the *Matelote* are eel, carp, tench, bream, perch, etc.

It may be prepared from one or many kinds of fish.

Put the fish, cut into sections, into a saucepan. For two lbs. of it, add one minced onion, one herb bunch, two cloves of garlic, one pint of red wine, a pinch of salt, and another of pepper or four peppercorns.

Set to boil; add three tablespoons of heated and burnt brandy; cover the saucepan, and complete the cooking of the fish.

This done, transfer the pieces to another saucepan; strain the cooking-liquor, reduce it by a third, and thicken it with *manié* butter (consisting of one and one-half oz. of butter and two tablespoons of flour), cut into small pieces.

When the binding has been properly done, pour the resulting

sauce over the pieces of fish; heat, and serve in a earthenware *timbale*.

1038—MATELOTE WITH WHITE WINE   *Matelote au Vin Blanc*

Prepare the fish as above, but use red wine instead of white, and burn the brandy as before. When the pieces of fish are cooked, transfer them to another saucepan with small onions, previously cooked in butter, and small, cooked mushrooms. Strain the cooking-liquor, reduce it to a little less than half, thicken it with fish velouté (26a), and finish with one oz. of butter.

Pour this sauce over the fish and the garnish; put it in a *timbale* or a deep dish, and surround with crayfish, cooked in *court-bouillon*, and little *croutons* in the shape of hearts, fried in butter.

1039—BOUILLABAISSE A LA MARSEILLAISE
Bouillabaisse à la Marseillaise

The fish for Bouillabaisse are rascasse, chapon, dory, whiting, fielas, boudreuil, spiny lobster, red mullet, gurnet, etc.

Cut the larger fish into slices; leave the smaller ones whole, and with the exception of the whiting and the mullet, which cook more speedily than the others, put them all into a saucepan.

For two lbs. of fish, add one small onion, the chopped white of one leek, one small, peeled, pressed and chopped tomato, two crushed cloves of garlic, a large pinch of chopped parsley, a pinch of powdered saffron, a bit of bay leaf, a little savory and fennel, and two tablespoons of oil.

Moisten the fish with just enough cold water to cover it, and season with one-third oz. of salt and a pinch of pepper per quart of water.

Set to boil, and cook over a brisk fire. At the end of eight minutes add the pieces of whiting and mullet, and leave to cook for a further seven minutes.

Pour the liquor of the bouillabaisse over some slices of French crust bread lying on the bottom of a deep dish; set the fish on another dish with the sections of spiny or rock lobster all round, and serve.

(Although it is impossible to make a bouillabaisse exactly like the French product, because most of the fish used in the French preparation can be found only along the shores of the Mediterranean Sea, still we have an ample supply of cod slices, small whitings, mullet, etc., that will suit the purpose.—Ed.)

1040—QUENELLES OF PIKE LYONNAISE

Quenelles de Brochet à la Lyonnaise

Grind separately one lb. of the meat of pike, cleared of all skin and bones, and one lb. of the fat of beef kidney, very dry, cleaned, and cut into small pieces. If desired, half of the weight of the fat of beef kidney may be replaced by one-half lb. of beef marrow.

Put the pounded meat of the pike and the kidney fat on separate plates. Now pound one lb. of frangipane *Panada* (192) and add, little by little, the whites of four small eggs. Put the pike meat and the fat back into the grinder, and grind the whole until a fine, smooth paste is obtained. Rub it through a sieve; put the resulting *purée* into a bowl, and work it well with a wooden spoon in order to smooth it.

With this *forcemeat* mould some *quenelles* with a spoon, and *poach* them in salted water.

If these *quenelles* are to be served with an ordinary fish sauce, put them into it as soon as they are *poached* and drained, and simmer them in it for ten minutes that they may swell.

If the sauce intended for them is to be thickened with egg-yolks, and buttered at the last moment, put them into a saucepan with a few tablespoons of *fumet,* and simmer them as directed in the case of an ordinary fish sauce, taking care to keep the saucepan well covered that the concentrated steam may assist the swelling of the *quenelles.* In this case they are added to the sauce at the last moment.

N.B.—Slices of truffle may always be added to the sauce. The *quenelles* are served either in a silver *timbale,* in a shallow *timbale-crust,* or in a fine vol-au-vent crust (2390), in accordance with the arrangement of the menu.

1041—FISH CAKES   *Fish Cakes*

Fish cakes or balls, which are greatly appreciated in both United States and England, but not in France, are made from any boiled fish. Salted cod, however, is best suited to their preparation, and is therefore used much more often than other kinds of fish.

Flake one lb. of cooked salt cod, and clear it of all skin and bones; grind it and mix with one-half lb. of freshly-cooked, mealy potatoes, two tablespoons of reduced Béchamel sauce (28), and two whole eggs. Season with salt and pepper. When the paste has been well blended and is smooth, divide it into portions weighing about two oz. Roll these portions into balls upon a flour-dusted mixing-board, flatten them out to the shape of thick round cakes, and treat them *à l'anglaise.*

Fry them at the last moment in very hot fat, and serve them on a napkin with fried parsley all round.

1042—WATERZOIE (BELGIAN FISH SOUP)   *Waterzoie*

In order to prepare Waterzoie, it is best, when possible, to have live fish at one's disposal, not only because these are better able to resist the cooking process, but also owing to the fact that they are richer in gelatine in the live state.

The fish more generally used are the eel, the perch, the tench, the carp, the pike, etc.

After having scaled and cleaned them, trim them and cut off their heads and tails. Cut the fish into sections; moisten these with just enough cold water to cover; add a piece of butter, sufficient parsley roots or sprigs to produce a decided taste, a few peppercorns, and some salt.

Set to cook on a brisk fire, and take care that the cooking-liquor be reduced and sufficiently thickened when the fish are cooked.

Serve in an earthenware *timbale* or on a deep dish, and send some slices of bread and butter to the table at the same time.

CHAPTER XV

RELEVÉS AND ENTRÉES

THE difference between Relevés and Entrées needs only to be examined very superficially in order for it to be seen how entirely the classification depends on the question of bulk. Indeed, with very few exceptions, the same food products—meat, fish, poultry, and game—may be used with perfect propriety in the preparation of either Relevés or Entrées. And if the mode of preparation and the nature of the garnishing ingredients are sometimes dissimilar, it is owing to that difference in bulk referred to above, on account of which the Relevés, being more voluminous, are usually *braised, poëled, poached,* or roasted; while the Entrées, consisting of smaller pieces, are chiefly *sautéd, poached,* or grilled.

In the menus of old-fashioned dinners à la Française, the line of demarcation between Relevés and Entrées was far more clearly defined, the latter being generally twice, if not three times, as numerous as the former. The first service of a dinner for twenty people, for instance, comprised eight or twelve Entrées and four soups, all of which were set on the dining-table before the admission of the diners. As soon as the soups were served, the Relevés, to the number of four, two of which consisted of fish, took the place of the soups on the table; they *relieved* the soups; hence their name, which now, of course, is quite meaningless.

The Russian method of serving greatly simplified the practice just described. Nowadays a formal dinner rarely consists of more than one soup, two Relevés (one of which is fish), and two Entrées for the first service. Very often the fish Relevé, instead of being a large piece of fish, only consists of fillets of sole, of chicken-turbots, or crusted *timbales,* which are real Entrées; while the Relevés (consisting of large pieces of meat or game), are served after the fish Relevé, when the diner's appetite is still keen.

Thus, as the two above examples show, the parts played by the Relevés and Entrées respectively are very far from being clearly defined; and I therefore resolved to treat them both in the same chapter, and to append a few grills (usually accompanied by various sauces and garnishes), which are really only luncheon-roasts. The indications given concerning the class to which the recipes belong will suffice to avoid confusion.

Relevés and Entrées of Beef

1043—FILLET OF BEEF   *Filet de Boeuf (Relevé)*

Fillet of beef for a Relevé may consist either of the whole piece, trimmed, *studded,* or *larded,* or a more or less large piece cut from the whole, and treated after one of the methods suited to the whole fillet. The fillet may be *braised, poêled,* or roasted; but the last two methods of preparation suit it best, as it is generally pre-ferred underdone and somewhat red towards the center.

The garnishes for a Relevé of fillet of beef are as numerous as they are varied; and, as they are applicable not only to fillet of beef but to all Relevés of meat, I give them here in preference, since fillet of beef may be considered the choicest of Relevés.

1044—ANDALUSIAN FILLETS OF BEEF   *Filets de Boeuf Andalouse*

Having removed all the connective tissue from the fillet, *lard* it with thin strips of bacon, and *poêle* or roast it. *Glaze* it at the last moment; set it on a long dish, and surround it with:—Some grilled half-peppers, filled with rice à la grecque (2253); slices of egg-plant, two inches in diameter and one inch thick, hollowed out to form cases, fried in oil, and garnished with chopped tomatoes tossed in oil. Arrange the half-peppers and the egg-plant alternately round the fillet, and place a grilled *chipolata* (Italian) sausage between each.

Sauce to be sent separately.—The gravy taken from the *poêled-* stock, strained, cleared of all grease, and thickened.

1045—BOUQUETIERE FILLET OF BEEF   *Filet de Boeuf Bouquetière*

Having *larded* the fillet and *poêled* or roasted it, set it on a long dish and surround it with small heaps of carrots and turnips, cut by means of a small fancy knife, and cooked in consommé; small heaps of little potatoes cut to the size of olives and cooked in butter; small heads of peas and of string beans, cut and mixed with butter; five cauliflowerettes.

Arrange these different products in such wise as to vary their colors and throw them into relief.

Serve the gravy of the fillet separately, after having cleared it of all grease and strained it.

1046—CAMARGO FILLET OF BEEF   *Fillet de Boeuf Camargo*

Trim the fillet; remove the long muscle lying on its thicker side (Fr. chaîne), and open the fillet lengthwise from the same side. Remove the meat from the inside of the fillet so as to leave a wall of meat only one-half inch thick all round. Finely grind the withdrawn meat and combine with it, per lb., little by little, from four to five tablespoons of cream and four oz. of fresh *foie gras*. Season with salt and pepper, correct the consistency of the meat mixture, and add, per lb., two oz. of chopped truffles.

Fill the hollowed out fillet with this stuffing, thereby returning it to its original shape, and *stud* its top surface with pointed pieces of truffle one inch long by one-quarter inch wide, stuck into the meat slantwise. In order to facilitate this operation, make incisions in the meat, before the insertion of the pieces of truffles, by means of a small sharp knife.

Now cover the fillet with slices of bacon and tie them across, leaving a space of one inch between each string.

Poële the meat carefully, and take care that the *forcemeat* inside be well, but not over-done. This may be checked by thrusting a testing needle into the thickest part of the fillet, as soon as the meat seems resisting and gives to the touch. If the needle comes out clean, the fillet is ready.

Now *glaze* it, after having cut away the string and removed the slices of bacon; place on a dish, and surround it with the following garnish:—Small *tartlet-crusts* filled with noodles with cream; a slice of *foie gras* stamped out with a round cutter and tossed in butter, upon the noodles; and a fine slice of truffle on the *foie gras*.

Sauce to be sent to the table separately.—The reduced *poëled*-liquor of the fillet, cleared of all grease, and added to a Périgueux sauce (47).

1047—CHATELAINE FILLET OF BEEF   *Filet de Boeuf Châtelaine*

Lard the fillet, *poële* it, and *glaze* it just before preparing to serve. Set it on a long dish, and surround it with the following garnish:—Medium-sized artichoke-bottoms garnished with thick Soubise (104); fine, peeled chestnuts cooked in the *poëled*-liquor; small heaps of lightly browned potatoes, cooked in butter at the last moment.

Sauce to be sent separately.—The reduced *poëlé*-liquor of the fillet, cleared of all grease and added to a Madeira sauce (44).

1048—CLAMART FILLET OF BEEF　　　*Filet de Boeuf Clamart*

Lard the fillet and roast it.

Set it on a long dish and surround it with:—Little *tartlet-crusts* garnished with peas, prepared à la Française (2193), combined with the shredded lettuce used in their cooking-process, and mixed with butter; small flat round cakes of "Pommes Macaire" (2228). Arrange the *tartlet-crusts* and the potato cakes alternately.

Sauce to be sent separately.—The gravy slightly thickened.

1049—DAUPHINE FILLET OF BEEF　　　*Filet de Boeuf Dauphine*

Lard the fillet and *poële* it.

Glaze it at the last moment; set it on a long dish, and surround it with a garnish of potato *croquettes* à la Dauphine, moulded to the shape of corks, and fried just before serving up.

Sauce to be sent separately.—Pale half-*glaze* with Madeira.

1050—DU BARRY FILLET OF BEEF　　　*Filet de Boeuf Du Barry*

Lard the fillet with bacon, and roast it.

Set it on a long platter, and surround it with small heaps of cauliflower moulded to the shape of balls, coated with Mornay sauce (91), sprinkled with grated cheese, and put in the oven for the *gratin* to form just in time for serving.

Send a thickened gravy to the table separately.

1051—DUCHESS FILLET OF BEEF　　　*Filet de Boeuf Duchesse*

Either roast or *poële* the *larded* fillet. If it be *poëléd, glaze* it at the last moment.

Set it on a long dish and surround it with potatoes à la Duchesse (221) (the shape of which may be varied according to fancy), lightly browned in the oven for a few minutes before serving.

Sauce to be sent separately.—Half-*glaze* (23) with Madeira.

1052—FINANCIER FILLET OF BEEF　　　*Filet de Boeuf Financière*

Poële the *larded* fillet.

Glaze it at the last moment and set it on a platter.

Surround it with a garnish consisting of *quenelles* of ordinary *forcemeat;* cut in grooves and cooked button-mushroom heads; cocks' combs and kidneys; turned and *blanched* olives. Each garnish should be placed on the dish in distinct heaps.

Cover the garnish with a little *financière* sauce, and send the same sauce separately.

1053—GASTRONOME FILLET OF BEEF   *Filet de Boeuf Gastronome*

Insert truffles, cut in the shape of ordinary larding-bacon (thin finger length), into the fillet, and set the latter to *marinate* for four or five hours in one-quarter pint of Madeira.

This done, thoroughly wipe it; cover it with slices of bacon, and *braise* it in Madeira. When about to serve it, remove the slices of bacon; *glaze* it slightly, and set it on a meat platter.

Surround it with a garnish consisting of large and thick slices of truffle, cooked in a fine *mirepoix* with champagne; fine chestnuts cooked in consommé and *glazed;* fine cocks' kidneys, rolled in pale, thin meat-*glaze* (15); noodles tossed in butter. These different garnishes should be arranged in alternate heaps, and connected by means of medium-sized truffles cooked in Madeira.

Sauce to be sent separately.—Half-*glaze* (23) combined with the cooking-liquor of the truffles, strained through linen and reduced to two-thirds.

1054—GODARD FILLET OF BEEF   *Filet de Boeuf Godard*

Lard the fillet with alternate strips of bacon and salted tongue, and *poële* it. *Glaze* it a few minutes before serving; set it on a long dish, and surround it with a garnish consisting of *quenelles* of ordinary *forcemeat* with chopped mushrooms and truffles added, moulded by means of a teaspoon, and *poached* just before serving; turned and cooked button-mushroom caps; *glazed* lamb sweet-breads; cocks' combs and kidneys; truffles fashioned like olives.

Slightly coat these garnishes, which should be arranged in heaps, with sauce; finish the dish with four oval *quenelles* decorated with tongue and truffle, and place one of these at either end and side of the dish.

Sauce to be sent separately.—A Godard sauce combined with the cooking-liquor of the fillet, cleared of all grease and reduced.

1055—HUNGARIAN FILLET OF BEEF   *Filet de Boeuf Hongroise*

Lard the fillet and roast it.

Set it on a long dish and surround it with a garnish consisting of medium-sized onions, cooked in white consommé (1), and *glazed* in butter at the last minute.

Sauce to be sent separately.—Thin Soubise (104) with paprika.

1056—JAPANESE FILLET OF BEEF   *Filet de Boeuf Japonaise*

Lard the fillet and *poêle* it.

Glaze it just before serving; set it on a long platter, and surround it with a garnish consisting of small *croustades* baked in fluted *brioche-moulds* and garnished with Japanese artichokes mixed with velouté (25); potato *croquettes* moulded to the shape of eggs and fried just before serving. Arrange the *croustades* and the *croquettes* alternately.

Send the gravy of the fillet, strained and cleared of all grease, to the table separately.

1057—JARDINIERE FILLET OF BEEF   *Filet de Boeuf Jardinière*

Lard the fillet and roast it.

Set it on a meat platter and surround it with the following garnishes, which should be arranged in distinct heaps in such a way as to alternate their colors:—Carrot and turnip balls done with a grooved ball-cutter and cooked separately in consommé; peas, string beans cut in one inch pieces and small young kidney beans; each vegetable should be cooked in a manner in keeping with its nature, and separately mixed with butter; portions of freshly-cooked cauliflower, kept very white.

Send some Hollandaise sauce (30) for the cauliflower, and some clear gravy, to the table, separately.

1058—LORETTE FILLET OF BEEF   *Filet de Boeuf Lorette*

Lard the fillet and *poêle* it.

Glaze it at the last moment; set it on a long dish, and surround it with a garnish as follows:—A small pyramid of Lorette potatoes (2226) at either end of the fillet; fine heaps of asparagus tips, mixed with butter, on either side.

Send some tomatoed half-*glazed* sauce (23) separately.

1059—MACEDOINE FILLET OF BEEF   *Filet de Boeuf Macédoine*

Prepare the fillet as directed under "Filet de Bœuf Jardinière" (1057). Set it on a long dish and surround it with a *Macédoine* garnish. The latter comprises the same ingredients as the "*Jardinière*"; but, instead of their being heaped separately, they are mixed together with butter.

1060—FILLET OF BEEF IN MADEIRA WITH MUSHROOMS

Filet de Boeuf au Madère et aux Champignons

Lard and *poële* the fillet.

Glaze it; serve it as before, and surround it with fine mushrooms-caps, turned and grooved.

Send to the table, separately, a Madeira sauce (44) finished with the *poële*-liquor, cleared of all grease and reduced.

1061—FILLET OF BEEF MODERN STYLE   *Filet de Boeuf Moderne*

Lard the fillet alternately with bacon and tongue, and *poële* it.

Glaze it just before serving; set it on a long dish, and surround it with garnish as follows:—On either side of the fillet lay a row of small *"chartreuses,"* made in small, hexagonal moulds.

To make these *"chartreuses,"* butter the moulds and decorate the bottom of each with a slice of truffle, large enough to almost entirely cover it. Now line the sides of the moulds with various vegetables, such as carrots, turnips, peas, and string beans; each vegetable should be cooked as its nature requires.

Arrange them in such a way as to vary their colors, and spread over the whole a thin layer of rather flimsy *forcemeat*.

Fill the moulds with *braised* cabbage, which should be well pressed with the view of ridding it of all its moisture, and put the *chartreuses* in a *bain-marie* (water-bath) ten minutes before serving the fillet.

At either end of the fillet set some *braised* lettuce halves, arranging them so that they frame the ends of the fillet in half-circles.

Between the lettuce and the *chartreuses* set four round *quenelles,* decorated with salted tongue and *poached* in time to be ready for the serving of the meat.

Send to the table, separately, the *poële*-liquor of the fillet, cleared of all grease, strained, and slightly thickened with arrowroot or flour.

1062—MONTMORENCY FILLET OF BEEF   *Filet de Boeuf Montmorency*

Lard the fillet and *poële* it.

Glaze it just before setting it on a platter.

Send to the table, separately, a Madeira sauce (44) finished with the *poële*-liquor of the fillet, to which add (per pint of the sauce) three tablespoons of red-currant jelly; two tablespoons of finely-grated horse-radish; thirty moderately-sweetened cherries, set to soak in tepid water seven or eight minutes beforehand, and drained just before being added to the sauce.

1063—NIVERNAISE FILLET OF BEEF   *Filet de Boeuf Nivernaise*

Lard the fillet and *poële* it.

Glaze it at the last moment; set it on a long dish, and surround it with garnish as follows:—Heaps of small carrots, shaped like elongated olives, cooked in white consommé and a little butter and sugar, and rolled in their cooking-liquor (reduced to the consistency of syrup), with the view of *glazing* them.

Send the *poële*-liquor (cleared of all grease and strained) to the table separately.

1064—ORIENTAL FILLET OF BEEF   *Filet de Boeuf Orientale*

Roast the fillet without previously *larding* it.

Set it on a platter, and surround it with the following garnish, taking care to alternate the ingredients: *timbales* of rice à la grecque (2253) moulded in buttered *dariole-moulds,* each *timbale* being placed on a medium-sized half-tomato, seasoned and tossed in butter; *croquettes* of sweet potatoes, moulded to the shape of corks (cylinders), and fried just before serving.

Send to the table, separately, a highly seasoned tomato sauce (29).

1065—PERIGOURDINE FILLET OF BEEF   *Filet de Boeuf Périgourdine*

Lard the fillet and *poële* it.

Glaze it just before serving; set it on a long dish, and surround it with medium-sized truffles, freshly cooked in Madeira and fine *mirepoix,* and *glazed.* Send a Périgueux sauce (47) separately.

1066—LITTLE DUKE FILLET OF BEEF   *Filet de Boeuf Petit Duc*

Lard the fillet and *poële* it.

Glaze it in good time; set it on a platter, and surround it with the following garnish:—crisp, small patties of puff paste garnished with asparagus tips mixed with a cream sauce (79); medium-sized artichoke-bottoms, prepared in the usual way, and garnished with slices of truffle.

Send, separately, a light, meat *glaze* (15), combined with four oz. of butter per one-half pint.

1067—PORTUGUESE FILLET OF BEEF   *Filet de Boeuf Portugaise*

Lard the fillet and roast it.

Set it on a platter, and garnish it as follows:—

A row of medium-sized, stuffed tomatoes on either side.

And at either end a nice heap of potatoes, shaped like long olives, and cooked in butter just before serving.

Send a light, Portugaise sauce (659) separately.

1068—PROVENCALE FILLET OF BEEF   *Filet de Boeuf Provençale*

Lard the fillet and *poële* it.

Glaze it at the last minute; set it on a platter, and surround it with the following alternated:—Tomatoes and mushrooms stuffed à la Provençale (2266 and 2075).

Send a tomatoed half-*glaze* (23) sauce, separately.

1069—REGENCY FILLET OF BEEF   *Filet de Boeuf Régence*

Marinate the fillet in Rhine wine two or three hours in advance; cover it with a *Matignon* (227); envelop the fillet and the *Matignon* in slices of bacon, and set to *braise* with its *marinade*.

A few minutes before serving, remove the slices of bacon and the *Matignon,* and glaze the fillet.

Set it on a long dish, and surround it with the following garnish, which, except for the decorated *quenelles,* which are left plain, should be arranged in distinct heaps, and slightly coated with sauce:—*quenelles* of ordinary *forcemeat,* combined with chopped tongue, moulded by means of a teaspoon, and *poached* at the last minute; slices of *foie gras* tossed in butter; fine cocks' combs; very white, cooked mushroom caps, and truffles shaped like large olives.

Send, separately, the *braising*-liquor of the fillet, cleared of all grease, strained, reduced, and added to a half-*glaze* (23) sauce.

1070—RENAISSANCE FILLET OF BEEF   *Filet de Boeuf Renaissance*

Lard the fillet and *poële* it.

Glaze it at the last minute; set it on a long dish, and surround it with a garnish of early Spring vegetables, comprising carrots and turnips, cut by means of a large, round, grooved ball-cutter, cooked in consommé and *glazed;* very green peas; small string beans; small bundles of asparagus tips; portions of cauliflowers, and small potatoes cooked in butter.

Renaissance garnish is, however, subject to no fixed rules, and it may consist of all the available early Spring vegetables, small artichoke-bottoms included.

Send a clear gravy separately.

1071—RICHELIEU FILLET OF BEEF   *Filet de Boeuf Richelieu*

Lard the fillet, and either *poêle* or roast it.

If it be *poêled*, *glaze* it in good time; set it on a platter, and surround it with the following garnish, which should be arranged in distinct heaps and in such a way as to contrast the coloring:— Small tomatoes and medium-sized mushrooms, stuffed; small or halved-lettuces, *braised* and well trimmed; small new potatoes, the size of pigeons' eggs, cooked in butter and prepared just in time for the serving.

Send the cooking-liquor, cleared of all grease, and slightly thick-ened, separately.

1072—ST. FLORENTIN FILLET OF BEEF

Filet de Boeuf Saint-Florentin

Lard the fillet and roast it.

Set it on a long dish, and surround it with the following garnish. At either end, a heap of *cèpes*, prepared à la Bordelaise (2068) at the last minute; *croquettes* of potatoes à la Saint-Florentin (2243), on either side. These *croquettes* are prepared from the same potato-paste as "Pommes Duchesse" (2210), but in this case the paste receives a copious addition of chopped tongue. Mould them to the shape of diamonds, and treat them *à l'anglaise,* using for the pur-pose very finely broken vermicelli instead of bread-crumbs.

Fry the *croquettes* just before serving.

Send, separately, a Bordelaise sauce (67) with white wine, kept somewhat light.

1073—ST. GERMAIN FILLET OF BEEF   *Filet de Boeuf Saint-Germain*

Lard the fillet and roast it.

Set it on a long dish, and surround it with the following garnish. At either end of the fillet a nice heap of *glazed* carrots, cut in the shape of olives; a heap of very small potatoes, cooked in butter, on either side of the carrots; a row of small *timbales* of very green peas *purée* (2196) on either side of the fillet.

1074—TALLEYRAND FILLET OF BEEF   *Filet de Boeuf Talleyrand*

Cut up the necessary number of raw truffles or mushrooms for the garnishing of the fillet. The pieces should be one inch long and one-quarter inch wide, and so pointed as to enable them to be easily stuck into the meat.

To stick them in, make small incisions in the fillet, and in these set the bits of truffle or mushroom. *Marinate* the fillet for three hours in Madeira; wrap it in slices of bacon; tie it, and set it to *braise* with its *marinade*.

This done, remove the slices of bacon; *glaze* it, and set it on a platter. Send the following garnish separately. *Poached* macaroni, cut into pieces one and one-half inches long, and combined per lb. with three oz. of grated Gruyère and Parmesan cheese, one and one-half oz. of butter, three oz. of a *julienne* of truffles, and three oz. of cooked *foie gras,* cut into large dice.

As an accompaniment, send a Périgueux sauce (49) with a fine *julienne* of truffles or mushrooms instead of the latter chopped.

1075—COLD FILLET OF BEEF   *Filet de Boeuf Froid (Relevé)*

Fillet of beef, when properly prepared, makes an excellent cold Relevé

For this purpose *lard* it, roast it (keeping it somewhat under-done towards the center), and, when it is quite cold, trim, and coat it with half-melted aspic-jelly.

Then set it either directly upon a dish or upon a bed of bread or moulded rice, which makes the dish more appetizing when the garnish is added.

Before setting the fillet on the dish or on the bed of rice, it is well to cut a slice one-fifth inch thick from the whole of its length of the bottom side of one fillet; leave this slice under the fillet when serving; by this means, when the carving is proceeded with, each slice will be found to be neatly trimmed.

Cold fillet of beef permits every possible cold vegetable garnish. The vegetables should be cooked with the greatest care and be left to cool naturally.

When they are quite cold, either paste them on the fillet with aspic-jelly, or set them round the fillet in neat heaps, taking care to alternate their shades, and coat them with almost melted aspic.

Finally, between each heap of vegetables lay a little chopped and very clear aspic, and, round the whole, arrange a border consisting of bits of aspic (round, oval, square, diamond-shaped, etc.) very regularly cut.

I see no reason for devoting any further space to this subject. What has been said should, I think, suffice to show how varied and numerous are the possible ways of dishing cold fillet of beef, the minute details of which may, with advantage, be left to the ingenuity of the cook.

FILLET OF BEEF FOR ENTRÉES

**1076—TENDERLOIN STEAK—*Le Bifteck*; THICK TENDERLOIN—
Châteaubriand; TOURNEDOS—*Tournedos*; FILET MIGNON—
*Filet Mignon***

The French method of cutting meat is not the same as the
method used in the United States. Therefore if it is desired to cook
the cuts indicated herein, ask your butcher to cut the piece according to the methods described below.

The large beef tenderloin is cut across in different thicknesses.
These slices of tenderloin weighing about four and one-half to
six pounds have different names according to the section of the
tenderloin from which they are cut and according to their thickness.

The "head" end of the tenderloin is cut from the fillet steak
called *le bifteck* in France. These steaks are usually not thick, and
weigh about five or six ounces.

Next comes the Châuteaubriand, procured from the center of
the tenderloin. Its weight is often two or three times that of the
ordinary fillet steak. It is cut thick and weighs twelve ounces or
more.

Tournedos are the small steaks according to weight. They are
cut from the narrower part of the tenderloin, and are cut and
trimmed to about two to one slice. They could be called the
"kernels" or "noisettes." They should be about one and one-half
inches thick, but trimmed round and small. Usually two or three
tournedos are served as a portion, weighing about two and one-half
ounces each. They are tied together to hold their shape.

The filet mignon comes from the narrowest pointed flat end of
the tenderloin of beef and they are cut in various thicknesses according to desire. They also may be tied if necessary.

The fillet steak, as a rule, especially when grilled, constitutes a
special meat dish for luncheons; when it is cooked in the saucepan,
or *sautéd,* it is more often served as a Relevé.

The same garnishes suit fillet steaks, Châteaubriands, and tournedos, the only necessary modifications being in respect of size and
arrangement, which should be subject to the size of the piece of
meat.

The garnishes detailed hereafter are for the tournedos, which
supply the greatest number of the dishes prepared from the three

different cuts of fillet. If a fillet steak be prepared after one of the following recipes, the garnish should be made a little stronger, and its ingredients modified in the serving, neither of which changes need in any way alter the recipe.

The same holds with regard to a Châteaubriand. Thus, for example, if it be required to prepare a fillet steak or a Châteaubriand, after the recipe "Tournedos à l'Algérienne" (1077), the number of *croquettes* and tomatoes should be half as much again, and they should be arranged alternately round the meat, instead of the latter being placed on the *croquettes*, as in the case of the tournedos.

If the fillet steaks are to be treated "à l'Alsacienne" (1078), after the recipe for tournedos, the sauerkraut should be served in an earthenware *timbale* instead of in *tartlet-crusts*, etc.

It should be borne in mind that nearly all the garnishes given under fillet of beef, served whole, may be applied to Châteaubriands, fillet steaks, tournedos and filet mignon, provided they be made in proportion to the size of the different pieces. I see no need, therefore, to repeat these vegetable recipes in so far as they relate to the various cuts of fillet of beef. Plain vegetable garnishes are best.

Whole fillets, fillet steaks, and tournedos may thus be served with garnishes of *braised* celery, tuberous fennel, Swiss chard with gravy, chayote and Belgian endives, *braised* lettuce, various *purées*, etc., and, generally, with all the vegetable preparations given in Chapter XVII.

IMPORTANT REMARKS RELATIVE TO THE SAUCES SUITED TO ENTRÉES OF MEAT, GARNISHED WITH VEGETABLES

The derivative sauces of the Espagnole are not, as a rule, suited to entrées garnished with vegetables. Thickened gravy is better.

The finest addition, however, is meat-*glaze* (15), which should have an addition of four oz. of butter per pint, and should be slightly acidulated by means of a few drops of lemon juice. This *glaze* ought to be so light as not to make the vegetables sticky.

Such vegetables as asparagus tips, peas, string beans, *macédoines*, etc., have a disintegrating action upon the sauces, and this is owing either to their natural moisture or to their thickening. As a result of this action the preparation has an unappetizing appearance when served.

With Châteaubriand sauce (71) or buttered meat-*glaze* this objection does not hold true, seeing that this sauce does not separate, but combines admirably with the garnish, and lends the latter a certain noticeable mellowness.

I therefore emphasize this point, that the derivative sauces of the Espagnole and tomato sauces should be exclusively used with such preparations garnished with truffles, cocks' combs and kidneys, *quenelles* and mushrooms, as "la Financière," "la Godard," etc.

TOURNEDOS

1077—ALGERIAN TOURNEDOS   *Tournedos Algérienne*
Season the tournedos, and fry them in clarified butter (175).

Arrange them in the form of a crown on a round dish, and set a *croquette* of sweet potato, moulded to a round shape, upon each.

Around the whole lay some small, emptied, and seasoned half-tomatoes, stewed in oil.

1078—ALSACIAN TOURNEDOS   *Tournedos Alsacienne*
Season and grill the tournedos.

There should have been prepared in advance as many *tartlet-crusts* of the same size as there are tournedos.

Fill these *tartlets* with well-drained, *braised* sauerkraut, and set on each a round slice of lean ham, stamped out with a plain cutter. Arrange them in the form of a crown on a dish, and set a tournedos upon each *tartlet*.

1079—TOURNEDOS ARLES STYLE   *Tournedos Arlésienne*
Fry the tournedos in butter and oil.

When about to serve, set the tournedos on a dish, and surround them with fried slices of egg-plant and *sautéd* tomatoes, alternating the two garnishes, and placing slices of fried onions on the tournedos.

1080—BALTIMORE TOURNEDOS   *Tournedos Baltimore*
Season the tournedos, and fry them in clarified butter (175).

Set them in the form of a crown on small *tartlets* garnished by means of corn with cream.

Upon each tournedos set a slice of tomato, seasoned and fried in butter, and a smaller slice of green pepper, also fried in butter, on each slice of tomato.

Accompanying sauce: a Châteaubriand (71).

1081—TOURNEDOS BEARNAISE *Tournedos Béarnaise*

Season the tournedos, and grill them.

Set them on round bread slices, half an inch thick, fried in clarified butter (175); slightly coat the surface of the tournedos with meat-*glaze* (15), and surround them with a ribbon of Béarnaise sauce (62).

In the center arrange a heap of small potatoes cooked in butter and kept very soft, and sprinkle on a pinch of chopped parsley.

N.B.—The tournedos may be simply coated with *glaze* and the Béarnaise sauce served separately.

1082—BELLE-HELENE TOURNEDOS *Tournedos Belle-Hélène*

Prepare as many small *croquettes* of asparagus tips, shaped in flat cakes, as there are tournedos, and fry them while the latter are being cooked. Season the tournedos, and fry them in clarified butter (175).

Arrange them, in the form of a crown, on a dish; place a *croquette* on each tournedos, and a large, *glazed* slice of truffle on each *croquette*.

1083—BERCY TOURNEDOS *Tournedos Bercy*

Grill the tournedos, and coat them lightly with pale meat-*glaze* (15).

Serve them in the form of a crown, and serve a half-melted "Beurre à la Bercy" (139) separately.

1084—BORDELAISE TOURNEDOS *Tournedos Bordelaise*

Grill the tournedos, and arrange them in the form of a crown

Set a large slice of *poached* marrow on each, and serve a Bordelaise sauce (32) separately.

1085—BRABANCONNE TOURNEDOS *Tournedos Brabançonne*

Prepare as many *tartlet-crusts* as there are tournedos.

Fill them with very small parboiled Brussels sprouts, stewed in butter; cover these with Mornay sauce (91), and set to *glaze* a few moments before serving.

Season the tournedos, and fry them in butter; set them on the prepared *tartlets* of sprouts, and surround with a border of small fondant potatoes (2214).

1086—TOURNEDOS CASTILLANE *Tournedos Castillane*

Prepare as many *tartlet-crusts* as there are tournedos; peeled, pressed, and seasoned tomatoes, cooked in butter; these should be in the proportion of one tablespoon per *tartlet;* rings of onion, fried in oil as for "Tournedos à l'Arlésienne"; a garnish of one table-spoon of small string beans, mixed with butter, per *tartlet.*

Season the tournedos; fry them in butter, and arrange them in the form of a crown on fried bread slices.

Place a *tartlet,* filled with a *fondue* of tomatoes, on each tourne-dos; all round arrange a border of the fried slices of onion, and serve the string beans, either in the middle of the dish or separately in an earthenware *timbale.*

1087—CINDERELLA TOURNEDOS   *Tournedos Cendrillon*

Prepare as many fine artichoke-bottoms as there are tournedos; a Soubise *purée* (104), combined with chopped truffles, and well-buttered.

A few moments before the tournedos are ready, garnish the artichoke-bottoms with the Soubise, and set them to *glaze* in a hot oven.

Season the tournedos; fry them in clarified butter (175), and set them on the artichoke-bottoms, which should be arranged in a circle round the dish.

1088—TOURNEDOS WITH MUSHROOMS
Tournedos aux Champignons

Season the tournedos, and fry them in butter.

Arrange them in the form of a crown; drain the butter from the saucepan; swirl into it some mushroom cooking-liquor, and add a proportional quantity of mushroom sauce. Set to boil for a few minutes, and pour the sauce, with the mushrooms, in the midst of the circle of tournedos.

1089—TOURNEDOS HUNTERS' STYLE   *Tournedos Chasseur*

Season the tournedos; fry them in butter, and arrange them in the form of a crown.

Drain the butter away; swash the saucepan with white wine, and add to this a quantity of Chasseur sauce (33), which should be in proportion to the number of tournedos.

Set to boil for a moment or two, and pour the sauce over the tournedos.

1090—CHORON TOURNEDOS   *Tournedos Choron*

Season the tournedos, and fry them in butter.

Set them on fried bread slices in butter; around the top of each lay a ribbon of Choron sauce (64), and in the middle of each set a medium-sized artichoke-bottom garnished with peas or asparagus tips mixed with butter.

All around, arrange a border of potatoes, lightly browned in butter, or heap them in the middle of the crown of tournedos.

N.B.—The sauce may be served separately.

1091—COLIGNY TOURNEDOS   *Tournedos Coligny*

With a preparation of sweet potatoes, made after the manner of "Duchesse potatoes" (221), make as many small flat patties as there are tournedos, and of the same size as the latter.

Place them on a tray; brush them with egg, and set them to brown in the oven a few minutes before the tournedos are ready.

Cut some chayotes in thick, *paysanne* fashion; parboil them; stew them in butter, and add an equal quantity of Provençale sauce (51).

Season the tournedos, and fry them in butter; arrange them in the form of a crown, on the patties of potato, and cover them with the *paysanne* of chayotes.

1092—TOURNEDOS WITH TARRAGON   *Tournedos à l'Estragon*

Season the tournedos, and fry them in butter.

Arrange them in the form of a crown, and on each set a spray of parboiled tarragon leaves. Send separately a thickened gravy with tarragon (41).

1093—FAVORITE TOURNEDOS   *Tournedos Favorite*

Season the tournedos; fry them in clarified butter (175), and arrange them, in the form of a crown, on bread slices stamped out with a scalloped cutter and fried in butter.

On each tournedos place a round slice of *foie gras*, a little smaller than the piece of meat; the slice should be seasoned, dredged, and tossed in butter. On each slice of *foie gras* put a fine, *glazed* slice of scalloped truffle. Garnish the center of the dish with a fine heap of asparagus tips mixed with butter, or merely set these in small heaps around the tournedos.

Serve separately a *timbale* of potato balls (of the size of hazel-nuts) cooked in butter, rolled in pale meat-*glaze* (15), and slightly sprinkled with chopped parsley.

1094—TOURNEDOS A LA FLORENTINE   *Tournedos à la Florentine*

Prepare as many *subrics* of shredded spinach as there are tourne-dos; make them of the same size, and cook them at the same time as the tournedos; also small, round *croquettes* of semolina the size of walnuts; these should be fried a few minutes before the tournedos are ready.

Grill the tournedos, and arrange them, in the form of a crown, on the spinach *subrics*. The *croquettes* of semolina may be arranged either in the middle or all around.

1095—FORESTIERE TOURNEDOS   *Tournedos Forestière*

Season the tournedos, and *sauté* them. Set them on bread slices fried in butter. Surround them with alternate heaps of noodles and potatoes cut into large dice and *sautéd* in butter.

The potatoes may also be placed in the midst of the tournedos with the noodles all around, or vice versa.

1096—GABRIELLE TOURNEDOS   *Tournedos Gabrielle*

Make a preparation from the white meat of a chicken and truffles —both cut into dice and combined with the necessary quantity of somewhat light "Duchesse-potatoes" paste (221).

With this preparation make as many small patty-shaped *croquettes* as there are tournedos, and fry them while the latter are being cooked.

Season the tournedos, and fry them with oil and butter in equal quantities. Arrange them, in the form of a crown, on the prepared *croquettes,* and on each tournedos set a fine slice of *poached* marrow and one slice of truffle.

Around the tournedos arrange some very small, *braised,* and well-trimmed lettuce heads.

1097—TOURNEDOS HENRI IV   *Tournedos Henri IV*

Grill the tournedos, and set them on bread slices fried in butter.

Around the edge of each tournedos lay a ribbon of Béarnaise sauce (62), and on top of each an artichoke-bottom garnished with very small potato balls (of the size of hazel-nuts) cooked in butter.

N.B.—Instead of putting the sauce on the edge of the tournedos, it may be served separately.

1098—JUDIC TOURNEDOS   *Tournedos Judic*

Season the tournedos; fry them in butter, and arrange them in the form of a crown on bread slices fried in butter. On each tournedos set a crown of truffle slices, with a cock's kidney in the center, and surround with *braised,* trimmed, and quartered lettuce.

1099—TOURNEDOS LAKME   *Tournedos Lakmé*

Prepare as many small *tartlet-crusts* as there are tournedos; the same number of grilled, medium-sized mushrooms; a garnish of one tablespoon of broad beans (large, flat and white) with cream per *tartlet.*

Season the tournedos, and fry them in clarified butter (175).

Arrange them in the form of a crown, each on a *tartlet* garnished with broad beans, and set a grilled mushroom on each tournedos.

1100—LESDIGUIERES TOURNEDOS   *Tournedos Lesdiguières*

Select onions sufficiently large to permit of placing the tournedos upon them, and of an equal number.

Trim their tops, and parboil them almost long enough to cook them.

Then, by means of a small knife, cut out their insides so that they may form little cases. Fill, two-thirds full, with spinach prepared with cream, cover the spinach with Mornay sauce (91), and set them to *glaze* in a hot oven a few moments before the tournedos are ready.

Grill the tournedos; arrange them in the form of a crown, each on an onion.

1101—TOURNEDOS LILI   *Tournedos Lili*

Season the tournedos, and fry them in butter.

Arrange them, in the form of a crown, each on a crust of "Potatoes Anna" (2203), stamped out with a round, even cutter of the same size as the tournedos.

On each tournedos set an artichoke-bottom garnished with a slice of *foie gras* tossed in butter, and on the *foie gras* place a slice of truffle. Send, separately, a reduced and well-buttered Périgueux sauce (47).

1102—LUCULLUS TOURNEDOS   *Tournedos Lucullus*

Season the tournedos; fry them in clarified butter (175), and arrange them, in the form of a crown, on fried slices of bread. Surround them with a garnish consisting of *quenelles* of chicken *force-meat*, cocks' combs, truffles, and *blanched* olives, and coat the whole with half-*glaze* sauce (23) prepared with truffle *essence.*

1103—TOURNEDOS MADELEINE   *Tournedos Madeleine*

For ten tournedos prepare ten *timbales* of a *purée* of white dried beans. For these *timbales* the *purée* of white dried beans must be combined per lb. with one egg and three yolks, finished with two

oz. of butter, put into well-buttered *dariole-moulds,* and set these
to *poach* fifteen minutes in advance.

Ten small artichoke-bottoms garnished with reduced Soubise
(104).

Season the tournedos; fry them in butter; arrange them, and
surround them with the *timbales* and the artichoke-bottoms, alternating the two garnishes.

1104—TOURNEDOS MARECHALE *Tournedos Maréchale*

Season the tournedos; fry them in butter, and arrange them upon
fried bread slices. On each of the tournedos set a large, *glazed* slice
of truffle, and surround them with little heaps of asparagus tips
mixed with butter.

1105—TOURNEDOS MARIE-LOUISE *Tournedos Marie-Louise*

Season the tournedos, and fry them in butter.

Arrange them, in the form of a crown, upon bread slices one-third
inch thick, fried in butter. On each tournedos set a small artichoke-
bottom, stewed in butter, filled in the shape of a dome, by means of
a pastry-bag, with a *purée* of mushrooms combined with a quart of
very reduced Soubise (104).

1106—TOURNEDOS MASCOTTE *Tournedos Mascotte*

Season the tournedos, and fry them in butter.

Have a garnish ready consisting of raw, quartered artichoke-
bottoms fried in butter; small, olive-shaped potatoes, also cooked
in butter; and olive-shaped truffles.

When about to serve, arrange the tournedos in a *cocotte* with the
garnish above described.

Swash the saucepan with white wine; add a little gravy; reduce
the whole, strain it into the *cocotte,* and put the latter in the front
of the oven for a minute or two.

1107—TOURNEDOS MASSENA *Tournedos Masséna*

Season the tournedos and fry them in butter; arrange them on
fried bread slices of the same size, and, in the middle of each tournedos, set a large slice of *poached* marrow.

Surround with a row of small artichoke-bottoms, garnished with
very stiff Béarnaise sauce (62).

1108—TOURNEDOS A LA MENAGERE *Tournedos à la Ménagère*

Put into an earthenware *cocotte* the following vegetables, which
should be in proportion to the number of tournedos:—Printanier

butter (157) cut into small pieces, and some minced new carrots, very small new onions, and very fresh peas.

All these vegetables should be equally apportioned.

Add salt, butter, and a very little water, for the vegetables should be cooked mainly by the concentration of steam inside the *cocotte,* which, for the purpose, should therefore be covered.

Fry the tournedos in butter, and arrange them upon the vegetables in the *cocotte* at the last moment.

1109—TOURNEDOS MEXICAN STYLE   *Tournedos à la Mexicaine*

Prepare a *fondue* of peeled and pressed tomatoes, cooked in butter, well reduced, and in the proportion of one tablespoon per mushroom; grill as many large mushrooms as there are tournedos, while the latter are being fried; some grilled or fried peppers in the proportion of half a one per tournedos.

Season the tournedos, and fry them in oil and butter in equal quantities. Place each on a mushroom filled with the *fondue* of tomatoes, and cover them with the grilled or fried peppers.

1110—MIKADO TOURNEDOS   *Tournedos Mikado*

Select some fine, rather firm tomatoes—"Ponderosas," as they are called—and cut them in two across. Squeeze them to take out all their juice and seeds; season them inside, and grill them so that they may be ready at the same time as the tournedos.

Season tournedos and fry them in butter.

Arrange them in the form of a crown, each on a grilled half-tomato, and garnish the center of the dish with Jerusalem artichokes tossed in butter.

1111—MIRABEAU TOURNEDOS   *Tournedos Mirabeau*

Grill the tournedos.

Lay eight fine strips of anchovy fillets upon each, crossing them after the manner of a lattice. Cover the edges with a crown of *blanched* tarragon leaves, and set a large pitted olive in the middle of each tournedos.

Send some half-melted anchovy butter (281) separately, and allow two-thirds oz. of it for each tournedos.

1112—MIREILLE TOURNEDOS   *Tournedos Mireille*

For ten tournedos, prepare in advance five *croustades* from the preparation used for "Potatoes Duchesse" (221). To make these *croustades,* fill some buttered *dariole-moulds* or muffin tins with the preparation referred to, taking care to press it snugly into them. Dip the moulds into tepid water, turn out, treat the potato forms *à l'anglaise,* fry them, hollow out their centers, and keep them hot.

A *fondue* of tomatoes in the proportion of one heaped tablespoon per *croustade.*

Five *timbales* of pilaff rice (2255), made after the same manner as the *croustades,* and kept hot until required for serving.

Season the tournedos, fry them in butter, and serve them as soon as they are ready.

Surround them with *timbales* of rice, and the *croustades* garnished with the *fondue,* the two garnishes to be alternated.

1113—TOURNEDOS MIRETTE   *Tournedos Mirette*

Prepare as many small *timbales* of "potatoes Mirette" (2234) as there are tournedos.

Turn them out on a dish, sprinkle with grated Parmesan cheese and a few drops of melted butter, and set them to *glaze* a few minutes before the tournedos are ready. Grill the tournedos, arrange them in the form of a crown, and set a *timbale* of Mirette potatoes upon each.

Swash the saucepan with white wine and add a little meat-*glaze* (15), finish with butter, and pour the resulting sauce over the tournedos.

1114—TOURNEDOS WITH MARROW   *Tournedos à la Moëlle*

Grill the tournedos and arrange them in the form of a crown.

Lay on each of them a large slice of *poached* marrow, and either surround them with Bordelaise sauce (32) or send the latter to the table separately.

1115—TOURNEDOS MONTGOMERY   *Tournedos Montgomery*

Season the tournedos and fry them in butter.

Place them upon a pancake of spinach (2138), cooked in a flat *tartlet-mould.* Decorate each tournedos with a rosette of reduced Soubise (104), made by means of a pastry-bag fitted with a fluted tube, and put a fine slice of truffle in the center of the rosette.

1116—TOURNEDOS MONTPENSIER   *Tournedos Montpensier*

Prepare as many *tartlet-crusts* as there are tournedos and a garnish of asparagus tips, mixed with butter, in the proportion of one heaped tablespoon per *tartlet.*

Fry the tournedos in butter, and arrange them upon fried bread slices.

On each of them set a *tartlet* garnished with asparagus tips, with a slice of truffle in the middle.

1117—TOURNEDOS WITH MORELS   *Tournedos aux Morilles*

Grill the tournedos or fry them in butter.

Arrange them in the form of a crown; in the center put a heap of morels (French mushrooms) *sautéd* in butter, and sprinkle them moderately with chopped parsley.

1118—TOURNEDOS NICOISE   *Tournedos à la Niçoise*

Fry the tournedos in butter, and arrange them in the form of a crown.

In the center of each tournedos set a small heap, consisting of one half-tablespoon of peeled, pressed, and chopped tomatoes, tossed in butter, together with a little crushed garlic and chopped tarragon.

Surround with small heaps of string beans mixed with butter, and also heaps of small potatoes, cooked in butter, alternating the two garnishes.

1119—TOURNEDOS NINON   *Tournedos Ninon*

Fry the tournedos in butter, and arrange them upon crusts of "potatoes Anna," stamped out with a round fancy-cutter of the same size as the tournedos. On each of the tournedos set a small patty, garnished with asparagus tips, mixed with butter and combined with a fine and short *julienne* of truffles.

1120—TOURNEDOS PARMENTIER   *Tournedos Parmentier*

Fry the tournedos in butter, and arrange them in the form of a crown.

In the middle of the dish or around it set a fine heap of potatoes, cut into regular cubes of two-thirds of an inch, or balls cut with an oval, grooved spoon. The potatoes should be cooked in butter and kept very soft.

Slightly sprinkle the potatoes with chopped parsley.

1121—TOURNEDOS PERSIAN STYLE   *Tournedos Persane*

Prepare as many green peppers, stuffed with rice moulded to the shape of balls and *braised,* and as many grilled tomatoes cut in half as there are tournedos. Also have some fried slices of banana ready, and allow three for each tournedos.

Fry the tournedos in butter and arrange them, in the form of a crown, on the grilled tomatoes. On each tournedos set a stuffed and *braised* sweet pepper.

In the center of the dish arrange the fried slices of banana in a nice heap. Send separately to the table a Châteaubriand sauce (71), combined with the reduced *braising*-liquor of the peppers.

1122—PERUVIAN TOURNEDOS   *Tournedos Péruvienne*

Prepare, after the manner described, as many *oxalis roots* (similar to potatoes) as there are tournedos.

Peel the *oxalis roots;* cut a slice from underneath them, in order to make them stand straight, and hollow them out to form little cases.

Chop up the pulp extracted from them, and add it to a preparation of *duxelles,* made as for stuffed mushrooms.

Fill the *oxalis* cases with this preparation, shaping it above their edges after the manner of a dome; sprinkle with *raspings* and oil, and put them in the oven in good time for them to be ready at the same time as the tournedos.

Grill the tournedos, arrange them in the form of a crown, and surround them with the *oxalis* cases.

1123—TOURNEDOS PIEDMONT STYLE   *Tournedos Piémontaise*

Butter as many *tartlet-moulds* as there are tournedos; fill them with Rizotto à la Piémontaise (2258), combined with white truffles cut into dice, and keep them hot.

Fry the tournedos in clarified butter (175); arrange them, in the form of a crown, on the *rizotto tartlets,* turned out at the last minute.

1124—TOURNEDOS PROVENCE STYLE   *Tournedos Provençale*

For ten tournedos, prepare ten medium-sized mushrooms, stuffed with *duxelles,* slightly flavored with garlic, and put in the oven in good time; ten half-tomatoes à la Provençale (2266).

Fry the tournedos in equal quantities of butter and oil; arrange them, in the form of a crown, on fried bread slices, with a half-tomato upon each, and around them set the stuffed mushrooms

1125—TOURNEDOS RACHEL   *Tournedos Rachel*

Fry the tournedos in butter, and arrange them, in the form of a crown, on fried bread slices one-third inch thick.

On each tournedos set a small artichoke-bottom, garnished with a large slice of *poached* marrow.

Send a Bordelaise sauce (32) separately.

1126—TOURNEDOS ROSSINI   *Tournedos Rossini*

Fry the tournedos in butter, and arrange them, in the form of a crown, upon fried bread slices.

On each tournedos set a round slice of *foie gras,* just a little smaller than the former; the slices should be seasoned, dredged, and fried in butter.

On each slice of *foie-gras,* set a fine slice of truffle.

1127—ROUMANILLE TOURNEDOS   *Tournedos Roumanille*

Cut the tournedos a little smaller than usual. Season them; fry them in butter, and arrange them in a circle on grilled half-tomatoes.

Coat the tournedos with Mornay sauce (91), and set them to *glaze* quickly.

In the middle of each tournedos set a large stuffed and *poached* olive, encircled by a ring of anchovy fillet.

In the center of the dish arrange a fine heap of egg-plant slices, seasoned with salt and pepper, dredged, fried in oil, and kept very crisp.

1128—ST. MANDE TOURNEDOS   *Tournedos Saint-Mande*

Fry the tournedos in butter, and arrange them, in the form of a circle, each on a little mound of "potatoes Macaire" (2228), moulded in ordinary *tartlet-moulds.*

In the center of the dish set a garnish consisting of peas mixed with butter.

1129—TOURNEDOS A LA SARDE   *Tournedos à la Sarde*

Prepare a garnish of hollowed, parboiled, and *braised* sections of cucumber, stuffed with *duxelles,* and *gratined;* also small tomatoes, similarly treated; small round *croquettes* of rice flavored with saffron, thickened with egg-yolks, treated *à l'anglaise,* and fried.

Fry the tournedos in butter, and arrange them in the form of a crown.

Set a *croquette* of rice upon each tournedos, and frame the whole with the stuffed cucumber cases and the stuffed tomatoes, laid alternately.

1130—TOURNEDOS SOUBISE   *Tournedos Soubise*

Grill the tournedos and arrange them in the form of a crown.

Serve a light Soubise (104) *purée* separately.

1131—TIVOLI TOURNEDOS   *Tournedos Tivoli*

For ten tournedos, prepare ten small grilled mushrooms, and allow one-half tomato tossed in butter for each mushroom.

Fry the tournedos in butter and arrange them, in the form of a crown, upon fried bread slices. On each tournedos set a grilled mushroom, garnished with a tossed half-tomato, and all around set some fine "potato *soufflé*" (2221), made in ribbon-form, of a round shape, and in the proportion of one potato to each tournedos.

Send a Béarnaise sauce (62) separately.

1132—TYROLEAN TOURNEDOS   *Tournedos Tyrolienne*

For ten tournedos, prepare the following sauce:—Gently cook one chopped onion in butter; add two peeled, pressed, and roughly-chopped tomatoes, salt, pepper, chopped parsley, and a little crushed garlic.

When the tomatoes are sufficiently cooked, add a few tablespoons of poivrade sauce (49) and set to boil for five minutes.

Fry the tournedos in butter; arrange them in the form of a crown, and cover them with the prepared sauce.

1133—TOURNEDOS VALENCAY   *Tournedos Valençay*

Fry the tournedos in butter; arrange them in the form of a crown, each on a small, round, and flat *croquette* of noodles and ham, fried just before serving.

Send a Châteaubriand sauce (71) separately.

1134—TOURNEDOS VALENTINO   *Tournedos Valentino*

Prepare as many slices of turnips, of the same diameter as the tournedos and one and one-half inch thick, as tournedos. Cut them neatly round, stamp them with a plain, round cutter, and parboil them until they are almost completely cooked. Hollow them out, by means of a spoon, inside the mark left by the fancy-cutter, and stuff them with a preparation of semolina with Parmesan cheese.

Put these stuffed pieces of turnip in a saucepan; add a little water, butter, and sugar, and *glaze* them while finishing their cooking-process.

Fry the tournedos in butter, and arrange them in a circle, each on a stuffed turnip.

1135—TOURNEDOS VERT-PRE
Tournedos Vert-Pré

Grill the tournedos, and serve them simply with half-melted butter à la Maître-d'Hôtel (150) on them.

Surround them with alternate heaps of water-cress and freshly-fried shoestring potatoes.

1136—TOURNEDOS VICTORIA
Tournedos Victoria

Fry the tournedos in butter.

Arrange them in a circle, each on a little round and flat *croquette* of chicken-meat. On each tournedos set a half-tomato tossed in butter.

1137—TOURNEDOS VILLARET
Tournedos Villaret

Prepare as many *tartlet-crusts* as there are tournedos; and a sufficient quantity of very smooth small kidney bean *purée* to fill the *tartlets;* also a fine grilled tomato per each tournedos.

Grill the tournedos, and place them on the filled *tartlets*. On each tournedos set a grilled mushroom cap, the hollow of which should have been filled with Châteaubriand sauce (71).

1138—VILLENEUVE TOURNEDOS
Tournedos Villeneuve

Fry the tournedos in butter, and arrange them in a circle on little patty-shaped *croquettes* of chicken-meat, fried at the last moment.

On each tournedos set a crown of small slices of tongue and truffle, laid alternately, and a small grooved mushroom in the middle.

Send a Châteaubriand sauce (71) separately.

1139—VILLEMER TOURNEDOS
Tournedos Villemer

Grill the tournedos, and arrange them in a circle, each on a fried, hollowed-out bread crust, filled with truffled Soubise (104).

On each tournedos set a large slice of truffle coated with meat-glaze (15).

1140—BEEF FILLETS VENISON STYLE
Filets en Chevreuil

For "venison" treatment, the meat used is generally cut from the narrowest end of the fillet of beef. The weight of the pieces cut should average about three oz. each.

After having slightly flattened and trimmed them, *lard* them with very thin strips of bacon, and *marinate* them for a few hours in the raw *marinade* given under (169). When about to cook them, dry them thoroughly, and fry them quickly in hot oil, taking care that the latter be smoking, and therefore hot enough to set the meat and to cause its surface moisture to evaporate.

The fillets may be accompanied by all vegetable *purées* and highly-seasoned sauces, the most suitable of the latter being the Poivrade (49) and the Chasseur (33).

1141—SIRLOIN OF BEEF   *Aloyau de Boeuf (Relevé)*

Sirloin of beef is that part of the steer's back reaching from the haunch to the floating ribs, which is equivalent to the saddle in veal and mutton. This piece, however, cannot properly be called "sirloin," except when it comprises the fillet or undercut, and the upper fillet (Fr.: contrefilet), so-called to distinguish it from the undercut. If this joint be treated whole, it need only be shortened by removing the flank, and by cutting the ligament lying alongside of the backbone on the upper fillet, in different places.

A little fat is left on the undercut, but none whatever must be removed from the upper fillet. As a rule, when sirloin of beef is *braised,* it is cut across into pieces weighing from six to seven lbs. If it is to be roasted, it is best to keep it whole.

When served as a *relevé,* it is *braised* or roasted, and is kept underdone if so desired. Unless it be of excellent quality, however, *braised* sirloin generally turns out to be dry.

All garnishes given for "Fillet of Beef" may be served with sirloin; but, as a rule, the bulkiest, such as the "Richelieu" (1071), the "Provençale" (1124), the "Godard" (1054), etc., are selected.

The accompanying sauce is that indicated for the above garnishes.

1142—PORTERHOUSE STEAK (GRILL)   *Le Steak Porterhouse*

Porterhouse steak is a slice from the sirloin of beef, which may be more or less thick. It is cleared of the flank and of the bones of the chine, and it is always grilled.

It may be served with any of the various garnishes and sauces suited to grills; but it is more often served plain.

(Porterhouse steak is a thick slice from that part of the beef, near the sirloin, which has the shortest rib and the longest part of the beef tenderloin. In the United States it is considered the choicest cut of meat as it has only a short rib-bone, and it is always grilled. —Ed.)

1143—UPPER FILLET AND RIBS OF BEEF
Filet et Côtes de Boeuf (Relevé)

The upper fillet is that part of beef which lies between the top of the haunch and the floating ribs, alongside of the backbone. It may be treated like the fillet, and all the garnishes suited to the latter may also be applied here.

If the piece is to be *braised*, it should be completely boned; if intended for roasting, it is best to retain the bones. In the latter case, the large ligament should be cut at various points so it won't lose its shape, while the rib bones should be cracked close to the point where they join the backbone, that they may be easily removed when the meat is being carved.

The upper fillet, especially when it is of good quality, is best roasted.

Ribs of beef may likewise be *braised* or roasted.

In either case, the meat should be properly trimmed and boned.

This piece should only be used after having been well hung (seasoned), in order that it may be as tender as possible.

1144—GRILLED SIRLOIN STEAKS AND RIBS OF BEEF
Aloyau et Côtes de Boeuf Grillé

The sirloin steak may be cut either from the upper fillet or the ribs of beef, between two rib-bones. In order that its cooking may be just right, it should not weigh more than from two to three lbs.

Ribs of beef may also be grilled, provided they be sufficiently tender.

They may be *braised,* too, and in this case they are served with any of the various garnishes given under Fillet of Beef.

1145—BRAISED TOP ROUND OR RUMP OF BEEF
Pièce de Boeuf Braisée (Relevé)

The piece of beef called rump is the one preferred for boiling and *braising*. Whatever be the use for which the meat is intended, the weight of the pieces should not be more than six or eight lbs. at the most, and they should be cut in the length rather than in the thickness, that the cooking process may be facilitated.

All the garnishes of *braised* sirloin of beef are suited to *braised* rump of beef.

Boiled beef is generally accompanied by the vegetables used in its cooking-process, by *purées,* green or dry vegetables, pastes, macaroni, etc.

1146—TOP ROUND OR RUMP OF BEEF BOURGUIGNONNE
Pièce de Boeuf à la Bourguignonne

Lard the rump of beef, and *marinate* it for three hours in brandy and red wine. *Braise* it after the manner described under (247);

moisten first with the wine of the *marinade,* and, when the latter is reduced, with some veal gravy and one-half pint of Espagnole sauce (24) per quart of liquid, taking care that the liquid reaches the top of the piece of meat. Add an herb bunch and some mushrooms peelings; set to boil, and cook gently in the oven.

When the meat is two-thirds cooked, transfer it to another saucepan, and surround it with mushrooms cut into two or four, according to their size, and tossed in butter; bacon, cut into dice, *blanched* and tossed in butter, and some small onions half-*glazed* with butter.

Strain the sauce through a sieve over the piece of beef and its garnish, and complete the cooking gently.

A few minutes before serving, put the meat on a platter and *glaze* it in the oven. Transfer the meat to the dish intended for the table; quickly reduce the sauce if necessary, and pour it over the piece of beef and the garnish.

1147—TOP ROUND OR RUMP OF BEEF A LA CUILLER

Pièce de Boeuf à la Cuiller

Select a very square or oval cut of beef, and bear in mind, in selecting it, that it will have to be fashioned to the shape of a mould when it has been cooked.

Tie it, and *braise* it after the manner described under (247), almost entirely covering it with moistening liquor.

Set it to cook gently; remove the piece when the meat is still somewhat firm, and let it cool under a slight weight.

This done, cut out the meat from the inside; leave a thickness of about half-inch around the sides and on the bottom, and the piece thus emptied should constitute a square or oval mould, in accordance with the shape originally adopted.

Coat the outside of the whole piece with a mixture of beaten eggs and fine bread-crumbs, combined with Parmesan cheese; sprinkle melted butter over it with a brush, and put the case into a sufficiently hot oven to allow of a crust forming around it.

Meanwhile chop up the meat extracted from the inside of the piece; add a little salted tongue, some *braised* slices of sweet-bread, and mushrooms; put the whole into a saucepan with an Italian (40) or a half-*glaze* sauce (23), according to the requirements, and heat this garnish.

N.B.—This preparation was quite common in old-fashioned cookery, but though it is still served occasionally, it is now looked upon more as a curiosity than anything else. As a curiosity, therefore, I chose to include it among these recipes; but it does not follow from this that I in any way recommend it.

1148—TOP ROUND OR RUMP OF BEEF FLEMISH STYLE
Pièce de Boeuf à la Flamande

Lard the piece of beef, and *braise* it as explained under (247).

Meanwhile prepare the following garnish:—Cut a nice firm cabbage into four, remove the heart, and parboil it for seven or eight minutes. Drain it; cool it; divide up the quarters, leaf by leaf, so as to remove the hard ribs, and season with salt and pepper.

Mould them to the shape by pressing them in the corner of a towel into balls weighing about three oz. each, or simply put them into a saucepan with a quartered carrot, an onion stuck with a clove, an herb bunch, six oz. of *blanched* salt pork, and a little Italian raw sausage with garlic, which must be taken out after cooking has gone on for one and one-half hours.

Moisten the cabbage with just sufficient consommé to cover it; add a few tablespoons of good stock-fat (drippings); set to boil, and cook gently in the oven for one and one-half hours.

Cut the required quantity of carrots and turnips to the shape of olives; cook them in consommé, and reduce the latter for the purpose of *glazing*.

Prepare some potatoes *à l'anglaise* (2202).

Set the piece of beef on a platter large enough to allow its being surrounded with the moulded or plainly-heaped cabbages, the *glazed* carrots and turnips, and the potatoes *à l'anglaise*. The last two vegetables should be set in alternate heaps with the cabbages and the bacon (cut into small rectangles) and the sausage (cut into slices) should be distributed all around.

Serve separately the gravy from the beef, cleared of all grease, reduced to a half-*glaze* and strained.

1149—HOT BEEF A LA MODE   *Pièce de Boeuf à la Mode Chaude*

Lard the top round piece of beef, which should not, if possible, weigh more than from four to five lbs. The strips of bacon used for *larding* ought to have been prepared fifteen or twenty minutes in advance, *marinated* in a few tablespoons of brandy, and sprinkled with parsley just before being used.

Rub the piece with salt, pepper, and nutmeg, and put it into a bowl with one bottle of red wine and one-fifth pint of brandy, and set it to *marinate* for four or five hours, taking care to turn it over from time to time.

Then set it to *braise* after the manner described under (247); add its *marinade* to the moistening, and surround it with three small, boned, *blanched*, and tied calf's feet.

When the cooking is three-quarters done, transfer the piece of beef to another saucepan, and surround it with the following garnish:—

About one-quarter lb. of carrots cut in the shape of elongated olives, and already two-thirds cooked. Small onions browned in two-thirds lb. of butter.

The calf's feet cut into small, square, or rectangular pieces.

Strain the *braising*-liquor over the whole, and complete the cooking gently. When about to serve, either *glaze* the piece of beef, or serve it plain; coat it lightly with sauce, and send what remains of the latter, with the garnish, in an earthenware *timbale*.

1150—COLD BEEF A LA MODE *Pièce de Boeuf à la Mode Froide*

Beef à la mode is very rarely prepared specially for cold serving, the remains of a fine piece being generally used for this purpose. The piece of meat must first be well trimmed. If the quantity of sauce does not seem enough, or if the sauce itself seems too stiff, add a third of its volume of aspic jelly to it.

For moulding, take a *terrine à pâté*, earthenware mould, or other utensil large enough to hold the piece of meat, its garnish, and its sauce. Decorate the bottom of the utensil in any suitable way with the carrots and the onions, and surround the meat with what remains of the vegetables and the dice of calf's feet.

Add the sauce, combined with the jelly, after having passed it through a strainer, and let chill for a few hours. Turn out just before serving, and surround with very light, chopped aspic-jelly.

1151—TOP ROUND OR RUMP OF BEEF A LA NOAILLES
Piè de Boeuf à la Noailles

Lard the piece of beef, and *marinate* it in brandy and red wine.

This done, dry it thoroughly, and brown it evenly in butter all over; moisten it with its *marinade* and an equal quantity of veal gravy, and set to cook gently.

When the meat is half-cooked, surround it with two lbs. of minced onions, tossed in butter, and three oz. of rice. Complete the cooking of the meat with onions and rice.

Now remove the beef, and quickly rub the onions and the rice through a fine sieve. Reduce this Soubise with rice for a few moments.

Neatly trim the beef; cut it into even slices; reconstruct it on a dish, and between each slice pour a tablespoon of Soubise *purée* (104).

Cover the reconstructed piece of beef with the remainder of the Soubise; sprinkle the surface with two tablespoons of bread-crumbs fried in butter, and some melted butter, and put the whole in the oven, that the *gratin* may form speedily.

RUMPSTEAK AND BEEFSTEAK

1152—THE RUMP *Culotte de Boeuf*

The rump is that portion of the sirloin of beef which touches the top of the haunch, known as *le* beefsteak in France.

It may be *braised,* but it is more often grilled in slices from one inch to one and one-half inches thick, which are called "rump-steaks."

Rumpsteak is either grilled or *sautéd,* but whatever be the method of cooking it, it is generally served plain.

All garnishes suited to fillets, however, may be served with it, as also the various butters and sauces generally used with grills.

1153—BEEF OR OX TONGUE *Langue de Boeuf*

Beef or ox tongue is served fresh or salted, but, even when it is to be served fresh, it is all the better for having been put in salt a few days previously. In order to salt it, put it into a special brine, as explained under (172). When salted, it is cooked in boiling water; when fresh, it is *braised* exactly after the manner of any other piece of meat.

Beef or ox tongue may be served with almost all the garnishes suited to *relevés* of fillet of beef, but more particularly with the following:—Bourgeoise; Flamande; Milanaise; Noodles or Macaroni with cream, cheese or tomatoes; and all vegetable *purées.*

The most suitable sauces are:—Madeira sauce (44), Piquante sauce (48), Tomato sauce (29), or their derivatives.

1154—BEEF OR OX TONGUE WITH SAUERKRAUT

Langue de Boeuf Choucroûte

Braise the tongue as described under (247), and *glaze* it at the last moment. Place it on a dish and send to the table separately a *timbale* of well-*braised* saukerkraut; a *timbale* of potato *purée;* a Madeira sauce (44), combined with the *braising*-liquor of the tongue, cleared of all grease, and reduced.

1155—BEEF OR OX TONGUE BOURGEOISE

Langue de Boeuf Bourgeoise

Braise the tongue in the usual way.

When it is two-thirds cooked, surround it with carrots fashioned to the shape of olives and already two-thirds cooked, and small onions browned in butter.

Complete the cooking gently, and for the rest of the operation, proceed as for "Piece de Bœuf à la Mode chaude" (1149).

1156—BEEF OR OX TONGUE WITH BROAD BEANS

Langue de Boeuf aux Fèves

Tongue intended for this preparation should be put in salt a few days in advance.

Boil it in the usual way very gently; *glaze* it when about to serve. Send to the table separately a *timbale* of very fresh, shelled, broad beans (large flat white beans), cooked in salted water with a sprig of savory, and mixed with butter at the last moment and a Madeira sauce (44).

1157—BEEF OR OX TONGUE FLEMISH STYLE

Langue de Boeuf Flamande

Braise the tongue, and *glaze* it at the last moment. Surround it with the garnish "à la Flamande" (1148) given under the beef recipe of that name, *braised* cabbages, *glazed* carrots and turnips, potatoes *à l'anglaise,* rectangles of lean bacon, and slices of sausage.

1158—COLD BEEF OR OX TONGUES   *Langues de Boeuf Froides*

Beef or ox tongues intended for cold serving should be kept in brine (172) for eight or ten days. When about to use them, put them to soak in cold water for a few hours, and then cook them plain in water for three hours.

This done, remove them from their cooking-liquor; skin them; cover them with buttered paper or vegetable parchment, and let them cool. The object of the paper is to keep off the air, which has the tendency to blacken the surface of the tongue.

When quite cool, coat the tongues with a *glaze* composed of about eight ounces of gelatine dissolved in one pint of water; the latter is given a scarlet tint by means of carmine and caramel coloring.

Cold tongues are served amid aspic jelly dice and curly leaf parsley.

Ox Tails

Ox tails, sectioned or unsectioned, are usually *braised,* and only the thicker half of the tail is ever used.

1159—OX TAIL A L'AUVERGNATE   *Queue de Boeuf à l'Auvergnate*

Section the tail and *braise* it in white wine, after recipe (247).

Prepare a garnish of rectangles of lean bacon, large chestnuts cooked in consommé and *glazed,* and small onions cooked in butter.

Put the sections of the tail in an earthenware *cocotte* with the garnish.

1160—OX TAIL A LA CAVOUR   *Queue de Boeuf à la Cavour*

Section the tail, and *braise* it in a moistening two-thirds of which is brown stock (7) and one-third white wine. It is well for the liquid to be somewhat abundant. Set to cook very gently, until the meat falls from the bones, or about four and one-half or five hours.

This done, put the sections of the tail in a *cocotte;* add some small, cooked mushrooms; clear the cooking-liquor of grease; reduce it, and thicken it slightly with *fecula,* flour, etc. Strain this thickened cooking-liquor over the sections of the tail and the mushrooms, and set to boil very gently for ten minutes.

Serve in the *cocotte* set on a dish, and send a *timbale* of chestnut *purée* to the table at the same time.

1161—STUFFED OX TAIL   *Queue de Boeuf Farcie*

Choose a large ox tail, and bone it carefully without breaking it.

Lay it on a napkin, and stuff it with a *forcemeat* consisting of the following ingredients:—Three-quarters lb. of very lean beef and one-half lb. of chopped fat bacon, the two mixed with four oz. of bread-crumbs soaked in milk and pressed; two whole eggs; three oz. of truffle peel; one-half oz. of salt, a pinch of pepper, and a very little seasoning.

Sew up the tail, cover it with a piece of cloth after the manner of a *galantine,* and cook it gently for three hours in a very light stock with vegetables as for boiled beef.

At the end of the three hours take it out of the cloth; put it into a saucepan, the bottom of which should be garnished as for a *braising;* add a little of the cooking-liquor of the tail, and complete the cooking, basting often. Take care to baste more frequently towards the close of the cooking with the view of properly *glazing* the meat.

When about to serve, put it on a dish, after having removed all string, and lightly coat the bottom of the dish with a sauce consisting of the cooking-liquor, reduced and thickened with arrow-root or flour, etc. Send what remains of the cooking-liquor in a sauceboat.

Serve separately either a *purée,* a garnish of *braised* vegetables, or one of the sauces suited to pieces of beef.

1162—GRILLED OX TAIL   *Queue de Boeuf Grillé*

Cut the tail into sections twice the usual length, and cook these in a pot for five hours with slightly salted water and *aromatics* (herbs and seasoning).

Drain the sections; dry them well; dip them in melted butter, and roll them in very fine bread-crumbs. Sprinkle with melted butter, and set to grill gently.

Grilled ox tail may be served with any vegetable *purée.* An ordinary Soubise (104), or one prepared "à la Noailles" (1151), as explained under the piece of beef of that name, also suits very well.

In any case, the Soubise should be sufficiently thick.

Such sauces as à la Diable, Hachée, Piquante, Robert, Tomato, Italienne, etc., are also suited to grilled ox tail.

N.B.—When the accompaniment to grilled ox tail is a highly-seasoned sauce, the sections should first be covered with a coat of mustard, then dipped in melted butter, and finally rolled in bread-crumbs.

1163—OX TAIL HODGEPODGE   *Queue de Boeuf en Hochepot*

Cut the tail into sections, and put these into a pot of convenient size, with two pig's feet, each of which must be cut into four or five pieces, and one pig's ear. Cover with cold water; add salt to the extent of one-third oz. per quart of the liquid; set to boil; skim, and leave to cook gently for two hours.

This done, add one small cabbage, cut into quarters, parboiled and cooled; ten small onions; five oz. of carrots, and the same weight of turnips, cut to the shape of large garlic cloves.

Set the whole to cook for a further two hours at least.

When about to serve, arrange the sections of tail in a circle; put the vegetable garnish in the center, and surround the latter with the pig's ear cut into small, narrow strips, and ten grilled chipolata (Italian) sausages.

Serve, separately, a *timbale* of potatoes cooked *à l'anglaise*.

Various Preparations of Beef

1164—STEWED STEAKS AND ONIONS
Daube de Biftecks et d'Oignons

Select some steaks one and one-third inches thick; fry them in butter on both sides, and set them to *braise* in a little moistening, with a sufficient quantity of quartered and browned onions to constitute an abundant garnish.

Leave the whole to cook gently for three hours.

When serving the steak, surround it with the onions and the *braising*-liquor cleared of all grease and reduced.

1165—CORNED BEEF
Plat-de-Côte

The pieces of beef chiefly selected for salting are brisket, plate, and round of beef, and these are always boiled for a more or less lengthy period, according to their size.

To the cooking-liquor is added a copious garnish of carrots and turnips. These are served with the meat, together with a sauceboat of cooking-liquor and suet dumplings, prepared as follows below.

1166—SUET DUMPLINGS
Pâté Cuite à Graisse de Boeuf

Finely chop up some suet; add to it an equal quantity of flour and about one-quarter oz. of salt per lb. of suet and flour.

Moisten with just enough water to make a thick paste of about the same consistency as *brioche*-paste. Cut this paste into portions weighing about one oz., and roll them into small balls. Put the dumplings in a saucepan containing some boiling beef stock, which need not have been cleared of grease, and let them *poach* for one and one-half hours.

Now drain the dumplings, and arrange them around the meat with the garnish of carrots and turnips, as explained above.

1167—COLD CORNED BEEF
Plat-de-Côte Froid

Salt beef, served cold, constitutes an excellent buffet dish for luncheons.

It need only be neatly trimmed all round, care being taken to preserve all the fat so highly esteemed by some. Indeed, a piece of cold corned fat is sometimes added to that already in the meat, in which case the extra quantity is fixed to the beef by means of an ornamental skewer.

1168—PRESSED BEEF *Pressed Beef*

Salt beef also serves in the preparation of "Pressed Beef," but, for this purpose, the brisket or plate is generally used.

After having thoroughly cooked the salted beef in accordance with the procedure indicated for salt beef (1165), cut it into large pieces of the same size as the moulds into which the meat is going to be pressed. Lay the pieces of beef one on top of another in a square or rectangular mould, and cover with a thick board, cut flush with the inside edge of the mould. Now apply pressure, either by means of a strong press or heavy weight, and leave the beef to cool under the applied pressure.

When the meat is quite cold, turn it out; trim it carefully on all sides, and *glaze* it, by covering it entirely with a coating of rather firm, clarified aspic-jelly, darkened a reddish brown with red and caramel vegetable coloring.

1169—STEAK AND KIDNEY PUDDING
Pudding de Biftecks et de Rognons

Cut three lbs. of very lean beef into slices one-third inch thick.

Season these slices with salt, pepper, and nutmeg, and add a little chopped onion and parsley. Take a pudding-bowl; line it with a firm layer of suet-dough (1166), and garnish the bottom and sides of the bowl with the slices of beef.

In the middle put one lb. of kidney of beef, of veal, or of mutton, cut up as for *sautéing,* and seasoned like the steaks. Moisten with just sufficient water to cover.

Now close up the bowl with a layer of the same paste as that used in lining, pinching it with the latter, all round, that it may stick thoroughly. In order to do this with greater certainty, the edges of the two layers of paste may be moistened.

This done, cover the bowl with a buttered and floured napkin, fastened on by means of string tied round just beneath the rim of the utensil. Cook for five hours, either in boiling water or in steam, and, after having removed the napkin, serve the pudding as it stands.

1170—STEAK PUDDING *Pudding de Biftecks*

Make some rather stiff paste with two lbs. of flour, one and one-quarter lbs. of the chopped fat of beef kidney, a pinch of salt, and one-quarter pint of water.

With the rolling-pin, roll out this paste to a round layer one-quarter inch thick, and line a buttered dome-mould or pudding-bowl.

Cut the lean beef into pieces, and season them, exactly as for steak and kidney pudding. Fill up the bowl with the pieces arranged in layers; moisten with just enough water to cover, and close up the bowl with a layer of the same paste as that used for its lining.

Carefully pinch together the edges of the two layers of paste, moistening the edges with a brush; wrap the bowl in a buttered pudding-cloth or vegetable parchment, and tie it firmly with string on top of the bowl.

Put the pudding in a saucepan of boiling water or a steamer, and leave it to cook for three hours if the beef has been cut from the fillet, and for four hours if cut from any other piece.

At the end of the required time take the pudding out of the saucepan and remove the cloth.

Serve on a folded napkin.

1171—STEAK AND OYSTER PUDDING
Pudding de Biftecks et d'Huîtres

Proceed exactly as for steak and kidney pudding, but take only two lbs. of beef, and replace the odd pound with forty oysters.

1172—HOT BEEF STEW PROVENCALE *Daube Chaude à la Provençale*

Cut four lbs. of shoulder round of beef into cubes weighing about four oz. each. *Lard* each piece of meat with a strip of bacon two inches long by one-half inch wide, and put the cubes or pieces into a bowl with salt, pepper, a very little spice, five or six tablespoons of vinegar, and a glass of red wine. Leave to *marinate* for two or three hours, and toss the pieces, from time to time, in the *marinading* liquor, in order that each may be well saturated with it. Heat six oz. of grated bacon in an *earthenware* saucepan, and brown in it twelve small onions, fifteen carrots in the shape of olives, two stalks of celery cut into pieces the same as the carrots, and four cloves of garlic. Add the *marinated* pieces of meat, which should have been properly dried; fry the meat and vegetables for a further seven or eight minutes, and moisten with the *marinade* and two glasses more of red wine.

Complete with one-half lb. of fresh bacon rind, *blanched* and cut into cubes of two-thirds inch; an herb bunch made of parsley sprigs, thyme, bay leaf, and, in the center, a small piece of dry

lemon rind. Set to boil, close the saucepan tightly, and leave to cook
in a moderate oven for six or seven hours.

When about to serve, remove the herb bunch, clear all grease
from the gravy, and put in a hot *timbale,* or serve the stew in the
saucepan itself.

1173—COLD BEEF STEW PROVENCALE

Daube Froide à la Provençale

A stew is rarely prepared specially for cold dishing; generally
the remains of one already served hot are used.

Take the pieces, one by one, with a fork, and place them in a
terrine à pâté (earthenware paté dish) with the carrots, onions,
and squares of bacon rind, which have remained almost untouched.

Strain the gravy over them through an ordinary strainer, pressing
lightly with a wooden spoon, and leave to cool.

When about to serve, turn out the stew on a cold dish, and
surround with chopped aspic jelly.

1174—FLEMISH CARBONADES   *Carbonnades Flamande*

Cut three lbs. of lean shoulder round of beef into thin, short slices.
Season the latter with salt and pepper, and brown them quickly
on both sides in stock fat. At the same time toss one and one-quarter
lbs. of minced onions in butter, until they are well browned.

Put the slices of beef and the onions in alternate layers into a
saucepan, and in their midst place an herb bunch.

Drain the grease from the saucepan in which the slices were
fried; then swirl into it one and one-half pints of beer (old Lambic,
Belgian beer in preference); add the same quantity of brown stock
(7), thicken with four oz. of brown *roux;* finish the seasoning with
one and one-half oz. of powdered sugar; set to boil, stirring the
while, and strain this sauce over the slices of beef and the onions.

Cover and cook gently in the oven for from two and one-half to
three hours.

N.B.—*Carbonades* are served thus, mingled with the onions;
but they may also be put in a *timbale* and covered with a Soubise
(104) consisting of the onion and the sauce rubbed through a fine
sieve.

1175—MINCED BEEF   *Emincé de Boeuf*

Cold roast or boiled meats may be warmed up in many different
ways.

In their preparation, however, the reader should follow one rule, the non-observance of which invariably leads to failure.

Whatever the meat be, it should first be cut into the thinnest possible slices; set on a dish, and covered with a boiling sauce or garnish, which should warm it. If the meat boils in the sauce or garnish, it toughens, and this, above all, should be avoided when roast meat is used.

Sauces suited to *Emincés* are the Bordelaise, the Piquante, the Italienne, the Chasseur, the Poivrade, the Périgueux, and the Tomato.

1176—MINCED BEEF EN MIROTON   *Emincé de Boeuf en Miroton*

For one lb. of cooked or roast beef, mince two fine onions somewhat finely, and toss them in butter until they are evenly and well browned.

Sprinkle with one-half tablespoon of flour; set to cook for a moment, and then moisten with one-half glassful of white wine and one-half pint of consommé; season with a pinch of pepper; boil, and leave to cook gently for seven or eight minutes.

The flour may be dispensed with, but, in this case, the white wine is reduced to two-thirds, one-half pint of half-*glaze* (23) is added, and the whole is cooked for seven or eight minutes.

Cut the roast or cooked beef into very thin slices, and lay these on a dish.

A minute before serving, add a few drops of vinegar to the onions; cover the meat with the onions and the sauce; stand the dish for a moment on the side of the fire, and sprinkle it slightly with chopped parsley.

N.B.—When the *miroton* is prepared with boiled beef, the slices should be cut somewhat more thickly, and left to simmer gently in the sauce for as long as possible—an hour or more if necessary.

The *miroton* is then served with some minced gherkins, sprinkled with *raspings*, and placed in the oven at the last moment for the *gratin* to form.

1177—HUNGARIAN BEEF GOULASH   *Goulash de Boeuf à la Hongroise*

Cut three lbs. of ribs or shoulder of beef into squares weighing about three oz. each. Fry these pieces on a moderate fire in four oz. of lard, together with one-half lb. of onions cut into large dice, until they acquire a nice, even, golden brown. Season with one-third oz. of salt and the necessary quantity of paprika; add one and one-quarter lbs. of peeled, pressed, and quartered tomatoes, and one-sixth pint of water.

Cover and cook in the oven for one and one-half hours.

This done, add one-third pint of water and one and one-quarter lbs. of quartered potatoes to the Goulash.

Continue the cooking in the oven, basting often, and do not stop until the liquid is entirely reduced. When about to serve, dish up the Goulash in an earthenware *timbale*.

1178—BEEF HASH AMERICAN STYLE   *Hachis de Boeuf à l'Americaine*

Cut the meat into small cubes.

Also cut into dice the same weight of potatoes as of meat.

Season these potatoes and toss them in butter.

This done, put half of them into a saucepan with the meat dice, and combine the whole with a few tablespoons of tomato sauce (29) and reduced veal gravy (42). Heat without allowing to boil; serve in a silver dish; distribute the remainder of the potatoes, which should be crisply fried, over the hash, and sprinkle with a pinch of freshly-chopped parsley.

1179—BEEF HASH PARMENTIER   *Hachis de Boeuf Parmentier*

Bake some fine potatoes in the oven.

The moment they are done, slice off a piece of their shell, and remove the pulp from the inside with a spoon.

Crush this pulp with a fork, and toss it in butter as for "Potatoes Macaire." Then add to it as much beef in dice as there is pulp; two tablespoons of chopped onion cooked in butter per lb. of the mixture; a pinch of chopped parsley, and a few drops of vinegar. Now toss the whole together for a few minutes, and then fill the empty potato shells with it.

Sprinkle with Lyonnaise sauce (43) rubbed through a fine sieve, and add as much as the hash will absorb.

Replace the portion of shell cut off so that the potatoes may seem whole; arrange them on a dish, and put the latter in the oven for ten minutes. When about to serve, serve the stuffed potatoes on a napkin.

1180—TRIPE CAEN STYLE   *Tripes à la Mode de Caen*

In the preparation of this culinary specialty of Normandy, a very common mistake is often made; namely, that of using calves feet instead of those of the ox, an innovation to which there are many objections.

In the first place, the gravy of the tripe cannot absorb so much gelatine, and is improperly thickened in consequence; secondly, since calves' feet are much more tender than those of the ox, the former get boiled to shreds before the cooking of the tripe has been properly finished. This supposed improvement on the old method is thus seen to actually run counter to the end in view; but methods there are, nevertheless, whereby those who insist upon the use of calves' feet may be satisfied. It is only necessary to *braise* a number of calves' feet beforehand, the number being in proportion to the quantity of tripe, and to add these to the latter a quarter of an hour before serving.

Another mistake which persists somewhat widely in respect of this dish is the serving of it in a silver utensil—a method quite as unreasonable as that of serving a Chaud-froid in an earthenware dish.

By virtue of its simplicity, tripe should be served in special *earthenware saucepans,* where the heat is best retained; and the cook should rather direct his attention to the serving of tripe as hot as possible, than to this or that fanciful method of dishing it up, which really has no reason for being in this case.

The Preparation of Tripe.—Under the head of "beef tripe" are understood: (1) The feet; (2) tripe proper, which comprises the Paunch (first stomach), the Honey-comb Bag (second stomach), the Manyplies (third stomach), and the Reed (real stomach).

First soak the tripe in cold water for some considerable time; then cut it into two inch squares.

For the seasoning and flavoring of whole tripe, complete in all its parts, take: (Seasoning) one-quarter oz. of salt and a pinch of pepper per lb.; (flavoring) four lbs. of onions stuck with four cloves; three lbs. of carrots; one herb bunch, comprising two lbs. of leeks, one-third lb. of parsley stalks, a sprig of thyme, and a bay leaf.

Moisten with two quarts of good cider (not likely to turn black while cooking, otherwise use water); one-half pint of apple brandy or liqueur-cider.

The quantity of the liquid largely depends upon the shape of the utensil; a little less will be needed in the case of a narrow one, and a little more in the case of a wide one.

In any case, however, the tripe should be just covered.

Treatment and Cooking-process.—Take a saucepan or pot, just large enough to hold the tripe and the garnish.

On the bottom of this lay carrots, onions, seasoning, and the four ox feet, bound and cut into fair-sized pieces.

Add the tripe, placing the herb bunch in its midst; upon the tripe lay the bones of the feet, cracked lengthwise; some slices of beef-fat, well soaked in cold water; and, finally, the liquid.

Cover the whole with a round cover of paste, consisting of flour mixed with hot water and kept somewhat stiff, and press down the paste well on to the edges of the pot.

Place in the oven, and, when about two hours have elapsed and the paste is well baked, close the utensil with its own cover.

In a regular and moderate oven, allow about ten hours for the cooking.

The Dishing and Serving.—After taking the tripe out of the oven, remove the cover of paste, the bones, the fat, the carrots, the onions, and the herb bunch, and by means of a draining spoon remove the pieces of tripe and lay them in the special earthenware bowls, taking care to distribute the pieces, coming from different portions of tripe, in such a way as to meet the demands or fancies of the various diners.

When the tripe has been transferred to the bowls, clear the gravy of all grease, and dole it out evenly among the number of receptacles. It is best, now, to put the latter in a *bain-marie* (water-bath), for they must only be served quite hot.

N.B.—To make the dish to perfection, the tripe should be put into special earthenware pots (wherein the heat is more effectively concentrated), and cooked in a baker's or pastry-cook's oven.

I dealt with the alternative of cooking tripe in a saucepan in order to make provision for those who can avail themselves of neither special pots nor a baker's oven.

The measures I prescribe, namely, those of first laying the slices of beef-suet upon the tripe, and then covering the whole with a lid of paste, are intended to stop a too rapid evaporation of the liquid— a possibility that must be guarded against, more particularly in a kitchen oven—and to preserve the whiteness of the tripe.

The cover of paste would be quite useless if a baker's oven were available, for the latter not only ensures perfectly regular heat, but also slows down.

2. VEAL

With the exception of veal sweetbreads, it cannot be denied that this meat is considerably less popular in America and England than abroad, nor does it ever seem to appear on important menus in this country.

It is difficult to state whether the unpopularity of veal in the United States causes the quality of veal to be, on the whole, inferior to European veal or whether the lack of care and attention to veal causes the unpopularity. For it is inconceivable that a country so famous for cattle-raising as the United States undoubtedly is could not produce veal equal in quality to its beef, mutton, and pork, if cattle breeders thought it worth their while to perfect that special branch of their business. I not only refer to the larger joints, but to those odd parts such as the head. the liver, the sweetbreads, etc., the continental quality of which is likewise very superior to that of the American product.

1181—LOINS OF VEAL   *Selle de Veau (Relevé)*

Loins of veal are the only *Relevé* of this meat which is sometimes allowed to appear on an important menu, and it is, in fact, a splendid and succulent joint if the two loins are left together.

(The reference to the loins in the following recipes really means the entire loin, both sides, or the saddle.—Ed.)

It may be roasted, but I should urge the adoption of the *braising* treatment, not only as a precaution against dryness, but because of the fine stock yielded by the cooking.

Whatever be the method, trim the loin on one side, flush with the bones of the pelvis, and up to the first ribs on the other side. Then cut out the kidneys, leaving a thick layer of fat on the tenderloin; pare the flank on either side, in such a way that what is left of it, when drawn under the loin on either side, may just cover the tenderloin above referred to. This flank should only be drawn over the tenderloin after the inside of the joint has been salted; then cover the top surface of the joint with slices of bacon, and tie it round with string, five or six times, that the bacon and the flank may not shift.

When the loin roast is intended for only a small number of people, half of it may be used at a time; that is to say, one tenderloin, in which case the joint may be cut in two, lengthwise.

The procedure for *braising* this piece is in keeping with the directions given under "The Braising of White Meats" (248).

The process of *braising*, whether it pertain to the loins or other veal *Relevés*, such as the round, the shoulder, the breast, etc., de-

mands particular care, must be frequently based, and should always
be done with very little liquid.

1182—LOINS OF VEAL A LA CHARTREUSE

Selle de Veau à la Chartreuse

Braise the loins, and *glaze* it at the last moment, after having
removed the slices of bacon. Set it on a long platter, and, at each
end of it, place a *chartreuse* of vegetables.

Around the joint put a few tablespoons of the *braising*-liquor,
cleared of all grease, reduced, and well-strained; and serve what
remains in a sauceboat.

Chartreuses of Vegetables.—Take two dome or *Charlotte-moulds*,
capable of holding two-thirds of a quart. Butter them liberally; line
them with buttered or vegetable paper, and on the latter, over the
bottom and sides of the utensil, lay carrots, turnips, peas, and string
beans; each of which vegetables should be cooked in a way suited to
its nature. This operation, which is somewhat tedious, may either
be done on the style of a checkerboard, or the different vegetables
may be superimposed in alternate rows of varying colors.

When the moulds are garnished in this way, spread, over the
vegetables, a layer of *forcemeat* softened with beaten white of egg;
the object of this is to keep the vegetable decoration in position, and
this is done by the *poaching* of the *forcemeat* before the *chartreuse*
is filled with its filling.

This finished, fill the moulds to within one-third inch of their
brims with a *Macédoine* of vegetables combined with a stiff Béchamel (28) and cream, and cover with a layer of *forcemeat*.

Set these *chartreuses* to *poach* thirty-five minutes before serving,
and take care to let them set for five minutes before unmoulding
them on either side of the loins.

1183—LOINS OF VEAL A LA METTERNICH

Selle de Veau à la Metternich

Braise the loins, and, when it is ready, put it on a dish. Now draw
a line within one-half inch of its extreme edge on either side and
end, pressing the point of a small knife along the meat in so doing.

Proceed in the same way on either side of the backbone, and remove the tenderloins from the joint, severing them from the bone
with care.

Cut the tenderloins into regular slices, keeping the knife somewhat at a slant.

In the double cavity left by the tenderloins spread a few table-spoons of Béchamel (28) with paprika; return the tenderloin slices to their respective places in the joint, reconstructing them in such a way as to make them appear untouched; and between the slices pour one-half tablespoon of Béchamel (28) and lay two slices of truffle.

This done, cover the whole surface of the joint with the Béchamel sauce with paprika, and set to *glaze* quickly at the *salamander*. Now, with a large spatula, carefully transfer the loins to a dish.

Serve separately the *braising*-liquor of the loins, cleared of all grease and reduced; and a *timbale* of pilaff rice (2255).

1184—LOINS OF VEAL A LA NELSON   *Selle de Veau à la Nelson*

Braise the loins. When it is ready, remove the tenderloin, pro-ceeding exactly as described under "Selle à la Metternich" (1183), and cut the tenderloin in a similar manner.

In the cavity left by the tenderloin spread a few tablespoons of Soubise (104); return the sliced tenderloin to their place, and, be-tween the slices, place a thin slice of ham, of the same size and shape as the next piece of meat, and a little Soubise sauce.

Having reconstructed the joint, cover its surface with a layer, about one inch thick, of "Soufflé au Parmesan" (2259a), combined with one quart of truffle *purée*.

Bind the joint with a strong band of buttered paper, for the purpose of holding in the *soufflé,* and set it to cook in a moderate oven for fifteen minutes. After having taken the loins out of the oven, remove the paper band, and send it to the table without changing the dish.

Send the *braising*-liquor, cleared of all grease, reduced and strained, to the table separately.

1185—LOINS OF VEAL ORIENTAL STYLE   *Selle de Veau à l'Orientale*

Braise the loins; remove the tenderloins, and cut them into slices as for "Selle à la Metternich" (1183). Fill the cavities with Soubise sauce with curry (104); reconstruct the tenderloins, putting a little of the same sauce between the slices, and coat the surface of the whole with the sauce already referred to.

Surround the joint with *braised* celery, and serve its cooking liquor and a *timbale* of pilaff rice (2255) separately.

1186—LOINS OF VEAL PIEDMONT STYLE

Selle de Veau à la Piémontaise

Braise the loins, and cut the tenderloins into slices as before. When reconstructing the tenderloins, between the slices put a little Béchamel sauce (28), combined with three and one-half oz. of grated Parmesan cheese and three and one-half oz. of grated white truffles per quart of the sauce.

Coat the surface of the joint with the same sauce, and set to *glaze* quickly.

Serve the *braising*-liquor, cleared of all grease and strained, separately; as also a *timbale* of *rizotto* à la Piémontaise (2258).

1187—LOINS OF VEAL PRINCE ORLOFF   *Selle de Veau Prince Orloff*

Braise the loins and proceed as above, placing between the slices of tenderloin a little Soubise sauce (104) and a fine slice of truffle.

Coat the surface of the joint with Mornay sauce (91), combined with one quart of highly-seasoned Soubise, and set to *glaze* quickly.

N.B.—The loins may be accompanied either by a garnish of asparagus tips or by cucumbers with cream.

1188—LOINS OF VEAL A LA ROMANOFF

Selle de Veau à la Romanoff

Braise the loins; remove the tenderloin, and cut the latter into slices as for "Selle à la Metternich" (1183). Reconstruct the tenderloin, placing a small quantity of minced mushrooms, mixed with a few tablespoons of cream, between the slices, and coat the surface of the joint with highly-seasoned Béchamel sauce (28), finished with four oz. of crayfish butter (147) per quart.

Surround the piece with a border of *braised* half-finocchios. Serve the *braising*-liquor, cleared of all grease, reduced and strained, separately.

1189—LOINS OF VEAL A LA TOSCA   *Selle de Veau à la Tosca*

Braise the loins, and then prepare it as for (1183). Almost completely fill the cavities left by the tenderloins with a garnish of macaroni, cut into short lengths, mixed with cream, and combined with a *julienne* of truffles.

Reconstruct the tenderloin upon this garnish and coat the slices with Mornay sauce (91), placing a slice of truffle between the slices. The reconstructed tenderloins thus appear raised on either side of the backbone.

Coat the surface of the joint with the same sauce as that already used, and set to *glaze* quickly. Send the *braising*-liquor, cleared of all grease and strained, to the table separately.

1190—LOINS OF VEAL A LA RENAISSANCE
Selle de Veau à la Renaissance

Braise the loins, and *glaze* it at the last moment. Put it on a dish and surround it with a large heap of cauliflower at either end; on either side, nice heaps of carrots and turnips, cut by means of an oval, grooved ball-cutter, cooked in consommé and *glazed;* peas; string beans cut in one-half inch lengths; asparagus tips mixed with butter; and some small potatoes cooked in butter.

Send the *braising*-liquor of the joint, cleared of grease and strained, separately.

1191—LOINS OF VEAL A LA TALLEYRAND
Selle de Veau à la Talleyrand

Prepare twenty pieces of truffle, about one inch long and one-third oz. in weight. Stick them upright and symmetrically into the meat of the joint, making for them little incisions cut with a small knife. Now wrap the joint in slices of *larding* bacon, tie it, *braise* it, and *glaze* it at the last moment.

Serve it with some of its *braising*-liquor, cleared of all grease and reduced.

Serve separately what remains of the *braising*-liquor; and a garnish of macaroni, cut into half-inch lengths, mixed with one and one-half oz. of butter, three oz. of grated Gruyère and Parmesan cheese, combined with three oz. of *foie gras*, cut into large dice, and three oz. of a *julienne* of truffles, per lb. of macaroni.

1192—COLD LOINS OF VEAL
Selle de Veau Froide

Cold loin of veal makes an excellent buffet dish which permits all cold-dish garnishes, such as *Macédoines* of vegetables combined with jelly or mayonnaise sauce; artichoke-bottoms and tomatoes, variously garnished; small, moulded vegetable salads, etc.

Decorate it with fine, regular, aspic-jelly dice; but its usual and essential accompaniment is its own *braising*-liquor, cooked, cleared of grease poured carefully away, and served in a sauceboat without having been either clarified or cleared.

All the pieces of veal given as *Relevés,* the kidney roast, the tenderloin, and the *fricandeau* or round, may be served cold like the loins, and are generally much appreciated, more particularly in summer.

1193—LOINS OF VEAL (KIDNEY ROAST)   *Selle de Veau*
1194—NECK AND BREAST OF VEAL   *Poitrine et Tendrons de Veau*
1195—VEAL RIB ROAST   *Côte de Veau*
1196—RUMP OR ROUND STEAK OF VEAL   *Fricandeau*
1197—RUMP OR ROUND ROAST OF VEAL   *Noix de Veau*

I have grouped these various *Relevés* together owing to their same garnishes.

The directions I give for round roast of veal are, with a very few exceptions which I shall point out, applicable to all other large veal joints. In the circumstances, therefore, it would be quite unnecessary to repeat the recipe in each case.

Kidney Roast or *Loin of Veal* is that piece which corresponds with the sirloin in beef. It extends from the floating ribs to the extreme end of the haunch, the latter being cut flush with the pelvic bone at its junction with the thigh bone, and following the direction of the former bone. The loin thus consists of two distinct parts:— the tail region (called the rump or round end), which comprises the bones of the pelvis and the haunch, up to the level of the latter, and is one of the best pieces of veal for *braising;* and the region extending from the rump to the floating ribs, comprising the tenderloin and the loins. This last portion called kidney roast also constitutes a choice joint, to which the kidneys are generally left attached. after all their superfluous fat has been removed.

Veal rib roast consists of the first eight or nine ribs, cut two inches above the kernel "noix" of meat. The ends of the rib-bones are cleared of meat about two-thirds of an inch, and the bare bone is then called the "handle" of the chop, which ultimately holds the ornamental frill of paper.

The backbone is then cut away, so that the bones of the ribs alone remain; the yellow ligament is removed; and the bared parts are covered with slices of bacon, tied on by means of string.

Rump or *Fricandeau of Veal* consists of an enormous muscle, which represents almost half of the haunch or leg and all the inside part of it, from the pelvis to its junction with the inner bone. A certain quantity of white fat will always be found to lie over the rump, and it should be carefully reserved.

If the rump roast is to be *larded,* a procedure which I do not advise, it should be done on the bared part adjoining the fat-covered region.

The various pieces of veal named above may be roasted, but, as in the case of the loins, I prefer *braising,* owing to the greater succulence of the dish resulting from this process, and its accompanying gravy, which has an incomparable flavor. (See Braising of White Meats, 248.)

1198—ACCOMPANIMENTS TO ROUND ROAST OR RUMP OF VEAL

Rump or round roast of veal, like the other large pieces of veal, permit an almost unlimited number of vegetable garnishes, simple or compound, as also garnishes of various pastes.

From among these garnishes the following may be quoted:—Bouquetière, Bourgeoise, Chartreuse, Choisy, Chicorée, Cardoons, Clamart, Braised Celery, Japanese Artichokes, Chayotes, Endives, Spinach, Braised Lettuce, à la Vichy, à la Nemours, etc.; Jardinière, Macédoine, Renaissance, etc.

Among the paste garnishes:—Noodles, Macaroni, Spaghetti, variously prepared; various Gnocchi, dumplings, etc.

And, in addition to all these, the garnishes already given under Beef *Relevés,* which need not be repeated here.

I shall, therefore, give only three recipes which are proper to the round roast of veal; though even these should be regarded as mere curiosities, seeing that, far from recommending them, I consider them rather as gastronomical mistakes. But some provision must be made for outlandish tastes, and, for this reason alone, I include the following recipes.

1199—RUMP OR ROUND ROAST OF VEAL EN SURPRISE

Noix de Veau en Surprise

Braise the round roast of veal, keeping it somewhat firm. This done, set it on a dish, and let it almost cool.

Then cut a slice across it, at a point one-third inch of its height from the top; and, within one-half inch of its edges, make a circular incision, pressing the point of a sharp knife into the meat, and remove the center of the roast. Take care to leave the same thickness of meat on the sides as on the bottom, that is to say, about one-half inch. The round roast of veal, thus emptied, should have the appearance of a round or oval mould.

If the meat taken from the center of the round roast is to serve for the garnish, or is to be used sliced to surround the case or mould, cut the parts to be removed in the largest possible pieces, so that slices may easily be cut from these.

The inside of the emptied round roast of veal is then garnished according to fancy; the top of the piece that was cut off at the start is returned, with the view of giving the piece an untouched appearance, and the whole is put in the oven for a few minutes that it may be hot for serving.

The *braising*-liquor, cleared of grease and strained, should be sent to the table separately.

1200—RUMP OR ROUND ROAST OF VEAL EN SURPRISE A LA
MACEDOINE   *Noix de Veau en Surprise à la Macédoine*

Braise the rump or round roast of veal, and hollow it out as explained above.

Meanwhile prepare a *Macédoine* garnish, or mixed *Jardinière* (combined with butter or cream), the quantity of which should be in proportion to the size of the case; cut the meat, taken from the center of the round roast, into thin rectangles.

Garnish the bottom of the roast with a layer of *Macédoine,* and put over this a layer of the rectangles of meat. Cover with *Macédoine;* spread over this another layer of the pieces of meat, and repeat the operation until the hollowed out roast is filled. Finish up with a layer of *Macédoine.*

Replace the slice cut from the roast at the start; put the whole in the oven for a few minutes; serve, and send the *braising*-liquor separately.

1201—RUMP OR ROUND ROAST OF VEAL EN SURPRISE A LA
PITHIVIERS   *Noix de Veau en Surprise à la Pithiviers*

Braise the round roast of veal, and prepare the roast as directed above.

Stuff fifteen larks without boning them; that is to say, put some stuffing about the size of a hazel-nut into each. Fry them in butter with one-half lb. of mushrooms and three oz. of truffles, each vegetable should be raw and minced. Combine the whole with the necessary quantity of half-*glazed* sauce (23), flavored with game *essence;* put this filling in the case; return the sliced piece to its place; seal the cover to the case by means of a band of almost liquid *forcemeat,* and set in the oven for seven or eight minutes.

When taking the roast out of the oven, surround with the removed meat, which should have been cut into thin slices and kept warm until required.

The larks may be replaced by quails or thrushes, or other small birds, but the name of the particular bird used must be referred to in the title of the dish.

1202—RUMP OR ROUND ROAST OF VEAL EN SURPRISE TOULOUSE
STYLE   *Noix de Veau en Surprise à la Toulousaine*

Braise the round roast and cut it to the shape of a case as explained above. Pour in a filling consisting of *quenelles* of chicken *forcemeat;* lamb sweetbreads, or slices of veal sweetbreads, *braised* without browning; cocks' combs; small mushrooms, cooked and very white; and slices of truffle; the whole to be combined by means of an Allemande sauce (27), flavored with mushroom *essence.*

Return the meat sliced off at the start to its place, and surround with slices of the meat taken from the inside of the round of veal.

N.B.—All the fillings suited to Vol-au-vent (2390) and *timbales* may be served with round roast of veal case, which stands instead of the Vol-au-vent and *timbale* crusts.

Finally, I must ask the reader to bear in mind that methods like those described above have no place in really good cookery, the ruling principle of which should always be simplicity.

1203—COLD RUMP OR ROUND ROAST OF VEAL CAUCASIAN STYLE
Noix de Veau Froide a la Caucasienne

Cut a cold round roast of veal into slices two inches long by one-half inch wide by one-sixth inch thick.

On each slice spread a little butter seasoned with salt and pepper, combined with finely-chopped chives and anchovy fillets cut into dice.

Put the slices together as for sandwiches; round off their edges and put them under a light weight. Prepare a *purée* of tomatoes with aspic-jelly; mould it in a *dome* or *Bombe-mould,* and let it set on ice.

When this moulding of tomatoes is quite firm, turn it out in the middle of a round, cold dish; arrange the meat slices all round, and border the dish with cubes of very clear veal jelly (158).

1204—COLD RUMP OR ROUND ROAST OF VEAL SWEDISH STYLE
Noix de Veau Froide à la Suédoise

From the widest part of a cold round roast of veal, cut a slice across one and one-third inch thick, and trim it nicely round.

Then let a coating of aspic jelly set on the bottom of a round dish, and upon this jelly, when it is quite firm, lay the slice of veal.

Cut what remains of the piece of veal into slices two inches long, by one and one-half inch broad, by one-eighth inch thick. Prepare the same number of rectangles of smoked tongue, of the same size, though slightly thinner than those of veal.

Mix a nice vegetable salad with cleared mayonnaise; mould it in an oiled, *Bombe-shaped* or narrow *pyramid* mould, and put it on ice to set.

Coat the rectangles of veal with horse-radish butter (290); place a rectangle of tongue on each, and finish off these sandwiches by rounding their corners.

For Serving.—By means of a pastry-bag fitted with a fluted tube, garnish the edges of the slices of veal with a ribbon of previously softened butter.

Turn out the vegetable salad in the center of the piece of meat; set on it the heart of a small lettuce (nicely opened), and arrange the veal and tongue sandwiches all round.

Serve a cold sauce, made from the mayonnaise, separately.

1205—COLD TENDERLOIN, CROWN, RUMP OR ROUND ROAST OF VEAL   *Longes, Carrés, et Noix de Veau Froids*

What was said in respect of cold loins of veal likewise applies to the different pieces mentioned in the above. They may be coated with aspic jelly and served with *Macédoines* of vegetables, combined with jelly; small salads, mixed with cleared mayonnaise; garnished artichoke-bottoms, etc.

The dishes should always be bordered with chopped clear aspic. jelly.

1206—RUMP STEAK OF VEAL   *Frincandeau (Relevé)*

Fricandeau is a lateral cut across from the rump or round of veal; that is to say, a piece cut with the grain of the meat. It should not be thicker than one and one-half inches.

After beating it with the flat side of a cleaver, to break the fibres of the meat, finely *lard* the piece of meat on the cut side with strips of bacon, somewhat smaller than those used for tenderloin of beef. Only when the piece is *larded* may it be called *"Fricandeau"*; for, when not thus treated, it is nothing else than an ordinary piece of veal. *Fricandeau* is invariably *braised;* but it differs from other *braisings* of white meat in this respect, namely, that it must be so cooked as to be easily cut with a spoon. Connoisseurs maintain that *Fricandeau* should never be touched with a knife.

It is *glazed* at the last moment, like other *braisings,* and, in view of its prolonged cooking, should be served with great care.

All the garnishes enumerated for round roast of veal may be adapted to *Fricandeau*.

1207—COLD RUMP STEAK OF VEAL Fricandeau Froid

Cold *fricandeau* constitutes an excellent luncheon dish. It is served and surrounded with its *braising*-liquor, cleared of grease and strained. This *braising*-liquor sets to a jelly, and is the finest accompaniment to *fricandeau* that could be found.

The piece may be *glazed* with half-melted jelly, coating it with a brush.

1208—STUFFED BREAST OF VEAL Poitrine de Veau Farcie

This is really a family dish, admirably suited for a luncheon *relevé*. It is accompanied chiefly by vegetable *purées,* but all the vegetables and other garnishes given under rump or round roast of veal may be served with it.

Breast of veal is prepared thus:—After having boned it, open it where it is thickest, without touching the ends. A kind of pocket is thus made, into which put the previously-prepared stuffing, taking care to spread it very evenly.

Now, with coarse thread, sew up the opening, and remember to withdraw the thread when the veal is cooked.

Stuffing for Breast of Veal.—For a piece weighing four lbs., add to one lb. of very fine sausage-meat (196), two oz. of dry *duxelles,* two oz. of butter, a pinch of chopped parsley, tarragon and chives, a small beaten egg, and a little salt and pepper.

Cooking.—Breast of veal is usually *braised;* the moistening should be short and the cooking process gentle. For a piece weighing four lbs. when stuffed, allow three hours in a moderate and regular oven. *Glaze* the breast of veal at the last moment, as in the case of other *braised* meats.

1209—CALF'S HEAD Tête de Veau (Relevé et Entrée)

Nowadays, calf's head is rarely served whole, as was the custom formerly. Still more rarely, however, is it served at a dinner of any importance; and it has now, by almost general consent, been relegated to luncheon menus where, indeed, it has found its proper place.

After having boned the head, soak it or hold it under running water, for a sufficiently long enough time to permit of its being entirely cleared of blood. Then *blanch* it for a good half-hour; cool it in cold water; drain it, and rub it with a piece of lemon to avoid its blackening.

If it is to be cooked whole, as sometimes happens, wrap it in a napkin, that it may be easily handled; if not, cut it into pieces. In either case, plunge it immediately into a boiling *blanc* (167).

With a view of keeping the calf's head from contact with the air, which would blacken it, cover it with a napkin, or cover the liquid with chopped suet. A layer of chopped suet is the best possible means of keeping the air from the calf's head.

Whatever the method of serving calf's head, it is the rule to send slices of tongue and slices of brain to the table with it.

The tongue may be cooked simultaneously with the head, and the brain is *poached* as described under (1289).

1210—CALF'S HEAD A L'ANGLAISE   *Tête de Veau à l'Anglaise*

Calf's head *à l'anglaise* is cooked in a *blanc,* as explained above; but in halves and unboned.

Put it on a napkin with sprays of very green parsley and a piece of boiled bacon.

Send a sauceboat of parsley sauce (119a) to the table at the same time.

1211—CALF'S HEAD A LA FINANCIERE   *Tête de Veau à la Financière*

Cook the calf's head in a *blanc* as already directed. Remove portions of the meat, where the latter is thick, in such a way as to leave only a very little on the skin.

Cut the pieces into squares of one, two or three inches; and put them in a *timbale,* and cover them with a financière garnish (1052); adding a few slices of tongue and brain.

1212—CALF'S HEAD A LA POULETTE   *Tête de Veau à la Poulette*

Cook the calf's head in a *blanc* (167).

Cut the pieces of the head into small slices, somewhat slantwise, and toss them into a previously-prepared poulette sauce (101).

Serve in a *timbale,* and sprinkle with a pinch of chopped parsley.

1213—CALF'S HEAD EN TORTUE   *Tête de Veau en Tortue*

With a round cutter one, two, or three in. in diameter, cut up the pieces of calf's head, the meat of which must be entirely removed. For this preparation, only the skin of the head should be used.

Put the pieces of head in a *timbale* or on a dish, and cover them with a Tortue garnish.

Tortue garnish consists of: Small *quenelles* of veal *forcemeat* with butter; cocks' combs and kidneys; small mushrooms; pitted, stuffed and *poached* olives; slices of truffle; gherkins cut to the shape of olives (these should only be put into the sauce at the last moment); and Tortue sauce (56).

This garnish comprises, besides, among unsauced ingredients: Slices of tongue and calf's brain; small, trussed crayfish, cooked in *court-bouillon;* fried eggs, the half of whose raw whites should be removed; and small *croûtons* of bread, fried in butter at the last moment.

1214—CALF'S HEAD WITH VINAIGRETTE OR OIL SAUCE
Tête de Veau à la Vinaigrette où à l'Huile

Set the boiled pieces of calf's head on a napkin, lying on a dish. Surround them with slices of tongue, slices of brain, and sprigs of very green, curley-leaf parsley.

Serve separately, on an hors-d'œuvre dish, without mixing them, capers, chopped onion and parsley.

Send to the table at the same time a sauceboat of vinaigrette or sauce à l'huile, prepared by mixing one part of vinegar, two parts of oil, and one part of the calf's-head cooking-liquor, together with the necessary salt and pepper.

1215—VEAL CUTLETS   *Escalopes de Veau*

Cutlets of veal may be cut from either the tenderloin or the loin; but they are more often cut from the rump. Their weight varies from three to four oz., and they should always be cleared of all connective tissue. They may be fashioned to the shape of ovals, or triangles, and they should be more or less flattened out, according to their use. Thus, when they are to be plainly *sautéd,* to be afterwards served with a sauced garnish or with a sauce, they are beaten in order to break the fibers of the meat, without flattening too much; but if, on the contrary, they are to be treated *à l'anglaise,* they should be beaten very thin with the moistened meat mallet.

In either case, they should be cooked somewhat quickly in clarified butter (175); for, if their cooking slowed up, the meat hardens.

All the garnishes of veal chops, and a large number of those of the round, may be served with hese pieces. These garnishes may be set on the same dish with the slices when the latter are plainly cooked; but, in the case of cutlets treated *à l'anglaise,* the garnish or sauce which accompanies them should be served separately, lest its moisture soften the crisp coating of the cutlets.

1216—GRENADINS OF VEAL *Grenadins*

Grenadins are small veal cutlets larded with rows of very thin bacon strips, and cut somewhat thicker than ordinary pieces. They are really small *fricandeaux*, the *braising* of which is a comparatively lengthy operation; for their cooking must be the same as that of the *fricandeaux*, and needs quite as much attention. In order that the *grenadins* be not too dry, they should be frequently basted with their *braising*-liquor.

When they are cooked, *glaze* them rapidly, and serve them with one of the garnishes given for the round roast of veal.

1217—COLD GRENADINS EN BELLEVUE *Grenadins Froids en Bellevue*

This dish may be prepared in several more or less complicated ways; here is a simple way:—

Take as many shell-shaped hors-d'œuvre dishes as there are *grenadins*. Let a thin coat of jelly set on the bottom of each, and set on a slight decoration composed of bits of carrot, turnip, peas, string beans in diamond shapes, etc. Put a *grenadin, larded,* upside down into each hors-d'œuvre dish; add enough melted aspic jelly to reach half-way up the thickness of the *grenadin*.

When this aspic-jelly has set, lay on it, all round the *grenadin,* a border consisting of carrots, turnips, string beans and peas. Sprinkle these vegetables with a few drops of jelly, so as to fix them, and keep them from floating, and then fill up the hors-d'œuvre dishes with jelly.

When about to serve, dip the hors-d'œuvre dishes into hot water; turn out the *grenadins* on a very cold dish, and arrange them on it to form a crown.

Surround with a border of very clear, chopped aspic jelly.

1218—VEAL SWEETBREADS *Ris de Veau*

Veal sweetbreads may be looked upon as one of the greatest delicacies in meats, and may be served at any dinner, however sumptuous. Select them very white, entirely free of blood stains, and leave them to soak in fresh water, which should be frequently changed, for as long as possible; or, better still, place them under the running water.

To *blanch* them (an operation the purpose of which is to harden the surface) put them in a saucepan with enough cold water to cover them completely, and bring to the boil gently. Let them boil for ten minutes; take them out and plunge them into a bowl of fresh water.

When the sweetbreads are cold, trim them; that is to say, cut away all cartilage and connective tissue; lay them between two pieces of cloth, and put them under a light weight for two hours.

Now *lard* them with fine bacon, tongue or truffles, subject to the way in which they are to be served. They may also be *studded* with either tongue or truffles, or they may be left *unlarded* and *unstudded,* and plainly *braised,* just as they are.

Certain it is, that neither *studding* nor *larding* helps in any way whatsoever their appetizing quality.

Veal sweetbread consists of two parts, as unequal in quality as in shape. They are: the *"kernel"* or heart sweetbread, which is the round and most delicate part, and the *"throat,"* or throat sweetbread, which is the elongated part, and not of such fine quality as the former.

There are three ways of cooking sweetbreads:—*Braising* (248), *poaching* (249), and grilling (259). In the following recipes, therefore, the reader will kindly refer to the directions given under one of the numbers just mentioned, according as to whether the dish is to be a *braising,* a *poaching,* or a grill.

1219—SKEWERS OF VEAL SWEETBREADS VILLEROY

Atteraux de Ris de Veau à la Villeroy

Cut some veal sweetbreads (preferably the throat kind) into slices one and one-third in. in diameter and one-third in. thick. Prepare an equal number of mushrooms and truffle slices, somewhat thinner than those of sweetbread.

Stick these slices on little metal skewers about four in. long; alternating the different foods in so doing. Dip these skewers into a Villeroy sauce (108), and set them on a dish. When the sauce is quite cold, remove the attereaux or skewered sweetbreads; clear them of any superfluous sauce that may have fallen on to the dish; dip them in an *anglaise* (174); roll them in very fine and fresh breadcrumbs, and turn them with the fingers, so as to shape them like small cylinders. Plunge them into plenty of hot fat eight minutes before serving; drain them on a piece of linen or paper. Serve the attereaux or skewered sweetbreads on a folded napkin, with fried parsley in the center; or set them upright in a circle, on a rice or semolina bed lying on a dish, and put some very green, fried parsley in the middle.

Serve a Périgueux sauce (47) separately.

1220—VEAL SWEETBREADS CHARTREUSE

Chartreuse de Ris de Veau

Prepare one and one-quarter lbs. of fine *forcemeat* with cream (194); two *poached,* veal sweetbreads, cut into slices; one-half lb. of cooked mushrooms, cut into large slices, and three oz. of sliced truffles; a garnish of carrots and turnips, cut with a ball spoon-cutter, or cut into grooved slices two-thirds inch in diameter; and peas and string beans. Each of these vegetables should be cooked in a way befitting its nature, and kept somewhat firm.

Liberally butter a quart *Charlotte-mould.* Line its bottom and sides with the vegetables, arranged in alternate and varicolored rows, and spread on a layer of *forcemeat,* one-half inch thick.

This done, set upon the layer of *forcemeat* just spread, another of slices of sweetbread, mushrooms, and truffles; cover with a coat of *forcemeat;* start the operation again with sweetbread, mushroom, and truffle slices, and proceed as before until the mould is filled. Finish with a layer of *forcemeat.* Cover with a round piece of buttered paper, and set to *poach* in a *bain-marie* (water-bath) and in the oven, for from forty-five to fifty minutes.

When taking the *chartreuse* out of the *bain-marie,* let it stand for seven or eight minutes, that the ingredients inside may settle, and then turn it out in the center of a round dish; place a large, cooked, grooved, and very white mushroom on the top of it, and encircle its base with a crown of small *braised* and well-trimmed lettuce halves.

Send to the table, separately, a sauceboat of Velouté (25) flavored with mushroom *essence.*

1221—VEAL SWEETBREADS BONNE MAMAN

Ris de Veau Bonne Maman

Cut the vegetables intended for the *braising* stock into a short and coarse *julienne,* and add an equal quantity of similarly-cut celery.

Braise the veal sweetbreads with this *julienne,* after the manner described under (248), and moisten with excellent veal stock (10). Take particular care of the vegetables, that they do not burn.

When the sweetbreads are ready, *glaze* them and serve them in a shallow, round *cocotte* with the *julienne* of vegetables and the *braising*-liquor all around.

Cover the *cocotte,* and place it on a folded napkin.

1222—CREPINETTE OF VEAL SWEETBREAD

Crépinette de Ris de Veau

For this dish take either some fine sweetbreads, or some left-over ones, from which slices have already been cut.

Chop up the sweetbreads, together with their weight of uncooked calf's udder.

Season with one-half oz. of salt and a pinch of pepper; add five oz. of chopped truffles and two whole eggs per lb. of the minced-meat. Mix well; divide it up into portions weighing three oz., and wrap each portion in a piece of very soft *pig's caul.*

Sprinkle with melted butter and bread-crumbs, and grill gently.

Arrange in the form of a crown, and serve a Périgueux sauce (47) at the same time.

1223—VEAL SWEETBREADS CEVENOLE   *Ris de Veau à la Cévénole*

Braise the veal sweetbreads and *glaze* them at the last moment.

Serve them with a heap of small *glazed* onions at either end, and serve, at the same time, a *purée* of chestnuts and a sauceboat of thickened gravy.

1224—VEAL SWEETBREADS DEMIDOFF   *Ris de Veau Demidoff*

· *Lard* the sweetbreads with bacon and truffles; *braise* them brown, and only half-cook them. Then place them in a shallow *cocotte,* and surround them with the following garnish:—Two oz. of carrots and the same weight of turnips, both cut in grooved crescents; an equal quantity of small onions, cut in thick slices, and some celery cut *paysanne*-fashion. All these vegetables should be first stewed in butter.

Add the *braising*-liquor of the sweetbreads, and one oz. of minced truffles, and complete the cooking of the former. Clear of all grease and serve in the *cocotte.*

1225—VEAL SWEETBREADS IN SLICES BERENGERE

Escalopes de Ris de Veau Bérengère

Braise the veal sweetbreads and cut each piece into four medium-sized slices. Trim each slice with an even, oval fancy-cutter; and, by means of a pastry-bag fitted with a plain tube, one-sixth inch in diameter, garnish the edge of each slice with a thick border of *mousseline forcemeat,* combined with chopped smoked tongue. Set the slices in a pan, and put them in a moderate oven to *poach* the *forcemeat.*

Now, by means of another pastry-bag fitted with a fancy tube, garnish the center of the slices with a nice rosette of fine and very white Soubise *purée;* and, in the middle of each rosette, place a little ball of very black truffle.

Set each slice on a thin, oval *croûton* of the same size, fried in butter. Serve at the same time, in a sauceboat, the *braising*-liquor of the sweetbreads, cleared of all grease, and a dish of fresh peas.

1226—VEAL SWEETBREADS IN SLICES A LA FAVORITE
Escalopes de Ris de Veau à la Favorite

Blanch the veal sweetbreads; cool them under pressure, and cut them into slices. Season and toss them in clarified butter (175).

At the same time, toss an equal number of slices of *foie gras* of the same size as those of the sweetbread, after having seasoned and dredged them.

Arrange in a circle, alternating the *foie gras* and the sweetbread slices; put a crown of sliced truffle on the circle already arranged; and, in the center, pour a garnish of asparagus tips buttered.

Send, separately, a Madeira sauce (44) flavored with truffle *essence.*

1227—VEAL SWEETBREADS IN SLICES GRAND DUC
Escalopes de Ris de Veau Grand Duc

Blanch and cool the sweetbreads, and cut them into slices. Season and cook them in butter without browning. Arrange them in the form of a crown, placing a large slice of truffle between each; coat with Mornay sauce (91), and *glaze* quickly.

When taking the dish out of the oven, arrange a heap of asparagus tips mixed with butter, in the middle of the dish, and serve at once.

1228—VEAL SWEETBREADS IN SLICES JUDIC
Escalopes de Ris de Veau Judic

Blanch and cool the sweetbreads, and cut them into slices.

Prepare and *poach* a roll of chicken *forcemeat,* large enough to allow slices to be cut from it of the same size as those of the sweet-breads.

Season, dredge, and toss the slices of sweetbread in butter, and arrange them in the form of a crown, each on a slice of the *poached* chicken *forcemeat.*

On each slice place a very small, *braised,* and well-trimmed lettuce, a slice of truffle, and a cock's kidney.

Send a sauceboat of thickened gravy separately.

1229—VEAL SWEETBREADS IN SLICES A LA MARECHALE
Escalopes de Ris de Veau à la Maréchale

Braise the veal sweetbreads, keeping them somewhat firm, and cut them into slices.

Treat the latter *à l'anglaise;* brown them in clarified butter (175), and arrange them in a circle, placing a fine slice of truffle between each.

In the middle of the dish arrange a fine heap of buttered asparagus tips.

1230—BROILED VEAL SWEETBREADS   *Ris de Veau Grillés*

After having *blanched,* cooked, and trimmed the sweetbreads, set them to get quite cold under pressure. Then cut them in two, across, at their thickest point; dip each piece into melted butter, and grill gently, basting frequently with melted butter.

The sweetbreads may also be grilled whole, but the process is a more lengthy one.

1231—BROILED VEAL SWEETBREADS CARMAGO
Ris de Veau Grillés Carmago

Bake a *brioche,* without sugar, in a *fluted mould,* the opening of which is a little larger than the veal sweetbreads. Carefully remove the top of the *brioche,* following the direction of the fluting, and remove all the crumbs from the inside.

Fill this kind of *croustade,* two-thirds full, with a garnish consisting of peas, prepared "à la française" (2193), and carrots "à la Vichy" (2061), in equal quantities.

Set the grilled veal sweetbreads on this garnish, and cover it with slices of grilled bacon.

Place on a napkin and serve at once.

1232—BROILED VEAL SWEETBREADS GISMONDA
Ris de Veau Grillés Gismonda

Prepare a shallow *croustade,* without browning, in an oval dome of the same length as the veal sweetbread. Grill the veal sweetbread after the manner already described.

Garnish the bottom of the *croustade* with equal quantities of artichoke-bottoms and mushrooms, minced raw, tossed in butter, and combined with cream sauce (79).

Set the grilled sweetbread on the garnish, and place the *croustade* on a folded napkin.

Serve, separately, a slightly buttered meat-*glaze* (15).

1233—BROILED VEAL SWEETBREADS JOCELYNE

Ris de Veau Grillés Jocelyne

Cut some potatoes into slices one and one-half inch thick and of the same size as the veal sweetbread. Stamp the slices, close up to their edges, with a round, even cutter, and cook them in butter. Grill the sweetbread at the same time.

When the potatoes are cooked, take out all insides in such a way as to give them the appearance of shells, and fill them with Soubise (105) prepared with curry.

Put on a dish and set the grilled sweetbread upon them. On the sweetbread lay a small half-tomato and a green half-pepper, both grilled.

1234—BROILED VEAL SWEETBREADS ST. GERMAIN

Ris de Veau Grillés Saint-Germain

Blanch, prepare, and grill the veal sweetbreads as already explained. Set them on a long dish, and surround them with alternate heaps of small potatoes cooked in butter and of a nice golden color, and carrots cut to the shape of elongated olives, cooked in consommé and *glazed*.

Serve a Béarnaise sauce (62) and a *purée* of fresh peas, separately.

1235—VEAL SWEETBREADS DES GOURMETS

Ris de Veau des Gourmets

Braise the veal sweetbreads, and, as soon as they are ready, set them in a round, flat *cocotte*, just large enough to hold them. Cover them with raw truffles, cut into thick slices; strain the *braising-*liquor over the whole; cover the *cocotte*, and seal the cover to the edges of the utensil by means of a band of soft paste, made simply from a mixture of flour and water.

The object of this last precaution is to prevent the escape of steam, and to hold the aroma of the truffles within.

Put the *cocotte* into a very hot oven for ten minutes; set it on a dish, and serve it as it stands. The cover should be removed only when the dish reaches the table.

1236—VEAL SWEETBREADS WITH CRAYFISH TAILS

Ris de Veau aux Queues d'Ecrevisses

Stud the sweetbreads with truffles and *braise* them without browning. Place on a dish and, on either side, set a heap of crayfish tails (in the proportion of four to each person), combined with cream.

At either end place some crayfish shells (in the proportion of two to each sweetbread), filled with chicken *forcemeat* combined with crayfish butter (147), and *poached*.

Serve, separately, an Allemande sauce (27) prepared with crayfish butter.

1237—REGENCY VEAL SWEETBREADS   *Ris de Veau à la Régence*

Stud the sweetbreads with truffles, and *braise* them without browning.

Place on a dish and pour their reduced *braising*-liquor around the dish.

Surround them with a Régence garnish, arranged in alternate heaps consisting of the following: *quenelles* of fine truffled chicken *forcemeat;* small grooved mushrooms; curled cocks' combs, and truffles cut to the shape of olives. Serve separately an Allemande sauce (27), flavored with truffle *essence*.

1238—VEAL SWEETBREADS UNDER ASHES

Ris de Veau sous la Cendre

Stud the veal sweetbreads with truffles and tongue, and three-quarters *braise* them.

Cut some slices of tongue of the same size as the sweetbreads, garnish them with slices of truffle, and set a sweetbread on each.

Cover each sweetbread with a layer of short paste (2358); set them on a tray; brush with egg; pinch paste together to close; make a small incision on the top of the paste to allow the escape of steam, and bake in a hot oven for thirty minutes.

When taking them from the oven, pour in some half-*glaze* (23) sauce with Madeira, and place them on a napkin.

1239—VEAL SWEETBREADS TOULOUSAINE

Ris de Veau à la Toulousaine

Stud the sweetbreads with truffles and *braise* them without browning.

Serve them with the Toulousaine garnish, arranged in heaps all around, and surround the latter with a ribbon of meat-*glaze* (14).

Toulousaine garnish comprises small chicken-*forcemeat quenelles;*

cocks' combs and kidneys; very white button-mushroom caps, and slices of truffle.

Serve, separately, an Allemande (147) flavored with mushroom *essence.*

1240—CROUSTADE OF VEAL SWEETBREADS FINANCIERE

Croustade de Ris de Veau à la Financière

Prepare the required number of small, fluted *croustades,* baked without browning in rather large *tartlet-moulds.* The same number of slices of *braised* veal sweetbread as there are *croustades,* and of the same size.

A Financière garnish, consisting of very small chicken-*forcemeat quenelles;* grooved button-mushrooms, and sliced cocks' combs and kidneys. The whole covered by half-*glaze* (23) with Madeira, in the proportion of one tablespoon per *croustade.* As many fine slices of truffle as there are *croustades.*

Put a tablespoon of the filling into each *croustade;* set on a slice of sweetbread; put a slice of truffle upon that, and serve the *croustades* on a folded napkin.

1241—HOT PATE OF VEAL SWEETBREADS

Pâté Chaud de Ris de Veau

Butter an ordinary round hot deep pie plate, or a *Charlotte· mould.* Take about one and one-half lbs. of short paste and roll it into round covers, one-third inch thick; fold the paste over after having dredged it slightly; draw the two ends gently towards the center, to form a kind of skullcap, which, when placed in the mould, immediately lines the latter. Avoid making folds in the paste while preparing the round pastry, for they would spoil the looks of the patty when turned out.

Press the dough on the bottom and sides of the mould, that the latter may impart its shape to its lining, and cut the projecting dough to within half inch of the brim. Now coat the bottom and sides of the paste lining with a layer of chicken *forcemeat,* of an even thickness of two-thirds of an inch.

Pour into the center of the mould a filling composed of slices of *poached* veal sweetbread; sliced and cooked mushrooms and sliced truffles; the whole covered with reduced and somewhat stiff Allemande sauce (27) flavored with mushroom *essence.*

Cover the garnish with a coating of *forcemeat,* and close the patty with a layer of paste, the edges of which should be moistened and sealed down all around the brim of the mould. Pinch the rim of pastry inside and outside, and finish off with leaves of paste stamped out with a fancy-cutter, ribbed with the back of a knife, and laid upon the paste cover. Brush with beaten egg; make a central slit for the escape of steam, and set to bake in a hot oven, for from forty-five to fifty minutes.

When taking the patty out of the oven, turn it out and serve it on a napkin.

1242—TIMBALE OF VEAL SWEETBREADS *Timbale de Ris de Veau*

Butter a *timbale* mould and decorate its sides with thin pieces of fresh noodle paste (2391), in the shape of diamonds, crescents, scalloped rings, discs and imitation-leaves. Excellent ornamental arrangements may be thus made; but the reader should bear in mind that the simplest are the best.

Prepare a round pastry lining as explained under (1241); slightly moisten the ornamentation in the mould, so that it may cling to the dough in the *timbale,* and line the latter with paste which should be well pressed, that it may take the shape of the mould.

Then prick the paste on the bottom, to prevent its blistering during the baking process; line the bottom and sides with buttered paper, and fill the *timbale,* three-quarters full, with split peas or lentils.

Cover the latter with a round piece of paper, and close the *timbale* with a round layer of pastry, which should be sealed down around the edges. Make and trim the edge of the *timbale;* pinch it inside and out, and finish the cover with imitation-leaves of paste, superimposed to form a kind of dome.

Set in a moderate oven, and when the *timbale* is baked, remove its cover to take out the lentils or peas and the paper, the object of which was to provide a support for the cover. Brush the inside of the *timbale* with the beaten white of an egg; keep it for a minute or two in front of the oven, with the view of drying it inside; turn it out, and spread upon its bottom and sides a very thin coat of chicken or ordinary *forcemeat,* the purpose of which is to protect the crust from the softening effects of the juices of the garnish.

Put the *timbale* in the front of the oven for a moment or two, that this coating of *forcemeat* may *poach.*

Filling.—Veal sweetbreads, *braised* without browning and cut into pieces; small mushrooms; cocks' combs and kidneys; small *quenelles* of chicken, *mousseline forcemeat,* or slices of chicken *forcemeat* rolls one-third inch thick, trimmed with the fancy-cutter;

and slices of truffles, half of which should be kept for the purposes of decoration.

Cover this garnish with Allemande sauce (27), prepared with mushroom *essence*. Pour it into the *timbale,* just before serving; upon it set the reserved slices of truffle, in the form of a crown; replace the cover; place upon a folded napkin, and serve.

N.B.—As already stated the filling of the *timbale* may be mixed with a half-*glaze* sauce (23), flavored with Madeira or truffle *essence*.

In this filling, whether it be combined with a white or brown sauce, the slices of veal sweetbreads are always the principal ingredient; but, subject to the circumstances, the other details may be altered or modified.

1243—VOL AU VENT OF VEAL SWEETBREADS

Vol au Vent de Ris de Veau

Vol au vent, which formerly held the place of honor on bourgeois menus, has now fallen somewhat into the background; nevertheless, I wished it to appear among the recipes in this work.

The preparation of the pastry: Make the vol au vent crust as explained under (2390).

Filling.—Prepare it exactly as explained under "Timbale de ris de Veau" (1242). This garnish may also be combined with a brown sauce, and its minor ingredients may be modified; but the slices of veal sweetbread must always stand as the dominating element.

Whatever be the selected kind of garnish or filling, vol au vent should always be accompanied by medium-sized, trussed crayfish, cooked in *court-bouillon*.

Serving.—Set the vol au vent crust upon a dish covered with a napkin; pour the filling into it; decorate with slices of truffle; arrange the crayfish round the edge, and lay the cover upon the crayfish.

1244—VEAL SWEETBREADS RICHELIEU   *Ris de Veau à la Richelieu*

Braise the veal sweetbreads exactly as described under "Ris de Veau Bonne Maman" (1221), taking care to keep the *braising*-liquor sufficiently plentiful to well cover the sweetbreads in the *cocotte*.

When the sweetbreads are in the *cocotte,* together with the *julienne* of vegetables and a *julienne* of truffles, strain the *braising*-liquor over the whole; leave to cool, and, when the liquid has turned to a jelly, remove the grease that has risen to the surface.

Serve the *cocotte* on a napkin.

1245—SWEDISH STYLE VEAL SWEETBREADS

Ris de Veau à la Suédoise

Poach the veal sweetbreads without browning, and, when they are quite cold, cut them into thin and regular slices. Spread some horse-radish butter (290) over the latter, and cover with a slice of tongue of the same size as the underlying slice.

Bake a pastry shell without browning in a spring-form, of a size in proportion to the number of slices, and fill it with a vegetable salad mixed with mayonnaise. This shell must necessarily be made in advance.

Upon the salad now set the pieces, either in the form of a crown or in that of a small turban; in the middle place a fine lettuce heart, the leaves of which should be slightly opened out.

1246—VEAL SWEETBREAD ROUNDS A L'ECARLATE

Palets de Ris de Veau à l'Ecarlate

Poach the sweetbreads; when they are cold, cut them into slices half-an-inch thick, and trim them with a round, even cutter. Stamp out some round slices of tongue with the same cutter, but let them be only one-eighth inch thick, and twice as many as the slices of veal sweetbread.

Coat the latter, on either side, with butter prepared with mustard; and cover with a round slice of tongue.

Set the prepared pieces on a tray; let the butter harden, coat with jelly, and decorate the middle of each with a fine slice of truffle.

Arrange the sweetbreads in a circle on a round dish; put some chopped jelly in the center, and border the dish with very regularly-cut aspic-jelly dice.

Serve a horse-radish sauce (119) and an Italian salad (2008) separately.

CALF'S LIVER

Calf's liver is served chiefly as a breakfast or luncheon entrée.

Nevertheless, in ordinary menus, it is sometimes served as a *relevé, braised* and whole.

1247—BRAISED CALF'S LIVER BOURGEOISE

Foie de Veau Braisé à la Bourgeoise

Lard the piece with large, seasoned strips of bacon, as for "Bœuf à la Mode" (1149). Brown it slightly in the oven, and then put it into a saucepan prepared for *braising* (247).

Moisten with one pint of white wine, and reduce it completely. This done, moisten again with brown stock, adding one pint of Espagnole sauce (22) per quart of the moistening.

It is sufficient if the moistening and the sauce reach a little above the middle of the piece of liver.

When the cooking is two-thirds completed, transfer the liver to another saucepan; surround it with carrots, shaped like elongated olives and half-cooked in consommé; and some small onions, half-cooked in butter.

The amount of this garnish of carrots and onions should naturally be in proportion to the size of the piece of liver.

Strain the sauce over the whole, and complete the cooking gently in the oven. Serve the liver with the carrots and onions all round; reduce the sauce if necessary, and pour it over the garnish.

N.B.—The latter need not be arranged symmetrically.

On the contrary simplicity should be made a feature of these bourgeois dishes.

1248—ENGLISH STYLE CALF'S LIVER   *Foie de Veau à l'Anglaise*

Cut the calf's liver into fairly thin slices, from two-and-a-half oz. to three oz. in weight. Season them with salt and pepper; dredge them, and toss them in butter. Grill an equal number of rashers of bacon.

Serve the slices of liver and the rashers of bacon alternately, and sprinkle them with the butter in which the liver was cooked, or with a brown butter (154).

1249—CALF'S LIVER BROCHETTES   *Brochettes de Foie de Veau*

Select a pale piece of calf's liver and cut it into square pieces two-thirds of an inch thick. Season with salt and pepper, and toss the pieces in butter, just to set them.

Put them into a bowl with an equal quantity of *blanched* salt pork, cut into squares, and of slices of cooked mushrooms. Add a few tablespoons of stiff *Duxelles* sauce (223), and toss together, that each particle of the various ingredients may become coated with *Duxelles*.

This done, stick the squares of liver and pork and the slices of mushrooms on skewers, alternating them; sprinkle copiously with fine *raspings* and melted butter, and set to grill gently.

These brochettes are served, either with a maître-d'hôtel butter (150), or a *Duxelles, Fines Herbes,* an Italian or other sauce.

1250—SPANISH STYLE CALF'S LIVER   *Foie de Veau à l'Espagnole*

Cut the calf's liver into slices weighing three and a half oz.; season these with salt and pepper; dredge them; sprinkle them with oil, and grill them gently.

Meanwhile, prepare as many grilled half-tomatoes as there are pieces of liver; onions cut into thin round slices, seasoned, dredged, and fried in oil; a proportionate quantity of fried parsley.

Arrange the grilled slices of liver along the center of an oval dish; place a half-tomato upon each; and, on one side, set the fried onions, on the other, the fried parsley.

1251—CALF'S LIVER SAUTE WITH HERBS

Foie de Veau Sauté aux Fines Herbes

Cut the calf's liver into slices, as above; season these with salt and pepper; dredge them, and toss them in butter.

Arrange the slices in a circle on a round dish; and either pour the herb sauce (83) over the slices, or serve it separately.

1252—CALF'S LIVER LOAF   *Pain de Foie de Veau*

For a calf's liver loaf made in a loaf pan, cut one lb. of calf's liver into dice, and finely grind these together with one-third oz. of salt, a pinch of pepper, and a little nutmeg. Add, little by little, five oz. of very cold *frangipane panada,* and two eggs.

Rub through a sieve; put this *forcemeat* in a bowl; work it over ice, and finish it with two tablespoons of chopped onions, cooked in butter, without browning; the yolks of two eggs, and a quarter pint of thick cream, added by degrees.

Pour this mixture into the well-buttered loaf pan; knock the pan gently on a folded napkin, with the view of settling its contents, and put it to *poach* in the oven in a *bain-marie* (water-bath), for about forty-five minutes.

When taking the loaf out of the oven, let it stand for five minutes, that the loaf inside may thoroughly settle; turn it out on a round dish, and cover it with a *Duxelles,* Italienne (40), Bordelaise (32), brown caper (68), or other sauce.

VEAL RIB CHOPS, KIDNEYS, ETC.

1253—VEAL RIB CHOPS   *Côtes de Veau*

Veal rib chops may either be grilled or *sautéd,* but the second method of cooking them is, in most cases, preferable.

When they are *sautéd,* the chops should be cooked in clarified butter (175), over a somewhat hot fire and in a utensil large enough to hold them without crowding.

This done lay the meat dish; pour away the butter in which they have been cooked; swash the saucepan, dissolving the concentrated gravy adhering to the sides and bottom of it with a liquid in keeping with the garnish; either mushroom cooking-liquor, white or red wine, or Madeira, etc.; and add this liquid, reduced, to the accompanying sauce. The latter is generally a buttered half-*glaze* (23), but the best accompaniment to veal rib chops is a pale meat *glaze* (15), moderately buttered.

All vegetables and paste garnishes, given under Rump or Round Roast of Veal, suit veal chops. I must therefore ask the reader to refer to those recipes, as circumstances may dictate; and restrict myself to a few which, in my opinion, are suited more particularly to veal rib chops.

1254—VEAL RIB CHOPS BONNE FEMME

Côte de Veau à la Bonne Femme

Put the veal chop into an earthenware saucepan, with one and one-half oz. of butter, and brown it well on both sides. Add six small onions cooked in butter, three oz. of potatoes cut into slices; and complete the cooking gently in the oven, keeping the saucepan covered. Serve the preparation in the saucepan as it stands.

1255—VEAL RIB CHOPS IN CASSEROLE   *Côte de Veau en Casserole*

Heat one oz. of butter in an earthenware saucepan; add the veal rib chop, seasoned, and cook it gently, taking care to turn it over from time to time.

At the last moment, add a tablespoon of excellent veal gravy (41), and serve in the saucepan or casserole.

1256—VEAL RIB CHOPS IN COCOTTE A LA PAYSANNE

Côte de Veau en Cocotte à la Paysanne

Toss the rib chop cutlet in butter, in the *cocotte,* with two small slices of *blanched* salt pork. Add four small onions, and two small, long potatoes, cut *paysanne*-fashion; and complete the cooking of the chops and the garnish very gently in the oven.

Send the preparation to the table in the *cocotte.*

1257—VEAL RIB CHOPS A LA DREUX   *Côte de Veau à la Dreux*

Stud the kernel of the veal chop with tongue, ham and truffle, and cook it gently in butter. This done, trim it on both sides, that the *studding* may be clean and neat; serve it with a frill on the bare bone, and, beside it, arrange a small garnish of *quenelles,* mushrooms, cocks' combs and kidneys, and turned and *blanched* olives.

Pour a little half-*glaze* sauce (23), flavored with truffle *essence,* over the garnish.

1258—VEAL RIB CHOPS MILANAISE   *Côte de Veau Milanaise*

With a moistened butcher's mallet, flatten the meat in suchwise as to reduce it to half its normal thickness. Dip the veal chop into beaten egg; roll it in bread-crumbs, mixed with half as much grated Parmesan cheese, and cook it in clarified butter (175), or butter and oil in equal quantities.

Serve it with a frill on the bare bone, and the garnish beside it.

Milanaise garnish consists of cooked macaroni, seasoned with salt, pepper and nutmeg, and combined with butter, grated Gruyère and Parmesan cheeses, and very red tomato *purée* (29); and combined with a *julienne* of very lean cooked ham, tongue, mushrooms and truffles, heated in Madeira.

1259—VEAL RIB CHOPS IN PAPER   *Côte de Veau Papillote*

Toss the veal chop in butter, and prepare, meanwhile:—

Two tablespoons of *Duxelles* sauce (223), combined with a cooked and sliced mushroom.

Two heart-shaped slices of ham, of about the same size as the chop.

A doubled sheet of strong paper (vegetable parchment) cut to the shape of a heart and well-oiled.

Spread out the sheet of paper, and, in the middle, lay a slice of ham; spread a tablespoon of *Duxelles* on the latter; put the chop on the sauce; cover it with the remainder of the *Duxelles,* and finish with the other slice of ham.

Fold the sheet of paper so as to enclose the whole; pleat the edges nicely; put the chop in a pan, and the *papillote* in a fairly hot oven. When taking it out of the oven, transfer it to a dish, and serve instantly.

1260—VEAL RIB CHOPS POJARSKI   *Côte de Veau Pojarski*

Completely separate the meat of the veal chop from the bone; clear it of all skin and gristle, and chop it up with half its weight of butter, salt and pepper. Mold this minced-meat close up to the bone, shaping it like a cutlet, and cook in clarified butter (175), turning it over very carefully in the process.

Serve with a suitable garnish.

1261—VEAL RIB CHOPS ZINGARA   *Côte de Veau Zingara*

Cook the veal chop in butter; at the same time prepare a slice of cured ham, cut to the shape of the chop, and likewise tossed in butter.

Put on a dish; set the slice of ham upon it, and surround with a few tablespoons of Zingara sauce.

Zingara sauce is prepared thus: Reduce a few tablespoons of white wine and mushroom cooking-liquor to half. Add one-fifth pint of half-*glaze* (23), two tablespoons of tomato sauce (29), one tablespoon of veal stock, one oz. of a *julienne* of tongue, mushrooms and truffles; and set to boil for a few seconds.

1262—COLD VEAL RIB CHOPS EN BELLE VUE

Côte de Veau Froide en Belle Vue

Let a little aspic-jelly set in a form somewhat resembling a chop in shape. Trim the veal chop; decorate it with various little vegetables, and sprinkle the latter with half-melted jelly, so as to fix them.

Put the chop on the layer of set jelly, inside the form, with its decorated side under.

Add enough jelly to cover the chop, and let the former set. This done, pass the blade of a small knife (dipped in hot water) round the chop; set the form for a moment upon a napkin dipped in hot water, turn out the chop with care, and set it on a cold dish, with a border of chopped aspic, and a paper frill on the bone.

1263—COLD VEAL RIB CHOPS RUBENS

Côte de Veau Froide Rubens

Trim the veal chop; coat it with half-melted aspic, and cover it with young hop shoots, combined with tomato sauce (29) cleared by means of aspic.

Let the sauce thoroughly set, and then put the chop between two layers of aspic as explained above.

N.B.—Cold veal chops may also be served Bellevue fashion, after the very simple manner described under "Grenadins en Bellevue" (1217).

1264—VEAL KIDNEY   *Rognon de Veau*

When *sautéd* after the usual manner, veal kidney permits all the preparations given for lamb's kidney. (See the chapter on Mutton (1298).)

I shall now, therefore, only give those recipes which are proper to veal kidney.

1265—VEAL KIDNEY IN CASSEROLE *Rognon de Veau en Casserole*

Trim the veal kidney and only leave a very slight layer of fat all round it.

Heat one oz. of butter in a small, earthenware saucepan, called a *cocotte;* put the seasoned kidney into it, and cook it gently for about thirty minutes, taking care to turn it often.

At the last minute sprinkle it with a tablespoon of good veal gravy. Serve it in the *cocotte* as it stands.

1266—VEAL KIDNEY IN COCOTTE *Rognon de Veau en Cocotte*

Prepare the veal kidney and fry it in butter, as in the case of the *"en casserole"* dish. Surround it with one and one-half oz. of small pieces of *blanched* bacon, *sautéd* in butter; one and one-half oz. of raw, quartered mushrooms, also *sautéd,* and one and one-half oz. of small *blanched* potatoes, of the size and shape of garlic cloves, and the same quantity of small, *glazed* onions. Complete the cooking of the whole gently.

At the last minute, add a tablespoon of good, veal gravy, and serve the *cocotte* as it stands.

1267—BROILED VEAL KIDNEY *Rognon de Veau Grillé*

Trim the veal kidney, and leave a slight layer of fat all round it. Cut it in half lengthwise, without completely separating the two halves, and pierce it with a small skewer, with the view of keeping it in shape.

Season with salt and pepper, and grill it gently; basting it often the while with melted butter.

Send separately, either a Maître-d'hôtel (150), a Bercy (139), or other butter suited to grills.

1268—VEAL KIDNEY LIEGEOISE *Rognon de Veau à la Liègeoise*

Prepare the veal kidney as for *"en casserole."* One minute before serving, add one small wineglassful of burned gin, two crushed juniper berries, and one tablespoon of good veal gravy (42). Serve in the cooking-utensil.

1269—VEAL KIDNEY A LA MONTPENSIER

Rognon de Veau à la Montpensier

Trim the veal kidney, leaving a slight coating of fat all round it, and cut into five or six slices. Season and toss them in butter over a brisk fire, and transfer them to a plate.

Swirl into the saucepan one tablespoon of Madeira, and add three tablespoons of melted meat *glaze* (15), a few drops of lemon juice, one and one-half oz. of butter, and a pinch of chopped parsley.

Put on a dish the pieces of kidney, or set them in a *timbale;* sprinkle them with the sauce, and in their midst set a heap of asparagus tips, mixed with butter, and one and one-half oz. of truffle slices.

1270—VEAL KIDNEY PORTUGUESE STYLE

Rognon de Veau Portugaise

Cut up the veal kidney, and toss it in butter, after the manner described under (1269).

Arrange the pieces in a circle on a dish; set a very small, stuffed half-tomato upon each, and garnish the center of the dish with a very reduced tomato *fondue.* Surround the kidney with a sauce prepared as directed above.

1271—VEAL KIDNEY A LA ROBERT   *Rognon de Veau à la Robert*

Heat one oz. of butter in a small *cocotte;* put the seasoned veal kidney in; fry it over a brisk fire, and set it to cook in the oven for about fifteen minutes. Serve the kidney as it leaves the oven, and complete the procedure, at the table, in the following manner:—

Transfer the kidney to a hot plate. Place the *cocotte* over a chafing dish lamp; pour into it one glassful of excellent liqueur brandy, and reduce to half. Meanwhile, quickly cut the kidney into extremely thin slices, and cover these with an overturned plate.

Add to the reduced liqueur brandy one teaspoon of mustard, one oz. of butter cut into small pieces, the juice of a quarter of a lemon, and a pinch of chopped parsley; and work well with a fork, mix it thoroughly.

Put the sliced kidney into this sauce, together with the gravy that has drained from it; heat the whole well, without boiling, and serve on very hot plates.

1272--BREAST OF VEAL   *Tendrons de Veau*

The tendrons are cut from breast of veal. They are, in fact, the extreme ends of the ribs, including the cartilage of the breast bone.

If the tendrons are *braised,* treat them after the manner described under "The Braising of White Meats" (248); or, simply stew them in butter; moisten them with excellent veal stock (9), and baste them frequently while cooking them. They may also be treated like an ordinary veal *sauté,* from which they only differ in shape, and the various preparations of which may be adapted to them.

The garnishes best suited to them are those of early-season vegetables, and, as a matter of fact, the latter, together with such pastes as noodles, macaroni, spaghetti, etc., are the garnishes most often served with them.

1273—OLD-FASHIONED BLANQUETTE VEAL BREAST
Blanquette de Veau à l'Ancienne

Cut the veal breast tendrons into pieces weighing about three oz. Then, slightly *blanch* them; cool them, and put them into a saucepan with enough white stock (10) to cover; add a very little salt: set to boil, and skim.

For two lbs. of tendrons, add one small carrot; one fair-sized onion, stuck with a clove; an herb bunch, consisting of one leek, parsley stalks, and a fragment of thyme and bay leaf; and set to cook gently for one and one-half hours.

Prepare a white *roux* from one and one-half oz. of butter and one and one-half oz. of flour; moisten with one pint of veal cooking-liquor; add one oz. of mushroom peelings, and cook for a quarter of an hour, skimming the sauce the while.

Transfer the pieces of tendron, one by one, to a saucepan with twelve small onions cooked in consommé, and fifteen small, cooked and very white mushrooms. Finish the sauce with a binder of two egg-yolks, mixed with three tablespoons of cream and a few drops of lemon juice; strain it over the veal and its garnish; heat without boiling; serve in a *timbale,* and sprinkle with a pinch of chopped parsley.

N.B.—This *blanquette* may also be prepared with noodles or *cèpes,* instead of with ordinary mushrooms.

1274—BLANQUETTE OF VEAL BREAST WITH CELERY KNOBS AND ENDIVES
Blanquette de Veau aux Céleris et Endives

Prepare the *blanquette* exactly as explained above, and set it to cook with the veal and the vegetable selected for the garnish, either small tops of celery well *blanched,* cut into two or four, or Belgian endives cut. The endives are not *blanched;* they need only be well washed and put with the veal.

When cooked, drain the vegetables, trim them, and serve them in a *timbale* with the veal and the sauce; the latter prepared as directed and strained over the meat.

1275—BLANQUETTE OF BREAST OF VEAL WITH NOODLES
Blanquette de Veau aux Nouilles

Proceed as for "Blanquette à l'ancienne" (1273), but omit the garnish of onions and mushrooms.

When the blanquette is served, set on heaps of noodles, parboiled and mixed with butter, and cover these with fresh home made noodles tossed quickly in butter; allow three oz. of tossed noodles per lb. of those buttered.

1276—FRICASSEE OF VEAL
Fricassée of Veau

Fricassée differs from *blanquette* in this, namely, that the pieces of veal in the former are seared in butter without browning.

When the meat has been well seared, sprinkle it with about one oz. of flour per lb.; cook this flour with the meat for a few minutes; then moisten the fricassée with white stock (10); season, and set to boil, stirring the while. All the garnishes of mushrooms and vegetables given for *blanquette* may be served with fricassée; but in the case of the latter, both the meat and the garnish are cooked in the sauce, which is thickened with egg-yolks and cream, as for *blanquette*.

1277—FRICADELLES
Fricadelles

Fricadelles are a kind of meat balls, somewhat like those commonly prepared in private households. They are made from fresh or cooked meat, in the following manner:—

Fricadelles with Fresh Meat.—For ten fricadelles, each weighing three and one-half oz., chop up or grind one lb. of very lean veal, cleared of all fat and gristle, together with two-thirds of a lb. of butter. Put into a bowl, and add five oz. of soaked and well-pressed bread crumbs, two eggs, half an oz. of salt, a pinch of pepper and a little nutmeg, and two oz. of chopped onion cooked in butter without browning.

Mix well, and divide it up into portions weighing three and one-half oz.

Fashion these portions to the shape of small patties, by first rolling them into balls on a flour-dusted board, and afterwards flattening them out with the flat of a knife.

Heat some butter of very pure fat in a saucepan; put the fricadelles in; brown them on both sides, and then complete their cooking in the oven.

This done, set them on a round dish, and serve them, either with a vegetable *purée*, a Piquante (48) or a Robert sauce (53).

Fricadelles with Cooked Meat.—For ten fricadelles, each weighing two and one-half oz., chop or grind one lb. of cooked veal, fat and lean, somewhat finely.

Put it into a bowl with a large pinch of salt, another of pepper, and a little nutmeg. Add the pulp from three fair-sized potatoes, baked in the oven; three oz. of chopped onions, cooked in butter without browning; one large egg, and one tablespoon of chopped parsley. Mix well; divide up into portions of the weight already given, and shape and cook them as in the previous case.

The fricadelles are served with vegetable *purées* and the sauces suited to those prepared from raw meat.

1278—VEAL BIRDS   *Paupiettes de Veau*

Paupiettes or rolls are made from extremely thin slices of veal, four in. long by two in. wide. After having seasoned them, cover them with *forcemeat* or very fine minced-meat; roll them, with the *forcemeat*-coat inside, into rolls, and tie them round, once or twice, with string, that they may keep their shape while cooking. They are sometimes covered with thin rashers of bacon. Veal birds are always *braised,* gently and a long time.

They are generally garnished with vegetable *purées;* but they may be served just as well with all vegetable garnishes.

By making them half the usual size, they may, after having been *braised,* serve as the garnish for a *timbale,* together with noodles, gnochi, spaghetti, or with Financière, Milanaise or Napolitaine garnish, etc.

1279—VEAL STEWS   *Sautés de Veau*

The pieces best suited to veal stews or *sautés* are: the breast and the shoulder, as also parts of the shank or knuckle.

1280—VEAL STEW A LA MARENGO   *Sauté de Veau à la Marengo*

Heat one pint of oil in a saucepan, until it smokes. Put in two lbs. of veal, cut into pieces, each weighing two oz., and fry until the latter are well seared. Add a chopped half onion and a crushed half-clove of garlic, and fry again for a few moments.

Drain away the oil, tilting the saucepan with its lid on, for the purpose; moisten with a quarter of a pint of white wine; reduce, and add two-thirds of a quart of thin Espagnole sauce (22), one and one-half lbs. of tomatoes, pressed and cut into pieces (or one pint of tomato sauce (29)), and a herb bunch.

Set to boil, and cook in the oven gently for one and one-half hours.

At the end of that time, transfer the pieces of veal, one by one, to another saucepan with fifteen small *glazed* onions, and five oz. of mushrooms. Reduce the sauce; strain it over the veal and its garnish, add two large pinches of chopped parsley, and cook for a quarter of an hour more.

When about to serve, clear it of all grease, put in a *timbale*, and surround with small heart-shaped *croûtons* of bread fried in oil.

1281—VEAL STEW CHASSEUR   *Sauté de Veau Chasseur*

Cut the veal into pieces as above, and fry these well in butter or oil.

Drain away the grease; moisten with one quart of brown stock, add two tablespoons of tomato *purée,* and a herb bunch; set to boil, and cook in the oven gently for one and one-half hours.

Transfer the pieces to another saucepan; strain; reduce the cooking-liquor by a quarter, and add it to one-quarter of a pint of Chasseur sauce (33).

Pour this sauce over the pieces of veal, and cook again for a quarter of an hour. Serve in a *timbale,* and sprinkle with chopped parsley.

1282—VEAL STEW SPRING STYLE   *Sauté de Veau Printanier*

Fry the pieces of veal in butter. Moisten with two-thirds of a quart of brown stock and one-fifth of a pint of half-*glaze* (23); add a herb bunch; boil, and cook in the oven gently for one hour.

This done, transfer the pieces to another saucepan; add a garnish of carrots, new turnips, and small, new potatoes; strain the sauce over the veal and the garnish, and cook for three-quarters of an hour more.

Put in a *timbale* and distribute over the *sauté* a few tablespoons of peas and string beans, both cooked *à l'anglaise.*

1283—CATALAN VEAL STEW   *Sauté de Veau à la Catalane*

Cut up, *sauté,* and cook the veal gently for one and one-half hours, as for (1280).

Transfer the pieces of veal to another saucepan, and add to them three small peeled and pressed tomatoes, quartered and tossed in butter: ten small onions cooked in butter; six oz. of raw, quartered mushrooms; ten chestnuts, three-parts cooked in consommé, and eight chipolata (Italian) sausages.

Reduce the sauce to one-third of a pint; strain it over the veal and its garnish; cook for a further quarter of an hour, and serve in a *timbale*.

1284—VARIOUS VEAL STEWS   *Sautés de Veau Divers*

Veal or stew *sauté* may also be prepared with mushrooms, *fines herbes*, eggplant, tomatoes, or "Currie à l'Indienne" (1345), etc.

1285—VEAL LOAF   *Pain de Veau*

Prepare "Pain de Veau" exactly as directed under (1252); but substitute for the liver some very white young veal.

Veal loaf is generally accompanied by a white sauce, such as velouté (25) prepared with mushroom *essence*, Allemande sauce (27) prepared with mushrooms, Suprême sauce (106a), etc.

1286—CALF'S FEET   *Pieds de Veau*

Calf's feet serve chiefly in supplying the gelatinous element of aspics, and the body of *braising* stock. They are rarely used in the preparation of a special dish; but, should they be so used, they may be cooked and served after the manner directed in the recipes treating of calf's head (1209).

1287—CALF'S TONGUES   *Langue de Veau*

Provided the difference of size be allowed for, calf's tongue may be prepared like ox tongue, and served with the same garnishes. (See Ox Tongue, Nos. 1153 to 1158 inclusive.)

1288—CALF'S BRAINS AND SPINAL MARROW
Cervelle de Veau et Amourettes

Calf's brains form the most wholesome and rebuilding diet for all those who are weakened by excessive head-work; and the same remark applies to the brains of the ox and the sheep.

The amourettes (marrow) mentioned here, which almost always accompany ox brains, are only the spinal marrow of the ox or the calf. This may be used in the preparation of a few special dishes; but all the recipes dealing with brains may be applied to it.

1289—THE COOKING OF BRAINS   *Le Cuisson de Cervelles*

Carefully remove the membrane enveloping the brains or the amourettes (marrow), and put them to soak in fresh water, until they are quite white. Put the brains in a saucepan with enough boiling *court-bouillon* (163) to cover them well; skim and then set to cook gently.

Brains have this peculiarity, namely, that prolonged cooking only sets them; thus, calf's brains only take half an hour to cook; but they may cook for two hours more without harm, seeing that the process only tends to make them firmer.

1290—CALF'S BRAINS BEAUMONT   *Cervelle à la Beaumont*

Cut the brains into slices; on each slice put a layer of *gratin force-meat* (202) prepared from *foie gras* and softened by means of a little cold, brown sauce, and a slice of truffle. Reconstruct the brains by putting the coated slices together again.

Roll some puff-paste remains into a round cake one-fifth of an inch thick, the diameter of which should be in proportion to the size of the brains under treatment. Put the brains in the middle of the round, and cover them with the same *forcemeat* as that laid on the slices; sprinkle with chopped truffles; moisten the edges of the paste, and draw these over the brain so as to enclose the latter completely.

Brush with egg; make a slit in the top for the escape of steam, and bake in a hot oven for fifteen minutes. After taking the pastry out of the oven, pour a few tablespoons of Périgueux sauce (47) into the former, and serve on a napkin.

1291—CALF'S BRAINS WITH BLACK BUTTER

Cervelle au Beurre Noir

Slice the brains; set the slices on a dish, and season them with salt and pepper.

Cook two oz. of butter in the frying-pan until it is slightly blackened; throw in a pinch of shredded parsley, and sprinkle the brains with this butter. Pour a few drops of vinegar into the hot frying-pan, and add it to the brains.

1292—CALF'S BRAINS WITH BUTTER   *Cervelle au Beurre Noisette*

Slice and season the brains as above. Cook the butter until it has acquired a golden brown and has a nutty odor; pour it over the brains, and finish with a few drops of lemon juice and a pinch of chopped parsley.

1293—CALF'S BRAINS MARECHALE   *Cervelle à la Maréchale*

Cut the brains into regular slices, one-third of an inch thick; treat them *à l'anglaise* with very fine bread-crumbs, and brown them in clarified butter (175).

Arrange them in the form of a circle, with a slice of truffle on each, and garnish the center of the dish with a fine heap of asparagus tips mixed with butter.

1294—CALF'S BRAINS POULETTE   *Cervelle à la Poulette*

Prepare half a pint of poulette sauce (101), combined with three oz. of small, cooked, and very white mushrooms.

Add the brains, cut into slices; toss them gently in the sauce, taking care lest they break; serve them in a *timbale,* and sprinkle with a pinch of chopped parsley.

1295—CALF'S BRAINS VILLEROY   *Cervelle à la Villeroy*

Cut the raw brains into slices; season them, and *poach* them in butter.

Dip the slices into an almost cold Villeroy sauce (108), in such a way as to cover them with a thick coating of it. Leave to cool, and treat them *à l'anglaise.* Set to cook for a few minutes before serving, and place on a napkin with fried parsley.

Serve a light Périgueux sauce (47) separately.

1296—VOL AU VENT OF BRAINS   *Vol au Vent de Cervelle*

Prepare a vol-au-vent crust, as explained under (2390). Slice the brains, and put the slices into half-a-pint of Allemande sauce (27), with twelve *quenelles* of ordinary *forcemeat, poached* just before serving; four oz. of small, cooked mushrooms, and one oz. of truffle slices, five or six of which should be reserved.

Pour the garnish into the vol au vent; set upon the latter the reserved slices of truffle, and serve on a folded napkin.

1297—SPINAL MARROW TOSCA   *Amourettes à la Tosca*

Poach one lb. of amourettes (spinal marrow), as explained above, and cut them into lengths of one in.

Prepare a garnish of macaroni mixed with butter and grated Parmesan cheese, and add four tablespoons of a crayfish *cullis* per four oz. of macaroni; three crayfish tails for each person, and two-thirds of the pieces of amourettes. Toss well, in order to thoroughly mix the whole; serve in a *timbale;* cover the macaroni with what remains of the pieces of amourettes, and cover them slightly with crayfish *cullis*.

MUTTON, GRASS LAMB AND HOUSE LAMB

Relevés and Entrées

From the culinary standpoint, the sheep supplies three kinds of meat:—

Mutton—Properly so-called when the meat is derived from the adult animal.

Grass or Winter Lamb—The name Grass or Winter Lamb indicates that the young animal has grazed and lived through a winter, making it about six or eight months old before being sent to market.

Hot House Lamb—Hot House or Spring Lamb is a young unweaned sheep which has never grazed, and being born around January, is ready for the March and April trade, and it never leaves the place where it has been housed. It is also called Baby Spring Lamb and the best ones are shipped from California to all over the United States.

Except for its greater delicacy and tenderness, grass lamb, which corresponds with what the French call "agneau de présalé" is scarcely distinguishable from mutton. The recipes suited to it are the same as those given for mutton; and all that is necessary is to allow for differences of quality in calculating the time of cooking.

Hot house or spring lamb, the white flesh of which is quite different, permits some of the mutton recipes; but it is generally prepared after special recipes, the details of which I shall give hereafter.

When served roasted, hot or cold, mutton and grass and house lamb are always accompanied by mint sauce, the recipe for which I gave under (136).

In view of the similarity of their preparations, and in order to avoid tedious repetitions, I have refrained from giving separate recipes for lamb and mutton, respectively. The reader will therefore bear in mind that the recipes relating to mutton also applies to grass or winter lamb.

1298—SADDLE OF MUTTON *Selle de Mouton*

1299—PAIR OF HIND QUARTERS OF MUTTON WITH LEGS AND LOINS *Baron de Mouton*

1300—PAIR OF LEGS OF MUTTON   *Double de Mouton*

1301—FILLETS OR TENDERLOINS OF MUTTON   *Noisettes de Mouton*

1302—NECK OF MUTTON   *Collet de Mouton*

Saddle of mutton is that part of the sheep which reaches from the bone of the haunch to the floating ribs.

Baron of mutton comprises the loins and the two legs, and a pair of hind-quarters.

"Double" consists of the two unseparated legs, minus the loins. The Baron and the Double are almost always cuts of lamb.

The fillet is one half of the saddle, when the latter is cut into two, lengthwise; that is to say, divided down the middle in such a way as to separate the backbone. These fillets are sometimes boned, rolled over with the kernel of meat in the center, and tied, in which case the skin should be removed before rolling. Saddle of mutton, before being roasted, should be cleared of all its superfluous underlying fat; and the flanks should be so shortened as to just meet when drawn over the fillets. The overlying skin should be removed, and the saddle should be tied in five or six places to keep it in shape.

In the case of a saddle of spring lamb, the skin need not be completely removed, but slit in various places. As to neck of mutton, this should be shortened as for the cutting of ordinary chops; the skin and the backbone should be removed, also the meat at the end of the rib-bones, down to two-thirds in. from the end of each. The shoulder piece is then covered with slices of bacon, tied on with string.

When the piece is roasted and ready to serve, a frill should be placed on the end of each bared bone. Neck of mutton ought never to comprise more than nine to ten ribs, counting from the floating ones; it should consist of rather less if anything.

Mutton *relevés* lend more particularly to vegetable and rice garnishes.

Garnishes with sauces do not suit them so well, even when the pieces are *braised*. As for paste garnishes, such as macaroni, noodles, gnochi; they are seldom used.

Garnishes for mutton *relevés* should therefore be chosen, in preference, from among the following, the details of which I gave under "Filet de Bœuf" (1044 to 1074) and which I recall hereafter:—

Andalouse, Bouquetière, Châtelaine, Clamart, Dauphine, Du-

barry, Duchesse, Japonaise, Jardinière, Lorette, Macédoine, Mont-morency, Moderne, Nivernaise, Orientale, Petit-Duc, Provençale, Renaissance, Richelieu, St. Germain.

Apart from these compound garnishes, the following simple garnishes also suit admirably, either alone, or separated by some kind of potato preparation:—

Braised Lettuce, stuffed with ordinary *forcemeat* or rice.

Cabbages, moulded to the shape of small balls, *braised* and stuffed with fine minced-meat or rice.

Dried White Beans, Peas and *String Beans,* mixed with butter.

Asparagus Tips, white or green, cooked and mixed with butter.

Celery, Endives, and *Chicory,* all *braised. Brussels Sprouts, Cauliflower, Broccoli,* etc.

Finally, the garnishes and modes of preparation termed: *à l'Anglaise, à la Boulangère, Braisés, Mariné en Chevreuil,* which I give below for the leg and the shoulder, may be applied to other large pieces of mutton.

1303—LARGE COLD JOINTS OF MUTTON
Grandes Pièces Froides de Mouton

Refer to Cold Beef; in all cases keep the serving simple.

The garnishing is optional.

1304—LEG AND SHOULDER OF MUTTON   *Gigot et Epaule de Mouton*

Legs of mutton or lamb ought never to appear on any menu other than an ordinary luncheon one. Although, strictly speaking, they should always be served after one of the ways described, all the garnishes given above may be applied to them.

Shoulders may be roasted whole; but they may also be boned, seasoned inside, rolled, and firmly tied. They may be treated like the legs, and the same garnishes are suited to them.

1305—BOILED LEG OF MUTTON ENGLISH STYLE
Gigot Bouilli à l'Anglaise

Trim the leg, shorten it in the region of the tibia (inner) bone, and plunge it into a pan of boiling water, salted in the proportion of one-third oz. of salt per quart of water.

For an ordinary leg, add: three medium-sized carrots, two onions, each stuck with a clove, a herb bunch, and two cloves of garlic.

Let the leg cook for a quarter of an hour for each two lbs. of its weight.

Serve with vegetables all round, and at the same time a butter sauce with capers.

N.B.—Leg of mutton *à l'anglaise* may be accompanied by *purées* of white turnips, celery, etc., and these vegetables should cook with the meat. A *purée* of potatoes or of dried white beans may be sent to the table with the meat; but, in this case, of course, the vegetables would be served separately.

1306—BRAISED FRENCHED LEG OF MUTTON

Gigot de Mouton à la Braise

Cut out the pelvic bone, shorten the end bone and brown the leg in the oven.

Now, put it in an oval utensil, garnished for *braising;* add just enough white stock to barely cover the joint, and cook gently, allowing forty minutes per lb. of meat.

Transfer the leg to a pan; strain the *braising*-liquor; clear it of all grease, and reduce it to half. Sprinkle the meat with a few table-spoons of this reduced gravy, and set it to *glaze* in the oven.

Serve at the same time:—

Either a *purée* of potatoes, of turnips, of dried white beans, of cauliflower, etc., or

The reduced *braising*-liquor.

1307—LEG OF MUTTON BOULANGERE   *Gigot à la Boulangère*

The leg may either be boned, seasoned inside and tied; or the end-bone may simply be shortened and that of the pelvis removed.

In either case, put it in an earthenware dish, and brown it well in the oven, on both sides; then complete its cooking, all but a third.

This done, set round the joint four large, sliced onions, just tossed in butter, that they may brown, and eight large, peeled potatoes cut into slices one half in. thick. Sprinkle this garnish with the gravy fat of the joint, and then complete the cooking of the leg and its garnish.

Serve in the dish in which the joint has cooked.

1308—LEG OF MUTTON MARINATED AS VENISON

Gigot Mariné en Chevreuil

Shorten the end-bone; remove the bone of the pelvis, and skin the top of the leg, leaving the meat in that region quite bare. *Lard* with very small strips of bacon, and put the meat into a *marinade* prepared after the manner described under (170). The length of its stay in the *marinade* should be based upon the tenderness of the meat and atmospheric conditions. In winter the time averages about three or four days, and in summer two days.

To Roast the Joint.—Remove it from the *marinade* and dry it thoroughly; set it on a rack in the baking pan; and put it into a very hot oven, that the meat may sear immediately. The object of the very hot oven is to prevent the juices absorbed from the *marinade* escaping in steam and hardening the meat.

Towards the close of the operation, *rissole* the *larding* bacon well.

Set on a long platter; fix a paper frill to the bone, and serve a Chevreuil sauce separately.

Chevreuil Sauce à la Française.—With the *marinade* of the joint and a *Mirepoix* with ham, prepare a sufficient quantity of Poivrade sauce (49) to obtain two-thirds of a pint of it after it has been strained through a colander—an operation which should be done with the application of great pressure to the seasoning herbs.

Skim this sauce for thirty minutes, and add, little by little, half a wine-glassful of excellent red wine. Finish the seasoning with a little cayenne and a pinch of powdered sugar, and once more rub the whole through a fine sieve or a fine strainer.

1309—LEG OF MUTTON A LA SOUBISE *Gigot à la Soubise*

Braise the leg of mutton as under (247). When it is two-thirds done, transfer it to another pot; strain the *braising*-liquor over it, and add three lbs. of sliced onions and two-third lb. of rice.

Gently complete the cooking of the joint, together with the onions and the rice. This done, put it on a baking-pan and *glaze* it in the oven; quickly rub the onions and the rice through a fine sieve.

Set the leg of mutton on a long platter; put a paper frill on the bone, and serve, separately, the well-heated Soubise, finished with one oz. of butter.

N.B.—This Soubise may be prepared separately; but in this case it has much less flavor than when it is made from the onions and the rice which have cooked in the *braising*-liquor. I therefore urge the adoption of the recipe as it stands.

1310—COLD LEG OF MUTTON *Gigot de Mouton Froid*

Serve it very simply, like other cold large joints of mutton.

1311—MUTTON CHOPS *Côtelettes de Mouton*

Mutton and lamb chops are sometimes *sautéd;* but grilling is the most suitable method of cooking them. When the nature of their preparation requires that they should be treated *à l'anglaise,* fry them in clarified butter (175). All the garnishes, given under "Tournedos" (1076), except those served with sauces, may be applied to chops.

The latter also allow of a few special garnishes, and these I give in the following recipes.

1312—MUTTON CHOPS CHAMPVALLON   *Côtelettes à la Champvallon*

Take some chops from the region underlying the shoulder; that is, those uncovered by the removal of this joint. And do not clear the bone-ends of their meat, as when paper frills are to be fixed to them.

Season them with salt and pepper, and brown them in butter on both sides. This done, put them in an earthenware dish with half lb. of sliced onions, tossed in butter without browning; moisten with enough white stock to almost cover the chops and the onions; add the quarter of a clove of garlic, crushed, and a herb bunch; boil, and set in the oven. At the end of twenty minutes, add one and one-half lbs. of potatoes, fashioned to the shape of corks, and cut into thin round slices; season, and complete the cooking, basting often.

When the chops are cooked, the moistening should be almost entirely reduced.

1313—LAURA MUTTON CHOPS   *Côtelettes Laura*

Grill the chops, and, meanwhile, prepare a garnish (the quantity of which should be such as to allow two and one-half oz. of it per chop) of parboiled macaroni, cut into half-inch lengths, combined with cream, and mixed, per lb., with three and one-half oz. of peeled, pressed, and chopped tomatoes, tossed in butter.

Or, when white truffles are in season, prepare some macaroni with cream, as above, combined with the peelings of raw, white truffles.

Cut some very soft *pig's caul* into triangles, proportionate in size to the chops; spread a little macaroni on each triangle; on each set a chop; cover the chops with some more macaroni, and enclose the whole in the *caul.* Lay the chops on a dish.

Sprinkle with fine *raspings* and melted butter, and set to grill at the *salamander,* or in a hot oven, for seven or eight minutes.

Arrange the chops in the form of a crown, and surround them with a ribbon of clear half-*glaze* sauce (23), combined with tomatoes.

1314—MUTTON CHOPS MAINTENON   *Côtelettes à la Maintenon*

Fry the chops in butter, on one side only. This done, put a heaping tablespoon of a *maintenon* preparation (226) on each; shape it like a dome, by means of the blade of a small knife dipped in tepid water, and put the chops, one by one, on a pan. The *Maintenon* preparation should be laid on the cooked side of each chop and sprinkled with fine *raspings* and melted butter. Now put the chops in a rather hot oven for seven or eight minutes in order to allow a *gratin* to form over the surface of the garnish, and finish the cooking of the chops.

Arrange in the form of a crown, and serve, separately, a sauceboat of meat *glaze* (15) finished with butter.

1315—MUTTON CHOPS MURILLO   *Côtelettes à la Murillo*

Fry the chops in butter, on one side only; and garnish the cooked side, dome-fashion, with a fine mince of mushrooms, mixed with a little very reduced Béchamel sauce (28).

Set them on a pan; sprinkle with grated Parmesan cheese and a few drops of melted butter, and *glaze* in a hot oven. Arrange the chops in the form of a crown; fix a paper frill to each, and surround them with sweet peppers and tomatoes, both of which should be sliced, tossed in butter, and mixed.

1316—MUTTON CHOPS PROVENCALE   *Côtelettes à la Provençale*

For ten chops reduce one-half pint of Béchamel sauce (28) to a third, and add the third of a garlic clove, crushed, and the yolks of three eggs; prepare at the same time as the chops, ten grilled mushrooms; and ten pitted, stuffed and *poached* olives, encircled by a strip of anchovy fillet.

Fry the chops in butter, on one side only. Cover the cooked side of each with the preparation described above; set them on a pan; sprinkle them with a few drops of melted butter, and put them in the oven, that their garnish may be *glazed* and that their cooking may be completed.

Arrange in the form of a circle; place a grilled mushroom in the middle of each chop, and, on each mushroom, a stuffed olive.

1316a—MUTTON CHOPS REFORME

Côtelettes de Mouton à la Reforme

Trim six mutton chops; season them; dip them in melted butter, and roll them in bread-crumbs, combined with finely-chopped ham

in the proportion of a third of the weight of the bread-crumbs.
Now cook them gently in clarified butter (175).

Dish them in a circle on a hot dish, and send the following sauce
to the table with them:—

Take a small saucepan, and mix three tablespoons of half-*glaze*
sauce (23), the same quantity of Poivrade sauce (49), and one teaspoon of red-currant jelly; add one teaspoon of each of the following
short *julienne* garnishes to the sauce: hard-boiled white of egg; very
red, cured tongue; gherkins; mushrooms, and truffles.

1317—MUTTON CHOPS SEVIGNE   *Côtelettes à la Sévigné*

Have ready a preparation of mushroom and artichoke-bottom
croquettes, in the proportion of one heaped tablespoon for each
chop.

Fry the chops in butter, on one side only. Garnish the fried side
of each, dome-fashion, with the above preparation; treat them
à l'anglaise, and sprinkle them with melted butter.

Put them in the oven to complete their cooking.

Serve in the form of a crown.

1318—MUTTON CHOPS SUEDOISE   *Côtelettes à la Suédoise*

Place the chops on a dish, and drop on some minced onions and
shallots, bits of parsley stalks, thyme and bay leaf. Sprinkle them
with the juice of a lemon and a few drops of oil, and leave them to
marinate for thirty minutes, turning them over, from time to time.

This done, dry them; dip them in melted butter, sprinkle them
with bread-crumbs, and grill them.

Arrange them in the form of a crown, and garnish the center of
the dish with the following, which may be sent separately: one-half
lb. of peeled and finely-sliced apples, quickly stewed to a *purée* with
the third of a wineglassful of white wine. When about to serve, add
to this *purée* two and one-half oz. of finely-grated horse-radish.

1319—MUTTON CHOPS EN BELLE VUE   *Côtelettes en Belle Vue*

Proceed after one of the recipes given for veal chops and *grenadins*
"en Belle Vue" (1217).

1320—MUTTON NECK CHOPS IN CHAUD-FROID
    Côtelettes en Chaud-froid

Cut some very regular chops from the neck of mutton or lamb,
which should have been trimmed as explained, *braised,* and left to

cook in its *braising*-liquor. Clear all grease from it; strain it; reduce it, and add to it a brown chaud-froid sauce (34).

Dip the chops in the sauce when it is almost cold; set them in a pan; decorate the kernel of meat in each with a fine slice of truffle, and sprinkle with cold, melted aspic. When the sauce has set well, pass the point of a small knife round the chops, with the view of removing the superfluous sauce; and either arrange them round a vegetable salad, mixed and moulded, or simply serve them in a circle and place a pyramid of mixed, vegetable salad in their midst.

1321—MUTTON OR LAMB FILLET STEAKS   *Noisettes de Mouton*

Mutton *noisettes* or fillet steak, and especially those of lamb, may be classed among the choicest of entrées. They are cut from either the fillet or the neck; but, in the latter case, only the first six or seven ribs are used.

Fillet steaks *noisettes* are grilled or *sautéd,* and all the recipes given for Tournedos (1077 to 1139) and for chops, may be applied to them.

1322—FILETS MIGNON OF MUTTON OR LAMB   *Filets Mignon*

The tenderloin of mutton or lamb consist of the two muscles which lie under the rack. Their mode of preparation changes according to their size. Thus, if they are small, they are served whole, after having been trimmed, sometimes *larded;* and *sautéd.*

If they are large, they are divided into two or three parts, cut across and on the slant; they are flattened, trimmed to the shape of ovals, seasoned, dipped in melted butter, sprinkled with fine bread-crumbs, and finally, gently grilled.

Filets mignon of beef, obtained from the narrow extremity or head of the fillet, are also used occasionally; and these are generally flattened, dipped in butter and fine bread-crumbs, and grilled.

These fillets are served chiefly with vegetable *purées* or with *macédoines* of fresh vegetables.

The sauces best suited to them are the Béarnaise (62) and the Robert Escoffier (53).

1323—SHEEP'S TONGUES   *Langues d'Agneau*

Salted or fresh sheep's tongues make an excellent luncheon entrée.

They are cooked after the manner of ox and calf's tongues (1153 to 1158), due allowance being made for the difference of size.

The various garnishes given for ox and calf's tongues may also be used in this case.

1324—SHEEP'S TROTTERS AND SHANKS *Pieds de Mouton*

Sheep's trotters and shanks, as they reach us from the butcher, should first be well singed, and then rubbed with a clean piece of linen. The little tuft of hair in the cleft of the hoof is next removed, the hoof itself is taken off, and the trotters and shanks are split open lengthwise and boned. Sheep's trotters and shanks are cooked like calf's feet, in the special *court-bouillon* or *blanc,* given under (167).

1325—FRY OF SHEEP'S TROTTERS AND SHANKS

Fritot de Pieds de Mouton

Fifteen minutes before frying them, put the sheep's trotters and shanks, which were parcooked in a *blanc* (167), into a bowl with lemon juice, a few drops of oil and some chopped parsley; keeping the quantity of these ingredients in proportion to the number of trotters and shanks. Be careful to toss the latter from time to time in the *marinade.*

A few moments before serving, dip the half-trotters and shanks into batter (232) and plunge them into an abundant and hot frying fat.

Drain them when the batter is nicely dry and golden; and serve on a napkin with a border of very green fried parsley.

Serve a tomato sauce (29) separately.

1326—SHEEP'S TROTTERS AND SHANKS POULETTE

Pieds de Mouton Poulette

For this dish the trotters and shanks should, as far as possible, be freshly cooked. For twenty trotters and shanks prepare two-thirds of a pint of poulette sauce (101); add the trotters and shanks, well drained; toss them in the sauce, and serve them in a *timbale* with a sprinkling of chopped parsley.

1327—SHEEP'S TROTTERS AND SHANKS ROUENNAISE

Pieds de Mouton Rouennaise

Instead of cooking the sheep's trotters and shanks in a *blanc,* *braise* them; add a little Madeira to their *braising*-liquor, and cook them thoroughly.

Prepare a *forcemeat,* consisting of one and one-half lbs. of very fine sausage-meat; three oz. of chopped onions, cooked in butter without browning, and a large pinch of parsley.

When the trotters and shanks are cooked, transfer them to a dish; almost entirely reduce their *braising*-liquor; add to this two liqueur-glassfuls of burnt brandy, for each ten trotters and shanks, and add this reduced *braising*-liquor to the *forcemeat*. Cut ten rectangles six inches long by four inches wide out of *pig's caul*.

Spread a tablespoon of *forcemeat* over each; set two trotters and shanks on the *forcemeat* of each rectangle; cover up with *forcemeat*, and draw the ends of the *caul* together in such a way as to enclose the whole.

Sprinkle with bread-crumbs and melted butter; grill gently, and serve.

1328—SHEEP'S TROTTERS AND SHANKS TYROLIENNE

Pieds de Mouton Tyrolienne

Cook a fair-sized chopped onion in butter, together with three peeled, pressed, and roughly-chopped tomatoes. Season with salt and pepper; add a pinch of chopped parsley, a little crushed garlic, one-sixth of a pint of Poivrade sauce (49), and twenty freshly-cooked and well-drained sheep's trotters and shanks.

Simmer for ten minutes and serve in a *timbale*.

1329—MUTTON KIDNEYS   *Rognons de Mouton*

Mutton kidneys are either grilled or *sautéd*. When they are to be grilled, first remove the fine skin enveloping them, cut them in halves, without completely severing them, and stick them on a small skewer, with the view of keeping them open during the grilling. Before grilling they may or may not be dipped in melted butter and rolled in bread-crumb.

When they are to be *sautéd*, clear the kidneys, as before, of the thin skin which envelops them; cut them into halves, and then into slices one-quarter in. thick.

Kidneys, of any kind, should be cooked very quickly, otherwise they harden. After having seasoned them, put them into very hot butter, and toss them over a hot fire in order to set them. This done, drain them; and let them stand for a few minutes, that they may give off the blood they contain, which sometimes has a distinct ammonia smell.

Meanwhile, swash the utensil in which they have been *sautéd*, and finish the sauce, to which they are added when ready to serve. Never let the kidneys boil in the sauce, for they would immediately harden.

1330—SAUTED KIDNEYS BERCY   *Rognons Sautés Bercy*

Slice, season, and quickly toss the mutton kidneys in butter, and drain them.

For six kidneys put one tablespoon of finely-chopped shallots into the saucepan, and just heat it. Moisten with one-sixth of a pint of white wine; reduce to half; add two tablespoons of melted meat *glaze* (15), and a few drops of lemon juice, and put the kidneys in this sauce. Add two and one-half oz. of butter, cut into small pieces; melt this on a low flame, tossing and rolling the pan the while; serve in a *timbale,* and sprinkle a pinch of chopped parsley over the kidneys.

1331—SAUTED KIDNEYS BORDELAISE   *Rognons Sautés Bordelaise*

Fry the mutton or lamb kidneys, and drain them as above.

Put into the saucepan one-third of a pint of Bordelaise sauce (32) combined with *poached* dice of marrow, a pinch of chopped parsley, and three oz. of sliced *cèpes,* tossed in butter and oil and well drained.

Return the kidneys to the saucepan; toss them in the sauce, and serve in a *timbale.*

1332—SAUTED KIDNEYS CARVALHO   *Rognons Sautés Carvalho*

Fry the skinned, halved and seasoned mutton or lamb kidneys in butter, and place them, each on a small *croûton* of bread, cut to the shape of a cock's comb and fried in butter. On each half-kidney, set a small cooked mushroom and a slice of truffle.

Swirl into the saucepan Madeira; add a little half-*glaze* (23); put in a small quantity of butter, away from the fire, and pour this sauce over the kidneys.

1333—SAUTED KIDNEYS IN CHAMPAGNE

Rognons Sautés au Champagne

Remove the outer skin from the mutton or lamb kidneys; cut them in two lengthwise; season them; fry them quickly in butter, and place in a *timbale.*

Swirl into the saucepan one-half pint of champagne per six kidneys; reduce almost entirely; add two tablespoons of melted meat *glaze* (23); add a small quantity of butter, and pour this sauce over the kidneys.

N.B.—The preparation of kidneys *sautéd* with wine always follows the same principle; that is to say, the saucepan in which the kidneys have cooked is always swashed with a quantity of wine, in proportion to the number of kidneys; a proportionate amount of meat *glaze* (23) is then added, and after the sauce has been slightly buttered, the kidneys are tossed in it.

1334—HUNGARIAN SAUTED KIDNEYS　　*Rognons Sautés Hongroise*

Remove the outer skin from the mutton or lamb kidneys; cut them into halves; slice and season them; fry them in butter, and drain them.

In the saucepan that has served in the cooking of the kidneys, fry a chopped onion with butter, and add a pinch of paprika.

Moisten with a tablespoon of cream, and reduce; add one-sixth of a pint of velouté (25), boil for a moment, and rub through a fine sieve.

Heat this sauce; put the kidneys into it, toss them for a minute. so as to heat without boiling, and serve in a *timbale*.

1335—SAUTED KIDNEYS CHASSEUR　　*Rognons Sautés Chasseur*

Quickly fry the sliced mutton or lamb kidneys in butter and drain them.

Swash the saucepan with white wine and almost entirely reduce; add one-third of a pint of Chausseur sauce (33) for each six kidneys; put the kidneys in this sauce, toss them for an instant; serve them in a *timbale,* and sprinkle with a pinch of chopped parsley.

1336—SAUTED KIDNEYS A L'INDIENNE

Rognons Sautés à l'Indienne

For six mutton or lamb kidneys: fry a chopped onion in butter and add a large pinch of curry. Moisten with one-sixth pint of velouté (25); cook for a few minutes, and rub through a fine sieve.

Clear the kidneys of their outer skin; slice and season them, and fry them quickly in butter. Put them into the sauce; put them in a *timbale,* and serve some rice "à l'Indienne" (2254) separately.

1337—SAUTED KIDNEYS TURBIGO　　*Rognons Sautés Turbigo*

Clear the mutton kidneys of their outer skin and cut them in halves; season them; fry them quickly in butter, and place them in a circle in a *timbale.*

In their midst set a garnish of small, cooked mushrooms, and grilled chipolata (Italian) sausages; and pour on a highly-seasoned, tomatoed half-*glaze* sauce (23).

1338—BREAD CROUSTADES WITH KIDNEYS　　*Croûte aux Rognons*

Cut some bread slices two and one-half in. in diameter and one and one-third in. thick, from a baked loaf, and allow one for each person. Remove the crumb from their insides, leaving only a slight thickness at the bottom; butter them, and dry them in the oven.

Fill these crusts with mutton kidneys *sautéd* with mushrooms, and combined with small, ordinary *forcemeat quenelles,* and slices of truffle.

Arrange on a napkin, and serve very hot.

1339—TURBAN OF KIDNEYS PIEMONTAISE

Turban de Rognons à la Piémontaise

Fill a ring with *"rizotto à la Piémontaise"* (2258), press into the mould, and keep it hot.

Clear the mutton or lamb kidneys of their outer skin; cut them into halves; season them, and fry them quickly in butter.

Turn out the *rizotto* ring on a round dish, set the half-kidneys in a circle on the "Turban," alternating them with fine slices of truffle, and pour a tomatoed half-*glaze* sauce (23), flavored with truffle *essence,* in the center.

1340—KIDNEYS ON SKEWERS   *Rognons à la Brochette*

Cut the mutton or lamb kidneys into halves, as explained, without dividing them; stick them two or four at a time, on a skewer; season them, and grill them in a somewhat hot oven. Place them, after removing the skewers, upon a hot dish, and put into the cavity of each a piece of softened, Maître-d'hôtel butter (150), the size of a hazel nut.

1341—KIDNEYS ON SKEWERS ESPAGNOLE

Rognons Brochette à l'Espagnole

Prepare the mutton or lamb kidneys as above.

Grill the same quantity of small, pressed and seasoned half-tomatoes. Garnish these tomatoes with a piece, the size of a walnut, of Maître-d'hôtel butter (150), combined with two-thirds oz. of chopped pimento per three oz. of butter. Arrange these tomatoes in a circle; set a kidney on each, and surround with a border consisting of rings of onion, seasoned, dredged and crisply fried in oil.

1342—KIDNEYS ON SKEWERS AU VERT PRE

Rognons Brochette au Vert Pré

Prepare the mutton or lamb kidneys exactly as explained under the first of these recipes, and surround them with small heaps of shoestring potatoes and bunches of very green parsley.

1343—BROCHETTES OF KIDNEYS   *Brochettes de Rognons*

Remove the outer skin from the mutton or lamb kidneys, and cut them into slices one-third in. thick. Season these slices and cook them in butter over a very hot fire. Stick them on skewers, alternating them with squares of *blanched* lean bacon and slices of *sautéd* mushrooms. Sprinkle with melted butter and *raspings,* and grill.

These *brochettes* are generally served as they stand.

VARIOUS PREPARATIONS OF MUTTON

1344—CASSOULET *Cassoulet*

Set one quart of dried white beans to cook with two quarts of water, one-third oz. of salt, one carrot, one onion stuck with a clove, one herb bunch, six garlic cloves, and two-thirds lb. of fresh pork rind, *blanched* and tied together. Boil; skim; cover, and cook gently for one hour. At the end of this time, add two-thirds lb. of breast or belly of pork, and a sausage with garlic, of the same weight as the pork. Salt the beans very moderately, allowing for the reduction which they have ultimately to undergo.

Complete the cooking of the whole gently.

Or fry gently in lard one lb. of shoulder of mutton, and the same weight of breast of mutton; both cut into pieces one and one-half oz. in weight.

This done, drain away half the grease; add two chopped onions and two crushed cloves of garlic, and fry again until the onions have acquired a slight color. Now pour in one-sixth pint of good tomato *purée;* moisten the meat, enough to cover, with the cooking-liquor of dried white beans, and cook gently in the oven for one and one-half hours at least.

Or garnish the bottom and sides of some *cocottes* or deep dishes with bacon rind; fill these with alternate layers of the pieces of mutton, the beans, the bacon cut into dice, and the sausage cut into round slices.

Sprinkle the surface with *raspings,* and set the *gratin* to form in a moderate oven for one hour; taking care to baste from time to time with some reserved dried white beans cooking-liquor.

1345—INDIAN CURRY *Currie à l'Indienne*

Cut two lbs. of lean mutton into cubes of one and one-third in. size, and fry these in three oz. of lard, with one chopped onion, salt, and a pinch of powdered curry. When the meat is frizzled and the onions begin to brown, sprinkle with one and one-third oz. of flour; cook the latter a while; moisten with one and one-third pints of water or stock; boil, stirring to dissolve the *roux,* and then cook gently in the oven for one and one-half hours. When about to serve, clear of all grease and serve in a *timbale*.

Send a *timbale* of rice à l'indienne (2254) separately.

1346—MUTTON STEW A L'AVIGNONNAISE   *Daube à l'Avignonnaise*

Bone a medium-sized leg of mutton, and cut the meat into squares, three oz. in weight. *Lard* each square with a large, seasoned strip of bacon, insert with the grain of the meat. Put the pieces into an oval saucepan with a sliced half of carrot and onion, three cloves of garlic, a little thyme, bay leaf, and parsley stalks. Moisten with one and one-third pints of good, red wine and four tablespoons of oil, and *marinate* in a cool place for two hours.

Prepare:—Three chopped onions mixed with two crushed garlic cloves; one-half lb. of lean bacon, cut into dice and *blanched;* one-half lb. of fresh, bacon rind, *blanched* and cut into squares of one in.; a large bunch of parsley, containing a small piece of dry, orange peel. Garnish the bottom and sides of an earthenware saucepan with thin slices of bacon; set the pieces of mutton in layers inside, and alternate them with layers of onion, bacon and bacon rind; sprinkle a pinch of powdered thyme and bay leaf on each layer of meat. Put the herb bunch in the middle.

Moisten with the *marinate,* strained through a sieve, and one-fifth pint of brown stock; cover with slices of bacon; cover the saucepan, and seal down the lid by means of a ribbon of soft paste, in order that the steam may be concentrated inside.

Boil on the side of the stove; put the pan in an oven of regular heat (slow oven) so that the cooking process may be gentle and steady, and cook for five hours.

When about to serve, uncover the saucepan; remove the top slices of bacon; clear of grease; remove the herb bunch, and place the saucepan on a napkin.

N.B.—According to the household method, the stew is served in the *daubière* itself; but, subject to the demands of the service and in order that the preparation may keep its pleasant character, it may be served in small earthenware pots.

1347—COLD MUTTON STEW   *Daube Froide*

Cold stew constitutes an excellent luncheon dish. All that is needed is to put what is left into a small *daubière,* where, as a result of the binding properties of the pork rinds, it will set into a mass.

When about to serve, turn out on a round dish; surround with very light, chopped aspic-jelly; and carve into very thin slices.

1348—MINCES AND HASHES *Emincés et Hachis*

An unalterable principle governs the preparation of minces and hashes, which is that the meats constituting these dishes should never boil if it be desired that they not be tough.

They should, therefore, only be heated in their accompanying garnish or sauce, and in the case of minces, cut as finely as possible.

For the various recipes under this head, see the Chapter on Beef. (1175, 1178 and 1179.)

1349—MUTTON AND BEANS *Haricot de Mouton*

Heat three oz. of lard in a saucepan. Put in one-half lb. of lean bacon, cut into dice and *blanched,* and twenty small onions. When the bacon is frizzled and the onions have acquired a good color, drain both on a dish. In the same fat, fry three lbs. of breast, neck and shoulder of mutton, all three being cut into pieces weighing about three oz. Keep the meat in the fat until each piece of it has acquired a fried crust.

Drain away half of the grease; add three crushed cloves of garlic; dust with two tablespoons of flour, and cook the latter, while stirring.

Moisten with one quart of water; season with one-third oz. of salt and a pinch of pepper; boil and stir; add an herb bunch, and cook in the oven for thirty minutes.

This done, transfer the pieces to another saucepan; add the bacon and the onions and a quart of half-cooked dried white beans; strain the sauce over the whole, and complete the cooking in the oven for one hour.

Serve in a *timbale* or in small *cocottes.*

1350—IRISH STEW *Irish Stew*

Cut two lbs. of boned breast and shoulder of mutton into pieces, as above.

Slice two lbs. of potatoes and chop four medium-sized onions.

Take a saucepan just large enough to hold these ingredients and the moistening; line the bottom of the utensil with a layer of the pieces of meat, and season the latter with salt and pepper. Upon the meat spread a layer of sliced potatoes and chopped onions; repeat the operation, again and again, until all the ingredients are used up, and remember to place an herb bunch in the center.

Moisten with one and one-third pint of water, and cook gently

in the oven for one and one-half hours. The potatoes in this preparation answer the double purpose of garnish and thickening.

Serve in a *timbale* and have it boiling hot.

1351—MUSAKA   *Moussaka*

Cut six fine egg-plants into halves, lengthwise; score the pulp
somewhat deeply with the point of a small knife, and fry them until
their pulp may be easily removed. Do this with a spoon, and put
the pulp aside with the skins of the egg-plants.

Peel two fair-sized egg-plants; cut them into round slices one-
third in. thick; season them, dredge them; fry them in oil, and put
them aside.

Chop up the pulp taken from the egg-plants, and put it into a
bowl with one and one-half lbs. of very lean, cooked mutton,
chopped or cut into very small dice; two tablespoons of very finely-
chopped onion, fried in butter; a pinch of parsley; a piece of crushed
garlic as large as a pea; three oz. of roughly-chopped raw mushrooms, fried in butter; two eggs; two tablespoons of cold Espagnole
sauce (22); one tablespoon of tomato *purée;* a pinch of salt, and
another of pepper. Mix the whole well.

Butter a low-bordered quart *Charlotte mould;* line it all round
with egg-plant skins, and lay these black side uppermost. Fill the
bottom of the mould with a layer of minced-meat, one in. thick; on
this layer a few fried slices of egg-plant and continue thus with
alternate layers of meat and egg-plant. Cover the last layer of
minced-meat with the remains of the egg-plant skins and cook in a
bain-marie (water-bath) for one hour.

When taking the mould out of the oven, let it stand for five
minutes in order that the ingredients may set; turn out on a round
dish, and sprinkle the surface of the Moussaka with chopped parsley.

1352—MUTTON PUDDING   *Mutton Pudding*

Follow the directions given under beefsteak pudding (1170) exactly. The preparation is just the same, but for the substitution of
mutton for the beef.

1353—NAVARIN PRINTANIER   *Navarin Printanier*

Heat four oz. of clarified fat in a saucepan, and put into it four
lbs. of breast, neck and shoulder of mutton or lamb; all three cut
into pieces weighing two and one-half oz. Fry over a very brisk fire;
season with one-third oz. of salt, a pinch of ground pepper, and
another of sugar.

The sugar settles slowly on the bottom of the saucepan, where it turns to caramel; it is then dissolved by the moistening, and thus gives the sauce the required color.

When the meat is well fried, remove almost all the fat; sprinkle with one and one-half oz. of flour; cook for a few minutes, and moisten with one and one-half quarts of water or stock.

Boil, stirring the while, and add two-thirds lb. of fresh chopped tomatoes or one-fifth pint of tomato *purée;* one crushed clove of garlic, and a large herb bunch. Cover and cook in the oven for one hour.

This done, transfer the pieces of mutton, one by one, to another saucepan with twenty small, new onions; twenty pieces of new trimmed carrots; twenty pieces of new turnips, cut in the shape of long olives and tossed with butter in a frying-pan; twenty small, new potatoes, cut in two, and trimmed, or whole; one-sixth pint of fresh peas, and an equal quantity of fresh string beans, cut in pieces. Strain the sauce over the whole; set to boil, and continue cooking slowly in the oven for one hour; taking care from time to time to baste the topmost vegetables with sauce.

Put in a *timbale* and serve very hot.

N.B.—When put into the sauce, the vegetables cook much slower than in boiling water. In the Navarin, moreover, they are cooked by means of gradual penetration; thus, by lowering the cooking speed of the Navarin, they are slowly cooked to the required extent.

1354—TURKISH PILAFF OF MUTTON   *Pilaw de Mouton à la Turque*

Mutton Pilaff is, in fact, nothing but a Navarin in which the tomatoes dominate the other ingredients; it is flavored with ginger or saffron, according to taste, and the usual vegetables are replaced by rice. Prepared in this way, it does not lend itself very well to the demands of a restaurant service.

More often, therefore, it is treated like curried mutton; but, instead of serving it with rice à l'Indienne (2254), it is dished in the midst of a pilaff-rice (2255) border. Sometimes, too, the rice is served separately, after the manner of a curry dish.

SPRING OR HOUSE LAMB

1355—PAIR OF HIND QUARTERS WITH LEGS AND LOINS OF LAMB
Baron d'Agneau

1356—PAIR OF LEGS OF LAMB   *Double d'Agneau*

1357—LEG AND HALF LOIN OF LAMB   *Quartier d'Agneau*

1358—FILLETS OR TENDERLOIN OF LAMB   *Noisettes d'Agneau*

1359—RACK AND NECK OF LAMB   *Selle d'Agneau*

Large joints of lamb for *relevés* are cut like those of mutton.

One joint, however, should be added, which is "The Quartier"; and this consists of one leg and half the loin attached.

Large joints of house lamb should be *poëled* or roasted. Their most suitable accompaniment is either their own stock, or a thickened, highly seasoned and clear gravy.

Spring or House Lamb *Relevés* are chiefly garnished with early-season or new vegetables; but all the garnishes given under Mutton *Relevés* may also be served with them, provided the difference in size be taken into account. In addition to these garnishes, rack of lamb permits all the preparations given under loins of veal (1181 to 1191).

1360—BONED RACK OF BABY LAMB EDWARD VII
Selle d'Agneau de Lait Edouard VII

Completely bone the rack from underneath, in such a way as to leave the skin intact; season it inside, and place in the middle a fine *foie gras, studded* with truffles and *marinated* in Marsala.

Reconstruct the rack, and wrap it tightly in a piece of muslin; put it in a saucepan just large enough to hold it, on a layer of pieces of bacon rind, cleared of all fat and *blanched*. Moisten, enough to cover, with the *braising*-liquor of a rump of veal; add the Marsala used in *marinating* the *foie gras,* and *poach* for about forty-five minutes.

Before taking out the rack, make sure that the *foie gras* is sufficiently cooked. Remove the muslin, and put the rack in an oval *terrine à pâté* just large enough to hold it. Strain the cooking-liquor over it, without clearing the former of fat, and set it to cool.

When the rack is quite cold, carefully clear away the fat that is on top, first by a spoon and then by means of boiling water. Serve it very cold, in the *terrine* as it stands.

1361—SQUARE SHOULDER OF LAMB BEAUCAIRE
Carré d'Agneau Beaucaire

Having trimmed the square cut shoulder of lamb, as explained, brown it in butter; surround it with eight small, very young artichokes, halved, and cook gently in the oven. The artichokes in question have no chokes and are very tender.

Meanwhile, peel, press, chop and season four or five tomatoes, and fry them in butter. When they are ready, add a large pinch of chopped tarragon to them.

Put the tomatoes on a dish; set the square shoulder upon them, and surround it with the stewed artichoke halves.

1362—SQUARE SHOULDER OF LAMB IN COCOTTE A LA BONNE FEMME   *Carré d'Agneau en Cocotte à la Bonne Femme*

Fry a shortened and well-trimmed square shoulder of lamb, in butter.

This done, transfer it to an oval *cocotte* with ten small onions browned in butter, and two medium-sized potatoes, cut into large pieces, shaped like garlic cloves, and *blanched*. Sprinkle the whole with melted butter and cook gently in the oven.

Serve the preparation as it stands, in the *cocotte,* placing the latter on a folded napkin.

1363—SQUARE SHOULDER OF LAMB BOULANGERE
Carré d'Agneau à la Boulangère

Fry the square shoulder of lamb with butter, in an earthenware dish, and surround it with sliced onions, tossed in butter, and sliced potatoes; both of which vegetables should be in quantities in proportion to the size of the piece of meat. The "à la Boulangère" procedure is always the same, and was explained under (1307), but allowances should always be made for the particular size and tenderness of the piece of meat.

1364—GRILLED SQUARE SHOULDER OF LAMB
Carré d'Agneau Grillé

Having shortened and well trimmed the square shoulder, season it; sprinkle it with melted butter, and grill it gently.

When it is almost cooked, sprinkle it again with melted butter and bread-crumbs, and let it acquire a golden brown color while completely cooking it.

Serve very hot with mint sauce (136) and a suitable garnish.

1365—MIREILLE SQUARE SHOULDER OF LAMB
Carré d'Agneau Printanier

Prepare some Anna potatoes (2203) in an oval earthenware dish, and add a third of the quantity of potatoes of raw, minced artichoke-bottoms.

When the potatoes are three-parts cooked, brown the shoulder in butter; place it on the potatoes, and complete the cooking of the two, basting often with melted butter.

Send the preparation to the table on the same dish that has served in the cooking process.

1366—PRINTANIER SQUARE SHOULDER OF LAMB
Carré d'Agneau Printanier

Prepare the following garnish: eight small onions, half-cooked in butter; ten carrots the size and shape of garlic cloves, cooked in consommé and *glazed;* and ten turnip pieces cut the same shape and size, similarly treated.

Put these vegetables into a *cocotte* with three tablespoons of fresh peas; the same quantity of fresh string beans, cut into pieces; two or three tablespoons of good and very clear stock, and complete the cooking.

Meanwhile, *poële* the shoulder of lamb, which should have been shortened and trimmed in the usual way. Lay the shoulder of lamb and serve the vegetables in the *cocotte*.

1367—SOUBISE SQUARE SHOULDER OF LAMB
Carré d'Agneau Soubise

Having shortened and trimmed the square of lamb, brown it in butter; surround it with one-half lb. of finely-minced and well-*blanched* onions, and complete the cooking of both by stewing.

This done, transfer the meat to a dish and keep it hot. Add one-quarter pint of boiling Béchamel sauce (28) to the onions, and rub them quickly through a fine sieve. Heat this Soubise; finish it with one and one-half oz. of butter, and pour it over the shoulder.

Border the dish with a ribbon of rather light meat-*glaze* (23), and serve.

1368—SQUARE SHOULDER OF LAMB A LA TUSCANE
Carré d'Agneau à la Tuscane

Shorten the square shoulder of lamb; remove the bones and brown it in butter. Garnish the bottom of an oval earthenware dish, of the same size as the shoulder, with a layer of Anna potatoes (2203). Set the meat on this layer, and cover it over with a second layer of the same potato preparation. Sprinkle with grated Parmesan cheese; cook in the oven as for Anna potatoes, and take care that the bottom

be so well covered as to prevent any of the juices of the joint from
escaping and depositing on it.

Serve the dish as it stands.

1369—LEG AND SHOULDER OF LAMB   *Gigot et Epaule d'Agneau*

All the recipes given under "Quartier" and "Double" (pair of
legs), may be applied to the legs and shoulders of Spring or house
lamb.

The shoulders are often grilled, the operation being done over
a moderate fire after the joints have been cut lattice-fashion, and
the same applies to the breast. The "à la Boulangère" treatment
(1307) admirably suits the legs and shoulders of Spring lamb.

1370—LAMB CHOPS   *Côtelettes d'Agneau*

According to custom, lamb chops are usually served like *"noisettes,"* and two are allowed for each person.

As a rule, when they are to be grilled, they are previously dipped
in melted butter and sprinkled with fine bread-crumbs.

When they are to be *sautéd* they are treated *à l'anglaise* (egg and
bread-crumbs) except when, subject to their mode of preparation,
they have to be served plain or stuffed.

1371—SPRING LAMB CHOPS A LA BULOZ

Côtelettes d'Agneau à la Buloz

Prepare a *rizotto* (2238) with truffles, in proportion to the number
of chops; some very reduced Béchamel sauce (28), combined with
one-half oz. of grated Parmesan cheese per one-fifth pint of the
sauce, and allowing one small tablespoon of it for each chop.

Half-grill the chops; dry them, and cover them, on both sides,
with the reduced sauce. As soon as the chops have received their
coat of sauce, dip them, one by one, into beaten egg *anglaise;* roll
them in very fine bread-crumbs mixed with grated Parmesan cheese.
Thoroughly press this coating of bread-crumbs with the flat of a
knife, so that it may stick well to the egg and produce a crust.
This done, set the chops in a saucepan of very hot, clarified butter
(175), and brown them on both sides.

Place the *rizotto* in a very even layer; set the chops in a circle
on the rice, and fix a paper frill to the bone of each.

1372—MARECHALE SPRING LAMB CHOPS

Côtelettes d'Agneau de Lait Maréchale

Treat the chops *à l'anglaise,* and cook them in clarified butter
(175).

Dish them in a circle, with a fine slice of truffle upon each; and, in their midst, set a nice heap of buttered asparagus tips.

1373—MILANAISE SPRING LAMB CHOPS
Côtelettes d'Agneau de Lait Milanaise

Treat the chops *à l'anglaise*, but add to the bread-crumbs the quarter of their weight of grated Parmesan cheese.

Cook the chops in clarified butter (175). Arrange them in a circle, and, in their midst, put a garnish "à la milanaise" (Côte de Veau à la Milanaise" (1258).

1374—MORLAND SPRING LAMB CHOPS
Côtelettes d'Agneau de Lait Morland

Slightly flatten the chops, dip them in beaten egg, and roll them in finely-chopped truffle, which in this case answers the purpose of bread-crumbs. Press the truffle with the flat of a knife, that it may thoroughly combine with the egg, and cook the chops in clarified butter (175). Arrange them in a circle; fill the center of the dish with a mushroom *purée* (2059), and surround the chops with a ribbon of buttered meat *glaze* (14).

1375—NAVARRAISE SPRING LAMB SHOPS
Côtelettes d'Agneau de Lait Navarraise

For twelve chops, make a preparation consisting of four oz. of ham, four oz. of cooked mushrooms, and one-half oz. of chopped, red peppers; the whole being combined by means of a very reduced Béchamel sauce (28), flavored with truffle *essence*.

Grill the chops on one side only, and garnish them on their grilled side with a tablespoon of the above preparation, which should be shaped like a dome.

Set the chops upon a pan as soon as they are garnished; sprinkle the surface of them with grated cheese and melted butter, and place them in the oven, that their cooking may be completed and the *gratin* formed. Meanwhile, toss twelve seasoned half-tomatoes in oil. Put these tomatoes in a circle; set a chop upon each, and border with a ribbon of tomato sauce (29).

1376—NELSON SPRING LAMB CHOPS
Côtelettes d'Agneau de Lait Nelson

Grill the chops, and, at the same time, prepare as many bread *croútons* as there are chops, and of exactly the same shape as the latter. Fry the *croûtons* in butter, and coat them with *foie-gras purée.*

Place a grilled chop on each coated *croûton,* and a slice of truffle on the kernel of each chop. Now, by means of a pastry-bag, fitted with a plain tube, cover the chops with some *soufflé* au Parmesan (2295a); arrange them in a circle, and put them in the oven for five minutes, that the *soufflé* may *poach.*

After taking them from the oven, garnish the center of the dish with a heap of asparagus tips, mixed with butter.

1377—STUFFED SPRING LAMB CHOPS A LA PERIGUEUX
Côtelettes d'Agneau de Lait Farcies à la Périgueux

Cook the chops in butter on one side only, and cool them under slight pressure.

Garnish the cooked side of each with a tablespoon of *forcemeat* with butter (193), which should have received a copious addition of chopped truffles. Shape this *forcemeat* dome-fashion, by means of the flat of a small knife, dipped in tepid water, and set the chops, one by one, in a pan. Now put them in the front of the oven for seven or eight minutes that the *forcemeat* may be *poached.*

Arrange them in a circle, and pour a Périgueux sauce (47) in their midst.

1378—EPIGRAMMES OF SPRING LAMB   *Epigrammes d'Agneau*

A lamb "epigram" consists of a chop, and a piece of *braised* breast, cooled under a light weight and cut to the shape of a heart of the same size as the chops. The chops and the pieces of breast must be treated *à l'anglaise,* and *sautéd* or grilled according to circumstance.

Epigrams should be arranged in a circle, the cutlets and the pieces being alternated.

They are usually garnished with *braised* chicory, or *macédoines* of early-season vegetables.

1379—LAMB SWEETBREADS   *Ris d'Agneau*

Lamb sweetbreads are, according to circumstances, either used as the principal ingredient of various preparations, or they answer the purpose of a garnish.

Due allowance having been made for their size, they may be treated after the same manner as veal sweetbreads; that is to say, once they have been cleared of blood, they are *blanched* and *braised* according to the nature of the selected method.

If they are to form part of a large garnish, combined by means of a brown sauce, they are *braised* brown and *glazed.* If they stand as an accompaniment to *poached* fowl, they may be either *studded* or plain, and *braised* white.

Apart from their two uses as ingredient and garnish the under-mentioned methods of preparation, explained in the various preceding series, may be applied to them: *Attereaux, Brochettes, Croustades, Paté chaud, Vol au vent,* etc.

1380—LAMB STEW PRINTANIER *Sauté d'Agneau Printanier*

Prepare the following garnish of twenty new carrots, cut to the shape of large olives, cooked in consommé and *glazed;* twenty pieces of turnip, similarly treated; fifteen small, new onions, cooked in butter; twenty very small new potatoes, cooked in butter or *à l'anglaise* if desired; three tablespoons of peas; the same quantity of string beans cut into one inch pieces, and an equal quantity of small kidney beans. The three last vegetables should be cooked *à l'anglaise,* and kept rather firm.

Cut two lbs. of shoulder and breast of lamb into pieces weighing two oz., and completely *sauté* them in butter without any moistening.

This done, transfer them to a dish. Swash the saucepan with three tablespoons of water; add five tablepoons of pale meat *glaze* (23); heat without boiling, and finish with two and one-half oz. of butter.

Put the pieces of lamb and the vegetables into this sauce, and gently rock the saucepan back and forth, that all the ingredients may absorb the sauce.

Serve in a hot *timbale.*

1381—PILAFF OF LAMB *Pilaw d'Agneau*

Proceed exactly as explained under "Pilaw de Mouton" (1354), only bear in mind that the time allowed for cooking should be proportionately shortened in view of the greater tenderness of lamb's meat.

1382—CURRY OF LAMB *Currie d'Agneau*

Proceed as for "Currie de Mouton" (1345), after allowing, as above, for the greater tenderness of the meat.

PORK

Relevés and Entrées

1383—FRESH HAM *Jambe de Porc*

1384—FRESH PORK TENDERLOIN *Filets de Porc*

1385—FRESH SHOULDER OF PORK *Epaule de Porc*

Relevés of fresh pork are only served at family and bourgeois meals. They are always roasts and permit all the dry or fresh vegetable garnishes, as well as the various vegetable *purées,* and the pastes, such as macaroni, noodles, polenta, gnochi, etc. I shall, therefore, give only a few recipes, and shall select fresh shoulder of pork as the typical joint.

1386—FRESH SHOULDER OF PORK WITH SAUERKRAUT

Carré de Porc à la Choûcroute

Roast the shoulder of pork and take it from the oven a few minutes before it is done.

Keep it in the stove for an hour, that its cooking may be completed gently; but remember, the cooking of the pork should be well finished in the oven; for pork is indigestible when it is not thoroughly cooked.

Meanwhile, prepare a garnish of sauerkraut (2097), and, during the last hour of its cooking, sprinkle it frequently with the fat of the shoulder.

Put the shoulder on a dish; clear the sauerkraut of any superfluous fat, and set it round the roast in spoons; slightly pressing it in so doing.

1387—FRESH SHOULDER OF PORK WITH BRUSSELS SPROUTS

Carré de Porc aux Choux de Bruxellet

Roast the shoulder of pork. Three-quarters cook the Brussels sprouts; completely drain them, and put them round the meat, that they may complete their cooking in its gravy and fat, frequently basting.

For this preparation it is well to roast the shoulder in an earthenware dish, in which it may be served with its garnish—a much better plan than that of transferring it to another dish.

1388—FRESH SHOULDER OF PORK WITH RED CABBAGE A LA FLAMANDE   *Carré de Porc aux Choux Rouges à la Flamande*

Roast the shoulder of pork; place it on a dish and surround it with a garnish of red cabbages, prepared à la Flamande (2098).

Sprinkle the garnish of vegetables with the gravy of the roast, three-quarters cleared of grease.

1389—FRESH SHOULDER OF PORK WITH STEWED APPLES
Carré de Porc à la Marmalade de Pommes

Roast the shoulder of pork and make certain that it is well done.

Meanwhile, peel and mince one lb. of apples; put them in a saucepan with one oz. of sugar and a few tablespoons of water; seal the lid of the saucepan down, so as to concentrate the steam inside, and cook quickly. When about to serve, thoroughly work the apple *purée* with a wire whisk, in order to smooth it. Serve the shoulder with its gravy, three-quarters cleared of grease, and serve the apple sauce separately in a *timbale*.

1390—FRESH SHOULDER OF PORK A LA SOISSONNAISE
Carré de Porc à la Soissonnaise

Roast the shoulder in a *casserole* that may be sent to the table.

When it is three-parts done, set one quart of cooked and well-drained white beans round it, and complete the cooking gently. Serve the dish as it stands.

1391—BOILED SALT PORK A L'ANGLAISE
Porc Salé Bouilli à l'Anglaise

Cook plainly in water three lbs. of shoulder, breast, or belly, and add a garnish of vegetables as for boiled beef, and six parsnips.

Serve the vegetables round the piece of meat, and send a pease-pudding (prepared as directed below) separately.

Pease-pudding: put one lb. of a *purée* of yellow or green, split peas into a bowl, and mix with three oz. of melted or softened butter, three eggs, a pinch of salt, another of pepper, and a little nutmeg. Pour this *purée* into a pudding bowl, and *poach* it in steam or in a *bain-marie* (double-boiled).

This preparation may also be put into a buttered and flour-dusted napkin; in which case, close the napkin up tightly, tying it up securely with string, and cook the pudding in the same saucepan with the pork. This procedure is simpler than the first and quite as good.

Very often a *purée* prepared from split, yellow or green peas, is used instead of the pudding given above.

1392—PORK PIE *Pâté de Porc à l'Anglaise*

Completely line the bottom and sides of a pie-dish with thin slices of uncooked cured ham, and prepare, for a medium-sized dish one and one-half lbs. of fresh pork in pieces, seasoned with salt and pepper, and sprinkle with two tablespoons of dry *Duxelles* (223), a pinch of parsley and another of chopped sage; one and one-half lbs. of raw, sliced potatoes, and one large, chopped onion.

Garnish the bottom of the dish with a layer of pork pieces; cover with potatoes and onions; spread another layer and begin again in the same order. Add one-quarter pint of water; cover with a layer of fine paste or puff-paste trimmings, which should be well sealed down round the edges; brush with beaten egg; mark the paste with the prongs of a fork; make a slit in the center of the covering of paste for the escape of steam, and bake in a moderate oven for about two hours.

Fresh-pork Cutlets

1393—PORK CHOPS A LA CHARCUTIERE

Côtes de Porc à la Charcutière

Season the chops; dip them in melted butter, and sprinkle them with fine *raspings*. Grill them gently, and baste them from time to time.

Arrange them in a circle; pour a Charcutière sauce in their midst, and serve a *timbale* of potato *purée* separately.

Charcutière sauce for eight or ten chops: prepare one pint of Robert sauce (52) and mix with it, just before serving, two oz. of gherkins, cut in short *julienne*-fashion or minced.

1394—PORK CHOPS A LA FLAMANDE *Côtes de Porc à la Flamande*

Season the chops, and fry them on both sides in butter or fat.

Meanwhile, peel and slice some eating apples, allowing three oz. of the latter for each chop, and put them in an earthenware dish. Set upon them the half-fried chops; sprinkle with fat, and complete their cooking, as well as that of the apples, in the oven.

Serve the dish as it stands.

1395—PORK CHOPS A LA MILANAISE *Côtes de Porc à la Milanaise*

Treat the chops *à l'anglaise,* but remember to add one quart of grated Parmesan cheese to the bread-crumbs. Cook them gently in butter.

Arrange in a circle; set a milanaise garnish (1258) in the center, and serve a tomato sauce (29) separately.

1396—PORK CHOPS WITH PIQUANTE SAUCE OR ROBERT SAUCE
Côtes de Porc Sauce Piquante ou Sauce Robert

Season and grill or *sauté* the chops. Arrange them in a circle, with Piquante (48) or Robert sauce (52) in their midst.

N.B.—Chops accompanied by either of the two above-mentioned sauces, may be treated with melted butter and bread-crumbs and grilled (257) or *sautéd* (251); but, in this case, the sauce should be served separately.

For chops with Piquante sauce (48), border the dish on which they are served with gherkins, and send the sauce either separately or on the dish.

All the garnishes given under fresh shoulder of pork may accompany grilled or *sautéd* pork chops.

1397—SUCKLING PIG *Cochon de Lait*

Stuffed or not stuffed, suckling pigs are always roasted whole, and the essential point of the procedure is that they should be just done when their skin is crisp and golden.

While cooking, they should be frequently basted with oil; the latter being used in preference to any other fatty substance owing to the greater crispness it gives to the skin of the suckling pig.

Serve a sauceboat of good gravy at the same time.

1398—ROAST STUFFED SUCKLING PIG A L'ANGLAISE
Cochon de Lait Farci et Rôti à l'Anglaise

For a suckling pig of medium weight, prepare the following *forcemeat:*—Cook three lbs. of large onions with their skins on, and let them cool. This done, peel and finely chop them, and put them in a bowl with one lb. of the chopped suet of beef kidney, one lb. of soaked and well-pressed bread-crumbs, four oz. of parboiled and chopped sage, two eggs, one oz. of salt, a pinch of pepper and a little nutmeg.

Mix well, and put this stuffing inside the suckling pig. Sew up the belly; put it on the spit, and roast as directed above.

Serve separately, either a *timbale* of apple sauce (112) or of mashed potatoes (2248). Four oz. per lb. of selected raisins, washed and plumped in tepid water, are sometimes combined with the apple sauce.

1399—ZAMPINO (STUFFED FRESH HAM) *Zampino de Modène*

This stuffed fresh ham is a product of Italian pork-butchery. It is cooked like a ham, after having been tied in a cloth lest its skin break.

Served hot, it is accompanied by a Madeira or tomato sauce (29), a garnish of boiled, *braised* (274), or *gratined* cabbages; of string beans, or of potato *purée* (658).

1400—COLD ZAMPINO (STUFFED FRESH HAM) *Zampino Froid*

Zampino is served cold, alone, or mixed with other meats; but it is used more particularly as an hors-d'œuvre. For this purpose, cut it into the thinnest possible slices.

1401—PIG'S EARS ROUENNAISE *Oreilles à la Rouennaise*

After having singed and well cleaned the inside of the pig's ears, cook them in water, salted to the extent of one-third oz. of salt per quart, together with a garnish of vegetables as for pot-au-feu (599). This done, cut them across in such a way as to have the end where the flesh is thickest on one side, and the thinnest end on the other side of the strips.

Chop up the thick portion; cut the other into pieces, and put the whole into a saucepan with one-quarter pint of *half-glaze* (23) with Madeira.

Cook gently for thirty minutes. This done, add to the minced ears one and one-half lbs. of sausage meat and a pinch of chopped parsley. Divide up into portions, each weighing three oz.; wrap each portion in a piece of *pig's caul,* insert a piece of ear into the wrapping, and give the latter the shape of ordinary *crépinettes.* Grill gently, until the cooking is three-parts done; sprinkle with butter and *raspings,* and complete the cooking of the *crépinettes,* browning them in so doing.

Arrange in a circle, and serve a Madeira sauce (44) at the same time.

1402—PIG'S EARS SAINTE MENEHOULD
Oreilles à la Sainte Menehould

Cook the ears as explained above, and let them cool.

Cut them in two, lengthwise; coat them with mustard; sprinkle them with melted butter and *raspings,* and grill them gently

Ears are usually served plain, but they may be accompanied by apple sauce.

1403—TRUFFLED PIG'S FEET *Pieds de Porc Truffés*

Truffled pig's feet may be bought already prepared; all that remains to be done, therefore, is to grill them.

Sprinkle them with melted butter; grill them very gently, basting them from time to time the while, and serve them with a Périgueux Sauce (47).

1404—BREADED PIG'S FEET *Pieds de Porc Panés*

Sprinkle the pig's feet copiously with melted butter, and put them on the grill, which should be very hot.

Grill them very gently, turning them with care; and serve them plain, or with a tomato *purée* separately.

PUDDINGS

1405—WHITE PORK PUDDING *Boudin Blanc Ordinaire*

Cut in pieces and grind one-half lb. of very lean fresh pork, and three-quarters lb. of fresh pork fat. Add one and one-half oz. of *foie gras* and rub through a fine sieve.

Put this *forcemeat* into a bowl, and finish it with two fresh eggs; one and one-half oz. of chopped onion, cooked in butter without browning; one-sixth pint of thick cream; one-half oz. of salt, a pinch of white pepper, and a little nutmeg.

Mix the whole well; put it into the casing, without overstuffing, and tie round with string at regular intervals. Now set the puddings in a wire basket, and plunge them into a pot full of boiling water. From this moment keep the water at 203° F., and let the puddings *poach* for twelve minutes. This done, take them out, and let them cool.

Before serving them, grill them very gently, and, as a precautionary measure, wrap them in buttered paper. Do not cut them, but prick them with a pin.

Serve a *purée* of potatoes with cream at the same time.

1406—WHITE CHICKEN PUDDING *Boudins Blancs de Volaille*

Grind separately one lb. of raw chicken fillets and three-quarters lb. of fresh pork fat.

Combine the two until thoroughly mixed, and add three oz. of chopped onion, cooked in butter without browning, together with a little thyme and bay leaf; one-half oz. of salt, a pinch of white pepper, and a little nutmeg.

Mix the whole well, and add four eggs, one by one, beating the *forcemeat* vigorously the while.

Rub through a fine sieve; return the *forcemeat* to the bowl, and add, little by little, one pint of boiled and very cold milk.

Put the *forcemeat* into the casing; *poach* it in the *bain-marie* (water-bath), and set it to grill, observing the same precautions as in the preceding recipe.

Serve a *purée* of potatoes with cream at the same time as the puddings.

1407—BLOOD PUDDING OR BLACK PUDDING Boudins Noirs

Make the following preparation, putting the various ingredients into a bowl:—One lb. of very fresh pork fat, cut into large dice, and half-melted; one sixth pint of thick cream; two eggs; six oz. of chopped onions, cooked in lard without browning; two-thirds oz. of salt, a pinch of pepper, and a little spice; a pinch of wild-thyme leaves, and a bay leaf, both chopped.

Mix well with one pint of pork blood, and put it into the casing without over-filling it, for it should be borne in mind that the preparation swells in *poaching*.

Set the puddings in wire baskets; plunge them into boiling water, and, from that time, keep the latter at 203° F.

Let them *poach* for twenty minutes, and remember to prick all those that, by rising to the surface, show they contain air, which might burst their skins. When about to serve them, cut them on both sides, and grill them very gently.

They are generally accompanied by a potato *purée* with cream.

1408—ENGLISH BLOOD OR BLACK PUDDING

Boudins Noirs à l'Anglaise

Have ready the same preparation as for black puddings, given above, and add to it three-quarters lb. of rice, cooked in consommé and kept somewhat firm. *Poach* as before, and leave to cool. Cut the puddings, and grill them over a moderate fire.

Serve very hot with an apple sauce.

1409—BLOOD OR BLACK PUDDING FLAMANDE

Boudins Noirs à la Flamande

Have ready the same preparation as for black puddings, and add to it three oz. of moist sugar, two oz. of raisins, and the same quantity of currants, washed and plumped in lukewarm water.

Put the preparation into the casing, and *poach* in the usual way.

When about to serve, grill these puddings gently, after the manner to black puddings (1407), and send them to the table with a sweetened apple sauce.

CRÉPINETTES AND SAUSAGES

1410—TRUFFLED CREPINETTES

Crépinettes Truffés

Add to two lbs. of very good sausage-meat, four oz. of chopped truffles, and two tablespoons of truffles cooking-liquor. Mix well; divide into portions weighing two and one-half oz., and wrap each portion in a square of *pig's caul*. Shape the *crépinettes* thus formed rectangularly. Sprinkle with melted butter, and grill gently.

Arrange them in a circle; pour a Périgueux Sauce (47) in their midst, and serve a potato *purée* with cream separately.

1411—CREPINETTES CINDERELLA STYLE

Crépinettes Cendrillon

Prepare the *crépinettes* as above (1410); wrap them in a double sheet of buttered vegetable parchment; over them set a heap of glowing charcoal embers, and keep the latter alive for a space of twenty minutes, when the cooking operation should be completed.

Formerly, the above was the mode of procedure, but nowadays the *crépinettes* are merely enclosed, each in an oval layer of paste. They are then brushed with egg and their tops streaked with a fork; and, after having been laid on a pan, they are baked in a warm oven for twenty minutes.

This done, they are served on a napkin.

1412—SAUSAGES

Saucisses

The most known sausages of many nations are cooked like the French kind, and are often served at breakfasts as an accompaniment to bacon. Sometimes they serve as a garnish to roast fowls, young turkeys, etc.

Their seasoning is often excessive.

1413—SAUSAGES IN WHITE WINE *Saucisses au Vin Blanc*

First Method.—Put the sausages in a well-buttered saucepan; *poach* them gently in the oven, and place them on thin crusts of bread fried in butter.

For twelve sausages, swirl into the saucepan one-sixth pint of white wine; reduce this to half; add one-sixth pint of *half-glaze* (23) sauce; boil for a few minutes, and finish, away from the fire, with one and one-half oz. of butter. Pour this sauce over the sausages.

Second Method.—Brown the sausages in butter; add one-third pint of white wine, and complete their *poaching*. Set them on fried bread crusts; reduce the wine by two-thirds, and add to it the yolk of one egg, a few drops of lemon juice, two tablespoons of pale melted meat-*glaze* (23), and three oz. of butter. Pour the sauce over the sausages.

1414—FRANKFORT AND STRASBURG SAUSAGES

Saucisses de Francfort et de Strasbourg

Plunge the sausages into a saucepan of boiling water, and then *poach* them for no more than ten minutes; should they be allowed to cook for a longer time, they would lose their quality.

They may be served with a hors-d'œuvre dish of grated horse-radish, and an apple sauce separately; but their proper accompaniment is *braised* sauerkraut.

Cured Ham

However deservedly pork may be praised, it could never have been included among the preparations of first-class cookery (except subsidiarily) had it not been for the culinary value of hams.

With the latter it triumphs, and, be they of Bayonne or York, of Prague or Westphalia, of Virginia or Kentucky, no other joints enjoy more favor than these as *relevés*.

Though it is somewhat difficult to decide which one of the various kinds of ham should be adopted, in my opinion that of Bohemia known as Prague ham, is best for a warm dish, and that of York for a cold dish.

The latter is also excellent when served hot, but, even so, for this purpose it is inferior to the Prague kind, the delicacy of which is incomparable.

Still, York ham ranks first in the opinion of many, for it should be remembered that England has no rival in the preparation of seasoned pork, and her famous bacon, the renown of which is enormous, constitutes one of the greatest discoveries in the science of gastronomy.

(The meats, especially the cured hams and bacons, of the United States have gained world-wide fame since the above paragraphs were written. No one could ask for better material to work with than a hot or cold baked Virginia or Kentucky ham.—Ed.)

1415—HOT HAM—ITS PREPARATION Jambon Chaud

After having soaked the ham in cold water for six hours, brush it and remove the pelvic bone; put it into a pot of cold water, and set to boil. This done, keep the water just simmering, that the ham may cook after the *poaching* method.

There is no need of any seasoning or *aromatic* garnish. As often as possible, leave the ham to cool in its cooking-liquor. If the ham is to be *braised,* take it out of the water thirty minutes before it is cooked. Skin it; clear it of any superfluous fat, and put it in a *braising*-pan, just large enough to hold it, with two-thirds pint of some such wine as Madeira, Port, Xeres, Chypre, etc. Select the wine in accordance with the name of the dish on the menu.

Having thoroughly sealed down the lid of the pan, put it in the oven, and continue the cooking of the ham gently for one hour, turning it over from time to time during the operation. If it has to reach the table whole, *glaze* it at the last moment.

Its usual accompaniment is a light and highly seasoned *half-glaze* (23) sauce, combined with some of the *braising*-liquor cleared of all fat.

1416—CURED HAM CHANOINESSE Jambon à la Chanoinesse

Having *poached* the ham as explained above, *braise* it in white wine, adding three oz. of mushroom peelings.

Put it on a dish and send separately a garnish of large, fresh noodles, mixed with butter and a Soubise *purée,* and completed with a *julienne* of truffles.

Serve separately a *half-glaze* sauce (23), combined with the *braising*-liquor, cleared of all grease and reduced.

1417—CURED HAM WITH SAUERKRAUT Jambon à la Choûcroute

Completely cook the ham by *poaching;* skin and trim it.

If served whole, send separately some *braised* sauerkraut and potatoes, freshly cooked *à l'anglaise.* Serve a *half-glaze* sauce (23) with Rhine wine at the same time.

If served already carved, arrange the slices in a circle on a round dish; put the sauerkraut in their center, and border with the potatoes.

Serve, separately, the same sauce as before.

1418—CURED HAM MAILLOT — *Jambon à la Maillot*

Poach the ham; *braise* it, and *glaze* it at the last moment. Set it on a long dish, and surround it with the following garnish, arranged in alternate heaps:—Carrots and white turnips, cut to the shape of large, elongated olives, cooked separately in consommé, and *glazed;* small onions cooked in butter; *braised* and trimmed lettuce halves; separately buttered peas and string beans.

Serve apart a thickened gravy combined with some of the *braising-liquor*, cleared of all grease.

1419—PRAGUE STYLE HAM UNDER ASHES
Jambon à la Prague sous la Cendre

Poach the ham and drain it on a dish. Remove the skin and all the black, outside parts. Prepare a piece of patty paste (2392) large enough to enclose the ham. Sprinkle the surface of the ham with powdered sugar; *glaze* quickly at the *salamander,* and place the ham *glazed* side under on the layer of paste.

Draw the ends of the paste towards each other; seal them together, with the help of a little moistening, in such a way as to enclose the ham completely; turn the ham over, and put it on a pan with the sealed side of the paste lying underneath. Brush with egg yolk and streak with fork, make a slit in the middle of the paste for the escape of steam, and put it in the oven.

Leave it there until the paste is dry and well browned. After taking the ham out of the oven, inject into it, through a prepared hole, a large wineglassful of Port wine or Sherry. Plug up the hole with a little piece of paste; put on a dish, and serve immediately.

Serve at the same time a garnish of gnochi, spinach, or *Soufflé au Parmesan* (2295a).

The best accompaniment to Prague ham is a very light *glaze* (23) prepared with Port wine, and buttered at the last minute.

1419a—PRAGUE HAM METTERNICH
Jambon de Prague à la Metternich

Prepare a ham underneath the ashes as described above.

Send to the table with it as many *fine* slices of *foie-gras,* tossed in butter and each covered with a nice slice of truffle, as there are diners. Send also a *timbale* of asparagus tips.

The waiter in charge then puts a slice of ham, a slice of *foie-gras,* and a tablespoon of asparagus tips on each plate and serves.

The sauce should be a Madeira (44) flavored with truffle *essence.*

1419b—VIRGINIA HAM NORFOLK   *Jambon de Virginie à la Norfolk*

Prepare a ham as in (1419). Serve each slice of it with one slice of *braised* veal sweetbread and one tablespoon of fresh peas *à la paysanne.*

Send as an accompaniment the *braising*-liquor of the veal sweetbread.

1420—VARIOUS GARNISHES FOR BRAISED HAM
Garnitures Diverses pour Jambon à la Braise

The garnishes best suited to ham *relevés* are:—

Spinach; new broad beans; braised lettuce; endives; fresh peas à la paysanne.

Noodles; spaghetti; various macaronis; gnochi; purées of fresh beans, broad beans.

The most usual accompanying sauce is *half-glaze* (23) with Madeira.

1421—HAM SOUFFLE   *Jambon Soufflé*

This is a variety of the ham *soufflés* given hereafter. The preparation used is the same, and it may be made either from uncooked or from cooked cured ham.

After having completely boned it, but for the end bone, which must be kept, cook the ham, and cool it.

Now cut it horizontally, one-half inch above the bone, from the extremity of the end bone to the head of the latter. At the last-mentioned point, make a vertical incision meeting and ending at the first; remove the cushion of ham, which should by now be quite separated from the rest of the joint, and put aside for some future purpose.

All that remains of the ham, therefore, is a thick piece adhering to the end-bone. Carefully trim this piece, and surround it with a strong band of buttered paper, tied on with string, the purpose of which is to hold in the *soufflé.*

This done, put a sufficient quantity of *soufflé de Jambon* (described later) on the remaining meat of the ham to reconstruct it entirely. Smooth the surface of the preparation with the flat blade of a knife (dipped in cold water), and so finish off the contour of the ham. Decorate according to fancy; place the dish containing the ham in a saucepan of boiling water, and put the two in the oven with the view of obtaining the maximum amount of steam, which latter helps to *poach* the *soufflé*. This *souffléd* ham may be *poached* just as well in a steamer.

When the preparation is properly *poached*, remove the band of paper. Put the ham on a dish and send separately one of the garnishes or sauces given for *braised* ham.

1422—SOUFFLES OF HAM   *Soufflés de Jambon*

Ham *soufflés* are prepared after two recipes; in the first, cooked ham is used, and in the second the ham is raw. This last procedure is derived from *mousseline forcemeat*, and, inasmuch as the preparation resulting from it is less flimsy than that of the first, it is preferred when a large number of people have to be served.

1423—THE PREPARATION OF THE SOUFFLE WITH COOKED CURED HAM   *Appareil de Soufflé avec Jambon Cuit*

Finely grind one lb. of lean, cooked ham, and add to it, one after the other, three tablespoons of very cold Béchamel sauce (28). Rub through a fine sieve; put the resulting *purée* into a saucepan, and finish with one-quarter pint of very creamy and boiling Béchamel Sauce, flavored with ham *essence;* four egg yolks, and the whites of six eggs, beaten to a stiff froth.

This preparation may be combined with three oz. of grated Parmesan cheese, and the two flavors will be found to blend very agreeably.

Prepared in this way, it is particularly well suited to the Jambon Soufflé.

1424—THE PREPARATION OF THE SOUFFLE WITH UNCOOKED CURED HAM   *Appareil de Soufflé avec Jambon Cru*

Following the quantities given under Farce Mousseline (195), make the *soufflé* preparation, and add four tablespoons of reduced and very cold Béchamel sauce (28) per lb. of raw cured ham.

Keep the *forcemeat* somewhat stiff, and finish it with the whites of four eggs, beaten to a stiff froth, per lb. of ham.

1425—HAM SOUFFLE ALEXANDRA   *Soufflé de Jambon Alexandra*

Make the *soufflé* preparation after one of the methods given. Spread it in layers in a buttered *timbale,* alternating the layers of *soufflé* with others of asparagus tips mixed with butter. Smooth the surface to the shape of a dome; decorate with a fine slice of truffle, and cook in a moderate oven, of a temperature suited to this kind of preparation. Serve the *soufflé* as soon as it is ready. If it be small, spread only one layer of asparagus tips in the middle of it.

If it be large, spread two or three layers of asparagus-tips.

1426—HAM SOUFFLE CARMEN — *Soufflé de Jambon Carmen*

Add to the selected one of the two *soufflé* preparations—either will do—for one lb. of ham, the *purée* of one-half lb. of pressed tomatoes, cooked in butter with one-half pimento rubbed through a sieve and very much reduced.

Place the *soufflé* in a buttered *timbale;* sprinkle the surface with a pinch of red pimento, cut in fine *julienne*-fashion, and cook as described above.

1427—HAM SOUFFLE GASTRONOME — *Soufflé de Jambon Gastronome*

Place the selected ham *soufflé* preparation in layers in a buttered *timbale,* and between each layer spread a litter of noodles, tossed in butter.

Sprinkle the surface with chopped truffles; set a ball of truffle well in the center of the *soufflé,* and cook in the usual way.

1428—HAM SOUFFLE MILANAISE — *Soufflé de Jambon Milanaise*

Place the ham *soufflé* preparation in a buttered *timbale,* and spread in alternate layers with a fine garnish à la Milanaise (1258).

Decorate the surface with small pieces of *poached* macaroni, fried in butter; sprinkle with grated cheese, and cook the *soufflé* in a moderate oven.

1429—HAM SOUFFLE PERIGOURDINE — *Soufflé de Jambon Périgourdine*

Place the *soufflé* preparation in layers in a buttered *timbale,* and between each layer spread a layer of truffle slices. Sprinkle the surface with chopped truffles, and cook the *soufflé* in the usual way.

1430—HOT MOUSSES AND MOUSSELINES OF CURED HAM
Mousses et Mousselines Chaudes de Jambon

Mousses and *Mousselines* are made from the same preparation as *Farce Mousseline de Jambon,* in the recipe given under (195).

The need of differentiating the terms arises from the fact that *mousses* are *poached* in a mould the contents of which are sufficient for a number of people, whereas *mousselines* are spoon-moulded *quenelles,* shaped like eggs (205).

In the preparation of *Farce Mousseline de Jambon* it is necessary to allow, in the salt seasoning, for the amount of salting the ham has already received.

If the meat of the ham is not very red, the color of the *forcemeat* may be intensified by means of a little vegetable red (2343), in order that it may be of a distinct pink shade.

1431—TREAMENT OF CURED HAM MOUSSE
Traitement de la Mousse de Jambon

Put the *forcemeat* in a deep ring-mould, somewhat like a *Charlotte,* and *poach* it under cover in a *bain-marie* (water-bath).

That the *poaching* may be regular, keep in water at a constant temperature of 205° or 208° Fahrenheit, and allow forty-five minutes for the *poaching* of a *mousse* made in a quart mould.

The preparation is cooked when it swells and rises in the mould.

As soon as this occurs, take it out of the *bain-marie;* let it stand for five minutes to settle; turn it upside-down on a dish, and wait two minutes before removing the mould. In any case, do not take off the mould until the liquid which has drained from it, all round the dish, has been soaked up. Ham *mousses* are chiefly accompanied by *Suprême* sauce (106a), or *Veloutés* (25) with curry or paprika; sometimes, also, a highly-seasoned and buttered *half-glaze* sauce (23), with Madeira, Port, or Marsala may be used. The most suitable garnishes for ham *mousses* are those I have already given for ham.

1432—TREATMENT AND POACHING OF CURED HAM MOUSSELINES
Traitement et le Poché des Mousselines de Jambon

As I have already stated, *mousselines,* like *quenelles* (205), are moulded with a spoon.

They may also be laid, by means of a pastry-bag, on the bottom of the well-buttered wide saucepan in which they are to be *poached;* they are shaped like *meringue* tarts, plain or fluted, and, in either case, they are decorated with diamonds, crescents, discs, etc., of ham or truffle.

Having carried out the selected method of preparation, cover them with boiling water, salted to the extent of one-third oz. per quart, and *poach* them for from eighteen to twenty minutes, taking care to keep the water at a constant temperature of 208° F. These *mousselines* may also be *poached* dry in a steamer or in a drying oven.

1433—MOUSSELINE OF CURED HAM ALEXANDRA
Mousselines de Jambon Alexandra

Decorate the *mousselines,* prepared according to one of the two methods above described, with one diamond shaped piece of ham and another of truffle. *Poach* them; drain them well, and arrange them in the form of a crown. Cover them with an Allemande sauce (27), flavored with ham *essence,* and combined with two oz. of grated Parmesan per pint of the sauce, and *glaze* quickly.

After taking the *mousselines* out of the oven, set in their midst a heap of buttered asparagus tips.

1434—MOUSSELINE OF CURED HAM FLORENTINE
Mousselines de Jambon à la Florentine

Spread a layer of shredded spinach, fried in butter, on a dish.

Upon it set the *poached* and well-drained *mousselines;* cover them with the same sauce as that prescribed for the *Mousselines* Alexandra, and *glaze* them quickly.

1435—MOUSSELINE OF CURED HAM HONGROISE
Mousselines de Jambon à la Hongroise

Poach the *mousselines.* the *forcemeat* of which must be flavored with paprika. Drain them; arrange them in a circle; cover them with Hongroise Sauce, and *glaze* them quickly.

On taking the dish from the oven, set a fine heap of baked cauliflower with cheese in the middle of it.

1436—MOUSSELINE OF CURED HAM WITH GREEN PEAS
Mousselines de Jambon aux Petits Pois

Proceed exactly as described under (1433), but substitute for the asparagus tips a garnish of very small buttered peas.

Cold Ham

1437—COLD CURED HAM IN JELLY   *Jambon Froid à la Gelée*

When ham is to be served cold, it should, if possible, be allowed to cool in its cooking-liquor, except when it has to be boned. In the latter case, take it out as soon as it is cooked; incise it underneath, following the edge of the cushion; detach and remove the bones.

Now roll up the ham; bind it tightly in a piece of linen, and cool it while pressing it.

Whether boned or unboned. skin it when it is cold; remove some of its fat, and sprinkle it with cold, melted aspic until the latter covers it evenly.

Put it on a dish; fix a paper frill to it, and surround it with fine chopped aspic.

1438—COLD CURED HAM SOUFFLE   *Jambon Soufflé Froid*

Proceed exactly as in (1421), but substitute for the *soufflé* preparation the cold ham *mousse* below.

1439—COLD CURED HAM MOUSSE   *Mousse Froide de Jambon*

The Preparation of the Mousse.—Finely grind one lb. of very lean, cooked ham; add to it one-third pint of cold *Velouté* (242), and rub through a fine sieve.

Put the resulting *purée* into a bowl; season it; work it on ice for a few minutes, and mix in, little by little, one-quarter pint of melted aspic. Finally combine two-thirds pint of lightly beaten cream with it.

The *mousse* may be moulded, either in an aspic-coated mould, decorated with truffles, as explained under (956), or in small *cassolettes*, lined with a thin strip of paper inside their brims, after the manner of small, cold *soufflés*.

As the dishing and serving of *mousses* are always the same, the reader is asked to refer to those recipes (1430–1431) dealing with the question.

1440—COLD CURED HAM MOUSSE ALSACIENNE
Mousse Froide de Jambon à l'Alsacienne

Take a deep, square dish and garnish it, half-full, with fine, ham *mousse*. Even the surface of this layer of *mousse,* and, when it has set, arrange upon it some shells, cut by means of a spoon dipped in hot water, from a *foie-gras Parfait*. As soon as this is done, pour over the *foie-gras* shells a sufficient quantity to cover them of half-melted succulent chicken aspic (159) with Madeira, and let this jelly set.

When about to serve, incrust the dish in a block of ice.

1441—MOUSSE OF CURED HAM WITH CHICKEN BREASTS
Mousse de Jambon au Blanc de Poulet

Garnish a deep, square dish with some ham *mousse*. When the latter has set, arrange on it the *suprêmes* (breasts) of a very white, *poached* fowl. These *suprêmes,* cut into regular slices, should be coated with a white *chaud-froid* sauce (73).

Cover with aspic, as directed under *Mousse à l'Alsacienne* (1440), and serve.

N.B.—If desired, the slices of breast need not be coated with *chaud-froid* sauce, but, in this case, they should be covered with aspic.

1442—COLD MOUSSELINES OF CURED HAM

Mousselines Froides de Jambon

These *mousselines* are made from the same preparation as that used for the *mousse,* and, but for the basic ingredient, which is not the same, they are treated after the manner described under *Petites Mousses de Homard* (958). To avoid needless repetition, therefore, the reader will kindly substitute the word ham for lobster in the recipe just referred to.

CHAPTER XVI

POULTRY (VOLAILLE)

ALTHOUGH the term "poultry" in its general sense, implies Turkeys, Geese, Ducks and Pigeons, just as well as Chickens, only the latter are meant, from the culinary standpoint, when the word "Volaille" appears on a menu.

Four qualities of fowl are recognized in cookery, and each plays its part, has its uses, and is quite distinct from the other three. We have:—

(1) *Pullets* (young, fat hens called poulardes) *and capons;* usually served whole, either as *relevés* or roasts.

(2) *Chickens,* so-called "à la Reine" (roasting or frying); used for *sautés* and chiefly for roasts—called poulets.

(3) *Spring chickens or broilers;* best suited to *en cocotte* or grilled preparations.

(4) *Chicks or squab chickens;* served only *en cocotte* or grilled.

Suprêmes and *ailerons* of fowl, which are among the finest entrées, are supplied by chickens à la Reine or by Spring chickens.

Finally, there are the giblets, consisting of the pinions (ends of the wings), necks, gizzards, and livers of fowl, which give rise to a number of preparations, the recipes of which I shall give briefly at the end of the series.

1443—PULLETS AND CAPONS FOR RELEVES

Poulets et Chapons pour Relevés

Pullets (fat hens) and capons for *relevés* and entrées are *poached* or *poêled;* sometimes, but more rarely, they are *braised.*

The birds to be cooked by *poaching* are trussed with the feet folded back and inserted into the belly; their fillets (breasts) and legs are rubbed with lemon, so as to keep them white, and they are then covered with thin slices of *larding* bacon.

The ingredients for chicken *poaching* stock were given under (249). The bird is cooked when the blood which issues from a fork prick on the leg is white or faintly pink.

These fowls are sometimes *larded* or *studded*. When this is to be done, dip the legs and breast of a trussed and lemon-rubbed fowl into boiling white stock; this will be found to sufficiently harden the flesh to permit it being treated in the required way. The products used for *studding* and *larding* are, according to circumstances, ham or tongue, truffles or mushrooms, and sometimes, the outer part of a carrot for the *larding*. Only truffles, ham and tongue are used for *studding*.

Poëled fowls are trussed as above; they are covered with slices of bacon in order that the breasts may be protected during the first stages of the cooking; then they are cooked in butter on *poëlé-aromatics,* under cover and in a deep, thick saucepan. When the piece is almost cooked, just moisten it a little, either with rich poultry-stock, with the cooking-liquor of truffles or mushrooms, with Madeira, red or white wine, etc. This moistening serves in the basting of the fowl and must therefore be renewed if it reduces too quickly. After having been cleared of all grease, it is always added to the sauce which accompanies the piece of poultry.

Braised fowls are always treated after the manner described under (248); they are not rubbed with lemon, but they are covered with slices of bacon. The latter should only cover the breast, but be thick, notwithstanding; for they protect the belly, which, without them, would shrivel by the time the legs cooked.

The covering of bacon is essential to all pieces of poultry, whether these be *poached, poëled, braised* or roasted.

1444—THE WAY TO SERVE POULTRY RELEVES QUICKLY AND HOT
Façon de Servir les Relevés de Volaille Rapidement et Chauds

I feel bound to call the reader's attention to this very important point in culinary work:—

Owing to the difficulties involved in the carving of the fowl and the placing and arranging of the pieces and their garnish upon the diners' plates—both of which operations require dexterity and expertness, which those in charge very often do not possess, or thanks to the inefficiency of particular installations, or what not, I have noticed for some considerable time, that the method of serving large pieces of poultry is, in many cases, very far from being the right one.

For, indeed, how often does not the diner find himself presented with a plate of fowl which is neither appetizing or sufficiently hot! It follows from this, that all the care and trouble devoted by a chef to the preparation of the dish are entirely wasted. Now, I have tried to improve this state of affairs, by planning a method of serving which would be at once simple and quick, without necessarily detracting from its tastefulness and presentability.

In the first place, it is my practice to remove the fowl's two *suprêmes,* breast fillets, in the kitchen, and to keep them warm in a little cooking-liquor until the last minute. Secondly, I remove all the bones of the breast, and I reconstruct the fowl with a stuffing in keeping with the dish. Either a *mousseline forcemeat,* pilaff rice combined with cream (2256), *foie gras* and truffles, spaghetti, or noodles with cream.

Having properly smoothed and arranged the selected stuffing, the fowl may now be placed, either at one end of a long platter, or on a low bed of fried bread, on which it may be set firmly.

It may also be entirely coated with Mornay sauce (91), sprinkled with grated cheese, and speedily *glazed.*

When the bird is ready to serve, its stuffing should be set round it in fine, *tartlet crusts;* its breasts, quickly sliced, should be distributed among the *tartlets,* and the platter sent to the table with the sauce separately.

By this means, it reaches the table hot, it is served quickly and cleanly; and every person gets a slice of meat, and not the stuffing only, as was so often the case formerly.

Instead of *tartlets,* one may use thin *croûtons* of bread, of the size of the slices of chicken, and fried in fresh butter.

Thus, for a "Poularde à la Derby" (1465), after having stuffed the pullet with rice, remove the bones of the breast, and the breasts; all that is necessary is to properly shape the rice, and to serve the fowl on a bed of fried bread, etc.

This done, prepare as many *croûtons* and slices of *foie-gras, sautéd* in butter, as there are diners, and arrange them round the pullet— the slices of *foie-gras* lying on the *croûtons.* Now, quickly cut the *suprêmes* into slices; put one of these on each slice of *foie-gras,* and on each of the latter put a slice of truffle. Put the pullet, thus prepared, in the oven for a few minutes; let it get very hot, and send it to the table with the sauce separately.

In the dining-room the Maître-d'hôtel, or at home whoever is waiting on the table, quickly serves the garnished *croûtons* on hot plates, beside each *croûton* he puts a tablespoon of the rice with which the pullet has been stuffed, and, finally, a tablespoon of sauce.

In less than two minutes after its entrance into the dining-room, the pullet is thus served warm to each person.

Of course, the above measures refer to the fowl that has to be served whole; but, when this is not required, the rice removed from the cooked bird need only be set in the center of a deep, square entrée dish (fitted with a cover), and surrounded by the sliced *suprêmes,* with inserted slices of *foie-gras* and truffle. The sauce is also served separately in this case. Cover the dish, so that it may stand and keep hot a few minutes, if necessary, without spoiling.

The legs, which are rarely served at a well-ordered dinner, remain in the kitchen together with the remains.

I cannot too strongly recommend the system just described, whenever the circumstances allow of its being put into practice. It is the only one that ensures an efficient service, calculated to give entire satisfaction to all concerned.

(For convenient carving and serving of poultry or roasts, it is best to have the piece repose on a bed of bread or rice. This will keep any food indicated from slipping on the platter.—Ed.)

1445—ALBUFERA PULLET — *Poularde Albufera*

Stuff the pullet with the rice (2256), and *poach* it. Put it on a dish and coat with Albuféra sauce (87).

Surround with small *tartlet crusts,* filled with truffles cut with a spoon the size of a pea; *quenelles* of the same shape; small button mushrooms, and cocks' kidney. Mix this garnish with the Albuféra sauce.

Between each *tartlet,* place a slice of tongue, cut to the shape of a cock's comb.

1446—ALEXANDRA PULLET — *Poularde Alexandra*

Having *larded* the pullet with tongue and truffle, *poach* it.

This done, remove the *suprêmes,* breasts, and replace them by *mousseline forcemeat;* smooth this *forcemeat,* giving it the shape of the pullet in so doing, and set to *poach* in the front of the oven.

Now, coat the piece with Mornay sauce (91), and *glaze* quickly. Put on a dish, and surround with *tartlet crusts* filled with asparagus tips, mixed with butter; place a slice of the reserved *suprêmes* (which should have been kept hot) on each *tartlet,* and border the dish with a ribbon of pale *glaze* (16).

1447—AMBASSADRICE PULLET   *Poularde Ambassadrice*

Stud the pullet with truffles, cover it with a Matignon (227), wrap it in muslin, and *braise* it.

Remove the *suprêmes;* remove the bones of the breast; fill the bird with a stuffing of asparagus tips, mixed with butter, and arrange as already described under (1444).

Slice the *suprêmes,* and put them back on the stuffing in such a way as to reconstruct the breast of the fowl. Coat the bird with somewhat stiff and fine Suprême sauce (106a); put it on a dish, and surround it with lamb sweetbreads, *studded* with truffles, *braised* and *glazed,* and alternate the sweetbreads with little bundles of asparagus tips.

1448—ANDALUSIAN PULLET   *Poularde Andalouse*

Poële the pullet. Put it on a dish, and coat it with its *poëlé*-liquor, combined with tomatoed half-*glaze* sauce (23). On either side of it set some peppers, stuffed with rice, and some slices of egg-plant, seasoned, dredged and tossed in butter; alternating the two.

1449—PULLET ANGLAISE   *Poularde à l'Anglaise*

Poach the pullet, and coat it with a Béchamel sauce (28) flavored with chicken-*essence.*

Put it on a dish and surround it with slices of cured tongue, laid tile-fashion on either side; and heaps of carrots and turnips (cut to the shape of balls) and peas and celery, at either end. All these vegetables should be cooked *à l'anglaise;* either in boiling water or steamed.

1450—PULLET A L'AURORE   *Poularde à l'Aurore*

Poach the pullet without browning; put it on a dish and coat it with an "Aurore Sauce" (60). Surround it with medium-sized, decorated *quenelles;* and trimmed oval slices of cured tongue, arranged according to fancy.

1451—PULLET BEAUFORT   *Poularde à la Beaufort*

Stuff the pullet with a fine *foie-gras,* browned in the oven for twenty minutes with a little Madeira, and cooled.

Fill up the pullet with a little, fine sausage-meat; *stud* it with truffles, and *braise* it in very little moistening.

Serve it on a low bed, and surround it with *braised* lambs' tongues, alternated with artichoke-bottoms, garnished with a rosette of Soubise *purée* (104). As an accompaniment, use the *braising*-liquor, cleared of all fat.

1452—BOILED PULLET ANGLAISE   *Poularde Bouillie à l'Anglaise*
Cook the pullet in light, white stock with one lb. of salt pork and a garnish of vegetables as for *pot-au-feu* (599). Serve, surrounded with the bacon, cut into slices.

Serve, separately, an English parsley sauce (119a), and a sauceboat of the pullet's cooking-liquor.

1453—PULLET WITH CELERY   *Poularde aux Céleris*
Poêle the pullet, and baste it towards the close of the cooking with strong veal stock.

Prepare a garnish of *braised* celery.

Serve the pullet surrounded with the *braised* celery, and cover it with the *poêlé*-liquor.

1454—PULLET WITH MUSHROOMS IN HALF-GLAZE
Poularde aux Champignons à Brun
Poêle the pullet, and swirl into the saucepan mushroom *essence*. Add this liquid (reduced) to one-quarter pint of half-*glaze* (23) with Madeira.

Place the pullet on a dish, and surround it with twenty grooved and cooked mushroom caps. Serve separately the reduced half-*glaze*, to which add two oz. of fresh butter.

1455—PULLET WITH MUSHROOMS IN WHITE SAUCE
Poularde aux Champignons à Blanc
Poach the pullet.

Put it on a dish, and coat it with an Allemande sauce (27) flavored with mushroom *essence*.

Surround it with twenty grooved, cooked and very white mushroom caps.

1456—CHANOINESSE PULLET   *Poularde Chanoinesse*
Prepare a *"Poularde Soufflée"* after recipe (1518). Surround it with small heaps of crayfish tails, alternated with small *croûtons* of fried bread, on each of which place a slice of the breast. Finish with a slice of truffle on each slice of the *suprêmes*.

Serve a Mornay sauce (91), finished with crayfish butter (147), separately.

1457—CHATELAINE PULLET   *Poularde Châtelaine*

Poële the pullet without letting it brown too much.

Serve it, surrounded with small artichoke-bottoms, stewed in butter and garnished with Soubise (104).

Alternate the artichoke-bottoms with small heaps of chestnuts cooked in consommé and *glazed*.

Pour a little thickened *poëlé*-liquor on the bottom of the dish, and serve what remains of it, separately, in a sauceboat.

1458—CHEVALIERE PULLET   *Poularde Chevalière*

Remove the *suprêmes,* and the *minion fillets. Lard* the former with two rows of truffles and two rows of tongue; trim the *minion fillets;* make five or six slits in each; insert a thin slice of truffle half-way into each slit, and draw the respective ends of the two fillets together in such a way as to form two rings. Put the *suprêmes* and the *minion fillets* each into a buttered saucepan, and cover.

Remove the pullet's legs, keeping the skin as long as possible; bone them to within one and one-third inches of the joints, and cut off the feet, slantwise, just below the same joints. Fill the boned regions with *godiveau* prepared with cream, close the opening by means of a few stitches with strong cotton, and truss each leg in such a manner as to imitate a small duck.

Poach these stuffed legs in stock made from the pullet's remains.

Also *poach the suprêmes* and the *minion fillets* in good time, with a little mushroom cooking-liquor, and a few drops of lemon juice.

With a pinch of flour mixed with water to a paste, stick a fried *croûton* (the shape of a pyramid, three inches high and of two inch base) in the middle of a dish.

Around this pyramid, arrange the two stuffed legs and the two *suprêmes;* putting each of them on a decorated *quenelle* with the view of slightly raising them. Set the *minion fillets* on the legs, and, between the latter and the *suprêmes,* lay small heaps of cocks' combs and kidneys, and some very white mushroom caps. Pierce the *croûton* with an ornamental skewer garnished with one truffle, one fine cock's comb, and a large mushroom.

Serve a Suprême sauce (106a) separately.

N.B.—This dish is generally bordered either with noodle-paste (2291), white English paste (biscuit dough). or with just the chased silver border of the dish.

1459—CHIMAY PULLET   *Poularde Chimay*

Stuff the pullet with one-half lb. of *half-poached* noodles, tossed in butter, and combined with a little cream and three oz. of *foie-gras* cut into large dice.

Poêle it gently; coat it with some of its *poêlé*-liquor, thickened.

Spread over the pullet a copious amount of fresh homemade noodles (2291), *sautéd* in clarified butter (175); and serve the remainder of the thickened *poêlé*-liquor separately

1460—CHIPOLATA PULLET   *Poularde Chipolata*

Poêle the pullet and put it into a *terrine à pâté* with a garnish consisting of small, *glazed* onions; chipolata (Italian) sausages, *poached* in butter; chestnuts cooked in consommé; fried pieces of bacon; and, if desired, some small *glazed* carrots.

Add the pullet's cooking stock, and simmer for ten minutes before serving.

1461—CHIVRY PULLET   *Poularde à la Chivry*

Poach the pullet. Put it on a platter and coat it with Chivry sauce (78).

Serve a *Macédoine* of fresh vegetables, mixed with butter or cream, separately.

1462—CUSSY PULLET   *Poularde Cussy*

Braise the pullet. Put it on a platter and surround it with whole truffles, cooked in *Mirepoix* with Madeira, and alternated with fine, grilled mushrooms, garnished with artichoke *purée*.

In front of the pullet set a small, silver shell, in which put a pyramid of large cocks' combs, heated in butter.

1463—PULLET IN DEMI-DEUIL (IN HALF MOURNING)

Poularde en Demi-Deuil

Between the skin and the breasts of the fowl insert a few fine slices of raw truffle. *Lard* the pullet and *poach* it.

When it is ready, strain the cooking-liquor through a napkin; reduce it, and add it to a very white Suprême sauce (106a), containing slices of truffle.

Cook it with some of the sauce, and serve what remains, separately, in a sauceboat.

1464—DEMIDOFF PULLET   *Poularde Demidoff*

Poêle the pullet. When it is three-quarters done, put it into a *cocotte* and surround it with the following garnish, prepared in advance and stewed in butter: one-half lb. of carrots and five oz. of turnips, cut into grooved crescents, one inch in diameter; five oz. of small onions cut into thin slices, and five oz. of celery.

Complete the cooking of the pullet with this garnish, and add to it, when about to serve, three oz. of truffles, cut in the shape of crescents, and one-sixth pint of chicken stock (10).

Serve the preparation in the *cocotte,* after having cleared the liquor of all fat.

1465—DERBY PULLET *Poularde Derby*

Stuff the pullet with rice (2256), and *poêle* it. Surround it with slices of *foie-gras,* tossed in butter (each set on a small, fried *croûton*), and alternate these with large, whole truffles, cooked in champagne.

As an accompaniment, serve the pullet's cooking-liquor, cleared of all grease, combined with the cooking-liquor of the truffles and one-sixth pint of veal gravy (41). Reduce the whole to one-sixth pint and thicken with arrow-root, cornstarch, etc.

1466—DIVA PULLET *Poularde Diva*

Stuff the pullet with rice, prepared after recipe (2256), and *poach* it without browning and coat it with Suprême sauce (106a), flavored with paprika.

Send a garnish consisting of *cèpes* with cream, separately.

N.B.—This dish was served for the first time to Mme. Adelina Patti, the great singer.

1467—DEVONSHIRE PULLET *Poularde Devonshire*

Bone the breast of a fine pullet; season it inside, and fill it with a chicken *forcemeat,* prepared with cream and mixed with half its weight of very fine sausage-meat.

In the middle of the pullet set a nice cured and cooked calf's tongue, trimmed and cleared of all cartilage; and place it so that its thin end lies in the region of the bird's tail.

Sew up the pullet with thin string, allowing the skin sufficient play not to tear under the pressure of the *forcemeat,* which swells while cooking. Truss, cover the pullet with a slice of *larding* bacon, *poach,* and drain it.

When about to serve, make an incision around the breast with the point of a knife; detach the stuffing with the blade of a knife, passed horizontally on a level with the spine, and cut off, at a stroke, the piece consisting of the pullet's breast, the stuffing, and the calf's tongue.

Put the bird, with the legs and wings still attached, on a low bed. Cut the breast, lengthwise, into two; and, if the fowl has been properly stuffed, the tongue should then be found neatly cut in two. Slice each half, and return them to the bird in such a way as to reconstruct the breast and give it an untouched appearance.

Coat lightly with Allemande sauce (27), combined with very red tongue, cut into dice; and surround with a border of *timbales* made from a *purée* of fresh peas (2196), each set on an artichoke bottom. Serve a sauceboat of the same sauce as that with which the pullet was coated.

1468—SCOTCH PULLET   *Poularde Ecossaise*

Stuff the pullet with pearl barley cooked in white consommé, well drained, and combined, per lb., with an equal quantity of fine sausage-meat (to which has been added a chopped onion, cooked in butter), and two tablespoons of cream.

Poach the pullet in the usual way; put it on a dish and coat it with Écossaise sauce (118) or an Allemande sauce (27), combined with a *brunoise* of vegetables: carrots, onions, leeks, and celery, and a large part of the reduced pullet's *poaching*-liquor.

Serve a garnish of string beans with cream, separately.

1469—EDWARD VII PULLET   *Poularde Edouard VII*

Stuff the pullet with rice (2256), and *poach* it without browning. Put it on a dish, and coat it with a curry sauce (81), combined with two oz. of red peppers in dice, per pint of sauce.

Serve a garnish of cucumbers with cream, separately.

N.B.—This dish was originated at the Carlton Hotel on the occasion of His Majesty King Edward VII's Coronation.

1470—PULLET EN ESTOUFFADE   *Poularde en Estouffade*

Partly *poêle* the pullet in a saucepan.

Line the bottom and sides of an oval *cocotte* with thin slices of ham. Put the pullet into this *cocotte*, together with one lb. of carrots, onions, and celery, all three sliced, fried in butter and moderately seasoned with salt and pepper.

Swirl into the saucepan one-third pint of strong veal stock; reduce to half; put this reduced stock into the *cocotte;* cover the latter; seal down the lid with a ribbon of paste, and complete the cooking of the pullet in a somewhat hot oven for three-quarters of an hour.

1471—TARRAGON PULLET   *Poularde à l'Estragon*

Poach the pullet, and add to the ordinary garnish a bunch of five or six sprigs of tarragon.

Put on a dish, and decorate the pullet's breast with a nice spray of *blanched* tarragon leaves.

Reduce and strain the pullet's cooking-liquor, and serve it separately.

1472—FAVORITE PULLET   *Poularde à la Favorite*

Stuff the pullet with one-half lb. of rice (2256).

Poach it and coat with a Suprême sauce (106a).

Surround with a garnish of cocks' combs and kidneys, and slices of truffle.

1473—FERMIERE PULLET   *Poularde à la Fermière*

Prepare the pullet as for (1470); but, instead of lining the *cocotte* with slices of ham, cut the latter into dice and add these to the garnish, together with four oz. of peas and four oz. of string beans, cut into small pieces.

1474—FINANCIERE PULLET   *Poularde à la Financière*

Braise the pullet.

Put it on a dish and surround it with a garnish consisting of small heaps of *quenelles* made from chicken, *mousseline forcemeat;* grooved, button-mushroom caps; cocks' combs and kidneys; slices of truffle, and *blanched* olives. Add a small quantity of half-*glaze* sauce (23) prepared with truffle *essence*.

Send a sauceboat of the same sauce separately.

1475—GASTRONOME PULLET   *Pullet à la Gastronome*

Stuff the pullet with one-half lb. of noodles, slightly tossed in butter, and *poêle* it.

Swirl into the saucepan one-quarter pint of champagne. Arrange the pullet and surround it with medium-sized truffles, cooked in champagne, alternated with small heaps of cooked and *glazed* chestnuts, and place a cock's kidney between each heap.

Serve, separately, a half-*glaze* sauce (23), flavored with truffle *essence* and combined with the reduced champagne-liquor.

1476—GODARD PULLET   *Poularde à la Godard*

Braise the pullet brown and surround it with spoon-moulded *quenelles* of *forcemeat,* combined with chopped mushrooms and truffles; large oval *quenelles,* decorated with tongue and truffle; grooved button-mushroom caps; cocks' combs and kidneys; *glazed* small lambs' sweetbreads; and olive-shaped truffles.

Slightly coat this garnish with Godard sauce (1054), combined with some reduced *braising*-liquor, and serve what remains in a sauceboat.

1477—GRAMMONT PULLET   *Poularde à la Grammont*

Poach the pullet, and let it half-cool.

Now remove the *suprêmes* and the bones of the breast; fill up the cavity in the bird with a stuffing consisting of larks' breasts, *sautéd* just before serving; grooved button-mushroom caps; cocks' combs and kidneys; and combine the whole by means of Béchamel sauce (28), finished with truffle *essence.*

Slice the *suprêmes,* and return them to their place, setting a slice of truffle between each. Coat the pullet with a stiff Allemande sauce (27); sprinkle with grated Parmesan cheese and melted butter; *glaze* quickly, and serve at once.

1478—PULLET GRAND HOTEL   *Poularde Grand Hôtel*

Cut up the fowl as for a *sauté,* and cook it in butter, covered. Then set the pieces in a very hot *cocotte,* and spread on five oz. of raw truffles cut into thick slices and slightly salted and peppered.

Swirl into the saucepan a few tablespoons of white wine; add a little chicken stock; pour this liquor into the *cocotte;* close the cover, and put it in a very hot oven for eight or ten minutes to cook the truffles.

Serve the preparation as it stands in the *cocotte.*

N.B.—The dish was invented at the Grand Hotel at Monte Carlo, as a means of offering to those who could not wait for the preparation of truffled pullets a substitute of a somewhat similar nature to the latter.

1479—PULLET WITH COARSE SALT   *Poularde au Gros Sel*

Poach the pullet, and add to it ten small olive-shaped carrots and ten small onions.

Put it on a dish, and surround the bird with the carrots and the onions, arranged in small heaps.

Serve, separately, a sauceboat containing the pullet's cooking-liquor, and a shaker of kitchen salt.

1480—PULLET GREEK STYLE   *Poularde à la Grecque*

Stuff the pullet with rice, prepared after recipe (2253), and *poële* it.

Arrange it on a dish, and coat it with very strong reduced chicken stock, thickened by means of arrowroot or flour, etc.

1481—PULLET HUNGARIAN STYLE   *Poularde à la Hongroise*

Poële the pullet.

Put it on a dish; coat it with Hongroise sauce (85), and surround it with *timbales* of pilaff rice (2255), combined with tomatoes, cut into dice.

Send the Hongroise sauce separately.

1482—PULLET WITH OYSTERS   *Poularde aux Huîtres*

Boil the pullet gently in light, white stock, until it is well cooked. With the cooking-liquor prepare a Suprême Sauce (106a), and add the almost entirely reduced *poaching*-liquor of twenty-four oysters, one-half pint of cream, and the twenty-four oysters, bearded.

Serve the pullet with this sauce poured over it.

1483—INDIA PULLET   *Poularde à l'Indienne*

Poach the pullet.

Put it on a dish; coat with Indienne sauce (1483), and serve a *timbale* of rice à l'Indienne, prepared after recipe (2254), separately.

1484—ISABELLE DE FRANCE PULLET   *Poularde Isabelle de France*

Stuff the pullet with *rizotto,* combined with two oz. of truffle slices and eighteen crayfish tails, and *poach* it in white stock containing one bottle of Chablis wine.

With the pullet's cooking-liquor prepare a highly-seasoned Suprême sauce (106a). Place the bird on a small bed of fried bread. etc.; coat it with the sauce, and surround it with fine black truffles, cooked in champagne, and set each on a small, round, and slightly hollowed *croûton* of fried bread.

Serve the remainder of the sauce separately.

1485—PULLET IVOIRE   *Poularde à l'Ivoire*

Poach the pullet, keeping it very white. Serve it very plain.

Send, separately, an ivory sauce (87), a sauceboat of the pullet's cooking-liquor, and some kind of garnish, such as macaroni or noodles with cream *cèpes,* cucumber, etc.

1486—LADY CURZON PULLET   *Poularde Lady Curzon*

Stuff the pullet with rice (2256), and *poach* it.

Put it on a dish, and coat it with an Indienne sauce (1486).

A garnish of *cèpes* or cucumber with cream may be served at the
same time.

1487—LOUISE D'ORLEANS PULLET   *Poularde Louise d'Orléans*

Insert a whole *foie gras* into the pullet, the former having been
studded with truffles, *poached* for fifteen minutes in some succulent
veal stock, and one glassful of old Madeira, and afterwards cooled.

Brown the pullet for twenty minutes in the oven, sprinkling it
with butter the while.

Cover it entirely with thick slices of truffles; cover these with
slices of bacon, and envelop the whole in a layer of plain dough
(2356), which should be well sealed. Set the pullet, prepared in this
way, in a pan; make a slit in the top of the paste for the escape
of steam during the cooking process, and cook in a moderate oven
for one and three-quarter hours.

This pullet is served as it stands, cold or hot.

1488—LOUISIANA PULLET   *Poularde à la Louisiane*

Stuff the pullet with one lb. of sweet corn with cream, combined
with one and one-half oz. of peppers cut into dice, and *poêle* it.
Put it on a dish and border it, on either side, with *timbales* of rice
and fried bananas, arranged alternately. At either end of the dish
set a *croustade* or crust of short dough, garnished with creamed corn.

1489—LUCULLUS PULLET   *Poularde à la Lucullus*

Braise the pullet.

Put it on a dish and surround it with fine truffles, cooked in
champagne, alternated with large, round *quenelles* of *mousseline
forcemeat*. At either end of the dish, set a small silver shell of the
same height as the bed on which the pullet lies.

Garnish these shells with very white, curled cocks' combs and
cocks' kidneys. Add the reduced *braising*-liquor to a half-*glaze*
sauce, flavored with truffle *essence;* cover the bottom of the dish
with some of this sauce, and send what remains, separately, in a
sauceboat.

1490—MANCINI PULLET   *Poularde à la Mancini*

Poach the pullet.

Remove the *suprêmes;* remove the bones of the breast without

touching either the wings or the legs, and set the bird, thus prepared, on a very low bed of bread or rice, so that it may be steady.

Fill the bird with macaroni, combined with cheese and cream
and three oz. of *foie gras* in dice, and one-half oz. of a *julienne*
of truffles.

Slice the *suprêmes* or breasts, and reconstruct them on the macaroni, placing a fine slice of truffle between each. Coat the pullet with
a stiff and smooth cream sauce; sprinkle with grated cheese, and
glaze quickly at the *salamander*.

Serve separately a creamy Suprême Sauce (106a).

1491—MARGUERITE DE SAVOIE PULLET
Poularde Marguerite de Savoie

Fry quickly ten larks in butter, insert these into a fine pullet,
and *braise* the latter in veal stock and white Savoy wine, in equal
quantities. Prepare a milk polenta (2294); spread it on a tray in
layers one inch thick, and let it cool. Now stamp it with a round
cutter one and one-half inches in diameter, and, a few minutes
before serving, dredge these slices of polenta, and brown them in
clarified butter (175).

Just before serving, sprinkle them with grated Parmesan cheese,
and *glaze* them quickly at the *salamander*.

Place the pullet on a very low bed of fried bread; surround it
with the *glazed* slices of polenta; pour a little of the fowl's cooking-
liquor, thickened, over the dish, and send what remains of it in a
sauceboat.

Serve at the same time a vegetable-dish of white Piedmont truffles,
slightly heated in a little butter and some consommé.

1492—MENAGERE PULLET   *Poularde à la Ménagère*

Poach the pullet in some rather gelatinous white stock. Slice six
carrots, six new potatoes, six new onions; put the whole into a
saucepan, and cook gently in the fowl's *poaching*-liquor or stock,
with the lid of the saucepan off. When the vegetables are cooked,
and the liquor is sufficiently reduced, place the pullet in a special
oval *cocotte,* and cover it with the prepared vegetables and their
cooking-liquor.

1493—MIREILLE PULLET   *Poularde Mireille*

Poêle the pullet.

Put it on a dish; surround it with small *timbales* of rice with saffron, alternated with *tartlet crusts,* filled with chopped tomatoes cooked in butter, and set a fine, pitted olive on each *tartlet.*

Serve a tomato sauce (29) separately.

1494—MONTBAZON PULLET   *Poularde à la Montbazon*
Stud the pullet with truffles, and *poach* it.

Put it on a dish; coat it with Suprême Sauce (106a), and surround it with *poached* lamb sweetbreads, spoon-moulded *quenelles* of *mousseline,* chicken *forcemeat,* and grooved mushroom caps, arranged alternately.

Serve a Suprême Sauce (106a) separately.

1495—MONTE CARLO PULLET   *Poularde à la Monte Carlo*
Poach the pullet.

Put it on a dish; coat it with Suprême sauce (106a), and surround it on the one side with *quenelles* of pink, *mousseline,* chicken *forcemeat,* and on the other with a border of fair-sized, very black truffles.

1496—MONTMORENCY PULLET   *Poularde à la Montmorency*
Lard the pullet with truffles, and *braise* it in Madeira.

Set it on an oval dish, and, at either end, place a fine, decorated *quenelle;* on either side of the fowl arrange some artichoke-bottoms, garnished with asparagus tips, mixed with butter.

Serve separately a half-*glaze* sauce (23) with Madeira, to which the *braising*-liquor of the pullet has been added.

1497—NANTUA PULLET   *Poularde à la Nantua*
Poach the pullet.

Put it on a dish; coat it with a Suprême sauce (106a), finished with crayfish butter (147), and surround it with small heaps of *quenelles* with crayfish butter, crayfish tails, and slices of truffle.

1498—ORIENTALE PULLET   *Poularde à l'Orientale*
Stuff the pullet with one lb. of pilaff rice with saffron (2257), and *poach* it.

Remove its *suprêmes* or breasts; cut out the breast-bones by means of scissors, without touching the rice, and coat the latter with Béchamel sauce (28) colored with tomato sauce (29) and flavored with saffron.

To serve: reconstruct the sliced *suprêmes* on the rice, and set between each slice another of chayote stewed in butter. Cover the pullet with the same sauce as that indicated above, and surround it with quarters of chayote cooked in butter, or serve this garnish separately.

1499—PULLET AUX OEUFS D'OR (WITH GOLDEN EGGS)
Poularde aux Oeufs d'Or

Poële the pullet without letting it get too brown.

Strain the *poëlé*-liquor; clear it of all grease; add a little tomato *purée,* and thicken it with arrowroot or flour. Finish with three oz. of butter, the juice of half a lemon, and a little cayenne.

Put the pullet on a platter; surround it with a border of egg-shaped *croquettes* of egg with truffles, and serve the sauce separately.

1500—PULLET PARISIENNE   *Poularde à la Parisienne*
Poach the pullet.

Place on a dish; cover it with Allemande sauce (27), and decorate it on top with slices of truffles and cured tongue cut to the shape of cocks' combs.

Surround with spoon-moulded *quenelles* of chicken *forcemeat,* half of which should have been combined with chopped truffles, and the other half with chopped, cured ox-tongue.

Arrange the *quenelles* round the fowl, alternately, and border the dish with a ribbon of pale *glaze* (16).

1501—ADELINA PATTI PULLET   *Poularde Adelina Patti*
Stuff the pullet with rice (2256), and *poach* it in white, chicken stock. Place it on a low bed; cover it with a Suprême sauce (106a), flavored with paprika, and surround it with fair-sized artichoke-bottoms, each garnished with a fine truffle, coated with pale meat-glaze (16).

Serve separately a sauceboat of the same sauce as that already used in coating the pullet.

1502—PAYSANNE PULLET   *Poularde à la Paysanne*
Brown the pullet in butter, and put it into an oval *cocotte.*

Around it set a garnish consisting of four oz. of the outer part of a carrot, three oz. of onion, and two oz. of celery, all three minced somewhat finely. Complete the cooking of the pullet with the vegetables, sprinkling it often the while with good veal stock (9).

Serve the preparation as it stands in the *cocotte.*

1503—PERIGORD PULLET *Poularde à la Perigord*

Stuff the pullet with one-half lb. of truffles in the shape of large olives, cooked in two oz. of melted pork fat, and mixed, while hot, with one lb. of fresh, grated pork fat, rubbed through a sieve. Tie the bird, taking care to close all its openings, and *poële* it gently.

Put it on a dish; coat it with a very fine half-*glaze* sauce (23), made from the *poëlé*-liquor and finished with truffle *essence*.

1504—PETITE MARIEE (HONEYMOONERS) PULLET

Poularde Petite Mariée

Poach the pullet in a little white stock, and surround it (when setting it to cook) with six small new onions, six small carrots, six small new potatoes, and one-quarter pint of freshly-shelled peas.

Set the pullet in a *cocotte* with the garnish of vegetables, and coat it with its reduced cooking-liquor, combined with some excellent Suprême Sauce (106a).

1505—PIEMONTAISE PULLET *Pullet à la Piémontaise*

Stuff the pullet with two-thirds lb. of *rizotto* combined with one-half lb. of white sliced truffles, and *poële* it in the usual way.

Put it on a dish, and serve at the same time a thickened chicken gravy to which has been added the reduced *poëlé*-liquor.

1506—PORTUGAISE PULLET *Poularde à la Portugaise*

Stuff the pullet with three-quarters lb. of rice, combined with five oz. of peeled and chopped tomatoes, cooked in butter.

Poële the pullet. Put on a dish; coat it with a Portugaise sauce (659), combined with the *poëlé*-liquor, and surround it with a garnish of medium-sized tomatoes, stuffed with rice "à la Portugaise" (2267).

1507—PRINCESSE PULLET *Poularde à la Princesse*

Poach the pullet.

Put it on a dish, and coat it with an Allemande sauce (27), flavored with mushroom *essence* and finished with two oz. of asparagus tips buttered per pint of sauce. Surround it with *croustades* of Duchesse potatoes (221), rolled in breadcrumbs and melted butter, fried, emptied, then garnished with asparagus tips mixed with butter, and each surmounted by a fine slice of truffle. Between each *croustade* set a bundle of very green asparagus tips.

1508—PRINCESSE HELENE PULLET　　*Poularde Princesse Hélène*

Stuff the pullet with rice (2256), and *poach* it. Place on a dish; coat it with Suprême Sauce (106a), and surround it with spinach *subrics* (2137), cooked at the last moment; add to this garnish some shavings of white truffles, barely heated in butter, and set in a shell placed behind the fowl.

1509—REGENCE PULLET　　*Poularde à la Régence*

Stuff the pullet with one lb. of *mousseline forcemeat* of chicken, combined with three oz. of crayfish *purée* (662), and *poach* it.

Put on a dish; coat it with Allemande sauce (27), flavored with truffle *essence,* and surround it with the following garnish, arranged in small heaps:—Spoon-moulded *quenelles* of *mousseline,* chicken *forcemeat;* white, curled cocks' combs; slices of raw *foie gras,* stamped out with a round cutter, and tossed in butter; small, grooved, cooked, and very white mushrooms; olive-shaped truffles, and one round *quenelle* decorated with truffles at either end of the dish.

1510—QUEEN ANNE'S PULLET　　*Poularde de la Reine Anne*

Poêle the pullet.

When it is ready, remove the *suprêmes* or breasts and the breast bones, and fill the bird with a garnish of macaroni and cream, combined with *foie gras* and truffle dice. Cover the macaroni with Mornay sauce (91); *glaze* quickly, and place the pullet on a low bed of bread.

Surround it with small *tartlet crusts* garnished with cocks' combs and kidneys, combined with Allemande sauce (27), and set a slice of the *suprêmes* on each *tartlet.* Put a silver shell containing a pyramid of truffles behind the fowl.

Serve the Allemande sauce, flavored with truffle *essence,* separately.

1511—REINE MARGOT PULLET　　*Poularde Reine Margot*

Stuff the pullet with two-thirds lb. of *mousseline forcemeat* of chicken, combined with two oz. of almond *purée,* and *poach* it.

Place on a dish; coat it with Suprême Sauce (106a), finished with a little almond milk (2506), and surround it with *quenelles* prepared with pistachio butter (156) and *quenelles* prepared with crayfish butter (147), arranged alternately.

1512—REINE MARGUERITE PULLET *Poularde Reine Marguerite*

Poach the pullet.

Remove the *suprêmes* or breasts, and the breast-bone, without touching either the wings or the legs, and set the bird, thus trimmed, on a low bed of bread or rice. Finely slice the *suprêmes;* add as many slices of truffle as there are slices of *suprêmes;* and combine the whole with a *soufflé* preparation with Parmesan cheese, which should not be too light.

Reconstruct the pullet with this preparation; smooth the surface, and surround the base of the pullet with a band of parchment paper, so that it may keep its form. Lay some thin slices of Gruyère cheese on it; set it in an earthenware dish, and cook it in a moderately hot oven.

1513—PULLET WITH RICE *Poularde au Riz*

Poach the pullet.

Put it on a dish, and coat it with an Allemande sauce (27), flavored with chicken *essence.* Surround it with a garnish of rice, cooked in the pullet's *poaching*-liquor, and moulded in small, buttered, *timbale* moulds.

1514—ROSSINI PULLET *Poularde Rossini*

Poële the pullet.

Remove the *suprêmes* or breasts; slice them, and arrange them in the form of a crown upon a round dish; alternating them with slices of *foie gras,* tossed in butter. Pour a very strong chicken stock finished with truffle *essence* in their midst.

Serve, separately, a *timbale* of noodles with butter sprinkled with freshly made noodles *sautéd* in butter to a crisp brown.

1515—SAINTE ALLIANCE PULLET *Poularde Sainte Alliance*

Heat in butter ten fine truffles seasoned with salt and pepper; sprinkle them with a glassful of excellent Madeira, and leave them to cool in a thoroughly sealed utensil. Now put these truffles into a fine pullet, and *poële* it just in time for it to be sent to the table.

When the pullet is ready, quickly cook as many ortolans, and toss in butter as many slices of *foie gras* as there are diners, and send them to the table at the same time as the pullet, together with the latter's *poëlé*-liquor, strained and in a sauceboat.

The waiter in charge should be ready for it with three assistants at hand, and he should have a very hot chafing dish on the buffet. The moment it arrives he quickly removes the *suprêmes* (breasts), cuts them into slices, and sets each one of these upon a slice of *foie gras,* which assistant No. 1 has placed ready on a plate, together with one of the truffles inserted into the pullet at the start.

Assistant No. 2, to whom the plate is handed, adds an ortolan and a little sauce, and then assistant No. 3, places the plate before the diner.

The pullet is thus served very quickly, and in such a way as to make it a dish of very exceptional gastronomical quality.

N.B.—The name "Sainte Alliance" which I give to this dish (a name that Brillat-Savarin employs in his "Physiology of Taste" in order to identify a certain famous toast) struck me as an admirable title for a preparation in which four such veritable gems of cookery are found united—the *suprêmes* of a fine pullet, *foie gras,* truffles, and ortolans.

1516—SANTA-LUCIA PULLET   *Poularde Santa-Lucia*

Stuff the pullet with truffles, prepared as for (1515), and *braise* it in Marsala. Serve it on a low bed, and surround it with small *tartlets* of gnochi "à la Romaine" (2381), alternated with slices of *foie gras,* tossed in butter.

1517—SICILIENNE PULLET   *Poularde Sicilienne*

Poach the pullet.

Lift out the fillets or breasts, leaving the wing-bones on the bird; remove the breast bones, and fill the cavity with macaroni, mixed with the strong liquor of *braised* beef "à la Napolitaine," and combined with dice of truffles and *foie gras,* cocks' combs and kidneys.

Envelop the bird in a *pig's caul,* giving the chicken its natural shape; sprinkle with *raspings* and melted butter, and set in the oven that the *pig's caul* may cook and brown.

Serve on a low bed of rice, etc., and coat with chicken *glaze* (16) with butter.

Surround with *tartlet crusts,* each garnished with a slice of the *suprêmes,* covered with a slice of *foie gras* tossed in butter, and surmounted by a slice of truffle.

Serve chicken *glaze* with butter separately.

1518—PULLET SOUFFLE   *Poularde Soufflé*

Poach the pullet.

Lift off the *suprêmes* (breasts), and cut them into thin slices; cut out the breast-bones by means of scissors, and stuff the bird with one lb. two oz. of *mousseline forcemeat* of chicken, combined with one-third lb. of *foie-gras purée*. Spread this preparation in layers, and between each of the latter set alternate slices of *suprême* and truffle.

Reconstruct the bird exactly; smooth its surface; decorate it with bits of truffle, tongue, and hard-boiled white of egg; place the dish in a deep pan containing a little boiling water, the steam of which assists the *poaching* of the preparation, and *poach* in a moderate oven.

When about to serve, coat the pullet with Allemande sauce (27) flavored with truffle *essence*.

N.B.—The use of a *bain-marie* (water-bath) consisting of a deep pan containing boiling water, where the dish which holds the pullet is placed, is highly recommended, but the ideal method of *poaching* this sort of preparation is by means of a steamer.

1519—STANLEY PULLET *Poularde Stanley*

Stuff the pullet with one-half lb. of rice, three oz. of mushrooms, and three oz. of a *julienne* of truffles. *Poach* it with one lb. two oz. of sliced and *blanched* onions, seasoned with a pinch of curry. When the pullet is ready, rub the cooking-liquor and the onions through a fine sieve. Add one-third pint of velouté (242) and one-third pint of cream to this *cullis;* reduce to a stiff consistency; rub once more through a sieve, and finish with one-sixth pint of cream.

1520—SOUVAROFF PULLET *Poularde Souvaroff*

Stuff the pullet with one-half lb. of *foie gras* and five oz. of truffles cut into large dice, and three-parts *poêle* it.

Now put it into a *cocotte* with ten fair-sized truffles stewed in Madeira for a few minutes in the same saucepan as that in which the pullet was *poêléd*. Moisten with one-sixth pint of veal stock; close the *cocotte;* seal the cover with a band of flour paste, and complete the cooking in a moderate oven for thirty minutes.

Serve the fowl as it stands in the *cocotte*.

1521—SYLVANA PULLET *Poularde Sylvana*

Stuff the pullet with one lb. of mushrooms, tossed in brown butter, and half-brown it in the oven.

Meanwhile put one pint of fresh peas into a saucepan, together with ten small new onions, one small lettuce cut *julienne*-fashion, and an herb bunch consisting of parsley stalks, chervil, and a sprig of mint. Add salt, sugar, two oz. of butter, and mix the whole together.

Moisten with two small tablespoons of water; cover and half-cook, taking care to toss from time to time during the operation. When the pullet is half-cooked, put it into a *cocotte* lined with a thin layer of paste, reaching over the edges of the *cocotte* by about two inches.

Surround it with a garnish of peas; cover it with a slice of bacon, and close the *cocotte* with its cover. Draw the overlapping paste over the latter; seal it down with some white of egg, that it may be hermetically sealed, and set in the oven for about forty-five minutes.

Serve the preparation as it stands in the *cocotte* A sauceboat of good chicken gravy may be served separately.

1522—TALLEYRAND PULLET *Poularde Talleyrand*

Poële the pullet; lift out the *suprêmes,* breasts, and cut these into large dice. Mix them with an equal quantity of macaroni, cut small, and thickened with cream sauce combined with Parmesan cheese, and add enough *foie gras* and truffles, cut into large dice, to equal half the weight of the *suprêmes.*

Remove the breast-bones; fill the fowl with the above preparation, and cover it with a layer of *mousseline forcemeat,* reconstructing the bird naturally in so doing. Decorate the surface with a crown of truffle slices; cover with buttered paper, and set in the oven and *poach* the *forcemeat,* to thoroughly heat the preparation beneath.

Lay it on a dish; pour a little half-*glaze* sauce (23), flavored with truffle *essence* and combined with slices of truffle, over the dish, and serve what remains of the sauce separately.

1523—TOSCA PULLET *Poularde Tosca*

Stuff the pullet with rice, prepared after (2256), and *poële* it in a little moistening. Serve it on a low bed of fried bread, and surround it with a garnish of *braised* finocchi.

Send the pullet's *poëlé*-liquor separately, after having reduced and finished it with butter.

1524—TOULOUSE PULLET *Poularde Toulousaine*

Poach the pullet.

Coat it with Allemande sauce (27), flavored with mushroom *essence,* and surround it with the following garnish, arranged in heaps:—*Quenelles* of *mousseline* chicken *forcemeat;* slices of *poached,* veal sweetbreads; cocks' combs and kidneys; cooked and very white button-mushroom caps, and slices of truffle.

Serve the Allemande sauce, flavored with mushroom *essence,* separately.

1525—TRIANON PULLET   *Poularde Trianon*
Poach the pullet.

Arrange on a dish and surround it with *quenelles* of chicken *forcemeat,* stuffed with *foie-gras purée.* Arrange these *quenelles* in heaps, and set a nice, whole truffle between each heap.

Pierce the pullet with a decorative skewer garnished with one grooved mushroom, one fair-sized *glazed* truffle, and a *quenelle* decorated with tongue.

Serve a Suprême Sauce (106a) at the same time.

1526—VALENCIENNE PULLET   *Poularde Valencienne*
Poële the pullet.

Put it on a dish, and surround it with a garnish of *rizotto,* combined with ham dice. Set a crown of grilled slices of ham upon the *rizotto.*

Serve a well-seasoned tomatoed Suprême Sauce (106a) separately.

1527—PULLET AU VERT-PRE   *Poularde au Vert-Pré*
Poach the pullet.

Put it on a dish; coat it with a Suprême Sauce (106a), finished with printanier butter (157), in the proportion of two oz. per pint of sauce; and surround it with a garnish consisting of peas, string beans, and asparagus tips, mixed with butter.

1528—VICHY PULLET   *Poularde Vichy*
Stuff the pullet with ordinary pilaff rice (2256), and *braise* it white. Put it on a dish; coat it with a Suprême Sauce (106a), combined with the reduced *braising-*liquor, and surround with small *tartlet crusts,* garnished with carrots à la Vichy (2061).

1529—VICTORIA PULLET   *Poularde Victoria*
Stuff the pullet with truffles and *foie gras,* and three-quarters *poële* it, exactly as directed under "Poularde Souvaroff" (1520).

Put it into a *cocotte* with one lb. of potatoes, cut into large dice and tossed in butter, and complete its cooking and that of the potatoes in the oven.

1530—PULLET WASHINGTON   *Poularde Washington*

Stuff the pullet with ten oz. of green corn, three-quarters cooked, and combined with one chopped onion cooked in butter and three oz. of good sausage-meat, fried in butter for one moment with the onion. *Braise* the pullet, and *glaze* it at the last minute.

Serve separately and at the same time a *timbale* of corn with cream.

1531—FINE CAPON WITH TRUFFLE BALLS FROM PERIGORD

Chapon Fin aux Perles du Périgord

Stuff the capon with fine truffles, and envelop it in very thin slices of rump of veal. *Braise* it with best liqueur-brandy.

Place on a dish and serve separately the *braising*-liquor in a sauceboat; a *timbale* of cardoons with gravy.

1532—CHICKEN SAUTES   *Poulets Sautés*

As I pointed out previously, in an earlier part of this chapter, the chickens best suited to the *sauté* treatment are "à la Reine" (roasters or fryers); they should be of medium size, very fleshy, and tender. In an extreme case, small pullets or large chickens might be used, but neither of these are so eminently suited to the procedure in question as chickens "à la Reine" (roasters or fryers).

The fowl which is to be *sautéd* should be cut up thus: after having been drawn singed, and thoroughly cleaned; cut off its legs—quite a simple matter, since all that is necessary is the disjointing of the thigh-bones, after having cut the skin. Cut off the feet just below the joint of the inner leg bone, and cut the spurs. Now cut the inner leg bone above the joint, and remove the thigh-bone.

Cut the wings at the first joint; remove the wing ends, after having cut round a portion of the breast in such a way that each wing holds one-half of it; finally detach the breast-bone, which should be left whole if the fowl be small and cut into two if it be otherwise.

Cut the remains of the bird into two, and trim each piece on both sides.

Before setting them to cook, moderately season the pieces of fowl with salt and pepper. Whatever the demands of a particular recipe may be, the preparatory principle of *sautéd* chickens is always as follows:—

Take a saucepan just large enough to hold the pieces of fowl, and heat in it two oz. of clarified butter (175); or, according to circumstances, half butter and half good oil. When the selected fat is quite hot, put in the pieces of fowl; let them brown quickly, and turn them over from time to time, that it may be done evenly. Now cover the utensil, and put it in a sufficiently hot oven to ensure the complete cooking of the fowl. Some tender pieces, such as the wings and the breast, should be taken out after a few minutes have elapsed, and kept warm; but the legs, the meat of which is firmer and thicker, should cook seven or eight minutes more at least.

When all the pieces are cooked, withdraw them; drain away their butter, and swirl into the prescribed liquor, which is either some kind of wine, mushroom cooking-liquor, or chicken stock, etc. This swirling or swashing forms, as I have already pointed out, an essential part of the procedure, inasmuch as its object is to dissolve those portions of solidified gravy which adhere to the bottom of the saucepan.

Reduce the swirling-liquor or pan gravy to half, and add the sauce given in the recipe. Put the pieces of fowl, the feet, the wing tips and the legs into this sauce, and simmer for a few minutes. The other pieces, the wings and breast, are then added, but when the sauce is sufficiently reduced, it must stop boiling. When the pieces are completely cooked, it is obviously unnecessary for the sauce to boil, since the former would only be hardened thereby.

A few minutes before serving, put the pieces into a deep entrée dish (fitted with a cover) in the following order:—the pieces of the bird, the feet and the ends of the wings on the bottom of the dish, upon these the legs and the breast, and, last of all, the wings.

The sauce is then finished according to the directions of the recipe, and is poured over the pieces of fowl.

Some chickens are prepared without browning—that is to say, the pieces are merely cooked in butter without browning and their cooking is completed in the oven as above. In this case the swashing-liquor is invariably white, as also the supplementary sauces, and the latter are finished with cream.

1533—ARCHDUKE CHICKEN SAUTE   *Poulet Sauté Archiduc*

Fry the pieces of fowl without browning and merely stiffen them. Add four oz. of onions, previously cooked in butter, and complete the cooking of the onions and the fowl together.

Withdraw the pieces; put on a dish; cover, and keep it hot. Moisten the onions with a small glassful of liqueur brandy; reduce the latter; add one-sixth pint of cream and one-sixth pint of velouté (242), and rub through a fine sieve.

Reduce this sauce to a stiff consistency; finish it, away from the fire, with one and one-half oz. of butter, the juice of the quarter of a lemon, and a tablespoon of Madeira, and pour it over the fowl.

Set about ten slices of truffle on the latter, and serve.

1534—ARLESIENNE CHICKEN SAUTE   *Poulet Sauté Arlésienne*

Sauté the chicken in oil, and take out the pieces.

Swirl it with one-quarter pint of white wine; add a piece of crushed garlic as large as a pea, one-sixth pint of tomatoed half-*glaze* sauce (23), and reduce by a third. Arrange the chicken, and surround with alternate heaps of onion and eggplant slices, seasoned, dredged, and fried in oil, and chopped tomatoes cooked in butter.

1535—ARMAGNAC CHICKEN SAUTE   *Poulet Sauté Armagnac*

Cook the pieces of chicken in butter without browning; add three and one-half oz. of raw slices of truffle, and serve in a shallow *cocotte*.

Swirl into it a small glassful of old liqueur brandy; add a few drops of lemon juice and one-sixth pint of cream; heat; finish this sauce, away from the fire, with two oz. of crayfish butter (147), and pour it over the fowl.

Serve in the *cocotte*.

1536—ARTOIS CHICKEN SAUTE   *Poulet Sauté d'Artois*

Sauté the chicken in butter, and place the pieces on a dish.

Swirl it with three tablespoons of Madeira, and add one-seventh pint of light, pale meat-*glaze* (15), four small quartered artichoke-bottoms, tossed in butter, ten carrots shaped like olives, cooked in consommé and *glazed,* and eight small onions cooked in butter.

Finish with one and one-half oz. of butter and a pinch of chopped chives, and pour this sauce over the pieces of fowl.

1537—BEAULIEU CHICKEN SAUTE   *Poulet Sauté Beaulieu*

Sauté the chicken in butter, and add to it five oz. of new potatoes (the size of hazel-nuts) and the same quantity of small quartered artichoke-bottoms, cooked in butter beforehand with the potatoes.

Keep the whole in the oven, under cover, for ten minutes.

Set the pieces of fowl, the potatoes and the artichoke-bottoms in an earthenware saucepan, and add twelve black olives.

Swirl the saucepan with a few tablespoons of white wine and a little lemon juice; complete with a tablespoon of veal stock, and pour into the *cocotte*.

Simmer for five minutes, in the utensil, and serve the preparation as it stands.

1538—BORDELAISE CHICKEN SAUTE   *Poulet Sauté Bordelaise*

Sauté the chicken in butter, and put it on a dish. Surround it with small quartered artichoke-bottoms stewed in butter; sliced potatoes cooked in butter, and slices of fried onions, arranged in small heaps, with a small bunch of fried parsley between each heap.

Swirl the saucepan with a few tablespoons of chicken gravy, and sprinkle the fowl with it.

1539—BOIVIN CHICKEN SAUTE   *Poulet Sauté Boivin*

Fry the chicken in butter and add twelve small onions; three quartered artichokes, small and very tender; twenty-four small potatoes of the size of hazel-nuts. Cover and cook the whole together, in the oven.

Serve the chicken with the onions and potatoes over it, and surround it with artichokes.

Swirl the saucepan with two tablespoons of consommé; add three tablespoons of pale *glaze* (15), a few drops of lemon juice, and one and one-half oz. of butter; and pour this sauce over the chicken.

1540—BRETON CHICKEN SAUTE   *Poulet Sauté Bretonne*

Cook the pieces without browning them, and add three oz. of the white of a leek and the half of an onion, both sliced and stewed in butter beforehand. Cover and set in the oven.

About five minutes before the fowl is quite cooked, add three oz. of mushrooms, minced raw and tossed in butter.

Put the pullet on a dish, add one-sixth pint of Suprême Sauce (106a) and as much cream to the vegetables; reduce to half, and pour the sauce and the vegetables over the chicken.

1541—CHICKEN SAUTE WITH CEPES   *Poulet Sauté aux Cèpes*

Sauté the chicken in oil. When it is cooked, drain away the oil; heat three chopped shallots in the saucepan; swirl with one-quarter pint of white wine; reduce, and complete with one and one-half oz. of butter.

Pour this sauce over the chicken, and surround the latter with eight oz. of *cèpes, sautéd* à la Bordelaise (2068).

Sprinkle a pinch of chopped parsley over the chicken.

1542—CHAMPEAUX CHICKEN SAUTE   *Poulet Sauté Champeaux*

Sauté the chicken in butter and surround it with small onions and potatoes (the size of hazel-nuts), both cooked in butter beforehand. Swirl it with a little white wine; add one-sixth pint of veal gravy and one tablespoon of meat-*glaze* (15); reduce; finish with one and one-half oz. of butter; and pour this sauce over the chicken.

1543—CHASSEUR CHICKEN SAUTE   *Poulet Sauté Chasseur*
Sauté the chicken in equal quantities of butter and oil, and place it on a dish. Swirl the saucepan with a few tablespoons of white wine, and reduce; add one-quarter pint of Chasseur Sauce Escoffier (33); heat; pour over the chicken, and sprinkle the latter with a pinch of chopped parsley.

1544—CYNTHIA CHICKEN SAUTE   *Poulet Sauté Cynthia*
Sauté the chicken in butter and put it on a dish.

Swirl the saucepan with a glass of dry champagne; reduce to half; add one tablespoon of light poultry *glaze* (15); finish with two and one-half oz. of butter, the juice of half a lemon, and one tablespoon of dry curaçao; pour this sauce over the chicken.

Surround with three oz. of grapes, cleared of all skin and seeds, and ten sections of an orange, peeled in such a way that the pulp of the fruit is raw.

1545—DEMIDOFF CHICKEN SAUTE   *Poulet Sauté Demidoff*
Brown the chicken in butter; add the vegetable garnish given for "Poularde à la Demidoff" (1464), and put to stew in the oven. About ten minutes before the cooking is completed, add two oz. of truffles, cut to the shape of crescents like the carrots and turnips, and three tablespoons of good veal stock (10).

Serve the pieces of chicken covered with the garnish.

1546—DORIA CHICKEN SAUTE   *Poulet Sauté à la Doria*
Brown the pieces of chicken in oil and butter; add one-half lb. of cucumber cut to the shape of garlic cloves; and complete the cooking by stewing in the oven.

Serve the chicken with the cucumber upon it. Swirl into the saucepan with one tablespoon of veal gravy and a few drops of lemon juice; and sprinkle the chicken and its garnish with this pan gravy, to which add one and one-half oz. of brown butter (154).

1547—DURAND CHICKEN SAUTE   *Poulet Sauté à la Durand*
Dredge the seasoned pieces of chicken, and *sauté* them in oil.

Arrange them in the form of a crown; garnish their center with a fine heap of round slices of fried onion; and, in the center of the latter, set a cone, made from a very thin slice of ham and filled with chopped tomatoes cooked in butter.

1548—EGYPTIAN CHICKEN SAUTE *Poulet Sauté à l'Egyptienne*

Brown the pieces of chicken in oil. Toss in oil, together, three oz. of onion, and two oz. of mushrooms, sliced; and six oz. of raw cured ham, cut into dice.

Set the pieces of chicken in a *cocotte,* alternating them with the garnish, which should have been well-drained; cover with two tomatoes, cut into thick slices; cover the *cocotte,* and complete the cooking in the oven for twenty minutes.

When about to serve, sprinkle with a tablespoon of veal stock (10).

1549—SPANISH CHICKEN SAUTE *Poulet Sauté à l'Espagnole*

Sauté the chicken in oil. Drain the latter away, and add one-half lb. of pilaff rice (2256), combined with one and one-half oz. of peppers in dice; three oz. of large green peas, cooked *à l'anglaise,* and two sliced and *poached* Spanish sausages.

Cover the saucepan, and set the whole to stew in the oven for ten minutes.

Place on a dish and cover the chicken with the garnish, and surround it with six small grilled tomatoes.

1550—CHICKEN SAUTE WITH TARRAGON *Poulet Sauté à l'Estragon*

Toss the chicken in butter.

Swirl the saucepan with one-sixth pint of white wine; reduce to half; add one-sixth pint of gravy in which tarragon has been infused, and thicken with arrowroot, flour, etc.

Pour this sauce over the chicken, and decorate its wings with sprays of parboiled tarragon leaves.

1551—FEDORA CHICKEN SAUTE *Poulet Sauté Fedora*

Sauté the chicken in butter, without browning, with four oz. of raw, sliced truffles; and place on a dish.

Swirl with one-sixth pint of cream; add three tablespoons of Béchamel sauce (28), and reduce to half. Finish, away from the fire, with one and one-half oz. of crayfish butter (147), a few drops of lemon juice, and a little cayenne; add four oz. of parboiled asparagus tips to this sauce, and pour it over the chicken. Or, after having mixed them with butter, the asparagus tips may be arranged in heaps round the fowl.

1552—CHICKEN SAUTE WITH FENNEL *Poulet Sauté au Fenouil*

Sauté the chicken in butter, without browning; swirl with cream; add three quartered finocchio, trimmed to the shape of garlic cloves and parboiled, and complete the cooking of the finocchios and the chicken, together.

Set the pieces of fennel in the form of a crown on a special earthen-ware dish, and put the chicken in their midst, placing the pieces side by side. Coat with Mornay sauce (91), flavored with chicken *essence,* and set to *glaze.*

1553—FERMIERE CHICKEN SAUTE   *Poulet Sauté à la Fermière*

Slice three oz. of the outer part of a carrot, the same quantity of turnip, two oz. of celery, and half an onion. Season with a little salt and sugar, and half-stew in butter.

Brown the pieces of chicken in butter; put them in the *cocotte* with the garnish of vegetables; add two and one-half oz. of ham cut into dice, and complete the cooking of both the chicken and the vegetables in the oven.

When about to serve, sprinkle with four or five tablespoons of veal stock (10).

1554—CHICKEN SAUTE WITH HERBS   *Poulet Sauté aux Fines Herbes*

Sauté the chicken in butter, and two minutes before serving it, sprinkle with one-half oz. of chopped shallots. Swirl the saucepan with one-sixth pint of white wine; reduce; add three tablespoons of strong, veal gravy (41) and as much half-*glaze* sauce (23); and finish the sauce, away from the fire, with one and one-half oz. of butter and a teaspoon of chopped parsley, chervil, and tarragon. Pour it over the chicken.

1555—FORESTIERE CHICKEN SAUTE   *Poulet Sauté Forestière*

Sauté the chicken in butter; sprinkle it with a tablespoon of chopped shallots; add five oz. of quartered morels (French mush-rooms); stew in the oven for ten minutes, and put the chicken on a dish.

Swirl with white wine; add one-sixth pint of veal stock (10); re-duce, and pour over the chicken with the morels. Surround with four small heaps of potatoes, cut into large dice and tossed in butter; put a rectangle of frizzled bacon between each heap, and sprinkle a pinch of chopped parsley over the chicken.

1556—GABRIELLE CHICKEN SAUTE   *Poulet Sauté Gabrielle*

Sauté the chicken in butter, without browning, and place it on a dish.

Swirl with one-eighth pint of mushroom cooking-liquor; add three tablespoons of Béchamel sauce (28), and three tablespoons of cream; reduce, and finish the sauce, away from the fire, with one and one-half oz. of butter.

Pour this sauce over the chicken; sprinkle on it some very black truffle, cut *julienne*-fashion, and surround it with little leaves of puff-paste, baked without browning.

1557—GEORGINA CHICKEN SAUTE   *Poulet Sauté Georgina*

Sauté the pullet in butter with twelve small new onions and a small herb bunch, containing a sprig of fennel. Put the chicken on a dish.

Swirl with three tablespoons of mushroom cooking-liquor and as much Rhine wine; add one-fifth pint of cream; twelve mushroom caps, sliced; and reduce the cream to half.

Complete with a pinch of chopped chervil and tarragon, and pour over the chicken.

1558—HUNGARIAN CHICKEN SAUTE   *Poulet Sauté Hongroise*

Prepare a sufficient quantity of pilaff rice (2255), combined with chopped tomatoes, to make a border.

Sauté the chicken in butter, without browning, with a chopped half-onion and a little paprika. When the onion is slightly browned, add three peeled and quartered tomatoes, and complete the cooking. Mould the rice to form a border, and set the chicken in the middle.

Add one-sixth pint of cream to the tomatoes; reduce to half; rub through a fine sieve; heat this sauce, and pour it over the chicken.

1559—CHICKEN SAUTE INDIENNE OR CHICKEN CURRY

Poulet Sauté à l'Indienne ou Currie de Poulet

Cut the chicken into small pieces, and fry them in oil with a sliced onion and a large pinch of curry powder. Swirl with one-sixth pint of cocoanut milk or water or, failing this, almond milk; add one-third pint of velouté (242), and complete the cooking of the chicken while reducing the sauce to half. Set in a deep dish, and serve a *timbale* of rice à l'Indienne (2254) separately.

1560—JAPANESE CHICKEN SAUTE   *Poulet Sauté Japonaise*

Fry the chicken in butter; add one lb. of cleaned and parboiled Japanese artichokes and complete the cooking of the whole, chicken and artichokes, in the oven.

Serve the chicken with the artichokes on it. Swirl with one-sixth pint of slightly thickened veal stock (10); complete, away from the fire, with one and one-half oz. of butter, and pour this over the chicken.

1561—JURASSIENNE CHICKEN SAUTE   *Poulet Sauté Jurassienne*

Sauté the chicken in butter and, when it is ready, add to it one-half lb. of *blanched* fresh pork fat, cut into strips and well fried in butter. Drain away three-quarters of the chicken's grease; swirl with one-sixth pint of light half-*glaze* sauce (23), and put the chicken on a dish.

Complete the sauce with a pinch of chopped chives, and pour it over the chicken with the strips of bacon.

1562—LATHUILE CHICKEN SAUTE   *Poulet Sauté Lathuile*

Heat three oz. of butter in a saucepan, just large enough to hold the chicken and its garnish. Set the pieces of chicken in this butter, together with one-half lb. of potatoes and five oz. of raw artichoke-bottoms, both cut into fair-sized dice.

When the chicken and the vegetables are browned underneath, flip it over at one stroke and complete the cooking on the other side; sprinkle the chicken with three tablespoons of meat-*glaze* (15) and a pinch of chopped parsley containing a bit of crushed garlic, and set the chicken and the garnish on a dish, after the manner of "Potatoes Anna" (2203).

Pour two and one-half oz. of nut-brown butter (154) over the whole, and surround with round slices of seasoned onions, dredged and fried in oil, and very green, fried parsley, arranged in alternate heaps.

1563—LYONNAISE CHICKEN SAUTE   *Poulet Sauté Lyonnaise*

Sauté the chicken in butter and, when it is half-cooked, add three fair-sized onions, finely sliced, tossed in butter and slightly browned.

Complete the cooking of the chicken and the onions together, and put it on a dish. Swirl with one-sixth pint of veal gravy (41); reduce; pour this liquor and the onions over the chicken, and sprinkle the whole with a pinch of chopped parsley.

1564—MARENGO CHICKEN SAUTE   *Poulet Sauté Marengo*

Sauté the chicken in oil. Swirl the saucepan with white wine; add two peeled and chopped tomatoes, or one and one-half tablespoons of tomato *purée,* a bit of crushed garlic, ten small mushrooms, and ten slices of truffle.

Put it on a dish; cover it with sauce and garnish; surround it with heart-shaped *croûtons,* fried in butter; small, fried eggs, and trussed crayfish cooked in *court-bouillon,* and sprinkle the whole with a pinch of chopped parsley.

1565—MARYLAND CHICKEN SAUTE *Poulet Sauté Maryland*

Season the pieces of chicken; dip them in butter; roll them in bread-crumbs, and cook them in clarified butter (175). Place a slice of grilled bacon between each piece of chicken; surround with small, fried cakes of cornmeal, and fried slices of banana.

Serve a horse-radish sauce (119) with cream, separately.

1566—MARSEILLAISE CHICKEN SAUTE *Poulet Sauté Marseillaise*

Sauté the chicken in oil, and, when it is half-cooked, add two crushed cloves of garlic; three oz. of finely chopped, green peppers, and the same weight of quartered tomatoes—all three tossed in oil.

When the chicken is cooked, drain away the oil; swirl the pan with one-sixth pint of white wine and a few drops of lemon juice, and reduce almost entirely.

Put the chicken on a dish; cover it with the garnish, and sprinkle with a pinch of chopped parsley.

1567—MEXICAN CHICKEN SAUTE *Poulet Sauté Mexicaine*

Sauté the chicken in oil; swirl the saucepan with a few table-spoons of white wine; reduce, and add one-sixth pint of tomatoed veal gravy (42).

Place the chicken on a dish; pour the sauce over it, and surround it with grilled peppers and mushrooms, garnished with chopped tomatoes cooked in butter.

1568—MIREILLE CHICKEN SAUTE *Poulet Sauté Mireille*

Sauté the chicken in oil and add to it, when half-cooked, one chopped onion, four chopped tomatoes, and one pimento cut into dice. Ten minutes before serving, flavor with a small piece of crushed garlic.

Put the chicken on a dish; pour the juice of the tomatoes into the saucepan; reduce to half, and strain over the chicken.

Serve a *timbale* of rice, flavored with saffron, separately.

1569—CHICKEN SAUTE WITH MORELS *Poulet Sauté aux Morilles*

Brown the chicken in butter and three-quarters cook it; add to it two-thirds lb. of morels (French mushrooms), stewed in butter, and complete the cooking of the chicken, covered, in the oven.

Serve the chicken with the morels on it; swirl the saucepan with a tablespoon of brandy; add the juice of the morels, two tablespoons of meat-*glaze* (15), and one and one-half oz. of butter, and pour this sauce over the chicken.

1570—NORMANDY CHICKEN SAUTE   *Poulet Sauté Normande*

Half-*sauté* the chicken in butter, and set the pieces in a *cocotte* with one lb. of peeled and sliced russet apples. Swirl with a small glassful of liqueur cider (apple brandy); put this liquor in the *cocotte;* cover, and set in the oven, that the chicken may be completely cooked and the apples as well.

Serve the preparation, as it stands, in the *cocotte.*

1571—PARMENTIER CHICKEN SAUTE   *Poulet Sauté Parmentier*

Brown the chicken in butter, and add one lb. of potato balls, cut by means of an oval spoon, or cut into large dice, and already slightly browned in butter.

Complete the cooking in the oven, and serve the chicken with the potatoes arranged in heaps all round. Swirl with a few tablespoons of white wine; add to it a tablespoon of veal gravy (41); pour this over the chicken, and sprinkle the latter with a pinch of chopped parsley.

1572—PIEMONTAISE CHICKEN SAUTE   *Poulet Sauté Piémontaise*

Sauté the chicken in butter and arrange it on a dish.

Swirl with a few tablespoons of white wine; add a tablespoon of melted pale meat-*glaze* (16), and pour this over the chicken. Sprinkle it at the last moment with two oz. of nut-brown butter (154), and finally with chopped parsley, and serve a *timbale* of *rizotto* with white truffles separately.

1573—PORTUGUESE CHICKEN SAUTE   *Poulet Sauté Portugaise*

Sauté the chicken in butter and oil, and put it on a dish. Drain away a portion of the butter used in the cooking, add to the remainder a bit of crushed garlic and a chopped half-onion; and, when the latter is fried, add four oz. of peeled and chopped tomatoes, two oz. of sliced mushrooms, a few drops of white wine, and a pinch of chopped parsley.

Complete the cooking of the whole, taking care to reduce all moisture.

Cover the chicken with its garnish, and surround it with half-tomatoes or tomatoes stuffed with rice.

1574—PROVENCALE CHICKEN SAUTE *Poulet Sauté Provençale*

Sauté the chicken in oil and put it on a dish. Swirl with white wine and add a bit of crushed garlic, three oz. of chopped tomatoes, four anchovy fillets cut into dice, twelve black olives pitted and parboiled, and a pinch of chopped sweet basil.

Leave the whole to simmer for five minutes, and cover the chicken with it.

1575—STANLEY CHICKEN SAUTE *Poulet Sauté Stanley*

Brown the chicken in butter, and complete its cooking under cover with one-half lb. of minced onions. Place it in a flat, earthenware *cocotte,* setting a heap of mushrooms on either side of it; add one-third pint of cream to the onions; simmer for ten minutes; rub through a fine sieve, and reduce.

Finish this sauce with one oz. of butter, a little curry powder, and pour it over the chicken.

Set ten slices of truffle on the latter.

1576—CHICKEN SAUTE WITH TRUFFLES *Poulet Sauté aux Truffes*

Half-*sauté* the chicken in butter; add six oz. of raw truffles, cut into slices, and complete the cooking under cover. Swirl with a few tablespoons of Madeira; reduce; add three tablespoons of half-*glaze* sauce (23); finish with one and one-half oz. of butter, ad pour this sauce over the chicken.

1577—VAN DYCK CHICKEN SAUTE *Poulet Sauté Van Dyck*

Cook the chicken in butter without letting it brown; swirl with one-sixth pint of cream; add one-sixth pint of Suprême Sauce (106a), and reduce by a third.

Mix one-half lb. of young parboiled hop-sprouts to the sauce; simmer for two minutes, and pour over the chicken, which should be served in a *cocotte.*

1578—VICHY CHICKEN SAUTE *Poulet Sauté Vichy*

Brown the chicken in butter; add one-half lb. of half-cooked carrots à la Vichy (2061) to it, and complete the cooking of the chicken and the carrots covered in the oven.

Swirl with a few tablespoons of veal stock (10); place on a dish, and cover with the garnish of carrots.

1579—VERDI CHICKEN SAUTE *Poulet Sauté Verdi*

Prepare a border of *rizotto* à la Piémontaise (2258).

Sauté the chicken in butter; set it in the center of the border, and on the latter arrange a crown of slices of *foie-gras*, tossed in butter, alternated with slices of truffle, resting against the chicken.

Swirl with Asti wine; reduce; add three tablespoons of veal stock (10) and one and one-half oz. of butter, and pour this sauce over the pieces of chicken.

1580—FILLETS (OR BREASTS) OF CHICKEN   *Filets de Poulet*

1581—BREASTS OF CHICKEN   *Suprêmês de Poulet*

1582—CHICKEN CUTLETS   *Côtelettes de Poulet*

1583—CHICKEN WINGS   *Ailerons de Poulet*

The terms *"Fillet"* and *"Suprême"* are synonymous, and either one or the other may be used for variety to express the same thing on a menu. They are names given to the breast of the fowl, divided into two along the breast bone, and cleared of all skin. Each *fillet* or *suprême* comprises the large and the *minion fillets* (small).

When *suprêmes* are taken from a small chicken, the *minion fillets* are not removed; if the chicken be an ordinary one or a pullet, the *minion fillets* are removed, cleared of all tendons, and twisted into rings or crescents, after having been *studded* with slices of truffle that are half-inserted into the little incisions, made at regular intervals in the meat with the point of a knife.

Prepared in this way, these fillets are generally included in the garnish of the *suprêmes*. Chicken *ailerons* (wings) and cutlets (the latter must not be mistaken for those prepared from the cooked meat and which are only a kind of *croquette*) are *suprêmes* to which the first joint of the wing is left.

Cutlets are always cut from very fleshy, spring chickens. The same rule applies to *suprêmes* (breasts); though, sometimes, the latter are cut from pullets. But, in that case, as they would be too large, they are cut into three or four very regular pieces, which are slightly flattened, and trimmed to the shape of hearts or ovals; except when they have to be stuffed.

In the latter case, they are opened in the thickness, by means of the point of a small knife, to form pockets; and, in the cavity the selected stuffing is inserted, with the help of a pastry-bag fitted with a little, even tube, and in a sufficient quantity to fill out the *suprêmes* well.

Suprêmes and cutlets are always cooked without liquor, or almost so; for should any moistening liquid even approach the boil, it would immediately harden them. If they be desired *poached,* it would be best to cook the whole fowl, and cut them off when it is cooked.

This is how they are prepared, according to whether they be required white or *sautéd;* though the brown method of preparing them is applied more particularly to cutlets.

Cutlets or *suprêmes sautéd:* Season them with salt; roll them in flour; set them in a pan containing some very hot clarified butter (175), and quickly brown them on both sides. These pieces of fowl are so tender that they are cooked and browned at the same time.

Cutlets or suprêmes prepared without browning: Season them, and set them in a pan containing some fresh, melted butter. Roll the *suprêmes* in this butter; add a few drops of lemon juice; thoroughly seal the pan, and put it in a very hot oven.

Allow a few minutes for the *poaching* of the *suprêmes,* which are known to be ready when they seem springy to the touch, and are perfectly white.

Important remarks: Chicken *suprêmes* or cutlets should never be allowed to stand, lest they harden. They should be cooked quickly, at the last moment and served immediately. The shortest delay is enough to spoil them, and to make an insipid and dry preparation of what should be an exquisite dish.

N.B.—The recipes given hereafter for *suprêmes* may of course be applied to fillets, cutlets, wings, *blanc de poulet,* etc.

1584—AGNES SOREL CHICKEN BREASTS
Suprêmes de Volaille Agnes Sorel

Line some oval buttered *tartlet-moulds* with *mousseline forcemeat.* Upon the latter, put some raw, sliced mushrooms, tossed in butter; cover with *forcemeat* so as to fill the mould, and *poach* in the *bain-marie* (water-bath).

Turn out in a circle on a round dish; put a *poached suprême* on each *tartlet;* coat with Allemande sauce (28); decorate with a truffle with a ring of very red tongue, and surround the *suprême* with a ribbon of pale, meat-*glaze* (15).

1585—ALEXANDRA CHICKEN BREASTS
Suprêmes de Volaille Alexandra

Poach the *suprêmes* dry. Serve with a few slices of truffle set on them; coat them with Mornay sauce (91), flavored with chicken *essence,* and *glaze* quickly. Surround with small heaps of asparagus tips, mixed with butter.

1586—AMBASSADRICE CHICKEN BREASTS
Suprêmes de Volaille Ambassadrice

Poach the *suprêmes* dry. Put on a dish; coat them with *Suprême* Sauce (106a), and surround them with lamb sweetbreads, *studded* with truffles and cooked without browning, alternated with bundles of asparagus tips.

1587—ARLESIENNE CHICKEN BREASTS
Suprêmes de Volaille Arlésienne

Season and dredge the *suprêmes,* and toss them in clarified butter (175).

Meanwhile, fry in oil some eggplant slices and some seasoned and dredged round slices of onion. Also prepare a garnish of tomatoes tossed in oil. Place the eggplant slices in a circle on a round dish; set the *suprêmes* on, and garnish with the tossed tomatoes and the fried onions, set in small heaps upon them.

Serve a delicate, tomatoed half-*glaze* sauce (23) separately.

1588—BOISTELLE CHICKEN BREASTS   *Suprêmes de Volaille Boistelle*

Cut the *suprêmes* into heart shapes, and stuff them with *mousseline forcemeat* combined with half its bulk of mashed raw mushrooms.

Put the *suprêmes* in a buttered pan, with two-thirds lb. of peeled, minced, raw mushrooms; season with salt, white pepper and lemon juice, and set to *poach* slowly in a moderate oven.

Arrange in the form of a crown, in a *timbale,* with the mushrooms in the center.

Add to the liquor, which should only consist of the moisture of the mushrooms, two and one-half oz. of butter and a few drops of lemon juice; pour this sauce over the *suprêmes,* and complete with a pinch of chopped parsley.

1589—CHICKEN BREASTS WITH MUSHROOMS IN WHITE SAUCE
Suprêmes de Volaille aux Champignons, à Blanc

Poach the *suprêmes* in a little mushroom cooking-liquor.

Arrange them in the form of a crown, with some fine very white cooked mushroom caps. Coat them moderately with Allemande sauce (28), combined with the cooking-liquor of the *suprêmes.*

Serve what remains of the sauce separately.

1590—CHICKEN BREASTS WITH MUSHROOM SAUCE
Suprêmes de Volaille aux Champignons, à Brun

Cook the *suprêmes* in clarified butter (175), as already described.

Place on a dish and surround them with mushrooms, minced raw and tossed in butter, and coat them with a light mushroom sauce.

1591—CHIMAY CHICKEN BREASTS   *Suprêmes de Volaille Chimay*

Cook the *suprêmes* in clarified butter (175).

Place on a dish; garnish them with *sautéd* morels (French mushrooms) and asparagus tips, mixed with butter, and surround with a ribbon of good thickened gravy.

1592—CUSSY CHICKEN BREASTS   *Suprêmes de Volaille Cussy*

Slice the *suprêmes;* slightly flatten each slice; trim them round, dredge them, and toss them in butter.

Set each slice of *suprême* upon an artichoke-bottom about equal in size; put a thick slice of *glazed* truffle on each slice, and a *blanched* cock's kidney upon each slice of truffle.

Serve a thickened gravy separately.

1593—DORIA CHICKEN BREASTS   *Suprêmes de Volaille Doria*

Season and dredge the *suprêmes,* and toss them quickly in clarified butter (175). Place on a dish and surround them with pieces of cucumber, shaped like garlic cloves and cooked in butter.

When about to serve, sprinkle them with a little nut-brown butter (154), and a few drops of lemon juice.

1594—DREUX CHICKEN BREASTS   *Suprêmes de Volaille Dreux*

Make some incisions, at short intervals, in the *suprêmes,* and halfway insert into these, alternate round slices of truffle and salted tongue. *Poach* them dry. Place on a dish and surround with a garnish of cocks' combs and kidneys, and slices of truffle, and pour a moderate quantity of Allemande sauce (28) over this garnish.

1595—ECARLATE CHICKEN BREASTS *Suprêmes de Volaille Ecarlate*

Cut the *suprêmes* as above; but garnish them only with slices of tongue. *Poach* them dry, and set them on oval, flat *quenelles* of *mousseline forcemeat,* sprinkled with very red chopped tongue.

Coat with clear Suprême Sauce (106a), so that the red of the tongue may be seen.

1596—SCOTCH CHICKEN BREASTS   *Suprêmes de Volaille Ecossaise*

Poach the *suprêmes.*

Place them on a dish; coat them with Écossaise sauce (118), and surround them with small heaps of string beans, mixed with butter.

1597—FAVORITE CHICKEN BREASTS   *Suprêmes de Volaille Favorite*

Sauté the *suprêmes* in clarified butter (175).

Arrange them in a crown, on tossed slices of *foie-gras,* with three slices of truffle on each *suprême.*

In their midst set a heap of asparagus tips, mixed with butter, and serve, separately, a sauceboat of light meat-*glaze* (15), buttered.

1598—FINANCIERE CHICKEN BREASTS

Suprêmes de Volaille Financière

Sauté the *suprêmes* in clarified butter (175).

Arrange them in the form of a crown, upon fried *croûtons* of the same size; in their midst arrange a garnish à la financière (1474), and coat the *suprêmes* and their garnish with financière sauce.

1599—CHICKEN BREASTS WITH ARTICHOKE BOTTOMS

Suprêmes de Volaille aux Fonds d'Artichauts

Sauté the *suprêmes* in clarified butter (175).

Arrange them with a garnish of raw artichoke-bottoms, sliced, tossed in butter, and sprinkled with *fine herbs.* Sprinkle a few drops of nut-brown butter (154) over the *suprêmes,* and serve a thickened gravy separately.

1600—GEORGETTE CHICKEN BREASTS

Suprêmes de Volaille Georgette

Prepare as many "Potatoes Georgette" as there are *suprêmes,* and take care to choose potatoes of the same size as the *suprêmes.*

Poach the *suprêmes.* Set one on each potato, with a fine slice of truffle in the middle, and arrange in the form of a crown on a round dish.

1601—HENRI IV CHICKEN BREASTS   *Suprêmes de Volaille Henri IV*

Slice the *suprêmes;* slightly flatten the slices, and trim them round. Season and dredge them; *sauté* them in clarified butter (175), and set each slice on an artichoke bottom, slightly garnished with buttered meat-*glaze* (15).

Serve a Béarnaise sauce (62) separately.

1602—HUNGARIAN CHICKEN BREASTS

Suprêmes de Volaille Hongroise

Prepare some pilaff rice (2255), combined with chopped tomatoes, and place it in a shallow *timbale*.

Season the *suprêmes* with paprika; toss them in clarified butter (175), and set them in a *timbale,* upon the pilaff rice.

Swirl the pan with a few tablespoons of cream; add the necessary quantity of Hongroise sauce (85), and coat the *suprêmes* with this sauce.

1603—INDIA CHICKEN BREASTS *Suprêmes de Volaille à l'Indienne*

Sauté the *suprêmes* in butter, and put them for a few minutes in a curry sauce à l'Indienne, but without letting it boil.

Serve the *suprêmes* in a *timbale* with the curry sauce (81).

Serve a *timbale* of rice à l'Indienne (1345), separately.

1604—JARDINIERE CHICKEN BREASTS

Suprêmes de Volaille Jardinière

Sauté the *suprêmes* in butter. Put it on a dish and surround with small heaps of vegetables, arranged very neatly, as explained in the case of the *Jardinière* garnish.

Sprinkle the *suprêmes* with a few drops of nut-brown butter (154), just before serving.

1605—JUDIC CHICKEN BREASTS *Suprêmes de Volaille Judic*

Cut the *suprêmes* into heart shapes; season them, and *poach* them dry.

Arrange them in a crown, upon little *braised* lettuces; and set a slice of truffle and a cock's kidney upon each heart of *suprême*. Coat slightly with thickened gravy.

1606—MARECHALE CHICKEN BREASTS

Suprêmes de Volaille Maréchale

It is the rule that all preparations termed "à la Maréchale" should be treated with chopped truffle; that is to say that the latter takes the place of the customary bread-crumbs.

For the sake of economy the *à l'anglaise* treatment (egg and bread-crumbs) is more commonly applied; so the cook may choose which of the two he prefers. In any case, *sauté* the *suprêmes* in butter; arrange them in the form of a crown, with a fine slice of truffle on each, and set in their midst a garnish of asparagus tips, mixed with butter.

N.B.—Formerly, these *suprêmes,* like all preparations "à la Maréchale," were gently grilled upon buttered paper.

1607—MARYLAND CHICKEN BREASTS *Suprêmes de Volaille Maryland*

Proceed exactly as directed under "Poulet sauté à la Maryland" (1565).

1608—MONTPENSIER CHICKEN BREASTS
Suprêmes de Volaille Montpensier

Roll the *suprêmes* in beaten egg and bread-crumbs, and *sauté* them in clarified butter (175). Arrange them in a crown with a slice of truffle on each, and surround with small heaps of asparagus tips, mixed with butter.

Sprinkle the *suprêmes* with a few drops of nut-brown butter (154).

1609—ORLY CHICKEN BREASTS *Suprêmes de Volaille Orly*

Take some *suprêmes* of a roasting chicken, and set them on a dish with parsley sprigs and finely sliced onions; sprinkle with a little oil and lemon juice, and set to *marinate* for an hour.

When about to prepare them, dry them by means of a piece of cloth; dip them into light batter, and put them in a very hot frying fat that they may cook quickly.

Drain; place on a napkin with a border of very green fried parsley, and serve a tomato sauce (29) separately.

1610—ORIENTAL CHICKEN BREASTS
Suprêmes de Volaille à l'Orientale

Sauté the *suprêmes* in butter, and place each on a thick slice of chayote, cut to the same shape, parboiled, and stewed in butter beforehand. Coat with Suprême Sauce (106a), combined with a quarter of its bulk of tomato *purée,* and flavored moderately with saffron.

1611—CHICKEN BREASTS IN PAPER CASES
Suprêmes de Volaille en Papillote

Cut out as many heart-shaped pieces of kitchen paper as there are *suprêmes,* and either butter or oil them.

Quickly brown the *suprêmes* in butter. In the center of each parchment paper heart, set a slice of ham cut to the shape of a triangle; cover the ham with a tablespoon of reduced Italienne sauce (40); set the *suprêmes* on the sauce, and cover with the same sauce and another triangle of ham. Close the pieces of paper, and pleat their edges in such a way as to entirely enclose their contents; set the *papillotes,* thus prepared, on a pan; and put them in a sufficiently hot oven to permit completing the cooking of the *suprêmes* and puffing out the *papillotes.*

1612—CHICKEN BREASTS WITH PARMESAN
Suprêmes de Volaille au Parmesan

Season the *suprêmes;* dip them in beaten egg and roll them in grated Parmesan cheese. *Sauté* them in butter, and place them on *croûtons* of *polenta* (2294), shaped somewhat like the *suprêmes* and browned in clarified butter (175). When about to serve, sprinkle the *suprêmes w*ith nut-brown butter (154).

1613—POLIGNAC CHICKEN BREASTS *Suprêmes de Volaille Polignac*

Poach the *suprêmes* dry, and put them on a dish.

Coat them with Suprême Sauce (106a), combined with a *julienne* of truffles and mushrooms.

1614—POJARSKI CHICKEN BREASTS *Suprêmes de Volaille Pojarski*

Mince the *suprêmes,* and, in so doing, combine with them, first, the quarter of their weight of bread-crumbs dipped in milk and squeezed dry, and the same weight of fresh butter; and then an equal quantity of fresh cream, which should be added little by little. Season with salt, pepper, and nutmeg.

Divide up this preparation into portions equal in size to the *suprêmes,* and reconstruct the *suprêmes* exactly with this minced-meat.

Dredge; cook in clarified butter (175), and serve as soon as ready.

There is no hard and fast rule for the garnishing of these *suprêmes;* the garnish is therefore optional.

1615—REGENCY CHICKEN BREASTS *Suprêmes de Volaille Régence*

Cut the *suprêmes* into heart shapes; flatten them slightly, and *poach* them. Set each *suprême* on a *quenelle* of chicken *forcemeat,* prepared with crayfish butter (147), and arrange in the form of a crown. Coat with Allemande sauce (27) flavored with truffle *essence,* and, on each *suprême,* set an olive-shaped truffle and a cock's kidney —the two separated by a cock's comb.

1616—RICHELIEU CHICKEN BREASTS *Suprêmes de Volaille Richelieu*

Treat the *suprêmes à l'anglaise,* and cook them in clarified butter (175).

Place on a dish; coat them with half-melted butter à la Maître-d'hôtel (150), and set four fine slices of truffle on each *suprême*.

1617—ROSSINI CHICKEN BREASTS   *Suprêmes de Volaille Rossini*

Sauté the *suprêmes* in butter, and serve them on slices of *foie-gras,* arranged in the form of a crown and also tossed in butter. Coat with a strong Madeira sauce (44), combined with slices of truffle.

1618—TALLEYRAND CHICKEN BREASTS
Suprêmes de Volaille Talleyrand

Prepare a *croustade* of lining paste, of a size in proportion to the garnish to be put inside it, just as the garnish should be in proportion to the number of *suprêmes.* Also a garnish of macaroni with cream, combined with three oz. of *foie-gras* and three oz. of truffles in dice, per one-half lb. of macaroni.

Cut the *suprêmes* to the shape of hearts; stuff them with *godiveau* with cream (198), mixed with half its bulk of a *purée* of *foie-gras,* and *poach* them dry.

Put the macaroni in the *croustade,* shaping it like a dome in so doing; coat the *suprêmes* with Allemande sauce (27), and set them in a crown on the *timbale* and round the dome of macaroni.

Send a sauceboat of velouté (25) to the table separately.

1619—VALENCAY CHICKEN BREASTS   *Suprêmes de Volaille Valençay*

Stuff the *suprêmes* with truffles, cut into small dice and mixed with very reduced Allemande sauce (27). Treat them *à l'anglaise* and cook them in butter.

Prepare some fried *croûtons,* shaped like cocks' combs, in the proportion of two for each *suprême;* cover these with a dome of fine truffled *forcemeat,* and put them in a moderate oven that the *forcemeat* may *poach.*

Serve the *suprêmes* in the form of a crown; surround them with the *croûtons;* and, in their midst, pour a *purée* of mushrooms.

1620—VALOIS CHICKEN BREASTS   *Suprêmes de Volaille Valois*

Treat the *suprêmes à l'anglaise,* and cook them in clarified butter (175).

Serve them with a garnish of small, pitted olives, stuffed and *poached* at the last moment.

Serve a Valois sauce (63) separately.

1621—VERNEUIL CHICKEN BREASTS *Suprêmes de Volaille Verneuil*

Marinate the *suprêmes* as for (1609); treat them *à l'anglaise,* and cook them in clarified butter (175). Arrange them in the form of a crown, and coat them with Colbert sauce (141).

Serve separately a *purée* of artichokes, combined with finely-minced truffles.

1622—VILLEROY CHICKEN BREASTS *Suprêmes de Volaille Villeroy*

Poach the *suprêmes* without completely cooking them.

Dip them in a Villeroy sauce (108), in such a way that they may be well coated with it. Leave them to cool; treat them *à l'anglaise;* and, a few minutes before serving, put them in some very hot frying fat. Arrange them in the form of a crown, and serve a Périgueux sauce (47) separately.

1623—CHICKEN BREASTS WITH OYSTERS

Suprêmes de Volaille aux Huîtres

Lift out the *suprêmes* of two small chickens; *poach* them in butter and lemon juice, and coat them with Suprême Sauce (106a).

Arrange them around a low, very cold bed of bread, placed on the dish at the last moment. Upon this bed, quickly set a dozen shucked oysters, which should have been kept in ice for at least two hours.

Serve very quickly in order that the *suprêmes* may be very hot and the oysters very cold. Send a Suprême sauce separately.

1624—TURBAN OF CHICKEN BREASTS *Turban de Filets de Poulet*

Take the required number of *fillets,* which is determined by the size of the mould to be used. Flatten these *fillets* out somewhat thinly, and trim them neatly on both sides.

With these *fillets,* line a buttered *savarin-mould;* setting a row of thin slices of truffle between each of the *fillets,* and allowing the latter to hang over the edge of the mould. Over the *fillets* spread a layer of *mousseline forcemeat,* two-thirds in. thick.

Three-parts fill the remaining space with a large cured tongue, truffles and mushrooms *salpicon,* combined with a reduced Allemande sauce (27).

Cover this *salpicon* with *forcemeat,* so as to fill the mould, and then draw the overlapping ends of the *fillets* across the *forcemeat.*

Set to *poach* in the *bain-marie* (water-bath) for about forty minutes; and, upon taking out the mould, let it stand for five minutes, that it may settle. Turn out upon a round dish; pour a Toulousaine garnish (1524) in the middle, and surround the turban with a ribbon of Allemande sauce (27).

1625—MIGNONETTES OF CHICKEN BREASTS   *Mignonettes de Poulet*

Take the required number of small, *minion fillets* of pullet; trim them; make six incisions in each, and half-way insert into each of these incisions alternate thin slices of truffle and tongue.

Set these *minion fillets* on a buttered dish, and shape them like rings.

Trim and scallop the edges of as many artichoke-bottoms as there are *minion fillets,* and heat them in butter. Garnish these artichoke-bottoms, dome-fashion, with a very white and somewhat stiff chicken *purée.* Sprinke the *minion fillets* with a little mushroom cooking-liquor, and *poach* them in the oven for from five to six minutes.

Set the artichoke-bottoms in a circle on a round dish, and set a *minion fillet* upon each.

Serve a very delicate Suprême sauce (106a), separately.

1626—AGNES SOREL NONNETTES OF CHICKEN
Nonnettes de Poulet Agnes Sorel

Truss twelve ortolans for entrées, and cook them in butter for a moment.

Lift out the *fillets* (breasts) of twelve spring chickens; trim them; flatten them slightly and pair them off, putting the edges of one on the other, that a larger surface may be obtained.

In the middle of these joined *suprêmes* of chicken, put an ortolan; wrap it in them, and tie them round once or twice with string, that they may keep the shape of a *paupiette* or *roulade.*

Set these *paupiettes* in a shallow saucepan, and, five minutes before serving, sprinkle them with four oz. of boiling butter; salt moderately, and cook in a hot oven.

After having removed the string, set each nonnette on a square, hollowed *crouton* of bread, fried in butter, and coated inside with *foie-gras purée.* Coat moderately with a light chicken *glaze* (16), finished with butter, and squeeze a drop of lemon juice on each nonnette.

1627—URSULINES DE NANCY   *Ursulines de Nancy*

Prepare some *barquette* crusts.

Mould some chicken *forcemeat* into large, round, regular *quenelles,* and *poach* them in some white consommé, in time for them to be ready when the Ursulines are finished.

A few moments before serving, garnish the *barquette* crusts with *foie-gras purée,* thinned with a little good half-*glaze* (23), flavored with port or sherry wine. In the middle of each garnished *barquette,* set a well-drained *mousseline quenelle;* decorate each quenelle with a thin and wide slice of truffle; set a small heap of asparagus tips, mixed with butter, at either end of the *barquettes,* that is to say, on either side of the *quenelle;* and slightly coat the latter with chicken *glaze* (16), finished with butter.

Serve, separately, a sauceboat containing some of the same chicken *glaze* with butter.

1628—ST. GERMAIN BREASTS OF CHICKEN
Filets de Poulet Saint-Germain

Season the *fillets,* dip them in melted butter and roll them in bread-crumbs; grill them gently, each on a sheet of oiled paper, and sprinkle with clarified butter (175) during the cooking.

Arrange the grilled *fillets,* and serve at the same time a Béarnaise sauce (62); a *timbale* containing a *purée* of *foie gras* with cream.

1629—MIREILLE BREASTS OF CHICKEN   *Filets de Poulet Mireille*

Prepare a garnish as for (1365), sliced, raw potatoes and artichoke-bottoms, set in a small earthenware dish and cooked as "Potatoes Anna."

Sauté the *fillets* in butter at the last moment; put them on the garnish, and sprinkle them with nut-brown butter (154).

Spring Chickens (Poulets de Grains)

Spring chickens are usually either grilled or prepared *"en casse-role"* in accordance with one or another of the many recipes applicable to them.

1630—BELLE-MEUNIÈRE SPRING CHICKEN
Poulet de Grains à la Belle-Meunière

Stuff the chicken with four sliced chickens' livers and three oz. of raw, quartered mushrooms, slightly tossed in butter. Slip five or six fine slices of truffle under the skin of the breast; truss the chicken as for an entrée, and brown it in butter.

This done, put it into an oval *cocotte,* with two oz. of butter, four rectangles of *blanched* salt pork, and three oz. of raw quartered mushrooms, quickly tossed in butter beforehand.

Cook in the oven, covered, and add two tablespoons of veal gravy (41), just before serving.

1631—BERGERE SPRING CHICKEN   *Poulet de Grains à la Bergère*

Fry in butter four oz. of *blanched* salt pork, cut into dice, and one-half lb. of small, whole mushrooms. Drain, and set to brown in the same butter, the chicken stuffed with a half-onion and three oz. of mushrooms, chopped and fried in butter, and mixed with three oz. of butter and a teaspoonful of chopped parsley.

When the chicken is well browned, put the salt pork and the mushrooms round it; swirl it with one-sixth pint of white wine; reduce by two-thirds; add four tablespoons of veal gravy (41), and complete the cooking of the chicken in the oven.

Set it on a round dish; thicken the cooking-liquor with a piece of *manié* butter, the size of a hazel-nut, or a little arrow-root, flour, etc.; pour the sauce and the garnish round the chicken, and surround it with a border of freshly-fried shoestring potatoes.

1632—BONNE FEMME SPRING CHICKEN

Poulet de Grains Bonne Femme

Fry in butter four oz. of fresh or salted pork fat, cut into slices and *blanched*. Drain; brown the chicken in the same fat, and put it in an oval *cocotte* with the slices of bacon.

With the same fat, fry in a frying-pan two-thirds lb. of potatoes cut to the shape of corks and divided into slices; put these round the chicken, and set to cook in the oven, covered.

When about to serve, sprinkle the fowl with a few tablespoons of veal gravy (41).

Serve the preparation in the *cocotte*.

1633—SPRING CHICKEN IN CASSEROLE

Poulet de Grains en Casserole

Poële the chicken with butter in an earthenware saucepan, and baste it often. When about to serve, clear of all grease, and add a tablespoon of veal gravy (41).

This chicken is served plain, without any garnish.

1634—SPRING CHICKEN IN COCOTTE   *Poulet de Grains en Cocotte*

Brown the chicken in butter, in a *cocotte,* and covered.

When it is half-done, surround it with two oz. of frizzled pieces of fresh or salt pork cut in dice, twelve small onions partly cooked in butter, and twenty small potatoes, the size and shape of olives.

Complete the cooking of the whole together, and, when about to serve, sprinkle with a little veal gravy (41).

1635—CLAMART SPRING CHICKEN   *Poulet de Grains Clamart*

Brown the chicken in butter; half-cook it, and put it in a *cocotte* with one-half pint of half-cooked peas à la Française (2193), the cooking-liquor of which should be very short. Complete the cooking of the whole, together, and serve the preparation as it stands, without mixing the peas.

1636—BROILED DEVILLED SPRING CHICKEN
Poulet de Grains Grillé Diable

Truss the chicken as for an entrée; split it open lengthwise along the middle of the back; flatten it with a butcher's mallet, and remove as many bones as possible. Season it; baste it with melted butter, and half-cook it in the oven.

This done, coat it with mustard strengthened with cayenne; sprinkle copiously with bread-crumbs; press upon the latter with the flat of a knife, that they may adhere to the mustard; sprinkle a little melted butter over the bird, and complete the cooking gently on the grill.

Set on a round dish, bordered with thin slices of lemon, and serve a Devilled Sauce Escoffier (37) separately.

1637—GRILLED SPRING CHICKEN ANGLAISE
Poulet de Grains Grillé à l'Anglaise

Split the chicken open, lengthwise, proceeding from the extremity of the belly to the wing-joints. Open it without separating the two halves, flatten it so as to break the joints and the bones, and remove the fragments of bones with great care.

Fasten the wings by means of a skewer; sprinkle the chicken with melted butter, season it, and half-cook it in the oven.

This done, sprinkle it with bread-crumbs and melted butter, and complete its cooking on the grill. Set it on a round dish, bordered with gherkins, and serve it as it stands.

1638—SPRING CHICKEN WITH ARTICHOKE BOTTOMS
Poulet de Grains aux Fonds d'Artichauts

Brown the chicken in butter, and put it in a *cocotte* with five fair-sized artichoke bottoms, sliced while raw, and tossed in butter. Complete its cooking gently in the oven, and, when about to serve, add a tablespoon of veal gravy (41) and a few drops of lemon juice.

1639—HOTELIERE SPRING CHICKEN   *Poulet de Grains à l'Hotelière*

Bone the chicken's breast; stuff it with one-half lb. of good sausage-meat, and truss it as for an entrée. Brown it with butter in an earthenware saucepan, and put it in the oven.

When it is two-thirds done, add to it four oz. of quartered mushrooms, *sautéd* in butter, complete its cooking, and, when about to serve, finish it with three tablespoons of veal gravy (41).

1640—KATOFF SPRING CHICKEN   *Poulet de Grains à la Katoff*

Split the chicken open along the back, and half-cook it in the oven as in (1636). This done, complete its cooking on the grill.

Meanwhile, mould on a round, buttered dish a sort of cake of Duchesse potatoes (2212), one inch thick. Brush with egg, and brown in the oven.

Serve the grilled chicken on this potato cake, and surround with a ribbon of strong veal gravy (41).

1641—LIMOUSINE SPRING CHICKEN   *Poulet de Grains à la Limousine*

Stuff the chicken with one-half lb. of good sausage-meat, combined with two oz. of chopped mushrooms fried in butter. Put the chicken in a *cocotte* with one oz. of butter and six rectangles of *blanched* bacon, and cook gently in the oven.

When about to serve, add two or three tablespoons of veal gravy (41).

Send, separately, six fine chestnuts cooked in consommé.

1642—MASCOTTE SPRING CHICKEN   *Poulet de Grains Mascotte*

Brown the chicken in butter, and cook it *"en casserole"* with four oz. of potatoes the size and shape of olives and tossed in butter.

When the chicken is almost cooked, put it in a *cocotte* with the potatoes all round, two tablespoons of veal gravy (41), and two oz. of sliced truffles set upon it.

Cover the *cocotte;* put the chicken in the front of the oven for ten minutes, and serve it as it stands.

1643—SPRING CHICKEN WITH MORELS
Poulet de Grains aux Morilles

Prepare this chicken like the one *"en casserole,"* and surround it with one-half lb. of morels (French mushrooms), tossed in butter for a moment. Complete the cooking under cover, and, when about to serve, finish with one tablespoon of veal gravy (41).

1644—SOUVAROFF SPRING CHICKEN   *Poulet de Grains Souvaroff*
Proceed exactly as explained under (1520), but reduce the garnish by half.

1645—TARTARE POULET DE GRAINS   *Poulet de Grains Tartare*
Proceed as for (1636), but serve a Tartar sauce at the same time.

SQUAB CHICKENS (POUSSINS)

When they are bred rationally, the squab chickens are a great delicacy. They are the youngest chickens used in cookery and are usually wheat or milk fed. They are as small as a Jumbo squab, but a bit heavier. They are admirably used for very elegant service and are prepared one for each person.

1646—CINDERELLA SQUAB CHICKENS   *Poussins Cendrillon*
Open the squab chicks along the back, and brown them in butter. This done, season them with salt and cayenne, and put them between two layers of pork *forcemeat*. Wrap them in very soft *pig's caul*. Dip them in melted butter; roll them in bread-crumbs, and grill them gently for twenty or twenty-five minutes.

Arrange on a dish, and serve a Périgueux sauce (47) separately.

1647—PIEMONTAISE SQUAB CHICKENS   *Poussins à la Piémontaise*
Stuff each squab chick with one and one-half oz. of white Piedmont truffles, ground with an equal weight of very fresh pork fat. Now truss them as for an entrée; tie them and fry them in butter over a hot fire. At the end of ten minutes put them in a *cocotte;* partly surround and cover them with *rizotto* à la Piémontaise (2258), and complete the cooking in the oven with lid off.

A few minutes before serving, sprinkle the *rizotto* with grated Parmesan cheese; *glaze;* and, at the last minute, sprinkle with nut-brown butter (154).

1648—POLISH SQUAB CHICKENS   *Poussins à la Polonaise*
Stuff each squab chick with one and one-half oz. of *gratin forcemeat,* two-thirds oz. of soaked and pressed bread-crumbs, one-third oz. of butter, and a pinch of chopped parsley. Truss as for entrées;

tie up; quickly fry the chicks in butter in a very hot oven; put them in a *cocotte,* and complete their cooking in the oven.

At the last moment sprinkle them with a few drops of lemon juice and nut-brown butter (154), combined with one oz. of bread-crumbs per four oz. of butter.

1649—TARTARE SQUAB CHICKENS   *Poussins à la Tartare*
Proceed exactly as for "Poulet a la Tartare."

1650—TORTE OF SQUAB CHICKENS PAYSANNE
Tourte de Poussins à la Paysanne

Prepare a round layer of short paste, ten inches in diameter. Upon this paste spread two-thirds lb. of sausage-meat, combined with five oz. of dry *duxelles,* taking care to leave a margin two inches wide of bare paste all round.

Upon this coating of *forcemeat* set ten split squab chicks, browned in butter; sprinkle two-thirds lb. of chopped mushrooms, *sautéd* in butter, over them; spread a second coating of sausage-meat and *duxelles* over the whole; cover with a very thin slice of bacon, and close the whole with a layer of paste a little larger than the under-lying one, the edges of which should have been moistened. Seal the two edges, and pleat regularly; brush with egg; make a slit in the top, and bake in a moderate oven for about forty minutes.

When taking the pie out of the oven, pour into it, through the slit in its cover, a few tablespoons of half-*glaze* sauce (23).

1651—VIENNESE SQUAB CHICKENS   *Poussins à la Viennoise*
Cut the squab chicks each into four pieces; season them; dredge them; dip them in beaten egg, and roll them in bread-crumbs.

A few minutes before serving, put them in hot fat; drain them, and arrange them in pyramid form on a folded napkin. Surround with fried parsley and sections of lemon, and serve very hot.

VARIOUS PREPARATIONS OF FOWL

1652—CHICKEN GIBLETS WITH WHITE TURNIPS *Abatis aux Navets*
Fry one-half lb. of *blanched* salt pork, cut into dice, in butter. Drain, and fry in the same saucepan three lbs. of giblets, cut into pieces (all except the livers, which are only added one-quarter hour before serving). Sprinkle with two and one-half oz. of flour; mix the latter with the pieces, and cook it in the oven for seven or eight minutes; moisten with three pints of white stock (10). Season

with a pinch of pepper; add an herb bunch and a crushed garlic clove; set to boil, stirring the while; cover, and place in a somewhat hot oven, that the preparation may boil gently.

At the end of thirty-five minutes transfer the pieces to another saucepan; put back the pork fat; add twenty-four small onions, tossed in butter, one lb. of turnips shaped like elongated olives and *glazed,* and strain the sauce over the whole.

Complete the cooking gently, and serve in a *timbale.*

N.B.—With the same procedure, the giblets may be prepared with peas; with mixed, new vegetables; à la *chipolata* (with Italian sausages).

1653—GIBLET PIE *Abatis en Croûte*

Fry the giblets, cut into pieces, in butter; sprinkle them moderately with flour; cook and moisten with just sufficient consommé to make a clear sauce which will just cover the pieces. Three-quarters cook, and leave to cool.

This done, pour the whole into a pie-dish; cover with a layer of puff-paste (2366), which should be sealed down to a strip of paste, on to the edge of the dish; crease with a fork; brush with egg, and bake in a moderately warm oven for from twenty-five to thirty minutes.

1654—STUFFED BALLS AND LEGS OF CHICKEN *Ballotines et Jambonneaux*

These preparations are useful for disposing of any odd legs of fowls, the other parts of which have been already used. The legs are boned and stuffed, and the skin, which should be purposely left long if this preparation be contemplated, is then sewn up. The stuffing used varies according to the kind of dish in preparation, but good sausage-meat is most commonly used.

Ballotines or Jambonneaux are *braised,* and they may be accompanied by any garnish suited to fowl.

If they be prepared for serving cold, coat them with aspic, or cover them with brown (34) or white chaud-froid sauce (72), and garnish them according to fancy.

CHICKEN PUDDINGS, CROQUETTES, ETC.

1655—BOUDINS OF CHICKEN RICHELIEU *Boudins de Volaille à la Richelieu*

Take the required amount of chicken *forcemeat,* prepared with *panada* and cream. and divide it into three-oz. portions. Roll these portions into sausage-form, and open them so as to stuff them with some white chicken-meat, truffle and mushroom *salpicon,* combined with reduced Allemande sauce (27). These *quenelles* may also be moulded in little, rectangular cases, used in biscuit-making, as follows:—Line the bottom and sides of the moulds, which should be well buttered, with a thickness of one-third inch of *forcemeat;* garnish the center with *salpicon;* cover with *forcemeat* up to the edges, and smooth with the blade of a small knife dipped in tepid water.

Whichever way they are made, however, the boudins (puddings) are *poached* like *quenelles,* and are afterwards drained on a piece of linen. They are then dipped in beaten egg and rolled in bread-crumbs, and, finally, gently browned in clarified butter (175), that their inside may get heated at the same time.

Arrange them in a circle on a folded napkin, and serve a Périgueux sauce (47) separately.

1656—BOUDINS OF CHICKEN SOUBISE　　*Boudins de Volaille Soubise*

Prepare the boudins (puddings) with some *forcemeat* as above, but replace the *salpicon* inside by a very reduced and cold truffled Soubise *purée.*

Poach, dip in beaten egg, and roll in bread-crumbs, and brown as before in clarified butter (175).

Serve a clear Soubise separately.

1657—QUENELLES OF CHICKEN MORLAND
Quenelles de Volaille Morland

Mould some portions of somewhat firm chicken *mousseline forcemeat* into the shape of oval *quenelles,* three oz. in weight. Dip them in beaten egg; roll them in finely minced truffle, and press lightly on the latter with the blade of a knife, in order that it may combine with the egg.

Poach gently in clarified butter (175), and cover, so that the *forcemeat* may be well cooked.

Arrange in a circle, and in the middle pour a mushroom *purée.*

1658—QUENELLES OF CHICKEN D'UZES　*Quenelles de Volaille d'Uzès*

Line the bottom and sides of some oval buttered *quenelle* moulds with chicken *forcemeat* prepared with *panada* and cream. Garnish the middle with a mince of the white of chicken meat combined with reduced Allemande sauce (27), and cover with *forcemeat.*

Poach the *quenelles* in good time; drain them on a piece of linen;

set them in a circle on a round dish, and coat with Aurore sauce (60).
Garnish the center of the circle with a fine *Julienne* of truffles.

1659—CAPILOTADE OF CHICKEN *Capilotade de Volaille*

Prepare an Italienne sauce (40), combined with cooked, sliced mushrooms. Add to this sauce some thin slices of cold fowl remains, and heat without allowing to boil.

Serve in a *timbale,* and sprinkle a little chopped parsley over the preparation.

1660—CHICKEN PIE *Chicken Pie*

Cut a fowl into pieces as for a fricassée; season the pieces, and sprinkle them with three finely-chopped onions, one and one-half oz. of chopped mushrooms cooked in butter, and a pinch of chopped parsley.

Line the bottom and sides of a pie-dish with thin slices of veal; set the pieces of fowl inside, putting the legs in first; add five oz. of thin slices of bacon; the yolks of four hard-boiled eggs cut into two; and moisten sufficiently to three-quarters cover with chicken consommé. Cover with a layer of puff-paste (2366), which should be sealed down to a strip of paste stuck to the edges of the pie-dish; brush with egg; streak with a knife; make a slit in the middle of the paste, and bake in a moderate oven for one and one-half hours.

When taking the pie out of the oven, pour a few tablespoons of strong gravy into it.

1661—COCKS' COMBS AND KIDNEYS *Crêtes et Rognons de Coq*

In order to prepare cocks' combs and kidneys, they should be first set to soak in cold water for a few hours.

If the combs are fresh, they should be put in a saucepan of cold water and then heated; then drained and rubbed in a towel so that their skins may be removed. This done, they are trimmed, and kept in fresh water, which ought to be frequently changed until they are quite white.

They may then be cooked in a very light Blanc (167).

The kidneys are merely soaked in cold water for a few hours, and put to cook with the combs a few minutes before the latter are ready.

Cocks' combs and kidneys are mostly used as garnish; nevertheless, they also serve in the preparation of special dishes, for which I shall now give a few recipes.

1662—COCKS' COMBS AND KIDNEYS A LA GRECQUE
Crêtes et Rognons de Coq à la Grecque

About twenty-five minutes before serving, prepare a pint of pilaff rice (2256), combined with one-half pepper cut into dice, and a very little saffron.

Also prepare ten round slices of egg-plant, seasoned, dredged, and fried in oil just before serving. The moment the rice is cooked, add thereto twenty-four very fresh cocks' kidneys, frizzled in butter, and twelve fine *blanched* cocks' combs, *poëled* after the manner of lambs' sweetbreads.

Set the whole in a silver saucepan, arrange the egg-plant slices in a circle on the rice, and serve instantly.

1663—DESIRS DE MASCOTTE   *Désirs de Mascotte*

Put three oz. of butter in a pan, and fry it nut-brown.

Add to this butter twenty-four fine cocks' kidneys (it is essential that these should be fresh); season them with salt, pepper, and a little cayenne, and cook them for from five to six minutes, which should prove sufficient.

Meanwhile, prepare twelve *croûtons* of bread, one-third inch thick, stamped out with a round cutter two-thirds inch in diameter. Fry these *croûtons* in butter at the last minute.

Put four fine, very black truffles, cut into somewhat thick slices, into the required quantity of reduced half-*glaze* sauce (23); add the kidneys, drained of their butter, as well as the fried *croûtons,* one and one-half oz. of very best butter, and a few drops of lemon juice, and roll the saucepan gently, that the butter may thoroughly combine with the sauce.

Place immediately in a very hot, silver *timbale,* and serve instantly.

1664—STUFFED COCKS' KIDNEYS FOR COLD ENTREES AND GARNISHINGS
Rognons de Coq Farcis pour Entrées Froides et Garnitures

Choose some fine, cooked kidneys, and cut them in two lengthwise. Trim them slightly underneath, that they may lie flat.

Stuff them by means of a pastry-bag with a highly seasoned *purée* of *foie gras,* or of ham, the white of a chicken and truffles, combined with an equal weight of fresh butter.

Coat them with a pink or white chaud-froid sauce (72), according to the requirements; set them in a low *timbale,* and cover them with light aspic.

They may also be put into *petits-fours* moulds, surrounded with the jelly, and used as a garnish for cold fowls.

1664a—CHICKEN CROQUETTES AND CUTLETS
Crochettes et Côtelettes de Volaille

The *croquettes* and cutlets with which we are now concerned are made up of exactly the same ingredients, and only differ in the matter of shape, the croquettes, as a rule, being shaped either like corks or rectangles; sometimes, too, like patties; whereas the cutlets, as their name implies, are made in cutlet-shaped moulds.

The preparation from which they are made is as follows:—One lb. of the meat of a *poached* or roast fowl, thoroughly cleared of all skin, cartilage, and bones, and cut into small regular dice [1]; six oz. of cooked mushrooms; an equal amount of cured ox-tongue or ham, and four oz. of truffles. Cut these various products like the chicken, and mix them; then add one-half pint of very reduced and finished Allemande sauce (27) to the whole; set the preparation to dry for a few minutes over the fire; this done, remove it, and thicken it with the yolks of four raw eggs, which should be quickly mixed with it. Now pour the preparation into a very clean, buttered tray, and butter its surface, lest a crust form during the cooling.

When the preparation is quite cold, transfer it, by means of a spoon, in pieces weighing about two oz., to a flour-dusted mixing board. Make the *croquettes* and cutlets about the desired shape; dip them into an *anglaise,* and roll them in fine bread-crumbs. Definitely shape them; plunge them into very hot fat; keep them in until they have acquired a fine golden color; drain them, and arrange them in a crown on a napkin, with a heap of fried parsley in the middle.

Croquettes and cutlets may be garnished as fancy suggests, but the accompaniment should always be served separately. Tomato (29) and Périgueux (47) sauces are the most commonly used, and the best garnishes for the purpose are all the *purées,* peas, string beans, and *jardinières.*

---

[1] When prepared as directed above, all meats, whether of poultry, game, fish, lobsters, shrimp, etc. or oysters, clams, etc., may serve in the preparation of croquettes or cutlets.

CHICKENS' LIVERS (FOIES DE VOLAILLE)

1665—BROCHETTES OF CHICKEN LIVERS
Brochettes de Foies de Volaille

Slice the livers; quickly cook them in butter, and then treat them exactly as explained under "Brochettes de Rognons" (1343).

1666—CHICKEN LIVER AND KIDNEY SAUTE WITH RED WINE
Foies de Volaille et Rognons Sautés au Vin Rouge

Proceed according to the recipe given under "Rognons Sautés au Champagne" (1333), using sliced chickens' livers and cocks' kidneys in equal quantities, and substituting excellent red wine for the Champagne.

N.B.—Chickens' livers are also prepared *sautés* chasseur; *sautés fines herbes,* au *gratin;* en coquilles; en pilaw, etc. Refer to sheeps' kidneys for these preparations (1329).

1667—OLD-FASHIONED CHICKEN FRICASSEE
Fricassée de Poulet à l'Ancienne

For a fricassée cut up the chicken as for a *sauté,* but divide the legs in two. The procedure is exactly that of "Fricassée de Veau" (1276)—that is to say, the chicken is cooked in the sauce.

About ten minutes before serving, add ten small onions cooked in white consommé, and ten small grooved mushroom-heads. Finish at the last moment with a pinch of chopped parsley and chives. Thicken the sauce at the last moment with the yolks of two eggs, four tablespoons of cream, and one oz. of best butter.

Place in a *timbale,* and surround the fricassée with little flowerets of puff-paste, baked without browning.

1668—CHICKEN FRICASSEE WITH CRAYFISH
Fricassée de Poulet aux Ecrevisses

Prepare the fricassée as above, and add as garnish ten small, cooked mushrooms, and the shelled tails of twelve crayfish, cooked as for *bisque.* When about to serve, finish the fricassée with two and one-half oz. of crayfish butter (147), made from the crayfish shells and their cooking-liquor rubbed through linen.

Serve in a *timbale.*

1669—DEEP FRY OR MARINADE OF CHICKEN
Fritôt ou Marinade de Volaille

Cut some boiled or roast fowl into slices, and *marinate* these in a few drops of oil, lemon juice, and some chopped herbs for one-quarter hour. Boiled fowl is preferable, in that the greater porousness of its meat aids the penetration of the *marinade* through it.

A few minutes before serving, dip the slices into a very light batter, and put them into very hot fat. Drain, the moment the batter is golden brown; set on a napkin with fried parsley, and serve a tomato sauce (29) separately.

N.B.—Nowadays Fritôt and Marinade of fowl are identically the same dish, but formerly they differed in this, namely, that the Fritôt was prepared from cooked fowl, and the Marinade from pieces of uncooked fowl which were *marinated* beforehand.

1670—MOUSSES AND MOUSSELINES OF CHICKEN
Mousses et Mousselines de Volaille

Both these preparations have for basic ingredient the *mousseline forcemeat* of (195). They differ in that the *"Mousses"* are prepared in one dish for several people, and that the *"Mousselines,"* which are virtually special *quenelles,* are prepared in the proportion of one or two for each person.

In different parts of this book, especially under (797), the preparation has already been exhaustively explained; there is no need now, therefore, to go over the ground again.

1671—ALEXANDRA MOUSSELINES OF CHICKEN
Mousselines de Volaille Alexandra

Mould and *poach* the Mousselines. Drain them, and set them in a circle on a round dish; place on each a fine slice of cooked fowl, and upon it a slice of truffle. Coat with Mornay sauce (91), *glaze* quickly, and, in the middle of the *mousselines,* set a heap of asparagus tips or small peas, mixed with butter.

1672—INDIA MOUSSELINES OF CHICKEN
Mousselines de Volaille à l'Indienne

Prepare the *mousselines* as above; set them in a circle on a round dish; coat with Indienne sauce (1345), and serve a *timbale* of rice à l'Indienne (2254) separately.

1673—PAPRIKA MOUSSELINES OF CHICKEN
Mousselines de Volaille au Paprika

When the *mousselines* are *poached,* set upon each a fine slice of breast, and coat with Suprême Sauce (106a) with paprika. Surround them with small *timbales* of pilaff rice (2256) combined with chopped tomatoes cooked in butter.

1674—PATTI MOUSSELINES OF CHICKEN
Mousselines de Volaille à la Patti

Proceed as for *"Mousselines Alexandra,"* but coat them with Suprême Sauce (106a), finished with crayfish butter (147). In their midst set a heap of asparagus tips, mixed with butter, and upon these lay some fine slices of *glazed* truffles.

1675—SICILIENNE MOUSSELINES OF CHICKEN
Mousselines de Volaille à la Sicilienne

Prepare the *mousselines* as above, and set them, each on an oval *tartlet,* filled with macaroni à la Napolitaine (2289). Coat them with Suprême Sauce (106a); besprinkle with grated Parmesan cheese, and *glaze* quickly.

1676—SYLPHIDES OF CHICKEN   *Sylphides de Volaille*

Prepare and *poach* the *mousselines* in the usual way. Fill the bottom of some *barquettes* with Mornay sauce (91), and put a *mousseline* into each *barquette.*

Set a slice of fowl on each *mousseline,* and cover them with a somewhat stiff preparation of soufflé au Parmesan (2295a), applied ornamentally with a pastry-bag fitted with a plain tube. Put the sylphides in the oven, in order to cook the *soufflé,* and serve instantly.

1677—FLORENTINE MOUSSELINES OF CHICKEN
Mousselines de Volaille à la Florentine

Proceed as for the sylphides; taking note only of this difference, viz., that the bottom of the *barquettes* must be filled with shredded spinach stewed in butter. For the other details of the operation the procedure is the same.

1678—PILAFF OF CHICKEN   *Pilaw de Volaille*

Pilaff (rice), which is the national dish of Orientals, gives rise to an endless number of recipes. The various curries of veal, lamb, and fowl are "pilaffs," and all except the one "à la Parisienne," which I give below, follow the same method of preparation—namely, that of curry; but for a change in the condiments and the treatment of the rice, which is not the same as that of "Riz à l'Indienne."

1679—GREEK PILAFF OF CHICKEN   *Pilaw de Volaille à la Grecque*

Cut the fowl into small pieces, and fry it in mutton fat with three oz. of chopped onions. Sprinkle with one oz. of flour; moisten with one pint of white consommé; add two-thirds of a green pepper, cut into dice, and one and one-half oz. of currants and sultanas (raisins), and cook gently.

Place in a *timbale,* and serve some pilaff rice (2255) separately.

1680—ORIENTAL PILAFF OF CHICKEN *Pilaw de Volaille à l'Orientale*

Prepare the fowl as above, only flavor it with a little powdered ginger, and add three green *braised* and quartered peppers to the sauce.

Serve a *timbale* of pilaff rice (2255) at the same time.

1681—PARISIAN PILAFF OF CHICKEN *Pilaw de Volaille à la Parisienne*

Cut up the fowl as for a fricassée; season it; fry it in butter, and add three and one-half oz. of rice, browned in butter, with one chopped onion, a bay leaf, and two peeled and chopped tomatoes. Moisten with enough white broth to more than cover, and cook in a very hot oven for twenty-five minutes. At the end of this time the fowl and rice are cooked, and the rice should be quite dry.

Sprinkle then with one-sixth pint of veal stock (10); mix it with the pilaff by means of a fork, and place with care in a *timbale.*

Serve a sauceboat of tomato sauce (29) separately.

1682—TURKISH PILAFF OF CHICKEN   *Pilaw de Volaille à la Turque*

Prepare the fowl as for "Pilaw à la Parisienne," and flavor with a little pinch of cayenne and another of saffron. Serve in a *timbale.*

N.B.—Pilaff may also be prepared with cooked fowl, cut into slices which are heated in butter. In this case, garnish the bottoms and sides of a *timbale* with *tomatoed* pilaff rice (2255); put the slices of fowl in the middle; cover with rice, and turn out the *timbale* on the dish.

Surround the *timbale* with a ribbon of tomato sauce (29).

1683—SOUFFLES OF CHICKEN *Soufflés de Volaille*

For dinners on a large scale, it is preferable to use raw chicken-meat. For small ones, cooked chicken-meat suits perfectly.

N.B.—The time allowed for cooking chicken *soufflées* with cooked chicken-meat is comparatively long, and it is better to cook them a little too much than not enough.

For a *soufflé* made in a quart *timbale,* and cooked in a moderate oven as directed, allow from about twenty-five to thirty minutes.

1684—SOUFFLE OF CHICKEN WITH RAW MEAT
Soufflé de Volaille avec Chair de Volaille Crue

Prepare two lbs. of *mousseline forcemeat* of chicken, according to recipe (195); add to this the whites of four eggs beaten to a stiff froth.

Place in buttered *timbales,* and cook in a moderate oven.

1685—SOUFFLE OF CHICKEN WITH COOKED MEAT
Soufflé de Volaille avec Chair de Volaille Cuite

Finely pound one lb. of the white of cooked chicken-meat; add six tablespoons of cold, reduced, Béchamel sauce (28). Rub through a fine sieve.

Heat this preparation in a saucepan, without allowing it to boil, and add to it one and one-half oz. of butter, the yolks of five eggs, and the whites of six, beaten to a stiff froth.

Place in a buttered *timbale,* and cook in a moderate oven.

Suprême sauce (106a) and the other derivatives of Allemande sauce form the best accompaniments to chicken *soufflés.*

1686—PERIGORD SOUFFLE OF CHICKEN
Soufflé de Volaille à la Périgord

This may be made from either one of the two above-mentioned preparations, but there must be added to it three and one-half oz. of chopped truffles. The preparation is then spread in layers separated by slices of truffle, which should weigh about three and one-half oz. in all, in order to be in proportion to the quantities already given.

Cold Preparations of Fowl

1687—PULLET CARMELITE *Poularde à la Carmelite*

Poach the pullet; lift out *suprêmes* breasts and remove their skin; slice them; coat them with white chaud-froid sauce (72), and decorate them plainly with pieces of truffle. Trim the bird; coat it outside with white chaud-froid sauce, and fill with a fine crayfish *mousse,* reconstructing to the shape of bird.

Put a *mousse* to set in a refrigerator; place the slices of *suprême* neatly upon it, in two rows, and between each row lay a dozen fine crayfish tails shelled and trimmed.

Coat the whole with half-melted aspic-jelly; set in a deep dish; incrust the latter in a block of ice, and pour enough very good, melting aspic-jelly (159) over the pullet to half cover it.

1688—PULLET IN CHAMPAGNE   *Poularde au Champagne*

Stuff a pullet two days beforehand with a whole *foie-gras studded* with truffles and browned in butter for twenty minutes. *Poële* it in champagne; put it in a *cocotte;* cover it with its *poëlé*-liquor, containing a sufficient addition of melted jelly, and leave it to cool.

On the morrow remove, by means of a spoon, the grease that has settled on the jelly, and scald the latter twice or three times with boiling water, in order to remove the last traces of grease.

Serve this pullet very cold, in the same *cocotte* in which it has cooled.

1689—CHAUD-FROID OF PULLET   *Poularde en Chaud-Froid*

Poach the pullet; let it cool in its cooking-liquor; cut it up, and clear the pieces of all skin. Dip the pieces in chaud-froid (72) sauce, already prepared from the pullet's cooking-liquor if possible, and arrange them in a pan. Decorate each piece with a fine slice of truffle; *glaze* with cold, melted jelly; leave to set, and trim the edges of the pieces, just before serving them.

Old method of serving: Formerly, chaud-froids were placed on a bed of bread or rice, placed in the middle of a border of aspic-jelly; and, between each piece, cocks' combs and mushrooms, covered with chaud-froid sauce or jelly, were set.

They were also served on suet platters, made in special moulds; but these methods, however much they may have been honored by old cookery, are generally overlooked at the present day.

The method of serving detailed hereafter is steadily eliminating the old methods; it permits the serving of much more delicate and more agreeable chaud-froids in the simplest possible way, and was inaugurated at my suggestion at the Savoy Hotel.

Modern method of serving: Set the decorated pieces, coated with chaud-froid sauce, side by side on a layer of excellent aspic-jelly, lying on the bottom of a deep square dish. Cover them with the same aspic, which should be half melted, and leave to set. When about to serve, incrust the dish in a block of carved ice, or surround it with cracked ice.

This procedure permits the using of less gelatinous products in the preparation of the aspic, and it is therefore much more delicate, mellow, and melting.

1690—SCOTCH CHAUD-FROID OF PULLET
Poularde en Chaud-Froid à l'Ecossaise

Having *poached* and cooled the pullets, lift out *suprêmes,* and cut each into three or four slices. Fill these slices, dome-fashion, with a *salpicon* consisting of the meat cut from the bird, combined with an equal quantity of tongue and truffle, and combined with reduced chicken jelly.

Coat these slices with white chaud-froid sauce (72); sprinkle them immediately with very red tongue, truffle, gherkins, and hard-boiled white of egg; all chopped, mixed, and *glazed* with jelly.

Now set the slices in a deep, square silver dish, alternating them with oval slices of salted tongue.

Garnish their midst with a salad of string beans, cut in short pieces and combined with aspic.

1691—FELIX FAURE CHAUD-FROID
Chaud-Froid Felix Faure

Lift out *suprêmes* (breasts) of a fine pullet; cut them in two in the thick part, without separating them, and slightly flatten them. Lay them on a piece of linen; season them; and, on one of their halves, spread a layer of *foie-gras purée* thickened with a little chicken *force-meat.* Upon this layer set some rectangles of raw *foie-gras,* one-third in. thick; cover with *purée,* set some slices of truffle upon the latter; coat again with *purée;* moisten with white of egg, and over the whole press the other half of the *suprême.* Wrap each *suprême,* prepared in this way, in a piece of muslin; *poach* them in a moderate oven, after having moistened them to within half their height with chicken stock; and leave them to cool in their cooking-liquor under slight pressure.

This done, take off the muslin, and cut each *suprême* into ten or twelve medallions (about the size of a half-dollar). Envelop each medallion in a *mousse* of chicken made with the meat of the *poached* eggs, and leave to set. Then coat each medallion with white chaud-froid sauce (72), and decorate each with a fine slice of truffle.

Coat a dome-mould with a fine chicken jelly, and decorate it with slices of truffle; put the medallions inside, proceeding as for an aspic, and leave to set.

When about to serve, turn out on a napkin.

1692—CHAUD-FROID OF PULLET GOUNOD
Chaud-Froid de Poularde à la Gounod

Lift out *suprêmes* of a *poached* pullet, and cool them under pressure.

Then cut them into rectangles of equal sizes; and, if necessary, split them in half.

Prepare a slab of *mousse* (made from the legs and the trimmings), twice as thick as the rectangles. Smooth this *mousse* neatly, and put it in the refrigerator that it may get firm. This done, cut it into pieces exactly equal in size to the *suprêmes;* to do this, all that is necessary is to stick it on the *mousse* by means of jelly.

Now coat each *suprême* garnished with *mousse* with white chaud-froid sauce (72), and decorate with a bar of notes (the music scale), imitated with truffles.

Set in a square, deep silver dish; cover with transparent and melting chicken jelly; leave to set, and serve the dish incrusted in a block of ice.

1693—CHAUD-FROID OF PULLET ROSSINI
Chaud-Froid de Poularde à la Rossini

Prepare the pieces as for ordinary chaud-froid (1689), and coat them with chaud-froid sauce (72) combined with a quarter of its bulk of very smooth *foie-gras purée*. Decorate each piece with a lyre composed of truffle stamped out with a "lyre" fancy-cutter, set them on a deep, square dish, and cover with chicken jelly as above.

1694—PULLET DAMPIERRE
Poularde à la Dampierre

Completely bone the pullet's breast, and stuff it with a preparation of chicken *forcemeat* (200). Sew up the bird, truss it as for an entrée, and *poach* it in a chicken stock.

When it is cold, trim it, and coat it with a white chaud-froid sauce (72), combined with a little almond milk (2506). *Glaze* with aspic-jelly, and set it, without decorating it, on a low bed lying on a long dish.

Surround it with six small, ham *mousses* and six small, chicken *mousses,* moulded in deep *dariole-moulds,* and arranged alternately.

Border the dish with *croûtons* of aspic-jelly, cut very neatly.

1695—CHICKEN A L'ECARLATE *Poulets à l'Ecarlate*

Bone the breasts of three fair-sized chickens; stuff and *poach* them as explained above. When they are quite cold, cover them with white chaud-froid sauce (72); decorate with pieces of truffle; *glaze* with aspic-jelly, and leave to set.

This done, set them upright on a dish, letting them lean one against the other. Between each chicken set a cured calf's tongue, upright, with the tip of the tongue pointing upwards; and, on either side of the tongues, a large *glazed* truffle.

Border the dish with fine *croûtons* of aspic-jelly, and serve a mayonnaise sauce at the same time.

1696—LAMBERTYE PULLET *Poularde à la Lambertye*

Poach the pullet and let it cool thoroughly.

Lift out *suprêmes*, remove the bones of the breast and fill the cavity with a cold chicken *mousse*, combined with a quarter of its volume of *foie-gras purée*, shaping it in such a way as to reconstruct the bird.

Cut the *suprêmes* into thin, long slices; coat them with white chaud-froid sauce (72), and place them on the *mousse*, pressing them lightly one upon the other. Decorate with pieces of truffle; *glaze* with chicken aspic-jelly; set in a square, entrée dish, and sur-round with melted jelly.

When about to serve, incrust the dish in a block of ice.

1697—NEVA PULLET *Poularde à la Neva*

Stuff the pullet with chicken *forcemeat* (200), combined with *foie-gras* and truffles, cut into dice; *poach* it in chicken stock and let it cool. This done, coat the piece with white chaud-froid sauce (72), decorate with jelly, and leave to set.

Set the pullet on a bed of rice, lying on a long dish. Behind the bird, arrange a fine, vegetable salad in a shell of molded rice, or in a large, silver shell.

Border the dish with neatly-cut *croûtons* of pale aspic-jelly.

1698—ROSE DE MAI PULLET *Poularde Rose de Mai*

Poach the pullet and, when it is quite cold, lift out its *suprêmes* and remove the bones of the breast. Coat the bird with a white chaud-froid sauce (72); decorate as fancy may dictate; garnish with a *mousse* of tomatoes (814), and arrange the latter in such a way as to reconstruct the bird.

Slice the *suprêmes;* coat them with the white chaud-froid sauce;

decorate with truffles, and *glaze* with chicken jelly. Fill with the same *mousse* as that already used for the pullet, as many small, *barquette*-moulds as there are chaud-froid-coated slices, and leave to set.

Put the pullets on a low bed of rice, placed on a long dish; surround it with the *barquettes* of *mousse,* turned out at the last moment; set a chaud-froid-coated slice on each *barquette,* and distribute *croûtons* of aspic-jelly over the dish.

1699—ROSE MARIE PULLET *Poularde Rose Marie*

Having *poached* and cooled the pullet, lift out its *suprêmes;* cut these into slices, and coat them with white chaud-froid sauce (72). Trim the bird, leaving the wings attached; fill it with very smooth and pink ham *mousse,* re-shape the pullet, and put to set in the refrigerator.

Mould in small, oval moulds, as many *barquettes* of the same ham *mousse* as there are slices.

When the *mousse* in the fowl has properly set, coat it with chaud-froid sauce (72), prepared with paprika of a fine, tender, pink shade; decorate according to fancy, and *glaze* with chicken jelly.

Set the pullet on a low bed of rice, placed on a dish; place the *barquettes* of ham *mousse* around it; set a slice on each *mousse* and a fine slice of truffle on each slice, and border the dish with *croûtons* of aspic-jelly.

1700—ST. CYR PULLET *Poularde à la Saint-Cyr*

Poêle the pullet in white wine, and leave it to cool in its cooking-liquor. This done, lift out *fillets,* breasts; cut them into regular slices; coat them with white chaud-froid sauce (72) and decorate.

Meanwhile, *sauté* fifteen larks in a *mirepoix;* remove the breasts of six of them; *glaze* them with brown, chaud-froid sauce (34), and decorate them with bits of hard-boiled white of egg.

With the remainder of the larks and five oz. of *foie-gras,* prepare a *mousse,* and use the latter for reconstructing the pullet as explained in the preceding recipes. When the *mousse* has set properly, coat it with brown chaud-froid sauce. Arrange the chicken breasts, coated with white chaud-froid sauce (72), on either side of the *mousse;* in the middle put the larks' breasts, coated with brown chaud-froid sauce, and let them slightly overlap one another.

Set the pullet in a deep, square dish; surround it with melted chicken jelly; let the latter set, and serve the dish incrusted in a block of ice.

1701—PULLET IN TERRINE WITH ASPIC

Poularde en Terrine à la Gelée

Bone the pullet all but the legs, and stuff it with a *forcemeat* consisting of: three and one-half oz. of veal; three and one-half oz. of fresh pork fat; three and one-half oz. of *gratin forcemeat,* prepared from chicken livers; two tablespoons of brandy; two table-spoons of truffle *essence,* and the yolk of an egg.

In the midst of the stuffing, set half of a raw *foie-gras* and one raw, quartered truffle on each side. Reconstruct the pullet; truss it as for an entrée; cover it with slices of bacon, and *poële* in Madeira for one and one-half hours.

Leave to half-cool in the cooking-liquor; take out the pullet; remove the slices of bacon, and put it in an earthenware dish just large enough to hold it.

Add a little chicken aspic-jelly to the bird's cooking-liquor, which should not have been cleared of grease, but merely strained through a napkin; and pour this sauce over the pullet.

Do not serve until twenty-four hours have elapsed, and clear of grease as directed under "Poularde au Champagne" (1688).

Serve the *terrine* in a block of ice, or on a dish with cracked ice all round.

1702—TERRINE OF PULLET IN CONSERVE

Terrine de Poularde en Conserve

Prepare the pullet as explained above, and put it in a box just large enough to hold it. Seal up the box; mark the top with a bit of tin; put it in a pot with enough water to cover it, and boil for two hours.

This done, take out the box and cool it, placing it upside down, that the grease may be at the bottom and the breast coated with jelly.

1703—CARMELITE CHICKEN WINGS *Ailerons de Poulet à la Carmelite*

Poach a roasting chicken; let it cool; lift off its *suprêmes* and leave the wing bones attached, after having cleared them of all meat; skin the *suprêmes,* and coat them with a little jelly.

Fill a *timbale,* just large enough to hold the two wings, half-way up with crayfish *mousse* (976). Upon this *mousse,* set the two *suprêmes,* opposite one another, and between them set a row of shelled and trimmed crayfish tails, cooked as for *bisque.* Cover the whole with a succulent half-set chicken aspic-jelly, and place in the refrigerator for two hours.

1704—LADY WILMER CHICKEN WINGS

Ailerons de Poulet Lady Wilmer

Poach three fleshy, spring chickens, taking care to have the *suprêmes* just cooked. Leave to cool, and cut off the wings as in the preceding recipe, trim them and coat them with aspic-jelly.

With the meat of three chicken legs, prepare a chicken *mousse,* and mould it in a *dome-mould.* When the *mousse* is set, turn it out on a dish, and place the wings all round, fixing them on the *mousse,* with their points upwards, by means of a little half-set jelly.

Cover the *mousse* on top, and the gaps between the points of the *suprêmes* with chopped truffle and chopped tongue, laid alternately. In the middle of the *mousse,* set a fine, *glazed* truffle, pierced by a small decorative skewer.

1705—ITALIAN CHICKEN ASPIC   *Aspic de Poulet à l'Italienne*

Coat a border mould with aspic-jelly, in accordance with the procedure described under "Aspic de Homard" (954), and decorate it with large slices of truffles. Fill the mould with a coarse *julienne* of chicken breasts, cured tongue and truffles, spread in successive layers and besprinkled with cold, melted aspic.

When about to serve, turn out the aspic on a very cold dish; set a salad "à l'Italienne" (2008) in its midst, and serve a Rémoulade sauce (130) separately.

1706—GAULOISE CHICKEN ASPIC   *Aspic de Poulet à la Gauloise*

Coat an ornamented mould with aspic-jelly, and decorate its bottom and sides with truffles. Fill it with successive and alternate layers of: aspic-jelly, slices of chicken breasts, cocks' combs coated with brown chaud-froid sauce (34), fine cocks' kidneys, coated with white chaud-froid sauce (72), and slices of cured tongue cut into oval shapes.

When about to serve, turn out, and surround with fine *croûtons* of aspic.

1707—MEDALLIONS OF CHICKEN RACHEL

Medaillons de Poulet Rachel

Prepare some chicken *suprêmes* as explained under "Chaud-froid Félix Faure" (1671), and cut them into slices. Trim these slices with a round, even cutter, and coat them with aspic.

Prepare a *mousse* from the meat of the legs. Spread this *mousse* on a tray in a layer one-third in. thick and leave it to set. When it is quite firm, stamp it out with a round, even cutter, dipped in hot water, and a little larger than the one used in trimming the slices.

Set a medallion about the size of a half-dollar on each slice of *mousse*, fixing it there by means of a little half-set jelly, and arrange the medallion prepared in this way on a square dish.

In their midst set a fine bundle of asparagus tips; fill the gaps between the medallions with a garnish consisting of a salad of asparagus tips with cream.

Serve on a block of ice or surround the dish with cracked ice.

1708—GALANTINE OF CHICKEN　　　　*Galantine de Poulet*

For *galantines*, fowls may be used which are a little too tough to be roasted, but old fowls should be discarded. The latter invariably yield a dry *forcemeat*, whatever measures one may take in the preparation.

The fowl should be cleaned but not emptied, and it should be carefully boned; the process beginning from an incision down the skin of the back, from the head to the tail.

This done, carefully remove the meat with the point of a small, sharp knife, until the bird is quite bare. Cut off the wings and the legs, flush with the joints of the trunk; remove all the meat that the skin may be quite clean, and spread the skin on a clean piece of linen. Trim the meat of the breast, cut it into pieces one-third inch square, and put the trimmings aside.

Season these pieces and *marinate* them in a few drops of brandy; prepare other pieces of the same size and length from four oz. of truffles; six oz. of fat salt pork; four oz. of cooked ham, and four oz. of cured and cooked ox-tongue. Then clear the meat of the legs of all tendons; add to it the trimmings cut from the breast, as much very white veal and twice as much very fat, fresh pork; season these meats with salt, pepper and nutmeg; chop them up very finely; grind them, and rub them through a sieve. Add the brandy in which the breasts were *marinated*.

Spread a layer, three in. wide, of this *forcemeat* along the whole of the middle of the chicken's skin; upon this layer of *forcemeat* set the strips of bacon, fowl, truffle, ham, and tongue, arranging them alternately and regularly; upon them spread another layer of *forcemeat*, equal to the first; then another layer of the various pieces, and finally cover and envelop the whole in what remains of the *forcemeat*.

Draw the skin of the fowl over the whole and completely wrap the former round the latter. Carefully sew up the edges of the skin, and roll the *galantine* in a napkin, either end of which should be tightly tied.

With six lbs. of shin of veal, one-half lb. of fresh *blanched* pork rind, and the fowl's skeleton, prepare a white veal stock (10). When this stock has cooked for about five hours, add the *galantine* to it, and gently cook the latter for about one and one-quarter hours.

At the end of this time take the *galantine* off the fire; drain it on a dish, and let it cool for ten minutes; remove the napkin in which it has cooked, and roll it in another one which should be similarly tied at both ends. This done, put the *galantine* to cool under a weight not exceeding five or six lbs.

The cooking-liquor, once it has been cleared of grease and clarified as for an aspic (158), constitutes a jelly which accompanies the *galantine*. When the latter is quite cold, remove the napkin covering it, trim it neatly at either end; coat it with half-melted jelly, and arrange it on a low bed of moulded rice. Finally, decorate it as fancy may dictate with pieces of aspic-jelly.

1709—COLD CHICKEN LOAF *Pain de Volaille Froid*

Poële a very tender chicken; do not brown it and have it only just barely done. Take it out and leave it to cool. Add two tablespoons of strong veal stock and one tablespoon of burned brandy to the *poëlé*-liquor.

Simmer for ten minutes. Strain this stock through a sieve, and slightly press the vegetables in so doing, that all their juices may be removed.

Clear of grease, and reduce until the liquor does not measure more than two tablespoons. Put it on the side of the fire, add the yolks of three eggs, stirring briskly, and add, little by little, six oz. of very good, fresh butter, just as for a Hollandaise sauce. Finally, add a little more than an ounce of gelatine, dissolved in two tablespoons of boiling water, and rub the whole through a fine sieve.

Meanwhile, lift out the chicken's breasts and cut them into wide and thin slices, after having cleared them of skin. Cover each slice with a slice of truffle dipped in good, half-melted jelly, and with them line the bottom and sides of a *timbale*-mould, already coated with jelly and incrusted in ice.

Then completely bone the chicken; finely grind the remainder of its meat as well as the skin; rub the whole through a fine sieve, and add the resulting *purée* to the prepared sauce. Mix the whole well, and fill the mould with it. Allow to set well, and turn out on a bed of rice surrounded by fine *croûtons* of aspic-jelly.

N.B.—By substituting young ducks, young pigeons, or some kind of game such as pheasant, woodcock, etc., for the chicken, this recipe may be applied to any piece of poultry or game.

1710—JEANNETTE SUPREME OF CHICKEN

Suprême de Volaille Jeannette

Poach a fowl; let it cool; lift out its *suprêmes,* and cut each into four slices, trimmed to the shape of ovals. Coat these slices with white chaud-froid sauce (72), and decorate them with tarragon leaves, *blanched,* cooled, well-drained and very green.

Let a layer of aspic-jelly one-half in. thick set on the bottom of a *timbale* or a square dish; upon his layer set some slices of *foie-gras Farfait,* cut to the shape of the slices, and place one of the latter on each slice of the *Parfait.* This done, cover with fine half-melted chicken jelly.

When about to serve, incrust the dish or the *timbale* in a block of carved ice.

1711—COLD MOUSSE OF CHICKEN   *Mousse de Volaille Froide*

The carefully boned and skinned meat of a *poached* fowl may be used in the preparation of this *mousse,* but a freshly-roasted fowl, scarcely cooled, is preferable; the latter's flavor being more delicate and more distinct.

The quantities and the mode of procedure for cold fowl *mousse* are those given under *"mousse de tomates"* (814).

The various *mousse* recipes which I gave for trout (813 and 815) may be applied to cold fillets of fowl. In this case, the latter may be coated with some kind of chaud-froid sauce, or simply *glazed* with jelly, and plainly decorated.

These *mousses* constitute excellent dishes for suppers, and from a very long list of them I may quote:—

Mousse of Ham with White Meat of Chicken.
Mousse of Foie-Gras with White Meat of Chicken.
Mousse of Tongue with White Meat of Chicken.
Mousse of Tomatoes with White Meat of Chicken.
Mousse of Crayfish with White Meat of Chicken.
Mousse of Whortleberries or Cranberries with White Meat of Chicken.
Mousse of Physalis with White Meat of Chicken.

1712—MAYONNAISE OF CHICKEN *Mayonnaise de Volaille*

Fill the bottom of a salad-bowl with shredded lettuce, arranging it in the shape of a dome. Season with a little salt and a few drops of vinegar. Upon this salad arrange the cold slices of boiled or roast fowl, carefully cleared of all skin.

Cover with mayonnaise sauce; smooth the latter and decorate with capers; small pitted olives; anchovy fillets; quartered hard-boiled eggs; small quartered or whole lettuce hearts.

Arrange these decorating ingredients according to fancy, as no hard and fast rule can be given.

When about to serve, mix as for a salad.

1713—CHICKEN SALAD *Salade de Poulet*

This dish consists of the same ingredients as the preceding one, except for the mayonnaise, which is replaced by an ordinary dressing added just before mixing and serving.

1714—PATE OF CHICKEN *Pâté de Poulet*

Line a raised-pie mould with patty paste (2359), taking care to leave a fine rim.

Bone a fowl weighing about four or five lbs. Set the *suprêmes* (each cut into three slices) to *marinate* in a glass of brandy, salt, pepper, nutmeg, and five medium-sized peeled truffles, each cut into four or five thick slices.

With what remains of the fowl's meat, as much lean pork and veal (mixed in equal quantities) and twice as much fresh, pork fat (i.e., a quantity equal in weight to all the other meats put together), prepare a very smooth *forcemeat;* chopping the whole first, then grinding it and rubbing it through a sieve. Add to this *forcemeat* a little truffle *essence;* the *marinade* of the breasts; one raw egg, and the necessary salt, pepper, and nutmeg.

Line the bottom and sides of the pie with this *forcemeat;* on this first layer of *forcemeat* lay a thin slice of bacon and thick slices or tongue, beef, or ham. Place on another slice of bacon, followed by a thin layer of *forcemeat,* a layer of truffle slices, another layer of *forcemeat,* the slices of fowl, another layer of *forcemeat,* one more layer of truffles, one more layer of *forcemeat,* one more layer of tongue or ham (between two thin slices of bacon); and finally cover the whole with what remains of the *forcemeat* and a slice of *larding* bacon topped by a bay leaf. Now close the pie with a cover of the same paste as that already used, carefully seal down the cover to the edge of the underlying paste, trim and pinch the rim, and decorate this cover of paste with imitation-leaves of the same paste.

Make a slit in the top of the pie, for the escape of steam; carefully brush with egg the cover and the rim, and bake in a moderate oven for about one and one-quarter hours. On taking the pie from the oven, let it half cool, and fill it with a succulent, chicken aspic-jelly. Allow this dish to cool for at least twenty-four hours before serving.

N.B.—With this recipe as model, and by substituting another piece of poultry or game for the fowl, raised pies may be prepared from every kind of game or poultry, except fish, which only yields mediocre results.

In the case of game pies, the *forcemeat* is combined with one-sixth of its weight of *gratin forcemeat* (202) and an equal quantity of fat bacon is eliminated. The chicken jelly is also replaced by a jelly prepared from the remains of the birds under treatment.

Serve these raised pies plainly, on napkins, and very cold.

1714a—CHICKEN PIE *Chicken Pie*
See (1660).

1715—YOUNG TURKEY *Dindonneau*
Young turkeys, served as *relevés* or entrées, admit of all the recipes given for pullets; therefore, in order to avoid unnecessary repetition, the reader is asked to refer to those recipes.

Those most generally applied to young turkeys are the ones termed "à l'Anglaise"—with celery, à la Financière, à la Godard, and à la Jardinière.

In addition to these preparations, there are others which are better suited and are more proper to young turkeys, and these I give below.

1716—YOUNG TURKEY STUFFED WITH CHESTNUTS
Dindonneau Farci aux Marrons

Cut open the shells of two and one-quarter lbs. of chestnuts; immerse them for a few seconds in hot smoking fat; peel them, and almost completely cook them in consommé. Then mix them with two lbs. of very finely-chopped pork, rubbed through a fine sieve. Fill the bird with this preparation; truss it, and roast it on the spit or in the oven, basting frequently.

Serve with the gravy separately, which should be somewhat fat.

1717—CATALANE YOUNG TURKEY   *Dindonneau à la Catalane*

Cut up the young turkey as for a fricassée, and fry the pieces in three oz. of butter. When the pieces are nicely browned, swirl into the utensil one pint of white wine; season with salt and pepper; add a piece of crushed garlic, and completely reduce. Then moisten with sufficient tomato *purée* and equal quantities of Espagnole and brown stock (7) to just cover the pieces.

Cook in the oven for forty minutes; transfer the pieces to another dish after having trimmed them, and add one-half lb. of raw, quartered mushrooms, *sautéd* in butter; twenty chestnuts cooked in consommé; twenty small, *glazed* onions; five quartered tomatoes, and ten sausages.

Strain the sauce over the pieces of turkey; complete the cooking for twenty-five minutes, and serve in a *timbale*.

1718—CHIPOLATA YOUNG TURKEY   *Dindonneau Chipolata*

This may be prepared in two ways, according as to whether it be intended for lunch or for dinner.

Cut up the young turkey and fry the pieces in butter as above. Swirl the pan with one glassful of white wine; add a sufficient quantity of tomatoed half-*glaze* sauce, just to cover, and cook in the oven for forty minutes.

This done, transfer the pieces to another saucepan and add twenty small, *glazed* onions, twenty chestnuts cooked in consommé, ten chipolata (Italian) sausages, one-third lb. of frizzled pieces of fresh pork cut into dice, and twenty olive-shaped and *glazed* carrots. Strain the sauce over the whole, complete the cooking and serve in a *timbale*.

Or *braise* the young turkey; *glaze* it at the last moment, and set on a long dish. Surround it with the garnish given above, combined with the reduced *braising*-liquor.

1719—YOUNG TURKEY EN DAUBE   *Dindonneau en Daube*

Bone the young turkey's breast, and stuff it, arranging its meat as for a *galantine,* with very good sausage-meat combined with a glassful of liqueur brandy per two lbs. of the former; bacon, truffles; and a very small and red ox-tongue, covered with slices of bacon and set in the center of the garnish.

Reconstruct the young turkey; sew it up; truss it, and put it in a *terrine* (earthenware dish) just large enough to hold it and its moistening.

With the bones and the trimmings of the young turkey, two slices of veal, two lbs. of frizzled beef, *aromatics,* one pint of white wine, and two quarts of water, prepare a brown stock after recipe (9). Reduce this stock to one and one-half quarts; put it into the *terrine;* cover and thoroughly close up the latter with a strip of paste, and cook in a hot oven for two and one-half hours.

Leave to cool in the *terrine,* and, when about to serve, slightly heat the latter in order to turn out the stew.

1720—BREASTS OF YOUNG TURKEY DAMPIERRE
Blanc de Dindonneau à la Dampierre

Remove and bone the young turkey's legs. With the meat, carefully cleared of all tendons, prepare a *mousseline forcemeat;* spread the latter in a pan in a layer one-third in. thick, and *poach* it. Stamp it out with an even, oval fancy-cutter, about three in. by two in.

Braise or *poële* the young turkey's breasts with the greatest care, keeping it underdone. This finished, lift out the two *suprêmes,* skin them, and cut them into slices of a size that will permit their being trimmed with the fancy-cutter already used. With a little raw *forcemeat,* stick a slice to each oval of *poached forcemeat;* then, by means of a pastry-bag fitted with a plain tube, garnish the borders of the slices with the same *forcemeat* combined with twice its bulk of chopped cured tongue. Set the medallions (about the size of a half-dollar) thus prepared in a covered pan, and put them in the steamer that the *forcemeat* may *poach.*

When about to serve, take the pastry-bag and make a fine rosette of a *purée* of peas in the center of each medallion. Set these medallions in a circle on a round dish, around a little bowl of carved, fried bread, garnished with the same *purée* of peas.

Serve separately a veloutè (242) prepared from the bones of the turkey.

1721—BREASTS OF YOUNG TURKEY TOULOUSAINE
Blanc de Dindonneau à la Toulousaine

Poële the young turkey. When it is cooked, lift out its *suprêmes,* skin them, and cut them into somewhat thick slices.

Arrange these slices in a circle, and set a slice of *foie-gras, sautéd* in butter, between each.

Pour a Toulousaine garnish in their midst, and surround with a ribbon of light *glaze* (15).

1722—YOUNG TURKEY WINGS DORES WITH PUREE OF CHEST-
NUTS   *Ailerons de Dindonneau Dorés à la Purée de Marrons*

The pinions referred to in this recipe are pinions properly so called; that is to say, they consist of the two last joints of the wing. When they are properly prepared, they constitute one of the most savory luncheon entrées that can be served.

The pinions of large pullets may be treated in this way.

Clear and singe the pinions, and set them in a buttered saucepan, just large enough to hold them. Brown gently on both sides and drain.

In the same butter, gently brown a sliced carrot and onion, to which add a few parsley stalks and a little thyme and bay leaf. Set the pinions on these *aromatics;* season moderately with salt and pepper; cover the saucepan, and continue cooking gently in a very slow oven, basting often the while.

The dish will be all the better for having been cooked slowly and regularly. Do not moisten, if possible, or, at the most, only do so with a few drops of water, in order to keep the butter from separating—not an unusual occurrence when the heat is too high.

When the pinions are cooked, arrange in a circle, and cover them that they may keep warm. Add a few tablespoons of light stock or some water to the cooking butter, and set to boil gently for fifteen minutes. When this stock is sufficiently reduced to only half, cover the pinions, pass it through a fine strainer and clear of some of the grease if necessary; remember, however, that this stock should be somewhat fat.

Pour it over the pinions, and serve a *timbale* of a fine *purée* of chestnuts separately.

1722a—COLD YOUNG TURKEY   *Dindonneau Froid*

All the recipes given for cold pullets may be applied to this bird.

Goose (Oie) and Gosling (Oison)

The principal value of the goose from the culinary point of view lies in the fact that it supplies the best, most delicate and firmest *foie gras.*

Apart from this property, the preciousness of which is truly inestimable, goose is really only served at family tables.

1722b—GOSLING ALLEMANDE. *Oison à l'Allemande*

Completely bone the gosling's breast; season it inside, and stuff it with quartered, peeled and cored apples, half-cooked in butter. Sew up the openings, and *braise* gently, basting with fat the while.

When the gosling is cooked, lay it on a dish and surround it with peeled apples, cored, cooked in butter, and garnished with red-currant jelly. Drain away three-quarters of the grease; swirl into the *braising*-pan with required quantity of good gravy for roasts; strain this gravy, and serve it separately.

1722c—GOSLING ALSACIENNE *Oison à l'Alsacienne*

Stuff the gosling with very good sausage-meat; truss; brown in butter and *poêle*. Lay it on a dish and surround with sauerkraut *braised* in goose grease, and rectangles of lean bacon, cooked with the sauerkraut.

1723—GOSLING ANGLAISE *Oison à l'Anglaise*

Cook one lb. of unpeeled onions in the oven. When they are cold, peel them; chop them, and add to them an equal weight of soaked and pressed bread, one oz. of fresh or chopped sage, salt, pepper and nutmeg.

Stuff the gosling with this preparation; truss it, and roast it on the spit or in the oven.

Set it on a dish; surround it with the gravy, which should be somewhat fat, and serve a sauceboat of slightly-sugared_applesauce, separately.

1724—JUGGED GOSLING *Oison en Civet*

When killing the gosling, carefully collect its blood. Add the juice of a lemon and beat it, so as to prevent coagulation, until it is quite cold.

Cut the gosling into pieces and proceed exactly as for "Civet de Lièvre" (1821).

1725—GOSLING WITH HORSERADISH *Oison au Raifort*

Braise the gosling.

Put it on a dish and surround it, either with noodles with butter, or rice au gras (2252). Sprinkle the garnish with the reduced *braising*-liquor, and serve a horse-radish sauce with cream (138), separately.

N.B.—Besides these various recipes, goslings may also be prepared like young turkeys with chestnuts, à la Chipolata, en Daube; or with turnips, peas, and "en Salmis," like Duck.

1726—FOIE GRAS (FAT GOOSE LIVER) *Foie Gras*

Foies gras are the extremely large livers of either especially fed geese or ducks. Goose liver is larger, firmer and less readily melted than that of the duck. As a rule the former should be selected in preference, more particularly in the matter of hot dishes. Nevertheless, lacking goose liver, duck liver may be used and with very good results when its quality is good.

Foies gras are used in the preparation of *terrines,* raised pies, *parfaits* and *mousses,* which are among the most delicate and richest of cold dishes.

They may also be used as a garnishing ingredient, in the form of pieces or *mousseline quenelles.* Finally, they may also be served as hot entrées.

When a whole *foie gras* of goose (it may weigh two lbs. or more) is to be served hot, it must first be trimmed, *studded* with raw truffles which have been previously peeled, quartered, seasoned with salt and pepper, set in a glassful of brandy, together with a bay leaf, and cooled in a thoroughly closed *terrine.*

When the *foie gras* has been *studded* with truffles, wrap it in thin slices of bacon or a piece of *pig's caul,* and set it in a thoroughly-sealed *terrine* before cooking it.

The best way to cook *foie gras,* when it is to be served whole and hot, is to bake it in a crust of paste that can absorb the excess of grease produced by the melting of the fat in the liver. For this purpose prepare two layers of patty paste (2350), a little larger than the liver.

On one of these layers, set the liver wrapped in slices of bacon; and, if possible, surround it with whole fair-sized truffles, peeled. Set half a bay leaf on the liver; moisten the edges of the paste; cover the whole with the other layer of paste; seal it down with the thumb, and fold over the edges of the paste to form a regular, ornamented border which, besides finishing off the preparation, also increases the strength of the closing edges.

Brush the top with beaten egg; streak with a fork; make a slit in the top for the escape of the steam; and, in the case of a medium-sized liver, cook in a good, moderate oven for from forty to forty-five minutes.

Serve this crust as it stands, and send the garnish separately.

In the dining-room, the waiter in charge removes the top of the crust, cuts out the liver with a spoon, setting a piece on each plate, and arranges around each piece the garnish mentioned on the menu.

I am not partial to the cooking of *foie gras* in a *terrine* when it is to be served hot. In any case the method described above strikes me as being much the best, whatever be the garnish that is served with the liver.

I particularly recommend a garnish of noodles, macaroni, lazagnes, spaghetti and even rice, with hot *foie gras*.

These pastes should simply be cooked in water and finished with cream.

This accompaniment makes the *foie gras* much more digestible and palatable. The best garnishes for hot *foie gras,* besides those given above, are truffles, whole or in slices, or a Financière (1240). In the matter of brown sauces, a Madeira sauce (44) suits admirably, provided it be of great delicacy and not too much Madeira; but a very light buttered veal or chicken *glaze* (16), combined with a little old Sherry or old Port, is even superior. A Hongroise sauce (85) with paprika or an excellent Suprême Sauce (106a) may also be served when the garnish permits it.

1727—FOIE GRAS COOKED IN A BRIOCHE

Foie Gras Cuit dans une Brioche

For this dish the *foie gras* is cooked differently; the result is almost the same as that yielded by the crust method described above, except that it is much more delicate. This method, moreover, allows of obtaining a *foie gras* clear of all grease (the latter being completely absorbed by the paste), and is therefore best suited to cold serving.

After having *studded* the *foie gras* with truffles and placed it in a closed *terrine* as above, wrap it in slices of bacon, set it to *poach* in a moderate oven for twenty minutes, and leave it to cool.

Line a buttered *timbale*-mould, of a size in proportion to that of the liver, with a thick layer of ordinary unsweetened brioche paste (2370).

Put the *foie gras* upright in the mould, which it should almost fill; close the *timbale* with a cover of the same paste; make a slit in the top; surround the top of the mould with a band of strong, buttered paper, that the dough may be prevented from running over, and let it rest for about thirty minutes in a temperature of 86° F. to allow the dough to rise.

Bake in a rather hot oven, until a needle inserted through the center comes out quite clean.

Serve the dish as it stands with one of the ordinary *foie-gras* garnishes.

1728—ESCALOPES OF FOIE GRAS PERIGUEUX

Escalopes de Foie Gras à la Périgueux

Cut some slices two and one-half oz. in weight from a raw *foie gras*. Season them with salt and pepper; dip in beaten egg; roll in finely-chopped truffle, and *sauté* in clarified butter (175).

Arrange in a circle, and, in the middle, pour a Madeira sauce (44) flavored with truffle *essence*.

1729—ESCALOPES OF FOIE GRAS RAVIGNAN

Escalopes de Foie Gras à la Ravignan

From a layer of unsweetened brioche paste, one-third in. thick, cut twenty slices two and one-half in. in diameter. On ten of these round slices, spread a coating of chicken *forcemeat*, leaving a margin one-third in. wide of bare paste on each slice.

Set a slice of truffle in the middle, a thick round slice of raw *foie gras* on the truffle, another slice of truffle upon that, a coat of *forcemeat* over the whole; and cover with the ten remaining round slices, after having slightly moistened them, so that the two edges of paste may be sealed. Press with the back of a round cutter; brush with egg, and cook in a hot oven for fifteen minutes.

Arrange in a circle, and serve a Périgueux sauce (47) at the same time.

1730—ESCALOPES OF FOIE GRAS TALLEYRAND

Escalopes de Foie Gras à la Talleyrand

Prepare a crust made in a spring pan, six in. in diameter; a filling of *blanched* macaroni, cut into lengths of one in., combined with four oz. of grated Gruyère and Parmesan cheese per lb. of macaroni, and combined with two oz. of butter, four oz. of a *julienne* of truffles and four oz. of *foie gras* cut into large dice.

Arrange in a circle in the crust ten slices of *foie gras sautéd* in butter, alternating them with fine slices of truffle. Put the macaroni in the middle, shaping it like a dome, sprinkle with grated cheese and *glaze* quickly.

Put on a napkin, and serve separately a clear chicken *glaze* (16), flavored with truffles and well buttered.

1731—SOUFFLE OF FOIE GRAS

Soufflé de Foie Gras

Rub two-thirds lb. of *foie gras* and three and one-half oz. of raw truffles through a fine sieve. Mix the two *purées* in a bowl, and add two-thirds lb. of raw chicken-meat, ground with the whites of four eggs, and rubbed through a fine sieve. Season; work the preparation on ice, and add to it, little by little, one-half pint of rich, thick, and very fresh cream, then the well-stiffened whites of four eggs.

Put in a buttered *soufflé* saucepan, and *poach* under cover in the *bain-marie* (water-bath) for from thirty to thirty-five minutes.

Serve a Madeira sauce (44), flavored with truffle *essence*, separately.

1732—TIMBALE OF FOIE GRAS ALSACIENNE
Timbale de Foie Gras à l'Alsacienne

Prepare an ordinary *timbale* crust (2394). When about to serve, fill it with layers of noodles with cream, separated by alternate layers of *foie-gras* slices, *sautéd* in butter, and slices of truffles. Complete with some homemade raw noodles, *sautéd* in butter and sprinkled over the last layer of noodles.

Cover the *timbale*, and serve a Suprême Sauce (106a), flavored with truffle *essence*, separately.

1733—TIMBALE OF FOIE GRAS CAMBACERES
Timbale de Foie Gras Cambacerès

Line a buttered *dome-mould* with rings of large *poached* macaroni.

These rings should be one-fifth inch thick, and should be filled inside with very black truffle *purée*, combined with a little *forcemeat*.

When the mould is lined, coat it inside with a layer of chicken *forcemeat* combined with truffle *purée*. Put the mould for a few minutes in a moderate oven, that the *forcemeat* may *poach*.

Reduce one-third pint of Béchamel sauce (28), combined with four to five tablespoons of truffle and chicken *essence*, to half; mix with one-half lb. of *poached* macaroni, cut into lengths of one inch, and four tablespoons of *foie-gras* and truffle *purée*, made from trimmings. Mix the whole thoroughly.

Fill the *timbale* with this macaroni, spreading it in layers, separated by other alternate layers of *foie-gras* slices, *poached* in Madeira, and slices of truffle. Cover the garnish with a layer of *forcemeat*, and *poach* in the *bain-marie* (water-bath), allowing forty-five minutes for a quart-mould.

Let the mould stand for a few minutes before emptying it; turn out the *timbale* upon a round dish; surround it with a border of Périgueux sauce (47), and serve a sauceboat of Périgueux sauce separately.

1734—TIMBALE OF FOIE GRAS MONTESQUIEU

Timbale de Foie Gras Montesquieu

Spread a very even layer, one-third inch thick, of chicken *force-meat* upon a sheet of buttered paper. Moisten the surface with some white of egg; sprinkle with chopped truffle, and press on the latter by means of the flat of a knife.

Set to *poach* gently; cool, and then stamp out with a round, even cutter, one inch in diameter. With the round slices, garnish the bottom and sides of a *Charlotte mould,* placing their truffled sides against the mould. Then, with the view of binding these round slices together, as they are to constitute the outside of the *timbale,* coat the whole of the mould inside with some fairly firm chicken *forcemeat,* combined with a quarter of its bulk of *foie-gras purée.*

Fill the mould with a *foie-gras Parfait* with truffles cut into very large dice and combined with a *mousseline* chicken *forcemeat.*

Cover the whole with a layer of the same *forcemeat* as that used for the purpose of binding the slices, and set to *poach* under cover.

Turn out, following the same precautions as above; surround the *timbale* with a border of nice, pink, Hungarian sauce (85) with paprika, and send a sauceboat of this sauce to the table at the same time.

COLD FOIE GRAS (FOIE GRAS FROID)

1735—ASPIC OF FOIE GRAS
Aspic de Foie Gras

Coat an even or ornamented mould (fitted with a central tube) with aspic, and decorate it with *poached* white of egg and truffle. Fill it with rows of well-trimmed *foie-gras* rectangles, or shells cut out with a spoon dipped in hot water, separating each row with a coat of aspic.

Except for its principal ingredient, which may vary, the preparation of aspic is always the same as that described under "Aspic de Homard" (954).

For the turning out and serving, proceed in exactly the same way.

1736—GASTRONOME FOIE GRAS
Foie Gras Gastronome

Take a plain *foie-gras Parfait* without a crust; trim it neatly to the shape of an egg, and completely cover it with a chaud-froid sauce (72) with paprika. Decorate it according to fancy, and *glaze* it with cold melted aspic-jelly.

Cut out a crust, proportionate in size to the egg, and shape it like a cushion. Coat it with a chaud-froid sauce (34) of a different color; decorate it with softened butter, applied by means of a pastry-bag fitted with a narrow, fancy tube; set it on the dish, and place the *foie-gras* egg upon it.

Surround the cushion with fine fair-sized truffles, *glazed* with aspic-jelly.

1737—FOIE GRAS WITH PAPRIKA *Foie Gras au Paprika*

Trim a fine, fresh *foie gras;* salt it; sprinkle it with a teaspoon of paprika; put it into a saucepan with a large sliced Spanish onion and a bay leaf, and cook in the oven for thirty minutes.

This done, set it instantly in an oval *terrine,* after having carefully removed every bit of onion; cover it with its own grease; fill up the *terrine* with jelly, and leave to cool.

Keep in a cool place until ready for serving.

N.B.—In Vienna, where this dish is usually served as a hors-d'œuvre, with baked potatoes, the onion is not removed. The *foie gras* is left to cool in the *terrine* in which it has cooked, with all its grease, and it is served thus, very cold.

This piece of information was kindly given to me by Madame Katinka.

1738—ESCALOPES OF FOIE GRAS MARECHALE

Escalopes de Foie Gras Maréchale

From a *terrine* of very firm *foie gras* cut the required number of slices, giving them an oval shape. Make a preparation of "pain de foie gras" (1741) with the remains of the *foie gras,* and cover the slices with the preparation, shaping the latter in a dome upon them. Coat these garnished slices with cream chaud-froid sauce (73); decorate with a slice of truffle, and *glaze* with aspic.

With some *foie-gras purée* prepare some balls (of the shape of large cherries); in the center of each place a little ball of truffle in imitation of the stone of the fruit, and coat them with a reddish-brown chaud-froid sauce (34). This done, *glaze* them with aspic-jelly.

Arrange the slices round a circular bed, set upon a very cold dish; arrange the balls in a pyramid on the bed, and border the dish with fine, aspic-jelly *croûtons.*

1739—MOUSSE OF FOIE GRAS *Mousse de Foie Gras*

For the preparation of the *mousse,* see (814). The procedure and the quantities are always the same, and only the principal ingredient changes. The moulding is also done in the same way in an aspic-jelly coated and decorated mould, generally just large enough to hold the required amount for one service, or in a silver *timbale,* incrusted in ice.

1740—MOUSSELINES OF FOIE GRAS   *Mousselines de Foie Gras*

I have oftentimes explained that the substance is the same from which *mousses* and *mousselines* are prepared, and I have pointed out where the difference between them lies.

Just like the other *mousselines,* those of *foie gras* are made in *egg* or *quenelle-moulds,* or others of the same kind. *Foie-gras mousselines* are, according to circumstances, either simply *glazed* with aspic, or coated with chaud-froid sauce and served in a *timbale* with aspic. They may also be moulded in little fluted paper cups.

1741—LOAF OF FOIE GRAS   *Pain de Foie Gras*

From a cold *foie gras, braised* in Madeira, cut a few slices and put them aside. Clear the cooking-liquor of all grease, reduce to half, and add the yolks of four eggs and one-half lb. of butter, proceeding as for a Hollandaise sauce. Complete with a grilled, crushed, hazel-nut, about one ounce of dissolved gelatine, and, when the preparation is only lukewarm, mix (without working too much) what remains of the *foie gras,* rubbed through a sieve.

Spread this preparation in layers in an aspic-coated and decorated mould, separating each layer with other alternate layers consisting of the reserved *foie gras* slices, and some slices of truffle.

Cover the last layer with aspic, and set the mould in a refrigerator for a few hours.

When about to serve, turn out, and border the dish with fine, aspic jelly *croûtons.*

1742—PARFAIT OF FOIE GRAS   *Parfait de Foie Gras*

Fresh *foie gras* do not bear transport very well, and, when sent from a distance, often reach their destination tainted. It is, therefore, difficult, whatever care may have been taken in their preparation, to obtain the results which are achieved by manufacturers who are renowned for this kind of produce. Consequently, it is preferable to buy the *Parfait* of *foie gras* readymade from a good firm rather than to try to make it oneself.

1743—PAVE OF FOIE GRAS LUCULLUS   *Pavé de Foie Gras Lucullus*

Let a coat of aspic, one-half inch thick, set on the bottom of a *square timbale,* and lay on a few slices of truffle. Upon this jelly spread a layer, two-thirds inch thick, of *foie-gras purée,* thinned by means of a little melted jelly. When this *purée* has set, lay on it a few *foie-gras* slices and slices of truffle; cover with aspic, and continue with alternate layers of *purée,* slices, and aspic. Fill up the mould with a layer of aspic jelly; put it in the refrigerator for a few hours, and serve on a block of ice, cut to the shape of a flagstone.

1744—TIMBALE OF FOIE GRAS TZARINA

Timbale de Foie Gras Tzarine

Line a *timbale-mould* with ordinary patty paste (2359), and cover the inside all over with slices of *larding* bacon. Just in the middle set a fresh *foie gras,* seasoned with salt, pepper, and allspice; surround it with quails stuffed with a piece of truffle, and set upright with their breasts against the slices of bacon. Fill up the mould with whole, raw, and peeled truffles; cover the whole with a round slice of the same bacon; cover the *timbale* with a layer of paste, well sealed down round the edges; make a slit in the top for the escape of steam, and bake in a good, moderate oven for one and one-quarter hours.

On taking out the *timbale* from the oven, pour into it some succulent veal stock, flavored with Madeira, and sufficiently gelatinous to form a nice jelly.

Keep the *timbale* in a cool place for one or two days before serving it.

DUCKS AND DUCKLINGS (CANARDS ET CANETONS)

Three varieties of the duck family are recognized in cookery in France, viz., the Nantes duck, the Rouen duck, and the different kinds of wild duck. The latter are generally used for roasts and in salmis.

The Rouen duck in France is also served more often as a roast than as an entrée. The characteristic trait of its preparation lies in its being kept very underdone, and it is very rarely *braised.* It is killed by suffocation, and not by bleeding, which is the usual mode of killing other birds.

The Nantes duck, which is similar to the English Aylesbury one, is not so fleshy as the Rouen duck, and may be roasted, *poëléd,* or *braised.*

(There are three principal types of ducks in the United States. The two better types are the Long Island ducklings and the Long

Island Pekin type. The ordinary duckling found all over the country is the third type. For the following recipes, it is advisable to use the meaty and larger Long Island Pekin type to take the place of the *Rouennais*.—Ed.)

1745—NANTAIS DUCKLING WITH SAUERKRAUT
Caneton Nantais à la Choûcroute

Take a piece of *manié* butter the size of an egg, and insert it into the duckling with chopped parsley and shallots. Truss the bird as for an entrée; brown it in the oven, and put it in a saucepan already lined for *braising*.

Moisten, just enough to cover, with white veal stock and Rhine wine (in the proportion of two-thirds of the former to one-third of the latter), or ordinary good white wine, and *braise* slowly until cooking is completed.

Meanwhile, *braise* in the usual way two lbs. of sauerkraut with one-half lb. of salt pork.

When it is three-quarters done, drain it, and complete its cooking with one-third pint of veal gravy and one-sixth pint of white wine, until this moistening is completely reduced.

Set the sauerkraut in a border round a dish, and surround it with the pork cut into small rectangles. Place the carved duck in the center, and coat it moderately with half-*glaze* (23) sauce combined with the reduced *braising*-liquor. Send the remains of this sauce separately.

1746—ROAST PEKIN DUCKLING WITH MINT
Caneton de Pekin Poëlé à la Menthe

Stuff the duckling with one oz. of butter combined with a pinch of chopped mint, and *poële* it. Dish it; swirl into the saucepan with one-sixth pint of clear, veal gravy and a little lemon juice; strain, add a pinch of chopped mint, and pour this sauce over the duckling.

1747—MOLIERE DUCKLING   *Caneton Molière*

Bone the duckling, and stuff it with one lb. of *gratin foie-gras forcemeat*, combined with two-thirds lb. of good sausage-meat. Set two rows of truffles in the middle of the thickest part of the *forcemeat*, lengthwise, along the duckling. Reconstruct; sew up the skin, wrap in a napkin, after the manner of a *galantine*, and *poach* in a stock made from the bones.

Glaze the duckling with some of this stock, strained, cleared of all grease, and reduced. With what remains prepare a Madeira sauce (44), and add' two oz. of sliced truffles.

Serve the duckling, after having removed all stitches from it, and coat it with this sauce.

1748—BRAISED DUCKLING WITH WHITE TURNIPS
Caneton Braisé aux Navets

Brown the duckling well in butter, and take it from the saucepan.

Drain away the butter; swirl it with a little white wine; add two-thirds pint of brown stock (7), as much Espagnole (22), and an herb bunch; return the duck to this sauce, and *braise* gently.

With the reserved butter brown one lb. of turnips, shaped like elongated garlic-cloves, and sprinkle them with a large pinch of powdered sugar, that they may be *glazed* to a nice, light brown color. Also have ready twenty small onions, which should have been gently cooked in butter.

When the duckling is half cooked, transfer it to another saucepan; put the turnips and the onions round it; strain the sauce over the whole, and complete the cooking gently.

Serve with the garnish of turnips and onions, arranged round the bird.

1749—DUCKLING WITH OLIVES
Caneton aux Olives

Prepare the duckling as above, and keep the sauce short and juicy. A few minutes before serving, add one-half lb. of pitted and *blanched* olives. *Glaze* the duckling at the last moment, and serve it surrounded with the olives and the sauce.

1750—BRAISED DUCKLING WITH ORANGE
Caneton Braisé à l'Orange

This *braised* duckling must not be confused with roast duckling, which is also served "a l'orange," for the two dishes are quite distinct.

As in the case of the roast, this duckling may be prepared with Seville oranges; but, in this case, the sections of orange must not appear as garnish, owing to their bitterness, and only the juice is used for the sauce.

Braise the duckling in one-third pint of brown stock (7) and two-thirds pint of Espagnole sauce (22), and cook it sufficiently to permit its being cut with a spoon.

Clear the sauce of grease; reduce it to a stiff consistency; rub it through a fine sieve, and add the juice of two oranges and one half-lemon to it, which should bring the sauce back to its original consistency.

Now add a *julienne* of the *blanched* yellow part only of the rind of a half-orange and a half-lemon, but remember that the addition of the juice and rind of the orange and the half-lemon only takes place at the last moment, after which the sauce must not boil again. *Glaze* the duckling, put it on a dish, coat it slightly with sauce, and surround it with sections of orange, skinned.

Serve what remains of the sauce separately.

1751—DUCKLING WITH GREEN PEAS   *Caneton aux Petits Pois*

Brown in butter six oz. of salt pork, cut into large dice and *blanched,* and fifteen small onions. Drain the pork and the onions, and set the duckling to fry in the same butter. When it is well browned, remove the butter; swirl the pan with a little brown stock, and add one-half pint of thin, half-*glaze* sauce (23), one and one-half pints of fresh peas, one herb bunch, the pork dice and the onions, and complete the cooking of the whole gently.

Arrange the duckling on a dish, and cover it with the garnish and the sauce, after having taken out the herb bunch and reduced the sauce so that it only just covers the garnish.

1752—HOT PATE OF DUCKLING   *Pâté Chaud de Caneton*

Roast the duckling, keeping it somewhat underdone, and cut the whole of the breast into long, very thin slices. Line a buttered *Charlotte mould* with short paste (2356), and cover the whole of the inside with a layer of *gratin forcemeat* (202), combined with four tablespoons of very reduced half-*glaze* (23) sauce per one and two-thirds lb. of *forcemeat*—the necessary quantity for this pie.

On the layer of *forcemeat* arrange a bed of the slices of breast; sliced, cooked mushrooms, and slices of truffle; and fill the mould in this way, taking care to alternate the layers of *forcemeat,* slices of breast, etc. Complete with a coat of *forcemeat,* upon which sprinkle a pinch of powdered thyme and bay leaf; close the mould with a thin layer of paste, sealed down round the edges; make a slit in the top; brush with egg, and bake in a moderate oven for one hour.

When taking the pie out of the oven, turn it upside-down on a dish; take off the bottom crust; cut it into triangles, and set these triangles round the pie. Cover the *forcemeat,* thus bared, with a few tablespoons of Madeira sauce (44); set a large, grooved, cooked mushroom just in the middle, and surround it with a crown of sliced truffle.

Serve a Madeira sauce separately.

1753—STUFFED BALLS OF DUCKLING Ballotines de Caneton

Bone the duckling, and completely clear the bones of all meat.

Remove all tendons from it, and chop it, together with half its weight of veal, as much fresh pork fat, a third as much panada (190), the yolks of four eggs, one-half oz. of salt, and a little pepper and nutmeg. Grind; rub through a sieve, and mix with this *forcemeat*, three oz. of *gratin foie-gras forcemeat* and three oz. of chopped mushrooms, *sautéd* in butter. Divide up into portions weighing two oz.; wrap each portion in a piece of the duckling's skin; envelop in muslin, and *poach* in a stock prepared from the duckling's bones. At the last moment, remove the pieces of muslin and *glaze* the ballotines (balls).

Arrange in a circle, and set the selected garnish, which may be turnips, peas, olives, or sauerkraut, etc., in the middle.

1754—ROUENNAIS DUCKLING Caneton Rouennais

Except for the one case when they are served cold "à la cuiller," Pekin, Rouen ducklings are not *braised:* they are roasted and always kept underdone. When they have to be stuffed, the *forcemeat* is prepared as follows:—Fry four oz. of larding bacon, cut into dice, with one oz. of chopped onion, and add one-half lb. of sliced ducks' livers, a pinch of chopped parsley, salt, pepper, and a little spice.

Keep the livers underdone, merely browned; let the whole half-cool; grind it, and rub through a fine sieve.

1755—ROUENNAIS DUCKLING WINGS BIGARRADE
Aiguillettes de Caneton Rouennais à la Bigarrade

Poële the duckling and only just cook it, bearing in mind that twenty minutes is the time allowed for cooking a fair-sized bird. Remove the fillets of breast lengthwise, each in ten slices, and set the latter on a lukewarm dish.

Add a few tablespoons of veal gravy to the *poëlé*-liquor; set to boil for a few minutes; strain clear of grease, and finish as directed under sauce Bigarrade claire (31).

Cover the slices of breast with some of the sauce, and serve the remainder separately. *"Aiguillettes"* (or thin slices of breast cut lengthwise) à l'orange are prepared in the same way, except that they are surrounded with sections of orange, skinned.

1756—ROUENNAIS DUCKLING WINGS WITH CHERRIES
Aiguillettes de Caneton Rouennais aux Cerises

Prepare the duckling as above, but add a little Madeira to the *braising*-liquor. Clear the latter of grease; thicken with arrowroot or flour, etc.; strain through muslin, and add one-half lb. of pitted Morella cherries, at the last moment. Set the cherries round the *aiguillettes* (1755); coat the latter thinly with sauce, and serve what remains, separately.

1757—ROUENNAIS DUCKLING WINGS WITH TRUFFLES
Aiguillettes de Caneton Rouennais aux Truffes

Poëlé the duckling, and only just cook it.

Add one-sixth pint of Chambertin wine to the *poëlé*-liquor, and cook in it five medium-sized, peeled truffles. This done, reduce the liquor, clear of grease, strain it, and add it to a somewhat light Rouennaise sauce (54).

Remove the duckling's *aiguillettes* (1755), slice the truffles, and set on a lukewarm dish, alternating the *aiguillettes* with the slices of truffle.

Coat thinly with sauce, and send what remains of the latter separately.

1758—ROUENNAIS DUCKLING IN CHAMPAGNE
Caneton Rouennais au Champagne

Poële the duckling as above.

Add one-half pint of dry Saint Marceaux champagne to the *poëlé*-liquor; reduce, and complete with one-sixth pint of thickened, veal stock.

Strain this sauce through muslin; clear it of grease, and serve it in a sauceboat at the same time as the duckling.

1759—ROUENNAIS DUCKLING EN CHEMISE
Caneton Rouennais en Chemise

Stuff the duckling with the preparation given under (1754); truss it as for an entrée; insert it into a well-soaked pig's bladder and string the end of it close to the bird's tail. Wrap the bladder in a napkin, also tied, and *poach* gently for about forty-five minutes in a very strong brown stock. When about to serve, remove the napkin, and leave the duckling in the bladder.

Serve a Rouennaise sauce (54) as an accompaniment.

1760—ROUENNAIS DUCKLING IN PORT WINE

Caneton Rouennais au Porto

Roast the duckling *"en casserole,"* keeping it only just done.

Swirl into the pan with one-fifth pint of port wine; reduce to half, and add this reduced pan gravy to one-half pint of duckling gravy, thickened with arrowroot, flour, etc.

1761—ROUENNAIS DUCKLING A LA PRESSE

Caneton Rouennais à la Presse

Roast the duckling for twenty minutes, and send it instantly to the table, where it should be treated as follows:—Remove the legs, which are not served; carve the breasts into fine slices, laid one against the other on a lukewarm dish.

Chop up the bird and press it, sprinkling it the while with a glassful of good red wine. Collect the gravy; add a few drops of brandy, and with this liquor sprinkle the slices of breast, which should have been well seasoned.

Put on a chafing dish, and thoroughly heat without allowing to boil.

Serve instantly.

1762—STUFFED DUCKLING A LA ROUENNAISE

Caneton Farci à la Rouennaise

Stuff the duckling with the *forcemeat* given under (1754), and roast it in a hot oven for from twenty-five to thirty minutes, according to its size.

Send a Rouennaise sauce (54) to the table with it.

If it be served carved, remove the legs, roughly cut them inside, season them well with salt and pepper, and grill them.

Cut the breasts into thin slices, set these on either side of a long dish, and, in the middle, place the *forcemeat* taken from the inside.

Set the grilled legs at either end of the dish.

Roughly chop up the bird and press it, sprinkling it with a glass of liqueur-brandy and a few drops of lemon juice. Add the collected gravy to the Rouennaise sauce; coat the slices of breast thinly with sauce, and serve what remains of the sauce separately.

1763—SALMIS OF DUCKLING ROUENNAISE

Salmis de Caneton à la Rouennaise

After having removed the breast bone, truss the duckling.

Put it in a very hot oven, where it should only stay eight minutes, four minutes each side.

If possible, let it cool for a few minutes, that it may be more easily carved. Take care, also, to wipe it, for, as a rule, the extreme heat of the oven blackens it. Remove the legs; roughly cut them inside; season and grill them.

Sprinkle a long, buttered dish with chopped shallots, kitchen salt not too fine, freshly-ground pepper, nutmeg, and allspice.

Cut the breasts into very thin slices lengthwise, fifteen from each breast, and set them one against the other on the dish. Sprinkle them with the same seasoning as that lying on the dish, except for the shallots.

Remove the remaining stumps of the wings, also the small, remaining skin of the breast; season both, and set them to grill by the side of the legs. Roughly chop up the bird; press it while sprinkling it with half a glassful of red wine, and sprinkle the slices of breast with the collected gravy.

When about to serve, set a few small pieces of butter on the slices of breast; heat for a moment on the stove, and put the dish in a very hot oven, or at the *salamander,* that the *glazing* may be instantaneous.

Take out the dish the moment the edges of the *aiguillettes,* the breast slices, begin to curl, set the grilled legs at either end of the dish, the two wing-stumps, with the skin of the breast, in the middle, and serve immediately.

1764—SOUFFLE OF ROUENNAIS DUCKLING

Soufflé de Caneton Rouennais

Poëlé the duckling, and only just cook it.

Lift out the *suprêmes,* and keep them hot, and cut the bones from the bird in such a way as to imitate a case, as I described in a number of pullet recipes. With the duckling's liver, the raw meat of another half-duckling, the white of an egg, and three oz. of raw *foie gras,* prepare a *mousseline forcemeat.*

Fill the case with this *forcemeat,* shaping it so as to reconstruct the bird. Surround it with a band of strong, buttered paper, to prevent loss of shape, and *poach* gently, under cover, for twenty minutes.

With some reserved *forcemeat,* combined with an equal weight of *foie-gras purée,* garnish some *tartlet* crusts, and *poach* them at the same time as the *soufflé.*

Put the bird on a dish; surround it with the *tartlets;* set a slice of *suprême* on each of the latter, and serve a Rouennaise sauce (54) separately.

COLD DUCKLINGS—CANETONS FROIDS

1765—DUCKLING A LA CUILLER *Caneton à la Cuiller*

Braise the duckling with Madeira, and cook it well.

Put into a *terrine* just large enough to hold it; cover with the *braising*-liquor, strained through a napkin, and combined with enough aspic jelly to completely coat the duckling. Leave to cool.

When about to serve, clear the surface of grease, first by means of a spoon, then with boiling water, and serve on a napkin.

1766—GLAZED DUCKLING WITH TANGERINES

Caneton Glacé aux Mandarines

Poële the duckling, and let it cool in its liquor.

When it is quite cold, set it on its back; *glaze* it with aspic jelly, and place it on a low rice or carved-bread bed lying on a long dish.

Surround it with emptied tangerines, filled with cold *mousse* made from ducklings' livers and *foie gras*. Alternate the tangerines with small *timbales* of aspic, combined with the *poëlé*-liquor and the juice squeezed from the sections of the tangerines.

1767—GLAZED DUCKLING WITH CHERRIES

Caneton Glacé aux Cerises

Roast the duckling, and keep it underdone.

When it is quite cold, remove the breast, and the bones in such a way as to form a case with the bird. Cut each breast into eight thin slices; coat them with a brown chaud-froid sauce (34), and decorate with truffles. Fill the bird with a *mousse* made from the remains of the meat, the duckling's liver, and some *foie gras,* and shape it so as to imitate the breast of the bird.

Glaze with aspic, and set in the refrigerator, that the *mousse* may harden. When the latter is firm, lay the chaud-froid-coated slices on it, and set the piece in a deep, square dish. Surround with cold, pitted, Morella cherries, *poached* in Bordeaux wine, and cover these with an aspic jelly flavored with duckling *essence.*

1768—DUCKLING WINGS ECARLATE

Aiguillettes de Caneton à l'Ecarlate

Poële a Rouen duckling until it is just cooked, and let it cool in its liquor. Lift out the breasts; skin them, and cut them each into eight thin slices. Coat them with a brown chaud-froid sauce (34), and decorate with truffles. Prepare an equal number of slices of tongue the size and shape of the slices of duckling, and coat them with aspic.

With the remains and the meat of the legs, prepare a *mousse,* and pour it into a square or oval silver dish; let it cool, and then set the *aiguillettes* of duckling and the slices of tongue upon it, alternating them in so doing, and cover the *mousse* with aspic.

1769—MOUSSE AND MOUSSELINES OF ROUENNAIS DUCKLING

Mousse et Mousselines de Caneton Rouennais

These are prepared with the same quantities as the chicken *mousses* and *mousselines,* but they permit no other sauce than the Rouennaise (54) or the Bigarrade (31), nor of any other garnishes than sections of orange, cherries, vegetable *purées,* or creams.

1770—MOUSSE OF ROUENNAIS DUCKLING

Mousse de Caneton Rouennais

With the exception of the nature of the principal ingredient, the preparation, quantities, and moulding of this *mousse* are the same as for chicken *mousse.* The reader is, therefore, begged to refer to (1670), which may be applied perfectly well to Rouen duckling.

1771—COLD SOUFFLE OF DUCKLING WITH ORANGE

Soufflé Froid de Caneton à l'Orange

Proceed as for the "Caneton aux cerises" (1767), but with this difference, that the entire duckling is used entirely for the *mousse.*

Serve, similarly, in a square dish, and surround with sections of oranges skinned. Cover with an aspic jelly flavored with the juice of Seville oranges, and combined with a liqueur-glassful of curaçao per pint of aspic-jelly.

1772—TERRINE OF ROUENNAIS DUCKLING IN ASPIC

Terrine de Caneton Rouennais à la Gelée

First prepare the following *forcemeat:*—Heat three oz. of fat bacon, cut into small dice, and three oz. of butter in a frying-pan. Throw six fine ducks' livers (seasoned with salt and pepper, and sprinkled with a pinch of powdered thyme, bay leaf, and half an onion chopped) into this fat. Toss them over a hot fire, just long enough to heat them; leave them to cool, and rub them through a sieve.

Bone the breast of a Rouen duckling and its back as far as the region of the legs, and remove the tail. Stuff it with the preparation given above; truss as for an entrée, and put it in a *terrine* just large enough to hold it. Sprinkle it with a glassful of brandy; cover with a slice of bacon, and cook it in the *bain-marie* (water-bath), in the oven, and cover for forty minutes.

With the bird's remains and some strong veal stock, prepare two-thirds pint of excellent aspic, and, after taking the duckling from the oven, cover it with this aspic, and let it cool. When about to serve, remove all grease, first by means of a spoon, and then by means of boiling water, and set the *terrine* on a napkin lying on a long dish.

1773—TIMBALE OF DUCKLING VOISIN

Timbale de Caneton à la Voisin

Roast a Rouen duckling, and keep it underdone; let it cool, and lift out its breasts. With the bird prepare a Salmis sauce (55), and thicken it with aspic as for a chaud-froid sauce.

Cut the breasts into slices, coat them with the Salmis sauce, and leave this to set. Let a thickness of sauce set on the bottom of a *timbale*.

Upon this sauce lay some of the coated slices, alternating them with slices of truffle, and cover with a thin layer of aspic jelly. Lay another row of slices of breasts and of truffles, followed as before by a layer of aspic, and continue thus in the same order. Complete with a somewhat thick layer of aspic, and keep it cool until ready for serving.

N.B.—This old and excellent cold entrée is really only a cold Salmis. The procedure may be applied to all game suited to the Salmis method of preparation. It is the simplest and certainly the best way of serving them cold.

1774—GUINEA-FOWL   *Pintades*

The guinea-fowl is not equal to the pheasant from the gastro-nomical standpoint, though it often takes the place of the latter among the roasts after the shooting season. But, though it has neither the fine flavor nor the delicate meat of the pheasant, it does serve well as an alternative. The majority of pheasant recipes may be applied to it, especially à la Bohémienne, à la crême, en Char-treuse, en salmis, à la choucroûte, etc.

1775—PIGEONS AND SQUABS   *Pigeons et Pigeonneaux*

Young pigeons are not very highly esteemed by gourmets, and this is more particularly to be regretted, since when the birds are of excellent quality, they are worthy of the best tables.

1776—BORDELAIS SQUABS   *Pigeonneaux à la Bordelais*

Open the squabs down the back; season them; slightly flatten them, and toss them in butter. They may just as well be split as left whole. Serve, and surround with the garnish given under "Poulet à la Bordelaise" (1538).

1777—SQUABS IN CASSEROLE PAYSANNE

Pigeonneaux en Casserole à la Paysanne

Cook the squabs in the oven in an earthenware saucepan.

When they are two-thirds done, surround them with one and one-half oz. of salt pork, cut into small dice and *blanched,* and two oz. of sliced and *sautéd* potatoes for each pigeon. Complete the cooking of the whole gently, and, when about to serve, add a little good gravy.

1778—CHARTREUSE OF SQUABS   *Pigeonneaux en Chartreuse*

Prepare the *Chartreuse* in a *Charlotte mould,* as explained under (1182). Line the the bottom and sides with a layer of *braised,* drained, and pressed cabbages; in the center set the squabs, cooked *"à la casserole"* and cut into two lengthwise, and alternate them with small rectangles of *blanched,* salt pork, and sausage slices. Cover with cabbages, and steam in a *bain-marie* (water-bath) for thirty minutes.

Let the *Chartreuse* stand for five minutes after taking it from the *bain-marie;* turn out on a round dish, and surround with a few tablespoons of half-*glaze* sauce (23).

1779—SQUABS EN CRAPAUDINE   *Pigeonneaux en Crapaudine*

Split the young pigeons lengthwise in two, from the apex of the breast to the wings. Open them; flatten them slightly; season them; dip them in melted butter, roll them in bread-crumbs and grill them gently.

Serve a devilled sauce (36) at the same time.

1780—SQUABS EN COMPOTE   *Pigeonneaux en Compôte*

Fry in butter two oz. of *blanched,* salt pork and two oz. of raw mushrooms, peeled and quartered. Drain the bacon and the mushrooms, and set the squabs, trussed as for an entrée, to fry in the same butter.

Take out when they are brown; drain them of butter; swirl with half a glass of white wine; reduce the latter, and add sufficient brown stock and tomatoed half-*glaze* sauce (23), in eanal quantities, to cover the birds. Plunge them into this sauce, with a herb bunch, and simmer until they are cooked and the sauce is reduced to half.

This done, transfer the squabs to another saucepan; add the pieces of bacon, the mushrooms, and six small onions, *glazed* with butter, for each bird; strain the sauce over the whole through a fine sieve; simmer for ten minutes more, and serve very hot.

1781—PIGEON PIE *Pigeon Pie*

Line the bottom and sides of a pie-dish with very thin, flattened slices of lean beef, seasoned with salt and pepper, and sprinkled with chopped shallots.

Set the quartered pigeons inside the dish, and separate them with a halved hard-boiled egg-yolk for each pigeon. Moisten half-way up with good gravy; cover with a layer of puff paste (2366); brush with egg; press down the rim; make a slit in the top, and bake for about one and one-half hours in a good, moderate oven.

1782—VOL AU VENT OF SQUABS *Vol au Vent de Pigeonneaux*

Remove the feet and the pinions (wing tips); *poële* the squabs, and only just barely cook them.

Cut each bird into four, and mix them with a garnish "à la Financière" (1474) combined with the *poëlé*-liquor. Pour the whole into a vol-au-vent crust (2390), and dish on a napkin.

1783—SQUAB CUTLETS NESLES *Côtelettes de Pigeonneaux à la Nesles*

Split them in two, and reserve the feet, which serve as the bone of the cutlet. Flatten them slightly; season, and fry them in butter on one side only. Cool them under slight pressure; coat their fried side, dome-fashion, with some *godiveau* (198) with cream, combined with a third of its bulk of *gratin forcemeat* and chopped truffles. Set them in a pan, and place in a moderate oven to complete the cooking, and *poach* the *forcemeat*. Arrange in a circle, and separate the cutlets with slices of veal sweetbreads, dipped in beaten eggs, rolled in bread-crumbs, and tossed in butter. Garnish their midst with mushrooms and sliced chicken livers, tossed in butter and combined with a few tablespoons of Madeira sauce.

1784—SQUAB CUTLETS IN PAPER CASES
Côtelettes de Pigeonneaux en Papillotes

Split the pigeons in two, as above; brown them in butter, and enclose them in *papillotes* as explained under "Côtelettes de Veau en Papillotes" (1259).

1785—SQUAB CUTLET SEVIGNE
Côtelettes de Pigeonneaux à la Sévigné

Sauté the half-pigeons in butter, and leave them to cool under slight pressure. Fill their cut sides dome-fashion with a *salpicon* of white chicken-meat, mushrooms, and truffles, the whole combined by means of a cold Allemande sauce (27).

Dip them in beaten egg, roll them in bread-crumbs, and cook them gently in clarified butter (175).

Arrange them in a circle; fill their center with asparagus tips mixed with butter, and serve a light, Madeira sauce (44) separately.

1786—BREASTS OF SQUABS DIPLOMATE
Suprêmes de Pigeonneaux à la Diplomate

Lift out the breasts and slightly flatten them; brown them in butter, and leave them to cool under slight pressure. This done, dip them in a Villeroy sauce (108), combined with chopped herbs and mushrooms, and cool them. Dip each breast in beaten egg; roll them in bread-crumbs, and fry just before serving.

Arrange in a circle, and in their center set a heap of fried parsley. Send separately a garnish of pigeon *quenelles,* mushrooms, and small, olive-shaped truffles, to which a half-*glaze* sauce (23) flavored with pigeon *essence* has been added.

1787—BREASTS OF SQUABS ST.-CLAIR
Suprêmes de Pigeonneaux à la Saint-Clair

With the meat of the legs prepare a *mousseline forcemeat,* and, with the latter, make some *quenelles* the size of small olives, and set them to *poach*. *Poële* the breasts, without browning, on a thick litter of sliced onions, and keep them underdone. Add a little *velouté* (25) to the onions; rub them through a fine sieve, and put the *quenelles* in this sauce.

In the middle of a shallow *croustade,* set a pyramid *cèpes* tossed in butter. Lift off the breasts; skin them, and set them on the *cèpes;* coat them with the prepared sauce; surround with a ribbon of meat *glaze* (15), and place the *quenelles* all round.

1788—BREASTS OF SQUABS MARIGNY
Suprêmes de Pigeonneaux à la Marigny

Cut off the legs, and, with their meat, prepare a *forcemeat. Poach* the latter in a pan, and stamp it out with an oval cutter into pieces the size of the *suprêmes*.

Cover the breasts with slices of bacon, and *poële* them, taking care to only just cook them.

Quickly lift off the breasts, skin them, and set each upon an oval of *forcemeat*, sticking them on by means of a little *gratin forcemeat*.

Put the *suprêmes* in the oven for a moment, that this *forcemeat* may *poach*. Arrange the *suprêmes* round a pyramid consisting of a smooth *purée* of peas, and coat with a velouté sauce (26), finished with an *essence* prepared from the remains and the *poëlé*-liquor of the breasts.

1789—BREASTS OF SQUABS WITH TRUFFLES
Suprêmes de Pigeonneaux aux Truffes

Lift off the *suprêmes*, flatten them slightly; toss them in clarified butter (175), and set them on a border of smooth *forcemeat* laid on a dish by means of a pastry-bag, and *poached* in the front of the oven.

Swash the pan with Madeira; add four fine slices of truffle for each *suprême* (breast), and a little pale melted meat *glaze,* and finish with a moderate amount of butter.

Coat the *suprêmes* (breasts), with this sauce, and set the slices of truffle upon it.

1790—MOUSSELINES OF SQUABS A L'EPICURIENNE
Mousselines de Pigeonneaux à l'Epicurienne

Prepare and *poach* these *mousselines* like the chicken ones, but make them a little smaller. Arrange them in the form of a crown; set thereon a young pigeon's fillet (breast) roasted, and in their midst arrange a garnish of peas with lettuce. Coat with a *fumet* prepared from the bird remains and combined with a few table-spoons of *velouté*.

N.B.—Pigeons and squabs may also be prepared after the recipes given for squab chickens.

RELEVÉS AND ENTRÉES OF

GAME

VENISON AND GROUND GAME

The stag (Fr. Cerf) and the fallow deer (Fr. Daim) supply the only venison that is consumed in England, where the roebuck (Fr. Chevreuil) is not held in very high esteem. True, the latter's flesh is very often mediocre in quality, and saddles and legs of roebuck often have to be imported from the Continent when they are to appear on an important menu.

On the other hand, venison derived from the stag or red deer and the fallow deer proper is generally of superior quality. The former has perhaps more flavor, but the latter, which is supplied by animals bred in herds on large private estates, has no equal as far as delicacy and tenderness are concerned, while it is covered with white and scented fat, which is greatly appreciated by English connoisseurs.

Venison (game for cooking) is procured from the white tail, mule, or fallow deer, the stag, and the reindeer. Bear is also available in the United States, but wild boar and roebuck are not, except when imported.

Although these types of venison are generally served as *relevés,* they belong more properly to the roasts, and I shall give their recipes a little later on. In any case, only half of the hind-quarters (leg and loin) is served at high class tables.

I shall now, therefore, only give the various recipes dealing with roebuck (as used in France), it being understood that these, if desired, may be applied to corresponding joints of the stag, white tail or mule, deer or in certain cases reindeer.

(Furred game is not nearly so plentiful in the United States as in France and other parts of Europe. It is also not so much appreciated, not only because of its scarcity, but also because people in general do not know how to prepare and cook it. It is important that all game be hung in a cool place for a time in order that it may become seasoned (high).

The following recipes often mention cuts of venison not used by America hunters or in the American markets. It is well to remember that the available cuts in the markets are the leg, the loins, the rack and the shoulder of venison. The hunter may follow the directions in the recipes and butcher his own kill.—Ed.)

1791—SADDLE AND HAUNCH OF ROEBUCK

Selle de Chevreuil et Cuissot

Saddles and legs of roebuck may be prepared after the same recipes, and allow of the same garnishes. The recipes for saddle which I give hereafter may therefore be applied equally well to legs.

Whichever joint be selected, it must first be cleared of all tendons and then *larded* with larding bacon. The last operation is no more essential than is the *marinading* which in France has become customary with such pieces. It might even be said with justice that *marinading* is not only useless, but harmful, more particularly in the case of young animals whose meat has been well hung (seasoned).

Unlike many other specimens of game, roebuck has to be eaten fresh; it does not suit it to be in the least tainted. I should like to point out here that game shot in ambush is best, owing to the fact that animals killed after a chase decompose very quickly, and thereby lose a large proportion of their flavor.

The saddle of the roebuck generally consists of the whole of the back, from the shoulder to the tail, in which case the bones of the ribs are cut very short, that the joint may lie steady at all points.

At the rump-end, cut the joint on either side diagonally, from the point of the haunch to the root of the tail. Sometimes, however, the saddle only consists of the loin portion of the back, and, in this case, the ribs are cut up to be cooked as chops.

1792—SADDLE OF ROEBUCK ALLEMANDE

Selle de Chevreuil à l'Allemande

Marinate the saddle for two or three days in raw *marinade* (169), and roast it, in a narrow baking-pan, upon the vegetables of the *marinade*.

As soon as the joint is cooked, take it out; swirl into the pan a little *marinade,* and almost entirely reduce. Clear of grease; add two-thirds pint of cream and one powdered juniper berry; reduce by a third; complete with a few drops of melted *glaze* (14), and rub through a fine sieve.

Serve this sauce at the same time as the saddle, which set on a long dish.

1793—SADDLE OR BACK OF ROEBUCK BADEN-BADEN

Selle de Chevreuil à la Baden-Baden

The saddle should be *marinated* and well dried before being set to cook.

Poêle it on the vegetables of the *marinade*.

When it is cooked, put it on a long dish, and, at either end of it, set a garnish of stewed pears, unsugared, but flavored with cinnamon and lemon-rind. Pour one-third pint of game stock (8) into the pan in which the joint was cooked; cook for ten minutes; strain; clear of grease, and thicken with arrowroot, or flour, etc.

Serve this thickened stock separately, and send some red-currant jelly to the table at the same time.

1794—SADDLE OR BACK OF ROEBUCK WITH CHERRIES
Selle de Chevreuil aux Cerises

Keep the saddle for twelve hours in *marinade* (169) made from *verjuice* instead of vinegar. Roast it on the spit, basting it with the *marinade,* and keep it slightly underdone.

At the same time, serve a cherry sauce consisting of equal quantities of Poivrade sauce (50) and red-currant jelly, to each pint of which add three oz. of semi-candied cherries, set to soak in hot water thirty minutes beforehand.

N.B.—This saddle need not be *marinated* if it be desired plain.

1795—SADDLE OR BACK OF ROEBUCK CUMBERLAND
Selle de Cheuvreuil à la Cumberland

Roast it like a haunch of venison, without *marinading* it. Send it to the table with a *timbale* of string beans, mixed with butter, and serve a Cumberland sauce (134) separately.

1796—SADDLE OR BACK OF ROEBUCK CREOLE
Selle de Chevreuil à la Créole

Marinate it for a few hours only, and roast it on the spit, basting it the while with the *marinade.*

Set it on a long dish, and surround it with bananas tossed in butter.

At the same time serve a Robert sauce (52), combined with a third of its bulk of Poivrade sauce (50), and one oz. of fresh butter per pint.

1797—SADDLE OR BACK OF ROEBUCK BEAUJEU
Selle de Chevreuil à la Beaujeu

Lard and roast it. Set it on a long dish, and surround it with artichoke-bottoms, garnished with lentil *purée,* and alternated with chestnuts cooked in a small quantity of consommé and *glazed.*

Serve a venison sauce separately.

1798—SADDLE OR BACK OF ROEBUCK WITH GINGER
Selle de Chevreuil au Genièvre

Lard the saddle, and roast it. Swirl into the roasting pan with a small glass of burned gin; add one powdered juniper berry and one-sixth pint of heavy cream. Reduce the cream to half; complete with a few tablespoons of Poivrade sauce (50) and a few drops of lemon juice. Serve this sauce with the saddle, and send separately some hot stewed apples, very slightly sugared.

1799—SADDLE OR BACK OF ROEBUCK WITH VARIOUS SAUCES
Selle de Chevreuil avec Sauces Diverses

Saddle of roebuck may also be served with the following sauces:—
Poivrade, Venison, Grand-Veneur, Moscovite, Robert, etc. The
selected accompaniment determines the title of the dish.

1800—ROEBUCK NOISETTES AND CHOPS
Noisettes et Côtelettes de Chevreuil

The same recipes may be applied to both. Trim them after the
manner of lamb noisettes or chops. They may be moderately
marinated, but they may also be used fresh. In the latter case, fry
them in butter over a somewhat hot fire, like the lamb rib chops.

If they have been *marinated,* it is better to toss them very quickly
in very hot oil, and then to dry them before serving them.

It is in the serving only that the noisettes and the chops differ;
for, whereas the latter are always served in a crown, one overlapping
the other, or each separated from the rest by *croûtons* of bread
fried in butter, the noisettes are always arranged in a circle on
small, oval *croûtons* fried in butter, or on *tartlet crusts* containing
some kind of garnish.

1801—ROEBUCK CHOPS CONTI   *Côtelettes de Chevreuil Conti*

Sauté the chops in very hot oil; dry them; arrange them in a
crown, and separate them by similarly-shaped slices of cured tongue.

Swirl into the saucepan a little white wine; add this liquor to a
Poivrade sauce (50), and coat the chops with it.

Serve a light, buttered *purée* of lentils at the same time.

1802—ROEBUCK CHOPS DIANE   *Côtelettes de Chevreuil Diane*

Spread an even layer, one-third inch thick, of *mousseline* game
forcemeat in a pan. *Poach* this *forcemeat* in a steamer or in a very
moderate oven, and cut it into triangles equal in size to the chops.

Toss the latter as already explained; arrange them in a crown, and
separate them by *croûtons* of *forcemeat* already prepared.

Coat the whole with Poivrade sauce (50), thinned by means of a
little beaten cream, and garnished with crescents of truffle and hard-
boiled white of egg, and serve a *purée* of chestnuts at the same time.

1803—NOISETTES OF ROEBUCK WITH GINGER
Noisettes de Chevreuil au Genièvre

Cook the noisettes (rib chops) in hot smoking oil. Dry them, put on a dish and coat them with the same sauce as that given under "Selle au Genièvre" (1798).

Serve some stewed apples at the same time.

1804—ROMANOFF NOISETTES OF ROEBUCK
Noisettes de Chevreuil Romanoff

Cook the noisettes (rib chops); set them on stuffed sections of cucumber, prepared after (2124a), and place a slice of truffle on each *noisette*. Coat with a Poivrade sauce (50) with cream, and serve a mushroom *purée* separately.

1805—VALENCIA NOISETTES OF ROEBUCK
Noisettes de Chevreuil Valencia,

Cook the noisettes (rib chops), and dish them in a circle, each on a round *croûton* of brioche fried in butter, and coat lightly with Bigarrade sauce (31).

Serve a sauceboat of Bigarrade sauce and an orange salad at the same time.

1806—VILLENEUVE NOISETTES OR ROEBUCK
Noisettes de Chevreuil Villeneuve

Carefully clear the meat of the roebuck of all tendons, and chop it up with a knife, combining with it the third of its weight of fresh butter, as much bread-crumbs, soaked in milk, and pressed, and one-third pint of fresh cream per lb. of meat. Season, divide into portions weighing two oz., mould to a nice round shape, wrap in *pig's caul,* cook quickly at the last moment, and arrange in the form of a crown.

Coat with Chasseur sauce (33), and serve a *timbale* of celery *purée* separately.

1807—VALKYRIE NOISETTES OR ROEBUCK
Noisettes de Chevreuil Valkyria

Sauté the noisettes (rib chops) in the usual way, and arrange them in the form of a crown, each on a small patty of "Potatoes Berny" (2205). On each noisette lay a fine, grilled mushroom, garnished with a rosette of Soubise *purée*, made by means of a pastry-bag fitted with a fancy tube. Pour a little venison sauce over the dish, and send a sauceboat of it separately.

N.B.—Roebuck *noisettes* and chops are still served with *purées* of chestnuts or celery, with truffles, *cèpes*, mushrooms, etc.

The sauces best suited to them are Poivrade sauce and its derivatives, such as Venison sauce, Grand-Veneur sauce, Romaine sauce, etc., also Robert sauce Escoffier.

1808—CIVET OR STEW OF ROEBUCK   *Civet de Chevreuil*

For "Civet Stew of Roebuck" the shoulders, the neck, and the breasts are used, and these pieces are cut up and set to *marinate* six hours beforehand with the *aromatics* and the same red wine as that with which the stew will be moistened.

When about to prepare the *civet*, or stew of hare, drain and dry these pieces, and proceed exactly as for "Civet de Lièvre" (1821), except for the thickening by means of blood, which the difficulty of obtaining the blood of the roebuck does not permit.

This *civet*, which should be classed among dishes for the home, is usually served in the form of a potted stew; for, inasmuch as the final thickening with blood is lacking, it can only be an imitation of the true *civet*. When, therefore, hare's blood is available, it should always be used in finishing this dish exactly after the manner of (1821)—that is to say, the preparation should be given the characteristic stamp of *civet* (which means "jugged hare") by means of a final thickening with blood.

1809—BOAR AND YOUNG BOAR   *Sanglier et Marcassin*

When the wild boar is over two years of age, it is no longer fit to be served as food. Between one and two years it should be used with caution, and the various roebuck recipes may then be applied to it. But only the young boar less than twelve months old should be cooked.

The hams of a young boar, salted and smoked, supply a very passable *relevé*, which gives variety to the ordinary menu. They are treated exactly like cured pork hams.

The saddle and the shoulders may be prepared after the recipes given for saddle of roebuck, and the same holds good with the loin chops and the rib chops.

Finally, the saddle may be served cold, in a stew, prepared after (1173).

As the various parts of the young boar are covered with fat, it is understood that they do not need to be larded.

1810—HARE AND LEVERET (OR YOUNG HARE)   *Lièvre et Levraut*

As a result of one of those freaks of taste, of which I have already pointed out some few examples, hare is not nearly so highly esteemed as it deserves in the United States; and the fact seems all the more strange when one remembers that in many of her states excellent specimens of the species can be found.

Whatever be the purpose for which it is required, always select a young hare, five or six lbs. in weight. The age may be ascertained as follows:—Grasp one ear close to its tip with both hands, and pull in opposite directions; if the ear tears, the beast is young; if it resists the strain, the hare is old, and should be set aside for soups and the preparation of *fumets* and *forcemeats*.

(In the United States we can get the Canadian hare, the jack-rabbit, the cotton-tail (the smallest of the species), the Australian hare, which is imported, and the Belgian hare, which is the common tame rabbit. Hares of the size found in Europe, particularly Belgium and France, are not procurable in this country. However, our types of hare lend themselves to the recipes given for hare, leveret, etc.— Ed.)

1811—STUFFED HARE PERIGOURDINE

Lièvre Farci à la Périgourdine

Take care to collect all the blood when drawing the hare; break the bones of the legs, that they may be easily trussed; clear the legs and the loins of all tendons, and *lard* them. Chop up the liver, the lungs, the heart, and four chicken livers, together with five oz. of fat bacon.

Add to this minced-meat five oz. of soaked and pressed bread-crumbs, the blood, two oz. of chopped onion, cooked in butter and cooled; a pinch of chopped parsley, a piece of crushed garlic the size of a pea, and three oz. of raw truffle parings. Mix up well; fill the hare with this stuffing; sew up the skin of the belly; truss the animal, and *braise* it in white wine for about two and one-half hours, basting it often the while. *Glaze* at the last moment. Serve the hare on a platter.

Add two-thirds pint of half-*glaze* game sauce (23) to the *braising-* liquor; reduce; clear of grease; strain, and add three oz. of chopped truffles to this sauce.

Pour a little sauce over the platter on which the hare has been set, and serve what remains of the sauce separately.

1812—SADDLE OR BACK OF HARE   *Râble de Lièvre*

The French term *"râble"* (saddle) means the whole of the back of the hare, from the root of the neck to the tail, with the ribs cut very short.

Often, however, that piece which corresponds with the saddle in other meats is the piece reaching from the rump to the floating ribs. Whatever be the particular cut, the piece should be well cleared of all tendons, and finely *larded* before being set to *marinate*; and this last operation may even be dispensed with when the *râble* is taken from a young hare.

Marinating would only become necessary if the piece had to be kept some considerable time.

1813—SADDLE OR BACK OF HARE ALLEMANDE

Râble de Lièvre à l'Allemande

Set the *râble* (saddle) well dried on the vegetables of the *marinade,* which should be laid on the bottom of a long, narrow dish. When it is nearly cooked, remove the vegetables, pour one-quarter pint of cream into the dish, and complete the cooking of the saddle, basting it the while with that cream.

Finish at the last minute with a few drops of lemon juice.

Serve the saddle on a platter, surrounded with the cream gravy, strained through a fine sieve.

1814—SADDLE OR BACK OF HARE WITH GINGER

Râble de Lièvre au Genièvre

Roast it, as above, on the vegetables of the *marinade* (169).

Swirl into the dish a small glass of gin and two or three tablespoons of *marinade,* and reduce to half. Add one-sixth pint of cream, two tablespoons of Poivrade sauce (50), and four powdered juniper berries.

Strain and serve this sauce separately at the same time as the *râble* (saddle).

1815—HIND-QUARTERS OF HARE   *Cuisses de Lièvre*

Use the hind-quarters or both legs of young hares only; those of old animals may be used for the *"civet"* (stew) and *forcemeat* alone. After having cleared them of tendons and *larded* them with very thin strips of bacon, treat them like the *râble.*

1816—FILLETS OR LOINS OF YOUNG HARE DAMPIERRE
Filets de Levraut à la Dampierre

Take five leverets' (young hares') fillets or loins; *lard* them with slices of truffle, after the manner directed for "Suprêmes de Volaille à la Chevalière" (1458); shape them like crescents, and set them on a buttered dish.

Lard the small tenderloins with a rosette consisting of strips of cured tongue, and set them also on a buttered dish.

With what remains of the meat of the leverets, prepare a *mousseline forcemeat,* and add some truffle *essence* and some chopped truffles.

Arrange this *forcemeat,* shaping it like a blunt cone two and one-half inches high, the radius of which should be the length of a leveret's loin.

Set this *forcemeat* to *poach* in the oven.

Sprinkle the fillets or loins and tenderloins with a little brandy and melted butter; cover them, and *poach* them likewise in the oven. This done, arrange them in a sunburst around the cone of *forcemeat,* alternating the fillets or loins and the tenderloins. Place a fine, *glazed* truffle in the middle of the rosette, and surround the base with mushrooms, separated by chestnuts cooked in consommé and *glazed,* and small onions cooked in butter.

Serve a Poivrade sauce (50) a the same time, combined with the hare's cooking-liquor.

1817—FILLETS OF YOUNG HARE MORNAY
Filets de Levraut à la Mornay

Trim two leverets' (young hares') fillets (loins and tenderloins), and cut them into slices, one inch in diameter and one-third inch thick. Prepare the same number of bread *croûtons* as there are slices, and make them of the same size as the latter, though half as thick; and the same number of thick slices of truffle, cooked at the last minute in a little Madeira.

Toss the slices of fillet or loin quickly in clarified butter (175); color the *croûtons* in butter at the same time, and mix them with the slices and the truffles in a saucepan.

Swirl in the saucepan the Madeira in which the truffles have cooked; add a little juicy pale *glaze* (17); reduce sufficiently; strain the sauce through a sieve; finish it liberally with butter; add it to the *sautéd* slices, and serve the latter in a very hot *timbale.*

N.B.—This recipe was given by the Comte de Mornay himself to the proprietors of the famous Parisian restaurant, and for a long while the dish was one of the specialties of a house no longer in existence.

1818—FILLETS OR LOINS OF YOUNG HARE VENDOME

Filets de Levraut à la Vendome

After having *larded* the young hare's fillets or loins, roll them round a buttered tin mould, and fasten them with a string so that they may form rings.

Set to *poach*. Meanwhile, spread on a buttered pan a layer one-half inch thick of game *forcemeat; poach* the latter; stamp it out by means of an even cutter into rounds of the same size as the rings, and set one of these on each of the *forcemeat* rounds, fixing it by means of a little raw *forcemeat*.

Cut the tenderloins into slices, and quickly toss them in butter with an equal quantity of mushrooms and five oz. of raw, sliced truffles.

Swirl in the saucepan a little brandy and the *poaching*-liquor of the fillet-rings; add a little Poivrade sauce (50); finish this sauce with butter, and plunge therein the slices of breast, the mushrooms, and the truffles.

Set the rings in a circle on a dish, and fill them with this garnish. Serve separately a sauceboat of Poivrade sauce and a *timbale* of chestnut *purée*.

1819—MOUSSES AND MOUSSELINES OF HARE

Mousses et Mousselines de Lièvre

Proceed exactly as for all other *mousses* and *mousselines*, except, of course, in regard to the basic ingredient, which in this case is the meat of a hare.

1820—SOUFFLE OF HARE
Soufflé de Lièvre

With one lb. of the meat of a hare, prepare a light *mousseline forcemeat;* add the whites of two eggs, beaten to a stiff froth; *poach* the *mousseline* in a *soufflé* saucepan.

Cut the hare's tenderloins into slices, and toss them in butter at the last moment.

Cook the *soufflé* in a moderate oven; coat the top lightly with half-*glaze* sauce (23) flavored with hare *fumet,* and surround it with the tenderloin slices, alternated with slices of truffles.

The tenderloin slices and the slices of truffles may be added to the sauce, and this garnish is served separately in another *timbale.*

1821—CIVET OR JUGGED HARE
Civet de Lièvre

Skin and clean the hare, taking care to collect all the blood in so doing. Put the liver aside, after having carefully freed it from the gall-bladder and those portions touching it.

Cut up the hare, and put the pieces in a bowl with a few table-spoons of brandy and an equal quantity of olive oil, salt, pepper, and an onion cut into thin slices. Cover and leave to *marinate* for a few hours in the very red wine used for the moistening. Fry one-half lb. of lean bacon, cut into large dice, in butter, and drain it as soon as it is brown. In the same butter brown two fair-sized, quartered onions; add two tablespoons of flour, and cook this *roux* gently until it acquires a golden tinge. Put the pieces of hare into this *roux*, after having well dried them, and brown them.

Moisten with the wine used for the *marinade*. Add a large herb bunch, in which place a garlic clove; cover, and leave to cook gently.

A few minutes before serving, thicken the *civet* or stew with the reserved blood, which should be slowly heated, and mix with a few tablespoons of sauce. Then transfer the pieces of hare, one by one, to another saucepan with the fried pieces of bacon, twenty small, *glazed* onions, and twenty cooked mushrooms.

Strain the sauce over the whole through a strainer.

Serve in a warm *timbale*, and surround with heart-shaped *croûtons* fried in butter at the last moment.

COLD PREPARATIONS OF HARE

1822—HARE EN DAUBE
Lièvre en Daube

Take a fresh hare, and bone it from the back without cleaning it, so that the skin of the belly may be untouched.

Detach the shoulders and the legs; do not touch the head; season with salt and pepper; sprinkle with a few drops of brandy, and leave to *marinate*. With the hare's liver, some fat bacon, and some truffle parings, prepare a *gratin forcemeat*. Prepare another *forcemeat* with the meat of the shoulders and the legs, an equal weight of fat bacon, one egg, a pinch of wild thyme, salt, pepper, spices, and the brandy of the *marinade*. Rub this *forcemeat* through a sieve, and add to it the *gratin forcemeat*, one-half lb. of fat bacon, and five oz. of truffles cut into dice.

Fill the boned hare with this preparation; sew it up, and tie the head to the back in such a way as to give it the appearance of the complete animal.

Wrap it in slices of bacon, and set it in a *terrine* lined with the latter; sprinkle with a glass of brandy, and place in the oven for thirty minutes uncovered.

Then pour into the *terrine* a *fumet* prepared with red wine from the hare's bones; cover, and then cook in the oven gently for three hours.

Leave to partly cool; drain off the cooking-liquor, and carefully remove the slices of bacon. Strain the cooking-liquor through muslin; return it to the *terrine,* and fill up the latter with savoury aspic.

Keep in a cool place for two hours before serving.

1823—LOAF OF HARE   *Pain de Lièvre*

This Loaf is prepared according to (1689), and it may be served in "Bellevue," after the manner described for cold pieces prepared in this way.

1824—PATE OF HARE   *Pâté de Lièvre*

Clear the loins, the tenderloins, and the legs of all tendons; moderately *lard* them; season them; set them in a dish with an equal quantity of truffles and fat bacon strips; sprinkle with some brandy, and leave to *marinate* for one hour. With what remains of the meat, some loins of veal and pork, in the proportion of six oz. per lb. of hare; fresh, fat bacon in the proportion of one and one-half lbs. per lb. of hare; and spiced salt, prepare a *forcemeat,* and finish it with one egg and three tablespoons of brandy per lb. of *forcemeat.*

Rub through a fine sieve, and add a portion of the hare's blood.

Line a round or oval buttered mould with raised-pie dough, and completely cover the dough with slices of bacon. Then coat inside with *forcemeat,* and fill up the mould with alternate layers of *forcemeat,* hares' loins, truffle, and fat bacon strips.

Finish with a layer of *forcemeat;* cover with a slice of bacon; sprinkle a pinch of powdered thyme and bay leaf over the latter; close the pie with a layer of dough, which should be sealed down round the moistened edges; pinch the edge inside and out, and finish off the pie by means of imitation leaves made from the dough.

Brush with egg; bake in a moderate oven, and, when the pie is almost cold, pour some aspic jelly flavored with hare *fumet* into it.

1825—TERRINE OR PATE OF HARE   *Terrine de Lièvre*

A *"Terrine"* or Patty is only a pie without a crust, and it permits of the same *forcemeat* and of the same garnish of bacon strips as the latter. The *terrine* should first be lined with slices of bacon, whereupon it is garnished like the pie with alternate layers of *forcemeat,* bacon strips, hares' loins, and truffles.

Cover with a slice of bacon; sprinkle the center with a little powdered thyme and bay leaf, and a little spice. Put the lid on the *terrine,* place it in a saucepan containing a little water, and set it to cook in the oven.

The time allowed for cooking is naturally subject to the size of the *terrine.* It is known to be quite cooked when the grease which rises to the surface is quite clear.

As long as this grease is cloudy, raw juices are still issuing from the *forcemeat* and the garnish inside. Another method of telling is by the insertion of a testing needle. If the latter comes out evenly heated throughout its length, the *terrine* is cooked.

If the patty is to be served immediately, add some aspic to it when it is just tepid, and set it to cool under slight pressure. When quite cold, clear it of grease; trim its surface, and slice it up in the utensil.

If it is to be served whole, set it to cool under greater pressure; turn it out, and trim it all around. This done, put a layer of aspic-jelly to set on the bottom of the *terrine;* return the trimmed patty to the *terrine,* and surround it with melted aspic jelly.

When about to serve, turn it out after the manner of an aspic; set it on a platter, and border with aspic *croûtons.*

If it must be kept some time, proceed as above, but use lard instead of aspic, and keep it well covered and in the refrigerator.

1826—YOUNG WILD RABBIT   *Laperaux*

Use the wild cotton-tail or jack-rabbit rather than the tame young rabbit, and test its age after the manner described in regard to the hare (1810), and also by means of a little lentil-shaped bone, which is to be found in the region of the leg joint.

As the wild rabbit ages, this bone shrinks and finally combines with the other bones of the joint.

When the wild rabbit is old, it is tough, and can only be used for stock or *forcemeats.*

All the recipes given for *"Poulet Sauté,"* and those given for hare, may be applied to wild rabbit: the reader is, therefore, asked to refer to these.

1827—FEATHERED GAME   *Gibier à Plume*

Feathered game comprises all edible birds that live in freedom.

The number of species involved, therefore, is considerable, but from the culinary standpoint game birds may be grouped into ten principal classes, which are:—

1. The various pheasants, grey and red partridges, the Tetras Californias.
2. The hazel-hen, grouse, prairie fowls, ganga, sand-grouse.
3. The various wild ducks and mallards.
4. The woodcocks and snipes.
5. The various plovers, lapwings, sandpipers, water-rails, water-hens.
6. The quails, land-rails, Virginia quails.
7. The various thrushes, Corsican blackbirds.
8. The various larks.
9. The warblers.
10. The ortolans.

The birds of Classes 1 and 4 are better high (seasoned)—that is to say, they should be hung for a few days, before being plucked, in a moderately cool place, that they may begin to decompose, and that the particular flavor of their flesh may be accentuated, a process which increases their culinary value. Whatever opinion may be held in regard to the gaminess of these birds, one thing is quite certain—namely, that the meat of a fresh pheasant and that of a high one are totally different. When fresh, the meat is flavorless, whereas when it is reasonably high it is tender, full of taste, and of an incomparable flavor.

Formerly, it was the custom to *lard* the birds of Class 1, especially when they were to be roasted. But this practice should be discarded, for, if the bird is young, it can only impair the flavor, and, if it is old, it cannot possibly restore those qualities to it which it has already lost.

Besides, an old bird should never be served; it ought only to be used in the preparation of game stock or *forcemeats*.

The birds belonging to the remaining classes are prepared fresh; or, if it is thought necessary to let them hang for a few days, at least they should not be allowed to get high (seasoned), more particularly the aquatic ones, because gaminess is, if anything, injurious to the flavor of their flesh.

In the United States it is forbidden to shoot many of these birds. Only in those states in which small birds such as the bob-white

quail become a nuisance do laws permit of their being shot. Therefore the recipes given here for larks, ortolans, etc., will merely
serve to give the reader an idea of what can be done with them.
Aside from those birds which may be shot here, there are a number
of imported birds on the market, to the joy of diners who know
how delicious a whole brochette of tiny fried birds can be.

(The feathered game which may be shot in the United States
includes the ruffed grouse, the partridge, the pheasant, the quail,
the prairie hen, the wild goose, the wild turkey (in some regions),
and about fifty different breeds of wild duck and mallard. The birds
mentioned above which are not native to the United States are
usually available, as imports, in the game markets.—Ed.)

1828—PHEASANT   *Faisan*

When this bird is young, its legs are grey and the belly end of
the breast-bone is tender and flexible. But with pheasants, as with
partridges, an infallible sign of youth may be discovered at the extremity of the last large feather in the wing. If this feather is pointed,
the bird is young; if it is round, the reverse is the case.

(This fine game bird is frequently found wild in the United
States and also often raised on pheasant farms.—Ed.)

1829—PHEASANT ALCANTARA   *Faisan à la Mode d'Alcantara*

This recipe comes from the famous Alcantara convent. History
tells us that at the beginning of the Portuguese campaign in 1807
the convent's library was pillaged by Junot's soldiers, and its pre-
cious manuscripts were used in the making of cartridges.

Now it happened that an officer of the commissariat who was
witnessing the event found, among a collection of recipes selected
by the monks, the particular one now under our notice, which was
applied only to partridges.

It struck him as interesting, and after trying it when he returned
to France in the following year, he surrendered it to the Duchess
of Abrantès, who noted it in her memoirs.

It represents, perhaps, the only good thing the French derived
from that unfortunate campaign, and it would tend to prove that
foie gras and truffles, which had been known for so long in Langue-
doc and Gascony, were also known in Estremadura, where, even at
the present day, tolerably good truffles are to be found.

The procedure is as follows:

Draw the pheasant from the front; bone its breast, and stuff it with fine ducks' *foies gras* (livers), mixed with quartered truffles, cooked in port wine.

Marinate the pheasant for three days in port wine, taking care that it be well covered therewith. This done, cook it *"en casserole"* (the original recipe says "on the spit," but the saucepan is more suitable). Reduce the port wine of the *marinade;* add to it a dozen medium-sized truffles; set the pheasant on these truffles, and heat for a further ten minutes.

N.B.—This last part of the recipe may be advantageously replaced by the "à la Souvaroff" treatment—that is to say, having placed the pheasant and the truffles in a *terrine,* sprinkle them with the reduced port combined with slightly buttered game *glaze* (17); then hermetically seal down the lid of the *terrine,* and complete the cooking in the oven.

1830—PHEASANT A L'ANGOUMOISE   *Faisan à l'Angoumoise*

Stuff the pheasant with a preparation consisting of two-thirds lb. of very fresh pork fat, rubbed through a sieve; four oz. of raw, peeled, and quartered truffles, and four oz. of fine chestnuts, cooked in consommé.

This preparation, which should be seasoned as for the ordinary truffling (1956), ought to be quite cold when stuffed into the pheasant.

Wrap the bird in slices of bacon; roast it gently for three-quarters of an hour, and take care to remove the slices of bacon seven or eight minutes before the cooking is completed, that the outside of the pheasant may be browned.

Set on a platter, and serve a Périgueux sauce (47) at the same time.

1831—BOHEMIAN PHEASANT   *Faisan à la Bohémienne*

Season a small *foie gras* with salt and paprika; *stud* it with raw quartered truffles, and *poach* it in Madeira for twenty minutes.

When it is cold, insert it into the pheasant, which should be high (seasoned). Truss the bird, and cook it in butter in a saucepan or a *cocotte* for forty-five minutes. When about to serve, remove some of the butter used in cooking; sprinkle the pheasant with a glass of burnt brandy, and add a few tablespoons of reduced game gravy to the cooking-liquor.

Serve the pheasant in its cooking utensil.

1832—PHEASANT IN CASSEROLE *Faisan en Casserole*

Truss the pheasant as for an entrée, and *poële* it in butter only. This done, swirl in the saucepan a few drops of brandy and table-spoon of game gravy.

Cover the utensil, and serve the dish burning hot.

1833—PHEASANT IN COCOTTE *Faisan en Cocotte*

Proceed exactly as for pheasant *"en casserole,"* and, when the cooking is two-thirds done, surround it with a garnish of small onions cooked in butter and small, cooked mushroom-caps and olive-shaped truffles, the latter taking the place of the potatoes, which are one of the garnishing ingredients of fowls *"en cocotte."*

1834—CHARTREUSE OF PHEASANT *Faisan en Chartreuse*

Parboil a fine, round-headed, quartered cabbage, and *braise* it as directed in (2100), adding an old, oven-browned pheasant.

The *chartreuse* may be made with the pheasant kept whole or cut into pieces, but in any case, roasted or *poëled*, it should be very tender and just cooked. The old pheasant put in with the cabbage only serves in imparting its flavor to the latter, but it must not and cannot be used for the *chartreuse*.

If the *chartreuse* is made with a cut-up pheasant, proceed as in the case of (1778). If whole, line an oval mould *chartreuse*-fashion; coat the inside with a portion of the *braised* cabbage, which should be slightly pressed; set the pheasant, breast down, in the mould; cover it with what remains of the cabbage, and then turn it out on a dish.

Serve a sauceboat of excellent half-*glaze* (23) flavored with pheas-ant *fumet*, separately.

1835—PHEASANT WITH SAUERKRAUT *Faisan à la Choûcroute*

Prepare the sauerkraut after (2097), and bear in mind that when it is specially prepared to accompany a pheasant, it is considerably improved by being *braised* with *foie-gras* fat.

Poële a very tender pheasant, and just barely cook it. Lay the well-drained sauerkraut on a platter; set the pheasant on it, and surround it with a border of rectangles of bacon, cooked in the sauerkraut.

Serve separately the *poële*-liquor combined with a little game *fumet*, strained and kept somewhat greasy.

1836—PHEASANT WITH CREAM   *Faisan à la Crème*

Cook the pheasant in butter, in a saucepan, with a medium-sized, quartered onion. When the cooking is three-quarters done, sprinkle the bird with one-quarter pint of cream (sour if possible), or with ordinary cream, acidulated by means of a few drops of lemon juice.

Finish the cooking, basting the piece with cream, and serve in the saucepan.

1837—DEMIDOFF PHEASANT   *Faisan Demidoff*

Proceed exactly as directed under "Poulet à la Demidoff" (1464).

1838—GEORGIENNE PHEASANT   *Faisan à la Georgienne*

Truss the pheasant as for an entrée, and put it into a saucepan with thirty fresh, halved, and well-peeled walnut meats; the juice of two lbs. of grapes and of four oranges, pressed through a sieve; a wineglass of Malmsey wine; a glass of strong, green tea; one and one-half oz. of butter, and the necessary seasoning.

Poach the pheasant in this preparation for about thirty minutes, and brown it when it is almost cooked.

When about to serve, surround it with fresh walnuts.

Strain the cooking-liquor through a napkin; add one-third pint of game *Espagnole* (22), and reduce to half.

Slightly coat the pheasant and its garnish with the sauce, and serve what remains of the latter separately.

1839—GRILLED DEVILLED PHEASANT   *Faisan Grillé Diable*

For this preparation only young pheasants are used; although, provided they are tender, older pheasants will answer the purpose. The procedure is precisely the same as that described under "Poulet Grillé (1636).

1840—KOTSCHOUBEY PHEASANT   *Faisan Kotschoubey*

Cook the pheasant *"en casserole,"* and add to it, when it is almost done, two oz. of fine, raw truffle slices, and a little excellent game *glaze* (17), clear and well buttered.

Serve the following garnish separately:—Fry in butter four oz. of *blanched,* fresh bacon fat, cut into dice. When the pieces are properly frizzled, add to them one lb. of freshly-cooked, well-drained, uncooled, and roughly-chopped Brussels sprouts. Add two oz. of fresh butter, a little pepper and grated nutmeg, and stew gently for one-half hour, that the garnish may just be ready in time for serving

1841—NORMANDY PHEASANT   *Faisan à la Normande*

Brown the pheasant in butter.

Meanwhile quarter, peel, mince, and slightly toss in butter six medium-sized apples.

Garnish the bottom of a *terrine* with a layer of these apples; set the browned pheasant on top; surround it with what remains of the apples; sprinkle it with a few tablespoons of fresh cream; cover the *terrine,* and cook in the oven for from twenty to twenty-eight minutes.

Serve the preparation in the *terrine.*

1842—PERIGUEUX PHEASANT   *Faisan à la Périgueux*

Stuff the pheasant with truffles, proceeding as for ordinary truffling (1956). *Poële* it in Madeira; put it on a dish, and surround it with a border of *quenelles* consisting of truffled game *forcemeat,* moulded by means of a teaspoon, and *poached* at the last moment.

Serve separately a *Périgueux Sauce* (47) combined with the reduced *poëlé*-liquor, cleared of all grease.

1843—REGENCE PHEASANT   *Faisan à la Régence*

Poële the pheasant, and place it on a low *croûton* bed, carved from a sandwich-loaf and fried in butter.

Surround it with small, decorated, round game *quenelles;* large, grooved, cooked mushrooms; and cocks' kidneys; all three arranged alternately.

Serve separately a *Salmis Sauce* (55), flavored with truffle essence, and combined with the strained and reduced *poëlé*-liquor, cleared of all grease.

1844—SAINTE ALLIANCE PHEASANT   *Faisan à la Sainte-Alliance*

Bone two woodcocks, and put their livers and intestines aside.

Chop up their meat, together with a quarter of its weight of *poached* and cooled beef-marrow, and as much fresh, fat bacon; salt, pepper, and herbs. Add to this hash six oz. of raw, peeled, and quartered truffles, slightly cooked in butter.

Stuff the pheasant with this preparation; truss it; wrap it in slices of bacon, and keep it in a cool place for twenty-four hours, so that the fragrance of the truffles may be concentrated.

Roast the pheasant on the spit, or, if in the oven, set it on a somewhat high rack in a baking-pan. Cut a large *croûton* from a sandwich-loaf, and fry it in clarified butter (175).

Grind the woodcocks' livers and intestines with an equal weight of grated fresh, fat bacon, the well-washed fillets of an anchovy, one oz. of butter, and one-half oz. of raw truffle. When this *force-meat* is very smooth and all its ingredients thoroughly mixed, spread it over the fried *croûtons*.

When the pheasant is two-thirds cooked, set this coated *croûton* under the bird in such a way as to allow the juices escaping from it to fall upon the *croûton*. Complete the cooking, and serve the pheasant on the *croûton*. Surround with slices of bitter orange, and serve the gravy separately.

When serving, accompany each piece of pheasant with a slice of orange and a small slice of the coated *croûton*.

1845—SOUVAROFF PHEASANT　　　　　　*Faisan Souvaroff*

Cook six fair-sized truffles for five minutes in a glass of Madeira and an equal quantity of light meat *glaze* (15). Take out the truffles and put them in the *terrine* in which the pheasant will complete its cooking.

Cut one-half lb. of *foie gras* into large dice; stiffen these in the truffles' cooking-liquor, and stuff the pheasant with them. Truss the bird; wrap it in slices of bacon, and two-thirds *poële* it.

This done, put it into the *terrine* containing the truffles; add the *poële*-liquor, a small glass of Madeira, and the same quantity of game gravy; tightly close the *terrine,* and continue cooking for about a quarter of an hour.

Serve the preparation as it stands.

1846—SUPREMES (BREASTS), CUTLETS, AND FILLETS OF PHEASANT
Suprêmes, Côtelettes, et Filets de Faisan

Pheasant Suprêmes, Cutlets and Fillets, take the same garnishes as those of fowl. But, whereas in the case of the latter, they are lifted out raw, and then *poached,* my advice in regard to pheasant is, that it should be previously roasted or *poële* (keeping it just underdone) and that the *suprêmes* be only lifted out at the last moment.

By this means, a much better result is obtained than by the *poaching* of raw fillets; which, once cooked, are generally dry if they have to wait but a few seconds.

I also advise, when the garnish consists only of *foie-gras* slices and truffles (as in the case of the Rossini garnish), the serving separately of a small *timbale* of noodles with cream.

1847—SALMIS OF PHEASANT
Salmis de Faisan

Salmis is perhaps the most delicate and most perfect of the game preparations given us by old-fashioned cookery. If it is less highly esteemed nowadays, it is owing to the fact that this recipe has been literally spoiled by the haphazard fashion in which it has been applied right and left to game already cooked, and cooked again for the purpose.

But the *Salmis* given above may always be included in any menu, however sumptuous. It is applied more particularly to game of the 1st and 2nd classes (see 1827), which should be somewhat high (seasoned) when treated.

The recipe I give may be applied to all the birds in the two classes referred to.

Roast the pheasant, keeping it moderately underdone. Quickly cut it into eight pieces, thus: two legs, two wings (separated from the pinions or wing tips), and the breast cut into four lengthwise pieces. Skin the pieces; trim them neatly, and keep them at a low heat in a covered pan, with a few drops of burnt brandy and a little clear melted meat *glaze* (15).

Pound the bones and the trimmings, and add to them half a bottle of red wine (almost entirely reduced), three chopped shallots and a few mignonette peppers or peeled peppercorns. Add one-quarter pint of good game *Espagnole Sauce;* cook for ten minutes; rub through a sieve, pressing well, and then strain.

Reduce this sauce to about one-third, and skim it; strain it once more through a fine mesh strainer; add a small quantity of butter, and pour it over the pieces of pheasant, to which add a fine, sliced truffle and six fluted mushroom-heads.

I advise the discarding of the old method of serving on a bed of bread fried in butter, as also of the triangular *croûtons* fried in butter and coated with *gratin forcemeat,* which usually accompanied the *Salmis.*

A speedy preparation and a simple method of serving, which hastens the service and permit the *Salmis* being eaten hot, are the only necessary conditions. Moreover, the richness of this preparation is such as to make it independent of an ornate method of serving.

1848—SAUTE OF PHEASANT
Sauté de Faisan

Unless it is prepared with the greatest care, *sauté* of pheasant is always dry. I therefore do not recommend it; but, should it be necessary to make it, care should be observed in selecting a young, plump bird. It should be cut up like a fowl, cooked in butter on a moderate fire and kept somewhat underdone.

Cook it after the manner of a "chicken *sauté*" and cover it. Swash the saucepan and prepare a sauce after the recipe in common use.

This sauce must always be rich, and it should be poured over the pheasant just before serving it.

1849—HOT PATE OF PHEASANT   *Pâté Chaud de Faisan*

The preparation of hot, raised pheasant pies is the same as usual; the ingredients alone changing. The reader will, therefore, kindly refer to "*Paté chaud de Canard*" (1752), and note the following modifications:—

(1) Use a *gratin forcemeat* (202) prepared from game livers and meat.

(2) Roast the pheasant, keeping it underdone, and mix the pieces of cooked mushroom with the sliced truffles.

(3) Accompany the pie by a *Salmis Sauce* (55), prepared from the pheasant's bones and pickings.

1850—MOUSSES AND MOUSSELINES OF PHEASANT

Mousses et Mousselines de Faisan

As already stated in various parts of this work, the ingredients and their quantities are the same for *mousses* and *mousselines,* and but for the basic ingredient, which is pheasant in this case, the procedure does not differ from that already described.

The base of the sauces served with these *mousses* and *mousselines* is a *fumet* made from the bones and remains.

1851—SOUFFLE OF PHEASANT   *Soufflé de Faisan*

Prepare a very light, *mousseline forcemeat* of pheasant.

Set in a buttered *soufflé* saucepan, and cook in a moderate oven.

Serve a fine, half-*glaze* sauce (23), flavored with game essence, at the same time.

COLD PHEASANT

1852—BOHEMIAN PHEASANT   *Faisan à la Bohémienn.*

Proceed as for "*Faisan à la Bohémienne*" (1831). Cook it in an earthenware *terrine,* and add, at the same time as the prescribed brandy, enough juicy, savoury aspic to fill up the *terrine.*

Leave to cool for a day or two, and, when about to serve, remove with a spoon the grease that has settled on the surface. Remove the last bits of grease by repeated scaldings; carefully wipe the *terrine,* and serve it incrusted in a block of ice.

1853—CHAUD-FROID OF PHEASANT   *Chaud-Froid de Faisan*

Proceed exactly as for *"Chaud-froid de Volaille"* (1689), and use a brown chaud-froid sauce (34), flavored with pheasant *fumet.*

In regard to the decoration, serving, etc., follow the recipe already referred to.

1854—CHAUD-FROID OF PHEASANT A LA BULOZ
Chaud-Froid de Faisan à la Buloz

Poële a pheasant, keeping it underdone; lift out its *suprêmes* (breasts), and cut these into thin slices.

With a *fumet* prepared from the bird and the *poëlé*-liquor, pre-pare a brown chaud-froid sauce (34). Coat the slices with this sauce, and also coat ten cooked and fluted mushrooms with a white chaud-froid sauce (72).

Coat a *dome-mould* with clear aspic jelly, and decorate it with truffles.

Set the slices of pheasant and the chaud-froid-coated truffles in-side, alternating the two in so doing; fill up the mould with the same aspic jelly, and let it set on ice. When about to serve, turn out after the manner of an aspic, on a low bed of rice or semolina, lying on a round dish.

Border with neatly-cut *croûtons* of very clear aspic.

1855—PHEASANT A LA CROIX DE BERNY   *Faisan à la Croix de Berny*

Roast the pheasant and keep it underdone. When it is quite cold, lift out its breasts and leave the legs and the wings attached to the bird.

By means of scissors, completely bone the bird; garnish it inside with a truffled *foie-gras Parfait,* and cover it with a thin coat of *foie-gras Mousse.*

Replace the breasts upon this *Mousse,* after having sliced them, and fill any gaps that may exist between the slices with some of the same *Mousse,* thus reconstructing the bird.

Let the *Mousse* set thoroughly, and *glaze* with aspic jelly.

Meanwhile, coat eight boned, stuffed, *poached* and cold larks with brown chaud-froid sauce (34). Decorate them with pieces of truffle and tongue, and *glaze* them with aspic jelly.

Serve the pheasant on a low bed; surround it with the larks. and garnish the gaps between with chopped and very clear aspic.

1856—PHEASANT EN DAUBE   *Faisan en Daube*

Proceed as for *"Terrine de Poularde à la gelée"* (1701), making due allowance, in the cooking, for the difference between the sizes of the two birds.

1857—CUTLETS OF PHEASANT   *Côtelettes de Faisan*

Proceed as for *"Côtelettes froides de Volaille."*

1858—GALANTINE OF PHEASANT   *Galantine de Faisan*

See *"Galantine de Volaille"* (1708).

1859—MOUSSE OF PHEASANT   *Mousse de Faisan*

Prepare the *Mousse* according to the usual procedure, and mould it after the manner of *"Mousse de Volaille"* (1711).

1860—PHEASANT LOAF EN BELLE VUE   *Pain de Faisan en Belle Vue*

The procedure follows that of (1709), but for the difference in the basic ingredient, which in this case is pheasant.

1861—BREASTS OF PHEASANT CHATELAINE

Suprêmes de Faisan Châtelaine

Lift out the *suprêmes* (breasts) and prepare them exactly like the *suprêmes* of fowl in *"Chaud-froid Félix Faure"* (1691). *Poach* them; cool them, and cut them into medallions (about the size of a half dollar) as explained.

Cover half of these medallions with Chicken *Mousse,* and the other half with Pheasant *Mousse.* Keep on ice for some time that the *Mousse* may set. This done, coat the first lot with brown chaud-froid sauce (34) and the second lot with white chaud-froid sauce (72). Decorate each medallion with small pieces of truffle. Set them in a deep, square dish (alternating the two colors), and cover with very clear, juicy aspic jelly. Leave to set and serve on a block of ice.

1862—BREASTS OF PHEASANT GASTRONOME

Suprêmes de Faisan Gastronome

Poêle the pheasant in Madeira and let it cool. Lift out the breasts; cut them into thin, regular slices; coat them with brown chaud-froid sauce (34), and decorate according to fancy. With the trimmings and the meat of the legs, prepare a Pheasant *Mousse* after the manner described under (1711), and mould it in a *Parfait mould* which should have the depth of the chaud-froid-coated slices.

When this *Mousse* has set, turn it out on a dish and place the slices all round, standing them upright and letting them lean one against the other.

Surround with a crowd of fine, fair-sized, peeled truffles, cooked in Champagne, and set one of them on the top of the *Mousse,* fixing it there by means of an ornamental skewer.

Border the dish with fine *croûtons* of aspic.

1863—TERRINE OR PATE OF PHEASANT   *Terrine de Faisan*

Prepare it after the manner of the *"Terrine de Lièvre"* (1825), and take care to make due allowance, in the cooking, for the difference, in the matter of tenderness, between the two meats. But the explanations already given on this subject ought to suffice for ascertaining whether or not the patty has cooked sufficiently.

PARTRIDGE (PERDRIX ET PERDREAUX)

Three kinds of partridges are used in European Cookery:—the Grey Partridge, which is commonest in flat country, and which is also the most highly esteemed; the Red Partridge, which is to be found in hilly and wooded country; and the Bartavelle (perdix vertevella), which is a somewhat larger species than the two former. To these three kinds may be added the American.

All the recipes given for pheasants may be applied to partridge, and below, I shall only give those which are proper to the latter.

(Partridge is an excellent bird easily procured. It may be shot in the United States or bought in the market as a South American import.—Ed.)

1864—BOURGUIGNONNE PARTRIDGE   *Perdreau à la Bourguignonne*

Truss the partridge as for an entrée; three-quarters *poële* it, and place it in a *terrine* with six small *glazed* onions and as many small, cooked mushroom heads. Swirl in the saucepan a glass of red wine; reduce it two-thirds, and add a tablespoon of game half-*glaze* (17). Strain; clear of fat; pour this sauce over the partridge, and complete the cooking for seven or eight minutes.

1865—DEMI-DEUIL PARTRIDGE   *Perdreau en Demi-Deuil*

Bone the breast and fill the partridge with truffled partridge *forcemeat,* prepared with *panada* (189) or butter. Between the skin and the fillets (breasts) slip a few slices of very black truffle; truss as for an entrée; wrap the pieces in muslin, and *poach* it for thirty minutes in a game *fumet.*

When about to serve, remove the muslin; take the string off, and put the partridge on a dish. Reduce the *fumet* in which the partridge has *poached;* strain it; add a liqueur-glass of burnt liqueur-brandy, and serve this reduced *fumet* separately.

1866—ESTOUFFADE OF PARTRIDGE   *Perdreau en Estouffade*

Brown the partridge in the oven and set in a *terrine* just large enough to hold it, with a tablespoon of Matignon (227) and one crushed juniper berry, on top and underneath.

Add one-half oz. of butter, a liqueur-glass of burnt brandy, and twice that amount of game *fumet*. Close the *terrine;* seal down the lid with a strip of paste (flour and water); bake in a hot oven for twenty-five minutes and serve the dish as it stands.

1867—LAUTREC PARTRIDGE   *Perdreau à la Lautrec*

Select a young partridge; split open its back; slightly flatten it with a butcher's beater or cleaver; pierce it through with a skewer; season it with salt, pepper and melted butter, and gently grill.

At the same time broil six small mushroom-caps.

Arrange the partridge; on either side of it set the mushrooms, each of which should be garnished with a teaspoon of Maître-d'hôtel butter (150); surround the mushrooms with a ribbon melted meat *glaze* (23) and sprinkle the partridge with a few drops of lemon juice.

1868—LADY CLIFFORD PARTRIDGE   *Perdreau Lady Clifford*

Cook the partridge in butter in a saucepan. When it is three-quarters done, surround it with two oz. of fine slices of raw truffle; add a liqueur-glass of burnt brandy and one tablespoon of clear melted meat *glaze* (15).

Serve a Soubise sauce (104) at the same time and separately.

1869—PARTRIDGE WITH CABBAGE   *Perdreau aux Choux*

Prepare a garnish of *braised* cabbages as explained under (2100), and add an old partridge, browned in the oven or on the spit. Meanwhile, roast or *poêle* a very tender young partridge and keep it underdone.

Put the cabbages, which should be well drained, on a dish; set the young partridge upon them, and surround with small rectangles of very lean bacon, cooked with the cabbages, and a ribbon of half-*glaze* sauce (23), flavored with game *fumet*.

Chartreuse: This dish may be given a more decorative appearance by means of a *Chartreuse,* which is prepared as follows:—Line a large bowl or a buttered, round-bottomed *timbale* with slices of sausages; slices of carrots arranged in rows, separated by a line of string beans or peas; and small rectangles of bacon, laid side by side.

Line the inside of the *timbale* with a thick layer of cabbages, and put the young partridge, breast down, in the middle (the partridge may also be carved up). Cover the cabbages and press the latter with a fork; turn the *timbale* out on a dish and tilt the latter so that all the grease may drain off before withdrawing the *timbale,* which answers the purpose of a mould.

Surround with a ribbon of half-*glaze* sauce (23), flavored with game *fumet.*

1870—CREPINETTES OF PARTRIDGE   *Crépinettes de Perdreau*

After substituting the meat of a young partridge, cleared of all tendons, for the veal sweetbreads, and fresh bacon for calf's udder, proceed exactly as directed (as regards quantities and other particulars) under *"Crépinettes de Ris de Veau"* (1222), taking care to add three oz. of chopped truffles per lb. of the *forcemeat.*

Divide up the *forcemeat* into portions one and one-half oz. to two oz. in weight; wrap them in *pig's caul;* roll them first in melted butter and then in bread-crumbs, and grill them gently.

The usual accompaniment to these *crépinettes* is a light chestnut or lentil *purée.*

1871—EPIGRAMMES OF PARTRIDGE   *Epigrammes de Perdreau*

Lift out the young partridge's breasts, leaving the wing-bone attached to the bird, and put them aside. From the smaller breasts and the meat of the legs, prepare a *mousseline forcemeat;* mould the latter in very small buttered *cutlet moulds,* and set to *poach.*

Roll the breasts in melted butter and bread-crumbs, and grill them gently. Dip the cutlets in beaten egg; roll them in finely-chopped truffles; press upon the latter with the flat of a knife, that they may combine with the egg; shape the cutlets, and toss them in butter.

Arrange in the form of a circle, alternating the breasts and the cutlets; pour in their midst a *cullis* prepared from the partridge's remains, and serve a chestnut *purée* separately.

1872—TIMBALE OF PARTRIDGE DIANE   *Timbale de Perdreau Diane*

Line a liberally-buttered, shallow mould with crescents of truffle arranged in rows one upon the other, and then completely cover the bottom and sides of the mould with a layer, two-thirds in. thick, of raw partridge *forcemeat*.

Place the mould in the oven that the *forcemeat* may be *poached;* and then spread another layer of *gratin forcemeat* of game.

Fill the utensil with a garnish of small *quenelles* consisting of truffled partridge *forcemeat*, mushrooms and slices of truffles, mixed with a reduced Madeira sauce. Cover the garnish with a small coat of *forcemeat*, and *poach* in the *bain-marie* (water-bath) for from thirty to thirty-five minutes.

When about to serve, turn out on a dish, and decorate the *timbale* with a crown of partridges' *suprêmes* (breasts), lifted off from birds fresh from the spit or the oven. Surround the base of the *timbale* with a thread of Diane sauce, and serve a sauceboat of the latter separately.

1873—COLD PARTRIDGE *Perdreaux Froids*

The various recipes given for cold pheasant also suit cold partridge; it is only necessary therefore to replace the word "pheasant" by "partridge" in the recipes referred to.

1874—WOODCOCK AND SNIPE *Bécasse et Bécassines*

If grouse, which can only be thoroughly appreciated in its native country, were extinct, woodcock would be the leading feathered game. But the latter have this advantage over the former, namely: that their *fumet* is not so fugitive, and that they may be kept much longer. Woodcock does not yield its full quality unless it be moderately high (seasoned).

1875—WOODCOCK CAREME *Bécasse de Carême*

Sprinkle the woodcock with a few drops of oil, and roast it, keeping it underdone. As soon as it is cooked, split it into two lengthwise, and cut each half of the breast into two slices. Mix half a teaspoon of French mustard in a small pan, with a few drops of lemon juice. Roll the pieces of woodcock in this mustard, and keep them hot.

Chop up the bird and the intestines; sprinkle with a glass of burnt liqueur brandy; reduce; add a tablespoon of game *fumet,* and cook for five minutes.

Strain, pressing on the pieces of woodcock in so doing, and tilt the saucepan back and forth, that the pieces may be coated with the *cullis*. Serve in a hot *timbale,* and, upon the pieces, set the woodcock's head.

N.B.—*Bécasse à la fine Champagne* is prepared in the same way, but without mustard. Cut it into six pieces: wings, legs and two halves of the breast, and put these pieces into a round *cocotte*. Swirl in the saucepan burnt liqueur brandy; add the chopped intes-tines, mixed with the juices of the pressed bird; add a tablespoon of *fumet*, a little lemon juice, and a little cayenne, and pour this *cullis* (heated but not boiled) over the pieces.

Bécasse à la Riche is prepared in the same way, but the pieces are placed on a *croûton* of fried bread, coated with *gratin forcemeat* of game: the sauce is thickened with a little *foie-gras purée* and one oz. of butter, and then strained over the pieces through a coarse sieve, during which process the cook should press it with a spoon.

1876—WOODCOCK FAVART   *Bécasse à la Favart*

Proceed as for *"Caneton Rouennais Soufflé"* (1764), and remem-ber to add the woodcock's intestines to the *forcemeat*.

When the bird is stuffed, set the sliced *suprêmes* (breasts) on the *forcemeat*, with a row of sliced truffles in the middle. The *forcemeat* should *poach* for about twenty minutes.

Serve at the same time a half-*glaze* sauce (23), flavored with wood-cock *fumet*.

1877—SALMIS OF WOODCOCK   *Salmis de Bécasse*

Under the article "Pheasant," I gave the general recipe for *Salmis*, which may be applied to all feathered game. In regard to the Wood-cock Salmis, the cook should remember to add the bird's intestines, fully minced, to the sauce, and to keep the meat rather rare than overdone.

1878—WOODCOCK SOUVAROFF   *Bécasse Souvaroff*

Proceed exactly as for *"Faisan Souvaroff"* (1845), after making due allowance for the size of the bird in regard to the quantity of truffles and *foie gras*.

1879—MOUSSES AND MOUSSELINES OF WOODCOCK
Mousses et Mousselines de Bécasse

Proceed as indicated in (1850).

1880—TIMBALE OF WOODCOCK METTERNICH
Timbale de Bécasse Metternich

Prepare a somewhat shallow, decorated *timbale* crust.

Roast the woodcocks and keep them underdone.

Lift off the *suprêmes* (breasts) and put them in the *timbale*, separating them by slices of fresh *foie gras, sautéd* at the last moment.

Grind the remains of the woodcocks, including their bones; thin the *purée* with truffle *essence;* rub it through a strainer, pressing heavily, and then rub it through a very fine sieve.

Heat the *cullis* thus obtained, without letting it boil; finish it with a little lemon juice, liqueur-brandy and butter, and pour it into the *timbale* over the pieces of woodcock and the *foie gras* slices.

Serve the *timbale* on a folded napkin on a round dish.

1881—TIMBALE OF WOODCOCK NESSELRODE

Timbale de Bécasse Nesselrode

Poële the woodcocks and keep them underdone.

As soon as they are cooked, lift out their fillets (breasts) and put these aside.

Bone the remains, and grind the meat, together with a quarter of its weight of raw *foie gras.*

Rub through a sieve, and add an equal weight of game *forcemeat,* prepared with *panada* and butter (193). Add the chopped birds and a glass of liqueur brandy to the *poëlé*-liquor; cook for a few minutes; strain, and in this stock *poach* five oz. of olive-shaped truffles (for an ordinary *timbale*).

Line a buttered *Charlotte-mould* with short paste (2356); cover its bottom and sides with the prepared *forcemeat,* and against this *forcemeat* set the woodcock's *suprêmes* (breasts), cut into slices. Garnish the center with the truffles, and cover these with a few tablespoons of *Espagnole,* reduced with some of the *fumet.* Close the *timbale* with a layer of paste, as explained in the various preceding *timbale* recipes, and bake in a good, moderate oven for about forty-five minutes.

When about to serve, turn out the *timbale* on a dish; pour into the former some half-*glaze* (23) sauce combined with what remains of the *fumet,* and serve a sauceboat of the same sauce separately.

N.B.—This *"Timbale Nesselrode"* may be prepared after the same recipe from Pheasant, Partridge, Woodcock or Hazel-Hen, but the name of the selected bird should, of course, appear on the menu.

1882—COLD WOODCOCKS AND SNIPES

Bécasses et Bécassines Froides

All the recipes given for cold pheasant and partridge may be applied to woodcocks and snipes.

1883—QUAILS
Cailles

Quails should always be chosen plump, and their fat should be white and very firm. Besides the spit, which should always be used in preference to the oven for roasting, they permit of two other methods of cooking: they may be cooked in butter, in a saucepan; or they may be *poached* in excellent strong and gelatinous veal stock.

This last mode of procedure greatly improves the quail's quality and is frequently used.

1884—QUAILS IN CASSEROLE
Cailles en Casserole

Cook them in butter, in the saucepan in which they will be served.

Swirl in the pot a few drops of brandy; add a little game *fumet;* cover, and serve very hot.

1885—QUAILS WITH CHERRIES
Cailles aux Cerises

For four quails:—Truss them as for an entrée and cook them with butter in a saucepan. Swash and swirl with a little brandy and a glass of port, in which a piece of orange rind should have soaked.

Add three tablespoons of excellent veal stock, three tablespoons of red-currant jelly and about forty cherries, previously *poached* in a boiling syrup of about 18° (Saccharometer) and cooled in the syrup.

Drain them before adding them to the quail, and, if the sauce is too insipid, sharpen it with a few drops of lemon juice.

1886—QUAILS DAUPHINOISE
Cailles à la Dauphine

Wrap each quail in a buttered vine-leaf and a thin, square slice of bacon, and roast them for ten minutes.

Meanwhile, prepare a well-seasoned *purée* of fresh peas with lettuce, and reduce it to a somewhat stiff consistency.

Line the bottom and sides of a deep dish with very thin slices of ham; pour the *purée* into it; smooth the surface, and plunge the quails half way up into this *purée.*

Place in the oven for ten minutes, and this done, send the dish to the table immediately.

1887—QUAILS FIGARO
Cailles Figaro

Insert a piece of truffle into each quail, and wrap them each in a piece of casing with a bit of pale veal *glaze,* the size of a pigeon's egg. Tie the pieces of casing at two points one in. from either end of the quails, that the casing may not burst while cooking. *Poach* the quails in good veal stock, so that they may not be *blanched* as they would be if the casing happened to burst in a *poaching*-liquor consisting of salted water.

Serve the quails as soon as they leave their cooking-liquor.

1888—QUAILS GREEK STYLE　　　　*Cailles à la Grecque*

Cook the quails in a saucepan, and set them in a *timbale*, half-garnished with *"Riz à la Grecque"* (2253). Swirl and scrape the saucepan with a few tablespoons of game *fumet*, and pour this liquor over the quails, without clearing it of grease.

1889—QUAILS JULIETTE　　　　*Cailles Juliette*

Split the quails into two along the back and do not separate the two halves; season them; sprinkle them with melted b.ttter and finely-chopped truffle. Wrap each quail in a piece of *pig's caul;* sprinkle again with melted butter and fine *raspings,* and grill gently.

Put the quails on a dish and sprinkle them with a few drops of *verjuice.*

1890—QUAILS JUDIC　　　　*Cailles Judic*

Poêle the quails.

Arrange them in the form of a crown, each on a small, *braised* lettuce, with a cock's kidney on either side and a truffle on top. Coat with a half-*glaze* sauce (23) prepared with quail *fumet.*

1891—QUAILS LUCULLUS　　　　*Cailles Lucullus*

Cook the quails in butter. Arrange them in a circle on a round dish, each on an oval or rectangular fried *croûton,* and between each set a fine truffle cooked in Champagne and chicken *glaze.*

1892—QUAILS NORMANDE　　　　*Cailles à la Normande*

Peel, mince and toss some apples in butter, as explained under *"Faisan à la Normande."* Allow half an apple per quail. Garnish the bottom of a *cocotte* with some of these apples; upon them set the quails, browned in butter; add what remains of the apples; sprinkle with a few tablespoons of cream, and complete the cooking in the oven.

1893—QUAILS WITH GREEN PEAS A LA ROMAINE
Cailles aux Petits Pois à la Romaine

Cook the quails in butter. At the same time, fry in butter one small new onion and two-thirds oz. of raw, chopped ham, for each quail. Add some peas, shelled at the last moment, and cook without any liquid whatsoever.

The moisture contained in the ham and peas is sufficient for the cooking. The peas should be ready simultaneously with the quails.

Serve the quails and the peas separately, in little, closed *timbales*.

1894—QUAILS WITH GRAPES   *Cailles aux Raisins*

Cook the quails in butter. Swirl in the utensil a few drops of dry, white wine and a little *verjuice;* add half a tablespoon of strong game *fumet* for each quail; and serve in a very hot *cocotte* with about one oz. of fresh peeled grapes for each quail.

1895—QUAILS RICHELIEU   *Cailles Richelieu*

Select some fresh and plump quails; remove their gizzards; season them inside with a few grains of salt and a few drops of brandy; insert a piece of raw truffle into each bird, and truss them as for an entrée. Set them in a saucepan, snugly pressed one against the other, and season them with salt. Cover them with a coarse *julienne* of carrots, onions and celery, cooked in butter, and prepared as far as possible from new vegetables.

Moisten, just enough to cover, with some juicy amber-colored veal stock, gelatinous and fine; cover, boil, and then *poach* gently for twelve minutes.

This done, add a *julienne* of truffles (raw if possible) which should equal only half of the vegetable *julienne,* and *poach* for a further two minutes, that the truffles may cook and the quails be done.

Set in a *timbale,* cleared of fat, and pour the cooking-liquor and the *julienne* over the quails.

Pilaff rice (2255) is often served with quails prepared in this way.

1896—RISOTTO OF QUAILS   *Rizotto de Cailles*

Into each quail insert a piece of fresh, ground pork fat, the size of a hazel nut, combined with an equal quantity of white truffle; and cook them in a saucepan with butter.

Add the quail parfait fat to a previously-prepared *rizotto.* Place this *rizotto* in a *timbale,* and hollow it out so as to make a nest for the quails.

Sprinkle the latter with the saucepan scrapings and gravy, consisting of game *fumet;* and send the dish to the table at once.

1897—QUAILS SOUS LA CENDRE (UNDER THE ASHES)
Cailles sous la Cendre

Stuff the quails with a little smooth truffled game *forcemeat,* and wrap them each in a buttered vine-leaf, followed by a slice of bacon, and finally by two sheets of buttered parchment paper.

Place them on the hearth-stone; cover them with very hot cinders, and cook thus for thirty-five minutes, taking care to renew the hot cinders from time to time.

When about to serve them, remove the outside covering of paper which is charred, but leave the other coverings.

N.B.—A log fire is essential for this recipe.

1898—QUAILS SOUVAROFF
Cailles Souvaroff

Prepare these as described under *"Faisan à la Souvaroff"* (1845).

1899—QUAILS TURKISH STYLE
Cailles à la Turque

Truss the quails as for an entrée; brown them in butter, and complete their cooking in pilaff rice (2255), combined with a quarter of its weight of cooked and chopped eggplant pulp.

Set the rice in a pyramid on a dish; place the quails all round (upright against the rice), and surround with a ribbon of quail *fumet.*

1900—TIMBALE OF QUAILS ALEXANDRA
Timbale de Cailles Alexandra

Coat a well-buttered *timbale mould* with patty paste (2356), and line it with slices of bacon so as to completely cover the paste. The slices of bacon in this case are there to prevent the moistening of the *timbale* from reaching the pastry. Insert a piece of *foie gras* into each quail; brown them in butter, and set them against the sides of the *timbale.*

Completely fill the center with small, peeled truffles; add one-quarter pint of excellent stock with Madeira (per six quails), and a few bits of bay leaf. Close the *timbale* with a layer of pastry and cook in a moderately hot oven for one and one-quarter hours.

Turn out upon taking from the oven, and serve the dish as it stands.

N.B.—The shell of pastry merely serves to hold in the quails and their filling and is not eaten.

Or the same *timbale* may be prepared with ortolans (small song-
birds), except that these need only forty-five minutes' cooking.

COLD QUAILS

1901—CHAUD-FROID OF QUAILS EN BELLE VUE
Chaud-Froid de Cailles en Belle Vue

The quails should be boned for a chaud-froid, and stuffed with
gratin forcemeat of game with a round strip of *foie gras* and another of truffle set in the middle. This done, reshape them; wrap
them each in a square of muslin; *poach* them for twenty minutes
in an excellent veal stock, and let them cool in it.

When they are quite cold, dry them; and dip them, so as to cover
them all over, in a good brown chaud-froid sauce (34), prepared
with quail *fumet*. Decorate the breast of each quail with bits of
truffle and *poached* white of egg; sprinkle with cold melted savory
jelly, so as to fix the decoration; and leave to set.

Remove the excess of sauce from around the quails; set them in
a square, deep dish; cover them with very good transparent savory
aspic, and place them in a refrigerator until they are required.

1902—QUAILS IN CASES   *Cailles en Caisses*

Prepare the quails as for a chaud-froid (34), as above; but set
each in an oval, fluted case of delicate porcelain or paper. Border
with a ribbon of chopped aspic, and on each quail set a glazed
quail's head, the eyes of which may be imitated by means of a ring
of white of egg and a bit of truffle.

1903—GLAZED QUAILS GRANITE   *Cailles Glacées au Granité*

I shall only give a few recipes of this class; for the series is a long
one, and I recommend them more particularly on account of their
quaintness. These dishes wherein a sweetened preparation and a
glazed one are introduced together are highly esteemed in summer;
but they really belong in the culinary repertory of hot countries.

1904—GLAZED QUAILS CERISETTE   *Cailles Glacées Cerisette*

Prepare the quails as for an entrée and *poach* them for 12 minutes in a strong veal stock, with Champagne. This done, put them
each into a small, oval mould; fill up these moulds with cooking-
liquor, cleared of all grease and strained, and leave them to set on
ice.

This preliminary procedure applies to all quail dishes in this series.

Now prepare a *Granité* with cherry juice (2930).

Set this *Granité* in a pyramid on a dish inserted in cracked ice. Turn out the quails and place them round the *Granité;* fill up the gaps between them with small heaps of pitted cherries, *poached* in syrup for a few minutes and quite cold.

1905—GLAZED QUAILS CARMEN   *Cailles Glacées Carmen*

Prepare the quails as above, and place them round a rock of *Granité* made from pomegranates.

1906—GLAZED QUAILS MARYLAND   *Cailles Glacées Maryland*

Set them round a rock of *Granité* made with pineapple.

1907—GLAZED QUAILS QUEEN AMELIE   *Cailles Glacées Reine Amélie*

Prepare the quails in the usual way, and lay them round a rock of *Granité* prepared with tomatoes.

1908—GLAZED QUAILS ROMANEE   *Cailles Glacées au Romanée*

Poach the quails in stock combined with Romanée wine, and set them round a rock of *Granité* made with *verjuice*.

1909—BREASTS OF QUAILS AUX POMMES D'OR
Filets de Cailles aux Pommes d'Or

Lift out the quails' *suprêmes* (breasts), after having *poached* and cooled them. Set these *suprêmes* (breasts) in the rinds of small oranges or tangerines, and fill up the rinds with aspic jelly prepared with Port. When about to serve, decorate each orange or tangerine, by means of the pastry-bag, with a small ornament of *Granité*, prepared with the juice of the fruit used.

1910—QUAILS CECILIA   *Cailles Cecilia*

Roast the quails, keeping them juicy, and leave them to cool.

This done, lift out their breasts and skin these; then, with the remains of the meat and an equal quantity of *foie gras*, prepare a *purée*.

Set each breast of quail on a similarly-shaped slice of *foie gras*, causing it to adhere by means of the prepared *purée*, and coat with brown chaud-froid sauce (34).

When the sauce has quite set, place these breasts in an even *border-mould*, coated with very transparent aspic, and decorated with truffles. Fill up the mould with the same aspic jelly, and let it set.

When about to serve, turn out on a napkin after the manner of an aspic.

1911—QUAILS WITH CHATEAU-YQUEM   *Cailles au Château-Yquem*

Prepare the quails like those "à la Richelieu" (1895). After having added the *julienne*, sprinkle them with Château-Yquem wine; cover; reduce, and complete their cooking as directed.

When they are *poached*, transfer them to another saucepan; add ten slices of truffle per quail; strain their cooking-liquor through muslin over them, and *poach* them for a further two minutes.

This done, place the quails in a *timbale;* cover them with the cooking-liquor cleared of all grease; leave it to set, and serve on a block of ice.

1912—TANGERINES OF QUAILS   *Mandarines de Cailles*

Remove the tangerine rinds at their stem-ends with an even round cutter; take out the sections; let them dry, and skin them.

Three-quarters fill the tangerine shells with a quail *Mousse,* combined with *foie gras,* cut into dice; set a roasted quail's breast on the *Mousse;* coat with brown chaud-froid sauce (34), and cover with the sections of tangerine, *glazed* with aspic jelly. Keep in a cool place for some time and serve on a napkin.

1913—QUAILS NILLSON   *Cailles Nillson*

Proceed as for "*Cailles au Château-Yquem*," and set each quail in a small, silver *cassolette.* Cover with the cooking-liquor, cleared of grease and strained, and surround each quail with four small very white (blanched) cocks' kidneys.

1914—COLD QUAILS RICHELIEU   *Cailles Richelieu Froides*

Prepare these like the "*Hot Cailles Richelieu*"; place them in a square, deep dish; cover with the cooking-liquor and the garnish and let them cool until the cooking-liquor sets. Then clear the dish of all grease and serve on a block of ice.

1915—TIMBALE OF QUAILS TZARINA   *Timbale de Cailles Tzarine*

Line a round pie-dish with ordinary pastry (2356), and coat it inside with slices of bacon. In the middle, place a fresh *foie gras* seasoned with salt, pepper and allspice, and surround it with quails, stuffed with quarters of truffles, set upright with their breasts against the bacon.

Fill up the *timbale* with whole raw and peeled truffles; cover with a round slice of bacon; close the *timbale* with a layer of pastry sealed down round the edges; make a slit in the top, and bake in a hot oven for one and one-quarter hours.

When taking the *timbale* from the oven, pour into it some veal stock (9) flavored with Madeira, and let it be sufficiently gelatinous to set like an aspic.

Keep the *timbale* in a cool place for one or two days before serving it.

1916—QUAILS VENDANGEUSE   *Cailles à la Vendangeuse*

Roast the quails; let them cool, and set them, each in a little basket of dry pastry, resting against a bed lying on a round dish. On top of the bed plant a leafy vine-branch with a bunch of grapes. Surround the quails with white and black grapes (peeled and seeded) and cover with a slightly gelatinous aspic, prepared with liqueur brandy.

1917—MOUSSES OF QUAILS   *Mousses de Cailles*

See the various remarks made concerning this subject, under Pheasant, Partridge and Woodcock.

1918—LAND RAIL, KING OF QUAILS   *Râle de Genêts, Roi de Cailles*

The Land Rail, which must not be confused with the Water Rail, is most often served roasted, but all the quail recipes, hot or cold (except those in which *Granité* forms an accompaniment) may be applied to it.

1919—HAZEL-HENS   *Gelinottes*
1920—BLACK GAME   *Petit Coq de Bruyère*
1921—PRAIRIE-HENS   *Poules de Prairie*
1922—PTARMIGAN   *Lagopède*
1923—GROUSE   *Grand Coq de Bruyère*
1924—GANGAS   *Gangas*

These birds, one or two of which, such as grouse and the hazel-hen, are of incomparable delicacy and high culinary value, are mostly served roasted.

Mousses, Mousselines and *Salmis* are also prepared from them, after the directions already given. But I must remind the reader that when they are served in the preparation of a salmis, their skins and legs, which are bitter, must be discarded.

All these birds must be treated while still very fresh.

1925—THRUSHES AND CORSICAN BLACKBIRDS
Grives et Merles de Corse

The greater part of the quail recipes, more particularly the *"en casserole"* and *"sous la cendre"* ones, may be applied to these excellent birds.

The two following recipes are proper to them.

1926—THRUSHES OR BLACKBIRDS BONNE FEMME
Grives ou Merles à la Bonne Femme

Cook the birds in butter, with one oz. of very small dice of salt bacon to each bird. Put them into a hot *cocotte* with two-thirds oz. of butter per bird; heat; add some square *croûtons* fried in butter; sprinkle with the saucepan-swirlings, which should include a few drops of brandy; cover, and serve very hot immediately.

1927—THRUSHES OR BLACKBIRDS LIEGEOISE
Grives ou Merles à la Liègeoise

Cook the birds in butter in an uncovered earthenware saucepan. When they are nearly done, sprinkle them with two finely-chopped juniper berries per bird; add some round *croûtons* of bread fried in butter; cover, and serve very hot.

This procedure particularly suits thrushes.

1928—COLD THRUSHES AND BLACKBIRDS   *Grives et Merles Froids*

The various, cold preparations of quails, except those comprising a *Granité,* may be applied to thrushes.

LARKS

These birds are generally served two or three for each person.

1929—LARKS BONNE FEMME   *Mauviettes à la Bonne Femme*

Proceed exactly as directed for the thrushes.

1930—LARKS MERE MARIANNE   *Mauviettes à la Mère Marianne*

Slice some peeled and cored russet apples, and three-quarters cook them in butter. Spread this sauce in thick layers on a buttered dish. Simply brown the seasoned larks in nut-brown butter (154), and place them upon the apples, pressing them slightly into the latter. Sprinkle with very fine bread-crumbs and melted butter, and set to *glaze* in the oven or at the *salamander,* just long enough to complete the cooking of the larks.

1931—LARKS OF PERE PHILIPPE — *Alouttes du Père Philippe*

Clean some fine, medium-sized potatoes, allowing one to each lark; and cut a cover from each, scraping it until it is only one-sixth inch thick. With a ballspoon, hollow out the potatoes in such a way that they each enclose a lark.

Brown the larks in butter, and add thereto some salt pork belly, cut into small dice and *blanched,* and in the proportion of one-third oz. per lark. Place a lark in each potato, together with a few bacon dice and some of the cooking-fat; return cover of each potato to its original place; tie it by means of cotton, and wrap each potato in oiled paper.

Proceed as in (1897). (In the United States we would bake the larks in a hot oven.—Ed.)

1932—COLD LARKS — *Mauviettes Froides*

When cold, larks may be prepared in plain chaud-froid (34) fashion, in cases, in Bellevue, in Aspic, as *Mousses,* etc., according to the directions given under these various recipes.

1933—ORTOLANS — *Ortolans*

Serve ortolans as plainly as possible; but the best method of preparing them is roasting. However, for the sake of variety, they may be prepared as follows:—

1934—SYLPHIDES OF ORTOLANS — *Sylphides d'Ortolans*

Butter some very small porcelain or silver *cassolettes,* and fill them half-full with *mousseline forcemeat* of ortolans prepared with truffle *essence.*

Set these *cassolettes* in the oven, that the *forcemeat* may *poach.* Cook in butter, for three minutes only, as many ortolans as there are garnished *cassolettes,* and proceed so as to have them just ready when the *forcemeat* is *poached.*

Place an ortolan in each *cassolette,* and sprinkle them with nut brown butter (154), combined with a little pale melted *glaze* (16) and pineapple juice.

1935—FIG PECKERS   *Becs-Figues et Beguinettes*

These birds are not met with in American markets; it is therefore useless to give the recipes concerning them. I will only say that they may be prepared like the larks.

1936—WILD DUCK   *Canards Sauvages*
1937—TEAL   *Sarcelles*
1938—PINTAILS AND WIDGEONS   *Pilets*

Birds of this class are mostly served roasted.

They may, however, be used in preparing excellent *Salmis,* which may be made after "Salmis de Faisan" (1847) or after "Salmis à la Rouennaise" (1763).

They may also be prepared after all the recipes of "Caneton à la Rouennaise."

1939—GOLDEN PLOVER   *Pluviers Dorés*
1940—LAPWINGS   *Vanneaux*
1941—VARIOUS SANDPIPERS   *Chevaliers Divers*

These various birds are generally served roasted.

They may also be served *"en Salmis,"* but in that case the skin must be discarded in the preparation of the *cullis.*

They only appear on very ordinary menus, and could not be served at an important dinner.

CHAPTER XVII

ROASTS AND SALADS

IN THE first part of this work I explained the fundamental principles governing the treatment of Roasts, and I now have to add only a few words to what has already been said. Recipes may be complete in detail and in accuracy, and still they will be found wanting in the matter of Roasts; for experience alone can tell the cook whether the joint he is treating be old or young, fresh or stale; whether it must be cooked quickly or slowly, and all the theories that I might advance on this subject, though perhaps they might not be useless, would at least prove impracticable nine times out of ten.

I shall not prescribe any limit of time for Roasts, except in very special cases, and even so that limit will only be approximate.

Nothing can be made precise in the matter; long practice alone, away from books, will teach it; for book-rules can only be understood when the light of practical knowledge is focussed upon them.

1942—ACCOMPANIMENT OF ROASTS   *Accompagnement des Rôtis*

It struck me as desirable that I should give in this chapter also those recipes of the various preparations which, in England, famous for its Roasts, are served with Roasts:—Yorkshire Pudding, Veal Stuffing, etc. Having treated of the accompanying sauces to Roasts in Part I, I need only recall them here.

1943—YORKSHIRE PUDDING (FOR BEEF ROASTS)
Yorkshire Pudding (Pour Rôtis de Boeuf)

Mix one-half lb. of sifted flour with six eggs and one quart of boiled milk, adding the eggs one by one and the milk little by little. Season with salt, pepper and nutmeg.

Pour this preparation into a deep baking-pan, containing some very hot dripping, and bake in the oven. If the joint is roasted on the spit, put the Yorkshire pudding under it, on taking the pudding out of the oven, and let it thus become saturated with the gravy and fat that fall from the roast.

Cut into squares or diamond shapes, and set these round the Roast or serve them separately.

1944—SAGE AND ONION STUFFING (FOR TURKEYS, DUCKS, AND GEESE) *Farce à la Sauge (Pour Dindes, Canards, et Oies)*

Bake four large onions in the oven with their skins on. This done, peel them and finely chop them; fry them in butter with a pinch of dry green chopped sage. Add bread-crumbs, soaked in milk and pressed, equal in weight to the onions, and half the weight of chopped veal fat.

1945—VEAL STUFFING (FOR VEAL AND PORK) *Farce de Veau (Pour le Veau et le Porc)*

This stuffing is made from equal quantities of chopped suet, sifted bread-crumbs, and chopped parsley. Season with salt and pepper as for an ordinary *forcemeat*, and be liberal with the nutmeg.

Combine this *forcemeat* with three small eggs per two lbs. of the above preparation.

1946—ROASTS OF MEAT *Rôtis des Viandes*

I must remind the reader of this principle, that (according to formal French ideas of the early century) however natural it may seem in a dinner to serve a roasted joint as a *Relevé*, a piece of meat of a four-footed animal must never stand as a Roast.

Roasts, in my opinion, really only comprise *Fowl and Feathered Game*, provided the menu only announces one roast. If two are announced, the second generally consists of some kind of crustacean, such as a *Lobster*, a *Spiny Lobster* or *Crayfish*, generally served in the form of a *Mousse*; or of a preparation of *foie gras*, either a *Pâté*, a *Terrine*, a *Mousse* or a *Parfait*; sometimes, too, by a very good ham or a derivative preparation thereof.

BEEF ROASTS

1947—ROAST RIBS OF BEEF *Côte de Boeuf Rôti*

Clear the joint of the backbone and the yellow ligaments. Roast in a moderately hot oven, and place the joint if possible in an uncovered roasting-pan, the sides of which may protect the meat during the cooking process.

1948—ROAST UPPER-FILLET   *Filet de Boeuf Rôti*

Bread the projecting rib bones of the backbone, and sever the yellow ligament at various points. For this joint the heat should be hotter than in the previous case, the limit of time being less.

1949—ROAST SIRLOIN   *Contre-filet de Boeuf Rôti*

These enormous pieces are scarcely trimmed; the excess of flank alone is removed; but the fillet must remain covered by a considerable thickness of fat, which protects it while roasting.

Without this precautionary measure, the under-cut would be cooked long before the upper-fillet, and would dry out.

The fire should be concentrated, regular and not too hot for this joint. The flat ribs of the backbone must be broken at their base, but not detached.

1950—FILLET OF BEEF   *Aloyau de Boeuf Rôti*

Fillet of beef intended for roasting should be carefully trimmed of its two sinewy coverings. But, since this trimming tends to let it dry while cooking, were the meat left as it stands, it is customary to *lard* it with strips of fresh fat bacon, which protect it; or it may be wrapped in slices of bacon. In certain circumstances, it is covered on top and beneath with slices of beef fat, flattened to the thickness of a rasher of bacon by means of a mallet or cleaver, and tied on with string.

Fillet of beef should be cooked with a somewhat hot fire, and is usually kept rare towards the center.

N.B.—Large roast joints of beef may be accompanied by Yorkshire pudding, grated Horse-radish or Horse-radish Sauce (119 or 138).

1951—VEAL ROASTS   *Rôtis de Veau*

In my opinion, the spit does not suit veal of any quality. *Poëling* (250) is preferable and suits it better.

The quality of meat can but be enhanced under the treatment I suggest, more particularly as the *poëlé*-liquor constitutes a much richer gravy than that which generally accompanies veal roasted on the spit. In some countries roast veal is accompanied by boiled ham or bacon. *Veal Stuffing* (1945) *poached* in steam in a special mould, and cut into slices, is served at the same time.

Roast joints of veal are generally the *Loin*, the *Rump*, the *Breast* or the *Tenderloin*.

Sometimes, too, but more rarely, the *Shoulder* is roasted.

1952—MUTTON AND LAMB ROASTS   *Rôtis de Mouton et d'Agneau*

Mutton and Lamb are the best possible meats to roast, and, as far as they are concerned, the culinary treatment might be limited to roasting.

True, good results are obtained from *poaching* mutton and *poêlé* spring lamb; but it is advisable only to have recourse to these methods when a menu requires varying.

The Mutton joints roasted are the *Leg, the Double or Pair of Hind-legs, the Baron* or *Hindquarters, the Saddle* and *the Neck.*

The *Shoulder* also makes an excellent roast, but it may only appear on more or less unimportant menus.

Roast joints of mutton and lamb are always accompanied by Mint Sauce (136).

1953—PORK ROAST   *Rôtis de Porc*

Pork roasts may only appear on very ordinary menus, and really belong to domestic cookery. The pork joints for roasting are *the Hams, the Tenderloins,* and *the Shoulder.*

The joints selected should be those from very young animals, and the rind should be left on them, and cut deeply in criss-cross lines, so as to form a diamond pattern.

Pork should always be roasted before a hot fire, and it is accompanied by its gravy and Sage and Onions (1944) or Apple Sauce (112). Sometimes Apple Sauce is replaced by Cranberry Sauce (115); while Robert Sauce *Escoffier* (53) is also admirably suited to these roasts.

1954—VENISON ROASTS   *Rôtis de Venaison*

I have already pointed out that Roebuck is not much eaten in the United States. This excellent ground game must be used without having been *marinated.* Every piece of roebuck must be trimmed and cleared of tendons, *larded* with larding bacon, or, at least, carefully wrapped in the latter; and roasted in a hot oven and kept rare towards the center.

The joints of roebuck most commonly roasted are *the Legs* and *the Saddle.*

The fallow white tail and *mule Deer* and *the Stag* supply the greater part of the venison consumed in the United States; and when these animals are of good quality their flesh is covered by a thick coat of white fat, which is very highly esteemed by connoisseurs. Only the neck and the haunch should be roasted, and the latter consists of one leg with half of the saddle attached.

This venison is never *marinated,* but it should be kept for as long as possible in a dry and well-aired place, that the meat may be seasoned (high).

Before hanging the joint, dredge it well with a mixture of flour and pepper, that it may keep dry and free from the flies.

When about to prepare this venison, scrape off the coating of flour; wrap it in an envelope of firm dough or paste made with suet. Cover the whole with oiled vegetable parchment, tied on with string; and roast the joint before a very hot oven.

When the joint is thought to be cooked, peel off its pastry envelope; season it with salt; sprinkle it with a few pinches of flour, and plenty of melted butter, and brown it as quickly as possible.

Large joints of venison allow of the following accompaniments: —*Poivrade Sauce* and its derivatives, such as *Venison Sauce* and *Grand-Veneur Sauce;* also *the Cumberland* and *Oxford Sauces* of English cookery. Generally a sauceboat of red-currant jelly is served with these joints, unless the accompanying sauce already contains some of it.

Fowl Roasts

FOWL ROASTS　　　　　　　　　　　　　　*Rôtis de Volaille*
1955—PULLETS　　　　　　　　　　　　　　　　*Poulardes*

Large birds, when roasted, should always be salted inside, trussed and covered with slices of bacon. They should be cooked in a concentrated and moderately hot oven. About ten minutes before completing the cooking, remove their covering of bacon, so that their breasts may brown.

A bird is known to be cooked when the juice which issues from it, if it be held over a plate, is white. Having ascertained that it is cooked, set it on a very hot dish and serve it instantly.

In England particularly (rarely in other countries), it is customary to surround the fowl with grilled sausages or slices of bacon, and to serve a sauceboat of bread sauce (113) at the same time as the gravy.

1956—TRUFFLED PULLET　　　　　　　　　　*Poularde Truffée*

Draw the pullet intended for truffling through a little hole on the side of the belly, and remember to keep the skin of the neck whole. This done, remove the collar bone at the top of the breast, and detach the skin from the whole of the breast.

For a fine pullet, there will be needed one and one-half lbs. of truffles.

After having well brushed and washed the truffles, carefully peel them; select one of the largest; cut it into slices, and put these aside.

Now quarter the other, letting each piece weigh about three oz.

Grind the truffle peel with two lbs. of very fresh pork fat, and rub the whole through a sieve. Take about one-half lb. of this fat; melt it, together with a bay leaf; and, when it is quite liquid, add the quartered truffles to it (seasoned with salt and pepper), and simmer for about ten minutes.

This done, take it off the fire; leave to cool slightly covered, and mix with what remains of the truffled fat.

Stuff the pullet with this preparation, and slip between the bird's skin and the flesh of its breast some thin slices of bacon. Upon the slices of bacon place the reserved slices of truffle; carefully sew up all the openings in the pullet with thread; wrap it in one or two sheets of buttered parchment paper; put it on the spit, and stand it before a concentrated fire which should be kept at an even heat throughout the process of roasting.

About one-quarter of an hour before serving, remove the paper and the slices of bacon, so that the breast may brown. Set on a hot platter, and serve the gravy, which should be kept rather fat, separately.

The time allowed for roasting a fine fowl is somewhere between one and one-quarter to one and one-half hours.

1957—CHICKEN A LA REINE AND SPRING CHICKENS
Poulet à la Reine et Poulets de Grains

The directions given for the pullet also apply to other kinds of fowl, provided the difference in size be taken in account.

1958—SPRING CHICKENS A LA RUSSE *Poulets de Grains à la Russe*

Truss the chicken and soak its breast for five minutes in boiling water, that the flesh and the skin may be stiff.

Lard it with thin strips of bacon and anchovy fillets; fill it with smooth, truffled sausage-meat, and roast it on the spit.

At the last moment, when the bird is cooked, baste it using a special funnel, with very hot melted bacon fat, which should frizzle the fowl's skin as it falls upon it.

Serve a *Rémoulade Sauce* (130) separately.

1959—ROAST SQUAB CHICKENS *Poussins Rôtis*

These birds should, if possible, be cooked *"en casserole."*

1960—ROAST YOUNG TURKEYS *Dindonneaux Rôtis*

Before trussing the young turkey, clear its legs of all tendons; an operation done by means of two incisions made on the inside of the legs, above and below the last joint. Seize the tendons one by one; fasten them to a large needle or skewer, and gently turn it, thus rolling the tendons round it.

Young turkey is covered with slices of bacon and roasted like the Pullet.

It may be stuffed with sage and onions (1944), or it may be accompanied by veal stuffing (1945), *poached* in steam in a special mould, and cut into slices set around the bird.

It is often accompanied, also, by boiled or grilled bacon, or grilled sausages. A bread sauce or a cranberry sauce may be served in addition to the gravy.

1961—TRUFFLED YOUNG TURKEY *Dindonneaux Truffés*

Proceed as for truffled pullet, after taking the difference of size into account in order to increase the quantity of truffles and fat, as also the time limit.

1962—ROAST GOSLING *Oison Rôti*

The Gosling, in order to be roasted, should just have reached its full growth. The bird is stuffed with sage and onions (1944), and it is always accompanied by apple sauce (112).

This roast must not stand waiting, and ought to be served very hot.

1963—ROAST DUCKLING *Caneton Rôti*

Long Island duckling, of which the Pekin variety is best known, is generally stuffed with sage and onions before being roasted.

Its most usual accompaniment is apple sauce, which is sometimes replaced by melted, red-currant jelly or a cranberry sauce.

1964—ROAST DUCKLING ROUENNAIS *Caneton Rouennais*

See the various recipes dealing with this bird (1761 and 1762).

1965—GUINEA FOWL *Pintade*

This bird is only roasted when quite young, and it is treated like the pheasant, with which it has some points in common.

1966—YOUNG PIGEONS (SQUABS) *Pigonneaux*

Select them fresh from the nest and very plump. They must be roasted in a very hot oven and only barely done. Their skin must be kept crisp.

Ground Game Roasts

1967—ROAST HARE *Lièvre Rôti*

The piece supplied by the hare for roasting is the *"râble"* (the saddle and back), which constitutes that part of the animal reaching from the root of the neck to the tail, the latter being included.

The *"râble"* should be cleared of all tendons, and delicately *larded* with bacon.

Roast in a hot oven for twenty minutes, and have it only just done. The usual accompaniment to this piece is Poivrade Sauce (102). In Northern countries the sauces and the accompaniment most common are slightly-sugared, stewed apples, or red currant jelly.

In Germany, the pan in which the *râble* (saddle) is roasted is swished with sour cream, and this cream constitutes the accompaniment. Sometimes a few drops of lemon juice or a tablespoon of melted meat *glaze* is added.

1968—ROAST YOUNG RABBIT *Levraut Rôti*

The various recipes for Hare also apply to the young wild rabbit.

Feathered Game Roasts

1969—ROAST PHEASANT *Faisan Rôti*

Everything I said in the preceding chapter concerning the classification of feather game applies in this instance.

All birds intended for roasting should be young, plump, and fat. They should also be high (seasoned) in the case of pheasants, partridges, and the various kinds of woodcock and snipe.

A pheasant for roasting should always be covered with slices of bacon.

An excellent practice which greatly improves the bird is that of stuffing it with a piece of fresh pork fat, ground with peelings of fresh truffles if possible.

Instead of well-ground fresh pork fat, an equal weight of fresh butter may be used.

This fatty substance penetrates the meat when it melts, and

keeps the bird from becoming dry while cooking. The method also applies to partridge. Roast pheasant is generally accompanied by two trimmed half-lemons and a dish of potato chips. The gravy, which should be fat, is served in a sauceboat, and bread sauce or some bread-crumbs fried in butter are served at the same time.

1970—PERIGOURDINE ROAST PHEASANT

Faisan Rôti à la Périgourdine

Stuff the pheasant with two oz. of ground fresh pork fat, two oz. of *foie-gras* trimmings, and a similar quantity of raw truffle parings, the whole ground together and combined with one-half lb. of raw truffles, cut into large dice.

After having covered the pheasant with slices of bacon, roast it in accordance with the directions given under Truffled Pullet. It is better, however, to cook and serve it in a *cocotte*.

1971—GUNZEBOURG ROAST PHEASANT　　*Faisan à la Gunzebourg*

Bone two fine snipes; take out their intestines; fry these in butter, and crush them on a plate. Chop up the meat of the snipes, combining half its weight of cream with it, and as much butter; season with salt and pepper, and add the crushed intestines and four oz. of truffles cut into large dice.

Stuff a fine pheasant with this preparation; roast it *"en casserole,"* or rather in a *cocotte*.

At the last moment sprinkle with a little *fumet,* prepared from the snipes' remains.

1972—ROAST PARTRIDGE　　　　　　　　*Perdreau Rôti*

The above recipes, dealing with pheasants, may be applied to partridges.

1973—ROAST QUAILS　　　　　　　　　*Cailles Rôtis*

Select them white, very fat, and with the fat firm.

Wrap them in a buttered vine-leaf and a thin slice of bacon, and roast them in a hot oven for ten or twelve minutes.

Serve on small bread *croûtons,* fried in butter with half-lemons.

Serve their gravy, which, of course, should be very rich, separately.

1974—ROAST ORTOLANS　　　　　　　　*Ortolans Rôtis*

Wrap each in a vine-leaf; set them on a pan, moistened with salted water. and cook them in a very hot oven for four or five minutes.

The small amount of water lying on the bottom of the utensil produces an evaporation which prevents the ortolans' fat from melting; consequently there is no need of slices of bacon, butter, or gravy.

Each ortolan may be served in a half-lemon, shaped like a basket.

N.B.—The ortolan is sufficient in itself, and it ought only to be eaten roasted. The products sometimes served as accompaniments to it, such as truffles and *foie gras,* are injurious, if anything, to its quality, for they modify the delicacy of its flavor, and this modification is more particularly noticeable the more highly flavored the additional products may be.

With its accompaniments it becomes a sumptuous dish, for the simple reason that it is expensive; but it does not follow that the true connoisseur will like it; it must be plainly roasted to suit him.

1975—ORTOLANS WITH PRUNES　　　　*Ortolans aux Questches*

Cut two very large prunes into halves, and allow one half for each ortolan. Garnish the inside of each with a piece of butter the size of a hazel-nut; set them in a pan, and put them in the oven. When they are almost cooked, on each half of prune place a moistened ortolan, wrapped in a vine-leaf, and bake them in a very hot oven for four minutes.

Salt them when taking them out of the oven, and baste them, by means of a brush, with *verjuice.*

Serve them as they stand, but the prunes are not eaten; they only serve as a support for the ortolan.

1976—ORTOLANS WITH PINEAPPLE JUICE　　*Ortolans au Suc d'Ananas*

Heat some fresh butter in a flat, earthenware *cocotte,* and allow one-quarter oz. of it to each ortolan. Roll the previously salted ortolans in this butter, and put them in a very hot oven for three minutes.

When taking them out of the oven, sprinkle them with a few tablespoons of very cold pineapple juice. Cover the *cocotte,* and serve immediately.

The *cocotte* should be just large enough to hold the ortolans.

1977—ROAST WOODCOCK　　　　　　*Bécasses Rôtis*

It should be just sufficiently high (seasoned). Remove its gizzard; truss it, piercing the legs with the beak, after having drawn the eyes; cover it with slices of bacon, and cook it in a hot oven for from fifteen to eighteen minutes. Serve on a bed of fried bread *croûtons*, and serve the swirling-liquor, which in this case should be brandy and a few drops of good game gravy, separately.

1978—ROAST SNIPES AND BECOTS   *Bécassines Rôtis*

For the preparation, proceed as for the woodcock.

Cook in a very hot oven for nine minutes.

1979—ROAST THRUSHES AND CORSICAN BLACKBIRDS
Grives et Merles de Corse Rôtis

Truss them, and wrap them in slices of bacon. Insert a juniper berry into each thrush. Roast in a moderately hot oven for ten or twelve minutes, and set on small beds of fried bread *croûtons*.

Serve a very rich gravy separately.

1980—ROAST LARKS   *Mauviettes Rôtis*

Wrap them in very thin slices of bacon, and stick them on a skewer, or discard the slices of bacon, and merely stick the larks on a skewer, separating them by *blanched* squares of bacon.

Roast for ten minutes in a hot oven.

Serve on small fried *croûtons*, with quarters of lemon and bunches of watercress around them.

1981—ROAST WILD DUCKS   *Canards Sauvages Rôtis*

These birds are not covered with slices of bacon, but simply roasted in a hot oven.

Wild duck must be kept underdone, and, in view of this, twenty minutes suffice for its roasting. Serve with lemons and bunches of watercress around it.

Wild duck, roasted English-fashion.—Treat it as above; serve an apple sauce with it.

Wild duck à la Bigarrade.—This is roasted in a similar manner.

Surround it with sections of skinned raw orange, and serve a clear *Bigarrade Sauce* (31) separately.

The *teal*, which is a small, wild duck, is roasted in a hot oven for from ten to twelve minutes, and is surrounded with lemons and watercress.

Widgeons and *pintails* are treated like the teal, but they are allowed three or four minutes more in the roasting.

1982—ROAST TEAL *Sarcelles Rôtis*
ROAST GOLDEN PLOVERS *Pluviers Dorés Rôtis*
ROAST LAPWINGS *Vanneaux Rôtis*
ROAST SANDPIPERS *Chevaliers Divers Rôtis*

These birds are not covered with slices of bacon; they must be roasted in a very hot oven, and kept somewhat underdone. They must be served as soon as ready, as waiting is injurious to them.

They permit of no accompaniment or garnish, except a very rich gravy.

1983—ROAST WIDGEONS AND PINTAILS *Pilets Rôtis*
ROAST GROUSE, BLACK GAME, AND HAZEL-HENS
Coqs de Bruyère et Gelinottes Rôtis

These birds must be very fresh when roasted, and should be kept moderately underdone.

They take the same accompaniments as pheasant—bread sauce, *croûtons,* potato chips, and gravy; and their breasts alone are served as a rule. Grouse and hazel-hens, when they are young, make incomparably fine roasts.

SALADS

Salads are of two kinds: simple, or compound. Simple, or raw salads always accompany hot roasts; compound salads, which generally consist of cooked vegetables, accompany cold roasts.

1984—THE SEASONING OF SALADS *Assaisonnement des Salades*

1. *Oil Dressing* may be applied to all salads, and is made up of three parts of oil to one part of vinegar, with salt and pepper.

2. *Cream Dressing* is particularly well suited to salads of early-season lettuce and romaine lettuce, and is made of three parts of very fresh and not very thick cream to one part of vinegar.

3. *Egg Dressing* is prepared from crushed hard-boiled yolks of egg mashed through a sieve and mixed in the salad-bowl with oil, vinegar, salt, and pepper. The whites of egg, cut into thin strips, are added to the salad. This dressing may also be a light mayonnaise sauce.

4. *Bacon Dressing* is used especially for dandelion, red-cabbage, and corn salad or field salad. In this case the oil is replaced by the grease of the bacon dice, which are melted and frizzled in the omelet-pan. This grease is poured while hot, with the bacon dice, over the salad, which should be in a hot salad-bowl and already

seasoned with salt, pepper, and the vinegar which has served in swashing the omelet-pan.

5. *Mustard with Cream Dressing* is used particularly with beet salads, with salads of celeriac or knob celery, and with green salads wherein beet plays a major part. It is made up of a small tablespoon of mustard, mixed with one-third pint of fresh and somewhat thin cream, the juice of a fair-sized lemon, salt, and pepper.

N.B.—I should like to point out that mayonnaise sauce must only be used in very small quantities in the dressing of salads. It is indigestible, and many constitutions cannot suffer it, especially at night at the end of a dinner.

Raw onion should likewise only be used in salads with great moderation, in view of the fact that so many do not like it. In any case, it should be finely shredded or sliced, washed in fresh water, and pressed in the corner of a towel.

1985—SIMPLE SALADS *Salades Simples*

They comprise, in the first place, those salads known under the name of green salads. Such as lettuce, romaine lettuce, chicory, endive, batavia (similar to water-cress), celery, corn-salad or field salad, dandelion, purslain, dittander, rampion, salsify (oyster plant) leaves, *blanched* dandelion, etc.

1986—BEET SALAD *Salade de Betterave*

Beets are really the accompaniment of compound and simple salads, and it is always best to cook it in the oven. If it is prepared especially as a salad, cut it into a *julienne* or into thin slices; flavor it with onions, first baked in coals and then finely chopped, and season it with mustard sauce or with oil, according to fancy. Always add some chopped herbs.

1987—CELERY SALAD *Salade de Céleri*

For salads, only the fibreless, white celery hearts are used. Cut it into pieces, and shred these into very thin strips without completely separating them at their base. Place in cold water for a few hours, that the strips may curl; drain and season with a mustard sauce with cream (299a).

1988—CELERIAC SALAD *Salade de Céleri-râve*

Cut the celery root into a fine *julienne* or *paysanne*.

Season, according to fancy, with a mustard sauce (299a) with cream, or a clear mayonnaise sauce containing plenty of mustard.

1989—CAULIFLOWER SALAD *Salade de Choûx-fleurs*

Divide the cooked and somewhat firm cauliflowers into flower-ettes, cleared of all the stalk. Season with oil and vinegar, and flavor with chopped chervil.

1990—RED CABBAGE SALAD *Salade de Choûx Rouges*

Remove the midribs of the leaves; cut the leaves into a *julienne,* and season them with oil and vinegar six hours in advance. The *julienne* of cabbages may be parboiled for a few minutes to modify the rawness of the vegetable; it should then be cooled and seasoned as above.

1991—CUCUMBER SALAD *Salade de Conconbres*

Peel and thinly slice them; sprinkle the slices with table-salt, and let them stand for two hours. Dry, and season them with oil, vinegar, and chopped chervil.

1992—HARICOT BEANS AND LENTIL SALADS
Salades d'Haricots Secs et de Lentilles

Thoroughly drain the vegetable, whatever its kind; season with oil and vinegar, and add some chopped parsley. Serve separately some thinly sliced, washed, and pressed onion.

1993—POTATO SALAD *Salade de Pommes de Terre*

Cut some long, fair-sized potatoes, cooked in salted water and lukewarm, to the shape of corks, and divide up the latter into thin slices.

Season with oil and vinegar, and add some chopped herbs.

1994—PARISIENNE POTATO SALAD
Salade de Pommes de Terre à la Parisienne

Select potatoes which are not mealy, such as the new kidney potatoes. Cook them in salted water; cut them to the shape of corks, and slice them (while still lukewarm) into thin slices. Put them into a salad-bowl, and sprinkle them with two-thirds pint of white wine per two lbs. of potatoes. Then season with oil and vinegar, add some chopped chervil and parsley, and stir with care lest the slices break.

1995—TOMATO SALAD *Salade de Tomates*

Select some medium-sized and rather firm tomatoes, and scald them. Then skin them; cut them in two crosswise; press them to clear them of juice and seeds; cut them into thin strips; season them with oil and vinegar, and add some chopped tarragon.

1996—COMPOUND SALADS   *Salades Composées*

Unless they leave the kitchen to be served immediately, compound salads are served without their ingredients being mixed. As the latter are generally of various colors, they are seasoned and set in distinct heaps of contrasted shades.

The serving of compound salads is finished by means of borders consisting of pieces of very red beet, gherkins, truffles, roundels of potatoes, and radishes. The method of arranging these vegetables constitutes the decoration, and the latter, being subject to no rules, is merely a matter of taste.

I do not advise the moulding of compound salads, for the increased appetizing look resulting therefrom is small compared with the loss in the taste of the preparation. The simplest form of serving is the best, and fancifulness should not be indulged in, beyond the arrangement of the vegetables in a pyramid, surrounded by a decorated border of aspic-jelly.

1997—GERMAN SALAD   *Salade Allemande*

Take equal quantities of potatoes and apples, gherkins, and herring-fillets, all cut into dice and arranged in heaps. Season with hard-boiled egg sauce, and decorate with very red beets.

1998—AMERICAN SALAD   *Salade Américaine*

Peel and press some tomatoes, and cut them into thin slices; cut some potatoes into thin slices, and prepare a short *julienne* of celery.

Decorate with slices of hard-boiled eggs and thin onion rings.

Season with oil and vinegar.

1999—ANDALUSIAN SALADE   *Salade Andalouse*

Peel and quarter some small tomatoes; cut some mild peppers *julienne*-fashion; cook some rice plainly in salted water, keeping each grain separate; add a little crushed garlic and chopped onion and parsley.

Season with oil and vinegar.

2000—BELLE-FERMIERE SALAD   *Salade Belle-Fermière*

This salad consists of celery and equal quantities of plain-boiled potatoes, beets, and green peppers—all these vegetables cut *julienne* ᴌashion, the celery measuring one-third, and the other ingredients two-thirds of the whole.

Season with mustard sauce with cream (299a).

2001—CRESSONNIERE SALAD   *Salade Cressonnière*

This consists of potatoes à la Parisienne (2017) and watercress, in equal quantities. Sprinkle with parsley, chervil, and hard-boiled egg, mixed.

2002—ISABELLE SALAD   *Salade Isabelle*

Thinly slice equal quantities of raw mushrooms, celery, cooked potatoes, and artichoke-bottoms. Arrange in distinct heaps.

Season with oil and vinegar, and add some chopped chervil.

2003—DANICHEFF SALAD   *Salade Danicheff*

Take equal quantities of sliced and *blanched* celeriac or knob celery, thin rounds of potatoes, slices of artichoke-bottoms, strips of raw mushrooms, and green asparagus-tips, and arrange them in heaps.

Decorate with crayfish tails, hard-boiled eggs, and truffles. Season with mayonnaise sauce (126).

2004—DEMI-DEUIL SALAD   *Salade Demi-Deuil*

Take equal quantities of a *julienne* of potatoes and a *julienne* of very black truffles. Decorate with rings of truffle girding small rounds of potato, and rings of potato girding small rounds of truffle. Alternate the two forms of rings.

Season with a mustard sauce with cream (299a).

2005—ESTREES SALAD   *Salade d'Estrées*

Take equal quantities of celery curls and a moderately small *julienne* of raw truffles. Season, when about to serve, with a mayonnaise sauce with mustard (126), slightly flavored with cayenne.

2006—FLAMANDE SALAD   *Salade à la Flamande*

This consists of a coarse *julienne* of endives, a similar *julienne* of potatoes, an onion baked in its skin, cooled, peeled, and chopped, and some fillets of herring cut into dice, the quantities being in the proportion of one-half of the whole for the endives, one-quarter of the whole for the potatoes, and the remaining quarter for the onion and fillets of herring.

Season with oil and vinegar, and add some chopped parsley and chervil.

2007—FRANCILLON SALAD
Salade Francillon

Take some potato salad "à la Parisienne" (2017), previously *marinated* in Chablis wine, some mussels (bearded and *poached* with celery), and slices of very black truffle, the three ingredients being in the proportion of one-half, one-quarter, and one-quarter respectively.

Set the potato salad on the bottom of the salad bowl, and lay thereon, by way of decoration, the mussels and the truffles in alternate layers.

2008—ITALIAN SALAD
Salade Italienne

Take equal quantities of carrots, turnips, potatoes, tomatoes, and string beans—all cut into regular dice; also peas, small pitted olives, capers, anchovy fillets in small dice, and herbs for the seasoning.

Use hard-boiled eggs for the decoration.

Season with mayonnaise sauce (126).

2009—JOCKEY CLUB SALAD
Salade Jockey Club

Take equal quantities of asparagus-tips and a *julienne* of raw truffles; the two should be seasoned separately some time in advance.

Combine with a very little highly-seasoned mayonnaise sauce (126).

2010—LAKME SALAD
Salade Lakmé

Take equal quantities of red peppers and tomato sauce; plain-boiled rice, kept very white, and with each grain distinct; and chopped, washed, and pressed onion.

Season with oil and vinegar, and flavor with curry powder.

2011—VEGETABLE SALAD
Salade de Légumes

Take equal quantities of carrots and turnips, cut with a fancy cutter; potato dice; cut string beans; peas; small kidney beans, and asparagus-tips; arrange them in distinct heaps, and set a fine head of cauliflower in the middle.

Season with oil and vinegar, and add some chopped parsley and chervil.

N.B.—For vegetable salad, use freshly-cooked and uncooled vegetables as much as possible.

2012—LORETTE SALAD
Salade Lorette

Take equal quantities of corn or field salad, and a *julienne* of beets and celery. Season with oil and vinegar.

2013—MIGNON SALAD   *Salade Mignon*

Take equal quantities of shelled shrimp tails, artichoke-bottoms, cut into dice, and very thin slices of black truffle arranged to form a border. Season with highly-seasoned mayonnaise sauce with cream (126).

2014—MONTE-CRISTO SALAD   *Salade Monte-Cristo*

Take equal quantities of lobster-meat, cooked truffles, and potatoes and hard-boiled eggs in dice, and arrange them in distinct heaps.

In their midst place the very white heart of a lettuce. Season with mayonnaise sauce with mustard (126), and add some chopped tarragon.

2015—NICOISE SALAD   *Salade Niçoise*

Take equal quantities of string beans, potato dice, and quartered tomatoes. Decorate with capers, small, pitted olives, and anchovy fillets.

Season with oil and vinegar.

2016—OPERA SALAD   *Salade Opéra*

Take equal quantities of white chicken meat, very red tongue, celery stalks cut *julienne*-fashion, and a *julienne* of truffles. Arrange these ingredients in very regular heaps, and in the middle of them set a heap of asparagus-tips. Decorate with a border consisting of rounds of cocks' kidneys and rounds of gherkins, laid alternately.

Season with very thin mayonnaise sauce (126).

2017—PARISIAN SALAD   *Salade Parisienne*

Coat a *Charlotte-mould* with very clear jelly, and garnish its bottom and sides with thin slices of spiny-lobster's tail decorated with truffles. Fill the mould with a vegetable salad (2011) mixed with a quarter of its volume of lobster or spiny-lobster remains, cut into dice, and bound by means of a cleared mayonnaise (127).

Leave to set in a cool place, and when about to serve turn out on a napkin.

2018—MASCOTTE SALAD   *Salade Mascotte*

Take some green asparagus-tips, some hard-boiled plovers' eggs, some sliced cocks' kidneys, some slices of truffle, and some crayfish tails.

Decorate according to fancy, making use of the ingredients of the salad for the purpose.

Season with mustard sauce with cream (299a).

2019—RACHEL SALAD   *Salade Rachel*

Take equal quantities of stalks of celery, raw artichoke-bottoms, truffles, potatoes, and asparagus-tips, all, except the latter, being cut *julienne*-fashion.

Slightly mix the salad with mayonnaise sauce (126).

2020—REGENCY SALAD   *Salade Régence*

Take equal quantities of sliced cocks' kidneys, shavings of raw truffles, asparagus-tips, and celery cut lengthwise into extremely thin strips.

Season strongly with oil and lemon juice.

2021—RUSSIAN SALAD   *Salade Russe*

Take equal quantities of carrots, potatoes, string beans, peas, truffles, capers, gherkins, sliced and cooked mushrooms, lobster meat, and lean ham—all cut *julienne*-fashion, and add some anchovy fillets.

Mix the whole with mayonnaise sauce (126); put on a dish, and decorate with some of the ingredients of the salad, together with beets and caviar.

2022—SICILIAN SALAD   *Salade Sicilienne*

Take equal quantities of celeriac (knob celery), russet apples, tomatoes, and artichoke-bottoms—all four cut into dice.

Season with oil and lemon juice.

2023—TREDERN SALAD   *Salade Tredern*

Take twenty-four crayfish tails, cooked as for *bisque,* and cut lengthwise; twenty-four oysters (bearded), *poached* in lemon juice; and three tablespoons of asparagus-tips. The three ingredients should have barely cooled. Complete with fine shavings of raw truffles.

Season with highly spiced mayonnaise sauce, combined with a *purée* made from the crayfishes' remains, pounded with two table-spoons of fresh cream.

2024—TRUFFLE SALAD *Salade de Truffles*

Cut some raw, peeled truffles into very thin shavings.

Season with a sauce consisting of hard-boiled egg-yolks, seasoned with salt and freshly-ground pepper, and finished with oil and lemon juice.

2025—WHITE TRUFFLE SALAD *Salade de Truffles Blanches*

Cut some raw, white, Piedmont truffles into thin shavings.

Season with a sauce consisting of hard-boiled egg-yolks seasoned with salt and pepper, and finished with mustard, oil, and vinegar.

2026—VICTORIA SALAD *Salade Victoria*

Take equal quantities of spiny-lobster trimmings, asparagus-tips, truffles, and cucumbers—all cut into dice.

Season with a mayonnaise sauce (126), combined with the spiny-lobster's creamy parts and a *purée* of coral.

2027—WALDORF SALAD *Salade Waldorf*

Take equal quantities of russet apples and celeriac (knob celery), both cut into dice, and halved and peeled walnuts, soaked in fresh water for one-quarter hour, and well drained.

Season with clear mayonnaise sauce (126).

CHAPTER XVIII

THE preparatory treatment of vegetables—parboiling and *braising,* etc.—having been explained in Chapter X, as also the preparation of *purées,* creams, and vegetable garnishes, it is now only necessary to deal with each vegetable separately.

ARTICHOKES (ARTICHAUTS)

2028—BARIGOULE ARTICHOKES   *Artichauts à la Barigoule*

Take some very fresh and tender artichokes. After having trimmed their tops, take off the outermost leaves; parboil the artichokes; remove their hearts, and completely clear them of their chokes. Season them inside, and fill them with a preparation of *Duxelles* (224), combined with a quarter of its weight of fresh, grated, fat bacon, and as much butter.

Wrap the stuffed artichokes in thin slices of bacon; tie them, and set them in a saucepan prepared for *braising. Braise* them gently with white wine, and cook them well.

When about to serve them, remove the string and the bacon, and dish them.

Strain the *braising*-liquor, and clear it of grease; thicken it with the necessary quantity of good half-*glaze* sauce (23); reduce it sufficiently to produce only a very little sauce, and pour the latter over the artichokes.

2029—CLAMART HEARTS OF ARTICHOKES

Coeurs d'Artichauts à la Clamart

Select some very tender small artichokes, and trim them.

Set them in a buttered *cocotte,* with a small quartered carrot and three tablespoons of freshly-shelled peas to each artichoke, add a large herb bunch and a little water, and salt moderately. Cover and cook gently in a steamer. When about to serve, withdraw the herb

648

bunch, and slightly thicken the liquor with a little *manié* butter. Serve the preparation in the *cocotte*.

2030—ARTICHOKES WITH VARIOUS SAUCES

Artichauts aux Sauces Diverses

Cut the artichokes evenly to within two-thirds of their height; trim them all round; tie them, and plunge them into slightly-salted boiling water. Cook them rather quickly; drain them well, just before serving them, and remove the string.

Place on a napkin, and send a butter, a Hollandaise, or a *mousseline* sauce, etc., at the same time.

When artichokes, cooked in this way, are to be served cold, remove their chokes, serve them on a napkin, and send a Vinaigrette (129) sauce separately.

2031—PROVENCALE ARTICHOKES   *Artichauts à la Provençale*

Select some very small Provençal artichokes; trim them, and put them in an earthenware saucepan containing some very hot oil. Season with salt and pepper; cover the saucepan, and leave to cook for about ten minutes.

Then add, for each twelve artichokes, one pint of very tender, freshly-shelled peas, and a coarse *julienne* of one lettuce.

Cover once more, and cook gently without moistening. The moisture of the peas and the lettuce suffices for the moistening, provided the saucepan be well covered and the fire be not too hot— both of which conditions are necessary to prevent evaporation on too large a scale.

2032—ITALIENNE QUARTERED ARTICHOKES

Quartiers d'Artichauts à l'Italienne

Cut, trim, and quarter some fair-sized artichokes. Trim the quarters, removing the chokes; rub them with a piece of lemon to prevent their blackening; plunge them one by one into fresh water; parboil and drain them. This done, set them in a saucepan on a bed of *aromatics,* as for *braising;* make them sweat in the oven for seven or eight minutes; moisten with white wine; reduce the latter; and moisten again, to within half their height, with brown stock (7). Cook gently in oven until the quarters of artichoke are very tender.

When about to serve, set them in a vegetable dish; strain the cooking-liquor; clear it of grease, and reduce it; add an Italian sauce (40) to it, and pour this sauce over the quartered artichokes

2033—STUFFED ARTICHOKE BOTTOMS   *Fonds d'Artichauts Farcis*

Select some medium-sized artichokes; clear them of their leaves and their chokes; trim their bottoms, rub them with lemon to prevent their blackening, and cook them in a *Blanc* (167), keeping them somewhat firm.

After having drained them, stuff them with a little *Duxelles*, prepared according to (224). Arrange them on a buttered dish; sprinkle the *Duxelles* with fine *raspings* and a little melted butter, and set in a hot oven for a *gratin* to form.

Serve a Madeira sauce (44) at the same time.

2034—FLORENTINE ARTICHOKE BOTTOMS

Fonds d'Artichauts à la Florentine

Prepare the artichoke bottoms as above.

Meanwhile fry a large, chopped onion in butter; add two-thirds lb. of parboiled and chopped spinach per twelve artichokes. Stir over an open fire, that all moisture may evaporate, and add salt and pepper, a piece of crushed garlic the size of a pea, a tablespoon of anchovy *purée*, and two tablespoons of Velouté (25). Cook gently for ten minutes.

Stuff the artichoke-bottoms with this preparation; arrange them on a buttered dish; coat with Mornay sauce (91); sprinkle with Gruyère cheese, cut *brunoise*-fashion, and set to *glaze* in a hot oven.

Upon taking the dish from the oven, sprinkle the artichoke-bottoms with a few drops of melted anchovy butter (281).

2035—ARTICHOKE BOTTOMS WITH ASPARAGUS TIPS

Fonds d'Artichauts aux Pointes d'Asperges

Prepare the artichoke bottoms as above; stew them in butter, and garnish them with asparagus tips, mixed with cream, and heaped in pyramid-form.

Lay them on a buttered dish; coat with Mornay sauce (91), and set to *glaze* quickly.

2036—ARTICHOKE BOTTOMS SAUTE   *Fonds d'Artichauts Sautés*

Remove the leaves and the chokes from the artichokes, trim the bottoms, and slice them up raw. Season them with salt and pepper; toss them in butter; set them in a vegetable-dish, and sprinkle them with herbs.

2037—PUREE OR CREAM OF ARTICHOKES

Purée ou Crème d'Artichauts

Take some very tender artichokes; trim and turn the bottoms, and half-cook them, keeping them very white. Complete their cooking in butter, and rub them through a fine sieve, together with the butter used in cooking.

Put the *purée* obtained in a saucepan, and add to it the half of its bulk of mashed, very smooth, and creamy potatoes.

Finish the *purée* with a little fresh and a little hazel-nut butter (155), the latter being used to increase the flavor of the artichokes.

2038—ASPARAGUS   *Asperges*

The best-known varieties of asparagus in Europe are:—

1. The Lauris asparagus, which is par excellence the early-season kind.

2. The green, Parisian asparagus, which is very small, and of which the most diminutive sticks serve for garnishes.

3. The Argenteuil asparagus—very much in demand while it is in season.

4. English asparagus, which is somewhat delicate in quality, but inclined to be small. During the season there are, besides, several other kinds of asparagus imported from Spain or France, which, though not equal to the four kinds above mentioned, may nevertheless be used for soups or garnishes instead of asparagus-tips.

(Asparagus is grown all over the United States but the best kind comes from California. There are two varieties grown, the green and the white. The taste of most Americans goes to the green asparagus which grows to be as thick as any of the white type, so much appreciated in Europe. The tips of both kinds are used for salads and garnishes. If the asparagus is not absolutely young it is best to peel the stalks thinly and remove the ends that are tough.—Ed.)

Asparagus should be had as fresh as possible; it should be cleaned with care, quickly washed, tied into bunches, and cooked in plenty of salted water.

Asparagus is served on special silver drainers, or on napkins.

2039—FLAMANDE ASPARAGUS   *Asperges à la Flamande*

According to Flemish custom, asparagus is served with one hot, hard-boiled egg, cut in half, and one oz. of melted butter per person. The egg-yolk is crushed, seasoned, and finished with the butter by the diners themselves. This accompaniment may also be prepared beforehand and served in a sauceboat.

2040—ASPARAGUS AU GRATIN *Asperges au Gratin*

Lay the asparagus in rows, and coat the heads of each row with a little Mornay sauce (91). When all are placed, two-thirds cover the bunch with a band of buttered parchment paper, and coat the uncovered portion with the Mornay sauce. Sprinkle with grated Parmesan cheese; *glaze* quickly at the *salamander,* remove the paper, and serve at once.

2041—MILANAISE ASPARAGUS *Asperges à la Milanaise*

Having thoroughly drained the asparagus, set it on a long, buttered dish sprinkled with grated Parmesan cheese; arrange it in successive rows, sprinkling the heads with grated Parmesan cheese. When about to serve, cover the cheese-sprinkled parts copiously with nut-brown butter (154), and set to *glaze* slightly at the *salamander.*

2042—POLONAISE ASPARAGUS *Asperges à la Polonaise*

Thoroughly drain the asparagus; set it on a long dish, in rows, and sprinkle the heads with hard-boiled egg-yolk and chopped parsley, mixed. When about to serve, cover the heads with nut-brown butter (154), combined with one oz. of very fresh and fine bread-crumbs per four oz. of butter.

2043—ASPARAGUS WITH VARIOUS SAUCES

Asperges aux Sauces Diverses

Butter sauce, Hollandaise, *Mousseline,* and Maltese sauces are the most usual accompaniments to asparagus. Béarnaise sauce without herbs is also served occasionally, likewise melted butter.

When eaten cold, it may be served with oil and vinegar or a mayonnaise—more particularly a Chantilly mayonnaise, one to which whipped cream has been added.

2044—ASPARAGUS TIPS WITH BUTTER *Pointes d'Asperges*

Green asparagus is chiefly used for garnishing or as a garnishing ingredient, but it may also be served as a vegetable with perfect propriety. Cut the asparagus into two-inch lengths, and tie them together in bundles.

Cut what remains of them into bits the size of peas. After having washed the latter, plunge them into boiling salted water, and cook them quickly, that they may keep green.

This done, thoroughly drain them; let their moisture evaporate by tossing them over the fire; mix them with butter, away from the fire, and serve them in a *timbale* with the asparagus bunches on top.

They are usually served in small patty crusts, or in small *tartlet crusts,* with a few tips on each small patty or *tartlet.*

2045—ASPARAGUS TIPS IN CREAM   *Pointes d'Asperges à la Crème*

Prepare them, and cook them in salted water as above.

Their mixture with cream is the procedure common to other vegetables similarly prepared, and they are served like those of (2044).

EGGPLANT (AUBERGINES)

2046—EGYPTIENNE EGGPLANT   *Aubergines à l'Egyptienne*

Cut them into two lengthwise; trim them round the edges; slice the center of each criss-cross with the view of facilitating the cooking process, and cook them.

Drain them; remove the pulp from their insides, and set the shells on a buttered *gratin* dish.

This done, chop up the removed pulp; add a little chopped onion cooked in oil, and the same quantity of very lean, chopped, and cooked mutton as there is eggplant pulp.

Fill the eggplant shells with this preparation; sprinkle with a few drops of oil, and set in the oven for fifteen minutes. On taking the dish from the oven, set on each eggplant a few slices of tomato, tossed in oil; sprinkle with chopped parsley, and serve.

2047—EGGPLANT AU GRATIN   *Aubergines au Gratin*

Fry the eggplants as above; empty them, chop up their pulps, and add to it an equal weight of dry *Duxelles* (223). Garnish the shells with this preparation, set them on a *gratin* dish, sprinkle them with *raspings* and a few drops of oil, and cause the *gratin* to form.

Surround the eggplants with a border of light half-*glaze* (23) sauce when serving.

2048—FRIED EGGPLANT   *Aubergines Frites*

Cut the eggplants into thin round slices; season and dredge them, and fry them in hot smoking oil. Place them on a napkin, and serve immediately, that they may be eaten crisp. If they wait at all, they soften, and thereby lose quality.

2049—PROVENCALE EGGPLANT   *Aubergines à la Provençale*

Proceed as for (2047), but replace the *Duxelles* by tomatoes tossed in oil and flavored with a little garlic.

Set the *gratin* to form in the same way, and surround the egg plants with a border of tomato sauce (29) when taking them out of the oven.

2050—EGGPLANT SOUFFLE   *Aubergines Soufflées*

Cut some fine eggplants into two; criss-cross the pulp, and fry them in the usual way; remove the pulp from their insides, and set the shells on a buttered *gratin* dish. Finely chop the removed pulp, and mix an equal quantity of reduced Béchamel sauce (28), combined with grated Parmesan cheese.

Add some white of egg beaten to a stiff froth, allowing as much of it as for an ordinary *soufflé*.

Garnish the eggplant shells with this preparation, and cook in a moderate oven, as for ordinary *soufflé*. On taking the dish from the oven, serve instantly.

2051—TURKISH EGGPLANT   *Aubergines à la Turque*

Peel the eggplants and cut them, each lengthwise, into six slices.

Season, dredge, and fry these slices in oil; pair them off, and join them together by means of a very firm preparation of raw egg-yolks and grated, fresh cheese. When about to serve, dip them into batter, and fry them in smoking oil.

Place on a napkin with very green fried parsley.

These stuffed slices of eggplant may be treated *à l'Anglaise* instead of with batter.

2052—CARDOONS   *Cardons*

Treatment and Cooking Process.—After having removed the green outside leaf-stalks, detach the white ones all round, and cut these into three-inch lengths. Peel these lengths, rub them with lemon, that they may not blacken, and throw them, one by one, into fresh water, acidulated with lemon juice.

Prepare the heart of the cardoon in the same way, after having removed the fibrous parts, and cook the whole in a *Blanc* (167), with one lb. of chopped veal fat, sprinkled over its surface, that the cardoon may be kept from blackening by exposure to the air.

Cook gently for about one and one-half hours.

2053—CARDOONS WITH PARMESAN
Cardons au Parmesan

After having well drained the sections, build them into a pyramid in successive layers. Sprinkle each row with a few drops of good half-*glaze* sauce (23), and with grated Parmesan cheese. Cover the whole with the same sauce; sprinkle with grated Parmesan cheese, and set to *glaze* quickly.

2054—CARDOONS MORNAY
Cardons à la Mornay

Proceed exactly as above, but replace half-*glaze* sauce by Mornay sauce (91). *Glaze* quickly, and serve immediately.

2055—MILANAISE CARDOONS
Cardons à la Milanaise

Proceed as for "Asperges à la Milanaise" (2041).

2056—CARDOONS WITH VARIOUS SAUCES
Cardons aux Sauces Diverses

They may be served either with gravy, or half-*glaze,* cream, Hollandaise, *Mousseline,* Italienne, or Bordelaise sauces.

The sauce is either poured over them or served separately.

If the sauce be poured over the cardoons, they are served in a *timbale;* if the sauce be sent separately, they may be served on a silver drainer, like asparagus.

2057—CARDOONS WITH MARROW
Cardons à la Moëlle

Arrange the cardoons in a pyramid on a round dish; cover them with a marrow sauce (45), and surround them with very small puff-paste patties filled with *poached* marrow dice. Or serve the cardoons in a *timbale,* and set on the heart cut into slices and arranged in a crown, with a slice of *poached* marrow on each slice of heart.

Cover the whole with marrow sauce (45).

2058—HEARTS OF CARDOONS WITH FINE HERBS
Coeur de Cardon aux Fines Herbes

Having cooked the heart of the cardoon, trim it all round so as to give it the cylindrical shape, and cut it across into slices one-third inch thick.

Roll these slices in some pale, thin, buttered meat *glaze* (15), combined with chopped herbs. Prepared in this way, the heart of a cardoon constitutes an excellent garnish for Tournedos and *sautéd* chickens.

Carrots (Carottes)

2059—GLAZED CARROTS FOR GARNISHINGS
Carottes Glacées pour Garnitures

New carrots are not parboiled; they are cut with a fancy knife. whole, halved, or quartered, according to their size, and then trimmed. If old, they should be cut to the shape of elongated olives, and parboiled before being set to cook.

Put the carrots in a saucepan with enough water to cover them well, one-half oz. of salt, one oz. of sugar, and two oz. of butter per pint of water.

Cook until the water has almost entirely evaporated, so that the reduction may have the consistency of a syrup. *Sauté* the carrots in this reduction, that they may be covered with a glossy coat.

Whatever be the ultimate purpose for which the carrots are intended, they should be prepared in this way.

2060—CREAMED CARROTS
Carottes à la Crème

Prepare the carrots as above, and, when the moistening is reduced to the consistency of a syrup, cover them with boiling cream.

Sufficiently reduce the cream, and serve in a *timbale*.

2061—VICHY CARROTS
Carottes à la Vichy

Slice the carrots, and, if they be old, parboil them.

Treat them exactly after the manner of the *"glazed* carrots" of (2059); serve them in a *timbale,* and sprinkle them with chopped parsley.

2062—PUREE OF CARROTS
Purée de Carottes

Slice the carrots, and cook them in slightly-salted water, with sugar and butter, as for *"glazed* carrots," and a quarter of their weight of rice. Drain them as soon as they are cooked; rub them through a fine sieve; transfer the *purée* to a saucepan, and dry it over a hot fire, together with three oz. of butter per lb. of *purée.*

Now add a sufficient quantity of either milk or consommé to give it the consistency of an ordinary *purée.* Serve in a *timbale* with triangular *croûtons* of bread, fried in butter at the last moment.

This *purée* is very commonly served as a garnish with *braised* pieces of veal.

2063—DEEP CARROT PIE   *Flan aux Carrots*

This is served either as a vegetable or a sweet.

Line a spring-form mould with good, short paste (2358); coat the inside of the ring with a round piece of paper, and fill it with rice or split peas. Bake it without letting it brown; remove the split peas or the rice (just to keep the form), as also the paper, and fill the crust with a slightly sugared *purée* of carrots. Cover this *purée* with half-slices of carrot cooked as for (2059), and kept unbroken. Coat with the cooking-liquor of the carrots reduced to a syrup, and put the flan in the oven for five minutes.

2064—CELERY   *Céleri*

Celery for *braising* should be non-fibrous, white, and very tender. Cut the stalks till they measure only eight inches from their roots; remove the green leaves; trim the root; wash with great care, parboil for one-quarter hour, and cool.

This done, *braise* them after recipe (275). When they are cooked, cut each stalk into three pieces, and double up each section before serving.

2065—VARIOUS PREPARATIONS OF STALK CELERY
Préparations Diverses de Céleri en Branches

The recipes given for cardoons may be applied to celery. On referring to the respective recipes, therefore, celery may be prepared:—

Au Parmesan, Sauce Mornay, à la Milanaise, Italienne, Hollandaise, with gravy, etc.

2066—PUREE OF CELERY   *Purée de Céleri*

Slice the celery; parboil it, and stew it, until it is quite cooked, in a little very fat consommé.

Drain as soon as cooked; rub through a sieve, adding the cooking-liquor cleared of all grease; thicken the *purée* with about one quart of very white and firm potato *purée;* heat; add butter at the last moment, and serve in a *timbale.*

2067—PUREE OF KNOB CELERY (CELERIAC)   *Purée de Céleri-Rave*

Peel the celeriac (knob celery); cut it into sections, and cook it in salted water.

Drain and rub it through a fine sieve, adding plain-boiled, quartered potatoes the while in the proportion of one-third of the weight of the *purée* of celeriac.

Put the *purée* in a saucepan; add to it three oz. of butter per lb.; dry it over a hot fire, and bring it to its normal consistency by means of milk. When about to serve, add butter, away from the fire, and serve in a *timbale*.

Cèpes

Those *cèpes* which are barely opened or not opened at all are not parboiled. But, those which are open should be washed, parboiled, and stewed in butter, after having been well dried.

(*Cèpes* are a delicious meaty mushroom (fungus) with a large brown cap and a white fleshy stem. They grow wild only in shady woods or forests, in many parts of the United States, and the quantities picked would not warrant their commercial use.—Ed.)

2068—BORDELAISE CEPES   *Cèpes à la Bordelaise*

Slice the *cèpes;* season them with salt and pepper; put them into very hot oil, and toss them until they are thoroughly frizzled. Almost at the last moment add, per one-half lb. of *cèpes,* one oz. of *cèpe* stalks, which should have been put aside and chopped up, one teaspoon of chopped shallots, and a tablespoon of bread-crumbs— the object of which is to absorb any excess oil, once the *cèpes* have been served.

Toss the whole together for a few minutes; serve in a *timbale,* and complete with a few drops of lemon juice and some chopped parsley.

2069—CREAMED CEPES   *Cèpes à la Crème*

Slice the *cèpes,* and stew them in butter with a teaspoon of chopped onion per one-half lb. of *cèpes;* the onion should have been cooked in butter, without browning.

When they are stewed, drain them; cover them with boiling cream, and boil gently until the latter is completely reduced. At the last moment finish with a little thin cream, and serve in a *timbale.*

2070—PROVENCALE CEPES   *Cèpes à la Provençale*

Proceed as for (2068), but substitute for the shallots some chopped onion and a bit of crushed garlic.

Serve in a *timbale,* and complete with a few drops of lemon juice and some chopped parsley.

2071—ROSSINI CEPES *Cèpes à la Rossini*

Proceed as for (2069), and add to the *cèpes* one-third of their weight of thickly-sliced, raw truffles, stewed at the same time as the former. When about to serve, finish with a little pale melted meat *glaze* (15), and put in a *timbale*.

MUSHROOMS (CHAMPIGNONS)

Cookery includes under this head only the white cultivated Parisian mushroom and the field mushroom, which is the kind so commonly used.

The other kinds are always identified by special and proper terms.

(The cultivated kinds are the only mushrooms (fungi) which are for sale in the markets of the United States for about nine months of the year. They are also available in cans, and the imported types can be purchased dried.—Ed.)

2072—CREAMED MUSHROOMS *Champignons à la Crème*

Proceed as described under (2069).

2073—MUSHROOMS SAUTE *Champignons Sautés*

After having washed the mushrooms, dried, and sliced them, and seasoned them with salt and pepper, toss them with butter in a frying-pan over a hot fire. Sprinkle them with chopped parsley at the last moment, and serve them in a *timbale*.

2074—BROILED MUSHROOMS *Champignons Grillés*

Take some large cultivated or field mushrooms. Carefully peel them; season them; brush them with oil, and grill them gently.

Set them on a round dish, and garnish them with well-softened, Maître-d'Hôtel butter (150).

2075—STUFFED MUSHROOMS *Champignons Farcis*

Select some fine, medium-sized mushroom caps; wash them, and dry them well. Set them on a dish; season them; sprinkle them with a few drops of oil; put them in the oven for five minutes, and garnish their midst with *Duxelles* (224) shaped like a dome, and thickened or not, with bread-crumbs.

Sprinkle the surface with fine *raspings* and a few drops of oil or melted butter, and set the *gratin* to form in a somewhat hot oven.

2076—LATTICED DEEP MUSHROOM PIE
Flan Grillé aux Champignons

Line a buttered *spring*-form mould with good lining paste (2358).

Fill it with very fresh button mushrooms, tossed in butter with a little chopped onion, combined with cream, and cooled.

Moisten the edges of the *flawn-mould* pastry, and decorate it with criss-cross strips of short paste, as for a latticed apple-flawn.

Brush the lattice work with egg; bake the pie in a very hot oven, and serve it the moment it is finished.

2077—LATTICED MUSHROOM TARTLETS
Tartlettes Grillées aux Champignons

These *tartlets* constitute an excellent and beautiful garnish, more particularly for Tournedos and Noisettes. Proceed exactly as for (2076), but use *tartlet* moulds the size of which is determined by the dimensions of the meat or preparation which they are to accompany.

2078—TURNED OR GROOVED MUSHROOMS FOR GARNISHINGS
Champignons Tournés ou Cannelés pour Garnitures

Take some very fresh mushrooms; wash and drain them quickly.

Cut their stalks flush with their heads; turn or groove the latter with the point of a small knife, and throw them, one by one, into a boiling liquor prepared as follows:—

For two lbs. of mushrooms, put one-sixth pint of water, one-third oz. of salt, two oz. of butter, and the juice of one and one-half lemons, in a saucepan. Boil; add the mushrooms, and cook for five minutes. Transfer to a bowl immediately, and cover with a piece of buttered parchment paper.

2079—PUREE OF MUSHROOMS   Purée de Champignons

Clean, wash, and dry two lbs. of mushrooms. Quickly peel them, and rub them through a sieve. Put this *purée* of raw mushrooms into a saucepan with two-thirds pint of reduced Béchamel sauce (28), and one-sixth pint of cream. Season with salt, white pepper, and nutmeg; reduce over an open fire for a few minutes, and finish, away from the fire, with three oz. of best butter.

2080—MORELS   Morilles

The Spring mushroom or Morel is the one most preferred by connoisseurs. There are two kinds of morels—the pale and the brown kind—both excellent, though some prefer the former to the latter, and vice versa.

In spite of what connoisseurs may say regarding the error of washing morels, I advocate the operation, and urge the reader to do it carefully, and without omitting to open out the underneath parts, so as to wash away any sand particles that may be lodged therein.

This type of mushroom does not generally grow in the United States.

The Cooking of Morels.—If they be small, leave them whole; if large, halve or quarter them. After having properly drained them, put them in a saucepan with two oz. of butter, the juice of a lemon, and a pinch of salt and another of pepper per lb. of morels. Boil, and then stew for ten or twelve minutes. Never forget that the vegetable juices produced by the morels should be reduced and added to their accompanying sauce.

2081—CREAMED MORELS   *Morilles à la Crème*
Proceed as for *Cèpes* and Mushrooms with Cream.

2082—STUFFED MORELS   *Morilles Farcies*
Select some large morels, and wash them well.

Remove their stems; chop them up, and prepare them like a *Duxelles* (223).

Add to this *Duxelles* half of its bulk of very smooth sausage-meat.

Open the morels on one side; fill them with the prepared *forcemeat,* and set them on a buttered dish, opened side up.

Sprinkle with fine *raspings,* and use plenty of melted butter; cook for twenty minutes in a moderate oven, and serve the dish as it stands.

2083—POULETTE MORELS   *Morilles à la Poulette*
Cook them as described under (2080), and add them to a Poulette sauce (101), together with their cooking-liquor reduced.

Serve in a *timbale,* and sprinkle with a pinch of chopped parsley.

2084—MORELS SAUTE   *Morilles Sautées*
After having thoroughly washed the morels, dry them well in a towel, and halve or quarter them according to their size.

Season them with salt and pepper, and *sauté* them with butter in an omelet-pan, over a very hot fire, to avoid the evaporation of their vegetable moisture. Put them in a *timbale;* squeeze a few drops of lemon juice over them, and sprinkle them with chopped parsley.

2085—TORTE OF MORELS   *Tourte de Morilles*

Cook the morels as explained under (2080), and drain them well.

Reduce their cooking-liquor by a quarter, and add to it two tablespoons of very thick cream and one oz. of butter per lb. of morels.

Heat this sauce without boiling it, toss the morels in it, and set them in a *tourte* crust, or merely in the center of a crown of puff-paste, lying on a dish.

Morels prepared in this way may also be served in a Vol-au-vent crust (2390).

2086—MOUSSERONS, ORONGES, CHANTARELLES

Mousserons, Oronges, Giroles

These varieties of edible fungi are not known or well liked in the United States, but are much appreciated in the Scandinavian and Central European countries.

The best way to prepare them is to toss them quickly in butter.

2087—CHAYOTE   *Brionne*

This excellent vegetable, which has only become known quite recently, is beginning to be appreciated by connoisseurs. It is in season from the end of October to the end of March—that is to say, at a time when cucumbers and squash are over. It greatly resembles these last-named vegetables, and is prepared like them, while the recipes given for cardoons (2052) may also be applied to it.

2088—CHICORY, ENDIVE, AND BELGIAN ENDIVE

Chicorée Frisée, Escarole, and Endive Belge

Three kinds of chicory are used for cooking:

1. Curled chicory, improperly termed "Endive" in the United States.

2. Flemish chicory, which is genuine endive in its primitive state, grown in the open air. It greatly resembles Escarole.

3. Belgian chicory, called endive; obtained from cultivating the root of Flemish chicory in the dark.

This last kind is quite different from the first two, with regard to both its quality and its culinary treatment, and it will be dealt with later under the name of "Endive."

2089—CHICORY OR ESCAROLE IN CREAM   *Chicorée à la Crème*

Parboil the chicory for ten minutes in plenty of boiling water. Cool it; press the water out of it, and chop it up.

Combine it with four and one-half oz. of pale *roux* per two lbs. of chicory; moisten with one quart of consommé; season with salt and a pinch of powdered sugar, and *braise* in the oven, under cover, for one and one-half hours.

Upon taking it from the oven, transfer it to another saucepan; add three-fifths pint of cream and two oz. of butter, and serve in a *timbale*.

2090—CHICORY OR ESCAROLE LOAF   *Pain de Chicorée*
Braise the chicory as described above.

Upon taking it from the oven, mix with it per lb.) five stiffly-beaten eggs; put it into an even, buttered mould, and set to *poach* in a *bain-marie* (water-bath).

Before unmoulding the "loaf," let it rest awhile, that the middle may settle. Turn out just before serving, and cover with a cream sauce (79).

2091—PUREE OF CHICORY   *Purée de Chicorée*
Braise the chicory, and rub it through a sieve. Mix it with one-third of its bulk of smooth mashed potatoes with cream; heat; add butter away from the fire, and serve in a *timbale*.

2092—SOUFFLE OF CHICORY OR ESCAROLE *Soufflé de Chicorée*
Braise about one-half lb. of chicory or escarole, keeping it somewhat stiff, and rub it through a sieve. Add to it the yolks of three eggs, also two oz. of grated Parmesan cheese and the whites of three eggs, beaten to a stiff froth.

Serve in a buttered *timbale;* sprinkle with grated Parmesan cheese, and cook after the manner of an ordinary *soufflé*.

N.B.—This *soufflé* of chicory may also be cooked in small paper cases or small moulds, and it makes an excellent stuffing for large pieces of veal or ham.

2093—FLAMANDE CHICORY OR ESCAROLE *Chicorée à la Flamande*
Cut the chicory into two-inch lengths; parboil it; cool it, and then proceed for the rest of the operation as described under (2089)—the only difference being that it is not chopped.

2094—ENDIVE OR BELGIAN ENDIVE   *Endives ou Endives Belges*
Whatever the purpose for which they are intended, endives should always be cooked as follows:—

After having washed and cleaned them, put them in a well-lined saucepan containing (per three lbs. of endives) a liquor prepared from the juice of a lemon, a pinch of salt, one oz. of butter, and one-fifth pint of water. Cover the saucepan; boil quickly, and complete the cooking on the side of the fire for from thirty to thirty-five minutes.

Endives may be served plain, and constitute a favorite vegetable or garnish. They may accompany all *relevés* of meat.

Some cardoon recipes may also be applied to them, more particularly *à la Mornay, à la Crème,* and *à la Milanaise*—all of which suit them admirably.

2095—CABBAGE   *Choûx*

From the culinary standpoint, cabbages may be divided into seven classes, as follows:—

1. White cabbage: used almost solely in the preparation of sauerkraut.

2. Red cabbage: used as a vegetable, as a hors-d'œuvre, or as a condiment.

3. Round-headed, Crinkled or Savoy cabbage: especially suited to *braising* and boiling.

4. Scotch Kale and spring cabbage: always boiled.

5. Cauliflower and broccoli: the flower of these is most commonly used, but the leaves are cooked in boiling water when they are tender.

6. Brussels sprouts.

7. Kohlrabi: the roots of these may be served as turnips, and the leaves cooked in boiling water, provided they are young and tender.

2096—WHITE CABBAGE   *Choûx Blancs*

In an extreme case, these cabbages may be *braised* like the green Savoys, but they are usually too firm, and they are therefore only used in the preparation of sauerkraut.

2097—SAUERKRAUT   *Choûcroute*

If the sauerkraut is somewhat old, set it to soak in cold water for a few hours. It is best, however, to avoid this measure, if possible, and to use only fresh sauerkraut.

When about to cook it, drain it, if it has been soaked, and press all the water out of it. Then pull it to pieces in such a way as to leave no massed leaves; season it with salt and pepper, and put it into a *braising*-pan lined with slices of bacon. Add, for ten lbs. of sauerkraut, three quartered carrots, three medium-sized onions, each stuck with a clove, a large herb-bunch, three oz. of juniper berries and one-half oz. of peppercorns contained in a bag, six oz. of goose drippings or lard, and one lb. of *blanched* breast of bacon, the latter to be taken out after one hour's cooking.

Moisten, just enough to cover, with white consommé; cover with slices of bacon; boil, and then cook in the oven for five hours with the lid on.

To serve Sauerkraut.—Take out the vegetables, the herb-bunch, and the juniper berries, and set the sauerkraut in a *timbale,* after having well drained it.

Surround it with thin slices of ham, rectangles of bacon, and some *poached* Frankfort sausages.

RED CABBAGE (CHOUX ROUGES)

2098—FLAMANDE RED CABBAGE   *Choûx Rouges à la Flamande*

Quarter the cabbages, remove the outside leaves and the core, and cut the trimmed leaves into a fine *julienne.* Season with salt, pepper, and nutmeg; sprinkle with vinegar, and put this *julienne* into a well-buttered earthenware *cocotte.* Cover and cook in a moderate oven.

When the cooking is three-quarters done, add four peeled and quartered russet apples and a tablespoon of brown or powdered sugar.

Take note that the cooking must be gentle from start to finish, and that the only moistening should be the vinegar.

2099—MARINATED RED CABBAGE FOR HORS D'OEUVRE
Choûx Rouges Marinées pour Hors-d'Oeuvre

Cut the cabbage into a small *julienne* as above, and put them into a bowl or deep dish. Sprinkle with table salt, and leave to steep for two days, stirring frequently.

Then drain, and put it into a pot with garlic cloves, peppercorns, and one bay leaf. Cover with raw or boiled and cooled vinegar, and leave to *marinate* for a day or two.

This *marinated* cabbage forms an excellent addition to boiled beef.

Savoy Cabbages (Choux Verts Pommés)

2100—BRAISED CABBAGE *Choûx Braisé*

Quarter the cabbage; parboil and cool it.

Strip the leaves from the quarters; remove the outside leaves and the midribs of the remaining leaves; season with salt and pepper, and put the cabbage in a saucepan garnished with slices of bacon, and containing one quartered carrot, one onion stuck with a garlic clove, one herb-bunch, two-thirds pint of consommé and three tablespoons of stock fat per two lbs. of cabbage. Cover with slices of bacon; boil, and then *braise* gently for two hours.

2101—CABBAGE ENGLISH STYLE *Choûx à l'Anglaise*

Plainly boil or steam the cabbage. Press all the water out of it, between two plates, and cut it into diamond shapes or squares.

2102—STUFFED CABBAGE *Choûx Farci*

Take a medium-sized crinkly or Savoy cabbage; parboil it; cool it, and remove its core. Slightly open out its leaves, and insert between them raw or cooked minced-meat, combined with chopped onion and parsley, and highly seasoned. Reconstruct the cabbage, pressing it closely together; wrap it in slices of bacon; tie it, and *braise* it gently for three hours with stock and stock fat.

When about to serve, drain the cabbage; remove the string and the slices of bacon; set it on a dish, and cover it with a few tablespoons of the *braising*-liquor, cleared of all grease, reduced, and thickened with some half-*glaze* sauce (23).

Serve what remains of the *braising*-liquor separately.

N.B.—The preparation is improved if the minced-meat with which the cabbage is stuffed is combined with a quarter of its bulk of pilaff rice (2255) and the same quantity of *foie-gras* fat.

2103—SOU-FASSUM PROVENCALE *Sou-Fassum Provençale*

Parboil and cool the cabbage as in (2102); remove the outer large leaves, and set them in vegetable parchment.

Upon this layer of cabbage leaves place the following products, mixed:—

The inside leaves of the cabbage, chopped up and seasoned; one-half lb. of chopped and *blanched* white of a leek; one and three-quarter lbs. of sausage-meat; six oz. of lean bacon, cut into dice and frizzled; one chopped onion, fried in butter; two chopped tomatoes;

a crushed clove of garlic; three oz. of *blanched* rice and four oz. of fresh young peas.

Gather up the ends of the parchment, and close it in such a way as to reconstruct the cabbage.

Cook it in mutton broth or in ordinary stock for three and one-half or four hours.

Serve the sou-fassum plain, on a round dish.

2104a—STUFFED CABBAGE   *Choûx pour Garnitures*

Parboil, cool, and thoroughly drain the cabbage. Remove as many large leaves as there are balls of stuffed cabbage required, and, if the leaves are too small, use two for each ball.

Chop up the remains of the cabbage; season it with salt and pepper; put a small portion on each of the leaves; fold in the shape of balls, and set them one by one in a saucepan.

Then proceed, for the cooking, as directed under *"Braised Cabbage"* (2100).

2105b—STUFFED CABBAGE   *Choûx pour Garnitures*

Prepare the cabbage as above; insert into the center of each ball a portion of smooth pork *forcemeat,* the size of a pigeon's egg, and *braise* in the same way.

2106c—STUFFED CABBAGE   *Choûx pour Garnitures*

Parboil the necessary quantity of cabbage leaves, in accordance with the number of balls required. Cool them; spread them out; garnish the middle of each with one tablespoon of pilaff rice (2255), mixed with *foie-gras purée,* and fold the leaves to form small packets.

Braise as in (2104).

2107—SCOTCH KALE, SPRING CABBAGE, BROCCOLI LEAVES, TURNIP-TOPS

Choû Frisé, Choûx de Printemps, Broccoli-rave, Choûx-navets

These various kinds of greens are boiled, as described above, or prepared with butter, like Brussels sprouts. These two methods of preparation are the only ones that suit them.

2108—CAULIFLOWER AND BROCCOLI   *Choû-Fleur et Broccoli*

Broccoli differs from cauliflower in the color and the arrangement of the parts of the flower. In the broccoli the flower is of a deep violet. English broccoli never reach the size of those grown in the

South of France. But in the United States such violet-colored broccoli is widely sold.

Some kinds do not even grow to a head, while their flowers—the
size of hazel-nuts—are scattered among the surrounding leaves. This
type is called Broccoli-rave by the Italians in the United States.

Cauliflower and large broccoli allow for the same treatment.

2109—CAULIFLOWER IN CREAM　　　*Choû-Fleur à la Crème*

Separate the cauliflowers into flowerets; remove the small leaves
which are attached, and cook the cauliflower in salted water.

Thoroughly drain; set the flowerets in a *timbale,* reconstructing
the cauliflower in so doing, or on a dish covered with a folded
napkin, and serve a cream sauce (79) separately.

2110—CAULIFLOWER AU GRATIN　　　*Choû-Fleur au Gratin*

Having well drained the cauliflower, set it in butter for a few
minutes; mould it in a bowl, and pour a few tablespoons of Mornay
sauce (91) into it.

Coat the bottom of a dish with the same sauce, and turn out the
cauliflower on the dish; completely cover with Mornay sauce; sprinkle with grated cheese mixed with *raspings;* sprinkle with melted
butter, and set the *gratin* to form.

2111—MILANAISE CAULIFLOWER　　　*Choû-Fleur à la Milanaise*

Set the cauliflower on a buttered dish sprinkled with grated
cheese. Also sprinkle the cauliflower with cheese; add a few pieces
of butter, and set the *gratin* to form.

On taking the dish out of the oven, sprinkle the cauliflower with
nut-brown butter (154) and serve immediately.

2112—POLONAISE CAULIFLOWER　　　*Choû-Fleur à la Polonaise*

Thoroughly drain the cauliflower, and set it on a buttered dish.

Sprinkle it with chopped, hard-boiled egg-yolks and chopped
parsley, mixed. When about to serve, sprinkle with nut-brown but
ter (154), in which one-half oz. of fine bread-crumbs (per three oz.
of butter) should have been fried.

2113—CAULIFLOWER WITH VARIOUS SAUCES
Choûx-Fleur aux Sauces Diverses

Cook the cauliflower in salted water. Drain it thoroughly, and set
it in a *timbale.* Serve at the same time either a sauceboat of *Melted
Butter* or *a Butter, a Hollandaise,* or *a Mousseline* sauce, etc.

2114—PUREE OF CAULIFLOWER, CALLED DU BARRY

Purée de Choû-fleur dite à la Du Barry

Cook the cauliflower in salted water; drain it well; rub it through a fine sieve, and combine the resulting *purée* with one quarter of its bulk of somewhat firm, mashed potatoes with cream. Heat; add butter away from the fire, and serve in a *timbale*.

BRUSSELS SPROUTS (CHOUX DE BRUXELLES)

2115—ANGLAISE BRUSSELS SPROUTS

Choûx de Bruxelles à l'Anglaise

Cook them in salted water; drain them well, and serve them on a drainer or in a *timbale*.

2116—BRUSSELS SPROUTS IN CREAM   *Choûx de Bruxelles à la Crème*

Cook the sprouts; drain them well without cooling them; stew them in butter, and chop them up. Then combine them with as much fresh cream as possible.

2117—BRUSSELS SPROUTS SAUTE   *Choûx de Bruxelles Sautés*

Cook them and, after having thoroughly drained them, throw them into an omelet-pan containing some very hot butter. Toss them until they are nicely frizzled; serve them in a *timbale,* and sprinkle them with chopped parsley.

2118—BRUSSELS SPROUTS IN BUTTER

Choûx de Bruxelles au Beurre

Cook them, keeping them somewhat firm, and drain without cooling them.

Put them into a saucepan; season them with salt and pepper; add two oz. of butter (per lb. of sprouts) cut into small pieces; cover, and stew in the oven for one-quarter hour.

2119—PUREE OF BRUSSELS SPROUTS CALLED FLAMANDE

Purée de Choûx de Bruxelles dite Flamande

Three-quarters cook the sprouts; drain them well without cooling them, and complete their cooking by stewing them in butter. Rub them through a fine sieve, and add to the resulting *purée* one-third of its bulk of mashed potatoes.

Heat, add butter away from the fire, and dish in a *timbale*.

2120—SEA KALE *Choû Marin*

This is one of the best and most delicate of vegetables.

It is trimmed with great care, washed, and then tied into bunches of from five to six plants, which are plainly cooked in salted water.

All cardoon recipes, and sauces given for asparagus, may be applied to sea kale.

2121—CUCUMBER AND SQUASH *Conconbres et Courgettes*

Though of different shapes, these two vegetables permit of almost the same treatment when they are cooked. They are especially used as garnishes.

2122—CUCUMBERS IN CREAM *Conconbres à la Crème*

Peel, and cut the cucumber to shapes resembling olives; parboil and drain these pieces. This done, three-quarters cook them in butter; moisten with boiling cream, and finish the cooking in reducing the cream. At the very last moment add a little Béchamel Sauce (28) to slightly thicken the preparation, and serve in a *timbale*.

2123—GLAZED CUCUMBERS *Conconbres Glacés*

After having shaped the cucumbers like large garlic cloves, quickly parboil them. This done, treat them as directed under *"Carottes glacées"* (2059) and roll them sufficiently in their cooking-liquor, reduced to the consistency of a thick syrup, to thoroughly coat them with it.

2124a—STUFFED CUCUMBERS *Conconbres Farcis*

Cut the cucumbers into two-inch lengths; peel, parboil, and drain them. Then hollow them out to form small, round cases; set them side by side in a saucepan, and cook them in butter. When they are three-quarters cooked, fill them with a raw, chicken *forcemeat,* by means of a pastry-bag. The *forcemeat* should be slightly moulded in the cucumber cases.

Complete the cooking of the cucumber, gently, while *poaching* the *forcemeat.*

2125b—STUFFED CUCUMBERS *Conconbres Farcis*

Peel the cucumbers; split them open lengthwise, and empty them with a spoon. This done, parboil and drain without cooling them.

Fill each half-cucumber, level with the edges, with a chicken *forcemeat,* prepared with *frangipane,* and combined with a third of its weight of *Duxelles.* Reconstruct the cucumbers by placing the halves one against the other; wrap each in a slice of bacon, and then in a piece of muslin, and finally tie them. This done, *braise* them in the usual way. When they are cooked, remove their wrappings, and cut them into slices the thickness of which is determined by the size of the piece which they are to accompany.

2126—STACHYS OR JAPANESE ARTICHOKES   *Crosnes de Japon*

Whatever be their mode of preparation, Japanese artichokes must be cleaned, parboiled, and kept firm, and cooked in butter without browning.

2127—STACHYS OR JAPANESE ARTICHOKES IN CREAM
Crosnes à la Crème

After having parboiled the Japanese artichokes and three-quarters cooked them in butter, moisten with boiling cream, and complete their cooking while reducing the cream. Add a little thin, fresh cream at the last moment, and serve in a *timbale*.

2128—SAUTE OF STACHYS OR JAPANESE ARTICHOKES IN BUTTER
Crosnes Sautés au Beurre

After having parboiled, drained, and dried the Japanese artichokes, put them in an omelet-pan containing some very hot butter, and toss them over a hot fire, until they are well frizzled. Serve in a *timbale,* and sprinkle moderately with chopped parsley.

2129—STACHYS OR JAPANESE ARTICHOKES WITH VELOUTE
Crosnes au Velouté

Completely cook the Japanese artichokes in salted water. Drain them, and combine them with the required quantity of *Velouté* (25) flavored with mushroom *essence*.

2130—CROQUETTES OF STACHYS OR JAPANESE ARTICHOKES
Croquettes de Crosnes

Having cooked the Japanese artichokes in salted water, and kept them somewhat firm, thoroughly drain them and mix them with a very reduced Allemande sauce (27), in the proportion of one-fifth pint per lb. of Japanese artichokes. Spread this preparation on a buttered dish, and cool. Now cut this preparation into portions weighing about two oz.; shape these portions like balls, pears, cakes, or otherwise, dip them in beaten eggs, and roll them in very fine bread-crumbs.

Plunge these *croquettes* into very hot fat five or six minutes before serving; drain them on a piece of linen; salt moderately, and set them on a napkin with very green, fried parsley.

2131—PUREE OF STACHYS OR JAPANESE ARTICHOKES
Purée de Crosnes

Cook the Japanese artichokes in salted water, keeping them some-what firm, and add four oz. of quartered potatoes per lb. of Japanese artichokes.

As soon as they are cooked, drain the Japanese artichokes and the potatoes; rub them through a sieve, and dry the *purée* over a very hot fire. Add the necessary quantity of milk to bring the *purée* to its proper consistency; heat; add butter away from the fire, and serve in a *timbale*.

2132—SPINACH
Epinards

Spinach should only be prepared at the last moment, if possible.

After having parboiled it in plenty of boiling salted water, cool it, press out all the water, and, according to circumstances, either chop it up or rub it through a sieve.

If it has to be served with the leaves left whole, merely drain it through a sieve, without either pressing or cooling it.

2133—ANGLAISE SPINACH
Epinards à l'Anglaise

Cook it after having carefully shredded it; drain it well, and serve in a *timbale* without cooling.

2134—CREAMED SPINACH
Epinards à la Crème

Having chopped up or rubbed the spinach through a sieve, put it into a saucepan with two oz. of butter per lb., and dry it over a hot fire.

Now add the quarter of its bulk of cream sauce (79) to it, and simmer gently for ten minutes.

Put in a *timbale* when ready to serve, and sprinkle the surface with fresh cream.

2135—SPINACH AU GRATIN
Epinards au Gratin

Dry the spinach as above (2134) in three oz. of butter per lb., and then, in the same proportion, add two and one-half oz. of grated cheese.

Set on a buttered *gratin*-dish; sprinkle copiously with grated cheese and melted butter, and set the *gratin* to form in a hot oven.

2136—VIROFLAY SPINACH   *Epinards à la Viroflay*

Spread some large leaves of *blanched* spinach on a napkin, and in the middle of each lay a *subric,* the substance of which should have been combined with very small *croûtons* of bread fried in butter. Wrap the *subrics* in the spinach leaves; cover with Mornay Sauce (91); sprinkle with grated cheese and melted butter, and set to *glaze* in a hot oven.

2137—SPINACH SUBRICS OR PUFFS   *Subrics d'Epinards*

Dry the spinach in butter as described above, and add to each lb. of spinach (away from the fire) one-sixth pint of very reduced Béchamel Sauce (28); two tablespoons of thick cream; one egg and the yolks of three, well beaten; salt, pepper, and nutmeg.

Have a sufficient quantity of clarified butter (175) very hot in an omelet-pan.

Take up some of the spinach mixture with a spoon, and let it drop (propelled by the finger) into the butter. Proceed thus in the making of the *subrics,* and take care that they do not touch each other. When a minute has elapsed, turn them over with a spatula or a fork, that their other sides may brown.

Set on a dish or in a *timbale,* and serve a cream sauce (79) separately.

2138—PANCAKES WITH SPINACH   *Crêpes aux Epinards*

Parboil some well-shredded spinach; dry it in butter; season it, and add to it an equal quantity of Yorkshire-pudding paste (1943).

Cook this preparation in a small, well-buttered omelet-pan or in drop *tartlet-moulds.*

N.B.—These spinach pancakes constitute an excellent garnish for *relevés* of beef, veal, and ham.

2139—SOUFFLE OF SPINACH   *Soufflé d'Epinards*

Make a preparation after the directions given under (2092). Spread it in two or three layers, and set on each layer a layer of well-cleaned and soaked anchovy fillets, arranged to form a lattice. Finish with a layer of spinach shaped like a dome, and set on it two crossed rows of anchovy fillets. Cook after the manner of an ordinary *soufflé.*

2140—SOUFFLE OF SPINACH WITH TRUFFLES
Souffle d'Epinards aux Truffes

Proceed as directed in the above recipe, but substitute for the anchovy fillets some fine slices of truffle.

N.B.—Both these spinach *soufflés* may be served either as vege-tables, in which case they are moulded in large *timbales,* or as gar-nishes, when they are served in small *cassolettes* of appropriate size.

They are very delicate preparations, which may be varied by watercress *soufflé*—prepared in the same way.

2141—STUFFED VINE LEAVES OR DOLMAS
Feuilles de Vigne Farcies ou Dolmas

Provided the vine leaves are very tender, they may serve in the preparation of the following garnish:—Remove their stalks; parboil the leaves; drain them well, and arrange three or four at a time in the form of a circular tray, in the center of which lay a tablespoon of pilaff rice (2255) to which some *foie-gras purée* has been added. This done, fold the ends of the leaves over the rice, so as to enclose it and to form regular balls of equal size.

Put these balls, well-pressed, one against the other in a saucepan, the bottom of which should be garnished with slices of bacon; cover with thin slices of bacon; moisten just enough to cover, with good consommé; boil, and then *braise* gently.

2142—SWEET FENNEL OR FINOCCHIO   *Fenouil Tubereux*

This vegetable commonly known as sweet fennel or finochhi is not very well known. It is prepared like the cardoons and the squashes.

2143—BROAD BEANS OR POLE BEANS   *Fèves*

Broad beans should be shelled just before being cooked, and it is quite the rule to peel them. Boil them in salted water containing a bunch of savory, the size of which should be in proportion to the quantity of broad beans. When they are cooked and drained, add the leaves of savory (chopped) to them.

2144—BROAD BEANS IN BUTTER   *Fèves au Beurre*

Having well-drained and shelled the broad beans, toss them over a hot fire to dry, and then finish them, away from the fire, with three oz. of butter per lb. of beans.

2145—CREAMED BROAD BEANS   *Fèves à la Crème*

After having dried and shelled the broad beans, combine them (per lb.) with three tablespoons of thick, fresh cream.

2146—PUREE OF BROAD BEANS   *Purée de Fèves*

Proceed exactly as for *purée* of peas (2195). This *purée* constitutes a very delicate garnish, which is particularly well suited to ham.

2147—GUMBO OR OKRA   *Gombos*

This vegetable—so common in America and the East—is only very rarely used. However, it is now beginning to be better known.

There are two kinds of Gumbos: the long and the round kind. The latter is also called *Bamia* or *Bamiès*. Both kinds are prepared after the same recipes.

2148—CREAMED GUMBO OR OKRA   *Gombos à la Crème*

After having trimmed them, parboil them in salted water and drain them. Then cook them in butter, and, just before serving them, combine them with a cream sauce (79).

2149—GUMBO OR OKRA FOR GARNISHES   *Gombos pour Garnitures*

Parboil the gumbos until they are two-thirds cooked. Drain them well, and complete their cooking in the *braising*-liquor of the piece they are to accompany.

If they are to garnish a chicken *sauté*, complete their cooking in some thin veal gravy.

2150—HOP SPROUTS   *Jets de Houblon*

The edible part is separated from the fibrous part by breaking off the ends of the sprouts, as in the case of asparagus. After having rinsed them in several waters, cook them in salted water containing, per every quart, the juice of one half-lemon.

Hop sprouts may be prepared with butter, cream, *velouté* (242), etc. When served as a vegetable, they are invariably accompanied by *poached* eggs, which are laid in a crown round them and alternated by comb-shaped *croûtons* fried in butter.

HARICOT-BEANS (HARICOTS BLANCS)

2151—AMERICAN LIMA BEANS   *Haricots Blancs à l'Américaine*

Cook the beans as described under (274). But add to the prescribed ingredients one-half lb. of lean bacon per pint of dry beans.

When they are cooked and well drained, mix them with the bacon cut into dice, and combine them with some good tomato sauce (29).

2152—BUTTERED WHITE BEANS   *Haricots Blancs au Beurre*

Having well drained the dried white beans, season them with salt and pepper and add to them two oz. of butter per lb. of cooked beans. Serve in a *timbale* and sprinkle with chopped parsley.

2153—DRIED WHITE BEANS A LA BRETONNE

Haricots Blancs à la Bretonne

Drain them well and blend them with a Bretonne sauce, in the proportion of one-third pint of sauce per lb. of cooked dried white beans. Serve in a *timbale* with chopped parsley.

Bretonne Sauce is prepared as follows: To two medium-sized chopped onions slightly browned in butter add one and a quarter cups of white wine. Reduce to one-half; add one and three-quarters cup of Espagnole Sauce, the same amount of Tomato Sauce, and a small crushed clove of garlic. Keep on the fire for seven or eight minutes and finish by adding a pinch of chopped parsley. This sauce is used exclusively as a binding agent in *Haricots Blancs à la Bretonne*.

2154—PUREE OF DRIED WHITE BEANS CALLED SOISSONNAISE

Purée de Haricots Blancs dite Soissonnaise

Rub the dried white beans through a sieve while they are very hot. Add to the *purée* (per lb.) three oz. of butter; dry it over a very hot fire, and then add some milk to it, to bring it to its proper consistency.

2155—FLAGEOLETS: DRIED, DWARF KIDNEY BEANS, FRESH WAX BEANS   *Flageolets*

These beans are used fresh; but, when they are out of season, recourse is often had to preserved or dried *flageolets*. (Dwarf kidney beans.)

They are prepared in the same way as dried white beans. Their *purée*, which is very delicate, is known under the name of "Purée Musard" (636), and it is particularly suitable for the garnishing of mutton. It is also used as a thickening ingredient in the *purée* of string beans, and nothing can equal it for the purpose; for, not only is it a smooth thickening medium, but its flavor is peculiarly adapted to accentuating that of the string beans.

2156—RED KIDNEY BEANS   *Haricot Rouges*

Red beans are cooked in salted water with one-third lb. of lean bacon, one pint of red wine, one carrot, one onion stuck with a clove, and one herb-bunch per quart of beans. The bacon should be withdrawn as soon as cooked. These beans are bound together by means of *manié* butter, and they are then mixed with the bacon, which is cut into dice and frizzled in butter.

2157—STRING BEANS   *Haricots Verts*

String beans are among the greatest vegetable delicacies; but they have to be prepared with the utmost care.

Their quality is such that they are almost always good, in spite of faulty preparation—so common in their case; but, when they are cooked with care, no other vegetable can surpass them in perfection of flavor. They should be taken quite fresh, and they should not be cooked too long. They are best when they seem a little firm to the teeth, without, of course, being in the least hard.

They must not be cooled when cooked; they should only be *sautéd* over the fire with the view of causing the evaporation of their moisture.

After having seasoned them with salt and pepper, add to them (per lb.) about three oz. of very fresh butter, cut into small pieces; *sauté* them so that they combine, and serve them immediately.

Do not add chopped parsley to string beans, unless it is very tender and gathered and chopped at the last moment.

2158—HARICOTS PANACHES   *Haricots Panachés*

This consists of string beans and *flageolets* (wax beans), in equal quantities, mixed with butter.

2159—PUREE OF STRING BEANS   *Purée d'Haricots Verts*

Cook the string beans in salted water; drain them well, and stew them in butter for eight or ten minutes. Rub them through a fine sieve, and mix the resulting *purée* with half its bulk of very creamy *flageolet* (wax bean) *purée*.

LETTUCES (LAITUES)

2160—BRAISED LETTUCE AU JUS   *Laitues Braisées au Jus*

After having parboiled, cooled, and pressed the water out of the lettuce, tie the small heads together in twos or threes, and *braise* them as directed under (275). This done, cut them in two, unfold the end of each half, and set them on a dish, in the form of a crown; alternating them with heart-shaped *croûtons* fried in butter. Or, merely serve them in a *timbale*.

Coat them with the reduced *braising*-liquor combined with some thickened veal gravy.

N.B.—*Braised* lettuce heads may also be stuffed after the manner described under (2106).

2161—LETTUCE WITH MARROW
Laitues à la Moëlle

Braise and serve the lettuce as above.

Upon the *turban* of lettuce, set a crown of large slices of *poached* marrow, and coat with a moderately thick buttered gravy.

2162—STUFFED LETTUCE
Laitues Farcies

Parboil, cool, and press the lettuce heads.

This done, open them in the middle without touching their stems, and fill them with good *forcemeat*, combined with half its bulk of dry *Duxelles* (223). Shape the lettuce; tie them; *braise* them, and serve them as directed under (2160).

2163—STUFFED LETTUCE FOR GARNISHING
Laitues Farcies pour Garniture

Proceed as directed under (2104 to 2106).

2164—CREAMED LETTUCE
Laitues à la Crème

Proceed as directed under (2089).

2165—SOUFFLE OF LETTUCE
Soufflé de Laitues

Proceed as directed under (2139).

LENTILS (LENTILLES)

Lentils are cooked as directed under the "preparation of dry vegetables" (274).

2166—BUTTERED LENTILS
Lentilles au Beurre

Carefully drain the lentils; dry them by tossing them over the fire, and bind them with two oz. of butter per lb. of lentils.

Serve in a *timbale,* and sprinkle with a little chopped parsley.

2167—PUREE OF LENTILS
Purée de Lentilles

Proceed as for the *purée* of dried white beans.

2168—VERONICA (SPEEDWELL)
Véronique (Laver)

As this vegetable is sold already cooked, it is only necessary to add enough good Espagnole Sauce (22), when heating it, to make a properly consistent *purée*.

2169—SWEET CORN *Maïs*

Take the corn when it is quite fresh and still milky, and cook it either in steam or salted water; taking care to leave the husks on. When cooked, the husks are drawn back so as to represent stems, and the ears are bared if served whole. This done, set the ears on a napkin, and send a hors-d'œuvre dish of fresh butter to the table with them.

If the corn is to be grilled, put the ears on a grill in the oven, and, when they have swollen and are of a golden color, remove the kernels and put on a napkin. Sometimes, too, the ears are served whole.

When corn is served as an accompaniment, to other dishes, the kernels are cut from the stalk and mixed with butter or cream, exactly like peas.

If fresh corn is not on hand, excellent canned or frozen kinds are to be found on the market.

(In the United States, the silk and the husks are removed, and corn-holders are sent to the table with the ears of corn.—Ed.)

2170—SOUFFLE OF CREAMED CORN *Soufflé de Maïs à la Crème*

Cook the cut corn in water or steam; rub it quickly through a sieve; put it into a saucepan with a small piece of butter, and quickly dry it.

This done, add sufficient fresh cream to this *purée* to make a somewhat soft paste. Thicken this paste with the yolks of three eggs, per lb. of *purée,* and combine it with the whites of four eggs beaten to a stiff froth. Pour into a *soufflé form* and cook after the manner of an ordinary *soufflé* (2519).

2171—SOUFFLE OF CORN WITH PAPRIKA

Soufflé de Maïs au Paprika

Before crushing the corn through a sieve, add to it two tablespoons of chopped onion fried in butter, and a large pinch of paprika per lb. of corn. Proceed for the rest of the cooking as in (2170).

N.B.—These two *soufflés* are served as a garnish and may be cooked either in a *timbale* or in small *cassolettes.* They constitute excellent accompaniments to large, *poached* fowls.

2172—CHESTNUTS *Marrons*

Slightly split open the shell on the convex sides of the nuts, and put them in the oven for from seven to eight minutes, in a pan containing a little water, that they may be shelled with ease.

Or, split them open in the same way; put them in small quantities at a time in a frying-basket, and plunge them into very hot fat. Peel them while they are still quite hot.

2173—STEWED CHESTNUTS   *Marrons Etuvés*

As soon as they are peeled, cook them in enough consommé to just cover them, and add half a stalk of celery per lb. of chestnuts.

If they are intended for the stuffing of a goose or a turkey, keep them somewhat firm.

2174—BRAISED AND GLAZED CHESTNUTS   *Marrons Braisés et Glacés*

Take some very large chestnuts, and dip them in hot fat in order to peel them. Then set them in one layer, one against the other in a saucepan. If they were heaped, a poor result would be obtained.

Moisten them, just enough to cover, with strong veal stock, and stir them as little as possible while they are cooking, so as to avoid breaking them.

When they are three-quarters cooked, reduce the stock, and gently roll the chestnuts in the *glaze* resulting from this reduction, that they may be covered with a glossy coating.

Chestnuts prepared in this way serve more particularly as a garnish.

2175—PUREE OF CHESTNUTS   *Purée de Marrons*

Having thoroughly peeled the chestnuts, cook them in white consommé, with a celery stalk as in the case of (2173), and one-half oz. of sugar per lb. of chestnuts. Continue cooking until they may be easily crushed; rub them through a fine sieve, and treat the *purée* as directed in the preceding ones.

2176—TURNIPS   *Navets*

Whether served as vegetables or as a garnish, white turnips are prepared like carrots. They may, therefore, be served either *glazed*, or "à la Crème," etc.

They may also be served stuffed, after the following recipes:—

2177a—STUFFED TURNIPS   *Navets Farcis*

Take some round, medium-sized white turnips, fairly equal in size. Peel them, and, in so doing, shape them nicely; then, by means of a round fancy-cutter, cut them at their base, pressing deeply into the pulp.

This done, thoroughly parboil and empty them.

With the pulp, prepare a *purée,* to which add an equal quantity of mashed potatoes. Fill the turnips with this *purée,* and shape the top dome-fashion.

Set the stuffed turnips in a saucepan, and complete their cooking in butter, taking care to baste them frequently.

2178b—STUFFED TURNIPS   *Navets Farcis*

Prepare the turnips as above; but stuff them with a preparation of semolina cooked in consommé and combined with grated Parmesan cheese.

Complete the cooking as directed in the preceding recipe (2177).

N.B.—Proceeding in the same way, turnips may be stuffed with spinach, chicory, and even with starchy vegetables or rice, kept very creamy. All these garnishes are at once sightly and excellent.

2179—WHITE TURNIP PUREE   *Purée de Navets*

Slice the white turnips and cook them in a little butter, salt, sugar, and the necessary amount of water. Rub through a fine sieve, and thicken the *purée* with just the required quantity of very good mashed potatoes.

2180—TURNIP-TOPS   *Pousses ou Feuilles de Navets*

Young turnip-tops are very much liked as a luncheon vegetable. They should be prepared like "Choux verts cooked *à l'anglaise*" (2101).

Onions (Oignons)

2181—STUFFED ONIONS   *Oignons Farcis*

Take some medium-sized, mild, Spanish onions; cut them at a point one-quarter of their height from the top, and parboil them.

Empty them, leaving only a wall one-third inch thick; chop up the parts taken out, and mix them with an equal quantity of *Duxelles* (225).

Garnish the emptied onions with this preparation; complete their cooking by *braising* them, and *glaze* them at the last moment, simultaneously with the formation of the *gratin.*

N.B.—Proceed in the same way for onions stuffed with spinach, *Rizotto,* or semolina, etc., as suggested under (2177 and 2178).

Onions may also be garnished with a *soufflé* preparation of spinach, tomatoes, chicory, etc. There is scope for a great variety of excellent and unusual garnishes.

2182—FRIED AND FRENCH FRIED ONIONS *Oignons Frits*

Cut them into round slices one-fifth inch thick; separate the rings; season them with salt and pepper; dredge them and fry them in very hot oil. Drain on a piece of linen and salt slightly.

For "French Fried" onions, dredge in seasoned flour and fry in deep fat or oil. To make them crisper, dip the onion rings in milk before dredging in flour.

2183—GLAZED ONIONS *Oignons Glacés*

For the preparation without browning: Peel some small onions of equal size without cutting into them. Set them to cook in enough white consommé to almost cover them, and two oz. of butter per pint of consommé.

At the last moment roll them in their cooking-liquor, reduced to a *glaze*.

For the preparation with browning: Cook the onions very gently in butter, with a pinch of powdered sugar, so that the cooking and the browning may be done at one time.

2184—PUREE OF ONIONS, CALLED SOUBISE
Purée d'Oignons, dite Soubise

See (104), in the chapter on sauces.

2185—SORREL *Oseille*

Having shredded the sorrel and washed it in several waters, set it to cook gently in a little water. This done, thoroughly drain it on a sieve and mix it with a pale *roux*, consisting of two oz. of butter and one oz. of flour. Add one and one-quarter pints of consommé, salt, and a pinch of sugar to it, and *braise* it in the oven for two hours.

Then rub it through a fine sieve; thicken it with the yolks of six eggs or three whole eggs beaten to a stiff froth and strained. Heat, and finish with one-sixth pint of cream and five oz. of butter.

Serve in a *timbale,* and sprinkle with strong, veal stock.

2186—OXALIS (Roots Like Potatoes) *Oxalis (Crenata)*

Cook this in boiling salted water after having well cleaned and washed it. It may then be prepared "à la Crème," stuffed, or "au Gratin."

Oxalis *purée* is called *Purée Brésilienne,* and is prepared in the same way as turnip *purée.*

(Oxalis roots are very similar to potatoes.—Ed.)

2187.—SWEET POTATOES   *Patates Douces*

Sweet potatoes are generally served, baked in their skins, and accompanied by fresh butter. They may also be prepared according to the majority of potato-recipes, especially the following:—*Sautées, Gratinées, Mashed, Duchesse,* etc.

They may also be fried; but, in that case, they should be served the moment they are ready, for they soften very quickly.

Finally, they may be prepared *soufflé*-fashion, after the directions given under "Soufflé de Pommes de Terre."

2188—PEAS   *Petits Pois*

Whatever be the treatment to which peas are to be subjected, always take them very green and freshly gathered, and shell them only at the last minute. Peas are one of the vegetables most prone to lose their quality through want of care. If prepared with care, the delicacy of their flavor is incomparable; but the slightest neglect on the part of the cook makes them savorless and commonplace.

2189—ANGLAISE GREEN PEAS   *Petits Pois à l'Anglaise*

Cook them quickly in salted boiling water; drain them, and dry them by tossing them over a hot fire. Serve them in a *timbale,* with some pats of very fresh butter separately.

2190—GREEN PEAS IN BUTTER   *Petits Pois au Beurre*

As soon as the peas are cooked, drain them and toss them over a hot fire, to dry. Then season them with a pinch of powdered sugar, and mix them, away from the fire, with butter, in the proportion of three oz. per pint of peas.

2191—BONNE-FEMME GREEN PEAS   *Petits Pois à la Bonne-Femme*

Fry twelve oz. of small onions and four oz. of breast of bacon, cut into dice and *blanched* in butter; add one-half oz. of flour to the latter; cook the *roux* for a moment; moisten with one-half pint of consommé and boil.

Put one quart of freshly-shelled peas into this sauce; add the onions and the bacon, together with a bunch of parsley; and cook, reducing the sauce to half in so doing.

2192—FLAMANDE GREEN PEAS   *Petits Pois à la Flamande*

Prepare one-half lb. of new carrots as though they were to be *glazed.*

When half-cooked, add two-thirds pint of freshly-shelled peas to them. Complete the cooking of the two vegetables together, and, at the last moment, add butter away from the fire.

2193—GREEN PEAS FRANCAISE   *Petits Pois à la Française*

Take a saucepan, of a size a little larger than would be necessary to just hold the following products, and put into it one quart of freshly-shelled peas; a herb-bunch containing a heart of lettuce, two sprigs of parsley, and two of chervil; twelve small onions, four oz. of butter, one-third oz. of salt, and two-thirds oz. of sugar. Mix the whole together until it forms a compact mass, and place in the cool until ready for cooking. Add three tablespoons of water, when about to cook the peas, and cook gently with lid on.

When about to serve, take the herb-bunch; shred the lettuce; add it to the peas, and combine the whole with butter, away from the fire.

N.B.—Raw, shredded lettuce may be added to the peas; but, as various tastes must be allowed for, it is better to insert the lettuce whole, and to mix it with the peas afterwards, if it be so desired. The lettuce may also be quartered and laid on the peas without being mixed with them.

2194—GREEN PEAS A LA MENTHE   *Petits Pois à la Menthe*

Cook the peas in salted water, together with a bunch of fresh mint.

Then prepare them in the English way (2189) or "au Beurre" (2190), and lay a few parboiled mint leaves upon them when serving.

2195—PUREE OF GREEN PEAS CALLED ST. GERMAIN
Purée de Pois Frais, dite Saint-Germain

Cook the peas with just enough boiling water to cover them, and season it with one-half oz. of salt, and one-sixth oz. of sugar per quart. Add a lettuce and a few parsley sprigs (tied together). When the peas are cooked, drain them; and reduce their cooking-liquor while they are being rubbed through a sieve.

Work the *purée* with four oz. of fresh butter per quart, and finally add to it the cooking-liquor, reduced almost to a *glaze*.

2196—MOULDED PEASE PUREE FOR GARNISH
Purée de Petits Pois en Moules pour Garnitures

Prepare the *purée* as above; but keep it a little creamier. Mix with it, per quart, two whole eggs and the yolks of three, beaten and strained through muslin. With this preparation, fill some *dariole* or *baba*-moulds, according to the piece for which the *timbales* are intended, and *poach* them in a *bain-marie* (water-bath) for from twenty to twenty-five minutes.

Remember to let them stand for five minutes before unmoulding them.

N.B.—*Timbales* of dried white beans, dwarf kidney beans, or lentil *purée,* are prepared similarly.

2197—SWEET PEPPERS OR PIMENTOS   *Poivrons doux*

Peppers used in cookery are of various kinds: the Chilian and Cayenne kinds (Chili and Cayenne peppers) which have a strong, burning taste, are only used as condiments.

The large or mild peppers, green, red, or yellow, are used more particularly as garnishes. Although the difference in their coloration is accompanied by a difference of quality, they are not easily distinguished in this respect; and, although the large, red Spanish peppers are the best, the other varieties may be treated in the same way.

Whatever be the kind of peppers used, either grill or scald them in order to skin them, and clear them of their seeds. According to the purpose they are intended for, they are either cut up or left whole.

2198—STUFFED PIMENTOS   *Pimentos Farcis*

For this purpose take some small, green long-shaped peppers.

Remove their stems, after having skinned them; empty them, and half-fill them with half-cooked, pilaff rice (2255).

Then set them in a saucepan, and carefully *braise* them with excellent stock.

2199—SWEET PEPPERS FOR GARNISHING   *Poivrons pour Garnitures*

For this purpose, the large red, Spanish peppers are best.

Braise them when they are peeled, and, when cooked, cut them up as the requirements may suggest.

2200—PUREE OF PIMENTOS   *Purée de Pimentos*

Braise some large, red sweet peppers, with two-thirds of their weight of rice. When the whole is well cooked, rub it through a sieve, and add butter to the extent of two oz. per quart of the preparation.

N.B.—This *purée* is particularly well suited to *poached* fowls and white meats, and it is well to keep it thin.

2201—POTATOES　　　　　　*Pommes de Terre*

Ordinary potatoes are rarely of good quality in England, and they do not lend themselves as well as certain Continental varieties do to the various culinary uses to which this valuable tuber may be put.

The very best kinds of potato are almost unknown in England, and the Dutch and Vitelotte potatoes have to be imported.

(Many varieties of potato are grown in the United States, the best known of which are probably the Idaho, the Maine, and the Long Island potatoes. It is a question whether they compare favorably with those raised in Europe, principally Germany, where unusually fine types have been developed. The waxy, yellowish oblong type of potato which is generally used for salads in the European and French recipes can be replaced by the small, early, rose potato with slightly pink skin, if the latter is not overcooked.—Ed.)

2202—ANGLAISE POTATOES　　　*Pommes de Terre à l'Anglaise*

Cut the potatoes to the shape of large garlic cloves, and cook them in salted water or steam. They accompany especially boiled fish.

2203—ANNA POTATOES　　　　*Pommes de Terre Anna*

Cut them to the shape of small cylinders; cut these into thin slices; wash them, and dry them in a piece of linen.

Set these slices in circles on the bottom of the mould proper to this potato preparation, or in a well-buttered thick-bottomed saucepan; let them overlap one another, and reverse each circle.

Season; spread a coat of butter upon the first layer, and proceed in the same way with a second layer.

Make five or six layers in this way, seasoning and spreading butter over each.

Cover the utensil; cook in a good oven for thirty minutes, turn the whole over, if necessary, to equalize the browning; turn out upon a saucepan-lid, to drain off the butter, and then tilt onto a dish.

2204—ANNA POTATOES FOR GARNISHING
Pommes Anna pour Garnitures

Either *dariole* or *baba*-moulds may be used for this purpose; but they should be tinned copper ones if possible. After having thoroughly buttered them, garnish them with thin slices of potato, cut to the diameter of the moulds, seasoned, and set one upon the other. Set the moulds in a pan containing enough very hot fat to reach half-way up to their brims, and cook in a very hot oven for twenty-five minutes.

Turn out just before serving.

2205—BERNY POTATOES   *Pommes de Terre Berny*

Add chopped truffles to some *"croquette"* paste (219), in the pro portion of two oz. of the former to one lb. of the latter; and divide up this preparation into two-oz. portions. Mould these to shapes resembling apricots; dip them in beaten eggs (174), and roll them in almonds cut into the thinnest possible slivers. Plunge the potato balls into hot fat five or six minutes before serving.

2206—BOULANGERE POTATOES   *Pommes de Terre à la Boulangère*

This preparation has been given in various recipes (1307).

2207—BYRON POTATOES   *Pommes de Terre Byron*

Prepare the required amount of "Pommes Macaire" (2228), and cook in butter in a small frying-pan. Put on a dish; sprinkle copi· ously with cream and grated cheese, and set to *glaze* quickly.

2208—CHATEAU POTATOES   *Pommes de Terre Château*

Cut them to the shape of large olives; season them; cook them gently in clarified butter (175), that they may be golden and very soft; and, just before serving, sprinkle them moderately with chopped parsley.

2209—CREAMED POTATOES   *Pommes de Terre à la Crème*

Vitelotte or new kidney potatoes are needed for this preparation.

Cook them in salted water; peel them as soon as this is done, and cut them into rather thick slices. Put them in a saucepan; moisten, enough to cover them, with boiling cream; season, and reduce the cream.

At the last moment, finish with raw cream.

2210—POTATO CROQUETTES   *Croquettes de Pommes de Terre*

Prepare the necessary quantity of "croquette" paste (219), and divide it into two-oz. portions. Roll these to the shape of corks or pears; treat them *à l'anglaise,* and put them into very hot fat, five or six minutes before serving.

2211—DAUPHINE POTATO CROQUETTES

Croquettes de Pommes de Terre à la Dauphine

Take the required amount of "Pommes Dauphine" preparation (220); divide it into two-oz. portions; mould these to the shape of corks; treat them *à l'anglaise,* and fry them like ordinary *croquettes.*

2212—DUCHESSE POTATOES   *Pommes de Terre à la Duchesse*

Use the same preparation as for (2210). Mould the portions to the shape of small brioches, patties or small loaves, or shape them by means of the pastry-bag. Arrange them in a buttered pan; brown them with beaten egg, and brown them in a hot oven for seven or eight minutes before serving them.

2213—DUCHESS OF CHESTER POTATOES

Pommes de Terre Duchesse de Chester

Use the same preparation as for (2210), and combine it with two oz. of grated sharp cheese per lb. Mould it to the shape of very small cakes; set these portions in a buttered pan; brush them with beaten eggs; cover each with a thin slice of cheese, and set them in the oven for seven or eight minutes before serving.

2214—FONDANTES POTATOES   *Pommes de Terre Fondantes*

Cut the potatoes to the shape of large, elongated olives, and let each weigh about three oz. Gently cook them in butter, in a sauce-pan, and take care to turn them over.

When they are cooked, take them out, so as to slightly flatten them with a fork without breaking them. Drain away their butter; return them to the saucepan with three oz. of fresh butter per every two lbs. of their weight, and cook them with lid on until they have entirely absorbed the butter.

2215—SHOESTRING POTATOES   *Pommes de Terre en Allumettes*

Trim the potatoes square, and then cut them into small sticks, of one-fifth in. Put them in hot fat, and let them dry well before draining them.

2216—CHATOUILLARD POTATOES   *Pommes de Terre Chatouillard*

Trim the potatoes, and cut them into long even ribbons one-eighth in. thick. Treat these ribbons like "Pommes soufflées" (2221).

2217—CHIPPED POTATOES   *Pommes de Terre "Chip"*

Cut the potatoes into thin slices, with a vegetable slicer; put them into cold water for ten minutes; drain them; dry them in linen, and fry them, keeping them very crisp. Serve them cold or hot, with roasted game.

2218—COLLERETTE POTATOES   *Pommes de Terre Collerette*

Cut the potatoes to the shape of corks, and slice them with a vegetable cutter. Treat them like chipped potatoes.

2219—JULIENNE POTATOES   *Pommes de Terre Paillés*

Cut the potatoes into a long, thin *julienne;* wash them and thoroughly dry them on a piece of linen.

Put them into hot fat; and, at the end of a few minutes, drain them in a frying-basket. Just before serving them, plunge them again into smoking fat, that they may be very crisp; drain them on a piece of linen, and salt them moderately.

2220—PONT-NEUF POTATOES (FRENCH FRIED POTATOES)
Pommes de Terre Pont-Neuf

Trim the potatoes square, and cut them into sticks of half-inch. Plunge them into hot fat, and leave them there until they are crisp outside and creamy in.

This preparation represents the general type of fried potatoes.

2221—POTATO SOUFFLE   *Pommes de Terre Soufflées*

Trim the potatoes square, and carefully cut them into slices one-eighth inch thick. Wash them in cold water; thoroughly dry them, and put them into moderately hot fat. As soon as the potatoes are in it, gradually heat the fat until they are cooked—which they are known to be when they rise to the surface of the frying fat.

Drain them in the frying-basket, and at once immerse them in fresh and hotter fat. This final immersion effects the puffing, which results from the sudden contact with intense heat.

Leave the potatoes to dry; drain them on a stretched piece of linen; salt them moderately, and serve them.

2222—DAUPHINOISE POTATOES GRATIN
Gratin de Pommes de Terre à la Dauphinoise

Finely slice two lbs. of fair-sized Irish potatoes. Put them in a bowl, and add salt, pepper, grated nutmeg, one beaten egg, one and one-half pints of boiled milk, and four oz. of fresh, grated Gruyère cheese.

Thoroughly mix up the whole.

Pour this preparation into earthenware dishes, rubbed with garlic and well buttered; copiously sprinkle with grated Gruyère cheese; add a few pieces of butter, and cook in a moderate oven for from forty to forty-five minutes.

2223—HUNGARIAN POTATOES *Pommes de Terre à la Hongroise*

Fry four oz. of chopped onion in butter, together with a teaspoon of paprika. Add two peeled, pressed, and sliced tomatoes; two lbs. of potatoes, cut into somewhat thick slices, and moisten, just enough to cover, with consommé. Cook, while almost entirely reducing the moistening, and sprinkle with chopped parsley at the last moment.

2224—GRATIN POTATOES *Pommes de Terre Gratinées*

This preparation may be made in two ways as follows:—

Make a smooth potato *purée;* this done, put it into a deep, buttered *gratin*-dish; smooth its surface; sprinkle with grated cheese mixed with fine *raspings;* coat with melted butter, and set the *gratin* to form in a hot oven.

Or bake some fine, well-washed, baking potatoes in the oven. As soon as they are cooked, open them lengthwise; scoop out their pulp; rub the latter through a sieve while it is still quite hot, and finish it after the manner of an ordinary *purée.*

Fill the shells with *purée;* sprinkle with grated cheese and *raspings;* lay the half-shells in a pan, and set the *gratin* to form as above.

On taking the potatoes out of the oven, put them on a napkin, and serve them immediately.

2225—POTATOES WITH SALT PORK *Pommes de Terre au Lard*

Frizzle in butter one-half lb. of salt pork, cut into dice and *blanched,* and twelve small onions. Drain the bacon and the onions; mix one oz. of flour with the butter; brown for a few minutes, and moisten with one and one-quarter pints of consommé. Season with a pinch of pepper, and add two lbs. of medium-sized, quartered and well-trimmed potatoes, the bacon and the onions, and a herb-bunch. Cover and cook gently.

Serve in a *timbale,* and sprinkle moderately with chopped parsley.

2226—LORETTE POTATOES *Pommes de Terre Lorette*

Add some grated cheese to the preparation for "Pommes Dauphine" (2211), in the proportion of one oz. of the former per lb. of the latter.

Divide up this mixture into one and one-half oz. portions; mould these to the shape of crescents, and dredge them moderately.

Plunge these crescents into very hot fat about six minutes before serving.

2227—LYONNAISE POTATOES   *Pommes de Terre à la Lyonnaise*

Cut some peeled and plain-boiled potatoes into slices, and toss these in butter in a frying-pan. Likewise toss some sliced onions in butter, the quantity of the former measuring one-fourth of that of the potatoes. When the onions are a nice golden brown, add them to the *sautéd* potatoes; season with salt and pepper; *sauté* the two together for a few minutes, that they may mix thoroughly, and serve them in a *timbale* with chopped parsley.

2228—MACAIRE POTATOES   *Pommes de Terre Macaire*

Bake some potatoes in the oven. As soon as they are done, empty them and scoop out their pulp on a dish; season it with salt and pepper, and work it with a fork; adding to it, the while, one and one-half oz. of butter per lb.

Spread this preparation in the form of a pancake on the bottom of an omelet-pan containing some very hot, clarified butter (175), and brown it well on both sides.

2229—MAIRE POTATOES   *Pommes de Terre Maire*

Prepare these exactly like "Pommes à la Crème" (2209).

2230—MAITRE-D'HOTEL POTATOES *Pommes de Terre Maitre-d'Hôtel*

Cook some medium-sized potatoes in salted water; peel them; cut them into round slices while they are still quite hot, and cover them with boiling milk.

Season them with salt and white pepper; completely reduce the milk, and serve them in a *timbale* with chopped parsley.

2231—MARQUISE POTATOES   *Pommes de Terre Marquise*

Mix some very reduced and very red tomato *purée* (659) with the preparation for "Pommes Duchesse," in the proportion of three tablespoons of the former per lb. of the latter.

Set this preparation on buttered tins (by means of a pastry-bag fitted with a large, fancy tube) in shapes resembling half-eggs.

Brush them slightly with beaten eggs, and set them in a somewhat hot oven seven or eight minutes before serving.

2232—POTATOES WITH MINT   *Pommes de Terre à la Menthe*

Boil some fair-sized new potatoes, and add a bunch of mint to them. Serve them in a *timbale,* and set a mint-leaf upon each potato.

2233—MIREILLE POTATOES　　　　*Pommes de Terre Mireille*

Cut some medium-sized, raw potatoes into round slices. Season them and *sauté* them in butter. When they are ready, add to them, per lb., four oz. of sliced artichoke-bottoms, tossed in butter, and one and one-half oz. of truffle slices.

Sauté so as to ensure a complete mixture, and serve in a *timbale*.

2234—MIRETTE POTATOES　　　　*Pommes de Terre Mirette*

Cut some raw potatoes into a *julienne* one-eighth inch wide, and cook them in butter, keeping them very creamy. Add to them, per lb., two oz. of a *julienne* of truffles and three tablespoons of melted meat *glaze* (15).

Mix; put in a *timbale;* sprinkle with grated Parmesan cheese and melted butter, and set to *glaze* quickly.

2235—MOUSSELINE POTATOES　　　　*Pommes de Terre Mousseline*

Prepare a flawn-crust (2395), baked without browning.

Meanwhile, bake a few potatoes in the oven; scoop out their pulp; season it with salt and white pepper, and work it over the fire with four oz. of butter and the yolks of two eggs per lb. of its weight. Add one-sixth pint of whipped cream, and set the preparation in the crust, shaping it like a dome. Decorate by means of a pastry-bag, fitted with a fancy tube, with some of the preparation which should have been put aside; sprinkle with melted butter, and set to *glaze* quickly.

2236—NOISETTE POTATOES　　　　*Pommes de Terre Noisette*

Cut the potatoes, by means of a round ball-cutter, into balls the size of hazel-nuts. Season and cook them in butter, and take care to keep them nicely golden and creamy.

2237—PARISIENNE POTATOES　　　　*Pommes de Terre Parisienne*

Prepare some "Pommes Noisettes" as above; but cut them a little smaller. When they are cooked, roll them in melted meat *glaze* (15), and sprinkle them with chopped parsley.

2238—PARMESAN POTATOES　　　　*Pommes de Terre au Parmesan*

Proceed as directed under "Pommes au Chester" (2213), but substitute Parmesan cheese for the latter.

2239—PARSLEY POTATOES　　　　*Pommes de Terre Persilées*

Boil the potatoes plainly; drain them well, and roll them in melted butter and chopped parsley.

2240—ROBERT POTATOES   *Pommes de Terre Robert*

Prepare a composition of "Pomme Macaire" (2228), and add, per lb., three eggs and a large pinch of chopped chives. Cook in the frying-pan as for "Pomme Macaire."

2241—ROXELANE POTATOES   *Pommes de Terre Roxelane*

Bake six fine potatoes in the oven. Scoop out the pulp from their insides, and work it, together with one-third lb. of butter and four egg-yolks, and enough fresh cream to thin it. Complete with the whites of two eggs, beaten to a stiff froth.

Set this preparation in small *timbales,* made from brioches (2370) the tops of which have been removed, and which have been emptied of all crumbs. Sprinkle with chopped truffle, and bake in a mild oven as for a *soufflé.*

2242—SAVOYARDE POTATOES   *Pommes de Terre à la Savoyarde*

Proceed as for (2222); but replace the milk by some consommé.

2243—ST. FLORENTIN POTATOES   *Pommes de Terre Saint-Florentin*

Prepare some "Pommes Croquettes" paste (219). Combine therewith (per lb.) two oz. of chopped, lean ham. Roll the portions into the shape of corks; dip them in beaten eggs, and roll them in vermicelli. This done, flatten so as to give them a rectangular shape, and fry them in very hot fat.

2244—SCHNEIDER POTATOES   *Pommes de Terre Schneider*

Proceed as directed under (2230); but for the milk substitute some consommé. Reduce in the same way, and finish with butter, melted meat *glaze* (15), and chopped parsley.

2245—SUZETTE POTATOES   *Pommes de Terre Suzette*

Peel some fine potatoes, and turn them to the shape of eggs. Cut them flat at one end that they may stand upright, and bake them in a pan in the oven.

Open them like a hard boiled egg; put aside the pieces thus cut off, and take out the pulp from their insides. Season this pulp, and work it; adding to it, per lb., two oz. of butter, two egg-yolks, a few tablespoons of thick cream, and a little *salpicon* of the white of a chicken, tongue, truffles, and mushrooms. Fill the potato-shells with this preparation; put back the covers, and set them in the oven for ten minutes.

On taking them from the oven, set the potatoes on a dish, and *glaze* them with melted butter.

2246—VOISIN POTATOES *Pommes de Terre Voisin*

Prepare these exactly like "Pommes Anna" (2204), but sprinkle each layer of potato slices with grated cheese. The cooking is the same.

2247—NANA POTATOES FOR GARNISHING

Pommes Nana pour Garniture

Cut the potatoes into a *julienne;* season them, and mould them by heaping them into well-buttered, *dariole*-moulds. Cook them, like "Pommes Anna" (2204) (for garnishing), in a pan containing some very hot fat.

On taking them out of the oven, turn them out and sprinkle them with Château sauce.

2248—MASHED POTATOES *Purée de Pommes de Terre*

Peel and quarter some fine potatoes, and quickly cook them in salted water. When they feel soft to the touch, drain them; rub them through a sieve, and work the *purée* vigorously with three oz. of butter per lb. of potatoes. Then add, little by little, about one-half pint of boiling milk, in order to bring the *purée* to the required consistency. Heat without boiling, and serve.

Remember that mashed potatoes should be only just cooked, and that if they be allowed to wait they lose all their quality.

2249—QUENELLES OF POTATOES *Quenelles de Pommes de Terre*

Prepare a mixture as for "Pommes Duchesse" (2212), and add (per two lbs.) three whole eggs and one-third lb. of flour. Divide up the preparation into one and one-half oz. portions; mould these to the shape of corks or patties, or mould them by means of a spoon, and set them in a buttered saucepan. *Poach* them in salted water; drain them; set them on a buttered dish sprinkled with grated cheese; dredge with the grated cheese; sprinkle with melted butter, and set the *gratin* to form.

On taking the dish out of the oven, sprinkle the *quenelles* with nut-brown butter (154).

2250—SOUFFLE OF POTATOES *Soufflé de Pommes de Terre*

Prepare a pint of mashed potatoes with cream; add the raw yolks of three eggs and their whites beaten to a stiff froth. Set in a buttered *soufflé* saucepan, or in small porcelain dishes, and cook like an ordinary *soufflé.*

RICE (RIZ)

2251—PLAIN RICE (FOR FOWLS AND EGGS)   *Riz au Blanc*

Wash one-half lb. of Carolina or Southern rice; put it into a saucepan; cover it with plenty of cold water; salt it, and parboil it for one-quarter hour.

This done, drain it and put it into a saucepan with two and one-half oz. of butter cut into small pieces. Mix with a fork; cover, and place in a moderate oven for fifteen minutes.

2252—RICE WITH FAT   *Riz au Gras*

Parboil one-half lb. of Carolina or Southern rice; drain it; fry it in butter, and moisten it with twice as much white and rather fat consommé as would be needed just to cover it. Set to boil, and then cook it gently in the oven for fifteen minutes.

2253—RICE GREEK STYLE   *Riz à la Grecque*

Prepare some "Pilaff" rice (2255). Add to it, per lb. of its weight one-half onion, chopped and fried in butter, together with two oz. of fat sausage-meat, divided into small portions, and two oz. of shredded lettuce; cook the whole, and complete with one-quarter pint of peas, cooked "à la Française" (2193), and one and one-half oz. of red sweet peppers cut into dice.

This garnish is mixed with the rice seven or eight minutes before serving.

2254—INDIA RICE   *Riz à l'Indienne*

Parboil one-half lb. of Patna (Persian) rice in salted water, for fifteen minutes; stirring it from time to time the while.

Drain it; wash it in several cold waters; lay it on a napkin, and set the latter on a tray or on a sieve. Dry for fifteen minutes in a steamer or in a very moderate oven.

2255—RICE PILAFF   *Riz Pilaw*

Fry one chopped half-onion and one-half lb. of Carolina or Southern rice in two oz. of butter. Stir over the fire, until the rice is well mixed; moisten with one quart of white consommé; cover, and cook in a moderate oven for eighteen minutes. Transfer it to another saucepan as soon as it is cooked.

2256—RICE PILAFF (FOR STUFFING OF FOWLS)
Riz Pilaw pour Garniture de Volaille

Pilaff rice is frequently used in stuffing fowls.

For this purpose, when it is cooked, it is combined (per quart) with a little cream, four oz. of *foie-gras* dice, and as much truffle, also in dice. The rice should only be three-quarters cooked for stuffings; for it completes its cooking inside the bird. For this reason the cream is added, that the rice may absorb it while its cooking is being completed.

2257—TURKISH RICE PILAFF   *Riz Pilaff à la Turque*

Prepare some pilaff rice as directed under (2255), and, while it is cooking, add to it enough saffron to make it of a nice, golden color. When cooked, add four oz. of peeled and chopped tomatoes to it.

2258—PIEMONTAISE RIZOTTO   *Rizotto à la Piémontaise*

Fry a medium-sized onion in butter, and add to it one-half lb. of Italian rice. Put the rice on the side of the stove; add some saffron to it and stir it until it is well saturated with butter. Moisten the rice with about one quart of consommé per lb. The consommé should be added to the rice seven or eight times, and as fast as it becomes absorbed, more should be added. When adding the consommé, stir the rice with a wooden spoon.

Cook the rice covered, and, to the preparation, which should be creamy, add a few pieces of fresh butter and some grated Parmesan cheese.

The dish may be finished, either with shavings of white truffles or ham cut into dice.

2259—SALSIFY OR OYSTER PLANT   *Salsifis*

There are two kinds of salsify:—the white and the black, which is also called "viper's grass."

After having carefully scraped and washed it, cook it in a *blanc*. The same preparations suit the two kinds.

2260—FRIED SALSIFY OR OYSTER PLANT   *Salsifis Frit*

After having thoroughly drained it, cut it into three and one-half lengths, and put these on a dish.

Season with salt and pepper; add lemon juice, a few drops of oil, some chopped parsley, and leave to *marinate* for from twenty-five to thirty minutes, taking care to toss the salsify from time to time.

This done, drain the lengths of salsify, dip them in some thin batter; plunge them in very hot fat, and drain them when the batter is quite dry. Serve them on a napkin with fried parsley.

N.B.—It is not absolutely necessary to *marinate* salsify; the question is one of taste.

2261—SAUTE OF SALSIFY OR OYSTER PLANT   *Salsifis Sauté*

Cut it into two-inch lengths; dry them very well, and toss these in butter in an omelet-pan, until they are of a nice golden brown. Season, and serve in a *timbale* with fried parsley.

2262—CREAMED SALSIFY OR OYSTER PLANT   *Salsifis à la Crème*

Proceed as directed in the case of other vegetables prepared in this way.

TOMATOES

2263—GRILLED TOMATOES   *Tomates Grillées*

Take some whole tomatoes, if possible; oil them copiously, and grill them gently.

2264—STUFFED TOMATOES   *Tomates Farcies*

If the tomatoes to be stuffed are large, cut them in two; if they be medium-sized or small, a slice cut from their stem-ends is sufficient. In any case, press them slightly in order to exude their juice and seeds; season them inside with salt and pepper; set them in an oiled pan, and only half-cook them in the oven.

Finally, stuff them as their recipe requires.

2265—STUFFED TOMATOES AU GRATIN   *Tomates Farcies au Gratin*

Having prepared the tomatoes as above, stuff them with somewhat stiff *Duxelles;* sprinkle with *raspings* and a few drops of oil, and set the *gratin* to form in a hot oven.

On taking the dish out of the oven, surround the tomatoes with a ribbon of clear tomatoed half-*glazed* (23) sauce.

2266—PROVENCALE STUFFED TOMATOES
Tomates Farcies à la Provençale

Prepare the tomatoes as follows:—Cut them in two; remove their seeds; season them, and place them, cut side down, in an omelet-pan containing very hot oil. Turn them over when they are half-cooked; cook them for a little while longer; lay them on a *gratin*-dish, and stuff them with the following preparation:—For six tomatoes, fry two tablespoons of chopped onion in oil; add four peeled, pressed, and chopped tomatoes, a pinch of chopped parsley, and a crushed clove of garlic, and cook covered for twelve minutes. Complete with four tablespoons of bread-crumbs, soaked in consommé and rubbed through a sieve; two anchovies also rubbed through a sieve, and finish with some somewhat fat, *braised*-beef gravy. When the tomatoes are stuffed, sprinkle them with bread-crumbs combined with grated cheese; sprinkle with oil, and set the *gratin* to form.

These tomatoes may be served either hot or cold.

2267—PORTUGAISE STUFFED TOMATOES

Tomates Farcies à la Portugaise

Stuff the tomatoes with pilaff rice (2255) combined with a quarter of its volume of chopped tomatoes. Serve this rice in the shape of a round dome, and sprinkle it with chopped parsley.

N.B.—In addition to the above recipes, tomatoes prepared as already directed may also be garnished with minced chicken or lamb meat, or with scrambled eggs, sprinkled with grated Parmesan cheese and then set to *glaze* at the *salamander*.

2268—PROVENCALE SAUTE OF TOMATOES

Tomates Sautés à la Provençale

Having halved, pressed, and seasoned the tomatoes, put them, cut side down, in an omelet-pan containing very hot oil. Turn them over when they are half-cooked, and sprinkle them with a little chopped parsley, together with a bit of garlic, and some bread-crumbs. Place them in a moderate oven in order to finish their cooking, and serve the tomatoes the moment they are taken from the oven.

2269—PUREE OF TOMATOES　　　　　　*Purée de Tomates*
See Tomato Sauce (29).

2270—NEAPOLITAN TOMATO SOUFFLE

Soufflé de Tomates à la Napolitaine

Prepare one-half pint of very reduced tomato purée, and combine therewith two oz. of grated Parmesan cheese, two tablespoons of very stiff Béchamel sauce (28), and the yolks of three eggs.

Add the three whites, beaten to a stiff froth, and spread the preparation in layers in a buttered, *soufflé timbale;* setting upon each layer a bed of freshly-cooked macaroni, combined with butter and grated Parmesan cheese. Cook like an ordinary *soufflé*.

JERUSALEM ARTICHOKES (TOPINAMBOURS)

2271—JERUSALEM ARTICHOKES ANGLAISE

Topinambours à l'Anglaise

Cut the Jerusalem artichokes to the shape of large olives, and gently cook them in butter, without browning. Season them, and combine them with a little thin Béchamel sauce (28).

2272—FRIED JERUSALEM ARTICHOKES   *Topinambours Frits*

Peel and cut the Jerusalem artichokes into thick slices. Cook these in butter; dip them in batter, and fry them at the last moment.

2273—PUREE OF JERUSALEM ARTICHOKES   *Purée de Topinambours*

Peel, slice, and cook the Jerusalem artichokes in butter. Rub them through a sieve, and work the *purée* over the fire, with two oz. of butter per lb. Add enough mashed potatoes to thicken the preparation, and complete with a few tablespoons of boiling milk.

2274—SOUFFLE OF JERUSALEM ARTICHOKES

Soufflé de Topinambours

Proceed as for (2250).

TRUFFLES (TRUFFES)

(Truffles, a kind of fungus, growing underground and ferreted out by pigs, are a true French delicacy; they are raised in no other part of the world except for a few inferior ones in the French African colonies. None can compare with the Périgord truffles. Truffles are of various colors; there are white, deep brown, and black ones. Those in the recipes are black unless otherwise indicated. Truffles have never been successfully raised in the United States, although attempts have been and are still being made. Those available in this country are imported, packed either in jars or cans. They may be purchased in special food shops.—Ed.)

Truffles are used especially as a garnish; but they may also be served as a vegetable or an hors-d'œuvre.

When so served, they should be prepared very simply; for they require no refining treatment to make them perfect.

2275—TRUFFLES SOUS LA CENDRE (UNDER THE ASHES)
Truffes sous la Cendre

Take some large truffles, and clean them well. Season them with salt and pepper and a few drops of liqueur brandy; completely enclose them in a layer of patty paste (2374), and bake them in the oven from twenty-five to thirty minutes.

Serve them in the patty

2276—TRUFFLES IN CHAMPAGNE
Truffes au Champagne

Take some fine, well-cleaned truffles; season them, and cook them, covered, in champagne.

This done, set them in a *timbale,* or in small silver saucepans.

Almost completely reduce the champagne; add a little thin, strong, veal stock; strain through muslin; pour it over the truffles, and place these on the side of the stove for ten minutes without allowing the stock to boil.

2277—TRUFFLES IN CREAM
Truffes à la Crème

Cut one lb. of raw, peeled truffles into thick slices. Season them with salt and pepper, and cook them very gently in two oz. of butter and a few drops of burnt liqueur brandy.

Reduce to a stiff consistency one-half pint of cream with three tablespoons of Béchamel sauce (28); add some truffle cooking-liquor and the necessary quantity of cream; complete with two oz. of best butter; mix the truffles with this sauce, and serve in a vol-au-vent crust (2390).

2278—TRUFFLES ON THE SERVIETTE
Truffes à la Serviette

Under this head are served "Truffes au Champagne," the recipe for which is given above, but the champagne should be replaced by Madeira.

Put them in a *timbale,* set in a napkin folded to represent an artichoke. But it would be much better to serve "Truffes à la cendre" under this head, serving them under a folded napkin, as for "Pommes de terre en robe de chambre" (potatoes in their skins).

2279—TIMBALE OF TRUFFLES
Timbale de Truffes

Line a buttered *timbale* mould with ordinary patty-paste (2374).

Line its bottom and sides with slices of bacon, and fill up the mould with raw, peeled truffles, seasoned with salt and pepper.

Add a glass of Madeira, two tablespoons of pale chicken or veal *glaze;* cover with a slice of bacon, and close up the *timbale,* in the usual way, with a layer of paste.

Brush with beaten eggs, and bake in a hot oven for fifty minutes. When about to serve, turn out and serve on a napkin.

STARCHY PRODUCTS

2280—GNOCHI AU GRATIN   *Gnochi au Gratin*

Prepare a "pâte à choux" after recipe (2374), from the following ingredients:—one pint of milk, a pinch of salt, and a little nutmeg, four oz. of butter, two-thirds lb. of flour, and six eggs. When the paste is ready, combine with it four oz. of grated Parmesan cheese. Divide this paste into portions the size of walnuts; drop them into boiling, salted water, and *poach* them.

As soon as the gnochi rise to the surface of the water, and seem springy to the touch, drain them on a piece of linen.

Coat the bottom of a *gratin*-dish with Mornay sauce (91); set the gnochi upon the latter; cover them with the same sauce; sprinkle with grated cheese and melted butter, and set the *gratin* to form in a moderate oven for from fifteen to twenty minutes.

2281—GNOCHI A LA ROMAINE   *Gnochi à la Romaine*

Scatter two-thirds lb. of semolina (farina) over a quart of boiling milk. Season with salt, pepper, and nutmeg, and cook gently for twenty minutes. Take the utensil off the fire; thicken the semolina with the yolks of two eggs, and spread it in a moistened pan, in a layer one-half in. thick.

When it is quite cold stamp it out with a round cutter, two in. in diameter. Set the gnochi in shallow, buttered *timbales;* sprinkle with grated Gruyère and Parmesan cheese, and with a little melted butter, and set the *gratin* to form.

2282—POTATOES GNOCHI   *Gnochi de Pommes de Terre*

Cook two lbs. of potatoes (2202). Drain them as soon as they are cooked, and work the *purée,* while it is very hot, with one and one-half oz. of butter, two small eggs, two egg-yolks, one-third lb. of flour, salt, pepper, and nutmeg. Divide up this preparation into portions the size of walnuts; roll them into balls; press upon them lightly with a fork to give them a criss-cross pattern, and poach them in boiling water.

Drain them on a piece of linen; serve them in layers, sprinkling some grated cheese between each layer; sprinkle some grated cheese over the top surface; sprinkle liberally with melted butter, and set the *gratin* to form in a hot oven.

2283—NOCKERL WITH PARMESAN   *Noques au Parmesan*

Put into a previously-heated bowl one-half lb. of *manié* butter, and work the latter with salt, pepper, and nutmeg; adding to it, little by little, two eggs and two well-beaten egg-yolks, five oz. of flour, and the white of an egg, also beaten to a stiff froth.

Divide up the preparation into portions the size of hazel-nuts; drop these portions into a saucepan of boiling, salted water, and let them *poach*.

Drain the *noques* on a piece of linen; serve them in a *timbale;* sprinkle them copiously with grated cheese and with nut-brown butter (154).

2284—MACARONI   *Macaroni*

Under this head are included all tubular pastes from spaghetti, the size of which is not larger than thick vermicelli, to canneloni, the bore of which is one-half in. in diameter.

All these pastes are cooked in boiling water, salted to the extent of one-third oz. per quart. Macaroni, like other pastes of a similar nature, should not be cooled.

The most one can do, if the cooking has to be stopped at a given moment, is to pour a little cold water into the saucepan and then to take it off the fire.

2285—ITALIENNE MACARONI   *Macaroni à l'Italienne*

Cook the macaroni in boiling water; completely drain it; put it into a saucepan, and toss it over the fire to dry.

Season it with salt, pepper and nutmeg; combine it with five oz. of grated Gruyère and Parmesan cheese, in equal quantities, and two oz. of butter, cut into small pieces, per lb. of macaroni. *Saute* well to combine, and serve in a *timbale*.

2286—MACARONI AU GRATIN   *Macaroni au Gratin*

Prepare the macaroni after (2285), adding to it a little Béchamel sauce (28); and set it on a buttered *gratin*-dish, sprinkle with grated cheese. Sprinkle the surface of the preparation with grated cheese and *raspings,* mixed, and with melted butter, and set the *gratin* to form in a hot oven.

2287—MACARONI IN STOCK   *Macaroni au Jus*

Parboil the macaroni in salted water, keeping it somewhat firm; drain it, cut it into short lengths, and simmer it in beef *braising*-liquor, until the macaroni has almost entirely absorbed it.

Serve in a *timbale,* and sprinkle with a few tablespoons of the *braising*-liquor.

2288—NANTUA MACARONI   *Macaroni à la Nantua*

Having cooked, drained and dried the macaroni, mix it with crayfish *purée* (662), and mix twenty-four crayfish tails per lb. of macaroni.

Serve in a *timbale,* and cover the macaroni with a *julienne* of very black truffles.

2289—NEAPOLITAN MACARONI   *Macaroni à la Napolitaine*

Prepare a beef estouffade (7) with red wine and tomatoes; cook it for from ten to twelve hours, that it may be reduced to a *purée.*

Rub this stock through a sieve and put it aside.

Parboil some thick macaroni, keeping it somewhat firm; drain it; cut it into short lengths, and combine it with butter.

Sprinkle the bottom of a *timbale* with grated cheese; cover with a layer of estouffade *purée;* spread a layer of macaroni upon the latter, and proceed in the same order until the *timbale* is full. Serve the preparation as it stands.

2290—MACARONI WITH WHITE TRUFFLES

Macaroni aux Truffes Blanches

Prepare the macaroni as directed under (2285), and add to it six oz. of white Piedmont truffles (cut into thin shavings), per lb. of macaroni.

Leave the preparation covered for five minutes and serve in a *timbale.*

2291—NOODLES   *Nouilles*

These are generally bought ready-made. If one wishes to prepare them, the ingredients of the paste are:—one lb. of flour, one-half oz. of salt, three whole eggs, and five egg-yolks. Moisten as for an ordinary paste, roll it out twice on a board, and leave it to stand for one or two hours before cutting it up.

All macaroni recipes may be applied to noodles.

For "Nouilles à l'Alsacienne," it is usual, when the preparation is ready in the *timbale,* to sprinkle over it a few raw pieces of noodles *sautéd* in butter to a golden brown and kept very crisp.

KASHA

Kasha (buckwheat) is not a vegetable; but since this preparation has appeared either as an ingredient or an accompaniment of certain Russian dishes which occur in this work, I am obliged to refer to it.

2292—KASHA OF SEMOLINA FOR COULEBIAC
Kache de Semoule pour Coulibiac

Take some coarse, yellow semolina, and scatter it over three times its bulk of boiling consommé. Cook it gently for twenty-five minutes; drain it on a sieve; spread it in a pan, and place it in a moderate oven to dry. This done, rub it lightly through a coarse sieve with the view of separating the grains, and put it aside in the dry until wanted.

2293—KASHA OF BUCKWHEAT FOR SOUPS
Kache de Sarrasin pour Potages

Moisten one lb. of cracked buckwheat with enough tepid water to make a stiff paste; add the necessary salt, and put this paste in a large *Charlotte-mould.* Bake in a hot oven for two hours. Then remove the thick crust which has formed upon the preparation, and transfer what remains, by means of a spoon, to a bowl. Mix with two oz. of butter while it is still hot.

Kasha prepared in this way may be served in a special *timbale.* But it is more often spread in a thin layer in a buttered pan, and left to cool.

It is then cut into slices one in. in diameter, and these are rolled in flour and browned on both sides in very hot clarified butter (175).

2294—POLENTA   *Polenta*

In a quart of boiling water containing one-half oz. of salt, put two-thirds lb. of corn meal, stirring the while with a spoon, that the two may mix. Cook for twenty-five minutes; add two oz. of butter and two and one-half oz. of grated Parmesan cheese. If the Polenta be prepared for a vegetable or a garnish, it is spread in a thin layer in a moistened pan. When cold, it is cut into slices or diamond shapes, which are first browned in butter, placed on a dish, and then sprinkled with grated cheese and nut-brown butter (154).

2295—SOUFFLE PIEMONTAIS *Soufflé Piémontais*

Boil one pint of milk with one-fifth oz. of salt; sprinkle on it two oz. of corn meal; mix well; cover, and cook in a mild oven for twenty-five minutes.

Then transfer the paste to another saucepan; work it with one and one half oz. of butter and as much grated Parmesan cheese; mix with one egg, two egg-yolks, and the whites of three eggs beaten to a stiff froth.

Serve in a buttered *timbale;* sprinkle with grated cheese, and cook like an ordinary *soufflé.*

2295a—SOUFFLE WITH PARMESAN *Soufflé au Parmesan*

Mix one lb. of flour and two and one-half pints of milk in a saucepan. Add a little salt, pepper and nutmeg, and set the prepara- tion to boil, stirring it constantly.

As soon as the boil is reached, take the saucepan off the fire, and add one lb. of grated Parmesan cheese, three oz. of butter, and ten egg-yolks. Rub the whole through a fine sieve and then combine with it the whites of ten eggs whisked to a stiff froth.

Use a silver *timbale* mould lined with a band of buttered paper, and bake in the oven for from twenty to twenty-five minutes.

2296—RAVIOLI *Ravioli*

Whatever be their filling, *ravioli* are always prepared in the same way. The stuffings given below represent the most usual forms of filling.

Stuffing A

Mix one-half lb. of finely-chopped, cooked chicken-meat; five oz. of cooked and chopped brains; three oz. of pressed white cottage cheese; three oz. of chopped, pressed and *blanched* spinach; three oz. of parboiled green borage; a pinch of green sweet basil; five oz. of grated Parmesan cheese, two eggs; two egg-yolks; salt, pepper and nutmeg.

Stuffing B

Mix two-thirds lb. of well-cooked, cold and finely-chopped beef stew; two-thirds lb. of parboiled, pressed, and chopped spinach; one oz. of chopped shallots; five oz. of a *purée* of cooked brains; two whole eggs, salt, pepper and nutmeg.

STUFFING C

Toss one-half lb. of chickens' livers in butter; add to it two chopped shallots, a pinch of parsley, and a little crushed garlic. Finely pound or grind the livers, and add successively one-half lb. of parboiled, cooled and fresh spinach; two anchovy fillets; three oz. of butter; three eggs, salt, pepper, nutmeg, and a pinch of sweet basil. Rub the whole through a sieve.

2297—THE PREPARATION OF RAVIOLI   *La Préparation de Ravioli*

They may be made in various shapes as follows:—

Roll a piece of noodle paste to a thin layer and stamp it out with a fancy cutter, two and one-half in. in diameter. Moisten the edges of each piece of paste; fill the center of each with a ball of one of the above stuffings, the size of a hazel-nut, and fold over.

Or roll the paste into a rectangle of four-in. sides; fill with stuffing, leaving a gap between the portions of the latter; moisten the edges of the paste, and seal up by drawing these together. Finally stamp out with a grooved, fancy-cutter or wheel.

Or prepare a square layer of paste; garnish it with lines consisting of portions of paste; leave a space of two in. between the lines. Moisten; cover with a second layer of paste, of the same dimensions as the first, and divide up, by means of the *rotella,* into squares of two-in. sides. Whatever be the shape of the *ravioli,* plunge them into a saucepan of slightly salted boiling water; *poach* them for from eight to ten minutes, and drain them.

Set them on a buttered *gratin*-dish, sprinkled with grated cheese; sprinkle them with good beef gravy; then again with grated cheese, and set the *gratin* to form. Or, serve the *ravioli* in layers, sprinkling each layer with grated cheese and gravy. Complete with some grated cheese, and set the *gratin* to form in the usual way.

N.B.—The *ravioli* may also be served, merely sprinkled with grated cheese and nut-brown butter (154).

CHAPTER XIX

APPETIZERS AND SNACKS

2298—REMARKS UPON SAVORIES   *Remarques sur les Savorys*

I HAVE already expressed my opinion in regard to Savories. I consider their use opposed to gastronomical principles, and that they have no *raison d'être* on a good menu. But, not wishing to preach, I shall give, hereafter, a few savory recipes, selected from among those which are gastronomically the best, and which custom has sanctioned.

I resolved to make these recipes appear after the Vegetables and before the Ices, because I consider that Dessert alone is allowable after the Entremets and Ices.

There is much in common between Hors-d'œuvres and Savories. Many of the former, the recipes for which I have given, may appear as Savories, once their seasoning has been intensified. Among the latter class may be quoted the various *Tartlets* (387, etc.); the Barquettes (314); Frivolities (350); Éclairs à la Karoly (344); Allumettes aux Anchois (300); City Toasts (320), etc.

2299—CHEESE STICKS   *Allumettes*

Prepare a ribbon of puff-paste (2366) three inches wide by one-fifth inch thick, leaving the length to come as it will. Spread on it some very reduced Béchamel sauce (28), combined with two table-spoons of grated Gruyère cheese per one-half pint, and season with cayenne. Sprinkle the surface with grated Parmesan cheese; press into the sauce by means of the flat of a knife; cut into rectangles one inch wide; set these on a slightly-moistened pan, and bake them in a moderate oven for twelve minutes.

2300—CHEESE FRITTERS   *Beignets Soufflés au Fromage*

Prepare some ordinary "pâte à choux" without sugar (2375), and combine it, per lb., with five oz. of a *Brunoise* of Gruyère cheese.

Divide up this paste into portions the size of hazel-nuts, and fry them in fat like other Beignets *soufflés* (1935).

707

2301—BEURRECKS A LA TURQUE   *Beurrecks à la Turque*

Reduce the required amount of Béchamel sauce (28) to a thick consistency; mix it with an equal quantity of Gruyère cheese dice; season with cayenne, and spread the preparation on a dish to cool.

Then divide it up into portions the size of walnuts; shape these like cigars, wrap each portion in a very thin layer of noodle paste (2291); treat them *à l'anglaise,* and fry them at the last moment in very hot fat.

2302—CHEESE PUFFS   *Choux au Fromage*

By means of a pastry-bag, form some *"choux,"* a little larger than the Saint-Honoré ones, from ordinary paste (2375). Brush them with beaten eggs; bake them in a moderate oven, and keep them dry. When cold, cut them at the top; garnish them with *"Fondue au fromage"* (cheese and eggs) seasoned with cayenne, and complete with some whipped cream, combined with grated Parmesan cheese); this should be laid on by means of a pastry-bag, as in the case of *"choux à la crème."*

2303—FRIED CAMEMBERT   *Camembert Frit*

Clear the cheese of its crust, and cut it into elongated diamonds. Sprinkle with cayenne, treat them *à l'anglaise,* twice, and fry them at the last moment in hot fat.

2304—CANAPES   *Canapés ou Toasts*

These are nothing more than pieces of toast, slices of breads, trimmed according to fancy, grilled, buttered, and garnished in some way.

As the garnishes for toast are innumerable, I shall quote only a few typical examples.

Canapés Garnished with Scrambled Eggs.—Set the scrambled eggs in domes upon the Canapés; sprinkle with grated Parmesan cheese, and set to *glaze* quickly.

Or arrange the scrambled eggs as above, and cover them with a lattice of anchovy fillets.

Canapés de Haddock.—Cook the haddock; rub it through a sieve; add a little butter and Béchamel sauce (28) to the resulting *purée,* and set the latter in domes on the toast.

For Variety.—Sprinkle the *purée* with grated Parmesan cheese, and set to *glaze.*

Or garnish the *purée* with oysters *poached* in a little Worcestershire sauce.

Or again: cover the *purée* with a lattice of anchovy fillets.

Canapés with Kippers or Bloaters.—Grill them and make a *purée* from them like the haddock.

Canapés with Halved or Filleted Anchovies.—In the case of fillets, set them to form a grill upon the toast; if the anchovies be halved, lay them lengthwise on the toast.

Canapés with Sardines in Oil.—Clear the fish of their skins and bones, and set the fillets on the canapés.

Canapés with Grilled Sprats.—Proceed as for sardines.

Canapés of Salmon.—Toast may be garnished with thin slices of smoked or fresh salmon, or with the latter prepared in a *purée* like the haddock.

Various Canapés.—Once the pieces of toast or canapés are grilled and buttered, they may be garnished with chopped smoked tongue or ham, combined with a little butter and mustard, with grilled slices of mushrooms or tomatoes, etc.

A few of the preparations have names, while others are only distinguished by the nature of their garnish.

2305—CADOGAN CANAPES   *Canapés Cadogan*
Take oval and slightly hollowed pieces of toast, fried in butter and garnished with spinach prepared with butter. Lay two oysters on the spinach of each piece of toast; cover with Mornay sauce (91), and *glaze* quickly.

2306—CANAPES DES GOURMETS   *Canapés des Gourmets*
Prepare some very thin pieces of toast; fry them in butter, and garnish them with a cheese *fondue.* Pair them off, and sandwich a piece of grilled bacon between each of them.

2307—IVANHOE CANAPES   *Canapés Ivanhoe*
Take some round, buttered pieces of toast, garnished with haddock *purée,* and set a very small, grilled mushroom on the *purée* of each piece of toast.

2308—SCOTCH CANAPES   *Canapés à l'Ecossaise*
Take some round, buttered pieces of toast, garnished with haddock *purée,* and *glazed.*

N.B.—I see no use in extending this list any further; the above directions should suffice to show the variety to which these preparations lend themselves.

2309—SAVORY CHICKEN   *Carcasse de Volaille*

Take in preference the remains of fowls cooked without browning.

After having trimmed them, coat them with mustard and cayenne, and grill them.

2310—MUSHROOMS SOUS CLOCHE   *Champignons sous Cloche*

Trim the mushrooms; season them with salt and pepper, and garnish the hollow of each cap with a piece of Maître-d'hôtel butter (150), the size of a hazel-nut, and one-half teaspoon of cream.

Set a mushroom cap on each piece of toast, which should be two inches in diameter and fried in butter. Place them on an egg-tray, and cover them with a special, small, glass bell, four inches in diameter and two inches high, the rim of which must rest on the bottom of a dish, the diameter of which should be such as to fit the bell.

Cook in moderate heat for about twenty-five minutes.

2311—CHEESE CONDES   *Condés au Fromage*

Prepare a ribbon from puff-paste trimmings, as in the case of (2299).

Spread on a thick layer of very reduced Béchamel sauce (28), flavored with cayenne, and combined, when cold, with very small dice of Gruyère and Parmesan cheese. Cut up and cook as for (2299).

2312—FRIED CREAM WITH CHEESE   *Crème Frite au Fromage*

Mix together four oz. of flour, two and one-half oz. of rice cream (711), three eggs, and two egg-yolks. Dilute with one pint of milk; season with salt, cayenne, and nutmeg; boil, and cook for five minutes over an open fire, stirring continually.

Add four oz. of grated Gruyère cheese; spread this preparation on a buttered tin; leave it to cool, and then cut it into elongated diamonds. Roll the latter in beaten egg and bread-crumbs mixed with grated cheese, and fry them at the last moment. Serve them on a napkin.

2313—CAMEMBERT CROQUETTES   *Croquettes de Camembert*

Dilute two oz. of flour and two oz. of rice cream (711) with one-third pint of milk.

Add one lb. of Camembert cheese, crust removed, and cut into dice, five oz. of butter, salt, cayenne, and nutmeg.

Cook the preparation, stirring it the while; cool it; spread **it** on a tray; mould it to the shape of small patties; treat these twice *à l'anglaise,* and fry them.

2314—FOIE GRAS DELICES   *Délices de Foie Gras*

Take some fresh, well-seasoned *foie gras, studded* with truffles, and covered with slices of bacon, and *poach* it in a bowl with good aspic-jelly flavored with dry champagne or Rhine wine. Leave to cool for twenty-four hours; clear the jelly of grease, first by means of a spoon, and then with boiling water.

Serve the preparation as it stands, very cold, and accompany it with grilled, crisp, and very hot slices of toast.

2315—DIABLOTINS   *Diablotins*

These are very small, poached Gnochi (2280), sprinkled with grated cheese, flavored with a very little cayenne, and set for their *gratin* to form at the last moment.

2316—CHESTER FONDANTS   *Fondants au Chester*

Moisten one-half lb. of flour, an equal quantity of butter and grated cheese, a pinch of salt, and a very little cayenne, with a few tablespoons of water.

Cut the paste into small patties, two inches in diameter; brush them with beaten eggs; crease them with a fork, and bake them in a moderate oven.

When cold, pair the patties, and stick them together with a tablespoon of fondant cream, prepared thus:—

Mix six egg-yolks with two-thirds pint of cream; season with salt and cayenne; leave to set on moderate fire, like an English custard (2398), and, when the preparation is almost cold, finish it with five oz. of best butter and as much grated cheese.

2317—ANGELS ON HORSEBACK   *Anges à Cheval*

Wrap some fine oysters, each in a thin slice of bacon. Stick them on a skewer; season and grill them, and set them on small pieces of toast.

Sprinkle with bread-crumbs and cayenne when about to serve.

2318—SKEWERS OF OYSTERS LUCIFER   *Brochettes d'Huîtres Lucifer*

Poach some fine oysters, bearded, in their own liquor; dry them, and dip them in thin mustard. Stick them, six at a time, on skewers, and treat them *à l'anglaise.*

Fry them at the last moment, and serve them on a napkin.

2319—SCOTCH OMELET   *Omelette a l'Ecossaise*

Take some fresh herring *milts;* salt them; sprinkle them with cayenne and chopped chives, parsley, and chervil; wrap each in a thin slice of smoked salmon, and *poach* them gently in butter.

Set them slantwise in the center of an *"omelette aux fines herbes";* cover them well with the latter, and roll it up.

2320—OMELET WITH FINE HERBS   *Omelette aux Fines Herbes*

See (502).

2321—GRILLED BONES   *Os Grillés*

Take the trimmed bones of a roast sirloin, and let there be still some meat upon them. Sprinkle them with cayenne; coat them with mustard, and grill them.

2322—PARMESAN STRAWS   *Pailettes de Parmesan*

Prepare some puff-paste (2366) with two-thirds lb. of butter; roll it out ten times, dusting it again and again with grated Parmesan cheese and a little cayenne, that the paste may absorb as much of it as possible. Then roll it into square layers of four-inch sides and one-eighth inch thick; cut these up into ribbons one-eighth inch wide; set them on buttered tins; bake them in a very hot oven, and serve them on a napkin.

2323—MUSCOVITE PANNEQUETS   *Pannequets à la Muscovite*

Take some ordinary, unsugared Pannequets (2403); cut them into rectangles three inches long by one and one-half inches wide. Coat them with caviar, flavored with cayenne; roll them into cigarette forms, and serve them on crystal hors-d'œuvre dishes.

2324—BREAD PUDDING WITH CHEESE *Pudding de Fromage au Pain*

Set some thin slices of stale, buttered and cheese-sprinkled bread in a pie-plate. Having three-parts filled the dish with it, cover the slices with a preparation consisting of the yolks of four eggs mixed with one-quarter pint of broth—which quantities are suited to a pint dish.

Sprinkle copiously with grated cheese; bake in the oven, and *glaze* at the last moment.

2325—DEVILLED SARDINES   *Sardines à la Diable*

Take fresh sardines, if possible. Skin and bone them; coat them with mustard and cayenne; treat them *à l'anglaise;* fry them at the last moment, and dish them on small fried *croûtons,* the shape of sardines.

N.B.—Fresh anchovies and smelts may be prepared in the same way.

2326—SCOTCH WOODCOCK Scotch-Woodcock

Toast some large slices of bread, one-third inch thick, and cover them with a very thick English butter sauce (2397), combined with plenty of capers and anchovy *purée.*

Sprinkle with grated Parmesan cheese; *glaze* quickly at the *sala-mander;* speedily cut up into small rectangles, and serve very hot.

2327—AGNES TARTLETS Tartelettes Agnès

Line some fluted *tartlet* moulds with good paste (2356), and fill them with thin slices of bacon slightly fried in butter, alternating with thin slices of Gruyère cheese, as in a Quiche. Then sprinkle with a little cayenne. Cook them at the last moment, and, on taking them out of the oven, set a roundel of *poached* marrow rolled in pale melted meat *glaze* (15) and chopped parsley on each tartlet.

2328—SCOTCH TARTLETS Tartelettes à l'Ecossaise

Take some *tartlet crusts,* baked without browning, and garnish them at the last moment with a haddock *purée,* combined with Béchamel sauce (28).

2329—HADDOCK TARTLETS Tartelettes au Eglefin

Fill some unbrowned *tartlet crusts* with a *salpicon* of *poached* haddock, mixed with curry sauce (81). Sprinkle the surface of each with fine *raspings,* and serve them on a napkin.

2330—FLORENTINE TARTLETS Tartelettes à la Florentine

Fill some unbrowned *tartlet crusts* with Soufflé with Parmesan (2295a), combined with grated truffles and crayfish tails cut into dice, and strongly seasoned with *mignonette.*

Bake in the oven for about three minutes.

2331—MARQUISE TARTLETS Tartelettes à la Marquise

Line some *tartlet* moulds with good paste; garnish their bottom and sides with a thread of gnochis preparation, put on with a pastry-bag fitted with a plain tube, the opening of which should be equal in diameter to macaroni.

Fill up the tartlets with Mornay sauce (91) flavored with cayenne; sprinkle with grated cheese, and bake in a hot oven.

2332—RAGLAN TARTLETS   *Tartelettes à la Raglan*

Fill the bottom of some unbrowned tartlets with a smoked herring-*milt purée*. Cover the latter with haddock *soufflé*, shaped like a hive by means of a pastry-bag fitted with a small, plain tube. Place in the oven for six minutes, and serve instantly.

2333—TOSCA TARTLETS   *Tartelettes à la Tosca*

Fill some *tartlet crusts* with crayfish tails, prepared "à l'Améri-caine" (58). Cover with Soufflé with Parmesan (2295a), and place in the oven for three minutes.

2334—VENDOME TARTLETS   *Tartelettes à la Vendôme*

Line some *tartlet moulds* with good paste; prick the bottom of each, and garnish them with the following preparation.

For twelve *tartlets:*—One and one-half oz. of chopped shallots, heated in butter; three oz. of *sautéd* and finely chopped *cèpes;* one and one-half oz. of raw marrow in dice; one small hard-boiled and chopped egg; one oz. of bread-crumbs, salt, cayenne, a few drops of lemon juice, and three tablespoons of melted meat *glaze* (15). Set a large slice of marrow on each *tartlet,* and cook at the last moment.

2335—WELSH RABBIT   *Welsh Rabbit*

This may be prepared in two ways, but always on square or rectangular pieces of buttered toast, one-third inch thick.

The simplest way is to cover the pieces of toast with a thick layer of grated Canadian Cheddar or sharp American, to sprinkle them with cayenne, and then to place them in the oven for the cheese to melt and *glaze* their surfaces.

Or the original method consists in melting the dice or slices of cheese in a few tablespoons of pale ale and a little English mustard.

As soon as the cheese has melted, it is poured over the pieces of buttered toast, quickly smoothed with the flat of a knife, and sprinkled with cayenne. The pieces may be cut up if required.

2336—SANDWICHES   *Sandwiches*

Sandwiches are prepared in two ways, according to their purposes.

They generally consist of two slices of buttered bread, with mustard spread upon them, covering a slice of ham or tongue, etc. Sandwiches are usually rectangular, and they should measure about three inches by one and one-half inches. The kind served at elaborate functions are much smaller, and therefore it is best to cut the sandwiched product (whatever this be) into dice, and to mix it with an equal weight of butter containing mustard.

When sandwiches have to be kept, they should be wrapped and placed under a slight weight to prevent the bread from drying. Sandwiches may also be made from thick, toasted slices of bread, cut across into two, and then filled according to fancy.

Names of Common Sandwiches

Ham Sandwich	Foie-Gras Sandwich
Tongue Sandwich	Hard-boiled Egg Sandwich
Beef Sandwich	Caviar Sandwich
Pressed-beef Sandwich	Tomato Sandwich
Veal Sandwich	Cucumber Sandwich
Chicken Sandwich	Watercress Sandwich

Mustard-and-watercress Sandwich

2337—BOOKMAKER SANDWICHES   *Sandwich de Bookmaker*

In his book, "La Cuisine Anglaise," Mr. Suzanne gives the following kind of sandwich, which deserves attention:—

This kind of sandwich, which is liked by racing people, is a most substantial affair, and it will be seen from the following recipe that a sandwich of the nature prescribed might, in an emergency, answer the purpose of a meal.

Take a small loaf of bread, and cut off its two end crusts, then split in half leaving on them about one-third inch of crust. Butter these large slices. Meanwhile grill a thick steak, well seasoned with salt and pepper. When it is cooked, cool it; sprinkle it with grated horse-radish and mustard, and lay it between the two slices. Tie the whole together as for a *galantine,* and wrap it in several sheets of blotting paper. Then place the sandwich under a letter-press, the screw of which should be gradually tightened, and leave the sandwich thus for one-half hour.

At the end of this time the insides of the slices of bread have, owing to the pressure, become saturated with meat juice, which is prevented from escaping by the covering of crust.

Remove the blotting-paper, and pack the sandwich in a box or in several sheets of white waxed paper.

CHAPTER XX

PASTRY, Confectionery, and Ices are so closely allied to Cookery, and they are so surely its complements, that it is impossible to omit them when dealing with Entremets, even though the latter be limited to the kind proper to the kitchen.

However, these subjects, which could supply matter for voluminous works, are too complex for it to be possible to cope thoroughly with them here.

I shall therefore confine myself to the expounding of their fundamental principles and the essential operations relating thereto, a knowledge of which is absolutely necessary for the successful preparation of Kitchen Entremets and Ices. The directions given hereafter are certainly too inadequate to convert an ordinary cook into a pastry-cook, a confectioner, or an icing cook ("glacier"); but they will at least permit of his carrying out a complete dinner, if the necessity so to do should occur.

ELEMENTARY PREPARATIONS OF PASTRY WHICH MAY BE APPLIED TO ENTREMETS

2338—VARIOUS ALMOND PREPARATIONS
Préparations Diverses d'amandes

It is important that one should have shelled, skinned, slivered, and chopped almonds.

To Skin Almonds.—Throw them in a saucepan of boiling water, place the utensil on the side of the fire without allowing the boiling to continue, and let the almonds soak for seven or eight minutes. As soon as the skin slips when pressing them between one's fingers, turn them out into a strainer; cool them in cold water, and skin them. This done, wash them in cold water; drain them well; spread them on a very clean pan, and dry them in a mild oven.

Slivered Almonds.—Having skinned and washed the almonds,

716

split them in two, and cut each half into five or six lengthwise slivers. Dry the latter in the warming-oven, and place them in the front of the oven for a while to color slightly.

They serve for nougat, and sometimes take the place of pine-nuts.

Chopped Almonds.—Having skinned the almonds, slightly dry them and chop them; rub them through a sieve, the coarseness of which should be in accordance with that required for the chopped almonds.

Spread the almonds on a pan covered with a sheet of paper, and dry them in the warming-oven, stirring them from time to time.

Toasted Almonds.—These are either slivered or chopped almonds set to bake on a pan in a moderate oven. Be sure to stir them frequently, that they may brown evenly, and take them out when they are of a nice golden shade.

Pralined Almonds.—Proceed as for toasted almonds, but sprinkle them frequently with icing sugar, which turns to caramel under the influence of the heat of the oven, and covers the almonds in a pale-brown coat of sugar.

2339—VARIOUS PREPARATIONS OF FILBERTS AND HAZEL-NUTS

Préparations Diverses de Noisettes

Filberts are a large kind of hazel-nut, generally covered with reddish skins.

After having cracked and removed the shells, put the filberts in a pan, and place them in the oven until their skins are slightly grilled. They need then only be rubbed between the fingers in order to clear them of their skins. Chopped filberts are prepared like chopped almonds, and should be included on the permanent handy shelf of the pastry cook.

2340—VARIOUS BUTTERS   *Beurres Divers*

Softened Butter.—More particularly in winter, when it is very hard, butter should be softened by being thoroughly kneaded in a towel to extract the butter-milk, which is always present in more or less large quantities; and to make the butter sufficiently soft to mix with the various ingredients of which the pastes are made.

Creamy Butter.—After having well softened it as above, put it in a bowl, previously rinsed with hot water and thoroughly wiped.

Work the butter with a spatula or a wooden spoon until it acquires the consistency of a cream—a necessary condition for certain of its uses.

Clarified Butter.—In pastry, clarified butter is used more especially for the buttering of moulds. Put the butter to be clarified into a saucepan, and cook it over a very slow fire until the casein substances liberated in the cooking process have accumulated and solidified on the bottom of the saucepan and the butter appears transparent, of a golden color, and gives off a slight, nutty odor.

Strain it through muslin, and put it aside until required.

2341—THE BUTTERING AND GLAZING OF MOULDS
Pour Beurrer et Glacer des Moules

All moulds, large and small, should be buttered to ensure the easy turning-out of cakes cooked in them. Clarified butter, owing to its purity, is the best for the purpose. It may be applied with a brush, care being taken that all the inside surfaces get uniformly covered. One unbuttered spot is sufficient to make a moulding stick, or to completely spoil a cake.

For certain cakes, chopped or slivered almonds are sprinkled in the mould. For others, especially biscuits, the moulds are flour-dusted—that is to say, a film of very dry flour or *fecula* (cornstarch, etc.) is allowed to settle on the layer of butter, which, at the turning out, appears like a *glazed* crust upon the cake.

2342—HOW TO BEAT THE WHITES OF EGGS
Façon de Fouetter les Blancs d'Oeufs

The best utensil for the purpose is a copper or stainless steel bowl in which the whisk or beater may act at all points owing to the spherical shape of the receptacle. Tinned or enamelled utensils set up a kind of greasiness which does not permit the whites to stiffen enough for some purposes.

Before beating the whites gently, and draw them up with the beater until all their molecules have disintegrated and they begin to thicken. They may then be beaten until they are sufficiently stiff to be taken up bodily by the whisk or beater.

Preventive Methods.—To facilitate the beating of whites of eggs, there may be added to them at the start a pinch either of salt or alum per ten whites. When, towards the close of the operation, the whites begin to separate, owing to any one of the various causes, add immediately one tablespoon of powdered sugar per ten whites, and then beat briskly, to restore them to their normal state.

2343—·VEGETABLE COLORING MATTERS   *La coloration Végétale*

Every pastry-cook's stock should include a series of vegetable coloring matters, comprising carmine, liquid spinach green, yellow, etc.

When required, the blending of these colors yields the intermediate tones. The colors may be bought.

2344—THE COOKING OF SUGAR   *Le Cuisson du Sucre*

From the state of syrup to the most highly-concentrated state in which it is used in pastry, sugar passes through various stages of cooking, which are:—The small thread (215° F.) and the large thread (222° F.), the small ball (236° F.) and the large ball (248° F.), the small crack (285° F.) and the large crack (315° F.). When the last state is overreached, the sugar has become caramel (360° F.).

Put the necessary quantity of sugar in a small, copper or stainless steel pot; moisten with enough water to melt it, and boil. Carefully remove the scum which forms, and which might cause the sugar to granulate.

As soon as the sugar begins to move stiffly in boiling, it is a sign that the water has almost entirely evaporated, and that the real cooking of the sugar has begun.

From this moment, with moistened fingers or a little piece of moistened linen, take care to remove the crystallized sugar from the sides of the utensil, lest it make the remaining portion turn.

The cooking of the sugar then progresses very rapidly, and the states of its various stages, coming one upon the other in quick succession at intervals of a few minutes, may be ascertained as follows:—

It has reached the *small-thread stage,* when a drop of it held between the thumb and the first finger forms small resistless strings when the thumb and finger are drawn apart.

It has reached the *large-thread stage,* when, proceeding in the same way, the strings formed between the parted finger and thumb are more numerous and stronger.

From this moment care must be taken to use cold water in order to ascertain the state of the sugar.

When a few minutes have elapsed after the test for the large-thread state, dip the end of the first finger, first into cold water, then into the sugar, and plunge it again immediately into the bowl of cold water, which should be at hand. The sugar taken from the finger forms a kind of soft ball, and it is this state which is called the *small ball.*

When, upon repeating the procedure, the sugar removed from the finger rolls into a firmer ball, the *large-ball stage* is reached.

After the cooking has continued for a few seconds longer, the sugar lying on the finger peels off in the form of a thin, flexible film, which sticks to the teeth. This is the *small-crack stage*. Tests should then be made in quick succession, until the film taken from the end of the finger breaks "clean" in the teeth, like glass. This is the *large-crack state*, the last of the cooking stages, and as soon as it has been reached the utensil should be taken off the fire, lest a few seconds more turn the sugar to *caramel*.

To prevent the granulating of the sugar, a few drops of lemon juice may be added to it; or, better still, a tablespoon of glucose per lb.

2345—OLD-FASHIONED GLAZE   *Glace à l'Ancienne*

Put the required amount of *icing sugar* (2346a) in a small saucepan, the quantity used being in proportion to the object to be glazed.

If it be flavored with vanilla, orange, or lemon, dilute it with a little water, keeping it somewhat stiff; add some vanilla-flavored sugar or grated orange-rind, and stir it up well for a few minutes. Then make it lukewarm, so that it may run easily and dry quickly, and pour it over the object to be treated.

For the above-mentioned flavors, an infusion of vanilla or orange-rind may be prepared, and this may serve in diluting the *glaze*. The flavors may also be used in the form of *essences*, provided it be remembered that they are usually very strong, and must be used with caution.

If liqueur *glazes* are in question, such as Kirsch, Rum, Anisette, Maraschino, etc., the *glaze* is diluted with the liqueur and made lukewarm as directed above.

2346—FONDANT GLAZE   *Glace au Fondant*

Preparation of the "Fondant."—Put some granulated sugar into a small saucepan, the quantity being in accordance with the amount of "Fondant" required.

Moisten with just enough water to melt the sugar, and set to cook as directed under "The Cooking of Sugar" (2344).

Stop the cooking precisely at 230° F. between the *large-thread stage* and the *small-ball stage,* and pour the sugar on a moderately-oiled marble slab. Let it half cool for a few minutes; then, with a spatula, move it about well in all directions, taking care that no portion of the sugar on the marble is left untouched by the spatula, for any such portion would harden and form lumps in the Fondant.

After ten to fifteen minutes' work with the spatula, the sugar should have become a white, slightly granulated paste. Heap the latter together, and scrape the marble slab with the blade of a strong knife. Carefully knead this paste (2357) with the palm of the hand until it is very thin and smooth, whereupon the Fondant is ready for use.

It need now only be heaped in a bowl, covered with a damp cloth, and kept somewhat dry.

To Glaze with "Fondant."—Put the required amount of it into a saucepan; work it over a slow fire for a while, in order to soften it, and moisten it, little by little, with water when a dry flavor or an *essence* is used, or, otherwise, with the selected liqueur.

Warm slightly in order to make the *glaze* very liquid and to ensure its speedy drying, and pour it, in one motion, over the object to be *glazed*.

With the help of some color, the *glaze* is generally given the tint of the fruit which flavors it.

2346a—ICING SUGAR *Sucre en Glace*

(In the United States there is available every quality of finest confectioners' sugar for icing. In Europe the following method was used.—Ed.)

The sugar is strained through a taut and fine silk sieve. The sugar strained through this silk has the delicacy of starch. At times it is used instead of Fondant for the *glazing* of cakes, but it is mostly used for white and caramel *glazings*. For this purpose the sugar is held in a tin box, covered with a lid pierced with small holes, called a sugar dredger.

To glaze (or sprinkle) white is to cover a cake, a fritter, or another object with a coat of icing sugar. This operation is done by shaking the sugar dredger over the object to be sprinkled.

To glaze with caramel is to cover a *Soufflé*, a *souffléd* omelet, fruit fritters, a custard, or other objects with a coat of icing sugar, by placing the sugar-coated object in intense heat a few minutes, to melt the sugar, which is converted into a brilliant, glossy covering of caramel.

2347—SUGAR GRAINS   *Les Paillettes de Sucre*

These are used in pastry to border certain cakes, or to surround the sugared-paste bases on which cakes are set. For this purpose the parts to which the sugar is expected to adhere must be spread with cooked apricot syrup.

To make them, take some sugar and sift it, first through a coarse strainer and then through a finer one, according to the size the sugar grains are required to be. The powder will, of course, fall and leave the grains clean.

2348—COLORED SUGAR GRAINS   *Sucre Coloré*

To color sugar grains, spread them on a piece of paper, and add a drop of liquid vegetable-coloring or a very little colored paste per tablespoon of sugar. The amount of coloring matter may either be lessened or increased, according to the shade required.

Rub the sugar in the hand to color it evenly; dry in a moderately warm drying-pan, and keep in a dry place in well-closed boxes.

(Colored sugar ready prepared is available in good grocery stores. —Ed.)

2349—VANILLA SUGAR   *Sucre Vanille*

The vanilla beans which have served in preparing infusions still possess some flavor. Reserve them, therefore, for the making of vanilla sugar.

After having gently dried them out, pound them finely with twice their weight of lump sugar; sift through the finest sieve, and again pound the bits remaining in the sieve until every particle goes through. Keep the preparation in a well-closed jar in a dry place.

(It is easier to make a good vanilla sugar nowadays by pounding the vanilla bean with finely powdered sugar, a little, and then allowing the mixture to remain in a tightly closed glass jar until the sugar is needed. You can replace the vanilla flavored sugar by fresh sugar and repeat the process. The bean will gradually lose its strength, but it will last for quite a while.—Ed.)

2350—CANDIED FRUIT   *Fruits Crystalisés*

These are used in the decoration of certain cakes, and as the ingredients of others.

They comprise angelica, golden and green preserved kumquats, cherries, plums, red and white pears, etc.

Candied fruit may be bought ready-prepared.

2351—APPLE JELLY FOR DECORATING
Gelée aux Pommes pour Garnitures

Quarter, peel, and core the apples (preferably russets or tart apples), and throw them, one by one, in a bowl of fresh water to prevent their getting brown.

Then put them in a copper or stainless steel pot with one and one-half pints of water per two lbs. of apples, and cook them gently without touching them.

This done, pour off their juice, and return it to the pot together with two lbs. of sugar per quart. Boil; skim with great care, that the jelly may be clear, and cook over a hot fire until the jelly has reached a stage when, on taking the skimmer out of the pot, the jelly adhering to it seems to mass itself towards the middle of the skimmer; or when the jelly breaks up into large drops, separated one from the other.

Then take the jelly off the fire; add some carmine to it, drop by drop, until it acquires a rosy hue; strain it again through a fine piece of linen, that it may be transparent, and finally pour it into tin pans to cool.

Put aside until wanted.

2352—PRALIN
Pralin

If it be for the purpose of covering certain cakes, or for forming a *glaze* on a fruit *entremet,* prepare it thus:—Put the whites of two eggs and three tablespoons of icing sugar in a small pan. Mix and stir briskly with a small, wooden spoon, until the paste becomes somewhat thick. Then, subject to the purpose for which it is intended, add a more or less large quantity of chopped almonds, according to whether the *pralin* be required thick or slightly liquid for spreading. Cover it with a piece of white paper, moistened with white of egg, that it may remain moist if kept for some time.

If it is to be added to a *soufflé* preparation, to a *soufflé* omelet, to a preparation of ice, or to a custard, it is a nougat powder which is prepared as follows:—

Gently melt one lb. of powdered sugar in a small saucepan, taking care not to let it acquire a deeper shade than old gold. Mix twenty oz. of dried almonds with it; turn the whole out on to the corner of a slightly-oiled marble slab (or on an over-turned saucepan-lid), and leave to cool. When the nougat is quite cold, pound it and rub it through a sieve.

Pound and rub what remains in the sieve until the whole goes through.

Put the powder in a tightly closed jar, and place in a dry place.

2353—CURRANTS AND SULTANA RAISINS
Groseilles aux Grappes et Sultanas

Sultana raisins and currants should always be at hand, ready and cleaned. To clean them, first dredge them and then rub them in a towel, closed to form a sort of purse. Now, turn them into a sieve or colander, and shake vigorously, that the flour and the stems may be removed; then examine them, one by one, to make sure that no stems remain.

Currants should be examined with very particular care, as small stones often get in among them.

Put the currants and the sultana raisins aside, each in a canister or a jar.

2354—ESSENCES AND FLAVORINGS
Essences et Assaissonements

The various *essences* used in pastry are bought ready-made. The flavorings consist of those products treated by infusion, such as vanilla; of grated or infused products, such as lemon and orange peels; and liqueurs in general.

Fruit juices only become flavors when a liqueur in keeping' with the fruit from which they were extracted has been added to them.

2355—GILDING PREPARATION
La Préparation de la Dorure

This consists of beaten eggs. Its purpose is to ensure the golden top coloring of certain cakes, to which it is applied with a brush. In some cases the eggs may be combined with a little water, as, for instance, when the heat of the oven is too hot, and cakes are required of a light color. In some cases, especially in that of small, dry cakes, it consists entirely of egg-yolks diluted with a few drops of water.

The Pastes

2356—ORDINARY SHORT PASTE
La Pâte Ordinaire

Sift one lb. of flour over the mixing-board; make a hollow in the center, and put therein one-sixth oz. of salt, one-third pint of cold water, and one-half lb. of well softened butter. Mix the flour gradually with the butter and the water; mass the whole a moment or two, and knead it (2357) twice. Then roll it up in a ball; wrap it in a piece of linen that its surface may not dry, and put it aside in a cool place.

Remarks: A kneaded paste should be prepared either one day, or at least a few hours, in advance, in order that it may lose that elasticity which it acquires from the kneading.

Pastes, after they have rested awhile, are much more easily handled, and bake a much more definite and lighter brown, than those that are used as soon as they are prepared.

2357—THE KNEADING OF PASTES *La Manipulation des Pâtes*

The object of kneading paste is to combine the ingredients of which it is composed thoroughly, and also to smooth it. Proceed as follows:—

When the paste is mixed, roll it into a mass; put it on the board; then press it away from you, little by little, between the board and the palm of the hand. For the paste to be perfectly smooth, it ought to be treated twice in this way.

2358—FINE, SHORT, OR FLAWN PASTE *Pâte à Foncer Fine*

Sift one lb. of flour on the mixing-board, and hollow it in the center. Put in the hollow one-third oz. of salt, one and one-half oz. of powdered sugar, an egg, one-fourth pint of cold water, and ten oz. of butter. First, thoroughly mix the butter, the egg, the water, and the seasoning, and then gradually combine the flour with it.

Knead the paste; press it out twice; roll it into a ball; and wrap it up and set it aside in a cool place.

2359—PIE PASTE *Pâte à Pâtés*

Take one lb. of sifted flour, four oz. of butter, one egg, one-third oz. of salt, and one-fourth pint of water. Mix as already directed; knead twice; roll up the paste, and set it in a cool place to rest. This paste should be kept somewhat firm.

2360—PIE PASTE WITH LARD *Pâte pour Pâté au Lard*

Take one lb. of sifted flour, four oz. of lard, one-quarter pint of tepid water, one egg, one-third oz. of salt, and proceed exactly as in the case of (2359).

2361—DUMPLING AND PUDDING PASTES
Pâte à Dumplings et à Puddings

Break up ten oz. of very dry beef suet, and carefully clear it of all little pieces of skin and connective tissue. Chop it up as finely as possible; sift one lb. of flour on the mixing-board; hollow it out; and put into the hollow one-half oz. of salt, one and one-half oz. of sugar, one-third pint of water, and the chopped suet. Mix up these various ingredients, and, by degrees, combine the flour with them.

Mix the paste together, without kneading it, and put it aside in a cool place until it is wanted.

2362—DRY SUGARED PASTE FOR VARIOUS PURPOSES
Pâte Sèche Sucrée pour Différents Usages

Take one lb. of sifted flour, seven oz. of butter, five oz. of powdered sugar, three eggs, and one-half tablespoon of orange-flower water.

Mix in the usual way, knead it twice; roll it into a ball, and keep it wrapped up, in a cool place, until required.

2363—PASTE FOR SMALL TEA-CAKES *Pâte à Petits Gateaux*

Take one lb. of sifted flour, ten oz. of butter, ten oz. of sugar, one egg, the yolks of four, and a tablespoon of orange-flower water.

Mix up gradually; mass the paste together, and roll it out into a thin layer, twice. Roll it up, and let it rest awhile in a cool place before it is used.

2364—GUMMING *Gommer*

In the case of certain small cakes, especially those served at tea, it is possible to gum their surfaces in order to make them glossy. For this purpose a thin solution of gum arabic is used, and it is brushed over the cakes as they leave the oven, by means of a small brush.

Cakes may also be brushed with a syrup formed from milk and sugar, which mixture may be used instead of gum arabic with advantage.

2365—GALETTES PASTE *Pâte à Galette Ordinaire*

Hollow out one lb. of sifted flour and put in its midst one-third oz. of salt, two oz. of powdered sugar, one-quarter pint of water, and one-half lb. of softened butter.

Mix, taking care to put in the flour only by degrees, knead thoroughly, that the ingredients may be well combined, and mass the paste together without making it too elastic. Leave it in a cool place for at least an hour; then roll it out three times, at intervals of eight minutes, for the reasons given under the directions for puff-paste.

2366—PUFF-PASTE   *Feuilletage*

Sift one lb. of flour on to the mixing-board. Make a hollow in it, and put in one-third oz. of table salt and about one-half pint of cold water, and mix without kneading. Mass the paste together, and let it rest for twenty minutes, that it may lose its elasticity, which will be all the more pronounced for its having been very much worked. It is to avoid this elasticity, therefore, that the mixing of puff-paste should be done with the smallest amount of kneading possible.

Spread the prepared paste on a flour-dusted board, in the shape of an even thin cake. Spread on one lb. of softened butter, without completely covering the paste; draw the edges of the paste towards the center, in such a way as to enclose the butter completely, and to form a square thickness of paste.

Leave to rest for ten minutes, and then begin the working of the paste; rolling it out to the length of one and one-half feet, and keeping it one in. thick. Fold this layer over three times, and press upon it with the rolling pin to join the superimposed layers. The whole of this operation constitutes one movement.

Begin another movement immediately, turning the paste the reverse way, and folding it as before. Set it to rest in a cool place for eight or ten minutes, and then do the same thing over twice more.

Ten minutes after the two last folding over actions (there should be six in all), the puff-paste is ready to be cut up and used.

Remarks relative to puff-paste: Good puff-paste should be buttered to the extent of one lb. per one and one-half lbs., that is, one lb. of butter for every one lb. of flour mixed with one-half pint of water. The consistency of the paste and the butter should be exactly the same, if they are to be evenly mixed; the butter ought therefore to be softened—more particularly in winter.

In preparing puff-paste, remember to put it in a cool place while it is resting; but never directly upon ice; for, though the ice would not affect the paste, it might seriously affect the butter.

It would harden it to the extent of preventing its perfect mixture with the mass, and lumps would form. Puff-paste should be rolled out very regularly, with the view of thoroughly distributing the butter throughout the preparation, and thus ensuring its uniform rising.

Puff-paste should not be worked too speedily; for, if it be so worked, it will be found to acquire an elasticity which not only makes it difficult to cut up, but also tends to make it shrink in the baking.

2367—PUFF-PASTE TRIMMINGS OR HALF PUFF-PASTE
Rognures ou Demi-Feuilletage

These are very useful in pastry work of the cook, for *tartlets, barquettes, croûtons,* etc. When the puff-paste is cut up, the trimmings should be rolled into a ball, and put aside in a cool place. Nevertheless they must be used within the space of two days in summer and four days in winter.

(They keep longer if protected by paper, in refrigerators.—Ed.)

2368—ORDINARY BRIOCHE PASTE   *Pate à Brioche Ordinaire*

Sift one lb. of flour on the board; take a quarter of it, make a hollow in it, and put in one-quarter oz. of very fresh, dry yeast. Mix the yeast and the flour with a little tepid water, so as to obtain a soft paste which is the leaven. Roll this paste into a ball; make two slits in its top, at right angles to one another, and place it in a small bowl.

Cover, and put it in a somewhat warm place, that the leaven may be sure to ferment.

Then make a hollow in the remaining flour, and put into it one-quarter oz. of salt, and one and one-half oz. of sugar, together with two tablespoons of milk to moisten it, one-third of the whole amount of the butter to be used, namely, four oz., and four eggs.

Begin by thoroughly mixing the butter, eggs and seasoning, and then combine the flour with it by degrees. When the paste forms a compact mass, knead and pull it about with the hands, that it may be light. When, at the end of a few minutes, it has acquired a certain resilience, make a hole in the middle of it and add one egg. Mix it with the paste; work it again, and after an interval of two minutes add one more egg in the same way. The total number of eggs for the quantities of other ingredients given above should be six.

Add the remaining butter (eight oz.) to the paste; the former being *manié* and even softened, just sufficiently to make it of the same consistency as the paste.

Spread it on, and mix the two; kneading small portions at a time, and combining those portions so as to mix the two elements completely.

At this stage, overturn the paste and spread the leaven (which should now be equal to twice its original bulk) upon it.

Mix it well as in the case of the butter, without working the paste.

Finally, put the paste into a bowl; cover it, and place it in a temperate place.

For it to have the desired lightness, this paste should rise for from ten to twelve hours. However, at the end of five or six hours, the process is arrested by the working of the paste; that is to say, by turning it out upon a flour-dusted board and beating it with the palm of the hand.

It is then returned to the bowl to rise again, for five or six hours; and then it is once more beaten just before being used.

(For the very dry yeast mentioned in all of the yeast recipes, the same amount of compressed yeast may be used, the only difference being that compressed yeast works much faster and more efficiently. Therefore the time for the rising of the fermented dough will be shortened.—Ed.)

2369—MOUSSELINE BRIOCHE PASTE   *Pâte à Brioche Mousseline*

Mousseline brioche paste is made from the ordinary kind (2368), combined with a little butter and developed in the mould by rising before the baking process—which procedure makes it exceedingly light and delicate.

This paste is used in the preparation of certain *timbales* for fruit desserts, and it is prepared as follows:—

Take the required amount of ordinary brioche paste, and add to it, per lb. of paste, two oz. of best butter, softened to the consistency of an ointment, that it may thoroughly mix with the paste. Roll the paste into a ball, and put it in a liberally-buttered mould, only filling it two-thirds. The remaining third of the mould is filled by the rising of the paste. Place the mould in a temperate place, until the paste has risen to the edges of the mould; brush the surface of the paste with melted butter, and bake in a moderate oven.

2370—ORDINARY BRIOCHE PASTE (FOR RISSOLES, SMALL PATTIES A LA DAUPHINE, AND VARIOUS OTHER PREPARATIONS)
Pâte à Brioche Commune

Quantities: One lb. of flour, seven oz. of butter, four fair-sized eggs, salt, a pinch of powdered sugar; one-third oz. of very dry, fresh yeast (see note in 2367), and a little tepid milk.

Make the leaven with a quarter of the flour, the yeast and the lukewarm milk, and set it to rise while the paste is being prepared.

Prepare the paste as already directed, and keep it rising as before for ten hours, taking care to arrest the process once.

The work is the same as in the preceding case, in every particular, except in regard to the amount of butter, which in this instance is only half as much; in regard to the amount of sugar, which should be just enough to ensure the coloring of the paste; and finally in regard to its firmness, which should permit the paste being worked with a rolling-pin.

2371—SAVARIN PASTE   *Pâte à Savarin*

Quantities: One lb. of flour; twelve oz. of butter; one-half oz. of very dry, fresh yeast; eight eggs; about one-third pint of milk; one-half oz. of salt, and one oz. of sugar.

Procedure: Savarin paste may be prepared in several ways; but the one given below is as simple and quick as could be desired.

Sift the flour into a round wooden bowl; hollow it out; add the yeast, and dissolve by means of tepid milk, stirring slightly with the tip of the finger.

Add the eggs; mix and work the paste by hand for a few minutes; scrape off those portions of it which have adhered to the side of the bowl, and add them to the whole.

Distribute the softened butter in small quantities over the paste. Cover, and set in a temperate place until the paste has risen to twice its original bulk. Then add salt; knead the paste, that it may thoroughly absorb the butter, and pat it briskly until it is sufficiently elastic to be taken up in one lump.

At this stage add the sugar, and work the paste again that the former may thoroughly mix with it. The sugar should only be added at the close of the operation; for, since it weakens the consistency of the paste, it would make it much more difficult to work were it added at the start.

THE USES OF THIS PASTE

If it be for Savarins with syrup, it is customary to sprinkle the previously-buttered moulds with slightly-grilled, chopped or slithered almonds. Take the paste in small quantities at a time, and line the moulds with it to the extent of one-third of their height.

The remaining two-thirds of each mould become covered when the paste rises owing to fermentation.

Proceed in the same way for Savarins which are to be kept dry, for fruit crusts or other uses; but then the sprinkling of the moulds with almond may be omitted.

2372—BABA PASTE
Pâte à Baba

Quantities: One lb. of flour; one-half lb. of butter; seven eggs; two-thirds oz. of yeast; one-fifth pint of milk; one-third oz. of salt; two-thirds oz. of sugar; three oz. of currants and sultana raisins in equal quantities.

Procedure: Proceed exactly as for Savarin paste, and add the currants and sultana raisins at the last with the sugar. In moulding, a few seeded Malaga raisins may be laid on the bottom of the moulds. As in the case of the Savarin, the paste should only fill one-third of the mould.

2373—ORDINARY CREAM PUFF PASTE
Pâte à Chou Ordinaire

Quantities.—One pint of water; eight oz. of butter; one-third oz. of salt; one oz. of sugar; one lb. of sifted flour; sixteen fair-sized eggs, and a tablespoon of orange-flower water.

Procedure.—Put the water, butter, salt, and sugar in a saucepan and boil. When the liquid boils and rises, take the saucepan off the fire; add the flour, and mix. Return the saucepan to a moderate fire, and stir the paste until it ceases to stick to the spoon, and the butter begins to ooze slightly.

Take the saucepan off the fire; add the eggs, two at a time, taking care to mix them thoroughly with the paste before adding the succeeding ones. When all the eggs have been blended, finish the paste with orange-flower water.

2374—COMMON CREAM PUFF PASTE (FOR SOUFFLE FRITTERS, GNOCHI, POTATOES A LA DAUPHINE)
Pâte à Chou Commune

Proceed as directed above, but reduce the quantity of butter to three oz., and the number of eggs to twelve; avoid drying this paste too much.

2375—RAMEKINS AND GOUGERE PASTE
Pâte à Ramequins et à Gougère

This is prepared exactly like ordinary "Pâte à Choux" (2373), except that:—

Milk takes the place of water.

The sugar and orange-flower water are omitted.

For the quantities given (2373), eight oz. of fresh Gruyère cheese, cut into dice, are added to the paste, after all the eggs have been beaten into it.

2376—FINE PASTE FOR SPONGE OR GENOISE

Pâte à Genoise Fine

Put into a bowl one lb. of powdered sugar and sixteen eggs. Mix the two; place the basin upon hot coal cinders or on the side of the fire, and beat its contents until they reach the *"ribbon" stage* (see remarks below). Then add the selected flavoring (vanilla sugar, orange rind, or liqueur, in the proportion of one tablespoon of vanilla sugar or orange rind, and one liqueur-glass of liqueur, to the quantities given above), twelve oz. of sifted flour, and eight oz. of melted butter, the latter being carefully poured into the paste without allowing it to bubble. Mix these ingredients with the paste, raising the latter with a spatula that it may not get heavy.

Bake it in buttered and floured moulds.

Remarks.—A preparation of Biscuit— (sponge cake) or *Génoise* reaches the *"ribbon" stage* when it becomes thick, draws out in ribbon-form, and takes some time to level itself again when a spoon is pulled out of it. This state of the paste is also indicative of its lightness.

2377—ORDINARY GENOISE PASTE FOR CUTTING UP

Pâte à Genoise Ordinaire

Quantities.—One lb. of sugar, twelve eggs, thirteen oz. of flour, eight oz. of butter, and the quantity of flavoring thought sufficient.

Proceed exactly as in the preceding recipe, in everything pertaining to the working of the paste.

This paste is baked in buttered and paper lined pans, in which it is spread in layers one and one-quarter inches thick, that it may rise to about one and three-quarter inches thick, while baking.

2378—LADY FINGERS SPONGE PASTE *Pâte pour Biscuits à la Cuiller*

Stir one lb. of sugar and sixteen egg-yolks in a bowl until the preparation has whitened slightly and has reached the *ribbon* stage. Now add a tablespoon of orange-flower water; mix with twelve oz. of sifted flour, followed by sixteen egg-whites, beaten to a stiff froth. Take care to cut in the whites with the spatula, that they may remain quite light.

To Shape the Fingers.—Put the paste, little by little, into a canvas pastry-bag, fitted with a plain tube of one-half inch flat opening. Close the bag; pipe the biscuits on sheets of strong paper; sprinkle them with powdered sugar, and shake off any superfluous sugar by holding the sheets end upwards.

Sprinkle a few drops of water upon the biscuits by means of a moistened brush to aid the beading of the sugar, and remember that a very moderate oven is the best for the completion of this beading.

2379—SAVOY SPONGE PASTE   *Pâte pour Biscuit de Savoie*

Stir one lb. of sugar and fourteen egg-yolks in a bowl until the preparation reaches the *ribbon stage*. Flavor with vanilla sugar; add six oz. of very dry, sifted flour mixed with six oz. of cornstarch, and finally cut in the fourteen egg-whites, which should be beaten very stiff.

Carefully set the preparation in buttered and cornstarch-dredged moulds, filling the latter only two-thirds full, and leaving the remaining third to be filled by the rising of the paste while baking.

Bake in a regular, moderate oven.

2380—SPONGE BISCUIT PASTE   *Pâte à Biscuit Manqué*

Stir one lb. of sugar with eighteen egg-yolks in a bowl until the preparation is white and light. Add three tablespoons of rum, thirteen oz. of sifted flour, and ten oz. of melted butter, carefully poured into the mixture. Mix, raising the paste from the bottom of the bowl with the spatula.

Put the preparation in special buttered and floured moulds, filling the latter only two-thirds full. Bake in a moderate oven.

2381—PUNCH BISCUIT SPONGE PASTE   *Pâte à Biscuit Punch*

Stir one lb. of sugar, twelve egg-yolks, and three eggs in a bowl, until the whole becomes frothy. Flavor with a bare tablespoon of orange sugar, the same amount of lemon sugar, and three tablespoons of best rum, and add twelve oz. of sifted flour, ten oz. of melted butter, and the whites of eight eggs beaten to a stiff froth. Mix with the usual precautions, that the paste may not be heavy.

Bake the preparation in buttered moulds, in paper cases or in rings, according to the purpose it is intended for. Use a moderate oven.

2382—ORDINARY MERINGUE   *Meringue Ordinaire*

Whisk the whites of eight eggs until they are as stiff as it is possible to make them. Sprinkle them with one lb. of powdered sugar, and mix them with the latter carefully, that they may retain all their lightness.

2383a—ITALIAN STYLE MERINGUE   *Meringue à l'Italienne*

Cook one lb. of sugar to the *large-ball* stage, and meanwhile whisk the whites of eight eggs to a stiff froth, so as to have them ready simultaneously with the sugar.

Pour the cooked sugar into the egg-whites, slowly and without stopping, and mix up briskly with the wire whisk.

2384b—ITALIAN STYLE MERINGUE   *Meringue à l'Italienne*

Mix one lb. of very best powdered sugar and the whites of eight eggs in a copper bowl. Place the utensil on hot cinders or on the side of the stove, that the preparation may be lukewarm while in progress.

Whisk the meringue until it is of sufficient consistency to span the wires of the whisk. If it is not to be used at once, transfer the paste to a small bowl; cover it with a round piece of paper, and set it in a cool place.

2385—ALMOND PASTE   *Pâte d'Amandes*

Instead of the antiquated and difficult method of making almond pastes in the mortar, a crushing machine is now used which not only yields a much smoother paste, but also greatly simplifies the work. Almond paste, which consists of almonds, sugar, and egg-whites, in quantities varying in accordance with the purpose of the paste, is now sold ready-made. It has only to be finished with a little sugar, white of egg, and other ingredients, subject to the use to which it is to be put.

2386—MELTING ALMOND PASTE (FOR STUFFING AND IMITATING FRUIT)   *Pâte d'Amandes Fondante*

Pass eight oz. of dry, skinned almonds through the grinder.

Place them in the mortar, together with the selected flavoring *essence;* either a tablespoon of vanilla sugar or a small glass of liqueur; and add to them, little by little, working the while with the pestle, one lb. of sugar cooked to the *small-crack* stage.

With this general recipe, the melting paste may be varied at will by an increase or decrease in the quantity of sugar.

2387—PISTACHIOS *Pistaches*

These should belong to the pastry-cook's stock, but, as a rule, they are only prepared just before being served. To skin them, proceed as in the case of almonds (2338).

2388—PISTACHIO PASTE FOR INFUSIONS

Pâte de Pistaches pour Infusions

As soon as the pistachios are skinned, washed, and dried, crush them in the mortar to a very smooth paste, which set in boiled milk, to infuse.

As the color of pistachios is weak, it is strengthened in preparations containing them with a few drops of vegetable green, while its aroma is thrown into relief with a drop of vanilla.

2389—MELTING PISTACHIO PASTE *Pâte de Pistaches Fondante*

Put seven oz. of pistachios and two oz. of almonds through the grinder; both should have been just skinned. Put the paste into the mortar; add to it two tablespoons of syrup, strongly flavored with vanilla, followed by eight oz. of sugar, cooked to the *small-crack* stage, and added to the paste little by little.

Transfer the paste to a marble slab, and finish it by combining three tablespoons of icing sugar with it.

THE PREPARATION AND COOKING OF VARIOUS PASTRY CRUSTS USED IN COOKERY

2390—VOL-AU-VENT CRUST *Croûte de Vol-au-Vent*

Prepare the puff-paste as directed under (2366). Make the layer of paste of an even thickness of four-fifths inch; set on it an overturned plate or a saucepan-lid, the size of which should be that intended for the Vol-au-vent, and cut the paste obliquely, following round the edges of the lid or plate with a small knife. Turn the layer of paste over, and set it on a slightly moistened round baking sheet; groove it all round; brush it with egg, and describe a circle on top of it with the point of a knife, not cutting deeply, one and one-quarter inches away from the edge, to form the cover of the Vol-au-vent. Streak this cover criss-cross-fashion; also streak the body of the Vol-au-vent with the point of a small knife, and bake it in a rather hot oven.

Upon taking the Vol-au-vent from the oven, remove its cover, and clear it of the soft part of the paste which will be found on the inside.

2391—SMALL-PATTY CRUSTS *Croûte de Bouchées*

Bouchées are really small Vol-au-vents. Roll out the paste, making it a good one-third inch thick. Cut this layer with a grooved round cutter three inches in diameter; set the rounds of stamped-out paste on a moistened pan; brush with egg, and make a circular incision in each of them, one-half inch from their edges, either with the point of a small knife or with an even, round cutter dipped in hot water. But do not cut all the way down.

Bake in a hot oven, and remove the insides of the bouchées on taking them out of the oven. "Mignonnes Bouchées," which are used as a garnish, are stamped out with a round cutter two inches in diameter, and are slightly thicker than ordinary bouchées.

2392—SMALL HOT PATTIES *Croûte de Bouchées Mignonnes*

Roll out the puff-paste (2366) to a thickness of one-sixth inch, and stamp it out with an even round cutter three inches in diameter. With the trimmings from this operation, rolled somewhat more thinly, make an equal quantity of rounds, and lay them on a pan. Slightly moisten the edges of these rounds with a brush; fill their centers with some *forcemeat,* rolled to the size of a hazel-nut; cover the *forcemeat* with the rounds stamped out from the first; press upon these with the back of a round cutter two inches in diameter; brush them with egg, and bake them in a hot oven for twelve or fourteen minutes.

2393—TARTLET CRUSTS *Croûtes de Tartelettes*

For *tartlet crusts,* which are put to various uses, take either even or fluted, large or small moulds, subject to the requirements.

Roll out a piece of short paste (2356) to a thickness of one-fifth inch; stamp it out with a fluted or scalloped round cutter of a size in proportion to the moulds used; line the buttered moulds with these rounds of paste; pierce the paste on the bottom of each with the point of a small knife; line with good-quality paper; fill up with lentils, split peas, or rice, just to keep the form, and bake in a moderate oven. When the paste is baked, remove the dry vegetable used and the paper, and place the crusts in the warming-oven, that they may be quite dry; or brush with egg inside, and set them in the front of the oven for a few minutes.

2394—TIMBALE CRUST *Croûte de Timbale*

Butter a *Charlotte-mould,* and decorate its sides with some sort of design made from noodle-paste trimmings to which a little powdered sugar has been added. Shape a piece of short paste (2356), of a size in proportion to the mould, like a ball; roll it out to a disc; sprinkle it with flour, and fold it in two. Draw the ends gently towards the center, so as to form a kind of skullcap, and take care to not crease the paste. Make this skullcap of an even thickness of one-third inch, and place it in the mould.

Press it well upon the bottom and sides of the mould, that it may acquire the shape of the latter; line the mould inside with good buttered paper; fill up with lentils or split peas, just to keep the form, letting them project in a dome above the edges of the paste, and cover with a round sheet of paper.

Prepare a round layer of paste, one-fifth inch thick, a little larger diametrically than the *timbale* one. Slightly moisten the inside edges of the *timbale;* cover it with the prepared disc of paste, and seal it well down to the edges of the *timbale,* pressing it between the fingers in such a way as to form an edge reaching one-half inch beyond the brim of the mould all round.

Pinch this edge with paste-pincers inside and out.

With a round or oval grooved fancy-cutter stamp out some imitation leaves from a very thin layer of paste, and imitate the veins of the leaves with the back of a knife; or stamp out some triangles of paste; shape them like leaves, and set these (slightly overlapping one another) upon the dome of the *timbale* in superimposed rows.

Finish with three rounds of paste, stamped out with a grooved round cutter of a different size from the first, and make a hole in the center of each roundel with a round, even fancy-cutter. Brush with egg and bake in a moderate oven. When the outside of the *timbale* is well browned, detach and remove the cover formed by the leaves. Remove the split peas and the paper; brush with egg the inside of the *timbale,* and leave it to dry in the front of the oven or in the warming-oven.

2395—CRUST FOR DEEP PIES   *Croûte de Flan*

With short or any other kind of paste prepare a layer one-sixth inch thick, the diameter of which should be one-fourth as long again as that of the spring-form used. Lift this layer, and place it into the previously-buttered spring-form, pressing it with the fingers, that it may assume the shape of the mould. Then roll the rolling-pin across the top of the rim, so that the overlapping paste may be cut away; press the thickness of paste that has been formed at the top between the fingers in such a way as to make it project above the edges of the form, and make a regular edge. Pinch this edge with the pastry pincers, and set the spring-form on a round baking sheet.

Prick it with the point of a small knife; line the bottom and sides with slightly-buttered, white paper; fill the pastry with dry lentils or split peas, just to keep the form, and bake in a moderately hot oven for about twenty-five minutes.

Then remove the lentils and paper, as also the spring-form rim, and return the crust to the oven for a few minutes to brown, if it is not already sufficiently colored.

If the paste be required very dry, place the crust in the warming-oven for a little while, or brush the inside with egg, and set it in the front of the oven for a few minutes.

2396—THE LINING AND COVERING OF RAISED AND DRESSED PIES
Croûtes pour les "Pies"

The moulds for raised pies are oval or round. If they are round, make a layer of patty paste, one-half inch thick, in proportion to the size of the mould. (Deep dish pie mould.)

Sprinkle this paste with flour, fold it in two, and shape it like a skullcap, after the manner described under *"Timbale Crust"* (2394). It is only necessary to press this skullcap of paste into the buttered mould in order to give it the shape of the latter. If the mould is oval, proceed in the same way, giving the skullcap an oval shape.

When the raised pie is filled, first cover the filling with a somewhat thin, round, or oval layer of paste, in accordance with the shape of the mould, and seal it well down upon the moistened edges. Then cut away the superfluous paste of the edge, so as to make the latter even and neat, and pinch it outside and in. Raised pies are covered in two ways—either with a layer of puff-paste (2366), or with leaves of paste stamped out with a round cutter or a knife, the veins being imitated with the back of a knife.

In the first case, prepare a layer of puff-paste one-third inch thick, equal in size to the inside of the patty. Place this layer of paste upon the cover of the pie, after having slightly moistened it; brush with egg and decorate with lines made by back of knife, and make a slit in the top for the escape of steam.

In the second case, prepare the paste leaves as directed above, and lay them on the pie (slightly overlapping one another) in superimposed rows, starting from the bottom. On the top of the pie set three or four scalloped rounds of paste, graduated in size, and stuck one upon the other, each round having a hole in its center for the escape of steam.

Brush with egg and set the pie in the oven.

The baking of raised pies made with raw *forcemeat* is done in a moderately-heated oven. Bear in mind that the larger the pie is, the more moderate should be the oven.

VARIOUS CUSTARDS

HOT CUSTARDS

2397—ENGLISH CREAM *Crème Anglaise*

This custard permits of various methods of preparation which are subject to the purpose for which it is intended. It is the chief sauce for entremets (sweet dishes), and whether it be *poached* in a deep dish or in a mould, it constitutes one of the oldest and best-known desserts. This last kind of custard will be examined hereafter. At present I shall only deal with the variety used either as a sauce or an accompaniment, cold or hot. It is extremely difficult to prescribe fixed quantities for this custard, for the former depend a great deal upon the diners' tastes, and, whereas some like a thick custard, others go to the extreme of wishing it just liquid enough to be drunk like any other beverage.

The quantities given below are suited to a custard of medium consistency, but if a thicker custard were desired, the number of egg-yolks would have to be proportionately increased, and *vice-versa*.

The quantity of sugar also varies, subject to the diners' tastes, and, as the amount used (except in the case of unreasonable excess) does not affect the consistency of the custard, it may be graduated from three to ten or twelve oz. per quart, as taste may dictate. Six oz. of sugar per quart of milk constitutes a happy medium.

English custard permits of all the flavoring *essences* used for desserts, but the one which suits it best is vanilla. When this last-named flavor or that of filberts, almond *pralin,* or coffee is used, it is well to put the required quantity to infuse for twenty minutes in the boiling milk, after the latter has been measured. Chocolate is first melted and then gradually added to the custard before it is cooked. Other *aromatic essences* or liqueurs are added to the custard after it has been strained.

English custard permits of two methods of preparation:—

Recipe A.—Put twelve raw egg-yolks and three-quarters lb. of powdered sugar in a bowl. Mix the sugar a little with the yolks, and beat the latter with a beater until they have entirely absorbed the sugar, and the resulting mixture is white and has reached the *ribbon* stage (2376). Then pour one quart of boiling milk into the egg mixture, little by little, mixing the whole with a whisk. Then put the preparation on the fire, stirring it with a spatula, and cook it until it approaches the boil and properly coats the spoon. Take care not to let it boil, for this would separate the preparation. In any case, when the sauce is intended for hot sweets, by adding a tablespoon of arrowroot or cornstarch, it may be prevented from separating.

When the custard is cooked, as already explained, strain it, either through a strainer, into a *bain-marie* (water-bath), if it is to be served hot, or through a sieve into a large, enamelled bowl, where it should be frequently stirred to be kept smooth while cooling.

Custard prepared in this way forms the base of all ice creams, of which I shall speak later on. It may serve as an addition to all cold or hot desserts which call for a sauce. When, while it is still lukewarm, it is combined with its weight of best butter, it constitutes the delicious butter cream, which is the richest and most delicate of the pastry-cook's confections.

Finally, if about four oz. of dissolved gelatine per quart of cooled milk be added to it, and it be mixed with twice its volume of whipped cream, it represents the preparation for Bavarian Creams and Russian Charlottes.

Recipe B.—Dissolve six oz. of sugar in one quart of milk; boil, and pour the mixture, little by little, over twelve egg-yolks, whisking the latter briskly the while. When this custard is to be moulded, or is intended for a Cabinet Pudding, or some other similar preparation, which must be finally *poached,* strain it as soon as it is mixed, without cooking it.

If, on the other hand, it is intended for an accompaniment, or for the preparation of butter creams or ices, cook it as directed in Recipe A.

2398—ENGLISH CUSTARD (TO ACCOMPANY COLD OR HOT STEWED FRUIT)　　　*Crème Anglaise pour Compôtes*

For this purpose English custard (2397) is made from only ten egg-yolks per quart of milk. Serve it in shallow silver or porcelain dishes; sprinkle its surface copiously with *icing sugar* (2346a), and criss-cross it with a red-hot iron.

2399—FRANGIPAN CREAM *Crème Frangipan*

As in the case of English custard (2397), Frangipan custard varies in the quantities of its ingredients in accordance with its purpose and personal taste. The recipe given below is an average one, which the cook will be able to modify, in regard to consistency, by increasing or decreasing the amount of flour.

Mix one-half lb. of powdered sugar, two oz. of flour, two whole eggs, and the yolks of five in a bowl. Pour one pint of boiling milk over this paste, stirring it briskly the while; add a few grains of salt and the selected flavoring, and set the saucepan on the fire, that the *Frangipan* may cook. Do not cease stirring this cream while it is cooking, for it burns easily. (A double boiler might be useful here.)

Let it boil a few minutes; pour it into a bowl, and combine three oz. of fresh butter and two tablespoons of dry, crushed macaroons with it. When the whole is well mixed, smooth the surface of the custard with a well-buttered spoon, so that no crust may form while the cooling progresses.

2400—FRANGIPAN FOR FRIED CREAM *Frangipan pour Crèmes Frites*

Proceed as above, but so apportion the quantities as to obtain a very firm cream. The quantities should be as follows:—Six oz. of flour, six oz. of sugar, ten egg-yolks, four whole eggs, one quart of milk, and one oz. of butter.

When this cream is cooked, spread it in a layer one inch thick on a buttered tray or on a marble slab; carefully butter its surface, and let it cool before using it.

COLD CUSTARDS

2401—PASTRY CREAM *Crème St. Honoré*

Mix one lb. of powdered sugar with four oz. of flour and twelve egg-yolks, and dilute with one quart of boiling milk. Cook this cream, stirring it continually the while; and, as soon as it boils, add to it a few drops of orange-flower water and about two oz. of dissolved gelatine, softened in cold water. Boil the cream a few minutes; take it off the fire, and, while stirring it briskly, carefully combine with it twelve egg-whites, beaten to a stiff froth.

N.B.—Some chefs call this St. Honoré cream (for, as a matter of fact, it serves chiefly in the garnishing of sweet dishes bearing that name), and give the name of Pastry cream to the same preparation minus the egg-whites and the gelatine. I prefer to abide by the principle given above, and to consider the cream without whisked egg-whites merely as a *Frangipan,* with which it has many points in common.

Pastry cream may be flavored according to fancy. The addition of the gelatine is not necessary when the cream is to be served immediately, or when it only has a moment or two to wait. But it is indispensable to prevent the separation of the cream, especially in hot weather, if it has to wait at all.

2402—CHANTILLY WHIPPED CREAM *Crème Chantilly*

Nothing could be simpler or more exquisite than this preparation, which is obtained by whipping the best cream (kept fresh for twenty-four hours in the refrigerator). The cream speedily increases in volume and becomes frothy. The operation should then be stopped, lest the cream turn to butter, and there should be immediately added to it four oz. of powdered sugar (part of which should be the vanilla kind) per quart, and then the preparation should be placed in a cool place until required.

N.B.—The addition of a little dissolved or powdered tragacanth gum or gelatine to the cream results in a more frothy cream being obtained, but the result is neither as fresh nor as perfect in taste when it is not combined with a sweet or ice preparation.

Various Preparations for Entremets

2403—PREPARATIONS FOR PANCAKES AND PANNEQUETS
Compositions pour Crêpes et Pannequets

Preparation A.—Put into a basin one lb. of sifted flour, six oz. of powdered sugar, and a pinch of salt. Dilute with ten eggs and one quart of milk, added by degrees. Flavor with one heaped tablespoon of orange, lemon or vanilla sugar, which should form part of the total weight of sugar prescribed; or with one-eighth pint of some liqueur such as brandy, kirsch, rum, etc., which should form part of the total liquid.

Preparation B.—Mix one lb. of flour, three and one-half oz. of powdered sugar and a pinch of salt, with nine eggs and a half-pint of cream. Add one-eighth pint of brandy, two and a half-oz. of melted butter and one and a half-pints of milk. Pass the whole through a fine strainer, and finish it with one-eighth pint of *orgeat* syrup or almond milk (2506) and three oz. of finely-crushed macaroons.

Preparation C.—Mix one lb. of flour, three and a half oz. of powdered sugar and a pinch of salt with nine eggs. Stir the mixture well; add to it a half-pint of fresh cream and one pint of milk. Finish with a half-pint of whipped cream, and flavor as taste may suggest.

Preparation D.—Mix one lb. of flour, three and a half oz. of powdered sugar and a pinch of salt, with five eggs and the yolks of three. Add one and three-quarter pints of milk and five egg-whites beaten to a stiff froth.

Flavor according to taste.

2404—RICE PREPARATION FOR DESSERTS   *Riz pour Entremets*

Wash one lb. of Southern or Indian rice; cover it with plenty of cold water; allow it to come to a boil, and drain it the moment it has boiled. Wash it once more in lukewarm water; drain it, and set it to cook with two pints of boiled milk, two-thirds lb. of sugar, a pinch of salt and three oz. of butter.

Flavor with a stick of vanilla or a few strips of orange or lemon rind, tied together with a thread. When the liquid begins to boil, cover the saucepan; place it in the oven, and let it cook gently for twenty or twenty-five minutes, without once touching the rice.

On taking it from the oven, thicken it with the yolks of sixteen eggs, which should be mixed with it by means of a fork in such a way as not to break the rice grains, which ought to remain whole.

N.B.—In some cases, the milk and the sugar may be replaced (for the cooking process) by an equal amount of sugar and water syrup at 12° (Saccharometer).

2405—SOUFFLE PREPARATIONS   *Compositions pour Soufflés*

Soufflé preparations are of two kinds:—

Those prepared with cream, which if necessary may serve for all *soufflés;* and those with a fruit-*purée* base, which permit of a more pronounced flavor for fruit *soufflés* than if these were prepared with cream.

Cream-soufflé Preparation for Four People.—Boil one-sixth pint of milk with one oz. of sugar; add a tablespoon of flour diluted in a little cold milk; cook for two minutes, and finish, away from the fire, with a piece of butter the size of a walnut, and two egg-yolks with three whites beaten to a stiff froth.

Soufflé Preparation for a Big Party.—Thoroughly mix a half-lb. of flour, a half-lb. of sugar, four eggs and the yolks of three, in a saucepan. Mix with one quart of boiling milk; add a stick of vanilla; boil, and cook for two minutes, stirring constantly.

Finish, away from the fire, with four oz. of butter, five egg-yolks, and twelve whites, beaten to a very stiff froth.

Soufflé Preparation with a Fruit Base.—Take one lb. of sugar cooked to the *small-crack* stage; add one lb. of the pulp or *purée* of the fruit to be used, and ten egg-whites, beaten to a stiff froth.

Proceed thus: Having cooked the sugar to the extent stated above, add to it the fruit pulp. If the latter reduces the sugar a stage or two, cook it again in order to return it to the *small-crack* stage; and, when this is reached, pour it over the whites.

Dishing and Cooking of Soufflés.—Whatever the soufflés may consist of, cook them in a *timbale,* or in a special false-bottomed dish, buttered and sugared inside. Cook in a somewhat moderate oven, that the heat may reach the center of the *soufflé* by degrees.

Two minutes before taking the *soufflé* from the oven, sprinkle it with *icing sugar,* which, when it becomes caramel upon the surface of the *soufflé,* constitutes the *glazing.*

The decoration of *soufflés* is optional, and, in any case, should not be overdone.

Hot Sauces for Desserts

2406—ENGLISH SAUCE   *Sauce Anglaise*
   See the Custard recipe (2397).

2407—CHOCOLATE SAUCE   *Sauce au Chocolat*
   Dissolve half-lb. of grated chocolate in two-thirds pint of water. Add a tablespoon of vanilla sugar; cook gently for twenty-five minutes, and complete at the last moment with three tablespoons of cream and a piece of best butter, the size of a walnut.

2408—SABAYON   *Sabayon*
   Mix one lb. of powdered sugar with twelve egg-yolks, in a basin, until the mixture has whitened slightly. Dilute with one quart of dry, white wine; pour the whole in a narrow *bain-marie* (double-boiler), which should be placed in a receptacle containing boiling water, and whisk it until it is four times its former size, and is firm and frothy.

   N.B.—Sabayon may also be made with milk instead of white wine, and it may be flavored according to taste.

2409—FRUIT SAUCE   *Sauces aux Fruits*
   Apricots, red-currants, greengages, and mirabelle (yellow) plums are the best fruits for sweet sauces. Other fruits, such as peaches,

Bartlet pears, apples, etc., may also be used in the form of light *purées* or *cullises*.

2410—APRICOT SAUCE   *Sauce à l'Abricot*

Rub some very ripe or stewed apricots through a sieve, and thin the *purée* with the required quantity of syrup at 28° (Saccharom.). Boil, skimming carefully the while; take off the fire when the sauce coats the spoon, and flavor according to taste.

If this sauce is to be used with pastry crusts, a little best butter may be added to it.

2411—RED CURRANT SAUCE   *Sauce Groseilles*

Melt some red currant jelly and flavor it with kirsch.

This sauce may be slightly thickened with arrowroot or corn-starch.

2412—ORANGE SAUCE   *Sauce à l'Orange*

Rub some orange marmalade through a sieve; add one-third of its bulk of apricot sauce, and flavor with Curaçao.

2413—HAZEL-NUT SAUCE   *Sauce Noisette*

Flavor some English custard (2397) with an infusion of grilled hazel-nuts, and add two tablespoons of moulded filbert *pralin* per quart of custard.

2414—GREENGAGE OR MIRABELLE SAUCE

Sauce aux Reines Claude ou Mirabelles

Proceed as for apricot sauce and flavor with kirsch.

2415—CHERRY SAUCE   *Sauce aux Cerises*

Take the syrup of some stewed cherries, add an equal quantity of red-currant jelly, and flavor with kirsch.

2416—RASPBERRY SAUCE   *Sauce aux Framboises*

Take the required quantity of melted raspberry jelly; thicken it slightly with arrowroot or cornstarch, and flavor with kirsch.

2417—STRAWBERRY SAUCE   *Sauce aux Fraises*

Proceed as for (2416).

2418—THICKENED SYRUPS   *Sirops Liés*

These accompaniments of desserts, which are commonly used in Germany, have this in their favor, that they are economical; but they should be used in moderation. To make them, take some sugar syrup at 15°, thickened with arrowroot, potato flour, or cornstarch, colored according to the purpose for which it is required, and flavored with some liqueur or *essence* at the last moment.

It is with this kind of sauce that custards and all other sorts of *tartlets* are coated in northern European countries.

HOT SWEET DISHES

FRITTERS

The numerous fritter recipes for desserts may all be grouped into five leading classes, viz.:—

(1) Fruit fritters.

(2) Custard fritters.

(3) Viennese fritters.

(4) Souffléd fritters.

(5) Many other fritters which are more or less like the four former ones without entirely resembling them.

2419—FRESH FRUIT AND FLOWER FRITTERS
Pâte de Beignets de Fruits et de Fleurs

Subject to the treatment undergone by them, fruits for fritters are of two kinds: firm fruits, such as apples and pears, and juicy fruits, such as strawberries, etc.

2420—FRITTERS OF FRUITS WITH FIRM PULPS, SUCH AS APRICOT FRITTERS
Beignet de Fruits à Pulpe Compacte

Select some apricots that are not over-ripe; cut them in two; sprinkle them with sugar, and set them to steep for an hour in kirsch, brandy, or rum, subject to taste. A few minutes before serving, dry the halved apricots, dip them in batter (234), and fry them in hot fat. Drain them on a napkin; set the fritters on a pan; cover them with icing sugar, and *glaze* them in a hot oven or at the *salamander* or under a hot broiler flame. Place them on a napkin, and serve them at once.

N.B.—Proceed in precisely the same way for apple, pear, peach, or banana fritters.

2421—JUICY FRUIT FRITTERS, SUCH AS STRAWBERRY FRITTERS
Beignets de Fruits Aqueux

Select some large, somewhat firm strawberries; sugar them copiously; sprinkle them with kirsch, and let them steep on ice for thirty minutes.

It is most essential that the strawberries be well sugared before soaking, because the heat of the fat sours them while the fritters are being fried, and they consequently become tart.

A few minutes before serving, drain the strawberries, dip them in batter (234), and plunge them into very hot fat. Drain them, place them on lace paper, and sprinkle them with icing sugar, by means of a shaker.

N.B.—The procedure is the same for Raspberry, Red-currant, Cherry, Orange, and Tangerine fritters. For the last-named, it is better to quarter them and peel them raw, than to slice them.

2422—BLOSSOM FRITTERS, SUCH AS ACACIA-FLOWER FRITTERS
Beignets de Fleurs d'Acacia

Select some full-blown acacia flowers; sprinkle them with sugar and liqueur brandy, and leave them to steep for thirty minutes.

Dip them in batter (234); plunge them into plenty of hot fat; drain them; sprinkle them with sugar and serve them on a napkin.

N.B.—Proceed as above for Elder-Blossom, Lily, and Vegetable-Blossom fritters; but in the case of the last two, the quartered crowns of the flowers, alone, are used.

2423—CUSTARD FRITTERS OR FRIED CREAM   *Beignets de Crème*

Custard fritters may be prepared in the three following totally different ways.

1st Method.—Cut up preparation (2400) with a round, square, or diamond-shaped fancy cutter, as taste may dictate. Treat the resulting pieces of custard twice *à l'anglaise*, using very fine and fresh bread-crumbs for the purpose. Press upon the bread-crumbs with the blade of a knife that they may adhere properly, and fry the pieces of custard cream in very hot fat. On taking the fritters out of the fat sprinkle them with icing sugar, and serve them on a napkin.

N.B.—Instead of treating these fritters *à l'anglaise,* they may be dipped into batter and treated as directed in the case of Apricot fritters (2420).

2nd Method.—Prepare a custard as for a "crème renversée" (2639), using only whole eggs, that it may be firm; and *poach* it in a pan of a shape which will facilitate the cutting-up of the preparation. When the latter is quite cool, cut it up as fancy may suggest; dip the pieces in batter (234) and plunge them in plenty of hot fat. Drain them on a piece of linen or absorbent paper; sprinkle them with icing sugar; *glaze* them in a hot oven, and serve them on a napkin.

3rd Method.—Prepare some regular-shaped hollow *meringues,* and keep them very dry.

When they have cooled, open them slightly on top, and, through the hole in each, fill them either with a Bavarian cream preparation (2622), with some kind of ice-cream, or with a fruit *salpicon* thickened with stewed apricots or plums. Close the holes with the pieces that were cut out, and place the *meringues* in the refrigerator for an hour.

When about to serve them, quickly treat them *à l'anglaise;* set them (opened side uppermost) in a frying-basket, and dip them for a few seconds in smoking fat. Take them out as soon as their crusts have acquired a golden color; sprinkle them with icing sugar; place them on a napkin, and serve them immediately.

2424—VIENNESE FRITTERS   *Beignets Viennois*

Quantities for the paste of Viennese fritters: one lb. of flour; six oz. of butter; half oz. of yeast; five eggs; half oz. of salt; two-third oz. of sugar; and one-sixth pint of milk. This paste is prepared exactly like Brioche paste (2368).

In any case, as it has to be worked with the rolling-pin, always keep it a little firm.

2425—HOT VIENNESE FRITTERS   *Beignets Viennois Chauds*

Roll out a piece of the paste given above to a thickness of one-fifth inch.

Spread upon it, at regular intervals, small quantities (about the size of a large walnut) either of stewed fruit or jam. Moisten slightly; cover with a second layer of paste, of the same size and thickness as the former; press upon it with the back of a round cutter, so as to ensure the joining of the two layers of paste, and then stamp the whole out with an even cutter two and a half inches in diameter.

Set the fritters on a pan covered with a flour-dusted piece of linen; let the paste rise for thirty minutes, and then fry them in plenty of hot fat. Drain them; sprinkle them with icing sugar and serve them on a napkin.

N.B.—These fritters may be accompanied by frothy sauces, flavored with vanilla, lemon, orange, coffee, or kirsch, etc., the type of which is the Sabayon with cream (2408).

2426—COLD VIENNESE FRITTERS   *Beignets Viennois Froids*

Roll out a piece of the paste prescribed, which should be kept somewhat soft, and stamp it out with a round cutter two and a half inches in diameter. Set half of these rounds of paste on buttered sheets of paper, lying on trays; fill them either with stewed fruit or jam; slightly moisten their edges; cover them with the remaining rounds of paste, and let the paste rise for thirty minutes.

A few minutes before serving, grasp the ends of the sheets of paper; plunge the fritters into plenty of hot fat, and take out the sheets of paper as soon as the fritters fall from them.

Drain them as soon as they begin to brown; and plunge them immediately into a light, hot syrup, flavored as fancy may dictate. Take them out as soon as they begin to be saturated, and serve them cold.

N.B.—In the case of either of these two methods of serving Viennese fritters, the latter, which are served under the name of "fritters à la Dauphine," may be garnished with fruit *salpicons* or cream preparations.

Soufflé Fritters

2427—ORDINARY SOUFFLE FRITTERS   *Beignets Soufflés Ordinaires*

Put one pint of water, three and a half oz. of butter, a pinch of salt and two pinches of sugar into a saucepan. Boil; take the utensil off the fire in order to add two-thirds lb. of sifted flour, and mix up the whole. Then dry this paste as directed for *pâte à choux* or cream puff paste (2373); and finish it, away from the fire, with seven eggs, added one by one.

Flavor according to taste.

Take this paste in portions, the size of small walnuts; put these portions in moderately hot fat, and gradually increase the heat of the latter, so as to ensure the rising of the paste.

When the fritters are quite dry outside, drain them; serve them on a napkin, and sprinkle them with icing sugar (2346a).

2428—SURPRISE SOUFFLE FRITTERS   *Beignets Soufflés en Surprise*

Prepare the fritters exactly like the preceding ones. When taking them out of the fat, slit open slightly and fill them, by means of the pastry-bag, either with stewed fruit, jam, a very fine, thickened *salpicon* of fruit, or some kind of cream, especially *frangipan* or pastry cream (2399).

VARIOUS FRITTERS

2429—FAVORITE PINEAPPLE FRITTERS   *Beignets d'Ananas Favorite*

Cut the pineapple into slices, one-third inch thick; cut each slice in two; sprinkle the half-discs with sugar and kirsch, and let them steep for thirty minutes. Then dry them and dip them into a very thick and almost cold *frangipan cream* (2399), combined with chopped pistachios. Set the cream-coated slices on a tray, and let them cool completely.

A little while before serving, take the slices from the tray; dip them in somewhat thin batter, and fry them in plenty of hot fat.

Drain them; sprinkle them with icing sugar; *glaze* them in a hot oven, and serve them on a napkin.

2430—FRITTERS A LA BOURGEOISE   *Beignets à la Bourgeoise*

Cut a stale brioche crown into slices, one-third inch thick, and dip these into fresh, sugared cream, flavored according to taste. Drain them; dry them slightly; dip them into thin batter, and fry them in very hot fat.

Drain them; sprinkle them with sugar, and serve them on a napkin.

2431—SYLVANA FRITTERS   *Beignets Sylvana*

Hollow out some small round brioches (2368), preserving the crusts for covers, and dip them in some thin, sugared and flavored fresh cream. Then fill them with a small fruit *salpicon* (filling) with kirsch; cover this with the reserved covers; dip them into thin batter, and fry them in plenty of hot fat.

Drain them; set them on a napkin, and sprinkle them with icing sugar.

2432—FRITTERS "A LA GRAND'MERE"   *Beignets Grand'Mère*

Spread upon a moistened pan a layer half-inch thick of very reduced, stewed fruit. Cut it up according to fancy; dip the pieces in batter (234), and fry them in plenty of hot fat.

On taking the fritters from the fat, sprinkle them with icing sugar and set them to *glaze* in a hot oven.

2433—REGINA FRITTERS
Beignets Regina

Shape some lady-finger paste (2378) into large half-balls, one and a half-inch in diameter; bake these in a moderate oven and cool them. Then hollow out these half-balls; fill them with apricot or some other jam; join them in pairs, and dip them so as to thoroughly soak them in some fresh cream flavored with maraschino.

Drain them; treat them *à l'anglaise* with very fine bread-crumbs, and fry them in plenty of hot fat.

Drain them; set them on a napkin, and sprinkle them with icing sugar.

2434—MIGNON FRITTERS
Beignets Mignon

Proceed as above, but substitute for biscuit half-balls of soft macaroons, saturated with kirsch syrup. For the rest of the procedure, follow the method of (2433).

2435—SUZON FRITTERS
Beignets Suzon

Make a preparation of "rice for desserts" (2404), and spread it in a thin layer upon a pan to cool. Divide it up into rounds three and a half inches in diameter; fill the center of these with very stiff fruit filling *(salpicon);* roll the rounds into balls, to enclose the *salpicon;* dip these balls into thin batter, and fry them in plenty of hot fat.

Drain them; place them on a napkin, and sprinkle them with powdered sugar.

CHARLOTTES

2436—APPLE CHARLOTTE
Charlotte de Pomme

Copiously butter a quart *Charlotte-mould.* Fill its bottom with heart-shaped *croûtons* of bread slices, slightly overlapping one another; and garnish its sides with rectangles of bread of exactly the same height as the mould, and also slightly overlapping one another. The *croûtons* and the rectangles should be one-eighth inch thick, and ought to have been dipped in melted butter before taking their place in the mould.

Meanwhile, quarter twelve fine russet apples; peel, slice, and cook them in a saucepan with one oz. of butter, two tablespoons of powdered sugar, and half the rind of a lemon and a little cinnamon tied into a bundle.

When the apples are cooked, and reduced to a thick *purée,*

remove the bundle of lemon peel and cinnamon, and add three tablespoons of stewed apricots.

Fill up the mould with this mixture, and remember to mound the apples in a high dome above the mould; for it settles in cooking.

Bake in a good, moderate oven for from thirty to thirty-five minutes.

2437—APPLE CHARLOTTE EMILE GIRET

Charlotte de Pommes Emile Giret

Prepare the *Charlotte* as directed above (2436), but in a shallow mould.

When it is unmoulded on the dish, completely cover it with an even coat, half inch thick, of very firm pastry cream (2401), and take care not to spoil the shape of the *Charlotte*.

Sprinkle the cream copiously with icing sugar; then, with a red-hot iron, criss-cross the *Charlotte* regularly all round; pressing the iron upon the sugar-sprinkled cream.

Surround the base of the *Charlotte* with a row of beads made by means of the pastry-bag, from the same cream as that already used.

2438—VARIOUS CHARLOTTES   *Charlottes Diverses*

Charlottes may be made with pears, peaches, apricots, etc., after the same procedure as that directed under (2436). The most important point to be remembered in their preparation is that the stewed fruit used should be very thick; otherwise it so softens the shell of bread that the *Charlotte* collapses as soon as it is turned out.

It is no less important that the mould should be as full as possible of the preparation used; for, as already explained, the latter settles in the cooking process.

2439—REGENCE CREAM   *Crème Régence*

Saturate half a pound of Lady Fingers (2378) with Maraschino Kirsch, and then dip them into a quart of boiled milk. Rub them through a very fine sieve, and add eight eggs, ten egg-yolks, two-thirds pound of powdered sugar and a small pinch of salt. Pour the whole into a shallow, *Charlotte-mould,* and set to *poach* in a *bain-marie* (water-bath) for about thirty-five minutes.

Let the mould rest for a few minutes; turn out its contents on a dish and surround the base of the cream with a crown of stewed half-apricots, each filled with a preserved cherry. Coat the whole with an apricot syrup, flavored with Kirsch and Maraschino.

2440—MERINGUED CREAM
Crème Meringuée

Prepare some "Crème a la Régence" as above, and *poach* it in a buttered deep border-mould in a *bain-marie* (water-bath); turn it out on a dish, and fill the middle of the border with Italian *meringue* (2383), combined with a *salpicon* of preserved fruit, soaked in Kirsch.

Decorate the border by means of a pastry-bag, fitted with a fancy tube and filled with plain Italian *meringue,* without the fruit; and set to brown in a moderate oven.

Serve an orange-flavored English custard (2398) separately.

2441—VILLAGE CREAM
Crème Village

Saturate five ounces of dry sponge fingers with Kirsch and Anisette, and set them in a deep dish in layers, alternated with coatings of stewed, seasonable fruit, such as pears, apples, etc.

Cover the whole with the following preparation: one-half pound of powdered sugar mixed with eight eggs and the yolks of four, and diluted with one and three-quarter pints of milk. *Poach* in a *bain-marie* (water-bath), in the oven.

2442—CUSTARD PUDDING
Le Custard Pudding

Custard pudding is a form of the English custard mentioned under (2397).

The difference between the two is that for the former whole eggs are used instead of the yolks alone, and that it is prepared according to the second method only. The average quantities for the preparation are:

Six eggs and six ounces of sugar per quart of milk. The custard is cooked in small deep pie-dishes in a *bain-marie* (water-bath), which should be placed in the oven or in a steamer.

According to whether the custard be required milky or thick, the number of eggs is either lessened or increased. In regard to the sugar, the guide should be your taste. If necessary, it may be removed altogether, and saccharine or glycerine may be used in its stead, as is customary for diabetic patients.

Custard is generally flavored with vanilla, but any other flavor suited to sweets may be used with it.

PANCAKES. *(See preparations No. 2403.)*

2443—CONVENT PANCAKES
Crêpes du Couvent

Pour into a buttered and hot omelet-pan some preparation A, sprinkle on it some Bartlett pears, cut into small dice; cover the latter with some more preparation A; toss the pancake in order to turn it; sprinkle it with powdered sugar, place it on a napkin and serve it sizzling hot.

2444—GEORGETTE PANCAKES *Crêpes Georgette*

Proceed as for Convent pancakes (2443), but substitute for pear-dice some very thin slices of pineapple, soaked in Maraschino.

2445—GIL-BLAS PANCAKES *Crêpes Gil-Blas*

Make the following preparation: stir three ounces of best butter in a bowl until it acquires the consistency of a cream. Mix with this three ounces of powdered sugar, three tablespoons of liqueur brandy, a piece of butter the size of a filbert, and a few drops of lemon juice. Make pancakes with preparation C (2403); spread the prepared butter upon them; fold each pancake twice, and serve on a napkin.

2446—NORMANDE PANCAKES *Crêpes à la Normande*

Proceed as for *Convent Pancakes* (2443), but for the pear dice substitute fine slices of apple, previously *sautéd* in butter.

2447—PARISIENNE PANCAKES *Crêpes à la Parisienne*

These are made from preparation B, and are ungarnished.

2448—PAYSANNE PANCAKES *Crêpes à la Paysanne*

Make these from preparation B (the *orgeat* syrup and the maca-roons being removed), and flavor with orange-flower water.

2449—RUSSIAN PANCAKES *Crêpes à la Russe*

Add to preparation C, a quarter of its volume of broken wafers saturated with kümmel and liqueur brandy, and make as usual.

2450—SUZETTE PANCAKES *Crêpes Suzette*

Make these from preparation A, flavored with curaçao and tangerine juice. Coat them, like Gil-Blas pancakes (2445), with softened brandied butter, flavored with curaçao and tangerine juice.

The pancakes are fried and kept warm, but not stacked on top of each other. Now use the flat pan of a large chafing dish. Have a moderate flame under pan, and allow it gradually to heat up. Rub six lumps of sugar over one lemon and one orange-rind until the sugar has well absorbed the rind. Dilute the sugar in one-half cup of orange juice. Allow to stand. Cream one-half cup of sweet butter with two tablespoons of sugar and chill. When ready to use let this melt in the hot pan and strain orange juice over it. Let this reduce to half and lift the pancakes into this, fold them over twice, and ladle the sauce over them. In the meanwhile mix one quarter cup Cointreau or

Curaçao with two tablespoons of rum or Benedictine and pour this over the pancakes, the last of all one-third cup of Brandy or Grand Marnier. When this has heated up, which is essential, tilt the pan to the flame so the sauce catches fire, and stir the pancakes in this flaming sauce. Serve on heated plates while the sauce is still flaming.

CROQUETTES AND CRUSTS

2451—CHESTNUT CROQUETTES *Croquettes de Marrons*

Peel the chestnuts after one of the ways directed (2172), and cook them in a thin syrup, flavored with vanilla. Reserve one small, whole chestnut for each *croquette*. Rub the remainder through a sieve; dry the *purée* over a hot fire, and thicken it with five egg-yolks and one and a half oz. of butter per lb. of *purée*. Let it cool.

Then divide the preparation up into portions the size of pigeons' eggs, and roll these portions into balls, with a chestnut in the center of each. Treat them *a l'anglaise* (174), with some very fine bread-crumbs; fry them in some very hot fat, and serve them on a napkin.

Serve a vanilla-flavored apricot sauce, separately.

2452—RICE CROQUETTES *Croquettes de Riz*

Make a preparation as directed under (2404). Divide it up into two-oz. portions, moulded to the shape of such fruit as pears, apples, apricots, etc.; treat these *à l'anglaise* (174), like the Chestnut *Croquettes* (2451), and fry them in the same way. Serve an apricot sauce or a vanilla-flavored Sabayon (2408) separately.

2453—VARIOUS CROQUETTES *Croquettes Diverses*

Croquettes may also be made from tapioca, semolina, vermicelli or fresh noodles (2291), etc., in which case the procedure is that of the Rice Croquettes (2452).

The preparation may be combined with currants and sultana raisins, and the *croquettes* are served with any suitable sauce.

2454—CRUSTS WITH FRUITS *Croûte aux Fruits*

Cut some slices one-fifth inch thick from a stale Savarin (2371), which has not been moistened with syrup, and allow two for each person. Set these slices on a pan; sprinkle them with *icing sugar,* and put them in the oven so as to dry and *glaze* them at the same time. Arrange them in a circle round a bed of fried bread-crusts, and between each lay a slice of pineapple of exactly the same size as the cake slices.

Upon this crown of *croûtons,* set some quartered apples and some stewed pears. The pears may be stewed in a pinkish syrup, which by varying the color, makes the crust better looking.

Decorate with preserved cherries, angelica cut in diamond shapes, quartered yellow and green preserved kumquats, etc. Fix a small, peeled and white or pink pear on the top of the bed, by means of an ornamental skewer, coat with apricot sauce, flavored with Kirsch.

2455—CRUSTS LYONNAISE   *Croûte à la Lyonnaise*

Prepare the crusts as described above, and coat them with a smooth chestnut *purée,* flavored with vanilla; then, cover them with an apricot *purée,* cooked to the *small-thread* (215° F.) stage; sprinkle with finely-slivered and slightly-browned almonds, and arrange in a circle.

Fill the middle of the circle with chestnuts cooked in syrup, and seeded Malaga raisins, currants, and sultana raisins (washed and plumped in tepid water); the whole combined with an apricot *purée* thinned with a few tablespoons of Malaga wine.

2456—CRUSTS WITH MADEIRA   *Croûte au Madère*

Arrange the *glazed* crusts in a circle as already described (2454). Pour into their midst a filling consisting of equal parts of seeded, Malaga raisins, currants, and sultana raisins, plumped in tepid water and moistened with a Madeira-flavored, apricot syrup.

2457—CRUSTS A LA MARECHALE   *Croûte à la Maréchale*

Cut from a stale *mousseline brioche* (2369), some triangles of the same thickness as the ordinary crusts. Coat them with *pralin* (2352), and then set them on a pan; sprinkle them with sugar *glaze,* and dry the *pralin* in a moderate oven.

Place a bed of fried-bread slices four inches high on a dish, and surround it with a *salpicon* of pineapple, raisins, cherries, and crystallized orange-rind, mixed with some stiff stewed apples, combined with a little apricot *purée.* Set the pralin-coated triangles upright alongside of the *salpicon,* and surround them with a border of halved pears, stewed in syrup, half their quantity being white and the other pink.

On the top of the bread, set a small pear, cooked in pink syrup, fixed with a small ornamental skewer, and surround the border of halved pears with a band of apricot *purée,* flavored slightly with vanilla, and serve a sauceboat of the same *purée* separately.

2458—CRUSTS A LA NORMANDE   *Croûte à la Normande*

Prepare the crusts as indicated under (2454), coat them with very stiffly stewed apples, and arrange them in a circle.

Fill their center with stewed apples, prepared as for a *Charlotte* (2436), and upon the apples set a pyramid of quartered white and pink apples, cooked in syrup. Cover with reduced apple syrup, thickened with a little very smooth stewed apples flavored with Kirsch or cold rum.

2459—CRUSTS A LA PARISIENNE · · · · · · · · · *Croûte à la Parisienne*

Coat the crusts with *pralin,* as explained under (2457), and arrange them in a circle. In their midst set some thin slices of pire-apple, the ends of which should rest upon the circle of crusts; in the middle, pour a filling of various fruits, mixed with an apricot *purée,* flavored with Madeira, and coat the circle of crusts with apricot syrup flavored with Madeira.

2460—CRUSTS WITH APRICOTS IN MARASCHINO
Croûte aux Abricots au Marasquin

Bake some *Savarin paste* (2371) in buttered *tartlet moulds.* When these *tartlets* are cooked, hollow them out at the top taking care to leave a somewhat thick border all round.

Coat them inside with *pralin* (2352), and dry them in a moderate oven. Then garnish the center of the *tartlets* with *frangipan cream* (2399), combined with filbert *pralin.* Upon this cream set a pitted apricot *poached* in Maraschino.

Surround the apricot with small, candied half-cherries, alternated with diamonds of angelica. Serve an apricot sauce, flavored with Maraschino, separately.

2461—CRUSTS VICTORIA · · · · · · · · · · · · · · · *Croûte Victoria*

Prepare a crust after (2456), and fill the center with candied cherries and *glazed* chestnuts. Serve an apricot sauce flavored with rum, separately.

OMELETS

Sweet omelets may be divided into four distinct classes, which are:—

1. Liqueur omelets
2. Jam omelets

3. *Souffléd* omelets
4. Surprise omelets

OMELETS WITH LIQUEUR

2462—OMELET WITH RUM · · · · · · · · · · · · · · *Omelette au Rum*

Season the omelet (492) with sugar and a little salt, and cook it in the usual way. Set it on a long dish, sprinkle it with sugar and heated rum, and light the rum on bringing it to the table.

Jam Omelets

2463—APRICOT OMELET
Omelette à l'Abricot

Season the omelet as above, and, when about to roll it up, fill it inside with two tablespoons of apricot jam per six eggs. Set on a long dish; sprinkle with *icing sugar* (2436a), and either criss-cross the surface with a red-hot iron or *glaze* the omelet at the *salamander* or under a hot broiler flame.

2464—CHRISTMAS OMELET
Omelette de Noël

Beat the eggs with salt and sugar and add, per six eggs: two tablespoons of cream, a pinch of orange or lemon rind, and one tablespoon of rum. When about to roll up the omelet, garnish it copiously with mincemeat (2605), set it on a long dish; sprinkle it with heated rum, and light it at the table.

Souffléd Omelets

2465—SOUFFLE OMELET WITH VANILLA
Omelette Soufflée à la Vanille

Mix eight oz. of sugar and eight egg-yolks in a bowl, until the mixture has paled slightly, and draws up in ribbons when the spoon is pulled out of it. Add ten egg-whites, beaten to a very stiff froth, and mix the two preparations gently; cutting in and raising the whole with the spoon.

Set this preparation on a long, buttered and sugar-dusted dish, in the shape of an oval mound, and take care to put some of it aside in a pastry-bag.

Smooth it all round with the blade of a knife; decorate according to fancy with the contents of the pastry-bag, and cook in a good, moderate oven, for as long as the size of the omelet requires.

Two minutes before taking it from the oven, sprinkle it with *icing sugar,* that the latter, when melted, may cover the omelet with a glossy coat.

Flavor according to taste with vanilla, orange or lemon rind, rum, Kirsch, etc.; but remember to add the selected flavor to the preparation before the egg-whites are added to it.

SURPRISE OMELETS

2466—NORWEGIAN OMELET   *Omelette Norvègienne*

Place an oval bed of *Génoise* (2376) one and one-half in. thick upon a long dish, and let the bed be as long as the desired omelet. Upon it set a pyramid of ice-cream with fruit. Cover the ice-cream with ordinary *meringue* (2382); smooth it with a knife, making it of an even thickness of two-thirds of an inch in so doing; decorate it, by means of the pastry-bag, with the same *meringue,* and set in a very hot oven, that the *meringue* may cook and brown quickly, without the heat reaching the ice-cream inside.

2467—SURPRISE OMELET MYLORD   *Omelette en Surprise Mylord*

Proceed as directed above; but garnish the bed of *Génoise* with coatings of vanilla ice-cream, alternated with coatings of stewed pears. Cover with *meringue* (2382) and cook in the same way.

2468—TANGERINE SURPRISE OMELET
Omelette en Surprise aux Mandarines

The procedure is the same, but the vanilla ice-cream is replaced by tangerine ice. On taking the omelet out of the oven, surround it with tangerines *glazed* with sugar, cooked to the *large-crack* stage (248° F.).

2469—SURPRISE OMELET WITH CHERRIES
Omelette en Surprise aux Cerises

Garnish the bed of *Génoise* (2376) with red-currant ice (2768), flavored with raspberries and mixed with equal quantities of cherry ice (2764) and half-sugared cherries, steeped in Kirsch.

Finish it like the Norwegian Omelet (2466).

On taking it out of the oven, surround the omelet with drained cherries, preserved in brandy, sprinkle it with heated Kirsch, and fight at the table.

2470—SURPRISE OMELET MILADY, also called PEACH MILADY
Omelette en Surprise Milady

This is a surprise omelet, garnished with very firm raspberry ice (2767), in which are incrusted a circle of fine peaches, *poached* (249) in vanilla.

The whole is then covered with Italian *meringue* (2383) flavored with Maraschino, and laid in such a way that those portions of the peaches which project from the *glaze* remain bare.

Decorate the surface of the omelet with the same *meringue;* sprinkle it with *icing sugar* (2436a), and set it to a *glaze* quickly.

2471—NEAPOLITAN SURPRISE OMELET, also called BOMBE VESUVE
Omelette en Surprise à la Napolitaine ou Bombe Vesuve

Garnish the bed of *Génoise* (2376) with coatings of vanilla and strawberry ice (2766), alternated with layers of broken glacé-chestnut. Cover the whole with Italian *meringue* (2383) prepared with Kirsch. Keep this flat and somewhat thick towards the center. On top, set a *barquette* of a size in proportion to the omelet, made with the pastry-bag with ordinary *meringue* and baked in the oven without browning. Decorate with Italian *meringue,* covering the *barquette* in so doing, and quickly brown the omelet in the oven. When about to serve, garnish the omelet with Jubilee cherries (2566), and light at the last moment.

2472—SURPRISE OMELET ELIZABETH *Omelette en Surprise Elizabeth*

Garnish the bed of *Génoise* with vanilla ice and crystallized-violets.

Cover it with *meringue;* decorate its surface with crystallized-violets, and treat the omelet as in (2466).

When about to serve it, cover the omelet with a veil of spun sugar.

2473—SURPRISE OMELET NERON *Omelette en Surprise Néron*

Make the bed of *Génoise* round instead of oval; set it on a round dish, and fill it with some sort of ice, which should be shaped like a blunt cone. Cover with *meringue;* set a small case on the top, made from *meringue,* as explained under (2471), but round instead of oval; conceal all but its inside with *meringue,* decorating the omelet in so doing, and set to brown quickly.

When about to serve, pour a glass of heated rum into the *meringue* case and light it.

2474—SYLPHS' SURPRISE OMELET *Omelette en Surprise des Sylphes*

Dip a freshly-cooked *savarin* (2371) into a syrup of maraschino, and stick it on a base of dry paste equal in size.

In the center of the *savarin* set a bed of *Génoise* sufficiently thick to reach half-way up the former.

At the last moment, turn out upon this bed an iced strawberry *mousse* (2766), made in an iced *madeleine-mould,* the diameter of which should be that of the opening of the *savarin*. Cover the *mousse* with a coat of Italian *meringue* (2383) with kirsch, shaping it like a cone of which the base rests upon the top of the *savarin*.

With a pastry-bag, fitted with a small tube, quickly decorate the cone, as also the *suvarin*, with the same *meringue;* brown it in the oven, and serve it instantly.

2475—VARIOUS SURPRISE OMELETS   *Omelettes Diverses en Surprise*

With the general example given this kind of omelet may be indefinitely varied by changing the ice preparation inside.

The superficial appearance remains the same, but every change in the inside filling should be made known in the title of the dish.

PANNEQUETS

2476—PANNEQUETS WITH JAM   *Pannequets aux Confitures*

Prepare some very thin pancakes (2403); spread them with some kind of jam, roll them up, trim them at a slant at either end, and cut them into two diamond shapes.

Place these diamonds on a tray, sprinkle them with *icing sugar,* set them to *glaze* in a hot oven, and serve them on a napkin.

2477—CREAM PANNEQUETS   *Pannequets à la Crème*

Spread the pancakes (2403) with *frangipan cream* (2399), and sprinkle the latter with crushed macaroons. For the rest of the procedure follow (2476).

2478—MERINGUED PANNEQUETS   *Pannequets Meringuées*

Spread the pancakes (2403) with Italian *meringue* (2383), flavored with kirsch and maraschino; roll them up, cut them into diamond shapes as above, and set them on a tray. Decorate them by means of the pastry-bag with the same *meringue;* sprinkle them with *icing sugar,* and set them to brown quickly in the oven.

2479—PUDDINGS   *Puddings*

American and English puddings are almost innumerable; but many of them lie more within the pastrycook's than the cook's province, and their enumeration here could not serve a very useful purpose. The name Pudding is, moreover, applied to a whole host of preparations which are really nothing more than custards—as, for example, "custard pudding." If both of the foregoing kinds of puddings be passed over, puddings proper. which belong to hot sweets may be divided into eight classes, of which I shall first give the general recipes, from which all pudding desserts given hereafter are derived. The six classes are:—

(1) Puddings with cream.
(2) Fruit puddings.
(3) Plum puddings.
(4) Bread puddings.
(5) Rice and paste puddings.
(6) Soufflé puddings.

Puddings permit various accompanying sauces, which will be given in each recipe. The majority of puddings may be accompanied by stewed fruit, Melba sauce, or whipped cream "à la Chantilly."

PUDDINGS WITH CREAM

2480—ALMOND PUDDING   *Pudding aux Amandes*

Make a preparation for *soufflé pudding* (2505), moistened with *almond milk* (2506). Pour it into well-buttered moulds, sprinkled, inside with slivered and grilled almonds (2338).

Set to *poach* in the *bain-marie* (water-bath). As an accompaniment serve a *sabayon* (2408) prepared with white wine and flavored with *orgeat*.

2481—ENGLISH ALMOND PUDDING *Pudding aux Amandes à l'Anglaise*

Mix to the consistency of a cream four oz. of butter and five oz. of powdered sugar; add eight oz. of finely-chopped almonds, a pinch of salt, a half tablespoon of orange-flower water, two eggs, two egg-yolks, and one-sixth pint of cream. Pour this preparation into a buttered deep pie-dish or casserole, and cook in a *bain-marie* (water-bath) in the oven.

N.B.—English puddings of any kind are served in the dishes or bowls in which they have cooked.

2482—SPONGE CAKE PUDDING   *Pudding de Bisquit*

Crush eight oz. of sponge ladyfingers in a saucepan, and moisten them with one pint of boiling milk containing five oz. of sugar. Stir the whole over the fire, and add five oz. of candied fruit, cut into dice and mixed with currants (both ingredients having been steeped in kirsch), three egg-yolks, four oz. of melted butter, and the whites of five eggs beaten to a stiff froth.

Set to *poach* in a *bain-marie* (water-bath) in a low, even *Charlotte-*

mould, or in a deep pie-dish or casserole, and serve an apricot sauce (2410) at the same time.

2483—CABINET PUDDING *Pudding de Cabinet*

Garnish a buttered *cylinder-mould* with sponge ladyfingers or slices of buttered biscuit, saturated with some kind of liqueur, arranging them in alternate layers with a *salpicon* of candied fruit and currants, soaked in liqueur. Here and there spread a little apricot jam.

Fill up the mould, little by little, with preparation (2639), flavored according to taste. *Poach* in a *bain-marie* (water-bath).

Turn out the pudding at the last moment, and coat it with English custard flavored with vanilla.

2484—FRUIT PUDDING *Pudding de Fruits*

This pudding requires very careful treatment. The custard (2639) which serves as its base is the same as that of Cabinet Pudding, except that it is thickened by seven eggs and seven egg-yolks per quart of milk. This preparation is, moreover, combined with a *purée* of fruit suited to the pudding.

Procedure: Butter a mould; set it in a *bain-marie* (water-bath), and pour a few tablespoons of the custard into it. Let it set, and upon this set custard sprinkle a layer of suitable fruit, sliced. This fruit may be apricots, peaches, pears, etc. Cover the fruit with a fresh coat of custard, but more copiously than in the first case; let this custard set as before; cover it with fruit, and proceed in the same order until the mould is full.

It is, in short, another form of aspic-jelly preparation, but hot instead of cold. If the solidification of the layers of custard were not ensured, the fruit would fall to the bottom of the mould instead of remaining distributed between the layers of custard, and the result would be the collapse of the pudding as soon as it was turned out.

Continue the cooking in the *bain-marie* (water-bath); let the preparation stand a few minutes before turning it out, and serve at the same time a sauce made from the same fruit as that used for the pudding.

2485—APPLE PUDDING *Pudding aux Pommes*

Prepare a suet paste from one lb. of flour, ten oz. of finely-chopped beef suet, quarter of a pint of water and a pinch of salt.

Let the paste rest for an hour, and roll it out to a thickness of one-third of an inch.

With this layer of paste, line a well-buttered *dome-mould* or large pudding-bowl. Garnish with sliced apples mixed with powdered sugar and flavored with a chopped piece of lemon peel.

Close the mould with a well-sealed-down layer of paste; wrap the mould in a piece of linen, which should be firmly tied with string; plunge it into a saucepan containing boiling water, and in the case of a quart pudding-bowl or mould, let it cook for about three hours.

N.B.—This pudding may be made with other fleshy fruit, as also with certain vegetables such as the pumpkin, etc.

2486—PLUM PUDDING   *Plum Pudding*

Put into a bowl one lb. of chopped beef suet; one lb. of crumbed bread slices; half lb. of flour; half lb. of peeled and chopped apples; half lb. each of Malaga raisins, currants and sultana raisins; two oz. each of candied orange, lemon and citron peel, cut into small dice; two oz. of ginger; four oz. of chopped almonds; eight oz. of powdered sugar; the juice and the chopped rind of half an orange and half a lemon; one-third oz. of mixed spices, containing a large quantity of cinnamon; three eggs; quarter of a pint of rum or brandy, and one-third of a pint of stout. The fruit should, if possible, have previously steeped in liqueur for a long time.

Mix the whole thoroughly.

Pour the preparation into white earthenware pudding-bowls, with projecting rims; press it into them, and then wrap them in a buttered and flour-dusted cloth or dampened vegetable parchment which tie into a knot on top.

Cook in boiling water or in steam for four hours.

When about to serve, sprinkle the puddings with heated brandy or rum, and light them, or accompany them, either with a *sabayon* (2408) with rum, with Brandy Butter (as directed under "Gil-Blas pancakes" (2445) but without sugar), or with an English custard thickened with arrowroot or cornstarch.

2487—AMERICAN PUDDING   *Pudding à l'Américaine*

Put into a bowl two and a half oz. of soft bread-crumbs; three oz. of powdered sugar; three oz. of flour; two and a half oz. of marrow and an equal quantity of beef suet (both chopped); three oz. of candied fruit cut into dice; one egg and three egg-yolks, a pinch of grated orange or lemon rind; a little nutmeg and cinnamon, and a liqueur-glass of brandy or rum.

Mix the whole; pour the preparation into a buttered and floured mould or bowl, and cook in the *bain-marie* (water-bath).

Serve a *sabayon* (2408) with rum at the same time.

2488—MARROW PUDDING   *Pudding à la Moëlle*

Melt half a lb. of beef-marrow and two oz. of beef suet, in a double-boiler, and let it get tepid. Then work this fat in a bowl with half a lb. of powdered sugar; three oz. of bread-crumbs, dipped in milk and pressed; three whole eggs and eight egg-yolks; half a lb. of candied fruit, cut into dice; three oz. of sultana raisins and two oz. of seeded, Malaga raisins.

Pour this preparation into an even, deep, buttered and floured border-mould; and *poach* in the *bain-marie* (water-bath).

Serve a *sabayon* (2408) with rum at the same time.

BREAD PUDDINGS

2489—ENGLISH BREAD PUDDING   *Pudding au Pain à l'Anglaise*

Butter some thin slices of bread and distribute over them some currants and sultana raisins, plumped in tepid water and well drained. Set these slices in a deep pie-dish or casserole; cover with preparation (2638), and *poach* in the oven.

2490—FRENCH BREAD PUDDING   *Pudding au Pain à la Française*

Soak two-thirds of a lb. of soft white bread-crumb in one and three-quarter pints of boiled milk, flavored with vanilla and containing eight oz. of sugar. Rub through a sieve and add: four whole eggs, six egg-yolks, and four egg-whites, beaten stiff.

Pour this preparation into a deep, buttered *border-mould,* dusted with bread-crumbs; and *poach* in *bain-marie* (water-bath).

As an accompaniment, serve either an English custard, a vanilla-flavored *sabayon,* or a fruit sauce.

2491—GERMAN BREAD PUDDING   *Pudding au Pain Allemand*

Soak two-thirds of a lb. of soft brown bread-crumbs (whole rye, etc.), in one and three-quarter pints of Rhine wine, Moselle or beer, containing half a lb. of brown sugar and a little cinnamon. Rub through a sieve and add four eggs, six egg-yolks, five oz. of melted butter, and the whites of four eggs beaten stiff. *Poach* in a *bain-marie* (water-bath) as in the preceding case. The accompaniment to this pudding is invariably a fruit syrup.

2492—SCOTCH BREAD PUDDING   *Pudding au Pain d'Ecossaise*

Proceed exactly as for (2490), but add five oz. of sliced seasonable fruit. Mould and *poach* in the same way, and serve a red-currant sauce flavored with raspberries, as an accompaniment.

Paste Puddings

2493—TAPIOCA PUDDING   *Pudding au Tapioca*

Sprinkle eight oz. of tapioca into one and three-quarter pints of boiling milk, containing four oz. of sugar, a pinch of salt and three oz. of butter.

Cook in the oven for twenty minutes; transfer the preparation to another saucepan, and add to it six egg-yolks, two and a half oz. of butter, and the whites of four eggs beaten to a stiff froth.

Pour the whole into a well-buttered *cylinder-mould,* sprinkled with tapioca, and *poach* in the *bain-marie* (water-bath) until the preparation seems springy to the touch. Let the pudding stand for seven or eight minutes before turning it out. Serve an English custard, a *sabayon* or a fruit sauce as accompaniment.

2494—SAGO PUDDING   *Pudding au Sagon*

Proceed as above, but substitute sago for the tapioca, and sprinkle the inside of the mould with sago. The treatment and accompaniments are the same.

2495—SEMOLINA PUDDING   *Pudding à la Semoule*

Proceed as for (2493), but use semolina instead of tapioca, and sprinkle the mould with granulated semolina (fine farina).

2496—VERMICELLI PUDDING   *Pudding a Vermicelle*

Proceed as for (2493), but use vermicelli, and sprinkle the mould with bits of vermicelli, which should not be broken up too much.

2497—FRESH MADE NOODLE PUDDING

Pudding aux Nouilles Fraiches

Proceed in exactly the same way as for (2493).

2498—ENGLISH TAPIOCA, SAGO, AND SEMOLINA PUDDINGS

Puddings de Tapioca, Sagon, et Semoule à l'Anglaise

Whatever be the ingredient used, it should be cooked in very slightly-sugared milk, flavored according to fancy, and in the quantities given above. Thicken with two eggs per pint of the preparation; pour the whole into a buttered pie-dish or casserole, and cook in the oven in a *bain-marie* (water-bath).

N.B.—All English puddings of this class are made in the same way, and, as already stated, are served in the dish in which they have cooked.

2499—BRAZILIAN PUDDING   *Pudding Brésilien*

Make the preparation for tapioca pudding and pour it into a mould, coated with sugar cooked to the *caramel* stage (360° F.).

Poach in a *bain-marie* (water-bath) and serve plain.

2500—CHEVREUSE PUDDING   *Pudding à la Chevreuse*

This is semolina pudding served with a Sabayon (2408), flavored with kirsch.

2501—RICE PUDDING   *Pudding au Riz*

Prepare the rice as directed under (2404), and mix with it (per lb. of raw rice) the whites of fifteen eggs beaten to a stiff froth. Mould in buttered moulds sprinkled with *raspings*.

The cooking and the accompaniments are the same as for (2493, 2494), etc.

2502—ENGLISH RICE PUDDING   *Pudding au Riz à l'Anglaise*

The quantities for this pudding are: six oz. of rice, one quart of milk (flavored according to taste), two oz. of sugar and three oz. of butter. The grains of rice should be kept somewhat firm, but the whole should be rather liquid. Thicken with three eggs; cook the preparation in the oven, in a pie-dish or casserole; and on taking the pudding out of the oven sprinkle its surface with *icing sugar*.

2503—RICE AND CHOCOLATE PUDDING   *Pudding de Riz au Chocolat*

Add two oz. of chocolate to every lb. of the preparation of rice, made after (2404), and combine with the whites of three eggs beaten to a fairly stiff froth; pour the preparation into a buttered pie-dish or casserole, and cook in the oven.

Serve some chocolate custard (combined with its bulk of whipped cream) separately.

N.B.—This sweet may be served hot or cold.

SOUFFLÉD PUDDINGS

2504—SAXON PUDDING   *Pudding Saxon*

Work four oz. of butter to a cream in a bowl. Add four oz. of powdered sugar and four oz. of sifted flour, and dilute with two-thirds pint of boiled milk.

Boil this preparation, stirring it the while; and dry it over a hot fire as in the case of a *panada* for a "Pâte à choux" (2374).

Take off the fire; thicken with five egg-yolks; and then carefully mix with it the five whites beaten to a stiff froth. Pour into well-buttered moulds, and *poach* in a *bain-marie* (water-bath).

As an accompaniment serve an English custard or a Sabayon, flavored according to fancy.

2505—ALMOND SOUFFLE PUDDING   *Pudding Soufflé aux Amandes*

Make a preparation as for (2504), but use almond milk (2506) instead of cow's milk. Pour the preparation into buttered moulds, sprinkled with slivered and grilled almonds, and *poach* in a *bain-marie* (water-bath).

As an accompaniment serve a white-wine Sabayon (2408) flavored with *orgeat*.

2506—SOUFFLE PUDDING DENISE ALMOND MILK

Pudding Soufflé Denise au Lait d'Amandes

Finely pound four oz. of freshly-washed and peeled almonds, and add, from time to time, a few drops of fresh water. When the almonds form a smooth paste, add the necessary quantity of water to them to produce one pint of milk. Strain through muslin and slightly twist the latter in order to squeeze out all the liquid.

With this almond milk, dilute three oz. of flour and three oz. of rice cream, mixed in a saucepan, and take care that no lumps form. Strain the whole through a sieve, and add five oz. of sugar, three oz. of butter and a little salt.

Set the saucepan on the stove; boil, stirring the while, and then stir briskly with a spatula until the preparation acquires the consistency of a thick paste and falls from the spatula without leaving any portions sticking. Pour this paste into a bowl and combine with: first, little by little, two oz. of fresh butter; then, eight egg-yolks, two ounces of finely-pounded almonds moistened with a tablespoon of kirsch and as much maraschino, and the whites of five eggs beaten to a stiff froth.

This pudding is cooked in a *bain-marie* (water-bath) in one of the following ways:

In a buttered deep pie-dish. In this case, on taking the pudding out of the *bain-marie,* sprinkle its surface with icing sugar, and criss-cross it with a red-hot iron.

Or in a shallow, buttered and flour dredged, *Charlotte-mould.*

Or in fairly shallow, buttered *dome-moulds,* lined inside with slices one inch in diameter, stamped (by means of a fancy-cutter) out of a layer of *Génoise* or a layer of sponge cake preparation, about one-third of an inch thick.

In the two last cases, the pudding is coated with an apricot sauce (2410), mixed with the almond milk, and a sauceboat of the same sauce is served separately.

2507—LEMON SOUFFLE PUDDING *Pudding Soufflé au Citron*

Make the preparation for (2504), and flavor it with a piece of lemon rind. The treatment is the same.

Serve an English custard (2397), flavored with lemon separately.

2508—ORANGE, CURACAO, ANISETTE, AND BENEDICTINE PUDDINGS *Puddings Soufflés à l'Orange, au Curaçao, à l'Anisette, et à la Benedictine*

For all these puddings the procedure is the same as for (2504), and only the flavor changes.

Accompany each with an English custard (2397), flavored like the particular pudding.

2509—INDIAN SOUFFLE PUDDING *Pudding Soufflé à l'Indienne*

Take some soufflé-pudding preparation and add to it two oz. of powdered ginger, and five oz. of candied ginger, cut in small dice. Proceed in the same way as for (2504).

As an accompaniment, serve an English custard (2397) flavored with ginger.

2510—CHESTNUT SOUFFLE PUDDING *Pudding Soufflé aux Marrons*

Cook two lbs. of peeled chestnuts in a light, vanilla-flavored syrup.

Rub them through a sieve, add five oz. of powdered sugar and three oz. of butter to the *purée,* and dry it over a hot fire. Thicken it with eight egg-yolks and finish it with the whites of six eggs, beaten to a stiff froth.

Poach in buttered moulds in a *bain-marie* (water-bath).

As an accompaniment, serve, either an English custard (2397), or a vanilla-flavored apricot syrup (2410).

2511—MOUSSELINE PUDDING *Pudding Mousseline*

Work four oz. of butter and four oz. of powdered sugar to a cream, and add the yolks of ten eggs, one by one; meanwhile stirring the preparation.

Set the latter on a moderate fire until it coats the withdrawn spoon; then immediately add the whites of seven eggs beaten to a stiff froth.

Pour the whole into a deep, buttered *border-mould,* which only half fill, in view of the expansion of the preparation while cooking.

Poach in a *bain-marie* (water-bath) for about thirty minutes, and let the pudding stand for ten minutes before turning it out.

As an accompaniment serve a light Sabayon (2408) or a fruit sauce.

2512—REGENCE SOUFFLE PUDDING *Pudding Soufflé Régence*

Make a *soufflé*-pudding preparation flavored with vanilla, and *poach* it in a *bain-marie* (water-bath), in a mould coated with sugar cooked to the *caramel* stage (360° F.). Serve an English custard (2397), prepared with caramel, separately.

2513—SOUFFLE PUDDING A LA REINE *Pudding Soufflé à la Reine*

Take some vanilla-flavored, *soufflé*-pudding preparation. Take a mould with a central tube; butter it, and sprinkle it with chopped pistachios and crushed macaroons. Set the preparation in the mould in layers, alternated by coats of chopped pistachios and crushed macaroons; and *poach* in a *bain-marie* (water-bath).

As an accompaniment serve an English custard (2397) combined with *pralin.*

2514—SOUFFLE PUDDING A LA ROYALE *Pudding Soufflé à la Royale*

Line the bottom and sides of a buttered *Charlotte-mould* with thin slices of sponge cake spread with jam and rolled up. Fill the mould with a *soufflé*-pudding preparation, and *poach* in a *bain-marie* (water-bath).

Serve an apricot sauce (2410) flavored with Marsala, separately.

2515—SOUFFLE PUDDING SANS-SOUCI *Pudding Soufflé Sans-Souci*

Copiously butter a mould, and sprinkle its bottom and sides with well-washed and drained currants. Fill with a *soufflé*-pudding preparation, combined per two lbs. with one lb. of peeled apples, cut in dice and cooked in butter.

Poach in a *bain-marie* (water-bath).

2516—SOUFFLE PUDDING VESUVIENNE *Pudding Soufflé Vésuvienne*

Make a *soufflé*-pudding preparation, and add to it for the quantities given in the original recipe one and a half oz. of tomato jam and the same quantity of seeded Malaga raisins. *Poach* in a *bain-marie* (water-bath) in a mould with a central tube.

When the pudding is turned out, surround it with apricot sauce (2410), and pour in the middle some heated rum, and light when serving.

2517—ROLY-POLY PUDDING *Rolly Pudding*

Proceed as for (2361): prepare a firm paste from one lb. of flour, nine oz. of chopped suet, one and a half oz. of sugar, a pinch of salt, and one-sixth pint of water. Let this paste rest for one hour before using it.

Roll it out to the shape of a rectangle one-fifth of an inch thick; spread a layer of jam upon it, and roll it up like a jelly roll.

Wrap it in a buttered and flour dredged cloth or vegetable parchment, and cook it in boiling water or in steam for one and a half hours.

When about to serve, cut the roll into slices half an inch thick, and arrange them in a crown. As an accompaniment serve a fruit sauce.

2518—RISSOLES *Rissoles*

The preparation of *rissoles* for desserts is the same as that for *rissoles* served as hors-d'œuvres, except that the former are garnished with marmalade or jam, with a fruit *salpicon* or with stewed fruit, with plain or *pralined* creams, etc.

The best paste for the purpose is derived from puff-paste (2366) trimmings.

The shape of *rissoles* varies very much. They may be shaped like half-moons, turnovers, small, round or oval patties, etc.

Rissoles for desserts are also frequently made from ordinary *brioche* paste (2368), and constitute a variety of Viennese fritters. In this case they are invariably mentioned on the menu as "à la Dauphine."

2519—SOUFFLES *Soufflés*

Although *soufflés* are generally served unaccompanied, some stewed, seasonable fruit, or a *macédoine* of fresh fruit, may, nevertheless, be served with them. This, of course, only applies to *soufflés* with a fruit base.

I have already given the recipes for *soufflés* (2405); I need now, therefore, only give the peculiarities of each particular *soufflé*.

2520—FRUIT SOUFFLE IN A CROUSTADE
Soufflé de Fruits en Croustade

Line a round, shallow, well-buttered, *croustade-mould* with a very thin layer of sweetened paste. Spread some vanilla-flavored, stewed apples on the bottom, and upon it lay a filling of various seasonable fresh stewed fruits—quartered if large. The mould ought now to be half-filled.

Fill it up with a vanilla-flavored *soufflé* preparation, and cook it in a moderate oven for about twenty-five minutes.

On taking it from the oven, carefully turn it out on a dish; pour a few tablespoons of heated rum into it, and light it when serving.

2521—ALMOND SOUFFLE *Soufflé aux Amandes*

Make a preparation of *soufflé* with cream, but use almond milk (2506) instead of cow's milk, add one and a half oz. of slightly-grilled, chopped almonds, per half pint of almond milk. Put in a dish and cook in the usual way.

2522—SOUFFLE WITH FRESH ALMONDS
Soufflé aux Amandes Fraîches

Proceed exactly as above, but use fresh slivered almonds instead of grilled, chopped ones.

2523—SOUFFLE WITH FILBERT *Soufflé aux Avelines*

Make the *soufflé* preparation from milk in which two oz. of filbert *pralin* per one-sixth pint have previously been steeped.

Put on a dish and cook the *soufflé* in the usual way.

2524—CAMARGO SOUFFLE *Soufflé Camargo*

Make a *soufflé* preparation of tangerines, and another of filberts as above. Put the two preparations in layers, alternated by lady-fingers, saturated with Curaçao liqueur.

2525—PAULETTE SOUFFLE　　　　　Soufflé Paulette

Take vanilla-flavored *soufflé* preparation, thickened somewhat more than the ordinary kind, and add to it five tablespoons of strawberry *purée*. Serve some well-cooled strawberries, coated with raspberry *purée*, separately.

2526—CHERRY SOUFFLE　　　　　Soufflé aux Cerises

Prepare a *soufflé* with Kirsch, accompany it with some stewed pitted cherries, covered with a raspberry *purée*.

2527—STRAWBERRY SOUFFLE　　　　　Soufflé aux Fraises

This is a *soufflé* with Kirsch, accompanied by iced strawberries steeped in orange juice.

2528—ORIENTALE POMEGRANATE SOUFFLE
Soufflé aux Grenades à l'Orientale

Make a *soufflé* preparation, slightly flavored with vanilla. Arrange it in layers in a *timbale,* alternated by sponge ladyfingers saturated with Grenadine and Kirsch. On taking the *soufflé* from the oven, cover it with a veil of spun sugar, and sprinkle the *soufflé* with small candies, flavored with Grenadine, in imitation of pomegranate seeds.

2529—JAVA SOUFFLE　　　　　Soufflé Javanais

Make the *soufflé* preparation, but use tea instead of milk, and add one and a half oz. of chopped pistachios per one-sixth pint of the tea.

2530—CHARTREUSE SOUFFLE　　　　　Soufflé Lérina

Take some ordinary *soufflé* preparation, flavored with Lérina liqueur, which is a kind of Chartreuse, made in the Lérins islands.

2531—SOUFFLE WITH LIQUEUR　　　　　Soufflé aux Liqueurs

This *soufflé* may be made, either from the *soufflé* with cream preparation or from that with fruit, given in the note.

The *soufflés* made from cream are flavored with such liqueurs as rum, curaçao, anisette, vanilla, etc.

Those made from fruit are flavored with Kirsch, Kümmel, etc.

2532—LUCULLUS SOUFFLE　　　　　Soufflé Lucullus

Set a *savarin* (2371), saturated with kirsch-flavored syrup, upon a dish, and surround it with a band of paper, tied on with string, in order to prevent the *soufflé* from drying during the cooking process.

Make a *soufflé* preparation with a fruit base, set it in the center of the *savarin,* and cook it in the usual way.

2533—HILDA SOUFFLE   *Soufflé Hilda*

This is a lemon *soufflé,* accompanied by fine strawberries, well chilled and coated with a *purée* of fresh raspberries.

2534—ORLEANS SOUFFLE   *Soufflé à l'Orléans*

Take some cream *soufflé*-preparation, combined with pieces of Jeanne-d'Arc biscuits (kind of small sponge cakes), saturated with peach liqueur and kirsch, and one oz. each of half-sugared cherries and angelica, cut into dice.

2535—PALMYRA SOUFFLE   *Soufflé Palmyre*

Take some vanilla-flavored *soufflé* preparation. Set it in a *timbale,* in layers alternated by sponge ladyfingers saturated with anisette and Kirsch. Cook in the usual way.

2536—PRALINE SOUFFLE   *Soufflé Praliné*

Take some vanilla-flavored *soufflé* preparation; add to it two ounces of almond *pralin* which should have previously steeped in milk. When the *soufflé* is ready, sprinkle its surface with grilled chopped almonds or crushed, burnt almonds.

2537—ROTHSCHILD SOUFFLE   *Soufflê Rothschild*

Take some cream *soufflé*-preparation, combined with three ounces of candied fruit, cut into dice and steeped in Dantzig Gold Wasser, a brandy, containing plenty of gold leaf spangles.

When the *soufflé* is almost cooked, set on it a border of fine strawberries (in season), or half-sugared, preserved cherries.

It should be remembered, however, that the correct procedure demands the use of strawberries in full season.

2538—ROYALE SOUFFLE   *Soufflé à la Royale*

Take some vanilla-flavored *soufflé*-preparation. Put it in a *timbale* in alternate layers with sponge ladyfingers, saturated with Kirsch; and distribute over it such fruits as pineapple, cherries, angelica and grapes—all cut into dice, and previously steeped in Kirsch.

2539—VANILLA SOUFFLE   *Soufflé à la Vanille*

Take some cream *soufflé*-preparation, made from milk in which a stick of vanilla has been previously steeped or cooked.

2540—VIOLET SOUFFLE
Soufflé aux Violets

Take some vanilla-flavored *soufflé* preparation, combined with crushed crystallized violets. When the *soufflé* is ready, set on it a crown of large crystallized violets, and cook in the usual way.

2541—SUBRICS
Subrics

Into one pint of vanilla-flavored boiled milk, containing three and a half oz. of sugar, drop four oz. of semolina. Add one and a half oz. of butter and a few grains of salt; mix thoroughly, and gently cook in the oven under cover for twenty-five minutes.

Thicken with six egg-yolks, and spread the preparation in layers two-thirds of an inch thick on a buttered pan. Pass a piece of butter over the surface to prevent its drying, and leave to cool.

Then cut out this preparation into rounds three inches in diame-ter.

Heat some clarified butter (175) in a frying-pan; set the rounds in it; brown them on both sides, and arrange them in a circle. Garnish the center of each round with a tablespoon of red-currant jelly, or very firm quince jelly.

TIMBALES

2542—D'AREMBERG TIMBALE
Timbale d'Aremberg

Line a buttered *Charlotte-mould* with some fairly firm Brioche paste (2368). Fill the mould with quartered pears, cooked in vanilla-flavored syrup, kept rather firm and alternated by apricot jam.

Close the *timbale* with a layer of the same paste, well sealed down round the slightly-moistened edges, and cut a slit in the middle for the escape of steam. Cook in a good moderate oven for about forty minutes.

On taking the *timbale* out of the oven, turn it out on a dish, and accompany it with a maraschino-flavored apricot sauce (2410).

2543—BOURDALOUE TIMBALE
Timbale Bourdaloue

Prepare a dry paste (2362), combined with four ounces of finely-chopped almonds per one lb. of flour.

With this paste line a buttered *timbale* mould, and garnish it with various stewed fruits, alternated by layers of *frangipan* cream (2399). Cover with a layer of the same paste, and bake in a good moderate oven.

When the *timbale* is turned out, coat it with a vanilla-flavored apricot syrup.

2544—MARIE-LOUISE TIMBALE   *Timbale Marie-Louise*

Take a stale *Génoise* baked in a deep *Charlotte-mould;* press the blade of a knife into it and cut it all round, leaving a base.

Remove the inside in one piece which should resemble a large cork in shape. Cut this piece into slices half-inch thick; coat each slice with Italian *meringue* (2383), and, upon the latter, spread a *salpicon* of peaches, cherries and pineapple.

Coat the outside of the *timbale* with the same *meringue,* and decorate it; put the slices back inside, and set them one upon the other. Owing to the inserted filling these slices naturally project above the sides of the *timbale;* surround them with a border of *poached* peaches, separated by a bit of *meringue.*

Put the *timbale* in a mild oven to brown the *meringue,* and serve a Kirsch-flavored peach sauce (2368) at the same time.

2545—MONTMORENCY TIMBALE   *Timbale Montmorency*

Bake a brioche in a mould of the required size. When it is quite cold, remove all the soft crumb from its inside, leaving a thickness of three-quarters of an inch on the bottom and sides. Coat all round, by means of a brush, with apricot jam cooked to the *small-thread* stage (215° F.), and decorate with pieces of puff-paste in the shape of crescents, diamonds, circles, etc., baked without browning in a moderate oven. When about to serve, pour in a filling of pitted cherries, cooked in a thin syrup, thickened with raspberry-flavored red-currant jelly.

2546—PARISIENNE TIMBALE   *Timbale à la Parisienne*

Bake a brioche in a *Charlotte-mould,* and, when it is quite cold, remove the crumb from its inside as above. Coat the outside with apricot jam, and decorate with candied fruit. When about to serve, pour into it a filling consisting of peeled and quartered pears, apples, peaches and apricots, cooked in vanilla-flavored syrup; pineapple cut into large dice, diamond shapes of angelica; half-almonds; and raisins, plumped in tepid water. Mix this filling with a Kirsch-flavored apricot *purée* (2410).

2547—FAVART TIMBALE   *Timbale à la Favart*

Bake a brioche in a *Richelieu-mould,* and hollow it out and decorate it as above. The filling of this *timbale* consists of only whole or halved fruit, and vanilla-flavored chestnuts; and these are mixed with Kirsch-flavored apricot syrup (2410), combined with one quart of a *purée* of chestnut pieces.

Pour the filling into the *timbale* just before serving.

Hot Fruit Entremets

2548—APRICOTS   *Abricots*

Whether fresh or preserved, apricots used for desserts should always be peeled. When preserved apricots are used, it is well to cook them again before using them, for sometimes they are inclined to be too firm.

2549—BOURDALOUE APRICOTS   *Abricots Bourdaloue*

Prepare a flawn-crust for custards, and bake it without browning. Fill its bottom with a layer of thin *frangipan* cream (2399), combined with crushed macaroons. Upon this cream set some half-apricots, *poached* in vanilla-flavored syrup, and cover them with a layer of the same cream.

Sprinkle the surface with crushed macaroons and melted butter and *glaze* quickly.

N.B.—The above is the usual procedure, but fruit "à la Bourdaloue" may also be prepared in the following ways: Set the fruit in a shallow *timbale* between two layers of cream, the upper one of which should be covered with *gratin;* or set the fruit in a border of rice or semolina, with the same coat of *gratin* upon the cream; or set the fruit in a border of *Génoise,* combined with apricots.

2550—COLBERT APRICOTS   *Abricots Colbert*

Poach some fine half-apricots in syrup, keeping them somewhat firm.

Drain them; dry them, and fill their hollows with "rice for desserts" (2404) in such a way as to reconstruct the fruit. Treat them *à l'Anglaise,* with very fine bread-crumbs; fry just before serving, and drain. Stick a small piece of angelica into each apricot, in imitation of the stems, and set them on a napkin.

Serve a Kirsch-flavored apricot sauce (2410) separately.

2551—CONDE APRICOTS   *Abricots Condé*

On a round dish prepare a border of vanilla-flavored, sweet rice, either by means of a knife, or by means of an even, buttered, *ring-mould.*

Upon this ring set some apricots *poached* in syrup; decorate with candied fruit, and coat with a Kirsch-flavored apricot syrup (2410).

2552—CONDE APRICOTS (2nd METHOD)   *Abricots Condé*

Set a crown of small *Génoise* round slices on a dish; on each round slice set a fine *poached* half-apricot face up, and set a half-sugared cherry in the hollow of each half-apricot. In the middle of the crown arrange a pyramid of rice croquettes, the size and shape of apricots.

Serve a Kirsch-flavored apricot sauce (2410) separately.

2553—CUSSY APRICOTS   *Abricots Cussy*

Garnish the flat side of some macaroons with a layer of smooth fruit *salpicon,* mixed with an apricot *purée;* set a fine *poached* half-apricot on each macaroon, coat with Italian *meringue* (2383); arrange in the form of a crown, and place the dish in a moderate oven for a few minutes to dry, but not to brown, the *meringue.*

Serve a Kirsch-flavored apricot sauce separately.

2554—APRICOTS GRATIN   *Abricots Gratinés*

Spread an even layer, one inch thick, of stiff stewed apples or stewed semolina (prepared like rice for desserts) (2404) on a dish. Set on some fine half-apricots *poached* in syrup; entirely cover the latter with a somewhat thin preparation of "*Pralin* à Condé," sprinkle with icing sugar, and set the dish in the oven to slightly brown the *pralin.*

2555—MERINGUED APRICOTS   *Abricots Meringués*

Spread a layer of vanilla-flavored sweet rice on a dish, and set some *poached* half-apricots on it. Cover with ordinary *meringue;* shaping the latter like a dome or a *Charlotte* (2404); decorate with the same *meringue;* sprinkle with icing sugar, and place the dish in the oven in order to slightly cook the *meringue.*

On taking the dish from the oven, garnish the decorative portions alternately with apricot and red-currant jam.

2556—MERINGUED APRICOTS (2nd METHOD)   *Abricots Meringués*

Prepare an unbrowned-baked deep crust for custard. Fill the bottom either with a layer of *frangipan* cream or with vanilla-flavored semolina, or sweet rice. Set on this some *poached* half-apricots; cover with *meringue,* smooth the latter on top and all round with the blade of a knife, and decorate with *meringue* by means of a pastry-bag fitted with a small even tube. For the rest of the procedure follow the preceding recipe.

2557—SULTANA APRICOTS *Abricots Sultane*

Prepare a *Génoise,* cooked in a somewhat deep *border-mould,* and stick it by means of some apricot, cooked to the *small-thread* stage (215° F.), to a base of dry paste (2362) of the same size. Coat it all round with ordinary *meringue;* decorate it with a pastry-bag fitted with a small even tube, and brown it in a moderate oven.

Then fill the inside of the border with a preparation of vanilla-flavored rice, combined with a little *frangipan* cream and some slivered pistachios; taking care to keep the preparation sufficiently stiff to be able to shape it like a dome. Upon the rice set some fine half-apricots, *poached* in vanilla-flavored syrup, and sprinkle these with chopped pistachios.

As an accompaniment serve a syrup prepared with almond milk (2506), and finished with a piece of butter as big as a hazel-nut.

PINEAPPLE (ANANAS)

2558—PINEAPPLE FAVORITE *Ananas Favorite*

See (2429).

2559—CONDE PINEAPPLE *Ananas Condé*

Steep in sugar and Kirsch some half-slices of pineapple. Arrange them in a circle upon a border of rice, prepared as directed under (2551); decorate with half-sugared cherries and diamond shapes of angelica, and coat with a Kirsch-flavored apricot syrup (2410).

2560—CREOLE PINEAPPLE *Ananas à la Créole*

Cook a pineapple in a Kirsch-flavored syrup; cut it lengthwise in two, and cut each half into thin and regular slices.

Line a *dome-mould* with these half-slices, and fill it up with vanilla-flavored rice; leaving a hollow in the middle. Fill this hollow with the pineapple left overs, cut into dice, and custard apples and bananas, likewise cut into dice and cooked in syrup.

Turn out upon a round dish; decorate the top with large leaves of angelica, and surround the base with bananas *poached* in Kirsch-flavored syrup.

Serve a Kirsch-flavored apricot syrup (2410) separately.

BANANAS (BANANES)

2561—BOURDALOUE BANANAS   *Bananes Bourdaloue*

Peel the bananas and *poach* them gently in a vanilla-flavored syrup. For the rest of the operation, proceed as directed under (2549).

2562—CONDE BANANAS   *Bananes Condé*

Poach the bananas in vanilla-flavored syrup, and then treat them as directed under (2551).

2563—MERINGUED BANANAS   *Bananes Meringuées*

Poach the bananas in vanilla-flavored syrup, and then treat them as directed under the apricot recipes (2555 and 2556); leaving them either whole or cutting them into round slices.

2564—BANANAS A LA NORVEGIENNE   *Bananes à la Norvègienne*

Cut a slice of the peel from each banana, and remove the pulp from their insides. Fill the emptied peels, three parts full, with banana ice, and quickly cover the latter with a pastry-bag fitted with a small fancy tube, with an Italian *meringue* (2383) flavored with rum.

Lay the prepared bananas on a dish; set in a pan containing cracked ice, and place the pan in a sufficiently hot oven to ensure the speedy browning of the *meringue*.

2565—SOUFFLE BANANAS   *Bananes Soufflées*

Cut off a quarter of each banana, and remove the pulp from their insides without breaking the peel. Rub this pulp through a sieve; add it to a cream *soufflé*-preparation (2405); finish the latter with the necessary quantity of egg-whites, and fill the emptied peels with it.

Set the filled peels in a star on a dish, and put the latter in the oven for six minutes.

CHERRIES (CERISES)

2566—JUBILEE CHERRIES   *Cerises Jubilée*

Pit some fine cherries; *poach* them in syrup, and set them in small silver *timbales*. Reduce the syrup and thicken it with a little arrowroot or cornstarch, diluted with cold water; allowing one tablespoon of thickening per half-pint of syrup. Cover the cherries with the thickened syrup; pour a teaspoonful of heated Kirsch into each *timbale,* and light each one when serving.

2567—VALERIA CHERRIES *Cerises Valéria*

Prepare some *tartlet crusts* for sweetened paste. Fill the bottom of each with red-currant ice, combined with cream, and cover the latter with vanilla-flavored, Italian *meringue* (2383), piped on with a pastry-bag. Upon this *meringue* set the pitted cherries, *poached* in sugared Bordeaux wine, and arrange the *tartlets* on a dish.

Lay the dish on a tray containing cracked ice, and set the tray in the oven in order to dry the *meringue.* On taking the dish from the oven, quickly coat the cherries with red-currant syrup; sprinkle the latter with chopped pistachios, and serve the *tartlets* on a napkin.

2568—DEEP CHERRY MERINGUE PIE *Flan de Cerises Meringue*

Line a buttered spring-form with fine paste: prick the bottom; fill with pitted cherries after the manner of an ordinary pie, and fill up with custard (2397). Cook in the usual way.

On taking the pie out of the oven, remove the rim of the form, and finish the pie like an ordinary *meringue*-one.

N.B.—All fruits used in the preparation of ordinary deep pies may be similarly prepared for *meringue*-coated pies. Only such fruits as strawberries and grapes, which are not cooked with the crust, are unsuited to this kind of preparation.

2569—NECTARINES *Nectarines ou Brugnons*

Nectarines may be prepared after all the recipes given for peaches. I shall not, therefore, give any recipes which are proper to them. See peaches (2573).

ORANGES AND TANGERINES (ORANGES ET MANDARINES)

2570—ORANGES A LA NORVEGIENNE *Oranges à la Norvègienne*

Cut a slice of peel from the top of each of the oranges, and scoop out with a spoon. Fill the emptied scooped out skin shells three-parts with orange or tangerine ice, in accordance with the fruit being used, and cover the ice with Italian *meringue* (2383), with a pastry-bag.

Set the dish containing the garnished skin shells on a tray covered with cracked ice, and quickly brown the *meringue* at the *salamander.*

2571—TANGERINES A LA PALIKARE *Mandarines à la Palikare*

Cut the tangerines at the top and remove the sections without breaking the peel. Skin the sections. Fill the peels with rice for desserts (2404), containing a little saffron; mould some of the same rice in a little *dome-mould,* and set it upon a carved bed.

Cover this dome with the tangerine sections; coat the latter with some apricot syrup; and, all round, arrange the rice-garnished peels, opened side down.

2572—SURPRISE ORANGE OR TANGERINE SOUFFLE

Soufflé d'Oranges ou de Mandarines en Surprise

Without splitting them, empty the orange or tangerine peels.

Half-fill them with orange or tangerine ice, according to the fruit being used, and cover the ice with orange- or tangerine-flavored *soufflé*-preparation. Place the dish containing the filled peels upon a tray covered with cracked ice; set in the oven that the *soufflé* may cook quickly, and allow two minutes for tangerines and four minutes for oranges.

PEACHES (PÊCHES)

2573—BOURDALOUE PEACHES *Pêches Bourdaloue*

Poach the peaches (cut into two) in some vanilla-flavored syrup, and then proceed exactly as for (2549).

2574—CONDE PEACHES *Pêches Condé*

Nos. 2551 and 2552 may be applied in every respect to peaches.

2575—CUSSY PEACHES *Pêches Cussy*

Proceed exactly as for (2553).

2576—PEACHES FLAMBEES *Pêches Flambées*

These may be prepared in two ways as follows:—

Poach the peaches whole in a Kirsch-flavored syrup (2418), and set them each in a small *timbale*. Thicken the syrup slightly with arrowroot or cornstarch, and pour it over the peaches. Add some heated Kirsch, and light it when serving.

Or *poach* the peaches as above, and set them on a fresh-strawberry *purée*. Sprinkle the whole with heated Kirsch, and light it at the last moment.

2577—GRATIN PEACHES *Pêches Gratinées*

Proceed exactly as for (2554).

2578—MERINGUED PEACHES   *Pêches Meringuées*

Prepare an unbrowned crust for custard; fill the bottom of it with *frangipan* cream prepared with *pralin,* and upon this cream set whole or halved, *poached* peaches. Cover with *meringue* and finish as explained under (2555).

2579—MAINTENON PEACHES   *Pêches Maintenon*

Take a sponge cake, baked in a dome-mould and completely cooled. Cut it across into slices, and coat each of the latter with *frangipan* cream, combined with a *salpicon* of candied fruit and chopped, grilled almonds.

Join the slices together in such a way as to reconstruct the cake, and cover the latter with Italian *meringue* (2383). Decorate by means of the pastry-bag, and dry in the oven.

Surround the cake with a border of fine half-peaches *poached* in a vanilla-flavored syrup.

2580—VANILLA PEACHES   *Pêches à la Vanille*

Poach the halved or whole peaches in a vanilla-flavored syrup, and set them in a *timbale.* Cover them to within half their height with the syrup used in *poaching,* thickened with arrowroot or corn-starch slightly tinted with pink, and combined with vanilla cream.

PEARS (POIRES)

2581—BOURDALOUE PEARS   *Poires Bourdaloue*

If the pears be of medium size, halve them; if they are large, quarter them. Carefully trim the sections. Cook the pears in a vanilla-flavored syrup, and for the rest of the operation follow (2549).

The remarks appended to (2549) apply equally to pears and to all fruit prepared according to the particular recipe referred to.

2582—CONDE PEARS   *Poires Condé*

Very small pears cut with great care are admirably suited to this dessert. If they are of medium size, halve them. Cook them in vanilla-flavored syrup, and serve them on a border of rice as directed under (2551).

2583—IMPERATRICE PEARS   *Poires à l'Impératrice*

Quarter and properly trim the pears, and cook them in vanilla-flavored syrup. Arrange them in a shallow *timbale* between two

layers of vanilla-flavored rice for desserts, combined with a little
frangipan cream (2399).

Sprinkle the upper layer with crushed macaroons and melted
butter, and set the *gratin* to form.

2584—PARISIENNE PEARS *Poires à la Parisienne*

Bake a *Génoise* base in a spring form, and, when it is almost cold,
saturate it with Kirsch-flavored syrup.

In the middle of this base set a little dome of vanilla-flavored rice,
and surround it with pears, cooked in syrup and set upright.
Border them with a ribbon of ordinary *meringue,* squeezed from a
pastry-bag, fitted with a fair-sized, fancy tube; by the same means
make a fine rosette of *meringue* on top of the dome, and bake this
meringue in a mild oven.

On taking the dish out of the oven, *glaze* the pears with a brush
dipped in rather stiff apricot-syrup, and surround them with a
border of half-sugared cherries.

2585—SULTANA PEARS *Poires Sultane*

Halve or quarter the pears; trim them well, and cook them in
a vanilla-flavored syrup.

For the rest of the operation follow (2557).

2586—REGENCE PEARS *Poires à la Régence*

Peel the pears; cook them whole in a vanilla-flavored syrup, and
let them cool in the syrup. When they are cold cut them in two
lengthwise, slightly hollow out the inside of each half; garnish the
hollow with rice for desserts, combined with a quarter of its weight
of *frangipan* cream and a fine *salpicon* of candied fruit, steeped in
Kirsch.

Join the two halves of each pear, and treat them *à l'anglaise* with
very fine bread-crumbs.

Fry them at the last moment, and, on taking them out of the
fat, stick an angelica stalk as a stem into each. Set them on a napkin,
and serve a Kirsch-flavored apricot sauce separately.

2587—VALENCIENNES TIMBALE OF PEARS
Timbale de Poires à la Valenciennes

Two-thirds fill a buttered *Charlotte-mould* with Savarin paste
(2371). Let the paste rise by fermentation; bake it, and let it cool.

Remove the top which acts as a cover, and put it aside; then
remove all of the soft crumb from the inside, leaving only the out-

side crust, and coat it with apricot syrup. Decorate with alternate bands of sugar grains and chopped, very green pistachios.

Brush the cover with apricot syrup and decorate it in the same way. Quarter some "Duchesse," Beurré," "Doyenné," "Bartlett" or other creamy pears; peel them; cut them into somewhat thick slices, and cook them in butter after the manner of Pommes à Charlotte (2436). When the pears are well cooked, mix with them a quarter of their weight of apricot jam, and flavor with vanilla liqueur.

Serve the *timbale* with this preparation; put its cover on, and set it on a warm dish.

Serve a Kirsch-flavored apricot sauce (2410) separately.

APPLES (POMMES)

2588—APPLE FRITTERS   *Beignets de Pommes*

Take some russet apples, which are the best for the purpose, and make a hole through their centers with a corer. Peel them and cut them into round slices one-third of an inch thick, and steep them for twenty minutes in powdered sugar and brandy or rum.

A few minutes before serving, dry them slightly; dip the slices into thin batter, and plunge them into plenty of hot fat. Drain them, set them on a tray, sprinkle them with icing sugar, *glaze* them quickly, and serve them on a napkin.

2589—APPLES WITH BUTTER   *Pommes au Beurre*

Core some gray Calville baldwins, pippins or russet apples; peel them and parboil them for two minutes in boiling water, containing a little lemon juice. Then set them in a buttered saucepan; add a few tablespoons of vanilla-flavored syrup, and cook them covered in the oven. Serve them on little, round, brioche *croûtons, glazed* in the oven, and fill the hollow with butter kneaded with an equal weight of powdered sugar, and mixed with a little brandy.

Cover the apples with their own syrup, slightly thickened with apricot *purée*.

2590—BONNE-FEMME APPLES   *Pommes Bonne-Femme*

Core some russet apples and slightly cut them all round.

Place on a dish; fill the hollow of each with butter and powdered sugar mixed; pour a little water into the dish, and gently cook the apples in the oven.

Serve these apples as they stand.

2591—BOURDALOUE APPLES   *Pommes Bourdaloue*

Quarter, peel and trim the apples, and cook them in vanilla-flavored syrup, keeping them somewhat firm. Proceed for the rest of the operation as directed under (2549).

2592—APPLE CHARLOTTE   *Pommes en Charlotte*

See (2436).

2593—CHATELAINE APPLES   *Pommes Châtelaine*

Take some medium-sized apples, and prepare them like those of (2590). Set them on a buttered dish; fill the hollow in each with a *salpicon* of half-sugared cherries, combined with apricot *purée;* cover with thin, *frangipan* cream; sprinkle with crushed sponge cake and macaroons and melted butter, and set the *gratin* to form in a hot oven.

2594—CHEVREUSE APPLES   *Pommes Chevreuse*

On a dish, set a bed of a preparation for semolina croquettes (2453). All round arrange a close border of quartered apples cooked in vanilla-flavored syrup; fill the center with a *salpicon* of candied fruit and raisins, combined with an apricot *purée,* and cover with a thin coat of semolina.

Cover the whole with ordinary *meringue,* peaked; sprinkle some chopped pistachios upon the latter; dredge with icing sugar, and set to brown in a mild oven.

On taking the dish out of the oven decorate the top of the peak with a rosette of elongated angelica diamonds; place a small apple, cooked in pink syrup, in the middle of the rosette, and surround the base of the dessert with a circle of alternated white and pink, quartered apples.

2595—CONDE APPLES   *Pommes Condé*

Poach some fine, peeled and trimmed apples in vanilla-flavored syrup. Serve them on a border of rice, decorated with cherries and angelica, as explained under (2551).

2596—GRATIN APPLES   *Pommes Gratinées*

Set the quartered apples, *poached* in vanilla-flavored syrup, upon a base of minced apples prepared as for a *Charlotte* and kept somewhat stiff. Cover with fairly thin *pralin à Condé;* sprinkle with icing sugar, and place the dish in a mild oven, that the *pralin* may dry and color slightly.

2597—MERINGUED APPLES *Pommes Meringuées*

Set the quartered apples, *poached* in vanilla-flavored syrup, upon a base of rice for croquettes, or of a mince as for a *Charlotte*. Cover with ordinary *meringue,* and smooth the latter, giving it the shape of a dome or a *Charlotte;* decorate with the same *meringue;* sprinkle with icing sugar, and bake and brown in a mild oven.

2598—MUSCOVITE APPLES *Pommes Muscovite*

Take some well-shaped apples, uniform in size; trim to within two-thirds of their height, and take out the pulp from their insides in such a way as to make each resemble a kind of case.

Poach these cases in a thin syrup, keeping the pulp somewhat firm; drain them well, and set them on a dish.

Fill them, one-third full, with a *purée* made from the apple pulp, and fill them up with a Kümmel-flavored, apple-*soufflé* preparation (2405).

Cook in a mild oven for twenty minutes.

2599—PARISIENNE APPLES *Pommes à la Parisienne*

Proceed exactly as for (2584).

2600—PORTUGUESE APPLES *Pommes à la Portugaise*

Make cases of the apples as under (2598), and *poach* them in the same way, keeping them somewhat firm.

Fill them with stiff *frangipan* cream, combined with grated orange rind, crushed macaroons, and currants and sultana raisins (both washed and plumped in a Curaçao-flavored, lukewarm syrup).

Arrange these filled apples on a base of semolina-croquette (2453) preparation, and set them in the oven for ten minutes. On taking them out of the oven, coat their surface with melted red currant jelly, combined with a fine *julienne* of well-parboiled orange-*zest*.

2601—APPLE DUMPLING OR DOUILLON NORMAN
Rabotte de Pommes ou Douillon Norman

Prepare the apples like those "à la Bonne-femme" (2590), and enclose each in a layer of fine, short paste. Cover each dumpling with a scalloped round slice of the same paste; brush with egg; streak with a fork, and bake in a hot oven for fifteen minutes.

2602—APPLES IRENE *Pommes Irène*

Select some nice apples; peel them, and cook them in syrup, keeping them somewhat firm. When they are cold, carefully remove their pulp, that they may form cases.

Rub the pulp through a sieve, sugar it with vanilla sugar (2438), and spread a layer of it on the bottom of each apple. Fill up the apple-cases with vanilla ice, combined with a *purée* of cooked plums; the proportions being one-third of the latter to one of the former.

Cover this ice with Kirsch-flavored Italian *meringue* (2383); set the latter to brown quickly, and serve instantly.

2603—NINON HOT APPLE PIE   *Flan de Pommes Chaud Ninon*

Prepare a baked pie crust without browning. Fill it with apples stewed as for a *Charlotte,* and shape these in the form of a dome. Upon these stewed apples set pink and white quartered apples, alternating the latter regularly; and, with a brush delicately coat these quarters of apple with some reduced white syrup.

2604—APPLE PIE A LA BATELIERE   *Flan de Pommes à la Batelière*

Line a spring form with some short paste, and fill it with apples, stewed as for a *Charlotte.*

Cover the apples with a dome of somewhat creamy rice for desserts, combined with the whites of four eggs beaten to a stiff froth per lb. of cooked rice.

Bake the deep pie in the usual way, and, on taking it out of the oven, sprinkle it copiously with icing sugar, and *glaze* with a red-hot iron.

Various Hot Desserts

2605—MINCE PIES   *Mince Pies*

Ingredients.—One lb. of chopped beef suet; one and one-third lbs. of cold, cooked fillet of beef, cut into very small dice; one lb. of seeded raisins; one lb. of currants and an equal quantity of sultana raisins; one lb. of candied peel; half lb. of peeled and chopped raw apples; the chopped *zest* and the juice of an orange; two-thirds oz. of allspice; one-sixth pint of brandy; and the same measure of Madeira and rum.

Thoroughly mix the whole; pour it into an earthenware jar; cover the latter, and let the preparation steep for a month.

Preparation.—Line some deep, buttered *tartlet moulds* with ordinary short paste; fill them with the above preparation; cover with a thin layer of puff-paste, having a hole in its centre; seal down this layer. brush with egg, and bake in a hot oven.

2606—CELESTINE OMELET   *Omelette Célestine*

Make an omelet from two eggs, and fill it either with cream, stewed fruit or jam. Make a somewhat larger omelet, and stuff it with a different filling from the one already used; enclose the first omelet in the second, and roll the latter up in the usual way. Sprinkle with icing sugar, and *glaze* in the oven or with a red-hot iron.

2607—EGGS A LA RELIGIEUSE   *Oeufs à la Religieuse*

Bake a somewhat deep pie-crust without browning, and have it of a size in proportion to the number of eggs it has to hold. Coat it inside with a layer of *pralin,* and dry the latter well in a mild oven.

Meanwhile *poach* the required number of fresh eggs in boiling milk, sugared to the extent of a quarter lb. per quart, and keep them somewhat soft. Drain them, and set them in the crust. Between each egg place a small slice of pineapple, cut to the shape of a cock's comb. Thicken the *poaching*-milk with five eggs and six egg-yolks per quart; pass it through a strainer: pour the preparation over the eggs, and put the deep pie in a mild oven, that the cream may be *poached* and slightly browned.

2608—GILDED CRUST (PAIN PERDU)   *Pain Perdu*

Cut some slices one-half inch thick from a brioche or a stale loaf of bread and dip them in cold sugared and vanilla-flavored milk. Drain the slices; dip them in some slightly-sugared beaten eggs, and place them in a frying-pan containing some very hot clarified butter (175). Brown them on both sides; drain them; sprinkle them with vanilla sugar, and serve them on a napkin.

2609—GABRIELLE FRUIT SUPREME   *Suprême de Fruits Gabrielle*

Prepare a border of apples, stewed as for a *Charlotte* thickened with eggs, and *poached* in a buttered and ornamented border mould.

Also a *macédoine* of fruit, the quantity of which should be in proportion to the capacity of the mould and consisting of quartered pears, cooked in syrup; pineapple, cut into large diamonds; half-sugared cherries; angelica, stamped into leaf-shapes by means of the fancy-cutter; and currants and sultana raisins, plumped in syrup. Set all these fruits in a saucepan.

To every pint of the pear-syrup add one lb. of sugar, and cook the mixture to the *small-ball* (236° F.) stage. This done, reduce it by adding one-sixth pint of very thick almond milk (2506); pour this over the fruit, and simmer very gently for ten minutes. Turn out the border of apples, *poached* in a *bain-marie* (water-bath), upon a dish, and surround it with a border of candied cherries. Complete the *macédoine* away from the fire with a little very best butter; pour it into the border, and sprinkle on it some peeled and finely-slivered almonds.

2610—JEWISH SCHALETH   *Schâleth à la Juive*

Line a greased iron saucepan, or a large mould for "Pommes Anna," with a thin layer of ordinary noodle paste (2291), and fill it up with the following preparation:—For a utensil large enough to hold one and a half quarts:—one and three quarter lbs. of thickly stewed russet apples; one and a quarter lbs. in all of seeded Malaga raisins, currants, and sultana raisins (plumped in tepid water) in equal quantities; the finely grated *zests* of half an orange and a half lemon; a bit of grated nutmeg; four oz. of powdered sugar; four whole eggs and the yolks of six; and a quarter of a pint of Malaga wine. Mix the whole well, in advance.

Cover with a layer of the noodle paste; seal the latter well down round the edges; brush with egg, and make a slit in the top for the escape of steam. Bake it in a moderate oven for fifty minutes, and let it rest ten minutes before turning it out.

2611—ENGLISH FRUIT TARTS   *Tartes de Fruits à l'Anglaise*

These tarts are made in deep pie or pastry-dishes or forms. Whatever be the fruit used, clean it, peel it, or core it, according to its nature. Some fruits are sliced while others are merely quartered or left whole.

Set them in the dish, to within half inch of its brim; sprinkle them with moist or powdered sugar, and (in the case of fruit with firm pulps like apples) with a few tablespoons of water.

This addition of water is optional and, in any case, may be dispensed with for very juicy fruits. First cover the edges of the dish, which should be moistened slightly, with a strip of short paste, an inch wide. Then cover the dish with a layer of puff-paste, which seal down well to the strip of paste, already in position and slightly moistened for the purpose. With a brush moisten the layer of paste constituting the cover of the tart; sprinkle it with sugar, and set the tart to bake in a moderate oven.

All English tarts are made in this way, and all fruits may be used with them even when, as in the case of gooseberries, they are green.

Accompany these tarts by a sauceboat of fresh-cream or by a custard pudding (2406).

COLD DESSERTS

2612—SAUCES AND ACCOMPANIMENT OF COLD SWEETS
Sauces et Accompagnements d'Entremets Froids

Cold sweets allow of the following sauces:—

English Custard (2397), flavored according to taste.

Syrups of apricot, of mirabelle plums, of greengages, of red-currant, etc., the particular flavor of which should always be intensified by the addition of a liqueur in keeping with the fruit forming the base of the syrup. Kirsch and Maraschino are admirably suited to this purpose.

Purées of fresh fruit, such as strawberries, raspberries, red-currants, etc., combined with a little powdered sugar, and used plain or mixed with a little whipped cream.

Chantilly or Whipped Cream, flavored as taste may suggest.

Finally, certain desserts permit of the following sauce:—

2613—CHERRY SAUCE *Sauce aux Cerises*

Gently melt one lb. of raspberry-flavored red-currant jelly. Pour it into a cold bowl, and add to it an equal quantity of freshly-prepared cherry juice, the juice of two blood-oranges, a little powdered ginger, and a few drops of carmine; the latter with the view of giving the preparation a sufficiently strong and distinctive color. Finally add a quarter of a lb. of half-sugared cherries, softened in a tepid, Kirsch-flavored syrup (2418).

BAVARIAN CREAMS

These are of two kinds:—

Bavarian with cream, and Bavarian with fruit.

2614—BAVARIAN CREAM *Bavarois*

Preparation: Work one lb. of granulated sugar with fourteen egg-yolks in a saucepan, dilute with a pint and a half of boiled milk, in which a stick of vanilla has previously been steeped, and two-thirds of an oz. of gelatine dipped in cold water.

Put the preparation on a mild fire until it properly coats the withdrawn spoon, and do not let it boil. Pass it through the strainer into an enamelled bowl; let it cool, stirring it from time to time; and, when it begins to thicken, add one and a half pints of whipped cream, three oz. of powdered sugar, and two-thirds oz. of vanilla sugar (2349).

2615—BAVARIAN CREAM WITH FRUITS   *Bavarois aux Fruits*

Ingredients.—One pint of fruit *purée* diluted with one pint of syrup at 30° (saccharom.). Add the juice of three lemons, one oz. of dissolved gelatine, strained through linen, and one pint of whipped cream. The preparation for fruit Bavarians may be combined with fruit of the same nature as that used for the *purée;* and this fruit may be added raw in the case of strawberries, raspberries, red-currants, etc., and *poached* in the case of pulpy fruits, such as pears, peaches, apricots, etc.

2616—THE MOULDING AND DRESSING OF BAVARIAN CREAM
Moulage et Dressage de Bavarois

Bavarian creams are generally moulded in fancy moulds fitted with a central tube, slightly greased with sweet almond oil. When they are greased they are incrusted in cracked ice after the preparation has been covered with a round sheet of white paper.

When about to serve, the mould is quickly plunged into tepid water, wiped, and turned out upon a dish, which may or may not be covered with a folded napkin.

Instead of oiling the moulds they may be covered with a thin coat of sugar cooked to the *caramel* (360° F.) stage, which besides making the Bavarian cream appetizing, also gives it an excellent taste. Another very advisable method is that of serving the Bavarian cream in a deep silver *timbale* or dish, surrounded with ice. In this case, the dessert not having to be turned out, does not need to be so thick in consistency, and is therefore much more delicate.

When the Bavarian cream is served after this last method it is sometimes accompanied by stewed fruit or a *Macédoine* of fresh fruit; though, in reality, these fruit accompaniments are better suited to cold puddings, which, in some points, are not unlike Bavarian creams.

Finally, when the Bavarian cream is moulded, it may be decorated, just before being served, with whipped cream piped on with a pastry-bag fitted with a fancy tube.

2617—CLERMONT BAVARIAN CREAM *Bavarois Clermont*

Take some vanilla-flavored Bavarian cream preparation combined with three oz. of candied chestnut *purée* and three oz. of candied chestnuts, broken into small pieces, per pint of the preparation.

Having turned out the Bavarian cream, surround it with a crown of fine glacé chestnuts.

2618—DIPLOMAT BAVARIAN CREAM *Bavarois Diplomate*

Coat a *timbale mould* with a layer of vanilla-flavored Bavarian cream preparation. Fill it with chocolate and strawberry Bavarian cream preparations, spread in alternate and regular layers.

2619—MY QUEEN BAVARIAN CREAM *Bavarois My Queen*

Coat a Bavarian cream mould with a preparation of slightly-sugared fresh cream, combined with dissolved gelatine. Then fill up the mould with a Bavarian cream preparation, made from strawberry *purée* and combined with large strawberries, steeped in Kirsch. When the dessert is turned out surround it with a border of large strawberries, also steeped in sugar and Kirsch.

2620—BAVARIAN CREAM A LA RELIGIEUSE *Bavarois à la Religieuse*

Coat a mould with some chocolate dissolved in a syrup containing a somewhat large proportion of gelatine. Fill the inside of the mould with a vanilla-flavored Bavarian cream preparation, made from plain instead of whipped cream.

2621—"RUBANNE" BAVARIAN CREAM *Bavarois Rubanné*

This kind of Bavarian cream is made from differently-colored and differently-flavored preparations, spread in alternate layers in the mould.

It is therefore governed by no hard and fast rules, and every kind of Bavarian cream preparation may be used.

2622—VARIOUS BAVARIAN CREAMS *Bavarois Divers*

Almond, anisette, filbert, coffee, chocolate, Kirsch, fresh walnut, orange, and violet Bavarian creams, etc., may be prepared after (2614); the flavor alone undergoing any change.

2623—VARIOUS FRUIT BAVARIAN CREAMS
Bavarois aux Fruits Divers

After the general recipe, Bavarian cream may be prepared from pineapple, apricots, strawberries, raspberries, melon, etc.

2624—BLANC-MANGE   *Blanc-Manger*

Blanc-mange is scarcely ever served nowadays, and this is a pity; seeing that, when it is well prepared, it is one of the best desserts that can be set before a diner. Blanc-mange, as it is prepared in England, is quite different from that generally served; but it is nevertheless an excellent and very wholesome dessert, and that is why I have given its recipe below.

As a matter of fact, in order to justify its name, blanc-mange ought always to be beautifully white; but, for a long time since, the compound word has lost its original meaning. The adjective and noun composing it have fused one with the other to form a single general title, which may now be applied with equal propriety to both colored and white preparations; and the verbal error is so old, dating as it does from pre-Carême times, that it would be futile to try and correct it.

2625—FRENCH BLANC-MANGE   *Blanc-Manger à la Française*

Preparation.—Skin one lb. of sweet almonds and four or five bitter almonds, and soak them well in fresh water that they may be quite white.

Pound them as finely as possible; adding to them a spoonful at a time, one pint of water. Strain the whole through a strong towel, twisting the latter tightly; melt one lb. of sugar in the almond milk (about one and half pints); add a scant oz. of gelatine dissolved in tepid syrup; strain the whole through muslin, and flavor according to taste.

Moulding:—Mould the blanc-mange in oiled moulds with center-tubes (funnels) as for Bavarian creams. Incrust them in ice that their contents may set, and proceed for the turning-out as already directed.

N.B.—For the preparation of almond milk, modern Cookery has substituted for the procedure given above, which is antiquated, another which consists in pounding the almonds with only a few tablespoons of water and some very thin cream.

2626—BLANC-MANGE WITH FRUIT AND LIQUEURS
Blancs-Mangers aux Fruits et aux Liqueurs

All fruits, reduced to *purées,* may serve in the preparation of blanc-manges, and the apportioning of the ingredients should be as follows. The *purée* of the selected fruit and the preparation given above (including the same amount of gelatine) should be mixed in equal quantities.

These blanc-manges take the name of the fruit with which they are prepared: strawberries, raspberries, apricots, peaches, etc. They may also be prepared with liqueurs, which should be in the proportion of one liqueur glass to one quart of the preparation. The best liqueurs for the purpose are Kirsch, Maraschino and Rum.

Blanc-manges are also made from chocolate and coffee, although the flavor of the latter does not blend so well with that of almonds as do the other products.

2627—BLANC-MANGES "RUBANNES"　　*Blanc-Mangers Rubannés*

Prepare these as directed under (2621), spreading the differently flavored and colored blanc-mange preparations in alternate even and regular layers.

N.B.—Blanc-mange preparations may also be served in silver *timbales,* in good china or glass dishes, or in deep pie dishes. By this means, to the great improvement of the preparation, the gelatine may be reduced to a minimum quantity, just enough to ensure the setting of the blanc-mange and no more. And the thing is quite possible inasmuch as there is no question of turning out the dessert.

In his book "The Parisian Cook," Carême recommends the addition to the Blanc-mange of a quarter of its volume of very fresh, good cream; and the advice, coming as it does from such an authoritative source, is worth following.

2628—ENGLISH BLANC-MANGE　　*Blanc-Manger à l'Anglaise*

Boil one quart of milk, containing four oz. of sugar, and pour it over a quarter of a lb. of corn meal diluted with half a pint of cold milk; stirring briskly the while.

Smooth the preparation with the whisk, and cook it over an open fire for a few minutes, without ceasing to stir.

On taking it off the fire, flavor it according to taste; and pour it, very hot, into moulds previously moistened with syrup, that the mouldings may turn out glossy and smooth.

Let the contents of the moulds set; turn them out, and serve them very cold either plain or with an accompaniment of stewed fruit.

CHARLOTTES

2629— HARLEQUIN CHARLOTTE　　*Charlotte à l'Arléquine*

Line the bottom of a *Charlotte mould* with a round piece of paper, and fill the sides with upright pieces of *Génoise, glazed* white, pink and pale-green; alternating the colors and pressing them snugly one against the other. Meanwhile, take some strawberry, chocolate, pistachio and apricot Bavarian cream preparations, and let them set in flat spring forms, lying on pieces of oiled paper.

Cut the Bavarian cream preparations into large dice, and mix them with an ordinary, and somewhat liquid, Bavarian cream preparation. Pour the whole into the mould, and leave to cool. When about to serve, turn out the *Charlotte;* remove the piece of paper and replace it by a thin *Génoise* top, *glazed* with "fondant" (2346) and decorated with candied fruit.

2630—CARMEN CHARLOTTE   *Charlotte Carmen*

Line the *Charlotte* with thin wafers, and fill it with the following preparation:—eight oz. of stewed tomatoes; four oz. of stewed red-sweet peppers, a pinch of powdered ginger, three oz. of candied ginger cut into dice, the juice of three lemons, half a pint of hot syrup at 32° (saccharom.), and about three ounces of dissolved gelatine.

Mix up the whole, and, when the preparation begins to thicken, add to it one and three-quarter pints of whipped cream.

2631—CHANTILLY (WHIPPED CREAM) CHARLOTTE
Charlotte Chantilly

Prepare the *Charlotte* with *gaufrettes* (thin wafers), stuck directly upon a round base of dry paste, either with apricot jam cooked to the *small-thread* stage (215° F.) or with sugar cooked to the *small-crack* stage (285° F.). As a help, a *Charlotte mould* may be used for this operation; it may be laid on the dry-paste base and removed when the *gaufrettes* are all stuck.

Garnish with whipped, sugared and vanilla-flavored cream built up in pyramid-form, and decorate its surface, by means of a spoon, with the same cream, slightly tinted with pink.

2632—BUCKET AND BASKET WITH WHIPPED CREAM
Baquet et Panier Chantilly

A "bucket" is made with sponge lady's finger, well trimmed and stuck upon a base of dry paste with sugar cooked to the *large-crack* stage (315° F.).

In the middle, and on either side of the bucket, set a "lady finger," somewhat higher than the rest, with a hole in its top end, cut by means of a small round cutter; and surround the bucket with small bands of chocolate-flavored almond paste, in imitation of iron hoops.

The "basket" is made in the same way, but with sponge "lady fingers" all of the same size, and without the imitation iron-hoops. On the base and by means of sugar cooked to the *large-crack* stage (315° F.), fix a handle of pulled sugar, decorated with sugar flowers.

The "bucket" and the "basket" are filled with the same cream as the Chantilly Charlotte, and are finished in the same way, with a decoration of pink-tinted cream.

2633—MONTREUIL CHARLOTTE   *Charlotte Montreuil*

Line the bottom and sides of the mould with sponge lady fingers. Fill with a Bavarian cream preparation consisting of one pint of peach *purée* per quart of English custard (2624), and the usual quantity of whipped cream.

Add some very ripe, sliced and sugared peaches, on putting the preparation into the mould.

2634—OPERA CHARLOTTE   *Charlotte Opéra*

Line a mould with Perfetto or Nabisco sugar wafers and garnish it with a vanilla-flavored Bavarian cream preparation, combined with one-quarter of its bulk of a smooth *purée* of glacé chestnuts, and a *salpicon* of candied fruit, steeped in Maraschino.

2635—PLOMBIERE CHARLOTTE   *Charlotte Plombière*

Line the Charlotte with sponge lady fingers or with *gaufrettes*. When about to serve, garnish it with a Plombière ice (2795) and turn it out upon a napkin.

2636—RENAISSANCE CHARLOTTE   *Charlotte Renaissance*

Line the bottom of the mould with a round piece of white paper, and the sides with rectangles of *Génoise, glazed* white and pink. Set the *glazed* sides of the rectangles against the mould.

Fill the mould, thus lined, with a vanilla-flavored Bavarian cream preparation, combined with raw peeled and sliced apricots and peaches, pineapple cut into dice, and wild strawberries, all these fruits having been previously steeped in Kirsch. Let the preparation set in a cool place or on ice.

When the *Charlotte* is turned out, remove the round piece of paper, and in its place lay a slice of pineapple, cut from the thickest part of the fruit and decorated with candied fruit.

2637—CHARLOTTE RUSSE   *Charlotte Russe*

Make a rosette on the bottom of the mould with some heart-shaped sponge lady fingers, and line the sides with the same, trimmed, set upright and close together.

This *Charlotte* may be filled with a vanilla-, *pralin-*, coffee-, orange- or chocolate-flavored Bavarian cream preparation; or a Bavarian cream preparation made from a *purée* of such fruits as apricots, pineapple, bananas, peaches, strawberries, etc.

The flavor or product which determines the character of the *Charlotte* should always be referred to on the menu, thus: *Charlotte Russe à l'Orange* or *Charlotte Russe aux Fraises,* etc.

2638—CREAMS   *Crèmes*

Cold creams, served as desserts, belong to two very distinct classes: *Cooked Creams,* which are, in short, but a variety of custard.

The Creams derived from natural, fresh cream, whipped and sugared, the general type of which is Chantilly cream (2402).

Cooked Creams are prepared either in special little pots, in small silver or porcelain bowls, or in moulds. Those prepared in moulds are turned out when they are quite cold, and are called *"Crèmes renversées"* to distinguish them from the first two kinds which are always served in the utensil in which they have cooked.

For all that, the term *"Crème renversée"* has grown somewhat obsolete, and the modern expression for this kind of custard is *"Crème moulée."*

Crème au Caramel represents a perfect type of this class.

The custards served in their cooking-receptacles are more delicate than the others, because their preparation does not demand such a large quantity of eggs; but they are only served in the home. For a stylish luncheon or dinner, moulded custards (Fr. crèmes moulées) are best.

2639—MOULDED VANILLA CREAM   *Crème Moulée à la Vanille*

Boil one quart of milk containing one-half lb. of sugar; add a stick of vanilla, and let the latter steep for twenty minutes. Pour this milk, little by little, over three eggs and eight yolks, previously beaten in a bowl, and whisk briskly. Pass the whole through a fine sieve; let it rest for a moment or two; then completely remove all the froth on its surface, and pour the preparation into buttered custard cups or into little covered pots specially made for this purpose. Set to *poach* in a *bain-marie* (water-bath), in a moderate oven, keeping lids on the utensils.

Not for one moment must the water in the *bain-marie* boil while the *poaching* is in progress; for the air contained by the preparation would then become over-heated, and the result would be an innumerable amount of small holes throughout the depth of the custard, which would greatly mar its appearance.

As a matter of fact, the custard should *poach,* that is to say, coagulate, as the result of the surrounding water being kept at a constant temperature of 185° F. As soon as it is *poached,* let the custard cool.

When it is *poached* in the utensils in which it is served, one egg and eight yolks per quart of milk will be found sufficient. The utensils should be carefully wiped and placed on a napkin.

If the custard is to be turned out, carefully overturn the custard cup upon a dish, and pull it off a few minutes later. Moulded and potted custards permit of all the flavorings proper to desserts; but those which suit them best are vanilla, almond milk, almond and filbert *pralin,* coffee, chocolate, etc. Unless used in the form of very concentrated *essences,* fruit flavors are less suited to them.

2640—MOULDED CARAMEL CREAM   *Crème Moulée au Caramel*

Coat the bottom and sides of a mould with sugar cooked to the *golden-caramel* stage (360° F.), and fill it up with a vanilla-flavored, moulded-custard preparation. *Poach* and turn it out as directed.

2641—VIENNA MOULDED CREAM   *Crème Moulée à la Viennoise*

This is a custard with caramel, but instead of coating the mould with the latter, it is dissolved in the hot milk. The custard should be treated exactly like the vanilla-flavored kind.

2642—FLORENTINE MOULDED CREAM *Crème Moulée à la Florentine*

Make a preparation of *pralin*-flavored custard with caramel and *poach* it.

When it is quite cold, turn it out on a dish; decorate it with Kirsch-flavored whipped cream, and sprinkle its surface with chopped pistachios.

2643—OPERA MOULDED CREAM   *Crème Moulée Opéra*

Poach, in an ornamented *border-mould,* a preparation of *pralin*-flavored custard. When it is turned out, garnish its midst with a dome of whipped cream, perfumed with *pralined* violets. Upon the border set a crown of fine strawberries, steeped in a Kirsch-flavored syrup, and cover with a veil of sugar cooked to the *large-crack* stage (315° F.).

Cold Creams with a Whipped-Cream Base

2644—CHANTILLY CREAM   *Crème Chantilly*

Take some fresh and somewhat thick cream, and whisk it until it is sufficiently stiff to span the wires of the whisk. Add to it eight oz. of powdered sugar per quart of cream, and flavor with vanilla or fruit *essence*.

Whatever be the purpose of this cream, it should, if possible, be prepared only at the last moment.

2645—CHANTILLY WHIPPED CREAM WITH FRUIT
Creme Chantilly aux Fruits

The ingredients for this preparation are a *purée* of the selected fruit and whipped cream, in the proportion of one-third of the former to two-thirds of the latter.

The quantities of sugar and kind of flavor vary according to the nature of the fruit.

It is served either as a dessert garnish, or alone in a bowl, with a decoration of the same cream, piped with a pastry-bag fitted with a small even or grooved tube. Send some sponge lady fingers separately.

2646—CAPRICE CREAM   *Crème Caprice*

Take some whipped cream, and add to it one-quarter of its bulk of roughly broken-up *meringues*. Put the preparation in an iced *Madeleine-mould,* lined with white paper; seal up thoroughly; tie tightly, and keep the utensil in ice for two hours.

Turn out when about to serve; remove the paper; and decorate, with a pastry-bag fitted with a fancy tube, with whipped cream, tinted pink with strawberry and raspberry juice.

2647—BRISE DU PRINTEMPS (SPRINGTIME BREEZES)
Brise du Printemps

Take some violet-flavored, slightly-iced whipped cream, and set in small dessert-dishes, by means of a spoon.

2648—NUEES ROSES (SHOWER OF ROSES)   *Roses Nuées*

Take some whipped cream, scented with vanilla-flavored strawberry *purée,* and serve it in small dessert-dishes, by means of a spoon.

2649—FLAMRI *Flamri*

Boil one pint of white wine and as much water, and sprinkle in it eight oz. of small semolina. Cook gently for twenty-five minutes. Then add to the preparation two-thirds lb. of powdered sugar, a pinch of table-salt, two eggs, and the whites of six, beaten to a stiff froth.

Pour it into moulds with buttered sides; set these to *poach* in the *bain-marie* (water-bath), and leave them to cool. Turn out, and coat with a *purée* of raw fruit, such as strawberries, red-currants, cherries, etc., reasonably sugared.

2650—JELLIES *Gelées*

From the standpoint of their preparation, jellies are of two kinds: wine or liqueur-flavored jellies; or fruit jellies. But their base is the same in all cases, gelatine dissolved in a certain quantity of water.

The gelatine should be extracted from calf's foot, by boiling the latter; but, although this is the best that can be obtained, the means of obtaining it are the most complicated. The gelatine bought ready-made may also be used in the quantities given below.

2651—CALF'S-FOOT JELLY *Gelée de Pieds de Veau*

Take some fine soaked and *blanched* calves' feet, and set them to cook in one and three-quarters pints of water apiece. Skim as thoroughly as possible; cover, and then cook very gently for seven hours. This done, strain the cooking-liquor and clear it of all grease; test its strength, after having cooled a little of it on ice; correct it if too thick with sufficient filtered water, and once more test it by means of ice.

Per quart of calf's-foot jelly, add eight oz. of sugar, a bit of cinnamon, half the rind of an orange and lemon, and all their juice.

For the clarification, proceed as directed hereafter.

2652—JELLY WITH GELATINE BASE *Gelée à Base de Gélatine*

Dissolve one oz. of granulated gelatine in a quart of water. Add one-half lb. of sugar, one-sixth oz. of coriander, and the *zest* and juice of half a lemon and of a whole orange; boil, and then let the preparation stand for ten minutes away from the fire.

Whisk one and a half egg-whites in a very clean saucepan, together with a port wine-glass of white wine, and pour the cleared syrup, little by little, over the egg-whites, whisking briskly the while. Set the saucepan on the fire, and continue whisking until the boil is reached; then move the utensil to a corner of the stove, and keep the jelly only just simmering for one-quarter of an hour.

At the end of that time the clarification is completed; strain the jelly through a bag, placed over a very clean bowl, and, if the jelly is cloudy after the first time of straining, strain it again and again until it becomes quite clear. Let it almost cool before adding any flavor.

The Flavoring.—Whether the jelly be prepared from calves feet or from gelatine, the above preparation is nothing more than a combined syrup, to which the addition of some flavor lends the character of a jelly. The complementary ingredients for jellies are liqueurs, good wines, and the juice of fruit; and the quantity of water prescribed should be so reduced as to allow for the ultimate addition of the liquid flavoring.

Thus, every jelly of which the flavor is a liqueur ought to be prepared with only nine-tenths of a quart of water; and the remaining one-tenth of the measure is subsequently added in the form of Kirsch, Maraschino, Rum, or Anisette, etc.

A jelly flavored with a good wine, such as Champagne, Madeira, Sherry, Marsala, etc., should contain only seven-tenths of a quart of water and three-tenths of a quart of the selected wine.

In the case of *fruit jellies,* the procedure differs in accordance with the kind of fruit used.

For *red-fruit jellies,* prepared from strawberries, raspberries, red-currants, cherries, and canberries, these fruits, which should be very ripe, are rubbed through a sieve, and combined with one-tenth to three-tenths of a quart of water per lb., according to whether the fruit be more or less juicy.

This done, filter the resulting juice, and add it to the jelly in the proportion of one part of the former to two parts of the latter. The jelly should therefore be twice as strong as for the previous preparation, in order that it may remain sufficiently consistent in spite of the added juice.

When the fruit is too juicy, rub it through a sieve; let the juice ferment for a few hours, and only filter the clear juice which results from the fermentation.

Juicy-fruit jellies, prepared from grapes, oranges, lemons, and tangerines, are made in the same way. The filtering of these fruit juices is easily done, and, except for the grapes, they need not be set to ferment.

When these fruits are not quite ripe, their juices may be added to the jelly even before the clarification—a procedure which helps to modify their acidity. The apportionment of the fruit juices to the jelly is practically the same as that of the red-fruit juices.

Stone-fruit, such as apricots, peaches, nectarines, plums, etc., are often used as jelly garnishes, but seldom serve as the flavoring base of a jelly. Whenever they are treated in this way, they are first plunged in boiling water, that they may be peeled; they are then *poached* and left to cool in the syrup which goes towards preparing the jelly.

This jelly, after it has been clarified and three-parts cooled, should have a little Kirsch or Maraschino added to it, that its fruit flavor may be intensified.

2653—THE GARNISH AND ACCOMPANIMENTS OF JELLY
Garnitures et Accompagnement des Gelées

As a rule, jellies are served plain. Sometimes, however, they are garnished with variously-shaped, stewed fruits, symmetrically distributed in the jelly, with their colors nicely contrasted.

A jelly prepared in this way is called a "Suédoise of fruit."

2654—"RUBANE" JELLY
Gelées Rubanées

These are differently-flavored and differently-colored jellies moulded in alternate layers, even and equally thick.

They are generally served without garnish.

2655—JELLY A LA RUSSE
Les Gelées à la Russe

These are ordinary jellies which are whisked over ice until they begin to set. They are then speedily moulded. By skilfully mixing two or three of these jellies, of different shades and flavors, at the moment of moulding, very effective "Marbled Jellies" are obtained.

2656—JELLY A LA MUSCOVITE
Les Gelées à la Muscovite

These are ordinary jellies, poured into tightly-closing moulds, the sealing of which is ensured by a thread of butter, laid round the edges of the lids. The moulds are then surrounded with cracked ice, mixed with five lb. of freezing salt and eight oz. of saltpetre per twenty-five lb. of ice.

The cold produced by the salted ice causes a frosted coat to form round the jelly, the effect of which is exceedingly pretty. But the moulds should be removed from the ice as soon as the frosted coat is formed and the jelly is set; for a longer time in the cold would transform the jelly into an uneatable block of ice.

N.B.—Modern methods have greatly simplified the dishing and serving of jellies. They are now served in special silver bowls or deep dishes, and they are not, as a rule, moulded. The bottom of these utensils is sometimes decorated with stewed fruit or *macédoines* of fruit which are covered with the jelly; and, as the latter is served in the utensil itself, the quantity of gelatine may be reduced, and greater delicacy is the result.

2657—FRUIT LOAVES   *Pains de Fruits*

These "pains" (loaves) are made in ordinary *Charlotte*-moulds.

Coat the mould with a fairly thick layer of jelly, in keeping with the flavor of the fruit used, which may be apricots, strawberries, red-currants, cherries, peaches, etc. Fill up the mould with a prep-aration, made as for a fruit Bavarian, but without cream.

The amount of gelatine used should therefore be reduced.

2658—COLD PUDDINGS   *Puddings Froids*

Cold puddings have a great deal in common with Bavarians and, more often than not, these two kinds of desserts have the same base. Their distinguishing difference lies in the fact that Bavarians are generally served without a garnish or sauce, whereas puddings always have either one or the other, and sometimes both.

The sauces for puddings are those given at the beginning of this chapter.

Their garnishes always consist of fruit, and the latter is either stewed and served separately, or it is candied and combined with the pudding paste.

2659—BOHEMIENNE PUDDING   *Pudding Bohémienne*

Make some very small pancakes, and garnish them with a *salpicon* of candied fruits and currants plumped in tepid water, mixed with some fairly stiff, apple *purée*. Fold up the pancakes to the shape of balls or rectangles, and set them in a buttered border-mould. Fill up the mould with a moulded-custard preparation (2639), containing a good proportion of whole eggs, and *poach* in a *bain-marie* (water-bath).

Leave the whole to cool in the mould; turn out at the last mo-ment, and coat the pudding with a *sabayon*, flavored according to taste.

2660—DIPLOMAT PUDDING *Pudding Diplomate*

Decorate the bottom of an oiled deep Bavarian cream mould with pieces of candied fruit. Fill up the mould with alternate layers of vanilla-flavored Bavarian cream preparation and sponge lady fingers, saturated with Kirsch. On each layer of "lady-fingers" sprinkle some currants and raisins plumped in tepid water, and here and there place a tablespoon of apricot jam.

Let the contents of the mould set in a cool place or on ice, and turn out just before serving.

2661—DIPLOMAT FRUIT PUDDING *Pudding Diplomate aux Fruits*

Prepare the pudding as above, but spread a few extra layers of fresh fruit in the mould, such as very ripe pears, peaches, apricots, etc., all peeled, cut into thin slices, and previously steeped with powdered sugar and half a port wine-glass of either Kirsch, Maraschino, or Anisette, etc.

When the pudding is turned out, surround its base with some very cold stewed fruit the same as one of the kinds used inside the pudding, or some stewed, mixed fruit.

2662—MALAKOFF PUDDING *Pudding Malakoff*

Prepare a gelatinous English custard (2397), combined with one pint of very fresh cream per quart; a stew of apples and pears, prepared as for an apple *Charlotte;* currants and sultana raisins, plumped in tepid syrup; fresh slivered almonds; candied orange peel, cut into dice; slices of stale sponge cake, or sponge lady fingers, saturated with liqueur. Oil a *Charlotte* mould, and pour into it a layer of cream half an inch thick. Upon this cream lay a thickness of sponge cake or lady fingers, copiously coated with marmalade, and sprinkle with raisins, almonds and orange peel dice.

Cover with a layer of cream; lay a second thickness of sponge cake and proceed thus in the same order with a Kirsch-flavored cold *sabayon.*

2663—NESSELRODE PUDDING *Pudding Nesselrode*

To an English custard, prepared after (2397), add eight oz. of a smooth, chestnut *purée,* and four oz. of currants and sultana raisins plumped in tepid water, and candied orange peel and cherries, cut into dice; these four products should be in almost equal quantities, and should have been previously steeped in sweetened Madeira.

Add some Maraschino-flavored, whipped cream to the prepara
tion; apportioning it as for a Bavarian cream.

Line the bottom and sides of a *Charlotte* mould with white paper;
pour the preparation into the mould; completely close the latter,
sealing the lid down with a thread of butter, and surround the
utensil with plenty of salted ice. When about to serve, turn out on
a napkin; remove the paper, and surround the base of the pudding
with a crown of fine, glacé chestnuts, or balls of chocolate-iced, glacé
chestnut *purée*.

N.B.—The English custard may be packed in the freezer, mixed
with whipped cream when it is almost congealed, and then placed
in a mould.

2664—RICHELIEU PUDDING *Pudding Richelieu*

Rub some stewed prunes through a fine sieve, and add to the
purée equal quantities of very stiff, Kirsch-flavored jelly and the
reduced juice of the prunes. Let a layer three-quarters of an inch
thick, of the preparation set on the bottom of a *Charlotte* mould.
In the latter set a small mould, filled with broken ice, and either
fitted with handles that can rest on the brim of the first mould, or
else sufficiently deep to be easily grasped and removed when necessary. The space between the sides of the two moulds should measure
about three-quarters of an inch.

Fill up this space with what remains of the prune *purée*, thickened with jelly; leave the preparation to set; remove the ice from
the little mould; pour some tepid water into the latter, that it may
be immediately detached from the surrounding, iced preparation.

Fill the space left by the withdrawn mould with some vanilla-
flavored Bavarian cream preparation; leave to set, and turn out at
the last moment on a napkin.

2665—FAIRY QUEEN PUDDING OR CREAM

Pudding ou Crème Reine des Fées

Prepare the whites of four eggs as for Italian *meringue* (2383),
and add to the sugar, while cooking, its bulk of quince jelly, and,
at the last moment, one and a half ounces of candied fruit, cut into
dice, steeped in Kirsch and carefully drained. Set the *meringue*, in
shapes resembling large buttons, on a sheet of paper.

Boil in a utensil large enough to take the sheet of paper, four
quarts of water, containing two and a half lb. of sugar and one-
quarter pint of Kirsch. Slip the sheet of paper into this boiling
syrup; withdraw it as soon as it easily separates from the pieces

of *meringue; poach* them; drain them on a piece of linen and let them cool.

Meanwhile, make two Bavarian cream preparations; one white and vanilla-flavored, and the other pink and flavored with Curaçao. In these preparations the quantity of whipped cream should be twice as much as for ordinary Bavarian cream, whereas the quantity of gelatine should be reduced by half.

Set these preparations in even, alternate layers, in a slightly-oiled iced-*Madeleine mould,* distributing the *meringues* between each layer.

Cover the mould with a piece of paper and a lid, and keep it surrounded by ice for two hours. When about to serve, turn it out on a napkin.

COLD FRUIT ENTREMETS

Apricots (Abricots)

2666—PARISIENNE APRICOTS   *Abricots à la Parisienne*
Poach the halved apricots in vanilla-flavored syrup. Cool them and drain them; and reconstruct the apricots by joining the halves together with a piece of vanilla ice-cream, the size of a walnut, in the center.

Set these apricots upon some large overturned macaroons; cover with vanilla-flavored whipped cream, shaped like a cone and sprinkle with fine filbert *pralin.*

2667—ROYALE APRICOTS   *Abricots à la Royale*
Take some fairly deep *tartlet moulds,* and set in them some fine, cold, half-apricots, *poached* in vanilla-flavored syrup. Fill up the *tartlet* moulds with very transparent, Kirsch-flavored jelly.

Prepare a shallow, *Génoise* border, *glazed* with red-currant jelly, cooked to the *small-thread* stage (215° F.), and sprinkle with chopped pistachios.

Turn out the *tartlets* of apricot jelly and place them in a crown over the border. Fill the center of the latter with chopped anisette-flavored pink jelly.

PINEAPPLE (ANANAS)

2668—GEORGETTE PINEAPPLE　　　*Ananas Georgette*

Take a fine pineapple, and hollow it out to within half an inch of its outside all round and at the bottom. Put aside the slice cut from the top, on which is the bunch of leaves.

Fill the inside with a Bavarian cream preparation made from pineapple *purée,* combined with the removed pineapple, cut into thin slices, and leave to set. Place on a napkin, and return the top slice to the pineapple, that it may seem untouched.

2669—VIRGINIA PINEAPPLE　　　*Ananas Virginie*

Proceed exactly as above, but replace the pineapple Bavarian cream preparation by a strawberry kind, combined, as before, with the flesh removed from the inside of the pineapple, cut in dice.

2670—NINON PINEAPPLE　　　*Ananas Ninon*

Line the sides of a *soufflé timbale* with vanilla ice-cream, laying it in an oblique strip from the edge of the utensil to the center of the bottom of the *timbale.* Upon this layer of ice-cream set two or three rows of thin pineapple slices, in such a way as to make the slices of the last row project beyond the edge of the *timbale.*

In the center of the mould build a pyramid of wild strawberries; cover this with a raspberry *purée,* and sprinkle with chopped pistachios.

2670a—ROYALE PINEAPPLE　　　*Ananas à la Royale*

Take a fresh pineapple and cut a slice from its top, containing the bunch of leaves. Scoop the pulp from the inside, and leave a thickness of about half an inch all round and on the bottom.

Fill it with a *macédoine* of fresh fruit steeped in Kirsch; set it in the middle of a crystal bowl; and surround the base with a crown of fine peaches, *poached* in a vanilla-flavored syrup, alternated by large strawberries, steeped in Kirsch.

Return the bunch of leaves to its place upon the pineapple.

CHERRIES (CERISES)

2671—DU BARRY CHERRIES　　　*Cerises DuBarry*

Line a small round spring form with good, short paste; set it on baking-sheet; prick the paste on the bottom to prevent its blistering while baking, sprinkle with powdered sugar, and fill with fine, pitted cherries, pressed snugly one against the other.

Bake the crust with cherries in the usual way and let it cool.

When it is quite cold cover the cherries with whipped cream, combined either with ordinary *pralin* or with crushed macaroons.

Smooth the surface of the cream, as also the sides of the crust; cover it with crushed powdered macaroon, and then decorate by means of the pastry-bag with white and pink whipped cream.

2672—CHERRIES IN CLARET *Cerises au Vin Rouge*

Select some fine cherries; cut off the ends of their stems, and set them in a silver *timbale*. Pour sufficient sweetened Bordeaux wine (flavored with a bit of cinnamon) over them, to just cover them. Close the *timbale,* and keep it on the side of the fire for ten minutes, that the cherries may *poach*.

Let them cool in the syrup; drain the latter away; reduce it by a third, and add, in order to thicken it slightly, one tablespoon of red-currant jelly per six tablespoons of reduced syrup.

Serve the cherries quite cold, and some sponge lady fingers separately.

STRAWBERRIES (FRAISES)

2673—CREOLE STRAWBERRIES *Fraises à la Créole*

Set some fine strawberries and an equal amount of pineapple, cut into dice, to steep in powdered sugar and Kirsch.

Arrange a close crown of pineapple slices, also steeped in Kirsch, upon a large shallow compote dish. In the middle of the crown build a pyramid of the strawberries and pineapple, and sprinkle with a Kirsch-flavored syrup.

2674—FEMINA STRAWBERRIES *Fraises Fémina*

Select some fine strawberries; sprinkle them with sugar and Grand-Marnier Curaçao, and leave them to steep on ice for an hour.

When about to serve, spread on the bottom of a bowl or *timbale* a layer of orange-ice (which should be combined with the steeping liqueur) and set the strawberries on the ices.

2675—MARGUERITE STRAWBERRIES *Fraises Marguerite*

Set some wild strawberries to steep in sugar and Kirsch. Drain them; combine them with an equal quantity of pomegranate sher-

bet; set them in a silver *timbale,* already surrounded with ice, cover
the strawberries with Maraschino-flavored whipped cream, and
decorate with the latter.

2676—MARQUISE STRAWBERRIES   *Fraises Marquise*
Set in a *timbale* surrounded with ice some whipped cream, combined with half its bulk of a *purée* of wild strawberries. Completely
cover this cream with fine, fair-sized selected strawberries steeped
with Kirsch, rolled at the last minute in granulated sugar.

2677—MELBA STRAWBERRIES   *Fraises Melba*
Fill the bottom of a *timbale* with vanilla ice-cream. Upon this
arrange a layer of choice strawberries, and cover the latter with
a thick, slightly-sugared, fresh raspberry *purée.*

2678—NINA STRAWBERRIES   *Fraises Nina*
Prepare the strawberries as directed under (2675), and mix
them with pineapple sherbet. Serve them as before in a *timbale,*
and cover them with some whipped cream, tinted pink with a red-
pimento *purée* flavored with ginger.

2679—ROMANOFF STRAWBERRIES   *Fraises Romanoff*
Steep some fine strawberries with orange juice and Curaçao. Set
them in a *timbale* surrounded with ice, and cover them with
whipped cream, piped on with a pastry-bag, fitted with a large,
grooved pipe.

2680—WILHELMINA STRAWBERRIES   *Fraises Wilhelmine*
Steep some fine, large strawberries with Kirsch, powdered sugar,
and orange juice. Put them in a *timbale* and serve a vanilla-flavored whipped cream separately.

2681—LERINA STRAWBERRIES   *Fraises Lérina*
Take a small black melon of Carmes or a fine cantaloup; open it
by cutting out a bung-shaped piece containing the stalk, and remove
all its seeds. Then scoop out all the pulp, with a dessert-spoon, and
sprinkle it with powdered sugar.

Steep the required number of strawberries in Lérina (Chartreuse)
liqueur.

Fill the inside of the melon with these strawberries and the
scooped out flesh; close the melon by replacing the bung cut out at

the start, and keep in a refrigerator for two hours, surrounded by ice.

Serve on a napkin at the last moment.

2682—BABY'S DREAM STRAWBERRIES   *Fraises Rêve de Bébé*

Select a fair-sized, very ripe pineapple, cut off a slice of it at the top and scoop out all its flesh without breaking the rind.

Prepare a square bed of *Génoise,* about two inches thick; slightly hollow it out towards its center, that the emptied pineapple may be set upright upon it; and stick the cushion upon a dry-paste base, of the same size and shape as the former. *Glaze* the *Génoise* bed with pink *fondant,* decorate with "royale" *glaze,* and set a large strawberry at each corner.

Slice half of the scooped out pineapple flesh, and steep it with Kirsch, Maraschino and sugar. Pound the remaining pulp and press it in order to extract its juice.

Set to steep with this pineapple juice a sufficient quantity of strawberries to three-parts fill the pineapple.

When about to serve, fill the emptied pineapple with successive and alternate layers of pineapple with Kirsch and strawberries; and, between each layer, spread a coat of vanilla-flavored, whipped cream.

Close the pineapple with the slice cut off at the start, and set it upright in the hollow of the cake. Serve the preparation very cold.

2683—STRAWBERRIES A LA RITZ   *Fraises à la Ritz*

Put some well-sugared and cooled strawberries in a *timbale,* and cover them with the following preparation: rub half-pound of wild strawberries through a sieve; add a little raspberry sauce to the *purée,* that it may acquire a pink tint; and then add the same quantity of very stiff vanilla-flavored whipped cream.

Thoroughly cool these strawberries before serving them.

2684—CARDINAL STRAWBERRIES   *Fraises Cardinal*

Set some fine, cooled strawberries in a *timbale;* coat them with raspberry sauce, or a *purée* of fresh raspberries, and sprinkle the latter with slivered fresh almonds.

2685—ZELMA KUNTZ STRAWBERRIES   *Fraises Zelma Kuntz*

Put some fine, cooled strawberries in a *timbale.* Cover them with a raspberry *purée,* combined with an equal quantity of whipped cream.

Decorate, by means of the pastry-bag, with whipped cream, and sprinkle with a crushed *pralin* of filberts.

GOOSEBERRIES (GROSEILLES VERTES)

2686—GOOSEBERRY FOOL   *Gooseberry-fool*
Poach one pound of green gooseberries in some thin syrup. When they are cooked, drain them thoroughly; rub them through a sieve, and collect the *purée* in a flat saucepan.

Work this *purée* on ice, and add the necessary amount of icing sugar to it.

The amount of the icing sugar varies according to the acidity of the fruit and the sweetness of the *poaching*-syrup.

Combine with the *purée* an equal quantity of very stiffly whipped cream; set the preparation in the shape of a dome in a *timbale;* decorate its surface, by means of a pastry-bag, with whipped cream, and serve very cold.

TANGERINES (MANDARINES)

2687—ALMINA TANGERINES   *Mandarines Almina*
Cut a slice of the peel from the stem-end of the tangerines by means of a round, even cutter, one inch in diameter. Then empty them, and fill the peels with a preparation of Bavarian cream with violets, combined with crumbled lady-fingers, sprinkled with Maraschino. Close the tangerines with the slice cut off at the start; let them set in a cool place, and, at the last moment, lay them on a dish covered with a folded napkin.

2688—TANGERINES WITH CREAM   *Mandarines à la Crème*
Empty the tangerines, and fill their peels with a somewhat thick tangerine Bavarian cream preparation, combined with a third of its bulk of fresh, raw cream.

Place them in ice until they have to be served; serve them as directed in the preceding recipe.

2689—SURPRISE TANGERINES   *Mandarines en Surprise*
Proceed as for the oranges, but for the orange ice substitute tangerine jelly.

ORANGES

2690—ORANGES WITH BLANC-MANGE *Oranges au Blanc-Manger*

Cut the oranges and empty them as directed in the case of tangerines. Then fill them with French blanc-mange (2625), and let it set. Close the oranges with the slices cut off at the start, and serve them on a napkin.

2691—RUBANEES ORANGES *Oranges Rubanées*

Fill the empty orange-shells with regular layers of variously colored and flavored blanc-manges, or with alternated fruit jellies. When about to serve, quarter the oranges.

N.B.—These quartered oranges are sometimes used for the garnishing of cold desserts.

2692—SURPRISE ORANGES *Oranges en Surprise*

Cut a slice across each orange, representing about one-fourth of their height, and scoop them out. Fill the shells with orange ice; cover the latter with Italian *meringue* (2383); fill the shells with cracked ice, lying on a tray, and set them in a sufficiently hot oven, to quickly brown the *meringue*. On taking the oranges out of the oven, close each with the slices cut from tnem at the start, in which are stuck imitation leaves and stalks, made from pulled sugar. Serve them on a napkin.

2693—SURPRISE SOUFFLE OF ORANGES

Oranges Soufflées en Surprise

Empty the oranges as above; garnish the rinds with an orange *soufflé* preparation, and cook the latter.

On taking the oranges out of the oven, cover the *soufflé* with the slices cut off at the start; set the oranges on a napkin, and serve them instantly.

PEACHES AND NECTARINES (PÊCHES ET NECTARINES)

As nectarines may be prepared after the same recipes as peaches, there is no need to give special recipes for the former.

2694—AIGLON PEACHES *Pêches Aiglon*

After having peeled the peaches, *poach* them in a vanilla-flavored syrup, and leave them to cool. Drain them, serve them upon a layer of vanilla ice-cream, spread in a false-bottomed silver *timbale,* the inner compartment of which contains cracked ice. Sprinkle crystallized violets over the peaches; set the *timbale* in a block of ice, carved to represent an eagle, and cover the whole with a veil of spun sugar.

2695—AURORA PEACHES *Pêches à l'Aurore*

Poach the peeled peaches in a Kirsch-flavored syrup, and let them cool there. Drain them; set them in a silver *timbale,* upon a layer of "iced *mousse* with strawberries" (2917), and coat the whole with a Curaçao-flavored *sabayon.*

2696—ALEXANDRA PEACHES *Pêches Alexandra*

Poach the peaches in a vanilla-flavored syrup and let them cool completely. Set them in a *timbale* surrounded by ice containing on its bottom a layer of vanilla ice-cream, covered with a strawberry *purée.* Sprinkle the peaches with white and red rose-petals, and veil the whole with spun sugar.

2697—CARDINAL PEACHES *Pêches Cardinal*

Poach the peaches in vanilla-flavored syrup, and, when they are quite cold, serve them in a *timbale.* Cover them with a very red, sweetened, raspberry *purée,* flavored with Kirsch, and sprinkled with very white, slithered fresh almonds.

2698—DAME-BLANCHE PEACHES *Pêches Dame-Blanche*

Poach the peaches in vanilla-flavored syrup. When they are cold, set them in a *timbale* upon a layer of vanilla ice-cream, covered with thin slices of pineapple steeped in Maraschino and Kirsch.

Between each peach, and in every crevice, pipe some balls of whipped cream, laid by means of a pastry-bag, fitted with a fancy tube.

2699—MELBA PEACHES *Pêches Melba*

Poach the peaches in vanilla-flavored syrup. Put them in a *timbale* upon a layer of vanilla ice-cream, and coat them with a raspberry *purée.*

2700—PETIT-DUC PEACHES *Pêches Petit-Duc*

Prepare the peaches as under (2698), but use small heaps of red-currant jelly instead of rosettes of cream.

2701—SULTANA PEACHES
Pêches Sultana

Poach the peaches in vanilla-flavored syrup, and let them cool.

Set them in a *timbale* upon a layer of pistachio ice, and coat them w.th very cold, thickened syrup, flavored with rose *essence.*

Veil the whole with spun sugar, and set the *timbale* in a block of ice.

2702—CHATEAU-LAFITTE PEACHES
Pêches Château-Lafitte

Scald the peaches; peel them, and cut them in half.

Poach them in sufficient Château-Laffite wine to cover them, and sugar the wine to the extent of ten oz. of sugar per bottle of wine.

Leave them to cool in the syrup, and put them in a silver *timbale.*

Reduce the wine by three-quarters; thicken it with a little raspberry-flavored, red-currant jelly.

When this syrup is quite cold, sprinkle the peaches with it.

2703—IMPERATRICE PEACHES
Pêches à l'Impératrice

Cut the peaches in half; *poach* them in a vanilla-flavored syrup, and let them cool. Then drain and dry them; fill the cut side of each of the half-peaches with enough vanilla ice-cream to give them the appearance of whole fruit. Coat the peach-side of each with some stiff apricot sauce, and roll them in *pralined* slivered almonds.

Serve these peaches upon a cushion of *Génoise,* saturated with Kirsch and Maraschino, set upon a dry-paste base, and *glazed* with raspberry *glaze.*

Veil the whole with spun sugar.

2704—ROSE-CHERI PEACHES
Pêches Rose-Chéri

Poach the peaches in vanilla-flavored syrup, and let them cool. Put them in a *timbale;* cover them with a *purée* of pineapple with finest champagne, and serve very cold.

2705—ROSE-POMPOM PEACHES
Pêches Rose-Pompom

Scald and peel some fine peaches; *poach* them in vanilla-flavored syrup, and let them cool. Stone them without opening or breaking them too much, and in the place of the stone, put some very firm vanilla ice-cream.

Set these reconstructed peaches in a silver *timbale,* upon a layer of raspberry ice; cover them with *pralined* whipped cream; and before serving put them for thirty minutes in the refrigerator.

At the last moment, veil the *timbale* with pink, spun sugar.

Pears (Poires)

2706—ALMA PEARS   *Poires Alma*

Peel the pears and *poach* them in a syrup made from one quart of water, one-half pint of port wine, eight ounces of sugar, and the *blanched* and chopped *zest* of an orange. Cool: set them in a *timbale;* sprinkle them with powdered *pralin,* and serve a whipped cream at the same time.

2707—CARDINAL PEARS   *Poires Cardinal*

Poach the pears in a vanilla-flavored syrup, and then proceed as directed under (2697).

2708—CARIGNAN PEARS   *Poires à la Carignan*

Evenly peel some very fine dessert pears, and cook them in a vanilla-flavored syrup; keeping them fairly firm. Drain them on a dish and let them cool. This done, trim them flat at their base, and scoop them from underneath by means of a sharp spoon, after having outlined the circumference of the opening with a plain sharp knife.

Fill them with a preparation of "Bombe au chocolat praliné" (2826).

Close the pears with a little round of *Génoise,* stamped out with the same cutter as that used for the pears.

Set them on a tray; coat them speedily with apricot jam cooked to the *small-thread* stage (215° F.); *glaze* them with chocolate *fondant,* and keep them for three hours in a very cold refrigerator. Meanwhile, prepare as many small *Génoise* squares as there are pears; and make them one-quarter inch wider than the diameter of the pears. Saturate these square bases with Anisette, and by means of a little apricot jam cooked to the *small-thread* stage (215° F.), stick each of them on to very thin, dry-paste bases of the same size. Coat these prepared bases with the same apricot jam, and garnish them all round, as also their uncovered corners, with *pralined* slivered almonds.

When about to serve, take the pears out of the refrigerator, set them on these bases: stick into each a stalk and a leaf, made from pulled sugar; and serve on a napkin.

N.B.—Each pear should be cut vertically into two, three, or four pieces, subject to its size.

2709—FELICIA PEARS
Poires Félicia

Poach some quartered bartlett pears in vanilla-flavored syrup and let them cool. Cook also, in a pink syrup, some very small halved pears.

Arrange the quarters in the middle of a border of Viennese cream (2641) laid out upon a dish. Cover them with a pyramid of vanilla-flavored whipped cream, and sprinkle its surface with crushed, red *pralines*.

Surround the cream border with the pink half-pears.

2710—FLORENTINE PEARS
Poires à la Florentine

Fill an oiled ring-mould with a semolina Bavarian cream preparation, and let it set. Turn it out at the last moment, and fill the middle of the border with stewed pears, set on by means of a vanilla-flavored apricot *purée*.

2711—HELENE PEARS
Poires Hélène

Poach the pears in vanilla-flavored syrup and let them cool.

When about to serve, set them in a *timbale* upon a layer of vanilla ice-cream, sprinkled with crystallized violets.

Serve a hot, chocolate sauce separately.

2712—MARQUISE PEARS
Poires Marquise

Cook the pears in a vanilla-flavored syrup, and drain them that they may cool. This done, coat them again and again with some very stiff raspberry-flavored red-currant jelly, and sprinkle them instantly with chopped, burnt almonds.

Set the pears on a "Diplomat Pudding" (2660), made in a *manqué mould,* and turned out on a round dish. Surround the base of the pudding with a border of apple-jelly *croûtons,* neatly cut to triangular shapes.

2713—MARY GARDEN PEARS
Poires Mary Garden

Cook the pears in syrup; cool them, and put them in a *timbale,* upon a raspberry sauce, combined with half-sugared cherries softened in tepid water for a few minutes.

Decorate the pears with whipped cream.

2714—MELBA PEARS
Poires Melba

Poach the pears in a vanilla-flavored syrup, and proceed as directed under (2699).

2715—PRALINED PEARS   *Poires Pralinées*

Stew the pears and let them cool. Set them in a *timbale,* and coat with some *frangipan* cream, thinned by means of a little raw cream.

Between each pear, set a well-moulded tablespoon of whipped cream, and cover the whole with *chopped*-almond *pralin.*

Serve a cold or hot chocolate sauce at the same time.

2716—PEARS A LA RELIGIEUSE   *Poires à la Religieuse*

Stew the pears in a vanilla-flavored syrup; cool them, and serve them in a shallow porcelain *timbale* equal in depth to the length of the pears.

Cover them with a somewhat thin chocolate Bavarois preparation, and place the whole for two hours in the refrigerator before serving.

2717—PEARS WITH RUM   *Poires au Rhum*

Stew the pears and set them in a *timbale.*

Thicken the syrup with arrowroot or cornstarch, color it faintly with pink; flavor it with rum; pour it over the pears, and let them cool.

N.B.—These pears may also be served hot, after the same recipe; except that the rum is poured over the pears, hot, at the last moment, and lighted at the table.

2718—QUEEN EMMA PEARS   *Poires à la Reine Emma*

Mould a Flamri preparation (2649) in an even ring-mould, decorated with candied fruit. Set this to *poach,* and, when it is cold, turn it out on a round dish.

In the middle set a pyramid of quartered pears, stewed in a vanilla-flavored syrup; coat the quarters with *frangipan* (2399) cream, combined with a quarter of its bulk of crushed, dry macaroons, and with double its volume of very stiff whipped cream.

Decorate the top, by means of a pastry-bag, with whipped cream; and serve some Kirsch-flavored apricot sauce separately.

APPLES

2719—ROYALE APPLES   *Pommes à la Royale*

Peel some small apples, core them by means of a corer, and *poach* them in vanilla-flavored syrup. When they are quite cold, coat them with red-currant jelly, and arrange them in a circle, each upon a *tartlet* of blanc-mange. Fill their midst with chopped Maraschino jelly.

Various Cold Sweets (Entremets)

2720—SPONGE CAKE A LA REINE *Biscuit à la Reine*

Cook, in a *manqué mould*, a Savoy-biscuit preparation (2439), and let it cool.

With a little apricot jam, cooked to the *small-thread* stage (215° F.), stick this biscuit on a dry-paste base; saturate it with cold syrup, flavored with Kümmel, and by means of a pastry-bag decorate it all round and on its edges with royale icing.

Turn out upon it a Bavarian cream with Maraschino, moulded in a *Richelieu mould* of proportionate size.

2721—MEXICAINE CRUST *Croûte à la Mexicaine*

Cut some slices three inches long by one-third inch thick from a stale *Génoise*. Coat them with a Condé *pralin* (2352), and dry them in a moderate oven.

Set these crusts in a crown on a round dish, and garnish their midst with a rocky pyramid of Plombière ice (2614), projecting above them.

2722—DIPLOMATE WITH FRUITS *Diplomate aux Fruits*

Prepare a base of *Génoise* with fruit, *glazed* with apricot jam, cooked to the *small-thread* stage (215° F.); a Bavarois with fruits.

Turn out the latter upon the former, and surround the whole with stewed fruit of the same kind as those used for the Bavarian cream.

2723—FLOATING ISLAND *Ile Flottante*

Take a stale Savoy biscuit (2349), and cut it into thin slices.

Saturate it with Kirsch and Maraschino, coat them with apricot jam, and sprinkle the latter with currants and chopped almonds. Put the slices one upon the other, in such a way as to reconstruct the biscuit, and coat the whole with a layer of sweetened and vanilla-flavored whipped cream.

Sprinkle the cream with slithered pistachios and currants; set the whole on a long shallow compote dish, and surround it with vanilla-flavored English custard (2398), or raspberry syrup.

2724—MILK JUNKET   *Junket-Milk*

Gently heat one quart of milk. When it has reached 95° F. take it off the fire; add two and one-half oz. of sugar to it; flavor it as fancy may suggest; put into it six drops of russet-apple *essence* (or two pastils of russet-apple *essence,* dissolved in six drops of water); pour it into a *timbale,* and serve it very cold.

N.B.—This very delicate and simple dessert is little else, indeed, than flavored and sweetened milk, caused to set by the combined agencies of heat and russet-apple *essence,* nowadays accomplished with Rennet.

2725—MACEDOINE OF COOLED FRUITS

Macédoine de Fruits Rafraîchis

Take some fresh fruit of the season, such as ripe Bartlett pears and peaches, peeled and sliced apricots and bananas, and add to it some small or large strawberries, raspberries, white- and red-currants; skinned, fresh almonds, etc.

Set these fruits in a *timbale* surrounded by ice, mixing them well together; sprinkle them with a syrup at 30° (saccharom.), flavored with Kirsch or Maraschino, and let them steep for an hour or two; taking care to toss them from time to time.

2726—EUGENIA-ITALIAN CREAM   *Eugénia-Crème à l'Italienne*

Select some very ripe Eugenia or Rose apples; peel, slice, and set to steep in a bowl, with Maraschino-flavored syrup.

Set the fruit in a *timbale,* upon a layer of vanilla ice-cream; decorate them on top with whipped cream, and sprinkle the latter with crystallized violets.

2727—MARQUISE ALICE   *Marquise Alice*

Prepare a *pralin*-flavored Bavarian cream in a *manqué mould:* garnish the inside with sponge lady fingers, saturated with Anisette.

Turn it out on a dish, and completely cover it with an even coat of very stiff, sweetened and vanilla-flavored whipped cream.

On top, lay some parallel lines of red-currant jelly, by means of the pastry-bag; and then cut these lines at right angles, with the point of a small knife. Surround the base with small puff-paste triangles, coated with *Pralin,* dried in the oven.

2728—ORIENTALE MELON   *Melon à l'Orientale*

Take a melon that is just ripe; make a circular incision round its stalk, and remove the bung. Seed and scoop out the flesh by means of a silver spoon and cut in dice.

Copiously sprinkle the inside of the melon with icing-sugar and fill it up with wild strawberries and the melon dice, spread in alternate layers, sprinkled with sugar. Complete with one-sixth pint of Kirsch; close the melon with the bung, seal the joint with a thread of butter, and keep the melon in a cool place for two hours.

Place it on a napkin, and serve *gaufrettes* (thin wafers) at the same time.

2729—MELON FRAPPE *Melon Frappé*

Select two very ripe, medium-sized melons, and, with the entire flesh of one of them, cleared of all the rind and seeds and rubbed through a fine sieve, prepare a *Granité* after (2930).

Cut the other melon round the stalk and open it. Completely remove the seeds; and, by means of a silver spoon, scoop out the flesh pieces, and set it to steep on ice with a little sugar and one of the following wines or liqueurs: Port, Curaçao, Rum, Kirsch or Maraschino.

Keep the emptied shell for thirty minutes in a refrigerator.

When about to serve, set the emptied melon on a small block of fancifully carved ice, and fill it up with the *Granité* and the steeped pulp spread in alternate layers. When the melon is full, return the bung to its place.

N.B.—This melon is served, by means of a spoon, upon iced plates, and it often takes the place of ices at the end of a dinner.

2730—SURPRISE MELON *Melon en Surprise*

Empty the melon as above, and fill it with a *macédoine* of fresh fruits, combined with the scooped flesh of the melon, cut into dice and mixed with a sugared and Kirsch-flavored *purée* of wild strawberries.

Close the melon and keep it in the refrigerator for two hours.

2731—GARNISHED MERINGUES *Meringués Garnies*

Join the *meringue* shells together in pairs, by means of some stiff sugared and flavored whipped cream or with some sort of ice, and serve them on a napkin.

2732—MONT-BLANC WITH STRAWBERRIES *Mont-Blanc aux Fraises*

Add some small wild strawberries steeped in cold, vanilla-flavored syrup and drained, to some very stiff whipped cream; the proportions being four oz. of the former per quart of the latter.

Arrange in the shape of a dome; surround the base with large strawberries, rolled in beaten egg-whites and then in coarse crystallized sugar, and decorate the surface with large and very red halved-strawberries.

2733—MONT-BLANC WITH CHESTNUTS *Mont-Blanc aux Marrons*

Cook some chestnuts in sweetened and vanilla-flavored milk and rub them through a sieve, over a ring mould; in order that the chestnut *purée,* falling in the form of vermicelli, may garnish the mould naturally.

Fill up the mould with the *purée* that has fallen over the sides of the mould; turn out the ring on a dish, and in the midst set an irregular and jagged mound of sugared and vanilla-flavored whipped cream.

2734—MONT-ROSE *Mont-Rose*

Prepare a *Charlotte,* Plombière in a shallow *Madeleine* ice-mould.

Having turned out the Charlotte on a dish, cover it on top with tablespoons of whipped cream, combined with a *purée* of fresh raspberries, and so shaped as to imitate a pyramidic rock.

2735—EGGS IN SNOW (A LA NEIGE) *Oeufs à la Neige*

Mould some ordinary *meringue,* by means of a spoon, to represent eggs; and drop the mouldings into a saucepan containing some boiling sugared and vanilla-flavored milk. Turn the *meringues* over in the milk, that they may *poach* evenly, and, as soon as they are firm, drain them in a sieve.

Strain the milk through muslin; add six egg yolks, and with it prepare an English custard (2398).

Set the egg-shaped *meringues* on a large shallow compote dish and cover them with the prepared custard, kept very cold.

2736—MOULDED EGGS IN SNOW (A LA NEIGE)
Oeufs à la Neige Moulés

Prepare the *meringues* and the English custard as above; but to the latter add about five ounces gelatine leaves soaked in cold water. Set the egg-shaped *meringues* in an oiled border-mould; cover them with the very cold custard, which, however, should not have set; and let the preparation set in the cool, or surrounded by ice.

2737—REJANE MOUSSELINE OF EGGS *Mousseline d'Oeufs Réjane*

By means of a pastry-bag, fitted with a plain tube, lay some ordinary *meringues* upon sheets of white paper, in shapes resembling large macaroons.

Slip the sheets of paper into boiling, sugared and vanilla-flavored milk, and pull out the sheets of paper as soon as the *meringues* slip off. Complete the *poaching* of the *meringues,* and drain them.

Set these *meringues,* two by two, in silver or porcelain egg-dishes; place a fine, *poached* half apricot in the middle of each, and cover the whole with a few teaspoons of English custard.

2738—MIMI MOUSSELINE OF EGGS   *Mousseline d'Oeufs Mimi*

This is a preparation of ordinary Italian *meringue* (2383), *poached* in a *bain-marie* (water-bath), in a caramel-coated mould. Let the contents get quite cold before turning out, and serve some stewed, fresh fruit and an English custard (2398) separately.

2739—IMPERATRICE RICE   *Riz à l'Impératrice*

Make a vanilla-flavored preparation of rice for desserts, using the quantities of milk and sugar already prescribed. When the rice is cooked, and somewhat cold, add to it four oz. of a *salpicon* of candied fruit and four tablespoons of apricot jam, per one-half lb. of raw rice. Then combine with it an equal quantity of Kirsch-flavored Bavarian preparation, or one pint of thick English custard and one pint of whipped cream.

Let a layer of red-currant jelly set upon the bottom of a Bavarian cream mould; then pour the above preparation into the latter and let the whole set, either in a cool place or surrounded by ice.

When about to serve, turn out on a napkin.

2740—MALTESE RICE   *Riz à la Maltaise*

Prepare the rice with milk as above, but flavor it with orange rind, and omit the apricot jam and the candied fruit *salpicon*. Combine with it an equal quantity of orange Bavarian cream preparation; pour the whole into a *dome-mould,* and let it set on ice. When about to serve, turn out upon a round dish, and cover it with alternate rows of orange-sections, skinned and steeped in a syrup flavored with orange-rind.

2741—SUEDOISE OF FRUITS   *Suédoise de Fruits*

As I mentioned in my remarks upon the preparation of jellies, a Suédoise of fruit is a jelly moulded in an *aspic mould* and garnished with layers of stewed fruit, the colors and kinds of which should be contrasted as much as possible.

2742—FRAISALIA TIMBALE   *Timbale Fraisalia*

Prepare a *timbale* of Savarin paste (2371) in a *Charlotte mould.*

When it is baked and cooled, remove the crumbs from its inside leaving a thickness of half an inch on its bottom and sides; coat it thinly with Kirsch-flavored syrup, and return the *timbale* to the mould.

Now garnish it with alternate layers of vanilla-flavored, Bavarian cream preparation and wild strawberries, steeped in Kirsch. Let it set in a cool place, or surround the mould with ice. Turn out the *timbale* first upon a plate; overturn it on a dish, and upon it set a pyramid of vanilla-flavored whipped cream. *Stud* the latter all over with small, very red strawberries, or garnish it with large halved-strawberries.

Surround the *timbale* with fine dice of strawberry jelly.

2743—TIVOLI WITH STRAWBERRIES   *Tivoli aux Fraises*

Coat an ornamented mould, fitted with a central tube, with a thick coat of very clear, Kirsch-flavored jelly. Fill the mould with a Bavarian cream preparation, combined with plenty of wild strawberry *purée,* and let its contents set. Turn it out, when about to serve, and surround it with very clear, chopped Kirsch-flavored jelly.

CHAPTER XXI

ICES

ICES, with their accompanying "petits fours," bring the dinner to a close—at least as far as Cookery is concerned; and, when they are well prepared and daintily dished, they are the consummation of all that is delicate and good. In no other department of the work has the culinary artist so freely indulged his fancy, or created such delectable tid-bits; and, though Italy be the cradle of the ice-worker's art, though the Neapolitans have deservedly maintained their reputation as authorities in this matter, to French chefs, certainly, is due the credit of those innovations which have perfected this important branch of dietetic science.

2744—THE MAKING OF ICES   *La Préparation des Glaces*

Whatever be the kind of ices required, they should always be prepared in advance; for none of these preparations can be made ready at a moment's notice.

There are two distinct operations in the confection of ices:—

(1) The making of the preparation.

(2) The freezing and the moulding of the preparation. I shall begin by dealing with the second operation, which remains the same for all ices, and is the essential part of the procedure.

To freeze an ice preparation is to surround it with cracked ice, mixed with sodium chloride (sea-salt or freezing salt) and saltpetre. The action of these two salts upon the ice causes a considerable drop in the temperature, which speedily congeals any enclosed liquid. Subject to their nature, ices are either moulded and frozen directly in their moulds, like the light ices: iced Biscuits, iced *Soufflés*, Puddings, *Mousses*, Parfaits, Bombes, etc.; or first frozen in a special utensil called a freezer, and then moulded and frozen again. Cream and syrup ices are prepared by the second method; and this I shall now describe.

The freezers, in which the freezing takes place, are generally wielded by hand, either directly or by means of some mechanism. They should be of pure tin, and fitted at their base on to a central pivot which turns in a socket, fixed in the wooden case which holds the freezer.

Having hermetically closed the latter, surround it with cracked ice containing three lbs. of salt and eight oz. of saltpetre per twenty-five lbs.

The freezer should be one-third of its height out of the ice, in order that no particle of salted ice may accidently fall into the preparation while it is being frozen. The ice should be snugly massed, by means of a special pestle, round the freezer. This operation constitutes the packing, and should be done at least ten minutes in advance if possible.

Having thus prepared the freezer, pour into it the preparation to be frozen and then either keep it in motion by rocking the utensil to and fro, by grasping the handle on the cover (if the apparatus is worked by hand), or by turning the handle if the utensil is on a central axle, fitted with the usual mechanism. In either case, the rotary movement of the utensil causes the preparation to splash continually against the sides of the freezer, where it rapidly congeals and the congealed portions are removed by means of a special paddle, as quickly as they form, until the whole becomes a smooth and a completely frozen mass. The delicacy and creaminess of the ice depend a great deal upon the care with which this freezing operation is effected; hence the preference which is now given to freezers fitted with a mechanism whereby two fans revolve inside in a direction opposite to that of the body of the machine, and thus not only detach the congealed portions of the preparation under treatment from the sides of the receptacle, but also work it with a regularity impossible to human motion.

2745—THE MOULDING OF ICES　　*Le Moulage des Glaces*

Having thus frozen the preparation, it may now be set in rock-form on a napkin, as it used sometimes to be served in the past, or in glasses. But as a rule it is put into special moulds, having closely-fitting covers. These moulds should be carefully filled, and banged out on a folded napkin, that the ice may settle and drive out any air which might cause holes being found in the preparation. When it is filled, place the mould in a receptacle of a suitable size, and surround it with cracked ice, prepared as for the packing. The mould should remain at least an hour in the ice, in the case of an ordinary ice, and an extra two hours if the ice be light and not previously frozen as are the Bombes.

When about to serve, take the mould out of the ice; wash it to rid it of the taint of salt; dip it in tepid water for an instant, that the surface of the preparation inside may melt and separate easily from the mould. Overturn the mould; and turn out the ice upon a folded napkin lying on a dish.

2746—PREPARATIONS FOR SIMPLE ICES

Compositions pour Glaces Simples

Preparations for simple ices are of two kinds: those made from cream, and those made from syrup; the latter being principally used for fruit ices.

As the quantities of sugar and eggs used for these preparations vary exceedingly, the following recipes have been based upon a working average.

If creamier ices be required, all that is needed is an increase in the sugar and egg-yolks per quart of milk; while, if the ices be required harder but less creamy, the two ingredients above mentioned should be proportionately reduced.

As an example of the difference that may exist between cream preparations, I might instance the case of ice-cream, which may be made from seven to sixteen egg-yolks, and six oz. to one lb. of sugar per quart of milk. In regard to ices made from syrups and fruit, their preparations may measure from 15° to 30° or 32° (saccharometer) respectively.

(The use of the saccharometer for gauging the sugar content of syrups is still in use today by the manufacturers and probably by chefs in large establishments. In only a few dessert recipes are directions given for measuring the sugar mixture by degrees. If the reader, inspired by the combinations and the wonderful flavors the recipes suggest, wishes to use such an instrument he may put the instructions to profitable use by measuring with a Brix Hydrometer, which takes the place of a saccharometer.

The hydrometer is plunged into a hydrometer jar filled with syrup. The syrup must be 68 degrees Fahrenheit, since the instrument is regulated to measure at this temperature. According to the density of the sugar content, the hydrometer will sink into the syrup. The reading on the graduated scale indicates the amount of sugar in the syrup.

A Brix Hydrometer may be purchased in many stores and

through the Taylor Instrument Companies of Rochester, New York. They sell for a little more than two dollars.—Ed.)

2747—ICE CREAM PREPARATION (General Recipe)
Composition pour Glace-Crème

Work two-thirds lb. of sugar and ten egg-yolks in a saucepan until the mixture reaches the ribbon-stage (2376). Dilute it, little by little, with one quart of boiling milk, and stir over a moderate fire until the preparation coats the withdrawn spoon. Avoid boiling, as it might separate the custard.

Strain the whole into a basin and stir it from time to time until it is quite cold.

N.B.—For the various ice cream preparations, the amount of sugar and number of egg-yolks, as also the procedure, do not change. They are only distinguishable by the particular flavor or infusion which may happen to characterize them.

VARIOUS ICE CREAM PREPARATIONS

2748—ALMOND ICE CREAM
Glace-Crème aux Amandes

Finely pound three and a half oz. of freshly-skinned sweet almonds and five bitter almonds; adding to them, little by little, in order to facilitate the pounding, a few tablespoons of water.

Set this almond paste to steep, twenty minutes beforehand, in the boiling milk, and prepare the cream as directed above, with the same quantities of sugar and egg-yolks.

2749—ASPARAGUS ICE CREAM
Glace-Crème aux Asperges

Parboil six oz. of asparagus tips for two minutes. Thoroughly drain them; quickly pound them, together with a few tablespoons of milk, and set this asparagus paste to steep in the boiled milk.

2750—FILBERT ICE CREAM
Glace-Crème aux Avelines

Slightly grill three and half oz. of filberts; finely pound them, together with a few tablespoons of milk, and set this paste to steep for twenty minutes in the boiled milk.

2751—COFFEE ICE CREAM
Glace-Crème au Café

Add two oz. of freshly-grilled and crushed coffee beans to the boiled milk, and let them steep for twenty minutes.

Or, with an equivalent amount of ground coffee and half a pint of water, prepare a very strong infusion and add it to one and a half pints of boiled milk.

2752—CHOCOLATE ICE CREAM   *Glace-Crème au Chocolat*

Dissolve eight oz. of grated chocolate in half pint of water, and add one quart of boiled milk, in which a large stick of vanilla has previously been steeped. For this preparation, eight oz. of sugar and seven egg-yolks will be found sufficient, if the chocolate used be sweet.

2753—WALNUT ICE CREAM   *Glace-Crème aux Noix*

Finely pound three and a half oz. of well-peeled walnut meats with a few tablespoons of water, and set them to steep for twenty minutes in boiling milk.

2754—PISTACHIO ICE CREAM   *Glace-Crème aux Pistaches*

Pound two oz. of sweet almonds, and two and a half oz. of freshly-peeled pistachios; moistening them with a few drops of milk. Set the paste to steep for twenty minutes in the boiled milk.

2755—PRALINE ICE CREAM   *Glace-Crème au Pralin*

Pound and rub through a sieve four oz. of almond *pralin,* and add one quart of previously-prepared vanilla-flavored custard.

2756—TEA ICE CREAM   *Glace-Crème au Thé*

Add one pint of very strong tea to one and a half pints of boiled milk, and make the preparation in the usual way.

2757—VANILLA ICE CREAM   *Glace-Crème à la Vanille*

When the milk has boiled, steep in it one large stick of vanilla for twenty minutes.

N.B.—If these various preparations be required more creamy, the milk may be wholly or partly replaced by fresh cream. Also when the preparation is congealed, it may be combined with one-sixth pint of whipped cream per quart.

2758—PREPARATIONS FOR FRUIT ICES
Compositions pour Glaces aux Fruits

The base of these preparations is a syrup of sugar at 32° (saccharom.), to which a *purée* of fruit, a flavoring, or a liqueur is added, which will give the ice its character. All these preparations require lemon juice, the quantity of which varies according to the acidity of the fruit used, but which, even in the case of the tartest fruits, should not measure less than the amount that may be extracted from a whole lemon per quart of the preparation.

Orange juice may also be used, more especially for red-fruit ices; while the juices of the orange and the lemons combined throw the flavor of the fruit under treatment into remarkable relief.

In the season the juices are extracted from fresh fruit, pressed and rubbed through a fine sieve. When the season is over the pre-served juice of fruit is used.

All red-fruit ices are improved, once they are set, by an addition of half pint of raw, fresh cream per quart of the preparation.

2759—THE MAKING OF FRUIT ICE PREPARATIONS
Pour Faire les Preparations pour Glaces aux Fruits

These preparations are made in two ways as follows:—

Rub the fruit through a fine sieve, after having pounded it if its nature permit. Dilute the *purée* with an equal quantity of cold sugar syrup at 32° (saccharom.), and add lemon juice in a quantity subject to the acidity of the treated fruit.

This mixture of ingredients should always be cold, and should be tested with saccharom. (pèse-sirops). If the instrument marks more than the proper degree, dilute the preparation with a little water; if it marks less, add syrup until the required degree is reached.

Or pound the fruit with an average quantity of ten oz. of sugar per lb.; but remember that this proportion may be modified either way, subject to the sweetness of the fruit used.

Rub the whole through a sieve; and then, to obtain the proper degree of strength, add the necessary quantity of filtered water.

2760—LIQUEUR ICE PREPARATIONS
Compositions pour Glaces aux Liqueurs

These preparations are made by adding to the syrup or the cream which forms the base of the ice a given quantity of the selected liqueur, the latter being generally added when the preparation is cold.

The proportion of one-fifth pint of liqueur per quart of syrup may be taken as an average. Subject to the requirements this liqueur flavor may be intensified with strong tea for rum ices; with orange-rind for Curaçao-flavored ices, with fresh, crushed cherry-stones for Kirsch ices, etc.

These preparations should always contain some lemon-juice, and their strength should reach the average degree indicated for fruit ices.

Various Fruit-Ice Preparations

2761—APRICOT ICE *Glace à l'Abricot*

Take one pint of fresh apricot *purée,* one pint of syrup, and the juice of two lemons. The strength of the preparation should measure 18° or 19° (saccharometer).

2762—PINEAPPLE ICE *Glace à l'Ananas*

Set to steep for two hours one pint of grated or pounded pineapple in one pint of syrup. Rub the whole through a sieve, add the juice of one lemon and a few drops of Kirsch, and test the preparation, which should measure from 18° to 20°.

2763—BANANA ICE *Glace aux Bananes*

Set one pint of pounded banana pulp to steep for two hours in one pint of Maraschino-flavored syrup. Add the juice of three lemons, and rub through a sieve. This preparation should measure from 20° to 21°.

2764—CHERRY ICE *Glace aux Cerises*

Crush one pint of pitted cherries, and pound their stones. Set the whole to steep for one hour in one pint of syrup, flavored with Kirsch. Rub through a sieve and add the juice of half a lemon. The preparation should measure 21°.

2765—LEMON ICE *Glace au Citron*

Set the *zests* of three lemon peels to steep for three hours in one pint of cold syrup. Add the juice of four lemons and of two oranges and strain. The preparation should measure 22°.

2766—STRAWBERRY ICE *Glace aux Fraises*

Mix one pint of strawberry *purée* with one pint of syrup, and add the juice of two oranges and of two lemons. Or pound two lbs. of strawberries with one lb. of powdered sugar; add the juice of oranges and lemons as above; rub the whole through a sieve, and add the necessary amount of filtered water to bring the preparation to 16° or 18°.

2767—RASPBERRY ICE *Glace aux Framboises*

Proceed as for (2766), and use the same quantities.

2768—RED-CURRANT ICE   *Glace à la Groseille*

Mix one pint of red-currant juice with one pint of syrup. In view
of the natural acidity of the fruit, lemon-juice may be dispensed
with. The preparation should measure 20°.

2769—TANGERINE ICE   *Glace aux Mandarines*

Throw the *zests* of the rinds of four tangerines into one and one-
half pints of boiling syrup. Let the whole cool; rub it through a sieve,
and finish it with the juice of six tangerines, two oranges and one
lemon. The preparation should measure 21°.

2770—MELON ICE   *Glace au Melon*

Mix one pint of very ripe melon pulp with one pint of syrup,
the juice of two oranges and one lemon, and one tablespoon of
orange-flower water. Rub the whole through a sieve. The mixture
should measure 22°.

2771—ORANGE ICE   *Glace à l'Orange*

Throw the *zests* of the rinds of four oranges into one quart of
boiling syrup. Let the whole cool; add the juice of four oranges
and one lemon, and rub it through a sieve. It should measure 21°.

2772—PEACH ICE   *Glace aux Pêches*

Proceed as for (2761), using wall peaches (those grown on a tree
near a wall) if possible.

2773—PEAR ICE   *Glace aux Poires*

Peel, core, and pound some fine Bartlett pears, with one lb. of
powdered sugar per two-thirds lb. of the fruit; and add the juice
of two lemons per lb. of pears. Rub the whole through a sieve, and
add enough filtered water to bring it to 22°.

2774—PLUM ICE   *Glace aux Prunes*

Proceed as for (2761), bringing the preparation to 20°.

2775—GRAPE ICE   *Glace aux Raisins*

Add to one and one-half pints of the juice of sweet, pressed grapes
the juice of three lemons and the necessary quantity of powdered
sugar to bring the preparation to 20°. Rub the whole through a
sieve.

2776—VIOLET ICE *Glace aux Violettes*

Put half a lb. of cleaned violet petals into one and one-half pints of boiling syrup. Let them steep for ten minutes; strain the whole through a sieve; let it cool, and finish it with the juice of three lemons. The preparation should measure from 20° to 21°.

Various Ices

2777—ALHAMBRA ICE *Glace Alhambra*

Take a *Madeleine-mould;* coat its bottom and sides with vanilla ice-cream and fill it with whipped cream, combined with fresh strawberries, steeped for two hours in Kümmel, which should afterwards be added to the whipped cream.

2778—CARMEN ICE *Glace Carmen*

Take a fluted mould. Garnish it with vertical and alternate layers of raspberry ice, coffee ice, and vanilla ice-cream.

2779—COUNTESS MARIE ICE *Glace Comtesse-Marie*

Take a special *square mould,* even or ornamented on the top. Coat it with strawberry ice; fill it with vanilla ice-cream; and, after turning it out, decorate it, with a pastry-bag (fitted with a fancy tube), with vanilla ice-cream.

2780—SUNSET ICE *Glace Coucher de Soleil*

Select one pound of fine very ripe strawberries, and put them in a silver *timbale.* Sprinkle them with ten ounces of powdered sugar and one liqueur-glass of Grand-Marnier liqueur; cover the *timbale* and keep it on ice for half an hour.

Then rub the strawberries through a sieve; and, with their *purée,* make a preparation after the directions given under Fruit Ices. Freeze this preparation in the freezer, and, when it is set, combine with it one pint of whipped cream. Now cover the freezer; surround it again with ice if necessary, and keep it thus for thirty-five to forty minutes. This done, put the ice preparation with care in pyramid form in crystal bowls.

N.B.—This ice gets its name from its color, which should be that of the western sky during a fine sunset.

2781—DAME JEANNE ICE *Glace Dame-Jeanne*

Take a *Madeleine-mould;* coat it with vanilla ice-cream, and fill it with whipped cream, combined with *pralined* orange flowers.

2782—DORA ICE *Glace Dora*

Take a *Madeleine-mould;* coat it with vanilla ice-cream, and fill it with Kirsch-flavored whipped cream combined with pineapple dice and Bar red-currant jam.

2783—ETOILE DU BERGER ICE *Glace Etoile de Berger*

Take a *star-shaped* mould, or a *Madeleine-mould* with a star on its bottom. Coat it with raspberry ice, and fill it with Benedictine flavored *Mousse.*

Turn it out upon a regular disc, consisting of a thick layer of white spun sugar, lying on a dish. This spun sugar throws the ice into relief, and emits rays which dart out from between the points of the star.

2784—FLEURETTE ICE *Glace Fleurette*

Take a *square mould.* Garnish it with strawberry and pineapple ice, laid in very regular, superimposed layers. After turning it out decorate with lemon ice.

2785—FRANCILLON ICE *Glace Francillon*

Take a *square mould;* coat it with coffee ice, and fill it with liqueur-brandy ice.

2786—FROMAGE ICES *Glaces Fromages*

These ices are made in *fluted moulds,* and generally with two differently flavored and colored ices, set vertically in the mould.

2787—GOURMETS' ICE *Glace des Gourmets*

Take a *"bombe"* mould. Coat it with *pralined,* vanilla ice-cream. Fill it with alternate layers of chestnut ice flavored with rum, and vanilla-flavored whipped cream. When the ice is turned out, roll it in *pralined* slivered almonds.

2788—MOULDED ICES *Glaces Moulées*

These ices are made in large or small moulds.

The large ices are moulded in tin moulds, fitted with hinged covers, and ornamented with some design. The small ones, which are generally served at evening parties, or are used to garnish larger ices, are made in similar moulds, shaped like flowers, fruit, birds, leaf-sprays, etc.

Any ice preparation may be used for these ices; but, as a rule, the preparation should have something in keeping with the design of the mould used.

Small moulded ices may be kept packed until they are served. They may also be turned out in advance and kept in the refrigerator.

2789—ICE "DES ILES" *Glace des Iles*

Take a *Madeleine-mould;* coat it with vanilla ice-cream, and fill it with pineapple ice.

2790—MADELEINE ICE *Glace Madeleine*

Take a *Madeleine-mould.* Fill it with vanilla ice-cream, combined with half its bulk of whipped cream and candied fruit steeped in Kirsch.

2791—FROSTED TANGERINES *Mandarines Givrées*

Cut the tangerines on top, with a round, even cutter, in such a way as to remove a round slice of their peel with the stalk attached, and two leaves clinging to it.

With the juice of the tangerines prepare some tangerine ice, after the directions given under Fruit-ice Preparations. Fill the tangerines with this ice; cover them with the slices removed at the start; and, with a brush, sprinkle the rinds of the fruit with water, and place them in a refrigerator.

As soon as the tangerines are coated with frost, serve them on a napkin.

2792—ICED TANGERINES "AUX PERLES DES ALPES" (CHARTREUSE CANDY BALLS) *Mandarines Glacées aux Perles de Alpes*

Empty the tangerines as above, and garnish them inside with tangerine *mousse,* with which *Chartreuse* bon-bons have been mixed. Cover them, and frost them as directed above.

2793—MARIE THERESE ICE *Glace Marie-Thérèse*

Take a *Madeleine-mould;* coat it with chocolate ice, and fill it with vanilla-flavored whipped cream.

After turning out, decorate it with pineapple ice.

2794—ICED MERINGUES *Meringues Glacées*

Fill some *meringue* shells with some kind of spoon-moulded ice, and set them on a napkin.

Or, fill the shells more sparingly and join them together in pairs.

2795—PLOMBIERE ICE   *Glace Plombière*

Take a *parfait mould*. Garnish it with vanilla-ice cream combined with candied fruit, steeped in Kirsch; spreading the preparation in alternate layers with apricot jam.

COUPES

We are now concerned with bowls filled, either with differently-flavored ices, or with ices combined with whipped cream or candied fruit. The bowls used for this purpose should be of crystal.

2796—COUPES D'ANTIGNY   *Coupes d'Antigny*

Three-quarters fill the bowls with Alpine-strawberry ice, or, failing this, four-seasons strawberry ice, combined with very light and strongly-flavored raw cream. The two most perfect examples of this cream are the "Fleurette Normande," and that which in the South of France is called "Crême Niçoise," and which comes from Alpine pastures. (In the United States we have very fine rich cream from Jersey and Guernsey cows, and all cream is graded according to butter fat content. This recipe calls for a 24–30% cream.—Ed.)

Upon the ice of each bowl set a half-peach, *poached* in vanilla-flavored syrup; and veil the whole thinly with spun sugar.

2797—COUPES CLO-CLO   *Coupes Clo-Clo*

Fill the bottom of the bowls with vanilla ice cream, combined with fragments of candied chestnuts, steeped in Maraschino. Set a candied chestnut in the middle of the ice, and surround it by means of a pastry-bag with a border of whipped cream, containing strawberry *purée*.

2798—COUPES DAME BLANCHE   *Coupes Dame Blanche*

Three-quarters fill the bowls with almond-milk (2506) ice. Upon the ice in each bowl set an overturned half-peach, *poached* in vanilla-flavored syrup, the hollow of which should be filled with Bar red-currant jam. Surround the peaches with a ribbon of lemon ice, laid by means of a pastry-bag.

2799—COUPES DENISE   *Coupes Denise*

Fill the bowls with Mocha ice, and sprinkle the latter with sweets containing liqueur (preferably rum). Cover with whipped cream laid on by means of the spoon.

2800—COUPES EDNA MAY *Coupes Edna May*

Fill the bottom of the bowls with vanilla ice-cream, and upon the latter set some very cold stewed cherries. Cover the latter with a cone of whipped cream, tinted pink by means of a fresh raspberry *purée.*

2801—COUPES ELIZABETH *Coupes Elizabeth*

These coupes do not contain ice. They are filled with very cold stewed choice bigaroon (large) cherries, *poached* in a Kirsch- and cherry-brandy-flavored syrup. The fruit is covered with whipped cream which is laid on by means of a spoon, and sprinkled with powdered spices in which cinnamon should predominate.

2802—COUPES EMMA CALVE *Coupes Emma Calve*

Fill the bottom of the bowls with *pralined* vanilla ice-cream. Upon the latter set some Kirsch-flavored stewed cherries, and cover the latter with raspberry *purée.*

2803—COUPES EUGENIE *Coupes Eugenie*

Fill the bowls with vanilla ice-cream, combined with broken candied chestnuts. Cover the ice with whipped cream and upon the latter sprinkle some crystallized violets.

2804—COUPES A LA FAVORITE *Coupes à la Favorite*

Fill the bowls vertically, half with Kirsch-Maraschino-flavored ice, and half with vanilla ice-cream. Border them with a thread of pineapple ice, and in the middle set some whipped cream combined with strawberry *purée.*

2805—COUPES GERMAINE *Coupes Germaine*

Fill the bottom of the bowls with vanilla ice, and distribute over it half-sugared cherries, steeped in Kirsch. Cover the cherries with a dry *purée* of chestnuts, squeezed out to resemble vermicelli, and border the bowls with whipped cream.

2806—COUPES GRESSAC *Coupes Gressac*

Fill the bottom of the bowls with vanilla ice-cream, and upon the latter in each bowl set three small macaroons, saturated with Kirsch. Upon the macaroons set an overturned *poached* half-peach, the hollow of which should be garnished with Bar red-currant jam. Surround the peaches with a border of whipped cream.

2807—COUPES JACQUES   *Coupes Jacques*

Fill the bowls vertically, half with lemon and half with strawberry ice. Between the two ices, on top of the bowl, set a tablespoon of a *macedoine* of fresh fruit, steeped in Kirsch.

2808—COUPES A LA MALMAISON   *Coupes à la Malmaison*

Fill the bowls with vanilla ice-cream, combined with peeled Muscadel grapes. Veil with spun sugar.

2809—COUPES A LA MEXICAINE   *Coupes à la Mexicaine*

Fill the bowls with tangerine ice, combined with pineapple cut into very small dice.

2810—COUPES MIREILLE   *Coupes Mireille*

Fill the bowls, half with vanilla ice-cream, and half with red-currant ice with cream. In the middle of each bowl set a nectarine *poached* in vanilla-flavored syrup, the stone of which should be replaced by Bar white-currant jam.

Decorate with whipped cream, and cover with a veil of spun sugar.

2811—COUPES PETIT DUC   *Coupes Petit Duc*

Fill the bowls with vanilla ice-cream. Set in each a *poached* half-peach garnished with Bar red-currant jam. Surround the peaches with a ribbon of lemon ice.

2812—COUPES REVE DE BEBE   *Coupes Rêve de Bébé*

Fill the bowls, half with pineapple ice and half with raspberry ice.

Between the two ices set a line of small strawberries, steeped in orange juice. Border the bowls with whipped cream, and sprinkle the latter with crystallized violets.

2813—COUPES MADAME SANS-GENE   *Coupes Madame Sans-Gêne*

Fill the bottom and sides of the bowls with a layer of vanilla ice-cream. Fill them with Bar red-currant jam, and cover the latter, by means of a spoon, with whipped cream.

2814—COUPES TUTTI-FRUTTI   *Coupes Tutti-Frutti*

Sprinkle the bottom of the bowls with various fresh fruits cut into dice; garnish the bowls with strawberry, pineapple and lemon ices, spread alternately with layers of the same fruits.

2815—COUPES VENUS   *Coupes Vénus*

Half-fill the bowls with vanilla ice-cream.

In the middle of each bowl set a small peach, *poached* in vanilla-flavored syrup, with a very red, small cherry upon it.

Border the peaches with a ribbon of whipped cream.

2816—LIGHT ICES   *Glaces Légéres*

These ices differ from those dealt with above, in that they are moulded and frozen directly, without being kept in the freezer.

To this class belong the ices most commonly served and the best; and, since their preparation requires no special utensils, they may be served everywhere: such are the "Iced Biscuits," the "Bombes," the *"Mousses,"* the *"Parfaits,"* the "Puddings," and the "Iced *Souflés."*

These different kinds of ices greatly resemble one another, and their names, which are puzzling at times, are only a matter of fancy.

2817—VARIOUS PREPARATIONS   *Préparations Diverses*

The old iced-biscuit preparation consisted of an English custard (2398), prepared from one lb. of sugar, twelve egg-yolks, and one pint of milk.

When the custard was cooked, it used to be strained into a bowl, left to cool (being fanned the while), and then placed upon ice, and finished with the whisk. Originally this cream was moulded at this stage; but now it is customary to add one quart of whipped cream to it; which operation makes the recipe more like that of a Bombe, which, in its turn, resembles that of the preparation for *Mousses*.

ICED BISCUITS

2818—PREPARATION FOR ICED BISCUITS
Préparation pour Biscuits Glacés

Beat in a copper basin, in a *bain-marie* (water-bath), twelve egg-yolks and one lb. of powdered sugar, until the paste gets very firm and reaches the ribbon-stage (2376).

Take the basin off the fire, and whisk until the whole is quite cold. Then, add eight oz. of Italian *meringue* (2383) and one pint of whipped cream.

2819—THE MOULDING OF ICED BISCUITS
Moulage de Biscuits Glacés

These biscuits are moulded in rectangular brick-shaped cases, fitted with lids, top and bottom.

Generally, the preparation moulded in the covers is of a different flavor and color from the one filling the middle of the mould.

For example, one of the covers may be garnished with strawberry, and the other with violet preparation, while the central portion may hold a vanilla-flavored preparation. After having frozen them for three hours, in a pail filled with freezing ice, and turned them out, these bricks are cut up vertically into rectangles, on the cut sides of which the differently colored layers are distinctly marked. Place these rectangles in special paper cases; decorate them on top, if the directions permit it, and place them in a refrigerator until about to serve.

Nearly all Bombe preparations may become the base of biscuits, which are then named after them; *e.g.:* from Bombe Odessa, Odessa Iced Biscuits may be prepared.

Various Iced Biscuits

2820—BENEDICTINE ICED BISCUIT   *Biscuit Glacé Bénédictine*

Mould the base with strawberry ice, the middle with Bénédictine ice, and the top with violet ice. Freeze and cut up as directed.

2821—MARQUISE ICED BISCUIT   *Biscuit Glacé Marquise*

Mould with Kirsch and strawberry ices, alternated twice.

2822—MONT BLANC ICED BISCUIT   *Biscuit Glacé Mont-Blanc*

Mould the base with a rum-flavored preparation, the middle with a chestnut preparation, and the top with a vanilla-flavored preparation.

2823—NEAPOLITAN ICED BISCUIT   *Biscuit Glacé Napolitaine*

Mould the base with a vanilla-flavored preparation, the middle with strawberry ice, and the top with a preparation of *pralined* biscuit.

2824—PRINCESSE ICED BISCUIT   *Biscuit Glacé Princesse*

Mould and leave to set a biscuit-*pralined* preparation. After having cut up the moulding, surround it with slivered and *pralined* almonds.

Decorate the pieces with vanilla ice-cream and tangerine ice.

2825—SIGURD ICED BISCUIT   *Biscuit Glacé Sigurd*

Mould the base with strawberry and the top with pistachio biscuit preparation. When the biscuit is frozen, cut it into rectangular slices, and sandwich each slice between two sugar wafers.

2826—BOMBES (General Recipe)   *Bombes*

Originally, Bombes were made from an ordinary ice preparation, in spherical moulds; hence their name, which is once more justified by their arrangement, consisting as it used to do of superimposed and circular layers, the outermost of which was very thin. Nowadays, Bombes are more often moulded in the shape of shells, but the preparation from which they are made is much more delicate than it was formerly.

2827—PREPARATION FOR BOMBES   *Préparation pour Bombes*

Gradually mix thirty-two egg-yolks with one quart of syrup at 28°. Put the whole on a very moderate fire, whisking it as for a *Génoise*, and, when the preparation is firm enough and taken off the fire, continue whisking it over ice until it is quite cold. Then add the selected flavor, and one and one-third quarts of stiffly-whipped cream.

2828—THE MOULDING OF BOMBES   *Moulage de Bombes*

First coat the bottom and sides of a mould with the ice preparation denoted by the name of the Bombe. This coat, which should vary in thickness in accordance with the size of the mould, should be somewhat thin, and made from an ordinary ice preparation, which is suited better than any other kind to this class of dish.

The middle is then filled with a Bombe preparation, flavored as directed, or with a *Mousse* preparation. The whole is then covered with a round piece of white paper, and the mould is hermetically sealed with its cover, set to freeze, and left for two or three hours in the ice.

When about to serve, take the mould out of the ice; wash it with cold water; dip it quickly in tepid water; dry it with a towel, and overturn the mould on a napkin or on a block of ice.

VARIOUS BOMBES

2829—BOMBE ABOUKIR   *Bombe Aboukir*

Having coated the mould with pistachio ice, fill it with a *pralined* Bombe-preparation, combined with chopped pistachios.

2830—BOMBE AFRICAINE *Bombe Africaine*

Coat the mould with chocolate ice, and fill it with an apricot Bombe-preparation.

2831—BOMBE ABRICOTINE *Bombe Abricotine*

Coat the mould with apricot ice, and fill it with a Kirsch-flavored Bombe-preparation, laid in alternate layers with stewed apricots.

2832—BOMBE AIDA *Bombe Aïda*

Coat the mould with strawberry ice, and fill it with a Kirsch-flavored Bombe-preparation.

2833—BOMBE ALMERIA *Bombe Almeria*

Coat the mould with Anisette ice, and fill it with a pomegranate Bombe-preparation.

2834—BOMBE ALHAMBRA *Bombe Alhambra*

Coat the mould with vanilla ice-cream, and garnish it with a strawberry Bombe-preparation. After turning it out surround the Bombe with a crown of fine strawberries steeped in Kirsch.

2835—BOMBE AMERICAINE *Bombe Américaine*

Coat the mould with strawberry ice, and fill it with a tangerine Bombe-preparation. After turning out decorate the Bombe with pistachio ice.

2836—BOMBE ANDALOUSE *Bombe Andalouse*

Coat the mould with apricot ice, and fill it with a vanilla Bombe-preparation.

2837—BOMBE BATAVIA *Bombe Batavia*

Coat the mould with a pineapple ice and fill it up with a strawberry Bombe-preparation, combined with candied ginger cut into dice.

2838—BOMBE BOURDALOUE *Bombe Bourdaloue*

Coat the mould with vanilla ice-cream, and fill it up with an Anisette Bombe-preparation.

After turning out decorate the Bombe with crystallized violets.

2839—BOMBE BRESILIENNE *Bombe Brésilienne*

Coat the mould with pineapple ice, and fill it with a vanilla and rum Bombe-preparation combined with pineapple dice.

2840—BOMBE CAMARGO   *Bombe Camargo*
Coat the mould with coffee ice, and fill it with a vanilla Bombe-preparation.

2841—BOMBE CARDINAL   *Bombe Cardinal*
Coat the mould with a red-currant and raspberry ice, and fill it with a *pralined* vanilla Bombe-preparation.

2842—BOMBE CEYLAN   *Bombe Ceylan*
Coat the mould with coffee ice and fill it with a rum Bombe-preparation.

2843—BOMBE CHATEAUBRIAND   *Bombe Châteaubriand*
Coat the mould with apricot ice, and fill it with a vanilla Bombe-preparation.

2844—BOMBE CLARENCE   *Bombe Clarence*
Coat the mould with banana ice, and fill it with a violet Bombe-preparation.

2845—BOMBE COLOMBIA   *Bombe Colombia*
Coat the mould with Kirsch ice, and fill it with a pear Bombe-preparation. After turning out decorate the Bombe with half-sugared cherries.

2846—BOMBE COPPELIA   *Bombe Coppélia*
Coat the mould with coffee ice and fill it with a *pralined* Bombe-preparation.

2847—BOMBE CZARINE   *Bombe Czarine*
Coat the mould with vanilla ice, and fill it with a Kümmel Bombe-preparation. After turning out decorate it with crystallized violets.

2848—BOMBE DAME-BLANCHE   *Bombe Dame-Blanche*
Coat the mould with vanilla ice, and fill it with an almond milk Bombe-preparation.

2849—BOMBE DANICHEFF   *Bombe Danicheff*
Coat the mould with coffee ice, and fill it with a Kirsch Bombe-preparation.

2850—BOMBE DIABLE ROSE   *Bombe Diable Rose*
Coat the mould with strawberry ice, and fill it with a Kirsch Bombe-preparation, combined with half-sugared cherries.

2851—BOMBE DIPLOMATE *Bombe Diplomate*

Coat the mould with vanilla ice-cream, and fill it with a Maraschino Bombe-preparation, combined with candied fruit.

ICES

2852—BOMBE DUCHESSE *Bombe Duchesse*

Coat the mould with banana-ice, and fill it with a pear Bombe-preparation flavored with Kirsch.

2853—BOMBE FANCHON *Bombe Fanchon*

Coat the mould with *pralined* ice, and fill it with a Kirsch Bombe-preparation, containing some coffee-drops.

2854—BOMBE FEDORA *Bombe Fedora*

Coat the mould with orange ice, and fill it with a *pralined* Bombe-preparation.

2855—BOMBE FLORENTINE *Bombe Florentine*

Coat the mould with raspberry ice, and fill it with a *pralined* Bombe-preparation.

2856—BOMBE FORMOSA *Bombe Formosa*

Coat the mould with vanilla ice-cream, and fill it with a strawberry Bombe-preparation, combined with big strawberries.

2857—BOMBE FRANCILLON *Bombe Francillon*

Coat the mould with coffee ice, and fill it with a Bombe-preparation flavored with liqueur-brandy.

2858—BOMBE FROU-FROU *Bombe Frou-Frou*

Coat the mould with vanilla ice-cream, and fill it with a rum Bombe-preparation, combined with candied fruit.

2859—BOMBE GRANDE DUCHESSE *Bombe Grande Duchesse*

Coat the mould with pear ice, and fill it with a Chartreuse Bombe-preparation.

2860—BOMBE GISMONDA *Bombe Gismonda*

Coat the mould with *pralined* ice, and fill it with an Anisette Bombe-preparation, combined with Bar white-currant jam.

2861—BOMBE HAVANAISE *Bombe Havanaise*

Coat the mould with coffee ice, and fill it with a vanilla and rum Bombe-preparation.

2862—BOMBE HILDA *Bombe Hilda*

Coat the mould with filbert ice, and fill it with a Chartreuse Bombe-preparation, combined with filbert *pralin*.

2863—BOMBE HOLLANDAISE *Bombe Hollandaise*

Coat the mould with vanilla ice-cream, and fill it with a Curaçao Bombe-preparation.

2864—BOMBE JAFFA *Bombe Jaffa*

Coat the mould with *pralined* ice, and fill it with an orange Bombe-preparation.

2865—BOMBE JAPONAISE *Bombe Japonaise*

Coat the mould with peach ice, and fill it with a tea *mousse*-preparation.

2866—BOMBE JEANNE D'ARC *Bombe Jeanne D'Arc*

Coat the mould with vanilla ice-cream, and fill it with a chocolate *pralined* Bombe-preparation.

2867—BOMBE JOSEPHINE *Bombe Joséphine*

Coat the mould with coffee ice, and fill it with a pistachio Bombe-preparation.

2868—BOMBE MADELEINE *Bombe Madeleine*

Coat the mould with almond ice, and fill it with a vanilla and Kirsch Bombe-preparation, combined with candied fruit.

2869—BOMBE MALTAISE *Bombe Maltaise*

Coat the mould with blood-orange ice, and fill it with tangerine-flavored whipped cream.

2870—BOMBE A LA MARECHALE *Bombe a la Maréchale*

Coat the mould with strawberry ice, and fill it with alternate layers of pistachio, orange and vanilla Bombe-preparation.

2871—BOMBE MARGOT *Bombe Margot*

Coat the mould with almond ice, and fill it with pistachio Bombe-preparation. After turning out, decorate with vanilla ice-cream.

2872—BOMBE MARIE LOUISE *Bombe Marie Louise*
Coat the mould with raspberry ice, and fill it with a vanilla
Bombe-preparation.

2873—BOMBE MARQUISE *Bombe Marquise*
Coat the mould with apricot ice, and fill it with a Champagne
Bombe-preparation.

2874—BOMBE MASCOTTE *Bombe Mascotte*
Coat the mould with peach-ice, and fill it with a Kirsch Bombe-
preparation.

2875—BOMBE MATHILDE *Bombe Mathilde*
Coat the mould with coffee ice, and fill it with an apricot Bombe-
preparation.

2876—BOMBE MEDICIS *Bombe Médicis*
Coat the mould with brandy ice, and fill it with a raspberry
Bombe-preparation.

2877—BOMBE MERCEDES *Bombe Mercédês*
Coat the mould with apricot ice, and fill it with a Chartreuse
Bombe-preparation.

2878—BOMBE MIGNON *Bombe Mignon*
Coat the mould with apricot ice, and fill it with nut Bombe-
preparation.

2879—BOMBE MISS HELYETT *Bombe Miss Helyett*
Coat the mould with raspberry ice, and fill it with a vanilla
Bombe-preparation.

2880—BOMBE MOGADOR *Bombe Mogador*
Coat the mould with coffee ice, and fill it with a Kirsch Bombe-
preparation.

2881—BOMBE MOLDAVE *Bombe Moldave*
Coat the mould with pineapple ice, and fill it with a Curaçao
Bombe-preparation.

2882—BOMBE MONTMORENCY *Bombe Montmorency*
Coat the mould with Kirsch ice, and fill it with a cherry Bombe-
preparation. After turning out, surround it with half-candied
cherries.

2883—BOMBE MOSCOVITE *Bombe Moscovite*

Coat the mould with Kümmel ice, and fill it with a bitter-almond Bombe-preparation, combined with candied fruit.

2884—BOMBE MOUSSELINE *Bombe Mousseline*

Coat the mould with strawberry ice, and fill it with whipped cream, combined with strawberry *purée*.

2885—BOMBE NABAB *Bombe Nabab*

Coat the mould with *pralined* ice, and fill it with a liqueur-brandy Bombe-preparation, containing candied fruit.

2886—BOMBE NELUSKO *Bombe Néluskc*

Coat the mould with filbert *pralined* ice, and fill it with a chocolate Bombe-preparation.

2887—BOMBE NERO *Bombe Nero*

Take a *dome-mould* and coat it with vanilla ıce-cream with caramel; fill it with vanilla *mousse,* combined with small, imitation truffles, the size of small nuts, made from chocolate.

Turn out the Bombe on a thin cushion of Punch Biscuit (2381), of the same diameter as the Bombe. Cover the whole with a thin layer of Italian *meringue* (2383); and, on top, set a small receptacle made of Italian *meringue* dried in an almost cold oven. Decorate the sides by means of a pastry-bag with *meringue,* and set the whole in the oven to *glaze* quickly.

On taking the Bombe out of the oven, pour some hot rum into the bowl, and light it when serving.

2888—BOMBE SAINT LAUD *Bombe Saint Laud*

Coat the mould with raspberry ice, and fill it with alternate layers of melon Bombe-preparation and whipped cream.

2889—BOMBE NESSELRODE *Bombe Nesselrode*

Coat the mould with vanilla ice-cream, and fill it with whipped cream, combined with chestnut *purée*.

2890—BOMBE ODETTE *Bombe Odette*

Coat the mould with vanilla ice-cream, and fill it with a *pralined* Bombe-preparation.

2891—BOMBE ODESSA *Bombe Odessa*

Coat the mould with apricot ice, and fill it with a strawberry Bombe-preparation.

2892 —BOMBE ORIENTALE   *Bombe Orientale*
Coat the mould with ginger ice, and fill it with a pistachio Bombe-preparation.

2893—BOMBE PATRICIENNE   *Bombe Patricienne*
Coat the mould with vanilla ice-cream, and fill it with a *pralin* and chocolate Bombe-preparation.

2894—BOMBE PETIT DUC   *Bombe Petit Duc*
Coat the mould with strawberry ice, and fill it with a hazel-nut Bombe-preparation, combined with Bar red-currant jam.

2895—BOMBE POMPADOUR   *Bombe Pompadour*
Coat the mould with asparagus ice, and fill it with a pomegranate Bombe-preparation.

2896—BCMBE PROPHETE   *Bombe Prophête*
Coat the mould with strawberry ice, and fill it with pineapple preparation.

2897—BOMBE RICHELIEU   *Bombe Richelieu*
Coat the mould with rum ice; fill it with a coffee Bombe-preparation, and distribute coffee drops upon it after turning.

2898—BOMBE ROSETTE   *Bombe Rosette*
Coat the mould with vanilla ice-cream, and fill it up with red-currant-flavored whipped cream, combined with red-currants.

2899—BOMBE A LA ROYALE   *Bombe a La Royale*
Coat the mould with Kirsch ice, and fill it with a chocolate *pralined* Bombe-preparation.

2900—BOMBE SANTIAGO   *Bombe Santiago*
Coat the mould with Brandy ice, and fill it with a pistachio Bombe-preparation.

2901—BOMBE SELIKA   *Bombe Sélika*
Coat the mould with *pralined* ice, and fill it with a Curaçao Bombe-preparation.

2902—BOMBE SKOBELEFF   *Bombe Skobeleff*
Coat the mould with Vodka ice, and fill it with Kümmel-flavored whipped cream.

2903—BOMBE STROGOFF   *Bombe Strogoff*
Coat the mould with peach ice, and fill it with a Champagne
Bombe-preparation.

2904—BOMBE SUCCES   *Bombe Succès*
Coat the mould with apricot ice, and fill it with Kirsch-flavored
whipped cream, combined with candied apricots cut into dice.

2905—BOMBE SULTANE   *Bombe Sultane*
Coat the mould with chocolate ice, and fill it with a *pralined*
Bombe-preparation.

2906—BOMBE SUZANNE   *Bombe Suzanne*
Coat the mould with pink rum ice, and fill it with vanilla Bombe-
preparation, combined with Bar red-currant jam.

2907—BOMBE TORTONI   *Bombe Tortoni*
Coat the mould with *pralined* ice, and fill it with coffee Bombe-
preparation, containing coffee beans.

2908—BOMBE TOSCA   *Bombe Tosca*
Coat the mould with apricot ice, and fill it with a Maraschino
and fruit Bombe-preparation. After turning out, decorate the Bombe
with lemon ice.

2909—BOMBE TROCADERO   *Bombe Trocadéro*
Coat the mould with orange ice, combined with candied orange-
rind, cut into small dice; and fill with alternate layers of whipped
cream and slices of filbert *Génoise,* cut in graduated sizes, and saturated with Curaçao syrup. Sprinkle some orange-*zest* dice on each
slice of *Génoise.*

2910—BOMBE TUTTI-FRUTTI   *Bombe Tutti-Frutti*
Coat the mould with strawberry ice, and fill it with a lemon
Bombe-preparation, combined with various candied fruits, cut into
dice.

2911—BOMBE A LA VALENCAY   *Bombe a la Valençay*
Coat the mould with *pralined* ice, and fill it with whipped cream,
combined with raspberries.

2912—BOMBE VENITIENNE *Bombe Vénitienne*

Coat the mould half with vanilla and half with strawberry ice and fill it with a Maraschino and Kirsch Bombe-preparation.

2913—BOMBE VICTORIA *Bombe Victoria*

Coat the mould with strawberry ice, and fill it with Plombière ice.

2914—BOMBE ZAMORA *Bombe Zamora*

Coat the mould with coffee ice, and fill it with a Curaçao Bombe-preparation.

ICED MOUSSES

The composition for *mousses* is prepared either from English cream (2397) or from syrup. The last method is specially suited to fruit *mousses*.

2915—PREPARATION FOR ICED FRUIT MOUSSES
Composition de Mousse Glacée aux Fruits

This is a cold syrup at 35°, to which is added an equal quantity of a *purée* of the fruit under treatment, and twice that amount of very stiff whipped cream.

2916—PREPARATION OF ICED MOUSSE WITH CREAM
Composition de Mousse Glacée à la Crème

Make an English cream from one lb. of powdered sugar, sixteen egg-yolks, and one pint of milk, and leave it to cool.

When it is quite cold, add to it one pint of raw cream, two-thirds oz. of powdered tragacanth gum, and the flavor which is to characterize the preparation.

If the *mousse* be a fruit one, add to it one pint of a *purée* of fresh fruit.

Beat over ice, until the preparation gets very frothy; put it into moulds, lined with white paper; thoroughly close them, and keep them in a refrigerator for two or three hours, subject to their size.

2917—VARIOUS ICED MOUSSES *Mousses Glacées Diverses*

After the same procedure, *mousses* may be prepared with Anisette, Coffee, Chocolate, Kirsch, Maraschino, Rum, Tea, etc.; Apricots, Strawberries, Oranges and Tangerines, fresh Walnuts, Peaches, Vanilla, Violets, etc.

2918—PARFAIT (General Recipe) *Parfait*

Mix thirty egg-yolks with one quart of cold syrup at 28°. Put the mixture on a slow fire, and cook it as for an English cream; strain it and whisk it over ice until it is quite cold.

Add three pints of very stiff, whipped cream and one-fifth pint of brandy or rum, in order to finish it; mould the preparation in *Parfait moulds,* and pack them in a freezer for from two to three hours.

N.B.—The term *"Parfait,"* which, formerly, was applied only to *"Parfait au Café,"* has become the common name for uncoated ices, made from Bombe-preparations having but one flavor. And this is fairly logical, seeing that Bombe-preparations, but for a few insignificant distinctions, are exactly like *Parfait*-preparation.

It is therefore just as reasonable to make vanilla, chocolate, and *pralined Parfaits,* etc., as to make them with coffee.

2919—ICED PUDDINGS *Puddings Glacés*

Preparations of this class follow no hard and fast rules, and, in reality, they are not ices at all. They are nothing else than iced desserts, the bases of which generally consist of thick English custard, the same as that which serves in the preparation of Bavarois.

The few following recipes, however, are exceptions to this rule.

2920—PUDDING DE CASTRIES *Pudding de Castries*

Coat a Bombe mould with a thin layer of vanilla ice-cream, and fill it with two Bombe-preparations, spread in somewhat thick, alternate layers. One of the preparations should be of vanilla, on each thickness of which a layer of lady fingers, cut into dice and sprinkled with Anisette, should be spread; and the other preparation should be of tangerine.

Between the layers, sprinkle a few pinches of grated chocolate, and fill up the mould with a thickness of vanilla ice-cream.

Thoroughly close the utensil; pack it for about two or three hours. Turn it out on a folded napkin; sprinkle on a few red, crushed *pralins;* and serve an iced tangerine syrup separately.

2921—MARIE-ROSE PUDDING *Pudding Marie-Rose*

Line a *Charlotte-mould* with rolled *gaufrettes* (thin wafers); placing them snugly one against the other. By means of a pastry-bag, fill the *gaufrettes* with very stiff strawberry ice, and then fill the mould with a vanilla *pralined* Bombe-preparation. Keep the mould in the refrigerator for three hours, and turn out the pudding on a napkin. Decorate it on top with pink and white whipped cream. Serve a chocolate ice-cream separately.

2922—MIRAMAR PUDDING   *Pudding Miramar*

Fill an iced *Madeleine-mould* with lady fingers, saturated with Chartreuse, and alternate them with thin slices of fresh pineapple, saturated in Kirsch, and pipped sections of tangerine, skinned.

Fill up the mould with a Bombe-preparation of pomegranate juice, flavored with Kirsch; close the mould, keep it in ice for two hours, and turn out the pudding on a napkin when about to serve.

Serve an iced vanilla syrup separately.

2923—SEYMOUR PUDDING   *Pudding Seymour*

Cut a *Mousseline* Brioche into thin slices, and set these to soak in raw, sweetened and Kirsch-flavored cream. Peel and finely slice some peaches, and *poach* them in vanilla-flavored syrup; also peel some very ripe Bartlett pears.

Prepare a pink Bombe-preparation, flavored with Kirsch and *Orgeat;* and then fill up the mould with alternate layers of the slices of brioche and fruit, with Bar red-currant jam added; and the Bombe-preparation.

Close the mould, keep it in ice for two hours, and turn out the pudding on a napkin.

2924—ICED SOUFFLES   *Soufflés Glacés*

The preparation differs according as to whether the *Soufflés* be prepared with fruit, or with such flavors as vanilla, coffee, chocolate, etc.

The last named are made with the Iced-*Mousse* preparation (2916), which may also serve for the fruit *Soufflés;* but, in the case of the latter, the following preparation is preferable:—

Whip the whites of ten eggs to a very stiff froth, and add to this one and one-tenth lbs. of sugar cooked to the *small-crack* (285° F.) stage. Transfer the whole to a bowl; flavor according to fancy, and add one pint of a *purée* of fruit and one pint of very stiffly-whipped cream.

2925—THE MOULDING OF LARGE AND SMALL ICED SOUFFLES
Moulage des Gros et des Petits Soufflés Glacés

Mould the large ones in ordinary *Soufflé timbales,* which should be lined with bands of white paper, fixed with butter, and over-reaching the edges of the *timbales* by one and a half to two inches, that the preparation, in projecting above the brims of the utensils, may appear like a *Soufflé* when the paper is removed.

The small *Soufflés* are moulded in cases or in small silver *casso-lettes,* which are likewise wrapped in bands of paper, that the preparation may rise above their brims. As soon as they are moulded, put the *Soufflés* in a very cold refrigerator; and when about to serve them, carefully remove the bands of paper which, once the preparation has solidified, have served their purpose; and serve the cases or silver *cassolettes* on a napkin or on a carved block of ice.

Like the Bombes, and the Iced Biscuits, Iced *Soufflés* may be indefinitely varied, owing to the many combinations to which they lend themselves.

2926—SHERBETS *Sorbets*

Sherbets and their derivative preparations consist of very light and barely-congealed ices, served after the Entrées. They serve in freshening the stomach; preparing it to properly receive the roast.

They are appetizers and help to aid digestion.

2927—PREPARATION FOR SHERBETS *Préparation pour Sorbets*

Sherbets are made from any liqueur ice preparation at 15°; or they may be prepared as follows:—For one quart of preparation, take the juice of two lemons and one orange, half-a-pint of port wine, of Samos wine, of Sauterne, or other good wine; and add cold syrup at 22°, until the saccharometer registers 15°.

For liqueur sherbets, allow about one-fifth pint of liqueur per quart of the preparation; but remember that this is subject to the kind of liqueur used. For the quantity just prescribed, use syrup at 18° or 19°, which the subsequent addition of liqueur reduces to the proper degree. Whatever be the kind of liqueur, the latter should only be added when the Sherbet is completely frozen; that is to say, at the last moment.

Fruit sherbets are generally prepared from the juices and syrups of juicy fruits. Fruit *purées* are scarcely suited to this mode of procedure, and they are only resorted to in exceptional cases.

The Freezing of Sherbets.—Pour the preparation into the freezer, which should have been previously packed, and keep the utensil moving. Remove portions of the preparation from the sides of the receptacle as fast as they adhere, and mix them with the whole. until the latter is completely congealed; remembering not to stir at all during the freezing process. When the preparation is firm enough, mix with it, gently, the quarter of its weight of Italian *meringue* (2383) or very stiffly whipped cream; and finish by the addition of the liqueur.

The Serving of Sherbets.—Take some of the Sherbet preparation in a spoon, and set it in Sherbet or Sherry glasses, shaping it to a point.

When the Sherbet is prepared with wine, sprinkle the preparation when it is in the glasses with a tablespoon of the selected wine.

The consistency of a Sherbet, of any kind, should be such as to permit it being drunk.

2928—VARIOUS SHERBETS   *Sorbets Divers*

Having pointed out that Sherbets may be prepared from the juices of every fruit such as pineapple, cherries, strawberries, raspberries, red-currants, etc., and from every wine and liqueur such as Port, Samos wine, Marsala, Johannisburg, Rum, Kirsch, Liqueur-Brandy, etc., and since the procedure is the same in every case, there is no need to devote a special article to each.

2929—SICILIENNE SHERBERT   *Sorbet à la Sicilienne*

Keep a very green watermelon in the refrigerator for three hours.

One hour before serving, open it on top, as directed under "Surprise Melon" (2730), and take out the seeds.

Then, loosen the pulp with a silver spoon, without taking it from the fruit; sprinkle it with Maraschino, and put the whole back into the refrigerator.

Serve on cracked ice or on a block of it, and serve the pulp before the diners in Sherbet glasses.

2930—GRANITES   *Granités*

Granités answer the same purpose as Sherbets, while they may also be introduced into certain culinary preparations.

The bases of these preparations consist of very thin syrups made from fruit juices, and not overreaching fourteen degrees (saccharometer).

Granités consist only of iced syrups, and are not combined with any Italian or other *meringue*.

As in the case of the Sherbets, but more particularly in regard to these, the cook should remember not to stir the syrup during the freezing process, lest it separate; and, when it is congealed, it should form a light, granulated mass.

2931—MARQUISES *Marquises*

Marquises are generally made from strawberries or pineapple, with Kirsch. The preparation is that of a Sherbet with Kirsch, registering 17° by the saccharometer. The freezing is the same as for *Granités;* but it should be carried a little further.

When about to serve, mix the preparation per pint with half a pint of very stiff whipped cream, combined with a strawberry or pineapple *purée,* subject to the purpose of the Marquise.

2932—ROMAINE PUNCH *Punch à la Romaine*

Mix sufficient amount dry white wine, or dry champagne, with one pint of syrup at 22°, to reduce the latter to 17°; add the juice of two oranges and two lemons, a strip of orange and lemon *zest,* and let infusion proceed for one hour.

Strain the syrup and bring it to 18°.

Freeze until it is somewhat stiff, and mix it with the quarter of its volume of Italian *meringue* (2383) (prepared from two egg-whites and three and a half oz. of sugar).

When about to serve, complete with one-fifth pint of Rum, added little by little.

Serve the preparation in glasses, after the style of the Sherbets.

N.B.—For all Sherbets and Punches, one quart of the finished preparation should be allowed for every ten people.

2933—SPOOMS *Spooms*

Spoom is a kind of Sherbet prepared from a syrup at 20°. Add to it twice as much Italian *meringue* (2383) as was added to the Sherbets. Do not work it too briskly, that it may remain very light and ɹothy.

Spooms are made from fruit juices; but more often from such wines as Champagne, Samos, Muscat, Zucco, etc.

Serve it in glasses like the Sherbets.

CHAPTER XXII

N.B.—The quantities given below are calculated to be sufficient for fifteen glasses.

2934—BAVARIAN CREAM   *Bavaroise*

Work eight oz. of powdered sugar with eight egg-yolks in a saucepan, until the whole becomes white and reaches the *ribbon* stage (2344). Then add consecutively: one-fifth pint of *capillary* syrup, one pint of freshly made, boiling hot tea, and the same amount of boiling milk; whipping briskly the while, that the drink may be very frothy. Complete at the last moment with one-third pint of the liqueur which is to characterize the Bavaroise; either Kirsch or Rum.

If the Bavaroise is flavored with vanilla, orange or lemon, let the flavor steep in the milk for fifteen minutes beforehand. If it be flavored with chocolate, dissolve six oz. of the latter, and add the milk to it, flavored with vanilla.

If it be coffee-flavored, set three oz. of freshly roasted and ground coffee to steep in the milk or flavor with one pint of freshly-made coffee.

Bavaroise is served in special glasses, and it must be frothy.

2935—BISHOF   *Bischoff*

Put into a basin one bottleful of Champagne, one Sherry-glassful of "tilleul" (linden or lime) infusion, one orange and one lemon, cut into thin slices, and enough syrup at 32° to bring the preparation to 18°. Let the steeping proceed in a cool place for an hour. This done, strain; freeze it like a *Granité,* and finish it with four liqueur-glassfuls of liqueur-brandy.

Serve in bumpers.

2936—ICED COFFEE   *Café Glacé*

Pour one and a half pints of boiling water, gradually, over ten oz. of freshly-ground coffee, and strain it gently. Put this coffee into a bowl with 20 oz. of sugar, and let the latter dissolve while the coffee cools. Then add one quart of very cold, boiled milk, in which half a stick of vanilla should have infused, and one pint of very fresh cream.

Freeze the whole in a freezer, taking care to keep the preparation almost liquid, and serve it in very cold cups.

2937—LEMONADE *Citronade*

Dissolve half-lb. of sugar in one quart of filtered water. Add the juice and the *zests* of the rinds of two lemons, and let steeping proceed in the cool for three hours. Pass the whole through a fine strainer; add one syphon of seltzer water, and serve with a thin round slice of lemon in each glass.

2938—PINEAPPLE WATER *Eau d'Ananas*

Finely chop one and a half lbs. of fresh or preserved pineapple; put it into a bowl and pour over it one quart of boiling syrup at 20°. Let it cool, and steep for two hours.

Strain through a bag; add a piece of ice and sufficient seltzer water to reduce the liquid to 9°. Keep the preparation in a cool place for a further twenty minutes, and complete it, when about to serve, with three liqueur-glasses of Kirsch.

2939—CHERRY WATER *Eau de Cerises*

Pit two lbs. of very ripe cherries, and rub them through a sieve. Put the *purée* into a bowl with the stones, crushed in the mortar, and let the whole steep for one hour. Then moisten with one pint of filtered water, and strain the juice through a bag, or muslin folded in two and stretched.

Add a piece of well-washed ice and six oz. of sugar, and put the whole in a cool place for twenty minutes. Flavor, when about to serve, with four liqueur-glasses of Kirsch.

The saccharometer should register 9° when inserted into this preparation.

2940—RASPBERRY-FLAVORED RED CURRANT WATER
Eau de Groseilles Framboisées

Rub through a sieve, over a bowl, twelve oz. of red and white currants, and four oz. of very ripe raspberries. Add to the currant-water one pint of filtered water, six oz. of sugar, and one piece of washed ice. Keep the whole in a cool place for twenty minutes, and stir it from time to time with a silver spoon, that the sugar may dissolve.

Degree the same as in (2939).

2941—MELONADE
Eau de Melon

Rub one lb. of just-ripe melon pulp through a sieve. Put it into a bowl and pour over it one pint of boiling syrup at 20°. Let the whole cool and steep for two hours, and strain it through muslin or through a bag. Add a piece of very clean ice and sufficient seltzer water to reduce the syrup to 9°. Keep the preparation in a cool place for a further twenty minutes, and finish it, when about to serve, with two tablespoons of orange-flower water.

2942—KALTSCHALE
Kaltschale

Peel and slice one-half lb. of peaches and an equal quantity of pineapple; add four oz. of ripe, melon pulp, cut into dice, and four oz. of a mixture of raspberries and red and white currants, cleared of their stalks. Put these fruits in a *silver timbale* and keep the latter on ice. Set a little cinnamon to steep in a half-bottleful of boiling, white wine; add six oz. of sugar and the *zest* of one lemon; and let the whole cool. Then add half a pint of a mixed *purée* of strawberries and red-currants to this infusion.

Filter the whole, and complete it by the addition of a bottle of champagne.

Pour this preparation over the fruit, and serve the *timbale* very cold.

2943—ORANGEADE
Orangeade

Proceed as for lemonade, but use the juice and *zests* of orange rinds instead of those of lemons, and the juice of only half a lemon. Put very thin slices of orange in the glasses.

2944—PUNCH WITH KIRSCH
Punch au Kirsch

Throw a good half oz. of tea into one quart of boiling water, and let it steep for ten minutes. Put into a punch or salad-bowl one lb. of sugar; strain the infusion of tea over the sugar, and dissolve the sugar; stirring the while with a silver spoon.

Add one and a half pints of Kirsch, light it, and serve in glasses.

2945—PUNCH WITH RUM
Punch au Rhum

Make an infusion as above, with the same amount of tea and one quart of boiling water. Strain it over one lb. of sugar, in a punch-bowl, and let the sugar dissolve.

Add a few thin slices of lemon, and one and a half pints of rum, and light it. Serve with a slice of lemon in each glass.

2946—MARQUISE PUNCH   *Punch Marquise*

Put into a small, copper saucepan one quart of Sauterne wine, half-lb. of sugar, and the *zest* of the rind of one lemon bound round a clove. Dissolve the sugar; heat the wine until it becomes covered by thin white froth, and pour it into a punch-bowl after having removed the *zest* and the clove.

Add half a pint of burnt brandy; light it and let it burn itself out. Serve with a thin slice of lemon in each glass.

2947—ICED PUNCH   *Punch Glacé*

Prepare a Marquise Punch as above; when the wine is hot, take it off the fire; throw in a good half oz. of tea, and let the whole steep covered for ten minutes.

Pass the whole through a fine strainer; add one orange and one lemon, peeled and cut into slices, and some heated rum. Light it; leave to cool, and reduce to 15°. Then freeze like a *Granité,* and serve in glasses.

2948—HOT WINE   *Vins Chauds*

Pour one bottle of red wine over ten oz. of sugar, set in a small, copper basin. Dissolve the sugar. Add one orange *zest,* a bit of cinnamon and mace, and one clove. Heat the wine until it is covered by thin froth, and then pass it through a fine strainer.

Serve with a thin slice of lemon in each glass.

2949—HOT WINE WITH ORANGE   *Vin Chaud à l'Orange*

Pour half a pint of boiling water over ten oz. of sugar. Add the *zest* of one orange and let steeping proceed for fifteen minutes. Remove the *zest,* and mix one bottle of heated Burgundy wine with the infusion.

Serve with a round slice of orange in each glass.

2950—WINE A LA FRANCAISE   *Vin à la Française*

Put eight oz. of sugar into a salad-bowl, and sprinkle on a few tablespoons of water, that it may dissolve. Add one bottle of excellent Bordeaux wine or red Burgundy, and the half of a lemon cut into thin slices. Stir well with a silver spoon and serve with a slice of lemon in each glass.

N.B.—Always remember to free the lemons and oranges used of all seeds, which would lend a bitterness to the drink.

2951—CLARET CUP   *Le Cup de Vin Rouge*

Put into a crystal bowl one oz. of sugar, the rind of one lemon and three slices of the latter, an equal quantity of orange, one strip of cucumber peel, one tablespoon of Angostura Bitters, and a liqueur-glass of each of the following liqueurs:—Brandy, Maraschino and white Curaçao.

Complete with one and a half bottles of red wine and a bottle of Soda. Cover and let the whole infuse. Strain, add a few pieces of very clean ice and a few leaves of fresh mint.

CHAPTER XXIII

FRUIT PRESERVES AND JAMS

2952—PLAIN STEWED FRUIT *Compôtes Simples*

Fruit for stewing is used whole, halved or quartered, and cooked or *poached* in a syrup, of a flavor in keeping with the fruit.

Serve these preparations in bowls or deep dishes; cover them with their syrup, reduced or not; and, in certain cases, thicken the latter with arrowroot or cornstarch. They may be served hot or cold; but in any case, the fruit used should not be too ripe.

2953—MIXED STEWED FRUIT *Compôtes Composées*

These preparations generally consist of stewed, fresh fruit of one or several kinds; combined with fruit *purées*.

Quince and apple jellies are greatly used, either in coating the preparations or in bordering them with dice, etc.

With this class of stewed fruits, which are merely a matter of fancy and taste, candied and preserved fruits are almost always used as auxiliary constituents.

2954—JAMS *Confitures*

Under this general title the following preparations are classed:—

(1) Those in which the fruit is treated directly with the sugar:—

(2) Those in which the juice alone, owing to its gelatinous nature, produces, together with the sugar, jellies.

The amount of sugar used is subject to the nature of the fruit and its sweetness; but in the case of nearly all tart fruits, the weight of sugar should equal that of the fruit, or nearly so.

If too much sugar be used, the flavor is impaired; while crystallization will follow very shortly afterwards; if too little be used, the jam has to be overcooked in order to be made sufficiently thick, and the flavor is once more impaired by extended evaporation; finally if the time allowed for cooking be inadequate, rapid fermentation will be the result.

In making jam, therefore, the cook should base his measure of sugar upon the nature of the fruit he intends treating.

2955—THE COOKING, POTTING, AND SEALING OF JAMS

Cuisson de Confiture, Mise en Pot, Bouchage

The time allowed for cooking any jam whatsoever can only be approximately decided, and it is a gross mistake to suppose the case otherwise, since the matter is wholly dependent upon the heat of the fire, and the resulting speed of the evaporation of the vegetable moisture. Theoretically, a jam is all the better for having been cooked quickly, seeing that it may thus more easily preserve its color and flavor.

For all that, unless great care and attention be exercised, a whole-fruit jam ought not to be made on a too quick fire, lest it burn. It is just the opposite, when jellies are in question, where the juice alone of the fruit is treated, the fire should be as intense as possible; in order that the required degree of consistency, which marks the close of the operation, may be reached as speedily as possible.

The degree of consistency is the same for all jellies, and may be ascertained thus: when the steam given off by the preparation loses its density, and the boiling movement becomes perceptible, it may be concluded that evaporation has ceased, and that the real cooking-process, which is very rapid, has begun. At this stage frequently take the skimmer out of the saucepan.

The jam clinging to it falls off, at first very quickly; then, in a few minutes, it is seen to accumulate towards the center of the skimmer and to fall slowly at lengthy intervals, in large drops.

This stage, which is indubitably indicative of the cooking being at an end, is called the *"nappe"* and is equivalent to the *large-thread* stage (222° F.) in the cooking of sugar; and, as soon as it is reached the jam should be taken off the fire. Allow it to cool for seven or eight minutes, and pour it into pots, which, if of glass, should be gradually heated, lest they crack.

The following day, set a round piece of white paper saturated with rectified glycerine or wax, on each pot, and drop these pieces of paper directly upon the jam. Rectified glycerine will be found preferable by far to the commonly-used sugared brandy.

Then close the pots with a double sheet of paper, fastened on with string, and place them somewhere in the dry.

2956—APRICOT JAM   *Confiture d'Abricots*

Cut the apricots in two, and use very ripe fruit, grown in the open, if possible. Break the stones, skin the almonds, and cut them in two. Allow three-quarters lb. of sugar per lb. of fruit. Put this sugar in a preserving pan with one-third pint of water per two lbs. of sugar, and, when it is dissolved, boil for a few minutes, carefully skimming the while. Add the apricots, set the whole to cook on a moderate fire, and stir constantly, especially towards the end, when the jam is more particularly prone to burn on the bottom of the saucepan. Take the jam off the fire as soon as it reaches the *"nappe"* stage (222° F. *large thread*), as explained above, and mix the almonds with the jam.

2957—CHERRY JAM   *Confiture de Cerises*

Pit the cherries, and allow one and a half lbs. of sugar per two lbs. of the fruit; taking care to have equal weights of sugar and fruit if the latter be not over sweet. Put the sugar in the preserving pan; moisten it with water that it may dissolve, and boil it for five minutes, skimming carefully the while. Add the cherries and a half-pint of red-currant juice, and cook over a hot fire until the *"nappe"* stage (222° F., *large-thread*) is reached.

Remarks:—The addition of red-currant juice is advocated for this jam, seeing that by ensuring the proper consistency it eliminates prolonged cooking; and, as I have already pointed out, red fruit is all the better, and preserves a more perfect color, when it is cooked rapidly.

When the fruit begins to boil, carefully skim it, otherwise the scum hardens, and not only spoils the jam but often sets it to fermenting.

2953—STRAWBERRY JAM   *Confiture de Fraises*

This is one of the most difficult jams to make. There are several ways of preparing it, and the one I give strikes me as the quickest and simplest. Clean the fruit, which should be just ripe. Only wash it when absolutely necessary, as, for instance, when mould has stuck to it.

Allow twelve oz. of sugar per lb. of fruit. Put this sugar in a preserving pan, sprinkle it with water that it may dissolve, and cook it to the *large-ball* stage (248° F.), taking care to skim thoroughly when boiling begins. Throw the strawberries into the sugar, and set the preserving pan on the side of the fire for seven or eight minutes;

that is to say, until the moisture of the fruit has dissolved the sugar to a syrup.

Return the saucepan to a hot fire, and cook the strawberries for ten or twelve minutes, remembering to carefully remove the scum that forms.

Then remove the strawberries by means of a ladle and drain them in a basin. Continue cooking the syrup rapidly, until the *"nappe"* stage (222° F. *large-thread*) shows signs of appearing, then return the strawberries for five minutes; that is to say, until the *"nappe"* (222° F. *large thread*) stage is completely reached.

Fill the pots, little by little, that the strawberries may be well distributed in them and not rise in a mass to the top, as often happens when the receptacles are filled too quickly.

2959—ORANGE MARMALADE *Confiture d'Oranges*

Select some oranges about equal in size, of a good color, free from blemishes, and with thick and soft rinds. The latter consideration is important, since the parboiling operation is accomplished more perfectly when the rinds are thick and supple.

Prick them somewhat deeply with a small, pointed stick (in order to hasten the cooking process), and throw them into a preserving pan of boiling water. Boil for thirty minutes; drain the oranges, cool them, and put them under a running tap for twelve hours, or more if possible; or soak them in constantly changed, cold water for twenty hours. The object of this operation is to soften the rinds and extract their bitterness.

This done, drain the oranges; quarter them, remove their seeds and filaments, and rub them through a coarse sieve.

Take the same weight of sugar as of orange *purée*. Melt the former in the preserving pan, and boil it for five or six minutes, skimming carefully the while. Then add the orange *purée,* and one-quarter pint of good apple juice (cider) per lb. of the former.

During the first stage of the cooking process, skim with great care, and during the second stage, stir almost constantly until the *"nappe"* (220° F. *large thread*) stage is reached.

2960—PLUM JAM *Confiture de Prunes*

Allow twelve oz. of sugar per lb. of pitted plums.

Dissolve the sugar; skim, set it to boil for seven or eight minutes, and proceed for the cooking as directed under apricot jam.

Remarks:—It is a mistake to let the plums steep in the sugar for some hours previously, for the acid they contain causes them to blacken, and the color of the jam is thus spoiled. And in order to have greengage jam of a fine, green color, do not cook more than from six to eight lbs. of it at a time, and cook that quantity as quickly as possible.

2961—RHUBARB JAM   *Confiture de Rhubarbe*

Rhubarb jam is one of the most difficult and tedious to make owing to the abundant moisture contained by the vegetable; and it may start to burn on the bottom of the saucepan, especially towards the close of the cooking process.

If it be desired very green, select suitable natural rhubarb; if it be desired pink, only take the central stalks which are bordered with red, or use cultivated rhubarb. In any case, it is best not to make more than five or six lbs. at once.

Remove the ends of the stalks, cut what remains into pieces; by means of a small knife, scrape off the fibrous skin and cut the stalks into three-inch lengths. Allow thirteen oz. of sugar per lb. of rhubarb. Dissolve the former, boil it for seven or eight minutes and then throw the rhubarb into it. Cover the preserving pan and, put it on the side of the stove for about twelve minutes that the fibres of the rhubarb may disintegrate, and at the end of that time become like vermicelli.

Then set the saucepan upon a hot fire, and stir constantly until the preparation reaches the *"nappe"* (222° F. *large thread*) stage, whereupon the jam is finished.

2962—TOMATO JAM   *Confiture de Tomates*

There are also several ways of making this jam, of which the following seems the quickest:

The first fact that should be grasped is that the amount of pulp that can be used represents about one-fifth of the tomato, and this itself depends upon the kind of tomato used, and whether it be just ripe, nearly so, or very ripe.

In order to obtain one lb. of pulp, therefore, five lbs. of tomatoes should be used, or thereabouts.

Finely slice the tomatoes, and rub them through a sieve. Put the juice and the *purée* into the jam-saucepan, and boil for five minutes, stirring the while.

This done, pour the whole into a napkin, stretched over a frame, as for straining a jelly; and let it drain thoroughly.

At the end of the operation, therefore, all that remains on the napkin is the mere vegetable pulp, freed of all moisture.

Allow the same weight of sugar as of pulp. Put the former into the jam-saucepan, together with a small glass of water; let it dissolve, and cook it to the *small-ball stage* (236° F.); taking care to skim it well as soon as it begins to boil. A stick of vanilla may be put with the sugar before boiling it; or the jam may be flavored with a good tablespoon of vanilla sugar (2349) when it is taken off the fire; in any case, the jam ought to be flavored with vanilla.

When the sugar has reached the *small-ball stage* (236° F.), add the tomato pulp to it, and one-fourth pint of red-currant juice per lb. of pulp. Owing to the fact that tomato pulp of itself has no binding properties the mixing of red-currant juice with it is essential.

Set the preserving pan upon a hot fire, stirring constantly the while, until the *"nappe"* (222° F. large thread) *stage* is reached; then let the jam cook for a few more minutes.

2963—BLACK CURRANT JELLY *Gelée de Cassis*

Take some very ripe black-currants: clean them; put them into the preserving-kettle with half a glass of water per two lbs. of fruit, and let them boil.

While this preparatory operation is in progress, the skins of the currants burst, and their juice flows into the pan. At this stage, transfer the fruit to a sieve lying on a bowl—a much simpler method than crushing and pressing them in a twisted towel.

Allow as many lbs. of sugar as there are quarts of juice; put this sugar into the preserving-kettle; dissolve it, and cook it to the *small-ball stage* (236° F.); thoroughly skimming the while. Add the black-currant juice, combined per quart with half pint of white-currant juice.

Move the utensil to the side of the stove for a few minutes, that the sugar may dissolve, and then cook the jelly on a hot fire, carefully skimming the while, until the *"nappe"* (222° F. large thread) *stage* is almost reached.

Remarks: The object of adding the white-currant jelly is to modify the blackness of pure black-currant jelly.

2964—QUINCE JELLY *Gelée de Coings*

Select very ripe fruit; cut it into slices; peel and seed these, and throw them into a basin of fresh water.

Then put them into a preserving-kettle with three and a half pints of water per lb. of quinces, and cook them without stirring. This done, transfer them to a sieve, and let them drain. Return the juice to the pot, together with twelve oz. of sugar per lb.; dissolve the sugar; and set the whole to cook on a hot fire, meanwhile skimming with care, until the *"nappe"* (222° F. large thread) *stage* is almost reached.

As soon as the jelly is cooked, strain it through a piece of muslin stretched over a basin; and by this means, a perfectly clear jelly will be obtained.

2965—RED CURRANT JELLY (1st Method)   *Gelée de Groseilles*

Take some red and white currants, in the proportion of two-thirds of the former to one-third of the latter, and combine with them, per two lbs., three oz. of raspberries. Crush the three products together in a basin, and then press them in small quantities at a time, in a strong towel, in order to extract their juice. Put the juice in the preserving-kettle, together with eight oz. of sugar per pint. Thoroughly dissolve the sugar, and set the whole to cook over a very hot fire; meanwhile skimming carefully—more particularly at first, until the *"nappe"* (222° F. large thread) stage is reached.

N.B.—The yield of juice from red-currants equals about two-thirds or three-fourths of the weight of the raw fruit.

2966—RED CURRANT JELLY (2nd Method)   *Gelée de Groseilles*

Take the same quantities of white and red currants and of raspberries, as above. Carefully clean the fruit; wash it in cold water, and put it into the preserving-kettle, with one wineglass of water per lb.

Cook the whole gently on the side of the stove for ten or twelve minutes; transfer the fruit to a sieve, lying on a bowl, and let it drain.

Put the juice into the preserving-kettle, with twelve oz. of sugar per lb., and proceed with the cooking as before.

2967—RED CURRANT JELLY (3rd Method)   *Gelée de Groseilles*

Take the same quantities as above of white-currants, red-currants, and raspberries. Remove the currants from their stalks by means of a fork, and collect them in a bowl; clean the raspberries, and allow twelve oz. of sugar per lb. of the fruit.

Dissolve the sugar in the preserving-kettle with a little water and cook it to the *small-ball* stage (236° F.); meanwhile skimming carefully.

Throw the currants and the raspberries into it; put the pan on the side of the fire for seven or eight minutes, that the juice may exude from the fruit; and then cook on a hot fire, skimming very carefully the while, until the *"nappe"* (222° F. large thread) stage is reached.

2968—WHITE CURRANT JELLY   *Gelée de Groseilles Blanches*

This is made from fresh, very ripe white currants and two oz. of raspberries per lb. of the latter. Any one of the three methods given above may be followed in its preparation, although Method C will be found to yield the clearest jelly.

2969—RED CURRANT JELLY, PREPARED COLD
Gelée de Groseilles à Froid

Prepare the juice as directed under (2965). Add to it one lb. of icing-sugar (2346a) per quart, and keep the whole in a cool place for two or three hours, taking care to stir it frequently with a silver spoon in order to dissolve the sugar. Fill the pots and keep them uncovered for two or three days.

This done, cover them in the usual way, and set them in the sun for two or three hours per day for two days.

This jelly is as fragile as it is delicate, and should be kept in a dry place.

2970—ORANGE JELLY   *Gelée d'Oranges*

In order to make one quart of orange jelly, take twelve oranges, each weighing about five oz.; one-third pint of good apple juice (cider), one lb. of sugar, and a tablespoon of grated orange sugar. The latter is obtained by rubbing the rinds of the oranges with loaf-sugar, and then grating the sugar so colored and flavored with a hard knife.

If the jelly be desired garnished, insert a fair-sized, candied orange-rind cut into small strips.

Preparation:—Thoroughly press the oranges and filter the juice; prepare the apple juice, and set the sugar to dissolve with a few drops of water.

Add the orange and apple juice to the sugar, and cook the jelly like the preceding ones. Leave it to cool for ten minutes; mix with it the orange sugar and the candied rind, and pour it into pots.

2971—APPLE JELLY   *Gelée de Pommes*

Proceed exactly as for quince jelly, and strain the apple juice (cider) without pressing the fruit. Do not cook too much, lest the juice become mixed with pulp. Nevertheless, this should be very carefully poured away; for, in spite of the greatest care, there is always a certain amount of residue.

Put the juice into the preserving-kettle, with thirteen oz. of sugar and one-third of a stick of vanilla per quart.

Cook, and strain through muslin, as in the case of quince jelly.

2972—TOMATO JELLY (1st Method)   *Gelée de Tomates*

Prepare the tomatoes as directed under (2962).

Per lb. of drained juice allow one good pint of apple jelly, twenty oz. of sugar, and a large vanilla stick.

Put into the preserving-kettle the sugar, the apple jelly, and the vanilla-flavored tomato juice, and put the pot on the side of the fire for five minutes.

This done, set the whole to cook on a hot fire, until the *"nappe"* (222° F. *large thread*) stage is reached.

2973—TOMATO JELLY (2nd Method)   *Gelée de Tomates*

Take the same amount of juice as in the preceding case.

Use red currant jelly instead of apple jelly, and prepare the former from red and white currants in the proportion of one-third of the former to two-thirds of the latter. Use the same amount of vanilla as above. Put the latter into the preserving-kettle; dissolve it with a little water; add the vanilla, and cook it to the *small-crack stage* (285° F.); remembering to skim carefully at the start.

Add the tomato pulp and the red-currant jelly to the cooked sugar; put the whole on the side of the stove for a moment in order to reduce the sugar; and then proceed with the cooking on a very hot fire until the *"nappe"* (222° F. *large thread*) stage is reached.

CHAPTER XXIV

SNAILS, MUSSELS, SCALLOPS

2974—THE PREPARATION OF SNAILS *La Préparation des Escargots*

USE snails in their shells. Remove the protective membranes at the openings, wash them thoroughly several times, and allow them to absorb for two hours a mixture of clear cold water, salt, vinegar, and a pinch of flour.

Wash them again in clear cold water until they are thoroughly cleansed of any stickiness. Then blanch them in boiling water for five or six minutes.

After draining them, remove snails from shells, take off the black tips of their tails, and replace them in their shells. Then let them cook, on a bed of carrots, onions, chopped shallots, and an herb bunch, in a mixture of half white wine and half water, enough to cover them completely. Add one and three-quarters teaspoon of salt per quart of the liquid and cook over a very low fire for at least three hours. Allow them to get cold in the liquid in which they have cooked. Remove from shells when cold.

Put the empty shells in a mixture of water with bicarbonate of soda and let them boil for thirty minutes to bleach and cleanse them. Drain them, wash thoroughly in fresh water, and dry them.

2975—SNAILS ABBAYE *Escargots à la Mode de l'Abbaye*

For forty snails: Melt butter and *sauté* a heaping teaspoon of finely minced onion; do not brown. Add the snails, cooked and dried according to directions (2974), and a heaping teaspoon of flour.

Mix thoroughly in pan. Add seven-eighths cup of boiling fresh cream; let simmer from twelve to fifteen minutes. Finish at the last minute with a mixture of four egg yolks, cream, and three and one-half tablespoons of butter. Serve in a *timbale*.

870

2976—SNAILS BOURGUIGNONNE   *Escargots à la Bourguignonne*

Prepare the snails as indicated (2974). Fill the bottom end of each shell with Bourguignonne Sauce or Butter (2978).

Return the cooked snails to their shells, and close the shells with the same butter mixture, well pressed down. Lay them on a snail pan or other oven dish.

Put a little water on the bottom of the pan; sprinkle the snail butter with crumbs; and heat in a hot oven for seven or eight minutes.

2977—SNAILS CHABLISIENNE   *Escargots à la Chablisienne*

For sixty snails: Add two teaspoons of finely chopped shallots to one pint of good white wine; reduce this wine to three-quarters of a cup. Strain through a cloth or fine sieve. Add a teaspoon of melted meat *glaze* (14), and put in the bottom of each shell a little of this reduced wine.

Replace the snails in their shells; close these with butter and proceed to finish as in *Snails Bourguignonne* (2976).

2978—BOURGUIGNONNE SAUCE OR BUTTER   *Sauce Bourguignonne*

Reduce by one-half, a quart and a half of excellent red wine, flavored with five minced shallots, several sprigs of parsley and thyme, half a bay leaf, and three-quarters of an ounce of mushroom peelings. Strain through a fine sieve and thicken with two and three-quarters ounces of *manié* butter (151), four parts butter to three parts flour. When ready to serve, add five ounces of butter and season lightly with cayenne pepper.

Aside from being a special sauce for snails, *Bourguignonne* is well adapted to various egg dishes and other recipes.

2979—MUSSELS   *Moules*

For each person count one and a half quarts of mussels. After cleaning them thoroughly, lay mussels on a bed of chopped onions, a bunch of herbs, and a bit of bay leaf. Add a cup of cold water and allow to steam for eight or ten minutes. Remove one shell from each, and keep mussels hot in dish.

Reduce to one-third, seven eighths cup of white wine to which has been added a heaping teaspoon of minced shallots. Add seven-eighths cup of the mussel juice, finely strained and poured off from the residue at the bottom of the pot. Add a half cup of Fish *Velouté* (26a) and three tablespoons of butter.

Sauté the mussels in this sauce, with lemon juice added, for a few seconds. Put in a *timbale* and sprinkle with chopped parsley.

2980—MUSSELS POULETTE   *Moules Poulette*
Prepare mussels as in 2979, and remove one shell from each. Add one-half cup of reduced mussel liquor to one and a half cups of Poulette Sauce (101); season with a dash of lemon juice. Sauté the mussels in this sauce. Serve in a *timbale* and sprinkle with chopped parsley.

2981—MUSSELS VILLEROY   *Moules Villeroy*
Take very large *poached* and bearded mussels and dip them in Villeroy Sauce (108). Put them on a tray as soon as they have been dipped in sauce; let them chill; then bread them *à l'anglaise* and fry in deep fat. These serve as garnish to fish dishes rather than as separate dishes.

2982—SCALLOPS IN THEIR SHELLS (COQUILLES SAINT JACQUES)
Préparation de Coquilles Saint-Jacques ou Pélerines
Place large fresh unopened scallops on a pan in a hot oven; as they heat up they will open wide. Detach the scallop from the lower shell by passing a knife blade underneath. Wash and brush the shells thoroughly; let them bleach in bicarbonate of soda and water from eight to ten minutes; drain and dry.
Cut the scallop flesh into small round pieces, and use as indicated in the following recipes.

2983—SCALLOPS AU GRATIN   *Coquilles Saint-Jacques au Gratin*
After having scrubbed and cleaned the lower shells, cover the shell inside with Duxelles Sauce (223) and add a half teaspoon of white wine. On top of this sauce arrange the scallops; place slices of raw mushrooms around the edges of the shell, and cover the whole with a *gratin* sauce (270).
Sprinkle with herbs and bread-crumbs, brush with melted butter, and prepare a *gratin*, taking note that the *Complete Gratin* (269) should be used here.

2984—SCALLOPS PARISIENNE *Coquilles Saint-Jacques à la Parisienne*
Prepare the shells as in (2982). Wash and dry the scallops and *braise* them gently with white wine and mushroom liquor.
Border the shells with garnish of Duchess Potatoes (221), piped

on by means of a pastry-bag and fluted tube. Brush with egg and brown in oven before filling. Keep hot.

Cover bottom of each shell with a teaspoon of white wine sauce (45), to which a little chopped truffle has been added. Fill shells with prepared scallops, alternating these with slices of cooked mush. rooms. Cover with the same white wine sauce and *glaze*. Serve immediately.

MENUS

MENUS DE DEJEUNERS

Concombre mariné aux piments doux.
Duchesse au Caviar.
Œufs frits.
Pieds de mouton poulette.
Poulet Bonne femme.
Pâté de foie gras.
Pain grillé très chaud.
Asperges à l'huile.
Pêche Cardinal.
Pâtisserie.

Hors-d'Œuvres.
Œufs Cocotte.
Sole grillée Diable.
Faisan poêlé au Céleri.
Parfait de foie gras.
Salade Rachel.
Soufflé au Chocolat.
Tartelette aux fruits.

Kilkis. Olives de Lucques.
Crevettes roses.
Truite au bleu.
Agneau de lait Boulangère.
Terrine de Canard Rouennais
Cœurs de Romaine.
Asperges vertes.
Mousse à la Fraise.
Mille-feuilles.

Hors-d'Œuvre.
Merlan à l'anglaise.
Fricassée de poulet à l'ancienne.
Selle d'Agneau à la Broche.
Petits pois Française.
Soufflé au Kirsch.
Fromage à la Crème.
Confiture de groseille de Bar-le-Duc.

Figues nouvelles glacées.
Olives farcies.
Omelette aux fonds d'Artichauts.
Langoustine Ravigote.
Queue de bœuf en Daube.
Cardons au parmesan.
Alouette à la casserole.
Salade Lorette.
Fraises et pêches au Maraschino.
Pâtisserie.

Fenouil à la Grecque.
Salade de Salicoque.
Turbotin au vin rouge.
Pilau aux ris d'Agneau.
Caneton nouveau aux petits pois
Mousse de jambon à la gelée.
Salade d'asperges.
Coupe d'Antigny.
Fruits.

MENUS DE DEJEUNERS

Anguille fumée de Kiel.
Cerneaux au verjus.
Œufs brouillées aux truffes.
Homard Américaine.
Poulet poêlé Ménagère.
Selle de Pré-salé.
Petits pois au laitues.
Riz Impératrice.
Sablés Viennois.

Cantaloup rafraîchi.
Matelote de Sole.
Risotto de Volaille.
Râble de lièvre à la crème.
Purée de marrons.
Aspic de homard.
Salade de légumes.
Poire au vin rouge.
Pâtisserie.

———

Artichauts à la Grecque.
Sardines au Currie.
Truite à la Meunière.
Pudding de Bécassine aux truffes.
Selle d'Agneau de lait.
Haricots verts à l'anglaise, Pommes
Anna.
Soufflé aux Ecrevisses à la Florentine.
Crêpes Suzette.
Fruits.

Anchois de Collioure.
Tomates marinées.
Œufs à la Reine.
Whitebait Diablés.
Tournedos Béarnaise.
Pommes soufflées.
Faisan Casserole.
Salade d'Endives.
Pâté de foie gras.
Charlotte de pommes.
Crème Chantilly.

———

Colchester Natives.
Œufs frits.
Merlan sur le plat.
Noisette a'Agneau Rachel.
Pommes paille.
Perdreau à la Broche.
Salade de céleri aux truffes.
Bavarois au Chocolat.
Petits Condés.
Fruits.

Hors-d'Œuvres.
Moules à la Marinière.
Côtelette d'Agneau grillée.
Purée de pommes de terre.
Perdreau Périgourdine.
Salade de Céleri.
Soufflé au Paprika.
Mont Blanc aux marrons.
Pâtisserie Parisienne.

MENU

Hors-d'Œuvres.
Melon Cantaloup.
Tortue Claire.
Germiny.
Consommé Madrilène.
Truite d'Écosse au Vin du Rhin.
Mignonnettes de Sole.
Poularde Soufflé au Paprika Rose.
Concombres au Velouté.
Selle d'Agneau Rotie
ou
Selle de Chevreuil à la Bohémienne.
Suprêmes d'Écrevisses Moscovite.
Neige au Clicquot.
Cailles escortées d'Ortolans.
Salade de Cœurs de Romaine.
Jambon de Prague sous la Cendre.
Soufflé d'Asperges Rothschild.
Biscuit Glacé à l'Orientale.
Mille-Feuilles, Petit-Duc.
Diablotins.
Pêches, Nectarines et Raisin Muscat.

MENU

Hors-d' Œuvre Moscovite.
Tortue claire.
Germiny.
Truite au Chambertin.
Mignonettes de Sole.
Whitebait Diablés.
Cailles à la Turque.
Baron d'agneau de lait Soubise.
Petits pois à l'Anglaise.
Pommes Byron.
Suprêmes de Volaille Jeannette.
Nageoires de Tortue à la Maryland.
Sorbet fleur de Pêcher.
Caneton de Rouen à l'orange.
Jambon de Prague sous la cendre.
Fèves de Marais.
Asperges d'Argenteuil.
Biscuit glacé praliné.
Feuillantine.
Œufs de pluvier en Aspic.
Diablotins.
Fraises Chantilly.

MENU

Hors-d'Œuvre Suédoise.
Consommé glacé.
Tortue Claire.
Suprêmes de Sole au vin du Rhim.
Selle de Pré-salé aux Laitues à la
Grecque.
Petits Pois à la Bourgeoise.
Poularde au Paprika Rose.
Cailles aux Raisins.
Cœurs de Romaines.
Asperges Mousselines.
Écrevisses à la Moscovite.
Soufflé Surprise.
Mille-Feuilles, Petit-Duc, Friandises.
Pêches, Nectarines, Ananas, Muscat.

MENU

Hors-d'Œuvre.
Consommé Leopold.
Bisque d'Écrevisses.
Turbotin au Volnay.
Whitebait Diablé.
Poularde à la Diva.
Concombres au beurre.
Selle d'agneau Portugaise.
Haricots verts à l'Anglaise.
Faisan Périgourdine.
Salade d'Endives.
Pâté de foie gras.
Biscuit glacé aux marrons.
Savarin aux fruits.
Friandises.

MENU

Frivolités Orientales.
Cantaloup au Maraschino.
Figues Fraîches.
Gelée aux Paillettes dorées.

Consommé aux Nids d'Hirondelles.
Velouté au Blé Vert.

Sterlets du Volga à la Livonienne.
Nonats de la Méditerranée au Fenouil.

Chapon Fin à la Mode du Couven.
Mousse de Mai.
Jeune Venaison à la Châtelaine.
Petites Mascottes Printanière.
Sylphides Roses.

FLEURS DE PECHER.

Cailles escortées d'Ortolans Ste.
Alliance.
Cœurs de Romaine aux Pommes
d'Amour.

Asperges de France au Beurre d'Isigny.
Suprêmes d'Écrevisses au Champagne.

Belle de Nuit.
Bénédictines—Mignardises.
Huîtres Perlières en Surprise.
Fruits de Serre Chaude.
Café Turc.

Vins du Rhin.
Grands Crus de France.
Grandes Liqueurs.

MENU

Caviar frais—Œufs de pluvier.
Melon.
Tortue claire.
Rossolnick.
Truite au Chambertin.
Laitances Meunière.
Poularde Soufflée à la Catalane.
Morilles à la crème.
Selle d'Agneau de Galles aux laitues.
Petits pois à l'Anglaise.
Pommes Nana.
Suprême d'Écrevisses Moscovite.
Punch à la Mandarine.
Caneton de Rouen à la Rouennaise.
Cœurs de Romaine.
Asperges de France.
Biscuit glacé aux violettes.
Friandises.
Barquettes à l'Écossaise.
Fraises.
Pêches de Serre.

MENU

Œufs de pluvier.
Caviar frais.
Consommé Henri IV.
Bisque d'Écrevisses.
Truite au Chambertin.
Laitances Meunière.
Filet de poulet an beurre noisette.
Petits pois à l'Anglaise.
Selle de jeune Chevreuil aux cerises.
Terrine de Cailles à la Richelieu.
Punch glacé.
Caneton de Rouen au sang.
Salade Royale.
Asperges Sauce Mousseline.
Soufflé au Parmesan à la Florentine.
Bombe Algésiras.
Biscuit Génois.
Fraises Chantilly.

MENU

Caviar Blinis.
Royal Natives.
Velouté aux petits pois frais.
Filets de Sole Marie Stuart.
Barquettes de Laitances Florentine.
Suprême de poulet au beurre noisette.
Cœurs d'Artichauts au velouté.
Selle de Chevreuil Grand Veneur.
Mousse d'Écrevisse au Champagne.
Punch Napolitain.
Faisan truffé—Brochette d'Ortolans.
Salade Lorette.
Asperges vertes.
Parfait de foie gras.
Biscuit glacé à l'Orientale.
Mignardises.
Diablotins.
Pêches de Montreuil.
Raisins Muscat.

MENU

Melon Cantaloup.
Caviar.
Tortue Claire.
Consommé froid en gelée.
Truite au Champagne.
Côtelettes d'agneau de lait Maréchale
Concombres au velouté.
Jambon de Prague sous la cendre.
Petits pois à la Française.
Poularde Néva.
Poulet Rose Marie.
Caille au raisin.
Cœurs de Romaine.
Asperges d'Argenteuil.
Soufflé au Parmesan.
Pêches et fraises Melba.
Friandises.

MENU

Hors-d'œuvre Moscovite.
Melon Cantaloup—Figues fraîches.
Gelée Madrilene en tasse.
Tortue claire.
Truite Régina.
Mignonnettes de Sole.
Côtelettes d'agneau de lait Maréchale.
Petits pois à l'Anglaise.
Jambon de Prague sous la cendre.
Crème de Champignons.
Poularde Suédoise.
Punch Sicilien.
Caille au Muscat.
Brochette d'Ortolans.
Salade d'Asperges à la Toulousaine.
Mousseline d'Écrevisses.
Soufflé Hélène.
Gâteau Manqué.
Pêches. Nectarines.

MENU

Caviar de la Néva—Blinis.
Royal Natives.
Tortue claire.
Stchi à la Russe.
Suprême de sole au Château Yquem
Caille au nid.
Selle de Chézelles à la Broche.
Purée de Céleri.
Bécasse au fumet.
Salade Lorette.
Asperges vertes.
Parfait de foie gras au Clicquot.
Soufflé Rothschild.
Biscuit glacé aux perles des **Alpes.**
Corbeille de fruits.

CHRISTMAS DINNER

Frivolités.

Caviar frais.

Blinis de Sarrasin.

Oursins de la Méditerranée.

Consommé aux nids d'Hirondelle.

Velouté Dame Blanche.

Sterlet du Volga à la Moscovite.

Barquette de Laitance à la Vénitienne.

Chapon fin aux Perles du Périgord.

Cardon épineux à la Toulousaine.

Selle de Chevreuil aux Cerises.

Sylphide d'Ortolan Reine Alexandra.

Suprême d'Écrevisses au Champagne.

Mandarines Givrées.

Terrine de Caille sous la Cendre aux
Raisins.

Bécassine rosée au feu de sarments.

Salade Isabelle.

Asperges de France.

Délices de Foie gras.

Soufflé de Grenade à l'Orientale.

Biscuit glacé aux Violettes.

Mignardises.

Fruits de Serre chaude.

Grandes Liqueurs.

Fine Champagne.

BON VOYAGE

MENU

Caviar frais—Blinis.

Royal Natives.

Tortue Claire.

Rossolnick.

Suprême de Sole Marie Stuart.

Barquette de Laitance Meunière.

Filet de Poulet au Beurre Noisette.

Cœur d'artichaut aux Truffes.

Selle de Veau Braisée.

Puree de Châtaignes—Pommes Nana.

Mousse d'Écrevisse au Champagne.

Punch Sicilien.

Bécassine à la Broche.

Salade Lorette.

Asperges Vertes.

Pâté de Foie Gras.

Biscuit Glacé aux Violettes.

Mille-Feuilles.

Diablotins.

Corbeille de Fruits.

NEW YEAR'S EVE DINNER

MENU

Caviar de Sterlet.
Royal Natives.
Tortue claire.
Velouté Régina.
Suprême de Sole Clarence.
Poularae Alexandra.
Morilles des Alpes.
Mignonnette d'agneau à l'Écossaise.
Pommes Parisienne.
Crême de haricots verts.
Soufflé d'Écrevisse Moscovite.
Mandarines givrées.
Caille aux truffes.
Salade d'Endive et Céleri.
Asperges de France.
Parfait de Foie gras.
Plum pudding à la fine Champagne.
Mousse glacée Aurore 19—
Friandises.
Fruits.

CHRISTMAS DINNER

MENU

Crêpe aux œufs de Sterlet.
Consommé Santa-Maria.
Velouté aux Paillettes dorées.
Paupiette de Sole sous la cendre.
Caille à l'Orientale.
Jeune Chevreuil aux Cerises.
Crème de Marrons.
Suprême de Foie gras au Champagne,
Neige aux Perles des Alpes.
Chapon accompagné d'Ortolans Ste.
Alliance.
Salade Nazareth.
Asperges de France.
Le plum pudding des Rois Mages.
L'Étoile au Berger.
Bénédictins Blancs.

GARDEN PARTY

LUNCHEON

Melon Cantaloup Glacé.

Consommé froid Madrilène.
Consommé de Volaille chaud.

Truite d'Écosse à la Vénitienne.
Œuf Glacé au Jambon.

Noisette d'Agneau à l'Estragon.
Petits pois Bonne Femme.
Poutets nouveaux Mireille.

BUFFET FROID

Filet de Bœuf Printanière.
Chaud-froid de Caille à l'Alsacienne.
Galantine de Volaille aux Truffes.
Suprême de Caneton aux Cerises.
Cœurs de Romaine.
Pêche Melba.
Glace Napolitaine.
Biscuit Mousseline.
Petits-Fours.
Savarin au Kirsch.
Panier de Nectarines Raisins, Fraises.

SUPPER MENU

Velouté Ecossaise.
Filet de sole Meunière.
Côtelette d'Agneau Maréchale.
Pointes d'Asperges à la Crême.
Mignonnette de Poulet glacée au
Paprika.
Buffet Froid.
Salade Lorette.
Pêche Melba.
Friandises.

————

SUPPER MENU

Caviar frais.
Royal Natives.
Consommé Madrilène.
Paupiette de Sole Orientale.
Côtelette de volaille à la Maréchale.
Pointes d'asperges.
Noisette d'agneau Rachel.
Caille aux raisins.
Parfait de foie gras.
Pêche Alice.
Friandises.

————

SUPPER MENU

Natives.
Consommé de Volaille.
Filet de Sole Américaine.
Côtelette d'agneau grillée.
Concombres à la crème.
Mousse de Jambon au blanc de poulet.
Parfait de foie gras.
Perdreau Périgourdine.
Salade Rachel.
Macédoine de fruit glacée.
Friandises.

FANCY SUPPER MENU

Caviar de Sterlet.
Crêpes Moscovite.
Consommé aux Pommes d'Amour.
Sylphides à la crème d'Écrevisses.
Mignonnette de poulet Petit-Duc.
Velouté Favori.
Cailles dodues escortées d'Ortolans.
Nymphes roses—Désirs de Mascotte.
Pointes d'Asperges à l'huile Vierge.
Charmes de Vénus voilés à l'Orientale.
Plaisirs des Dames.
Étoiles Filantes—Frivolités.

————

MENU

Hors-d'œuvre Moscovite.
Melon-Cantaloup.
Tortue claire.
Velouté aux Pommes d'Amour.
Paupiette de sole à l'Ancienne.
Timbale de Ris de Veau Toulousaine.
Poularde Rose Marie.
Selle d' Agneau aux laitues à la
Grecque.
Petits pois à l'Anglaise.
Punch glacé.
Caille en cocotte.
Salade Romaine.
Asperges d'Argenteuil.
Terrine de Canard Rouennaise.
Bombe Néro.
Friandises.
Diablotins.
Fruits.

MENU

Hors-d'œuvre Moscovite.
Melon Cantaloup.
Consommé froid Madrilène.
Tortue claire.
Truite d'Écosse au Vin du Rhin.
Mignonnette de Sole.
Filet de poulet Alexandra.
Concombres au Paprika.
Selle de Chevreuil à la Bohémienne.
Suprême d'Écrevisse au Clicquot.
Neige aux Perles des Alpes.
Caille au raisin.
Salade d'Asperges vertes.
Aubergine au gratin.
Biscuit glacé Orientale.
Marcelin Anisette.
Diablotins.
Corbeille de Pêches et Nectarines.

MENU

Hors-d'œuvre.
Caviar frais—Crêpe Moscovite.
Nymphes roses.
Consommé de faisan au céleri.
Bisque d'Oursin.
Mousseline de Lavaret
au Vin de Savoie.
Mignonnette de Sole au poivre noir.
Salmi de perdreau à l'ancienne mode.
Selle d'agneau à l'Orientale.
Aubergine à la Grecque.
Crème de piment au blanc de poulet.
Coupe givrée au Suc de grenade.
Caille de vigne au vert-jus.
Salade des Capucins.
Soufflé de pomme à la Chantilly.
Parfait glacé aux Avelines.
Mignardises.
Paillettes Diablées.
Corbeille de fruits.

MENU

Hors-d'œuvre.
Huîtres au raifort.
Poutargue de Gènes.
Figues fraîches.
Cocky Leekie.
Velouté aux fleurs de courgette.
Truite au bleu.
Nonats de la Méditerranée au Fenouil.
Poularde à l'Aurore.
Selle de Chevreuil à la Bohémienne.
Pommes aigrelettes
à la gelée de groseille.
Suprêmes d'Écrevisse au Champagne.
Pastèque en Sorbet.
Perdreau aux raisins.
Salade Créole.
Cœur d'artichaut Petit-Duc.
Mousse Favorite.
Délices au Caramel.
Pêches Rose Chérie.

MENU

Hors-d'œuvre Moscovite.
Natives.
Consommé Marie Stuart.
Chicken Okra.
Timbale de Sole Orientale.
Poularde Favorite.
Concombre au beurre.
Baron d'agneau de lait.
Riz à la Grecque.
Laitues braisées.
Bécasse au fumet.
Salade d'asperges et d'artichauts.
Parfait de foie gras.
Biscuit glacé Alice.
Mille-feuilles.
Fruits.

INDEX

INDEX

(HD) Indicates Hors d'oeuvre.   (E) Indicates Entremet.